T0222367

Lecture Notes in Computer Science 13993

Advanced Research in Computing and Software Science
Subline of Lecture Notes in Computer Science

More information about this series at https://link.springer.com/bookseries/558

Sriram Sankaranarayanan ·
Natasha Sharygina
Editors

Tools and Algorithms for the Construction and Analysis of Systems

29th International Conference, TACAS 2023
Held as Part of the European Joint Conferences
on Theory and Practice of Software, ETAPS 2023
Paris, France, April 22–27, 2023
Proceedings, Part I

 Springer

Editors
Sriram Sankaranarayanan
University of Colorado
Boulder, CO, USA

Natasha Sharygina ⓘ
University of Lugano
Lugano, Switzerland

ISSN 0302-9743   ISSN 1611-3349   (electronic)
Lecture Notes in Computer Science
ISBN 978-3-031-30822-2   ISBN 978-3-031-30823-9   (eBook)
https://doi.org/10.1007/978-3-031-30823-9

This Springer imprint is published by the registered company Springer Nature Switzerland AG
The registered company address is: Gewerbestrasse 11, 6330 Cham, Switzerland

ETAPS Foreword

Welcome to the 26th ETAPS! ETAPS 2023 took place in Paris, the beautiful capital of France. ETAPS 2023 was the 26th instance of the European Joint Conferences on Theory and Practice of Software. ETAPS is an annual federated conference established in 1998, and consists of four conferences: ESOP, FASE, FoSSaCS, and TACAS. Each conference has its own Program Committee (PC) and its own Steering Committee (SC). The conferences cover various aspects of software systems, ranging from theoretical computer science to foundations of programming languages, analysis tools, and formal approaches to software engineering. Organising these conferences in a coherent, highly synchronized conference programme enables researchers to participate in an exciting event, having the possibility to meet many colleagues working in different directions in the field, and to easily attend talks of different conferences. On the weekend before the main conference, numerous satellite workshops took place that attracted many researchers from all over the globe.

ETAPS 2023 received 361 submissions in total, 124 of which were accepted, yielding an overall acceptance rate of 34.3%. I thank all the authors for their interest in ETAPS, all the reviewers for their reviewing efforts, the PC members for their contributions, and in particular the PC (co-)chairs for their hard work in running this entire intensive process. Last but not least, my congratulations to all authors of the accepted papers!

ETAPS 2023 featured the unifying invited speakers Véronique Cortier (CNRS, LORIA laboratory, France) and Thomas A. Henzinger (Institute of Science and Technology, Austria) and the conference-specific invited speakers Mooly Sagiv (Tel Aviv University, Israel) for ESOP and Sven Apel (Saarland University, Germany) for FASE. Invited tutorials were provided by Ana-Lucia Varbanescu (University of Twente and University of Amsterdam, The Netherlands) on heterogeneous computing and Joost-Pieter Katoen (RWTH Aachen, Germany and University of Twente, The Netherlands) on probabilistic programming.

As part of the programme we had the second edition of TOOLympics, an event to celebrate the achievements of the various competitions or comparative evaluations in the field of ETAPS.

ETAPS 2023 was organized jointly by Sorbonne Université and Université Sorbonne Paris Nord. Sorbonne Université (SU) is a multidisciplinary, research-intensive and worldclass academic institution. It was created in 2018 as the merge of two first-class research-intensive universities, UPMC (Université Pierre and Marie Curie) and Paris-Sorbonne. SU has three faculties: humanities, medicine, and 55,600 students (4,700 PhD students; 10,200 international students), 6,400 teachers, professor-researchers and 3,600 administrative and technical staff members. Université Sorbonne Paris Nord is one of the thirteen universities that succeeded the University of Paris in 1968. It is a major teaching and research center located in the north of Paris. It has five campuses, spread over the two departments of Seine-Saint-Denis and Val d'Oise: Villetaneuse, Bobigny, Saint-Denis, the Plaine Saint-Denis and Argenteuil. The university has more than 25,000 students in different fields, such as health, medicine, languages, humanities, and science. The local organization team consisted of Fabrice Kordon (general co-chair), Laure Petrucci (general co-chair), Benedikt Bollig (workshops), Stefan Haar (workshops), Étienne André (proceedings and tutorials), Céline Ghibaudo (sponsoring), Denis Poitrenaud (web), Stefan Schwoon (web), Benoît Barbot (publicity), Nathalie Sznajder (publicity), Anne-Marie Reytier (communication), Hélène Pétridis (finance) and Véronique Criart (finance).

ETAPS 2023 is further supported by the following associations and societies: ETAPS e.V., EATCS (European Association for Theoretical Computer Science), EAPLS (European Association for Programming Languages and Systems), EASST (European Association of Software Science and Technology), Lip6 (Laboratoire d'Informatique de Paris 6), LIPN (Laboratoire d'informatique de Paris Nord), Sorbonne Université, Université Sorbonne Paris Nord, CNRS (Centre national de la recherche scientifique), CEA (Commissariat à l'énergie atomique et aux énergies alternatives), LMF (Laboratoire méthodes formelles), and Inria (Institut national de recherche en informatique et en automatique).

The ETAPS Steering Committee consists of an Executive Board, and representatives of the individual ETAPS conferences, as well as representatives of EATCS, EAPLS, and EASST. The Executive Board consists of Holger Hermanns (Saarbrücken), Marieke Huisman (Twente, chair), Jan Kofroň (Prague), Barbara König (Duisburg), Thomas Noll (Aachen), Caterina Urban (Inria), Jan Křetínský (Munich), and Lenore Zuck (Chicago).

Other members of the steering committee are: Dirk Beyer (Munich), Luís Caires (Lisboa), Ana Cavalcanti (York), Bernd Finkbeiner (Saarland), Reiko Heckel (Leicester), Joost-Pieter Katoen (Aachen and Twente), Naoki Kobayashi (Tokyo), Fabrice Kordon (Paris), Laura Kovács (Vienna), Orna Kupferman (Jerusalem), Leen Lambers (Cottbus), Tiziana Margaria (Limerick), Andrzej Murawski (Oxford), Laure Petrucci (Paris), Elizabeth Polgreen (Edinburgh), Peter Ryan (Luxembourg), Sriram Sankaranarayanan (Boulder), Don Sannella (Edinburgh), Natasha Sharygina (Lugano), Pawel Sobocinski (Tallinn), Sebastián Uchitel (London and Buenos Aires), Andrzej Wasowski (Copenhagen), Stephanie Weirich (Pennsylvania), Thomas Wies (New York), Anton Wijs (Eindhoven), and James Worrell (Oxford).

I would like to take this opportunity to thank all authors, keynote speakers, attendees, organizers of the satellite workshops, and Springer-Verlag GmbH for their support. I hope you all enjoyed ETAPS 2023.

Finally, a big thanks to Laure and Fabrice and their local organization team for all their enormous efforts to make ETAPS a fantastic event.

April 2023

Marieke Huisman
ETAPS SC Chair
ETAPS e.V. President

Preface

We are pleased to present the proceedings of TACAS 2023, the 29th edition of the International Conference on Tools and Algorithms for the Construction and Analysis of Systems held as part of the 26th European Joint Conferences on Theory and Practice of Software (ETAPS 2023), April 24–28, 2023 in Paris, France. TACAS brings together a community of researchers, developers, and end-users who are broadly interested in rigorous algorithmic techniques for the construction and analysis of systems. The conference is a venue that interleaves various disciplines including formal verification of software and hardware systems, static analysis, program synthesis, verification of machine learning/autonomous systems, probabilistic programming, SAT/SMT solving, constraint solving, static analysis, automated theorem proving and Cyber-Physical Systems.

There were five submission categories for TACAS 2023:

1. **Regular research papers** advancing the theoretical foundations for the construction and analysis of systems.
2. **Case study papers** describing the application of state-of-the-art research techniques on real-world applications.
3. **Regular tool papers** presenting a new tool, a new tool component, or novel extensions to an existing tool of interest to the community.
4. **Tool demonstration papers** focusing on the usage aspects of tools.
5. **SV-COMP competition tool papers** organized as a separate conference track.

Regular research, case study, and regular tool papers were restricted to a total of sixteen pages, and tool demonstration papers to six pages, exclusive of references.

This year 169 papers were submitted to TACAS, consisting of 119 regular research papers, 34 regular tool and case study papers, and 16 tool demonstration papers. Each paper was reviewed by three Program Committee (PC) members, who made use of sub-reviewers. As a result, the PC accepted in total 62 papers, among which there were 45 regular papers, 11 regular tool/case-study papers and 6 tool demonstration papers. The PC members were pleasantly surprised by an unusually large number of strong submissions. Almost all accepted papers had either all positive reviews or a "championing" program committee member who argued in favor of accepting the paper. Furthermore, all accepted papers had a positive average score. One paper was accepted conditionally and successfully "shepherded" by the PC.

Similarly to previous years, it was possible to submit an artifact alongside a paper, which was mandatory for regular tool and tool demonstration papers. An artifact might consist of tools, models, proofs, or other data required for validation of the results of the paper. The Artifact Evaluation Committee (AEC) reviewed the artifacts based on their documentation, ease of use, and, most importantly, whether the results presented in the corresponding paper could be accurately reproduced. The evaluation was carried out using a standardized virtual machine to ensure consistency of the results, except for 4 artifacts that had special hardware or software requirements. The evaluation had two rounds. The first round was carried out in parallel with the work of the PC and evaluated the artifacts for all the submitted regular tool and tool demo papers. The judgment of the AEC was communicated to the PC and weighed in their discussion (the PC rejected a total of 4 papers in this phase). The second round took place after the paper acceptance notifications were sent out so the authors of accepted research and case-study papers could submit their artifacts. In both rounds, the AEC provided 3 reviews per artifact and communicated with the authors to resolve apparent technical issues. In total, 69 artifacts were submitted (51 in the first round and 18 in the second), and the AEC evaluated a total of 64 artifacts regarding their availability, functionality, and/or reusability. Finally, among the 62 accepted papers, the AEC awarded 32 functional badges, 21 reusable badges, and 33 available badges. Such badges appear on the first page of each paper to certify the properties of each artifact.

As a separate conference track, TACAS 2023 hosted the 12th Competition on Software Verification (SV-COMP 2023). SV-COMP is the annual comparative evaluation of tools for automatic software verification and witness validation. The TACAS proceedings contain a selection of 13 short papers that describe participating verification systems and a report presenting the results of the competition. These papers were reviewed by a separate program committee (the competition jury); each of the papers was assessed by at least three reviewers. A total of 52 verification systems were systematically evaluated, with 34 developer teams from ten countries, including five submissions from industry. Two sessions in the TACAS program were reserved for the competition: presentations by the competition chair and the participating development teams in the first session and an open community meeting in the second session.

We would like to thank all the people who helped to make TACAS 2023 successful. First, we would like to thank the authors for submitting their papers to TACAS 2023. The PC members and additional reviewers did a great job in reviewing papers: they contributed informed and detailed reports and engaged in the PC discussions. We also thank the steering committee, and especially its chair, Joost-Pieter Katoen, for his valuable advice. Lastly, we would like to thank the overall organization team of ETAPS 2023.

April 2023

Sriram Sankaranarayanan
Natasha Sharygina
Grigory Fedyukovich
Sergio Mover
Dirk Beyer

Organization

Program Committee Chairs

Sriram Sankaranarayanan | University of Colorado Boulder, USA
Natasha Sharygina | University of Lugano, Switzerland

Program Committee

Christel Baier | TU Dresden, Germany
Haniel Barbosa | Universidade Federal de Minas Gerais, Brazil
Ezio Bartocci | TU Wien, Austria
Dirk Beyer | LMU Munich, Germany
Armin Biere | Freiburg, Germany
Nikolaj Bjørner | Microsoft, USA
Roderick Bloem | Graz University of Technology, Austria
Ahmed Bouajjani | IRIF, Université Paris Cité, France
Hana Chockler | King's College London, UK
Alessandro Cimatti | Fondazione Bruno Kessler, Italy
Rance Cleaveland | University of Maryland, USA
Javier Esparza | TU Munich, Germany
Chuchu Fan | MIT, USA
Grigory Fedyukovich | Florida State University, USA
Bernd Finkbeiner | CISPA Helmholtz Center for Information Security, Germany
Martin Fränzle | Carl von Ossietzky Universität Oldenburg, Germany
Khalil Ghorbal | Inria, France
Laure Gonnord | Grenoble-INP/LCIS, France
Orna Grumberg | Technion - Israel Institute of Technology, Israel
Kim Guldstrand Larsen | Aalborg University, Denmark
Arie Gurfinkel | University of Waterloo, Canada
Ranjit Jhala | University of California, San Diego, USA
Laura Kovacs | TU Wien, Austria
Alexander Kulikov | St. Petersburg Department of Steklov Institute of Mathematics, Russia
Bettina Könighofer | Graz University of Technology, Austria
Wenchao Li | Boston University, USA
Sergio Mover | Ecole Polytechnique, France
Peter Müller | ETH Zurich, Switzerland
Kedar Namjoshi | Nokia Bell Labs, USA
Aina Niemetz | Stanford University, USA
Corina Pasareanu | CMU, NASA, KBR, USA
Nir Piterman | University of Gothenburg, Sweden

Philipp Ruemmer	University of Regensburg, Germany
Krishna S.	Indian Institute of Technology Bombay, India
Cesar Sanchez	IMDEA Software Institute, Spain
Sharon Shoham	Tel Aviv University, Israel
Fabio Somenzi	University of Colorado Boulder, USA
Cesare Tinelli	University of Iowa, USA
Stavros Tripakis	Northeastern University, USA
Frits Vaandrager	Radboud University, Netherlands
Yakir Vizel	Technion, Israel
Tomas Vojnar	Brno University of Technology, Czechia
Naijun Zhan	Chinese Academy of Sciences, China
Lijun Zhang	Chinese Academy of Sciences, China
Florian Zuleger	Vienna University of Technology, Austria

Artifact Evaluation Committee Chairs

Grigory Fedyukovich	Florida State University, USA
Sergio Mover	Ecole Polytechnique, France

Artifact Evaluation Committee

Timothy A. Thijm	Princeton University, USA
Leonardo Alt	Ethereum Foundation, Germany
Pedro H. A. de Amorim	Cornell University, USA
Martin Blicha	University of Lugano, Switzerland
Alexander Bork	RWTH Aachen, Germany
Priyanka Darke	Tata Consultancy Services, India
Emanuele De Angelis	IASI-CNR, Rome, Italy
Jip J. Dekker	Monash University, Australia
Zafer Esen	Uppsala University, Sweden
Aleksandr Fedchin	Tufts University, USA
Hadar Frenkel	CISPA – Helmholtz Center for Information Security, Germany
Pamina Georgiou	Vienna University of Technology, Austria
Thomas Møller Grosen	Aalborg University, Denmark
Ahmed Irfan	SRI International, USA
Martin Jonas	Fondazione Bruno Kessler, Italy
Dongjoo Kim	Seoul National University, South Korea
Satoshi Kura	National Institute of Informatics, Japan
Denis Mazzucato	Ecole Normale Superieure, France
Baoluo Meng	GE Global Research, USA
Federico Mora	University of California, Berkeley, USA
Dmitry Mordvinov	Saint-Petersburg State University, JetBrains Research, Russia
Srinidhi Nagendra	Chennai Mathematical Institute, India
Andres Noetzli	Stanford University, USA

Jiří Pavela	FIT VUT, Czechia
Sumanth Prabhu	TRDDC, India
Felipe R. Monteiro	Amazon Web Services, USA
Olli Saarikivi	Microsoft Research, USA
Saeid Tizpaz Niari	University of Texas at El Paso, USA
Hari Govind Vediramana Krishnan	University of Waterloo, Canada
Jingbo Wang	University of Southern California, USA
Anton Xue	University of Pennsylvania, USA
Hansol Yoon	Republic of Korea Air Force, South Korea

Program Committee and Jury—SV-COMP

Dirk Beyer (Chair)	LMU Munich, Germany
Viktor Malík (2LS)	TU Brno, Czechia
Lei Bu (BRICK)	Nanjing University, China
Marek Chalupa (Bubaak)	ISTA, Austria
Michael Tautschnig (CBMC)	Queen Mary University London, UK
Henrik Wachowitz (CPAchecker)	LMU Munich, Germany
Hernán Ponce de León (Dartagnan)	Huawei Dresden Research, Germany
Fei He (Deagle)	Tsinghua University, China
Fatimah Aljaafari (EBF)	University of Manchester, UK
Rafael Sá Menezes (ESBMC-kind)	University of Manchester, UK
Martin Spiessl (Frama-C-SV)	LMU Munich, Germany
Falk Howar (GDart, GDart-LLVM)	TU Dortmund, Germany
Simmo Saan (Goblint)	University of Tartu, Estonia
William Leeson (Graves-CPA, Graves-Par)	University of Virginia, USA
Soha Hussein (Java-Ranger)	University of Minnesota, USA
Peter Schrammel (JBMC)	University of Sussex/Diffblue, UK
Gidon Ernst (Korn)	LMU Munich, Germany
Tong Wu (LF-checker)	University of Manchester, UK
Vesal Vojdani (Locksmith)	University of Tartu, Estonia
Lei Bu (MLB)	Nanjing University, China
Raphaël Monat (Mopsa)	Inria and University of Lille, France
Cedric Richter (PeSCo-CPA)	University of Oldenburg, Germany
Jie Su (PIChecker)	Xidian University, China
Marek Trtik (Symbiotic)	Masaryk University, Brno, Czechia
Levente Bajczi (Theta)	Budapest University of Technology and Economics, Hungary

Matthias Heizmann (UAutomizer)	University of Freiburg, Germany
Dominik Klumpp (UGemCutter)	University of Freiburg, Germany
Frank Schüssele (UKojak)	University of Freiburg, Germany
Daniel Dietsch (UTaipan)	University of Freiburg, Germany
Priyanka Darke (VeriAbs, VeriAbsL)	Tata Consultancy Services, India
Raveendra Kumar M. (VeriFuzz)	Tata Consultancy Services, India
HaiPeng Qu (VeriOover)	Ocean University of China, China

Steering Committee

Dirk Beyer	LMU Munich, Germany
Rance Cleaveland	University of Maryland, USA
Holger Hermanns	Universität des Saarlandes, Germany
Joost-Pieter Katoen (Chair)	RWTH Aachen, Germany and Universiteit Twente, Netherlands
Kim G. Larsen	Aalborg University, Denmark
Bernhard Steffen	Technische Universität Dortmund, Germany

Additional Reviewers

Abd Alrahman, Yehia
Ahmad, H. M. Sabbir
An, Jie
Asarin, Eugene
Azzopardi, Shaun
Bacci, Giorgio
Baier, Daniel
Balakrishnan, Gogul
Balasubramanian, A. R.
Baumeister, Jan
Becchi, Anna
Ben Shimon, Yoav
Berger, Guillaume
Beutner, Raven
Bily, Aurel
Blicha, Martin
Bombardelli, Alberto
Brieger, Marvin
Brizzio, Matías
Bunk, Thomas
Caillaud, Benoît
Cano Córdoba, Filip

Ceresa, Martin
Ceska, Milan
Chen, Mingshuai
Chen, Xin
Chen, Yilei
Chiari, Michele
Czerner, Philipp
Dardinier, Thibault
Dawson, Charles
De Masellis, Riccardo
Debrestian, Darin
Di Stefano, Luca
Egolf, Derek
Elad, Neta
Elashkin, Andrey
Esen, Zafer
Fazekas, Katalin
Feng, Shenghua
Ferres, Bruno
Fiedor, Jan
Fleury, Mathias
Fontaine, Pascal

Frenkel, Eden
Frenkel, Hadar
Froleyks, Nils
Fu, Feisi
Garcia-Contreras, Isabel
Garg, Kunal
Georgiou, Pamina
Gianola, Alessandro
Gigerl, Barbara
Goorden, Martijn
Gorostiaga, Felipe
Goyal, Srajan
Griggio, Alberto
Grosen, Thomas Møller
Gstrein, Bernhard
Gupta, Ashutosh
Habermehl, Peter
Hader, Thomas
Hadzic, Vedad
Hagemann, Willem
Hamza, Ameer
Haring, Johannes
Hausmann, Daniel
Havlena, Vojtěch
Hermo, Montserrat
Holík, Lukáš
Hozzová, Petra
Huang, Chao
Huang, Chengchao
Hyvärinen, Antti
Itzhaky, Shachar
Jacobs, Swen
Jaeger, Manfred
Jansen, David N.
Jensen, Nicolaj Østerby
Jha, Prabhat
Jonas, Martin
Junges, Sebastian
Kaki, Gowtham
Kaufmann, Daniela
Kenison, George
Kettl, Matthias
Khalimov, Ayrat
Kifetew, Fitsum
Kiourti, Panagiota
Klüppelholz, Sascha

Kröger, Paul
Käfer, Nikolai
Lal, Akash
Larrauri, Alberto
Larraz, Daniel
Lazic, Marijana
Le, Nham
Lee, Nian-Ze
Lengal, Ondrej
Li, Renjue
Lidell, David
Liu, Jiaxiang
Lopez-Miguel, Ignacio D.
Luttenberger, Michael
Macías, Fernando
Maderbacher, Benedikt
McClurg, Jedidiah
Meng, Yue
Metzger, Niklas
Michelland, Sebastien
Monniaux, David
Moosbrugger, Marcel
Nadel, Alexander
Nam, Seunghyeon
Nesterini, Eleonora
Neufeld, Emery
Nickovic, Dejan
Noetzli, Andres
Oliveira Da Costa, Ana
Otoni, Rodrigo
Parthasarathy, Gaurav
Paxian, Tobias
Pluska, Alexander
Poli, Federico
Pontiggia, Francesco
Prandi, Davide
Pranger, Stefan
Preiner, Mathias
Radanne, Gabriel
Rakow, Astrid
Rappoport, Omer
Rauh, Andreas
Rawson, Michael
Rebola Pardo, Adrian
Reynolds, Andrew
Riley, Daniel

Rodriguez, Andoni
Rogalewicz, Adam
Román Calvo, Enrique
Rubio, Rubén
Rutledge, Kwesi
Sallinger, Sarah
Sankaranarayanan, Sriram
Schlichtkrull, Anders
Schoisswohl, Johannes
Schultz, William
Schupp, Stefan
Schwammberger, Maike
Sextl, Florian
Siber, Julian
So, Oswin
Sogokon, Andrew
Spiessl, Martin
Steen, Alexander
Su, Yusen
Susi, Angelo
Síč, Juraj
Tappler, Martin
Thibault, Joan
Ting, Gan
Treml, Lilly Maria
Trivedi, Ashutosh

Turrini, Andrea
Varanasi, Sarat Chandra
Vediramana Krishnan, Hari Govind
Visconti, Ennio
Wachowitz, Henrik
Wand, Michael
Wardega, Kacper
Weininger, Maximilian
Wendler, Philipp
Wienhöft, Patrick
Wu, Hao
Wu, Haoze
Xue, Anton
Yadav, Drishti
Yang, Pengfei
Yang, Ruixiao
Yu, Chenning
Yu, Mingxin
Zavalia, Lucas
Zhan, Bohua
Zhang, Hanwei
Zhang, Songyuan
Zhou, Weichao
Zhou, Yuhao
Zimmermann, Martin
Zlatkin, Ilia

Contents – Part I

Machine Learning/Neural Networks

Automata

Proofs

Contents – Part II

Invited Talk

A Learner-Verifier Framework for Neural Network Controllers and Certificates of Stochastic Systems*

Krishnendu Chatterjee[1], Thomas A. Henzinger[1]([✉]),
Mathias Lechner[2], and Đorđe Žikelić[1]

[1] Institute of Science and Technology Austria (ISTA), Klosterneuburg, Austria
{krishnendu.chatterjee,tah,djordje.zikelic}@ist.ac.at
[2] Massachusetts Institute of Technology (MIT), Cambridge, MA, USA
mlechner@mit.edu

Abstract. Reinforcement learning has received much attention for learning controllers of deterministic systems. We consider a learner-verifier framework for stochastic control systems and survey recent methods that formally guarantee a conjunction of reachability and safety properties. Given a property and a lower bound on the probability of the property being satisfied, our framework jointly learns a control policy and a formal certificate to ensure the satisfaction of the property with a desired probability threshold. Both the control policy and the formal certificate are continuous functions from states to reals, which are learned as parameterized neural networks. While in the deterministic case, the certificates are invariant and barrier functions for safety, or Lyapunov and ranking functions for liveness, in the stochastic case the certificates are supermartingales. For certificate verification, we use interval arithmetic abstract interpretation to bound the expected values of neural network functions.

Keywords: Learning-based control · Stochastic systems · Martingales. · Formal verification

1 Introduction

Learning-based control and verification of learned controllers. Learning-based control and reinforcement learning (RL) were empirically demonstrated to have enormous potential to solve highly non-linear control tasks. However, their deployment in safety-critical scenarios such as autonomous driving or healthcare requires safety assurances. Most safety-aware RL algorithms optimize expected reward while only empirically trying to maximize safety probability. This together with the non-explainable nature of neural network controllers obtained via deep RL raise questions about the trustworthiness of learning-based methods for safety-critical applications [9,27]. To that end, formal verification of learned

*This work was supported in part by the ERC-2020-AdG 101020093, ERC CoG 863818 (FoRM-SMArt) and the European Union's Horizon 2020 research and innovation programme under the Marie Skłodowska-Curie Grant Agreement No. 665385.

S. Sankaranarayanan and N. Sharygina (Eds.): TACAS 2023, LNCS 13993, pp. 3–25, 2023.
https://doi.org/10.1007/978-3-031-30823-9_1

controllers as well as learning-based control with formal safety guarantees have become very active research topics.

Learning certificate functions. A classical approach to formally proving properties of dynamical systems is to compute a certificate function. A *certificate function* [26] is a function that assigns real values to system states and its defining conditions imply satisfaction of the property. Thus, in order to prove the property of interest, it suffices to compute a certificate function for that property. For instance, Lyapunov functions [46] and barrier functions [50] are standard certificate functions for proving reachability of some target set and avoidance of some unsafe set of system states, respectively, when the system dynamics are deterministic. While both Lyapunov and barrier functions are well-studied concepts in dynamical systems theory, early methods for their computation either required designing the certificates by hand or using computationally intractable numerical procedures. A more recent approach reduces certificate computation to a semi-definite programming problem by using sum-of-squares (SOS) techniques [33,49,37]. However, a limitation of this approach is that it is only applicable to polynomial systems and computation of polynomial certificate functions, whereas it is not applicable to systems with general non-linearities. Moreover, SOS methods do not scale well with the dimension of the system.

Learning-based methods are a promising approach to overcome these limitations and they have received much attention in recent years. These methods jointly learn a neural network control policy and a neural network certificate function, e.g. a Lyapunov function [53,18,3,17] or a barrier function [38,58,52,1], depending on the property of interest. The neural network certificate is then formally verified, ensuring that these methods provide formal guarantees. Both learning and verification procedures developed for verifying neural network certificates are not restricted to polynomial dynamical systems. See [26] for an overview of existing learning-based control methods that learn a certificate function to verify a system property in deterministic dynamical systems.

Prior works – deterministic dynamical systems. While the above works present significant advancements in learning-based control and verification of dynamical systems, they are predominantly restricted to *deterministic* dynamical systems. In other words, they assume that they have access to the exact dynamics function according to which the system evolves. However, for most control tasks, the underlying models used by control methods are imperfect approximations of real systems inferred from observed data. Thus, control and verification methods should also account for model uncertainty due to the noise in observed data and the approximate nature of model inference.

This survey – stochastic dynamical systems. In this work, we survey recent developments in learning-based methods for control and verification of discrete-time *stochastic* dynamical systems, based on [44,68]. Stochastic dynamical systems use probability distributions to quantify and model uncertainty. In stochastic dynamical systems, given a property of interest and a probability parameter $p \in [0,1]$, the goal is to learn a control policy and a formal certificate which guarantees that the system under the learned policy satisfies the property of interest with probability at least p.

Supermartingale certificate functions. Lyapunov functions and barrier functions can be used to prove properties in deterministic dynamical systems, however they are not applicable to stochastic dynamical systems and do not allow reasoning about the probability of a property being satisfied. Instead, the learning-based methods of [44,68] use *supermartingale certificate functions* to formally prove properties in stochastic systems. Supermartingales are a class of stochastic processes that decrease in expected value at every time step [66]. Their nice convergence properties and concentration bounds allow their use in designing certificate functions for stochastic dynamical systems. In particular, *ranking supermartingales (RSMs)* [15,44] were used to verify probability 1 reachability and *stochastic barrier functions (SBFs)* [50] were used to verify safety with the specified probability $p \in [0,1]$. *Reach-avoid supermartingales (RASMs)* [68] unify and extend these two concepts and were used to verify reach-avoidance properties with the specified probability $p \in [0,1]$, i.e. a conjunction of reachability and safety properties. We define and compare these concepts in Section 3.

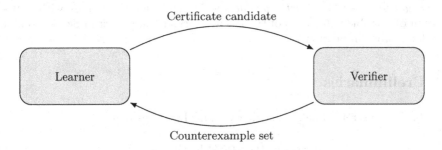

Certificate candidate

Learner

Verifier

Counterexample set

Fig. 1: Schematic illustration of the learner-verifier loop.

Learner-verifier framework for stochastic dynamical systems. In Section 4, we then present a *learner-verifier framework* of [44,68] for learning-based control and for the verification of learned controllers in stochastic dynamical systems in a counterexample guided inductive synthesis (CEGIS) fashion [55]. The algorithm jointly learns a neural network control policy and a neural network supermartingale certificate function. It consists of two modules – the learner, which learns a policy and a supermartingale certificate function candidate, and the verifier, which then formally verifies the candidate supermartingale certificate function. If the verification step fails, the verifier computes counterexamples and passes them back to the learner, which tries to learn a new candidate. This loop is repeated until a candidate is successfully verified, see Fig. 1.

   This framework builds on the existing learner-verifier methods for learning-based control in deterministic dynamical systems [18,2,26]. However, the extension of this framework to stochastic dynamical systems and the synthesis of supermartingale certificate functions is far from straightforward. In particular, the methods of [18,2] use knowledge of the deterministic dynamics function to reduce the verification task to a decision procedure and use an off-the-shelf solver. However, verification of the expected decrease condition of supermartingale certificates by reduction to a decision procedure would require being able to compute a closed-form expression of the expected value of a neural network function over a probability distribution and provide it to the solver. It is not clear how the closed-form expression can be computed, and it is not known whether the closed-form expression exists in the general case.

This challenge is solved by using a method for efficient computation of tight *upper and lower bounds on the expected value* of a neural network function. The verifier module then verifies the expected decrease condition by *discretizing* the state space and formally verifying a slightly stricter condition at the discretization points by using the computed expected value bounds. By carefully choosing the mesh of the discretization and adding an additional error term, we obtain a sound verification method applicable to general Lipschitz continuous systems. The expected value bound computation for neural network functions relies on interval arithmetic and abstract interpretation, and since it is of independent interest, we discuss it in detail in Section 5. We are not aware of any existing methods that tackle this problem.

Extension to general stochastic certificates. We conclude this survey with a discussion of possible extensions of the learner-verifier framework in Section 6 and of related work in Section 7.

2   Preliminaries

We consider discrete-time stochastic dynamical systems defined via

$$\mathbf{x}_{t+1} = f(\mathbf{x}_t, \mathbf{u}_t, \omega_t), \ \mathbf{x}_0 \in \mathcal{X}_0.$$

The function $f : \mathcal{X} \times \mathcal{U} \times \mathcal{N} \to \mathcal{X}$ is the dynamics function of the system and $t \in \mathbb{N}_0$ is the time index. We use $\mathcal{X} \subseteq \mathbb{R}^m$ to denote the system state space, $\mathcal{U} \subseteq \mathbb{R}^n$ the control action space and $\mathcal{N} \subseteq \mathbb{R}^p$ the stochastic disturbance space. For each $t \in \mathbb{N}_0$, $\mathbf{x}_t \in \mathcal{X}$ the state of the system, $\mathbf{u}_t \in \mathcal{U}$ the action and $\omega_t \in \mathcal{N}$ the stochastic disturbance vector at time t. The set $\mathcal{X}_0 \subseteq \mathcal{X}$ is the set of initial states. In each time step, $\mathbf{u}_t$ is chosen according to a control policy $\pi : \mathcal{X} \to \mathcal{U}$, i.e. $\mathbf{u}_t = \pi(\mathbf{x}_t)$, and ω_t is sampled according to some specified probability distribution d over $\mathbb{R}^p$. The dynamics function f, control policy π and probability distribution d together define a stochastic feedback loop system.

A trajectory of the system is a sequence $(\mathbf{x}_t, \mathbf{u}_t, \omega_t)_{t \in \mathbb{N}_0}$ such that, for each $t \in \mathbb{N}_0$, we have $\mathbf{u}_t = \pi(\mathbf{x}_t)$, $\omega_t \in \mathsf{support}(d)$ and $\mathbf{x}_{t+1} = f(\mathbf{x}_t, \mathbf{u}_t, \omega_t)$. For each initial state $\mathbf{x}_0 \in \mathcal{X}$, the system induces a Markov process. This gives rise to the probability space over the set of all trajectories of the system that start in $\mathbf{x}_0$ [51]. We denote the probability measure and the expectation in this probability space by $\mathbb{P}_{\mathbf{x}_0}$ and $\mathbb{E}_{\mathbf{x}_0}$, respectively.

Assumptions. We assume that $\mathcal{X} \subseteq \mathbb{R}^m$, $\mathcal{X}_0 \subseteq \mathbb{R}^m$, $\mathcal{U} \subseteq \mathbb{R}^n$ and $\mathcal{N} \subseteq \mathbb{R}^p$ are all Borel-measurable. This is necessary for the probability space of the set of all system trajectories starting in some initial state to be mathematically well-defined. We also assume that $\mathcal{X} \subseteq \mathbb{R}^m$ is compact (i.e. closed and bounded) and that the dynamics function f is Lipschitz continuous, which are common assumptions in control theory. Finally, we assume that the probability distribution d is a product of independent univariate probability distributions, which is necessary for efficient sampling and expected value computation.

2.1 Brief Overview of Martingale Theory

In this subsection, we provide a brief overview of definitions and results from martingale theory that lie at the core of formal reasoning about supermartingale certificate functions. We assume that the reader is familiar with the mathematical definitions of probability space, measurability and random variables, see [66] for the necessary background. The results in this subsection will help in building an intuition on supermartingale certificate functions, but omitting them would not prevent the reader from following the rest of this paper.

Probability space. A probability space is a triple $(\Omega, \mathcal{F}, \mathbb{P})$ where Ω is a state space, $\mathcal{F}$ is a sigma-algebra and $\mathbb{P}$ is a probability measure which is required to satisfy Kolmogorov axioms [66]. A random variable is a function $X : \Omega \to \mathbb{R}$ that is $\mathcal{F}$-measurable. We use $\mathbb{E}[X]$ to denote the *expected value* of X. A *(discrete-time) stochastic process* is a sequence $(X_i)_{i=0}^{\infty}$ of random variables in $(\Omega, \mathcal{F}, \mathbb{P})$.

Conditional expectation. Let X be a random variable in a probability space $(\Omega, \mathcal{F}, \mathbb{P})$. Given a sub-$\sigma$-algebra $\mathcal{F}' \subseteq \mathcal{F}$, a *conditional expectation* of X given $\mathcal{F}'$ is an $\mathcal{F}'$-measurable random variable Y such that, for each $A \in \mathcal{F}'$, we have

$$\mathbb{E}[X \cdot \mathbb{I}(A)] = \mathbb{E}[Y \cdot \mathbb{I}(A)].$$

Here, $\mathbb{I}(A) : \Omega \to \{0, 1\}$ is an *indicator function* of A defined via $\mathbb{I}(A)(\omega) = 1$ if $\omega \in A$, and $\mathbb{I}(A)(\omega) = 0$ if $\omega \notin A$. Intuitively, conditional expectation of X given $\mathcal{F}'$ is an $\mathcal{F}'$-measurable random variable that behaves like X whenever its expected value is taken over an event in $\mathcal{F}'$. Conditional expectation of a random variable X given $\mathcal{F}'$ is guaranteed to exist if X is real-valued and nonnegative [66]. Moreover, for any two conditional expectations Y and Y' of X given $\mathcal{F}'$, we have that $\mathbb{P}[Y = Y'] = 1$. Therefore, the conditional expectation is almost-surely unique and we may pick one such random variable as a canonical conditional expectation and denote it by $\mathbb{E}[X \mid \mathcal{F}']$.

Supermartingales. Let $(\Omega, \mathcal{F}, \mathbb{P})$ be a probability space and $\mathcal{F}_0 \subseteq \mathcal{F}_1 \subseteq \cdots \subseteq \mathcal{F}$ be an increasing sequence of sub-σ-algebras in $\mathcal{F}$ with respect to inclusion. A nonnegative *supermartingale* with respect to $(\mathcal{F}_i)_{i=0}^{\infty}$ is a stochastic process $(X_i)_{i=0}^{\infty}$ such that each X_i is $\mathcal{F}_i$-measurable, and $X_i(\omega) \geq 0$ and $\mathbb{E}[X_{i+1} \mid \mathcal{F}_i](\omega) \leq X_i(\omega)$ hold for each $\omega \in \Omega$ and $i \geq 0$. Intuitively, the second condition says that the expected value of X_{i+1} given the value of X_i has to decrease. This condition is formalized by using conditional expectation.

The following two results that will be key technical ingredients in our design of supermartingale certificate functions. The first theorem shows that nonnegative supermartingales have nice convergence properties and converge almost-surely to some finite value. The second theorem bounds the probability that the value of the supemartingale ever exceeds some threshold, and it will allow us to bound from above the probability of occurrence of some bad event.

Theorem 1 (Supermartingale convergence theorem [66]). *Let $(X_i)_{i=0}^{\infty}$ be a nonnegative supermartingale with respect to $(\mathcal{F}_i)_{i=0}^{\infty}$. Then, there exists a random variable X_∞ in $(\Omega, \mathcal{F}, \mathbb{P})$ to which the supermartingale converges to with probability 1, i.e. $\mathbb{P}[\lim_{i \to \infty} X_i = X_\infty] = 1$.*

Theorem 2 ([41]). *Let $(X_i)_{i=0}^{\infty}$ be a nonnegative supermartingale with respect to $(\mathcal{F}_i)_{i=0}^{\infty}$. Then, for every real $\lambda > 0$, we have $\mathbb{P}[\sup_{i \geq 0} X_i \geq \lambda] \leq \mathbb{E}[X_0]/\lambda$.*

2.2 Problem Statement

We now formally define the properties and control tasks that we focus on in this work. In what follows, let $\mathcal{X}_t, \mathcal{X}_u \subseteq \mathcal{X}$ be disjoint Borel-measurable sets and $p \in [0, 1]$ be a lower bound on the probability with which the system under the learned controller needs to satisfy the property:

- *Reachability.* Let $\mathrm{Reach}(\mathcal{X}_t) = \{(\mathbf{x}_t, \mathbf{u}_t, \omega_t)_{t \in \mathbb{N}_0} \mid \exists t \in \mathbb{N}_0 . \mathbf{x}_t \in \mathcal{X}_t\}$ be the set of all trajectories that reach the target set $\mathcal{X}_t$. The goal is to learn a control policy under which the system reaches $\mathcal{X}_t$ with probability at least p, i.e. $\mathbb{P}_{\mathbf{x}_0}[\mathrm{Reach}(\mathcal{X}_t)] \geq p$ holds for every initial state $\mathbf{x}_0 \in \mathcal{X}_0$.
- *Safety (or avoidance).* Let $\mathrm{Safe}(\mathcal{X}_u) = \{(\mathbf{x}_t, \mathbf{u}_t, \omega_t)_{t \in \mathbb{N}_0} \mid \forall t' \leq t . \mathbf{x}_{t'} \notin \mathcal{X}_u\}$ be the set of all trajectories that do not visit the unsafe set $\mathcal{X}_u$. The goal is to learn a control policy under which the system stays away from $\mathcal{X}_u$ with probability at least p, i.e. $\mathbb{P}_{\mathbf{x}_0}[\mathrm{Safe}(\mathcal{X}_u)] \geq p$ holds for every initial state $\mathbf{x}_0 \in \mathcal{X}_0$.
- *Reach-avoidance.* Let $\mathrm{ReachAvoid}(\mathcal{X}_t, \mathcal{X}_u) = \{(\mathbf{x}_t, \mathbf{u}_t, \omega_t)_{t \in \mathbb{N}_0} \mid \exists t \in \mathbb{N}_0 . \mathbf{x}_t \in \mathcal{X}_t \wedge (\forall t' \leq t . \mathbf{x}_{t'} \notin \mathcal{X}_u)\}$ be the set of all trajectories that reach $\mathcal{X}_t$ without reaching $\mathcal{X}_u$. The goal is to learn a control policy under which the system reaches $\mathcal{X}_t$ while staying away from $\mathcal{X}_u$ with probability at least p, i.e. $\mathbb{P}_{\mathbf{x}_0}[\mathrm{ReachAvoid}(\mathcal{X}_t, \mathcal{X}_u)] \geq p$ holds for every initial state $\mathbf{x}_0 \in \mathcal{X}_0$.

3 Supermartingale Certificate Functions

We now overview three classes of supermartingale certificate functions that formally prove reachability, safety and reach-avoidance properties. *Supermartingale certificate functions* do not refer to a single class of certificate functions. Rather, we use this term to refer to all certificate functions that exhibit a supermartingale-like behavior and can formally verify properties in stochastic dynamical systems. In what follows, we assume that the control policy π is fixed. In the following section, we will then present a learner-verifier framework for jointly learning a control policy and a supermartingale certificate function.

RSMs for probability 1 reachability. We start with *ranking supermartingales (RSMs)*, which can prove probability 1 reachability of some target set $\mathcal{X}_t$. Intuitively, an RSM is a continuous function that maps system states to nonnegative real values and is required to strictly decrease in expectation by some $\epsilon > 0$ in every time step until the target $\mathcal{X}_t$ is reached. Due to the strict expected decrease as well as the Supermartingale Convergence Theorem (Theorem 1), one can show that the existence of an RSM guarantees that the system under policy π reaches $\mathcal{X}_t$ with probability 1. RSMs can be viewed as a stochastic extension of Lyapunov functions. Note that RSMs can only be used to prove probability 1 reachability, but cannot be used to reason about probabilistic reachability. RSMs were originally used for proving almost-sure termination in probabilistic programs [15] and were used to certify probability 1 reachability in stochastic dynamical systems in [44].

Definition 1 (Ranking supermartingales [44]). *Let $\mathcal{X}_t \subseteq \mathcal{X}$ be a target set. A continuous function $V : \mathcal{X} \to \mathbb{R}$ is a* ranking supermartingale (RSM) *with respect to $\mathcal{X}_t$ if it satisfies:*

1. *Nonnegativity condition. $V(\mathbf{x}) \geq 0$ for each $\mathbf{x} \in \mathcal{X}$.*
2. *Expected Decrease condition. There exists $\epsilon > 0$ such that, for each $\mathbf{x} \in \mathcal{X} \backslash \mathcal{X}_t$, we have $V(\mathbf{x}) \geq \mathbb{E}_{\omega \sim d}[V(f(\mathbf{x}, \pi(\mathbf{x}), \omega))] + \epsilon$.*

Theorem 3 ([44]). *Suppose that there exists an RSM with respect to $\mathcal{X}_t$. Then, for every $\mathbf{x}_0 \in \mathcal{X}_0$, we have $\mathbb{P}_{\mathbf{x}_0}[\mathrm{Reach}(\mathcal{X}_t)] = 1$.*

SBFs for probabilistic safety. On the other hand, *stochastic barrier functions (SBFs)* can prove probabilistic safety. Given an unsafe set $\mathcal{X}_u$ and probability $p \in [0, 1)$, an SBF is also a continuous function mapping system states to nonnegative real values, which is required to decrease in expectation at each time step. However, unlike RSMs, the expected decrease need not be strict and there is no target set. In addition, its initial value must be at most 1, whereas its value upon reaching an unsafe set must be at least $1/(1 - p)$. Thus, for the system under policy π to violate the safety constraint, the value of the SBF needs to increase from at most 1 to at least $1/(1-p)$ even though it is required to decrease in expectation. The probability of this event can be bounded from above and shown to be at most $1-p$ by using Theorem 2. We highlight the assumption that $p < 1$, which is necessary for the safety constraint to be mathematically defined. As the name suggests, SBFs are a stochastic extension of barrier functions.

Definition 2 (Stochastic barrier functions [50]). *Let $\mathcal{X}_u \subseteq \mathcal{X}$ be an unsafe set and $p \in [0, 1)$. A continuous function $V : \mathcal{X} \to \mathbb{R}$ is a* stochastic barrier function (SBF) *with respect to $\mathcal{X}_u$ and p if it satisfies:*

1. *Nonnegativity condition. $V(\mathbf{x}) \geq 0$ for each $\mathbf{x} \in \mathcal{X}$.*
2. *Initial condition. $V(\mathbf{x}) \leq 1$ for each $\mathbf{x} \in \mathcal{X}_0$.*
3. *Safety condition. $V(\mathbf{x}) \geq \frac{1}{1-p}$ for each $\mathbf{x} \in \mathcal{X}_u$.*
4. *Expected Decrease condition. For each $\mathbf{x} \in \mathcal{X}$, if $V(\mathbf{x}) \leq \frac{1}{1-p}$ then $V(\mathbf{x}) \geq \mathbb{E}_{\omega \sim d}[V(f(\mathbf{x}, \pi(\mathbf{x}), \omega))]$.*

Theorem 4 ([50]). *Suppose that there exists an SBF with respect to $\mathcal{X}_u$ and p. Then, for every $\mathbf{x}_0 \in \mathcal{X}_0$, we have $\mathbb{P}_{\mathbf{x}_0}[\mathrm{Safe}(\mathcal{X}_u)] \geq p$.*

RASMs for probabilistic reach-avoidance. Finally, *reach-avoid supermartingales (RASMs)* unify and extend RSMs and SBFs in the sense that they allow simultaneous reasoning about reachability and safety and proving a conjunction of these properties, i.e. reach-avoid properties. Let $\mathcal{X}_t$ and $\mathcal{X}_u$ be disjoint target and unsafe sets and let $p \in [0, 1)$. Similarly to SBFs, an RASM is a continuous nonnegative function which is required to be initially at most 1 but needs to attain a value that is at least $1/(1-p)$ for the unsafe region to be reached. On the other hand, similarly to RSMs, it is required to strictly decrease in expectation by $\epsilon > 0$ at every time step until either the target set $\mathcal{X}_t$ or a state in which the value is at least $1/(1-p)$ is reached. Thus, RASMs can be viewed as a stochastic extension of both Lyapunov functions and barrier functions, which combines the strict decrease of Lypaunov functions and the level-set reasoning of barrier functions.

Definition 3 (Reach-avoid supermartingales [68]). *Let $\mathcal{X}_t \subseteq \mathcal{X}$ and $\mathcal{X}_u \subseteq \mathcal{X}$ be a target set and an unsafe set, respectively, and let $p \in [0, 1]$ be a probability threshold. Suppose that either $p < 1$ or that $p = 1$ and $\mathcal{X}_u = \emptyset$. A continuous function $V : \mathcal{X} \to \mathbb{R}$ is a reach-avoid supermartingale (RASM) with respect to $\mathcal{X}_t$, $\mathcal{X}_u$ and p if it satisfies:*

1. *Nonnegativity condition. $V(\mathbf{x}) \geq 0$ for each $\mathbf{x} \in \mathcal{X}$.*
2. *Initial condition. $V(\mathbf{x}) \leq 1$ for each $\mathbf{x} \in \mathcal{X}_0$.*
3. *Safety condition. $V(\mathbf{x}) \geq \frac{1}{1-p}$ for each $\mathbf{x} \in \mathcal{X}_u$.*
4. *Expected Decrease condition. There exists $\epsilon > 0$ such that, for each $\mathbf{x} \in \mathcal{X} \backslash \mathcal{X}_t$ at which $V(\mathbf{x}) \leq \frac{1}{1-p}$, we have $V(\mathbf{x}) \geq \mathbb{E}_{\omega \sim d}[V(f(\mathbf{x}, \pi(\mathbf{x}), \omega))] + \epsilon$.*

Theorem 5 ([68]). *Suppose that there exists an RASM with respect to $\mathcal{X}_t$, $\mathcal{X}_u$ and p. Then, for every $\mathbf{x}_0 \in \mathcal{X}_0$, we have $\mathbb{P}_{\mathbf{x}_0}[\mathrm{ReachAvoid}(\mathcal{X}_t, \mathcal{X}_u)] \geq p$.*

Note that RASMs indeed unify and generalize the definitions of RSMs and SBFs. First, by setting $\mathcal{X}_u = \emptyset$ and $p = 1$ (so $1/(1-p) = \infty$), RASMs reduce to RSMs as the Initial condition that can be enforced without loss of generality by rescaling. Second, by setting $\mathcal{X}_t = \emptyset$, RASMs reduce to SBFs. In this case, the Expected Decrease condition is strengthened as it requires strict decrease by $\epsilon > 0$. However, the proof of Theorem 5 which we outline below also implies Theorem 4 and $\epsilon > 0$ is only necessary to reason about the reachability of $\mathcal{X}_t$.

We also note that RASMs strictly extend the applicability of RSMs, since RASMs can be used to prove reachability with any lower bound $p \in [0, 1]$ on probability and not only probability 1 reachability. Indeed, if we set $\mathcal{X}_u = \emptyset$ and $p \in [0, 1]$, in order to prove reachability of $\mathcal{X}_t$ with probability at least p the RASMs require strict expected decrease in expectation by $\epsilon > 0$ until either $\mathcal{X}_t$ is reached or the RASM value exceeds $1/(1-p)$ (with $1/(1-p) = \infty$ if $p = 1$).

In the rest of this section, we outline the proof of Theorem 5 that was presented in [68]. This proof also implies Theorem 3 and Theorem 4. We do this to highlight the connection of RSMs, SBFs and RASMs to the mathematical notion of supermartingale processes. We also do this to illustrate the tools from martingale theory that are used in proving soundness of supermatingale certificate functions, as we envision that they may be useful in designing supermatingale certificate functions for more general classes of properties.

Proof (proof sketch of Theorem 5). Here we outline the main ideas behind the proof, and for the full proof we refer the reader to [68]. Let $\mathbf{x}_0 \in \mathcal{X}_0$. We need to show that $\mathbb{P}_{\mathbf{x}_0}[\text{ReachAvoid}(\mathcal{X}_t, \mathcal{X}_u)] \geq p$. To do this, we consider the probability space $(\Omega_{\mathbf{x}_0}, \mathcal{F}_{\mathbf{x}_0}, \mathbb{P}_{\mathbf{x}_0})$ of trajectories that start in $\mathbf{x}_0$ and for each time step $t \in \mathbb{N}_0$ define a random variable in this probability space via

$$X_t(\rho) = \begin{cases} V(\mathbf{x}_t), & \text{if } \mathbf{x}_i \notin \mathcal{X}_t \text{ and } V(\mathbf{x}_i) < \frac{1}{1-p} \text{ for each } 0 \leq i \leq t \\ 0, & \text{if } \mathbf{x}_i \in \mathcal{X}_t \text{ for some } 0 \leq i \leq t, V(\mathbf{x}_j) < \frac{1}{1-p} \text{ for each } 0 \leq j \leq i \\ \frac{1}{1-p}, & \text{otherwise} \end{cases}$$

for each trajectory $\rho = (\mathbf{x}_t, \mathbf{u}_t, \omega_t)_{t \in \mathbb{N}_0} \in \Omega_{\mathbf{x}_0}$. Hence, $(X_t)_{t=0}^{\infty}$ defines a stochastic process whose value at each time step is equal to the value of V at the current system state unless either the target set $\mathcal{X}_t$ has been reached after which future values of $\mathcal{X}_t$ are set to 0, or a state in which V exceeds $1/(1-p)$ has been reached after which future values of $\mathcal{X}_t$ are set to $1/(1-p)$. It can be shown that $(X_t)_{t=0}^{\infty}$ is a nonnegative supermartingale $(\Omega_{\mathbf{x}_0}, \mathcal{F}_{\mathbf{x}_0}, \mathbb{P}_{\mathbf{x}_0})$. This claim can be proved by using the Nonnegativity and the Expected Decrease condition of RASMs. Here we do not yet need that the expected decrease is strict, i.e. $\epsilon \geq 0$ in the Expected Decrease condition of RASMs is sufficient.

Since $(X_t)_{t=0}^{\infty}$ is a nonnegative supermartingale, substituting $\lambda = 1/(1-p)$ into the inequality in Theorem 2 shows that

$$\mathbb{P}_{\mathbf{x}_0}\left[\sup_{i \geq 0} X_i \geq \frac{1}{1-p}\right] \leq (1-p) \cdot \mathbb{E}_{\mathbf{x}_0}[X_0] \leq 1 - p.$$

The second inequality follows since $X_0(\rho) = V(\mathbf{x}_0) \leq 1$ for every $\rho \in \Omega_{\mathbf{x}_0}$ by the Initial condition of RASMs. Hence, by the Safety condition of RASMs it follows that the system under policy π reaches the unsafe set $\mathcal{X}_u$ with probability at most $1 - p$. Note that here we can already conclude the claim of Theorem 4.

Finally, as $(X_t)_{t=0}^{\infty}$ is a nonnegative supermartingale, by Theorem 1 its value converges with probability 1. One can then prove that this value has to be either 0 or $\geq 1/(1-p)$ by using the fact that the expected decrease in the Expected Decrease condition of RASMs is strict. But we showed above that a state in which V is $\geq 1/(1-p)$ is reached with probability at most $1 - p$. Hence, the probability that the system under policy π reaches the target set $\mathcal{X}_t$ without reaching the unsafe set $\mathcal{X}_u$ is at least p, i.e. $\mathbb{P}_{\mathbf{x}_0}[\text{ReachAvoid}(\mathcal{X}_t, \mathcal{X}_u)] \geq p$. $\square$

4   Learner-Verifier Framework for Stochastic Systems

We now present the learner-verifier framework of [44,68] for the learning-based control and verification of learned controllers in stochastic dynamical systems. We focus on the probabilistic reach-avoid problem, assume that we are given a target set $\mathcal{X}_t$, unsafe set $\mathcal{X}_u$ and a probability parameter $p \in [0, 1]$, and learn a control policy π and an RASM which certifies that $\mathbb{P}_{\mathbf{x}_0}[\text{ReachAvoid}(\mathcal{X}_t, \mathcal{X}_u)] \geq p$ for all $\mathbf{x}_0 \in \mathcal{X}_0$. The algorithm for learning RSMs and SBFs can be obtained analogously, since we showed that RASMs unify and generalize RSMs and SBFs.

The algorithm behind the learner-verifier framework consists of two modules – the learner, which learns a neural network control policy π_θ and a neural network supermartingale certificate function V_ν, and the verifier, which then formally verifies the learned candidate function. If the verification step fails, the verifier produces counterexamples that are passed back to the learner to fine-tune its loss function. Here, θ and ν are vectors of neural network parameters. The loop is repeated until either a certificate function is successfully verified, or some specified timeout is reached. By incorporating feedback from the verifier, the learner is able to tune the policy and the certificate function towards ensuring that the resulting policy meets the desired reach-avoid specification.

Applications. As outlined above, the learner-verifier framework can be used for *learning-based control* with formal guarantees that a property of interest is satisfied by jointly learning a control policy and a supermartingale certificate function for the property. On the other hand, it can also be used to *formally verify* a previously learned control policy by fixing policy parameters and only learning a supermartingale certificate function. Finally, if one uses a different method to learn a policy that turns out to violate the desired property, one can use the learner-verifier framework to *fine-tune an unsafe policy* towards repairing it and obtaining a safe policy for which a supermartingale certificate function certifies that the property of interest is satisfied.

4.1   Algorithm Initialization

As mentioned in Section 1, the key challenge for the verifier is to check the Expected Decrease condition of supermartingale certificates. Our algorithm solves this challenge by discretizing the state space and verifying a slightly stricter condition at discretization vertices which we show to imply the Expected Decrease condition over the whole region required by Definition 3. On the other hand, learning two neural networks in parallel while simultaneously optimizing several objectives can be unstable due to inherent dependencies between two networks. Thus, proper initialization of networks is important. We allow all neural network architectures so long as all activation functions are continuous functions. Furthermore, we apply the softplus activation function to the output neuron of V_ν, in order to ensure that the value of V_ν is always nonnegative.

Discretization. A *discretization* $\tilde{\mathcal{X}}$ of $\mathcal{X}$ with mesh $\tau > 0$ is a set of states such that, for every $\mathbf{x} \in \mathcal{X}$, there exists a state $\tilde{\mathbf{x}} \in \tilde{\mathcal{X}}$ such that $||\mathbf{x} - \tilde{\mathbf{x}}||_1 < \tau$. The algorithm takes mesh τ as a parameter and computes a finite discretization $\tilde{\mathcal{X}}$ with mesh τ by simply taking a hyper-rectangular grid of the sufficiently small cell size. Since $\mathcal{X}$ is compact, this yields a finite discretization.

Network initialization. The policy network π_θ is initalized by running proximal policy optimization (PPO) [54] on the Markov decision process (MDP) defined by the stochastic dynamical system with a reward function $r_t = 1[\mathcal{X}_t](\mathbf{x}_t) - [\mathcal{X}_u](\mathbf{x}_t)$.

The discretization $\tilde{\mathcal{X}}$ is used to define three sets of states which are then used by the learner to initialize the certificate network V_ν and to which counterexamples computed by the verifier will be added later. In particular, the algorithm initializes $C_{\text{init}} = \tilde{\mathcal{X}} \cap \mathcal{X}_0$, $C_{\text{unsafe}} = \tilde{\mathcal{X}} \cap \mathcal{X}_u$ and $C_{\text{decrease}} = \tilde{\mathcal{X}} \cap (\mathcal{X} \backslash \mathcal{X}_t)$.

4.2 The Learner module

The Learner updates the parameters θ of the policy and ν of the neural network certificate function candidate V_ν with the objective of the candidate satisfying the supermartingle certificate conditions. The parameter updates happen incrementally via gradient descent of the form $\theta \leftarrow \theta - \alpha \frac{\partial \mathcal{L}(\theta,\nu)}{\partial \theta}$ and $\nu \leftarrow \nu - \alpha \frac{\partial \mathcal{L}(\theta,\nu)}{\partial \nu}$, where $\alpha > 0$ is the learning rate and $\mathcal{L}$ is a loss function that corresponds to a differentiable optimization objective of the supermartingle certificate conditions. Ideally, the global minimum of $\mathcal{L}$ should correspond to a policy π and a neural network V_ν that fulfills all certificate conditions. In practice, however, due to the non-convexity of the network V_ν, gradient descent is not guaranteed to converge to the global minimum. As a result, the learner is not monotone, i.e. a new iteration does not guarantee improvement over the previous iteration. The training process usually applies a fixed number of gradient descent iterations or, alternatively, continues until a certain threshold on the loss value is achieved.

Loss functions. The particular type of loss function $\mathcal{L}$ depends on the type of supermartingale certificate function that should be learned by the network, but is of the general form

$$\mathcal{L}(\theta,\nu) = \mathcal{L}_{\text{Certificate}}(\theta,\nu) + \lambda \cdot \left(\mathcal{L}_{\text{Lipschitz}}(\theta) + \mathcal{L}_{\text{Lipschitz}}(\nu) \right), \quad (1)$$

where $\mathcal{L}_{\text{Certificate}}$ is the specification-specific loss. The auxiliary loss terms $\mathcal{L}_{\text{Lipschitz}}$ regularize the training to obtain networks π_θ and V_ν that have a low upper bound of their Lipschitz constant. The purpose of this regularization is that networks with low Lipschitz upper bound are easier to check by the verifier module, i.e. requiring a coarser discretization grid. The value of $\lambda > 0$ decides the strength of the regularization that is applied. The regularization loss is based on the upper bound derived in [57] and defined as

$$\mathcal{L}_{\text{Lipschitz}}(\theta) = \max \left\{ L_{V_\theta} - \frac{\delta}{\tau \cdot (L_f \cdot (L_\pi + 1) + 1)}, 0 \right\}. \quad (2)$$

In the case of a reach-avoid specification, the RASM certificate loss is

$$\mathcal{L}_{\text{Certificate}}(\theta,\nu) = \mathcal{L}_{\text{Expected}}(\theta,\nu) + \mathcal{L}_{\text{Unsafe}}(\nu) + \mathcal{L}_{\text{Init}}(\nu), \quad (3)$$

with

$$\mathcal{L}_{\text{Expected}}(\theta,\nu) = \frac{1}{|C_{\text{decrease}}|} \cdot \sum_{\mathbf{x} \in C_{\text{expected}}} \left(\max \left\{ \right. \right.$$

$$\left. \left. \sum_{\omega_1,\ldots,\omega_N \sim \mathcal{N}} \frac{V_\nu \left(f(\mathbf{x}, \pi_\theta(\mathbf{x}), \omega_i) \right)}{N} - V_\theta(\mathbf{x}) + \tau \cdot K, 0 \right\} \right)$$

$$\mathcal{L}_{\text{Init}}(\nu) = \max_{\mathbf{x} \in C_{\text{init}}} \left\{ V_\nu(\mathbf{x}) - 1, 0 \right\}$$

$$\mathcal{L}_{\text{Unsafe}}(\nu) = \max_{\mathbf{x} \in C_{\text{unsafe}}} \left\{ \frac{1}{1-p} - V_\nu(\mathbf{x}), 0 \right\}.$$

The sets C_{expected}, C_{init} and C_{unsafe} are the training sets for achieving the expected decrease, initial and unsafe RASM conditions. Each of the three sets is initialized with a coarse discretization of the state space to guide the learning toward learning a correct RASM already in the first loop iteration. In the subsequent calls to the learner, these sets are extended by counterexamples computed by the verifier. In [68] it was shown that, if V_θ is a RASM and satisfies all conditions checked by the verifier below, then $\mathcal{L}_{\mathrm{Certificate}}(\theta, \nu) \to 0$ as the number of samples N used to estimate expected values in $\mathcal{L}_{\mathrm{Expected}}(\theta, \nu)$ increases.

4.3   The Verifier module

Verification task. The verifier now formally checks whether the learned RASM candidate V_ν satisfies the four RASM defining conditions in Definition 3. Since we applied the softplus activation function to the output neuron of V_ν, we know that the Nonnegativity condition is satisfied by default. Thus, the verifier only needs to check the Initial, Safety and Expected Decrease conditions in Definition 3.

Expected Decrease condition. To check the Expected Decrease condition, we utilize the fact that the dynamics function f is Lipschitz continuous and that the state space $\mathcal{X}$ is compact to show that it suffices to check a slightly stricter condition at the discretization points. Let L_f be a Lipschitz constant of f. Since π_θ and V_ν are continuous functions defined over the compact domain $\mathcal{X}$, we know that they are also Lipschitz continuous. Let L_π and L_V be their Lipschitz constants. We assume that L_f is provided to the algorithm, and use the method of [57] for computing neural network Lipschitz constants to compute L_π and L_V.

To verify the Expected Decrease condition, the verifier collects a subset $\tilde{\mathcal{X}}_e \subseteq \tilde{\mathcal{X}}$ of all discretization vertices whose adjacent grid cells contain a non-target state and over which V_ν attains a value that is smaller than $\frac{1}{1-p}$. To compute this set, the algorithm first collects all grid cells that intersect $\mathcal{X} \backslash \mathcal{X}_t$. For each collected cell, it then uses interval arithmetic abstract interpretation (IA-AI) [24,30] to propagate interval bounds across neural network layers towards bounding from below the minimal value that V_ν attains over the cell. Finally, it adds to $\tilde{\mathcal{X}}_e$ vertices of those cells at which the computed lower bound is less than $1/(1-p)$.

Finally, the verifier checks if the following condition is satisfied at each $\tilde{\mathbf{x}} \in \tilde{\mathcal{X}}_e$

$$\mathbb{E}_{\omega \sim d}\Big[V_\nu\Big(f(\tilde{\mathbf{x}}, \pi_\theta(\tilde{\mathbf{x}}), \omega)\Big)\Big] < V_\nu(\tilde{\mathbf{x}}) - \tau \cdot K, \tag{4}$$

where $K = L_V \cdot (L_f \cdot (L_\pi + 1) + 1)$. Note that this condition is a strengthened version of the Expected Decrease condition, where instead of strict decrease by arbitrary $\epsilon > 0$ we require strict decrease by at least $\tau \cdot K$ which depends on the discretization mesh τ and Lipschitz constants of f, π_θ and V_ν. To compute $\mathbb{E}_{\omega \sim d}[V_\nu(f(\tilde{\mathbf{x}}, \pi_\theta(\tilde{\mathbf{x}}), \omega))]$ in eq. (4), we cannot simply evaluate the expected value in state $\tilde{\mathbf{x}}$ by substituting $\tilde{\mathbf{x}}$ into some expression, as we do not know a closed-form expression for the expected value of a neural network function. Instead, the algorithm uses the method of [44] to compute upper and lower bounds on the expected value of a neural network function, which we describe in Section 5. This upper bound is then plugged it into eq. (4).

If no violations to eq. (4) are found, the verifier concludes that the Expected Decrease condition is satisfied. Otherwise, for any counterexample $\tilde{\mathbf{x}}$ to eq. (4), the algorithm checks if $\tilde{\mathbf{x}} \in \mathcal{X} \backslash \mathcal{X}_t$ and $V_\nu(\mathbf{x}) < 1/(1-p)$ and if so adds it to the counterexample set C_{decrease}.

Initial and safety conditions. The Initial and Safety conditions are checked using IA-AI. To check the Initial condition, the verifier collects the set $\text{Cells}_{\mathcal{X}_0}$ of all grid cells that intersect the initial set $\mathcal{X}_0$, and for each cell in $\text{Cells}_{\mathcal{X}_0}$ checks if

$$\sup_{\mathbf{x} \in \text{cell}} V_\nu(\mathbf{x}) > 1. \tag{5}$$

The supremum is bounded from above via IA-AI by propagating interval bounds across neural network layers. If no violations are found, the verifier concludes that V_ν satisfies the Initial condition. Otherwise, vertices of any grid cells which are counterexamples to eq. (5) and which are contained in $\mathcal{X}_0$ are added to C_{init}. Analogously, to check the Safety condition, the verifier collects the set $\text{Cells}_{\mathcal{X}_u}$ of all grid cells that intersect the unsafe set $\mathcal{X}_u$, and for each cell checks if

$$\inf_{\mathbf{x} \in \text{cell}} V_\nu(\mathbf{x}) < \frac{1}{1-p}. \tag{6}$$

If no violations are found, the verifier concludes that V_ν satisfies the Safety condition. Otherwise, vertices of any grid cells which are counterexamples to eq. (6) and which are contained in $\mathcal{X}_u$ are added to C_{unsafe}.

Algorithm output and correctness. If all three checks are successful and no counterexample is found, the algorithm concludes that π_θ guarantees reach-avoidance with probability at least p and outputs the policy p_θ. Otherwise, it proceeds to the next learner-verifier iteration where computed counterexamples are added to sets C_{init}, C_{unsafe} and C_{decrease} to be used by the learner. The following theorem establishes correctness of the verifier module, and its proof can be found in [68].

Theorem 6 ([68]). *Suppose that the verifier verifies that the certificate V_ν satisfies eq. (4) for each $\tilde{\mathbf{x}} \in \tilde{\mathcal{X}}_e$, eq. (5) for each cell $\in \text{Cells}_{\mathcal{X}_0}$ and eq. (6) for each cell $\in \text{Cells}_{\mathcal{X}_u}$. Then the function V_ν is an RASM for the system with respect to $\mathcal{X}_t$, $\mathcal{X}_u$ and p.*

Optimizations. The verification task can be made more efficient by a discretization refinement procedure. In particular, the verifier may start with a coarse grid and decomposes each grid cell on demand into a finer discretization in case the check when some RASM condition fails. This procedure can be used recursively to refine further in the case when elements of the decomposed grid cannot be verified. In case the recursion encounters a grid element that violates Eq. 4 even for $\tau = 0$, the refinement procedure terminates unsuccessfully with the grid center point as a counterexample of the RASM condition. This optimization with a maximum recursion depth of 1 has been applied in [68].

5   Bounding Expected Values of Neural Networks

We now present the method for computing upper and lower bounds on the expected value of a neural network function over a given probability distribution.

We are not aware of any existing methods for solving this problem, so believe that this is a result of independent interest.

To define the setting of the problem at hand, let $\mathbf{x} \in \mathcal{X} \subseteq \mathbb{R}^n$ be a system state and suppose that we want to compute upper and lower bounds the expected value $\mathbb{E}_{\omega \sim d}[V(f(\mathbf{x}, \pi(\mathbf{x}), \omega))]$. Here d is a probability distribution over the stochastic disturbance space $\mathcal{N} \subseteq \mathbb{R}^p$ from which the stochastic disturbance is sampled independently at each time step. As noted in Section 2, we assume that d is a product of independent univariate probability distributions. Alternatively, the method is also applicable if the support of d is bounded.

The method first partitions the stochastic disturbance space $\mathcal{N} \subseteq \mathbb{R}^p$ into finitely many cells $\text{cell}(\mathcal{N}) = \{\mathcal{N}_1, \ldots, \mathcal{N}_k\}$. Let $\text{maxvol} = \max_{\mathcal{N}_i \in \text{cell}(\mathcal{N})} \text{vol}(\mathcal{N}_i)$ and $\text{minvol} = \min_{\mathcal{N}_i \in \text{cell}(\mathcal{N})} \text{vol}(\mathcal{N}_i)$ denote the maximal and the minimal volume of any cell in the partition with respect to the Lebesgue measure over $\mathbb{R}^p$, respectively. Also, for each $\omega \in \mathcal{N}$ let $F(\omega) = V(f(\mathbf{x}, \pi(\mathbf{x}), \omega))$. The upper and the lower boundd on the expected value are computed as follows

$$\mathbb{E}_{\omega \sim d}\left[V\left(f(\mathbf{x}, \pi(\mathbf{x}), \omega)\right)\right] \leq \sum_{\mathcal{N}_i \in \text{cell}(\mathcal{N})} \text{maxvol} \cdot \sup_{\omega \in \mathcal{N}_i} F(\omega),$$

$$\mathbb{E}_{\omega \sim d}\left[V\left(f(\mathbf{x}, \pi(\mathbf{x}), \omega)\right)\right] \geq \sum_{\mathcal{N}_i \in \text{cell}(\mathcal{N})} \text{minvol} \cdot \inf_{\omega \in \mathcal{N}_i} F(\omega).$$

Each supremum (resp. infimum) in the sum is then bounded from above (resp. from below) via interval arithmetic abstract interpretation by using the method of [30].

If the support of d is bounded, then no further adjustments are needed. However, if the support of d is unbounded, maxvol and minvol may not be finite. In this case, since we assume that d is a product of univariate distributions, the method first applies the probability integral transform [48] to each univariate probability distribution in d in order to reduce the problem to the case of a probability distribution of bounded support.

6   Discussion on Extension to General Certificates

The focus of this survey has primarily been on three concrete classes of supermartingale certificate functions in stochastic systems, namely RSMs, SBFs and RASMs, and the learner-verifier framework for their computation. For each class of supemartingale certificate functions, the learner module encodes the defining conditions of the certificate as a differentiable loss function whose minimization leads to a candidate certificate function. The verifier module then formally checks whether the defining conditions of the certificate function are satisfied. These checks are performed by discretizing the state space and using interval arithmetic abstract interpretation and the previously discussed method for computing bounds on expected values of neural network functions.

It should be noted that the design of both the learner and the verifier modules was not specifically tailored to any of the three certificate functions. Rather, both the learner and the verifier follow very general design principles that we envision are applicable to more general classes of certificate functions. In particular, we hypothesize that as long as the state space of the system is compact and a certificate function can be defined in terms of

- exact and expected value evaluations of Lipschitz continuous functions, and
- inequalities between such evaluations imposed over state space regions,

then the learner-verifier framework in Section 4 may present a promising approach to learning and verifying the certificate function. In particular, the learner-verifier framework presents a natural candidate for automating the computation of *any supermartingale certificate function* that may be designed for other properties in the future. Furthermore, while RSMs, SBFs and RASMs exhibit a supermartingale-like behavior which is fundamental for their soundness, the learner-verifier framework does not rely or depend on their supermartingale-like behavior. Hence, we envision that the learner-verifier framework could also be used to compute other classes of *stochastic certificate functions*.

Even more generally, note that all certificate functions that we have considered so far are of the type $\mathcal{X} \to \mathbb{R}$. One could also consider extensions of the learner-verifier framework to learning certificate functions of different datatypes. For instance, the work [43] uses a learner-verifier framework to learn an inductive transition invariant of type $\mathcal{X} \times \mathcal{X} \to \mathbb{R}$ that certifies safety in deterministic systems. On the other hand, lexicographic ranking supermartingales are a multidimensional generalization of RSMs of type $\mathcal{X} \to \mathbb{R}^k$ that provide a more efficient and compositional approach to proving probability 1 termination in probabilistic programs [5,22]. Studying possible extensions of the learner-verifier framework for stochastic systems to learn certificate functions of different arity of both domain and codomain is a very interesting direction of future work.

7 Related Work

Existing learning-based methods for learning and verification of certificate functions in deterministic and stochastic systems have been discussed in Section 1. In this section, we overview some other existing methods for verification and control of stochastic dynamical systems, as well as some other uses of martingale theory in stochastic system verification.

Abstraction-based methods. Another class of approaches to stochastic dynamical system control with formal safety guarantees are abstraction based methods [56,42,14,63,60,25]. These methods consider finite-time horizon systems and approximate them via a finite-state Markov decision process (MDP). The control problem is then solved for the obtained MDP and the computed policy is used to exhibit a policy for the original stochastic dynamical system. The key difference in applicability between abstraction based methods and our framework is that abstraction based methods consider *finite-time horizon* systems, whereas we consider *infinite-time horizon* systems.

Safe control via shielding. Shielding is an RL framework that ensures safety in the context of avoidance of unsafe regions by computing two control policies – the main policy that optimizes the expected reward, and the backup policy that the system falls back to whenever the safety constraint may be violated [7,36,29].

Constrained MDPs. A standard approach to safe RL is to solve constrained MDPs (CMDPs) [8,28] which impose hard constraints on expected cost for one or more auxiliary cost functions. Several efficient RL algorithms for solving CMDPs have been proposed [59,4], however their constraints are only satisfied in expectation, hence constraint satisfaction is not formally guaranteed.

RL reward specification and neurosymbolic methods. There are several works on solving model-free RL tasks under logic specifications. In particular, several works propose methods for designing reward functions that encode temporal logic specifications [6,12,32,31,45,34,13,40,39]. Formal methods have also been used for extraction of interpretable policies [62,61,35] and safe RL [10,67,11].

Deterministic systems with stochastic controllers. Another way to give rise to a stochastic dynamical system is to consider a dynamical system with deterministic dynamics function and use a stochastic controller, which helps in quantifying uncertainty in the controller's prediction. Formal verification of deterministic dynamical systems with Bayesian neural network controllers has been considered in [43]. In particular, this work also uses a learner-verifier method to learn an inductive invariant for the deterministic system which formally proves safety.

Supermartingales for probabilistic program analysis. Supermartingales have also been used for the analysis of probabilistic programs (PPs). In particular, RSMs were originally introduced in the setting of PPs to prove almost-sure termination [15] and have since been extensively used, see e.g. [19,20,5,47,22]. The work [1] proposed a learner-verifier method to learn an RSM in the PP. Supermartingales were also used for safety [23,64,21], cost [65] and recurrence and persistence [16] analysis in PPs.

8   Conclusion

This paper presents a framework for learning-based control with formal reachability, safety and reach-avoidance guarantees in stochastic dynamical systems. We present a learner-verifier framework in which a neural network control policy is learned together with a neural network certificate function that formally proves that the property of interest holds with at least some desired probability $p \in [0,1]$. For certification, we use supermartingale certificate functions. The learner module encodes the defining certificate function conditions into a differentiable loss function which is then minimized to learn a candidate certificate function. The verifier then formally verifies the candidate by using interval arithmetic abstract interpretation and a novel method for computing bounds on expected values of neural networks.

The learner-verifier framework presented in this work opens several interesting directions for future work. The first is the design of supermartingale certificates for more general properties of stochastic systems and the use of our learner-verifier framework for their computation. The second is to study and understand the general class of certificate functions in stochastic systems that the learner-verifier can be used to compute, possibly going beyond supermartingale certificate functions. Finally, on the practical side, a venue for future work is to explore methods for reducing the computational cost of the framework and extensions that can handle more complex and higher dimensional systems.

References

1. Abate, A., Ahmed, D., Edwards, A., Giacobbe, M., Peruffo, A.: FOSSIL: a software tool for the formal synthesis of lyapunov functions and barrier certificates using neural networks. In: Bogomolov, S., Jungers, R.M. (eds.) HSCC '21: 24th ACM International Conference on Hybrid Systems: Computation and Control, Nashville, Tennessee, May 19-21, 2021. pp. 24:1–24:11. ACM (2021). https://doi.org/10. 1145/3447928.3456646, https://doi.org/10.1145/3447928.3456646
2. Abate, A., Ahmed, D., Giacobbe, M., Peruffo, A.: Formal synthesis of lyapunov neural networks. IEEE Control. Syst. Lett. **5**(3), 773–778 (2021). https://doi.org/10.1109/LCSYS.2020.3005328, https://doi.org/10. 1109/LCSYS.2020.3005328
3. Abate, A., Giacobbe, M., Roy, D.: Learning probabilistic termination proofs. In: Silva, A., Leino, K.R.M. (eds.) Computer Aided Verification - 33rd International Conference, CAV 2021, Virtual Event, July 20-23, 2021, Proceedings, Part II. Lecture Notes in Computer Science, vol. 12760, pp. 3–26. Springer (2021). https://doi.org/10.1007/978-3-030-81688-9_1, https://doi.org/10. 1007/978-3-030-81688-9_1
4. Achiam, J., Held, D., Tamar, A., Abbeel, P.: Constrained policy optimization. In: International Conference on Machine Learning. pp. 22–31. PMLR (2017)
5. Agrawal, S., Chatterjee, K., Novotný, P.: Lexicographic ranking supermartingales: an efficient approach to termination of probabilistic programs. Proc. ACM Program. Lang. **2**(POPL), 34:1–34:32 (2018). https://doi.org/10.1145/3158122, https://doi.org/10.1145/3158122
6. Aksaray, D., Jones, A., Kong, Z., Schwager, M., Belta, C.: Q-learning for robust satisfaction of signal temporal logic specifications. In: 55th IEEE Conference on Decision and Control, CDC 2016, Las Vegas, NV, USA, December 12-14, 2016. pp. 6565–6570. IEEE (2016). https://doi.org/10.1109/CDC.2016.7799279, https://doi.org/10.1109/CDC.2016.7799279
7. Alshiekh, M., Bloem, R., Ehlers, R., Könighofer, B., Niekum, S., Topcu, U.: Safe reinforcement learning via shielding. In: McIlraith, S.A., Weinberger, K.Q. (eds.) Proceedings of the Thirty-Second AAAI Conference on Artificial Intelligence, (AAAI-18), the 30th innovative Applications of Artificial Intelligence (IAAI-18), and the 8th AAAI Symposium on Educational Advances in Artificial Intelligence (EAAI-18), New Orleans, Louisiana, USA, February 2-7, 2018. pp. 2669–2678. AAAI Press (2018), https://www.aaai.org/ocs/index.php/AAAI/AAAI18/paper/view/17211
8. Altman, E.: Constrained Markov decision processes, vol. 7. CRC Press (1999)
9. Amodei, D., Olah, C., Steinhardt, J., Christiano, P.F., Schulman, J., Mané, D.: Concrete problems in AI safety. CoRR **abs/1606.06565** (2016), http://arxiv. org/abs/1606.06565
10. Anderson, G., Verma, A., Dillig, I., Chaudhuri, S.: Neurosymbolic reinforcement learning with formally verified exploration. In: Larochelle, H., Ranzato, M., Hadsell, R., Balcan, M., Lin, H. (eds.) Advances in Neural Information Processing Systems 33: Annual Conference on Neural Information Processing Systems 2020, NeurIPS 2020, December 6-12, 2020, virtual (2020), https://proceedings.neurips.cc/paper/2020/hash/ 448d5eda79895153938a8431919f4c9f-Abstract.html
11. Bacci, E., Giacobbe, M., Parker, D.: Verifying reinforcement learning up to infinity. In: Zhou, Z. (ed.) Proceedings of the Thirtieth International Joint Conference on Artificial Intelligence, IJCAI 2021, Virtual Event / Montreal, Canada, 19-27 August 2021. pp. 2154–2160. ijcai.org (2021). https://doi.org/10.24963/ijcai. 2021/297, https://doi.org/10.24963/ijcai.2021/297

12. Brafman, R.I., Giacomo, G.D., Patrizi, F.: Ltlf/ldlf non-markovian rewards. In: McIlraith, S.A., Weinberger, K.Q. (eds.) Proceedings of the Thirty-Second AAAI Conference on Artificial Intelligence, (AAAI-18), the 30th innovative Applications of Artificial Intelligence (IAAI-18), and the 8th AAAI Symposium on Educational Advances in Artificial Intelligence (EAAI-18), New Orleans, Louisiana, USA, February 2-7, 2018. pp. 1771–1778. AAAI Press (2018), https://www.aaai.org/ocs/index.php/AAAI/AAAI18/paper/view/17342

13. Camacho, A., Icarte, R.T., Klassen, T.Q., Valenzano, R.A., McIlraith, S.A.: LTL and beyond: Formal languages for reward function specification in reinforcement learning. In: Kraus, S. (ed.) Proceedings of the Twenty-Eighth International Joint Conference on Artificial Intelligence, IJCAI 2019, Macao, China, August 10-16, 2019. pp. 6065–6073. ijcai.org (2019). https://doi.org/10.24963/ijcai.2019/840, https://doi.org/10.24963/ijcai.2019/840

14. Cauchi, N., Abate, A.: Stochy-automated verification and synthesis of stochastic processes. In: Proceedings of the 22nd ACM International Conference on Hybrid Systems: Computation and Control. pp. 258–259 (2019)

15. Chakarov, A., Sankaranarayanan, S.: Probabilistic program analysis with martingales. In: Sharygina, N., Veith, H. (eds.) Computer Aided Verification - 25th International Conference, CAV 2013, Saint Petersburg, Russia, July 13-19, 2013. Proceedings. Lecture Notes in Computer Science, vol. 8044, pp. 511–526. Springer (2013). https://doi.org/10.1007/978-3-642-39799-8_34, https://doi.org/10.1007/978-3-642-39799-8_34

16. Chakarov, A., Voronin, Y., Sankaranarayanan, S.: Deductive proofs of almost sure persistence and recurrence properties. In: Chechik, M., Raskin, J. (eds.) Tools and Algorithms for the Construction and Analysis of Systems - 22nd International Conference, TACAS 2016, Held as Part of the European Joint Conferences on Theory and Practice of Software, ETAPS 2016, Eindhoven, The Netherlands, April 2-8, 2016, Proceedings. Lecture Notes in Computer Science, vol. 9636, pp. 260–279. Springer (2016). https://doi.org/10.1007/978-3-662-49674-9_15, https://doi.org/10.1007/978-3-662-49674-9_15

17. Chang, Y., Gao, S.: Stabilizing neural control using self-learned almost lyapunov critics. In: IEEE International Conference on Robotics and Automation, ICRA 2021, Xi'an, China, May 30 - June 5, 2021. pp. 1803–1809. IEEE (2021). https://doi.org/10.1109/ICRA48506.2021.9560886, https://doi.org/10.1109/ICRA48506.2021.9560886

18. Chang, Y., Roohi, N., Gao, S.: Neural lyapunov control. In: Wallach, H.M., Larochelle, H., Beygelzimer, A., d'Alché-Buc, F., Fox, E.B., Garnett, R. (eds.) Advances in Neural Information Processing Systems 32: Annual Conference on Neural Information Processing Systems 2019, NeurIPS 2019, December 8-14, 2019, Vancouver, BC, Canada. pp. 3240–3249 (2019), https://proceedings.neurips.cc/paper/2019/hash/2647c1dba23bc0e0f9cdf75339e120d2-Abstract.html

19. Chatterjee, K., Fu, H., Goharshady, A.K.: Termination analysis of probabilistic programs through positivstellensatz's. In: Chaudhuri, S., Farzan, A. (eds.) Computer Aided Verification - 28th International Conference, CAV 2016, Toronto, ON, Canada, July 17-23, 2016, Proceedings, Part I. Lecture Notes in Computer Science, vol. 9779, pp. 3–22. Springer (2016). https://doi.org/10.1007/978-3-319-41528-4_1, https://doi.org/10.1007/978-3-319-41528-4_1

20. Chatterjee, K., Fu, H., Novotný, P., Hasheminezhad, R.: Algorithmic analysis of qualitative and quantitative termination problems for affine probabilistic programs. In: Bodík, R., Majumdar, R. (eds.) Proceedings of the 43rd Annual ACM SIGPLAN-SIGACT Symposium on Principles of Programming Languages, POPL 2016, St. Petersburg, FL, USA, January 20 - 22, 2016. pp. 327–

342. ACM (2016). https://doi.org/10.1145/2837614.2837639, https://doi.org/10.1145/2837614.2837639
21. Chatterjee, K., Goharshady, A.K., Meggendorfer, T., Zikelic, D.: Sound and complete certificates for quantitative termination analysis of probabilistic programs. In: Shoham, S., Vizel, Y. (eds.) Computer Aided Verification - 34th International Conference, CAV 2022, Haifa, Israel, August 7-10, 2022, Proceedings, Part I. Lecture Notes in Computer Science, vol. 13371, pp. 55–78. Springer (2022). https://doi.org/10.1007/978-3-031-13185-1_4, https://doi.org/10.1007/978-3-031-13185-1_4
22. Chatterjee, K., Goharshady, E.K., Novotný, P., Zárevúcky, J., Zikelic, D.: On lexicographic proof rules for probabilistic termination. In: Huisman, M., Pasareanu, C.S., Zhan, N. (eds.) Formal Methods - 24th International Symposium, FM 2021, Virtual Event, November 20-26, 2021, Proceedings. Lecture Notes in Computer Science, vol. 13047, pp. 619–639. Springer (2021). https://doi.org/10.1007/978-3-030-90870-6_33, https://doi.org/10.1007/978-3-030-90870-6_33
23. Chatterjee, K., Novotný, P., Zikelic, D.: Stochastic invariants for probabilistic termination. In: Castagna, G., Gordon, A.D. (eds.) Proceedings of the 44th ACM SIGPLAN Symposium on Principles of Programming Languages, POPL 2017, Paris, France, January 18-20, 2017. pp. 145–160. ACM (2017). https://doi.org/10.1145/3009837.3009873, https://doi.org/10.1145/3009837.3009873
24. Cousot, P., Cousot, R.: Abstract interpretation: A unified lattice model for static analysis of programs by construction or approximation of fixpoints. In: Graham, R.M., Harrison, M.A., Sethi, R. (eds.) Conference Record of the Fourth ACM Symposium on Principles of Programming Languages, Los Angeles, California, USA, January 1977. pp. 238–252. ACM (1977). https://doi.org/10.1145/512950.512973, https://doi.org/10.1145/512950.512973
25. Crespo, L.G., Sun, J.: Stochastic optimal control via bellman's principle. Autom. 39(12), 2109–2114 (2003). https://doi.org/10.1016/S0005-1098(03)00238-3, https://doi.org/10.1016/S0005-1098(03)00238-3
26. Dawson, C., Gao, S., Fan, C.: Safe control with learned certificates: A survey of neural lyapunov, barrier, and contraction methods. CoRR abs/2202.11762 (2022), https://arxiv.org/abs/2202.11762
27. García, J., Fernández, F.: A comprehensive survey on safe reinforcement learning. J. Mach. Learn. Res. 16, 1437–1480 (2015), http://dl.acm.org/citation.cfm?id=2886795
28. Geibel, P.: Reinforcement learning for mdps with constraints. In: Fürnkranz, J., Scheffer, T., Spiliopoulou, M. (eds.) Machine Learning: ECML 2006, 17th European Conference on Machine Learning, Berlin, Germany, September 18-22, 2006, Proceedings. Lecture Notes in Computer Science, vol. 4212, pp. 646–653. Springer (2006). https://doi.org/10.1007/11871842_63, https://doi.org/10.1007/11871842_63
29. Giacobbe, M., Hasanbeig, M., Kroening, D., Wijk, H.: Shielding atari games with bounded prescience. In: Dignum, F., Lomuscio, A., Endriss, U., Nowé, A. (eds.) AAMAS '21: 20th International Conference on Autonomous Agents and Multiagent Systems, Virtual Event, United Kingdom, May 3-7, 2021. pp. 1507–1509. ACM (2021). https://doi.org/10.5555/3463952.3464141, https://www.ifaamas.org/Proceedings/aamas2021/pdfs/p1507.pdf
30. Gowal, S., Dvijotham, K., Stanforth, R., Bunel, R., Qin, C., Uesato, J., Arandjelovic, R., Mann, T.A., Kohli, P.: On the effectiveness of interval bound propagation for training verifiably robust models. CoRR abs/1810.12715 (2018), http://arxiv.org/abs/1810.12715
31. Hahn, E.M., Perez, M., Schewe, S., Somenzi, F., Trivedi, A., Wojtczak, D.: Omega-regular objectives in model-free reinforcement learning. In: Vojnar, T., Zhang,

L. (eds.) Tools and Algorithms for the Construction and Analysis of Systems - 25th International Conference, TACAS 2019, Held as Part of the European Joint Conferences on Theory and Practice of Software, ETAPS 2019, Prague, Czech Republic, April 6-11, 2019, Proceedings, Part I. Lecture Notes in Computer Science, vol. 11427, pp. 395–412. Springer (2019). https://doi.org/10.1007/978-3-030-17462-0_27, https://doi.org/10.1007/978-3-030-17462-0_27

32. Hasanbeig, M., Kantaros, Y., Abate, A., Kroening, D., Pappas, G.J., Lee, I.: Reinforcement learning for temporal logic control synthesis with probabilistic satisfaction guarantees. In: 58th IEEE Conference on Decision and Control, CDC 2019, Nice, France, December 11-13, 2019. pp. 5338–5343. IEEE (2019). https://doi.org/10.1109/CDC40024.2019.9028919, https://doi.org/10.1109/CDC40024.2019.9028919

33. Henrion, D., Garulli, A.: Positive polynomials in control, vol. 312. Springer Science & Business Media (2005)

34. Icarte, R.T., Klassen, T.Q., Valenzano, R.A., McIlraith, S.A.: Using reward machines for high-level task specification and decomposition in reinforcement learning. In: Dy, J.G., Krause, A. (eds.) Proceedings of the 35th International Conference on Machine Learning, ICML 2018, Stockholmsmässan, Stockholm, Sweden, July 10-15, 2018. Proceedings of Machine Learning Research, vol. 80, pp. 2112–2121. PMLR (2018), http://proceedings.mlr.press/v80/icarte18a.html

35. Inala, J.P., Bastani, O., Tavares, Z., Solar-Lezama, A.: Synthesizing programmatic policies that inductively generalize. In: 8th International Conference on Learning Representations, ICLR 2020, Addis Ababa, Ethiopia, April 26-30, 2020. OpenReview.net (2020), https://openreview.net/forum?id=S1l8oANFDH

36. Jansen, N., Könighofer, B., Junges, S., Serban, A., Bloem, R.: Safe reinforcement learning using probabilistic shields (invited paper). In: Konnov, I., Kovács, L. (eds.) 31st International Conference on Concurrency Theory, CONCUR 2020, September 1-4, 2020, Vienna, Austria (Virtual Conference). LIPIcs, vol. 171, pp. 3:1–3:16. Schloss Dagstuhl - Leibniz-Zentrum für Informatik (2020). https://doi.org/10.4230/LIPIcs.CONCUR.2020.3, https://doi.org/10.4230/LIPIcs.CONCUR.2020.3

37. Jarvis-Wloszek, Z., Feeley, R., Tan, W., Sun, K., Packard, A.: Some controls applications of sum of squares programming. In: 42nd IEEE international conference on decision and control (IEEE Cat. No. 03CH37475). vol. 5, pp. 4676–4681. IEEE (2003)

38. Jin, W., Wang, Z., Yang, Z., Mou, S.: Neural certificates for safe control policies. CoRR abs/2006.08465 (2020), https://arxiv.org/abs/2006.08465

39. Jothimurugan, K., Alur, R., Bastani, O.: A composable specification language for reinforcement learning tasks. In: Wallach, H.M., Larochelle, H., Beygelzimer, A., d'Alché-Buc, F., Fox, E.B., Garnett, R. (eds.) Advances in Neural Information Processing Systems 32: Annual Conference on Neural Information Processing Systems 2019, NeurIPS 2019, December 8-14, 2019, Vancouver, BC, Canada. pp. 13021–13030 (2019), https://proceedings.neurips.cc/paper/2019/hash/f5aa4bd09c07d8b2f65bad6c7cd3358f-Abstract.html

40. Jothimurugan, K., Bansal, S., Bastani, O., Alur, R.: Compositional reinforcement learning from logical specifications. In: Ranzato, M., Beygelzimer, A., Dauphin, Y.N., Liang, P., Vaughan, J.W. (eds.) Advances in Neural Information Processing Systems 34: Annual Conference on Neural Information Processing Systems 2021, NeurIPS 2021, December 6-14, 2021, virtual. pp. 10026–10039 (2021), https://proceedings.neurips.cc/paper/2021/hash/531db99cb00833bcd414459069dc7387-Abstract.html

41. Kushner, H.J.: A partial history of the early development of continuous-time nonlinear stochastic systems theory. Autom. 50(2), 303–334 (2014). https:

`//doi.org/10.1016/j.automatica.2013.10.013`, `https://doi.org/10.1016/j.`
`automatica.2013.10.013`
42. Lavaei, A., Khaled, M., Soudjani, S., Zamani, M.: AMYTISS: parallelized automated controller synthesis for large-scale stochastic systems. In: Lahiri, S.K., Wang, C. (eds.) Computer Aided Verification - 32nd International Conference, CAV 2020, Los Angeles, CA, USA, July 21-24, 2020, Proceedings, Part II. Lecture Notes in Computer Science, vol. 12225, pp. 461–474. Springer (2020). `https://doi.org/10.1007/978-3-030-53291-8_24`, `https://doi.org/10.1007/978-3-030-53291-8_24`
43. Lechner, M., Zikelic, D., Chatterjee, K., Henzinger, T.A.: Infinite time horizon safety of bayesian neural networks. In: Ranzato, M., Beygelzimer, A., Dauphin, Y.N., Liang, P., Vaughan, J.W. (eds.) Advances in Neural Information Processing Systems 34: Annual Conference on Neural Information Processing Systems 2021, NeurIPS 2021, December 6-14, 2021, virtual. pp. 10171–10185 (2021), `https://proceedings.neurips.cc/paper/2021/hash/544defa9fddff50c53b71c43e0da72be-Abstract.html`
44. Lechner, M., Zikelic, D., Chatterjee, K., Henzinger, T.A.: Stability verification in stochastic control systems via neural network supermartingales. In: Thirty-Sixth AAAI Conference on Artificial Intelligence, AAAI 2022, Thirty-Fourth Conference on Innovative Applications of Artificial Intelligence, IAAI 2022, The Twelveth Symposium on Educational Advances in Artificial Intelligence, EAAI 2022 Virtual Event, February 22 - March 1, 2022. pp. 7326–7336. AAAI Press (2022), `https://ojs.aaai.org/index.php/AAAI/article/view/20695`
45. Li, X., Vasile, C.I., Belta, C.: Reinforcement learning with temporal logic rewards. In: 2017 IEEE/RSJ International Conference on Intelligent Robots and Systems, IROS 2017, Vancouver, BC, Canada, September 24-28, 2017. pp. 3834–3839. IEEE (2017). `https://doi.org/10.1109/IROS.2017.8206234`, `https://doi.org/10.1109/IROS.2017.8206234`
46. Lyapunov, A.M.: The general problem of the stability of motion. International journal of control **55**(3), 531–534 (1992)
47. McIver, A., Morgan, C., Kaminski, B.L., Katoen, J.: A new proof rule for almostsure termination. Proc. ACM Program. Lang. **2**(POPL), 33:1–33:28 (2018). `https://doi.org/10.1145/3158121`, `https://doi.org/10.1145/3158121`
48. Murphy, K.P.: Machine learning - a probabilistic perspective. Adaptive computation and machine learning series, MIT Press (2012)
49. Parrilo, P.A.: Structured semidefinite programs and semialgebraic geometry methods in robustness and optimization. California Institute of Technology (2000)
50. Prajna, S., Jadbabaie, A., Pappas, G.J.: A framework for worst-case and stochastic safety verification using barrier certificates. IEEE Trans. Autom. Control. **52**(8), 1415–1428 (2007). `https://doi.org/10.1109/TAC.2007.902736`, `https://doi.org/10.1109/TAC.2007.902736`
51. Puterman, M.L.: Markov Decision Processes: Discrete Stochastic Dynamic Programming. Wiley Series in Probability and Statistics, Wiley (1994). `https://doi.org/10.1002/9780470316887`, `https://doi.org/10.1002/9780470316887`
52. Qin, Z., Zhang, K., Chen, Y., Chen, J., Fan, C.: Learning safe multi-agent control with decentralized neural barrier certificates. In: 9th International Conference on Learning Representations, ICLR 2021, Virtual Event, Austria, May 3-7, 2021. OpenReview.net (2021), `https://openreview.net/forum?id=P6_q1BRxY8Q`
53. Richards, S.M., Berkenkamp, F., Krause, A.: The lyapunov neural network: Adaptive stability certification for safe learning of dynamical systems. In: 2nd Annual Conference on Robot Learning, CoRL 2018, Zürich, Switzerland, 29-31 October 2018, Proceedings. Proceedings of Machine Learning Research, vol. 87, pp. 466–476. PMLR (2018), `http://proceedings.mlr.press/v87/richards18a.html`

54. Schulman, J., Wolski, F., Dhariwal, P., Radford, A., Klimov, O.: Proximal policy optimization algorithms. arXiv preprint arXiv:1707.06347 (2017)
55. Solar-Lezama, A., Tancau, L., Bodík, R., Seshia, S.A., Saraswat, V.A.: Combinatorial sketching for finite programs. In: Shen, J.P., Martonosi, M. (eds.) Proceedings of the 12th International Conference on Architectural Support for Programming Languages and Operating Systems, ASPLOS 2006, San Jose, CA, USA, October 21-25, 2006. pp. 404–415. ACM (2006). https://doi.org/10.1145/1168857.1168907, https://doi.org/10.1145/1168857.1168907
56. Soudjani, S.E.Z., Gevaerts, C., Abate, A.: FAUST ^{2} : Formal abstractions of uncountable-state stochastic processes. In: Baier, C., Tinelli, C. (eds.) Tools and Algorithms for the Construction and Analysis of Systems - 21st International Conference, TACAS 2015, Held as Part of the European Joint Conferences on Theory and Practice of Software, ETAPS 2015, London, UK, April 11-18, 2015. Proceedings. Lecture Notes in Computer Science, vol. 9035, pp. 272–286. Springer (2015). https://doi.org/10.1007/978-3-662-46681-0_23, https://doi.org/10.1007/978-3-662-46681-0_23
57. Szegedy, C., Zaremba, W., Sutskever, I., Bruna, J., Erhan, D., Goodfellow, I.J., Fergus, R.: Intriguing properties of neural networks. In: Bengio, Y., LeCun, Y. (eds.) 2nd International Conference on Learning Representations, ICLR 2014, Banff, AB, Canada, April 14-16, 2014, Conference Track Proceedings (2014), http://arxiv.org/abs/1312.6199
58. Taylor, A.J., Singletary, A., Yue, Y., Ames, A.D.: Learning for safety-critical control with control barrier functions. In: Bayen, A.M., Jadbabaie, A., Pappas, G.J., Parrilo, P.A., Recht, B., Tomlin, C.J., Zeilinger, M.N. (eds.) Proceedings of the 2nd Annual Conference on Learning for Dynamics and Control, L4DC 2020, Online Event, Berkeley, CA, USA, 11-12 June 2020. Proceedings of Machine Learning Research, vol. 120, pp. 708–717. PMLR (2020), http://proceedings.mlr.press/v120/taylor20a.html
59. Uchibe, E., Doya, K.: Constrained reinforcement learning from intrinsic and extrinsic rewards. In: 2007 IEEE 6th International Conference on Development and Learning. pp. 163–168. IEEE (2007)
60. Vaidya, U.: Stochastic stability analysis of discrete-time system using lyapunov measure. In: American Control Conference, ACC 2015, Chicago, IL, USA, July 1-3, 2015. pp. 4646–4651. IEEE (2015). https://doi.org/10.1109/ACC.2015.7172061, https://doi.org/10.1109/ACC.2015.7172061
61. Verma, A., Le, H.M., Yue, Y., Chaudhuri, S.: Imitation-projected programmatic reinforcement learning. In: Wallach, H.M., Larochelle, H., Beygelzimer, A., d'Alché-Buc, F., Fox, E.B., Garnett, R. (eds.) Advances in Neural Information Processing Systems 32: Annual Conference on Neural Information Processing Systems 2019, NeurIPS 2019, December 8-14, 2019, Vancouver, BC, Canada. pp. 15726–15737 (2019), https://proceedings.neurips.cc/paper/2019/hash/5a44a53b7d26bb1e54c05222f186dcfb-Abstract.html
62. Verma, A., Murali, V., Singh, R., Kohli, P., Chaudhuri, S.: Programmatically interpretable reinforcement learning. In: Dy, J.G., Krause, A. (eds.) Proceedings of the 35th International Conference on Machine Learning, ICML 2018, Stockholmsmässan, Stockholm, Sweden, July 10-15, 2018. Proceedings of Machine Learning Research, vol. 80, pp. 5052–5061. PMLR (2018), http://proceedings.mlr.press/v80/verma18a.html
63. Vinod, A.P., Gleason, J.D., Oishi, M.M.K.: Sreachtools: a MATLAB stochastic reachability toolbox. In: Ozay, N., Prabhakar, P. (eds.) Proceedings of the 22nd ACM International Conference on Hybrid Systems: Computation and Control, HSCC 2019, Montreal, QC, Canada, April 16-18, 2019. pp. 33–38.

ACM (2019). https://doi.org/10.1145/3302504.3311809, https://doi.org/10.1145/3302504.3311809

64. Wang, J., Sun, Y., Fu, H., Chatterjee, K., Goharshady, A.K.: Quantitative analysis of assertion violations in probabilistic programs. In: Freund, S.N., Yahav, E. (eds.) PLDI '21: 42nd ACM SIGPLAN International Conference on Programming Language Design and Implementation, Virtual Event, Canada, June 20-25, 2021. pp. 1171–1186. ACM (2021). https://doi.org/10.1145/3453483.3454102, https://doi.org/10.1145/3453483.3454102

65. Wang, P., Fu, H., Goharshady, A.K., Chatterjee, K., Qin, X., Shi, W.: Cost analysis of nondeterministic probabilistic programs. In: McKinley, K.S., Fisher, K. (eds.) Proceedings of the 40th ACM SIGPLAN Conference on Programming Language Design and Implementation, PLDI 2019, Phoenix, AZ, USA, June 22-26, 2019. pp. 204–220. ACM (2019). https://doi.org/10.1145/3314221.3314581, https://doi.org/10.1145/3314221.3314581

66. Williams, D.: Probability with Martingales. Cambridge mathematical textbooks, Cambridge University Press (1991)

67. Zhu, H., Xiong, Z., Magill, S., Jagannathan, S.: An inductive synthesis framework for verifiable reinforcement learning. In: McKinley, K.S., Fisher, K. (eds.) Proceedings of the 40th ACM SIGPLAN Conference on Programming Language Design and Implementation, PLDI 2019, Phoenix, AZ, USA, June 22-26, 2019. pp. 686–701. ACM (2019). https://doi.org/10.1145/3314221.3314638, https://doi.org/10.1145/3314221.3314638

68. Zikelic, D., Lechner, M., Henzinger, T.A., Chatterjee, K.: Learning control policies for stochastic systems with reach-avoid guarantees. To appear at the Thirty-Seventh AAAI Conference on Artificial Intelligence (AAAI-23) (2023)

Model Checking

Bounded Model Checking for Asynchronous Hyperproperties*

Tzu-Han Hsu[1], Borzoo Bonakdarpour[1]([✉]), Bernd Finkbeiner[2], and César Sánchez[3]

[1] Michigan State University, East Lansing, MI, USA {tzuhan,borzoo}@msu.edu
[2] CISPA Helmholtz Center, Saarbrücken, Germany finkbeiner@cispa.de
[3] IMDEA Software Institute, Madrid, Spain cesar.sanchez@imdea.org

Abstract. Many types of attacks on confidentiality stem from the nondeterministic nature of the environment that computer programs operate in. We focus on verification of confidentiality in nondeterministic environments by reasoning about *asynchronous hyperproperties*. We generalize the temporal logic A-HLTL to allow nested *trajectory* quantification, where a trajectory determines how different execution traces may advance and stutter. We propose a bounded model checking algorithm for A-HLTL based on QBF-solving for a fragment of A-HLTL and evaluate it by various case studies on concurrent programs, scheduling attacks, compiler optimization, speculative execution, and cache timing attacks. We also rigorously analyze the complexity of model checking A-HLTL.

1 Introduction

Motivation. Consider the concurrent program [10] shown in Fig. 1, where h is a secret variable, and `await` command is a conditional critical region. This program should satisfy the following information-flow policy: "Any sequences of observable outputs produced by an interleaving should be reproducible by some other interleaving for a different value of h". If this is the case, then an attacker cannot successfully guess the value of h from the sequence of observable outputs of the `print()` statements. For example, Fig. 2 shows how one can align two interleavings of threads T1 and T2 with respect to the observable sequence of outputs 'abcd', given two different values of secret h. Let us call such an alignment a *trajectory* (illustrated by the sequence of dashed lines). However, if

```
1  Thread T1() {
2    await sem>0 then
3      sem = sem - 1;
4      print('a');
5      v = v+1;
6      print('b');
7      sem = sem + 1;
8  }
9
10 Thread T2 (){
11   print('c');
12   if h then
13     await sem>0 then
14       sem = sem - 1;
15       v = v+2;
16       sem = sem + 1;
17   else
18     skip;
19   print('d');
20 }
```

Fig. 1: T1 and T2 leak the value of h.

---

* This research has been partially supported by the United States NSF SaTC Award 2100989, by the Madrid Regional Gov. Project BLOQUES-CM (S2018/TCS-4339), by Project PRODIGY (TED2021-132464B-I00) funded by MCIN/AEI/10.13039/501100011033/ and the EU NextGenerationEU/PRTR, by the German Research Foundation (DFG) as part of TRR 248 (389792660), and by the European Research Council (ERC) Grant HYPER (101055412)

S. Sankaranarayanan and N. Sharygina (Eds.): TACAS 2023, LNCS 13993, pp. 29–46, 2023.
https://doi.org/10.1007/978-3-031-30823-9_2

thread T1 holds the semaphore and executes the critical region as an atomic operation. Then, output 'acdb' arising due to concurrent execution of threads T1 and T2 reveals the value of h as 0, as the same output cannot be reproduced when h=1. Thus, the program in Fig. 1 violates the above policy.

The above policy is an example of a *hyperproperty* [5]; i.e., a set of sets of execution traces. In addition to information-flow requirements, hyperproperties can express other complex requirements such as linearizability [12] and control conditions in cyber-physical systems such as robustness and sensitivity. The temporal logic A-HLTL [1] can express hyperproperties whose sets of traces advance at different speeds, allowing stuttering steps. For example, the above policy can be expressed in A-HLTL by the following formula: $\varphi_{NI} = \forall \pi.\exists \pi'.E\tau.(h_{\pi,\tau} \neq h_{\pi',\tau}) \wedge \square(obs_{\pi,\tau} = obs_{\pi',\tau})$, where obs denotes the output observations, meaning that for all executions (i.e., interleavings) π, there should exist another execution π' and a trajectory τ, such that π and π' start from different values of h and τ can align all the observations along π and π' (see Fig. 2). A-HLTL can reason about *one* source of *nondeterminism* by the scheduler in the system that may lead to information leak. Indeed, the model checking algorithms proposed in [1] can discover the bug in the program in Fig. 1.

```
1   Thread T1 (){
2     while (true){
3       await sem>0 then
4         sem = sem - 1;
5         print('a');
6         v = v+1;
7         print('b');
8         sem = sem + 1;
9     }
10  }

12  Thread T2(){
13    while (true)
14      h = read(Channel1);
15  }

17  Thread T3(){
18    while (true){
19      print('c');
20      if (h == 1) then
21        await sem>0 then
22          sem = sem - 1;
23          v = v+2;
24          sem = sem + 1;
25      else
26        skip;
27        print('d');
28    }
29  }

31  Thread T4(){
32    while (true)
33      l = read(Channel2);
34  }
```

Fig. 3: T1 and T2 receive inputs from asynch. channels read by T3 and T4.

Now, consider a more complex version of the same program shown in Fig. 3 inspired by modern programming languages such as Go and P that allow CSP-style concurrency. Here, new threads T3 and T4 read the values of secret input h and public input l from two asynchronous channels, rendering two different sources of nondeterminism: (1) the scheduler that results in different interleavings, and (2) data availability in the channels. This, in turn, means formula φ_{NI} no longer captures the following specification of the program, which should be:

> *"Any sequence of observable outputs produced by an interleaving should be reproducible by some other interleaving such that for all alignments of public inputs, there exists an alignment of the public outputs".*

Satisfaction of this policy (not expressible in A-HLTL as proposed in [1]) prohibits an attacker from successfully determining the sequence of values of h.

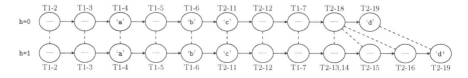

Fig. 2: Two secure interleavings for the program in Fig. 1

Contributions. In this paper, we strive for a general logic-based approach that enables model checking of a rich set of asynchronous hyperproperties. To this end, we concentrate on A-HLTL model checking for programs subject to multiple sources of nondeterminism. Our first contribution is a generalization of A-HLTL that allows nested *trajectory* quantification. For example, the above policy requires reasoning about two different trajectories that cannot be composed into one since their sources of nondeterminism are different. This observation motivates the need for enriching A-HLTL with the tools to quantify over trajectories. This generalization enables expressing policies such as follows:

$$\varphi_{\mathsf{NI_{nd}}} = \forall \pi.\exists \pi'.\mathsf{A}\tau.\mathsf{E}\tau'.\left(\Diamond (h_{\pi,\tau} \neq h_{\pi',\tau}) \wedge \Box (l_{\pi,\tau} = l_{\pi',\tau}) \right) \rightarrow \Box (\mathsf{obs}_{\pi,\tau'} = \mathsf{obs}_{\pi',\tau'}),$$

where A and E denote the universal (res., existential) trajectory quantifiers.

Our second contribution is a *bounded model checking* (BMC) algorithm for a fragment of the extended A-HLTL that allows an arbitrary number of trace quantifier alternations and up to one trajectory quantifier alternation. Following [15], we propose two bounded semantics (called *optimistic* and *pessimistic*) for A-HLTL based on the satisfaction of eventualities. We introduce a reduction to the satisfiability problem for quantified Boolean formulas (QBF) and prove that our translation provides decision procedures for A-HLTL BMC for *terminating systems*, i.e., those whose Kripke structure is acyclic. Our focus on terminating programs is due to the general undecidability of A-HLTL model checking [1]. As in the classic BMC for LTL, the power of our technique is in hunting bugs that are often in the shallow parts of reachable states.

Our third contribution is rigorous complexity analysis of A-HLTL model checking for terminating programs (see Table 1). We show that for formulas with only one trajectory quantifier the complexity is aligned with that of classic synchronous semantics of HyperLTL [4]. However, the complexity of A-HLTL model checking with multiple trajectory quantifiers is one step higher than HyperLTL model checking in the polynomial hierarchy. An interesting observation here is that the complexity of model checking a formula with two existential trajectory quantifiers is one step higher than one with only one existential quantifier

Multiple Traces – Single Trajectory		
$\exists^+ E \,/\, \forall^+ A$	NL-complete (Theorem 2)	
$[\exists(\exists/\forall)^+(A/E)]^k$	Σ^p_k-complete	Thm 3
$[\forall(\exists/\forall)^+(E/A)]^k$	Π^p_k-complete	Thm 3
Multiple Traces – Multiple Trajectories		
$[\exists(\exists/\forall)^+(E^+E)]^k$	Σ^p_{k+1}-complete	Thm 4
$[\forall(\forall/\exists)^+(A^+A)]^k$	Π^p_{k+1}-complete	Thm 4
$[\exists(\exists/\forall)^+A^+E^+]^k$	Σ^p_{k+1}-complete	Thm 5
$[\forall(\forall/\exists)^+E^+A^+]^k$	Π^p_{k+1}-complete	Thm 5
A-HLTL	PSPACE	

Table 1: A-HLTL model checking complexity for acyclic models.

although the plurality of the quantifiers does not change. Generally speaking, A-HLTL model checking for terminating programs remains in PSPACE.

Finally, we have implemented our BMC technique. We evaluate our implementation on verification of four case studies: (1) information-flow security in concurrent programs, (2) information leak in speculative executions, (3) preservation of security in compiler optimization, and (4) cache-based timing attacks. These case studies exhibit a proof of concept for the highly intricate nature of information-flow requirements and how our foundational theoretical results handle them.

Related Work. The concept of hyperproperties is due to Clarkson and Schneider [5]. HyperLTL [4] and A-HLTL are currently the only logics for which practical model checking algorithms are known [8,7,15,1]. For HyperLTL, the algorithms have been implemented in the model checkers MCHYPER and bounded model checker HYPERQB [14]. HyperLTL is limited to synchronous hyperproperties. The A-HLTL model checking problem is known to be undecidable in general [1]. However, decidable fragments that can express observational determinism, noninterference, and linearizability have been identified. This paper generalizes A-HLTL by allowing nested trajectory quantifiers and due to the general undecidability result focuses on terminating programs.

FOL[E] [6] can express a limited form of asynchronous hyperproperties. As shown in [6], FOL[E] is subsumed by HyperLTL with additional quantification over predicates. For $S1S[E]$ and H_μ, the model checking problem is in general undecidable; for H_μ, two fragments, the k-synchronous, k-context bounded fragments, have been identified for which model checking remains decidable [11]. Other logical extensions of HyperLTL with asynchronous capabilities are studied in [3], including their decidable fragments, but their model checking problems have not been implemented and the relative expressive power with respect to other asynchronous formalisms has not been studied.

2 Extended Asynchronous HyperLTL

Preliminaries. Given a natural number $k \in \mathbb{N}_0$, we use $[k]$ for the set $\{0, \ldots, k\}$. Let AP be a set of *atomic propositions* and $\Sigma = 2^{\mathsf{AP}}$ be the *alphabet*, where we call each element of Σ a *letter*. A *trace* is an infinite sequence $\sigma = a_0 a_1 \cdots$ of letters from Σ. We denote the set of all infinite traces by Σ^ω. We use $\sigma(i)$ for a_i and σ^i for the suffix $a_i a_{i+1} \cdots$. A *pointed trace* is a pair (σ, p), where $p \in \mathbb{N}_0$ is a natural number (called the *pointer*). Pointed traces allow to traverse a trace by moving the pointer. Given a pointed trace (σ, p) and $n > 0$, we use $(\sigma, p) + n$ to denote the resulting trace $(\sigma, p + n)$. We denote the set of all pointed traces by $\mathsf{PTR} = \{(\sigma, p) \mid \sigma \in \Sigma^\omega \text{ and } p \in \mathbb{N}_0\}$.

A *Kripke structure* is a tuple $\mathcal{K} = \langle S, s_{init}, \delta, L \rangle$, where S is a set of states, $s_{init} \in S$ is the initial state, $\delta \subseteq S \times S$ is a transition relation, and $L : S \to \Sigma$ is a labeling function on the states of $\mathcal{K}$. We require that for each $s \in S$, there exists $s' \in S$, such that $(s, s') \in \delta$.   □

A *path* of a Kripke structure $\mathcal{K}$ is an infinite sequence of states $s(0)s(1) \cdots \in S^\omega$, such that $s(0) = s_{init}$ and $(s(i), s(i+1)) \in \delta$, for all $i \geq 0$. A trace of $\mathcal{K}$ is a sequence $\sigma(0)\sigma(1)\sigma(2) \cdots \in \Sigma^\omega$, such that there exists a path $s(0)s(1) \cdots \in S^\omega$ with $\sigma(i) = L(s(i))$ for all $i \geq 0$. We denote by $\mathsf{Traces}(\mathcal{K}, s)$ the set of all traces of $\mathcal{K}$ with paths that start in state $s \in S$.

The directed graph $\mathcal{F} = \langle S, \delta \rangle$ is called the *Kripke frame* of the Kripke structure $\mathcal{K}$. A *loop* in $\mathcal{F}$ is a finite sequence $s_0 s_1 \cdots s_n$, such that $(s_i, s_{i+1}) \in \delta$, for all $0 \leq i < n$, and $(s_n, s_0) \in \delta$. We call a Kripke frame *acyclic*, if the only loops are self-loops on terminal states, i.e., on states that have no other outgoing transition. Acyclic Kripke structures model terminating programs.

Extended A-HLTL. The syntax of extended A-HLTL is:

$$\varphi ::= \exists \pi.\varphi \mid \forall \pi.\varphi \mid \mathsf{E}\tau.\varphi \mid \mathsf{A}\tau.\varphi \mid \psi$$
$$\psi ::= true \mid a_{\pi,\tau} \mid \neg\psi \mid \psi_1 \vee \psi_2 \mid \psi_1 \wedge \psi_2 \mid \psi_1 \, \mathcal{U} \, \psi_2 \mid \psi_1 \, \mathcal{R} \, \psi_2$$

where $a \in \mathsf{AP}$, π is a trace variable from an infinite supply $\mathcal{V}$ of trace variables, τ is a *trajectory variable* from an infinite supply $\mathcal{J}$ of trajectory variables (see formula $\varphi_{\mathsf{NI}_{\mathsf{nd}}}$ in Section 1 for an example). The intended meaning of $a_{\pi,\tau}$ is that proposition $a \in \mathsf{AP}$ holds in the current time in trace π and *trajectory* τ (explained later). Trace (respectively, trajectory) quantifiers $\exists \pi$ and $\forall \pi$ (respectively, $\mathsf{E}\tau$ and $\mathsf{A}\tau$) allow reasoning simultaneously about different traces (respectively, trajectories). The intended meaning of E is that there is a trajectory that gives an interpretation of the relative passage of time between the traces for which the temporal formula that relates the traces is satisfied. Dually, A means that all trajectories satisfy the inner formula. Given an A-HLTL formula φ, we use $\mathsf{Paths}(\varphi)$ (respectively, $\mathsf{Trajs}(\varphi)$) for the set of trace (respectively, trajectory) variables quantified in φ. A formula φ is *well-formed* if for all atoms $a_{\pi,\tau}$ in φ, π and τ are quantified in φ (i.e., $\tau \in \mathsf{Trajs}(\varphi)$ and $\pi \in \mathsf{Paths}(\varphi)$) and no trajectory/trace variable is quantified twice in φ. We use the usual syntactic sugar $false \triangleq \neg true$, and $\Diamond\varphi \triangleq true \, \mathcal{U} \, \varphi$, $\varphi_1 \to \varphi_2 \triangleq \neg\varphi_1 \vee \varphi_2$, and $\Box\varphi \triangleq \neg\Diamond\neg\varphi$, etc. We choose to add $\mathcal{R}$ (release) and $\wedge$ to the logic to enable negation normal form (NNF). As our BMC algorithm cannot handle formulas that are not invariant under stuttering, the *next* operator is not included.

Semantics. A *trajectory* $t : t(0)t(1)t(2) \cdots$ for a formula φ is an infinite sequence of subsets of $\mathsf{Paths}(\varphi)$, i.e., each $t_i \subseteq \mathsf{Paths}(\varphi)$, for all $i \geq 0$. Essentially, in each step of the trajectory one or more of the traces make progress or all may stutter. A trajectory is *fair* for a trace variable $\pi \in \mathsf{Paths}(\varphi)$ if there are infinitely many positions j such that $\pi \in t(j)$. A trajectory is fair if it is fair for all trace variables in $\mathsf{Paths}(\varphi)$. Given a trajectory t, by t^i, we mean the suffix $t(i)t(i+1)\cdots$. Furthermore, for a set of trace variables $\mathcal{V}$, we use $\mathsf{TRJ}_{\mathcal{V}}$ for the set of all fair trajectories for indices from $\mathcal{V}$. We also use a *trajectory assignment* $\Gamma : \mathsf{Trajs}(\varphi) \rightharpoonup \mathsf{TRJ}_{Dom(\Gamma)}$, where $Dom(\Gamma)$ is the subset of $\mathsf{Trajs}(\varphi)$ for which Γ is defined. Given a trajectory assignment Γ, a trajectory variable τ, and a trajectory t, we denote by $\Gamma[\tau \mapsto t]$ the assignment that coincides with Γ for every trajectory variable except for τ, which is mapped to t.

For the semantics of extended A-HLTL, we need asynchronous trace assignments $\Pi : \mathsf{Paths}(\varphi) \times \mathsf{Trajs}(\varphi) \to T \times \mathbb{N}$ which map each pair (π, τ) formed by a path variable and trajectory variable into a pointed trace. Given (Π, Γ) where Π is an asynchronous trace assignment and Γ a trajectory assignment, we use $(\Pi, \Gamma) + 1$ for the successor of (Π, Γ) defined as (Π', Γ') where $\Gamma'(\tau) = \Gamma(\tau)^1$, and $\Pi'(\pi, \tau) = \Pi(\pi, \tau) + 1$ if $\pi \in \Gamma(\tau)(0)$ and $\Pi'(\pi, \tau) = \Pi(\pi, \tau)$ otherwise. Note that Π can assign the same π to different pointed traces depending on the trajectory. We use $(\Pi, \Gamma) + k$ as the k-th successor of (Π, Γ). Given an asynchronous trace assignment Π, a trace variable π, a trajectory variable τ a trace σ, and a pointer p, we denote by $\Pi[(\pi, \tau) \mapsto (\sigma, p)]$ the assignment that coincides

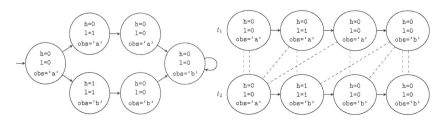

Fig. 4: Kripke structure $\mathcal{K}$ and traces t_1 and t_2 of $\mathcal{K}$, $\mathcal{K} \models \varphi_{\mathsf{NI}_{\mathsf{nd}}}$ but $\mathcal{K} \not\models \varphi_{\mathsf{NI}}$.

with Π for every pair except for (π, τ), which is mapped to (σ, p). The satisfaction of an A-HLTL formula φ over a trace assignment Π, a trajectory assignment Γ, and a set of traces T is defined as follows (we omit $\neg$, $\wedge$ and $\vee$ which are standard):

$$(\Pi, \Gamma) \models_T \exists \pi.\varphi \quad \text{iff} \quad \text{for some } \sigma \in T: \\ (\Pi[(\pi, \tau) \mapsto (\sigma, 0)], \Gamma) \models_T \varphi \text{ for all } \tau$$

$$(\Pi, \Gamma) \models_T \forall \pi.\varphi \quad \text{iff} \quad \text{for all } \sigma \in T: \\ (\Pi[(\pi, \tau) \mapsto (\sigma, 0)], \Gamma) \models_T \varphi \text{ for all } \tau$$

$$(\Pi, \Gamma) \models_T \mathsf{E}\tau.\psi \quad \text{iff} \quad \text{for some } t \in \mathsf{TRJ}_{Dom(\Pi)} : (\Pi, \Gamma[\tau \mapsto t]) \models \psi$$

$$(\Pi, \Gamma) \models_T \mathsf{A}\tau.\psi \quad \text{iff} \quad \text{for all } t \in \mathsf{TRJ}_{Dom(\Pi)}(\Pi, \Gamma[\tau \mapsto t]) \models \psi$$

$$(\Pi, \Gamma) \models a_{\pi,\tau} \quad \text{iff} \quad a \in \sigma(n) \text{ where } (\sigma, n) = \Pi(\pi, \tau)$$

$$(\Pi, \Gamma) \models \psi_1 \, \mathcal{U} \, \psi_2 \quad \text{iff} \quad \text{for some } i \geq 0 : (\Pi, \Gamma) + i \models \psi_2 \text{ and} \\ \text{for all } j < i : (\Pi, \Gamma) + j \models \psi_1$$

$$(\Pi, \Gamma) \models \psi_1 \, \mathcal{R} \, \psi_2 \quad \text{iff} \quad \text{for all } i \geq 0 : (\Pi, \Gamma) + i \models \psi_2, \text{ or} \\ \text{for some } i \geq 0 : (\Pi, \Gamma) + i \models \psi_1 \text{ and} \\ \text{for all } j \leq i : (\Pi, \Gamma) + j \models \psi_2$$

We say that a set T of traces satisfies a sentence φ, denoted by $T \models \varphi$, if $(\Pi_\emptyset, \Gamma_\emptyset) \models_T \varphi$. We say that a Kripke structure $\mathcal{K}$ satisfies an A-HLTL formula φ (and write $\mathcal{K} \models \varphi$) if and only if we have $\mathsf{Traces}(\mathcal{K}, S_{init}) \models \varphi$. An example is illustrated in Fig. 4.

3   Bounded Model Checking for A-HLTL

We first introduce the bounded semantics of A-HLTL (for at most one trajectory quantifier alternation but arbitrary trace quantifiers) which will be used to generate queries to a QBF solver to aid solving the BMC problem. The main result of this section is Theorem 1 which provides decision procedures for model checking A-HLTL for terminating systems.

3.1   Bounded Semantics of A-HLTL

The bounded semantics corresponds to the exploration of the system up to a certain bound. In our case, we will consider two bounds k and m (with $k \leq m$).

The bound k corresponds to the *maximum depth* of the unrolling of the Kripke structures and m is the *bound on trajectories length*. We start by introducing some auxiliary functions and predicates, for a given trace assignment and (Π, Γ). First, the family of functions $pos_{\pi,\tau} : \{0 \dots m\} \to \mathbb{N}$. The meaning of $pos_{\pi,\tau}(i)$ provides how many times π has been selected in $\{\tau(0), \dots, \tau(i)\}$. We assume that Kripke structures are equipped with an atomic proposition *halt* (one per trace variable π) which encodes whether the state is a halting state. Given (Π, Γ) we consider the predicate *halted* that holds whenever for all π and τ, $halt \in \sigma(j)$ for $(\sigma, j) = \Pi(\pi, \tau)$. In this case we write $(\Pi, \Gamma, n) \models halted$.

We define two bounded semantics which only differ in how they inspect beyond the (k, m) bounds: $\models_{k,m}^{hpes}$, called the *halting pessimistic semantics* and $\models_{k,m}^{hopt}$, called the *halting optimistic semantics*. We start by defining the bounded semantics of the quantifiers.

$$(\Pi, \Gamma, 0) \models_{k,m} \exists \pi. \ \psi \qquad \text{iff} \qquad \text{there is a } \sigma \in T_\pi, \text{ such that for all } \tau$$
$$(\Pi[(\pi, \tau) \to (\sigma, 0)], \Gamma, 0) \models_{k,m} \psi \tag{1}$$

$$(\Pi, \Gamma, 0) \models_{k,m} \forall \pi. \ \psi \qquad \text{iff} \qquad \text{for all } \sigma \in T_\pi, \text{ for all } \tau :$$
$$(\Pi[(\pi, \tau) \to (\sigma, 0)], \Gamma, 0) \models_{k,m} \psi \tag{2}$$

$$(\Pi, \Gamma, 0) \models_{k,m} \mathsf{E}\tau. \ \psi \qquad \text{iff} \qquad \text{there is a } t \in \mathsf{TRJ}_{Dom(\Pi)} :$$
$$(\Pi, \Gamma[\tau \to t], 0) \models_{k,m} \psi \tag{3}$$

$$(\Pi, \Gamma, 0) \models_{k,m} \mathsf{A}\tau. \ \psi \qquad \text{iff} \qquad \text{for all } t \in \mathsf{TRJ}_{Dom(\Pi)} :$$
$$(\Pi, \Gamma[\tau \to t], 0) \models_{k,m} \psi \tag{4}$$

For the Boolean operators, for $i \leq m$:

$$(\Pi, \Gamma, i) \models_{k,m} \mathtt{true} \tag{5}$$

$$(\Pi, \Gamma, i) \models_{k,m} a_{\pi,\tau} \qquad \text{iff} \qquad a \in (\sigma, j) \text{ where}$$
$$(\sigma, j) = \Pi(\pi, \tau)(i) \text{ and } j \leq k \tag{6}$$

$$(\Pi, \Gamma, i) \models_{k,m} \neg a_{\pi,\tau} \qquad \text{iff} \qquad a \notin (\sigma, j) \text{ where}$$
$$(\sigma, j) = \Pi(\pi, \tau)(i) \text{ and } j \leq k \tag{7}$$

$$(\Pi, \Gamma, i) \models_{k,m} \psi_1 \vee \psi_2 \qquad \text{iff} \qquad (\Pi, \Gamma, i) \models_{k,m} \psi_1 \text{ or } (\Pi, \Gamma, i) \models_{k,m} \psi_2 \tag{8}$$

$$(\Pi, \Gamma, i) \models_{k,m} \psi_1 \wedge \psi_2 \qquad \text{iff} \qquad (\Pi, \Gamma, i) \models_{k,m} \psi_1 \text{ and } (\Pi, \Gamma, i) \models_{k,m} \psi_2 \tag{9}$$

For the temporal operators, we must consider the cases of falling of the paths (beyond k) and falling of the traces (beyond m). We define the predicate *off* which holds for (Π, Γ, i) if for some (π, τ), $pos_{\pi,\tau}(i) > k$ and $halt_\pi \notin \sigma(k)$ where σ is the trace assigned to π. Note that *halted* implies that *off* does not hold because all paths (including those at k or beyond) satisfy *halt*.

We define two semantics that differ on how to interpret when the end of the unfolding of the traces and trajectories is reached. The *halting pessimistic* semantics, denoted by $\models_{k,m}^{hpes}$ take (1)-(9) above and add (10)-(13) together with $(\Pi, \Gamma, i) \not\models_{k,m} off$. Rules (10) and (11) define the semantics of the temporal operators for the case $i < m$, that is, before the end of the unrolling of the trajectories (recall that we do not consider $\bigcirc$):

$$(\Pi, \Gamma, i) \models_{k,m} \quad \psi_1 \, \mathcal{U} \, \psi_2 \ \text{iff} \ (\Pi, \Gamma, i) \models_{k,m} \psi_2, \text{ or } (\Pi, \Gamma, i) \models_{k,m} \psi_1, \text{ and}$$
$$(\Pi, \Gamma, i) + 1 \models_{k,m} \psi_1 \, \mathcal{U} \, \psi_2 \tag{10}$$

$$(\Pi, \Gamma, i) \models_{k,m} \quad \psi_1 \, \mathcal{R} \, \psi_2 \quad \text{iff} \quad (\Pi, \Gamma, i) \models_{k,m} \psi_2, \text{ and } (\Pi, \Gamma, i) \models_{k,m} \psi_1, \text{ or}$$
$$(\Pi, \Gamma, i) + 1 \models_{k,m} \psi_1 \, \mathcal{R} \, \psi_2 \qquad (11)$$

For the case of $i = m$, that is, at the bound of the trajectory:

$$(\Pi, \Gamma, m) \models_{k,m}^{hpes} \quad \psi_1 \, \mathcal{U} \, \psi_2 \quad \text{iff} \quad (\Pi, \Gamma, m) \models_{k,m} \psi_2 \qquad (12)$$
$$(\Pi, \Gamma, m) \models_{k,m}^{hpes} \quad \psi_1 \, \mathcal{R} \, \psi_2 \quad \text{iff} \quad (\Pi, \Gamma, m) \models_{k,m} \psi_1 \wedge \psi_2, \text{ or}$$
$$(\Pi, \Gamma, m) \models_{k,m} halted \wedge \psi_2 \qquad (13)$$

The *halting optimistic* semantics, denoted by $\models_{k,m}^{hopt}$ take rules (1)-(11) and (12′)-(13′), but now if $(\Pi, \Gamma, i) \models_{k,m}^{hopt}$ off then $(\Pi, \Gamma, i) \models_{k,m}^{hopt} \varphi$ holds for every formula. Again, rules (10) and (11) define the semantics of the temporal operators for the case $i < m$. Then, for $i = m$:

$$(\Pi, \Gamma, m) \models_{k,m}^{hopt} \quad \psi_1 \, \mathcal{U} \, \psi_2 \quad \text{iff} \quad (\Pi, \Gamma, m) \models_{k,m} \psi_2, \text{ or}$$
$$(\Pi, \Gamma, m) \not\models_{k,m} halted \wedge \psi_1 \qquad (12')$$
$$(\Pi, \Gamma, m) \models_{k,m}^{hopt} \quad \psi_1 \, \mathcal{R} \, \psi_2 \quad \text{iff} \quad (\Pi, \Gamma, m) \models_{k,m} \psi_2 \qquad (13')$$

Similar to [15] for the case of HyperLTL, the pessimistic semantics capture the case where we assume that pending eventualities will not become true in the future after the end of the trace (this is also assumed in LTL BMC). Dually, the optimistic semantics assume that all pending eventualities at the end of the trace will be fulfilled. Therefore, the following hold (proofs in [13]).

Lemma 1. *Let $k \leq k'$ and $m \leq m'$.*
1. *If $(\Pi, \Gamma, 0) \models_{k,m}^{hpes} \varphi$, then $(\Pi, \Gamma, 0) \models_{k',m'}^{hpes} \varphi$.*
2. *If $(\Pi, \Gamma, 0) \not\models_{k,m}^{hopt} \varphi$, then $(\Pi, \Gamma, 0) \not\models_{k',m'}^{hopt} \varphi$.*

Lemma 2. *The following hold for every k and m,*
1. *If $(\Pi, \Gamma, 0) \models_{k,m}^{hpes} \varphi$, then $(\Pi, \Gamma, 0) \models \varphi$.*
2. *If $(\Pi, \Gamma, 0) \not\models_{k,m}^{hopt} \varphi$, then $(\Pi, \Gamma, 0) \not\models \varphi$.*

3.2 From Bounded Semantics to QBF Solving

Let $\mathcal{K}$ be a Kripke structure and φ be an A-HLTL formula. Based on the bounded semantics introduced previously, our main approach is to generate a QBF query (with bounds k, m), which can use either the pessimistic or the optimistic semantics. We use $[\![\mathcal{K}, \varphi]\!]_{k,m}^{hpes}$ if the pessimistic semantics are used and $[\![\mathcal{K}, \varphi]\!]_{k,m}^{hopt}$ if the optimistic semantics are used. Our translations will satisfy that

(1) if $[\![\mathcal{K}, \varphi]\!]_{k,m}^{hpes}$ is SAT, then $\mathcal{K} \models \varphi$;
(2) if $[\![\mathcal{K}, \varphi]\!]_{k,m}^{hopt}$ is UNSAT, then $\mathcal{K} \not\models \varphi$;
(3) if the Kripke structure is unrolled to the diameter and the trajectories up to a maximum length (see below), then $[\![\mathcal{K}, \varphi]\!]_{k,m}^{hpes}$ is SAT if and only if $[\![\mathcal{K}, \varphi]\!]_{k,m}^{hopt}$ is SAT.

The first step to define $[\![\mathcal{K}, \varphi]\!]_{k,m}^{hopt}$ and $[\![\mathcal{K}, \varphi]\!]_{k,m}^{hpes}$ is to encode the unrolling of the models up-to a given depth k. For a path variable π corresponding to Kripke structure $\mathcal{K}$, we introduce $(k+1)$ copies $(x^0, \ldots, x^k)$ of the Boolean variables that define the state of $\mathcal{K}$ and use the initial condition I and the transition relation R of $\mathcal{K}$ to relate these variables. For example, for $k = 3$, we unroll the transition relation up-to 3 as follows:

$$[\![\mathcal{K}]\!]_3 = I(x^0) \wedge R(x^0, x^1) \wedge R(x^1, x^2) \wedge R(x^2, x^3).$$

Encoding positions. For each trajectory variable τ and given the bound m on the unrolling of trajectories, we add $\mathsf{Paths}(\varphi) \times (m+1)$ variables $t_\pi^0 \ldots t_\pi^m$, for each π. The intended meaning of t_π^j is that t_π^j is true whenever $\pi \in t(j)$, that is, when t dictates that π moves at time instant j. In order to encode sanity conditions on trajectories, that are crucial for completeness, it is necessary to introduce a family of variables that captures how much π has moved according to τ after j steps. There is a variable pos for each trace variable π, each trajectory τ and each $i \leq k$ and $j \leq m$. We represent this variable by $pos_{\pi,\tau}^{i,j}$. The intention is that pos is true whenever after j steps trajectory τ has dictated that trace π progresses precisely i times. Fig. 5 shows encodings t_π^j and $pos_{\pi,\tau}^{i,j}$ for the traces w.r.t. the blue trajectory, τ' in Fig. 4. We will use the auxiliary

Encodings of t_π^j and $t_{\pi'}^j$:

$[t_\pi^0, t_\pi^1, t_\pi^2, t_\pi^3, t_\pi^4, t_\pi^5, t_\pi^6]$
$[t_{\pi'}^0, t_{\pi'}^1, t_{\pi'}^2, t_{\pi'}^3, t_{\pi'}^4, t_{\pi'}^5, t_{\pi'}^6]$

Encodings of $pos_{\pi,\tau'}^{i,j}$ and $pos_{\pi',\tau'}^{i,j}$:

$[pos_{\pi,\tau'}^{0,0}, pos_{\pi,\tau'}^{0,1}, pos_{\pi,\tau'}^{0,2}, pos_{\pi,\tau'}^{0,3},$
$pos_{\pi,\tau'}^{1,1}, pos_{\pi,\tau'}^{1,2}, pos_{\pi,\tau'}^{1,3}, pos_{\pi,\tau'}^{1,4},$
$pos_{\pi,\tau'}^{2,2}, pos_{\pi,\tau'}^{2,3}, pos_{\pi,\tau'}^{2,4}, pos_{\pi,\tau'}^{2,5},$
$pos_{\pi,\tau'}^{3,3}, pos_{\pi,\tau'}^{3,4}, pos_{\pi,\tau'}^{3,5}, pos_{\pi,\tau'}^{3,6}]$

$[pos_{\pi',\tau'}^{0,0}, pos_{\pi',\tau'}^{0,1}, pos_{\pi',\tau'}^{0,2}, pos_{\pi',\tau'}^{0,3},$
$pos_{\pi',\tau'}^{1,1}, pos_{\pi',\tau'}^{1,2}, pos_{\pi',\tau'}^{1,3}, pos_{\pi',\tau'}^{1,4},$
$pos_{\pi',\tau'}^{2,2}, pos_{\pi',\tau'}^{2,3}, pos_{\pi',\tau'}^{2,4}, pos_{\pi',\tau'}^{2,5},$
$pos_{\pi',\tau'}^{3,3}, pos_{\pi',\tau'}^{3,4}, pos_{\pi',\tau'}^{3,5}, pos_{\pi',\tau'}^{3,6}]$

Fig. 5: Variables for encodings of the blue trajectory in Fig. 4, where green variables are *true* and gray variables are *false*.

definitions (for $i \in \{0 \ldots k\}$ and $j \in \{0 \ldots m\}$) to force that the path π has moved to position i after j moves from the trajectory and that π has not fallen off the trace (and does not change position when the paths fall off the trace):

$$setpos_{\pi,\tau}^{i,j} \stackrel{\text{def}}{=} pos_{\pi,\tau}^{i,j} \wedge \bigwedge_{n \in \{0..k\} \setminus \{i\}} \neg pos_{\pi,\tau}^{n,j} \wedge \neg off_{\pi,\tau}^j$$

$$nopos_{\pi,\tau}^j \stackrel{\text{def}}{=} off_{\pi,\tau}^j \wedge \bigwedge_{n \in \{0..k\}} \neg pos_{\pi,\tau}^{n,j}$$

Initially, $I_{pos} \stackrel{\text{def}}{=} \bigwedge_{\pi,\tau} setpos_{\pi,\tau}^{0,0}$, where $\pi \in \mathsf{Traces}(\varphi)$ and $\tau \in \mathsf{TRJ}_{Dom(\Pi)}$. I_{pos} captures that all paths are initially at position 0. Then, for every step $j \in \{0 \ldots m\}$, the following formulas relate the values of pos and off, depending on whether trajectory τ moves path π or not (and on whether π has reached the end k or halted):

$$step_{\pi,\tau}^j \stackrel{\text{def}}{=} \bigwedge_{i \in \{0..k-1\}} \left(pos_{\pi,\tau}^{i,j} \wedge t_\pi^j \to setpos_{\pi,\tau}^{i+1,j+1} \right)$$

$$stutters_{\pi,\tau}^{j} \stackrel{\text{def}}{=} \bigwedge_{i \in \{0..k\}} \left(pos_{\pi,\tau}^{i,j} \wedge \neg t_{\pi}^{j} \rightarrow setpos_{\pi,\tau}^{i,j+1} \right)$$

$$ends_{\pi,\tau}^{j} \stackrel{\text{def}}{=} \left(pos_{\pi,\tau}^{k,j} \wedge t_{\pi}^{j} \right) \rightarrow \left(\left(\neg halt_{\pi}^{k} \rightarrow nopos_{\pi,\tau}^{j+1} \right) \wedge \left(halt_{\pi}^{k} \rightarrow setpos_{\pi,\tau}^{k,j+1} \right) \right)$$

Then the following formula captures the correct assignment to the the *pos* variables, including the initial assignment:

$$\varphi_{pos} \stackrel{\text{def}}{=} I_{pos} \wedge \bigwedge_{j \in \{0..m\}} \bigwedge_{\pi,\tau} (step_{\pi,\tau}^{j} \wedge stutters_{\pi,\tau}^{j} \wedge ends_{\pi,\tau}^{j})$$

For example, Fig. 5 (w.r.t. Fig. 4) encodes the blue trajectory (τ') of π (i.e., t_1) and π' (i.e., t_2) as follows. First, for $j \in [0,3)$, it advances t_1 and stutters t_2. Therefore, $t_{\pi}^{0}, t_{\pi}^{1}, t_{\pi}^{2}$ are *true* and $t_{\pi'}^{0}, t_{\pi'}^{1}, t_{\pi'}^{2}$ are *false*. Notice that for *pos* encodings, the π position advances according to $step_{\pi,\tau'}^{j}$ (i.e., $pos_{\pi,\tau'}^{0,0}, pos_{\pi,\tau'}^{1,1}, pos_{\pi,\tau'}^{2,2}, pos_{\pi,\tau'}^{3,3}$,); while π' stutters according to $stutters_{\pi',\tau'}^{j}$ (i.e., $pos_{\pi',\tau'}^{0,0}, pos_{\pi',\tau'}^{0,1}, pos_{\pi',\tau'}^{0,2}, pos_{\pi',\tau'}^{0,3}$). Then, for $j \in [3,5]$, it alternatively advances t_2 which makes $t_{\pi}^{3}, t_{\pi}^{4}, t_{\pi}^{5}$ *false* and $t_{\pi'}^{3}, t_{\pi'}^{4}, t_{\pi'}^{5}$ *true*. Similarly, the movements becomes $pos_{\pi,\tau'}^{3,4}, pos_{\pi,\tau'}^{3,5}, pos_{\pi,\tau'}^{3,6}$ and $pos_{\pi',\tau'}^{1,4}, pos_{\pi',\tau'}^{2,5}, pos_{\pi',\tau'}^{3,6}$. At the halting point (i.e., $j = k$), both trajectory trigger $ends^{j}$ and do not advance anymore.

Encoding the inner LTL formula. We will use the following auxiliary predicates:

$$halted^{j} \stackrel{\text{def}}{=} \bigwedge_{\tau} halted_{\tau}^{j} \qquad off^{j} \stackrel{\text{def}}{=} \bigvee_{\pi,\tau} off_{\pi,\tau}^{j}$$

We now give the encoding for the inner temporal formulas for a fix unrolling k and m as follows. For the atomic and Boolean formulas, the following translations are performed for $j \in \{0 \ldots m\}$.

$$\llbracket p_{\pi,\tau} \rrbracket_{k,m}^{j} := \bigvee_{i \in \{0..k\}} (pos_{\pi,\tau}^{i,j} \wedge p_{\pi}^{i}) \qquad (14)$$

$$\llbracket \neg p_{\pi,\tau} \rrbracket_{k,m}^{j} := \bigvee_{i \in \{0..k\}} (pos_{\pi,\tau}^{i,j} \wedge \neg p_{\pi}^{i}) \qquad (15)$$

$$\llbracket \psi_1 \vee \psi_2 \rrbracket_{k,m}^{j} := \llbracket \psi_1 \rrbracket_{k,m}^{j} \vee \llbracket \psi_2 \rrbracket_{k,m}^{j} \qquad (16)$$

$$\llbracket \psi_1 \wedge \psi_2 \rrbracket_{k,m}^{j} := \llbracket \psi_1 \rrbracket_{k,m}^{j} \wedge \llbracket \psi_2 \rrbracket_{k,m}^{j} \qquad (17)$$

The halting pessimistic semantics translation uses $\llbracket \cdot \rrbracket_{hpes}$, taking (14)-(17) and (18)-(21) below. For the temporal operators and $j < m$:

$$\llbracket \psi_1 \, \mathcal{U} \, \psi_2 \rrbracket_{k,m}^{j} := \neg off^{j} \wedge \left(\llbracket \psi_2 \rrbracket_{k,m}^{j} \vee \left(\llbracket \psi_1 \rrbracket_{k,m}^{j} \wedge \llbracket \psi_1 \, \mathcal{U} \, \psi_2 \rrbracket_{k,m}^{j+1} \right) \right) \qquad (18)$$

$$\llbracket \psi_1 \, \mathcal{R} \, \psi_2 \rrbracket_{k,m}^{j} := \neg off^{j} \wedge \left(\llbracket \psi_2 \rrbracket_{k,m}^{j} \wedge \left(\llbracket \psi_1 \rrbracket_{k,m}^{j} \vee \llbracket \psi_1 \, \mathcal{R} \, \psi_2 \rrbracket_{k,m}^{j+1} \right) \right) \qquad (19)$$

For $j = m$:

$$\llbracket \psi_1 \, \mathcal{U} \, \psi_2 \rrbracket_{k,m}^{m} := \llbracket \psi_2 \rrbracket_{k,m}^{m} \qquad (20)$$

$$\llbracket \psi_1 \, \mathcal{R} \, \psi_2 \rrbracket_{k,m}^{m} := \left(\llbracket \psi_1 \rrbracket_{k,m}^{m} \wedge \llbracket \psi_2 \rrbracket_{k,m}^{m} \right) \vee \left(halted^{m} \wedge \llbracket \psi_2 \rrbracket_{k,m}^{m} \right) \qquad (21)$$

The halting optimistic semantics translation uses $\llbracket \cdot \rrbracket_{hopt}$, taking (14)-(17) and (18')-(21') as follows, For the temporal operators and $j < m$:

$$\llbracket \psi_1 \, \mathcal{U} \, \psi_2 \rrbracket^j_{k,m} := \mathit{off}^j \vee \left(\llbracket \psi_2 \rrbracket^j_{k,m} \vee \left(\llbracket \psi_1 \rrbracket^j_{k,m} \wedge \llbracket \psi_1 \, \mathcal{U} \, \psi_2 \rrbracket^{j+1}_{k,m} \right) \right) \qquad (18')$$

$$\llbracket \psi_1 \, \mathcal{R} \, \psi_2 \rrbracket^j_{k,m} := \mathit{off}^j \vee \left(\llbracket \psi_2 \rrbracket^j_{k,m} \wedge \left(\llbracket \psi_1 \rrbracket^j_{k,m} \vee \llbracket \psi_1 \, \mathcal{R} \, \psi_2 \rrbracket^{j+1}_{k,m} \right) \right) \qquad (19')$$

For $j = m$:

$$\llbracket \psi_1 \, \mathcal{U} \, \psi_2 \rrbracket^m_{k,m} := \llbracket \psi_2 \rrbracket^m_{k,m} \vee \left(\mathit{halted}^m \wedge \llbracket \psi_1 \rrbracket^m_{k,m} \right) \qquad (20')$$

$$\llbracket \psi_1 \, \mathcal{R} \, \psi_2 \rrbracket^m_{k,m} := \llbracket \psi_2 \rrbracket^m_{k,m} \qquad (21')$$

Combining the encodings. Let φ be a A-HLTL formula of the form $\varphi = \mathbb{Q}_A \pi_A . \dots . \mathbb{Q}_Z \pi_Z . \mathbb{Q}_a \tau_a . \dots . \mathbb{Q}_z \tau_z . \psi$. Combining all the components, the encoding of the A-HLTL BMC problem into QBF, for bounds k and m is:

$$\llbracket \mathcal{K}, \varphi \rrbracket_{k,m} = \mathbb{Q}_A \overline{x_A} . \cdots . \mathbb{Q}_Z \overline{x_Z} . \mathbb{Q}_a \overline{t_a} . \cdots . \mathbb{Q}_z \overline{t_z} . \, \exists \overline{pos} . \, \exists \overline{\mathit{off}} .$$

$$\left(\llbracket \mathcal{K} \rrbracket_k \circ_A \cdots \llbracket \mathcal{K} \rrbracket_k \circ_Z (\varphi_{pos} \wedge enc(\psi)) \right)$$

where $\circ_A = \rightarrow$ if $\mathbb{Q}_A = \forall$ (and $\circ_A = \wedge$ if $\mathbb{Q}_A = \exists$), and $\circ_B, \dots$ are defined similarly. The sets $\overline{pos}$ is the set of variables $pos^{i,j}_{\pi,\tau}$ that encode the positions and $\overline{\mathit{off}}$ is the set of variables $\mathit{off}^j_{\pi,\tau}$ that encode when a trace progress has fallen off its unrolling limit. We next define the encoding $enc(\psi)$ of the temporal formula ψ.

Encoding formulas with up to 1 trajectory quantifier alternations We consider the encoding into QBF of formulas with zero and one quantifier alternation separately. In the following, we say that at position j a collection of trajectories U "moves" whenever either all trajectories have moved all their paths to the halting state, or at least one of the trajectories in U makes one of the non-halted path move at position j. Formally,

$$moves^j_U \stackrel{\text{def}}{=} halted^j_U \vee \bigvee_{\tau \in U, \pi} (t^j_\pi \wedge \neg halt^j_{\pi,\tau})$$

– $E^+ U.\psi$: In this case, the formula generated for $enc(\psi)$ is

$$\left(\bigwedge_{j \in \{0 \dots m\}} moves^j_U \right) \wedge \llbracket \psi \rrbracket^0_{k,m}$$

This is correct since the positions at which all trajectories stutter all paths can be removed (obtaining a satisfying path), we can restrict the search to non-stuttering trajectory steps.

– $A^+ U.\psi$: In this case, the formula generated for $enc(\psi)$ is

$$\left(\bigwedge_{j \in \{0 \dots m\}} moves^j_U \right) \rightarrow \llbracket \psi \rrbracket^0_{k,m}$$

The reasoning is similar as the previous case.

– $\mathsf{A}^+ U_A \mathsf{E}^+ U_E.\psi$: In this case, the formula generated for $enc(\psi)$ is

$$(\bigwedge_{j\in\{0...m\}} moves^j_{U_A}) \rightarrow (\bigwedge_{j\in\{0...m\}} (halted^j_{U_A} \rightarrow moves^j_{U_E}) \wedge [\![\psi]\!]^0_{k,m})$$

Universally quantified trajectories must explore all trajectories, which must be responded by the existential trajectories. Assume there is a strategy for U_E for the case that universal trajectories U_A never stutter at any position. This can be extended into a strategy for the case where U_A can possible stutter, by adding a stuttering step to the U_E trajectories at the same position. This guarantees the same evaluation. Therefore, we restrict our search for the outer U_A to non-stuttering trajectories. Finally, U_E is obliged to move after U_A has halted all paths to prevent global stuttering.

– $\mathsf{E}^+ U_E \mathsf{A}^+ U_A.\psi$: In this case, the formula generated for $enc(\psi)$ is similar,

$$(\bigwedge_{j\in\{0...m\}} moves^j_{U_E}) \wedge (\bigwedge_{j\in\{0...m\}} (halted^j_{U_E} \rightarrow moves^j_{U_A}) \rightarrow [\![\psi]\!]^0_{k,m})$$

The rationale for this encoding is the following. It is not necessary to explore a non-moving step j for the existentially quantified trajectories U_E because if this stuttering step is successful it must work for all possible moves of the U_A trajectories at the same time step j. This includes the case that all trajectories in U_A make all paths stutter (which, if we remove j one still has all the legal trajectories for U_A). Since the logic does not contain the next operator, the evaluation for the given U_E and one of the trajectories for U_A that stutter at j will be the same as for $j+1$ for all logical formulas. Therefore, the trajectory that is obtained from removing step j from U_E is still a satisfying trajectory assignment. It follows that if there is a model for U_E there is a model that does not stutter. Finally, after all paths have halted according to the U_E trajectories, a step of U_A that stutters all paths that have not halted can be removed because, again the evaluation is the same in the previous and subsequent state. It follows that if the formula has a model, then it has a model satisfying the encoding.

Theorem 1. *Let φ be an A-HLTL formula with at most one trajectory quantifier alternation, let K be the maximum depth of a Kripke structure and let $M = K \times |\mathsf{Paths}(\varphi)| \times |\mathsf{Trajs}(\varphi)|$. Then, the following hold:*

– $[\![\mathcal{K}, \varphi]\!]^{hpes}_{K,M}$ is satisfiable if and only if $\mathcal{K} \models \varphi$.
– $[\![\mathcal{K}, \varphi]\!]^{hopt}_{K,M}$ is satisfiable if and only if $\mathcal{K} \models \varphi$.

Theorem 1 (proof in [13]) provides a model checking decision procedure. An alternative decision procedure is to iteratively increase the bound of the unrollings and invoke both semantics in parallel until the outcome coincides.

4   Complexity of A-HLTL Model Checking for Acyclic Frames

Our goal in this section is to analyze the complexity of the A-HLTL model checking problem in the size of an acyclic Kripke structure (all proofs in [13]).

Problem Formulation. We use MC[Fragment] to distinguish different variations of the problem, where MC is the model checking decision problem, i.e., whether or not $\mathcal{K} \models \varphi$, and Fragment is one of the following for φ:

- '$[\exists(\exists/\forall)^+A/E]^k$', for $k \geq 0$, is the fragment with a lead existential trace quantifier, one outermost universal or existential trajectory quantifier, and k (counting *all*) quantifier alternations, where $k = 0$ means the existential alternation-free fragment '$\exists^+E^+$'. Fragment '$[\forall(\forall/\exists)^+A/E]^k$' is defined similarly, where $k = 0$ is the universal alternation-free fragment '$\forall^+A^+$'.
- Fragments '$[\exists(\exists/\forall)^+(E^+A^+/A^+E^+/EE^+/AA^+)]^k$', for $k \geq 1$ denotes the fragment with a lead existential trace quantifier, multiple outermost trajectory quantifiers with at most one alternation, and k quantifier alternations (counting *all* quantifiers), where $k = 1$ means fragment '$\exists EA$'. Fragment '$[\forall(\forall/\exists)^+$ $(E^+A^+/A^+E^+/EE^+/AA^+)]^k$' is defined similarly, where $k = 1$ means fragment '$\forall AE$'.

The Complexity of A-HLTL Model Checking. We first show the A-HLTL model checking problem for the alternation-free fragment with only one trajectory quantifier is NL-complete. For example, verification of information leak in speculative execution in sequential programs renders a formula of the form $\forall^4 A$, which belongs to the alternation-free fragment (more details in Section 5).

Theorem 2. MC$[\exists^+E]$ *and* MC$[\forall^+A]$ *are* NL-complete.

We now switch to formulas with alternating trace quantifiers. The significance of the next theorem is that a single trajectory quantifier does not change the complexity of model checking as compared to the classic HyperLTL verification [2]. It is noteworthy to mention that several important classes of formulas belong to this fragment. For example, according to Theorem 3 while model checking *observational determinism* [20] ($\forall\forall E$), *generalized noninference* [16] ($\forall\forall\exists E$), and *non-inference* [5] ($\forall\exists E$) with a single initial input are all coNP-complete.

Theorem 3. MC$[\exists(\exists/\forall)^+(A/E)]^k$ *is* Σ_k^p-*complete and* MC$[\forall(\forall/\exists)^+(E/A)]^k$ *is* Π_k^p-*complete in the size of the Kripke structure.*

We now focus on formulas with multiple trajectory quantifiers. We first show that alternation-free multiple trajectory quantifiers bumps the class of complexity by one step in the polynomial hierarchy.

Theorem 4. MC$[\exists(\exists/\forall)^+EE^+]^k$ *is* Σ_{k+1}^p-*complete and* MC$[\forall(\forall/\exists)^+AA^+]^k$ *is* Π_{k+1}^p-*complete in the Kripke structure.*

Theorem 5. *For* $k \geq 1$, MC$[\exists(\exists/\forall)^+A^+E^+]^k$ *is* Σ_{k+1}^p-*complete and* MC$[\forall(\forall/\exists)^+E^+A^+]^k$ *is* Π_{k+1}^p-*complete in the size of the Kripke structure.*

Finally, Theorems 3, 4, and 5 imply that the model checking problem for acyclic Kripke structures and A-HLTL formulas with an arbitrary number of trace quantifier alternation and only one trajectory quantifier is in PSPACE.

5   Case Studies and Evaluation

We now evaluate our technique. The encoding in Section 3 is implemented on top of the open-source bounded model checker HYPERQB [15]. All experiments are executed on a MacBook Pro with 2.2GHz processor and 16GB RAM (https://github.com/TART-MSU/async_hltl_tacas23).

Non-interference in Concurrent Programs. We first consider the programs presented earlier in Figs. 1 and 3 together with A-HLTL formulas φ_{NI} and $\varphi_{\mathsf{NI}_{\mathsf{nd}}}$ from Section 1. We receive UNSAT (for the original formula and not its negation), which indicates that violations have been spotted. Indeed, our implementation successfully finds a counterexample with a specific trajectory that prints out 'acdb' when the high-security value h is equal to zero (entries of ACDB and $\mathtt{ACDB}_{\mathsf{ndet}}$ in Table 3). Our other experiment is an extension of the example in [10] for multiple asynchronous channels (see Fig. 6) and the following formula: $\varphi_{\mathsf{OD}_{\mathsf{nd}}} = \forall\pi.\forall\pi'.\mathsf{A}\tau.\ \mathsf{E}\tau'.\ \square\,(\mathsf{l}_{\pi,\tau} \leftrightarrow \mathsf{l}_{\pi',\tau}) \to \square\,(\mathsf{obs}_{\pi,\tau'} \leftrightarrow \mathsf{obs}_{\pi',\tau'})$. The results for this case are entries of ConcLeak and $\mathtt{ConcLeak}_{\mathsf{ndet}}$ in Table 3. Details of the counterexample can be found in [13].

```
Thread T1(){
  while (true){
    x := 0;
    y := 0;
    if ( h == 1) then
      x := 1;
      y := 1;
    else
      y := 1;
      x := 1;
  }
}
Thread T2(){
  while (true) {
    print x;
    print y;
  }
}
Thread T3(){
  while (true){
    h := 0||1;
    l := 0||1;
  }
}
```

Fig. 6: Program with nondeterministic sequence of inputs.

Speculative Information Flow. *Speculative execution* is a standard optimization technique that allows branch prediction by the processor. *Speculative non-interference* (SNI) [9] requires that two executions with the same *policy* p (i.e., initial configuration) can be observed differently in speculative semantics (e.g., a possible branch), if and only if their non-speculative semantics with normal condition checks are also observed differently; i.e., the following A-HLTL formula:

$$\varphi_{\mathsf{SNI}} = \underbrace{\forall\pi_1.\forall\pi_2.}_{\text{speculative}}\ \underbrace{\forall\pi_1'.\forall\pi_2'}_{\text{nonspeculative}}\ .\ \mathsf{A}\tau.\Big(\square(\mathsf{obs}_{\pi_1,\tau} \leftrightarrow \mathsf{obs}_{\pi_2,\tau}) \wedge$$

$$(\mathsf{p}_{\pi_1,\tau} \leftrightarrow \mathsf{p}_{\pi_2,\tau}) \wedge (\mathsf{p}_{\pi_1,\tau} \leftrightarrow \mathsf{p}_{\pi_1',\tau}) \wedge (\mathsf{p}_{\pi_2,\tau} \leftrightarrow \mathsf{p}_{\pi_2',\tau})\Big) \to \square\big(\mathsf{obs}_{\pi_1',\tau} \leftrightarrow \mathsf{obs}_{\pi_2',\tau}\big)$$

where obs is the memory footprint, traces π_1 and π_2 range over the (nonspeculative) C code and traces π_1' and π_2' range over the corresponding (speculative) assembly code. We evaluate SNI on the translation from a C program (details in [13]), where y is the input policy p and multiple versions of x86 assembly code [9]. The results of model checking speculative execution are in Table 3 (see entries from $\mathtt{SpecExcu}_{V1}$ to $\mathtt{SpecExcu}_{V7}$). Additional versions from $\mathtt{SpecExcu}_{V3}$ to $\mathtt{SpecExcu}_{V7}$ are under different compilation options. Our method correctly identify all the insecure and secure ones as stated in [9].

Compiler Optimization Security. Secure compiler optimization [17] aims at preserving input-output behaviors of a *source* program (original implementation) and a *target* program (after applying optimization), including security policies. We investigate the following optimization strategies: Dead Branch Elimination (DBE), Loop Peeling (LP), and Expression Flattening (EF). To verify a secure optimization, we consider two scenarios: (1) one single I/O event (one trajectory, similar to [1]), and (2) a sequences of I/O events (two trajectories):

$$\varphi_{\mathsf{SC}} = \forall \pi. \forall \pi'. \mathsf{E}\tau. \ (\mathsf{in}_{\pi,\tau} \leftrightarrow \mathsf{in}_{\pi',\tau}) \rightarrow \Box \ (\mathsf{out}_{\pi,\tau} \leftrightarrow \mathsf{out}_{\pi',\tau})$$

$$\varphi_{\mathsf{SC}_{\mathsf{nd}}} = \forall \pi. \forall \pi'. \mathsf{A}\tau. \ \mathsf{E}\tau'. \Box \ (\mathsf{in}_{\pi,\tau} \leftrightarrow \mathsf{in}_{\pi',\tau}) \rightarrow \Box \ (\mathsf{out}_{\pi,\tau'} \leftrightarrow \mathsf{out}_{\pi',\tau'}),$$

where in is the set of inputs and out is the set of outputs. Table 3 (cases DBE – EFLP$_{\mathsf{ndet}}$) shows the verification results of each optimization strategy and different combination of the strategies (details in [13]).

Cache-Based Timing Attacks. Asynchrony also leads to attacks when system executions are confined to a single CPU and its cache [18]. A cache-based timing attack happens when an attacker is able to guess the values of high-security variables when cache operations (i.e., evict, fetch) influence the scheduling of different threads. Our case study is inspired by the cache-based timing attack example in [18] and we use the formula of observational determinism $\varphi_{\mathsf{OD}_{\mathsf{nd}}}$ introduced earlier in this section to find the potential attacks (see cases of CacheTA and CacheTA$_{\mathsf{ndet}}$ in Table 3 with details in [13]).

5.1   Analysis of Experimental Results

Table 3 presents the diameter of the transition relation, length of trajectories m, state spaces, and the number of trajectory variables. We also present the total solving time of our algorithm as well as the break down: generating models (genQBF), building trajectory encodings (buildTr), and final QBF solving (solveQBF). Our two most complex cases are concurrent leak (ConcLeak$_{\mathsf{ndet}}$) and loop peeling (LP$_{\mathsf{ndet}}$). For concurrent leak, it is because there are three threads with many interleavings (i.e., asynchronous composition), takes longer time to build. For loop peeling, although there is no need to consider interleavings except for the nondeterministic inputs; however, the diameters of traces ($D_{\mathcal{K}_1}, D_{\mathcal{K}_2}$) are longer than other cases, which makes the length and size of trajectory variables (i.e., m and $|T|$) grow and increases the total solving time.

Our encoding is able to handle a variety of cases with one or more trajectories, depending on whether multiple sources of non-determinism is present. To see efficiency, we compare the solving time for cases of compiler optimization with one trajectory with the results in [1]. This

	MCHyper [1]	This paper	
Case	Total[s]	genQBF/ buildTr/ solveQBF[s]	Total[s]
DBE	0.8	0.9 / 0.07 / 0.01	0.98
LP	365.9	1.37 / 1.40 / 1.13	3.90
EFLP	1315.2	5.11 / 8.12 / 9.35	22.58

Table 2: Comparison of model checking compiler optimization with [1].

method reduces A-HLTL model checking to HyperLTL model checking for limited fragments and utilizes the model checker MCHyper. On the other hand, we directly handle asynchrony by trajectory encoding. Table 2 shows our algorithm considerably outperforms the approach in [1] in larger cases.

Models	φ	(model checking spec and data)							(time took for solving)			
		$D_{\mathcal{K}_1}$	$D_{\mathcal{K}_2}$	m	$|S_{\mathcal{K}_1}|$	$|S_{\mathcal{K}_2}|$	$|T|$	QBF	genQBF[s]	buildTr[s]	solveQBF[s]	Total[s]
ACDB	φ_{NI}	6	6	12	109	109	1378	UNSAT	2.80	0.32	0.23	**3.35**
ACDB$_{\mathsf{ndet}}$	$\varphi_{\mathsf{NI}_{\mathsf{nd}}}$	8	8	16	696	696	2754	UNSAT	7.74	2.54	3.73	**14.01**
ConcLeak	φ_{OD}	11	11	22	597	597	6118	UNSAT	14.85	7.10	8.29	**30.24**
ConcLeak$_{\mathsf{ndet}}$	$\varphi_{\mathsf{OD}_{\mathsf{nd}}}$	18	18	36	2988	2988	22274	UNSAT	127.09	53.14	731.48	**911.72**
SpecExcu$_{V1}$	φ_{SNI}	3	6	9	132	340	1112	UNSAT	7.45	1.72	3.07	**12.24**
SpecExcu$_{V2}$	φ_{SNI}	3	6	9	144	168	1112	SAT	5.61	1.28	2.44	**9.33**
SpecExcu$_{V3}$	φ_{SNI}	3	6	9	87	340	636	UNSAT	7.30	1.68	2.97	**11.95**
SpecExcu$_{V4}$	φ_{SNI}	3	6	9	93	340	636	UNSAT	7.37	1.71	4.50	**13.58**
SpecExcu$_{V5}$	φ_{SNI}	3	6	9	132	168	636	SAT	6.23	1.23	3.48	**10.94**
SpecExcu$_{V6}$	φ_{SNI}	3	7	10	132	340	766	UNSAT	7.47	1.82	3.26	**12.55**
SpecExcu$_{V7}$	φ_{SNI}	2	5	7	144	168	352	SAT	5.83	1.28	2.58	**9.69**
DBE	φ_{SC}	4	4	8	8	6	546	SAT	0.9	0.07	0.01	**0.98**
DBE$_{\mathsf{ndet}}$	$\varphi_{\mathsf{SC}_{\mathsf{nd}}}$	13	13	26	82	72	9414	SAT	1.60	0.56	9.61	**11.77**
DBE$_{\mathsf{ndet}}$ w/ bugs	$\varphi_{\mathsf{SC}_{\mathsf{nd}}}$	13	13	26	82	72	9414	UNSAT	1.36	0.49	2.05	**3.90**
LP	φ_{SC}	22	22	44	80	76	3870	SAT	1.37	1.40	1.13	**3.90**
LP$_{\mathsf{ndet}}$	$\varphi_{\mathsf{SC}_{\mathsf{nd}}}$	17	17	34	558	811	19110	SAT	7.37	3.86	48.15	**59.38**
LP$_{\mathsf{ndet}}$ w/ loops	$\varphi_{\mathsf{SC}_{\mathsf{nd}}}$	33	35	68	757	1591	128114	SAT	30.52	34.99	4165.54	**4231.05**
LP$_{\mathsf{ndet}}$ w/ bugs	$\varphi_{\mathsf{SC}_{\mathsf{nd}}}$	17	17	34	558	661	19110	SAT	6.51	3.60	20.75	**30.86**
EFLP	φ_{SC}	32	32	64	80	248	108290	SAT	5.11	8.12	9.35	**22.58**
EFLP$_{\mathsf{ndet}}$	$\varphi_{\mathsf{SC}_{\mathsf{nd}}}$	18	22	40	582	1729	28986	SAT	15.92	8.90	135.48	**160.30**
EFLP$_{\mathsf{ndet}}$ w/ loops	$\varphi_{\mathsf{SC}_{\mathsf{nd}}}$	33	45	78	295	1996	178894	SAT	36.98	62.89	121.60	**221.47**
CacheTA	φ_{OD}	13	13	26	48	48	9414	UNSAT	1.49	0.53	0.38	**2.40**
CacheTA$_{\mathsf{ndet}}$	$\varphi_{\mathsf{OD}_{\mathsf{nd}}}$	58	58	16	16	32	16258	UNSAT	1.95	1.33	1.02	**4.30**
CacheTA$_{\mathsf{ndet}}$ w/ loops	$\varphi_{\mathsf{OD}_{\mathsf{nd}}}$	35	35	70	88	88	139302	UNSAT	5.50	27.65	125.92	**159.07**

Table 3: Case studies break down for Kripke structures: $\mathcal{K}_1, \mathcal{K}_2$ (all case studies have two, e.g.,one for high-level and one for assembly code), formula: φ, diameter: D, state space: $|S|$, trajectory depth: m, and size of trajectory variables: $|T|$.

6   Conclusion and Future Work

In this paper, we focused on the problem of A-HLTL model checking for *terminating* programs. We generalized A-HLTL to allow nested *trajectory* quantification, where a trajectory determines how different traces may advance and stutter. We rigorously analyzed the complexity of A-HLTL model checking for acyclic Kripke structures. The complexity grows in the polynomial hierarchy with the number of quantifier alternations, and, it is either aligned with that of HyperLTL or is one step higher in the polynomial hierarchy. We also proposed a BMC algorithm for A-HLTL based on QBF-solving and reported successful experimental results on verification of information flow security in concurrent programs, speculative execution, compiler optimization, and cache-based timing attacks.

Asynchronous hyperproperties enable logic-based verification for software programs. Thus, future work includes developing different abstraction techniques such as predicate abstraction, abstraction-refinement, etc, to develop software model checking techniques. We also believe developing synthesis techniques for A-HLTL creates opportunities to automatically generate secure programs and assist in areas such as secure compilation.

References

1. J. Baumeister, N. Coenen, B. Bonakdarpour, B. Finkbeiner, and C. Sánchez. A temporal logic for asynchronous hyperproperties. In *Proc. of the 33rd Int'l Conf. on Computer Aided Verification (CAV'21), Part I*, volume 12759 of *LNCS*, pages 694–717. Springer, 2021.

2. B. Bonakdarpour and B. Finkbeiner. The complexity of monitoring hyperproperties. In *Proceedings of the 31st IEEE Computer Security Foundations Symposium CSF*, pages 162–174, 2018.

3. L. Bozzelli, A. Peron, and C. Sánchez. Asynchronous extensions of HyperLTL. In *Proc. of the 36th Annual ACM/IEEE Symposium on Logic in Computer Science (LICS'21)*, pages 1–13. IEEE, 2021.

4. M. R. Clarkson, F. Finkbeiner, K. Koleini, K. K. Micinski, M. N. Rabe, and C. Sánchez. Temporal logics for hyperproperties. In *Proceedings of the 3rd International Conference on Principles of Security and Trust (POST)*, pages 265–284, 2014.

5. M. R. Clarkson and F. B. Schneider. Hyperproperties. *Journal of Computer Security*, 18(6):1157–1210, 2010.

6. N. Coenen, B. Finkbeiner, C. Hahn, and J. Hofmann. The hierarchy of hyperlogics. In *2019 34th Annual ACM/IEEE Symposium on Logic in Computer Science (LICS)*, pages 1–13, 2019.

7. N. Coenen, B. Finkbeiner, C. Sánchez, and L. Tentrup. Verifying hyperliveness. In I. Dillig and S. Tasiran, editors, *Computer Aided Verification*, pages 121–139, Cham, 2019. Springer International Publishing.

8. B. Finkbeiner, M. Rabe, and C. Sánchez. Algorithms for model checking HyperLTL and HyperCTL*. In *In Proc. of the 27th Int'l Conf. on Computer Aided Verification (CAV'15)*, volume 9206 of *LNCS*, pages 30–48. Springer, 2015.

9. M. Guarnieri, B. Köpf, J. F. Morales, J. Reineke, and A. Sánchez. SPECTECTOR: Principled detection of speculative information flows. In *Proceedings of the 41st IEEE Symposium on Security and Privacy, S&P 2020*. IEEE, 2020.

10. G. L. Guernic. Automaton-based confidentiality monitoring of concurrent programs. In *Proceedings of the 20th IEEE Computer Security Foundations Symposium (CSF)*, pages 218–232, 2007.

11. J. O. Gutsfeld, M. Müller-Olm, and C. Ohrem. Automata and fixpoints for asynchronous hyperproperties. *Proc. ACM Program. Lang.*, 5(POPL):1–29, 2021.

12. M. Herlihy and J. M. Wing. Linearizability: A correctness condition for concurrent objects. *ACM Transactions on Programming Languages and Systems*, 12(3):463–492, 1990.

13. T. Hsu, B. Bonakdarpour, B. Finkbeiner, and C. Sánchez. Bounded model checking for asynchronous hyperproperties. *CoRR*, abs/2301.07208, 2023.

14. T. Hsu and C. Sánchez. Hyperqube: A qbf-based bounded model checker for hyperproperties. *CoRR*, abs/2109.12989, 2021.

15. T.-H. Hsu, C. Sánchez, and B. Bonakdarpour. Bounded model checking for hyperproperties. In *Proceedings of the 27th International Conference on Tools and Algorithms for Construction and Analysis of Systems (TACAS)*, pages 94–112, 2021.

16. J. McLean. A general theory of composition for trace sets closed under selective interleaving functions. In *Proceedings of the IEEE Symposium on Security and Privacy*, pages 79–93, Apr. 1994.

17. K. S. Namjoshi and L. M. Tabajara. Witnessing secure compilation. In *International Conference on Verification, Model Checking, and Abstract Interpretation*, pages 1–22. Springer, 2020.
18. D. Stefan, P. Buiras, E. Z. Yang, A. Levy, D. Terei, A. Russo, and D. Mazières. Eliminating cache-based timing attacks with instruction-based scheduling. In *European Symposium on Research in Computer Security*, pages 718–735. Springer, 2013.
19. S. Zdancewic and A. C. Myers. Observational determinism for concurrent program security. In *Proceedings of the 16th IEEE Computer Security Foundations Workshop (CSFW)*, page 29, 2003.

Model Checking Linear Dynamical Systems under Floating-point Rounding[*]

Engel Lefaucheux[1]([✉])[iD], Joël Ouaknine[2][iD], David Purser[3,4][iD], and
Mohammadamin Sharifi[5][iD]

[1] University of Lorraine, CNRS, Inria, LORIA, Nancy, France
`engel.lefaucheux@inria.fr`
[2] Max Planck Institute for Software Systems, Saarland Informatics Campus,
Saarbrücken, Germany
`joel@mpi-sws.org`
[3] University of Warsaw, Warsaw, Poland
[4] University of Liverpool, Liverpool, UK
`D.Purser@liverpool.ac.uk`
[5] Sharif University of Technology, Tehran, Iran
`sharifim689@gmail.com`

Abstract. We consider linear dynamical systems under floating-point rounding. In these systems, a matrix is repeatedly applied to a vector, but the numbers are rounded into floating-point representation after each step (i.e., stored as a fixed-precision mantissa and an exponent). The approach more faithfully models realistic implementations of linear loops, compared to the exact arbitrary-precision setting often employed in the study of linear dynamical systems.
Our results are twofold: We show that for non-negative matrices there is a special structure to the sequence of vectors generated by the system: the mantissas are periodic and the exponents grow linearly. We leverage this to show decidability of ω-regular temporal model checking against semi-algebraic predicates. This contrasts with the unrounded setting, where even the non-negative case encompasses the long-standing open Skolem and Positivity problems.
On the other hand, when negative numbers are allowed in the matrix, we show that the reachability problem is undecidable by encoding a two-counter machine. Again, this is in contrast with the unrounded setting where point-to-point reachability is known to be decidable in polynomial time.

Keywords: Model Checking · Floating-point · Dynamical Systems.

1 Introduction

Loops are a fundamental staple of any programming language, and the study of loops plays a pivotal role in many subfields of computer science, including automated verification, abstract interpretation, program analysis, semantics, etc. The focus of the present paper is on the algorithmic analysis of simple (i.e., non-nested) linear (or affine) while loops, such as the following:

[*] A long version of this paper is available as [19].

© The Author(s) 2023
S. Sankaranarayanan and N. Sharygina (Eds.): TACAS 2023, LNCS 13993, pp. 47–65, 2023.
https://doi.org/10.1007/978-3-031-30823-9_3

```
x = 3, y = 4, z = 2
while x+3y+z > 4:
    x = 3x +2z
    y = 3x + y
    z = y + z
```

We are interested in analysing how the loop evolves. A simple reachability query is to decide whether the loop variables ever satisfy a Boolean combination of polynomial inequalities, for example modelling a loop guard. More generally, one might seek to consider significantly more complex temporal properties, such as those expressible in linear temporal logic or monadic second-order logic: this gives rise to a model-checking problem.

Modelling the evolution of such a loop may require unbounded memory. That is, the number of bits needed to represent the numbers x, y, and z may grow larger and larger. However, most computer systems do not represent rational numbers to arbitrary precision, but rather use *floating-point rounding*, in which a number y is stored using two components: the mantissa $m \in \mathbb{Q}$ and the exponent $\alpha \in \mathbb{Z}$, such that $y = m \cdot 10^\alpha$.[6]

Typically floating-point numbers are specified using either 32 or 64 bits, with some of these reserved for the mantissa and some for the exponent, thus bounding both the mantissa and the exponent. **We do not do this**, and only place a bound on the number of bits representing the mantissa, allowing the exponent to grow unboundedly (in either direction). From a theoretical standpoint, bounding the number of bits of both the mantissa and the exponent would necessarily give rise to a finite-state system, for which essentially any decision problem would become decidable (at least in principle, if not necessarily in practice). Due to the unboundedness of exponents in our setting, we do not have to consider overflows ('NaN', 'infinity' or '-infinity' which are part of most floating-point specifications).

Formally, we model our programs using linear dynamical systems (LDS), which comprise a starting vector representing the initial state of each variable and a matrix describing the evolution of the program. An LDS generates an infinite sequence of vectors (the *orbit* of the system) by multiplying the matrix with the current vector and then applying floating-point rounding to the result.

Our results

We consider the *model-checking* problem for linear dynamical systems evolving under floating-point rounding. More formally, let $Y_1, \ldots, Y_k \subseteq \mathbb{R}^d$ be semi-algebraic targets. Given an orbit $(x^{(t)})_{t \in \mathbb{N}}$, we define the characteristic word $w = w_1, w_2, w_3, \ldots$ with respect to $Y_1, \ldots, Y_k$ over alphabet $2^{\{1, \ldots, k\}}$ such that $i \in w_t$ if and only if $x^{(t)} \in Y_i$. The model-checking problem asks whether w is in an ω-regular language, or equivalently satisfies a temporal specification given in monadic second-order logic (MSO).

---

[6] We work in base 10 throughout for simplicity of exposition. All our results carry over *mutatis mutandis* in any integer base, including base 2 as typically used in practice.

Our results show that analysing LDS under floating-point rounding is neither clearly easier nor harder than in the standard setting (without rounding). Our first contribution establishes *undecidability* of point-to-point reachability (and *a fortiori* model checking) under floating-point rounding, a surprising outcome given that point-to-point reachability is solvable in polynomial time without rounding [16]. On the other hand, in the standard setting neither decidability nor undecidability are known for full model checking (although mathematical hardness results exist); see [24,18,17].

Theorem 1. *The floating-point point-to-point reachability problem is undecidable.*

However, for non-negative matrices, we show that the full MSO model-checking problem is decidable in our setting, without restrictions on the dimensions of the predicates or the ambient space. This is in stark contrast to the standard setting, where assuming non-negativity does not simplify the problem. Model checking non-negative LDS without rounding would require (at a minimum) solving the longstanding open Skolem and Positivity problems [2].

Theorem 2. *Let (M, x) be a non-negative linear dynamical system, let $Y_1, \ldots, Y_k$ be semialgebraic targets and let ϕ be an MSO formula using predicates over $Y_1, \ldots, Y_k$. It is decidable whether the characteristic word under floating-point rounding satisfies ϕ.*

We place no dimension restriction on the predicates; in particular, showing that the Skolem and Positivity problems are *decidable* on non-negative systems under floating-point rounding. At this time we do not however have complexity upper bounds on our model-checking algorithm, or lower bounds on the model-checking problem.

Related work

There is a line of practical tools for the analysis, verification, and invariant synthesis for floating-point loops [7,20,1,22]. These tools typically work well in practice, but do not necessarily work in all cases. The analysis of concrete implementations of floating-point specifications requires careful analysis of edge cases around $\pm\infty$ and 'NaN'. In contrast to these tools which focus primarily on practical analysis, our work seeks to understand the theoretical possibilities and limitations of the exact analysis of (possibly long-running) floating-point loops in a generalised setting.

The study of linear dynamical systems explores the sequence of vectors induced by a matrix. Model checking is only known to be decidable for certain classes of semialgebraic predicates—in particular those with low dimension [18] or for prefix-independent properties [4]; see also [17]. The well-known Skolem and Positivity problems being special cases of model checking, they place technical limits on the dimensions that can be handled without first resolving longstanding open cases of these problems. Recent progress suggests that the Skolem problem may be yet be conquered, at least for diagonalisable matrices [8,21], but Positivity requires solving particularly difficult problems in analytic number theory [24,12]. The non-negative case can be used to model sequences of distributions induced by Markov chains [6], although all hardness limitations apply already in the probabilistic setting [2].

Baier et al. [5] consider LDS under rounding to fixed-decimal precision, showing reachability is PSPACE-complete for hyperbolic systems (when no eigenvalue has modulus one) and decidable for certain other constrained classes of rounding. A notable difference of fixed-decimal precision is that it cannot allow arbitrarily small numbers, unlike the floating-point numbers we consider.

A recent line of work focusses on linear dynamical systems with perturbations at every step, with a view to understanding the robustness of reachability problems [13,14,3]. However, unlike rounding, the perturbation is chosen in order to assist hitting the target and the perturbation is arbitrarily small.

For linear while loops the reachability problem can be rephrased as a halting problem, asking whether a guard condition is eventually met from a given initial state. The related termination problem asks whether a guard condition is met from *every* initial state [26,10]. Issues arising from implementations using floating-point representations to solve the termination problem of unrounded (arbitrary precision) loops are considered in [27]. In contrast, we are interested in analysing programs in which the intended behaviour is to round the numbers to fixed-precision floating-point numbers at every step of the loop.

Organisation In Section 2, we formalise the model and problems and discuss some of the properties of floating-point rounding. In Section 3, we present our undecidability result for the general case. Finally, in Section 4 we establish some special periodic structure associated with the orbit and use this structure in Section 5 to show that model checking is decidable for non-negative LDS.

2   Preliminaries

2.1   Linear dynamical systems and rounding functions

Definition 1. *A d-dimensional linear dynamical system (LDS) (M, x) comprises a matrix $M \in \mathbb{Q}^{d \times d}$ and an initial vector $x \in \mathbb{Q}^d$.*

Given a rounding function $[\cdot] : \mathbb{Q}^d \to \mathbb{Q}^d$, and an LDS (M, x) the rounded orbit $\mathcal{O}$ is the sequence $(x^{(t)})_{t \in \mathbb{N}}$ such that $x^{(0)} = [x]$ and $x^{(t)} = [Mx^{(t-1)}]$ for all $t \geq 1$.

Given $p \in \mathbb{N}$, we say that a number x is a floating-point number with precision p if $x = m \cdot 10^\alpha$ such that $m \in \mathbb{Q}$ is a decimal number in $\{0\} \cup [0.1, 1)$ with p digits in the fractional part (after the decimal point) and $\alpha \in \mathbb{Z}$. In particular, we associate by convention the number with mantissa $m = 0$ to the exponent $-\infty$. Given a number $x = m \cdot 10^\alpha$ we define $\mathsf{mantissa}(x) = m$ and $\mathsf{exponent}(x) = \alpha$.

We are interested in the floating-point rounding function $[\cdot]$ with precision $p \in \mathbb{N}$. Given a real number $x \in \mathbb{R}$, we define $[x]$, the floating-point rounding of

x, as the closest floating-point number with precision p based on the first $p + 1$ digits of x.

Where there are two possible choices, any deterministic choice that is consistent with the properties listed below is acceptable.[7] We denote by $\mathbb{FP}_{10}[p]$ the subset of $\mathbb{Q}$ representable in base 10 as a floating-point numbers with p digits. We use the following useful properties of the rounding function:

- it is *log-bounded*, *i.e.* there exists a constant $c \in \mathbb{R}_+$ such that $\forall x \in \mathbb{R}$, $\frac{|x|}{c} \leq |[x]| \leq c|x|$.
- it is *mantissa-based*, *i.e.* if $x = 10^{\alpha} x'$, then $[x] = 10^{\alpha}[x']$.
- it is $(p+1)$-*finite*, *i.e.* the output of the rounding is not dependent on the i-th digit of the mantissa, for each integer $i > p + 1$. In other words, if x and x' agree on the first $p + 1$ digits then $[x] = [x']$.
- it is *sign preserving*, *i.e.* $\text{sign}(x) = \text{sign}([x])$. The fact that $[x] = 0$ if and only if $x = 0$ also follows from the log-bounded property.

The floating-point rounding is defined above on a single real. It is extended straightforwardly to a vector x by applying it to each of its components $(x)_i$ where i ranges from 1 to the dimension of the vector. As such, the term $[Mx]$ is obtained by first computing exactly the the vector Mx and then by rounding each component $(Mx)_i$. An alternative approach could be to maintain each subcomputation in p-bits of precision, *but this is not the approach we take*. Such an orbit can be simulated in our setting by increasing the dimension so that operations can be staggered in a way that at most one operation (scalar product or variable addition) is used in each assignment.

2.2   Model checking

We consider the model-checking problem of an LDS over semialgebraic sets.

Definition 2. *A semialgebraic set $Y \subseteq \mathbb{R}^d$ is defined by a finite Boolean combination of polynomial inequalities.*

Let (M, x) be an LDS with rounded orbit $\mathcal{O}$ and $\mathcal{Y} = \{Y_1, \ldots, Y_k\}$ be a collection of semialgebraic sets. The characteristic word of $\mathcal{O}$ is $w = w_1 w_2 w_3 \ldots \in (2^{\{1,\ldots,k\}})^{\omega}$, such that $j \in w_t$ if and only if $x^{(t)} \in Y_j$.

The model-checking problem asks whether the characteristic word is contained within a given ω-regular language, usually specified in a temporal logic such as monadic second order logic (MSO), or often its LTL fragment. Without loss of generality we assume that the property is given as a Büchi automaton [11].

Problem 1 (Floating-point Model-checking Problem). Given an LDS (M, x) with rounded orbit $\mathcal{O}$, a collection of semialgebraic sets $\mathcal{Y} = \{Y_1, \ldots, Y_k\}$ and an ω-regular specification ϕ, the model-checking problem consists in deciding whether the characteristic word w of $\mathcal{O}$ satisfies the specification ϕ.

---

[7] For example, always rounding up, always rounding down, round to even, rounding towards zero, rounding away from zero are acceptable, providing the choice is fixed.

We will also consider the point-to-point reachability problem, which is a subcase of the model-checking problem (Problem 1):

Problem 2 (Floating-point Point-to-point Reachability Problem). Given a d-dimensional LDS (M, x), and a target vector $y \in \mathbb{Q}^d$, the point-to-point reachability problem consists in deciding whether y belongs to the rounded orbit $\mathcal{O}$.

Given a target $Y \subseteq \mathbb{R}^d$, we associate the set of hitting times $\mathcal{Z}(Y) = \{t \mid x^{(t)} \in Y\}$. Under this formulation, the reachability problem is reformulated as whether $\mathcal{Z}(Y)$ is empty. However, for model checking we will develop a more comprehensive understanding of the hitting times of each target $Y_1, \ldots, Y_k$.

2.3   Structure of M

Formally, M is a d-dimensional matrix indexed by the elements $\{1, \ldots, d\}$. However, we interpret M as an automaton over states $Q = \{q_1, \ldots, q_d\}$ and reference the entries of M by pairs of states. That is, we refer to M_{q_1,q_2} rather than $M_{1,2}$.

We denote by G_M the weighted directed graph whose adjacency matrix is M. That is, a graph with vertices Q and with an edge from q_j to q_i weighted by M_{q_i,q_j} if $M_{q_i,q_j} \neq 0$.[8]

Let $S_1, \cdots, S_s \subseteq Q$ be the strongly connected components (SCCs) of G_M. Our analysis will consider each strongly connected component separately, thus it will often be useful to consider the entries of $x \in \mathbb{FP}_{10}[p]^Q$ corresponding only to one strongly connected component. Without loss of generality, by re-ordering the states where necessary, we assume that the states in Q are ordered so that states within the same SCC appear next to one another, and the strongly connected components are topologically sorted, *i.e.* there is no edge from S_i to S_j where $i > j$. We split a vector x into s smaller vectors, denoted $x_{S_1}, \ldots, x_{S_s}$, each representing the entries of x corresponding to the SCC. Letting $x_{S_j} = (z_{1,j}, \cdots, z_{d_j,j})^T$ and $|S_j| = d_j$, we thus have x is partitioned as

$$x = (z_{1,1} \cdots z_{d_1,1}, \cdots, z_{1,s} \cdots z_{d_s,s})^T.$$

Moreover, for each pair of SCCs S_i, S_j, we denote by M_{S_i,S_j} the submatrix of M restricted to the rows related to S_i and columns related to S_j, which is a matrix with d_i rows and d_j columns. If $S_i = S_j$, we simply write M_{S_i}. In other words, M_{S_i,S_j} is the matrix that shows the dependency between S_i and S_j, and we have

$$M = \begin{pmatrix} M_{S_1} & M_{S_1,S_2} & \cdots & M_{S_1,S_s} \\ M_{S_2,S_1} & M_{S_2} & \cdots & M_{S_2,S_s} \\ \vdots & \vdots & \ddots & \vdots \\ M_{S_s,S_1} & M_{S_s,S_2} & \cdots & M_{S_s} \end{pmatrix}$$

We say S_i *feeds* S_j, and S_j is *fed by* S_i if there is some edge in G_M from some state in S_i to some state in S_j.

---

[8] Note that the orientation of the edge may appear switched from the reader's expectation. This is due to the convention that M is pre-multiplied with x at every step.

3   Undecidability of point-to-point reachability

In this section, we give a sketch of the proof of the undecidability of Problem 2 (and thus of Problem 1) in the general case. The full proof can be found in the long version of this paper [19].

Theorem 1. *The floating-point point-to-point reachability problem is undecidable.*

This result is obtained by reduction from the termination of a two-counter Minsky machine. We recall the definition of this model:

Definition 3. *A two-counter Minsky machine is defined by a finite set of states $\ell_1, \ldots, \ell_m$, a distinguished starting state (w.l.o.g. ℓ_1), a distinguished halting state (w.l.o.g. ℓ_m), two natural integer counters, here denoted as x and y, and a mapping deterministically associating to each state transition a particular action. Each transition takes one of the following forms: for $z \in \{x, y\}$,*

increment $\mathrm{inc}_z(\ell_j)$: *add 1 to counter z, move to state ℓ_j.*
decrement $\mathrm{dec}_z(\ell_j)$: *remove 1 from counter z if $z > 0$, move to state ℓ_j.*
zero test $\mathrm{zero?}_z(\ell_j, \ell_k)$: *if $z = 0$ move to state ℓ_j else move to state ℓ_k.*

The configuration of a two-counter Minsky machine consists of the current state and the values of x and y.

Without loss of generality (by first using a zero test), one can assume a decrementation operation is never used in a configuration where the counter to be decreased has value 0, hence removing the need to check whether $z > 0$.

The halting problem asks whether, starting in configuration $(\ell_1, 0, 0)$, that is, in the distinguished starting state with both counters set to 0, whether the state ℓ_m is reached. The problem is undecidable [23].

We build an LDS with mantissa length $p = 1$ and base 10 that simulates a run of a given Minsky machine. The reduction happens to maintain the invariant that each mantissa always has the value 0 or 1 after rounding (although, as we operate in base 10, there are 10 possible values the mantissa could have taken). For ease of readability, we describe this LDS using variables to represent the dimensions and linear functions to represent the transition matrix. For each state of the Minsky machine, we use two variables corresponding to the two counters. Throughout the simulation, if the Minsky machine is in state j, the counter values are stored in the exponents of the variables associated with state j, and all other variables are zero.

The crux of our reduction lies in the handling of the zero test. More precisely, suppose we need to branch depending on whether x is equal to 0, then we need to define linear transitions that transfer the values of the two counters from one pair of variables to the appropriate new pair of variables. This is done using filter functions: the function $\mathrm{filter}_+(u, v)$ (resp. $\mathrm{filter}_-(u, v)$) is equal to v if $v \geq u$ (resp. $v < u$) and to 0 otherwise. We end this sketch with the construction of these functions and proof that they operate as advertised.

Lemma 1. *Given u, v of the form 10^c with $c \in \mathbb{N}$, one can compute the value $w = \text{filter}_+(u, v)$ in three linear operations with floating-point rounding.*

Proof. We compute $w = \text{filter}_+(u, v)$ in three successive operations using two temporary variables, *temp* and *temp2*, initially set at 0 (recall, rounding is applied after each step):

$$temp \leftarrow u + v$$
$$temp2 \leftarrow temp - u$$
$$w \quad \leftarrow 1.1 * temp2$$

Let $c_1, c_2 \in \mathbb{N}$ such that $u = 10^{c_1}$ and $v = 10^{c_2}$. Recall that the notation $[\cdot]$ is the floating-point rounding function.

First observe that if $c_1 = c_2$:

$$temp \quad \leftarrow [10^{c_1} + 10^{c_2}] = 2 \cdot 10^{c_1}$$
$$temp2 \leftarrow [2 \cdot 10^{c_1} - 10^{c_1}] = 10^{c_1} (= v)$$
$$w \quad \quad \leftarrow [1.1 \cdot 10^{c_1}] = 10^{c_1} = v \quad \text{as required.}$$

Secondly, assume that $u > v$, and thus $c_1 > c_2$:

$$temp \quad \leftarrow [10^{c_1} + 10^{c_2}] = 10^{c_1} = u$$
$$temp2 \leftarrow [10^{c_1} - 10^{c_1}] = 0$$
$$w \quad \quad \leftarrow [1.1 \cdot 0] = 0 \quad \text{as required.}$$

We split the case that $v > u$, thus $c_2 > c_1$, into two cases. Suppose $c_2 > c_1 + 1$:

$$temp \quad \leftarrow [10^{c_1} + 10^{c_2}] = 10^{c_2} = v$$
$$temp2 \leftarrow [10^{c_2} - 10^{c_1}] = [0.\underbrace{99 \ldots 99}_{c_2 - c_1 \geq 2} \cdot 10^{c_2}] = 1 \cdot 10^{c_2} = v$$
$$w \quad \quad \leftarrow [1.1 \cdot 10^{c_2}] = 10^{c_2} = v \quad \text{as required.}$$

Finally, $c_2 = c_1 + 1$:

$$temp \quad \leftarrow [10^{c_1} + 10^{c_2}] = 10^{c_2} = v$$
$$temp2 \leftarrow [10^{c_2} - 10^{c_1}] = [0.9 \cdot 10^{c_2}] = 9 \cdot 10^{c_2 - 1}$$
$$w \quad \quad \leftarrow [1.1 \cdot 9 \cdot 10^{c_2 - 1}] = [9.9 \cdot 10^{c_2 - 1}] = 10 \cdot 10^{c_2 - 1} = 10^{c_2} = v$$

$$\text{as required.} \quad \square$$

Corollary 1. *Given u, v of the form 10^c with $c \in \mathbb{N}$, one can compute the value $w = \text{filter}_-(u, v)$ in four linear operations with floating-point rounding.*

Proof. Observe that $\text{filter}_-(u, v) = v - \text{filter}_+(u, v)$, which can be encoded in four steps by first computing $\text{filter}_+(u, v)$ in three steps. $\square$

4   Pseudo-periodic orbits of non-negative LDS

We shift our focus to proving that model checking is decidable for systems with non-negative matrices. We first establish the behaviour of the system in this section and then complete the proof of Theorem 2 in Section 5. Our main result is that the rounded orbit of an LDS is periodic in the following sense, which we call *pseudo-periodic*.

Definition 4. *A sequence $(x^{(t)})_{i \in \mathbb{N}}$ of d-dimensional vectors of floating-point numbers is called pseudo-periodic if and only if there exists a starting point $N \in$*

N, *period* $T \in \mathbb{N}$ *and growth rates* $\alpha_1, \ldots, \alpha_d \in \mathbb{Z}$ *such that*

$$\forall t \geq N, \forall j \in \{1, \ldots, d\}, (x^{(t+T)})_j = 10^{\alpha_j} (x^{(t)})_j.$$

We say the sequence is effectively pseudo-periodic if the defining constants $N, T, \alpha_1, \ldots, \alpha_d$ *can be computed.*

Theorem 3. *Let* (M, x) *be a d-dimensional LDS where* M *is non-negative and let* $(x^{(t)})_{t \in \mathbb{N}}$ *be its rounded orbit.*
The rounded orbit $(x^{(t)})_{t \in \mathbb{N}}$ *is effectively pseudo-periodic.*

In order to establish this result, we will find some partitions of the graph associated to M such that each part is effectively pseudo-periodic with the same increasing rate α for every state in the partition.

4.1 Preprocessing periodicity

The core of our approach is to show that, within each SCC of the graph associated to M, the values associated with states are of similar magnitude. This is however only true if the SCC is aperiodic. When a state is in a periodic SCC its value could change drastically depending on which phase the system is in. For example, consider a simple alternation between two states, in which the value is very large in one state and very small in the other; the states will alternate between big and small values.

We "hide" these periodic behaviours by blowing up the system so that each SCC of the new system describes only one of the periodic subsequence and we will subsequently show that the value of each state in an SCC is either zero or of a similar magnitude.

We apply the following construction to our system. Let P be the period, defined as the least common multiple of the length of every simple cycle in the graph. Let Q be the indices of M (*i.e.* the states of the generated automaton). We define new states $Q' = Q \times \{0, \ldots, P - 1\}$ by annotating each state in Q with the phase. To avoid cluttering notation we will regularly refer to states in Q' in the form $(q, i + \ell)$ for $\ell \in \mathbb{Z}$, on the understanding that the phase, $i + \ell$, is normalised into $\{0, \ldots, P - 1\}$ by taking the residue modulo P if necessary. We define a new matrix M' over the states Q' such that $M'_{(q,i+1),(q',i)} = M_{q,q'}$ for $i \in \{0, \ldots, P - 1\}$, and zero otherwise. We initialise a new starting vector $x^{(0)}_{(q,0)} = x^{(0)}_q$ and $x^{(0)}_{(q,i)} = 0$ for $i \in \{1, \ldots, P - 1\}$.

Intuitively, at each time step t the vector generated by the original system is equal to the vector of the new system restricted to the states indexed by $i \equiv t$ mod P and every state with another index is equal to 0.

Let $S \subseteq Q$ be a strongly connected component. In Q' there exists strongly connected components $S'_1, \ldots, S'_k \subseteq Q'$ with $k \leq |S|$ such that $\bigcup_{i=1}^{k} S'_i = S \times \{0, \ldots, P - 1\}$. Each set S'_j is periodic, with period P.

Henceforth in the rest of this section we work on the system (M', x') implicitly over states Q' which, by overloading of notation, we rename (M, x) over Q to avoid cluttering notation.

Note that this transformation also requires to marginally complicate the targets. Indeed, consider a set $Y \subseteq \mathbb{R}^Q$. We define the sets Y/i for $i < P$ such that $Y/i = \{y \in \mathbb{R}^{Q'} \mid \exists y' \in Y : y_{(q,i)} = y'_q$ for $q \in Q$ and $y'_{(q,j)} = 0$ for $j \neq i\}$. The hitting times of Y, $\mathcal{Z}(Y)$, in the original LDS can then be obtained in the new LDS as the disjoin union: $\bigcup_{i \in \{0,\dots,P-1\}} \mathcal{Z}(Y/i)$. It suffices to characterise the hitting times for each Y/i.

4.2   Pseudo-periodicity within top SCCs

Let us first consider top SCCs, these are SCCs with no incoming edges from states of other SCC, and therefore the value of each variable at each step depends only on the value of states in the same SCC.

Lemma 2. *Let S_j be a strongly connected component of (M, x). Let $S_{j,i} = \{(q, i) \in S_j\}$ be the states associated with S_j from the i-th phase.*

There exists $C \leq Pd^2$, such that, for every i, j, $(M^C)_{S_{j,i}}$ is positive.

Proof. The matrix $(M^P)_{S_{j,i}}$ is non-negative, irreducible (*i.e.*, its graph is strongly connected) and of period 1. As such, $(M^P)_{S_{j,i}}$ is primitive [9] which means that a power C' of this matrix is positive. The theorem follows with $C = PC'$. Moreover, C' is at most $d^2 - 2d + 2$ [25]. □

Our goal is to show that within an SCC, each of the non-zero entries are of a similar magnitude due to the presence of a relatively short path (C) between any two states in the SCC. To do this we introduce the notion of closeness and observe some useful properties.

Definition 5. *We say two numbers $x, x' \in \mathbb{FP}_{10}[p]$ are δ-close, denoted by $x \approx_\delta x'$ if $|\text{exponent}(x) - \text{exponent}(x')| < \delta$. In particular, for every $\delta > 0$, zero is assumed to be δ-close only to itself.*

We extend the notion to vectors $y, y \in \mathbb{FP}_{10}[p]^S$, indexed by $S \subseteq Q$, such that $y \approx_\delta y'$ if all entries of the same phase are δ-close to one another across both y and y', that is, for each phase $i \in \{0, \dots, P-1\}$ and all $(q,i), (q',i) \in S$: $y_{(q,i)} \approx_\delta y'_{(q',i)}$, $y_{(q,i)} \approx_\delta y_{(q',i)}$ and $y'_{(q,i)} \approx_\delta y'_{(q',i)}$.

Proposition 1. *Let $x, x' \in \mathbb{FP}_{10}[p]$ be non-zero floating-point numbers.*

(1) *If $x \approx_\delta x'$ then $10^{-\delta-1} \leq x/x' \leq 10^{\delta+1}$.*
(2) *If $10^{-\delta} \leq x/x' \leq 10^\delta$ then $x \approx_{\delta+2} x'$.*
(3) *If $x \approx_\delta x'$ and $x' \approx_\eta x''$ then $x \approx_{\delta+\eta+4} x''$.*

Lemma 3. *Let S_j be a top strongly connected component of (M, x), and let C be as given by Lemma 2.*

There exists $\beta \in \mathbb{N}$ such that for all $(q, i), (q', i) \in S_j$ and every $t \geq C$ then

- *if $t \not\equiv i \mod P$, then $x^{(t)}_{(q,i)} = 0$,*
- *otherwise, $x^{(t)}_{(q,i)} \approx_\beta x^{(t)}_{(q',i)}$.*

Proof. Let $t \in \mathbb{N}$. If $t \not\equiv i \mod P$ then $x_{(q,i)}^{(t)} = 0$ for all $(q,i) \in S_{j,i}$ by construction.

Otherwise, let $m \geq \max\limits_{q,q' \in Q : M_{q,q'} \neq 0} \max\left(M_{q,q'}, (M_{q,q'})^{-1}\right)$ be a constant larger than all values occurring in M and so that $\frac{1}{m}$ is smaller than all non-zero values appearing in M. Let c be the constant from the log bounded property of the rounding function $[\cdot]$ and d be the dimension of M.

Observe that for all $t \in \mathbb{N}$ with $t = i \mod P$ we have

$$x_{(q,i)}^{(t)} = \left[\sum_{(q',i-1)} M_{(q,i),(q',i-1)} x_{(q',i-1)}^{(t-1)} \right]$$

$$\geq \frac{1}{c} \sum_{(q',i-1)} M_{(q,i),(q',i-1)} x_{(q',i-1)}^{(t-1)} \qquad \text{(by log bounded)}$$

$$\geq \frac{1}{cm} \max_{(q',i-1) \text{ s.t. } M_{(q,i),(q',i-1)}>0} x_{(q',i-1)}^{(t-1)} \qquad \text{(by defn of } m\text{)}$$

In particular

$$x_{(q,i)}^{(t)} \geq \frac{1}{cm} x_{(q',i-1)}^{(t-1)} \text{ for all } (q',i-1) \text{ s.t. } M_{(q,i),(q',i-1)} > 0$$

Using induction we obtain:

$$x_{(q,i+k)}^{(t+k)} \geq \frac{1}{(cm)^{k-1}} x_{(q',i+1)}^{(t+1)} \geq \frac{1}{(cm)^{k}} x_{(q'',i)}^{(t)}$$

for all $(q',i+1), (q'',i)$ such that $M_{(q,i+k),(q',i+1)}^{k-1} > 0$ and $M_{(q',i+1),(q'',i)} > 0$.

In particular, we have $x_{(q,i)}^{(t+C)} \geq \frac{1}{(cm)^{C}} x_{(q',i)}^{(t)}$ for all q' (since $M_{(q,i),(q',i)}^{C} > 0$ for all q' by the previous lemma).

On the other hand we have

$$x_{(q,i+1)}^{(t+1)} = \left[\sum_{q' : M_{(q,i+1),(q',i)}>0} M_{(q,i+1),(q',i)} x_{(q',i)}^{(t)} \right] \leq mcd \max_{(q',i) \in S_j} x_{(q',i)}^{(t)}.$$

By induction we get that $x_{(q,i)}^{(t+C)} \leq (mcd)^{C} \max_{(q',i) \in S_j} x_{(q',i)}^{(t)}$. Hence, for all $q, q' \in S_j$ we have

$$\frac{1}{(mc)^{C}} \max_{(q'',i) \in S_j} x_{(q'',i)}^{(t)} \leq x_{(q',i)}^{(t+C)} \quad \text{and} \quad x_{(q,i)}^{(t+C)} \leq (mcd)^{C} \max_{(q'',i) \in S_j} x_{(q'',i)}^{(t)}.$$

Hence $\frac{x_{(q,i)}^{(t+C)}}{x_{(q',i)}^{(t+C)}} \leq d^{C}(mc)^{2C}$.

Setting $\gamma = \lceil \log_{10} d^{C}(mc)^{2C} \rceil$, we thus have that $10^{-\gamma} x_{(q',i)}^{(t+C)} \leq x_{(q,i)}^{(t+C)} \leq 10^{\gamma} x_{(q',i)}^{(t+C)}$ for all $(q,i), (q',i) \in S_{j,i}$ and $t \in \mathbb{N}$. Then $x_{(q',i)}^{(t)}$ and $x_{(q,i)}^{(t)}$ are $\beta = \gamma+2$ close by Proposition 1. $\qquad \square$

Lemma 4. *Let S_j be a top strongly connected component of (M, x). Then the sequence $(x_{S_j}^{(t)})_{t \in \mathbb{N}}$ is effectively pseudo-periodic.*

Proof. Let β and C be as in Lemma 3. Denote $q_1, \ldots, q_m$ the states of S_j. We define the sequence $(y^{(t)})_{t \geq C}$ such that for all $t \geq C$ and $q \in S_j$ denoting $(p^{(t)})_q = \mathsf{mantissa}([x_q^{(t)}])$ and $(\alpha^{(t)})_q = \mathsf{exponent}([x_q^{(t)}])$ we have that $y^{(t)} = (p_{q_1}, 0, p_{q_2}, \alpha_{q_2} - \alpha_{q_1}, \ldots, p_{q_m}, \alpha_{q_m} - \alpha_{q_1})$. Note that this sequence can only take finitely many values as the mantissas have a precision of p decimals and by Lemma 3, for all $k \leq m$, $\alpha_{q_k} - \alpha_{q_1} \in \{-\beta, \ldots, \beta\}$. As a consequence, the sequence $(y^{(t)})_{t \geq C}$ takes the same value multiple times. Let k_1 and k_2 be the two distinct minimal integers such that $y^{(k_1)} = y^{(k_2)}$. Setting $\alpha = \alpha_{q_1}^{(k_2)} - \alpha_{q_1}^{(k_1)}$ We have that $x^{(k_1)} = x^{(k_2)} \cdot 10^\alpha$. Since $[\cdot]$ is mantissa-based, one can show by induction that for all $t \geq 0$, $x^{(k_1 + t)} = x^{(k_2 + t)} \cdot 10^\alpha$. Therefore the sequence $(x_{S_j}^{(t)})_{t \in \mathbb{N}}$ is effectively pseudo-periodic with period $T = k_2 - k_1$ and starting point $N = C + k_1$.

Moreover, as the maximum number of different values taken by $(y^{(t)})_{t \geq C}$ is known, we can deduce that both k_1 and $k_2 - k_1$ are smaller than $10^{pm}(2\beta + 1)^m + 1$. □

Note that the increasing rate is the same for every state of the strongly connected component.

4.3 Pseudo-periodicity within lower SCCs

We consider a strongly connected component S_{me}, which is fed by at least one strongly connected components $F_1, \ldots, F_\ell$, $\ell \geq 1$. We let $S_F = F_1 \cup \cdots \cup F_\ell$ and assume every F_i is pseudo-periodic.

In this section we show

Theorem 4. *S_{me} is effectively pseudo-periodic and the growth rate of S_{me} is the same for all $q \in S_{me}$.*

We first observe that the difference between values in S_{me} is bounded. This is achieved with a proof similar to the one of Lemma 2 and Lemma 3 (though having to combine considerations of S_{me} and S_F).

Lemma 5. *There exists $\eta, N' \in \mathbb{N}$, such that for all $(q, i), (q', i) \in S_{me}$, all $t \geq N'$ and all $i \in \{0, \ldots, P - 1\}$ then*

- *if $t \not\equiv i \mod P$, then $x_{(q,i)}^{(t)} = 0$,*
- *otherwise, $x_{(q,i)}^{(t)} \approx_\eta x_{(q',i)}^{(t)}$.*

Definition 6. *We say that $x_q^{(t)}$ is influenced by S_F if*

$$x_q^{(t)} = \left[\sum_{q' \in S_F} M_{q,q'} x_{q'}^{(t-1)} + \sum_{q' \in S_{me}} M_{q,q'} x_{q'}^{(t-1)} \right] \neq \left[\sum_{q' \in S_{me}} M_{q,q'} x_{q'}^{(t-1)} \right]$$

and in particular $x_q^{(t)}$ is influenced by $u \in S_F$ if:

$$\left[\sum_{q' \in S_F \cup S_{me}} M_{q,q'} x_{q'}^{(t-1)} \right] \neq \left[\sum_{q' \in S_F \cup S_{me} \setminus \{u\}} M_{q,q'} x_{q'}^{(t-1)} \right].$$

We can restrict S_F to the F_i in S_F with the maximum growth rate. Indeed, from some point on, any F_i with non-maximal growth rate is much smaller than the maximal ones, and as by the proof of Lemma 5 the values within S_{me} are close to (or greater than) the maximum value within S_F, this F_i would not influence with any $x_q^{(t)}$ with $q \in S_{me}$. Let N_1 be the point from which we can assume, that the elements of S_F are much larger than any other feeding SCCs and are thus the only ones potentially influencing of S_{me}.

Since each F_i is assumed to be pseudo-periodic, we have that S_F pseudo-periodic. Let T be the period of S_F, N_2 be the starting point and α be the growth rate of every state of S_F (meaning the exponent of every state changes by α every T starting form the N-th step.) Let $N = \max\{N_1, N_2\}$, that is, the point from which we can assume S_F is both pseudo-periodic and dominating non-maximal SCCs feeding S_{me}.

As a direct consequence of having the same growth rate, the non-zero terms within S_F are close:

Proposition 2. *If a sequence of non-zero floating-point vectors $(v^{(t)})_{t \in \mathbb{N}}$ is pseudo-periodic with the same growth rate within a set Q, then there exists δ such that for all $q, q' \in Q$ and all $t \geq N$, $v_q^{(t)} \approx_\delta v_{q'}^{(t)}$.*

Moreover, either S_F does not influence S_{me}, or they are close.

Lemma 6. *There exists $\beta, N \in \mathbb{N}$ such that:*
For $t \geq N$ and $(q, i) \in S_{me}$, if $x_{(q,i)}^{(t)}$ is influenced by $(q', i - 1) \in S_F$, then
$x_{(r,i)}^{(t)} \approx_\beta x_{(r',i)}^{(t)}$ *for all $(r, i), (r', i) \in S_{me} \cup S_F$.*

We will show Theorem 4 through the following observation:

Observation 1. Observe that S_F either influences S_{me} infinitely many times or finitely many times. We have two cases:

- If S_F influences S_{me} infinitely often, then they are infinitely often β-close by Lemma 6. Then we will observe through a simultaneous version of Lemma 4 that S_{me} is pseudo-periodic.
- If S_F influences S_{me} only finitely often, then clearly from some point on S_{me} behaves like a top SCC, and thus is pseudo-periodic directly by Lemma 4.

It will then remain to show that we can detect which of the two cases applies, and place a bound on the time to detect this, which will effectively reveal the constants of the pseudo-periodic behaviour.

We now present a version of Lemma 4 to observe that if S_F and S_{me} are infinitely often β-close then S_{me} is pseudo-periodic:

Lemma 7. *Suppose $x_{S_F}^{(t)} \approx_\beta x_{S_{me}}^{(t)}$ for infinitely many t. Then there exists $t_1 < t_2$, such that $x_{S_F}^{(t_1)} \approx_\beta x_{S_{me}}^{(t_1)}$ and $x_{S_F}^{(t_2)} \approx_\beta x_{S_{me}}^{(t_2)}$, $x_{S_F}^{(t_2)} = 10^\gamma x_{S_F}^{(t_1)}$ and $x_{S_{me}}^{(t_2)} = 10^\gamma x_{S_{me}}^{(t_1)}$. In particular, the sequence $(x_{S_{me}}^{(t)})_{t \in \mathbb{N}}$ is pseudo-periodic with period $(t_2 - t_1)$, starting from t_1 with growth rate of γ in every state.*

Proof. At a time t such that $x_{S_F}^{(t)} \approx_\beta x_{S_{me}}^{(t)}$, we denote the vectors $x_{S_F}^{(t)} \in \mathbb{FP}_{10}[p]^{|S_F|}$ and $x_{S_{me}}^{(t)} \in \mathbb{FP}_{10}[p]^{|S_{me}|}$ respectively

$$(m_1^{(t)} 10^{\gamma_1^{(t)}}, m_2^{(t)} 10^{\gamma^{(t)} + \alpha_2^{(t)}}, \ldots, m_{|S_F|}^{(t)} 10^{\gamma^{(t)} + \alpha_{|S_F|}^{(t)}}) \text{ and}$$

$$(n_1^{(t)} 10^{\gamma^{(t)} + \zeta_1^{(t)}}, \ldots, n_{|S_{me}|}^{(t)} 10^{\gamma^{(t)} + \zeta_{|S_{me}|}^{(t)}}),$$

where m_i, n_i are taken from the finite set of mantissa values expressible in p bits, $\gamma^{(t)} \in \mathbb{Z}$ and $\alpha_i, \zeta_i \in \mathbb{Z} \cap [-\beta, \beta]$ denote the offset from $\gamma^{(t)}$.

Let F bound the number of possible values $m_i, n_i, \alpha_i, \zeta_i$ can take on, where $F \leq 10^{p(|S_F| + |S_{me}|)} \cdot (2\beta + 1)^{|S_F| + |S_{me}| - 1}$. By the pigeonhole principle, after at most $F + 1$ times in which $x_{S_F}^{(t)} \approx_\beta x_{S_{me}}^{(t)}$ there must exist two times $t_1 < t_2$ where the values of $m_i, n_i, \alpha_i, \beta_i$'s are equal (although the value of γ could be different), thus $x_{S_F \cup S_{me}}^{(t_2)} = \frac{10^{\gamma^{(t_2)}}}{10^{\gamma^{(t_1)}}} x_{S_F \cup S_{me}}^{(t_1)}$.

Since the rounding function is mantissa-based, the system evolution from $x^{(t_1)}$ is equivalent to the systems evolution from $x^{(t_2)} = 10^\gamma x^{(t_1)}$, where γ is the growth rate, $\gamma^{(t_2)} - \gamma^{(t_1)}$. $\qquad \square$

We can in fact decide whether $x_{S_F}^{(t)} \approx_\beta x_{S_{me}}^{(t)}$ for the last time:

Lemma 8. *Let β, N be defined as in Lemma 6. If $t \geq N$ then it is decidable whether there exists $t' > t$ such that $x_{S_F}^{(t')} \approx_\beta x_{S_{me}}^{(t')}$.*

Proof Sketch (Full proof available in [19]). If we considered S_{me} in isolation, without the effect of S_F, we know it would be pseudo-periodic. We can simulate one period of S_{me} with and without the effect of S_F and determine if S_F influences S_{me} within one period. If it does then they must be close at this point. If S_F does not influence S_{me} we know that S_{me} will behave pseudo-periodically at least until S_F is close to S_{me} again; having established a growth rate for S_{me}, we can compare the growth rates of S_F and S_{me} to see if S_{me} will ever be close to S_F again in the future. $\qquad \square$

Finally to conclude the proof of Theorem 4, we refine Observation 1 to show that the period is bounded and thus the growth rates are computable:

- either S_F is β-close to S_{me} infinitely often, in particular if they become close $F + 1$ times then by Lemma 7 it is pseudo-periodic.
- or the system is pseudo-periodic because it behaves like a top-SCC, in which Lemma 4 gives effective computation of the constants.

Which of these occurs is determined by at most $F + 1$ applications of Lemma 8.

5   Decidability of model checking

In this section we use the results obtained in the previous section to show that model checking is decidable. We use pseudo-periodicity to show that the characteristic word is eventually periodic, a case for which model checking is decidable.

Theorem 2. *Let (M, x) be a non-negative linear dynamical system, let $Y_1, \ldots, Y_k$ be semialgebraic targets and let ϕ be an MSO formula using predicates over $Y_1, \ldots, Y_k$. It is decidable whether the characteristic word under floating-point rounding satisfies ϕ.*

Consider a semialgebraic target Y, which can be expressed as a Boolean combination of polynomial inequalities over variables representing the dimensions. That is $Y = \{(x_1, \ldots, x_d) \mid \bigwedge_i \bigvee_j P_{ij}(x_1, \ldots, x_n) \rhd_{ij} 0\}$, where $\rhd_{ij} \in \{\geq, >, =\}$.

Given a linear dynamical system (M, x) defining the rounded orbit $(x^{(n)})_{n=1}^{\infty}$, recall that $\mathcal{Z}(Y) = \{n \mid x^{(n)} \in Y\}$ are the hitting times of Y. We claim that this set is semi-linear (equivalently eventually periodic) for semialgebraic Y.

Definition 7. *A 1-dimensional linear-set, defined by a base $b \in \mathbb{N}$ and period $p \in \mathbb{N}$, is the set $\{x \mid \exists k \in \mathbb{N} : x = b + k \cdot p\}$. A semi-linear set is the finite union of a finite set $F \subseteq \mathbb{N}$ and linear sets. It can be assumed that each linear-set has the same period. Hence a 1-dimensional semi-linear set X is defined by a finite set $F \subseteq \mathbb{N}$ and integers $m, p, b_1, \ldots, b_m \in \mathbb{N}$ such that $x \in X$ if and only if $x \in F$ or $x = b + k \cdot p$ for some $k \in \mathbb{N}$ and $b \in \{b_1, \ldots, b_m\}$.*

Theorem 5. *Let Y be a semialgebraic target, $\mathcal{Z}(Y)$ is a semi-linear set.*

Theorem 5 essentially completes the proof of Theorem 2. It is almost immediate that the characteristic word is eventually periodic (see the long version [19] for a formal proof) and thus the model-checking problem can be decided by checking $A \cap \overline{B} = \emptyset$, where A is an automaton representing the characteristic word and B encodes the language of ϕ.

It is standard that semi-linear sets are closed under intersection, union, and complementation (see [15] for a nice introduction to semi-linear sets). Thus in order to express the hitting times of $\mathcal{Z}(Y)$ it is sufficient to express the hitting times of $\{(x_1, \ldots, x_d) \mid P(x_1, \ldots, x_n) \geq 0\}$ for a finitely many polynomials P. Conjunction is found by taking the intersection of the hitting times, and disjunction by taking union. The hitting times of $P(x_1, \ldots, x_n) > 0$ can be rewritten as the complement of the hitting times of $-P(x_1, \ldots, x_n) \geq 0$. The hitting times of $P(x_1, \ldots, x_n) = 0$ is the conjunction (intersection) of $P(x_1, \ldots, x_n) \geq 0$ and $-P(x_1, \ldots, x_n) \geq 0$. Thus Theorem 5 is a consequence of the following lemma.

Lemma 9. *Assume $x^{(t)} = (z_1^{(t)}, \ldots, z_d^{(t)})_{i=1}^{\infty}$, is a pseudo-periodic sequence with start point N, period T and growth rates $\alpha_1, \ldots, \alpha_n$ and $P \in \mathbb{Q}[x_1, \cdots, x_d]$ a rational polynomial in d variables.[9] Then, $\{i \in \mathbb{N} \mid P(z_1^{(t)}, \cdots, z_d^{(t)}) \geq 0\}$ is a semi-linear set.*

---

[9] Some variables may be redundant, that is, if the polynomial does not depend on all dimensions of $x^{(t)}$ then some of the variables may not appear in P.

Proof. First, we show that pseudo-periodicity is closed under product. Suppose $x_i^{(N+Tn)} = m_i 10^{\beta_i + \alpha_i \cdot n}$ and $x_j^{(N+Tn)} = m_j 10^{\beta_j + \alpha_j \cdot n}$. Observe that $x_i^{(N+Tn)} \cdot x_j^{(N+Tn)} = m_i \cdot 10^{\beta_i + \alpha_i n} m_j \cdot 10^{\beta_j + \alpha_j n} = m_i m_j \cdot 10^{\beta_i + \beta_j + n(\alpha_i + \alpha_j)}$. We conclude that the vector $(x_i \cdot x_j)^{(t)}$ is pseudo-periodic with growth rate $\alpha_i + \alpha_j$. Observe that the mantissa precision increase by at most 2.

Secondly, we show that if two pseudo-periodic sequences have the same growth rate, then their sum is also pseudo-periodic with the same growth rate. Suppose $x_i^{(N+Tn)} = m_i 10^{\beta_i + \alpha \cdot n}$, and $x_j^{(N+Tn)} = m_j 10^{\beta_j + \alpha \cdot n}$. Observe that $(x_i + x_j)^{(N+Tn)} = m_i 10^{\beta_i + \alpha \cdot n} + m_j 10^{\beta_j + \alpha \cdot n} = (m_i + m_j \cdot 10^{\beta_j - \beta_i}) 10^{\beta_i + \alpha \cdot n}$. Observe that the mantissa precision increased by at most $10^{|\beta_j - \beta_i|}$.

Let $P(x_1, \ldots, x_n) = \sum_{i=1}^{N} c_i Z_i$, where Z_i is a product of $x_1, \ldots, x_n$. Consider each monomial Z_i occurring in P, since produce preserves pseudo-periodicity, we conclude that Z_i is pseudo-periodic. $P^{(t)}$ is thus a linear combination of these pseudo-periodic vectors. Note our prior observation does not immediately imply that $P^{(t)}$ is pseudo-periodic as we required taking the sum of elements with the same growth rate. However, from some point on, we are only interested in those with the maximal growth rate.

Without loss of generality, let $Z_1, \ldots, Z_r$ have the maximum-growth rate, and $Z_{r+1}, \ldots, Z_N$ have strictly smaller growth rate. For every $L \in \mathbb{N}$ there exists $N \in \mathbb{N}$ such that for all $t > N$, $\mathsf{exponent}(Z_1^{(t)}) - \mathsf{exponent}(Z_{r+1}^{(t)}) > L$.

Hence there exists $N \in \mathbb{N}$ such that for all $t > N$ if $\sum_{i=1}^{r} c_i Z_i > 0$ if and only if $\sum_{i=1}^{N} c_i Z_i = \sum_{i=1}^{r} c_i Z_i + \sum_{i=r+1}^{N} c_i Z_i > 0$ because $\left| \sum_{i=r+1}^{N} c_i Z_i \right| < \left| \sum_{i=1}^{r} c_i Z_i \right|$ from some point on. Hence $\mathsf{sign}(\sum_{i=1}^{N} c_i Z_i^{(t)}) = \mathsf{sign}(\sum_{i=1}^{r} c_i Z_i^{(t)})$.

Thus we restrict our attention to $\sum_{i=1}^{r} c_i Z_i^{(t)}$. Since each of the Z_i for $i \in \{1, \ldots, r\}$ have the same growth rate, we know that $\sum_{i=1}^{r} c_i Z_i^{(t)}$ is pseudo-periodic. Since $\mathsf{sign}(\sum_{i=1}^{r} c_i Z_i^{(t)})$ does not depend on the exponent, only the periodic mantissa, we have that the sign is periodic. The hitting times for $t \leq N$ can be determined exhaustively and included in the finite set of the semi-linear set. $\qquad\square$

Acknowledgements Partially funded by DFG grant 389792660 as part of TRR 248 – CPEC, see `perspicuous-computing.science`. Joël Ouaknine is also affiliated with Keble College, Oxford as `emmy.network` Fellow. David Purser was partially supported by the ERC grant INFSYS, agreement no. 950398.

References

1. Abbasi, R., Schiffl, J., Darulova, E., Ulbrich, M., Ahrendt, W.: Deductive verification of floating-point java programs in key. In: Groote, J.F., Larsen, K.G. (eds.) Tools and Algorithms for the Construction and Analysis of Systems - 27th International Conference, TACAS 2021, Part of ETAPS 2021. Part II. Lecture Notes in Computer Science, vol. 12652, pp. 242–261. Springer (2021). https://doi.org/10.1007/978-3-030-72013-1_13

2. Akshay, S., Antonopoulos, T., Ouaknine, J., Worrell, J.: Reachability problems for Markov chains. Inf. Process. Lett. **115**(2), 155–158 (2015). https://doi.org/10.1016/j.ipl.2014.08.013

3. Akshay, S., Bazille, H., Genest, B., Vahanwala, M.: On robustness for the Skolem and Positivity problems. In: Berenbrink, P., Monmege, B. (eds.) 39th International Symposium on Theoretical Aspects of Computer Science, STACS 2022. LIPIcs, vol. 219, pp. 5:1–5:20. Schloss Dagstuhl - Leibniz-Zentrum für Informatik (2022). https://doi.org/10.4230/LIPIcs.STACS.2022.5

4. Almagor, S., Karimov, T., Kelmendi, E., Ouaknine, J., Worrell, J.: Deciding ω-regular properties on linear recurrence sequences. Proc. ACM Program. Lang. **5**(POPL), 1–24 (2021). https://doi.org/10.1145/3434329

5. Baier, C., Funke, F., Jantsch, S., Karimov, T., Lefaucheux, E., Ouaknine, J., Pouly, A., Purser, D., Whiteland, M.A.: Reachability in dynamical systems with rounding. In: 40th IARCS Annual Conference on Foundations of Software Technology and Theoretical Computer Science, FSTTCS 2020. LIPIcs, vol. 182, pp. 36:1–36:17. Schloss Dagstuhl - Leibniz-Zentrum für Informatik (2020). https://doi.org/10.4230/LIPIcs.FSTTCS.2020.36

6. Baier, C., Funke, F., Jantsch, S., Karimov, T., Lefaucheux, E., Ouaknine, J., Purser, D., Whiteland, M.A., Worrell, J.: Parameter Synthesis for Parametric Probabilistic Dynamical Systems and Prefix-Independent Specifications. In: Klin, B., Lasota, S., Muscholl, A. (eds.) 33rd International Conference on Concurrency Theory (CONCUR 2022). Leibniz International Proceedings in Informatics (LIPIcs), vol. 243, pp. 10:1–10:16. Schloss Dagstuhl – Leibniz-Zentrum für Informatik, Dagstuhl, Germany (2022). https://doi.org/10.4230/LIPIcs.CONCUR.2022.10

7. Becker, H., Panchekha, P., Darulova, E., Tatlock, Z.: Combining tools for optimization and analysis of floating-point computations. In: Havelund, K., Peleska, J., Roscoe, B., de Vink, E.P. (eds.) Formal Methods - 22nd International Symposium, FM 2018, Held as Part of the Federated Logic Conference, FloC 2018. Lecture Notes in Computer Science, vol. 10951, pp. 355–363. Springer (2018). https://doi.org/10.1007/978-3-319-95582-7_21

8. Bilu, Y., Luca, F., Nieuwveld, J., Ouaknine, J., Purser, D., Worrell, J.: Skolem meets Schanuel. In: Szeider, S., Ganian, R., Silva, A. (eds.) 47th International Symposium on Mathematical Foundations of Computer Science, MFCS 2022. LIPIcs, vol. 241, pp. 20:1–20:15. Schloss Dagstuhl - Leibniz-Zentrum für Informatik (2022). https://doi.org/10.4230/LIPIcs.MFCS.2022.20

9. Boyle, M.: Notes on the Perron-Frobenius theory of nonnegative matrices (2005)

10. Braverman, M.: Termination of integer linear programs. In: Ball, T., Jones, R.B. (eds.) Computer Aided Verification, 18th International Conference, CAV 2006 Proceedings. Lecture Notes in Computer Science, vol. 4144, pp. 372–385. Springer (2006). https://doi.org/10.1007/11817963_34

11. Büchi, J.R.: On a decision method in restricted second order arithmetic. In: The collected works of J. Richard Büchi, pp. 425–435. Springer (1990)

12. Chonev, V., Ouaknine, J., Worrell, J.: On the complexity of the orbit problem. J. ACM **63**(3), 23:1–23:18 (2016). https://doi.org/10.1145/2857050

13. D'Costa, J., Karimov, T., Majumdar, R., Ouaknine, J., Salamati, M., Soudjani, S., Worrell, J.: The pseudo-Skolem problem is decidable. In: Bonchi, F., Puglisi, S.J. (eds.) 46th International Symposium on Mathematical Foundations of Computer Science, MFCS 2021. LIPIcs, vol. 202, pp. 34:1–34:21. Schloss Dagstuhl - Leibniz-Zentrum für Informatik (2021). https://doi.org/10.4230/LIPIcs.MFCS.2021.34

14. D'Costa, J., Karimov, T., Majumdar, R., Ouaknine, J., Salamati, M., Worrell, J.: The pseudo-reachability problem for diagonalisable linear dynamical systems. In: Szeider, S., Ganian, R., Silva, A. (eds.) 47th International Symposium on Mathematical Foundations of Computer Science, MFCS 2022. LIPIcs, vol. 241, pp. 40:1–40:13. Schloss Dagstuhl - Leibniz-Zentrum für Informatik (2022). https://doi.org/10.4230/LIPIcs.MFCS.2022.40

15. Haase, C.: A survival guide to Presburger arithmetic. ACM SIGLOG News **5**(3), 67–82 (2018). https://doi.org/10.1145/3242953.3242964

16. Kannan, R., Lipton, R.J.: Polynomial-time algorithm for the orbit problem. J. ACM **33**(4), 808–821 (1986). https://doi.org/10.1145/6490.6496

17. Karimov, T., Kelmendi, E., Ouaknine, J., Worrell, J.: What's decidable about discrete linear dynamical systems? In: Raskin, J., Chatterjee, K., Doyen, L., Majumdar, R. (eds.) Principles of Systems Design - Essays Dedicated to Thomas A. Henzinger on the Occasion of His 60th Birthday. Lecture Notes in Computer Science, vol. 13660, pp. 21–38. Springer (2022). https://doi.org/10.1007/978-3-031-22337-2_2

18. Karimov, T., Lefaucheux, E., Ouaknine, J., Purser, D., Varonka, A., Whiteland, M.A., Worrell, J.: What's decidable about linear loops? Proc. ACM Program. Lang. **6**(POPL), 1–25 (2022). https://doi.org/10.1145/3498727

19. Lefaucheux, E., Ouaknine, J., Purser, D., Sharifi, M.: Model checking linear dynamical systems under floating-point rounding. CoRR **abs/2211.04301** (2022). https://doi.org/10.48550/arXiv.2211.04301

20. Lohar, D., Jeangoudoux, C., Sobel, J., Darulova, E., Christakis, M.: A two-phase approach for conditional floating-point verification. In: Groote, J.F., Larsen, K.G. (eds.) Tools and Algorithms for the Construction and Analysis of Systems - 27th International Conference, TACAS 2021, Part of ETAPS 2021. Part II. Lecture Notes in Computer Science, vol. 12652, pp. 43–63. Springer (2021). https://doi.org/10.1007/978-3-030-72013-1_3

21. Luca, F., Ouaknine, J., Worrell, J.: Algebraic model checking for discrete linear dynamical systems. In: Bogomolov, S., Parker, D. (eds.) Formal Modeling and Analysis of Timed Systems - 20th International Conference, FORMATS 2022. Lecture Notes in Computer Science, vol. 13465, pp. 3–15. Springer (2022). https://doi.org/10.1007/978-3-031-15839-1_1

22. Maurica, F., Mesnard, F., Payet, E.: Optimal approximation for efficient termination analysis of floating-point loops. In: 2017 1st International Conference on Next Generation Computing Applications (NextComp). pp. 17–22. IEEE (2017)

23. Minsky, M.L.: Computation. Prentice-Hall Englewood Cliffs (1967)

24. Ouaknine, J., Worrell, J.: Positivity problems for low-order linear recurrence sequences. In: Chekuri, C. (ed.) Proceedings of the Twenty-Fifth Annual ACM-SIAM Symposium on Discrete Algorithms, SODA 2014. pp. 366–379. SIAM (2014). https://doi.org/10.1137/1.9781611973402.27

25. Schneider, H.: Wielandt's proof of the exponent inequality for primitive nonnegative matrices. Linear Algebra and its Applications **353**(1), 5–10 (2002)

26. Tiwari, A.: Termination of linear programs. In: Alur, R., Peled, D.A. (eds.) Computer Aided Verification, 16th International Conference, CAV 2004 Proceedings. Lecture Notes in Computer Science, vol. 3114, pp. 70–82. Springer (2004). https://doi.org/10.1007/978-3-540-27813-9_6

27. Xia, B., Yang, L., Zhan, N., Zhang, Z.: Symbolic decision procedure for termination of linear programs. Formal Aspects Comput. **23**(2), 171–190 (2011). https://doi.org/10.1007/s00165-009-0144-5

Efficient Loop Conditions for
Bounded Model Checking Hyperproperties*

Tzu-Han Hsu[1], César Sánchez[2], Sarai Sheinvald[3],
and Borzoo Bonakdarpour[1]([⊠])

[1] Michigan State University, East Lansing, MI, USA {tzuhan,borzoo}@msu.edu
[2] IMDEA Software Institute, Madrid, Spain cesar.sanchez@imdea.org
[3] Dept. of Software Engineering, Braude College, Karmiel, Israel
sarai@braude.ac.il

Abstract. Bounded model checking (BMC) is an effective technique for
hunting bugs by incrementally exploring the state space of a system. To
reason about infinite traces through a finite structure and to ultimately
obtain completeness, BMC incorporates *loop conditions* that revisit previously observed states. This paper focuses on developing loop conditions
for BMC of HyperLTL– a temporal logic for hyperproperties that allows
expressing important policies for security and consistency in concurrent
systems, etc. Loop conditions for HyperLTL are more complicated than
for LTL, as different traces may loop inconsistently in unrelated moments.
Existing BMC approaches for HyperLTL only considered linear unrollings
without any looping capability, which precludes both finding small infinite traces and obtaining a complete technique. We investigate loop
conditions for HyperLTL BMC, for HyperLTL formulas that contain up to
one quantifier alternation. We first present a general complete automata-
based technique which is based on bounds of maximum unrollings. Then,
we introduce alternative simulation-based algorithms that allow exploiting short loops effectively, generating SAT queries whose satisfiability
guarantees the outcome of the original model checking problem. We also
report empirical evaluation of the prototype implementation of our BMC
techniques using Z3py.

1 Introduction

Hyperproperties [13] have been getting increasing attention due to their power to
reason about important specifications such as information-flow security policies
that require reasoning about the interrelation among different execution traces.
HyperLTL [12] is an extension of the linear-time temporal logic LTL [31] that
allows quantification over traces; hence, capable of describing hyperproperties.
For example, the security policy *observational determinism* can be specified as

---

* This research has been partially supported by the United States NSF
SaTC Award 2100989, by the Madrid Regional Gov. Project BLOQUES-CM
(S2018/TCS-4339), by Project PRODIGY (TED2021-132464B-I00) funded by
MCIN/AEI/10.13039/501100011033/ and the EU NextGenerationEU/PRTR, and
by a research grant from Nomadic Labs and the Tezos Foundation.

S. Sankaranarayanan and N. Sharygina (Eds.): TACAS 2023, LNCS 13993, pp. 66–84, 2023.
https://doi.org/10.1007/978-3-031-30823-9_4

HyperLTL formula: $\forall \pi.\forall \pi'.(o_\pi \leftrightarrow o_{\pi'}) \, \mathcal{W} \, \neg(i_\pi \leftrightarrow i_{\pi'})$, which specifies that for every pair of traces π and π', if they agree on the secret input i, then their public output o must also be observed the same (here '$\mathcal{W}$' denotes the weak until operator).

Several works [14,22] have studied model checking techniques for HyperLTL specifications, which typically reduce this problem to LTL model checking queries of modified systems. More recently, [27] proposed a QBF-based algorithm for the direct application of bounded model checking (BMC) [11] to HyperLTL, and successfully provided a push-button solution to verify or falsify HyperLTL formulas with an arbitrary number of quantifier alternations. However, unlike the classic BMC for LTL, which included the so-called *loop conditions*, the algorithm in [27] is limited to (non-looping) linear exploration of paths. The reason is that extending path exploration to include loops when dealing with multiple paths simultaneously is not straightforward. For example, consider the HyperLTL formula $\varphi_1 = \forall \pi.\exists \pi'. \, \Box(a_\pi \rightarrow b_{\pi'})$ and two Kripke structures K_1 and K_2 as follows:

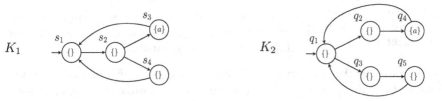

Assume trace π ranges over K_1 and trace π' ranges over K_2. Proving $\langle K_1, K_2 \rangle \not\models \varphi_1$ can be achieved by finding a finite counterexample (i.e., path $s_1 s_2 s_3$ from K_1). Now, consider $\varphi_2 = \forall \pi.\exists \pi'. \, \Box(a_\pi \leftrightarrow a_{\pi'})$. It is easy to see that $\langle K_1, K_2 \rangle \models \varphi_2$. However, to prove $\langle K_1, K_2 \rangle \models \varphi_2$, one has to show the absence of counterexamples in infinite paths, which is impossible with model unrolling in finite steps as proposed in [27].

In this paper, we propose efficient loop conditions for BMC of hyperproperties. First, using an automata-based method, we show that lasso-shaped traces are sufficient to prove infinite behaviors of traces within finite exploration. However, this technique requires an unrolling bound that renders it impractical. Instead, our efficient algorithms are based on the notion of *simulation* [32] between two systems. Simulation is an important tool in verification, as it is used for abstraction, and preserves ACTL* properties [6,24]. As opposed to more complex properties such as language containment, simulation is a more local property and is easier to check. The main contribution of this paper is the introduction of practical algorithms that achieve the exploration of infinite paths following a simulation-based approach that is capable of relating the states of multiple models with correct successor relations.

We present two different variants of simulation, SIM$_{EA}$ and SIM$_{AE}$, allowing to check the satisfaction of $\exists \forall$ and $\forall \exists$ hyperproperties, respectively. These notions circumvent the need to boundlessly unroll traces in both structures and synchronize them. For SIM$_{AE}$, in order to resolve non-determinism in the first model, we also present a third variant, where we enhance SIM$_{AE}$ by using *prophecy vari-*

ables [1,7]. Prophecy variables allow us to handle cases in which $\forall\exists$ hyperproperties hold despite the lack of a direct simulation. With our simulation-based approach, one can capture infinite behaviors of traces with finite exploration in a simple and concise way. Furthermore, our BMC approach not only model-checks the systems for hyperproperties, but also does so in a way that finds *minimal* witnesses to the simulation (i.e., by partially exploring the existentially quantified model), which we will further demonstrate in our empirical evaluation.

We also design algorithms that generate SAT formulas for each variant (i.e., $\mathsf{SIM_{EA}}$, $\mathsf{SIM_{AE}}$, and $\mathsf{SIM_{AE}}$ with prophecies), where the satisfiability of formulas implies the model checking outcome. We also investigate the practical cases of models with different sizes leading to the eight categories in Table 1. For example, the

Case	φ with $\square$	$\neg\varphi$ with $\Diamond$
$\forall_{\mathtt{small}}\ \exists_{\mathtt{big}}$	$\mathsf{SIM_{AE}} \rightarrow \models \forall\exists\square\varphi$	$\mathsf{BMC} \rightarrow \not\models \forall\exists\square\varphi$
$\forall_{\mathtt{big}}\ \exists_{\mathtt{small}}$	$\mathsf{SIM_{AE}} \rightarrow \models \forall\exists\square\varphi$	$\mathsf{BMC} \rightarrow \not\models \forall\exists\square\varphi$
$\exists_{\mathtt{small}}\ \forall_{\mathtt{big}}$	$\mathsf{SIM_{EA}} \rightarrow \models \exists\forall\square\varphi$	$\mathsf{BMC} \rightarrow \not\models \exists\forall\square\varphi$
$\exists_{\mathtt{big}}\ \forall_{\mathtt{small}}$	$\mathsf{SIM_{EA}} \rightarrow \models \exists\forall\square\varphi$	$\mathsf{BMC} \rightarrow \not\models \exists\forall\square\varphi$

Table 1: Eight categories of HyperLTL formulas with different forms of quantifiers, sizes of models, and different temporal operators.

first row indicates the category of verifying two models of different sizes with the fragment that only allows $\forall\exists$ quantifiers and $\square$ (i.e., *globally* temporal operator); $\forall_{\mathtt{small}}\exists_{\mathtt{big}}$ means that the first model is relatively smaller than the second model, and the positive outcome ($\models \forall\exists\square\varphi$) can be proved by our simulation-based technique $\mathsf{SIM_{AE}}$, while the negative outcome ($\not\models \forall\exists\square\varphi$) can be easily checked using non-looping unrolling (i.e., [27]). We will show that in certain cases, one can verify a $\square$ formula without exploring the entire state space of the big model to achieve efficiency.

We have implemented our algorithms[1] using Z3py, the Z3 [15] API in python. We demonstrate the efficiency of our algorithm exploring a subset of the state space for the larger (i.e., big) model. We evaluate the applicability and efficiency with cases including conformance checking for distributed protocol synthesis, model translation, and path planning problems. In summary, we make the following contributions: (1) a bounded model checking algorithm for hyperproperties with loop conditions, (2) three different practical algorithms: $\mathsf{SIM_{EA}}$, $\mathsf{SIM_{AE}}$, and $\mathsf{SIM_{AE}}$ with prophecies, and (3) a demonstration of the efficiency and applicability by case studies that cover through all eight different categories of HyperLTL formulas (see Table 1).

Related Work. Hyperproperties were first introduced by Clarkson and Schneider [13]. HyperLTL was introduced as a temporal logic for hyperproperties in [12]. The first algorithms for model checking HyperLTL were introduced in [22] using alternating automata. Automated reasoning about HyperLTL specifications has received attention in many aspects, including static verification [14,20,21,22] and monitoring [2,8,10,18,19,26,33]. This includes tools support, such as MCHy-

---

[1] Available at: https://github.com/TART-MSU/loop_condition_tacas23

per [22,14] for model checking, EAHyper [17] and MGHyper [16] for satisfiability checking, and RVHyper [18] for runtime monitoring. However, the aforementioned tools are either limited to HyperLTL formulas without quantifier alternations, or requiring additional inputs from the user (e.g., manually added strategies [14]).

Recently, this difficulty of alternating formulas was tackled by the bounded model checker HyperQB [27] using QBF solving. However, HyperQB lacks loop conditions to capture early infinite traces in finite exploration. In this paper, we develop simulation-based algorithms to overcome this limitation. There are alternative approaches to reason about infinite traces, like reasoning about strategies to deal with $\forall\exists$ formulas [14], whose completeness can be obtained by generating a set of prophecy variables [7]. In this work, we capture infinite traces in BMC approach using simulation. We also build an applicable prototype for model-check HyperLTL formulas with models that contain loops.

2 Preliminaries

Kripke structures. A *Kripke structure* K is a tuple $\langle S, S^0, \delta, \mathsf{AP}, L \rangle$, where S is a set of *states*, $S^0 \subseteq S$ is a set of *initial states*, $\delta \subseteq S \times S$ is a total *transition relation*, and $L : S \to 2^{\mathsf{AP}}$ is a *labeling function*, which labels states $s \in S$ with a subset of atomic propositions in AP that hold in s. A *path* of K is an infinite sequence of states $s(0)s(1) \cdots \in S^\omega$, such that $s(0) \in S^0$, and $(s(i), s(i+1)) \in \delta$, for all $i \geq 0$. A *loop* in K is a finite path $s(n)s(n+1) \cdots s(\ell)$, for some $0 \leq n \leq \ell$, such that $(s(i), s(i+1)) \in \delta$, for all $n \leq i < \ell$, and $(s(\ell), s(n)) \in \delta$. Note that $n = \ell$ indicates a *self-loop* on a state. A *trace* of K is a trace $t(0)t(1)t(2) \cdots \in \Sigma^\omega$, such that there exists a path $s(0)s(1) \cdots \in S^\omega$ with $t(i) = L(s(i))$ for all $i \geq 0$. We denote by *Traces*(K, s) the set of all traces of K with paths that start in state $s \in S$. We use *Traces*(K) as a shorthand for $\bigcup_{s \in S^0}$ *Traces*(K, s), and $\mathcal{L}(K)$ as the shorthand for *Traces*(K).

Simulation relations. Let $K_A = \langle S_A, S_A^0, \delta_A, \mathsf{AP}_A, L_A \rangle$ and $K_B = \langle S_B, S_B^0, \delta_B, \mathsf{AP}_B, L_B \rangle$ be two Kripke structures. A *simulation relation* R from K_A to K_B is a relation $R \subseteq S_A \times S_B$ that meets the following conditions:
1. For every $s_A \in S_A^0$ there exists $s_B \in S_A^0$ such that $(s_A, s_B) \in R$.
2. For every $(s_A, s_B) \in R$, it holds that $L_A(s_A) = L_B(s_B)$.
3. For every $(s_A, s_B) \in R$, for every $(s_A, s'_A) \in \delta_A$, there exists $(s_B, s'_B) \in \delta_B$ such that $(s'_A, s'_B) \in R$.

The Temporal Logic HyperLTL. HyperLTL [12] is an extension of the linear-time temporal logic (LTL) for hyperproperties. The syntax of HyperLTL formulas is defined inductively by the following grammar:

$$\varphi ::= \exists\pi.\varphi \mid \forall\pi.\varphi \mid \phi$$
$$\phi ::= \mathsf{true} \mid a_\pi \mid \neg\phi \mid \phi \vee \phi \mid \phi \wedge \phi \mid \phi \, \mathcal{U} \, \phi \mid \phi \, \mathcal{R} \, \phi \mid \bigcirc\phi$$

where $a \in \mathsf{AP}$ is an atomic proposition and π is a *trace variable* from an infinite supply of variables $\mathcal{V}$. The Boolean connectives $\neg$, $\vee$, and $\wedge$ have the usual meaning, $\mathcal{U}$ is the temporal *until* operator, $\mathcal{R}$ is the temporal *release* operator, and $\bigcirc$ is the temporal *next* operator. We also consider other derived Boolean connectives, such as $\rightarrow$ and $\leftrightarrow$, and the derived temporal operators *eventually* $\Diamond \varphi \equiv \mathsf{true} \, \mathcal{U} \, \varphi$ and *globally* $\Box \varphi \equiv \neg \Diamond \neg \varphi$. A formula is *closed* (i.e., a *sentence*) if all trace variables used in the formula are quantified. We assume, without loss of generality, that no trace variable is quantified twice. We use $Vars(\varphi)$ for the set of trace variables used in formula φ.

Semantics. An interpretation $\mathcal{T} = \langle T_\pi \rangle_{\pi \in Vars(\varphi)}$ of a formula φ consists of a tuple of sets of traces, with one set T_π per trace variable π in $Vars(\varphi)$, denoting the set of traces that π ranges over. Note that we allow quantifiers to range over different models, called the *multi-model semantics* [23,27][2]. That is, each set of traces comes from a Kripke structure and we use $\mathcal{K} = \langle K_\pi \rangle_{\pi \in Vars(\varphi)}$ to denote a *family* of Kripke structures, so $T_\pi = Traces(K_\pi)$ is the traces that π can range over, which comes from $K_\pi \in \mathcal{K}$. Abusing notation, we write $\mathcal{T} = Traces(\mathcal{K})$.

The semantics of HyperLTL is defined with respect to a trace assignment, which is a partial map $\Pi \colon Vars(\varphi) \rightharpoonup \Sigma^\omega$. The assignment with the empty domain is denoted by $\Pi_\emptyset$. Given a trace assignment Π, a trace variable π, and a concrete trace $t \in \Sigma^\omega$, we denote by $\Pi[\pi \to t]$ the assignment that coincides with Π everywhere but at π, which is mapped to trace t. The satisfaction of a HyperLTL formula φ is a binary relation $\models$ that associates a formula to the models $(\mathcal{T}, \Pi, i)$ where $i \in \mathbb{Z}_{\geq 0}$ is a pointer that indicates the current evaluating position. The semantics is defined as follows:

$$
\begin{aligned}
(\mathcal{T}, \Pi, 0) &\models \exists \pi. \, \psi & \text{iff} \quad & \text{there is a } t \in T_\pi, \text{ such that } (\mathcal{T}, \Pi[\pi \to t], 0) \models \psi, \\
(\mathcal{T}, \Pi, 0) &\models \forall \pi. \, \psi & \text{iff} \quad & \text{for all } t \in T_\pi, \text{ such that } (\mathcal{T}, \Pi[\pi \to t], 0) \models \psi, \\
(\mathcal{T}, \Pi, i) &\models \mathsf{true} \\
(\mathcal{T}, \Pi, i) &\models a_\pi & \text{iff} \quad & a \in \Pi(\pi)(i), \\
(\mathcal{T}, \Pi, i) &\models \neg \psi & \text{iff} \quad & (\mathcal{T}, \Pi, i) \not\models \psi(\mathcal{T}, \Pi, i) \\
(\mathcal{T}, \Pi, i) &\models \psi_1 \vee \psi_2 & \text{iff} \quad & (\mathcal{T}, \Pi, i) \models \psi_1 \text{ or } (\mathcal{T}, \Pi, i) \models \psi_2, \\
(\mathcal{T}, \Pi, i) &\models \psi_1 \wedge \psi_2 & \text{iff} \quad & (\mathcal{T}, \Pi, i) \models \psi_1 \text{ and } (\mathcal{T}, \Pi, i) \models \psi_2, \\
(\mathcal{T}, \Pi, i) &\models \bigcirc \psi & \text{iff} \quad & (\mathcal{T}, \Pi, i+1) \models \psi, \\
(\mathcal{T}, \Pi, i) &\models \psi_1 \, \mathcal{U} \, \psi_2 & \text{iff} \quad & \text{there is a } j \geq i \text{ for which } (\mathcal{T}, \Pi, j) \models \psi_2 \text{ and} \\
& & & \text{for all } k \in [i, j), (\mathcal{T}, \Pi, k) \models \psi_1, \\
(\mathcal{T}, \Pi, i) &\models \psi_1 \, \mathcal{R} \, \psi_2 & \text{iff} \quad & \text{either for all } j \geq i, \, (\mathcal{T}, \Pi, j) \models \psi_2, \text{ or,} \\
& & & \text{for some } j \geq i, (\mathcal{T}, \Pi, j) \models \psi_1 \text{ and} \\
& & & \text{for all } k \in [i, j] : (\mathcal{T}, \Pi, k) \models \psi_2.
\end{aligned}
$$

We say that an interpretation $\mathcal{T}$ satisfies a sentence φ, denoted by $\mathcal{T} \models \varphi$, if $(\mathcal{T}, \Pi_\emptyset, 0) \models \varphi$. We say that a family of Kripke structures $\mathcal{K}$ satisfies a sentence φ, denoted by $\mathcal{K} \models \varphi$, if $\langle Traces(K_\pi) \rangle_{\pi \in Vars(\varphi)} \models \varphi$. When the same Kripke structure K is used for all path variables we write $K \models \varphi$.

Definition 1. A *nondeterministic Büchi automaton* (NBW) is a tuple $A = \langle \Sigma, Q, Q_0, \delta, F \rangle$, where Σ is an *alphabet*, Q is a nonempty finite set of

---

[2] In terms of the model checking problem, multi-model and (the conventional) single-model semantics where all paths are assigned traces from the same Kripke structure [12] are equivalent (see [23,27]).

states, $Q_0 \subseteq Q$ is a set of *initial states*, $F \subseteq Q$ is a set of *accepting states*, and $\delta \subseteq Q \times \Sigma \times Q$ is a *transition relation*.

Given an infinite word $w = \sigma_1 \sigma_2 \cdots$ over Σ, a *run of A on w* is an infinite sequence of states $r = (q_0, q_1, \ldots)$, such that $q_0 \in Q_0$, and $(q_{i-1}, \sigma_i, q_i) \in \delta$ for every $i > 0$. The run is *accepting* if r visits some state in F infinitely often. We say that A *accepts* w if there exists an accepting run of A on w. The *language* of A, denoted $\mathcal{L}(A)$, is the set of all infinite words accepted by A. An NBW A is called a *safety* NBW if all of its states are accepting. Every safety LTL formula ψ can be translated into a safety NBW over 2^{AP} such that $\mathcal{L}(A)$ is the set of all traces over AP that satisfy ψ [29].

3 Adaptation of BMC to HyperLTL on Infinite Traces

There are two main obstacles in extending the BMC approach of [27] to handle infinite traces. First, a trace may have an irregular behavior. Second, even traces whose behavior is regular, that is, lasso shaped, are hard to synchronize, since the length of their respective prefixes and lassos need not to be equal. For the latter issue, synchronizing two traces whose prefixes and lassos are of lengths p_1, p_2 and l_1, l_2, respectively, is equivalent to coordinating the same two traces, when defining both their prefixes to be of length $\max\{p_1, p_2\}$, and their lassos to be of length $\operatorname{lcm}\{l_1, l_2\}$, where 'lcm' stands for 'least common multiple'. As for the former challenge, we show that restricting the exploration of traces in the models to only consider lasso traces is sound. That is, considering only lasso-shaped traces is equivalent to considering the entire trace set of the models.

Let $K = \langle S, S^0, \delta, \mathsf{AP}, L \rangle$ be a Kripke structure. A *lasso path* of K is a path $s(0)s(1) \ldots s(\ell)$ such that $(s(\ell), s(n)) \in \delta$ for some $0 \leq n < \ell$. This path induces a *lasso trace* (i.e., a *lasso*) $L(s_0) \ldots L(s_{n-1}) (L(s_n) \ldots L(s_\ell))^\omega$. Let $\langle K_1, \ldots, K_k \rangle$ be a multi-model, we denote the set of lasso traces of K_i by C_i for all $1 \leq i \leq k$, and we use $\mathcal{L}(C_i)$ as the shorthand for the set of lasso traces of K_i.

Theorem 1. *Let* $\mathcal{K} = \langle K_1, \ldots, K_k \rangle$ *be a multi-model, and let* $\varphi = \mathbb{Q}_1 \pi_1 \cdots \mathbb{Q}_k \pi_k.\psi$ *be a* HyperLTL *formula, both over* AP, *then* $\mathcal{K} \models \varphi$ *iff* $\langle C_1, \ldots, C_k \rangle \models \varphi$.

Proof. (sketch) For an LTL formula ψ over $\mathsf{AP} \times \{\pi_i\}_{i=1}^k$, we denote the translation of ψ to an NBW over $2^{\mathsf{AP} \times \{\pi_i\}_{i=1}^k}$ by A_ψ [34]. Given $\alpha = \mathbb{Q}_1 \pi_1 \cdots \mathbb{Q}_k \pi_k$, where $\mathbb{Q}_i \in \{\exists, \forall\}$, we define the satisfaction of A_ψ by $\mathcal{K}$ w.r.t. α, denoted $\mathcal{K} \models (\alpha, A_\psi)$, in the natural way: $\exists \pi_i$ corresponds to the existence of a path assigned to π_i in K_i, and dually for $\forall \pi_i$. Then, $\mathcal{K} \models (\alpha, A_\psi)$ iff the various k-assignments of traces of $\mathcal{K}$ to $\{\pi_i\}_{i=1}^k$ according to α are accepted by A_ψ, which holds iff $\mathcal{K} \models \varphi$.

For a model K, we denote by $K \cap_k A_\psi$ the intersection of K and A_ψ w.r.t. $\mathsf{AP} \times \{\pi_k\}$, taking the projection over $\mathsf{AP} \times \{\pi_i\}_{i=1}^{k-1}$. Thus, $\mathcal{L}(K \cap_k A_\psi)$ is the set of all $(k-1)$-words that *an extension* (i.e., $\exists$) by a word in $\mathcal{L}(K)$ to a k-word in $\mathcal{L}(A_\psi)$. Oppositely, $\mathcal{L}(\overline{K \cap_k \overline{A_\psi}})$ is the set of all $(k-1)$-words that *every extension* (i.e., $\forall$) by a k-word in $\mathcal{L}(K)$ is in $\mathcal{L}(A_\psi)$.

We first construct NBWs $A_2, \ldots, A_{k-1}, A_k$, such that for every $1 < i < k$, we have $\langle K_1, \ldots, K_i \rangle \models (\alpha_i, A_{i+1})$ iff $\mathcal{K} \models (\alpha, A_\psi)$, where $\alpha_i = \mathbb{Q}_1 \pi_1 \ldots \mathbb{Q}_i \pi_i$.

For $i = k$, if $\mathbb{Q}_k = \exists$, then $A_k = K_k \cap_k A_\psi$; otherwise if $\mathbb{Q}_k = \forall$, $A_k = \overline{K_k \cap_k \overline{A_\psi}}$. For $1 < i < k$, if $\mathbb{Q}_i = \exists$ then $A_i = K_i \cap_i A_{i+1}$; otherwise if $\mathbb{Q}_i = \forall$, $A_i = \overline{K_i \cap_i \overline{A_{i+1}}}$. Then, for every $1 < i < k$, we have $\langle K_1, \ldots, K_i \rangle \models (\alpha_i, A_{i+1})$ iff $\langle K_1, \ldots, K_k \rangle \models \varphi$.

We now prove by induction on k that $\mathcal{K} \models \varphi$ iff $\langle C_1, \ldots C_k \rangle \models \varphi$. For $k = 1$, it holds that $\mathcal{K} \models \varphi$ iff $K_1 \models (\mathbb{Q}_1 \pi_1, A_2)$. If $\mathbb{Q}_1 = \forall$, then $K_1 \models (\mathbb{Q}_1 \pi_1, A_2)$ iff $K_1 \cap \overline{A_2} = \emptyset$. If $\mathbb{Q}_1 = \exists$, then $K_1 \models (\mathbb{Q}_1 \pi_1, A_2)$ iff $K_1 \cap A_2 \neq \emptyset$. In both cases, a lasso witness to the non-emptiness exists. For $1 < i < k$, we prove that $\langle C_1, \ldots, C_i, K_{i+1} \rangle \models (\alpha_{i+1}, A_{i+2})$ iff $\langle C_1, \ldots, C_i, C_{i+1} \rangle \models (\alpha_{i+1}, A_{i+2})$. If $\mathbb{Q}_i = \forall$, then the first direction simply holds because $\mathcal{L}(C_{i+1}) \subseteq \mathcal{L}(K_{i+1})$. For the second direction, every extension of $c_1, c_2, \ldots c_i$ (i.e., lassos in $C_1, C_2, \ldots C_i$) by a path τ in K_{i+1} is in $\mathcal{L}(A_{i+2})$. Indeed, otherwise we can extract a lasso c_{i+1} such that $c_1, c_2, \ldots c_{i+1}$ is in $\mathcal{L}(\overline{A_{i+2}})$, a contradiction. If $\mathbb{Q}_i = \exists$, then $\mathcal{L}(C_{i+1}) \subseteq \mathcal{L}(K_{i+1})$ implies the second direction. For the first direction, we can extract a lasso $c_{i+1} \in \mathcal{L}(C_{i+1})$ such that $\langle c_1, c_2, \ldots c_i, c_{i+1} \rangle \in \mathcal{L}(A_{i+2})$. □

One can use Theorem 1 and the observations above to construct a sound and complete BMC algorithm for both $\forall\exists$ and $\exists\forall$ hyperproperties. Indeed, consider a multi-model $\langle K_1, K_2 \rangle$, and a hyperproperty $\varphi = \forall\pi.\exists\pi'.\ \psi$. Such a BMC algorithm would try and verify $\langle K_1, K_2 \rangle \models \varphi$ directly, or try and prove $\langle K_1, K_2 \rangle \models \neg\varphi$. In both cases, a run may find a short lasso example for the model under $\exists$ (K_2 in the former case and K_1 in the latter), leading to a shorter run. However, in both cases, the model under $\forall$ would have to be explored to the maximal lasso length implicated by Theorem 1, which is doubly-exponential. Therefore, this naive approach would be highly inefficient.

4   Simulation-Based BMC Algorithms for HyperLTL

We now introduce efficient simulation-based BMC algorithms for verifying hyperproperties of the types $\forall\pi.\exists\pi'.\Box\mathsf{Pred}$ and $\exists\pi.\forall\pi'.\Box\mathsf{Pred}$, where Pred is a *relational predicate* (a predicate over a pair of states). The key observation is that simulation naturally induces the exploration of infinite traces without the need to explicitly unroll the structures, and without needing to synchronize the indices of the symbolic variables in both traces. Moreover, in some cases our algorithms allow to only partially explore the state space of a Kripke structure and give a conclusive answer efficiently.

Let $K_P = \langle S_P, S_P^0, \delta_P, \mathsf{AP}_P, L_P \rangle$ and $K_Q = \langle S_Q, S_Q^0, \delta_Q, \mathsf{AP}_Q, L_Q \rangle$ be two Kripke structures, and consider a hyperproperty of the form $\forall\pi.\exists\pi'.\ \Box\mathsf{Pred}$. Suppose that there exists a simulation from K_P to K_Q. Then, every trace in K_P is embodied in K_Q. Indeed, we can show by induction that for every trace $t_p = s_p(1)s_p(2)\ldots$ in K_P, there exists a trace $t_q = s_q(1)s_q(2)\ldots$ in K_Q, such that $s_q(i)$ simulates $s_p(i)$ for every $i \geq 1$; therefore, t_p and t_q are equally labeled. We generalize the labeling constraint in the definition of standard simulation by requiring, given Pred, that if (s_p, s_q) is in the simulation relation, then

$(s_p, s_q) \models$ Pred. We denote this generalized simulation by SIM$_{AE}$. Following similar considerations, we now have that for every trace t_p in K_P, there exists a trace t_q in K_Q such that $(t_p, t_q) \models \Box$Pred. Therefore, the following result holds:

Lemma 1. *Let K_P and K_Q be Kripke structures, and let $\varphi = \forall \pi. \exists \pi'. \Box Pred$ be a HyperLTL formula. If there exists SIM$_{AE}$ from K_P to K_Q, then $\langle K_P, K_Q \rangle \models \varphi$.*

We now turn to properties of the type $\exists \pi. \forall \pi'. \Box$Pred. In this case, we must find a single trace in K_P that matches every trace in K_Q. Notice that SIM$_{AE}$ (in the other direction) does not suffice, since it is not guaranteed that the same trace in K_P is used to match all traces in K_Q. However, according to Theorem 1, it is guaranteed that if $\langle K_P, K_Q \rangle \models \exists \pi. \forall \pi'. \Box$Pred, then there exists such a single lasso trace t_p in K_P as the witness of the satisfaction. We therefore define a second notion of simulation, denoted SIM$_{EA}$, as follows. Let $t_p = s_p(1) s_p(2) \ldots s_p(n) \ldots s_p(\ell)$ be a lasso trace in K_P (where $s_p(\ell)$ closes to $s_p(n)$, that is, $(s_p(\ell), s_p(n)) \in \delta_P$). A relation R from t_p to K_Q is considered as a SIM$_{EA}$ from t_p to K_Q, if the following holds:

1. $(s_p, s_q) \models$ Pred for every $(s_p, s_q) \in R$.
2. $(s_p(1), s_q) \in R$ for every $s_q \in S_Q^0$.
3. If $(s_p(i), s_q(i)) \in R$, then for every successor $s_q(i+1)$ of $s_q(i)$, it holds that $(s_p(i+1), s_q(i+1)) \in R$ (where $s_p(\ell+1)$ is defined to be $s_p(n)$).

If there exists a lasso trace t_p, then we say that there exists SIM$_{EA}$ from K_P to K_Q. Notice that the third requirement in fact unrolls K_Q in a way that guarantees that for every trace t_q in K_Q, it holds that $(t_p, t_q) \models \Box$Pred. Therefore, the following result holds:

Lemma 2. *Let K_P and K_Q be Kripke structures, and let $\varphi = \exists \pi. \forall \pi'. \Box Pred$. If there exists a SIM$_{EA}$ from K_P to K_Q, then $\langle K_P, K_Q \rangle \models \varphi$.*

Lemmas 1 and 2 enable sound algorithms for model-checking $\forall \pi. \exists \pi'. \Box$Pred and $\exists \pi. \forall \pi'. \Box$Pred hyperproperties with loop conditions. To check the former, check whether there exists SIM$_{AE}$ from K_P to K_Q; to check the latter, check for a lasso trace t_p in K_P and SIM$_{EA}$ from t_p to K_Q. Based on these ideas, we introduce now two SAT-based BMC algorithms.

For $\forall \exists$ hyperproperties, we not only check for the existence of SIM$_{AE}$, but also iteratively seek a small subset of S_Q that suffices to simulate all states of S_P. While finding SIM$_{AE}$, as for standard simulation, is polynomial, the problem of finding a simulation with a bounded number of K_Q states is NP-complete (see [28] for details). This allows us to efficiently handle instances in which K_Q is large. Moreover, we introduce in Subsection 4.3 the use of *prophecy variables*, allowing us to overcome cases in which the models satisfy the property but SIM$_{AE}$ does not exist.

For $\exists \forall$ hyperproperties, we search for SIM$_{EA}$ by seeking a lasso trace t_p in K_P, whose length increases with every iteration, similarly to standard BMC techniques for LTL. Of course, in our case, t_p must be matched with the states of K_Q in a way that ensures SIM$_{EA}$. In the worst case, the length of t_p may be doubly-exponential in the sizes of the systems. However, as our experimental results show, in case of satisfaction the process can terminate much sooner.

We now describe our BMC algorithms and our SAT encodings in detail. First, we fix the unrolling depth of K_P to n and of K_Q to k. To encode states of K_P we allocate a family of Boolean variables $\{x_i\}_{i=1}^n$. Similarly, we allocate $\{y_j\}_{j=1}^k$ to represent the states of K_Q. Additionally, we encode the simulation relation T by creating $n \times k$ Boolean variables $\{sim_{ij}\}_{i=1,j=1}^{n,\ k}$ such that sim_{ij} holds if and only if $T(p_i, q_j)$. We now present the three variations of encoding: (1) EA-Simulation (SIM$_{EA}$), (2) AE-Simulation (SIM$_{AE}$), and (3) a special variation where we enrich AE-Simulation with prophecies.

4.1   Encodings for EA-Simulation

The goal of this encoding is to find a lasso path t_p in K_P that guarantees that there exists SIM$_{EA}$ to K_Q. Note that the set of states that t_p uses may be much smaller than the whole of K_P, while the state space of K_Q must be explored exhaustively. We force x_0 be an initial state of K_P and for x_{i+1} to follow x_i for every i we use, but for K_Q we will let the solver fill freely each y_k and add constraints[3] for the full exploration of K_Q.

- **All states are legal states.** The solver must only search legal encodings of states of K_P and K_Q (we use $K_P(x_i)$ to represent the combinations of values that represent a legal state in S_P and similarly $K_Q(y_j)$ for S_Q):

$$\bigwedge_{i=1}^n K_P(x_i) \wedge \bigwedge_{j=1}^k K_Q(y_j) \tag{1}$$

- **Exhaustive exploration of K_Q.** We require that two different indices y_j and y_r represent two different states in K_Q, so if $k = |K_Q|$, then all states are represented, where $y_j \neq y_r$ captures that some bit distinguishes the states encoded by j and r (note that the validity of states is implied by (1)):

$$\bigwedge_{j \neq r} (K_Q(y_j) \wedge K_Q(y_r)) \rightarrow (y_j \neq y_r) \tag{2}$$

- **The initial S_P^0 state simulates all initial S_Q^0 states.** State x_0 is an initial state of K_P and simulates all initial states of K_Q (we use $I_P(x_0)$ to represent a legal initial state in K_P and $I_Q(y_j)$ for S_Q^0 of K_Q):

$$I_P(x_0) \wedge \big(\bigwedge_{j=1}^k I_Q(y_j) \rightarrow T(x_0, y_j) \big) \tag{3}$$

---

[3] An alternative is to fix an enumeration of the states of K_Q and force the assignment of $y_0 \ldots$ according to this enumeration instead of constraining a symbolic encoding, but the explanation of the symbolic algorithm above is simpler.

- **Successors in K_Q are simulated by successors in K_P.** We first introduce the following formula $succ_T(x, x')$ to capture one-step of the simulation, that is, x' follows x and for all y if $T(x, y)$ then x' simulates all successors of y (we use $\delta_Q(y, y')$ to represent that y and y' states are in δ_Q of K_Q, similarly for $(x, x') \in \delta_P$ of K_P we use $\delta_P(x, x')$) :

$$succ_T(x, x') \stackrel{\text{def}}{=} \bigwedge_{y=y_1}^{y_k} T(x, y) \rightarrow \left(\bigwedge_{y'=y_1}^{y_k} \delta_Q(y, y') \rightarrow T(x', y') \right)$$

We can then define that x_{i+1} follows x_i:

$$\bigwedge_{i=1}^{n-1} \left[\delta_P(x_i, x_{i+1}) \wedge succ_T(x_i, x_{i+1}) \right] \tag{4}$$

And, x_n has a jump-back to a previously seen state:

$$\bigvee_{i=1}^{n} \left[\delta_P(x_n, x_i) \wedge succ_T(x_n, x_i) \right] \tag{5}$$

- **Relational state predicates are fulfilled by simulation.** Everything relating in the simulation fits the relational predicate, defined as a function Pred of two sets of labels (we use $L_Q(y)$ to represent the set of labels on the y-encoded state in K_Q, similarly, $L_P(x)$ for the x-encoded state in K_P):

$$\bigwedge_{i=1}^{n} \bigwedge_{j=1}^{k} T(x_i, y_j) \rightarrow \mathsf{Pred}(L_P(x_i), L_Q(y_j)) \tag{6}$$

We use $\varphi_{\mathsf{EA}}^{n,k}$ for the SAT formula that results of conjoining (1)-(6) for bounds n and k. If $\varphi_{\mathsf{EA}}^{n,k}$ is satisfiable, then there exists $\mathsf{SIM}_{\mathsf{EA}}$ from K_P to K_Q.

4.2 Encodings for AE-Simulation

Our goal now is to find a set of states $S'_Q \subseteq S_Q$ that is able to simulate all states in K_P. Therefore, as in the previous case, the state space K_P corresponding to the $\forall$ quantifier will be explored exhaustively, and so $n = |K_P|$, while k is the number of states in K_Q, which increases in every iteration. As we have explained, this allows finding a small subset of states in K_Q which suffices to simulate all states of K_P (Note that here we guarantee soundness but not necessarily completeness, which will be further explained in Section 4.3).

- **All states in the simulation are legal states.** Again, every state guessed in the simulation is a legal state from K_P or K_Q:

$$\bigwedge_{i=1}^{n} K_P(x_i) \wedge \bigwedge_{j=1}^{k} K_Q(y_j) \tag{1'}$$

- **K_P is exhaustively explored.** Every two different indices in the states of K_P are different states[4]:

$$\bigwedge_{i \neq r} (K_P(x_i) \wedge K_P(x_r)) \to (x_i \neq x_r) \tag{2'}$$

- **All initial states in K_P must match with some initial state in K_Q.** Note that, contrary to the $\exists \forall$ case, here the initial state in K_Q may be different for each initial state in K_P:

$$\bigwedge_{i=1}^{n} \bigvee_{j=1}^{k} I_P(x_i) \to \big(I_Q(y_j) \wedge T(x_i, y_j) \big) \tag{3'}$$

- **For every pair in the simulation, each successor in K_P must match with some successor in K_Q.** For each (x_i, y_j) in the simulation, every successor state of x_i has a matching successor state of y_j:

$$\bigwedge_{i=1}^{n} \bigwedge_{t=1}^{n} \delta_P(x_i, x_t) \to \bigwedge_{j=1}^{k} \left[T(x_i, y_j) \to \bigvee_{r=1}^{k} \big(\delta_Q(y_j, y_r) \wedge T(x_t, y_r) \big) \right] \tag{4'}$$

- **Relational state predicates are fulfilled.** Similarly, all pairs of states in the simulation should respect the relational Pred:

$$\bigwedge_{i=1}^{n} \bigwedge_{j=1}^{k} T(x_i, y_j) \to \mathsf{Pred}(L_P(x_i), L_Q(y_j)) \tag{5'}$$

We now use $\varphi_{\mathsf{AE}}^{n,k}$ for the SAT formula that results of conjoining $(1')$-$(5')$ for bounds n and k. If $\varphi_{\mathsf{AE}}^{n,k}$ is satisfiable, then there exists $\mathsf{SIM}_{\mathsf{AE}}$ from K_P to K_Q.

4.3   Encodings for AE-Simulation with Prophecies

The AE-simulation encoding introduced in Section 4.2 is sound but not complete (i.e., the property is satisfied, yet no simulation exists). For example, when the system for the $\forall$ quantifier is non-deterministic, the simulation is required to match immediately the successor of the $\exists$ path without inspecting the future of the $\forall$ path. In this section, we incorporate our encodings with *prophecies* to resolve these kind of cases, which takes us one step towards completeness. We now illustrate with the following example.

Example 1. Consider Kripke structures K_1 and K_2 from Section 1, and HyperLTL formula $\varphi_2 = \forall \pi. \exists \pi'. \, \Box(a_\pi \leftrightarrow a_{\pi'})$. It is easy to see that the two models satisfy φ_2, since mapping the sequence of states $(s_1 s_2 s_3)$ to $(q_1 q_2 q_4)$ and $(s_1 s_2 s_4)$ to $(q_1 q_3 q_5)$ guarantees that the matched paths satisfy $\Box(a_\pi \leftrightarrow a_{\pi'})$. However, the technique in Section 4.2 cannot differentiate the occurrences of s_2 in the two different cases.   □

---

[4] As in the previous case, we could fix an enumeration of the states of S_P and fix $x_0 x_1 \ldots$ to be the states according to the enumerations.

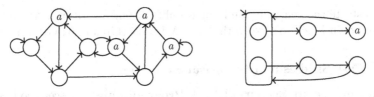

Fig. 1: Prophecy automaton for $\bigcirc\bigcirc a$ (left) and its composition with K_1 (right).

To solve this, we incorporate the notion of *prophecies* to our setting. Prophecies have been proposed as a method to aid in the verification of hyperliveness [14] (see [7] for a systematic method to construct prophecies). For simplicity, we restrict here to prophecies expressed as safety automata. A safety prophecy over AP is a Kripke structure $U = \langle S, S^0, \delta, \mathsf{AP}, L \rangle$, such that $Traces(U) = \mathsf{AP}^\omega$. The product $K \times U$ of a Kripke structure K with a prophecy U preserves the language of K (since the language of U is universal). Recall that in the construction of the product, states $(s, u) \in (K \times U)$ that have incompatible labels are removed. The direct product can be easily processed by repeatedly removing dead states, resulting in a Kripke structure K' whose language is $Traces(K') = Traces(K)$. Note that there may be multiple states in K' that correspond to different states in K for different prophecies. The prophecy-enriched Kripke structure can be directly passed to the method in Section 4.2, so the solver can search for a SIM_AE that takes the value of the prophecy into account.

Example 2. Consider the prophecy automaton shown in Fig. 1 (left), where all states are initial. Note that for every state, either all its successors are labeled with a (or none are), and all successors of its successors are labeled with a (or none are). In other words, this structure encodes the prophecy $\bigcirc\bigcirc a$. The product K_1' of K_1 with the prophecy automaton U for $\bigcirc\bigcirc a$ is shown in Fig. 1 (right). Our method can now show that $\langle K_1', K_2 \rangle \models \varphi_2$, since it can distinguish the two copies of s_1 (one satisfies $\bigcirc\bigcirc a$ and is mapped to $(q_1 q_2 q_4)$, while the other is mapped to $(q_1 q_3 q_5)$).   □

5   Implementation and Experiments

We have implemented our algorithms using the SAT solver Z3 through its python API Z3Py [15]. The SAT formulas introduced in Section 4 are encoded into the two scripts `simEA.py` and `simAE.py`, for finding simulation relations for the SIM_EA and SIM_AE cases, respectively. We evaluate our algorithms with a set of experiments, which includes all forms of quantifiers with different sizes of given models, as presented earlier in Table 1. Our simulation algorithms benefit the most in the cases of the form $\forall_\mathsf{small} \exists_\mathsf{big}$. When the second model is substantially larger than the first model, SIM_AE is able to prove that a $\forall\exists$ hyperproperty holds by exploring only a subset of the second model. In this section, besides $\forall_\mathsf{small} \exists_\mathsf{big}$ cases, we also investigate multiple cases on each category in Table 1 to demonstrate the generality and applicability of our algorithms. All case studies are run on a MacBook Pro with Apple M1 Max chip and 64 GB of memory.

5.1 Case Studies and Empirical Evaluation

Conformance in Scenario-based Programming. In scenario-based programming, scenarios provide a big picture of the desired behaviors of a program, and are often used in the context of program synthesis or code generation. A synthesized program should obey what is specified in the given set of scenarios to be considered *correct*. That is, the program *conforms* with the scenarios. The conformance check between the scenarios and the synthesized program can be specified as a $\forall\exists$-hyperproperty:

$$\varphi_{\mathsf{conf}} = \forall\pi.\exists\pi'. \bigwedge_{p\in\mathsf{AP}} \square\,(p_\pi \leftrightarrow p_{\pi'}),$$

where π is over the scenario model and π' is over the synthesized program. That is, for all possible runs in the scenarios, there must exists a run in the program, such that their behaviors always match.

We look into the case of synthesizing an *Alternating Bit Protocol (ABP)* from four given scenarios, inspired by [3]. ABP is a networking protocol that guarantees reliable message transition, when message loss or data duplication are possible. The protocol has two parties: sender and receiver, which can take three different actions: *send, receive,* and *wait*. Each action also specifies which message is currently transmitted: either a *packet* or *acknowledgment* (see [3] for more details). The correctly synthesized protocol should not only have complete functionality but also *include all scenarios*. That is, for every trace that appears in some scenario, there must exist a corresponding trace in the synthesized protocol. By finding $\mathsf{SIM_{AE}}$ between the scenarios and the synthesized protocols, we can prove the conformance specified with φ_{conf}. Note that the scenarios are often much smaller than the actual synthesized protocol, and so this case falls in the $\forall_{\mathsf{small}}\,\exists_{\mathsf{big}}$ category in Table 1. We consider two variations: a correct and an incorrect ABP (that cannot handle packet loss). Our algorithm successfully identifies a $\mathsf{SIM_{AE}}$ that satisfies φ_{conf} for the correct ABP, and returns UNSAT for the incorrect protocol, since the packet loss scenario cannot be simulated.

Verification of Model Translation. It is often the case that in model translation (e.g., compilation), solely reasoning about the source program does not provide guarantees about the desirable behaviors in the target executable code. Since program verification is expensive compared with repeatedly checking the target, alternative approaches such as *certificate translation* [4] are often preferred. Certificate translation takes inputs of a high-level program (source) with a given specification, and computes a set of verification conditions (certificates) for the low-level executable code (target) to prove that a model translation is safe. However, this technique still requires extra efforts to map the certificates to a target language, and the size of generated certificates might explode quickly (see [4] for retails). We show that our simulation algorithm can directly show the correctness of a model translation more efficiently by investigating the source and target with the same formula φ_{conf} used for ABP. That is, the specifications from the source runs π are always preserved in some target runs π', which infers a correct model translation. Since translating a model into executable code implies adding extra instructions such as writing to registers, it also falls into the $\forall_{\text{small}} \exists_{\text{big}}$ category in Table 1.

We investigate a program from [4] that performs *matrix multiplication (MM)*. When executed, the C program is translated from high-level code (C) to low-level code RTL (Register Transfer Level), which contains extra steps to read from/write to memories. Specifications are triples of $\langle Pre, annot, Post \rangle$, where *Pre*, and *Post* are assertions and *annot* is a partial function from labels to assertions (see [4] for detailed explanations). The goal is to make sure that the translation does not violate the original verified specification. In our framework, instead of translating the certification, we find a simulation that satisfies φ_{conf}, proving that the translated code also satisfies the specification. We also investigate two variations in this case: a correct translation and an incorrect translation, and our algorithm returns SAT (i.e., finds a correct SIM_{AE} simulation) in the former case, and returns UNSAT for the latter case.

Compiler Optimization. Secure compiler optimization aims at preserving input-output behaviors of an original implementation and a target program after applying optimization techniques, including security policies. The conformance between source and target programs guarantees that the optimizing procedure does not introduce vulnerabilities such as information leakage. Furthermore, optimization is often not uniform for the same source, because one might compile the source to multiple different targets with different optimization techniques. As a result, an efficient way to check the behavioral equivalence between the source and target provides a correctness guarantee for the compiler optimization.

Imposing optimization usually results in a

```
// Source program S
L1: if (j < arr_size) {
L2:     a := arr[0];
L3:     b := arr[j];
L4: } else {
L5:     a := arr[0];
L6:     b := arr[arr_size - 1];
L7: }
// Target program T
L1: a := arr[0];
L2: if (j < arr_size) {
L3:     b := arr[j];
L4: } else {
L5:
L6:     b := arr[arr_size - 1];
L7: }
```

Fig. 2: The common branch factorization example [30].

smaller program. For instance, *common branch factorization* (CBF) finds common operations in an if-then-else structure, and moves them outside of the conditional so that such operation is only executed once. As a result, for these optimization techniques, checking the conformance of the source and target falls in the $\forall_{\text{big}} \exists_{\text{small}}$ category. That is, given two programs, source (**big**) and target (**small**), we check the following formula:

$$\varphi_{\text{sc}} = \forall \pi . \exists \pi'. (\text{in}_\pi \leftrightarrow \text{in}_{\pi'}) \rightarrow \square (\text{out}_\pi \leftrightarrow \text{out}_{\pi'}).$$

In this case study we investigate the strategy CBF using the example in Figure 2 inspired by [30]. We consider two kinds of optimized programs for the strategy, one is the correct optimization, one containing bugs that violates the original behavior due to the optimization. For the correct version, our algorithm successfully discovered a simulation relation between the source and target, and the simulation relation returns a smaller subset of states in the second model (i.e., $|S'_Q| < |S_Q|$). For the incorrect version, we received UNSAT.

Robust Path Planning. In robotic planning, *robustness planning (RP)* refers to a path that is able to consistently complete a mission without being interfered by the uncertainty in the environment (e.g., adversaries). For instance, in the 2-D plane in Fig. 3, an agent is trying to go from the starting point (blue grid) to the goal position (green grid). The plane also contains three adversaries on the three corners other than the starting point (red-framed grids), and the adversaries move trying to catch the agent but can only move in one direction (e.g., clockwise). This is a $\exists_{\text{small}} \forall_{\text{big}}$ setting, since the adversaries may have several ways to cooperate and attempt to catch the agent. We formulate this planning problem as follows:

Fig. 3: A robust path.

$$\varphi_{\text{rp}} = \exists \pi. \forall \pi'. \; \Box \; (\text{pos}_\pi \not\leftrightarrow \text{pos}_{\pi'}).$$

That is, there exists a robust path for the agent to safely reach the goal regardless of all the ways that the adversaries could move. We consider two scenarios, one in which there exists a way for the agent to form a robust path and one does not. Our algorithm successfully returns SAT for case which the agent can form a robust path, and returns UNSAT for which a robust path is impossible to find.

Plan Synthesis. The goal of *plan synthesis (PS)* is to synthesize a single comprehensive plan that can simultaneously satisfy all given small requirements has wide application in planning problems. We take the well-known toy example, *wolf, goat, and cabbage*[5], as a representative case here. The problem is as follows. A farmer needs to cross a river by boat with a wolf, a goat, and a cabbage. However, the farmer can only bring one item with him onto the boat each time. In addition, the wolf would eat the goat, and the goat would eat the cabbage, if they are left unattended. The goal is to find a plan that allows the farmer to successfully cross the river with all three items safely. A plan requires the farmer to go back and forth with the boat with certain possible ways to carry different items, while all small requirements (i.e., the constraints among each item) always satisfied. In this example, the overall plan is a big model while the requirements form a much smaller automaton. Hence, it is a $\exists_{\text{big}} \forall_{\text{small}}$ problem that can be specified with the following formula:

$$\varphi_{\text{ps}} = \exists \pi. \forall \pi'. \; \Box \; (\text{action}_\pi \not\leftrightarrow \text{violation}_{\pi'}).$$

---

[5] https://en.wikipedia.org/wiki/Wolf,_goat_and_cabbage_problem

Type	Quants	Cases	$|S_P|$	$|S_Q|$	Z3	Outcome	solve[s]
SIM$_{AE}$	$\forall_{small} \exists_{big}$	ABP	11	14	sat	$|S_Q'|$=11	9.37
		ABP$_{w/ bug}$	11	14	unsat	-	9.46
		MM	27	27	sat	$|S_Q'|$=27	67.74
		MM$_{w/ bug}$	27	27	unsat	-	66.85
	$\forall_{big} \exists_{small}$	CBF	15	9	sat	$|S_Q'|$=8	3.49
		CBF$_{w/ bug}$	15	9	unsat	-	3.51
SIM$_{EA}$	$\exists_{small} \forall_{big}$	RP 3^3	8	9	sat	$|S_P'|$=5	1.09
		RP $3^3_{no sol.}$	8	9	unsat	-	1.02
	$\exists_{big} \forall_{small}$	GCW	16	4	sat	$|S_P'|$=8	3.36
		GCW$_{no sol.}$	16	4	unsat	-	2.27

Table 2: Summary of our case studies. The outcomes with simulation discovered show how our algorithms find a smaller subset for either K_P or K_Q.

5.2 Analysis and Discussion

The summary of our empirical evaluation is presented in Table 2. For the $\forall\exists$ cases, our algorithm successfully finds a set $|S_Q'| < |S_Q|$ that satisfies the properties for the cases ABP and CBF. Note that case MM does not find a small subset, since we manually add extra *paddings* on the first model to align the length of both traces. We note that handling this instance without padding requires asynchornicity— a much more difficult problem, which we leave for future work. For the $\exists\forall$ cases, we are able to find a subset of S_P which forms a single lasso path that can simulate all runs in S_Q for all cases RP and GCW. We emphasize here that previous BMC techniques (i.e., HyperQB) cannot handle most of the cases in Table 2 due to the lack of loop conditions.

6   Conclusion and Future Work

We introduced efficient loop conditions for bounded model checking of fragments of HyperLTL. We proved that considering only lasso-shaped traces is equivalent to considering the entire trace set of the models, and proposed two simulation-based algorithms SIM$_{EA}$ and SIM$_{AE}$ to realize infinite reasoning with finite exploration for HyperLTL formulas. To handle non-determinism in the latter case, we combine the models with prophecy automata to provide the (local) simulations with enough information to select the right move for the inner $\exists$ path. Our algorithms are implemented using Z3py. We have evaluated the effectiveness and efficiency with successful verification results for a rich set of input cases, which previous bounded model checking approach would fail to prove.

As for future work, we are working on exploiting general prophecy automata (beyond safety) in order to achieve full generality for the $\forall\exists$ case. The second direction is to handle asynchrony between the models in our algorithm. Even though model checking asynchronous variants of HyperLTL is in general undecidable [25,5,9], we would like to explore semi-algorithms and fragments with decidability properties. Lastly, exploring how to handle infinite-state systems with our framework by applying *abstraction* techniques is also another promising future direction.

References

1. Martin Abadi and Leslie Lamport. The existence of refinement mappings. *Theoretical Computer Science*, 82:253–284, 1991.
2. Shreya Agrawal and Borzoo Bonakdarpour. Runtime verification of k-safety hyperproperties in HyperLTL. In *Proc. of the 29th IEEE Computer Security Foundations Symp. (CSF'16)*, pages 239–252. IEEE, 2016.
3. Rajeev Alur, Milo Martin, Mukund Raghothaman, Christos Stergiou, Stavros Tripakis, and Abhishek Udupa. Synthesizing finite-state protocols from scenarios and requirements. In *Proc. of the 10th Int'l Haifa Verification Conf. (HVC'14)*, volume 8855 of *LNCS*, pages 75–91. Springer, 2014.
4. Gilles Barthe, Benjamin Grégoire, Sylvain Heraud, César Kunz, and Anne Pacalet. Implementing a direct method for certificate translation. In *Proc. of the 11th Int'l Conf. on Formal Engineering Methods (ICFEM'09)*, volume 5885 of *LNCS*, pages 541–560. Springer, 2009.
5. Jan Baumeister, Norine Coenen, Borzoo Bonakdarpour, Bernd Finkbeiner, and César Sánchez. A temporal logic for asynchronous hyperproperties. In *Proc. of the 33rd Int'l Conf. on Computer Aided Verification (CAV'21), Part I*, volume 12759 of *LNCS*, pages 694–717. Springer, 2021.
6. Saddek Bensalem, Ahmed Bouajjani, Claire Loiseaux, and Joseph Sifakis. Property preserving simulations. In *Proc. of the Fourth Int'l Workshop on Computer Aided Verification (CAV'92)*, volume 663 of *LNCS*, pages 260–273. Springer, 1992.
7. Raven Beutner and Bernd Finkbeiner. Prophecy variables for hyperproperty verification. In *Proc. of 35th IEEE Computer Security Foundations Symp. (CSF'22)*, pages 471–485. IEEE, 2022.
8. Borzoo Bonakdarpour, César Sánchez, and Gerardo Schneider. Monitoring hyperproperties by combining static analysis and runtime verification. In *Proc. of the 8th Int'l Symp. on Leveraging Applications of Formal Methods, Verification and Validation (ISoLA'18), Part II*, volume 11245 of *LNCS*, pages 8–27. Springer, 2018.
9. Laura Bozzelli, Adriano Peron, and César Sánchez. Asynchronous extensions of HyperLTL. In *Proc. of the 36th Annual ACM/IEEE Symp. on Logic in Computer Science (LICS'21)*, pages 1–13. IEEE, 2021.
10. Noel Brett, Umair Siddique, and Borzoo Bonakdarpour. Rewriting-based runtime verification for alternation-free HyperLTL. In *Proc. of the 23rd Int'l Conf. on Tools and Algorithms for the Construction and Analysis of Systems (TACAS'17), Part II*, volume 10206 of *LNCS*, pages 77–93. Springer, 2017.
11. Edmund M. Clarke, Armin Biere, Richard Raimi, and Yunshan Zhu. Bounded model checking using satisfiability solving. *Formal Methods in System Design (FMSD)*, 19(1):7–34, 2001.
12. Michael R. Clarkson, Bernd Finkbeiner, Masoud Koleini, Kristopher K. Micinski, Markus N. Rabe, and César Sánchez. Temporal logics for hyperproperties. In *Proc. of the 3rd Int'l Conf. on Principles of Security and Trust (POST'14)*, volume 8414 of *LNCS*, pages 265–284. Springer, 2014.
13. Michael R. Clarkson and Fred B. Schneider. Hyperproperties. *Journal of Computer Security*, 18(6):1157–1210, 2010.
14. Norine Coenen, Bernd Finkbeiner, César Sánchez, and Leander Tentrup. Verifying hyperliveness. In *Proc. of the 31st Int'l Conf. on Computer Aided Verification (CAV'19)*, volume 11561 of *LNCS*, pages 121–139. Springer, 2019.

15. Leonardo M. de Moura and Nikolaj Bjørner. Z3: An efficient SMT solver. In *Proc. of 14th Int'l Conf. on Tools and Algorithms for the Construction and Analysis of Systems (TACAS'08)*, volume 4963 of *LNCS*, pages 337–340. Springer, 2008.
16. Bernd Finkbeiner, Cristopher Hahn, and Tobias Hans. MGHyper: Checking satisfiability of HyperLTL formulas beyond the ∃*∀* fragment. In *Proc. of the 16th Int'l Symp. on Automated Technology for Verification and Analysis (ATVA'18)*, volume 11138 of *LNCS*, pages 521–527. Springer, 2018.
17. Bernd Finkbeiner, Cristopher Hahn, and Marvin Stenger. EAHyper: Satisfiability, implication, and equivalence checking of hyperproperties. In *Proc. of the 29th Int'l Conf. on Computer Aided Verification (CAV'17)*, *Part II*, volume 10427 of *LNCS*, pages 564–570. Springer, 2017.
18. Bernd Finkbeiner, Cristopher Hahn, Marvin Stenger, and Leander Tentrup. RVHyper: A runtime verification tool for temporal hyperproperties. In *Proc. of the 24th Int'l Conf. on Tools and Algorithms for the Construction and Analysis of Systems (TACAS'18)*, *Part II*, volume 10806 of *LNCS*, pages 194–200. Springer, 2018.
19. Bernd Finkbeiner, Cristopher Hahn, Marvin Stenger, and Leander Tentrup. Monitoring hyperproperties. *Formal Methods in System Design (FMSD)*, 54(3):336–363, 2019.
20. Bernd Finkbeiner, Cristopher Hahn, and Hazem Torfah. Model checking quantitative hyperproperties. In *Proc. of the 30th Int'l Conf. on Computer Aided Verification (CAV'18)*, *Part I*, volume 10981 of *LNCS*, pages 144–163. Springer, 2018.
21. Bernd Finkbeiner, Christian Müller, Helmut Seidl, and Eugene Zalinescu. Verifying security policies in multi-agent workflows with loops. In *Proc. of the 15th ACM Conf. on Computer and Communications Security (CCS'17)*, pages 633–645. ACM, 2017.
22. Bernd Finkbeiner, Markus N. Rabe, and César Sánchez. Algorithms for model checking HyperLTL and HyperCTL*. In *Proc. of the 27th Int'l Conf. on Computer Aided Verification (CAV'15)*, *Part I*, volume 9206 of *LNCS*, pages 30–48. Springer, 2015.
23. Ohad Goudsmid, Orna Grumberg, and Sarai Sheinvald. Compositional model checking for multi-properties. In *Proc. of the 22nd Int'l Conf. on Verification, Model Checking, and Abstract Interpretation (VMCAI'21)*, volume 12597 of *LNCS*, pages 55–80. Springer, 2021.
24. Orna Grumberg and David E. Long. Model checking and modular verification. *ACM Transactions on Programming Languages and Systems (TOPLAS)*, 16(3):843–871, 1994.
25. Jens Oliver Gutsfeld, Markus Müller-Olm, and Christoph Ohrem. Automata and fixpoints for asynchronous hyperproperties. *Proc. ACM Program. Lang.*, 5:1–29, 2021.
26. Cristopher Hahn, Marvin Stenger, and Leander Tentrup. Constraint-based monitoring of hyperproperties. In *Proc. of the 25th Int'l Conf. on Tools and Algorithms for the Construction and Analysis of Systems (TACAS'19)*, volume 11428 of *LNCS*, pages 115–131. Springer, 2019.
27. Tzu-Han Hsu, César Sánchez, and Borzoo Bonakdarpour. Bounded model checking for hyperproperties. In *Proc. of the 27th Int'l Conf on Tools and Algorithms for the Construction and Analysis of Systems (TACAS'21)*. *Part I*, volume 12651 of *LNCS*, pages 94–112. Springer, 2021.
28. Tzu-Han Hsu, César Sánchez, Sarai Sheinvald, and Borzoo Bonakdarpour. Efficient loop conditions for bounded model checking hyperproperties. *CoRR*, abs/2301.06209, 2023.

29. Orna Kupferman and Moshe Y. Vardi. Model checking of safety properties. In *Proc. of the 11th Int'l Conf. on Computer Aided Verification (CAV'99)*, volume 1633 of *LNCS*, pages 172–183. Springer, 1999.
30. Kedar S. Namjoshi and Lucas M. Tabajara. Witnessing secure compilation. In *Proc. of the 21st Int'l Conf. on Verification, Model Checking, and Abstract Interpretation (VMCAI'20)*, volume 11990 of *LNCS*, pages 1–22. Springer, 2020.
31. Amir Pnueli. The temporal logic of programs. In *Proc. of the 18th Symp. on Foundations of Computer Science (FOCS'77)*, pages 46–57. IEEE, 1977.
32. Amir Pnueli. Applications of temporal logic to the specification and verification of reactive systems: A survey of current trends. In *Proc. of Current Trends in Concurrency, Overviews and Tutorials*, volume 224 of *LNCS*, pages 510–584. Springer, 1985.
33. Sandro Stucki, César Sánchez, Gerardo Schneider, and Borzoo Bonakdarpour. Graybox monitoring of hyperproperties. In *Proc. of the 23rd Int'l Symp. on Formal Methods (FM'19)*, volume 11800 of *LNCS*, pages 406–424. Springer, 2019.
34. Moshe Y. Vardi and Pierre Wolper. Automata theoretic techniques for modal logic of programs. *Journal of Computer and System Sciences*, 32(2):183–221, 1986.

Reconciling Preemption Bounding with DPOR

Iason Marmanis[(✉)] ⓘ, Michalis Kokologiannakis ⓘ, and Viktor Vafeiadis ⓘ

MPI-SWS, Kaiserslautern and Saarbrücken, Germany
{imarmanis,michalis,viktor}@mpi-sws.org

Abstract. There are two major techniques for scaling up stateless model checking: *dynamic partial order reduction* (DPOR), which only explores executions that differ in the ordering of racy accesses, and *preemption bounding*, which only explores executions containing up to k preemptions (preemptive context-switches).
Combining these two techniques is challenging because DPOR-equivalent executions often contain a different number of preemptions, making it incorrect to cut explorations that exceed the preemption bound. To restore completeness, prior work has weakened the DPOR algorithm, which often results in the exploration of many redundant executions.
We propose an alternative approach. Starting from an optimal DPOR algorithm, we achieve completeness by allowing some slack on the preemption-bound of the explored executions. We prove that the required slack does not exceed the number of threads of the program (minus two), and that this upper limit is tight.

1 Introduction

Stateless model checking (SMC) [12] is an effective bug-finding technique for concurrent programs that systematically explores all interleavings of the given input program. As such, it suffers from the state-space explosion problem: the number of possible interleavings of a program grows rapidly with the program size. There are two main approaches to attack this problem in the literature.

Dynamic partial order reduction (DPOR) [11] is based on the idea that permutations of *independent* instructions in an interleaving lead to the same state. DPOR deems such interleavings equivalent and strives to explore only one representative interleaving from each equivalence class.

Preemption bounding (PB, a.k.a. context bounding) [25] is based on the idea that concurrency bugs in practice can be exposed with a small number of preemptions [24]. Leveraging this insight, PB only explores the interleavings that arise with at most k preemptions (for some fixed k), thereby guaranteeing a partial coverage of the state space.

Combining the two approaches is non-trivial. Simply modifying a DPOR algorithm to discard any explored executions that exceed the desired bound k is not complete, as executions with $\leq k$ preemptions are missed. To restore completeness, Coons et al. [10] weaken DPOR by adding extra backtracking points, but such an

S. Sankaranarayanan and N. Sharygina (Eds.): TACAS 2023, LNCS 13993, pp. 85–104, 2023.
https://doi.org/10.1007/978-3-031-30823-9_5

approach negates any optimality properties of the underlying DPOR algorithm, and can lead to the (redundant) exploration of multiple equivalent interleavings.

In this paper, we propose a different approach. We adapt a state-of-the-art optimal DPOR algorithm with polynomial memory requirements called TruSt [16] to support preemption-bounded search.

We first observe that the preemption-bound definition of Coons et al. [10] is overly pessimistic for incomplete executions (i.e., executions where at least one thread is enabled) in that an incomplete execution can often be extended to a complete one with a smaller preemption-bound. Updating the definition to be more optimistic, however, does not fully resolve the issue: an intermediate execution that exceeds the bound might still be needed in order to reveal a conflicting instruction that leads to the exploration of the desired execution.

Our solution is to allow the exploration of executions exceeding the bound, as long as they only exceed it by a small amount, which we call *slack*. For programs with $N \geq 2$ threads, we show that a slack value of $N - 2$ suffices to maintain completeness (up to the provided bound). Unlike Coons et al. [10], our approach is optimal in the sense that it does not explore equivalent executions more than once. Although it may explore executions with larger bound than the desired one, we argue that these executions are useful, because they can still reveal bugs.

We have implemented our bounding approach in GENMC [18], a state-of-the-art open-source stateless model checker. We show that for small preemption bounds (and despite the slack), bounded search can perform significantly faster than full search. Moreover, we experimentally confirm the literature observation that small bounds suffice to expose most concurrency bugs. We therefore argue that our combination of preemption bounding and DPOR is useful as a practical testing approach, which also provides certain coverage guarantees.

2   Background

In this section, we recall the basic DPOR approach and how prior work has tried to incorporate preemption-bounded search into it. Subsequently, we review the TruSt algorithm [16], which we later build upon to obtain our results.

2.1   The Basics of Dynamic Partial Order Reduction

DPOR starts by exploring one thread interleaving. In the process, it detects conflicting transitions, i.e., instructions that, if executed in the opposite order, will alter the state of the system. At each state, when an earlier transition t is in conflict with a possible transition t' that can be taken by another thread in this state, DPOR considers the execution where t' is fired before t. To accomplish this, DPOR adds the transition t' to the *backtrack set* of the state immediately before t was fired, to be explored later.

We illustrate DPOR by running it on the following example (Fig. 1).

$$\begin{array}{ll} (r_x)\ a := x \ \| & (w_1)\ y := 1 \\ (r_y)\ b := y \ \| & (w_2)\ y := 2 \end{array} \qquad (\text{RR+WW})$$

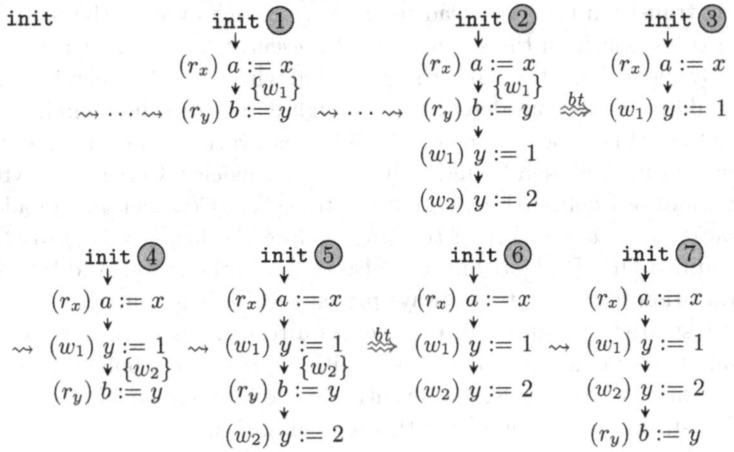

init

init ①
↓
$(r_x)\ a := x$
↓ $\{w_1\}$
⤳ … ⤳ $(r_y)\ b := y$

init ②
↓
$(r_x)\ a := x$
↓ $\{w_1\}$
⤳ … ⤳ $(r_y)\ b := y$
↓
$(w_1)\ y := 1$
↓
$(w_2)\ y := 2$

init ③
↓
$(r_x)\ a := x$
↓
$(w_1)\ y := 1$

init ④
↓
$(r_x)\ a := x$
↓
⤳ $(w_1)\ y := 1$
↓ $\{w_2\}$
$(r_y)\ b := y$

init ⑤
↓
$(r_x)\ a := x$
↓
⤳ $(w_1)\ y := 1$
↓ $\{w_2\}$
$(r_y)\ b := y$
↓
$(w_2)\ y := 2$

init ⑥
↓
$(r_x)\ a := x$
↓
$(w_1)\ y := 1$
↓
$(w_2)\ y := 2$

init ⑦
↓
$(r_x)\ a := x$
↓
⤳ $(w_1)\ y := 1$
↓
$(w_2)\ y := 2$
↓
$(r_y)\ b := y$

Fig. 1. Left-to-right DPOR exploration of RR+WW

After firing the transitions (r_x) and (r_y) (trace ①), DPOR adds transition (w_1) to the backtrack set of the state after the firing of transition (r_x), since transition (w_1) is in conflict with transition (r_y). When the initial exploration is finished (trace ②), DPOR backtracks to ① and considers the second exploration option, i.e., firing transition (w_1) and thus reaching ③.

Subsequently, DPOR fires (r_y) (trace ④) and notices that this is in conflict with (w_2); it then adds (w_2) as an alternative exploration option for the state before the firing of (r_y) in ④. Again, DPOR finishes with the exploration where the read instruction reads the value 1 (trace ⑤) and backtracks to ③. Now, (w_2) is fired (trace ⑥) and the algorithm continues with the remaining transition, leading to ⑦. DPOR now terminates since there is no other exploration option.

This way, DPOR manages to explores all three equivalence classes (representatives ②, ⑤, ⑦) of the 6 interleavings that correspond to this program.

2.2 Bounded Partial Order Reduction

Preemption bounding (PB) [25] prunes the state space by discarding executions that contain more preemptions than a given constant bound k. A preemption occurs at index i of a sequence of events τ whenever (1) events τ_i and τ_{i+1} originate from different threads and (2) the thread of τ_i remains enabled after τ_i; in particular, τ_i is not the last event of its thread.

Combining DPOR and PB is non-trivial. Specifically, simply pruning from DPOR's exploration space any trace with more than k preemptions is incorrect because their exploration might lead to exploring traces with up to k preemptions.

To see this, consider the run of RR+WW with $k = 0$. DPOR reaches the state where (r_x) is fired and (w_1) is considered as an alternative option in the backtrack set. Firing transition (w_1) will lead to trace ③, which exceeds the bound, since there is a transition from the second thread present, while the first thread is still enabled. By discarding this state, the execution where $b = 2$ (which is equivalent to ⑦) would never be considered, even though it respects the bound.

To address this issue, Coons et al. [10] conservatively add more backtrack points accounting for such bound-induced dependencies. Concretely, when the two transitions of the first thread are fired (trace ①), Coons et al. [10] adds (w_1) in the backtrack set not only of the state before the firing of (r_y) in ②, as in the unmodified DPOR algorithm, but also of the initial state. Additionally, the initial transition from a state is always picked so that it is from the same thread as of the last fired transition, if possible. As a result, when the state with only (w_1) being fired is reached (due to the additional backtrack point), (w_2) will be fired immediately afterwards, and eventually the interleaving that corresponds to the right-to-left execution of the threads will be explored.

While this solution guarantees that no execution within the bound is lost, it weakens DPOR, i.e., it leads to the exploration of equivalent interleavings that would otherwise not be considered. In RR+WW, for $k > 0$, Coons et al. [10] explore interleavings that only differ in the order of (r_x) and (w_1).

2.3   TruSt: Optimal Dynamic Partial Order Reduction

The basic DPOR algorithm described in §2.1 does not guarantee optimality, i.e., that only one execution from each equivalent class will be explored. There are several improvements of the basic algorithm, some of which achieve optimality (e.g., [2, 17]). Here, we follow the most recent such improvement, TruSt [16], which achieves optimality with polynomial memory consumption.

TruSt represents program executions as *execution graphs*, a concept that appeared in previous works for DPOR under weak memory models [15, 17]. An execution graph G consists of a set of nodes $G.\mathsf{E}$ (a.k.a. events) representing the individual thread instructions executed, such as read events R and write events W, and three kinds of directed edges encoding the ordering between events:

- the *program order* $G.\mathsf{po}$, which orders events of the same thread;
- the *coherence order* $G.\mathsf{co}$, which orders writes to the same location; and
- the *reads-from* mapping $G.\mathsf{rf}$, which shows where each read is reading from.

For an execution graph G, we define the following derived relations:

$$G.\mathtt{porf} \triangleq \left(G.\mathsf{po} \cup \left\{\langle G.\mathtt{rf}(r), r\rangle \,\middle|\, r \in G.\mathsf{R}\right\}\right)^{+} \qquad \text{(causality order)}$$
$$G.\mathtt{fr} \triangleq \left\{\langle r, w\rangle \,\middle|\, \langle G.\mathtt{rf}(r), w\rangle \in G.\mathsf{co}\right\} \qquad \text{(reads-before)}$$

The causality order, $\mathtt{porf}$, relates two events if there is a path of program order or read-from dependencies between them, while $\mathtt{fr}$ orders a read event before every write that is coherence after the one read by the read.

An execution graph is SC-consistent (sequentially consistent) if there is a total ordering of its events respecting po such that each read event reads from the immediately preceding same-location write in the total order. Equivalently, a graph is SC-consistent if porf ∪ co ∪ fr is acyclic.

Execution graphs enable the efficient reversal of many conflicting events. If a write or a read event is in conflict with a previous write event, there is no need to backtrack to the state before the write events is added. Instead, the new event can be directly added in the execution and either read from a co-earlier write in case of a read event, or be placed co-before the conflicting write in case of a write event.

The only reversals where backtracking is necessary are those between a write event and a previously added read event: when a read event is added, it does not have the option to read from a write that has not yet been added. These reversals are referred to as *backward revisits*. To avoid exponential memory consumption, TruSt considers each exploration option eagerly when the new event is added, instead of maintaining backtrack sets for later exploration. In the case of backward revisits, TruSt removes the part of the execution that was added after the read event but is not in the *prefix* of the write event. The prefix of an event is defined as the set of events that precede it in the porf order. This allows the write event to be directly added in the execution graph. Because there is the possibility that many different execution graphs can lead to the same execution after a backward revisit, TruSt only considers the revisit if the events to be removed respect a *maximality condition* which is defined in such a way so that there will always be exactly one such set of deleted events, achieving an optimal exploration.

3   Bounded Optimal DPOR: Obstacles

We discuss the two main obstacles that complicate the application of preemption-bounded search to a DPOR algorithm.

3.1   Pessimistic Bound Definition

The first problem concerns the definition of preemptions for incomplete executions. Recall in the RR+WW example why the naive adaptation of DPOR with preemption bound $k = 0$ (incorrectly) does not generate the execution reading $b = 2$. The partial trace ③ is discarded because it contains at least one preemption according to the definition of Musuvathi et al. [23]. (Both threads are enabled and have executed one instruction each.)

We argue that this trace should be deemed to have no preemptions because of monotonicity. Trace ③ can be extended to a full trace (namely, ⑦) that (is equivalent to one that) does not have any preemptions.

We therefore modify the definition of preemptions as follows. A preemption occurs at index i of an event sequence τ whenever (1) events τ_i and τ_{i+1} originate from different threads and (2) the thread of τ_i remains enabled after τ_i, and has further events in the trace $\tau_{i+1}\tau_{i+2} \ldots \tau_{|\tau|}$. According to our new definition, both

$$
\begin{array}{l}
a := x; \\
b := z;
\end{array}
\quad
\left\|
\begin{array}{l}
t_1 := x; \\
x := t_1 + 1; \\
t_2 := y; \\
y := t_2 + 1; \\
c := y; \\
\text{if } (c = 1)\; z := 1;
\end{array}
\right\|
\quad
\begin{array}{l}
t_3 := x; \\
x := t_3 + 1; \\
t_4 := y; \\
y := t_4 + 1;
\end{array}
\right\|
$$

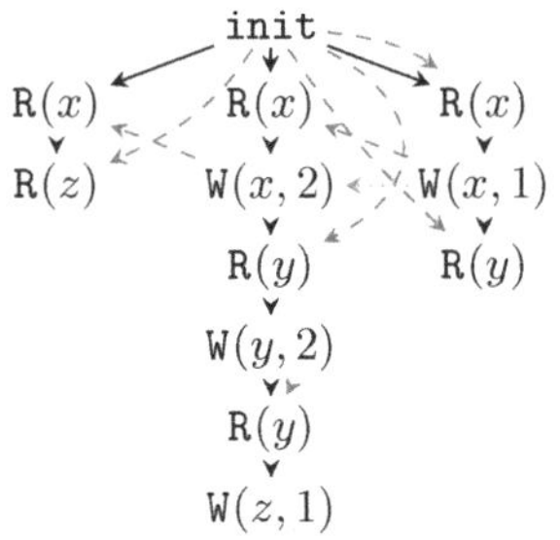

Fig. 2. A program and its intermediate execution that TruSt must explore in order to reach the right-to-left execution.

interleavings that are equivalent with ③ have zero preemptions, because when switching to another thread, the first thread has no further events in the trace.

Our new definition satisfies monotonicity and coincides with the original on complete executions. We note, however, that partial executions with k preemptions cannot always be extended to a complete execution with k preemptions. Consider, for example, trace ④ of RR+WW, which has no preemptions. Firing the only remaining transition leads to trace ⑤, which has one preemption. A DPOR algorithm that employs our definition of preemptions might thus reach states that are *bound-blocked*; the current explored execution respects the bound but there is no final execution reachable from this state that respects the bound. In our experience (see §6), bound-blocked executions do not seem to have a significant effect on the performance of our algorithm.

3.2   Need For Slack

Monotonicity alone is not enough to incorporate bounded search in an algorithm like TruSt, without still forfeiting completeness: some executions that respect the bound might still be lost. Intuitively, since DPOR algorithms operate by detecting conflicting instructions during an interleaving's exploration and reversing the conflict to obtain a new interleaving, it might be the case that for the conflict to be revealed, an execution that exceeds the bound needs to be explored.

We illustrate this point with the example in Fig. 2 where all the variables are initialized to zero. Consider a run of TruSt that always adds the next event from the left-most enabled thread. To reach the final execution that results from executing the threads from right to left, TruSt needs to pass through the execution depicted on the right of Fig. 2 before reaching this final execution. In the next step, the second write of the third thread will be added, which will reveal a conflict with the first read of y of the second thread. The algorithm will then perform a backward revisit, removing the events of the second thread after the first read of y, and change the read's incoming rf edge to the new write event. The desired final execution will be reached after the remaining events of the second thread are added again.

It is easy to see that, while the final execution has zero preemptions, the depicted intermediate execution has at least one preemption, and would thus be discarded. This example can in fact be generalized by adding more threads identical to the third one; to reach the final right-to-left execution that has zero preemptions, TruSt must visit an execution that has at least $N-2$ preemptions, where N is the total number of threads. In §4, we show that this is in fact an upper limit; a final execution with k preemptions is always reachable through a sequence of executions that never exceed $k + N - 2$ preemptions. This result directly enables us to incorporate preemption-bounded search into TruSt by allowing some *slack* to the bound.

4   Recovering Completeness via Slack

Our bounded DPOR algorithm, BUSTER, can be seen in Algorithm 1, where we have highlighted the differences w.r.t. to TruSt [16].

We first discuss some additional notation used in the algorithm. First, each execution graph generated by the algorithm keeps track of the order $<_G$ in which events were added to it. Second, given a graph G and a set of events E, we write $G|_E$ for the restriction of G to E. Third, let G.cprefix(e) be the causal prefix of an event e in an execution graph G, i.e., the set of all events that causally precede it (including e itself). Formally, G.cprefix$(e) \triangleq \{e' \,|\, \langle e', e \rangle \in G.\texttt{porf}^*\}$. Fourth, a subscript $\texttt{loc}(a)$ restricts a set of events to those that access the same location as event a. Fifth, the function $\mathsf{SetRF}(G, a, w)$ adds an $\texttt{rf}$ edge from w to a and $\mathsf{SetCO}(G, w_p, a)$ places a immediately after w_p in $\texttt{co}$. Finally, we define the *traces* of an execution graph as the linearizations of $(G.\texttt{porf} \cup G.\texttt{co} \cup G.\texttt{fr})$ on $G.\texttt{E}$. We lift the definition of preemptions to an execution graph G: $\texttt{preemptions}(G)$ is the minimum number of preemptions in the traces of G.

Apart from only exploring SC-consistent executions, BUSTER eagerly discards executions with more preemptions than the user-provided value k plus the slack (Line 5). If both tests fail, BUSTER continues by picking an new event to extend the current execution (Line 6). For correctness, we fix $\texttt{next}_P(G)$ to always return the event that corresponds to the left-most available thread. Depending on the type of the new event, the algorithm proceeds in a different way. We discuss the interesting cases of read and write events.

If the new event a is a read event, BUSTER simply considers every possible write event as an $\texttt{rf}$ option for a (Line 13), and eagerly explores the corresponding execution. If a is a write event, first every $\texttt{co}$ placement is considered and explored (Line 15). Afterwards, BUSTER considers possible backward-revisits; for every read r event that is not in the causal prefix of a, the execution where r reads from a is considered, after deleting the events added after r, that are not in the causal prefix of a (Line 19). To avoid redundant revisits, only when the set of deleted events satisfies a maximality condition (Line 18), is the backward-revisit performed (see [16] for more details).

Algorithm 1 A Bounded DPOR algorithm based on TruSt [16]

1: **procedure** VERIFY(P, k)
2:     VISIT$_{P,k}(G_\emptyset)$

3: **procedure** VISIT$_{P,k}(G)$
4:     **if** ¬consistent(G) **then return**
5:     **if** preemptions(G) $> k + N - 2$ **then return**
6:     **switch** $a \leftarrow$ next$_P(G)$ **do**
7:         **case** $a = \bot$
8:             **return** "Visited full execution graph G"
9:         **case** $a \in$ error
10:            **exit**("Visited erroneous execution graph G")
11:        **case** $a \in$ R
12:            **for** $w \in G.\text{W}_{\text{loc}(a)}$ **do**
13:                VISIT$_{P,k}(\text{SetRF}(G, a, w))$
14:        **case** $a \in$ W
15:            VISITCOS$_{P,k}(G, a)$
16:            **for** $r \in G.\text{R}_{\text{loc}(a)} \setminus G.\text{cprefix}(a)$ **do**
17:                $Deleted \leftarrow \{e \in G.\text{E} \mid r <_G e\} \setminus G.\text{cprefix}(a)$
18:                **if** $\forall e \in Deleted \cup \{r\}.$ ISMAXIMALLYADDED(G, e, a) **then**
19:                    VISITCOS$_{P,k}(\text{SetRF}(G|_{G.\text{E} \setminus Deleted}, r, a), a)$
20:        **case** _
21:            VISIT$_{P,k}(G)$

22: **procedure** VISITCOS$_{P,k}(G, a)$
23:     **for** $w_p \in G.\text{W}_{\text{loc}(a)}$ **do** VISIT$_{P,k}(\text{SetCO}(G, w_p, a))$

4.1   Properties of TruSt

We now present some key properties of the TruSt algorithm, i.e., Algorith 1 without Line 5, that are used to prove BUSTER's correctness (Theorem 1).

From TruSt's correctness argument, we know that every SC-consistent execution G_f has exactly one sequence of VISIT$_P$ calls that leads to it. We call the sequence of the corresponding graphs a *production sequence* for G_f.

Given two SC-consistent graphs G and G', we say that G is a *prefix* of G', and write $G \sqsubseteq G'$, if $G'|_{G.\text{E}} = G$. Intuitively, G is a prefix of G' if we can construct G' from G, by adding the missing events in some order for some rf and co.

Let a *maximal step* of an execution G be a execution that results from extending a thread of G by an event e in a *maximal* way, i.e., if $e \in$ R, then e is made to read from the co-latest event and if $e \in$ W, then e is placed at the end of co. We write $G \to G'$ when G' is a maximal step of G, and $G \to_e G'$ when $G \to G'$ and e is the added event. We say that a sequence of maximal steps is non-decreasing when the sequence of the thread identifiers of the added events is non-decreasing. Finally, we write tid(e) for the thread identifier of an event e.

A key property of TruSt (stated in Prop. 1) is that every execution G in the production sequence of an SC-consistent execution G_f is either a prefix of G_f, or it contains a read event r that does not read from the "correct" write, but there is a prefix $\hat{G}$ of G_f that can by extended to G by a non-decreasing sequence of maximal steps starting with r and not including events of at least one thread to the right of r.

Proposition 1. *Let S be the production sequence of an SC-consistent final execution G_f, and G be an execution in S. Then, either $G \sqsubseteq G_f$ or there exists an execution G_b that is before G in S, a read event $r = \mathsf{next}_P(G_b)$, a thread $t > \mathsf{tid}(r)$ and an execution $\hat{G}$ such that $G_b \sqsubseteq \hat{G} \sqsubseteq G_f|_{G_b.\mathrm{E} \cup G_f.\mathsf{cprefix}(r)}$, $G_f|_{G_f.\mathsf{cprefix}(G_f.\mathtt{rf}(r))} \not\sqsubseteq G$, there is a non-decreasing sequence of maximal steps s.t. $\hat{G} \to_r \to^* G$, and $\forall e \in G.\mathrm{E} \setminus \hat{G}.\mathrm{E}. \mathtt{tid}(e) \neq t$.*

Intuitively, TruSt tries to construct G_f by exploring an increasing sequence of its prefixes. This is not always possible, because when a read event r is added to G_b, the write event w that it should read from might not yet be present in G_b. In that case, r is made to read from another write and is later revisited by w leading to the execution $G'_b = G_f|_{G_b.\mathrm{E} \cup G_f.\mathsf{cprefix}(r)}$, which is a prefix of G_f. It is possible that additional backward revisit steps may happen between G_b and G'_b. Due to maximality, however, for every intermediate execution G in the production sequence between G_b and G'_b, there will be an execution $G_b \sqsubseteq \hat{G} \sqsubseteq G'_b$ that can be extended to G by a sequence of non-decreasing maximal steps. Execution $\hat{G}$ is exactly the part of G that is not deleted or revisited in a later step in S. Hence, if w is the first write that performed a backward revisit in S after G, then the events of thread $t = \mathtt{tid}(w)$ are already included in $\hat{G}$. Finally, it can be shown that t is to the right of r. The formal proof of this proposition can be found in the extended version of this paper [22].

4.2 Correctness of Slacked Bounding

To see why executions in the production sequence of a graph G_f can have at most $\mathtt{preemptions}(G_f) + N - 2$ preemptions, we start with a definition. A *witness* of a graph G is a trace of G that contains $\mathtt{preemptions}(G)$ preemptions.

Next, we observe that preemptions are monotone w.r.t. execution prefixes. That is, if an execution G requires a certain number of preemptions to be produced, a larger execution $G' \sqsupseteq G$ requires at least that many preemptions.

Lemma 1. *If G, G' are SC-consistent and $G \sqsubseteq G'$, then $\mathtt{preemptions}(G) \leq \mathtt{preemptions}(G')$.*

To prove this, take a witness of G' and restrict to the events of G, thereby obtaining a witness of G. The restriction can only remove preemptions.

Further, we note that the number of preemptions of an execution is unaffected if we extend its last executed thread with a maximal step; if a maximal step adds an event to a different thread, the number is increased by at most one.

Lemma 2. *Let G and G' be SC-consistent executions and $r \in G'.E$ such that $G \rightarrow_r \rightarrow^* G'$. Then, $\text{preemptions}(G') \leq \text{preemptions}(G) + S$, where S is the number of threads that where extended to obtain G' from G.*

Proof. Consider a witness w of G and extend by appending the missing events in the same order they were added in the sequence of maximal steps. Notice that, by construction of the maximal step, the resulting sequencing is a trace of G'. Each time we add an event e in the trace, such that the last event of of the trace was not in the thread of e, we increase the preemption-bound by one: a thread was previously considered as completed, but was now extended with a new event. However, this can only happen S times: the maximal steps keep adding events of the same thread and when another thread is picked, the first is not extended again (the maximal steps are non-decreasing). This gives us a trace of G' with at most $\text{preemptions}(G) + S$ preemptions, which concludes our proof. □

We can now prove that BUSTER is complete, i.e., it visits every full, SC-consistent execution that respects the bound.

Theorem 1. VERIFY(P, k) *visits every full, SC-consistent execution G_f of P with $\text{preemptions}(G_f) \leq k$.*

Proof. Consider a full, SC-consistent execution G_f of P with at most k preemptions. From the completeness of TruSt, we know that a run of Algorithm 1 without the test on Line 5 will visit G_f. It thus suffices to show that for every execution G in the production sequence of G_f has at most $k + N - 2$ preemptions, where N is the number of threads of P. If $G \sqsubseteq G_f$, then from Lemma 1 $\text{preemptions}(G) \leq \text{preemptions}(G_f) \leq k$.

Otherwise, from Prop. 1, there exists an execution G_b that is before G in the production sequence of G_f and an execution $\hat{G}$, such that $G_b \sqsubseteq \hat{G} \sqsubseteq G_f|_{G_b.E \cup G_f.\text{cprefix}(r)}$, $\text{next}_P(G_b) = r \in R$, $G_f|_{G_f.\text{cprefix}(G_f.\text{rf}(r))} \not\sqsubseteq G$, $\hat{G} \rightarrow_r \rightarrow^* G$, and no events in $G.E \setminus \hat{G}.E$ are in thread t, for some thread t to the right of r.

From the last two properties and Lemma 2 we have $\text{preemptions}(G) \leq k + N - 1$ since it is $\text{preemptions}(\hat{G}) \leq \text{preemptions}(G_f)$ ($\hat{G} \sqsubseteq G_f$ and Lemma 1) and at most $N - 1$ threads are extended from $\hat{G}$ to G.

To complete the proof, we will prove that $\text{preemptions}(G) = k + N - 1$ leads to contradiction. The equality implies that $\hat{G}$ had k preemptions and that $N-1$ threads were extended in the maximal steps from $\hat{G}$ to G, and all of them increased the preemptions by one. The sequence of maximal steps from $\hat{G}$ to G is non-decreasing and starts with the thread of r. Since there are at most N threads, $N-1$ are extended, and at least one thread to the right of t is not extended, r is in the leftmost thread.

Let t_r be the leftmost thread, $G'_b \triangleq G_f|_{G_b.E \cup G_f.\text{cprefix}(r)}$, and $w \triangleq G_f.\text{rf}(r)$. From the proof of TruSt, we can infer that all events of G_b are in the porf-prefix of the last event of t_r. It is $G_f|_{G_f.\text{cprefix}(w)} \not\sqsubseteq G_b$: the opposite, together with $G_b \sqsubseteq \hat{G} \sqsubseteq G$, contradicts $G_f|_{G_f.\text{cprefix}(w)} \not\sqsubseteq G$. Since G_b is in the production sequence of G_f, $G_b \sqsubseteq G_f$, $\text{next}_P(G_b) = r$, and $G_f|_{G_f.\text{cprefix}(w)} \not\sqsubseteq G_b$, TruSt will eventually add the write $w \triangleq G_f.\text{rf}(r)$ and revisit the read r, reaching the execution $G'_b \sqsubseteq G_f$ that contains all events added before r, i.e., the events of G_b, the events in the porf-prefix of r, and r. Hence, all events in $G'_b.E \setminus \{r\}$ are in the porf-prefix of r, which implies that any witness of G'_b ends with r.

Since $G'_b \sqsubseteq G_f$, any witness t of G'_b has at most k preemptions. Let G' be the execution G'_b without r, and G'' the unique execution s.t. $\hat{G} \rightarrow_r G''$. Removing the last event r from t gives us a trace t' of G' with at most k preemptions. If t' ends with an event of t_r, then we can restrict t' to the events of $\hat{G}$ and add r at the end, obtaining a trace of G'' with at most k preemptions. Otherwise, t' does not end with an event of t_r, and thus trace t has one more preemption than t, i.e., t' has at most $k-1$ preemptions. Then, we can again restrict t' to the events of $\hat{G}$ and add r a the end, obtaining again a trace of G'' with at most k preemptions. This contradicts our assumption that $\texttt{preemptions}(\hat{G}) = k$ and all $N-1$ threads that are extended from $\hat{G}$ increase the number of preemptions, since the first thread t_r can be extended without incurring any more preemptions. □

BUSTER inherits TruSt's optimality, as it only explores a subset of the executions that TruSt does. Here, optimality refers to avoiding redundant work; due to the slack, VERIFY(P, k) can also visit executions more than k preemptions.

Theorem 2. VERIFY(P, k) *explores each graph G of a program P at most once.*

5 Implementation

We have implemented BUSTER on top of the GENMC tool [18], which implements the TruSt algorithm [16]. Since GENMC supports weak memory models and the standard notion of preemption bounding only makes sense for sequential consistency, we enforce SC in our benchmarks by using only SC memory accesses and selecting GENMC's RC11 model [20].

The bulk of our modifications to GENMC concern the checking of whether the preemption-bound of an execution G exceeds a value k. Generally, deciding whether the preemption-bound of a Mazurkiewicz trace exceeds a value is an NP-complete problem [23]. We use an adaptation of the bound computation in Musuvathi et al. [23] to execution graphs, but instead of recursively computing $\texttt{preemptions}(G)$ (and cache computations across calls to amortize the cost), we recursively compute the predicate $\Phi(G, k) \triangleq \texttt{preemptions}(G) \leq k$. The benefit of this method is that we can avoid calculating $\texttt{preemptions}(G)$ exactly when its value exceeds the desired bound. Furthermore, there is no additional state that needs to be stored; BUSTER remains stateless.

As an optimization, we use as slack (Line 5) the minimum between $N-2$ and the number of threads that have no *deletable* events; an event is not deletable if it is in the porf-prefix of a write that backward revisited. Intuitively, the events that are added in G to reach $\hat{G}$ (Prop. 1) are the events that will later be deleted to eventually reach a graph that is a prefix of the final graph G_f.

Table 1. Buggy benchmarks. An ✗ indicates that an error was found.

Benchmark	$k=0$ Execs	Time	$k=1$ Execs	Time	$k=2$ Execs	Time	GENMC Execs	Time
account-bad	3 ✗	0.01	3 ✗	0.01	3 ✗	0.01	3 ✗	0.01
bluetooth-driver-bad	1	0.01	3 ✗	0.02	7 ✗	0.02	8 ✗	0.01
circular-buffer-bad	2	0.07	13 ✗	0.49	1 ✗	0.03	1 ✗	0.03
din-phil-sat	0 ✗	0.01	0 ✗	0.01	0 ✗	0.01	0 ✗	0.01
fsbench-bad	0 ✗	0.93	0 ✗	0.93	0 ✗	0.94	0 ✗	1.01
lazy01-bad	0 ✗	0.01	0 ✗	0.01	0 ✗	0.01	0 ✗	0.01
queue-bad	20	1.91	56 ✗	27.47	2 ✗	0.18	2 ✗	0.19
reorder-20-bad	⏱	⏱	⏱	⏱	⏱	⏱	10 ✗	0.05
stack-bad	11	0.44	10 ✗	0.35	10 ✗	0.35	10 ✗	0.37
token-ring-bad	12 ✗	0.02	12 ✗	0.02	12 ✗	0.02	12 ✗	0.02
twostage-100-bad	⏱	⏱	⏱	⏱	⏱	⏱	⏱	⏱
wronglock-bad	5914	164.46	2 ✗	0.02	2 ✗	0.02	2 ✗	0.02
lazy01-unsafe	0 ✗	0.01	0 ✗	0.01	0 ✗	0.01	0 ✗	0.01
sigma-unsafe	0 ✗	0.01	0 ✗	0.01	0 ✗	0.01	0 ✗	0.01
singleton-unsafe	5 ✗	0.01	5 ✗	0.01	5 ✗	0.01	5 ✗	0.01
stateful01-1-unsafe	0 ✗	0.01	0 ✗	0.01	0 ✗	0.01	0 ✗	0.01
triangular-2-unsafe	6	0.04	66	0.40	368	2.06	9069 ✗	29.44
stack-2-unsafe	6	0.06	5 ✗	0.05	5 ✗	0.05	5 ✗	0.05
read-write-lock-2-unsafe	68	0.51	53 ✗	0.25	132 ✗	0.59	276 ✗	0.96
reorder-2	417	0.14	6 ✗	0.01	2 ✗	0.01	2 ✗	0.01

6   Evaluation

To evaluate BUSTER, we answer the following questions:

§ 6.1 How many preemptions suffice to expose common concurrency bugs? Is BUSTER effective at finding such concurrency bugs?

§ 6.2 How good is preemption bounding at pruning the search space? Up to what bound does BUSTER run faster than vanilla DPOR?

§ 6.3 What is the overhead induced by the bound calculation?

§ 6.4 What is the overhead induced by bound-blocked executions?

To that end, we evaluate BUSTER against GENMC on a diverse set of benchmarks. Unfortunately, we cannot include the approach of Coons et al. [10] in our comparison because their implementation is not available.

We can draw two major conclusions from our evaluation. First, most bugs do manifest with a small number of preemptions (≤ 2), an observation that has been made in the literature before [25, 27]. Second, even though the bound calculation can be fairly expensive expensive, for small bounds BUSTER outperforms GENMC and can find bugs faster than GENMC.

Experimental Setup We conducted all experiments on a Dell PowerEdge M620 blade system with two Intel Xeon E5-2667 v2 CPU (8 cores @ 3.3 GHz) and 256GB of RAM. We used LLVM 11.0.1 for GENMC and BUSTER. All reported times are in seconds. We set a timeout limit of 30 minutes.

6.1   Bound and Bug Manifestation

To validate that most bugs require a small number of preemptions, we run BUSTER and GENMC on three sets of benchmarks:

Table 2. Buggy CD benchmarks. An ✗ indicates that the error was found.

Benchmark	$k = 0$ Execs	Time	$k = 1$ Execs	Time	$k = 2$ Execs	Time	GenMC Exec	Time
dglm-queue-bug(6)	48 ✗	2.55	305 ✗	102.25	810 ✗	272.71	☺	☺
dglm-queue-bug(7)	54 ✗	3.94	404 ✗	209.22	1259 ✗	628.52	☺	☺
dglm-queue-bug(8)	60 ✗	5.88	517 ✗	393.02	1854 ✗	1320.58	☺	☺
ms-queue-bug(6)	84 ✗	7.71	1366 ✗	155.08	9906 ✗	1057.28	☺	☺
ms-queue-bug(7)	103 ✗	12.87	1936 ✗	294.76	☺	☺	☺	☺
ms-queue-bug(8)	124 ✗	20.72	2636 ✗	530.04	☺	☺	☺	☺
bstack(7)	2	0.24	19 ✗	1.26	83 ✗	3.55	☺	☺
bstack(8)	2	0.34	22 ✗	2.06	111 ✗	6.41	☺	☺
bstack(9)	2	0.48	25 ✗	3.23	143 ✗	10.95	☺	☺
msq-bug2(5)	2	0.09	18 ✗	0.48	154 ✗	2.69	37420 ✗	280.64
msq-bug2(6)	2	0.12	22 ✗	0.87	232 ✗	6.29	☺	☺
stack-oe-bug(4)	77	0.64	1086	17.77	375 ✗	9.66	3523 ✗	97.65
stack-oe-bug(5)	92	1.04	1700	38.25	663 ✗	23.61	17032 ✗	763.96
stack-oe-bug(6)	107	1.58	2478	74.83	1076 ✗	50.38	☺	☺
stack-oe-bug(7)	122	2.32	3435	134.89	1638 ✗	97.52	☺	☺

- the unsafe concurrent benchmarks of the SCT suite [27],
- the unsafe benchmarks of the pthread category of SV-COMP [26] included in GenMC's test suite, and
- a set of concurrent data structures (CDs) from GenMC's test suite with randomly induced bugs.

In all cases, we configure BUSTER to disregard any errors that occur in executions that exceed the bound and are explored due to the slack. We note that this configuration may delay bug finding, since BUSTER may by chance quickly come across a buggy execution with more than k preemptions (due to slack) before finding any buggy execution with up to k preemptions. Nevertheless, we follow it to ensure that the bugs found arise in executions with up to the desired number of preemptions, so as to be able to validate the claim that bugs manifest in executions with a small number of preemptions.

Table 1 reports our outcomes on the first two classes of benchmarks. As can be seen, BUSTER was able to find most bugs using a bound of 1. In fact, for most benchmarks, BUSTER found the bug before exploring a complete execution, hence the "0 ✗" entries in the table. The only benchmarks, where BUSTER needs a bound greater that 1 are the synthetic benchmarks triangular, which needs a bound of 8, as it was specifically designed to make the bug discovery difficult and push model checkers to their limits; reorder-20 and twostage-100, which have a large number of threads (20 and 100, respectively). BUSTER times out on the latter two benchmarks because the large number of threads put a lot of stress in the bound checking procedure. We note that for twostage-100, GenMC also fails to terminate within the time limit.

Table 2 reports our results for our CD benchmarks. For these benchmarks, we have taken CD implementations from the GenMC test suite, and induced bugs into them by randomly dropping a synchronization instruction or replacing a CAS instruction with a normal write or an unconditional exchange instruction, thereby introducing a possible atomicity violation. We then construct medium-

Table 3. BUSTER and GENMC comparison on safe data structure benchmarks.

Benchmark	$k=0$ Execs	Time	$k=1$ Execs	Time	$k=2$ Execs	Time	$k=3$ Execs	Time	GENMC Execs	Time	Max k
dglm-queue(6)	2	0.61	12	3.05	62	11.30	162	27.14	924	104.47	7
dglm-queue(7)	2	0.97	14	5.78	86	25.65	266	71.73	3432	570.68	8
ms-queue(6)	2	0.30	18	2.23	128	8.46	513	29.46	18564	321.58	8
ms-queue(7)	2	0.46	21	4.16	177	18.53	840	78.13	⏱	⏱	
bstack2(8)	2	0.12	16	0.58	114	2.97	408	9.17	12870	159.27	9
bstack2(9)	2	0.15	18	0.88	146	5.08	594	17.75	48620	720.06	8
bstack(5)	2	0.12	20	0.53	92	2.98	310	7.87	4214	88.01	8
bstack(6)	2	0.18	24	0.97	134	6.84	549	21.35	26040	787.64	8
ms-queue(7)	2	0.19	14	1.19	86	5.77	266	16.41	3432	135.85	7
ms-queue(8)	2	0.26	16	1.85	114	10.29	408	33.78	12870	641.64	8
stack-oe(4)	77	0.64	1098	17.62	6208	139.81	23472	641.13	⏱	⏱	
stack-oe(5)	92	1.06	1713	39.55	11510	377.50	⏱	⏱	⏱	⏱	
ms-oe(6)	12	0.27	84	2.93	615	18.82	2039	57.58	10880	218.86	5
ms-oe(7)	14	0.34	100	3.97	800	27.42	2855	91.54	20823	458.09	5
dglm-oe(7)	5	0.20	29	2.14	129	9.27	238	19.53	248	20.88	3
dglm-oe(8)	5	0.23	31	2.62	146	11.77	294	26.33	306	28.50	3
dglm-fifo(7)	26	4.50	128	21.84	128	25.93	128	25.12	128	22.92	1
dglm-fifo(8)	29	6.81	162	35.43	162	42.66	162	41.59	162	37.91	1
ttas-lock2(7)	2	0.12	14	0.48	86	1.89	266	4.57	3432	28.50	7
ttas-lock2(8)	2	0.17	16	0.81	114	3.66	408	10.14	12870	121.94	8
ttas-lock3(4)	21	0.89	195	7.12	1041	29.94	3525	84.55	34650	387.36	5
ttas-lock3(5)	26	2.32	320	23.97	2274	130.62	10494	492.89	⏱	⏱	

sized clients (with 2-3 threads and up to 12 operations per thread) of these data structures that check for their intended semantics (for example, that a queue has FIFO semantics). In all cases, the induced bugs lead to violations of the assertions in the client programs, and occasionally even to memory errors. BUSTER can find these bugs easily; a bound of $k = 2$ suffices to expose them. By contrast, GENMC times out for most of these benchmarks, as their state space is enormous.

6.2   Comparison with Plain DPOR on Safe Benchmarks

We have already seen that modulo specially crafted synthetic benchmarks, a small preemption bound is sufficient for finding bugs in practice. Moreover, BUSTER is pretty good at finding such bugs in concurrent data structures. We now evaluate the application of BUSTER on a collection of safe benchmarks. For this purpose, we use different variations of the benchmarks of Table 2 (after repairing them so that no assertion is violated), as well as a few locking benchmarks.

Table 3 compares the performance of BUSTER for small values of k and GENMC. As it can be seen, GENMC struggles with these benchmarks, whereas BUSTER with $k = 2$ (and often also with $k = 3$) terminates fairly quickly. This is because only a small fraction of the total executions of sizeable benchmarks have few preemptions. Therefore restricting the search to only those executions makes BUSTER run much faster than GENMC, and guarantees that the program under consideration does not have any common bugs.

In the last column of Table 3 we include the maximum value of k such that BUSTER terminates faster than GENMC, for the benchmarks that terminate under GENMC. In most cases BUSTER is faster than GENMC even for $k > 3$. For the `dglm-fifo` benchmarks BUSTER is only faster for $k \in \{0, 1\}$, because for these benchmarks a small k suffices to fully explore the state space.

6.3 Bound Calculation Overhead

We now measure the cost of checking that each encountered execution is below the specified bound. As we discussed in §5, checking whether an execution graph's preemption-bound exceeds a value is a NP-complete problem, and thus we expect this calculation to threaten the performance of our tool.

To carefully account for this cost, we compare BUSTER against the baseline GENMC implementation on benchmarks where preemption bounding does not reduce the number of executions that are explored. In Line 4, we report results on simple CD clients that have only one operation per thread of the Treiber stack [28] and the TTAS lock [13]. The clients are designed so that BUSTER can explore the full set of program executions with a small bound k. We suffix the name of the benchmarks with the number of writer and reader threads for the Treiber stack and the total number of threads for TTAS.

Column b contains the minimal number of the bound k for which BUSTER explores the same number of executions as GENMC does. Note that since these benchmarks contain several threads, exploration up to a certain bound (e.g., $k = 0$) does not mean that only executions with k preemptions are visited; due to slack, executions with more preemptions may be visited, and so it is possible for the exploration to cover the entire state space for a smaller bound than intrinsically necessary. In the subsequent columns we report the time overhead (percentage) for bounds $k = b, k = b + 1$, and $k = b + 2$ w.r.t. to GENMC's execution time, which is visible on the last column. The maximum overhead is observed for $k = b$ (the minimal value sufficient to cover the entire state space). This is expected because $k = b$ places the most burden on the calculation of whether the number of preemptions in a given execution are below k. For larger k values, the overhead drops because it is easier to show that the number of preemptions are below the bound; one does not have to calculate the number of preemptions of an execution precisely. Overall, for the Treiber stack benchmark, the overhead introduced by calculating the bounds is fairly low and does not exceed the 23% of the execution time of GENMC. For the plain runs of ttas-lock, the maximal overhead is a bit larger, up to 38%. We note, however, that such overhead only occurs in clients with a large number of threads (7); smaller clients are not affected as much.

6.4 Overhead due to Bound-Blocked Executions

Finally, we measure the overhead caused by bound-blocked executions, by evaluating how often they arise in practice. Specifically, we ran BUSTER on GENMC's test suite for various preemption-bound values, as well as on the safe CD clients used in § 6.2, and counted the number of such bound-blocked executions.

Table 4. Overhead w.r.t. to GENMC (left) and blocking in benchmarks (right).

Benchmark	b	$k = b$	$k = b + 1$	$k = b + 2$	GENMC
treiber(6,0)	0	10%	6%	4%	30.81
treiber(7,0)	0	23%	12%	5%	529.42
treiber(3,2)	1	6%	5%	5%	2.75
treiber(3,3)	1	7%	6%	5%	31.15
treiber(3,4)	1	13%	8%	6%	332.76
treiber(4,2)	1	9%	7%	5%	47.50
treiber(4,3)	2	10%	7%	5%	777.44
ttas-lock(6)	0	20%	13%	11%	14.52
ttas-lock(7)	0	38%	25%	16%	231.91

# Blocked	# Benchmarks
0	72
1	143
2	45
3	3
4	14
5	4
6	1
8	69
>8	6

For GENMC's test suite, the results are summarized in table 4 (right). We have restricted out attention to the runs with at least 10 executions, so that our results are not skewed by benchmarks that have very few executions. We have also excluded 8 benchmarks from the test suite that use barriers because they are currently not supported by our tool. As it can be seen, bound-blocked executions are rare: most runs lead to one bound-blocked execution, and only 6 lead to more than 8 bound-blocked executions. Bound-blocked executions are on average no more than 6% of the total number of executions explored.

For the CDs clients, bound-blocked executions are even more rare; out of the 22 clients, BUSTER encounters bound-blocked executions in only 4 of them, for some k. We exclude again from the discussion runs with very few executions. From the remaining runs, only two encounter a considerable number of bound-blocked executions that become negligible as the bound is increased: around 10% for $k = 1$ and less than 1% for $k = 2$

7   Related Work

There is a large body of work that has improved the original DPOR algorithm of Flanagan et al. [11]. Abdulla et al. [2] introduced the first optimal DPOR algorithm, which, however, suffers from possibly exponential memory consumption. Kokologiannakis et al. [16] developed TruSt, which is the first optimal DPOR algorithm that consumes polynomial memory.

Agarwal et al. [6], Chalupa et al. [8], Chatterjee et al. [9], and Huang [14] have extended DPOR for partitions coarser than the one we have focused in this paper, i.e., Mazurkiewicz traces. Abdulla et al. [1, 4, 5] consider DPOR under various weak memory models, while the works of Kokologiannakis et al. [16, 17, 19] provide a DPOR algorithm that is parametric in the choice of the memory model, provided it respects some basic properties.

Qadeer et al. [25] showed the decidability of context-bound verification of concurrent boolean programs. Musuvathi et al. [24] propose *iterative* context bounding, a search algorithm that prioritizes executions with fewer preemptions. Musuvathi et al. [23] combine partial-order reduction with a preemption-bound search, and prove that judging whether the preemption-bound of a Mazurkiewicz trace exceeds a certain value is an NP-complete problem.

To our knowledge, the only attempt to combine DPOR and preemption bounding is by Coons et al. [10], who identify the difficulty of maintaining completeness of the exploration, and resolve it by weakening DPOR.

Abdulla et al. [3] and Atig et al. [7] have extended the notion of preemption bounding to weak memory models. We leave a possible extension of our approach to weak memory models for future work.

Acknowledgments We thank the anonymous reviewers for their valuable feedback. This work has received funding from the European Research Council (ERC) under the European Union's Horizon 2020 research and innovation programme grant agreement No. 101003349).

8 Data-Availability Statement

All supplementary material is available at [22]. The artifact is also available at [21].

References

[1] Parosh Aziz Abdulla, Stavros Aronis, Mohamed Faouzi Atig, Bengt Jonsson, Carl Leonardsson, and Konstantinos Sagonas. "Stateless model checking for TSO and PSO". In: *TACAS 2015*. Vol. 9035. LNCS. Berlin, Heidelberg: Springer, 2015, pp. 353–367. DOI: 10.1007/978-3-662-46681-0_28. URL: http://dx.doi.org/10.1007/978-3-662-46681-0_28.

[2] Parosh Aziz Abdulla, Stavros Aronis, Bengt Jonsson, and Konstantinos Sagonas. "Optimal dynamic partial order reduction". In: *POPL 2014*. New York, NY, USA: ACM, 2014, pp. 373–384. DOI: 10.1145/2535838.2535845. URL: http://doi.acm.org/10.1145/2535838.2535845.

[3] Parosh Aziz Abdulla, Mohamed Faouzi Atig, Ahmed Bouajjani, and Tuan Phong Ngo. "Context-Bounded Analysis for POWER". In: *TACAS 2017*. Ed. by Axel Legay and Tiziana Margaria. Berlin, Heidelberg: Springer Berlin Heidelberg, 2017, pp. 56–74. ISBN: 978-3-662-54580-5. DOI: 10.1007/978-3-662-54580-5_4.

[4] Parosh Aziz Abdulla, Mohamed Faouzi Atig, Bengt Jonsson, and Carl Leonardsson. "Stateless model checking for POWER". In: *CAV 2016*. Vol. 9780. LNCS. Berlin, Heidelberg: Springer, 2016, pp. 134–156. DOI: 10.1007/978-3-319-41540-6_8. URL: https://doi.org/10.1007/978-3-319-41540-6_8.

[5] Parosh Aziz Abdulla, Mohamed Faouzi Atig, Bengt Jonsson, and Tuan Phong Ngo. "Optimal stateless model checking under the release-acquire semantics". In: *Proc. ACM Program. Lang.* 2.OOPSLA (Oct. 2018), 135:1–135:29. ISSN: 2475-1421. DOI: 10.1145/3276505. URL: http://doi.acm.org/10.1145/3276505.

[6] Pratyush Agarwal, Krishnendu Chatterjee, Shreya Pathak, Andreas Pavlogiannis, and Viktor Toman. "Stateless Model Checking Under a Reads-Value-From Equivalence". In: *CAV 2021*. Ed. by Alexandra Silva and K. Rustan M. Leino. Cham: Springer International Publishing, July 2021, pp. 341–366. ISBN: 978-3-030-81685-8. DOI: 10.1007/978-3-030-81685-8_16.

[7] Mohamed Faouzi Atig, Ahmed Bouajjani, and Gennaro Parlato. "Context-Bounded Analysis of TSO Systems". In: *FPS 2014*. Ed. by Saddek Bensalem, Yassine Lakhneck, and Axel Legay. Berlin, Heidelberg: Springer Berlin Heidelberg, 2014, pp. 21–38. ISBN: 978-3-642-54848-2. DOI: 10.1007/978-3-642-54848-2_2.

[8] Marek Chalupa, Krishnendu Chatterjee, Andreas Pavlogiannis, Nishant Sinha, and Kapil Vaidya. "Data-centric dynamic partial order reduction". In: *Proc. ACM Program. Lang.* 2.POPL (Dec. 2017), 31:1–31:30. ISSN: 2475-1421. DOI: 10.1145/3158119. URL: http://doi.acm.org/10.1145/3158119.

[9] Krishnendu Chatterjee, Andreas Pavlogiannis, and Viktor Toman. "Value-Centric Dynamic Partial Order Reduction". In: *Proc. ACM Program. Lang.* 3.OOPSLA (Oct. 2019). DOI: 10.1145/3360550. URL: https://doi.org/10.1145/3360550.

[10] Katherine E. Coons, Madan Musuvathi, and Kathryn S. McKinley. "Bounded Partial-Order Reduction". In: *OOPSLA 2013*. Indianapolis, Indiana, USA: ACM, 2013, pp. 833–848. ISBN: 9781450323741. DOI: 10.1145/2509136.2509556. URL: https://doi.org/10.1145/2509136.2509556.

[11] Cormac Flanagan and Patrice Godefroid. "Dynamic partial-order reduction for model checking software". In: *POPL 2005*. New York, NY, USA: ACM, 2005, pp. 110–121. DOI: 10.1145/1040305.1040315. URL: http://doi.acm.org/10.1145/1040305.1040315.

[12] Patrice Godefroid. "Model checking for programming languages using VeriSoft". In: *POPL 1997*. Paris, France: ACM, 1997, pp. 174–186. DOI: 10.1145/263699.263717. URL: http://doi.acm.org/10.1145/263699.263717.

[13] Maurice Herlihy and Nir Shavit. *The art of multiprocessor programming*. 2008.

[14] Jeff Huang. "Stateless model checking concurrent programs with maximal causality reduction". In: *PLDI 2015*. New York, NY, USA: ACM, 2015, pp. 165–174. DOI: 10.1145/2737924.2737975. URL: http://doi.acm.org/10.1145/2737924.2737975.

[15] Michalis Kokologiannakis, Ori Lahav, Konstantinos Sagonas, and Viktor Vafeiadis. "Effective stateless model checking for C/C++ concurrency". In: *Proc. ACM Program. Lang.* 2.POPL (Dec. 2017), 17:1–17:32. ISSN: 2475-1421. DOI: 10.1145/3158105. URL: http://doi.acm.org/10.1145/3158105.

[16] Michalis Kokologiannakis, Iason Marmanis, Vladimir Gladstein, and Viktor Vafeiadis. "Truly stateless, optimal dynamic partial order reduction". In:

Proc. ACM Program. Lang. 6.POPL (Jan. 2022). DOI: 10.1145/3498711. URL: https://doi.org/10.1145/3498711.

[17] Michalis Kokologiannakis, Azalea Raad, and Viktor Vafeiadis. "Model checking for weakly consistent libraries". In: *PLDI 2019*. New York, NY, USA: ACM, 2019. DOI: 10.1145/3314221.3314609.

[18] Michalis Kokologiannakis and Viktor Vafeiadis. "GenMC: A model checker for weak memory models". In: *CAV 2021*. Ed. by Alexandra Silva and K. Rustan M. Leino. Vol. 12759. LNCS. Springer, 2021, pp. 427–440. DOI: 10.1007/978-3-030-81685-8_20.

[19] Michalis Kokologiannakis and Viktor Vafeiadis. "HMC: Model checking for hardware memory models". In: *ASPLOS 2020*. ASPLOS '20. Lausanne, Switzerland: ACM, 2020, pp. 1157–1171. ISBN: 9781450371025. DOI: 10.1145/3373376.3378480. URL: https://doi.org/10.1145/3373376.3378480.

[20] Ori Lahav, Viktor Vafeiadis, Jeehoon Kang, Chung-Kil Hur, and Derek Dreyer. "Repairing sequential consistency in C/C++11". In: *PLDI 2017*. Barcelona, Spain: ACM, 2017, pp. 618–632. ISBN: 978-1-4503-4988-8. DOI: 10.1145/3062341.3062352. URL: http://doi.acm.org/10.1145/3062341.3062352.

[21] Iason Marmanis, Michalis Kokologiannakis, and Viktor Vafeiadis. "Reconciling Preemption Bounding with DPOR (artifact)". In: (Apr. 2023). DOI: 10.5281/zenodo.7505917.

[22] Iason Marmanis, Michalis Kokologiannakis, and Viktor Vafeiadis. "Reconciling Preemption Bounding with DPOR (supplementary material)". In: (Apr. 2023). URL: https://plv.mpi-sws.org/genmc.

[23] Madalan Musuvathi and Shaz Qadeer. *Partial-Order Reduction for Context-Bounded State Exploration*. Tech. rep. MSR-TR-2007-12. Microsoft Research, 2007. URL: https://www.microsoft.com/en-us/research/wp-content/uploads/2016/02/tr-2007-12.pdf.

[24] Madanlal Musuvathi and Shaz Qadeer. "Iterative Context Bounding for Systematic Testing of Multithreaded Programs". In: *PLDI 2007*. San Diego, California, USA: ACM, 2007, pp. 446–455. ISBN: 9781595936332. DOI: 10.1145/1250734.1250785. URL: https://doi.org/10.1145/1250734.1250785.

[25] Shaz Qadeer and Jakob Rehof. "Context-Bounded Model Checking of Concurrent Software". In: *TACAS 2005*. Ed. by Nicolas Halbwachs and Lenore D. Zuck. Vol. 3440. LNCS. Springer, 2005, pp. 93–107. DOI: 10.1007/978-3-540-31980-1_7. URL: https://doi.org/10.1007/978-3-540-31980-1%5C_7.

[26] SV-COMP. *Competition on Software Verification (SV-COMP)*. 2019. URL: https://sv-comp.sosy-lab.org/2019/ (visited on 03/27/2019).

[27] Paul Thomson, Alastair F. Donaldson, and Adam Betts. "Concurrency testing using schedule bounding: an empirical study". In: *PPoPP 2014*. ACM, 2014, pp. 15–28. DOI: 10.1145/2555243.2555260. URL: https://doi.org/10.1145/2555243.2555260.

[28]   R. Kent Treiber. *Systems Programming: Coping with Parallelism.* Tech. rep. Technical Report RJ5118, IBM, 1986. URL: https://dominoweb.draco. res.ibm.com/58319a2ed2b10789852570030046l7ef.html.

Optimal Stateless Model Checking for Causal Consistency

Parosh Abdulla[1] , Mohamed Faouzi Atig[1] , S. Krishna[2] ,
Ashutosh Gupta[2], and Omkar Tuppe[2](✉)

[1] Uppsala University, Uppsala, Sweden
{parosh,mohamed_faouzi.atig}@it.uu.se
[2] IIT Bombay, Mumbai, India
{krishnas,akg,omkarvtuppe}@cse.iitb.ac.in

Abstract. We present a framework for efficient stateless model checking (SMC) of concurrent programs under three prominent models of causal consistency, CCv, CM, CC. Our approach is based on exploring traces under the program order po and the reads from rf relations. Our SMC algorithm is provably optimal in the sense that it explores each po and rf relation exactly once. We have implemented our framework in a tool called CONSCHECKER. Experiments show that CONSCHECKER performs well in detecting anomalies in classical distributed databases benchmarks.

1 Introduction

Traditionally, distributed shared memories ensure that all processes in the system agree on a common order of all operations on memory. Such guarantees are provided by sequential consistency (SC) [33], and by linearizable memory [26]. However, providing these consistency guarantees entails access latencies, making them inefficient for large systems. There is a tradeoff in providing strong consistency guarantees while ensuring low latency and this presents significant efficiency challenges. There is a large body of work which suggests that a systematic weakening of memory consistency can reduce the costs of providing consistency. Weakened consistency guarantees admit more concurrent behaviours than SC or linearizability. To this end, Lamport [32] proposed *causal consistency* which provides an ordering among events in a distributed system in which processes communicate via message passing. This has been adapted [7] to a setting of reads and writes in a shared memory environment. In this setting, the return values of reads must be consistent with causally related reads and writes. As causality only orders events partially, the reading processes can disagree on the relative ordering of concurrent writes. This makes concurrent writer processes independent, reducing the costs of synchronization.

Several efforts have been made to formalize causal consistency [16], [25], [39] [40], [7], [15], [10], [8], [38] and there are many implementations [9], [20], [21] satisfying this criterion as opposed to strong consistency (linearizability).

© The Author(s) 2023
S. Sankaranarayanan and N. Sharygina (Eds.): TACAS 2023, LNCS 13993, pp. 105–125, 2023.
https://doi.org/10.1007/978-3-031-30823-9_6

While strong consistency makes it easier to program than weak ones, they require costly implementations. Weak memories may be easier to implement, but much harder to program. An acceptable medium which has emerged over the years are three important notions in causal consistency, respectively *causal consistency* (CC) [15], [25], *causal convergence* (CCv) [16], [39], [15], [25] and *causal memory* (CM) [7], [39], [15], [25].

The focus of this paper is the verification of shared memory programs under causal consistency. We consider the three variants mentioned above. We propose a stateless model checking (SMC) framework that covers all three variants. SMC is a successful technique for finding concurrency bugs [23]. For a terminating program, SMC systematically explores all process schedulings that are possible during runs of the program. The number of possible schedulings grows exponentially with the execution length in SMC. To counter this and reduce the number of explored executions, the technique of *partial order reduction* [18,22] has been proposed. This has been adapted to SMC as DPOR (dynamic partial order reduction). DPOR was first developed for concurrent programs under SC [1,41]. Recent years have seen DPOR adapted to language induced weak memory models [28,37],[5], as well as hardware-induced relaxed memory models [3,46]. To the best of our knowledge, DPOR algorithms have not been developed for causal consistency models. The goal of this paper is to fill this gap.

DPOR is based on the observation that two executions are equivalent if they induce the same ordering between conflicting events, and hence it is sufficient to consider one such execution from each equivalence class. Under sequential consistency, these equivalence classes are called *Mazurkiewicz* traces [34], while for relaxed memory models, the generalization of these are called *Shasha-Snir* traces [42]. A Shasha-Snir trace characterizes an execution of a concurrent program by the relations (1) *po* program order, which totally orders events of each process, (2), *rf* reads from, which connects each read with the write it reads from, (3) *co* coherence order, which totally orders writes to the same shared variable. DPOR can be optimized further by observing that the assertions to be verified at the end of an execution does not depend on the coherence order of shared variables, and hence it suffices to consider traces over $po - rf$. Based on this observation, the DPOR algorithms for programs under the release-acquire semantics (RA) and SC [5], [4] explores traces with *po*, *rf* and *co* where the *co* edges are added on the fly. The equivalence classes are considered wrt $po - rf$, reducing the number of distinct traces to be analyzed.

Contributions. We propose a DPOR based SMC algorithm for all three consistency models CC, CCv, CM which explores systematically, all the distinct po-rf traces covering all possible executions of the program. We develop a uniform algorithm for all three models which is sound and complete : that is, all traces explored are consistent wrt the model $X \in \{CC, CCv, CM\}$ under consideration, and all such consistent traces are explored. Moreover, our algorithm is optimal in the sense that, each consistent po-rf trace is explored exactly once. One of the key challenges during the trace exploration is to maintain the consistency of the traces wrt the model under consideration. We tackle this by defining a *trace se-*

mantics which ensures that the traces generated in each step only contain edges which will be present in any consistent trace. We implement our algorithms in a tool CONSCHECKER which is, to the best of our knowledge, the first of its kind to perform SMC on the three prominent causal consistency models CC, CCv, CM. CONSCHECKER checks for assertion violation of programs under CC, CCv, CM. We evaluate the correctness of our tool on CC, CCv, CM by simulating these models on the memory model simulator Herd [8] and validating our outcomes with theirs. Then we proceed with experimental evaluation on a wide range of benchmarks from distributed databases. We showed that (i) CONSCHECKER correctly detects known consistency bugs [13], [14], [12] and [11] under CCv, CM, CC, (ii) CONSCHECKER correctly detects known assertion violations in applications [19], [27], [12], [36]. We also did a stress test of CONSCHECKER on some SV-COMP benchmarks and parameterized benchmarks which resulted in a large number (6 million) of traces.

Related Work. SMC has been implemented in many tools CHESS [35], Concuerror [17], VeriSoft [24], NIDHUGG [3], CDSChecker [37], RCMC[28], GenMC [30], rInspect [46] and Tracer [5]. While most of these work with either Mazurkiewicz traces or *po − rf* traces, [6] proposes a RVF-SMC algorithm where the value read is used to decide equivalence of two runs.

In recent years, there has been much interest in DPOR algorithms : [4] for SC, [30] for the release acquire semantics, [43] for C/C++, and [29] for TSO, PSO and RC11. It is known that CC is weaker than RA, CCv is stronger than RA while CM is incomparable with RA [31]. In conclusion, all the above memory models are different from CC, CCv, CM. Hence we cannot reuse any of the existing DPOR algorithms.

Recent work on causal consistency [15] studies the complexity of checking whether one execution (all executions) of a program under CC, CCv, CM is consistent. They show that checking if an execution is consistent is NP-completeness, while the question of checking if all executions are consistent is undecidable. [11], [12] explore the robustness wrt SC, of transactional programs under CC, CCv, CM. However, none of these papers propose a DPOR algorithm for CC, CCv, CM.

2   Preliminaries

Programs We consider a program $\mathcal{P}$ consisting of a finite set $\mathcal{T}$ of *threads* (*processes*) that share a finite set $\mathbb{X}$ of *(shared) variables*, ranging over a domain $\mathbb{V}$ of *values* that includes a special value 0.

A process has a finite set of local registers that store values from $\mathbb{V}$. Each process runs a deterministic code, built in a standard way from expressions and atomic commands, using standard control flow constructs (sequential composition, selection, and bounded loop constructs). Throughout the paper, we use x, y for shared variables, a, b, c for registers, and e for expressions. *Global statements* are either writes $x := e$ to a shared variable, or reads $a := x$ from a shared variable. *Local statements* only access and affect the local state of the process and include assignments $a := e$ to registers, and conditional control flow constructs.

Note that expressions do not contain shared variables, implying that a statement accesses at most one shared variable.

The local state of a process $proc \in \mathcal{T}$ is defined by its program counter and the contents of its registers. A *configuration* of $\mathcal{P}$ is made up of the local states of all the processes. The values of the shared variables are not part of a configuration. A program execution is a sequence of transitions between configurations, starting with the initial configuration γ^{init}. Each transition corresponds to one process performing a local or global statement. A transition between two configurations γ and γ' is of form $\gamma \overset{\ell}{\rightsquigarrow} \gamma'$, where the label ℓ describes the interaction with shared variables. The label ℓ is one of three forms: (i) $\langle proc, \varepsilon \rangle$, indicating a local statement performed by thread $proc$, which updates only the local state of $proc$, (ii) $\langle proc, \mathsf{wt}, x, v \rangle$, indicating a write of the value v to the variable x by the thread $proc$, which also updates the program counter of $proc$, and (iii) $\langle proc, \mathsf{rd}, x, v \rangle$ indicating a read of v from x by the thread $proc$ into some register, while also updating the program counter of $proc$. There is no constraint on the values that are used in transitions corresponding to read statements. This will allow some illegal program behaviors, which is sorted by associating runs with so-called *traces*, which represent how reads obtain their values from writes. A causal consistency model $X \in \{\mathsf{CC}, \mathsf{CCv}, \mathsf{CM}\}$ is formulated by imposing restrictions on traces, thereby also restricting the possible runs that are associated with them.

Since local statements are not visible to other threads, we will not represent them explicitly in the transition relation considered in our DPOR algorithm. Instead, we let each transition represent the combined effect of some finite sequence of local statements by a process followed by a global statement by the same process. For configurations γ and γ' and a label ℓ which is either of the form $\langle proc, \mathsf{wt}, x, v \rangle$ or of the form $\langle proc, \mathsf{rd}, x, v \rangle$, we let $\gamma \overset{\ell}{\rightarrow} \gamma'$ denote that we can reach γ' from γ by performing a sequence of transitions labeled with $\langle proc, \varepsilon \rangle$ followed by a transition labeled with ℓ. Defining the relation $\rightarrow$ in this manner ensures that we take the effect of local statements into account, while avoiding consideration of interleavings of local statements of different threads in the analysis.

We use $\gamma \rightarrow \gamma'$ to denote that $\gamma \overset{\ell}{\rightarrow} \gamma'$ for some ℓ and define $\mathsf{succ}(\gamma) := \{\gamma' \mid \gamma \rightarrow \gamma'\}$, i.e., it is the set of successors of γ wrt. $\rightarrow$. A configuration γ is said to be *terminal* if $\mathsf{succ}(\gamma) = \emptyset$, i.e., no thread can execute a global statement from γ. A *run* ρ from γ is a sequence $\gamma_0 \overset{\ell_1}{\longrightarrow} \gamma_1 \overset{\ell_2}{\longrightarrow} \cdots \overset{\ell_n}{\longrightarrow} \gamma_n$ such that $\gamma_0 = \gamma$. We say that ρ is *terminated* if γ_n is terminal. We let $Runs(\gamma)$ denote the set of runs from γ.

Events. An event corresponds to a particular execution of a statement in a run of $\mathcal{P}$. A *write event* ev is given by $(id, proc, \mathsf{wt}(x, v))$ where $id \in \mathbb{N}$ is the identifier of the event, $proc$ is the process containing the event, $x \in \mathbb{X}$ is a variable, and $v \in \mathbb{V}$ is a value. This event corresponds to a process writing the value v to variable x. Likewise, a *read event* ev is given by $(id, proc, \mathsf{rd}(x))$ where $x \in \mathbb{X}$. This event corresponds to a process reading some value to x. The read event ev does not specify the particular value it reads; this value will be defined in a trace by specifying a write event from which ev fetches its value. For each variable $x \in \mathbb{X}$, we assume a special write event $\mathsf{init}_x = \mathsf{wt}(x, 0)$ called the *initializer* event for x. This event is not performed by any of the processes in $\mathcal{T}$, and writes the value 0 to x. We define $\mathbf{E}_{init} := \{\mathsf{init}_x \mid x \in \mathbb{X}\}$ as the set of initializer events. If $\mathbf{E}$ is a set of events, we define subsets of $\mathbf{E}$ characterized by particular attributes of its events. For instance, for a variable x, we let $\mathbf{E}^{\mathsf{wt},x}$ denote $\{ev \in \mathbf{E} \mid ev.type = \mathsf{wt} \wedge ev.var = x\}$.

Traces. A *trace* τ is a tuple $\langle \mathbf{E}, po, rf \rangle$, where $\mathbf{E}$ is a set of *events* which includes the set $\mathbf{E}_{init}$ of initializer events, and po (program order), rf (read-from) are binary relations on $\mathbf{E}$ that satisfy:

- ev po ev' if $process(ev) = process(ev')$ and $ev.id < ev'.id$. po totally orders the events of each individual process.
- ev rf ev' if ev is a write event and ev' is a read event on the same variable, which obtains its value from ev.

We can view $\tau = \langle \mathbf{E}, po, rf \rangle$ as a graph whose nodes are $\mathbf{E}$ and whose edges are defined by the relations po, rf. po depicted by red solid edges captures the order in each process while rf edges are depicted as solid blue edges. We define the *empty trace* $\tau_\emptyset := \langle \mathbf{E}_{init}, \emptyset, \emptyset \rangle$, i.e., it contains only the initializer events, and all the relations are empty.

We define when a trace can be associated with a run. Consider a run ρ of form $\gamma_0 \xrightarrow{\ell_1} \cdots \xrightarrow{\ell_n} \gamma_n$, where $\ell_i = \langle proc_i, \mathsf{t}_i, x_i, v_i \rangle$, and let $\tau = \langle \mathbf{E}, po, rf \rangle$ be a trace. We write $\rho \models \tau$ to denote that the following conditions are satisfied: (i) $\mathbf{E} = \{ev_1, \ldots, ev_n\}$, i.e., each event corresponds exactly to one label in ρ. (ii) If $\ell_i = \langle proc_i, \mathsf{wt}, x_i, v_i \rangle$, then $ev_i = \langle id_i, proc_i, \mathsf{wt}, x_i, v_i \rangle$, and if $\ell_i = \langle proc_i, \mathsf{rd}, x_i, v_i \rangle$, then $ev_i = \langle id_i, proc_i, \mathsf{rd}, x_i \rangle$. An event and its label do the same (write or read) on identical variables, and for writes, they also agree on the written value. (iii) $id_i = |\{j \mid (1 \leq j \leq i) \wedge (proc_j = proc_i)\}|$. $ev.id$ shows how it is ordered relative to the other events of $process(ev)$. (iv) if ev_i rf ev_j then $x_i = x_j$ and $v_i = v_j$. (v) if init_x rf ev_i then $v_i = 0$, i.e., ev_i reads the initial value of x which is 0.

3   Causally Consistent Models

We study three variants [15] of causal consistency : $\mathsf{CC}, \mathsf{CCv}$ and CM. To define the three models formally, we introduce a function that, for each model, extends a given trace uniquely by a set of new edges. Then we define the model by requiring that the extended trace does not contain any cycles. A run of the program satisfies a consistency model X if its associated extended trace has no cycles.

Let CO, called *causality order* represent $(po \cup rf)^+$. Two events e_1, e_2 are *causally related* if either e_1 CO e_2 or e_2 CO e_1.

Causal Consistency CC. We start presenting the weakest notion of causal consistency, CC [25], [7]. First we give an intuitive description of CC. In CC, events which are not causally related can be executed in different orders in different processes; moreover decisions made about these orders can be revised by each process. To illustrate, consider the program Fig.1(b). The write events $\mathsf{wt}(x, 1), \mathsf{wt}(x, 2)$ are not causally related and hence can be ordered in any way.

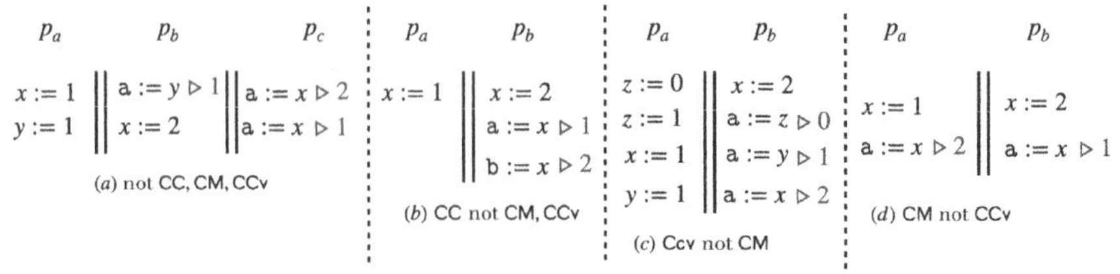

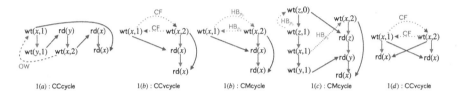

Fig. 1. Programs showing the differences between consistency models. The $\triangleright v$ denotes the expected return value of the read event.

Fig. 2. solid red, blue edges are po, rf, $\mathsf{wt}(x,v)$ and $\mathsf{rd}(x)$ are write, read events.

Note that p_b first orders $x := 1$ after $x := 2$ and reads 1 into a; it then revises this order, and orders $x := 2$ after $x := 1$ and reads 2 into b.

A trace τ does not violate CC as long as there is a causality order which explains the return value of each read event.

To capture traces violating CC, we define a relation OW (for overwrite) on writes to the same variable. For any two writes w_1, w_2 and a read r on a same variable, if w_1 CO w_2 CO r, and w_1 rf r, then w_2 OW w_1. This says that r reads the overwritten write w_1, resulting in a CO $\cup$ OW cycle. We refer to CO $\cup$ OW cycles as CCcycle. We define a function $\mathsf{extend}_{CC}(\tau)$ which extends a trace $\tau = \langle \mathsf{E}, po, rf \rangle$ by adding all possible OW edges between write events on the same variable. For a trace $\tau = \langle \mathsf{E}, po, rf \rangle$, we say that $\tau \models$ CC iff $\mathsf{extend}_{CC}(\tau)$ does not have a CCcycle.

Examples. Program Fig. 1(a) is not CC since there is no causality order which explains the return values of the read events. If we consider any trace (Fig. 2) of the program Fig.1(a), we find that $\mathsf{wt}(y,1)$ rf r where $r = \mathsf{rd}(y)$, $\mathsf{wt}(x,1)$ po $\mathsf{wt}(y,1)$, r po $\mathsf{wt}(x,2)$. Then we get $\mathsf{wt}(x,1)$ CO $\mathsf{wt}(x,2)$, $\mathsf{wt}(x,2)$ CO r' where $r' = \mathsf{rd}(x)$ and $\mathsf{wt}(x,1)$ rf r' giving $\mathsf{wt}(x,2)$ OW $\mathsf{wt}(x,1)$ witnessing CCcycle.

Causal Convergence CCv. Under CCv, we need a total order on all write events per variable. This order, called *arbitration order*, is an abstraction of how conflicts are resolved by all processes to agree upon one ordering among events which are not causally related. Thus, unlike CC, a process cannot revise its ordering of the events which are not causally related, and all processes must follow one ordering. This makes it stronger than CC.

To enforce a total order between all writes, we use a new relation CF called conflict relation on all write events per variable. For all variables $x \in \mathcal{V}$, and writes w_1, w_2 on x and a read $r = \mathsf{rd}(x)$, if w_1 CO r, and w_2 rf r then w_1 CF w_2.

We define a function $\mathsf{extend}_{\mathsf{CCv}}(\tau)$ which extends a trace $\tau = \langle \mathsf{E}, po, rf \rangle$ by adding all possible OW, CF edges between write events on the same variable. Traces violating CCv exhibit a $\mathsf{CO} \cup \mathsf{CF} \cup \mathsf{OW}$ cycle in $\mathsf{extend}_{\mathsf{CCv}}(\tau)$, which we refer to as $\mathsf{CCvcycle}$. We say that $\tau \models \mathsf{CCv}$ iff $\mathsf{extend}_{\mathsf{CCv}}(\tau)$ does not contain a $\mathsf{CCvcycle}$.

Examples. For the program Fig.1(b) and any trace τ, $\mathsf{extend}_{\mathsf{CCv}}(\tau)$ has a $\mathsf{CCvcycle}$ (see Fig.2) since in any trace, we have $w_1 = \mathsf{wt}(x, 1)$ CO r_2 where $r_2 = \mathsf{rd}(x)$ and w_2 rf r_2 for $w_2 = \mathsf{wt}(x, 2)$ giving w_1 CF w_2. We also have $\mathsf{wt}(x, 2)$ CO r_1 where $r_1 = \mathsf{rd}(x)$ with w_1 rf r_1 giving w_2 CF w_1. Intuitively, we cannot find a total order amongst the writes to justify the reads of 1 and 2.

However, the program Fig.1(c) has a trace τ s.t. $\mathsf{extend}_{\mathsf{CCv}}(\tau)$ does not have $\mathsf{CCvcycle}$. In the corresponding run, we first allow p_a to complete execution, followed by p_b.

Causal Memory CM. The CM model is stronger than CC and incomparable to CCv. Like CC, in CM also, a process can diverge from another one in its ordering of events which are not causally related. However, once a process chooses an ordering of such events, it cannot revise it; this makes it stronger than CC and incomparable to CCv.

A *happened before* relation per process fixes the per process ordering of events. For a read/write event e in a trace, the *Causal Past* of e, $\mathsf{CausalPast}(e) = \{e' \mid e'\ \mathsf{CO}\ e\}$ is the set of events which are in the causal past of e. For an event e, the happened before relation HB_e [15] is the smallest relation on events which is transitive, and is such that for all events $e_1, e_2 \in \mathsf{CausalPast}(e)$, e_1 CO e_2 $\Rightarrow$ e_1 HB_e e_2. In other words, $\mathsf{CO}_{|\mathsf{CausalPast}(e)} \subseteq \mathsf{HB}_e$: HB_e contains all pairs of events obtained by restricting CO to the events in the causal past of e. For any variable x, if we have writes w_1, w_2 on x and a read $r_2 = \mathsf{rd}(x)$ such that
(i) $r_2 = e$ or r_2 po e, w_2 rf r_2, and w_1 HB_e r_2, then w_1 HB_e w_2, and
(ii) if w_1 HB_e w_2 and w_1 rf r_2, then r HB_e w_2.

Let e_p be the po-last event of process p: that is, for all events e in process p, $e = e_p$ or e po e_p. Since $\mathsf{HB}_e \subseteq \mathsf{HB}_{e_p}$ for all events e in process p, HB_{e_p} fixes the ordering among all causally unrelated events for process p. We write HB_p instead of HB_{e_p}.

We define a function $\mathsf{extend}_{\mathsf{CM}}$ which extends a trace $\tau = \langle \mathsf{E}, po, rf \rangle$ by adding all possible $\mathsf{OW}, \mathsf{HB}_p$ edges for all processes p. Traces violating CM exhibit a $\mathsf{OW} \cup \mathsf{HB}_p$ cycle, called a $\mathsf{CMcycle}$ in $\mathsf{extend}_{\mathsf{CM}}(\tau)$ for some process p. We say that $\tau \models \mathsf{CM}$ iff $\mathsf{extend}_{\mathsf{CM}}(\tau)$ does not contain a $\mathsf{CMcycle}$. See Figure 3 which motivates conditions (i), (ii) to add HB edges so that $\mathsf{extend}_{\mathsf{CM}}(\tau)$ does not contain $\mathsf{CMcycle}$.

Examples. For the program Fig.1(c) and any trace τ, $\mathsf{extend}_{\mathsf{CM}}(\tau)$ contains CM cycle. Consider the read event $o_{p_b} = \mathsf{rd}(x)$ with $\mathsf{wt}(x, 2)$ rf o_{p_b}. Then $\mathsf{wt}(x, 1)$ po $\mathsf{wt}(y, 1)$ rf $\mathsf{rd}(y)$ po o_{p_b}, that is, $\mathsf{wt}(x, 1)$ CO o_{p_b}. This induces $\mathsf{wt}(x, 1)$ HB_{p_b} o_{p_b}, and $\mathsf{wt}(x, 1)$ HB_{p_b} $\mathsf{wt}(x, 2)$. This results in $\mathsf{wt}(z, 1)$ po $\mathsf{wt}(x, 1)$ HB_{p_b} $\mathsf{wt}(x, 2)$ po r where $r = \mathsf{rd}(z)$ with $\mathsf{wt}(z, 0)$ rf r. This gives $\mathsf{wt}(z, 1)$ HB_{p_b} $\mathsf{wt}(z, 0)$ resulting in a cycle. However, program Fig.1(d) has a trace τ s.t. $\mathsf{extend}_{\mathsf{CM}}(\tau)$ does not contain $\mathsf{CMcycle}$.

Fig. 3. Start with (a). In (b) we add the HB edge from rd(z) to wt(z, 2) following condition (ii). Then (c) is obtained on adding rd(x), wt(x, 1) *rf* rd(x). In contrast, (b)' does not follow condition (ii). Hence, when the rd(x) is added in (c)', wt(x, 2) is available to be read. Choosing wt(x, 2) *rf* rd(x) necessitates adding wt(x, 1) HB wt(x, 2) in (d)' by condition (i). This necessitates adding wt(z, 2) HB wt(z, 1) in (e)' creating CMcycle.

A run ρ satisfies a model $X \in \{\text{CC}, \text{CCv}, \text{CM}\}$ if there exists a trace τ such that $\rho \models \tau$ and $\tau \models X$. Define $\gamma_X := \{\tau_X \mid \exists \rho \in Runs(\gamma).\rho \models \tau_X \wedge \tau_X \models X\}$, the set of traces generated under X from a given configuration γ.

Note. Similar to our characterization of bad traces using cycles, [15] uses bad patterns in *differentiated histories* to capture violations of CC, CCv, CM. Differentiated histories are posets labeled with wt(x, v) and rd(x) $\triangleright$ v such that no two events wt(x, v_1) and wt(x, v_2) have $v_1 = v_2$. Bad patterns are characterized in [15] using the *po* and reads from relations on differentiated histories. Since we work with traces having *po* and *rf*, we do not require differentiated writes.

4   Trace Semantics

To analyse a program $\mathcal{P}$ under a model $X \in \{\text{CC}, \text{CCv}, \text{CM}\}$, all runs of $\mathcal{P}$ must be explored. We do this by exploring the associated traces. In fact, two runs having the same associated traces are equivalent since the assertions to be checked at the end of a run depend only on *po*, *rf*. We begin with the empty trace, and continue exploration by adding enabled read/write events to the traces generated so far. While doing this, we must ensure that the generated traces τ are s.t. $\tau \models X$. We present two efficient operations to add a new read/write event to a trace τ obtaining a trace τ' so that extend$_X(\tau')$ does not contain a Xcycle. We discuss two notions that are relevant while adding a new read event to a trace.

Readability and Visibility. For all 3 models, readability identifies the write events w from which a newly added read r can fetch its value. Visibility is used to add, in the case of CCv, new CF edges (and in the case of CM, new HB edges) that are implied by the fact that the new read event reads from w. Let $\tau = \langle \text{E}, po, rf \rangle$ be a trace, and $\tau_X = \text{extend}_X(\tau)$. Let τ_X^r denote adding r to τ_X. We define the readable set $\texttt{readable}(\tau_X^r, r, x)$ for read event r from process p on variable x.

1. For $X = \text{CC}$, $\texttt{readable}(\tau_X^r, r, x)$ is defined as the set of all write events $w \in \text{E}^{\text{wt}, x}$ s.t. there is no write $w' \in \text{E}^{\text{wt}, x}$, s.t. w CO w' CO r in τ_X^r.
2. For $X = \text{CCv}$, $\texttt{readable}(\tau_X^r, r, x)$ is defined as the set of all write events $w \in \text{E}^{\text{wt}, x}$ s.t. there is no write $w' \in \text{E}^{\text{wt}, x}$ s.t. w $(\text{CO} \cup \text{CF})^+$ w' CO r in τ_X^r.
3. For $X = \text{CM}$, $\texttt{readable}(\tau_X^r, r, x)$ is defined as the set of all write events $w \in \text{E}^{\text{wt}, x}$ s.t. there is no write $w' \in \text{E}^{\text{wt}, x}$ s.t. w HB$_p$ w' HB$_p$ r in τ_X^r.

Intuitively, $\mathtt{readable}(\tau_X^r, r, x)$ contains all write events which are not hidden in τ_X^r by other writes on x. The newly added read event r can fetch its value from a write in $\mathtt{readable}(\tau_X^r, r, x)$. The visible set $\mathtt{visible}(\tau_X^r, r, x)$ is defined as the set of events in $\mathtt{readable}(\tau_X^r, r, x)$ which can "reach" r in τ_X^r. Let τ^{rw} denote the trace obtained by adding r and w rf r to trace τ.

1. For $X = \mathtt{CCv}$, $\mathtt{visible}(\tau_X^r, r, x) = \{e \in \mathtt{readable}(\tau_X^r, r, x) \mid e \text{ CO } r\}$. The point of $\mathtt{visible}(\tau_X^r, r, x)$ is that when the new read r is added, which reads from a write w, $\mathtt{extend}_X(\tau^{rw})$ will not contain Xcycle on adding from each $e \in \mathtt{visible}(\tau_X^r, r, x)$ a CF edge to w. Then $\mathtt{extend}_X(\tau^{rw})$ contains $\{(e, w) \mid e \in \mathtt{visible}(\tau_X^r, r, x)\}$.
2. For $X = \mathtt{CM}$, $\mathtt{visible}(\tau_X^r, r, x) = \{e \in \mathtt{readable}(\tau_X^r, r, x) \mid e \text{ HB}_p r\}$ where r is a read in process p. The point of $\mathtt{visible}(\tau_X^r, r, x)$ is that when the new read r is added, which reads from a write w, $\mathtt{extend}_X(\tau^{rw})$ will not contain Xcycle on adding from each $e \in \mathtt{visible}(\tau_X^r, r, x)$ a HB$_p$ edge to w. Then $\mathtt{extend}_X(\tau^{rw})$ contains $\{(e, w) \mid e \in \mathtt{visible}(\tau_X^r, r, x)\}$.

The *trace semantics* for a model $X \in \{\mathtt{CC}, \mathtt{CCv}, \mathtt{CM}\}$ is given as the transition relation $\to_{X-\mathtt{tr}}$, defined as $\tau_X \xrightarrow{\alpha}_{X-\mathtt{tr}} \tau_X'$ where $\mathtt{extend}_X(\tau) = \tau_X, \mathtt{extend}_X(\tau') = \tau_X'$. The label α is one of $(read, r, w), (write, w)$ representing respectively, a read r reading from a write w, and a write event w. An important property of $\tau_X \xrightarrow{\alpha}_{X-\mathtt{tr}} \tau_X'$ is that if τ_X does not have Xcycle, then τ_X' also does not have Xcycle; in other words, if $\tau \models X$, then $\tau' \models X$. We now describe the transitions $\tau_X \xrightarrow{\alpha}_{X-\mathtt{tr}} \tau_X'$ where $\mathtt{extend}_X(\tau) = \tau_X, \mathtt{extend}_X(\tau') = \tau_X', \tau = \langle E, po, rf \rangle, \tau' = \langle E', po', rf' \rangle$. We start from the empty trace τ_0, $\mathtt{extend}_X(\tau_0) = \tau_0$.

- From τ_X, assume that we observe a write w in process p. In this case, the label α is $(write, w)$, and we add w, and a po edge from the po-latest event of process p in τ_X to w obtaining τ_X'.
- From τ_X, assume we observe a read event r on variable x in process p. In this case, the label α is $(read, r, w)$, where w is the write from which r reads. Add the read r, a po edge from the po-latest event of process p in τ_X to r obtaining τ_X^r. Add rf from a $w \in \mathtt{readable}(\tau_X^r, r, x)$ to r.
  - When $X = \mathtt{CCv}$. Add new CF edges from all $w'' \in \mathtt{visible}(\tau_X^r, r, x)$ to w to get τ_X'.
  - When $X = \mathtt{CM}$. Add new HB$_p$ edges from all $w'' \in \mathtt{visible}(\tau_X^r, r, x)$ to w. Adding these HB$_p$ edges can result in w_1 HB$_p$ w_2 for write events w_1, w_2 on a variable y. If we had w_1 rf r_1, r_1 po r, then add r_1 HB$_p$ w_2. When we are done adding all such HB$_p$ edges, we obtain τ_X'. (Figure 4(iv)).

Lemma 1. *If* $\tau_X = \mathtt{extend}_X(\tau)$ *with* $\tau \models X$, *and* $\tau_X \xrightarrow{\alpha}_{\mathtt{tr}} \tau_X' = \mathtt{extend}_X(\tau')$, *then* $\tau' \models X$ *for* $X \in \{\mathtt{CC}, \mathtt{CCv}, \mathtt{CM}\}$.

Efficiency and Correctness. Each step of $\xrightarrow{\alpha}_{\mathtt{tr}}$ is computable in polynomial time . This is based on the fact that readable and visible sets are computable in polynomial time. The correctness of the trace semantics for a model X stems from the fact that it generates only those X-extensions which do not have cycles (Lemma 1). The transitions ensure acyclicity of the resultant extended traces.

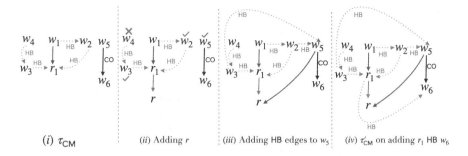

(i) τ_{CM} (ii) Adding r (iii) Adding HB edges to w_5 (iv) τ'_{CM} on adding r_1 HB w_6

Fig. 4. w_1, w_6 are writes on y, r_1 is a read on y, w_2, w_3, w_4, w_5 are writes on x in τ_{CM}. Add read r on x to τ_{CM}. $w_2, w_3, w_5 \in \texttt{readable}(\tau^r_{\text{CM}}, r, x)$. Choose w_5 rf r. Then we add w_2 HB w_5 and w_3 HB w_5. The addition of w_2 HB w_5 results in w_1 HB w_6. Since w_1 rf r_1, add the HB edge from r_1 to w_6 to obtain τ'_{CM}.

Algorithm 1: EXPLORETRACES(X, τ_X, π)

Input: $X \in \{\texttt{CC}, \texttt{CCv}, \texttt{CM}\}$ is a consistency model, τ_X is an X-extension, π is an observation sequence.

1 **if** $\exists w$ s.t. $\tau_X \xrightarrow{\langle write, w \rangle}_{X-\text{tr}} \tau'_X$ **then**   // handle a write event

2   let $w = \text{wt}(x, v)$ and perform $\tau_X \xrightarrow{\langle write, w \rangle}_{X-\text{tr}} \tau'_X$
                           // follow trace semantics write

3   EXPLORETRACES$(X, \tau'_X, \pi \bullet w)$

4   CREATESCHEDULE$(\tau'_X, \pi \bullet w)$

5 **else if** $\exists r$ s.t. $\tau_X \xrightarrow{\langle read, r, - \rangle}_{X-\text{tr}} \tau'_X$ **then**   // handle a read event

6     $Schedules(r) \leftarrow \emptyset$; $Swappable(r) \leftarrow \texttt{true}$

7   **for** $w, \tau'_X : \tau_X \xrightarrow{\langle read, r, w \rangle}_{X-\text{tr}} \tau'_X$ **do** EXPLORETRACES$(X, \tau'_X, \pi \bullet \langle r, w \rangle)$
                           // follow trace semantics read

8   **for** $\beta \in Schedules(r)$ **do** RUNSCHEDULE(X, τ_X, π, β)

---

5   DPOR Algorithm for CC, CCv, CM

We present our DPOR algorithm, which systematically explores, for any terminating program under the consistency models $X \in \{\texttt{CC}, \texttt{CCv}, \texttt{CM}\}$, all traces τ_X wrt X which can be generated by the trace semantics. Enabled write events from any of the processes are added to the trace generated so far, and we proceed with the next event. For a read event r, we add r to the trace, and explore in separate branches, all possible write events w from which r can read from. Each such branch is a sequence of events also called a *schedule*. There may be writes w' which will be added to the trace later in the exploration, from which r can also read. Such writes w' are called *postponed* wrt r; when w' is added to the trace later, the algorithm will have a branch where r can read from w'. In that branch, the algorithm reorders events in the sequence s.t. w' and r exchange places, and all events which are needed for w' to occur are also placed before w' (CREATESCHEDULE). All generated schedules will be executed

---

Algorithm 2: CREATESCHEDULE(X, τ_X, π)

Input: $X \in \{\text{CC}, \text{CCv}, \text{CM}\}$ is a consistency model, τ_X is an X-extension and π is an explored observation sequence.

1 let w be $last(\pi)$ and x be $\text{var}(w)$
2 **for** $i \leftarrow |\pi| - 1$ **to** 1 **do**   // look for reads r that have postponed w
3   let r be the element at $\pi[i]$
4   **if** r is a read on $x \wedge \neg (r \text{ CO } w) \wedge \text{Swappable}(r)$ **then**
5          $\beta \leftarrow \epsilon;\ flag = true;$
6   **for** $j \leftarrow i + 1$ **to** $|\pi| - 1$ **do**   // get all events after r in π and
                precedes w in CO
7   let ev be the element at $\pi[j]$
8   **if** ev CO w **then**
9   **if** r CO ev **then**
10                     $|\ flag = false;$ **break;**
11   **else**
12                     $|\ \beta \leftarrow \beta \bullet \pi[j]$
13   **if** $flag \wedge \nexists \beta' \in \text{Schedules}(r).\ \beta' \approx \beta \bullet w \bullet \langle r, w \rangle$ **then**
14             $\text{Schedules}(r) \leftarrow \text{Schedules}(r) \cup \{\beta \bullet w \bullet \langle r, w \rangle\}$ // r can read
                from w

Algorithm 3: RUNSCHEDULE(X, τ_X, π, β)

Input: $X \in \{\text{CC}, \text{CCv}, \text{CM}\}$ is a consistency model, τ_X is a X-extension, π is an explored-observation sequence, and β is a schedule.

1 **if** $\beta \neq \epsilon$ **then**   // explore the sequence of observations one by one
2   let β be $\alpha \bullet \beta'$ **choose** $\tau'_X : \tau_X \xrightarrow{\alpha} {}_{X-\text{tr}} \tau'_X$ // follow write and read
3   **if** $\alpha = (read, r, w)$ **then** $\text{Swappable}(r) \leftarrow \textbf{false}$
4   RUNSCHEDULE($X, \tau'_X, \pi \bullet \alpha, \beta'$)
5 **else** EXPLORETRACES(X, τ_X, π)

---

by RUNSCHEDULE. The algorithm is uniform across the models, with the main technical differences being taken care of by the respective trace semantics which guides the exploration of traces in each model.

The EXPLORETRACES Algorithm. This algorithm takes as input, a consistency model $X \in \{\text{CC}, \text{CCv}, \text{CM}\}$, an X-extension τ_X and an *observation sequence* π. π is a sequence of events of the form $(write, w)$ or $(read, r, w)$. The initial invocation is with the empty trace τ_0 and observation sequence $\pi = \epsilon$. The observation sequence is used to swap read operations with write operations that are *postponed* wrt them. From the initial τ_0, we choose an operation from any of the processes.

If a write operation is enabled, one such is chosen non deterministically from any process, and is added to the trace according to the trace semantics, and also appended to the observation sequence, whereafter EXPLORETRACES is called recursively to continue the exploration (line 3). After the recursive calls have returned, the algorithm calls CREATESCHEDULE, which finds read operations r in the observation sequence which can read from write operations w if w was performed before r. For each such read r, CREATESCHEDULE creates a *schedule* for r, an observation sequence that can be explored from the point when r was performed, allowing w to occur before r so that r can read from w. When a read operation r is enabled, the set Schedules(r) is initialized (line 6). This set is updated by CREATESCHEDULE when subsequent writes are explored. We also keep a Boolean flag Swappable(r) for each read event r. This is initialized to true, indicating that r is swappable, that is, subsequent writes can be considered for r. This flag is set to false for read events appearing in a schedule so that they are not swapped, eliminating redundant explorations. For each generated write event w from which r can read, EXPLORETRACES is called recursively (line 7)to continue the exploration. Once these recursive calls have returned, the set of schedules collected in Schedules(r) for the read r is considered. RUNSCHEDULE explores all schedules, where the read fetches its value from the respective write.

The CREATESCHEDULE algorithm. The input to this algorithm is a consistency model X, a trace τ_X wrt X, and an observation sequence π whose last element is a write. The algorithm looks for reads in π for which w is a postponed write. Indeed, this read r and w must be on the same variable, r must be swappable, and r must not precede w wrt CO (line 4). We begin with the closest (from the write w) such read r at position $\pi[j]$. After finding r, a schedule β is created. The schedule consists of all elements following r in π and preceding w wrt CO (line 12). It ends with $w \bullet (r, w)$, allowing r to read from w (line 13). This schedule is added to Schedules(r) if it does not already contain a schedule β' which has the same set of observations : Schedules(r) does not contain $\beta' \approx \beta$.

The RUNSCHEDULE Algorithm. The inputs are a consistency model X, a trace τ_X, an observation sequence π and a schedule β. The schedule of observations in β is explored one by one, by recursively calling itself, and updating the trace. The read events in the schedule are not swappable, preventing a redundant exploration for them (schedules where these are swapped with respective writes will be created by CREATESCHEDULE. All proofs and an illustrative example can be found in the extended version of the paper [2].

Theorem 1. *Our DPOR algorithms are sound, complete and optimal.*

Soundness, Optimality and Completeness. The algorithm is sound in the sense that, if we initiate Algorithm 1 from (X, τ_0, ϵ), then, all explored traces τ are s.t. $\tau \models X$. This follows from the fact that the exploration uses the $\rightarrow_{X-\text{tr}}$ relation. The algorithm is optimal in the sense that, for any two different recursive calls to Algorithm 1 with arguments (X, τ_X^1, π_1) and (X, τ_X^2, π_2), if τ_X^1, τ_X^2 are extendible, then $\tau_X^1 \neq \tau_X^2$. This follows from (i) for a given read r, each iteration of the for loop in line 7 will correspond to a different write, (ii) in each schedule $\beta \in$ Schedules(e) in line 8 of Algorithm 1, the read event r reads from a write w which is different from all writes it reads from in line 7 (iii) Any two schedules added to Schedules(e) at line 14 of Algorithm 2 will be different. The algorithm explores traces of all terminating runs, and is hence complete.

6   Experimental Evaluation

We describe the implementation of our optimal DPOR algorithm for the causal consistency models CC, CCv, CM as a tool CONSCHECKER, available at[45]. To the best of our knowledge, CONSCHECKER is the first stateless model checking tool for the causal consistency models CC, CCv, CM.

CONSCHECKER. CONSCHECKER extends NIDHUGG [3] and works at LLVM IR level accepting a C language program as input. At runtime, CONSCHECKER controls the exploration of the input program until it has explored all the traces using the DPOR algorithm. It can detect user-provided assertion violations by analyzing the generated traces. We conduct all experiments on a Ubuntu 22.04.1 LTS with Intel Core i7-1165G7 and 16 GB RAM. We evaluate CONSCHECKER on the following categories of benchmarks, as seen below.

Experimental Setup. We consider the following categories of benchmarks.

• A set of thousands of litmus tests (sec 6.1) generated from [8]. The main purpose of these experiments is to provide a sanity check of the correctness of CONSCHECKER on all three consistency models.

• A collection (sec 6.2) of concurrent benchmarks taken from the TACAS competition on software verification [44]. These are small programs with 50-100 lines of code used by many tools [4], [5].

• Five applications (sec 6.3) : Voter [19], Twitter clone [27], Fusion ticket [27], two versions of Auction [36], extracted from literature on databases, and verify against assertion violations wrt the three consistency models.

• Classical database benchmarks (sec 6.4) reported in recent papers on consistency models [13], [12] and [14]. We classify these benchmarks SAFE and UNSAFE on all three models depending on whether they witness an assertion violation.

• Eight parameterized programs (sec 6.5) from [5] and [4] to study the scalability of CONSCHECKER when increasing the number of processes, as well as read and write instructions in programs.

6.1   Litmus Benchmarks

We apply CONSCHECKER on a set of 9815 litmus benchmarks generated from [8]. Litmus tests are standard benchmark programs used by many tools running on weak memories. In these litmus tests, the processes execute concurrently, and we validate assertions on the underlying memory model, doing a sanity check for the correctness of CONSCHECKER. We compared the observed outcomes of CONSCHECKER on the litmus tests with expected outcomes generated from [8]. We generated the expected outcomes by simulating the CCv, and CC and CM semantics on [8] for these litmus tests. Out of the 9815 litmus tests, we found no assertion violations in 3810 under CC, CM and 3811 under CCv. Results obtained from CONSCHECKER matched with the expected outcomes. CONSCHECKER took <3 mins to execute on all litmus tests across models.

Table 1. Classical benchmarks

Program	CCv	CC	CM
Causality Violation [13]	UNSAFE	UNSAFE	UNSAFE
Causal Violation [14]	SAFE	SAFE	SAFE
Delivery Order [12]	UNSAFE	UNSAFE	SAFE
Long Fork [13]	UNSAFE	UNSAFE	UNSAFE
Lost Update [13]	UNSAFE	UNSAFE	UNSAFE
Message Passing [11]	SAFE	SAFE	SAFE
Conflict violation [14]	UNSAFE	UNSAFE	UNSAFE
Read Atomicity [14]	UNSAFE	UNSAFE	UNSAFE
Repeated Read [14]	UNSAFE	UNSAFE	UNSAFE
Load Buffer	SAFE	SAFE	SAFE
Store Buffer [11]	UNSAFE	UNSAFE	UNSAFE
Write Skew [13]	UNSAFE	UNSAFE	UNSAFE

Table 2. Applications.

App	Time
Vote [19]	1s
Twitter clone [27]	0.09s
FusionTicket [27]	0.75s
Auction [36]	0.11s
Auction-2 [36]	1.17s
Group	0.10s

Table 3. SV-Comp Benchmarks

	CCv		CC		CM	
Program	Traces	Time	Traces	Time	Traces	Time
Lamport	15669	3s	2904225	490s	299028	110s
Szymanski	1023397	131s	1023397	115s	1023397	190s
Peterson	5371	1s	13483	1s	12316	1.5s
Fibonacci	6224342	769s	6224342	695s	6224342	1796s
Dekker	86267	7s	1549862	155s	107698	18s

6.2   SV-COMP Benchmarks

These benchmarks [44] consist of five programs written in C/C++ having 2 processes each, with 50-100 lines of code per process (Table 3). The main challenge in these benchmarks is the large number of traces to be explored. These benchmarks have assertion checks, and under CCv, CM, and CC all these assertions are violated. CONSCHECKER stops exploration as soon as it detects the first assertion violation. To check the efficiency of CONSCHECKER, we removed all assertions and let CONSCHECKER exhaustively explore all $po\text{-}rf$ traces. Since these benchmarks have large number of traces, they serve as a stress test.

6.3   Database Applications

Table 2 reports the performance of CONSCHECKER on a set of programs inspired from five applications extracted from the literature on distributed systems [19], [27], [12], [36]. The applications we considered are

• Voter [19] : This application is derived from a software system used to record votes from a talent show. Users can vote for any of the n contestants from any one of the m sites (processes). The application asserts that users cannot vote from multiple sites and cannot vote for multiple contestants and checks for violations of this. [19] considers 3 sites and 3 users, and we follow suit.

Table 4. Parameterized Benchmarks from [5] and [4]

Program	CC Traces	CC Time	CCv Traces	CCv Time	CM Traces	CM Time
control-flow(6)	77	0.05s	77	0.05s	77	0.05s
control-flow(8)	273	0.07s	273	0.06s	273	0.10s
control-flow(10)	1045	0.16s	1045	0.12s	1045	0.33s
control-flow(12)	4121	0.60s	4121	0.45s	4121	1.80s
n-writers-a-read(5)	6	0.05s	6	0.05s	6	0.05s
n-writers-a-read(10)	11	0.05s	11	0.05s	11	0.05s
n-writers-a-read(15)	16	0.05s	16	0.05	16	0.05s
n-writers-a-read(20)	21	0.05s	21	0.05	21	0.05s
redundant-co(5)	91	0.07s	91	0.05s	91	0.05s
redundant-co(10)	331	0.09s	331	0.05s	331	0.08s
redundant-co(15)	721	0.11s	721	0.08s	721	0.12a
redundant-co(20)	1261	0.18	1261	0.13s	1261	0.20s
casrot(9)	8579	0.55s	8597	0.77s	8597	2s
casrot(10)	38486	2.50s	38486	3.16s	38486	9s
casrot(11)	182905	14s	182905	16s	182905	49s
floating-read(9)	10	0.05s	10	0.05s	10	0.05s
floating-read(11)	12	0.05s	12	0.05s	12	0.05s
floating-read(13)	14	0.05s	14	0.05s	14	0.05s
lastwrite(9)	9	0.04s	9	0.04s	9	0.04s
lastwrite(11)	11	0.04s	11	0.04	11	0.04s
lastwrite(13)	13	0.04	13	0.04	13	0.04s
lastzero(9)	1536	0.18s	1536	0.20s	1536	0.33s
lastzero(11)	7168	1s	7168	1s	7168	2s
lastzero(13)	32768	5s	32768	5s	32768	12s
readers(9)	512	0.10s	512	0.10s	512	0.18s
readers(11)	2048	0.40s	2048	0.35s	2048	1s
readers(13)	8192	1.5s	8192	1.5s	8192	6s

• Twitter clone [27] : This is based on a twitter like service where each user has some followers. The following assertion is checked : when the user tweets, the tweet ID must be added to the follower's time line exactly once if the user did not remove his tweet. We considered 3 users using 3 processes, each process has 10 tweet IDs and 6 followers.

• Fusion ticket [27] : There is a building having multiple concert rooms (venues). Tickets for venue i are sold by salesperson i who updates in the backend database, the sales for the day. The per venue ticket sale must be updated correctly in the database, so that the concert manager sees the correct total number of tickets sold. A discrepancy in this number is a violation. Each venue is represented by a process, and the communication across processes ensures the total sum is correct. We considered 4 venues and each venue had 10 tickets.

• Auction [36] and Auction-2 [36]: There are n bidders and an auctioneer participating in an auction, modeled using $n+1$ processes. The assertion to be checked is that the highest bidder must be declared winner. Auction is the buggy version for this application, while Auction-2 is the correct one.

• Group is a synthetic application created by us inspired from whatsapp groups. There is a group with n members, and a new person wants to be added to the group. This person must be added to the group only by one of the existing members. That is, a violation constitutes to adding a person more than once (by one or more members). We check with 6 processes(members).

6.4   Classical Benchmarks

Table 1 consists of classical benchmarks [13], [14], [12] and [11] which test for some assertion violations under the three models. Since the traces generated differ for each model $X \in \{CC, CCv, CM\}$, the violations also differ. For the ones marked SAFE under model $X \in \{CC, CCv, CM\}$, the assertion violation did not occur under any execution, while the unsafe ones reported the violation. We consider twenty such examples. We consider three different versions of each example, varying the number of processes and variables.

For each example, we have three versions by parameterizing the number of processes and instructions. In version 1, we have four processes per program and three to five instructions per process. Version 2 is obtained allowing each process to have seven-ten instructions. Version 3 expands version 2 by allowing each program to have up to five-six processes and up to 15-20 instructions. The number of instructions is increased by introducing fresh variables and having reads/writes on them. Versions 2,3 serve as a stress test for CONSCHECKER as increasing the number of instructions and processes increases the number of of consistent traces. CONSCHECKER took less than $3s$ to finish running all version 1 programs, about 30s to finish running all version 2 programs and about 200s to finish running all version 3 programs.

6.5   Parameterized Benchmarks

Table 4 reports experimental results of CONSCHECKER on 8 parameterized benchmarks. Out of these, in redundant-co(N) (taken from [5]), N is the number of loop iterations per process in a program with 3 processes. In all others, the parameterization is on the number of processes. This set of benchmarks serves to check the scalability of CONSCHECKER. As seen in Table 4, CONSCHECKER scales up to 20 processes (n-writers-a-read) and 13 variables (lastzero).

7   Conclusion

In this paper, we have provided a DPOR algorithm using the $po - rf$ equivalence for three prominent causal consistency models, and also implemented the same in a tool CONSCHECKER. This is the first tool for stateless model checking of causal consistency models. We plan to extend our work by developing a DPOR algorithm for transactional programs under CC, CCv, CM [12]. For these, the extra complication is the presence of transactions which must be executed atomically without interference in each process. The final notch is to handle snapshot isolation, the strongest among transactional consistency models.

8 Data-Availability Statement

The tool and experimental data for the study are available at the Zenodo repository: [45].

References

1. Abdulla, P., Aronis, S., Jonsson, B., Sagonas, K.: Optimal dynamic partial order reduction. SIGPLAN Not. **49**(1), 373–384 (jan 2014). https://doi.org/10.1145/2578855.2535845, https://doi.org/10.1145/2578855.2535845
2. Abdulla, P., Atig, M.F., S, K., Gupta, A., Tuppe, O.: Optimal Stateless Model Checking for Causal Consistency (Jan 2023). https://doi.org/10.5281/zenodo.7572282, https://doi.org/10.5281/zenodo.7572282
3. Abdulla, P.A., Aronis, S., Atig, M.F., Jonsson, B., Leonardsson, C., Sagonas, K.: Stateless model checking for tso and pso. In: Baier, C., Tinelli, C. (eds.) Tools and Algorithms for the Construction and Analysis of Systems. pp. 353–367. Springer Berlin Heidelberg, Berlin, Heidelberg (2015)
4. Abdulla, P.A., Atig, M.F., Jonsson, B., Lång, M., Ngo, T.P., Sagonas, K.: Optimal stateless model checking for reads-from equivalence under sequential consistency. Proc. ACM Program. Lang. **3**(OOPSLA) (Oct 2019). https://doi.org/10.1145/3360576, https://doi.org/10.1145/3360576
5. Abdulla, P.A., Atig, M.F., Jonsson, B., Ngo, T.P.: Optimal stateless model checking under the release-acquire semantics. Proc. ACM Program. Lang. **2**(OOPSLA) (Oct 2018). https://doi.org/10.1145/3276505, https://doi.org/10.1145/3276505
6. Agarwal, P., Chatterjee, K., Pathak, S., Pavlogiannis, A., Toman, V.: Stateless model checking under a reads-value-from equivalence. In: Silva and Leino [43], pp. 341–366. https://doi.org/10.1007/978-3-030-81685-8_16, https://doi.org/10.1007/978-3-030-81685-8_16
7. Ahamad, M., Neiger, G., Burns, J.E., Kohli, P., Hutto, P.W.: Causal memory: Definitions, implementation, and programming. Distrib. Comput. **9**(1), 37–49 (Mar 1995). https://doi.org/10.1007/BF01784241, https://doi.org/10.1007/BF01784241
8. Alglave, J., Maranget, L., Tautschnig, M.: Herding cats: Modelling, simulation, testing, and data mining for weak memory. ACM Trans. Program. Lang. Syst. **36**(2) (jul 2014). https://doi.org/10.1145/2627752, https://doi.org/10.1145/2627752
9. Bailis, P., Ghodsi, A., Hellerstein, J.M., Stoica, I.: Bolt-on causal consistency. In: Ross, K.A., Srivastava, D., Papadias, D. (eds.) Proceedings of the ACM SIGMOD International Conference on Management of Data, SIGMOD 2013, New York, NY, USA, June 22-27, 2013. pp. 761–772. ACM (2013). https://doi.org/10.1145/2463676.2465279, https://doi.org/10.1145/2463676.2465279
10. Batty, M., Owens, S., Sarkar, S., Sewell, P., Weber, T.: Mathematizing C++ concurrency. In: Ball, T., Sagiv, M. (eds.) Proceedings of the 38th ACM SIGPLAN-SIGACT Symposium on Principles of Programming Languages, POPL 2011,

Austin, TX, USA, January 26-28, 2011. pp. 55–66. ACM (2011). https://doi.org/10.1145/1926385.1926394, https://doi.org/10.1145/1926385.1926394

11. Beillahi, S.M., Bouajjani, A., Enea, C.: Checking robustness between weak transactional consistency models. Programming Languages and Systems **12648**, 87 (2021)

12. Beillahi, S.M., Bouajjani, A., Enea, C.: Robustness Against Transactional Causal Consistency. Logical Methods in Computer Science **Volume 17, Issue 1** (Feb 2021). https://doi.org/10.23638/LMCS-17(1:12)2021, https://lmcs.episciences.org/7149

13. Bernardi, G., Gotsman, A.: Robustness against consistency models with atomic visibility. In: 27th International Conference on Concurrency Theory (CONCUR 2016). Schloss Dagstuhl-Leibniz-Zentrum fuer Informatik (2016)

14. Biswas, R., Enea, C.: On the complexity of checking transactional consistency. Proc. ACM Program. Lang. **3**(OOPSLA) (oct 2019). https://doi.org/10.1145/3360591, https://doi.org/10.1145/3360591

15. Bouajjani, A., Enea, C., Guerraoui, R., Hamza, J.: On verifying causal consistency. In: Proceedings of the 44th ACM SIGPLAN Symposium on Principles of Programming Languages. p. 626–638. POPL 2017, Association for Computing Machinery, New York, NY, USA (2017). https://doi.org/10.1145/3009837.3009888, https://doi.org/10.1145/3009837.3009888

16. Burckhardt, S.: Principles of eventual consistency. Found. Trends Program. Lang. **1**(1-2), 1–150 (2014). https://doi.org/10.1561/2500000011, https://doi.org/10.1561/2500000011

17. Christakis, M., Gotovos, A., Sagonas, K.: Systematic testing for detecting concurrency errors in erlang programs. In: Sixth IEEE International Conference on Software Testing, Verification and Validation, ICST 2013, Luxembourg, Luxembourg, March 18-22, 2013. pp. 154–163. IEEE Computer Society (2013). https://doi.org/10.1109/ICST.2013.50, https://doi.org/10.1109/ICST.2013.50

18. Clarke, E.M., Grumberg, O., Minea, M., Peled, D.A.: State space reduction using partial order techniques. Int. J. Softw. Tools Technol. Transf. **2**(3), 279–287 (1999). https://doi.org/10.1007/s100090050035, https://doi.org/10.1007/s100090050035

19. Difallah, D.E., Pavlo, A., Curino, C., Cudre-Mauroux, P.: Oltp-bench: An extensible testbed for benchmarking relational databases. Proc. VLDB Endow. **7**(4), 277–288 (dec 2013). https://doi.org/10.14778/2732240.2732246, https://doi.org/10.14778/2732240.2732246

20. Du, J., Elnikety, S., Roy, A., Zwaenepoel, W.: Orbe: scalable causal consistency using dependency matrices and physical clocks. In: Lohman, G.M. (ed.) ACM Symposium on Cloud Computing, SOCC '13, Santa Clara, CA, USA, October 1-3, 2013. pp. 11:1–11:14. ACM (2013). https://doi.org/10.1145/2523616.2523628, https://doi.org/10.1145/2523616.2523628

21. Du, J., Iorgulescu, C., Roy, A., Zwaenepoel, W.: Gentlerain: Cheap and scalable causal consistency with physical clocks. In: Lazowska, E., Terry, D., Arpaci-Dusseau, R.H., Gehrke, J. (eds.) Proceedings of the ACM Symposium on Cloud Computing, Seattle, WA, USA, November 3-5, 2014. pp. 4:1–4:13. ACM (2014). https://doi.org/10.1145/2670979.2670983, https://doi.org/10.1145/2670979.2670983

22. Godefroid, P.: Partial-Order Methods for the Verification of Concurrent Systems - An Approach to the State-Explosion Problem, Lecture Notes in Computer Science, vol. 1032. Springer (1996). https://doi.org/10.1007/3-540-60761-7, https://doi.org/10.1007/3-540-60761-7

23. Godefroid, P.: Model checking for programming languages using verisoft. In: Proceedings of the 24th ACM SIGPLAN-SIGACT Symposium on Principles of Programming Languages. p. 174–186. POPL '97, Association for Computing Machinery, New York, NY, USA (1997). https://doi.org/10.1145/263699.263717, https://doi.org/10.1145/263699.263717

24. Godefroid, P.: Software model checking: The verisoft approach. Form. Methods Syst. Des. 26(2), 77–101 (Mar 2005). https://doi.org/10.1007/s10703-005-1489-x, https://doi.org/10.1007/s10703-005-1489-x

25. Hamza, J.: Algorithmic Verification of Concurrent and Distributed Data Structures. Ph.D. thesis, Université Paris Diderot (2015)

26. Herlihy, M., Wing, J.M.: Linearizability: A correctness condition for concurrent objects. ACM Trans. Program. Lang. Syst. 12(3), 463–492 (1990). https://doi.org/10.1145/78969.78972, https://doi.org/10.1145/78969.78972

27. Holt, B., Bornholt, J., Zhang, I., Ports, D., Oskin, M., Ceze, L.: Disciplined inconsistency with consistency types. In: Proceedings of the Seventh ACM Symposium on Cloud Computing. p. 279–293. SoCC '16, Association for Computing Machinery, New York, NY, USA (2016). https://doi.org/10.1145/2987550.2987559, https://doi.org/10.1145/2987550.2987559

28. Kokologiannakis, M., Lahav, O., Sagonas, K., Vafeiadis, V.: Effective stateless model checking for C/C++ concurrency. Proc. ACM Program. Lang. 2(POPL), 17:1–17:32 (2018). https://doi.org/10.1145/3158105, https://doi.org/10.1145/3158105

29. Kokologiannakis, M., Marmanis, I., Gladstein, V., Vafeiadis, V.: Truly stateless, optimal dynamic partial order reduction. Proc. ACM Program. Lang. 6(POPL), 1–28 (2022). https://doi.org/10.1145/3498711, https://doi.org/10.1145/3498711

30. Kokologiannakis, M., Vafeiadis, V.: Genmc: A model checker for weak memory models. In: Silva, A., Leino, K.R.M. (eds.) Computer Aided Verification. pp. 427–440. Springer International Publishing, Cham (2021)

31. Lahav, O.: Verification under causally consistent shared memory. ACM SIGLOG News 6(2), 43–56 (2019). https://doi.org/10.1145/3326938.3326942, https://doi.org/10.1145/3326938.3326942

32. Lamport, L.: Time, clocks, and the ordering of events in a distributed system. Commun. ACM 21(7), 558–565 (1978). https://doi.org/10.1145/359545.359563, https://doi.org/10.1145/359545.359563

33. Lamport, L.: How to make a multiprocessor computer that correctly executes multiprocess programs. IEEE Trans. Computers 28(9), 690–691 (1979). https://doi.org/10.1109/TC.1979.1675439, https://doi.org/10.1109/TC.1979.1675439

34. Mazurkiewicz, A.: Trace theory. In: Advances in Petri Nets 1986, Part II on Petri Nets: Applications and Relationships to Other Models of Concurrency. p. 279–324. Springer-Verlag, Berlin, Heidelberg (1987)

35. Musuvathi, M., Qadeer, S., Ball, T., Basler, G., Nainar, P.A., Neamtiu, I.: Finding and reproducing heisenbugs in concurrent programs. In: Draves, R., van Renesse, R. (eds.) 8th USENIX Symposium on Operating Systems Design and Implementation, OSDI 2008, December 8-10, 2008, San Diego, California, USA, Proceedings. pp. 267–280. USENIX Association (2008), http://www.usenix.org/events/osdi08/tech/full_papers/musuvathi/musuvathi.pdf

36. Nair, S.S., Petri, G., Shapiro, M.: Proving the safety of highly-available distributed objects. In: Müller, P. (ed.) Programming Languages and Systems. pp. 544–571. Springer International Publishing, Cham (2020)

37. Norris, B., Demsky, B.: A practical approach for model checking c/c++11 code. ACM Trans. Program. Lang. Syst. **38**(3) (May 2016). https://doi.org/10.1145/2806886, https://doi.org/10.1145/2806886

38. Owens, S., Sarkar, S., Sewell, P.: A better x86 memory model: x86-tso. In: Berghofer, S., Nipkow, T., Urban, C., Wenzel, M. (eds.) Theorem Proving in Higher Order Logics, 22nd International Conference, TPHOLs 2009, Munich, Germany, August 17-20, 2009. Proceedings. Lecture Notes in Computer Science, vol. 5674, pp. 391–407. Springer (2009). https://doi.org/10.1007/978-3-642-03359-9_27, https://doi.org/10.1007/978-3-642-03359-9_27

39. Perrin, M., Mostéfaoui, A., Jard, C.: Causal consistency: beyond memory. In: Asenjo, R., Harris, T. (eds.) Proceedings of the 21st ACM SIGPLAN Symposium on Principles and Practice of Parallel Programming, PPoPP 2016, Barcelona, Spain, March 12-16, 2016. pp. 26:1–26:12. ACM (2016). https://doi.org/10.1145/2851141.2851170, https://doi.org/10.1145/2851141.2851170

40. Raynal, M., Schiper, A.: From causal consistency to sequential consistency in shared memory systems. In: Thiagarajan, P.S. (ed.) Foundations of Software Technology and Theoretical Computer Science, 15th Conference, Bangalore, India, December 18-20, 1995, Proceedings. Lecture Notes in Computer Science, vol. 1026, pp. 180–194. Springer (1995). https://doi.org/10.1007/3-540-60692-0_48, https://doi.org/10.1007/3-540-60692-0_48

41. Sen, K., Agha, G.: A race-detection and flipping algorithm for automated testing of multi-threaded programs. In: Proceedings of the 2nd International Haifa Verification Conference on Hardware and Software, Verification and Testing. p. 166–182. HVC'06, Springer-Verlag, Berlin, Heidelberg (2006)

42. Shasha, D.E., Snir, M.: Efficient and correct execution of parallel programs that share memory. ACM Trans. Program. Lang. Syst. **10**(2), 282–312 (1988). https://doi.org/10.1145/42190.42277, https://doi.org/10.1145/42190.42277

43. Silva, A., Leino, K.R.M. (eds.): Computer Aided Verification - 33rd International Conference, CAV 2021, Virtual Event, July 20-23, 2021, Proceedings, Part I, Lecture Notes in Computer Science, vol. 12759. Springer (2021). https://doi.org/10.1007/978-3-030-81685-8, https://doi.org/10.1007/978-3-030-81685-8

44. SV-COMP: Competition on Software Verification. https://sv-comp.sosy-lab.org/2018 (2018), [Online; accessed 2017-11-10]

45. Tuppe, O.: Conschecker (Jan 2023). https://doi.org/10.5281/zenodo.7500551, https://doi.org/10.5281/zenodo.7500551

46. Zhang, N., Kusano, M., Wang, C.: Dynamic partial order reduction for relaxed memory models. In: Proceedings of the 36th ACM SIGPLAN Conference on Programming Language Design and Implementation. p. 250–259. PLDI '15, Association for Computing Machinery, New York, NY, USA (2015). https://doi.org/10.1145/2737924.2737956, https://doi.org/10.1145/2737924.2737956

Symbolic Model Checking for TLA+ Made Faster

Rodrigo Otoni[1]($\boxtimes$), Igor Konnov[2], Jure Kukovec[2], Patrick Eugster[1],
and Natasha Sharygina[1]

[1] Università della Svizzera italiana, Lugano, Switzerland
{otonir,eugstp,sharygin}@usi.ch
[2] Informal Systems, Vienna, Austria
{igor,jure}@informal.systems

Abstract. The need to provide formal guarantees about the behaviour
of the algorithms underpinning modern distributed systems became evident in recent years. This interest made apparent the complexities involved in applying verification techniques in a distributed setting, with
significant effort being made in both academia and industry to aid in
this endeavour. Many formalisms have been proposed to tackle the difficulties faced by practitioners, with one that has seen widespread use in
industry being TLA+, adopted, for instance, by Amazon Web Services.
TLA+ provides engineers with a way of specifying both systems and
desired properties, and is supported by a number of verification tools.
Despite their extensive use, such tools suffer considerably from lack of
scalability. To solve this, we propose a novel encoding of TLA+ into SMT
constraints to improve symbolic model checking efficiency. Our insight is
the need to provide the SMT solver with structural information about
the TLA+ specification encoded, i.e., how data structures and their component elements interact, which we do by relying on the SMT theory
of arrays. We implemented our approach by modifying the SMT-based
model checker APALACHE and evaluated it against comparable tools. Our
results show that our approach outperforms existing ones on a number of
benchmarks, with an order of magnitude improvement in checking time.

Keywords: Model checking · SMT arrays · Distributed algorithms

1 Introduction

Distributed systems are ubiquitous in the modern world, with many companies
directly relying on them to conduct business. Due to this, the ability to ensure
that a distributed system is operating correctly is paramount. The search for correctness guarantees led to an influx of interested parties adopting formal verification methodologies in recent years. One of the most famous example of this trend
is probably the adoption of TLA+ [17] by Amazon Web Services [19]. TLA+ is
a specification language based on the temporal logic of actions (TLA) which
allows users to describe the expected behaviour of a system, while abstracting

© The Author(s) 2023
S. Sankaranarayanan and N. Sharygina (Eds.): TACAS 2023, LNCS 13993, pp. 126–144, 2023.
https://doi.org/10.1007/978-3-031-30823-9_7

away implementation details that do not impact high-level properties, e.g., memory management. With TLA$^+$ specifications at hand, Amazon engineers rely on model checking for correctness guarantees of systems such as DynamoDB [23].

Despite recent interest and advances, the verification of distributed systems remains notoriously difficult. This is mainly due to the fact that, given their distributed nature, distributed algorithms' executions admit numerous potential interleavings of steps, with state-spaces generally growing exponentially with the number of participants. In the case of TLA$^+$, a handful of tools are available to aid in verification [14]. TLC [27] is an explicit-state model checker that enumerates all reachable states of the given system. APALACHE [13] is a symbolic bounded model checker that uses a satisfiability modulo theories (SMT) encoding of states in order to better tackle the state-space explosion problem. TLAPS [6] is an interactive proof system that enables the proving of properties without the need of exploring the state-space itself. Despite providing the benefit of verifying specifications with infinite state-spaces, and efforts being made towards partial automation [18], TLAPS adoption is still slow, with engineers favouring the push-button automation provided by model checkers.

In this work we focus on symbolic model checking for TLA$^+$, as spearheaded by the SMT encoding which underpins APALACHE, but provide insights into SMT-based model checking that may generalise to other contexts. The encoding of TLA$^+$ into SMT done by APALACHE removes all structural information present in the encoded specification, with all TLA$^+$ data structures being represented via uninterpreted constants in the generated SMT formula. The information not forwarded to the SMT solver has the potential to significantly improve solving efficiency. We propose an alternative SMT encoding that makes full use of the SMT theory of arrays [8] to encoded the main TLA$^+$ data structures, i.e., sets and functions, with the goal of improving solving performance, which is the determining factor in overall model checking performance.

Concretely, we modify APALACHE's abstract reduction system (ARS) to generate constraints in the SMT theory of arrays, while relying on its preprocessing infrastructure, as shown in Figure 1. APALACHE rewrites the input specification into the KerA$^+$ verification-friendly fragment of TLA$^+$ [13] and then applies ARS rules to generate the SMT formula to be solved. We implemented our encoding in APALACHE and compared it with APALACHE's constants encoding and TLC. Our experiments indicate that embedding structural information into the SMT formulas has a significant impact on performance. Our contributions are:

1. Formalisation of a TLA$^+$ encoding into the SMT theory of arrays;
2. Development of a robust open-source implementation of our encoding;
3. Evaluation via checking agreement on three asynchronous protocols.

The paper is structured as follows: background is given in Section 2, the arrays-based encoding and its evaluation are presented in Sections 3 and 4, related work is discussed in Section 5, and our final remarks are made in Section 6.

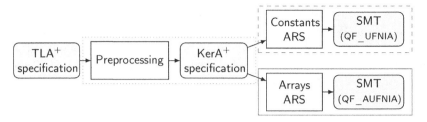

Fig. 1: Overview of the symbolic model checking for TLA$^+$. The dotted box high-lights the identification of symbolic transitions from [16] and the rewriting into KerA$^+$. The dashed box highlights the encoding based on uninterpreted con-stants from [13]. The solid box highlights the arrays-based encoding we propose.

2   Background

In this section we introduce the basics of TLA$^+$, its KerA$^+$ fragment used to represent TLA$^+$'s core, the approach to generate SMT constraints from KerA$^+$ via abstract reduction, and finally the SMT theory of arrays.

2.1   TLA+

We introduce TLA$^+$ via a specification of the asynchronous Byzantine agreement protocol by Bracha and Toueg [5], shown in Figure 2. Here we focus on the most relevant TLA$^+$ constructs, with further details being available in [17].

The first notable aspect of TLA$^+$ is that specifications may be parametrised, e.g., the number of processes and faults may not be fixed. In our example, the keyword CONSTANTS, in line 3, is used to declare its parameters: N, the total number of processes, and T and F, the maximal and actual number of faulty processes. It is important to understand, however, that while a specification may be parametrised, model checking can only be carried out for a specific instance of the protocol at a time, e.g., $N = 4$ and $T = F = 1$. Parameter declarations are followed by variable declarations, by the use of the VARIABLES keyword, in line 4. Variables define the states of the state-machine that the specification describes, with each state being defined by the combination of the values held by each variable. In our example, each state is defined by the values of $sentEcho, sentReady, rcvdEcho, rcvdReady$, and pc.

The remaining TLA$^+$ operators describe state-machine transitions or prop-erties to be checked, and are defined using $\triangleq$. Two operators are of special sig-nificance, one that defines the initial-state predicate and one that plays the role of the transition operator. In our example, these operators are $Init$, in line 8, and $Next$, in line 22. Concretely, $Init$ defines the starting point for state-space exploration and $Next$ defines the exploration itself. Transitions are guided by constraints that must hold in both pre-transition states, represented by non-primed variables, and post-transition states, represented by primed variables.

```
 1 ┌─────────────────────── MODULE ABA ───────────────────────┐
 2 │ EXTENDS Integers, FiniteSets
 3 │ CONSTANTS N, T, F
 4 │ VARIABLES sentEcho, sentReady, rcvdEcho, rcvdReady, pc
 5 │ Corr  ≜ 1 .. (N − F)        The set of correct processes
 6 │ Byz   ≜ (N − F + 1) .. N    The set of Byzantine processes
 7 │ Proc  ≜ 1 .. N              The set of all processes
 8 │ Init  ≜ ∧ pc ∈ [Corr → { "V0", "V1" }]
 9 │             ∧ rcvdEcho = [p ∈ Corr ↦ {}] ∧ rcvdReady = [p ∈ Corr ↦ {}]
10 │             ∧ sentEcho ∈ SUBSET Byz    ∧ sentReady ∈ SUBSET Byz
11 │ Receive(p, nextEcho, nextReady) ≜ ...   Omited for brevity
12 │ SendEcho(p, nextEcho, nextReady) ≜ ...  Omited for brevity
13 │ SendReady(p, nextEcho, nextReady) ≜
14 │     ∧ pc[p] = "EC"
15 │     ∧ ∨ Cardinality(nextEcho) ≥ (N + T + 2) ÷ 2
16 │       ∨ Cardinality(nextReady) ≥ T + 1
17 │     ∧ pc' = [pc EXCEPT ![p] = "RD"] ∧ sentReady' = sentReady ∪ {p}
18 │     ∧ UNCHANGED sentEcho
19 │ Decide(p, nextReady) ≜
20 │     ∧ pc[p] = "RD" ∧ Cardinality(nextReady) ≥ 2 * T + 1
21 │     ∧ pc' = [pc EXCEPT ![p] = "AC"] ∧ UNCHANGED ⟨sentEcho, sentReady⟩
22 │ Next ≜ ∃ p ∈ Corr, nextEcho ∈ SUBSET sentEcho, nextReady ∈ SUBSET sentReady :
23 │     ∧ Receive(p, nextEcho, nextReady)
24 │     ∧ ∨ SendEcho(p, nextEcho, nextReady) ∨ SendReady(p, nextEcho, nextReady)
25 │       ∨ Decide(p, nextReady) ∨ UNCHANGED ⟨pc, sentEcho, sentReady⟩
26 │ NoDecide ≜ ∀ p ∈ Corr : pc[p] ≠ "AC"   Invariant stating that processes never Decide
27 └───────────────────────────────────────────────────────────┘
```

Fig. 2: Example of a TLA$^+$ specification, based on the asynchronous Byzantine agreement protocol by Bracha and Toueg [5]; simplifications made for brevity.

Specifications may optionally define invariants, i.e., properties that should hold in every reachable state. There is no special syntax for invariants, and they are provided by name to model checkers at invocation time. In our example, we have one invariant, *NoDecide*, in line 26. A specification satisfies *NoDecide* if no state reachable from *Init* via any number of *Next* transitions has $pc[p] = $ "AC", for some $p \in Corr$. Abstractly, this invariant holds iff *Decide* can never be taken.

2.2   KerA+

TLA$^+$ provides users with a myriad of ways of specifying systems. This richness, although being one its strengths, adds significant difficulty to the generation of SMT constraints. To overcome this challenge, TLA$^+$ specifications are rewritten into a more compact language, KerA$^+$, before being checked. From KerA$^+$, the ARS can generate SMT constraints in a simpler and provably sound way.

The KerA$^+$ language consists of a small subset of TLA$^+$ conjoined with four additional constructs not originating from TLA$^+$, and is able to express almost all TLA$^+$ expressions. It contains constructs for the manipulation of sets,

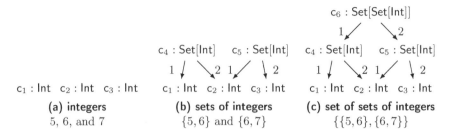

Fig. 3: Illustration of three arenas. The captions describe the modelled elements with the overapproximation $c_1 = 5$, $c_2 = 6$, $c_3 = 7$, $c_4 = \{5, 6\}$, $c_5 = \{6, 7\}$, and $c_6 = \{\{5, 6\}, \{6, 7\}\}$. Note that the concrete value of a cell can be given by any of the possible subtrees having said cell as a root, e.g., for c_6 we have that $\exists\, c_4 \in \mathcal{P}(\{5, 6\}), c_5 \in \mathcal{P}(\{6, 7\})\,.\, c_6 \in \mathcal{P}(\{c_4, c_5\})$; $\mathcal{P}$ stands for power set.

functions, records, tuples, and sequences, as well as integer arithmetic operators, Boolean and integer literals, and constants, with all data structures having a bounded size. The semantics of KerA^+ derive directly from the TLA^+ constructs it uses, with the non-TLA^+ based constructs, which help simplify the rewriting system, having simple control semantics. The correctness of the rewriting itself is guaranteed by construction. One example is the rewriting of $S \cup T$ into the set comprehension $\{x \in S : x \in T\}$. Further KerA^+ details are available in [13].

2.3   Abstract Reduction System

In order to verify a specification in KerA^+ we generate a SMT formula that is equisatisfiable to it. To do so, we use an abstract reduction system (ARS) which iteratively applies reduction rules that transform KerA^+ expressions into SMT constraints. The core of the ARS is the *arena*, a graph structure that overapproxiamtes the specification's data structures and guides rule application. The rules collapse KerA^+ expressions into *cells*, which represent the symbolic evaluation of these expressions, with the cells then being used as vertices in the arena. The arena edges represent the data structures overapproximation, e.g., a cell representing a set will have directed edges to the cells representing all its potential elements, as illustrated in Figure 3. The reduction process terminates when the initial KerA^+ expression e is collapsed into a single cell c, producing a SMT formula Φ in the process, such that $\mathsf{c} \wedge \Phi$ is equisatisfiable to e; equisatisfiability relies on the boundedness of the data structures and is detailed in Section 3.3. The satisfiability of e can then be checked by forwarding $\mathsf{c} \wedge \Phi$ to a SMT solver.

Formally, the ARS is defined as $(\mathcal{S}, \rightsquigarrow)$, with $\mathcal{S}$ being the set of ARS states and $\rightsquigarrow \,\subseteq\, \mathcal{S} \times \mathcal{S}$ being the transition relation. A state $(e, \mathcal{A}, \nu, \Phi) \in \mathcal{S}$ is a four-tuple containing a KerA^+expression e, an arena $\mathcal{A}$, a binding of names to cells ν, and a first-order formula Φ. ARS states' elements contain a number of cells, which are first-order terms annotated with a type τ. Cells of type Bool and Int are interpreted in SMT as Booleans and integers, while cells of the remaining types are encoded as uninterpreted constants in the constants encoding; the arrays encoding approach is discussed in Section 3. Cells are referred to via the notation c_{name} or c_{index}, and they can be seen as both KerA$^+$ constants and first-order terms in SMT. An arena is a directed acyclic graph $\mathcal{A} = (\mathcal{V}, \mathcal{E})$, with $\mathcal{V}$ being a finite set of cells and $\mathcal{E} \subseteq \mathcal{V} \times (1..|\mathcal{V}|) \times \mathcal{V}$ being a set of relations between the cells in $\mathcal{V}$. Every relation between cells is represented by an arena edge of form (c_a, i, c_b), also written $c_a \overset{i}{\to} c_b$, with no duplicates, i.e., for every pair $(c_{a_1}, i_1, c_{b_1}), (c_{a_2}, i_2, c_{b_2}) \in \mathcal{E}$ we have that $c_{a_1} = c_{a_2} \wedge c_{b_1} \neq c_{b_2}$ implies $i_1 \neq i_2$, and no gaps in the relation indexes, i.e., for every edge (c_a, i, c_b) and index $j \in 1..(i-1)$ we have that $\exists c_c \in \mathcal{V} \,.\, (c_a, j, c_c)$. A binding is a partial function from KerA$^+$ variables to $\mathcal{V}$ of $\mathcal{A}$, i.e., a mapping from variables to cells. Finally, Φ is a formula in the SMT fragment supported by the ARS and the target SMT solver, e.g., the quantifier-free uninterpreted functions and non-linear arithmetics (QF_UFNIA) fragment supported by the constants encoding.

A series of n reduction steps has the form $s_0 \rightsquigarrow ... \rightsquigarrow s_n$, with each step generating state s_{i+1} for state s_i, $0 \leq i < n$, by applying a reduction rule. The initial state $s_0 = (e_0, \mathcal{A}_0, \nu_0, \Phi_0)$ has e_0 as the initial KerA$^+$ specification, $\mathcal{A}_0 = (\emptyset, \emptyset)$, ν_0 containing no mappings, and $\Phi_0 = \text{true}$. The reduction steps end upon reaching a state $s_n = (e_n, \mathcal{A}_n, \nu_n, \Phi_n)$, with e_n being a single cell $c \in \mathcal{V}_n$ and $\mathcal{A}_n = (\mathcal{V}_n, \mathcal{E}_n)$. Below we give two examples of rules.

Integer literal reduction. One of the simplest rules has an integer literal *num* being rewritten into a cell c_{num}. This cell is added to the arena and a constraint equating c_{num} to the literal is conjoined with Φ; we use vertical lines to separate state elements and commas to indicate additions to $\mathcal{A}$ and conjunctions to Φ.

$$\frac{\langle num : \mathsf{Int} \mid \mathcal{A} \mid \nu \mid \Phi \rangle \qquad num \text{ is one of } 0, 1, -1, ...}{\langle c_{num} \mid \mathcal{A}, c_{num} : \mathsf{Int} \mid \nu \mid \Phi, c_{num} = num \rangle} \; (\text{INT})$$

The descriptions of rules can be given as inferences, with the premises above the bar and the resulting state below it. Inferences, although reasonable to express rules such as INT, are not suitable to give the intuition about how more complex rules work. In light of this, we will use a simplified notation moving forward. We inline inferences as $\rightarrowtail$ and omit nonessential information, e.g., propagated values. Below we can see rule INT in this simplified format. Note that only $\mathcal{A}$ and Φ updates are shown, without propagating them, and that ν is omitted.

$$\begin{array}{c} num : \mathsf{Int} \\ num \text{ is one of } 0, 1, -1, ... \end{array} \rightarrowtail c_{num} \mid c_{num} : \mathsf{Int} \mid c_{num} = num \qquad (\text{Int})$$

Picking. To pick a cell out of n cells we use an oracle θ, as per rule FromBasic. In addition to the FROM ... BY θ expression, this rule requires that all pickable cells are of the same basic type τ, e.g., Int. The resulting state has a new cell c_{pick}, which is equated to one of the n cells if $1 \leq \theta \leq n$ and is unconstrained otherwise. Picking among cells representing data structures, e.g., sets, can be done via a more general version of rule `FromBasic`, which we omit for brevity.

$$\text{FROM } c_1, ..., c_n \text{ BY } \theta : \tau \atop \tau \text{ is basic and } c_1 : \tau, ..., c_n : \tau \;\rightarrowtail\; c_{pick} \mid c_{pick} : \tau \mid \bigwedge_{1 \le i \le n} (\theta = i \to c_{pick} = c_i)$$

(FromBasic)

2.4 SMT Theory of Arrays

The theory of arrays provides a natural way to encode data structures and is thus a prime candidate as an encoding target for TLA$^+$constructs. Here we present the theory's operators relevant for our work, further details can be found in [8].

Given the set of sorts S, containing one sort s_τ for each type τ in KerA$^+$, an array sort s_{τ_1,τ_2} has the form $s_{\tau_1} \Rightarrow s_{\tau_2}$, with $s_{\tau_1} \in S$ being its *index sort* and $s_{\tau_2} \in S$ being its *value sort*. Each array sort is supported by two basic operators, $select : (s_{\tau_1} \Rightarrow s_{\tau_2}, s_{\tau_1}) \to s_{\tau_2}$, which handles array access at a given index, and $store : (s_{\tau_1} \Rightarrow s_{\tau_2}, s_{\tau_1}, s_{\tau_2}) \to s_{\tau_1} \Rightarrow s_{\tau_2}$, which updates an array for a given index and value. For brevity, we will write $select(a, i)$ as $a[i]$ in the remainder of the manuscript. Regarding equality between arrays, different interpretations are possible. We use arrays with extensionality [25], which are considered equal if they contain the same values in the same entries. Extensionality is formally defined as $\forall\, a, b : s_{\tau_1} \Rightarrow s_{\tau_2}\, .\, a = b \lor \exists\, i : s_{\tau_1}\, .\, a[i] \neq b[i]$. For access and update, consistency is ensured by the following property:

$$\forall\, a : s_{\tau_1} \Rightarrow s_{\tau_2},\, i : s_{\tau_1},\, j : s_{\tau_1},\, v : s_{\tau_2}\, . \atop \underbrace{store(a, i, v)[i] = v}_{\text{access consistency}} \land \underbrace{(i = j \lor store(a, i, v)[j] = a[j])}_{\text{update consistency}}$$

In addition to *select* and *store*, the theory of arrays can be extended with other operators, two of which are map_f and K_{s_τ}, whose signatures are shown below. The map_f operator applies a n-ary function $f : (s_{\tau_1}, ..., s_{\tau_n}) \to s_\tau$ to the values stored in each index of its array arguments, producing a new array whose values are the result of the function application, i.e., map_f is the pointwise array extension of f. The K_{s_τ} operator produces a constant array, with all its values being the constant provided as argument. The properties defining the behaviour of these two operators are shown after their signatures.

$$map_f : (s_\tau \Rightarrow s_{\tau_1}, ..., s_\tau \Rightarrow s_{\tau_n}) \to s_\tau \Rightarrow s_{\tau_f} \qquad K_{s_\tau} : s_{\tau_{const}} \to s_\tau \Rightarrow s_{\tau_{const}}$$

$$\forall\, a_1 : s_\tau \Rightarrow s_{\tau_1},\, ...,\, a_n : s_\tau \Rightarrow s_{\tau_n},\, i : s_\tau\, .\, map_f(a_1, ..., a_n)[i] = f(a_1[i], ..., a_n[i])$$

$$\forall\, i : s_{\tau_1},\, v : s_{\tau_2}\, .\, K_{s_{\tau_1}}(v)[i] = v$$

The *select* and *store* operators are part of theory of arrays with extensionality defined in version 2.6 of the SMT-LIB standard [3]. Other operators are provided on a solver-by-solver basis, e.g., Z3 [7] supports both map_f and K_{s_τ}, while CVC5 [2] supports K_{s_τ}; SMT-LIB updates may add them to the standard.

3   Encoding TLA+ using Arrays

Our goal is to encode TLA$^+$ data structures in a structure-preserving way. To do this, we use arrays to represent the main components of TLA$^+$, sets and functions, as SMT constraints. We follow the ARS structure described in Section 2.3, but update the reduction rules handling sets and functions. The remaining TLA$^+$ constructs, e.g., tuples, are represented as per the constants encoding.

The two efficiency benefits of the arrays encoding are the ease of access of data structures and the possibility of using SMT equality. The first benefit can be easily understood by the use of SMT *select*, which allows us to check a stored value by using a single constraint, in contrast to the amount of constraints used in the constants encoding, which is linear in the size of data structures' overapproximation. The second benefit affects the comparison of data structures, which can be done via a single SMT equality for sets and functions in the arrays encoding, since these structures are represented by a single SMT term, while the constants encoding requires a number of constraints that is quadratic in the size of data structures' overapproximation. A summary can be seen in Table 1. We first describe how to encode sets and functions, and then present the correctness argument for the reduction to arrays.

3.1   Encoding TLA+ Sets using Arrays

We use arrays to encode TLA$^+$ sets as characteristic functions, i.e., a set of type τ is represented by an array of sort $s_\tau \Rightarrow$ Bool. Set membership is encoded by storing true or false on a given array index. The reduction rules used to handle the main set operators are presented below.

Set Enumeration. The simplest way to create a set is to enumerate its elements. Rule Enum reduces an explicit set of cells to a fresh cell c_{set}, whose edges link it to its elements; $c_{set} \rightarrow c_1, \ldots, c_n$ is a shorthand for $c_{set} \overset{1}{\rightarrow} c_1, \ldots, c_{set} \overset{n}{\rightarrow} c_n$. There is no guarantee that the enumerated elements are unique, thus the arena may contain edges to repeated elements.

$$\{c_1, \ldots, c_n\} : \mathsf{Set}[\tau] \rightarrowtail c_{set} \mid c_{set} : \mathsf{Set}[\tau], c_{set} \rightarrow c_1, \ldots, c_n \mid EnumCtr \quad \text{(Enum)}$$

The constraints *EnumCtr* added by the arrays encoding create an empty set, by using a constant array with the value false, $\perp$, and updates the array by storing true, $\top$, on the appropriate indexes. The array resulting from the last update, $a_{c_{set}}^n$, is then equated to c_{set}. Since cells representing repeated elements lead to updates to the same index, we encode standard sets, in contrast the constants encoding, which encodes multisets due to the arena imprecision; multisets lead to multiple constraints being generated to encode membership of a single element.

$$\underbrace{a_{c_{set}}^0 = K_\tau(\perp)}_{\text{empty set}} \wedge \underbrace{\bigwedge_{1 \leq i \leq n} a_{c_{set}}^i = store(a_{c_{set}}^{i-1}, c_i, \top)}_{\text{set updates}} \wedge \underbrace{c_{set} = a_{c_{set}}^n}_{\text{cell equality}} \quad (EnumCtr)$$

Although the amount of constraints generated by the arrays encoding to model set enumeration is equal to that of the constants encoding, it has the benefit of generating a defined interpretation for c_{set}, the array $a_{c_{set}}^n$, which is not present in the constants encoding. This has a significant impact on set membership and cell equality, as described below.

Set Membership. The checking of a membership relation $c_x \in c_{set}$, given the presence of the arena edges $c_{set} \rightarrow c_1, ..., c_n$ and $1 \leq x \leq n$, is straightforward. A single fresh cell of Boolean type is introduced and is equated to $c_{set}[c_x]$.

Cell Equality. The constraints generated by encoding set membership and many other constructs assume that cells can be compared. When this is not directly the case the equalities are cached in preparation. For example, if a set of n tuples c_t of size two is being equated, the constraints $c_{t_i} = c_{t_j} \leftrightarrow c_{t_i}^1 = c_{t_j}^1 \wedge c_{t_i}^2 = c_{t_j}^2$, with $1 \leq i \leq n$ and $1 \leq j \leq n$, are added to Φ; here we use c_t^1 and c_t^2 to represent the values of the 2-tuple. The need for this caching of equalities only arises when data structures encoded as uninterpreted constants are compared. For the remaining rules we assume that caching was done, if needed, and cells can be compared via direct equality.

Table 1: Amount of constraints generated by each SMT encoding to model the main TLA$^+$ constructs.

Construct	Arrays	Constants
Set enumeration	$\mathcal{O}(n)$	$\mathcal{O}(n)$
Set membership	$\mathcal{O}(1)$	$\mathcal{O}(n)$
Set equality	$\mathcal{O}(1)$	$\mathcal{O}(n^2)$
Set filter	$\mathcal{O}(n)$	$\mathcal{O}(n)$
Set map	$\mathcal{O}(n)$	$\mathcal{O}(n)$
Fun. definition	$\mathcal{O}(n)$	$\mathcal{O}(n)$
Fun. domain	$\mathcal{O}(1)$	$\mathcal{O}(n)$
Fun. equality	$\mathcal{O}(1)$	$\mathcal{O}(n^2)$
Fun. update	$\mathcal{O}(1)$	$\mathcal{O}(n)$
Fun. application	$\mathcal{O}(n)$	$\mathcal{O}(n)$

Set Filter. In TLA$^+$, the elements of a set S can be filtered by a predicate p via the expression $\{x \in S : p\}$. This expression will create a set F which contains only the elements of S that satisfy p, e.g., $\{x \in \{-1, 0, 1\} : x \geq 0\} = \{0, 1\}$. Rule Filter reduces a filter to a new set cell, c_F, whose arena overapproximation contains the elements of S, but whose constraints ensure that only filtered elements are members of F; $p[y/x]$ means that x is replaced by y in p and parentheses indicate the application of another rule, the predicate resolution rule in this case.

$$\{x \in c_S : p\} : \mathsf{Set}[\tau] \text{ and } c_S \rightarrow c_1, ..., c_n$$
$$\rightarrowtail \big(p[c_1/x] : \mathsf{Bool}, ..., p[c_n/x] : \mathsf{Bool} \rightarrowtail c_1^p, ..., c_n^p \big)$$
$$\rightarrowtail c_F \mid c_F : \mathsf{Set}[\tau], c_F \rightarrow c_1, ..., c_n \mid FilterCtr$$

$$\text{(Filter)}$$

The constraints added use an array $a_{c_F}^0$ initially unconstrained, i.e., the values mapped by all the indexes of $a_{c_F}^0$ are unconstrained, as opposed to $a_{c_{set}}^0$ in *EnumCtr*. The values of $a_{c_F}^0$ mapped by indexes $c_1, ..., c_n$ are constrained by $c_1^p, ..., c_n^p$ via array access, i.e., $a_{c_F}^0[c_i]$ is asserted to be true or false based on c_i^p, with $1 \leq i \leq n$. We then apply pointwise conjunction to c_S and $a_{c_F}^0$ via the

map_f SMT operator; we go from a_F^0 to a_F^n to keep the array index in step with the arena overapproximation. Indexes whose values were false in S remain so in F, and indexes whose values were true in S store the filter's predicate evaluation.

$$\underbrace{\bigwedge_{1 \leq i \leq n} \text{ite}\left(c_i^p, a_{c_F}^0[c_i], \neg a_{c_F}^0[c_i]\right)}_{\text{predicate-based constraining}} \wedge \underbrace{a_{c_F}^n = map_\wedge(c_S, a_{c_F}^0)}_{\text{pointwise conjunction}} \wedge \underbrace{c_F = a_{c_F}^n}_{\text{cell equality}} \quad (\textit{FilterCtr})$$

Both encodings generate a linear amount of constraints, since n $p[c_i/x]$ predicates have to be considered. Unlike with *EnumCtr*, *FilterCtr* does not contain many *store* operations, due to the usage of map_f. This avoids the need to create intermediary arrays, and is not possible in *EnumCtr* due to its constant array.

Set Map. The expression $\{e : x \in S\}$ can be used to construct a set M from a set S, having all the elements of M as $e[y/x]$, with $y \in S$. For example, the expression $\{x \div 5 : x \in \{4, 5, 6\}\}$ yields the set $\{0, 1\}$, with $\div$ denoting standard integer division. To reduce set map we use rule Map.

$$\frac{\{e : x \in c_S\} : \mathsf{Set}[\tau] \text{ and } c_S \rightarrow c_1, \dots, c_n}{\begin{array}{l} \rightarrowtail \left(e[c_1/x] : \tau, \dots, e[c_n/x] : \tau \rightarrowtail c_1^e :, \dots, c_n^e\right) \\ \rightarrowtail c_M \mid c_M : \mathsf{Set}[\tau], c_M \rightarrow c_1^e, \dots, c_n^e \mid \textit{MapCtr} \end{array}}$$
$$(\text{Map})$$

The constraints added in rule Map are similar to those added in rule Enum. The difference between them is that set enumeration precisely defines the elements to be added to the new set cell, while set map is based on an existing set cell, which is a set overapproximation. Due to this, membership in M has to be guarded by membership in S, leading to a linear amount of constraints being generated.

$$\underbrace{a_{c_M}^0 = K_\tau(\bot)}_{\text{empty set}} \wedge \underbrace{\bigwedge_{1 \leq i \leq n} \text{ite}\left(\begin{array}{c} c_S[c_i], \\ a_{c_M}^i = store(a_{c_M}^{i-1}, c_i^e, \top), \\ a_{c_M}^i = a_{c_M}^{i-1} \end{array}\right)}_{\text{set updates}} \wedge \underbrace{c_M = a_{c_M}^n}_{\text{cell equality}} \quad (\textit{MapCtr})$$

3.2   Encoding TLA+ Functions using Arrays

We use arrays to encode TLA$^+$ functions directly as functions themselves. To do this, arrays are used in their general format, with a function $f : \mathsf{s}_{\tau_1} \to \mathsf{s}_{\tau_2}$ being encoded as an array of sort $\mathsf{s}_{\tau_1} \Rightarrow \mathsf{s}_{\tau_2}$. Since functions with a finite domain can rely on infinite sorts, e.g., the integer numbers, the encoding of each function also includes constraints defining its domain set, by means of the rules described in the previous section; the result of a function application to a value outside its domain is undefined in TLA$^+$. This approach allows us to generate SMT constraints that follow directly from TLA$^+$, making the encoding not only more efficient, but also more natural to describe. In contrast, the constants encoding represents functions explicitly as sets of pairs of form $\{\langle x, f(x) \rangle : x \in \text{DOMAIN} f\}$. Due to this, its function manipulation relies on set manipulation, e.g., function comparison is encoded as set comparison, leading to a quadratic amount of constraints. The reduction rules used to handle functions are presented below.

Function Definition. The definition of a function in TLA^+ is an expression of the form $[x \in S \mapsto e]$, which maps every domain value v to the expression $e[v/x]$. This definition is similar to that of set map $\{e : x \in S\}$, and thus generates constraints in a similar fashion to rule Map. The main difference is that the evaluations of the expression $e[v/x]$ are stored as array values, rather than array indexes, i.e., function definition uses $store(a, v, e[v/x])$ and set map uses $store(a, e[v/x], \top)$, with v being a value in the function's domain or the set being mapped. Every encoded function has a single argument, with multiple arguments being rewritten as tuples in preprocessing.

Unlike with set cells, a function cell c_F in the arena does not directly point to its values, with the arrays encoding adding two edges to c_F, $c_F \xrightarrow{1} c_{F_{dom}}$ and $c_F \xrightarrow{2} c_{F_{pairs}}$. Cell $c_{F_{dom}}$ represents the function's domain and cell $c_{F_{pairs}}$ represents the set of pairs $\{\langle x, f(x) \rangle : x \in \text{DOMAIN} f\}$. Cell $c_{F_{pairs}}$, despite being in the arena, has no SMT constraints modelling it in the arrays encoding, with its sole purpose being to help propagate the arena edges of the function's codomain elements.

Function Domain. Accessing a function's domain is trivial in the arrays encoding, since the domain set is generated during function definition. This results in a simple access to the array representing the domain.

Function Update. The update of a TLA^+ function f is done by changing the result of applying f to an argument arg, $f[arg]$, to be a given value v, via the expression $[f \text{ EXCEPT! } [arg] = v]$. The update will produce a new function g which is identical f, except that $g[arg] = v$ if $arg \in \text{DOMAIN} f$. The arrays encoding generates a single array update constraint in this case.

Function Application. The application of a function to an argument arg is conceptually simple, but is quite intricate to realize, as can be seen in rule FunApp. The arrays encoding uses an oracle to check that c_{arg} is in the domain and to gather the arena edges of c_{res}. The *FunAppCtr* constraints ensure that the oracle chooses the correct index and equates the result cell to an array access on c_F. Note that the value of c_{res} comes directly from the function application expression itself, with the oracle only been needed to gather the arena edges of c_{res}, if $m > 0$, via c^p. The need for an oracle is restricted to functions whose codomain contain structured data, e.g., $f : \text{Int} \to \text{Set}[\text{Int}]$. If this is not the case, e.g., $g : \text{Int} \to \text{Int}$, rule FunApp is simplified and *FunAppCtr* becomes $c_{res} = c_F[c_{arg}]$.

$$c_F[c_{arg}] : \tau \text{ and } c_F \xrightarrow{1} c_{F_{dom}} \rightarrow c_1^d, \ldots, c_n^d \text{ and } c_F \xrightarrow{2} c_{F_{pairs}} \rightarrow c_1^p, \ldots, c_n^p$$
$$\longmapsto \left(\text{FROM } c_1^p, \ldots, c_n^p \text{ BY } \theta : \langle \tau_{arg}, \tau \rangle \mid \theta : \text{Int} \mid 0 \leq \theta \leq n \longmapsto c^p \right)$$
$$\text{and } c^p[2] \rightarrow c_1, \ldots, c_m$$
$$\longmapsto c_{res} \mid c_{res} : \tau, c_{res} \rightarrow c_1, \ldots, c_m \mid FunAppCtr$$

(FunApp)

$$\bigwedge_{1 \leq i \leq n} \wedge \frac{(\theta = i \to c_{arg} = c_i^d \wedge c_{F_{dom}}[c_i^d])}{(\theta = 0 \to c_{arg} \neq c_i^d \vee \neg c_{F_{dom}}[c_i^d])} \wedge c_{res} = c_F[c_{arg}] \qquad (FunAppCtr)$$

oracle constraining   cell equality

3.3   Correctness of the Reduction to Arrays

Correctness of the ARS is given by four properties: finiteness of the models, compliance to the target SMT theories, termination of any reduction sequence, and soundness of the reductions. These properties have their correctness sketched for the constants encoding in [13], with detailed proofs present in [26]. Since we rely on the existing ARS and restrict our changes to mainly affect constraint generation, we have the same degree of overapproximation and the correctness arguments made for the constants encoding are in large part valid for the arrays encoding. We present below the definition of a KerA$^+$ model and detail, for each property, how the use of arrays affects the correctness arguments and how they can be adjusted to remain valid.

Models. Every satisfiable KerA$^+$ formula has a model $\mathcal{M} = \langle \mathcal{D}, \mathcal{I} \rangle$, where $\mathcal{D}$ is the model domain, consisting of a disjoint union of sets $\mathcal{D}_1, ..., \mathcal{D}_n$, with $\mathcal{D}_i$, $1 \leq i \leq n$, containing the values for type τ_i, and $\mathcal{I}$ is the model interpretation, consisting of assignments of domain values to KerA$^+$ constants. Models are used to access cell values, with the value of a KerA$^+$ expression e in model $\mathcal{M}$ being $[\![e]\!]^{\mathcal{M}}$. In $s_{before} \leadsto s_{after}$, we go from $\mathcal{M}_{before}$ to $\mathcal{M}_{after}$, with $\mathcal{M}_{after}$ containing the interpretation of additional constants and being thus an extension of $\mathcal{M}_{before}$.

Finiteness. This property states that every interpretation of a KerA$^+$ expression is defined only over finite values. Its proof is derived from the finiteness of the elements being modelled. In the arrays encoding, we potentially use arrays with infinite sorts, e.g., the integers, but all SMT interpretations that can be derived from such arrays are finite, since we encode only finite TLA$^+$ data structures. This guarantees finiteness of all KerA$^+$ models in the arrays encoding.

Theory Compliance. This property states that any sequence of states $s_0 \leadsto ... \leadsto s_n$ has the formulas Φ_i, $1 \leq i \leq n$, in the first-order logic fragment containing only quantifier-free expressions over uninterpreted functions and integer arithmetic. Its proof is done by induction on the constraints generated. The constraint Φ_0 is always true and is thus trivially compliant. The inductive case is proved by showing that the constraint added by each rule are compliant. The rules in the arrays encoding only add array constraints, in addition to constraints supported by the constants encoding, so theory compliance is straightforward to guarantee.

Termination. This property states that every sequence of ARS reductions is finite, i.e., the reduction process always terminates. Its proof is based on ensuring that every rule r applied to a given state s_{before} yields a state s_{after} with e_{after} being smaller than e_{before}. An expression's length is given based on the length of its sub-expressions. The arrays encoding mainly changes constraint generation, and in the cases where rules are slightly modified they generate resulting expressions of the same size, thus guaranteeing termination.

Soundness. This property is described in Theorem 1. Both e and Φ are KerA^+ expressions, but Φ is in the first-order logic fragment supported by SMT solvers. Fundamentally, the ARS is rewriting a formula to forward it to the solver. The soundness proof consists of case analysis of each reduction rule to establish that $e_{before} \wedge \Phi_{before}$ is equisatisfiable to $e_{after} \wedge \Phi_{after}$, no matter the rule applied in $s_{before} \leadsto s_{after}$. The case analysis, which describes how e_{after} and Φ_{after} can be derived from e_{before} and Φ_{before} for each rule, relies on six invariants of the reduction system. Three invariants, 1, 3, and 4, are encoding independent, and thus are the same as in [13], the remaining three, 2, 5, and 6, are changed due to the new representation of sets and functions. Below we show all six invariants, with the modifications needed to guarantee soundness for the arrays encoding.

Theorem 1. *Let* $s_0 \leadsto ... \leadsto s_n$ *be a sequence of states produced by the ARS, with* $s_i = \langle e_i \mid \mathcal{A}_i \mid \nu_i \mid \Phi_i \rangle$ *and* $1 \le i \le n$. *Assume that* e_0 *is a formula, i.e., it has type* Bool. *Then* e_0 *is satisfiable iff the conjunction* $e_n \wedge \Phi_n$ *is satisfiable.*

Invariant 1 (type correctness) *In every reachable state* $\langle e \mid \mathcal{A} \mid \nu \mid \Phi \rangle$ *of the ARS, the expression* e *is well typed.*

Invariant 2 (arena membership) *In every reachable state* $\langle e \mid \mathcal{A} \mid \nu \mid \Phi \rangle$ *of the ARS, every cell* c *in either the expression* e *or the formula* Φ *is also in* $\mathcal{A}$.

Invariant 3 (model suitability) *Let* $s_{before} \leadsto s_{after}$ *be a reachable transition in the ARS, and* $\mathcal{M}_{before}$ *be a suitable model for* s_{before}. *An extended model* $\mathcal{M}_{after}$ *from* $\mathcal{M}_{before}$ *is suitable for* s_{after}.

Invariant 4 (overapproximation) *Let* $\langle e \mid \mathcal{A} \mid \nu \mid \Phi \rangle$ *be a reachable state of the ARS, and* $\mathcal{M}$ *be its model. Assume that* c_{set} *is a set cell in the arena* $\mathcal{A}$ *and that* $c_{set} \rightarrow c_1, \ldots, c_n$ *are edges in* $\mathcal{A}$, *for some* $n \ge 0$. *Then, it holds that* $[\![c_{set}]\!]^{\mathcal{M}} \subseteq \{[\![c_1]\!]^{\mathcal{M}}, ..., [\![c_n]\!]^{\mathcal{M}}\}$.

Invariant 5 (function domain) *Let* $\langle e \mid \mathcal{A} \mid \nu \mid \Phi \rangle$ *be a reachable state of the ARS. Assume that* c_f *is a function cell of type* $\mathsf{s}_{\tau_1} \rightarrow \mathsf{s}_{\tau_2}$ *in the arena* $\mathcal{A}$. *Then, there is a cell* c_{dom} *of type* $\mathsf{s}_{\mathsf{Set}[\tau_1]}$ *such that* $c_f \xrightarrow{1}_{\mathcal{A}} c_{dom}$.

Invariant 6 (domain reduction) *Let* $\langle e \mid \mathcal{A} \mid \nu \mid \Phi \rangle$ *be a reachable state of the ARS, and* $\mathcal{M}$ *be its model. Assume that* c_f *is a function cell and that* $c_f \xrightarrow{1} c_{F_{dom}}$ *is in the arena* $\mathcal{A}$. *Then, it follows that* $[\![c_{F_{dom}}]\!]^{\mathcal{M}} = [\![\text{DOMAIN} f]\!]^{\mathcal{M}}$.

As described in sections 3.1 and 3.2, arrays precisely model TLA^+ sets and functions. The handling of sets revolves around membership constraints of form $c_{set}[c_i]$, which and can be set to true or false via *store*. Regarding functions, function application and update are trivially equivalent to array access and update. The more elaborate array operators also have a counterpart in TLA^+. Constant arrays are equivalent to a function definition for which all range values are the same constant, and array map is equivalent to set map. These equivalences explain how the changes in the arrays encoding do not invalidate the case analysis of the reduction rules used to prove Theorem 1, thus guaranteeing soundness.

4   Evaluation

In order to evaluate the performance impact of the arrays-based encoding, we implemented it in the APALACHE model checker, which currently supports the constants encoding. Given a TLA$^+$ specification containing a property P, APALACHE is capable of performing bounded model checking up to a length k and, if P is an inductive invariant, it can check if the property holds with an unbounded length. In both modes, APALACHE checks if the SMT formula encoding the specification is satisfiable when conjoined with $\neg P$, and if that is the case a counterexample (CEX) in the form of a trace is produced using the arena information and the satisfiable assignment provided by the SMT solver. Our implementation adds new reduction rules to APALACHE, which can be enabled via a CLI flag. When enabled, these rules replace the existing ones encoding sets and functions, as described in Section 3. In addition, we also extended APALACHE's CEX generation to handle assignments to SMT formulas containing arrays. We use Z3 [7] as our back-end solver. APALACHE is open-source and freely available[3].

We performed a number of experiments using APALACHE and the explicit-state model checker TLC. For APALACHE, we evaluated both its existing constants encoding and two versions of the arrays encoding we propose, called *arrays* and *funArrays*. The *arrays* version encodes both TLA$^+$ sets and functions as arrays, while the *funArrays* version encodes only TLA$^+$ functions as arrays. The purpose of having two versions of our encoding is to evaluate the impact of encoding sets and functions as arrays separately. Our evaluation setup consisted of a machine with 64 AMD EPYC 7452 processors and 256 GB of memory. We first present the benchmarks used and then discuss the results obtained.

4.1   Benchmarks

We consider the TLA$^+$ specifications of three asynchronous protocols as benchmarks. The first benchmark is a specification of the asynchronous Byzantine agreement protocol by Bracha and Toueg [5], showed in a simplified version in Figure 2, to which we refer as *aba*. The second benchmark is a specification of the consensus algorithm with Byzantine faults in one communication step by Dobre and Suri [9], to which we refer as *cab*. The third benchmark is a specification of the asynchronous non-blocking atomic commitment protocol by Guerraoui [12], to which we refer as *nac*. The common use of *aba* and *cba* is in replication scenarios with $N = 3F + 1$ replica nodes to tolerate F failures, while the *nac* protocol is typically used for partitioned databases. The specifications are available online[4].

4.2   Results

For each specification we check a variation of the agreement property. The results are shown in Figure 4. We can see that both *arrays* and *funArrays* scale in

---

[3] Available at https://github.com/informalsystems/apalache
[4] Available at https://github.com/informalsystems/apalache-bench

performance better that the constants encoding, with an order of magnitude improvement for some instances. It is also worth pointing out that *arrays* and *funArrays* were able to reach a result before the time limit in 29 and 28 instances, respectively, while the constants encoding was able to do so in only 20 instances. In regards to TLC, it performed worse than the three APALACHE encodings in the nontrivial cases, only reaching a result before the time limit in 8 instances.

5   Related Work

An extensive discussion of works related to symbolic model checking for TLA$^+$ can be found in [13]. Here we focus exclusively on closely related publications. The IVy Prover [20] was designed to tackle verification of distributed algorithms with a decidable fragment of relational first-order logic. Some distributed algorithms, such as the one in Figure 2, cannot be directly expressed in this fragment however, due to the use of power sets and set cardinalities. Recent efforts have focused on offering support to reason about set cardinalities [4], but limitations remain. Cut-off based techniques to automatically infer invariants of distributed algorithms in the IVy language, such as relational abstractions of Paxos and two-phase commit, have been recently proposed [10,11]. Similar benchmarks are used in [22] to infer generalized invariants from finite instances of TLA$^+$ and semi-automatically prove invariants with TLAPS. Specifications of fault-tolerant distributed algorithms encoded as threshold automata can be efficiently verified with ByMC [15,24]. The manual rewriting of an algorithm into threshold automata is, however, usually beyond the skills of a typical TLA$^+$ user. The work closest to ours involves the use of SMT arrays to encode EventB and TLA$^+$ specifications in ProB [21]. The focus on ProB aims at handling infinite data structures, in contrast to our choice to work with bounded overapproximations. Reasoning about infinite domains implies the use of quantifiers, which prevents the use of efficient decision procedures available for the decidable fragment of SMT, with this approach been shown to underperform when compared against APALACHE in checking the benchmarks from [13]. An important last point to mention is that CVC5 has its own non-standard SMT theory of sets [1]. This theory, however, cannot currently handle nested sets, which is a very commonly used TLA$^+$ construct. It remains as a viable alternative to the SMT theory of arrays for the encoding of flat sets, but whose use implies important restrictions to the input language and, consequentially, to practical application.

6   Conclusions

We propose an encoding of the main TLA$^+$ constructs into the SMT theory of arrays, with the goal of providing the SMT solver with the structural information it needs to efficiently reach a solution. We implemented our encoding into the APALACHE model checker and our evaluation indicates that our arrays-based encoding provides a significant performance improvement when compared against APALACHE's existing SMT encoding and the explicit-state model checker TLC.

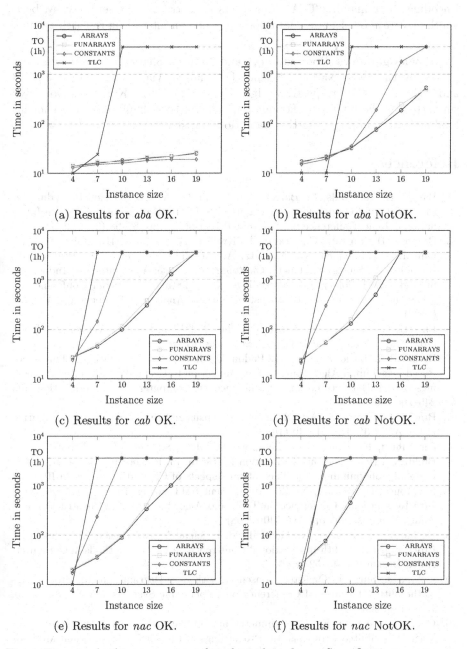

(a) Results for *aba* OK.

(b) Results for *aba* NotOK.

(c) Results for *cab* OK.

(d) Results for *cab* NotOK.

(e) Results for *nac* OK.

(f) Results for *nac* NotOK.

Fig. 4: Time in checking agreement for *aba*, *cab*, and *nac*. Specifications were ran in two configurations, one in which agreement is expected to hold (OK) and one in which it is not (NotOK). Instance size stands for the number of nodes used, and the time is given in seconds in logarithmic scale; Timeout (TO) is 1 hour.

Encoding the remaining TLA$^+$ constructs in a structure-preserving way, be it via SMT arrays or algebraic datatypes, remains an interesting research avenue.

Acknowledgements Rodrigo Otoni and Natasha Sharygina's work was supported by the Swiss National Science Foundation, via grants 200021_197353 and 200021_185031, respectively. Igor Konnov and Jure Kukovec's work was supported by the Interchain Foundation. The authors thank Shon Feder for his kind assistance in preparing the evaluation infrastructure.

References

1. Bansal, K., Reynolds, A., Barrett, C., Tinelli, C.: A New Decision Procedure for Finite Sets and Cardinality Constraints in SMT. In: Proceedings of the 8th International Joint Conference on Automated Reasoning. pp. 82–98 (2016)
2. Barbosa, H., Barrett, C., Brain, M., Kremer, G., Lachnitt, H., Mann, M., Mohamed, A., Mohamed, M., Niemetz, A., Nötzli, A., Ozdemir, A., Preiner, M., Reynolds, A., Sheng, Y., Tinelli, C., Zohar, Y.: CVC5: A Versatile and Industrial-Strength SMT Solver. In: Proceedings of the 28th International Conference on Tools and Algorithms for the Construction and Analysis of Systems. pp. 415–442 (2022)
3. Barrett, C., Fontaine, P., Tinelli, C.: The SMT-LIB Standard: Version 2.6. Tech. rep. (2021), Available at `https://smtlib.cs.uiowa.edu`
4. Berkovits, I., Lazic, M., Losa, G., Padon, O., Shoham, S.: Verification of Threshold-Based Distributed Algorithms by Decomposition to Decidable Logics. In: Proceedings of the 31st International Conference on Computer Aided Verification. pp. 245–266 (2019)
5. Bracha, G., Toueg, S.: Asynchronous Consensus and Broadcast Protocols. Journal of the ACM **32**(4), 824–840 (1985)
6. Chaudhuri, K., Doligez, D., Lamport, L., Merz, S.: The TLA+ Proof System: Building a Heterogeneous Verification Platform. In: Proceedings of the 7th International Colloquium on the Theoretical Aspects of Computing. p. 44 (2010)
7. De Moura, L., Bjørner, N.: Z3: An Efficient SMT Solver. In: Proceedings of the 14th International Conference on Tools and Algorithms for the Construction and Analysis of Systems. pp. 337–340 (2008)
8. De Moura, L., Bjørner, N.: Generalized, Efficient Array Decision Procedures. In: Proceedings of the 9th International Conference on Formal Methods in Computer-Aided Design. pp. 45–52 (2009)
9. Dobre, D., Suri, N.: One-step Consensus with Zero-Degradation. In: Proceedings of the 36th International Conference on Dependable Systems and Networks. pp. 137–146 (2006)
10. Goel, A., Sakallah, K.: On Symmetry and Quantification: A New Approach to Verify Distributed Protocols. In: Proceedings of the 13th NASA Formal Methods International Symposium. p. 131–150 (2021)
11. Goel, A., Sakallah, K.A.: Towards an Automatic Proof of Lamport's Paxos. In: Proceedings of the 21st Conference on Formal Methods in Computer-Aided Design. pp. 112–122 (2021)
12. Guerraoui, R.: On the Hardness of Failure-Sensitive Agreement Problems. Information Processing Letters **79**(2), 99–104 (2001)
13. Konnov, I., Kukovec, J., Tran, T.H.: TLA+ Model Checking Made Symbolic. Proc. ACM Program. Lang. **3**(OOPSLA), 123:1–123:30 (2019)

14. Konnov, I., Kuppe, M., Merz, S.: Specification and Verification with the TLA+ Trifecta: TLC, Apalache, and TLAPS. In: Proceedings of the 11th International Symposium On Leveraging Applications of Formal Methods, Verification and Validation. pp. 88–105 (2022)
15. Konnov, I., Lazić, M., Stoilkovska, I., Widder, J.: Tutorial: Parameterized Verification with Byzantine Model Checker. In: Proceedings of the 40th International Conference on Formal Techniques for Distributed Objects, Components, and Systems. pp. 189–207 (2020)
16. Kukovec, J., Tran, T.H., Konnov, I.: Extracting Symbolic Transitions from TLA+ Specifications. Science of Computer Programming **187**, 102361 (2020)
17. Lamport, L.: Specifying Systems: The TLA+ Language and Tools for Hardware and Software Engineers. Addison-Wesley Longman Publishing Co., Inc. (2002)
18. Merz, S., Vanzetto, H.: Encoding TLA+ into unsorted and many-sorted first-order logic. Science of Computer Programming **158**, 3–20 (2018)
19. Newcombe, C., Rath, T., Zhang, F., Munteanu, B., Brooker, M., Deardeuff, M.: How Amazon Web Services uses Formal Methods. Communications of the ACM **58**(4), 66–73 (2015)
20. Padon, O., McMillan, K.L., Panda, A., Sagiv, M., Shoham, S.: Ivy: Safety Verification by Interactive Generalization. In: Proceedings of the 37th ACM SIGPLAN Conference on Programming Language Design and Implementation. pp. 614–630 (2016)
21. Schmidt, J., Leuschel, M.: Improving SMT Solver Integrations for the Validation of B and Event-B Models. In: Proceedings of the 26th International Conference on Formal Methods for Industrial Critical Systems. pp. 107–125 (2021)
22. Schultz, W., Dardik, I., Tripakis, S.: Plain and Simple Inductive Invariant Inference for Distributed Protocols in TLA+. In: Proceedings of the 22nd Conference on Formal Methods in Computer-Aided Design. pp. 273–283 (2022)
23. Sivasubramanian, S.: Amazon DynamoDB: A Seamlessly Scalable Non-Relational Database Service. In: Proceedings of the 2012 ACM SIGMOD International Conference on Management of Data. p. 729–730 (2012)
24. Stoilkovska, I., Konnov, I., Widder, J., Zuleger, F.: Verifying Safety of Synchronous Fault-Tolerant Algorithms by Bounded Model Checking. International Journal on Software Tools for Technology Transfer **24**(1), 33–48 (2022)
25. Stump, A., Barrett, C., Dill, D., Levitt, J.: A Decision Procedure for an Extensional Theory of Arrays. In: Proceedings of the 16th Annual IEEE Symposium on Logic in Computer Science. pp. 29–37 (2001)
26. Tran, T.H.: Symbolic Verification of TLA+ Specifications with Applications to Distributed Algorithms. Ph.D. thesis, Technische Universität Wien (2023), upcoming thesis
27. Yu, Y., Manolios, P., Lamport, L.: Model Checking TLA+ Specifications. In: Proceedings of the 10th Advanced Research Working Conference on Correct Hardware Design and Verification Methods. pp. 54–66 (1999)

AutoHyper: Explicit-State Model Checking for HyperLTL

Raven Beutner[(✉)] and Bernd Finkbeiner

CISPA Helmholtz Center for Information Security, Saarbrücken, Germany
{raven.beutner,finkbeiner}@cispa.de

Abstract. HyperLTL is a temporal logic that can express hyperproperties, i.e., properties that relate multiple execution traces of a system. Such properties are becoming increasingly important and naturally occur, e.g., in information-flow control, robustness, mutation testing, path planning, and causality checking. Thus far, complete model checking tools for HyperLTL have been limited to alternation-free formulas, i.e., formulas that use only universal or only existential trace quantification. Properties involving quantifier alternations could only be handled in an incomplete way, i.e., the verification might fail even though the property holds. In this paper, we present AutoHyper, an explicit-state automata-based model checker that supports full HyperLTL and is complete for properties with arbitrary quantifier alternations. We show that language inclusion checks can be integrated into HyperLTL verification, which allows AutoHyper to benefit from a range of existing inclusion-checking tools. We evaluate AutoHyper on a broad set of benchmarks drawn from different areas in the literature and compare it with existing (incomplete) methods for HyperLTL verification.

1 Introduction

Hyperproperties [16] are system properties that relate multiple executions of a system. Such properties are of increasing importance as they naturally occur, e.g., in information-flow control [36], robustness [22], linearizability [30,31], path planning [39], mutation testing [27], and causality checking [18]. A prominent logic to express hyperproperties is HyperLTL, which extends linear-time temporal logic (LTL) with explicit trace quantification [15]. HyperLTL can, for instance, express generalized non-interference (GNI) [34], stating that the high-security input of a system does not influence the observable output.

$$\forall \pi. \forall \pi'. \exists \pi''. \square \Big(\bigwedge_{a \in H} a_\pi \leftrightarrow a_{\pi''} \Big) \wedge \square \Big(\bigwedge_{a \in L \cup O} a_{\pi'} \leftrightarrow a_{\pi''} \Big) \qquad \text{(GNI)}$$

Here, H is a set of high-security input, L is a set of low-security inputs, and O is a set of low-security outputs. The formula states that for any traces π, π' there exists a third trace π'' that agrees with the high-security inputs of π and with the low-security inputs and outputs of π'. Any observation made by a low-security attacker is thus compatible with every possible high-security input.

© The Author(s) 2023
S. Sankaranarayanan and N. Sharygina (Eds.): TACAS 2023, LNCS 13993, pp. 145–163, 2023.
https://doi.org/10.1007/978-3-031-30823-9_8

We are interested in the model checking (MC) problem of HyperLTL, i.e., whether a given (finite-state) system satisfies a given property. For HyperLTL, the structure of the quantifier prefix directly impacts the complexity of this problem. For alternation-free formulas (i.e., formulas that only use quantifiers of a single type), verification is well understood and is reducible to the verification of a trace property on a self-composition of the system [3]. This reduction has, for example, been implemented in MCHyper [29], a tool that can model check (alternation-free) HyperLTL formulas in systems of considerable size (circuits with thousands of latches).

Verification is much more challenging for properties involving quantifier alternations (such as GNI from above). While MC algorithms supporting full HyperLTL exist (see [15,29]), they have not been implemented yet. Instead, over the years, a number of approaches to the verification of such properties in practice have been made: Finkbeiner et al. [29] and D'Argenio et al. [22] manually strengthen properties with quantifier alternation into properties that are alternation-free and can be checked by MCHyper. Coenen et al. [19] instantiate existential quantification in a $\forall^*\exists^*$ property (i.e., a property involving an arbitrary number of universal quantifiers followed by an arbitrary number of existential quantifiers, such as GNI) with an explicit (user-provided) strategy, thus reducing to the verification of an alternation-free formula. Alternatively, the strategy that resolves existential quantification can be automatically synthesized [7]. Hsu et al. [31] present a bounded model checking (BMC) approach for HyperLTL that is implemented in HyperQube. See Section 4 for more details.

While all these verification tools can verify (or refute) interesting properties, they all suffer from the same fundamental limitation: they are *incomplete*. That is, for all the tools above, we can come up with verification instances where they fail, not because of resource constraints but because of inherent limitations in the underlying verification algorithm. Moreover, such instances are not rare events but are encountered regularly in practice. For example, many of the benchmarks used to evaluate HyperQube (by Hsu et al. [31]) do not admit a strategy to resolve existential quantification. Conversely, many of the properties verified by Coenen et al. [19] (such as GNI) cannot be verified using BMC [31].

AutoHyper. In this paper, we present AutoHyper, a model checker for HyperLTL. Our tool checks a hyperproperty by iteratively eliminating trace quantification using automata-complementations, thereby reducing verification to the emptiness check of an automaton [29]. Importantly – and different from previous tools for HyperLTL verification such as MCHyper [29,19] and HyperQube [31] – AutoHyper can cope with (and is *complete* for) arbitrary HyperLTL formulas. Model checking using AutoHyper does not require manual effort (such as writing an explicit strategy in MCHyper [19]), nor does a user need to worry if the given property can even be verified with a given method. AutoHyper thus provides a "push-button" model checking experience for HyperLTL.[1]

---

[1] The name of AutoHyper is derived from the fact that it is both **Auto**mata-based and **Auto**matic (i.e., it is complete and does not require any user intervention).

To improve `AutoHyper`'s efficiency, we make the (theoretical) observation that we can often avoid explicit automaton complementation and instead reduce to a language inclusion check on Büchi automata (cf. Proposition 1). On the practical side, this enables `AutoHyper` to resort to a range of mature language inclusion checkers, including `spot` [26], `RABIT` [17], `BAIT` [25], and `FORKLIFT` [24].

Evaluation. Using `AutoHyper`, we extensively study the practical aspects of model checking HyperLTL properties with quantifier alternations. To evaluate the performance of explicit-state model checking, we apply `AutoHyper` to a broad range of benchmarks taken from the literature and compare it with existing (incomplete) tools. We make the surprising observation that – at least on the currently available benchmarks – explicit-state MC as implemented in `AutoHyper` performs on-par (and frequently outperforms) symbolic methods such as BMC [31]. Our benchmarks stem from various areas within computer science, so `AutoHyper` should – thanks to its "push-button" functionality, completeness, and ease of use – be a valuable addition to many areas.

Apart from using `AutoHyper` as a practical MC tool, we can also use it as a complete baseline to systematically evaluate existing (incomplete) methods. For example, while it is known that replacing existential quantification with a strategy (as done by Coenen et al. [19]) is incomplete, it was, thus far, unknown if this incompleteness occurs frequently or is merely a rare phenomenon. We use `AutoHyper` to obtain a ground truth and evaluate the strategy-based verification approach in terms of its effectiveness (i.e., how many instances it can verify despite being incomplete) and efficiency.

Structure. The remainder of this paper is structured as follows. In Section 2, we introduce HyperLTL. We recap automata-based verification (which we abbreviate ABV) and our new approach utilizing language inclusion checks in Section 3. We discuss alternative verification approaches for HyperLTL in Section 4. In Section 6, we compare different backend solving techniques and study the complexity of HyperLTL MC with multiple quantifier alternations in practice; In Section 7, we evaluate ABV on a set of benchmarks from the literature and compare with the bounded model checker `HyperQube` [31]; In Section 8 we use `AutoHyper` for a detailed analysis of (and comparison with) strategy-based verification [19,7].

2 Preliminaries

We fix a set of atomic propositions AP and define $\Sigma := 2^{AP}$. HyperLTL [15] extends LTL with explicit quantification over traces, thereby lifting it from a logic expressing trace properties to one expressing hyperproperties [16]. Let $\mathcal{V}$ be a set of trace variables. We define HyperLTL formulas by the following grammar:

$$\psi := a_\pi \mid \neg\psi \mid \psi \wedge \psi \mid \bigcirc\psi \mid \psi\,\mathcal{U}\,\psi$$
$$\varphi := \exists\pi.\,\varphi \mid \forall\pi.\,\varphi \mid \psi$$

where $\pi \in \mathcal{V}$ and $a \in AP$.

We assume that the formula is closed, i.e., all trace variables that are used in the body are bound by some quantifier. The semantics of HyperLTL is given with respect to a trace assignment $\Pi : \mathcal{V} \rightharpoonup \Sigma^\omega$ mapping trace variables to traces. For $\pi \in \mathcal{V}$ and $t \in \Sigma^\omega$, we write $\Pi[\pi \mapsto t]$ for the trace assignment obtained by updating the value of π to t. Given a set of traces $\mathbb{T} \subseteq \Sigma^\omega$, a trace assignment Π, and $i \in \mathbb{N}$, we define:

$$
\begin{aligned}
\Pi, i &\models a_\pi && \text{iff} && a \in \Pi(\pi)(i) \\
\Pi, i &\models \neg\psi && \text{iff} && \Pi, i \not\models \psi \\
\Pi, i &\models \psi_1 \wedge \psi_2 && \text{iff} && \Pi, i \models \psi_1 \text{ and } \Pi, i \models \psi_2 \\
\Pi, i &\models \bigcirc\psi && \text{iff} && \Pi, i+1 \models \psi \\
\Pi, i &\models \psi_1 \mathcal{U} \psi_2 && \text{iff} && \exists j \geq i.\, \Pi, j \models \psi_2 \text{ and } \forall i \leq k < j.\, \Pi, k \models \psi_1
\end{aligned}
$$

$$
\begin{aligned}
\Pi &\models_\mathbb{T} \psi && \text{iff} && \Pi, 0 \models \psi \\
\Pi &\models_\mathbb{T} \exists\pi.\, \varphi && \text{iff} && \exists t \in \mathbb{T}.\, \Pi[\pi \mapsto t] \models_\mathbb{T} \varphi \\
\Pi &\models_\mathbb{T} \forall\pi.\, \varphi && \text{iff} && \forall t \in \mathbb{T}.\, \Pi[\pi \mapsto t] \models_\mathbb{T} \varphi
\end{aligned}
$$

A *transition system* is a tuple $\mathcal{T} = (S, S_0, \kappa, L)$ where S is a set of states, $S_0 \subseteq S$ is a set of initial states, $\kappa \subseteq S \times S$ is a transition relation, and $L : S \to \Sigma$ is a labeling function. We write $s \xrightarrow{\mathcal{T}} s'$ whenever $(s, s') \in \kappa$. A path is an infinite sequence $s_0 s_1 s_2 \cdots \in S^\omega$, s.t., $s_0 \in S_0$, and $s_i \xrightarrow{\mathcal{T}} s_{i+1}$ for all i. The associated trace is given by $L(s_0)L(s_1)L(s_2)\cdots \in \Sigma^\omega$. We write $\mathit{Traces}(\mathcal{T}) \subseteq \Sigma^\omega$ for the set of all traces generated by $\mathcal{T}$. We say $\mathcal{T}$ satisfies a HyperLTL property φ, written $\mathcal{T} \models \varphi$, if $\emptyset \models_{\mathit{Traces}(\mathcal{T})} \varphi$, where $\emptyset$ denotes the empty trace assignment.

3   Automata-based HyperLTL Model Checking

Given a system $\mathcal{T}$ and HyperLTL property φ, we want to decide whether $\mathcal{T} \models \varphi$. In this section, we recap the automata-based approach to the model checking of HyperLTL [29]. We further show how language inclusion checks can be incorporated into the model checking procedure to make use of a broad collection of mature language inclusion checkers.

3.1   Automata-based Verification

The idea of automata-based verification (ABV) [29] is to iteratively eliminate quantifiers and thus reduce MC to the emptiness check on an automaton. A non-deterministic Büchi automaton (NBA) is a tuple $\mathcal{A} = (Q, Q_0, \delta, F)$ where Q is a finite set of states, $Q_0 \subseteq Q$ is a set of initial states, $\delta : Q \times \Sigma \to 2^Q$ is a transition function, and $F \subseteq Q$ is a set of accepting states. We write $\mathcal{L}(\mathcal{A}) \subseteq \Sigma^\omega$ for the language of $\mathcal{A}$, i.e., all infinite words that have a run that visits states in F infinitely many times (see, e.g., [2]). For traces $t_1, \ldots, t_n \in \Sigma^\omega$, we write $\mathit{zip}(t_1, \ldots, t_n) \in (\Sigma^n)^\omega$ as the pointwise product, i.e., $\mathit{zip}(t_1, \ldots, t_n)(i) := (t_1(i), \ldots, t_n(i))$.

Let $\mathcal{T} = (S, S_0, \kappa, L)$ be a fixed transition system and let $\dot{\varphi}$ be some fixed closed HyperLTL formula (we use the dot to refer to the original formula and use φ, φ' to refer to subformulas of $\dot{\varphi}$). For some subformula φ that contains free trace variables $\pi_1, \ldots, \pi_n$, we say an NBA $\mathcal{A}$ over Σ^n is $\mathcal{T}$-equivalent to φ, if for all traces $t_1, \ldots, t_n$ it holds that $[\pi_1 \mapsto t_1, \ldots, \pi_n \mapsto t_n] \models_{Traces(\mathcal{T})} \varphi$ iff $zip(t_1, \ldots, t_n) \in \mathcal{L}(\mathcal{A})$. That is, $\mathcal{A}$ accepts exactly the zippings of traces that constitute a satisfying trace assignment for φ.

To check if $\mathcal{T} \models \dot{\varphi}$, we inductively construct an automaton $\mathcal{A}_\varphi$ that is $\mathcal{T}$-equivalent to φ for each subformula φ of $\dot{\varphi}$. For the (quantifier-free) LTL body of $\dot{\varphi}$, we can construct this automaton via a standard LTL-to-NBA construction [29,2]. Now consider some subformula $\varphi' = \exists \pi.\varphi$ where φ' contains free trace variables $\pi_1, \ldots, \pi_n$ and so φ contains free trace variables $\pi_1, \ldots, \pi_n, \pi$. We are given an inductively constructed NBA $\mathcal{A}_\varphi = (Q, Q_0, \delta, F)$ over Σ^{n+1} that is $\mathcal{T}$-equivalent to φ. We define the automaton $\mathcal{A}_{\varphi'}$ over Σ^n as $\mathcal{A}_{\varphi'} := (S \times Q, S_0 \times Q_0, \delta', S \times F)$ where δ' is defined as

$$\delta'\big((s,q), \langle l_1, \ldots, l_n \rangle\big) := \Big\{ (s', q') \mid s \xrightarrow{\mathcal{T}} s' \wedge q' \in \delta\big(q, \langle l_1, \ldots, l_n, L(s) \rangle\big) \Big\}.$$

Informally, $\mathcal{A}_{\varphi'}$ reads the zippings of traces $t_1, \ldots, t_n$ and guesses a trace $t \in Traces(\mathcal{T})$ such that $zip(t_1, \ldots, t_n, t) \in \mathcal{L}(\mathcal{A}_\varphi)$. It is easy to see that $\mathcal{A}_{\varphi'}$ is $\mathcal{T}$-equivalent to φ'. To handle universal trace quantification, we consider a formula $\varphi' = \forall \pi.\varphi$ as "$\varphi' = \neg \exists \pi.\neg \varphi$" and combine the construction for existential quantification with an automaton complementation.

Following the inductive construction, we obtain an automaton $\mathcal{A}_{\dot{\varphi}}$ over the singleton alphabet Σ^0 that is $\mathcal{T}$-equivalent to $\dot{\varphi}$. By definition of $\mathcal{T}$-equivalence, $\mathcal{T} \models \dot{\varphi}$ iff $\emptyset \models_{Traces(\mathcal{T})} \dot{\varphi}$ iff $\mathcal{A}_{\dot{\varphi}}$ is non-empty (which we can decide [21]).

3.2   HyperLTL Model Checking by Language Inclusion

The algorithm outlined above requires one complementation for each quantifier alternation in the HyperLTL formula. While we cannot avoid the theoretical cost of this complementation (see [36,15]), we can reduce to a, in practice, more tamable problem: *language inclusion*.

For a system $\mathcal{T}$, and a natural number $n \in \mathbb{N}$ we define $\mathcal{A}_{\mathcal{T}}^n$ as an NBA over Σ^n such that for any traces $t_1, \ldots, t_n \in \Sigma^\omega$ we have $zip(t_1, \ldots, t_n) \in \mathcal{L}(\mathcal{A}_{\mathcal{T}}^n)$ if and only if $t_i \in Traces(\mathcal{T})$ for every $1 \leq i \leq n$. We can construct $\mathcal{A}_{\mathcal{T}}^n$ by building the n-fold self-composition of $\mathcal{T}$ [3] and convert this to an automaton by moving the labels from states to edges and marking all states as accepting. We can now state a formal connection between language inclusion and HyperLTL MC (a proof can be found in the full version [9]):

Proposition 1. *Let $\dot{\varphi} = \forall \pi_1.\ldots.\forall \pi_n.\varphi$ be a HyperLTL formula (where φ may contain additional trace quantifiers) and let $\mathcal{A}_\varphi$ be an automaton over Σ^n that is $\mathcal{T}$-equivalent to φ. Then $\mathcal{T} \models \dot{\varphi}$ if and only if $\mathcal{L}(\mathcal{A}_{\mathcal{T}}^n) \subseteq \mathcal{L}(\mathcal{A}_\varphi)$.*

We can use Proposition 1 to avoid a complementation for the outermost quantifier alternation. For example, assume $\dot{\varphi} = \forall \pi_1.\forall \pi_2.\exists \pi_3.\psi$ where ψ is quantifier-free. Using the construction from Section 3.1, we obtain an automaton $\mathcal{A}_{\exists \pi_3.\psi}$

that is $\mathcal{T}$-equivalent to $\exists \pi_3.\psi$ (we can construct $\mathcal{A}_{\exists \pi_3.\psi}$ in linear time in the size of $\mathcal{T}$). By Proposition 1, we then have $\mathcal{T} \models \dot{\varphi}$ iff $\mathcal{L}(\mathcal{A}_{\mathcal{T}}^2) \subseteq \mathcal{L}(\mathcal{A}_{\exists \pi_3.\psi})$.

Note that complementation and subsequent emptiness check is a theoretically optimal method to solve the (PSPACE-complete) language inclusion problem. Proposition 1 thus offers no asymptotic advantages over "standard" ABV in Section 3.1. In *practice* constructing an explicit complemented automaton is often unnecessary as the language inclusion or non-inclusion might be witnessed without a complete complementation [26,25,17,24]. This makes Proposition 1 relevant for the present work and the performance of AutoHyper.

4   Related Work and HyperLTL Verification Approaches

HyperLTL [15] is the most studied logic for expressing hyperproperties. A range of problems from different areas in computer science can be expressed as Hyper-LTL MC problems, including (optimal) path panning [39], mutation testing [27], linearizability [31], robustness [22], information-flow control [36], and causality checking [18], to name only a few. Consequently, any model checking tool for HyperLTL is applicable to many disciples within computer science and provides a unified solution to many challenging algorithmic problems. In recent years, different (mostly incomplete) methods for the verification of HyperLTL have been developed. We discuss them below (see the full version [9] for details).

Automata-based Model Checking. Finkbeiner et al. [29] introduce the automata-based model checking approach as presented in Section 3.1. For alternation-free formulas, the algorithms corresponds to the construction of the self-composition of a system [3] and is implemented in the MCHyper tool [29]. MCHyper can handle systems of significant size (well beyond the reach of explicit-state methods) but is unable to handle any quantifier alternation (the main motivation for AutoHyper). htltl2mc [15] is a prototype model checker for HyperLTL$_2$ (a fragment of Hy-perLTL with at most one alternation) built on top of GOAL [38]. In contrast to htltl2mc, AutoHyper supports properties with arbitrarily many quantifier alternations and features automata with symbolic alphabets – which is important to handle large systems with many atomic propositions, cf. Footnote 7.

Strategy-based Verification. Coenen et al. [19] verify $\forall^*\exists^*$ properties by instantiating existential quantification with an explicit strategy. This method – which we refer to as strategy-based verification (SBV) – comes in two flavors: either the strategy is provided by the user or the strategy is synthesized automatically. In the former case, model checking reduces to checking an alternation-free formula and can thus handle large systems, but requires significant user effort (and is thus no "push-button" technique). In the latter case, the method works fully automatically [8,7] but requires an expensive strategy synthesis. SBV is incomplete as the strategy resolving existentially quantified traces only observes finite prefixes of the universally quantified traces. While SBV can be made complete by adding prophecy variables [7], the automatic synthesis of such prophecies is currently limited to very small systems and properties that are temporally safe [5]. We investigate both the performance and incompleteness of SBV in Section 8.

Bounded Model Checking. Hsu et al. [31] propose a bounded model checking (BMC) procedure for HyperLTL. Similar to BMC for trace properties [11], the system is unfolded up to a fixed depth, and pending obligations beyond that depth are either treated pessimistically (to show the satisfaction of a formula) or optimistically (to show the violation of a formula). While BMC for trace properties reduces to SAT-solving, BMC for hyperproperties naturally reduces to QBF-solving. As usual for bounded methods, BMC for HyperLTL is incomplete. For example, it can never show that a system satisfies a hyperproperty where the LTL body contains an invariant (as, e.g., is the case for GNI).[2] We compare `AutoHyper` and BMC (in the form of `HyperQube` [31]) in Section 7.

5   AutoHyper: Tool Overview

`AutoHyper` is written in `F#` and implements the automata-based verification approach described in Section 3.1 and, if desired by the user, makes use of the language-inclusion-based reduction from Section 3.2. `AutoHyper` uses `spot` [26] for LTL-to-NBA translations and automata complementations. To check language inclusion, `AutoHyper` uses `spot` (which is based on determinization), `RABIT` [17] (which is based on a Ramsey-based approach with heavy use of simulations), `BAIT` [25], and `FORKLIFT` [24] (both based on well-quasiorders). `AutoHyper` is designed such that communication with external automata tools is done via established text-based formats (opposed to proprietary APIs), namely the `HANOI` [1] and `BA` automaton formats. New (or updated) tools that improve on fundamental automata operations, such as complementation and inclusion checks, can thus be integrated easily. Internally we represent automata using symbolic alphabets (similar to `spot`). We store transition formulas as DNFs as this allows for very efficient SAT checks, which are needed during the product construction.

All experiments in this paper were conducted on a Mac Mini with an Intel Core i3 (i3-8100B) and 16GB of memory. We used `spot` version 2.11.1; `RABIT` version 2.4.5; `BAIT` commit 369e1a4; and `FORKLIFT` commit 5d519e3.

Input Formats. `AutoHyper` supports both explicit-state systems (given in a `HANOI`-like [1] input format) and symbolic systems that are internally converted

---

[2] BMC for trace properties can be made complete by using bounds on the unrolling depth (also called completeness thresholds) [14] and including loop conditions in the encoding [11]. As remarked by Hsu et al. [31], the same is much more challenging for hyperproperties, and no solutions have been proposed. Instead, Hsu et al. [31] propose an alternative unrolling semantics (which they call halting semantics) that can mitigate this incompleteness issue for programs that terminate after a *fixed* number of steps. This is a strong (and often unrealistic) assumption for general reactive systems.

to an explicit-state representation. The support for symbolic systems includes Aiger circuits, symbolic models written in a fragment of the NuSMV input language [13], and a simple boolean programming language [6].

Random Benchmarks. For our evaluation, we use both existing instances from various sources in the literature and randomly generated problems.[3] We generate random transition systems based on the Erdős–Rényi–Gilbert model [28]. Given a size n and a density parameter $p \in [0, 1]$, we generate a graph with n states, where for every two states s, s', there is a transition $s \to s'$ with probability p. To generate a graph with n edges and, in expectation, constant outdegree of k, we can choose $p = \frac{k}{n}$. We further ensure that the system is connected and all states have at least one outgoing edge. We generate random HyperLTL formulas (with a given quantifier prefix) by sampling the LTL matrix using spot's randltl.

6   HyperLTL Model Checking Complexity in Practice

Before we turn our attention to benchmarks found in the literature, we compare the different backend inclusion checkers supported by AutoHyper by evaluating them on a large set of synthetic (random) benchmarks (in Section 6.1). Moreover, the random generation of benchmarks allows us to peek at formulas with more than one quantifier alternation. The theoretical hardness of model checking properties with multiple alternations has been studied extensively [15,36], and we analyze, for the first time, how these results transfer to practice (in Section 6.2).

6.1   Performance of Inclusion Checkers

As the first set of benchmarks, we compare the different backend inclusion checkers supported by AutoHyper. In Figure 1, we depict how many instances can be solved using the inclusion checks of spot, BAIT, RABIT, and FORKLIFT within a timeout of 10s and give the median running time used on the instances that could be solved within the timeout. We observe that spot clearly outperforms RABIT, BAIT, and FORKLIFT in terms of the percentage of instances that can be checked within 10s.[4] While, in general, spot solves the most instances, a manual inspection reveals that there are also instances that can only be solved by RABIT

---

[3] The advantage of randomly generated instances is twofold. First, it allows for the easy generation of a large set of benchmarks. Second, the random generation is parameterized by multiple parameters (such as system size, transition density, formula size, etc.), enabling a comprehensive analysis of the exact impact of different parameters on the model checking complexity in practice.

[4] We remark that spot operates on automata with a symbolic alphabet (i.e., transitions are defined as boolean formulas over AP). In contrast, RABIT, BAIT, and FORKLIFT only support explicit alphabets (i.e., automata with one symbol for each element in 2^{AP}).

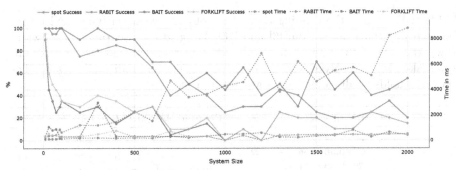

Fig. 1: We evaluate different backend solvers on instances of varying system size with an (on average) constant outdegree of 10 and a fixed property size of 20. We generate 20 samples per system size. We display both the success rate of each solver within a timeout of 10s (on the left axis) and the median running time on the solved instances (on the right axis).

or **BAIT/FORKLIFT**. This justifies why **AutoHyper** supports multiple backed inclusion checkers that implement different algorithms and thus excel on different problems (we will confirm this in Section 7). Moreover, our experiments provide evidence that HyperLTL MC is a natural source for challenging language inclusion benchmarks (see the full version [9]).

We remark that we set the timeout of 10s deliberately low to compute (and reproduce) the plots in a reasonable time (computing Figure 1 took about 3.5h). If a user wants to verify a given instance and does not require a result within a few seconds, running the solver for even longer will likely increase the success rate further (see also the evaluation in Section 7).

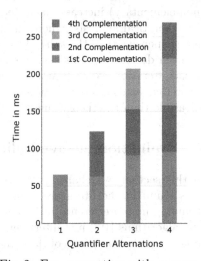

6.2 Model Checking Beyond ∀*∃*

Using randomly generated benchmarks, we can also peek at the practical complexity of model checking in the presence of multiple quantifier alternations. In *theory*, the model checking complexity of HyperLTL increases by one exponent with each quantifier alternation [15,36]. Using **AutoHyper**, we can, for the first time, investigate the model checking complexity in *practice*.

Fig. 2: For properties with a varying number of quantifier alterations, we display the average time spent on the automata complementation during model checking.

We model check randomly generated formulas with 1 to 4 quantifier alternations and visualize the total running time based on the cost of each complementation (using **spot**) in Figure 2 (recall that checking a formula with k alternations

Table 1: We depict the running time of `AutoHyper` when verifying GNI on the boolean programs taken from [6] and [10]. We give the program, the bitwidth (bw), the size of the intermediate explicit-state representation (Size), and the time taken by each solver. The timeout is set to 60s and indicated by a "-". The property holds in all cases. Times are given in seconds.

Program	bw	Size	t_{spot}	t_{RABIT}	t_{BAIT}	$t_{FORKLIFT}$
[6].1	1-bit	17	**0.52**	0.59	0.80	0.61
	3-bit	65	**0.56**	0.86	-	22.73
	4-bit	129	**0.99**	5.51	-	-
[6].2	1-bit	55	**0.53**	0.69	-	5.49
[6].3	1-bit	20	**0.52**	0.61	3.05	0.98
	3-bit	80	**0.61**	1.31	-	-
[6].4	1-bit	29	**0.52**	0.56	0.58	0.57
	3-bit	113	**0.67**	1.74	-	-

Program	bw	Size	t_{spot}	t_{RABIT}	t_{BAIT}	$t_{FORKLIFT}$
[10].1	1-bit	5	0.52	**0.56**	0.58	0.57
[10].2	1-bit	11	**0.51**	0.57	0.72	0.61
	2-bit	27	**0.52**	0.65	35.7	5.43
	4-bit	291	**1.46**	-	-	-
[10].3	1-bit	21	**0.52**	0.60	3.15	1.00
	3-bit	225	-	**45.2**	-	-
[10].4	1-bit	25	**0.52**	0.71	12.8	1.63
	3-bit	193	**0.98**	-	-	-

using ABV requires k automaton complementations). Although the number of quantifier alternations has an undeniable impact on the total running time (the cumulative height of each bar), the increase in runtime is not proportional to the (non-elementary) increase suggested by the theoretical analysis. Different from the theoretical analysis (where the $(k+1)$th complementation is exponentially more expensive than the kth), the cost of each complementation barely increases (or even decreases). This suggests that the $\mathcal{T}$-equivalent automata constructed in each iteration are, in practice, much smaller than indicated by the worst-case theoretical analysis. Verification of properties beyond one alternation is thus less infeasible than the theory suggests (at least on randomly generated test cases).

7 Evaluation on Symbolic Systems

In this section, we challenge `AutoHyper` with complex model checking problems found in the literature. Our benchmarks stem from a range of sources, including non-interference in boolean programs [6], symmetry in mutual exclusion algorithms [19], non-interference in multi-threaded programs [37], fairness in non-repudiation protocols [32], mutation testing [27], and path planning [39].

7.1 Model Checking GNI on Boolean Programs

We use `AutoHyper` to verify GNI on a range of boolean programs that process high-security and low-security inputs (taken from [6,10]). Table 1 depicts the runtime results using different backend solvers. We test each program with varying bitwidth and depict the largest bitwidth that can be solved by at least one solver (within a timeout of 60s). We, again, note that `spot` performs better than

Table 2: We evaluate `HyperQube` and `AutoHyper` on the benchmarks from [31]. We list the system and the property (as given in [31, Table 2]), the quantifier structure (Q^*), the verification result (Res) (✓ indicates that the property holds and ✗ that it is violated), and the total running time of either tool (t). For `HyperQube`, we additionally list the unrolling bound (k) and the unrolling semantics (Sem). For `AutoHyper`, we additionally list the size of the intermediate explicit state space (Size). Times are given in seconds.

| System | Spec | Q^* | Res | HyperQube [31] | | | AutoHyper | |
				k	Sem	t	Size	t
Bakery$_3$	φ_{S1}	∃∃	✗	7	pes	**1.9**	167	2.3
Bakery$_3$	φ_{S2}	∀∃	✗	12	pes	**2.0**	167	4.2
Bakery$_3$	φ_{S3}	∃∀	✗$^!$	20	pes	**2.8**	167	34.6
Bakery$_3$	φ_{sym1}	∀∃	✗	10	pes	**1.7**	167	16.2
Bakery$_3$	φ_{sym2}	∀∃	✗	10	pes	**1.6**	167	2.9
Bakery$_5$	φ_{sym1}	∀∃	✗	10	pes	**17.3**	996	282.1
Bakery$_5$	φ_{sym2}	∀∃	✗	10	pes	18.2	996	**18.0**
SNARK-bug1	φ_{lin}	∀∃	✗	26	hpes	618.0	4941	**96.1**
3-Thread$_{correct}$	φ_{NI}	∀∃	✓	10	hopt	1.6	64	**1.3**
3-Thread$_{incorrect}$	φ_{NI}	∀∃	✗	57	hpes	12.8	368	**7.7**
NRP : T$_{correct}$	φ_{fair}	∃∀	✓	15	hopt	1.3	55	**0.5**
NRP : T$_{incorrect}$	φ_{fair}	∃∀	✓$^!$	15	hopt	1.4	54	**0.8**
Mutant	φ_{mut}	∃∀	✓	8	hopt	1.1	32	**0.8**

other inclusion checkers and, in particular, scales better when the size of the system increases. Note that the number of atomic propositions is 3 in all instances, so `spot`'s support for symbolic alphabets has a negligible impact on the running time. We emphasize that not all instances in Table 1 can be verified using SBV [19,7] without a user-provided fixed lookahead. Likewise, BMC [31] can *never* verify GNI. This provides further evidence why complete model checking tools (of which `AutoHyper` is the first) are necessary.

7.2   Explicit Model Checking of Symbolic Systems

In this section, we evaluate `AutoHyper` on challenging symbolic models (NuSMV models [13]) that were used by Hsu et al. [31] to evaluate `HyperQube`.

The properties we verify cover a wide range of properties. For example, we verify that Lamport's bakery algorithm [33] does not satisfy various symmetry properties (as the algorithm prioritizes processes with a lower ticket ID); We check linearizability[5] [30] on the SNARK datastructure [23] and identify a previously known bug; And, we generate model-based mutation test cases using the approach proposed by Fellner et al. [27]. Further details on the benchmarks are provided in [31].

We check each instance using both `HyperQube` and `AutoHyper` and depict the results in Table 2.[6] When using `AutoHyper` we always apply `spot`'s inclusion checker.[7] For `HyperQube` we use the unrolling semantics and unrolling depth listed in [31, Table 2]. We observe that for most instances – despite using explicit state methods and thus being complete (cf. Section 7.4) – `AutoHyper` performs on par with `HyperQube`. On instances using Lamport's bakery algorithm, BMC only needs to unroll to very shallow depths, resulting in very efficient solving, whereas `AutoHyper`'s running time is dominated by `spot`'s LTL-to-NBA translation (consuming up to 98% of the total time). Conversely, on the large SNARK example, `AutoHyper` performs significantly better.

7.3   Hyperproperties for Path Planning

As a last set of benchmarks, we use planning problems for robots encoded into HyperLTL as proposed by Wang et al. [39]. For example, the synthesis of a shortest path can be phrased as a $\exists\forall$ property that states that there exists a path to the goal such that all alternative paths to the goal take at least as long. Wang et al. [39] propose a solution to check the resulting HyperLTL property by encoding it in first-order logic, which is then solved by an SMT solver. While not competitive with state-of-the-art planning tools, HyperLTL allows one to express a broad range of problems (shortest path, path robustness, etc.) in a very general way. Hsu et al. [31] observe that the QBF encoding implemented in `HyperQube` outperforms the SMT-based approach by Wang et al. [39]. In this section, we evaluate `AutoHyper` on these planning-hyperproperties and compare it with `HyperQube`[8].

We depict the results in Table 3. It is evident that `AutoHyper` outperforms `HyperQube`, sometimes by orders of magnitude. This is surprising as planning problems (which are essentially reachability problems) on symbolic systems should be advantageous for symbolic methods such as BMC. The large size of the in-

---

[5] Linearizability asserts that any execution of a concurrent data structure corresponds to a sequential execution, which is naturally expressed as a $\forall\exists$ hyperproperty.

[6] For the two verification instances (Bakery$_3$,φ_{S3}) and (NRP : $T_{incorrect}$, φ_{fair}) `HyperQube` provides the wrong verification result. We mark such instances with a "!" to avoid confusion when comparing Table 2 with [31, Table 2]. In particular, the supposedly unfair version of the NRP protocol is, in fact, fair.

[7] The automata use a symbolic alphabet with up to 18 letters. A conversion to an explicit alphabet – as required for `RABIT`, `BAIT`, and `FORKLIFT` – is thus infeasible (this would require 2^{18} symbols).

[8] `AutoHyper` is intended as a model checking tool, i.e., it only checks if a property holds or is violated. However, as we show in the full version [9], we could use the counterexamples returned by the inclusion checker to *synthesize* an actual plan.

Table 3: We evaluate HyperQube and AutoHyper on hyperproperties that encode the existence of a shortest path (φ_{sp}) and robust path (φ_{rp}). We give the specification (Spec), the size of the grid (Grid), and the times taken by HyperQube and AutoHyper (t). For HyperQube, we additionally give the unrolling depth used (k) and the file size of the QBF generated ($|QBF|$). For AutoHyper, we additionally give the size of the generated explicit state space (Size). Times are given in seconds. The timeout is set to 20 min and indicated by a "-".

| Spec | Grid | HyperQube [31] | | | AutoHyper | |
		k	$|QBF|$	t	Size	t
φ_{sp}	10×10	20	8 MB	4.6	146	**0.7**
	20×20	40	26 MB	168.1	188	**1.5**
	40×40	80	-	-	408	**22.7**
	60×60	120	-	-	404	**88.8**
φ_{rp}	10×10	20	13 MB	4.2	266	**0.6**
	20×20	40	84 MB	22.4	572	**0.7**
	40×40	80	419 MB	265.0	1212	**1.6**
	60×60	120	-	-	1852	**3.7**

termediate QBF indicates that a more optimized encoding (perhaps specific to path planning) could improve the performance of BMC on such examples.

7.4   Bounded vs. Explicit-State Model Checking

Bounded model checking has seen remarkable success in the verification of trace properties and frequently scales to systems whose size is well out of scope for explicit-state methods [20]. Similarly, in the context of *alternation-free* hyperproperties, symbolic verification tools such as MCHyper [29] (which internally reduces to the verification of a circuit using ABC [12]) can verify systems that are well beyond the reach of explicit-state methods. In contrast, in the context of model checking for hyperproperties that involve *quantifier alternations*, our findings make a strong case for the use of explicit-state methods (as implemented in AutoHyper):

First, compared to symbolic methods (such as BMC), explicit-state model checking is currently the only method that is *complete*. While BMC was able to verify or refute all properties in Tables 2 and 3, many instances cannot be solved with the current BMC encoding. As a concrete example, BMC can *never* verify formulas whose body contains simple invariants (such as GNI) and can thus not verify any of the instances in Table 1. The most significant advantage of explicit-state MC (as implemented in AutoHyper) is thus that it is both push-button and complete, i.e., it can – at least in theory – verify or refute all properties.

Second, the performance of `AutoHyper` seems to be *on-par* with that of BMC and frequently outperforms it (even by several orders of magnitude, cf. Table 3). We stress that this is despite the fact that for the evaluation of `HyperQube` we already fix an unrolling depth and unrolling semantics, thus creating favorable conditions for `HyperQube`.[9] While BMC for trace properties reduces to SAT solving, BMC of hyperproperties reduces to QBF solving; a problem that is much harder and has seen less support by industry-strength tools. It is, therefore, unclear whether the advance of modern QBF solvers can improve the performance of hyperproperty BMC, to the same degree that the advance of SAT solvers has stimulated the success of BMC for trace properties. Our findings seem to indicate that, at the moment, QBF solving (often) seems inferior to an explicit (automata-based) solving strategy.

8   Evaluating Strategy-based Verification

So far, we have used `AutoHyper` to check hyperproperties on instances arising in the literature. In this last section, we demonstrate that `AutoHyper` also serves as a valuable baseline to evaluate different (possibly incomplete) verification methods. Here we focus on strategy-based verification (SBV), i.e., the idea of automatically synthesizing a strategy that resolves existential quantification in $\forall^*\exists^*$ HyperLTL properties [19,7].

8.1   Effectiveness of Strategy-based Verification

SBV is known to be incomplete [19,7]. However, due to the previous lack of *complete* tools for verifying $\forall^*\exists^*$ properties, a detailed study into how effective SBV is in practice was impossible on a larger scale (i.e., beyond hand-crafted examples). With `AutoHyper`, we can, for the first time, rigorously evaluate SBV. We use the SBV implementation from [7], which synthesizes a strategy for the $\exists$-player by translating the formula to a deterministic parity automaton (DPA) [35] and phrases the synthesizes as a parity game.

We have generated random transition systems and properties of varying sizes and computed a ground truth using `AutoHyper`. We then performed SBV (recall that SBV can never show that a property does not hold and might fail to establish that it does). We find that for our generated instances, the property holds in **61.1%** of the cases, and SBV can verify the property in **60.4%** of the cases. Successful verification with SBV is thus possible in many cases, even without the addition of expensive mechanisms such as prophecies [7]. On the other hand, our results show that random generation produces instances (albeit not many)

---

[9] In Tables 2 and 3, we perform a single query with a fixed unrolling depth k and semantics, i.e., we already know if we want to show satisfaction or violation and the depth needed to show this (as done in [31]). In a classical BMC loop, we would check for satisfaction and violation with an incrementally increasing unrolling depth and thus perform roughly $2k$ many QBF queries where k is the least bound for which satisfaction or violation can be established (if this bound even exists).

on which SBV fails (so far, examples where SBV fails required careful construction by hand). Reverting to SBV as the default verification strategy is thus not possible, further strengthening the case for complete model checking tools (of which AutoHyper is the first).

8.2 Efficiency of Strategy-based Verification

After having analyzed the effectiveness of SBV (i.e., how many instances *can* be verified), we turn our attention to the efficiency of SBV. In theory, (automata-based) model checking of $\forall^*\exists^*$ HyperLTL – as implemented in AutoHyper – is EXPSPACE-complete in the specification and PSPACE-complete in the size of the system [15,36]. Conversely, SBV is 2-EXPTIME-complete in the size of the specification but only PTIME in the size of the system [19]. Consequently, one would expect that ABV fares better on larger specifications and SBV fares better on larger systems (the more important measure in practice).

However, in this section, we show that this does not translate into practice (at least using the current implementation of SBV [7]). We compare the running time of AutoHyper (ABV) (using

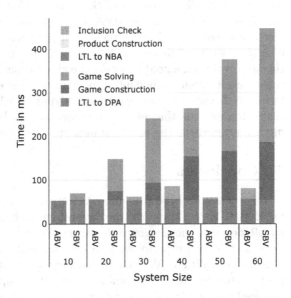

Fig. 3: We compare ABV (AutoHyper) and SBV ([7]) on instances of varying system size. We fix the property size to 20. We generate 100 random instances for each size and take the average over the fastest L instances, where L is the minimum number of instances solved within a 5s timeout by both methods.

spot's inclusion checker) and SBV. We break the running time into the three main steps for each method. For ABV, this is the LTL-to-NBA translation, the construction of the product automaton, and the inclusion check. For SBV, it is the LTL-to-DPA translation, the construction of the game, and the game-solving.

We depict the average cost for varying system sizes in Figure 3. We observe that SBV performs worse than ABV and, more importantly, scales poorly in the size of the system. This is contrary to the theoretical analysis of ABV and SBV. As the detailed breakdown of the running time suggests, the poor performance is due to the costly construction of the game and the time taken to solve the game. An almost identical picture emerges if we compare ABV in SBV relative to the property size (we give a plot in the full version [9]). While, in this case, the results match the theory (i.e., SBV scales worse in the size of the specification), we find that the bottleneck for SBV is not the LTL-to-DPA translation (which, in theory, is exponentially more expensive than the LTL-to-NBA translation used in ABV), but, again the construction and solving of the parity game.

We remark that the SBV engine we used [7] is not optimized and always constructs the full (reachable) game graph. The poor performance of SBV can be attributed to the fact that the size of the game does, in the worst case, scale quadratically in the size of the system (when considering $\forall^1 \exists^1$ properties). This is amplified in dense systems (i.e., systems with many transitions), as, with increasing transition density, the size of the parity games approaches its worst-case size (see the full version [9]). In contrast, the heavily optimized inclusion checker (in this case spot) seems to be able to check inclusion in almost constant time (despite being exponential in theory). This efficiency of mature language inclusion checkers is what enables AutoHyper to achieve remarkable performance that often exceeds that of symbolic methods such as BMC (cf. Section 7) and further strengthens the practical impact of Proposition 1.

9   Conclusion

In this paper, we have presented AutoHyper, the first complete model checker for HyperLTL with an arbitrary quantifier prefix. We have demonstrated that AutoHyper can check many interesting properties involving quantifier alternations and often outperforms symbolic methods such as BMC, sometimes by orders of magnitude. We believe the biggest advantage of AutoHyper to be its push-button functionality combined with its completeness: As a user, one does not need to worry whether AutoHyper is applicable to a particular property (different from, e.g., SBV or BMC) and does not need to provide hints (e.g., in the form of explicit strategies in SBV).

Apart from evaluating AutoHyper's performance on a range of benchmarks, we have used AutoHyper to (1) compare various backend language inclusion checkers, (2) explore practical verification beyond one quantifier alternation (which is not as infeasible as suggested by the theory), and (3) rigorously evaluate the effectiveness and efficiency of strategy-based verification in practice (which, different than suggested by a theoretical analysis, performs worse than automata-based methods).

Acknowledgments. This work was partially supported by the DFG in project 389792660 (Center for Perspicuous Systems, TRR 248), and by by the ERC Grant HYPER (No. 101055412). R. Beutner carried out this work as a member of the Saarbrücken Graduate School of Computer Science.

Data Availability Statement

AutoHyper and all experiments are available at [4].

References

1. Babiak, T., Blahoudek, F., Duret-Lutz, A., Klein, J., Kretínský, J., Müller, D., Parker, D., Strejcek, J.: The Hanoi omega-automata format. In: International Conference on Computer Aided Verification, CAV 2015. LNCS, vol. 9206. Springer (2015). https://doi.org/10.1007/978-3-319-21690-4_31
2. Baier, C., Katoen, J.P.: Principles of model checking. MIT press (2008)
3. Barthe, G., D'Argenio, P.R., Rezk, T.: Secure information flow by self-composition. Math. Struct. Comput. Sci. **21**(6) (2011). https://doi.org/10.1017/S0960129511000193
4. Beutner, R.: AutoHyper: Explicit-state model checking for HyperLTL (2023). https://doi.org/10.5281/zenodo.7309986
5. Beutner, R., Carral, D., Finkbeiner, B., Hofmann, J., Krötzsch, M.: Deciding hyperproperties combined with functional specifications. In: Annual ACM/IEEE Symposium on Logic in Computer Science, LICS 2022. ACM (2022). https://doi.org/10.1145/3531130.3533369
6. Beutner, R., Finkbeiner, B.: A temporal logic for strategic hyperproperties. In: International Conference on Concurrency Theory, CONCUR 2021. LIPIcs, vol. 203. Schloss Dagstuhl (2021). https://doi.org/10.4230/LIPIcs.CONCUR.2021.24
7. Beutner, R., Finkbeiner, B.: Prophecy variables for hyperproperty verification. In: IEEE Computer Security Foundations Symposium, CSF 2022. IEEE (2022). https://doi.org/10.1109/CSF54842.2022.00030, https://arxiv.org/abs/2206.01797
8. Beutner, R., Finkbeiner, B.: Software verification of hyperproperties beyond k-safety. In: International Conference on Computer Aided Verification, CAV 2022. LNCS, vol. 13371. Springer (2022). https://doi.org/10.1007/978-3-031-13185-1_17
9. Beutner, R., Finkbeiner, B.: AutoHyper: Explicit-state model checking for HyperLTL. CoRR **abs/2301.11229** (2023). https://doi.org/10.48550/arXiv.2301.11229
10. Beutner, R., Finkbeiner, B.: HyperATL*: A logic for hyperproperties in multi-agent systems. CoRR **abs/2203.07283** (2023). https://doi.org/10.48550/arXiv.2203.07283
11. Biere, A., Cimatti, A., Clarke, E.M., Zhu, Y.: Symbolic model checking without BDDs. In: International Conference on Tools and Algorithms for Construction and Analysis of Systems, TACAS 1999. LNCS, vol. 1579. Springer (1999). https://doi.org/10.1007/3-540-49059-0_14
12. Brayton, R.K., Mishchenko, A.: ABC: an academic industrial-strength verification tool. In: International Conference on Computer Aided Verification, CAV 2010. LNCS, vol. 6174. Springer (2010). https://doi.org/10.1007/978-3-642-14295-6_5
13. Cimatti, A., Clarke, E.M., Giunchiglia, E., Giunchiglia, F., Pistore, M., Roveri, M., Sebastiani, R., Tacchella, A.: NuSMV 2: An opensource tool for symbolic model checking. In: International Conference on Computer Aided Verification, CAV 2002,Copenhagen. LNCS, vol. 2404. Springer (2002). https://doi.org/10.1007/3-540-45657-0_29
14. Clarke, E.M., Kroening, D., Ouaknine, J., Strichman, O.: Completeness and complexity of bounded model checking. In: International Conference on Verification, Model Checking, and Abstract Interpretation, VMCAI 2004. LNCS, vol. 2937. Springer (2004). https://doi.org/10.1007/978-3-540-24622-0_9
15. Clarkson, M.R., Finkbeiner, B., Koleini, M., Micinski, K.K., Rabe, M.N., Sánchez, C.: Temporal logics for hyperproperties. In: International Conference on Principles of Security and Trust, POST 2014. LNCS, vol. 8414. Springer (2014). https://doi.org/10.1007/978-3-642-54792-8_15

16. Clarkson, M.R., Schneider, F.B.: Hyperproperties. In: IEEE Computer Security Foundations Symposium, CSF 2008. IEEE (2008). https://doi.org/10.1109/CSF. 2008.7

17. Clemente, L., Mayr, R.: Efficient reduction of nondeterministic automata with application to language inclusion testing. Log. Methods Comput. Sci. **15**(1) (2019). https://doi.org/10.23638/LMCS-15(1:12)2019

18. Coenen, N., Finkbeiner, B., Frenkel, H., Hahn, C., Metzger, N., Siber, J.: Temporal causality in reactive systems. In: International Symposium on Automated Technology for Verification and Analysis, ATVA 2022. LNCS, vol. 13505. Springer (2022). https://doi.org/10.1007/978-3-031-19992-9_13

19. Coenen, N., Finkbeiner, B., Sánchez, C., Tentrup, L.: Verifying hyperliveness. In: International Conference on Computer Aided Verification, CAV 2019. LNCS, vol. 11561. Springer (2019). https://doi.org/10.1007/978-3-030-25540-4_7

20. Copty, F., Fix, L., Fraer, R., Giunchiglia, E., Kamhi, G., Tacchella, A., Vardi, M.Y.: Benefits of bounded model checking at an industrial setting. In: International Conference on Computer Aided Verification, CAV 2001. LNCS, vol. 2102. Springer (2001). https://doi.org/10.1007/3-540-44585-4_43

21. Courcoubetis, C., Vardi, M.Y., Wolper, P., Yannakakis, M.: Memory-efficient algorithms for the verification of temporal properties. Formal Methods Syst. Des. **1**(2/3) (1992). https://doi.org/10.1007/BF00121128

22. D'Argenio, P.R., Barthe, G., Biewer, S., Finkbeiner, B., Hermanns, H.: Is your software on dope? - formal analysis of surreptitiously "enhanced" programs. In: European Symposium on Programming, ESOP 2017. LNCS, vol. 10201. Springer (2017). https://doi.org/10.1007/978-3-662-54434-1_4

23. Doherty, S., Detlefs, D., Groves, L., Flood, C.H., Luchangco, V., Martin, P.A., Moir, M., Shavit, N., Jr., G.L.S.: DCAS is not a silver bullet for nonblocking algorithm design. In: Annual ACM Symposium on Parallelism in Algorithms and Architectures, SPAA 2004. ACM (2004). https://doi.org/10.1145/1007912.1007945

24. Doveri, K., Ganty, P., Mazzocchi, N.: FORQ-based language inclusion formal testing. In: International Conference on Computer Aided Verification, CAV 2022. LNCS, vol. 13372. Springer (2022). https://doi.org/10.1007/978-3-031-13188-2_6

25. Doveri, K., Ganty, P., Parolini, F., Ranzato, F.: Inclusion testing of Büchi automata based on well-quasiorders. In: International Conference on Concurrency Theory, CONCUR 2021. LIPIcs, vol. 203. Schloss Dagstuhl (2021). https://doi.org/10.4230/LIPIcs.CONCUR.2021.3

26. Duret-Lutz, A., Renault, E., Colange, M., Renkin, F., Aisse, A.G., Schlehuber-Caissier, P., Medioni, T., Martin, A., Dubois, J., Gillard, C., Lauko, H.: From Spot 2.0 to Spot 2.10: What's new? In: International Conference on Computer Aided Verification, CAV 2022. LNCS, vol. 13372. Springer (2022). https://doi.org/10.1007/978-3-031-13188-2_9

27. Fellner, A., Befrouei, M.T., Weissenbacher, G.: Mutation testing with hyperproperties. Softw. Syst. Model. **20**(2) (2021). https://doi.org/10.1007/s10270-020-00850-1

28. Fienberg, S.E.: A brief history of statistical models for network analysis and open challenges. Journal of Computational and Graphical Statistics **21**(4) (2012)

29. Finkbeiner, B., Rabe, M.N., Sánchez, C.: Algorithms for model checking HyperLTL and HyperCTL*. In: International Conference on Computer Aided Verification, CAV 2015. LNCS, vol. 9206. Springer (2015). https://doi.org/10.1007/978-3-319-21690-4_3

30. Herlihy, M., Wing, J.M.: Linearizability: A correctness condition for concurrent objects. ACM Trans. Program. Lang. Syst. **12**(3) (1990). https://doi.org/10.1145/78969.78972
31. Hsu, T., Sánchez, C., Bonakdarpour, B.: Bounded model checking for hyperproperties. In: International Conference on Tools and Algorithms for the Construction and Analysis of Systems, TACAS 2021. LNCS, vol. 12651. Springer (2021). https://doi.org/10.1007/978-3-030-72016-2_6
32. Jamroga, W., Mauw, S., Melissen, M.: Fairness in non-repudiation protocols. In: International Workshop on Security and Trust Management, STM 2011. LNCS, vol. 7170. Springer (2011). https://doi.org/10.1007/978-3-642-29963-6_10
33. Lamport, L.: A new solution of dijkstra's concurrent programming problem. Commun. ACM **17**(8) (1974). https://doi.org/10.1145/361082.361093
34. McCullough, D.: Noninterference and the composability of security properties. In: IEEE Symposium on Security and Privacy, SP 1988. IEEE (1988). https://doi.org/10.1109/SECPRI.1988.8110
35. Piterman, N.: From nondeterministic Büchi and Streett automata to deterministic parity automata. Log. Methods Comput. Sci. **3**(3) (2007). https://doi.org/10.2168/LMCS-3(3:5)2007
36. Rabe, M.N.: A temporal logic approach to Information-flow control. Ph.D. thesis, Saarland University (2016)
37. Smith, G., Volpano, D.M.: Secure information flow in a multi-threaded imperative language. In: ACM SIGPLAN-SIGACT Symposium on Principles of Programming Languages, POPL 1998. ACM (1998). https://doi.org/10.1145/268946.268975
38. Tsai, M., Tsay, Y., Hwang, Y.: GOAL for games, omega-automata, and logics. In: International Conference on Computer Aided Verification, CAV 2013. LNCS, vol. 8044. Springer (2013). https://doi.org/10.1007/978-3-642-39799-8_62
39. Wang, Y., Nalluri, S., Pajic, M.: Hyperproperties for robotics: Planning via HyperLTL. In: IEEE International Conference on Robotics and Automation, ICRA 2020. IEEE (2020). https://doi.org/10.1109/ICRA40945.2020.9196874

Machine Learning/Neural Networks

Feature Necessity & Relevancy in ML Classifier Explanations

Xuanxiang Huang[1], Martin C. Cooper[2], Antonio Morgado[3],
Jordi Planes[4], and Joao Marques-Silva[5]($\boxtimes$)

[1] University of Toulouse, Toulouse, France xuanxiang.huang@univ-toulouse.fr
[2] Univ. Paul Sabatier, IRIT, Toulouse, France martin.cooper@irit.fr
[3] Universitat de Lleida, Lleida, Spain antonio.morgado@udl.cat
[4] Universitat de Lleida, Lleida, Spain jordi.planes@udl.cat
[5] IRIT, CNRS, Toulouse, France joao.marques-silva@irit.fr

Abstract. Given a machine learning (ML) model and a prediction, explanations can be defined as sets of features which are sufficient for the prediction. In some applications, and besides asking for an explanation, it is also critical to understand whether sensitive features can occur in some explanation, or whether a non-interesting feature must occur in all explanations. This paper starts by relating such queries respectively with the problems of relevancy and necessity in logic-based abduction. The paper then proves membership and hardness results for several families of ML classifiers. Afterwards the paper proposes concrete algorithms for two classes of classifiers. The experimental results confirm the scalability of the proposed algorithms.

Keywords: Formal Explainability · Abduction · Abstraction Refinement.

1 Introduction

The remarkable achievements in machine learning (ML) in recent years [12,32,47] are not matched by a comparable degree of trust. The most promising ML models are inscrutable in their operation. As a direct consequence, the opacity of ML models raises distrust in their use and deployment. Motivated by a critical need for helping human decision makers to grasp the decisions made by ML models, there has been extensive work on explainable AI (XAI). Well-known examples include so-called model agnostic explainers or alternatives based on saliency maps for neural networks [9,50,58,59]. While most XAI approaches do not offer guarantees of rigor, and so can produce explanations that are unsound given the underlying ML model, there have been efforts on developing rigorous XAI approaches over the last few years [40,54,63]. Rigorous explainability involves the computation of explanations, but also the ability to answer a wide range of related queries [7,8,36].

By building on the relationship between explainability and logic-based abduction [25,30,40,61], this paper analyzes two concrete queries, namely feature

© The Author(s) 2023
S. Sankararayanan and N. Sharygina (Eds.): TACAS 2023, LNCS 13993, pp. 167–186, 2023.
https://doi.org/10.1007/978-3-031-30823-9_9

necessity and relevancy. Given an ML classifier, an instance (i.e. point in feature space and associated prediction) and a target feature, the goal of feature necessity is to decide whether the target feature occurs in *all* explanations of the given instance. Under the same assumptions, the goal of feature relevancy is to decide whether a feature occurs in *some* explanation of the given instance. This paper proves a number of complexity results regarding feature necessity and relevancy, focusing on well-known families of classifiers, some of which are widely used in ML. Moreover, the paper proposes novel algorithms for deciding relevancy for two families of classifiers. The experimental results demonstrate the scalability of the proposed algorithms.

The paper is organized as follows. The notation and definitions used throughout are presented in Section 2. The problems of feature necessity and relevancy are studied in Section 3, and example algorithms are proposed in Section 4. Section 5 presents experimental results for a sample of families of classifiers, Section 6 relates our contribution with earlier work and Section 7 concludes the paper.

2   Preliminaries

Complexity classes, propositional logic & quantification.   The paper assumes basic knowledge of computational complexity, namely the classes of decision problems P, NP and Σ_2^P [6]. The paper also assumes basic knowledge of propositional logic, including the Boolean satisfiability (SAT) problem for propositional logic formulas in conjunctive normal form (CNF), and the use of SAT solvers as oracles for the complexity class NP. The interested reader is referred to textbooks on these topics [6, 13].

2.1   Classification Problems

Throughout the paper, we will consider classifiers as the underlying ML model. Classification problems are defined on a set of features (or attributes) $\mathcal{F} = \{1, \ldots, m\}$ and a set of classes $\mathcal{K} = \{c_1, c_2, \ldots, c_K\}$. Each feature $i \in \mathcal{F}$ takes values from a domain $\mathbb{D}_i$. Domains are categorical or ordinal, and each domain can be defined on boolean, integer/discrete or real values. Feature space is defined as $\mathbb{F} = \mathbb{D}_1 \times \mathbb{D}_2 \times \ldots \times \mathbb{D}_m$. The notation $\mathbf{x} = (x_1, \ldots, x_m)$ denotes an arbitrary point in feature space, where each x_i is a variable taking values from $\mathbb{D}_i$. The set of variables associated with the features is $X = \{x_1, \ldots, x_m\}$. Also the notation $\mathbf{v} = (v_1, \ldots, v_m)$ represents a specific point in feature space, where each v_i is a constant representing one concrete value from $\mathbb{D}_i$. A classifier $\mathbb{C}$ is characterized by a (non-constant) *classification function* κ that maps feature space $\mathbb{F}$ into the set of classes $\mathcal{K}$, i.e. $\kappa : \mathbb{F} \to \mathcal{K}$. An *instance* denotes a pair $(\mathbf{v}, c)$, where $\mathbf{v} \in \mathbb{F}$ and $c \in \mathcal{K}$, with $c = \kappa(\mathbf{v})$.

2.2   Examples of Classifiers

The results presented in the paper apply to a comprehensive range of widely used classifiers [28, 62]. These include, decision trees (DTs) [18, 42], decision graphs (DGs) [44] and diagrams (DDs) [1, 68], decision lists (DLs) [38, 60] and sets (DSs) [19, 41], tree ensembles (TEs) [37], including random forests (RFs) [17, 43] and boosted trees (BTs) [29], neural networks (NNs) [56], naive bayes classifiers (NBCs) [45, 52], classifiers represented with propositional languages, including deterministic decomposable negation normal form (d-DNNFs) [23, 35] and its proper subsets, e.g. sentential decision diagrams (SDDs) [22, 66] and free binary decision diagrams (FBDDs) [23, 31, 68], and also monotonic classifiers. In the rest of the paper, we will analyze some families of classifiers in more detail.

d-DNNF classifiers.   Negation normal form (NNF) is a well-known propositional language, where the negation operators are restricted to atoms, or inputs. Any propositional formula can de reduced to NNF in polynomial time. Let the *support* of a node be the set of atoms associated with leaves reachable from the outgoing edges of the node. Decomposable NNF (DNNF) is a restriction of NNF where the children of AND nodes do not share atoms in their support. A DNNF circuit is *deterministic* (referred to as d-DNNF) if any two children of OR nodes cannot both take value 1 for any assignment to the inputs. Restrictions of NNF including DNNF and d-DNNF exhibit important tractability properties [23]. Besides, we briefly introduce FBDDs which is a proper subset of d-DNNFs. An FBDD over a set X of Boolean variables is a rooted, directed acyclic graph comprising two types of nodes: *nonterminal* and *terminal*. A nonterminal node is labeled by a variable $x_i \in X$, and has two outgoing edges, one labeled by 0 and the other by 1. A terminal node is labeled by a 1 or 0, and has no outgoing edges. For a subgraph rooted at a node labeled with a variable x_i, it represents a boolean function f which is defined by the *Shannon expansion*: $f = (x_i \wedge f|_{x_i=1}) \vee (\neg x_i \wedge f|_{x_i=0})$, where $f|_{x_i=1}$ ($f|_{x_i=0}$) denotes the *cofactor* [16] of f with respect to $x_i = 1$ ($x_i = 0$). Moreover, any FBDD is *read-once*, meaning that each variable is tested at most once on any path from the root node to a terminal node.

Monotonic classifiers.   Monotonic classifiers find a number of important applications, and have been studied extensively in recent years [26, 48, 65, 70]. Let $\preccurlyeq$ denote a partial order on the set of classes $\mathcal{K}$. For example, we assume $c_1 \preccurlyeq c_2 \preccurlyeq \ldots c_K$. Furthermore, we assume that each domain D_i is ordered such that the value taken by feature i is between a lower bound $\lambda(i)$ and an upper bound $\mu(i)$. Given $\mathbf{v}_1 = (v_{11}, \ldots, v_{1i}, \ldots, v_{1m})$ and $\mathbf{v}_2 = (v_{21}, \ldots, v_{2i}, \ldots, v_{2m})$, we say that $\mathbf{v}_1 \leq \mathbf{v}_2$ if $\forall (i \in \mathcal{F}).(v_{1i} \leq v_{2i})$. Finally, a classifier is monotonic if whenever $\mathbf{v}_1 \leq \mathbf{v}_2$, then $\kappa(\mathbf{v}_1) \preccurlyeq \kappa(\mathbf{v}_2)$.

Running examples.   As hinted above, throughout the paper, we will consider two fairly different families of classifiers, namely classifiers represented with d-DNNFs and monotonic classifiers.

Example 1. The first example is the d-DNNF classifier $\mathbb{C}_1$ shown in Fig. 1. It represents the boolean function $(x_1 \wedge (x_2 \vee x_4)) \vee (\neg x_1 \wedge x_3 \wedge x_4)$. The instance considered throughout the paper is $(\mathbf{v}_1, c_1) = ((0, 1, 0, 0), 0)$.

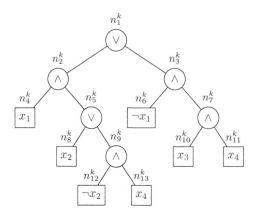

$$\mathcal{F}_1 = \{1, 2, 3, 4\}$$
$$\mathbb{D}_{1i} = \{0, 1\}, i = 1, \ldots, 4$$
$$\mathcal{K}_1 = \{0, 1\}$$

(b) Definition of $\mathcal{F}_1, \mathbb{D}_{1i}, \mathcal{K}_1$

IF $x_1 = 1 \wedge x_2 = 1$ THEN 1
ELSE IF $x_1 = 1 \wedge x_4 = 1$ THEN 1
ELSE IF $x_3 = 1 \wedge x_4 = 1$ THEN 1
ELSE   0

(c) Alternative representation of κ_1

(a) Graphical representation of d-DDNF, i.e. κ_1

Fig. 1: Example of d-DDNF classifier

$$\mathcal{F}_2 = \{1, 2, 3, 4\}$$
$$\mathbb{D}_{2i} = \{0, 1\}, i = 1, \ldots, 4$$
$$\mathcal{K}_2 = \{0, 1\}$$

$$\kappa_2(\mathbf{x}) = \begin{cases} 1 & \text{if } x_1 + x_2 + x_3 \geq 2 \\ 0 & \text{otherwise} \end{cases}$$

(a) Definition of $\mathcal{F}_2, \mathbb{D}_{2i}, \mathcal{K}_2$

(b) Definition of κ_2

Fig. 2: Example of a monotonic classifier

Example 2. The second running example is the monotonic classifier $\mathbb{C}_2$ shown in Fig. 2. The instance that is considered throughout the paper is $(\mathbf{v}_2, c_2) = ((1, 1, 1, 1), 1)$.

2.3   Formal Explainability

Prime implicant (PI) explanations [63] represent a minimal set of literals (relating a feature value x_i and a constant $v_i \in \mathbb{D}_i$) that are logically sufficient for the prediction. PI-explanations are related with logic-based abduction, and so are also referred to as abductive explanations (AXp's) [54]. AXp's offer guarantees of rigor that are not offered by other alternative explanation approaches. More recently, AXp's have been studied in terms of their computational complexity [7, 10]. There is a growing body of recent work on formal explanations [3–5, 14, 15, 24, 27, 33, 51, 54, 67].

Formally, given $\mathbf{v} = (v_1, \ldots, v_m) \in \mathbb{F}$, with $\kappa(\mathbf{v}) = c$, an AXp is any subset-minimal set $\mathcal{X} \subseteq \mathcal{F}$ such that,

$$\mathsf{WAXp}(\mathcal{X}) \quad := \quad \forall (\mathbf{x} \in \mathbb{F}). \left[\bigwedge_{i \in \mathcal{X}} (x_i = v_i) \right] \rightarrow (\kappa(\mathbf{x}) = c) \tag{1}$$

If a set $\mathcal{X} \subseteq \mathcal{F}$ is not minimal but (1) holds, then $\mathcal{X}$ is referred to as a *weak* AXp. Clearly, the predicate WAXp maps $2^{\mathcal{F}}$ into $\{\perp, \top\}$ (or $\{\textbf{false}, \textbf{true}\}$). Given $\mathbf{v} \in \mathbb{F}$, an AXp $\mathcal{X}$ represents an irreducible (or minimal) subset of the features which, if assigned the values dictated by $\mathbf{v}$, are sufficient for the prediction c, i.e. value changes to the features not in $\mathcal{X}$ will not change the prediction. We can use the definition of the predicate WAXp to formalize the definition of the predicate AXp, also defined on subsets $\mathcal{X}$ of $\mathcal{F}$:

$$\mathsf{AXp}(\mathcal{X}) \quad := \quad \mathsf{WAXp}(\mathcal{X}) \wedge \forall(\mathcal{X}' \subsetneq \mathcal{X}).\neg\mathsf{WAXp}(\mathcal{X}') \tag{2}$$

The definition of WAXp($\mathcal{X}$) ensures that the predicate is *monotone*. Indeed, if $\mathcal{X} \subseteq \mathcal{X}' \subseteq \mathcal{F}$, and if $\mathcal{X}$ is a weak AXp, then $\mathcal{X}'$ is also a weak AXp, as the fixing of more features will not change the prediction. Given the monotonicity of predicate WAXp, the definition of predicate AXp can be simplified as follows, with $\mathcal{X} \subseteq \mathcal{F}$:

$$\mathsf{AXp}(\mathcal{X}) := \mathsf{WAXp}(\mathcal{X}) \wedge \forall(j \in \mathcal{X}).\neg\mathsf{WAXp}(\mathcal{X} \setminus \{j\}) \tag{3}$$

This simpler but equivalent definition of AXp has important practical significance, in that only a linear number of subsets needs to be checked for, as opposed to exponentially many subsets in (2). As a result, the algorithms that compute one AXp are based on (3) [54].

Example 3. From Example 1, and given the instance $((0, 1, 0, 0), 0)$, we can conclude that the prediction will be 0 if features 1 and 3 take value 0, or if features 1 and 4 take value 0. Hence, the AXp's are $\{1, 3\}$ and $\{1, 4\}$. It is also apparent that the assignment $x_2 = 1$ bears no relevance on the fact that the prediction is 0.

Example 4. From Example 2, we can conclude that any sum of two variables assigned value 1 suffices for the prediction. Hence, given the instance $((1, 1, 1, 1), 1)$, the possible AXp's are $\{1, 2\}$, $\{1, 3\}$, and $\{2, 3\}$. Observe that the definition of κ_2 does not depend on feature 4.

Besides abductive explanations, another commonly studied type of explanations are contrastive or counterfactual explanations [8, 36, 39, 55]. As argued in related work [36], the duality between abductive and contrastive explanations implies that for the purpose of the queries studied in this paper, it suffices to study solely abductive explanations.

3   Feature Relevancy & Necessity: Theory

This section investigates the complexity of feature relevancy and necessity[6]. We are interested in membership results, which allow us to devise algorithms for the target problems. We are also interested in hardness results, which serve to confirm that the running time complexities of the proposed algorithms are within reason, given the problem's complexity.

3.1   Defining Necessity, Relevancy & Irrelevancy

Throughout this section, a classifier $\mathbb{C}$ is assumed, with features $\mathcal{F}$, domains $\mathbb{D}_i$, $i \in \mathcal{F}$, classes $\mathcal{K}$, a classification function $\kappa : \mathbb{F} \to \mathcal{K}$, and a concrete instance $(\mathbf{v}, c)$, $\mathbf{v} \in \mathbb{F}, c \in \mathcal{K}$.

---

[6] For the sake of brevity, we opt to only present sketches of some of the proofs.

Definition 1 (Feature Necessity, Relevancy & Irrelevancy). Let $\mathbb{A}$ denote the set of all AXp's for a classifier given a concrete instance, i.e. $\mathbb{A} = \{\mathcal{X} \subseteq \mathcal{F} \mid \mathsf{AXp}(\mathcal{X})\}$, and let $t \in \mathcal{F}$ be a target feature. Then, (i) t is necessary if $t \in \cap_{\mathcal{X} \in \mathbb{A}} \mathcal{X}$; (ii) t is relevant if $t \in \cup_{\mathcal{X} \in \mathbb{A}} \mathcal{X}$; and (iii) t is irrelevant if $t \in \mathcal{F} \setminus \cup_{\mathcal{X} \in \mathbb{A}} \mathcal{X}$.

Throughout the remainder of the paper, the problem of deciding feature necessity is represented by the acronym FNP, and the problem of deciding feature relevancy is represented by the acronym FRP.

Example 5. As shown earlier, for the d-DNNF classifier of Fig. 1, and given the instance $(\mathbf{v}_1, c_1) = ((0, 1, 0, 0), 0)$, there exist two AXp's, i.e. $\{1, 3\}$ and $\{1, 4\}$. Clearly, feature 1 is necessary, and features 1, 3 and 4 are relevant. In contrast, feature 2 is irrelevant.

Example 6. For the monotonic classifier of Fig. 2, and given the instance $(\mathbf{v}_2, c_2) = ((1, 1, 1, 1), 1)$, we have argued earlier that there exist three AXp's, i.e. $\{1, 2\}$, $\{1, 3\}$ and $\{2, 3\}$, which allows us to conclude that features 1, 2 and 3 are relevant, but that feature 4 is irrelevant. In this case, there are no necessary features.

The general complexity of necessity and (ir)relevancy has been studied in the context of logic-based abduction [25, 30, 61]. Recent uses in explainability are briefly overviewed in Section 6.

3.2   Feature Necessity

Proposition 2. If deciding $\mathsf{WAXp}(\mathcal{X})$ is in complexity class $\mathfrak{C}$, then FNP is in the complexity class co-$\mathfrak{C}$.

Given the known polynomial complexity of deciding whether a set is a weak AXp for several families of classifiers [54], we then have the following result:

Corollary 3. For DTs, XpG's[7], NBCs, d-DNNF classifiers and monotonic classifiers, FNP is in P.

3.3   Feature Relevancy: Membership Results

Proposition 4 (Feature Relevancy for DTs [36]). FRP for DTs is in P.

Proposition 5. If deciding $\mathsf{WAXp}(\mathcal{X})$ is in P, then FRP is in NP.

The argument above can also be used for proving the following results.

Corollary 6. For XpG's, NBCs, d-DNNF classifiers and monotonic classifiers, FRP is in NP.

Proposition 7. If deciding $\mathsf{WAXp}(\mathcal{X})$ is in NP, then FRP is in Σ_2^P.

Corollary 8. For DLs, DSs, RFs, BTs, and NNs, FRP is in Σ_2^P.

Additional results.   The following result will prove useful in designing algorithms for FRP in practice.

Proposition 9. Let $\mathcal{X} \subseteq \mathcal{F}$, and let $t \in \mathcal{X}$ denote some target feature such that, $\mathsf{WAXp}(\mathcal{X})$ holds and $\mathsf{WAXp}(\mathcal{X} \setminus \{t\})$ does not hold. Then, for any AXp $\mathcal{Z} \subseteq \mathcal{X} \subseteq \mathcal{F}$, it must be the case that $t \in \mathcal{Z}$.

---

[7] Explanation graphs (XpG's) have been proposed to enable the computation of explanations for decision graphs, and (multi-valued) decision diagrams [36].

3.4   Feature Relevancy: Hardness Results

Proposition 10 (Relevancy for DNF Classifiers [36]). Feature relevancy for a
DNF classifier is Σ_2^P-hard.

Proposition 11. Feature relevancy for monotonic classifiers is NP-hard.

Proof. We say that a CNF is trivially satisfiable if some literal occurs in all
clauses. Clearly, SAT restricted to nontrivial CNFs is still NP-complete. Let Φ
be a not trivially satisfiable CNF on variables $x_1, \ldots, x_k$. Let $N = 2k$. Let $\tilde{\Phi}$ be
identical to Φ except that each occurrence of a negative literal x_i ($1 \le i \le k$) is
replaced by x_{i+k}. Thus $\tilde{\Phi}$ is a CNF on N variables each of which occur only posi-
tively. Define the boolean classifier κ (on $N+1$ features) by $\kappa(x_0, x_1, \ldots, x_N) = 1$
iff $x_i = x_{i+k} = 1$ for some $i \in \{1, \ldots, k\}$ or $x_0 \wedge \tilde{\Phi}(x_1, \ldots, x_N) = 1$. To show
that Φ is monotonic we need to show that $\mathbf{a} \le \mathbf{b} \Rightarrow \kappa(\mathbf{a}) \le \kappa(\mathbf{b})$. This follows by
examining the two cases in which $\kappa(\mathbf{a}) = 1$: if $a_i = a_{i+k} \wedge \mathbf{a} \le \mathbf{b}$, then $b_i = b_{i+k}$,
whereas, if $a_0 \wedge \tilde{\Phi}(a_1, \ldots, a_N) = 1$ and $\mathbf{a} \le \mathbf{b}$, then $b_0 \wedge \tilde{\Phi}(b_1, \ldots, b_N) = 1$ (by
positivity of $\tilde{\Phi}$), so in both cases $\kappa(\mathbf{b}) = 1 \ge \kappa(\mathbf{a})$.

Clearly $\kappa(\mathbf{1}_{N+1}) = 1$. There are k obvious AXp's of this prediction, namely
$\{i, i + k\}$ ($1 \le i \le k$). These are minimal by the assumption that Φ is not
trivially satisfiable. This means that no other AXp contains both i and $i + k$ for
any $i \in \{1, \ldots, k\}$. Suppose that $\Phi(\mathbf{u}) = 1$. Let $\mathcal{X}_u$ be $\{0\} \cup \{i \mid 1 \le i \le k \wedge u_i = 1\} \cup \{i + k \mid 1 \le i \le k \wedge u_i = 0\}$. Then $\mathcal{X}_u$ is a weak AXp of the prediction
$\kappa(1) = 1$. Furthermore $\mathcal{X}_u$ does not contain any of the AXp's $\{i, i+k\}$. Therefore
some subset of $\mathcal{X}$ is an AXp and clearly this subset must contain feature 0. Thus
if Φ is satisfiable, then there is an AXp which contains 0.

We now show that the converse also holds. If $\mathcal{X}$ is an AXp of $\kappa(\mathbf{1}_{N+1}) = 1$
containing 0, then it cannot also contain any of the pairs $i, i + k$ ($1 \le i \le k$),
otherwise we could delete 0 and still have an AXp. We will show that this implies
that we can build a satisfying assignment $\mathbf{u}$ for Φ. Consider first $\mathbf{v} = (v_0, \ldots, v_N)$
defined by $v_i = 1$ if $i \in \mathcal{X}$ ($0 \le i \le N$) and $v_{i+k} = 1$ if neither i nor $i+k$ belongs
to $\mathcal{X}$ ($1 \le i \le k$), and $v_i = 0$ otherwise ($1 \le i \le N$). Then $\kappa(\mathbf{v}) = 1$ by definition
of an AXp, since $\mathbf{v}$ agrees with the vector 1 on all features in $\mathcal{X}$. We can also
note that $v_0 = 1$ since $0 \in \mathcal{X}$. Since $\mathcal{X}$ does not contain i and $i + k$ ($1 \le i \le k$),
it follows that $v_i \ne v_{i+k}$. Now let $u_i = 1$ iff $i \in \mathcal{X} \wedge 1 \le i \le k$. It is easy to verify
that $\Phi(\mathbf{u}) = \tilde{\Phi}(\mathbf{v}) = \kappa(\mathbf{v}) = 1$.

Thus, determining whether $\kappa(\mathbf{1}_{N+1}) = 1$ has an AXp containing the feature
0 is equivalent to testing the satisfiability of Φ. It follows that FRP is NP-hard
for monotonic classifiers by this polynomial reduction from SAT. $\qquad\square$

Proposition 12. Relevancy for FBDD classifiers is NP-hard.

Proof. Let ψ be a CNF formula defined on a variable set $X = \{x_1, \ldots, x_m\}$ and
with clauses $\{\omega_1, \ldots, \omega_n\}$. We aim to construct an FBDD classifier $\mathcal{G}$ (representing a classification function κ) based on ψ and a target variable in polynomial
time, such that: ψ is SAT iff for κ there is an AXp containing this target variable.

For any literal $l_j \in \omega_i$, replace l_j with l_j^i. Let $\psi' = \{\omega_1', \ldots, \omega_n'\}$ denote the
resulting CNF formula defined on the new variables $\{x_1^1, \ldots, x_m^1, \ldots x_1^n, \ldots, x_m^n\}$.
For each original variable x_j, let I_j^+ and I_j^- denote the indices of clauses con-

taining literal x_j and $\neg x_j$, respectively. So if $i \in I_j^+$, then $x_j^i \in \omega_i'$, if $i \in I_j^-$, then $\neg x_j^i \in \omega_i'$. To build an FBDD D from ψ': 1) build an FBDD D_i for each ω_i'; 2) replace the terminal node 1 of D_i with the root node of D_{i+1}; D is read-once because each variable x_j^i occurs only once in ψ'. Satisfying a literal $x_j^i \in \omega_i'$ means $x_j = 1$, while satisfying a literal $\neg x_j^k \in \omega_k'$ means $x_j = 0$. If both x_j^i and $\neg x_j^k$ are satisfied, then it means we pick inconsistent values for the variable x_j, which is unacceptable. Let us define ϕ to capture inconsistent values for any variable x_j:

$$\phi := \bigvee_{1 \le j \le m} \left(\left(\bigvee_{i \in I_j^+} x_j^i \right) \wedge \left(\bigvee_{k \in I_j^-} \neg x_j^k \right) \right) \tag{4}$$

If $I_j^+ = \emptyset$, then let $\left(\bigvee_{i \in I_j^+} x_j^i \right) = 0$. If $I_j^- = \emptyset$, then let $\left(\bigvee_{k \in I_j^-} \neg x_j^k \right) = 0$. Any true point of ϕ means we pick inconsistent values for some variable x_j, so it represents an unacceptable point of ψ. To avoid such inconsistency, one needs to at least falsify either $\bigvee_{i \in I_j^+} x_j^i$ or $\bigvee_{k \in I_j^-} \neg x_j^k$ for each variable x_j. To build an FBDD G from ϕ: 1) build FBDDs G_j^+ and G_j^- for $\bigvee_{i \in I_j^+} x_j^i$ and $\bigvee_{k \in I_j^-} \neg x_j^k$, respectively; 2) replace the terminal node 1 of G_j^+ with the root node of G_j^-, let G_j denote the resulting FBDD; 3) replace the terminal 0 of G_j with the root node of G_{j+1}; G is read-once because each variable x_j^i occurs only once in ϕ.

Create a root node labeled x_0^0, link its 1-edge to the root of D, 0-edge to the root of G. The resulting graph $\mathcal{G}$ is an FBDD representing $\kappa := (x_0^0 \wedge \psi') \vee (\neg x_0^0 \wedge \phi)$, κ is a boolean classifier defined on $\{x_0^0, x_1^1, \ldots, x_m^n\}$ and x_0^0 is the target variable. The number of nodes of $\mathcal{G}$ is $O(n \times m)$. Let $\mathcal{I} = \{(0,0), (1,1), \ldots (n,m)\}$ denote the set of variable indices, for variable x_j^i, $(i,j) \in \mathcal{I}$.

Pick an instance $\mathbf{v} = \{v_0^0, \ldots, v_j^i, \ldots\}$ satisfying every literal of ψ' (i.e. $v_j^i = 1$ and $v_j^k = 0$ for $x_j^i, \neg x_j^k \in \psi'$) and such that $v_0^0 = 1$, then $\psi'(\mathbf{v}) = 1$, and so $\kappa(\mathbf{v}) = 1$. Suppose $\mathcal{X} \subseteq \mathcal{I}$ is an AXp of $\mathbf{v}$: 1) If $\{(i,j), (k,j)\} \subseteq \mathcal{X}$ for some variable x_j, where $i \in I_j^+$ and $k \in I_j^-$, then for any point $\mathbf{u}$ of κ such that $u_j^i = v_j^i$ for any $(i,j) \in \mathcal{X}$, we have $\kappa(\mathbf{u}) = 1$ and $\phi(\mathbf{u}) = 1$. Moreover, if $\mathbf{u}$ sets $u_0^0 = 1$, then $\kappa(\mathbf{u}) = 1$ implies $\psi'(\mathbf{u}) = 1$, else if $\mathbf{u}$ sets $u_0^0 = 0$, then $\kappa(\mathbf{u}) = 1$ because of $\phi(\mathbf{u}) = 1$. $\kappa(\mathbf{u}) = 1$ regardless the value of u_0^0, so $(0,0) \notin \mathcal{X}$. 2) If $\{(i,j), (k,j)\} \not\subseteq \mathcal{X}$ for any variable x_j, where $i \in I_j^+$ and $k \in I_j^-$, then for some point $\mathbf{u}$ of κ such that $u_j^i = v_j^i$ for any $(i,j) \in \mathcal{X}$, we have $\phi(\mathbf{u}) \ne 1$, in this case $\kappa(\mathbf{u}) = 1$ implies $\psi'(\mathbf{u}) = 1$, besides, any such $\mathbf{u}$ must set $u_0^0 = 1$, so $(0,0) \in \mathcal{X}$.

If case 2) occurs, then ψ is satisfiable. (a satisfying assignment is $x_j = 1$ iff $\exists i \in I_j^+$ s.t. $(i,j) \in \mathcal{X}$). If case 2) never occurs, then ψ is unsatisfiable. It follows that FRP is NP-hard for FBDD classifiers by this polynomial reduction from SAT.   □

Corollary 13. Relevancy for d-DNNF classifiers is NP-hard.

4   Feature Relevancy: Example Algorithms

This section details two methods for FRP. One method decides feature relevancy for d-DNNF classifiers, whereas the other method decides feature relevancy for

Table 1: Encoding for deciding whether there is a weak AXp including feature t.

Conditions	Constraints	Fml #
$\mathsf{Leaf}(j), \mathsf{Feat}(j,i), \mathsf{Sat}(\mathsf{Lit}(j), v_i)$	n_j^k	(1.1)
$\mathsf{Leaf}(j), \mathsf{Feat}(j,i), \neg\mathsf{Sat}(\mathsf{Lit}(j), v_i), i = k$	n_j^k	(1.2)
$\mathsf{Leaf}(j), \mathsf{Feat}(j,i), \neg\mathsf{Sat}(\mathsf{Lit}(j), v_i), i \neq k$	$n_j^k \leftrightarrow \neg s_i$	(1.3)
$\mathsf{NonLeaf}(j), \mathsf{Oper}(j) = \vee$	$n_j^k \leftrightarrow \bigvee_{l \in \mathsf{children}(j)} n_l^k$	(1.4)
$\mathsf{NonLeaf}(j), \mathsf{Oper}(j) = \wedge$	$n_j^k \leftrightarrow \bigwedge_{l \in \mathsf{children}(j)} n_l^k$	(1.5)
$\kappa(\mathbf{v}) = 0$	$\neg n_1^0$	(1.6)
$\kappa(\mathbf{v}) = 0$	$s_i \leftrightarrow n_1^i$	(1.7)
	s_t	(1.8)

arbitrary monotonic classifiers. Based on Proposition 2 and Corollary 3, existing algorithm for computing one AXp [35, 36, 52, 53] can be used to decide feature necessity. Hence, there is no need for devising new algorithms. Additionally, the weak AXp returned from the proposed methods (if it exist) can be fed (as a seed) into the algorithms of computing one AXp [35, 53] to extract one AXp in polynomial time.

4.1 Relevancy for d-DNNF Classifiers

This section details a propositional encoding that decides feature relevancy for d-DNNFs. The encoding follows the approach described in the proof of Proposition 9, and comprises two copies ($\mathbb{C}^0$ and $\mathbb{C}^t$) of the same d-DNNF classifier $\mathbb{C}$, $\mathbb{C}^0$ encodes $\mathsf{WAXp}(\mathcal{X})$ (i.e. the prediction of κ remains unchanged), $\mathbb{C}^t$ encodes $\neg\mathsf{WAXp}(\mathcal{X} \setminus \{t\})$ (i.e. the prediction of κ changes). The encoding is polynomial in the size of classifier's representation.

The encoding is applicable to the case $\kappa(\mathbf{x}) = 0$. The case $\kappa(\mathbf{x}) = 1$ can be transformed to $\neg\kappa(\mathbf{x}) = 0$, so we assume both d-DNNF $\mathbb{C}$ and its negation $\neg\mathbb{C}$ are given. To present the constraints included in this encoding, we need to introduce some auxiliary boolean variables and predicates.

1. $s_i, 1 \leq i \leq m$. s_i is a selector such that $s_i = 1$ iff feature i is included in a weak AXp candidate $\mathcal{X}$.
2. $n_j^k, 1 \leq j \leq |\mathbb{C}|$ and $0 \leq k \leq m$. n_j^k is the indicator of a node j of d-DNNF $\mathbb{C}$ for replica k. The indicator for the root node of k-th replica is n_1^k. Moreover, the semantics of n_j^k is $n_j^k = 1$ iff the sub-d-DNNF rooted at node j in k-th replica is consistent.
3. $\mathsf{Leaf}(j) = 1$ if the node j is a leaf node.
4. $\mathsf{NonLeaf}(j) = 1$ if the node j is a non-leaf node.
5. $\mathsf{Feat}(j,i) = 1$ if the leaf node j is labeled with feature i.
6. $\mathsf{Sat}(\mathsf{Lit}(j), v_i) = 1$ if for leaf node j, the literal on feature i is satisfied by v_i.

The encoding is summarized in Table 1. As literals are d-DNNF leafs, the values of the selector variables only affect the values of the indicator variables of leaf nodes. Constraint (1.1) states that for any leaf node j whose literal is consistent with the given instance, its indicator n_j^k is always consistent regardless of the value of s_i. On the contrary, constraint (1.3) states that for any leaf node j whose literal is inconsistent with the given instance, its indicator n_j^k is consistent iff feature i is not picked, in other words, feature i can take any value. Because replica k $(k > 0)$ is used to check the necessity of including feature k in $\mathcal{X}$, we assume the value of the local copy of selector s_k is 0 in replica k. In this case, as defined in constraint (1.2), even though leaf node j labeled feature k has a literal that is inconsistent with the given instance, its indicator n_j^k is consistent. Constraint (1.4) defines the indicator for an arbitrary $\vee$ node j. Constraint (1.5) defines the indicator for an arbitrary $\wedge$ node j. Together, these constraints declare how the consistency is propagated through the entire d-DNNF. Constraint (1.6) states that the prediction of the d-DNNF classifier $\mathbb{C}$ remains 0 since the selected features form a weak AXp. Constraint (1.7) states that if feature i is selected, then removing it will change the prediction of $\mathbb{C}$. Finally, constraint (1.8) indicates that feature t must be included in $\mathcal{X}$.

Example 7. Given the d-DNNF classifier of Fig. 1 and the instance $(\mathbf{v}_1, c_1) = ((0, 1, 0, 0), 0)$, suppose that the target feature is 3. We have selectors $\mathbf{s} = \{s_1, s_2, s_3, s_4\}$, and the encoding is as follows:

1. $(n_1^0 \leftrightarrow n_2^0 \vee n_3^0) \wedge (n_2^0 \leftrightarrow n_4^0 \wedge n_5^0) \wedge (n_3^0 \leftrightarrow n_6^0 \wedge n_7^0) \wedge (n_5^0 \leftrightarrow n_8^0 \vee n_9^0) \wedge$
   $(n_7^0 \leftrightarrow n_{10}^0 \wedge n_{11}^0) \wedge (n_9^0 \leftrightarrow n_{12}^0 \wedge n_{13}^0) \wedge (n_4^0 \leftrightarrow \neg s_1) \wedge (n_6^0 \leftrightarrow 1) \wedge (n_8^0 \leftrightarrow 1) \wedge$
   $(n_{10}^0 \leftrightarrow \neg s_3) \wedge (n_{11}^0 \leftrightarrow \neg s_4) \wedge (n_{12}^0 \leftrightarrow \neg s_2) \wedge (n_{13}^0 \leftrightarrow \neg s_4) \wedge (\neg n_1^0) \wedge (s_3)$
2. $(n_1^3 \leftrightarrow n_2^3 \vee n_3^3) \wedge (n_2^3 \leftrightarrow n_4^3 \wedge n_5^3) \wedge (n_3^3 \leftrightarrow n_6^3 \wedge n_7^3) \wedge (n_5^3 \leftrightarrow n_8^3 \vee n_9^3) \wedge$
   $(n_7^3 \leftrightarrow n_{10}^3 \wedge n_{11}^3) \wedge (n_9^3 \leftrightarrow n_{12}^3 \wedge n_{13}^3) \wedge (n_4^3 \leftrightarrow \neg s_1) \wedge (n_6^3 \leftrightarrow 1) \wedge (n_8^3 \leftrightarrow 1) \wedge$
   $(n_{10}^3 \leftrightarrow 1) \wedge (n_{11}^3 \leftrightarrow \neg s_4) \wedge (n_{12}^3 \leftrightarrow \neg s_2) \wedge (n_{13}^3 \leftrightarrow \neg s_4) \wedge (s_3 \leftrightarrow n_1^3)$

Given the AXp's listed in Example 3, by solving these formulas we will either obtain $\{1, 3\}$ or $\{1, 4\}$ as the AXp.

4.2 Relevancy for Monotonic Classifiers

This section describes an algorithm for FRP in the case of monotonic classifiers. No assumption is made regarding the actual implementation of the monotonic classifier.

Abstraction refinement for relevancy. The algorithm proposed in this section iteratively refines an over-approximation (or abstraction) of all the subsets $\mathcal{S}$ of $\mathcal{F}$ such that: i) $\mathcal{S}$ is a weak AXp, and ii) any AXp included in $\mathcal{S}$ also includes the target feature t. Formally, the set of subsets of $\mathcal{F}$ that we are interested in is defined as follows:

$$\mathbb{H} = \{\mathcal{S} \subseteq \mathcal{F} \mid \mathsf{WAXp}(\mathcal{S}) \wedge \forall (\mathcal{X} \subseteq \mathcal{S}). [\mathsf{AXp}(\mathcal{X}) \rightarrow (t \in \mathcal{X})]\} \quad (5)$$

The proposed algorithm iteratively refines the over-approximation of set $\mathbb{H}$ until one can decide with certainty whether t is included in some AXp. The refinement step involves exploiting counterexamples as these are identified. (The approach is referred to as abstraction refinement FRP, since the use of abstraction refinement can be related with earlier work (with the same name) in model checking [20].) In practice, it will in general be impractical to manipulate such over-approximation of set $\mathbb{H}$ explicitly. As a result, we use a propositional formula (in fact a CNF formula) $\mathcal{H}$, such that the models of $\mathcal{H}$ encode the subsets of features about which we have yet to decide whether each of those subsets only contains AXp's that include t. (Formula $\mathcal{H}$ is defined on a set of Boolean variables $\{s_1, \ldots, s_m\}$, where each s_i is associated with feature i, and assigning $s_i = 1$ denotes that feature i is included in a given set, as described below.) The algorithm then iteratively refines the over-approximation by filtering out sets of sets that have been shown not to be included in $\mathbb{H}$, i.e. the so-called counterexamples.

Algorithm 1 summarizes the proposed approach[8]. Also, Algorithms 2 and 3 provide supporting functions. (For simplicity, the function calls of Algorithms 2 and 3 show the arguments, but not the parameterizations.) Algorithm 1 iteratively uses an NP oracle (in fact a SAT solver) to pick (or *guess*) a subset $\mathcal{P}$ of $\mathcal{F}$, such that any previously picked set is not repeated. Since we are interested in feature t, we enforce that the picked set must include t. (This step is shown in lines 4 to 7.) Now, the features not in $\mathcal{P}$ are deemed universal, and so we need to account for the range of possible values that these universal features can take. For that, we update lower and upper bounds on the predicted classes. For the features in $\mathcal{P}$ we must use the values dictated by $\mathbf{v}$. (This is shown in lines 8 and 9, and it is sound to do because we have monotonicity of prediction.) If the lower and upper bounds differ, then the picked set is not even a weak AXp, and so we can safely remove it from further consideration. This is achieved by enforcing that at least one of the non-picked elements is picked in the future. (As can be observed $\mathcal{H}$ is updated with a positive clause that captures this constraint, as shown in line 11.) If the lower and upper bounds do not differ (i.e. we picked a weak AXp), and if by allowing t to take any value causes the bounds to differ, then we know that any AXp in $\mathcal{P}$ must include t, and so the algorithm reports $\mathcal{P}$ as a weak AXp that is *guaranteed* to be included in $\mathbb{H}$. (This is shown in line 14.) It should be noted that $\mathcal{P}$ is not necessarily an AXp. However, by Proposition 9, $\mathcal{P}$ is guaranteed to be a weak AXp such that *any* of the AXp's contained in $\mathcal{P}$ *must* include feature t. From [53], we know that we can extract an AXp from a weak AXp in polynomial time, and in this case we are guaranteed to always pick one that includes t. Finally, the last case is when allowing t to take any value does not cause the lower and upper bounds to change. This means we picked a set $\mathcal{P}$ that is a weak AXp, but not all AXp's in $\mathcal{P}$ include the target feature t (again due to Proposition 9). As a result, we must prevent the same weak AXp from being re-picked. This is achieved by requiring that at least one of the picked features not be picked again in the feature set. (This is shown in line 16. As can be observed, $\mathcal{H}$ is updated with a negative clause that captures this constraint.)

As can be concluded from Algorithm 1 and from the discussion above, Proposition 9 is essential to enable us to use at most two classification queries per iter-

---

[8] Arguments can either represent actual arguments or some parameterization; these are separated by a semi-colon.

Algorithm 1 Deciding feature relevancy for a monotonic classifier

    Input: Instance $\mathbf{v}$, Target feature t; Feature Set $\mathcal{F}$, Monotonic Classifier κ

1: **function** DecideRelevant($\mathbf{v}, t; \mathcal{F}, \kappa$)
2:     $\mathcal{H} \leftarrow \emptyset$ ▷ $\mathcal{H}$ overapproximates $\mathbb{H}$
3:     **repeat**
4:         (outc, $\mathbf{s}$) $\leftarrow$ SAT($\mathcal{H}, s_t$)   ▷ Pick candidate weak AXp containing t
5:         **if** outc $=$ **true then**
6:             $\mathcal{P} \leftarrow \{i \in \mathcal{F} \mid s_i = 1\}$ ▷ $\mathcal{P}$ is the candidate weak AXp, and $t \in \mathcal{P}$
7:             $\mathcal{D} \leftarrow \{i \in \mathcal{F} \mid s_i = 0\}$ ▷ $\mathcal{D}$ contains the features not included in $\mathcal{P}$
8:             $\mathbf{v}_L \leftarrow (v_{L_1}, \ldots, v_{L_N})$, s.t. $v_{L_i} \leftarrow \text{ITE}(s_i, v_i, \lambda(i))$ ▷ $\mathbf{v}_L$: LB
9:             $\mathbf{v}_U \leftarrow (v_{U_1}, \ldots, v_{U_N})$, s.t. $v_{U_i} \leftarrow \text{ITE}(s_i, v_i, \mu(i))$ ▷ $\mathbf{v}_U$: UB
10:           **if** $\kappa(\mathbf{v}_L) \neq \kappa(\mathbf{v}_U)$ **then**   ▷ More than one value possible?
11:               $\mathcal{H} \leftarrow \mathcal{H} \cup \text{newPosCl}(\mathcal{D}, t)$ ▷ $\mathcal{P}$ is *not* a weak AXp; block set
12:           **else**   ▷ $\mathcal{P}$ is a weak AXp
13:               **if** $\kappa(\mathbf{v}_L[v_{L_t} \leftarrow \lambda(t)]) \neq \kappa(\mathbf{v}_U[v_{U_t} \leftarrow \mu(t)])$ **then** ▷ t needed?
14:                   reportWeakAXp($\mathcal{P}$)   ▷ t is included in any AXp $\mathcal{X} \subseteq \mathcal{P}$
15:                   **return true**
16:               $\mathcal{H} \leftarrow \mathcal{H} \cup \text{newNegCl}(\mathcal{P}, t)$ ▷ t unneeded; block set
17:     **until** outc $=$ **false**
18:     **return false**   ▷ If $\mathcal{H}$ becomes inconsistent, then *no* AXp contains t

---

Table 2: Example algorithm execution for $t = 4$

$\mathbf{s}$	$\mathcal{P}$	$\mathcal{D}$	$\kappa(\mathbf{v}_L)$	$\kappa(\mathbf{v}_U)$	Decision	New clause	Line
$(0,0,0,1)$	$\{4\}$	$\{1,2,3\}$	0	1	New pos clause	$(s_1 \vee s_2 \vee s_3)$	11
$(1,0,0,1)$	$\{1,4\}$	$\{2,3\}$	0	1	New pos clause	$(s_2 \vee s_3)$	11
$(1,1,0,1)$	$\{1,2,4\}$	$\{3\}$	1	1	New neg clause	$(\neg s_1 \vee \neg s_2)$	16
$(1,0,1,1)$	$\{1,3,4\}$	$\{2\}$	1	1	New neg clause	$(\neg s_1 \vee \neg s_3)$	16
$(0,1,1,1)$	$\{2,3,4\}$	$\{1\}$	1	1	New pos clause	(s_1)	11
—	—	—	–	–	$\mathcal{H}$ inconsistent	–	17

ation of the algorithm. If we were to use Proposition 5 instead, then the number of classification queries would be significantly larger.

Example 8. We consider the monotonic classifier of Fig. 2, with instance $(\mathbf{v}, c) = ((1,1,1,1), 1)$. Table 2 summarizes a possible execution of the algorithm when $t = 4$. Similarly, Table 3 summarizes a possible execution of the algorithm when $t = 1$. (As with the current implementation, and for both examples, the creation of clauses uses no optimizations.) In general, different executions will be determined by the models returned by the SAT solver.

With respect to the clauses that are added to $\mathcal{H}$ at each step, as shown in Algorithms 2 and 3, one can envision optimizations (shown lines 2 to 7 in both algorithms) that heuristically aim at removing features from the given sets, and so produce shorter (and so logically stronger) clauses. The insight is that any feature, which can be deemed irrelevant for the condition used for constructing

Algorithm 2 Create new pos. clause
Input: Set $\mathcal{D}$, t; κ, $\mathbf{v}_L$, $\mathbf{v}_U$
1: **function** newPosCl($\mathcal{D}, t; \kappa, \mathbf{v}_L, \mathbf{v}_U$)
2:   **for all** $i \in \mathcal{D}$ **do**
3:      $(v_{L_i}, v_{U_i}) \leftarrow (v_i, v_i)$
4:      **if** $\kappa(\mathbf{v}_L) \neq \kappa(\mathbf{v}_U)$ **then**
5:         $\mathcal{D} \leftarrow \mathcal{D} \setminus \{i\}$
6:      **else**
7:         $(v_{L_i}, v_{U_i}) \leftarrow (\lambda(i), \mu(i))$
8:   $\omega \leftarrow (\vee_{i \in \mathcal{D}} s_i)$
9:   **return** ω

Algorithm 3 Create new neg. clause
Input: Set $\mathcal{P}$, t; κ, $\mathbf{v}_L$, $\mathbf{v}_U$
1: **function** newNegCl($\mathcal{P}, t; \kappa, \mathbf{v}_L, \mathbf{v}_U$)
2:   **for all** $i \in \mathcal{P} \setminus \{t\}$ **do**
3:      $(v_{L_i}, v_{U_i}) \leftarrow (\lambda(i), \mu(i))$
4:      **if** $\kappa(\mathbf{v}_L) = \kappa(\mathbf{v}_U)$ **then**
5:         $\mathcal{P} \leftarrow \mathcal{P} \setminus \{i\}$
6:      **else**
7:         $(v_{L_i}, v_{U_i}) \leftarrow (v_i, v_i)$
8:   $\omega \leftarrow (\vee_{i \in \mathcal{P} \setminus \{t\}} \neg s_i)$
9:   **return** ω

Table 3: Example algorithm execution for $t = 1$

s	$\mathcal{P}$	$\mathcal{D}$	$\kappa(\mathbf{v}_L)$	$\kappa(\mathbf{v}_U)$	Decision	New clause	Line
$(1,0,0,0)$	$\{1\}$	$\{2,3,4\}$	0	1	New pos clause	$(s_2 \vee s_3 \vee s_4)$	11
$(1,1,0,0)$	$\{1,2\}$	$\{3,4\}$	1	1	Weak AXp: $\{1,2\}$	–	14

the clause, can be safely removed from the set. (In practice, our experiments show that the time running the classifier is far larger than the time spent using the NP oracle to guess sets. Thus, we opted to use the simplest approach for constructing the clauses, and so reduce the number of classification queries.)

Given the above discussion, we can conclude that the proposed algorithm is sound, complete and terminating for deciding feature relevancy for monotonic classifiers. (The proof is straightforward, and it is omitted for the sake of brevity.)

Proposition 14. For a monotonic classifier $\mathbb{C}$, defined on set of features $\mathcal{F}$, with κ mapping $\mathbb{F}$ to $\mathcal{K}$, and an instance $(\mathbf{v}, c)$, $\mathbf{v} \in \mathbb{F}$, $c \in \mathcal{K}$, and a target feature $t \in \mathcal{F}$, Algorithm 1 returns a set $\mathcal{P} \subseteq \mathcal{F}$ iff $\mathcal{P}$ is a weak AXp for $(\mathbf{v}, c)$, with the property that any AXp $\mathcal{X} \subseteq \mathcal{P}$ is such that $t \in \mathcal{X}$ (i.e. $\mathcal{P}$ is a witness for the relevancy of t).

5   Experimental Results

This section reports the experimental results on FRP for the d-DNNF and monotonic classifiers. The goal is to show that FRP is practically feasible. We opt not to include experiments for FNP as the complexity of FNP is in P. Besides, to the best of our knowledges, there is no baseline to compare with. The experiments were performed on a MacBook Pro with a 6-Core Intel Core i7 2.6 GHz processor with 16 GByte RAM, running macOS Monterey.

d-DNNF classifiers.   For d-DNNFs, we pick its subset SDDs as our target classifier. SDDs support polynomial time negation, so given a SDD $\mathbb{C}$, one can obtain its negation $\neg \mathbb{C}$ efficiently.

Table 4: Solving FRP for SDDs. Sub-Columns Avg. #var and Avg. #cls show, respectively, the average number of variables and clauses in a CNF encoding. Column Runtime reports maximum and average time in seconds for deciding FRP.

Dataset	SDD		%Y	CNF		Runtime (s)	
	#Features	#Nodes		Avg. #var	Avg. #cls	Max	Avg.
Accidents	415	8863	97	26513	78276	56.4	3.5
Audio	272	7224	88	31148	100972	663.1	22.0
DNA	513	8570	91	29155	91288	86.3	11.0
Jester	254	7857	85	35998	121508	362.1	22.7
KDD	306	8109	99	26402	83480	111.2	2.8
Mushrooms	248	7096	91	23874	82112	266.3	15.8
Netflix	292	7039	94	25520	83324	105.7	4.2
NLTCS	183	6661	100	19817	58494	1.4	0.5
Plants	244	6724	97	25356	84782	950.7	20.6
RCV-1	410	9472	90	33438	102500	153.6	11.2
Retail	341	3704	87	10601	28342	1.8	1.1

Monotonic classifiers.   For monotonic classifiers, we consider the Deep Lattice Network (DLN) [70] as our target classifier. Since our approach for monotonic classifier is model-agnostic, it could also be used with other approaches for learning monotonic classifiers [48, 69] including Min-Max Network [21, 64] and COMET [65].

Prototype implementation.   Prototype implementations of the proposed approaches were implemented in Python [9]. The PySAT toolkit [10] was used for propositional encodings. Besides, PySAT invokes the Glucose 4 [11] SAT solver to pick a weak AXp candidate. SDDs were loaded by using the PySDD [12]package.

Benchmarks & training.   For SDDs, we selected 11 datasets from Density Estimation Benchmark Datasets[13]. [34, 46, 49]. 11 datasets were used to learn SDD using LearnSDD [11] (with parameter *maxEdges=20000*). The obtained SDDs were used as binary classifiers. For DLNs, we selected 5 publicly available datasets: *australian* (aus), *breast_ cancer* (b.c.), *heart_ c, nursery* [57] and *pima* [2]. We used the three-layer DLN architecture: Calibrators → Random Ensemble of Lattices → Linear Layer. All calibrators for all models used a fixed number of 20 keypoints. And the size of all lattices was set to 3.

Results for SDDs.   For each SDD, 100 test instances were randomly generated. All tested instances have prediction 0. (We didn't pick instances predicted to class 1 as this requires the compilation of a new classifier which may have dif-

---

[9] https://github.com/XuanxiangHuang/frp-experiment
[10] https://github.com/pysathq/pysat
[11] https://www.labri.fr/perso/lsimon/glucose/
[12] https://github.com/wannesm/PySDD
[13] https://github.com/UCLA-StarAI/Density-Estimation-Datasets

Table 5: Solving FRP for DLN. Column Runtime reports maximum and average time in seconds for deciding FRP. Column SAT Time (resp. $\kappa(\mathbf{v})$ Time) reports maximum and average time in seconds for SAT solver (resp. calling DLN's predict function) to decide FRP. Column SAT Calls (resp. $\kappa(\mathbf{v})$ Calls) reports maximum and average number of calls to the SAT solver (resp. to the DLN's predict function) to decide FRP.

Dataset	%Y	Runtime (s)		SAT Time		SAT Calls		$\kappa(\mathbf{v})$ Time		$\kappa(\mathbf{v})$ Calls		$\frac{\kappa(\mathbf{v})\text{Time}}{\text{Runtime}}$
		Max	Avg.	Max	Avg.	Max	Avg.	Max	Avg.	Max	Avg.	
aus	61	40.4	8.31	0.02	0.01	291	65	40.0	8.15	424	98	97.8%
b.c.	45	5.4	1.93	0.00	0.00	53	20	5.3	1.89	78	30	98.0%
heart_c	35	31.5	6.67	0.02	0.00	171	54	31.1	6.52	249	80	97.7%
nursery	45	4.3	1.77	0.00	0.00	31	13	4.3	1.75	73	30	98.6%
pima	74	3.7	1.41	0.00	0.00	33	13	3.7	1.39	47	22	98.4%

ferent size). Besides, for each instance, we randomly picked a feature appearing in the model. Hence for each SDD, we solved 100 queries. Table 4 summarizes the results. It can be observed that the number of nodes of the tested SDD is in the range of 3704 and 9472, and the number of features of tested SDD is in the range of 183 and 513. Besides, the percentage of examples for which the answer is Y (i.e. target feature is in some AXp) ranges from 85% to 100%. Regarding the runtime, the largest running time for solving one query can exceed 15 minutes. But the average running time to solve a query is less than 25 seconds, this highlights the scalability of the proposed encoding.

Results for DLNs. For each DLN, we randomly picked 200 tested instances, and for each tested instance, we randomly pick a feature. Hence for each DLN, we solved 200 queries. Table 5 summarizes the results. The use of a SAT solver has a negligible contribution to the running time. Indeed, for all the examples shown, at least 97% of the running time is spent running the classifier. This should be unsurprising, since the number of the iterations of Algorithm 1 never exceeds a few hundred. (The fraction of a second reported in some cases should be divided by the number of calls to the SAT solver; hence the time spent in each call to the SAT solver is indeed negligible.) As can be observed, the percentage of examples for which the answer is Y (i.e. target feature is in some AXp and the algorithm returns **true**) ranges from 35% to 74%. There is no apparent correlation between the percentage of Y answers and the number of iterations. The large number of queries accounts for the number of times the DLN is queried by Algorithm 1, but it also accounts for the number of times the DLN is queried for extracting an AXp from set $\mathcal{P}$ (i.e. the witness) when the algorithm's answer is **true**. A loose upper bound on the number of queries to the classifier is $4 \times \text{NS} + 2 \times |\mathcal{F}|$, where NS is the number of SAT calls, and $|\mathcal{F}|$ is the number of features. Each iteration of Algorithm 1 can require at most 4 queries to the classifier. After reporting $\mathcal{P}$, at most 2 queries per feature will be required to extract the AXp (see Section 2.3). As can be observed this loose upper bound is respected by the reported results.

6 Related Work

The problems of necessity and relevancy have been studied in logic-based abduction since the early 90s [25, 30, 61]. However, this earlier work did not consider the classes of (classifier) functions that are considered in this paper.

There has been recent work on explainability queries [7, 8, 36]. Some of these queries can be related with feature relevancy and necessity. For example, relevancy and necessity have been studied with respect to a target class [7, 8], in contrast with our approach that studies a concrete instance, and so can be naturally related with earlier work on abduction. Recent work [36] studied feature relevancy under the name feature membership, but neither d-DNNF nor monotonic classifiers were discussed. Moreover, [36] only proved the hardness of deciding feature relevancy for DNF and DT classifiers and did not discuss the feature necessity problem. The results presented in this paper complement this work. Besides, the complexity results of FRP and FNP in this paper also complement the recent work [54] which summarizes the progress of formal explanations. [40] focused on the computation of one arbitrary AXp and one smallest AXp, which is orthogonal to our work. Computing one AXp does not guarantee that either FRP or FNP is decided, since the target feature t may not appear in the computed AXp. [53] studied the computation of one formal explanation and the enumeration of formal explanations in the case study of monotonic classifiers. However, neither FRP or FNP were identified and studied.

7 Conclusions

This paper studies the problems of feature necessity and relevancy in the context of formal explanations of ML classifiers. The paper proves several complexity results, some related with necessity, but most related with relevancy. Furthermore, the paper proposes two different approaches for solving relevancy for two families of classifiers, namely classifiers represented with the d-DNNF propositional language, and monotonic classifiers. The experimental results confirm the practical scalability of the proposed algorithms. Future work will seek to prove hardness results for the families of classifiers for which hardness is yet unknown.

Acknowledgements. This work was supported by the AI Interdisciplinary Institute ANITI, funded by the French program "Investing for the Future – PIA3" under Grant agreement no. ANR-19-PI3A-0004, and by the H2020-ICT38 project COALA "Cognitive Assisted agile manufacturing for a Labor force supported by trustworthy Artificial intelligence", and funded by the Spanish Ministry of Science and Innovation (MICIN) under project PID2019-111544GB-C22, and by a María Zambrano fellowship and a Requalification fellowship financed by Ministerio de Universidades of Spain and by European Union – NextGenerationEU.

References

1. Akers, S.B.: Binary decision diagrams. IEEE Transactions on computers **27**(06), 509–516 (1978)
2. Alcalá-Fdez, J., Fernández, A., Luengo, J., Derrac, J., García, S., Sánchez, L., Herrera, F.: Keel data-mining software tool: data set repository, integration of algorithms and experimental analysis framework. Journal of Multiple-Valued Logic & Soft Computing **17** (2011), https://sci2s.ugr.es/keel/dataset.php?cod=21
3. Amgoud, L., Ben-Naim, J.: Axiomatic foundations of explainability. In: IJCAI. pp. 636–642 (2022)
4. Arenas, M., Baez, D., Barceló, P., Pérez, J., Subercaseaux, B.: Foundations of symbolic languages for model interpretability. In: NeurIPS (2021)
5. Arenas, M., Barceló, P., Romero, M., Subercaseaux, B.: On computing probabilistic explanations for decision trees. CoRR **abs/2207.12213** (2022). https://doi.org/10.48550/arXiv.2207.12213, https://doi.org/10.48550/arXiv.2207.12213
6. Arora, S., Barak, B.: Computational Complexity - A Modern Approach. Cambridge University Press (2009), http://www.cambridge.org/catalogue/catalogue.asp?isbn=9780521424264
7. Audemard, G., Bellart, S., Bounia, L., Koriche, F., Lagniez, J., Marquis, P.: On the computational intelligibility of boolean classifiers. In: KR. pp. 74–86 (2021)
8. Audemard, G., Koriche, F., Marquis, P.: On tractable XAI queries based on compiled representations. In: KR. pp. 838–849 (2020)
9. Bach, S., Binder, A., Montavon, G., Klauschen, F., Müller, K.R., Samek, W.: On pixel-wise explanations for non-linear classifier decisions by layer-wise relevance propagation. PloS one **10**(7), e0130140 (2015)
10. Barceló, P., Monet, M., Pérez, J., Subercaseaux, B.: Model interpretability through the lens of computational complexity. In: NeurIPS (2020)
11. Bekker, J., Davis, J., Choi, A., Darwiche, A., den Broeck, G.V.: Tractable learning for complex probability queries. In: NeurIPS. pp. 2242–2250 (2015), https://github.com/ML-KULeuven/LearnSDD
12. Bengio, Y., LeCun, Y., Hinton, G.E.: Deep learning for AI. Commun. ACM **64**(7), 58–65 (2021), https://doi.org/10.1145/3448250
13. Biere, A., Heule, M., van Maaren, H., Walsh, T. (eds.): Handbook of Satisfiability - Second Edition, Frontiers in Artificial Intelligence and Applications, vol. 336. IOS Press (2021), https://doi.org/10.3233/FAIA336
14. Blanc, G., Lange, J., Tan, L.: Provably efficient, succinct, and precise explanations. In: NeurIPS (2021)
15. Boumazouza, R., Alili, F.C., Mazure, B., Tabia, K.: ASTERYX: A model-Agnostic SaT-basEd appRoach for sYmbolic and score-based eXplanations. In: CIKM. pp. 120–129 (2021)
16. Brayton, R.K., Hachtel, G.D., McMullen, C., Sangiovanni-Vincentelli, A.: Logic minimization algorithms for VLSI synthesis, vol. 2. Springer Science & Business Media (1984)
17. Breiman, L.: Random forests. Mach. Learn. **45**(1), 5–32 (2001). https://doi.org/10.1023/A:1010933404324, https://doi.org/10.1023/A:1010933404324
18. Breiman, L., Friedman, J.H., Olshen, R.A., Stone, C.J.: Classification and Regression Trees. Wadsworth (1984)
19. Clark, P., Boswell, R.: Rule induction with cn2: Some recent improvements. In: European Working Session on Learning. pp. 151–163. Springer (1991)

20. Clarke, E.M., Grumberg, O., Jha, S., Lu, Y., Veith, H.: Counterexample-guided abstraction refinement for symbolic model checking. J. ACM **50**(5), 752–794 (2003). https://doi.org/10.1145/876638.876643, https://doi.org/10.1145/876638.876643

21. Daniels, H., Velikova, M.: Monotone and partially monotone neural networks. IEEE Trans. Neural Networks **21**(6), 906–917 (2010)

22. Darwiche, A.: SDD: A new canonical representation of propositional knowledge bases. In: IJCAI. pp. 819–826 (2011)

23. Darwiche, A., Marquis, P.: A knowledge compilation map. J. Artif. Intell. Res. **17**, 229–264 (2002). https://doi.org/10.1613/jair.989

24. Darwiche, A., Marquis, P.: On quantifying literals in boolean logic and its applications to explainable AI. J. Artif. Intell. Res. **72**, 285–328 (2021)

25. Eiter, T., Gottlob, G.: The complexity of logic-based abduction. J. ACM **42**(1), 3–42 (1995), https://doi.org/10.1145/200836.200838

26. Fard, M.M., Canini, K.R., Cotter, A., Pfeifer, J., Gupta, M.R.: Fast and flexible monotonic functions with ensembles of lattices. In: NeurIPS. pp. 2919–2927 (2016)

27. Ferreira, J., de Sousa Ribeiro, M., Gonçalves, R., Leite, J.: Looking inside the blackbox: Logic-based explanations for neural networks. In: KR. p. 432–442 (2022)

28. Flach, P.A.: Machine Learning - The Art and Science of Algorithms that Make Sense of Data. CUP (2012)

29. Friedman, J.H.: Greedy function approximation: a gradient boosting machine. Annals of statistics pp. 1189–1232 (2001)

30. Friedrich, G., Gottlob, G., Nejdl, W.: Hypothesis classification, abductive diagnosis and therapy. In: ESE. pp. 69–78 (1990)

31. Gergov, J., Meinel, C.: Efficient boolean manipulation with OBDD's can be extended to FBDD's. IEEE Transactions on Computers **43**(10), 1197–1209 (1994). https://doi.org/10.1109/12.324545

32. Goodfellow, I.J., Bengio, Y., Courville, A.C.: Deep Learning. Adaptive computation and machine learning, MIT Press (2016), http://www.deeplearningbook.org/

33. Gorji, N., Rubin, S.: Sufficient reasons for classifier decisions in the presence of domain constraints. In: AAAI (February 2022)

34. Haaren, J.V., Davis, J.: Markov network structure learning: A randomized feature generation approach. In: AAAI (2012)

35. Huang, X., Izza, Y., Ignatiev, A., Cooper, M.C., Asher, N., Marques-Silva, J.: Tractable explanations for d-DNNF classifiers. In: AAAI. pp. 5719–5728 (2022)

36. Huang, X., Izza, Y., Ignatiev, A., Marques-Silva, J.: On efficiently explaining graph-based classifiers. In: KR. pp. 356–367 (2021)

37. Ignatiev, A., Izza, Y., Stuckey, P.J., Marques-Silva, J.: Using MaxSAT for efficient explanations of tree ensembles. In: AAAI. pp. 3776–3785 (2022)

38. Ignatiev, A., Marques-Silva, J.: SAT-based rigorous explanations for decision lists. In: SAT. pp. 251–269 (2021)

39. Ignatiev, A., Narodytska, N., Asher, N., Marques-Silva, J.: From contrastive to abductive explanations and back again. In: AIxIA. pp. 335–355 (2020)

40. Ignatiev, A., Narodytska, N., Marques-Silva, J.: Abduction-based explanations for machine learning models. In: AAAI. pp. 1511–1519 (2019)

41. Ignatiev, A., Pereira, F., Narodytska, N., Marques-Silva, J.: A SAT-based approach to learn explainable decision sets. In: IJCAR. pp. 627–645 (2018)

42. Izza, Y., Ignatiev, A., Marques-Silva, J.: On tackling explanation redundancy in decision trees. J. Artif. Intell. Res. **75**, 261–321 (2022), https://doi.org/10.1613/jair.1.13575

43. Izza, Y., Marques-Silva, J.: On explaining random forests with SAT. In: IJCAI. pp. 2584–2591 (2021)
44. Kohavi, R.: Bottom-up induction of oblivious read-once decision graphs: strengths and limitations. In: AAAI. pp. 613–618 (1994)
45. Kohavi, R., et al.: Scaling up the accuracy of naive-bayes classifiers: A decision-tree hybrid. In: Kdd. vol. 96, pp. 202–207 (1996)
46. Larochelle, H., Murray, I.: The neural autoregressive distribution estimator. In: AISTATS. pp. 29–37 (2011)
47. LeCun, Y., Bengio, Y., Hinton, G.: Deep learning. nature **521**(7553), 436–444 (2015)
48. Liu, X., Han, X., Zhang, N., Liu, Q.: Certified monotonic neural networks. In: NeurIPS (2020)
49. Lowd, D., Davis, J.: Learning Markov network structure with decision trees. In: ICDM. pp. 334–343 (2010)
50. Lundberg, S.M., Lee, S.: A unified approach to interpreting model predictions. In: NeurIPS. pp. 4765–4774 (2017)
51. Malfa, E.L., Michelmore, R., Zbrzezny, A.M., Paoletti, N., Kwiatkowska, M.: On guaranteed optimal robust explanations for NLP models. In: IJCAI. pp. 2658–2665 (2021)
52. Marques-Silva, J., Gerspacher, T., Cooper, M.C., Ignatiev, A., Narodytska, N.: Explaining naive bayes and other linear classifiers with polynomial time and delay. In: NeurIPS (2020)
53. Marques-Silva, J., Gerspacher, T., Cooper, M.C., Ignatiev, A., Narodytska, N.: Explanations for monotonic classifiers. In: ICML. pp. 7469–7479 (2021)
54. Marques-Silva, J., Ignatiev, A.: Delivering trustworthy AI through formal XAI. In: AAAI. pp. 12342–12350 (2022)
55. Miller, T.: Explanation in artificial intelligence: Insights from the social sciences. Artif. Intell. **267**, 1–38 (2019)
56. Müller, B., Reinhardt, J., Strickland, M.T.: Neural networks: an introduction. Springer Science & Business Media (1995)
57. Olson, R.S., La Cava, W., Orzechowski, P., Urbanowicz, R.J., Moore, J.H.: PMLB: a large benchmark suite for machine learning evaluation and comparison. BioData Mining **10**(1), 36 (2017), https://epistasislab.github.io/pmlb/index.html
58. Ribeiro, M.T., Singh, S., Guestrin, C.: "Why should I trust you?": Explaining the predictions of any classifier. In: KDD. pp. 1135–1144 (2016)
59. Ribeiro, M.T., Singh, S., Guestrin, C.: Anchors: High-precision model-agnostic explanations. In: AAAI. pp. 1527–1535 (2018)
60. Rivest, R.L.: Learning decision lists. Mach. Learn. **2**(3), 229–246 (1987)
61. Selman, B., Levesque, H.J.: Abductive and default reasoning: A computational core. In: AAAI. pp. 343–348 (1990)
62. Shalev-Shwartz, S., Ben-David, S.: Understanding Machine Learning - From Theory to Algorithms. Cambridge University Press (2014)
63. Shih, A., Choi, A., Darwiche, A.: A symbolic approach to explaining bayesian network classifiers. In: IJCAI. pp. 5103–5111 (2018)
64. Sill, J.: Monotonic networks. In: NIPS. pp. 661–667 (1997)
65. Sivaraman, A., Farnadi, G., Millstein, T.D., den Broeck, G.V.: Counterexample-guided learning of monotonic neural networks. In: NeurIPS (2020)
66. Van den Broeck, G., Darwiche, A.: On the role of canonicity in knowledge compilation. In: AAAI. pp. 1641–1648 (2015)

67. Wäldchen, S., MacDonald, J., Hauch, S., Kutyniok, G.: The computational complexity of understanding binary classifier decisions. J. Artif. Intell. Res. **70**, 351–387 (2021), `https://doi.org/10.1613/jair.1.12359`

68. Wegener, I.: Branching Programs and Binary Decision Diagrams. SIAM (2000), `http://ls2-www.cs.uni-dortmund.de/monographs/bdd/`

69. Wehenkel, A., Louppe, G.: Unconstrained monotonic neural networks. In: NeurIPS. pp. 1543–1553 (2019)

70. You, S., Ding, D., Canini, K.R., Pfeifer, J., Gupta, M.R.: Deep lattice networks and partial monotonic functions. In: NeurIPS. pp. 2981–2989 (2017), `https://github.com/tensorflow/lattice`

Towards Formal XAI: Formally Approximate Minimal Explanations of Neural Networks

Shahaf Bassan and Guy Katz[(✉)]

The Hebrew University of Jerusalem, Jerusalem, Israel
{shahaf.bassan,g.katz}@mail.huji.ac.il

Abstract. With the rapid growth of machine learning, deep neural networks (DNNs) are now being used in numerous domains. Unfortunately, DNNs are "black-boxes", and cannot be interpreted by humans, which is a substantial concern in safety-critical systems. To mitigate this issue, researchers have begun working on explainable AI (XAI) methods, which can identify a subset of input features that are the cause of a DNN's decision for a given input. Most existing techniques are heuristic, and cannot guarantee the correctness of the explanation provided. In contrast, recent and exciting attempts have shown that formal methods can be used to generate provably correct explanations. Although these methods are sound, the computational complexity of the underlying verification problem limits their scalability; and the explanations they produce might sometimes be overly complex. Here, we propose a novel approach to tackle these limitations. We (i) suggest an efficient, verification-based method for finding *minimal explanations*, which constitute a *provable approximation* of the global, minimum explanation; (ii) show how DNN verification can assist in calculating lower and upper bounds on the optimal explanation; (iii) propose heuristics that significantly improve the scalability of the verification process; and (iv) suggest the use of *bundles*, which allows us to arrive at more succinct and interpretable explanations. Our evaluation shows that our approach significantly outperforms state-of-the-art techniques, and produces explanations that are more useful to humans. We thus regard this work as a step toward leveraging verification technology in producing DNNs that are more reliable and comprehensible.

1 Introduction

Machine learning (ML) is a rapidly growing field with a wide range of applications, including safety-critical, high-risk systems in the fields of health care [18], aviation [38] and autonomous driving [12]. Despite their success, ML models, and especially deep neural networks (DNNs), remain "black-boxes" — they are incomprehensible to humans and are prone to unexpected behaviour and errors. This issue can result in major catastrophes [13,73], and also in poor decision-making due to brittleness or bias [7,24].

In order to render DNNs more comprehensible to humans, researchers have been working on *explainable AI* (*XAI*), where we seek to construct models for

S. Sankaranarayanan and N. Sharygina (Eds.): TACAS 2023, LNCS 13993, pp. 187–207, 2023.
https://doi.org/10.1007/978-3-031-30823-9_10

explaining and interpreting the decisions of DNNs [50,55–57]. Work to date has focused on heuristic approaches, which provide explanations, but do not provide guarantees about the correctness or succinctness of these explanations [14,32,44]. Although these approaches are an important step, their limitations might result in skewed results, possibly failing to meet the regulatory guidelines of institutions and organizations such as the European Union, the US government, and the OECD [51]. Thus, producing DNN explanations that are provably accurate remains of utmost importance.

More recently, the formal verification community has proposed approaches for providing formal and rigorous explanations for DNN decision making [27,31, 51,59]. Many of these approaches rely on the recent and rapid developments in DNN verification [1,8,9,39]. These approaches typically produce an *abductive explanation* (also known as a *prime implicant*, or *PI-explanation*) [31,58,59]: a minimum subset of input features, which by themselves already determine the classification produced by the DNN, regardless of any other input features. These explanations afford formal guarantees, and can be computed via DNN verification [31].

Abductive explanations are highly useful, but there are two major difficulties in computing them. First, there is the issue of scalability: computing locally minimal explanations might require a polynomial number of costly invocations of the underlying DNN verifier, and computing a globally minimal explanation is even more challenging [10, 31, 48]. The second difficulty is that users may sometimes prefer "high-level" explanations, not based solely on input features, as these may be easier to grasp and interpret compared to "low-level", complex, feature-based explanations.

To tackle the first difficulty, we propose here new approaches for more efficiently producing verification-based abductive explanations. More concretely, we propose a method for *provably approximating* minimum explanations, allowing stakeholders to use slightly larger explanations that can be discovered much more quickly. To accomplish this, we leverage the recently discovered dual relationship between explanations and contrastive examples [30]; and also take advantage of the sensitivity of DNNs to small adversarial perturbations [64], to compute both lower and upper bounds for the minimum explanation. In addition, we propose novel heuristics for significantly expediting the underlying verification process.

In addressing the second difficulty, i.e. the interpretability limitations of "low-level" explanations, we propose to construct explanations in terms of *bundles*, which are sets of related features. We empirically show that using our method to produce bundle explanations can significantly improve the interpretability of the results, and even the scalability of the approach, while still maintaining the soundness of the resulting explanations.

To summarize, our contributions include the following: (i) We are the first to suggest a method that formally produces sound and minimal abductive explanations that *provably approximate* the global-minimum explanation. (ii) Our three suggested novel heuristics expedite the search for minimal abductive explanations, significantly outperforming the state of the art. (iii) We suggest a novel approach for using bundles to efficiently produce sound and provable explanations that are more interpretable and succinct.

For evaluation purposes, we implemented our approach as a proof-of-concept tool. Although our method can be applied to any ML model, we focused here on DNNs, where the verification process is known to be NP-complete [39], and the scalable generation of explanations is known to be challenging [31, 58]. We used our tool to test the approach on DNNs trained for digit and clothing classification, and also compared it to state-of-the-art approaches [31, 32]. Our results indicate that our approach was successful in quickly producing meaningful explanations, often running 40% faster than existing tools. We believe that these promising results showcase the potential of this line of work.

The rest of the paper is organized as follows. Sec. 2 contains background on DNNs and their verification, as well as on formal, minimal explanations. Sec. 3 covers the main method for calculating approximations of minimum explanations, and Sec. 4 covers methods for improving the efficiency of calculating these approximations. Sec. 5 covers the use of *bundles* in constructing "high-level", provable explanations. Next, we present our evaluation in Sec. 6. Related work is covered in Sec. 7, and we conclude in Sec. 8.

2   Background

DNNs. A deep neural network (DNN) [46] is a directed graph composed of layers of nodes, commonly called *neurons*. In feed-forward NNs the data flows from the first (*input*) layer, through intermediate (*hidden*) layers, and onto an *output* layer. A DNN's output is calculated by assigning values to its input neurons, and then iteratively calculating the values of neurons in subsequent layers. In the case of *classification*, which is the focus of this paper, each output neuron corresponds to a specific *class*, and the output neuron with the highest value corresponds to the class the input is classified to.

Fig. 1 depicts a simple, feed-forward DNN. The input layer includes three neurons, followed by a weighted sum layer, which calculates an affine transformation of values from the input layer. Given the input $V_1 = [1,1,1]^T$, the second layers computes the values $V_2 = [6,9,11]^T$. Next comes a ReLU layer, which computes the function $\mathrm{ReLU}(x) = \max(0,x)$ for each neuron in the preceding layer, resulting in

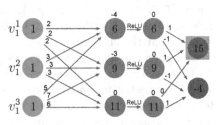

Fig. 1: A simple DNN.

$V_3 = [6,9,11]^T$. The final (output) layer then computes an affine transformation, resulting in $V_4 = [15, -4]^T$. This indicates that input $V_1 = [1,1,1]^T$ is classified as the category corresponding to the first output neuron, which is assigned the greater value.

DNN Verification. A DNN verification query is a tuple $\langle P, N, Q \rangle$, where N is a DNN that maps an input vector x to an output vector $y = N(x)$, P is a predicate on x, and Q is a predicate on y. A DNN verifier needs to decide whether there exists an input x_0 that satisfies $P(x_0) \wedge Q(N(x_0))$ (the SAT case) or not (the UNSAT case). Typically, P and Q are expressed in the logic of real arithmetic [49]. The DNN verification problem is known to be NP-Complete [39].

Formal Explanations. We focus here on explanations for classification problems, where a model is trained to predict a label for each given input. A classification problem is a tuple $\langle F, D, K, N \rangle$ where (i) $F = \{1, ..., m\}$ denotes the features; (ii) $D = \{D_1, D_2 ..., D_m\}$ denotes the domains of each of the features, i.e. the possible values that each feature can take. The entire feature (input) space is hence $\mathbb{F} = D_1 \times D_2 \times ... \times D_m$; (iii) $K = \{c_1, c_2, ..., c_n\}$ is a set of classes, i.e. the possible labels; and (iv) $N : F \to K$ is a (non-constant) classification function (in our case, a neural network). A classification instance is the pair (v, c), where $v \in \mathbb{F}$, $c \in K$, and $c = N(v)$. In other words, v is mapped by the neural network N to class c.

Looking at (v, c), we often wish to know why v was classified as c. Informally, an *explanation* is a subset of features $E \subseteq F$, such that assigning these features to the values assigned to them in v already determines that the input will be classified as c, regardless of the remaining features $F \setminus E$. In other words, even if the values that are *not* in the explanation are changed arbitrarily, the classification remains the same. More formally, given input $v = (v_1, ... v_m) \in \mathbb{F}$ with the classification $N(v) = c$, an explanation (sometimes referred to as an *abductive explanation*, or an *AXP*) is a subset of the features $E \subseteq F$, such that:

$$\forall(x \in \mathbb{F}). \quad \left[\bigwedge_{i \in E} (x_i = v_i) \to (N(x) = c) \right] \tag{1}$$

We continue with the running example from Fig. 1. For simplicity, we assume that each input neuron can only be assigned the values 0 or 1. It can be observed that for input $V_1 = [1, 1, 1]^T$, the set $\{v_1^1, v_1^2\}$ is an explanation; indeed, once the first two entries in V_1 are set to 1, the classification remains the same for any value of the third entry (see Fig. 2). We can prove this by encoding a verification query $\langle P, N, Q \rangle = \langle E = v, N, Q_{\neg c} \rangle$, where E is the candidate explanation, and $E = v$ means that we restrict the features in E to their values in v; and $Q_{\neg c}$ implies that the classification is not c. An UNSAT result for this query indicates that E is an explanation for instance (v, c).

Clearly, the set of all features constitutes a trivial explanation. However, we are interested in *smaller* explanation subsets, which can provide useful information regarding the decision of the classifier. More precisely, we search for *minimal explanations* and *minimum explanations*. A subset $E \subseteq F$ is a *minimal explanation* (also referred to as a *local-minimal explanation*, or a *subset-minimal explanation*) of instance (v, c) if it is an explanation that ceases to be an explanation if even a single feature is removed from it:

$$(\forall(x \in \mathbb{F}).[\wedge_{i \in E}(x_i = v_i) \to (N(x) = c)]) \wedge$$
$$(\forall(j \in E).[\exists(y \in \mathbb{F}).[\wedge_{i \in E \setminus j}(y_i = v_i) \wedge (N(y) \neq c)]) \tag{2}$$

Fig. 3 demonstrates that $\{v_1^1, v_1^2\}$ is a minimal explanation in our running example: removing any of its features allows mis-classification.

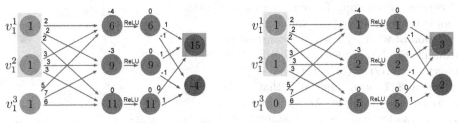

Fig. 2: $\{v_1^1, v_1^2\}$ is an explanation for input $V_1 = [1, 1, 1]^T$.

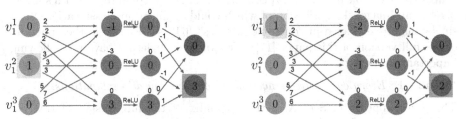

Fig. 3: $\{v_1^1, v_1^2\}$ is a minimal explanation for input $V_1 = [1, 1, 1]^T$.

A *minimum explanation* (sometimes referred to as a *cardinal minimal explanation* or a *PI-explanation*) is defined as a minimal explanation of minimum size; i.e., if E is a minimum explanation, then there does not exist a minimal explanation $E' \neq E$ such that $|E'| < |E|$. Fig. 4 demonstrates that $\{v_1^3\}$ is a minimum explanation for our running example.

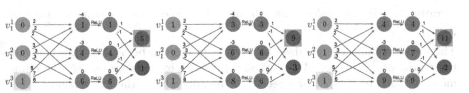

Fig. 4: $\{v_1^3\}$ is a minimum explanation for input $V_1 = [1, 1, 1]^T$.

Contrastive Example. A subset of features $C \subseteq F$ is called a *contrastive example* or a *contrastive explanation (CXP)* if altering the features in C is sufficient to cause the misclassification of a given classification instance (v, c):

$$\exists (x \in \mathbb{F}).[\wedge_{i \in F \setminus C}(x_i = v_i) \wedge (N(x) \neq c)] \tag{3}$$

A contrastive example for our running example is shown in Fig. 5. Notice that the question of whether a set is a contrastive example can be encoded into a verification query $\langle P, N, Q \rangle = \langle (F \setminus C) = v, N, Q_{\neg c} \rangle$, where a SAT result indicates that C is a contrastive example. As with explanations, smaller contrastive examples are more valuable than large ones. One useful notion is that of a *contrastive singleton*: a

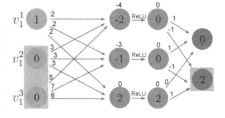

Fig. 5: $\{v_1^2, v_1^3\}$ is a contrastive example for $V_1 = [1, 1, 1]^T$.

contrastive example of size one. A contrastive singleton could represent a specific pixel in an image, the alteration of which could result in misclassification. Such singletons are leveraged in "one-pixel attacks" [64] (see Fig. 16 in the appendix of the full version of this paper [11]). Contrastive singletons have the following important property:

Lemma 1. *Every contrastive singleton is contained in all explanations.*

The proof appears in Sec. A of the appendix of the full version of this paper [11]. Lemma 1 implies that each contrastive singleton is contained in all minimal/minimum explanations.

We consider also the notion of a *contrastive pair*, which is a contrastive example of size 2. Clearly, for any pair of features (u, v) where u or v are contrastive singletons, (u, v) is a contrastive pair; however, when we next refer to contrastive pairs, we consider only pairs that *do not* contain any contrastive singletons. Likewise, for every $k > 2$, we can consider contrastive examples of size k, and we exclude from these any contrastive examples of sizes $1, \ldots, k - 1$ as subsets.

We state the following theorem, whose proof also appears in Sec. A of the appendix of the full version of this paper [11]:

Lemma 2. *All explanations contain at least one element of every contrastive pair.*

The theorem can be generalized to any $k > 2$; and can be used in showing that the *minimum hitting set (MHS)* of all contrastive examples is exactly the minimum explanation [29, 54] (see Sec. B of the appendix of the full version of this paper [11]). Further, the theorem implies a duality between contrastive examples and explanations [30, 34]: a minimal hitting set of all contrastive examples constitutes a minimal explanation, and a minimal hitting set of all explanations constitutes a minimal contrastive example.

3   Provable Approximations for Minimal Explanations

State-of-the-art approaches for finding minimum explanations exploit the MHS duality between explanations and contrastive examples [31]. The idea is to iteratively compute contrastive examples, and then use their MHS as an under-approximation for the minimum explanation. Finding this MHS is an NP-complete problem, and is difficult in practice as the number of contrastive examples increases [20]; and although the MHS can be approximated using maximum satisfiability (MaxSAT) or mixed integer linear programming (MILP) solvers [26, 47], existing approaches tackle simpler ML models, such as decision trees [33, 36], but face scalability limitations when applied to DNNs [31, 58]. Further, enumerating all contrastive examples may in itself take exponential time. Finally, recall that DNN verification is an NP-Complete problem [39]; and so dispatching a verification query to identify each explanation or contrastive example is also very slow, when the feature space is large. Finding *minimal* explanations may be easier [31], but may converge to larger and less meaningful explanations, while still requiring a linear number of calls to the underlying verifier. Our approach, described next, seeks to mitigate these difficulties.

Our overall approach is described in Algorithm 1. It is comprised of two separate threads, intended to be run in parallel. The *upper bounding thread* (T_{UB}) is responsible for computing a minimal explanation. It starts with the entire feature space, and then gradually reduces it, until converging to a minimal explanation. The size of the presently smallest explanation is regarded as an upper bound (UB) for the size of the minimum explanation. Symmetrically, the *lower bounding thread* (T_{LB}) attempts to construct small contrastive sets, used for computing a lower bound (LB) on the size of the minimum explanation. Together, these two bounds allow us to compute the approximation ratio between the minimal explanation that we have discovered and the minimum explanation. For instance, given a minimal explanation of size 7 and a lower bound of size 5, we can deduce that our explanation is at most $\frac{\text{UB}}{\text{LB}} = \frac{7}{5}$ times larger than the minimum. The two threads share global variables that indicate the set of contrastive singletons (Singletons), the set of contrastive pairs (Pairs), the upper and lower bounds (UB, LB), and the set of features that were determined not to participate in the explanation and are "free" to be set to any value (Free). The output of our algorithm is a minimal explanation (F\Free), and the approximation ratio ($\frac{\text{UB}}{\text{LB}}$). We next discuss each of the two threads in detail.

Algorithm 1 Minimal Explanation Search

Input N (Neural network), F (features), v (input values), c (class prediction)

1: Singletons, Pairs, Free ← ∅, UB ← |F|, LB ← 0   ▷ Global variables
2: Launch thread T_{UB}
3: Launch thread T_{LB}
4: **return** F\Free, $\frac{\text{UB}}{\text{LB}}$

The Upper Bounding Thread (T_{UB}). This thread, whose pseudocode appears in Algorithm 2, follows the framework proposed by Ignatiev et al. [31]: it seeks a minimal explanation by starting with the entire feature space, and then iteratively attempting to remove individual features. If removing a feature allows misclassification, we keep it as part of the explanation; otherwise, we remove it and continue. This process issues a single verification query for each feature, until converging to a minimal explanation (lines 2–8). Although this naïve search is guaranteed to converge to a minimal explanation, it needs not to converge to a *minimum* explanation; and so we apply a more sophisticated ordering scheme, similar to the one proposed by [32], where we use some heuristic model as a way for assigning weights of importance to each input feature. We then check the "least important" input features first, since freeing them has a lower chance of causing a misclassification, and they are consequently more likely to be successfully removed. We then continue iterating over features in ascending order of importance, hopefully producing small explanations.

Algorithm 2 T_{UB}: Upper Bounding Thread

1: Use a heuristic model to sort F's features by ascending relevance
2: **for each** $f \in F$ **do**
3:     Explanation ← F\Free
4:     **if** Verify((Explanation\{f})=v,N,$Q_{\neg c}$) is **UNSAT then**
5:         Free ← Free ∪ {f}
6:         UB ← UB − 1
7:     **end if**
8: **end for**

The Lower Bounding Thread (T_{LB}). The pseudocode for the lower bounding thread (T_{LB}) appears in Algorithm 3. In lines 1–6, the thread searches for contrastive singletons. Neural networks were shown to be very sensitive to adversarial attacks [25] — slight input perturbations that cause misclassification (e.g., the aforementioned one-pixel attack [64]) — and this suggests that contrastive sets, and in particular contrastive singletons, exist in many cases. We observe that identifying contrastive singletons is computationally cheap: by encoding Eq. 3 as a verification query, once for each feature, we can discover all singletons; and in these queries all features but one are fixed, which empirically allows verifiers to dispatch them quickly.

The rest of T_{LB} (lines 9–13) performs a similar process, but with contrastive pairs (which do not contain contrastive singletons as one of their features). We use verification queries to identify all such pairs, and then attempt to find their MHS. We observe that finding the MHS of all contrastive pairs is the 2-MHS problem, which is a reformalization of the *minimum vertex cover* problem (see Sec. B of the appendix of the full version of this paper [11]). Since this is an easier problem than the general MHS problem, solving it with MAX-SAT or MILP often converges quickly. In addition, the minimum vertex cover algorithm has a linear 2-approximating greedy algorithm, which can be used for finding a lower bound in cases of large feature spaces.

More formally, T_{LB} performs an efficient computation of the following bound:

$$\text{LB} = |\text{Singletons}| + |\text{MVC(Pairs)}| \leq \text{MHS(Cxps)} = E_M \qquad (4)$$

Algorithm 3 T_{LB}: Lower Bounding Thread

1: **for each** $f \in F$ **do**   ▷ Find all singletons
2:     **if** Verify$((F \setminus \{f\}=v,N,Q_{\neg c})$ is **SAT then**
3:         Singletons ← Singletons ∪ $\{f\}$
4:         LB ← LB +1
5:     **end if**
6: **end for**
7:
8: AllPairs ← Distinct pairs of F\Singletons
9: **for each** (a,b) ∈ AllPairs **do**   ▷ Find all pairs
10:     **if** Verify$((F \setminus \{a,b\}=v,N,Q_{\neg c})$ is **SAT then**
11:         Pairs ←Pairs ∪ $\{(a,b)\}$
12:     **end if**
13: **end for**
14: LB ← LB + MVC(Pairs)

---

where MVC is the minimum vertex cover, Cxps denotes the set of all contrastive examples, and E_M is the size of the minimum explanation.

It is worth mentioning that this approach can be extended to use contrastive examples of larger sizes ($k = 3, 4, \ldots$), as specified in Sec. C of the appendix of the full version of this paper. The fact that small contrastive examples, such as singletons, exist in large, state-of-the-art DNNs with large inputs [21, 64] suggests that useful approximations exist in large DNNs. In our experiments, we observed that using only singletons and pairs affords good approximations, without incurring overly expensive computations by the underlying verifier.

4   Finding Minimal Explanations Efficiently

Algorithm 1 is the backbone of our approach, but it suffers from limited scalability — particularly, in T_{UB}. As the execution of T_{UB} progresses, and as additional features are "freed", the quickly growing search space slows down the underlying verifier. Here we propose three different methods for expediting this process, by reducing the number of verification queries required.

Method 1: Using Information from T_{LB}. We suggest to leverage the contrastive examples found by T_{LB} to expedite T_{UB}. The process is described in Algorithm 4. In line 3, T_{LB} is queried for the current set of contrastive singletons, which we know must be part of any minimal explanation. These are subtracted from the RemainingFeatures set (features left for T_{UB} to query), and consequently will not be added to the Free set — i.e., they are marked as part of the current explanation. In addition, for any contrastive pair (a, b) found by T_{LB}, either a or b must appear in any minimal explanation; and so, our algorithm skips checking the case where both a and b are removed from F (Line 8). (the method could also be extended to contrastive sets of greater cardinality.)

Algorithm 4 T_{UB} using information from T_{LB}

1: Use a heuristic model to sort F by ascending relevance
2: RemainingFeatures ← F\Singletons
3: **for each** f ∈ RemainingFeatures **do**
4:     Explanation ← F\Free
5:     **if** Verify(($\mathrm{Explanation}\backslash\{f\}$)=v,N,$Q_{\neg c}$) is UNSAT **then**
6:         Free ← Free ∪ {f}
7:         UB ← UB − 1
8:         Delete all features in a pair with f from RemainingFeatures
9:     **end if**
10: **end for**

Method 2: Binary Search. Sorting the features being considered in ascending order of importance can have a significant effect on the size of the explanation found by Algorithm 2. Intuitively, a "perfect" heuristic model would assign the greatest weights to all features in the minimum explanation, and so traversing features in ascending order would first discover all the features that can be removed (UNSAT verification queries), followed by all the features that belong in the explanation (SAT queries). In this case, a sequential traversal of the features in ascending order is quite wasteful, and it is much better to perform a binary search to find the point where the answer flips from UNSAT to SAT.

Of course, in practice, the heuristic models are not perfect, leading to potential cases with multiple "flips" from SAT to UNSAT, and vice versa. Still, if the heuristic is good in practice (which is often the case; see Sec. 6), these flips are scarce. Thus, we propose to perform multiple binary searches, each time identifying one SAT query (i.e., a feature added to the explanation). Observe that each time we hit an UNSAT query, this indicates that all the queries for features with lower priorities would also yield UNSAT — because if "freeing" multiple features cannot change the classification, changing fewer features certainly cannot. Thus, we are guaranteed to find the first SAT query in each iteration, and soundness is maintained. This process is described in Algorithm. 6 and in Fig. 14 in the appendix of the full version of this paper [11].

Method 3: Local-Singleton Search. Let N be a DNN, and let x be an input point whose classification we seek to explain. As part of Algorithm 2, T_{UB} iteratively "frees" certain input features, allowing them to take arbitrary values, as it continues to search for features that must be included in the explanation. The increasing number of free features enlarges the search space that the underlying verifier must traverse, thus slowing down verification. We propose to leverage the hypothesis that input points nearby x that are misclassified tend to be clustered; and so, it is beneficial to *fix* the free features to "bad" values, as opposed to letting them take on arbitrary values. We speculate that this will allow the verifier to discover satisfying assignments much more quickly.

This enhancement is shown in Algorithm 5. Given a set Free of features that were previously freed, we fix their values according to some satisfying assignment previously discovered. Thus, the verification of any new feature that we consider is similar to the case of searching for contrastive singletons, which, as we already know, is fairly fast. See Fig. 15 in the appendix of the full version of this paper [11] for an illustration. The process can be improved further by fixing the freed features to small neighborhoods of the previously discovered satisfying assignment (instead of its exact values), to allow some flexibility while still keeping the query's search space small.

Algorithm 5 T_{UB} using local-singleton search

1: Use a heuristic model to sort F by ascending relevance
2: RemainingFeatures ← F\Singletons
3: **for each** f ∈ RemainingFeatures **do**
4:     Explanation ← F\Free
5:     **if** Verify$((\text{Explanation}\setminus\{f\})=v,N,Q_{\neg c})$ is UNSAT **then**
6:         Free ← Free ∪ {f}
7:         UB ← UB − 1
8:     **else**
9:         Extract counter example C
10:         LocalSingletons ← ∅
11:         **for each** f' ∈ RemainingFeatures **do**
12:             **if** Verify$(\text{Explanation}\setminus\{f'\} = C,N,Q_{\neg c})$ is SAT **then**
13:                 LocalSingletons ← LocalSingletons ∪ $\{f'\}$
14:             **end if**
15:         **end for**
16:         RemainingFeatures ← RemainingFeatures \ LocalSingletons
17:     **end if**
18: **end for**

---

5 Minimal Bundle Explanations

So far, we presented methods for generating explanations within a given approximation ratio of the minimum explanation (Sec. 3), and for expediting the computation of these explanations (Sec. 4) — in order to improve the scalability of our explanation generation mechanism. Next, we seek to tackle the second challenge from Sec. 1, namely that these explanations may be too low-level for many users. To address this challenge, we focus on *bundles*, which is a topic well covered in the ML [63] and heuristic XAI literature [50,55] (commonly known as "super-pixels" for computer-vision tasks). Intuitively, bundles are a partitioning of the features into disjoint sets (an

Fig. 6: Partition input's features into bundles.

illustration appears in Fig. 6). The idea, which we later validate empirically, is that providing explanations in terms of bundles is often easier for humans to comprehend. As an added bonus, using bundles also curtails the search space that the verifier must traverse, expediting the process even further.

Given a feature space $F = \{1, ..., m\}$, a bundle b is just a subset $b \subseteq F$. When dealing with the set of all bundles $B = \{b_1, b_2, ...b_n\}$, we require that they form a partitioning of F, namely $F = \cup b_i$. We define a *bundle explanation* E_B for a classification instance (v, c) as a subset of bundles, $E_B \subseteq B$, such that:

$$\forall (x \in \mathbb{F}).[\wedge_{i \in \cup E_B}(x_i = v_i) \rightarrow (N(x) = c)] \tag{5}$$

The following theorem then connects bundle explanations and explicit, non-bundle explanations:

Theorem 1. *The union of features in a bundle explanation is an explanation.*

The proof directly follows from Eqs. 1 and 5. We note that this definition of bundles implies that features that are not part of the bundle explanation (i.e. features contained in *"free"* bundles) are "free" to be set to any possible value. Another possible alternative for defining bundles could be to allow features in "free" bundles to only change in the same, coordinated manner. We focus here on the former definition, and leave the alternative definition for future work.

Many of the aforementioned results and definitions for explanations can be extended to bundle explanations. In a similar manner to Eq. 5, we can define the notions of minimal and minimum bundle explanations, a contrastive bundle singleton, and contrastive bundle pairs (see Sec. D of the appendix of the full version of this paper [11]). Theorems 1 and 2 can be extended to bundle explanations in a straightforward manner. It then follows that all bundle explanations contain all contrastive singleton bundles, and that all bundle explanations contain at least one bundle of any contrastive bundle pair.

Our method from Secs. 3 and 4 can be similarly performed on bundles rather than on features, and T_{UB} would then be used for calculating a minimal bundle explanation, rather than a minimal explanation. Regarding the aforementioned approximation ratio, we discuss and evaluate two different methods for obtaining it. The first, natural approach is to apply our techniques from Sec. 3 on bundle explanations, thus obtaining a provable approximation for a *minimum bundle explanation*. The upper bound is trivially derived by the size of the bundle explanation found by T_{UB}, whereas the lower bound calculation requires assigning a cost to each bundle, representing the number of features it contains. This is done via a known notion of *minimum hitting sets of bundles (MHSB)* [6] and using minimum *weighted* vertex cover for the approximation of contrastive bundle pairs. This method, which is almost identical to the one mentioned in Sec. 3, is formalized in Sec. D of the appendix of the full version of this paper [11].

The second approach is to calculate an approximation ratio with respect to a regular, non-bundle minimum explanation. The minimal bundle explanation found by T_{UB} is an upper bound on the minimum non-bundle explanation following theorem 5. For computing a lower bound, we can analyze contrastive bundle examples; extract from them contrastive non-bundle examples; and then use the duality property, compute an MHS of these contrastive examples, and derive lower bounds for the size of the minimum explanation. We formalize techniques for performing this calculation in Sec. E of the appendix of the full version of this paper [11].

6   Evaluation

Implementation and Setup. For evaluation purposes, we created a proof-of-concept implementation of our approach as a Python framework. Currently, the framework uses the Marabou verification engine [41] as a backend, although other engines may be used. Marabou is a Simplex-based DNN verification framework that is sound and complete [5,39–41,68,69], and which includes support for proof production [35], abstraction [15,16,52,60,67,72], and optimization [62]; and has been used in various settings, such as ensemble selection [3], simplification [22,43] repair [23,53], and verification of reinforcement-learning based systems [2,4,17]. For sorting features by their relevance, we used the popular XAI method LIME [55]; although again, other heuristics could be used. The MVC was calculated using the classic 2-approximating greedy algorithm. All experiments reported were conducted on x86-64 Gnu/Linux-based machines, using a single Intel(R) Xeon(R) Gold 6130 CPU @ 2.10GHz core, with a 1-hour timeout.

Benchmarks. As benchmarks, we used DNNs trained over the MNIST dataset for handwritten digit recognition [45]. These networks classify 28×28 grayscale images into the digits $0, \ldots, 9$. Additionally, we used DNNs trained over the Fashion-MNIST dataset [71], which classify 28×28 grayscale images into 10 clothing categories ("Dress", "Coat", etc.) For each of these datasets we trained a DNN with the following architecture: (i) an input layer (which corresponds to the image) of size 784; (ii) a fully connected hidden layer with 30 neurons; (iii) another fully connected hidden layer, with 10 neurons; and (iv) a final, softmax layer with 10 neurons, corresponding to the 10 possible output classes. The accuracy of the MNIST DNN was 96.6%, whereas that of the Fashion-MNIST DNN was 87.6%. (We note that we configured LIME to ignore the external border pixels of each input, as these are not part of the actual image.)

In selecting the classification instances to be explained for these networks, we targeted input points where the network was not confident — i.e., where the winning label did not win by a large margin. The motivation for this choice is that explanations are most useful and relevant in cases where the network's decision is unclear, which is reflected in lower confidence scores. Additionally, explanations of instances with lower confidence tend to be larger, facilitating the process of extensive experimentation. We thus selected the 100 inputs from the MNIST and the Fashion-MNIST datasets where the networks demonstrated the lowest confidence scores — i.e., where the difference between the winning output score and the runner-up class score was minimal.

Experiments. Our first goal was to compare our approach to that of Ignatiev et al. [31], which is the current state of the art in verification-based explainability of DNNs. Other approaches consider other ML types, such as decision trees [33,36], or focus on alternative definitions for abductive explanations [42,70] and are thus not comparable. Because the implementation used in [31] is unavailable, we implemented their approach, using Marabou as the underlying verifier for a fair comparison. In addition, we used the same heuristic model, LIME, for sorting

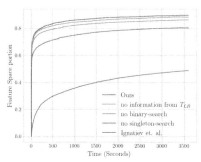
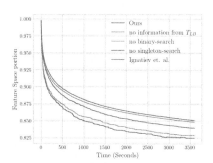

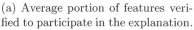

(a) Average portion of features veri-   (b) Average explanation size.
fied to participate in the explanation.

Fig. 7: Our full and ablation-based results, compared to the state of the art for finding minimal explanations on the MNIST dataset.

the input features' relevance. Fig. 7 depicts a comparison of the two approaches, over the MNIST benchmarks. The Fashion-MNIST results were similar, but since the Fashion-MNIST network had lower accuracy it tended to produce larger explanations with lower run-times, resulting in less meaningful evaluations (due to space limitations, these results appear in Fig. 12 in the appendix of the full version of this paper [11]). We compared the approaches according to two criteria: the portion of input features whose participation in the explanation was verified, over time (part (a) of Fig. 7), and the average size of the presently obtained explanation over time, also presented as a fraction of the total number of input features (part (b)). The results indicate that our method significantly improves over the state of the art, verifying the participation of 40.4% additional features, on average, and producing explanations that are 9.7% smaller, on average, at the end of the 1-hour time limit. Furthermore, our method timed out on 10% fewer benchmarks. We regard this as compelling evidence of the potential of our approach to produce more efficient verification-based XAI.

We also looked into comparing our approach to heuristic, non-verification-based approaches, such as LIME itself; but these comparisons did not prove to be meaningful, as the heuristic approaches typically solved benchmarks very quickly, but very often produced incorrect explanations. This matches the findings reported in previous work [14, 32].

Next, we set out to evaluate the contribution of each of the components implemented within our framework to overall performance, using an ablation study. Specifically, we ran our framework with each of the components mentioned in Sec. 4, i.e. (i) information exchange between T_{UB} and T_{LB}; (ii) the binary search in T_{UB}; and (iii) local-singleton search, turned off. The results on the MNIST benchmarks appear in Fig. 7; see Fig. 12 in the appendix of the full version of this paper [11] for the Fashion-MNIST results. Our experiments revealed that each of the methods mentioned in Sec. 4 had a favorable impact on both the average portion of features verified, and the average size of the discovered explanation, over time. Fig 7a indicates that the local-singleton search method, used for efficiently proving that features are bound to be *included* in the explanation, was the most significant in reducing the number of features remained for verifying, thus substantially increasing the portion of verified features. Moreover, Fig. 7b indicates that the binary search method, which is used for grouping UNSAT queries and proving the *exclusion* of features from the explanation, was the most significant for more efficiently obtaining smaller-sized explanations, over time.

Our second goal was to evaluate the quality of the *minimum* explanation approximation of our method (using the lower/upper bounds) over time. Results are averaged over all benchmarks of the MNIST dataset and are presented in Fig. 8 (similar results on Fashion-MNIST appear in Fig. 13 in the appendix of the full version of this paper [11]). The upper bound represents the average size of the explanation discovered by T_{UB} over time, whereas the lower bound represents the average lower bound discovered by T_{LB} over time. It can be seen that initially, there is a steep increase in

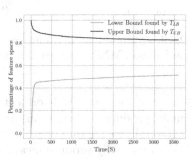

Fig. 8: Average approximation of *minimum* explanation over time.

the size of the lower bound, as T_{LB} discovered many contrastive singletons. Later, as we begin iterating over contrastive pairs, the verification queries take longer to solve, and progress becomes slower. The average approximation ratio achieved after an hour was 1.61 for MNIST and 1.19 for Fashion-MNIST.

For our third experiment, we set out to assess the improvements afforded by bundles. We repeated the aforementioned experiments, this time using sets of features representing bundles instead of the features themselves. The segmentation into bundles was performed using the *quickshift* method [65], with LIME again used for assigning relevance to each bundle [55]. We approximate the sizes of the bundle explanations in terms of both the minimum bundle explanation as well as the minimum (non-bundle) explanation (as mentioned in Sec. 5 and in Sec. E of the appendix of the full version of this paper [11]). The bundle configuration showed drastic efficiency improvements, with none of the experiments timing out within the 1-hour time limit, thus improving the portion of timeouts on the MNIST dataset by 84%. The efficiency improvement was obtained at the expense of explanation size, resulting in a decrease of 352% in the approximation ratios obtained for MNIST and 39% for Fashion-MNIST. Nevertheless, when calculating the approximation in terms of the *minimum bundle explanation*, an increase of 12% and 8% was obtained for MNIST and Fashion-MNIST (results are summarized in Table 1 in the appendix of the full version of this paper [11]). For a visual evaluation, we performed the same set of experiments for both bundle and non-bundle implementations, using instances with high confidence rates to obtain smaller-sized explanations that could be more easily interpreted. A

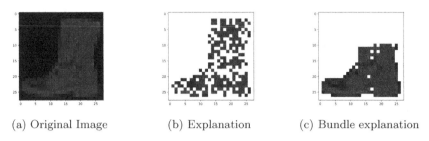

(a) Original Image   (b) Explanation   (c) Bundle explanation

Fig. 9: Minimal explanations and bundle explanations found by our method on the Fashion-MNIST dataset. White pixels are not part of the explanation.

sample of these results is presented in Fig. 9. Empirically, we observe that the bundle-produced explanations are less complex and more comprehensible.

Overall, we regard our results as compelling evidence that verification-based XAI can soundly produce meaningful explanations, and that our improvements can indeed significantly improve its runtime.

7 Related Work

Our work is another step in the ongoing quest for formal explainability of DNNs, using verification [19, 27, 31, 58]. Related approaches have applied enumeration of contrastive examples [30, 31], which is also an ingredient of our approach. Other approaches focus on producing abductive explanations around an epsilon environment [42, 70]. Similar work has been carried out for decision sets [33], lists [28] and trees [36], where the problem appears to be simpler to solve [36]. Our work here tackles DNNs, which are known to be more difficult to verify [39].

Prior work has also sought to produce approximate explanations, e.g., by using δ-relevant sets [37,66]. This line of work has focused on probabilistic methods for generating explanations, which jeopardizes soundness. There has also been extensive work in heuristic XAI [50, 55, 56, 61], but here, too, the produced explanations are not guaranteed to be correct.

8 Conclusion

Although DNNs are becoming crucial components of safety-critical systems, they remain "black-boxes", and cannot be interpreted by humans. Our work seeks to mitigate this concern, by providing formally correct explanations for the choices that a DNN makes. Since discovering the minimum explanations is difficult, we focus on approximate explanations, and suggest multiple techniques for expediting our approach — thus significantly improving over the current state of the art. In addition, we propose to use bundles to efficiently produce more meaningful explanations. Moving forward, we plan to leverage lightweight DNN verification techniques for improving the scalability of our approach [49], as well as extend it to support additional DNN architectures.

References

1. M. Akintunde, A. Kevorchian, A. Lomuscio, and E. Pirovano. Verification of RNN-Based Neural Agent-Environment Systems. In *Proc. 33rd AAAI Conf. on Artificial Intelligence (AAAI)*, pages 197–210, 2019.
2. G. Amir, D. Corsi, R. Yerushalmi, L. Marzari, D. Harel, A. Farinelli, and G. Katz. Verifying Learning-Based Robotic Navigation Systems, 2022. Technical Report. https://arxiv.org/abs/2205.13536.
3. G. Amir, G. Katz, and M. Schapira. Verification-Aided Deep Ensemble Selection. In *Proc. 22nd Int. Conf. on Formal Methods in Computer-Aided Design (FMCAD)*, pages 27–37, 2022.
4. G. Amir, M. Schapira, and G. Katz. Towards Scalable Verification of Deep Reinforcement Learning. In *Proc. 21st Int. Conf. on Formal Methods in Computer-Aided Design (FMCAD)*, pages 193–203, 2021.
5. G. Amir, H. Wu, C. Barrett, and G. Katz. An SMT-Based Approach for Verifying Binarized Neural Networks. In *Proc. 27th Int. Conf. on Tools and Algorithms for the Construction and Analysis of Systems (TACAS)*, pages 203–222, 2021.
6. E. Angel, E. Bampis, and L. Gourvès. On the Minimum Hitting Set of Bundles Problem. *Theoretical Computer Science*, 410(45):4534–4542, 2009.
7. J. Angwin, J. Larson, S. Mattu, and L. Kirchner. Machine Bias. *Ethics of Data and Analytics*, pages 254–264, 2016.
8. G. Avni, R. Bloem, K. Chatterjee, T. Henzinger, B. Konighofer, and S. Pranger. Run-Time Optimization for Learned Controllers through Quantitative Games. In *Proc. 31st Int. Conf. on Computer Aided Verification (CAV)*, pages 630–649, 2019.
9. T. Baluta, S. Shen, S. Shinde, K. Meel, and P. Saxena. Quantitative Verification of Neural Networks And its Security Applications. In *Proc. 26th ACM Conf. on Computer and Communication Security (CCS)*, pages 1249–1264, 2019.
10. P. Barceló, M. Monet, J. Pérez, and B. Subercaseaux. Model interpretability through the lens of computational complexity. *Advances in neural information processing systems*, 33:15487–15498, 2020.
11. S. Bassan and G. Katz. Towards Formally Approximate Minimal Explanations of Neural Networks, 2022. Technical Report. https://arxiv.org/abs/2210.13915.
12. M. Bojarski, D. Del Testa, D. Dworakowski, B. Firner, B. Flepp, P. Goyal, L. Jackel, M. Monfort, U. Muller, J. Zhang, X. Zhang, J. Zhao, and K. Zieba. End to End Learning for Self-Driving Cars, 2016. Technical Report. http://arxiv.org/abs/1604.07316.
13. CACM. A Case Against Mission-Critical Applications of Machine Learning. *Communications of the ACM*, 62(8):9–9, 2019.
14. O.-M. Camburu, E. Giunchiglia, J. Foerster, T. Lukasiewicz, and P. Blunsom. Can I Trust the Explainer? Verifying Post-Hoc Explanatory Methods, 2019. Technical Report. http://arxiv.org/abs/1910.02065.
15. Y. Elboher, E. Cohen, and G. Katz. Neural Network Verification using Residual Reasoning. In *Proc. 20th Int. Conf. on Software Engineering and Formal Methods (SEFM)*, pages 173–189, 2022.
16. Y. Elboher, J. Gottschlich, and G. Katz. An Abstraction-Based Framework for Neural Network Verification. In *Proc. 32nd Int. Conf. on Computer Aided Verification (CAV)*, pages 43–65, 2020.

17. T. Eliyahu, Y. Kazak, G. Katz, and M. Schapira. Verifying Learning-Augmented Systems. In *Proc. Conf. of the ACM Special Interest Group on Data Communication on the Applications, Technologies, Architectures, and Protocols for Computer Communication (SIGCOMM)*, pages 305–318, 2021.

18. A. Esteva, A. Robicquet, B. Ramsundar, V. Kuleshov, M. DePristo, K. Chou, C. Cui, G. Corrado, S. Thrun, and J. Dean. A Guide to Deep Learning in Healthcare. *Nature Medicine*, 25(1):24–29, 2019.

19. T. Fel, M. Ducoffe, D. Vigouroux, R. Cadène, M. Capelle, C. Nicodème, and T. Serre. Don't Lie to Me! Robust and Efficient Explainability with Verified Perturbation Analysis, 2022. Technical Report. `http://arXivpreprintarXiv:2202.07728`.

20. A. Gainer-Dewar and P. Vera-Licona. The Minimal Hitting Set Generation Problem: Algorithms and Computation. *SIAM Journal on Discrete Mathematics*, 31(1):63–100, 2017.

21. S. Garg and G. Ramakrishnan. BAE: Bert-Based Adversarial Examples for Text Classification, 2020. Technical Report. `https://arxiv.org/abs/2004.01970`.

22. S. Gokulanathan, A. Feldsher, A. Malca, C. Barrett, and G. Katz. Simplifying Neural Networks using Formal Verification. In *Proc. 12th NASA Formal Methods Symposium (NFM)*, pages 85–93, 2020.

23. B. Goldberger, Y. Adi, J. Keshet, and G. Katz. Minimal Modifications of Deep Neural Networks using Verification. In *Proc. 23rd Int. Conf. on Logic for Programming, Artificial Intelligence and Reasoning (LPAR)*, pages 260–278, 2020.

24. I. Goodfellow, J. Shlens, and C. Szegedy. Explaining and Harnessing Adversarial Examples, 2014. Technical Report. `http://arxiv.org/abs/1412.6572`.

25. S. Huang, N. Papernot, I. Goodfellow, Y. Duan, and P. Abbeel. Adversarial Attacks on Neural Network Policies, 2017. Technical Report. `http://arxiv.org/abs/1702.02284`.

26. IBM. The CPLEX Optimizer, 2018.

27. A. Ignatiev. Towards Trustable Explainable AI. In *Proc. 29th Int. Joint Conf. on Artificial Intelligence (IJCAI)*, pages 5154–5158, 2020.

28. A. Ignatiev and J. Marques-Silva. SAT-Based Rigorous Explanations for Decision Lists. In *Proc. 24th Int. Conf. on Theory and Applications of Satisfiability Testing (SAT)*, pages 251–269, 2021.

29. A. Ignatiev, A. Morgado, and J. Marques-Silva. Propositional Abduction with Implicit Hitting Sets, 2016. Technical Report. `http://arxiv.org/abs/1604.08229`.

30. A. Ignatiev, N. Narodytska, N. Asher, and J. Marques-Silva. From Contrastive to Abductive Explanations and Back Again. In *Proc. 19th Int. Conf. of the Italian Association for Artificial Intelligence (AIxIA)*, pages 335–355, 2020.

31. A. Ignatiev, N. Narodytska, and J. Marques-Silva. Abduction-Based Explanations for Machine Learning Models. In *Proc. 33rd AAAI Conf. on Artificial Intelligence (AAAI)*, pages 1511–1519, 2019.

32. A. Ignatiev, N. Narodytska, and J. Marques-Silva. On Validating, Repairing and Refining Heuristic Ml Explanations, 2019. Technical Report. `http://arxiv.org/abs/1907.02509`.

33. A. Ignatiev, F. Pereira, N. Narodytska, and J. Marques-Silva. A SAT-Based Approach to Learn Explainable Decision Sets. In *Proc. 9th Int. Joint Conf. on Automated Reasoning (IJCAR)*, pages 627–645, 2018.

34. A. Ignatiev, A. Previti, M. Liffiton, and J. Marques-Silva. Smallest MUS Extraction with Minimal Hitting Set Dualization. In *Proc. 21st Int. Conf. on Principles and Practice of Constraint Programming (CP)*, pages 173–182, 2015.

35. O. Isac, C. Barrett, M. Zhang, and G. Katz. Neural Network Verification with Proof Production. In *Proc. 22nd Int. Conf. on Formal Methods in Computer-Aided Design (FMCAD)*, pages 38–48, 2022.

36. Y. Izza, A. Ignatiev, and J. Marques-Silva. On Explaining Decision Trees, 2020. Technical Report. http://arxiv.org/abs/2010.11034.

37. Y. Izza, A. Ignatiev, N. Narodytska, M. Cooper, and J. Marques-Silva. Efficient Explanations with Relevant Sets, 2021. Technical Report. http://arxiv.org/abs/2106.00546.

38. K. Julian, M. Kochenderfer, and M. Owen. Deep Neural Network Compression for Aircraft Collision Avoidance Systems. *Journal of Guidance, Control, and Dynamics*, 42(3):598–608, 2019.

39. G. Katz, C. Barrett, D. Dill, K. Julian, and M. Kochenderfer. Reluplex: An Efficient SMT Solver for Verifying Deep Neural Networks. In *Proc. 29th Int. Conf. on Computer Aided Verification (CAV)*, pages 97–117, 2017.

40. G. Katz, C. Barrett, D. Dill, K. Julian, and M. Kochenderfer. Reluplex: a Calculus for Reasoning about Deep Neural Networks. *Formal Methods in System Design (FMSD)*, 2021.

41. G. Katz, D. Huang, D. Ibeling, K. Julian, C. Lazarus, R. Lim, P. Shah, S. Thakoor, H. Wu, A. Zeljić, D. Dill, M. Kochenderfer, and C. Barrett. The Marabou Framework for Verification and Analysis of Deep Neural Networks. In *Proc. 31st Int. Conf. on Computer Aided Verification (CAV)*, pages 443–452, 2019.

42. E. La Malfa, A. Zbrzezny, R. Michelmore, N. Paoletti, and M. Kwiatkowska. On Guaranteed Optimal Robust Explanations for NLP Models, 2021. Technical Report. https://arxiv.org/abs/2105.03640.

43. O. Lahav and G. Katz. Pruning and Slicing Neural Networks using Formal Verification. In *Proc. 21st Int. Conf. on Formal Methods in Computer-Aided Design (FMCAD)*, pages 183–192, 2021.

44. H. Lakkaraju and O. Bastani. "How do I Fool You?" Manipulating User Trust via Misleading Black Box Explanations. In *Proc. AAAI/ACM Conf. on AI, Ethics, and Society (AIES)*, pages 79–85, 2020.

45. Y. LeCun. The MNIST Database of Handwritten Digits, 1998. http://yann.lecun.com/exdb/mnist/.

46. Y. LeCun, Y. Bengio, and G. Hinton. Deep Learning. *Nature*, 521(7553):436–444, 2015.

47. C. Li and F. Manya. MaxSAT, Hard and Soft Constraints. In *Handbook of Satisfiability*, pages 903–927. IOS Press, 2021.

48. P. Liberatore. Redundancy in logic i: Cnf propositional formulae. *Artificial Intelligence*, 163(2):203–232, 2005.

49. C. Liu, T. Arnon, C. Lazarus, C. Barrett, and M. Kochenderfer. Algorithms for Verifying Deep Neural Networks, 2020. Technical Report. http://arxiv.org/abs/1903.06758.

50. S. M. Lundberg and S.-I. Lee. A Unified Approach to Interpreting Model Predictions. In *Proc. 31st Conf. on Neural Information Processing Systems (NeurIPS)*, 2017.

51. J. Marques-Silva and A. Ignatiev. Delivering Trustworthy AI through formal XAI. In *Proc. 36th AAAI Conf. on Artificial Intelligence (AAAI)*, pages 3806–3814, 2022.

52. M. Ostrovsky, C. Barrett, and G. Katz. An Abstraction-Refinement Approach to Verifying Convolutional Neural Networks. In *Proc. 20th. Int. Symposium on Automated Technology for Verification and Analysis (ATVA)*, 2022.

53. I. Refaeli and G. Katz. Minimal Multi-Layer Modifications of Deep Neural Networks. In *Proc. 5th Workshop on Formal Methods for ML-Enabled Autonomous Systems (FoMLAS)*, 2022.

54. R. Reiter. A Theory of Diagnosis from First Principles. *Artificial Intelligence*, 32(1):57–95, 1987.

55. M. Ribeiro, S. Singh, and C. Guestrin. "Why should I Trust You?" Explaining the Predictions of any Classifier. In *Proc. 22nd Int. Conf. on Knowledge Discovery and Data Mining (KDD)*, pages 1135–1144, 2016.

56. M. Ribeiro, S. Singh, and C. Guestrin. Anchors: High-Precision Model-Agnostic Explanations. In *Proc. 32nd AAAI Conf. on Artificial Intelligence (AAAI)*, 2018.

57. R. Selvaraju, M. Cogswell, A. Das, R. Vedantam, D. Parikh, and D. Batra. Grad-Cam: Visual Explanations from Deep Networks via Gradient-Based Localization. In *Proc. 20th IEEE Int. Conf. on Computer Vision (ICCV)*, pages 618–626, 2017.

58. W. Shi, A. Shih, A. Darwiche, and A. Choi. On Tractable Representations of Binary Neural Networks, 2020. Technical Report. http://arxiv.org/abs/2004.02082.

59. A. Shih, A. Choi, and A. Darwiche. A Symbolic Approach to Explaining Bayesian Network Classifiers, 2018. Technical Report. http://arxiv.org/abs/1805.03364.

60. G. Singh, T. Gehr, M. Puschel, and M. Vechev. An Abstract Domain for Certifying Neural Networks. In *Proc. 46th ACM SIGPLAN Symposium on Principles of Programming Languages (POPL)*, 2019.

61. D. Smilkov, N. Thorat, B. Kim, F. Viégas, and M. Wattenberg. Smoothgrad: Removing Noise by Adding Noise, 2017. Technical Report. http://arxiv.org/abs/1706.03825.

62. C. Strong, H. Wu, A. Zeljić, K. Julian, G. Katz, C. Barrett, and M. Kochenderfer. Global Optimization of Objective Functions Represented by ReLU Networks. *Journal of Machine Learning*, pages 1–28, 2021.

63. D. Stutz, A. Hermans, and B. Leibe. Superpixels: An Evaluation of the State-of-the-Art. *Computer Vision and Image Understanding*, 166:1–27, 2018.

64. J. Su, D. Vargas, and K. Sakurai. One Pixel Attack for Fooling Deep Neural Networks. *IEEE Transactions on Evolutionary Computation*, 23(5):828–841, 2019.

65. A. Vedaldi and S. Soatto. Quick Shift and Kernel Methods for Mode Seeking. In *Proc. 10th European Conf. on Computer Vision (ECCV)*, pages 705–718, 2008.

66. S. Waeldchen, J. Macdonald, S. Hauch, and G. Kutyniok. The Computational Complexity of Understanding Binary Classifier Decisions. *Journal of Artificial Intelligence Research*, 70:351–387, 2021.

67. S. Wang, K. Pei, J. Whitehouse, J. Yang, and S. Jana. Formal Security Analysis of Neural Networks using Symbolic Intervals. In *Proc. 27th USENIX Security Symposium*, 2018.

68. H. Wu, A. Ozdemir, A. Zeljić, A. Irfan, K. Julian, D. Gopinath, S. Fouladi, G. Katz, C. Păsăreanu, and C. Barrett. Parallelization Techniques for Verifying Neural Networks. In *Proc. 20th Int. Conf. on Formal Methods in Computer-Aided Design (FMCAD)*, pages 128–137, 2020.

69. H. Wu, A. Zeljić, G. Katz, and C. Barrett. Efficient Neural Network Analysis with Sum-of-Infeasibilities. In *Proc. 28th Int. Conf. on Tools and Algorithms for the Construction and Analysis of Systems (TACAS)*, pages 143–163, 2022.

70. M. Wu, H. Wu, and C. Barrett. VeriX: Towards Verified Explainability of Deep Neural Networks, 2022. Technical Report. https://arxiv.org/abs/2212.01051.

71. H. Xiao, K. Rasul, and R. Vollgraf. Fashion-MNist: a Novel Image Dataset for Benchmarking Machine Learning Algorithms, 2017. Technical Report. http://arxiv.org/abs/1708.07747.

72. T. Zelazny, H. Wu, C. Barrett, and G. Katz. On Reducing Over-Approximation Errors for Neural Network Verification. In *Proc. 22nd Int. Conf. on Formal Methods in Computer-Aided Design (FMCAD)*, pages 17–26, 2022.
73. Z. Zhou and L. Sun. Metamorphic Testing of Driverless Cars. *Communications of the ACM*, 62(3):61–67, 2019.

OccRob: Efficient SMT-Based Occlusion Robustness Verification of Deep Neural Networks

Xingwu Guo [1], Ziwei Zhou [1], Yueling Zhang [1], Guy Katz [2], Min Zhang [1(✉)]

[1] Shanghai Key Laboratory of Trustworthy Computing,
East China Normal University, Shanghai, China
zhangmin@sei.ecnu.edu.cn
[2] The Hebrew University of Jerusalem, Jerusalem, Isarel

Abstract. Occlusion is a prevalent and easily realizable semantic perturbation to deep neural networks (DNNs). It can fool a DNN into misclassifying an input image by occluding some segments, possibly resulting in severe errors. Therefore, DNNs planted in safety-critical systems should be verified to be robust against occlusions prior to deployment. However, most existing robustness verification approaches for DNNs are focused on non-semantic perturbations and are not suited to the occlusion case. In this paper, we propose the first efficient, SMT-based approach for formally verifying the occlusion robustness of DNNs. We formulate the occlusion robustness verification problem and prove it is NP-complete. Then, we devise a novel approach for encoding occlusions as a part of neural networks and introduce two acceleration techniques so that the extended neural networks can be efficiently verified using off-the-shelf, SMT-based neural network verification tools. We implement our approach in a prototype called OccRob and extensively evaluate its performance on benchmark datasets with various occlusion variants. The experimental results demonstrate our approach's effectiveness and efficiency in verifying DNNs' robustness against various occlusions, and its ability to generate counterexamples when these DNNs are not robust.

1 Introduction

Deep neural networks (DNNs) are computer-trained *programs* that can implement hard-to-formally-specify tasks. They have repeatedly demonstrated their potential in enabling artificial intelligence in various domains, such as face recognition [6] and autonomous driving [27]. They are increasingly being incorporated into safety-critical applications with interactive environments. To ensure the security and reliability of these applications, DNNs must be highly dependable against adversarial and environmental perturbations. This dependability property is known as *robustness* and is attracting a considerable amount of research efforts from both academia and industry, aimed at ensuring robustness via different technologies such as adversarial training [13,28], testing [40,33], and formal verification [34,10,5].

Occlusion is a prevalent kind of perturbation, which may cause DNNs to misclassify an image by occluding some segment thereof [38,25,8]. For instance, a "turn left" traffic sign may be misclassified as "go straight" after it is occluded by a tape, probably resulting in traffic accidents. A similar situation may occur in face recognition, where many well-trained neural networks fail to recognize faces correctly when they are partially occluded, such as when glasses are worn[37]. A neural network is called *robust against occlusions*

© The Author(s) 2023
S. Sankaranarayanan and N. Sharygina (Eds.): TACAS 2023, LNCS 13993, pp. 208–226, 2023.
https://doi.org/10.1007/978-3-031-30823-9_11

if small occlusions do not alter its classification results. Generally, we wish a DNN to be robust against occlusions that appear negligible to humans.

It is challenging to verify whether a DNN is robust or not on an input image if the image is occluded. On the one hand, the verification problem is non-convex due to the non-linear activation functions in DNNs. It is NP-complete even when dealing with common, fully connected feed-forward neural networks (FNNs) [20]. On the other hand, unlike existing perturbations, occlusions are challenging to encode using L_p norms. Most existing robustness verification approaches assume that perturbations need to be defined by L_p norms and then apply approximations and abstract interpretation techniques [34,10,5] as part of the verification process. The semantic effect of occlusions partially alters the values of some neighboring pixels from large to small or in the inverse direction, e.g., 255 to 0, when a black occlusion occludes a white pixel. Therefore, existing techniques for perturbations in L_p norms are not suited to occlusion perturbations.

SMT-based approaches have been shown to be an efficient approach to DNN verification [20]. They are both sound and complete, in that they always return definite results and produce counterexamples in non-robust cases. We show that, although it is straightforward to encode the occlusion robustness verification problem into SMT formulas, solving the constraints generated by this naïve encoding is experimentally beyond the reach of state-of-the-art SMT solvers, due to the inclusion of a large number of the piece-wise ReLU activation functions. Consequently, such a straightforward encoding approach cannot scale to large networks.

In this paper, we systematically study the occlusion robustness verification problem of DNNs. We first formalize and prove that the problem is NP-complete for ReLU-based FNNs. Then, we propose a novel approach for encoding various occlusions and neural networks together to generate new equivalent networks that can be efficiently verified using off-the-shelf SMT-based robustness verification tools such as Marabou [21]. In our encoding approach, although additional neurons and layers are introduced for encoding occlusions, the number is reasonably small and independent of the networks to be verified. The efficiency improvement of our approach comes from the fact that our approach significantly reduces the number of constraints introduced while encoding the occlusion and leverages the backend verification tool's optimization against the neural network structure. Furthermore, we introduce two acceleration techniques, namely input-space splitting to reduce the search space of a single verification, which can significantly improve verification efficiency, and label sorting to help verification terminates earlier. We implement a tool called OccRob with Marabou as the backend verification tool. To our knowledge, this is the first work on formally verifying the occlusion robustness of deep neural networks.

To demonstrate the effectiveness and efficiency of OccRob, we evaluate it on six representative FNNs trained on two benchmark datasets. The empirical results show that our approach is effective and efficient in verifying various types of occlusions with respect to the occlusion position, size, and occluding pixel value.

Contributions. We make the following three major contributions: (i) we propose a novel approach for encoding occlusion perturbations, by which we can leverage *off-the-shelf* SMT-based robustness verification tools to verify the robustness of neural networks against various occlusion perturbations; (ii) we prove the verification problem of the occlusion robustness is NP-complete and introduce two acceleration techniques, i.e., label sorting and input space splitting, to improve the efficiency of verification further; and (iii) we implement a tool called OccRob and conduct experiments extensively on a collection of benchmarks to demonstrate its effectiveness and efficiency.

Paper Organization. Sec. 2 introduces preliminaries. Sec. 3 formulates the occlusion robustness verification problem and studies its complexity. Sec. 4 presents our encoding approach and acceleration techniques for the verification. Sec. 5 shows the experimental results. Sec. 6 discusses related work, and Sec. 7 concludes the paper.

We omit the complete proofs and experimental results due to the page limit. Please refer to the technical report [15] for more details.

2 Preliminaries

2.1 Deep Neural Networks and the Robustness

As shown in Fig. 1, a deep neural network consists of multiple layers. The neurons on the input layer take input values, which are computed and propagated through the hidden layers and then output by the output layer. The neurons on each layer are connected to those on the predecessor and successor layers. We only consider fully connected, feedforward networks (FNNs) [11].

Given a λ-layer neural network, let $W^{(i)}$ be the weight matrix between the $(i-1)$-th

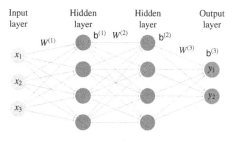

Fig. 1: A fully-connected feed-forward neural network (FNN).

and i-th layers, and $b^{(i)}$ be the biases of the corresponding neurons, where $i = 1, 2, \ldots, \lambda$. The network implements a function $F : \mathbb{R}^u \rightarrow \mathbb{R}^r$ that is recursively defined by:

$$z^{(0)} = x$$
$$z^{(i)} = \sigma(W^{(i)} \cdot z^{(i-1)} + b^{(i)}), \; for \; i = 1, \ldots, \lambda - 1 \qquad \text{(Layer Function)}$$
$$F(x) = W^{(\lambda)} \cdot z^{(\lambda-1)} + b^{(\lambda)} \qquad \text{(Network Function)}$$

where $\sigma(\cdot)$ is called an *activation function* and $z^{(i)}$ denotes the result of neurons at the i-th layer.

For example, Fig. 1 shows a 3-layer neural network with three input neurons and two output neurons, namely, $\lambda = 3$, $u = 3$ and $r = 2$.

For the sake of simplicity, we use $\Phi_F(x) = arg\,max_{\ell \in L} F(x)$ to denote the label ℓ such that the probability $F_\ell(x)$ of classifying x to ℓ is larger than those to other labels, where L represents the set of labels. The activation function σ usually can be a piece-wise Rectified Linear Unit (ReLU), $\sigma(x) = max(x, 0)$, or S-shape functions like Sigmoid $\sigma(x) = \frac{1}{1+e^{-x}}$, Tanh $\sigma(x) = \frac{e^x - e^{-x}}{e^x + e^{-x}}$, or Arctan $\sigma(x) = tan^{-1}(x)$. In this work, we focus on the networks that only contain ReLU activation functions, which are widely adopted in real-world applications.

(a) Multiform: 30km/h   (b) Origin 70km/h   (c) Uniform: 30km/h   (d) Origin 70km/h

Fig. 2: Two multiform and uniform occlusions to traffic signs causing mis-classifications.

A neural network is called *robust* if small perturbations to its inputs do not alter the classification result [39]. Specifically, given a network F, an input x_0 and a set Ω of perturbed inputs of x_0, F is called locally robust with respect to x_0 and Ω if F classifies all the perturbed inputs in Ω to the same label as it does x_0.

Definition 1 (Local Robustness [17]). *A neural network $F : \mathbb{R}^u \to \mathbb{R}^r$ is called locally robust with respect to an input x_0 and a set Ω of perturbed inputs of x if $\forall x \in \Omega$, $\Phi_F(x) = \Phi_F(x_0)$ holds.*

Usually, the set Ω of perturbed inputs is defined by an ℓ_p-norm ball around x_0 with a radius of ϵ, i.e., $\mathbb{B}_p(x_0, \epsilon) := \{x \mid \|x - x_0\|_p \le \epsilon\}$ [17,2].

2.2 Occlusion Perturbation

In the context of image classification networks, occlusion is a kind of perturbation that blocks the pixels in certain areas before the image is fed into the network. Existing studies showed that the classification accuracy of neural networks could be significantly decreased when the input objects are artificially occluded [23,44].

Occlusions can have various occlusion shapes, sizes, colors, and positions. The shapes can be square, rectangle, triangle, or irregular shape. The size is measured by the number of occluded pixels. The occlusion color specifies the colors occluded pixels can take. The coloring of an occlusion can be either uniform, where all occluded pixels share the same color, or multiform, where these colors can vary in the range of $[-\epsilon, \epsilon]$, where ϵ specifies the threshold between an occluded pixel's value and its original value.

Prior studies [8,3] showed that both the uniform and multiform occlusions could cause misclassification to neural networks. Fig. 2 shows two examples of multiform and uniform occlusions, respectively. The traffic sign for "70km/h speed limit" in Fig. 2(a) is misclassified to "30km/h" by adding a 5×5 multiform occlusion. Fig. 2(d) shows another sign, with different light conditions, where a 3×3 uniform occlusion (in Fig. 2(c)) causes the sign to be misclassified to "30km/h".

The occlusion position is another aspect of defining occlusions. An occlusion can be placed precisely on the pixels of an image, or between a pixel and its neighbors. Fig. 3 shows an example, where the dots represent image

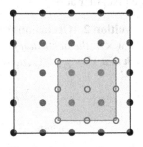

Fig. 3: An example occlusion on a 5×5 image at real number position.

pixels and the circles are the occluding pixels that will substitute the occluded ones. We say that an occlusion pixel $\vartheta_{i',j'}$ at location (i', j') surrounds an image pixel $p_{i,j}$ at location (i, j) if and only if $|i - i'| < 1$ and $|j - j'| < 1$. Note that i', j' are real numbers, representing the location where the occlusion pixel o is placed on the image. An image pixel can be occluded by the substitute occlusion pixels if the occlusion pixels surround the image pixel.

There are at most four surrounding occlusion pixels for each image pixel, as shown in Fig. 3. Let $\mathbb{I}_p$ be the set of the locations where the surrounding occlusion pixels of p are placed. After the occlusion, the value of pixel $p_{i,j}$ is altered to the new one denoted by $p'_{i,j}$, which can be computed by interpolation [19,22] such as next neighbour interpolation or Bi-linear interpolation based on occlusion pixels in $\mathbb{I}_p$. Besides that, we use a method based on L_1-distance to calculate how much a pixel is occluded. Since the L_1-distance of two adjacent pixels is 1, a surrounding occlusion pixel should not affect the image pixel if their L_1-distance is greater than 1. The formula $max(0, (|1 - i' + i|) + (1 - j' + j) - 1)$ indicates how much an image pixel at (i, j) is occluded by an occlusion pixel at (i', j'). For instance, occlusion pixel at $(i', j') = (0.9, 0.9)$ has no effect to image pixel $(i, j) = (0, 0)$ since their L_1-distance is larger than 1. Therefore, the occlusion factor $s_{i,j}$ for pixel p at (i, j) can be calculated based on all surrounding occlusion pixels in $\mathbb{I}_p$ as:

$$s_{i,j} = max(0, \sum_{i'_0, j' \in \mathbb{I}_p} (|1 - j + j'|) + \sum_{i', j'_0 \in \mathbb{I}_p} (|1 - i' + i|) - 1) \tag{1}$$

where (i'_0, j'_0) is the first element of $\mathbb{I}_p$. Notably, s is 1 for completely occluded pixel and 0 for the pixel that is not occluded, otherwise s has a value between $(0, 1)$. Also, it is a special case for Equation 1 when (i', j') are integers, where s can be reduced to 0 or 1.

3   The Occlusion Robustness Verification Problem

Let $\mathbb{R}^{m \times n}$ be the set of images whose height is m and width is n. We use $\mathbb{N}_{1,m}$ (resp. $\mathbb{N}_{1,n}$) to denote the set of all the natural numbers ranging from 1 to m (resp. n). A coloring function $\zeta : \mathbb{R}^{m \times n} \times \mathbb{R} \times \mathbb{R} \to \mathbb{R}$ is a mapping of each pixel of an image to its corresponding color value. Given an image $x \in \mathbb{R}^{m \times n}$, $\zeta(x, i, j)$ defines the value to color the pixel of x at (i, j).

Definition 2 (Occlusion function). *Given a coloring function ζ and an occlusion ϑ of size $w \times h$, the occlusion function is defined as function $\gamma_{\zeta, w \times h} : \mathbb{R}^{m \times n} \times \mathbb{R} \times \mathbb{R} \to \mathbb{R}^{m \times n}$ such that $x' = \gamma_{\zeta, w \times h}(x, a, b)$ if for all $i \in \mathbb{N}_{1,n}$ and $j \in \mathbb{N}_{1,m}$, there is,*

$$x'_{i,j} = x_{i,j} - s_{i,j} \times (x_{i,j} - \zeta(x, i, j)), \tag{2}$$

$$where, \; \zeta(x, i, j) = \frac{\sum_{(i',j') \in \mathbb{I}_{x_{i,j}}} \vartheta_{i',j'} \sqrt{(i - i')^2 + (j - j')^2}}{\sum_{(i',j') \in \mathbb{I}_{x_{i,j}}} \sqrt{(i - i')^2 + (j - j')^2}}. \tag{3}$$

s in Equation 2 is the occlusion factor for pixel at (i, j) as mentioned in Sec. 2.2. Note that when i', j' are integers, Equation 2 can be reduced to $x_{i,j} = \vartheta_{i,j}$, which represents that $x_{i,j}$ is completely occluded by the occlusion. In other words, the integer case is a special case of the real number case. Also, when pixel at (i, j) is not occluded, since $s_{i,j} = 0$. In this case, Equation 2 can be reduced to $x'_{i,j} = x_{i,j}$.

Interpolation is handled by ζ showed in Equation 3. It shows the standard form for the color of the new $x'_{i,j}$. A unique color value is specified for all the pixels in the occluded area for a uniform occlusion. Therefore, ζ in Equation 3 can be reduced to $\zeta(x, i, j) = \mu$ for some $\mu \in [0, 1]$. The coloring function in a multiform occlusion is defined as $\zeta(x, i, j) = x_{i,j} + \Delta_p$ with $\Delta_p \in [-\epsilon, \epsilon]$, where $\epsilon \in \mathbb{R}$ defines the threshold that a pixel can be altered.

Definition 3 (Local occlusion robustness). *Given a DNN $F : \mathbb{R}^{m \times n} \to \mathbb{R}^r$, an occlusion function $\gamma_{\zeta, w \times h} : \mathbb{R}^{m \times n} \times \mathbb{R} \times \mathbb{R} \to \mathbb{R}^{m \times n}$ with respect to coloring function ζ and occlusion size $w \times h$, and an input image x, F is called local occlusion robust on x with $\gamma_{\zeta, w \times h}$ if $\Phi_F(x) = \Phi_F(\gamma_{\zeta, w \times h}(x, a, b))$ holds for all $1 \le a \le n$ and $1 \le b \le m$.*

Intuitively, Definition 3 means that F is robust on x against the occlusions of $\gamma_{\zeta, w \times h}$, if on any occluded image of x by the occlusion function $\gamma_{\zeta, w \times h}$, F always returns the same classification result as on the original image x. Depending on the coloring function ζ, the definition applies to various occlusions concerning shapes, colors, sizes, and positions. We can also extend the above definition to the global occlusion robustness if F is robust on all images concerning $\gamma_{\zeta, w \times h}$.

We prove that even for the case of uniform occlusion, a special case of the multiform one, the local occlusion robustness verification problem is NP-complete on the ReLU-based neural networks.

4 SMT-Based Occlusion Robustness Verification

4.1 A Naïve SMT Encoding Method

The verification problem of FNNs' local occlusion robustness can be straightforwardly encoded into an SMT problem. In Definition 3, we assume that x is classified by Φ to the label ℓ_q, i.e., $\Phi(x) = \ell_q$, for a label $\ell_q \in L$. To prove F is robust on x after x is occluded by occlusion ϑ with size $w \times h$, it suffices to prove that F classifies every occluded image $x' = \gamma_{\zeta, w \times h}(a, b)$ to ℓ_q for all $1 \le a \le n$ and $1 \le b \le m$. This is equivalent to proving that the following constraints are not satisfiable:

$$1 \le a \le n, 1 \le b \le m, \tag{4}$$

$$\bigwedge_{i \in \mathbb{N}_{1,n}, j \in \mathbb{N}_{1,m}}$$

$$\left(((a - 1 < i < a + w + 1) \wedge (b - 1 < j < b + h + 1) \wedge x'_{i,j} = \gamma_{\zeta, w \times h}(x, a, b)_{i,j}) \vee \right. \tag{5}$$

$$\left. ((i \ge a + w + 1) \vee (i \le a - 1) \vee (j \ge b + h + 1) \vee (j \le b - 1)) \wedge x'_{i,j} = x_{i,j}) \right),$$

$$\bigvee_{l \in \mathbb{N}_{1,q-1} \cup \mathbb{N}_{q+1,r}} F(x')_l \ge F(x')_q. \tag{6}$$

The conjuncts in Eq. 5 define that x' is an occluded instance of x, and the disjuncts in Eq. 6 indicate that, when satisfiable, there exists some label ℓ_i which has a higher probability than ℓ_q to be classified to. Namely, the occlusion robustness of F on x is falsified, with x' being a witness of the non-robustness. Note that this naive encoding

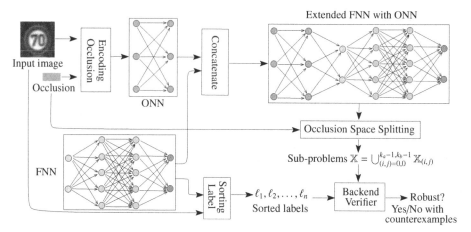

Fig. 4: The workflow of encoding and verifying FNN's robustness against occlusions.

considers the occlusion position's real number cases since function γ implicitly includes the interpolation.

Although the above encoding is straightforward, solving the encoded constraints is experimentally beyond the reach of general-purpose existing SMT solvers due to the piece-wise linear ReLU activation functions in the definition of F in the constraints of Eq. 6, and the large search space $m \times n \times (2\epsilon)^{w \times h}$ (see Experiment II in Sec. 5).

4.2   Our Encoding Approach

An Overview of the Approach. To improve efficiency, we propose a novel approach for encoding occlusion perturbations into four layers of neurons and concatenating the original network to these so-called *occlusion layers*, constituting a new neural network which can be efficiently verified using state-of-the-art, SMT-based verifiers.

Fig. 4 shows the overview of our approach. Given an input image and an occlusion, we first construct a 3-hidden-layer occlusion neural network (ONN) and then concatenate it to the original FNN by connecting the ONN's output layer to the FNN's input layer. The combined network represents all possible occluded inputs and their classification results. The robustness of the constructed network can be verified using the existing SMT-based neural network verifiers.

We introduce two acceleration techniques to speed up the verification further. First, we divide the occlusion space into several smaller, orthogonal spaces, and verify a finite set of sub-problems on the smaller spaces. Second, we employ the eager falsification technique [14] to sort the labels according to their probabilities of being misclassified to. The one with a larger probability is verified earlier by the backend tools. Whenever a counterexample is returned, an occluded image is found such that its classification result differs from the original one. If all sub-problems are verified and no counterexamples are found, the network is verified robust on the input image against the provided occlusion.

Encoding Occlusions as Neural Networks. Given a coloring function ζ, an occlusion size $w \times h$ and an input image x of size $m \times n$, we construct a neural network $O : \mathbb{R}^{4+ct} \rightarrow \mathbb{R}^{m \times n}$ to encode all the possible occluded images of x, where $c = 1$ if x is a grey image and $c = 3$ if x is an RGB image, $t = 0$ for the uniform occlusion and $t = w \times h$ for the multiform one.

Fig. 5 shows the neural network architecture for encoding occlusions. We divide it into a fundamental part and an additional part. The former encodes the occlusion position and the uniform occlusion color. The additional part is needed only by the multiform occlusion to encode the coloring function. Without loss of generality, we assume that the input layer takes the vector (a, w, b, h, ζ), where (a, b) is the top-left coordinate of occlusion area in x. The coloring function ζ is admitted by other $c \times t$ neurons in the input layer when the occlusion is multiform.

(1) Encoding occlusion positions.
We explain the weights and biases that are defined in the neural network to encode the occlusion position. On the connections between the input layer and the first hidden layer, the weights in matrices $W_{1,1}$, $W_{1,2}$ and $W_{1,3}$ are 1, -1 and -1, respectively. Note that we hide all the edges whose weights are 0 in the figure for clarity. The biases in $\overline{b}_{1,1}$ are $(-1, -2, \ldots, -m)$ for the first m neurons on the first hidden layer. Those in $\overline{b}_{1,2}$ are $(2, 3, \ldots, m + 1)$. The weights in $W_{1,4}$, $W_{1,5}$, $W_{1,6}$ and the biases in $\overline{b}_{1,3}$ and $\overline{b}_{1,4}$ are defined in the same way. We omit the details due to the page limitation.

For the second layer, the diagonals of weight matrices $W_{2,1}$ to $W_{2,4}$ are set to -1, and the rest of their entries are 0. The biases in $\overline{b}_{2,1}$ and $\overline{b}_{2,2}$ are 1. After the prop-

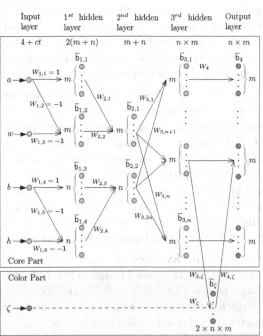

Fig. 5: An occlusion neural network for the occlusions on an image x with ζ and $w \times h$.

agation to the second hidden layer, a pixel at position (i, j) in the image x is occluded if and only if both the outputs of the ith neuron in the first m neurons and the jth neuron in the remaining n neurons on the second hidden layer are 1.

The third hidden layer represents the occlusion status of each pixel in the original image x. $2n$ weight matrices connect the second layer and the $n \times m$ neurons of the third layer. For example, we consider the weights in $W_{3,i}$ and $W_{3,n+i}$ which connect the ith group of m neurons in the third layer to the second layer. The size of $W_{3,i}$ is $m \times m$, and the weights in the ith row are 1 while the rest is 0. The size of $W_{3,n+i}$ is $m \times n$. The weights on its diagonal are set to 1, while the rest are set to 0. All the biases in $\overline{b}_{3,1}$ to $\overline{b}_{3,n}$ are -1. The output of the third layer indicates the occlusion status of all the pixels. If a pixel at (i, j) is occluded, then the output of the $(i \times m + j)^{th}$ neuron in the third layer is 1, and otherwise, 0.

(2) Encoding Coloring Functions. We consider the uniform and multiform coloring functions separately for verification efficiency, although the former is a special case of the latter. We first consider the general multiform case. In the multiform case, we introduce $2 \times n \times m$ extra neurons in the third hidden layer, as shown in the bottom part of Fig. 5. These neurons can be combined with the third layer, but it would be more clear to separate them. The weight matrix $W_{3,\zeta}$ connects the third layer to these neurons, with its first half of diagonal set to 1, and the second half set to -1. This helps retain the sign of the input ζ during propagation. The weight matrix W_ζ connects the input ζ to these neurons, whose diagonal are 1, and the biases $\bar{b}_\zeta$ are -1. These neurons work just like the third layer, except that they not only represent the occlusion status of pixels, but also preserve the input ζ. If a pixel at (i, j) is occluded and ζ has a positive value, then the $(i \times m + j)^{th}$ output in the first half of them is ζ. The $(i \times m + j)^{th}$ output in the second half is ζ when ζ has a negative value. Otherwise, the output is 0. In the uniform case, it can be encoded together with input images, and we thus explain it in the following paragraph.

(3) Encoding Input Images. In the fourth layer, we use W_4 to denote the weight matrix connecting the third layer. W_4 is used to encode pixel values of the input image x and the coloring function ζ of occlusions. In the uniform case, the weight $\mathsf{w}(i, i)$ in the diagonal of W_4 is $\mathsf{w}(i, i) = \zeta_i - x_i$ and the biases $\bar{b}_4 = \mathbf{x}$ where $\mathbf{x}$ is the flattened vector of the original input image. In the multiform case, the weight matrix $W_{4,\zeta}$ connects the neurons in the bottom part that preserves information of input ζ to the fourth layer. The first half of $W_{4,\zeta}$ is identical to W_4, and the second half of $W_{4,\zeta}$ has its diagonal set to -1. It provides the value of the coloring function ζ with any sign for each occluded pixel. The output of the jth neuron in the ith group of the fourth layer is the raw pixel value plus ζ if the pixel at (i, j) is occluded; otherwise, it is the raw pixel value of p.

An Illustrative Example. We show an example of constructing the occlusion network on a 2×2, single-channel image in Fig. 6. In this example, we assume that the input image is $x = [0.4, 0.6, 0.55, 0.72]$ and the occlusion applied to x has a size of 1×1, which means $w = 1$ and $h = 1$. For uniform occlusion, the coloring function ζ has a fixed value of 0, and for multiform case, the threshold ϵ that a pixel can be altered is 0.1.

We suppose the occlusion is applied at position $(1, 2)$, which means $a = 1$ and $b = 2$ for the input of occlusion network. In the forward propagation, we calculate the output of the first layer by $a \times W_{1,1} + \bar{b}_{1,1}$ and $a \times W_{1,2} + b \times W_{1,3} + \bar{b}_{1,2}$ and can get $(0, 0, 0, 1)$ for the first four neurons. Following the same process, we get the output of the second 4 neurons, $(1, 0, 0, 0)$. After propagation to the second layer, it outputs $(1, 0), (0, 1)$ based on $W_{2,1}, W_{2,2}$ and $\bar{b}_2$, representing the second column and the first

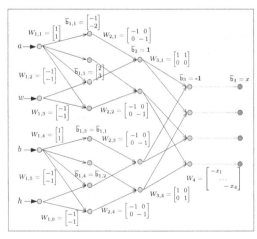

Fig. 6: An example of encoding a one-pixel uniform occlusion as a neural network.

row of x is under occlusion. Likely, the third layer outputs $(0, 1, 0, 0)$ based on its weight matrices and biases, representing that the second pixel in the first row is occluded. After propagation to the fourth layer, the occlusion network outputs an occluded image $x' = [0.4, 0, 0.55, 0.72]$ based on W_4 and $\overline{b}_4$. It is identical to the expected occluded image, where the second pixel is occluded, and other pixels stay unchanged. Suppose we change a to some real number, for instance, 1.5. After the same propagation, we will get an output of $(0, 0.5, 0, 0.5)$ in the third layer, representing that the neurons in the second column are affected by the occlusion by a factor of 0.5. The fourth layer then outputs $[0.4, 0.3, 0.55, 0.36]$, which is the corresponding occluded image x'.

In the multiform case, as mentioned at the first, we suppose the threshold $\epsilon = 0.1$, and keep all other settings. Then after the same propagation to the third layer, the third layer would output $(0, 1, 0, 0)$, representing that the second pixel is occluded. Those extra neurons then output $(0, 0.1, 0, 0, 0, 0, 0, 0)$ where the second neuron in the first half is 0.1 and 0 for the remaining. This indicates both that the second pixel in the first row is occluded, and has an epsilon of 0.1. After propagation to the fourth layer, the occlusion network outputs $x' = [0.4, 0.7, 0.55, 0.72]$ based on its W_4 and $\overline{b}_4$. As expected, the second pixel is occluded and increases by 0.1, and other pixels stay unchanged. For the case of a negative ϵ of -0.1, the extra neurons output $(0, 0, 0, 0, 0, 0.1, 0, 0)$. Note that the second neuron in the second half is 0.1 and the remaining are 0, which helps retain the sign of -0.1. The fourth layer then outputs $[0.4, 0.5, 0.55, 0.72]$, which is the expected occluded image where the second pixel decreases by 0.1.

4.3   The Correctness of the Encoding

Given an input image x, a rectangle occlusion of size $w \times h$, and a coloring function ζ, let O be the corresponding occlusion neural network constructed in the approach above. Let F be the FNN to verify. We concatenate O to F by connecting O's output layer to F's input layer. The combined network implements the composed function $F \circ O$. The problem of verifying the occlusion robustness of F on the input image x is reduced to a regular robustness verification problem of $F \circ O$.

Theorem 1 (Correctness). *An FNN F is robust on the input image x with respect to a rectangle occlusion in the size of $w \times h$ and a coloring function ζ if and only if* $\Phi_{F \circ O}((a, w, b, h, \zeta)) = \Phi_F(x)$ *for all $1 \le a \le n$ and $1 \le b \le m$.*

Theorem 1 means that all the occluded images from x are classified by F to the same label as x, which implies the correctness of our proposed encoding approach. To prove Theorem 1, it suffices to show that the encoded occlusion neural network represents all the possible occluded images. In other words, when being perceived as a function, the network outputs the same occluded image as the occlusion function for the same occlusion coordinate (a, b), as formalized in the following lemma.

Lemma 1. *Given an occlusion function* $\gamma_{\zeta,w\times h} : \mathbb{R}^{m\times n} \times \mathbb{R} \times \mathbb{R} \to \mathbb{R}^{m\times n}$ *and an input image* x, *let* $O_{\gamma,x} : \mathbb{R}^{4+cl} \to \mathbb{R}^{m\times n}$ *be the corresponding occlusion neural network. There is* $\gamma_{\zeta,w\times h}(x,a,b) = O_{\gamma,x}(a,w,b,h,\zeta)$ *for all* $1 \leq a \leq n$ *and* $1 \leq b \leq m$.

Proof (Sketch). It suffices to prove $\gamma_{\zeta,w\times h}(x,a,b)_{i,j} = O_{\gamma,x}(a,w,b,h,\zeta)_{i,j}$ for all $i \in \mathbb{N}_{1,n}$ and $j \in \mathbb{N}_{1,m}$. By Definition 2, we consider the following two cases:

Case 1: When a pixel p *at position* (i,j) *is fully occluded, we have* $\gamma_{\zeta,w\times h}(x,a,b)_{i,j} = \zeta(x,i,j)$. *We need to prove that* $O_{\gamma,x}(a,w,b,h,\zeta)_{i,j} = \zeta(x,i,j)$.

Suppose p is covered by an arbitrary uniform occlusion with size of $w_0 \times h_0$ at position (a_0,b_0). We can observe that for that pixel p, $i > a_0 \wedge i < a_0 + w_0 - 1$ and $j > b_0 \wedge j < b_0 + h_0 - 1$ hold since p is covered by the occlusion.

We show the output of $O_{\gamma,x}(a,w,b,h,\zeta)_{i,j}$ by inspecting the $(i*n+j)^{th}$ output of the occlusion network after propagation, starting from inspecting the output of the ith and $(i+m)^{th}$ neurons of the first layer. According to the network structure discussed in Sec. 4.2, we can tell that the ith neuron in the first layer is 0 only when $i > a_0$, the same property holds for the $(i+m)^{th}$ neuron when $i < a_0 + w_0 - 1$. Therefore, the output for the ith and $(i+m)^{th}$ neurons of the first layer is 0, which leads to the ith neuron in the first part of the second layer has output of value 1. Through the similar process, we can get that the value of $z_j^{(2)}$ in the second part of the second layer is also 1.

The $(i \times n + j)^{th}$ neuron in the third layer is based on the ith neuron and j^{th} neuron of the second layer that we just discussed. Therefore, the output of that neuron, $z_{i\times n+j}^{(3)}$, is 1. For uniform occlusion, suppose the coloring function ζ has a fixed value μ_0. By propagating the output $z_{i\times n+j}^{(3)}$ to the fourth layer, which is calculated as $W_4 \times z^{(3)} + \overline{b}_4$, the $(i \times n + j)^{th}$ output of the fourth layer is $1 \times (\mu_0 - p_{i,j}) + p_{i,j} = \mu_0$. Likely, for multiform occlusion, ζ indicates the threshold ϵ_0 that a pixel can change. The $(i \times n + j)^{th}$ extra neuron outputs ϵ_0, then the corresponding neuron in the fourth layer outputs $p_{i,j} + \epsilon_0$.

This output of $O_{\gamma,x}(a,w,b,h,\zeta)_{i,j}$ is identical to $\gamma_{\zeta,w\times h}(x,a,b)_{i,j}$, the expected pixel value at position (i,j), which also indicates that the color is correctly encoded.

Case 2: When a pixel p *at position* (i,j) *is not occluded, we have* $\gamma_{\zeta,w\times h}(x,a,b)_{i,j} = x_{i,j}$. *Then, we need to prove that* $O_{\gamma,x}(a,w,b,h,\zeta)_{i,j} = x_{i,j}$.

In this case, we can observe that $i < a_0 \vee i \geq a_0 + w_0$ and $j < b_0 \vee j \geq b_0 + h_0$ hold for pixel p. Then We can tell that the corresponding neuron in the third layer outputs 0 and the output of the $(i*n+j)^{th}$ neuron in the fourth layer is the origin pixel value of p following the similar process discussed in case 1.

For the occlusion with real number position, some more cases need to be discussed, but the proof has a very similar sketch as the normal occlusion with integer position. We leverage the equality of $a \times b = exp(log(a) + log(b))$ and add it to the propagation between the third layer and those extra neurons only when the occlusion is at real number positions in the multiform case. And we use $ReLU(a + b - 1)$ as an alternative to logarithms and exponents in implementation since Marabou does not support such operations. Due to the page limit, please refer to [15] for the details of the full proof.

Theorem 1 can be directly derived from Lemma 1 and Definition 3 by substituting $\gamma_{\zeta,w\times h}(x,a,b)$ for $O_{\gamma,x}(a,w,b,h,\zeta)$ in the definition.

4.4 Verification Acceleration Techniques

Existing SMT-based neural network verification tools can directly verify the composed neural network. The number of ReLU activation functions in the network is the primary factor in determining the verification time cost by the backend tools. In the occlusion part, the number of ReLU nodes is independent of the scale of the original networks to be verified. Therefore, our approach's scalability relies only on the underlying tools.

To further improve the verification efficiency, we integrate two algorithmic acceleration techniques by dividing the verification problem into small independent sub-problems that can be solved separately.

Occlusion Space Splitting. We observed that verifying the composed neural network with a large input space can significantly degrade the efficiency of backend verifiers. Even for small FNNs with only tens of ReLUs, the verifiers may run out of time due to the large occlusion space for searching. For instance, the complexity of Reluplex [20] can be derived from the original SMT method of Simplex [32]. It has a complexity of $\Omega(v \times m \times n)$, where m and n represent the number of constraints and variables, and v represents the number of pivots operated in the Simplex method. In the worst case, v can grow exponentially. Reduction in the search space can reduce the number of pivot operations, therefore significantly improving verification efficiency.

Based on the above observation, we can divide $[1, m]$ (*resp.* $[1, n]$) into $k_m \in \mathbb{Z}^+$ (*resp.* $k_n \in \mathbb{Z}^+$) intervals $[m_0, m_1], \ldots, [m_{k_m-1}, m_{k_m}]$ (*resp.* $[n_0, n_1], \ldots, [n_{k_n-1}, n_{k_n}]$) and verify the problem on the Cartesian product of the two sets of intervals.

$$\forall x' \in \mathbb{X}.\Phi(x') = \Phi(x) \equiv \bigwedge_{(i,j)=(0,0)}^{(k_m-1,k_n-1)} \forall x' \in \mathbb{X}_{(i,j)}.\Phi(x') = \Phi(x), \text{ where}$$

$$\mathbb{X} = \bigcup_{(i,j)=(0,0)}^{(k_m-1,k_n-1)} \mathbb{X}_{(i,j)} = \bigcup_{(i,j)=(0,0)}^{(k_m-1,k_n-1)} \{\gamma_{\zeta,w \times h}(x, a, b) | m_i \le a \le m_{i+1}, n_j \le b \le n_{j+1}\}. \tag{7}$$

In this way, we split the occlusion space into $k_m \times k_n$ sub-spaces. It is equivalent to prove $\forall x' \in \mathbb{X}.\Phi(x')$ for all $\mathbb{X}_{(i,j)}$ with $0 \le i < k_m$ and $0 \le j < k_n$, without losing the soundness and completeness. We call each verification instance a *query*, which can be solved more efficiently than the one on the whole occlusion space by backend verifiers. Furthermore, another advantage of occlusion space splitting is that these divided queries can be solved in parallel by leveraging multi-threaded computing.

Eager Falsification by Label Sorting. Another *Divide & Conquer* approach for acceleration is to divide the verification problem into independent sub-problems by the classification labels in L, as defined below:

$$\forall x' \in \mathbb{X}.\Phi(x') = \Phi(x) \equiv \forall x' \in \mathbb{X}. \bigwedge_{\ell' \in L} \Phi(x) = \ell' \vee \Phi(x') \ne \ell'. \tag{8}$$

The dual problem to disprove the robustness can be solved to find some label ℓ' such that $\Phi(x) \ne \ell' \wedge \Phi(x') = \ell'$. We can first solve those that have higher probabilities of being non-robust. Once a sub-problem is proved non-robust, the verification terminates, with no need to solve the remainder. Such approach is called *eager falsification* [14]. Based on this methodology, we sort the sub-problems in a descent order according to the probabilities at which the original image is classified to the corresponding labels by the neural network. A higher probability implies that the image is more likely to be classified to the corresponding label. Heuristically, there is a higher probability of finding

Table 1: Occlusion verification results on two medium FNNs trained on MNIST and GTSRB in different occlusion sizes 2×2 and 5×5 and occlusion radius ϵ.

Size	ϵ	Medium FNN (600 ReLUs) on MNIST					Medium FNN (343 ReLUs) on GTSRB				
		- / +	T_+	T_-	T_{build}	TO(%)	- / +	T_+	T_-	T_{build}	TO(%)
	0.05	**2** / 28	120.01	11.98	0.068	0.00	**8** / 13	103.64	24.18	0.089	0.00
	0.10	**3** / 27	121.37	19.18	0.067	0.00	**8** / 13	108.62	22.57	0.088	0.00
2×2	0.20	**4** / 26	122.12	39.57	0.067	0.00	**10** / 11	113.7	23.17	0.084	0.00
	0.30	**6** / 24	165.98	45.6	0.086	0.00	**11** / 10	117.97	26.41	0.089	0.00
	0.40	**7** / 23	183.65	47.32	0.098	4.75	**14** / 7	115.49	31.53	0.096	0.14
	0.05	**5** / 25	123.45	49.04	0.065	0.00	**9** / 12	123.99	26.02	0.101	0.00
	0.10	**6** / 24	124.13	44.09	0.073	0.00	**12** / 9	127.65	26.96	0.01	0.00
5×5	0.20	**10** / 20	179.89	52.51	0.073	3.26	**16** / 5	126.98	27.22	0.102	0.00
	0.30	**14** / 16	284.67	65.98	0.076	5.45	**18** / 3	146.68	29.11	0.100	0.04
	0.40	**22** / 8	339.78	97.28	0.074	7.33	**19** / 2	169.17	26.52	0.103	0.09

* - / +: the numbers of non-robust and robust cases; T_+ (*resp.* T_-): average verification time in robust (*resp.* non-robust) cases; T_{build}: the building time of occlusion neural networks; TO (%): the percentage of runtime-out cases among all the queries.

an occlusion such that the occluded image is misclassified to that label. We sequence the queries into backend verifiers until all are verified, or a non-robust case is reported. Our experimental results will show that this approach can achieve up to 8 and 24 times speedup in the robust and non-robust cases, respectively.

5   Implementation and Evaluation

We implemented our approach in a Python tool called OccRob, using the PyTorch framework. As a backend tool, we chose the Marabou [21] state-of-the-art, SMT-based DNN verifier. We evaluated our proposed approach extensively on a suite of benchmark datasets, including MNIST [24] and GTSRB [16]. The size of the networks trained on the datasets for verification is measured by the number of ReLUs, ranging from 70 to 1300. All the experiments are conducted on a workstation equipped with a 32-core AMD Ryzen Threadripper CPU @ 3.7GHz and 128 GB RAM and Ubuntu 18.04. We set a timeout threshold of 60 seconds for a single verification task. All code and experimental data, including the models and verification scripts can be accessed at https://github.com/MakiseGuo/OccRob.

We evaluate our proposed method concerning efficiency and scalability in the occlusion robustness verification of ReLU-based FNNs. Our goals are threefold:

1. To demonstrate the effectiveness of the proposed approach for the robustness verification against various types of occlusion perturbations.
2. To evaluate the efficiency improvement of the proposed approach, compared with the naive SMT-based method.
3. To demonstrate the effectiveness of the acceleration techniques in efficiency improvement.

Experiment I: Effectiveness. We first evaluate the effectiveness of OccRob in robustness verification against various types of occlusions of different sizes and color ranges. Table 1

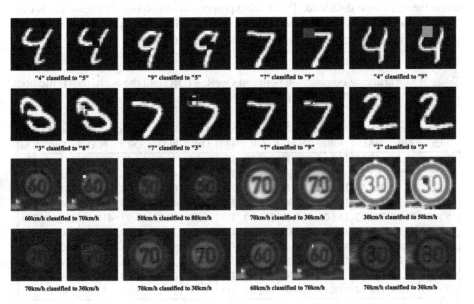

Fig. 7: Occlusive adversarial examples automatically generated for non-robust images.

shows the verification results and time costs against multiform occlusions on two medium FNNs trained on MNIST and GTSRB. We consider two occlusion sizes, 2×2 and 5×5, respectively. The occluding color range is from 0.05 to 0.40. In each verification task, we selected the first 30 images from each of the two datasets and verified the network's robustness around them, under corresponding occlusion settings. As expected, larger occlusion sizes and occluding color ranges imply more non-robust cases. One can see that OccRob can almost always verify and falsify each input image, except for a few time-outs. The robust cases cost more time than the non-robust cases, but all can be finished in a few minutes. Note that the time overhead for building occlusion neural networks is almost negligible, compared with the verification time. The effectiveness against uniform occlusions is shown in the following experiment.

Fig. 7 shows several occlusive adversarial examples that are generated by OccRob under different occlusion settings. These occlusions do not alter the semantics of the original images and should be classified to the same results as those non-occluded ones. However, they are misclassified to other results.

Experiment II: Efficiency improvement over the naive encoding method. We compare the efficiency of OccRob with that of a naive SMT encoding approach on verifying uniform occlusions since the naive encoding approach cannot handle verification against multiform occlusions. We apply the same acceleration techniques, such as parallelization and a variant of input space splitting, to the naive approach, which otherwise times out for almost all verification tasks even on the smallest model.

Table 2 shows the average verification time on six FNNs of different sizes against uniform occlusions. We can observe that OccRob affords a significant improvement in efficiency, up to 30 times higher than the naive approach. It can always finish before the preset time threshold, while the naive method fails to verify the two large networks under the same time threshold. The timeout proportion of two medium networks is over 70%. While the small network on MNIST only has an 8% of timeout proportion with the naive method, OccRob barely timeouts on every network.

Table 2: Performance comparison between OccRob (OR) and the naive (NAI) methods on MNIST and GTSRB under different occlusion sizes.

FNNs	MNIST						GTSRB					
	Small FNN		Medium FNN		Large FNN		Small FNN		Medium FNN		Large FNN	
Size	OR	NAI	OR	NAI	OR	NAI	OR	NAI	OR	NAI	OR	NAI
1×1	46.44	63.12	110.18	759.93	206.50	TO	29.76	472.23	69.28	989.08	173.62	TO
2×2	49.62	165.53	98.60	832.98	199.17	TO	21.04	340.89	42.16	680.81	103.42	TO
3×3	51.23	298.59	111.14	863.74	205.67	TO	11.93	169.35	32.00	499.31	81.17	TO
4×4	44.78	256.22	115.99	886.73	225.02	TO	8.90	141.85	31.24	419.62	106.41	TO
5×5	48.96	270.23	113.01	803.40	264.79	TO	6.11	190.81	27.97	418.56	118.99	TO
6×6	47.81	318.28	127.98	642.01	288.18	TO	7.49	213.35	21.70	282.04	60.02	TO
7×7	34.99	357.78	124.47	589.41	222.65	TO	6.02	153.81	31.96	404.18	62.60	TO
8×8	36.05	324.34	129.27	469.24	215.53	TO	5.99	123.07	28.44	250.97	54.37	TO
9×9	34.58	224.01	141.54	375.97	219.61	TO	6.42	102.39	31.30	160.84	59.87	TO
10×10	28.98	178.44	78.89	398.01	182.36	TO	6.61	127.20	28.59	153.96	40.69	TO

Experiment III: Effectiveness of the integrated acceleration techniques. We finally evaluate the effectiveness of the two acceleration techniques integrated with the tool. We evaluate each technique separately by excluding it from OccRob and comparing the verification time of OccRob and the corresponding excluded versions. Fig. 8 shows the experimental results of verifying the medium FNN trained on GTSRB against multiform occlusions by the tools. Fig. 8 (a) shows that label sorting can improve efficiency in both robust and non-robust cases. In particular, the improvement is more significant in the non-robust case, with up to 5 times speedup in the experiment. That is because solving each query is faster than solving all simultaneously, and further OccRob immediately stops dispatching queries once a counterexample is found in the non-robust case. Fig. 8 (b) shows that occlusion space splitting can also significantly improve the efficiency, with up to 8 and 24 times speedups in the robust and non-robust cases, respectively. In addition, Fig. 8 (b) also shows a significant reduction in the number of time-outs.

6 Related Work

Robustness verification of neural networks has been extensively studied recently, aiming at devising efficient methods for verifying neural networks' robustness against various types of perturbations and adversarial attacks. We classify those methods into two categories according to the type of perturbations, which can be semantic or non-semantic. Semantic perturbation has an interpretable meaning, such as occlusions and geometric transformations like rotation, while non-semantic perturbation means that noises perturb inputs with no particular meanings.

Non-semantic perturbations are usually represented as L_p norms, which define the ranges in which an input can be altered. Some robustness verification approaches for

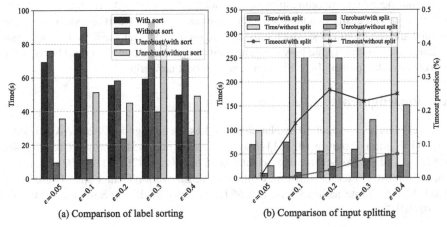

(a) Comparison of label sorting   (b) Comparison of input splitting

Fig. 8: Efficiency evaluation results of the two acceleration techniques.

non-semantic perturbations are both sound and complete by leveraging SMT [20,1] and MILP (mixed integer linear programming) [36] techniques, while some sacrifice the completeness for better scalability by over-approximation [29,2,7], abstract interpretation [34,10,5], interval analysis by symbolic propagation [43,42,26], etc.

In contrast to a large number of works on non-semantic robustness verification, there are only a few studies on the semantic case. Because semantic perturbations are beyond the range of L_p norms [9], those abstraction-based approaches cannot be directly applied to verifying semantic perturbations. Mohapatra et al. [30] proposed to verify neural networks against semantic perturbations by encoding them into neural networks. Their encoding approach is general to a family of semantic perturbations such as brightness and contrast changes and rotations. Their approach for verifying occlusions is restricted to uniform occlusions at integer locations. Sallami et al.[31] proposed an interval-based method to verify the robustness against the occlusion perturbation problem under the same restriction. Singh et al. [35] proposed a new abstract domain to encode both non-semantic and semantic perturbations such as rotations. Chiang et al. [4] called occlusions *adversarial patches* and proposed a certifiable defense by extending interval bound propagation (IBP) [12]. Compared with these existing verification approaches for semantic perturbations, our SMT-based approach is both sound and complete, and meanwhile, it supports a larger class of occlusion perturbations.

7   Conclusion and Future Work

We introduced an SMT-based approach for verifying the robustness of deep neural networks against various types of occlusions. An efficient encoding method was proposed to represent occlusions using neural networks, by which we reduced the occlusion robustness verification problem to a regular robustness verification problem of neural networks and leveraged *off-the-shelf* SMT-based verifiers for the verification. We implemented a resulting prototype OccRob and intensively evaluated its effectiveness and efficiency on a series of neural networks trained on the public benchmarks, including MNIST and GTSRB. Moreover, as the scalability of DNN verification engines continues to improve, our approach, which uses them as blackbox backends, will also become more scalable.

As our occlusion encoding approach is independent of target neural networks, we believe it can be easily extended to other complex network structures, such as convolutional and recurrent ones, which only depend on the backend verifiers. It would also be interesting to investigate how the generated adversarial examples could be used for neural network repairing [41,18] to train more robust networks.

Acknowledgments

This work has been supported by National Key Research Program (2020AAA0107800), NSFC-ISF Joint Program (62161146001, 3420/21) and NSFC projects (61872146, 61872144), Shanghai Science and Technology Commission (20DZ1100300), Shanghai Trusted Industry Internet Software Collaborative Innovation Center and "Digital Silk Road" Shanghai International Joint Lab of Trustworthy Intelligent Software (Grant No. 22510750100).

References

1. Amir, G., Wu, H., Barrett, C., Katz, G.: An smt-based approach for verifying binarized neural networks. In: TACAS'21. pp. 203–222. Springer (2021)
2. Boopathy, A., Weng, T.W., Chen, P.Y., Liu, S., Daniel, L.: Cnn-cert: An efficient framework for certifying robustness of convolutional neural networks. In: AAAI'19. vol. 33, pp. 3240–3247 (2019)
3. Brown, T.B., Mané, D., Roy, A., Abadi, M., Gilmer, J.: Adversarial patch. arXiv preprint arXiv:1712.09665 (2017)
4. Chiang, P.y., Ni, R., Abdelkader, A., Zhu, C., Studer, C., Goldstein, T.: Certified defenses for adversarial patches. arXiv preprint arXiv:2003.06693 (2020)
5. Cohen, J., Rosenfeld, E., Kolter, Z.: Certified adversarial robustness via randomized smoothing. In: ICML'19. pp. 1310–1320. PMLR (2019)
6. Coşkun, M., Uçar, A., Yildirim, Ö., Demir, Y.: Face recognition based on convolutional neural network. In: MEES'17. pp. 376–379. IEEE (2017)
7. Elboher, Y.Y., Gottschlich, J., Katz, G.: An abstraction-based framework for neural network verification. In: CAV'20. pp. 43–65. Springer (2020)
8. Eykholt, K., Evtimov, I., Fernandes, E., Li, B., Rahmati, A., Xiao, C., Prakash, A., Kohno, T., Song, D.: Robust physical-world attacks on deep learning visual classification. In: CVPR'18. pp. 1625–1634 (2018)
9. Fischer, M., Baader, M., Vechev, M.: Certified defense to image transformations via randomized smoothing. NeurIPS'20 **33**, 8404–8417 (2020)
10. Gehr, T., Mirman, M., Drachsler-Cohen, D., Tsankov, P., Chaudhuri, S., Vechev, M.: Ai2: Safety and robustness certification of neural networks with abstract interpretation. In: S&P'18. pp. 3–18. IEEE (2018)
11. Goodfellow, I., Bengio, Y., Courville, A.: Deep Learning, pp. 168–196. MIT Press (2016), http://www.deeplearningbook.org
12. Gowal, S., Dvijotham, K., Stanforth, R., Bunel, R., Qin, C., Uesato, J., Arandjelovic, R., Mann, T., Kohli, P.: On the effectiveness of interval bound propagation for training verifiably robust models. arXiv preprint arXiv:1810.12715 (2018)
13. Gowal, S., Dvijotham, K.D., Stanforth, R., Bunel, R., Qin, C., Uesato, J., Arandjelovic, R., Mann, T., Kohli, P.: Scalable verified training for provably robust image classification. In: ICCV'19. pp. 4842–4851 (2019)

14. Guo, X., Wan, W., Zhang, Z., Zhang, M., Song, F., Wen, X.: Eager falsification for accelerating robustness verification of deep neural networks. In: ISSRE'21. pp. 345–356. IEEE (2021)
15. Guo, X., Zhou, Z., Zhang, Y., Katz, G., Zhang, M.: OccRob: Efficient smt-based occlusion robustness verification of deep neural networks. arXiv preprint (2023)
16. Houben, S., Stallkamp, J., Salmen, J., Schlipsing, M., Igel, C.: Detection of traffic signs in real-world images: The German Traffic Sign Detection Benchmark. In: IJCNN'13 (2013)
17. Huang, X., Kwiatkowska, M., Wang, S., Wu, M.: Safety verification of deep neural networks. In: CAV'17. pp. 3–29. Springer (2017)
18. Islam, M.J., Pan, R., Nguyen, G., Rajan, H.: Repairing deep neural networks: Fix patterns and challenges. In: ICSE'20. pp. 1135–1146. IEEE (2020)
19. Jaderberg, M., Simonyan, K., Zisserman, A., et al.: Spatial transformer networks. In: Advances in neural information processing systems. pp. 2017–2025. PMLR (2015)
20. Katz, G., Barrett, C., Dill, D.L., Julian, K., Kochenderfer, M.J.: Reluplex: An efficient smt solver for verifying deep neural networks. In: CAV'17. pp. 97–117. Springer (2017)
21. Katz, G., Huang, D.A., Ibeling, D., Julian, K., Lazarus, C., Lim, R., Shah, P., Thakoor, S., Wu, H., Zeljić, A., et al.: The Marabou framework for verification and analysis of deep neural networks. In: CAV'19. pp. 443–452. Springer (2019)
22. Kirkland, E.J.: Bilinear Interpolation, pp. 261–263. Springer US, Boston, MA (2010)
23. Kortylewski, A., Liu, Q., Wang, A., Sun, Y., Yuille, A.: Compositional convolutional neural networks: A robust and interpretable model for object recognition under occlusion. International Journal of Computer Vision 129(3), 736–760 (2021)
24. LeCun, Y., Cortes, C.: MNIST handwritten digit database (2010), http://yann.lecun.com/exdb/mnist/
25. Lengyel, H., Remeli, V., Szalay, Z.: Easily deployed stickers could disrupt traffic sign recognition. Perner's Contacts 19(Special Issue 2), 156–163 (2019)
26. Li, J., Liu, J., Yang, P., Chen, L., Huang, X., Zhang, L.: Analyzing deep neural networks with symbolic propagation: Towards higher precision and faster verification. In: SAS'19. pp. 296–319. Springer (2019)
27. Lillicrap, T.P., Hunt, J.J., Pritzel, A., Heess, N., Erez, T., Tassa, Y., Silver, D., Wierstra, D.: Continuous control with deep reinforcement learning. arXiv preprint arXiv:1509.02971 (2015)
28. Lyu, Z., Guo, M., Wu, T., Xu, G., Zhang, K., Lin, D.: Towards evaluating and training verifiably robust neural networks. In: CVPR'21. pp. 4308–4317 (2021)
29. Lyu, Z., Ko, C.Y., Kong, Z., Wong, N., Lin, D., Daniel, L.: Fastened crown: Tightened neural network robustness certificates. In: AAAI'20. vol. 34, pp. 5037–5044 (2020)
30. Mohapatra, J., Weng, T.W., Chen, P.Y., Liu, S., Daniel, L.: Towards verifying robustness of neural networks against a family of semantic perturbations. In: ICCV'20. pp. 244–252 (2020)
31. Mziou Sallami, M., Ibn Khedher, M., Trabelsi, A., Kerboua-Benlarbi, S., Bettebghor, D.: Safety and robustness of deep neural networks object recognition under generic attacks. In: ICONIP'19. pp. 274–286. Springer (2019)
32. Nelder, J.A., Mead, R.: A simplex method for function minimization. The computer journal 7(4), 308–313 (1965)
33. Pei, K., Cao, Y., Yang, J., Jana, S.: Deepxplore: Automated whitebox testing of deep learning systems. In: SOSP'17. pp. 1–18 (2017)
34. Raghunathan, A., Steinhardt, J., Liang, P.: Certified defenses against adversarial examples. arXiv preprint arXiv:1801.09344 (2018)
35. Singh, G., Gehr, T., Püschel, M., Vechev, M.: An abstract domain for certifying neural networks. Proceedings of the ACM on Programming Languages 3(POPL), 1–30 (2019)
36. Singh, G., Gehr, T., Püschel, M., Vechev, M.: Robustness certification with refinement. In: ICLR'19 (2019)
37. Song, L., Gong, D., Li, Z., Liu, C., Liu, W.: Occlusion robust face recognition based on mask learning with pairwise differential siamese network. In: ICCV'19. pp. 773–782 (2019)

38. Su, J., Vargas, D.V., Sakurai, K.: One pixel attack for fooling deep neural networks. IEEE Transactions on Evolutionary Computation **23**(5), 828–841 (2019)
39. Szegedy, C., Zaremba, W., Sutskever, I., Bruna, J., Erhan, D., Goodfellow, I., Fergus, R.: Intriguing properties of neural networks. arXiv preprint arXiv:1312.6199 (2013)
40. Tian, Y., Pei, K., Jana, S., Ray, B.: Deeptest: Automated testing of deep-neural-network-driven autonomous cars. In: ICSE'18. pp. 303–314 (2018)
41. Usman, M., Gopinath, D., Sun, Y., Noller, Y., Păsăreanu, C.S.: Nn repair: Constraint-based repair of neural network classifiers. In: CAV'21. pp. 3–25. Springer (2021)
42. Wang, S., Pei, K., Whitehouse, J., Yang, J., Jana, S.: Efficient formal safety analysis of neural networks. In: NeurIPS'18. vol. 31. Curran Associates, Inc. (2018)
43. Wang, S., Pei, K., Whitehouse, J., Yang, J., Jana, S.: Formal security analysis of neural networks using symbolic intervals. In: USENIX Security'18. pp. 1599–1614 (2018)
44. Zhu, H., Tang, P., Park, J., Park, S., Yuille, A.: Robustness of object recognition under extreme occlusion in humans and computational models. arXiv preprint arXiv:1905.04598 (2019)

Neural Network-Guided Synthesis of Recursive List Functions

Naoki Kobayashi[✉][iD] and Minchao Wu

The University of Tokyo, Tokyo, Japan
`koba@is.s.u-tokyo.ac.jp`

Abstract. Kobayashi et al. have recently proposed NEUGUS, a framework of neural-network-guided synthesis of logical formulas or simple program fragments, where a neural network is first trained based on sample data, and then a logical formula over integers is constructed by using the weights and biases of the trained network as hints. The previous method was, however, restricted the class of formulas of quantifier-free linear integer arithmetic. In this paper, we propose a NEUGUS method for the synthesis of recursive predicates over lists definable by using the left fold function. To this end, we design and train a special-purpose recurrent neural network (RNN), and use the weights of the trained RNN to synthesize a recursive predicate. We have implemented the proposed method and conducted preliminary experiments to confirm the effectiveness of the method.

1 Introduction

Kobayashi et al. [12] have recently proposed a framework called *Neural-Network-Guided Synthesis (NEUGUS)* for the synthesis of quantifier-free logical expressions over integer variables, which may also be viewed as simple program expressions over integer variables. Given sample data (also called *training data* below, which consist of positive/negative samples and implication constraints [6] such as "if d_1 is a positive sample, so is d_2, but it is unknown whether d_1 is indeed a positive sample), NEUGUS first trains a feed-forward neural network with respect to the sample data, and then constructs a logical expression on integers (more precisely, a Boolean combination of inequalities on integer variables) by using the weights and biases of the neural network as hints. The main characteristic of NEUGUS is its *gray*-box use of neural networks. NEUGUS first trains a neural network, but instead of directly using the trained network as a classifier, it tries to construct a simple logical expression by using the trained network as a hint. Advantages of the gray-box approach over the white-box approach of using the network itself as a classifier include: (i) if successful, a simple classifier is obtained that is easier to understand (for human beings) and verify (for computers), and (ii) we need not worry too much about overfitting; even if the trained network is overfit to the given sample data, we may still be able to extract useful information such as features important for the classification, and use them to construct a simple classifier. Kobayashi et al. [12,13] have applied the proposed framework to automated program verification, where NEUGUS is

S. Sankaranarayanan and N. Sharygina (Eds.): TACAS 2023, LNCS 13993, pp. 227–245, 2023.
https://doi.org/10.1007/978-3-031-30823-9_12

used to find program invariants, and also to program synthesis where, given a program sketch containing holes called *oracles*, NEUGUS is used to find program expressions to fill the holes.

In this paper, we extend NEUGUS to enable the synthesis of *recursive* predicates over Booleans, integers, and lists of Booleans, and lists of integers from positive/negative samples and implication constraints. For example, in the case of the synthesis of a sortedness predicate, the extended NEUGUS (henceforth, simply called NEUGUSR) takes as inputs sample data like:

sorted($[1; 3; 4]$)   sorted($[2; 5; 6; 7]$)   ¬sorted($[3; 1; 4]$)   ¬sorted($[5; 2; 7; 6]$)
sorted($[1; 3; 5]$) $\Rightarrow$ sorted($[1; 3; 5; 6]$) $\cdots$.

Here, sorted($[1; 3; 5]$) $\Rightarrow$ sorted($[1; 3; 5; 6]$) means that if sorted($[1; 3; 5]$) is true, so is sorted($[1; 3; 5; 6]$). The goal of the synthesis is to construct a recursive program that satisfies the constraints specified by the sample data. In the case of the above example, we aim to construct a program (written in OCaml language: https://ocaml.org/) like:

```
let sorted l =
  let rec sorted_aux l b r =
    match l with [] -> b
               | x::l' -> sorted_aux l' (b && r <= x) x
  in sorted_aux l true 0
```

Here, the Boolean argument b of the auxiliary function sorted_aux denotes whether the elements of the list read so far are sorted (in the ascending order), and the integer argument r keeps the last element read (which is initially set to 0; hence, the function sorted judges the sortedness of a list consisting of non-negative integers), to compare it with the next element. The recursive programs constructed with our method are restricted to those definable by using the left fold function. Note that the function sorted above can be expressed as *foldl* $(\lambda(b, r).\lambda x.(b \wedge r \leq x, x))$ (true, 0) using the left fold function *foldl*.[1]

To synthesize recursive predicates, we first train a recurrent neural network (RNN), and construct a recursive program like the one above by using, as hints, the weights of the RNN and information about the executions of the RNN for the training data. We have designed a special-purpose RNN for that purpose, with the synthesis of recursive programs in mind. Figure 1 shows the overall structure of our RNN. The RNN has two kinds of inputs: Boolean lists and integer lists (where their elements are read one by one), and a Boolean output. The inputs and output correspond to those of the function to be synthesized, which takes m Boolean lists and n integer lists as arguments, and returns a Boolean value. Here, we assume that the lists are of equal length, by replicating integer arguments and padding short lists with dummy elements if necessary. For

---

[1] In fact, the program above is written so that it matches the computation of the left fold function. Otherwise, sorted_aux could alternatively be defined so that it returns false immediately when $r > x$ holds.

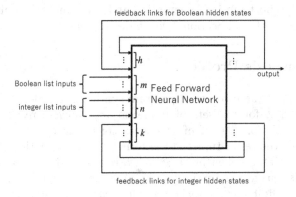

Fig. 1. The overall structure of the special-purpose RNN

example, if the argument of the function to be synthesized is $([1; 2; 3], 0, [1; 0])$, then the input for RNN will be $([1; 2; 3], [0; 0; 0], [1; 0; -1])$. The Boolean values **true** and **false** are respectively represented as 1 and -1. The RNN has also two kinds of hidden states: Booleans and integers. The Boolean hidden states are actually represented as numerical values, but they are constrained to range over $[-1, 1]$ by using the hyperbolic tangent function **tanh** as the activation function for those values inside the feed-forward network. The details of the feed-forward network will be discussed later.

After training the RNN, by using (i) the weights and biases of each link/node and (ii) the the input/output behavior of the trained feed-forward network as hints, we construct a function:

$$step : \mathbf{B}^m \times \mathbf{Z}^n \times \mathbf{B}^h \times \mathbf{Z}^k \to \mathbf{B}^h \times \mathbf{Z}^k,$$

which takes the current input (consisting of m Booleans and n integers) and the current values of Boolean and integer hidden states, and returns the next hidden states. Here, $\mathbf{Z}$ and $\mathbf{B}$ are the types of integers and Booleans respectively. We then construct the whole program as the one that "folds" the input lists by using the *step* function, where the base-case values correspond to the initial values of the hidden states; more details are discussed in later sections. Finally, we check whether the synthesized program conforms to the sample data and if so, output the program; otherwise we retrain the RNN and retry the program synthesis.

We have implemented a program synthesis tool based on the above idea. We have confirmed through experiments that the tool worked reasonably well; our tool could successfully synthesize the sortedness predicate above, as well as other non-trivial predicates, including the binary predicate $\mathtt{avge}(\ell, n)$, which means that the average value of the elements in the list ℓ is no less than n.

The rest of this paper is structured as follows. Section 2 defines the program synthesis problem considered in this paper. Section 3 introduces our special-purpose RNN. Section 4 explains how to synthesize a program from a trained

RNN. Section 5 reports an implementation and experimental results. Section 6 discusses related work and Section 7 concludes the paper.

2   The Synthesis Problem

This section defines the problem of program synthesis considered in this paper. We write $\mathbf{B}$ and $\mathbf{Z}$ for the sets of Booleans and integers respectively. For a set S, we write S^* for the set of sequences consisting of elements of S, and $S_1 \times \cdots \times S_k$ for the set of tuples of the form $(v_1, \ldots, v_k)$ with $v_i \in S_i$ for each i. We sometimes call an element of S^* a *list*, based on the terminology used in programming languages, and write $[a_1; \cdots ; a_n]$ instead of $a_1 \cdots a_n$.

We assume a finite set of variables called *predicate variables*. A *signature* maps each predicate variable to its domain of the form $T_1 \times \cdots \times T_k$, where $T_i \in \{\mathbf{B}, \mathbf{Z}, \mathbf{B}^*, \mathbf{Z}^*\}$. For example, for a signature $\mathcal{K}$ and a predicate variable p, $\mathcal{K}(p) = \mathbf{Z}^* \times \mathbf{Z}$ means that p is a binary predicate that takes an integer list and an integer as arguments.

For a signature $\mathcal{K}$, we write $\mathbf{Atoms}_\mathcal{K}$ for the set of pairs (p, v) where $v \in \mathcal{K}(p)$; we often write $p(v)$ for (p, v). An *implication constraint* is a formula of the form $a_1 \wedge \cdots \wedge a_k \Rightarrow b_1 \vee \cdots \vee b_\ell$, where $a_1, \ldots, a_k, b_1, \ldots, b_\ell \in \mathbf{Atoms}_\mathcal{K}$. Let Θ be an interpretation for predicate variables, i.e., a map that assigns a predicate $P \subseteq \mathcal{K}(p)$ to each predicate $p \in dom(\mathcal{K})$. We write $\Theta \models p(v)$ if $v \in \Theta(p)$. We write $\Theta \models a_1 \wedge \cdots \wedge a_k \Rightarrow b_1 \vee \cdots \vee b_\ell$ and say that Θ satisfies the implication constraint $a_1 \wedge \cdots \wedge a_k \Rightarrow b_1 \vee \cdots \vee b_\ell$, when $\Theta \models b_j$ for some $j \in \{1, \ldots, \ell\}$ if $\Theta \models a_i$ for every $i \in \{1, \ldots, k\}$.

The *synthesis problem* considered in this paper is the problem of, given a signature $\mathcal{K}$ and a set of implication constraints as input, finding (a description of) a predicate assignment Θ that satisfies all the implication constraints. As a description of the predicate assigned to each predicate variable, we consider the class of functions f defined by programs of the following form:

$$
\begin{aligned}
&\textbf{let } f(\widetilde{x} : T_1 \times \cdots \times T_n) = \\
&\qquad \textbf{let rec } g(y, \widetilde{r}) = \textbf{match } y \textbf{ with} \\
&\qquad\qquad \texttt{[]} \texttt{ -> } r_1 \\
&\qquad\qquad \texttt{| } (u_1, \ldots, u_n) :: y' \texttt{ -> let } \widetilde{r}' = step(u_1, \ldots, u_n, \widetilde{r}) \textbf{ in } g(y', \widetilde{r}') \\
&\qquad \textbf{in } g(ezip_{T_1 \times \cdots \times T_n}(\widetilde{x}), \widetilde{d}).
\end{aligned}
$$

Here, $\widetilde{x}$ denotes a sequence $x_1, \ldots, x_k$, and $\widetilde{d}$ denotes a sequence of default integer or Boolean values $d_1, \ldots, d_\ell$, where d_i is $\texttt{true}$ or 0; we write $d_\mathbf{B}$ for $\texttt{true}$ and $d_\mathbf{Z}$ for 0.[2] The function $ezip$ is an extended "zip" function, which maps a tuple

---

[2] The use of fixed default values slightly restricts the class of functions. In fact, the value of $f([])$ is restricted to $\texttt{true}$. To remove the restriction, it suffices to either (i) allow $\widetilde{d}$ to take other values and make them also learnable, or (ii) replace r_1 with $h(r_1)$ and make the Boolean function h also learnable.

consisting of lists, integers, and Booleans to a list of tuples. It is defined by:

$$ezip_{T_1 \times \cdots \times T_n}(v_1, \ldots, v_n) =$$
$$\begin{cases} [] & \text{if every } v_i \text{ is } [], \text{ an integer, or a Boolean} \\ (ehd_{T_1}(v_1), \ldots, ehd_{T_1}(v_n)) :: (etl_{T_1}(v_1), \ldots, etl_{T_n}(v_n)) & \text{otherwise} \end{cases}$$
$$ehd_{\mathbf{Z}^*}([]) = -1 \quad ehd_{\mathbf{Z}^*}(n :: v) = n \quad ehd_{\mathbf{B}^*}([]) = \mathtt{false} \quad ehd_{\mathbf{B}^*}(b :: v) = b$$
$$ehd_{\mathbf{Z}}(n) = n \quad ehd_{\mathbf{B}}(b) = b \quad etl_{\mathbf{Z}}(n) = n \quad etl_{\mathbf{B}}(b) = b$$
$$etl_{\mathbf{Z}^*}([]) = [] \quad etl_{\mathbf{Z}^*}(n :: v) = v \quad etl_{\mathbf{B}^*}([]) = [] \quad etl_{\mathbf{B}^*}(b :: v) = v.$$

For example, $ezip_{\mathbf{Z}^* \times \mathbf{Z}^* \times \mathbf{Z}}([1; 2; 3], [2; 3], 1) = [(1, 2, 1); (2, 3, 1); (3, -1, 1)]$. The function $step$ is the main target of the synthesis. It should be a function on integers and Booleans, consisting of (i) Boolean operations, (ii) affine expressions of the form $c_0 + c_1 x_1 + \cdots + c_k x_k$ and (iii) inequalities of the form $e \leq 0$, where e is an affine expression. The function g above can also be expressed as

$$\lambda \tilde{x}.\#_1(foldl \; step' \; (\tilde{d}) \; (ezip_{T_1 \times \cdots \times T_n}(\tilde{x}))),$$

where $foldl$ is the left fold function, $step'$ is the curried version of $step$, and $\#_1$ denotes the projection of a tuple to its first element.

In the case of the sortedness predicate discussed in Section 1, $T_1 = \mathbf{Z}^*$ with $k = 1$, the length $|\tilde{z}|$ of the auxiliary parameters of g is 2, and $step : \mathbf{Z} \times \mathbf{B} \times \mathbf{Z} \to \mathbf{B} \times \mathbf{Z}$ is given by $step(u, r_b, r_i) = (r_b \wedge (r_i \leq u), u)$.

For the predicate $\mathtt{avge}$ mentioned in Section 1, $T_1 = \mathbf{Z}^*$ and $T_2 = \mathbf{Z}$ with $k = 2$, and $step : \mathbf{Z} \times \mathbf{Z} \times \mathbf{B} \times \mathbf{Z} \to \mathbf{B} \times \mathbf{Z}$ is given by $step(u_1, u_2, r_b, r_i) = (r_i + u_1 - u_2 \geq 0, r_i + u_1 - u_2)$. Here, during the computation of $avge(\ell, m)$, the parameter z accumulates the sum of $\ell_i - m$ (where ℓ_i is the i-th element of ℓ). Whether the average of the elements of ℓ is no less than m can be determined by checking whether the final value of z is no less than 0.

Our synthesis problem subsumes the problem of learning automata (which is obtained as a special case, where the signature consists of a single predicate $p :$ $(\mathbf{B}^*)^m$ and $step : \mathbf{B}^{m+n} \to \mathbf{B}^n$; input symbols and states are encoded as elements of $\mathbf{B}^m$ and $\mathbf{B}^n$ respectively) and also that of symbolic automatic relations [19]. In fact, the automatic synthesis of symbolic automatic relations was one of the motivations behind the present paper, as explained below.

The motivations for the synthesis problem above come from automated program verification and synthesis. For automated program verification, we have CHC-based program verification [1] in mind, where various program verification problems are reduced to the satisfiability problem for Constrained Horn Clauses (CHCs). For programs using lists, the CHCs obtained by the reduction involve predicates over lists, but the current CHC solvers [10,14,2] are not very good at solving such CHCs. A solver for the synthesis problem above can be used as an important component in a CHC solver [2,4] based on the ICE-learning framework [6], to synthesize a candidate solution for CHCs involving lists. Another application is the oracle-based programming mentioned in Section 1, whose goal is to synthesize code fragments to fill the holes of a given program pattern. By solving the synthesis problem above, we can automatically synthesize code

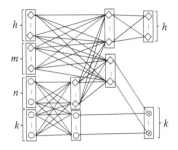

Fig. 2. The feed-forward network inside the RNN

fragments that involve recursive computation over lists. The roles of implication constraints in those applications are explained in [2,13].

In both of the applications above, the validity of a synthesized program is determined based on the whole verification or synthesis goal (in the case of verification, a synthesized predicate over lists is valid if it is indeed a solution for the CHC satisfiability problem). Thus, in the actual applications, the synthesis problem defined above needs to be repeatedly solved with the set of sample data being gradually expanded, until the end goal of program verification or synthesis is achieved.

3   The Design and Training of the RNN

This section describes the design of our special-purpose recursive neural network (RNN) tailored for our synthesis problem, and how to train it.

3.1   The Architecture of the RNN

The overall structure of the RNN is as already depicted in Figure 1. The structure of the feed-forward (FF) network inside the RNN is shown in Figure 2. The network consists of four layers of nodes, where the first layer (the leftmost one) consists of input nodes of the FF network, which hold the input values and hidden state values of the whole RNN, and the fourth layer (the rightmost one) consists of output nodes of the FF network, which hold the next states of the RNN. The nodes of the diamond shape take values in the range $[-1, 1]$ (either by the assumption on inputs or by the use of **tanh** as the activation function), and those of the circle shape take arbitrary floating point numbers. The value of each diamond-shaped node is computed by $\tanh(b + w_1 x_1 + \cdots + w_k x_k)$ and that of each circle node is computed by $b + w_1 x_1 + \cdots + w_k x_k$, where the bias b and the weight w_i vary for each node and link. Each $\otimes$ node in the fourth layer has exactly two inputs x and y, and outputs $\frac{x+1}{2}y$, where x is the output of the diamond-shaped node.

The part of the FF network to compute the diamond-shaped nodes in the fourth layer is analogous to the network in the previous NEUGUS framework [12] for the synthesis of logical formulas. Each diamond-shaped node in the second layer, whose output is $\tanh(b+w_1x_1+\cdots+w_kx_k)$, is intended to recognize linear inequalities of the form $c_0 + c_1x_1 + \cdots c_kx_k \geq d$ where $|d|$ is a small integer, and $c_i/c_0 = w_i/b$. The idea is that the value of the node $\tanh(b+w_1x_1+\cdots+w_kx_k) = \tanh((b/c_0)\cdot(c_0 + c_1x_1 + \cdots + c_kx_k))$ is close to -1 or 1 when both $|b/c_0|$ and $|c_0 + c_1x_1 + \cdots + c_kx_k|$ are large, so that the node carries only information about whether $c_0 + c_1x_1 + \cdots c_kx_k \geq d$ holds for each d such that $|d|$ is small. The diamond-shaped nodes in the third and fourth layers are intended to compute the Boolean combinations of those linear inequalities and Boolean inputs/hidden states.

The rest of the FF network, for computing the $\otimes$-nodes in the fourth layer, is intended to compute conditional expressions of the form

$$\textbf{if } b \textbf{ then } c_0 + c_1x_1 + \cdots + c_kx_k \textbf{ else } 0,$$

where b is a logical combination of linear inequalities and Boolean inputs/hidden states. Each circle node in the second layer compute the part $c_0+c_1x_1+\cdots+c_kx_k$, each node in the lower group of the third layer computes the Boolean value b, and each $\otimes$-node emulates the conditional expression. The idea is that the Boolean value b is actually represented as a value in $[-1, 1]$ where values close to -1 and 1 are respectively interpreted as $\texttt{false}$ and $\texttt{true}$. Thus, $\frac{b+1}{2}(c_0+c_1x_1+\cdots+c_kx_k)$ is close to $c_0+c_1x_1+\cdots+c_kx_k$ when b represents $\texttt{true}$, and it is close to 0 when b represents $\texttt{false}$. Note that the general conditional $\textbf{if } b \textbf{ then } e_1 \textbf{ else } e_2$ can be expressed by $(\textbf{if } b \textbf{ then } e_1 \textbf{ else } 0) + (\textbf{if } \neg b \textbf{ then } e_2 \textbf{ else } 0) = \frac{b+1}{2}e_1 + \frac{-b+1}{2}e_2$, which can be computed in the next cycle if we have hidden states that correspond to $\textbf{if } b \textbf{ then } e_1 \textbf{ else } 0$ and $\textbf{if } \neg b \textbf{ then } e_2 \textbf{ else } 0$.

Remark 1. As explained above, the internal structure of our RNN is specialized for the purpose of solving our synthesis problem, and quite different from other popular RNNs. The $\otimes$-node is a reminiscent of a multiplicative gate of LSTM [9], but its main role is to emulate a conditional expression, rather than to address the problems of conventional RNNs such as the gradient vanishing problem. In fact, we do not expect that our RNN scales for very long lists. Fortunately, however, training data with short lists would often suffice for our synthesis problem.

3.2   Training the RNN

Let $\mathbf{R}$ be the set of real numbers and $g \in [-1,1]^{h+m} \times \mathbf{R}^{n+k} \to [-1,1]^h \times \mathbf{R}^k$ be the function computed by the FF network. The function $f \in ([-1,1]^m \times \mathbf{R}^n)^* \to [-1, 1]$ computed by the whole RNN is defined by: $f(\ell) = f'(\tilde{1}, \ell, \tilde{0})$, where:

$$f'(b_1,\ldots,b_h,[],\tilde{0}) = b_1 \quad f'(\tilde{b}, x :: \ell', \tilde{z}) = f'(\tilde{b}', \ell', \tilde{z}') \text{ where } (\tilde{b}', \tilde{z}') = g(\tilde{b}, x, \tilde{z}).$$

Here, $f' \in [-1,1]^h \times ([-1,1]^m \times \mathbf{R}^n)^* \times \mathbf{R}^k \to [-1, 1]$.

For an atom $p(\widetilde{v}, \widetilde{w})$ with $\widetilde{v} \in \mathbf{B}^m$ and $\widetilde{w} \in \mathbf{Z}^n$, we write $O_{p(\widetilde{v}, \widetilde{w})}$ for $f(\widetilde{v}^\dagger, \widetilde{w})$, where $\mathtt{true}^\dagger = 1$ and $\mathtt{false}^\dagger = -1$. For an implication constraint $a_1 \wedge \cdots \wedge a_k \Rightarrow b_1 \vee \cdots \vee b_\ell$, we define the loss $loss_{a_1 \wedge \cdots \wedge a_k \Rightarrow b_1 \vee \cdots \vee b_\ell}$ for the implication constraint by:[3]

$$loss_{a_1 \wedge \cdots \wedge a_k \Rightarrow b_1 \vee \cdots \vee b_\ell} := \prod_{i \in \{1,\ldots,k\}} \left(\frac{1+O_{a_i}}{2}\right)^2 \cdot \prod_{j \in \{1,\ldots,\ell\}} \left(\frac{1-O_{b_j}}{2}\right)^2 .$$

Note that $loss_{a_1 \wedge \cdots \wedge a_k \Rightarrow b_1 \vee \cdots \vee b_\ell}$ is 0 just if one of the a_i's is $\mathtt{false}$ or one of the b_j's is $\mathtt{true}$, which matches the meaning of the implication constraint. For a set $C = \{\gamma_1, \ldots, \gamma_p\}$ of implication constraints, the overall loss is defined by: $loss_C := \sum_{i \in \{1,\ldots,p\}} loss_{\gamma_i}$. Using the loss function above, we train the RNN with a gradient descent method.

Adjusting the loss function. The diamond-shaped nodes in Figure 2 are intended to hold Boolean values (which correspond to 1 and -1), but those nodes in the actual RNN trained by using the above loss function may take values close to 0, which cannot be interpreted as $\mathtt{true}$ or $\mathtt{false}$. That is problematic during the program synthesis, because the behavior of the RNN may deviate too much from that of an ordinary program to be synthesized. To remedy the problem, we also use a modified version of the loss function, obtained by replacing O_a in the basic loss function above with $O'_a := O_a \cdot \prod_i \frac{1+\lambda v_i^2}{1+\lambda}$ where $\lambda \geq 0$ (note that the modified loss function coincides with the basic loss function when $\lambda = 0$), and v_i is the value of a diamond-shaped node in the second or fourth layer of the FF network in Figure 2. This penalizes the use of "non-Boolean values" in diamond-shaped nodes. Note that if v_i cannot be interpreted as $\mathtt{true}$ or $\mathtt{false}$, i.e., if $|v_i|$ is close to 0, then $\frac{1+\lambda v_i^2}{1+\lambda}$ is much smaller than 1; thus, $|O'_a|$ would also be much smaller than 1, causing a large loss.

4   Synthesis Based on the Trained RNN

This section discusses how to construct the function *step* in Section 2, by using the trained RNN as a hint. From the trained RNN and its runs for training data, we gather and use the following information.

- The weight and bias of each link and node in the FF network.
- A collection of the inputs given to the FF network and the corresponding outputs of each node.

The output of the function *step* consists of Booleans and integers. We first discuss how to construct the integer part. The integer part of *step* corresponds

---

[3] This loss function is different from the one used in [12]. The difference is partly due to the encoding of Boolean values; Kobayashi et al. [12] used 0 for $\mathtt{false}$ while we use -1. Another difference is the use of log vs squared loss. We preferred the latter for simplicity, but more experiments are necessary to tune the shape of the loss function.

to the $\otimes$-nodes of the FF-network in Figure 2, whose values are computed by a function of the form:

$$I(\widetilde{r}_{1,\ldots,m}, \widetilde{v}_{1,\ldots,m}, \widetilde{u}_{1,\ldots,n}, \widetilde{s}_{1,\ldots,k}) :=$$
$$B(\widetilde{r}_{1,\ldots,m}, \widetilde{v}_{1,\ldots,m}, \widetilde{u}_{1,\ldots,n}, \widetilde{s}_{1,\ldots,k}) \otimes (b_0 + \textstyle\sum_{i\in\{1,\ldots,n\}} w_i u_i + \sum_{j\in\{1,\ldots,k\}} w'_j s_j),$$

where $\widetilde{r}$, $\widetilde{v}$, $\widetilde{u}$, and $\widetilde{s}$ respectively represent the hidden Boolean states, Boolean inputs, integer inputs, and hidden integer states; the function B is the output of a node in the lower half in the third layer in Figure 2; the part $b_0 + \cdots$ is the output of a circle node in the second layer; and $x \otimes y = \frac{x+1}{2}y$ as defined before.

Since the value of I is $b_0 + \sum_{i\in\{1,\ldots,n\}} w_i x_i + \sum_{j\in\{1,\ldots,k\}} w'_j y_j$ if the value of B is 1, and 0 if the value of B is -1, one may be tempted to construct the corresponding program expression as:

$$\textbf{if } \varphi_B \textbf{ then } b_0 + \textstyle\sum_{i\in\{1,\ldots,n\}} w_i u_i + \sum_{j\in\{1,\ldots,k\}} w'_j s_j \textbf{ else } 0,$$

where φ_B is a Boolean expression corresponding to B. That is problematic, however, because we wish to construct an integer program expression, but the weights and bias (w_i, w'_j, b_0) may be arbitrary floating point numbers. We thus re-scale the coefficients w_i, w'_j, and b_0 as follows. We first pick integers $c_0, c_1, \ldots, c_n$ and a real number r so that $rb_0, rw_1, \ldots, rw_n$ are close to $c_0, c_1, \ldots, c_n$. For w'_j, we just pick an integer c'_j close to w'_j, and prepare the integer expression:

$$\textbf{if } \varphi_B \textbf{ then } c_0 + \textstyle\sum_{i\in\{1,\ldots,n\}} c_i u_i + \sum_{j\in\{1,\ldots,k\}} c'_j s_j \textbf{ else } 0,$$

and use it as the integer-part of the function $step$.

Before constructing Boolean expressions (including φ_B), we adjust (i) the hidden integer states in the run history of RNNs for training data and (ii) the weights for the hidden integer nodes accordingly, to reflect the re-scaling of the coefficients for computing hidden integer states. We multiply (i) with r, and divide (ii) by r. To see the need for the adjustment, let us recall the $step$ function for the sortedness:

$$step(u, r_b, r_i) = (r_b \wedge (r_i \leq u), u).$$

The RNN may actually learn the following function:

$$step(u, r_b, r_i) = (r_b \wedge (2r_i \leq u), 0.5u).$$

Suppose we have re-scaled $0.5u$ to u, to make the coefficient an integer. That would increase the value of the hidden integer state by a factor of 2, so that the coefficient of r_i in the inequality $2r_i \leq u$ should be decreased by half, to obtain $r_i \leq u$. We can thus obtain

$$step(u, r_b, r_i) = (r_b \wedge (r_i \leq u), u)$$

correctly.

Table 1. The value of each node of the FF-network for $[2; 3; 5]$.

	Before re-scaling.				After re-scaling.		
1st layer	2nd layer	3rd layer	4th layer	1st layer	2nd layer	3rd layer	4th layer
1.000	0.996	0.936	0.999	1.000	0.996	0.936	0.999
2.000	0.997	0.994		2.000	0.997	0.994	
0.000	-0.999	0.975	2.231	0.000	-0.999	0.975	1.978
	0.992	-0.969			0.992	-0.969	
	2.235	0.998			1.982	0.998	
0.999	1.000	0.936	0.999	0.999	1.000	0.936	0.999
3.000	0.977	0.992		3.000	0.977	0.992	
2.231	-1.000	0.967	3.256	1.978	-1.000	0.967	2.888
	0.924	-0.969			0.924	-0.969	
	3.262	0.998			2.893	0.998	
0.999	1.000	0.936	0.999	0.999	1.000	0.936	0.999
5.000	0.998	0.994		5.000	0.998	0.994	
3.256	-1.000	0.975	5.463	2.888	-1.000	0.975	4.844
	0.995	-0.969			0.995	-0.969	
	5.472	0.998			4.853	0.998	

Example 1. As a concrete example, consider the synthesis of a sortedness predicate *sorted*, which takes a list ℓ and returns whether ℓ is sorted in the ascending order. We set $h = n = k = 1$, and $m = 0$. The numbers of hidden nodes in the upper-half of the second layer and those in the upper-half of the third layer were both set to 4. We have trained the network by using 200 positive samples (like $\Rightarrow sorted([2; 3; 5])$) and 94 negative samples (like $sorted([9; 8]) \Rightarrow$). After the training, we re-ran the RNN for the training data, and collected the value of each node of the FF-network. For example, for the data $[2; 3; 5]$, we obtained the information shown on the left-hand side of Table 1. Here, the first group (separated by the horizontal line), shows the values of the nodes for the first element 2 of the list, and the second group shows those for the second element 3. We also look at the weights and biases of the FF-network to synthesize the target function *step*.

By inspecting the weights and bias for the the circle node in the second layer, we can find that the function computed by the node is: $-0.023 + 1.128u - 0.045s$, where u and s respective denote the values of the integer input and the hidden integer state. The ratio between the constant and the coefficient of u is about $0 : 1$, and the co-efficient of s is close to 0. Thus, we set the integer expression to compute the next hidden integer state to **if** φ_B **then** u **else** 0, where the condition φ_B is yet to be synthesized.

The replacement of $-0.023 + 1.128u - 0.045s$ with u results in the decrease of the value of the hidden integer state by a factor of $1/1.128$, as shown on the right-hand side of Table 1. The weights for the nodes in the second layer are also accordingly re-scaled.   □

It remains to construct Boolean expressions, consisting of linear inequalities on integer variables and Boolean variables. That can be achieved in a manner similar to [12]; we have, however, adopted the following procedure, which utilizes information about the value of each node in the FF network. In contrast, Kobayashi et al.'s method [12] uses only the weights and biases, in addition to the input and output for each training data; they did not utilize the values of internal nodes for each training data.

We synthesize linear inequalities corresponding to the diamond-shaped nodes in the second layer as follows. Let

$$\tanh(b_0 + w_1 u_1 + \cdots + w_n u_n + w_{n+1} s_1 + \cdots + w_{n+k} s_k)$$

be the value computed by a diamond-shaped node in the second layer (where we assume that the weights $w_{n+1}, \ldots, w_{n+k}$ have already been re-scaled). Let $c_0, c_1, \ldots, c_{n+k}$ be integers whose ratios are close to those of $b_0, w_1, \ldots, w_{n+k}$. Then we set the corresponding inequality to

$$c_0 + c_1 u_1 + \cdots + c_n u_n + c_{n+1} s_1 + \cdots + c_{n+k} s_k > e,$$

where $e \in \{-1, 0, 1\}$ is chosen so that the truth value of the inequality best-matches the actual input-output behavior of the node for training data; recall the discussion in Section 3.1.

Next, we construct Boolean functions corresponding to the diamond-shape nodes in the fourth layer and the lower-half of the third layer in Figure 2. This is performed by first constructing the truth tables for those functions based on the runs of the RNN for the training data, and then using a method for Boolean decision tree construction [7],[4] where Boolean variables and the inequalities synthesized above are used as qualifiers (i.e., atomic predicates that constitute Boolean functions). Those qualifiers are prioritized based on the weights for the nodes in the third and fourth layers. The synthesized functions may not completely match the truth tables if appropriate inequalities have not been found in the previous step. Even so, we proceed to the next step to construct the *step* function and test it; recall that in our *gray-box* use of the neural network, the internal behavior of the synthesized program need not completely match that of the RNN.

Example 2. Recall Example 1. The next step is to synthesize linear inequalities from the (re-scaled) weights of the nodes in the second layer. After the re-scaling of weights, the functions computed by the diamond-shaped nodes are:

$$\tanh(1.396 + 0.876u + 1.182s) \quad \tanh(1.066 + 1.084u - 1.052s) \quad \cdots$$

Based on the ratios between the constant and coefficients, we synthesize linear inequalities of the form:

$$4 + 3u + 4s > e_1 \qquad 1 + u - s > e_2 \qquad -6 - 4u - 3s > e_3 \qquad u - s > e_4.$$

---

[4] Kobayashi et al. [12] suggested using the Quine-McClusky method for this purpose, but we prefer the Boolean decision tree construction for two reasons. First, the Quine-McClusky method would not scale when the dimension is large. Second, we wish to give priorities to some qualifiers as explained below.

We then check the re-scaled trace information (such as the one in Table 1, but including the trace information for all the training data), we choose appropriate values for each e_i. In the present case, we obtain:

$$4 + 3u + 4s > 0 \qquad 1 + u - s > -1 \qquad -7 - 3u - 4s > 0 \qquad u - s > -1.$$

It remains to synthesize Boolean functions. To this end, for each diamond-shaped node in the fourth layer and in the lower-half of the third layer, we construct a truth table, where the inputs are Boolean values obtained by discretizing the values of the diamond-shaped nodes in the first and second layers. For example, from Table 2, we obtain the following truth table for the diamond-shaped node in the fourth layer. The duplicated rows can be removed before the synthesis of a logical function.

input					output
I_0	I_1	I_2	I_3	I_4	O
true	true	true	false	true	true
true	true	true	false	true	true
...	...	...	...	...	...

Here, I_0 corresponds to the value of the hidden Boolean node, and I_1–I_4 correspond to the diamond-shaped nodes in the second layer, which represent inequality constraints extracted above. We interpret values close to 1 (say, those greater than 0.5) as true, and those close to -1 (say, those less than -0.5) as false, ignoring the other values.

Once a truth table has been constructed, we can apply a classical method to synthesize a logical function that conforms to the truth table. In our implementation, we have employed a technique for Boolean decision tree construction; instead of computing the entropy [7], however, we have prioritized Boolean inputs (I_0–I_4, in the above case) based on the weights for the nodes in the third and fourth layer, which indicate which Boolean inputs affected the output node.

Suppose that the logical function $O = I_0 \wedge I_4$ has been synthesized in the above example. Suppose also that the constant function true has been synthesized for the diamond-shaped node in the third layer. Since I_0 corresponds to the hidden Boolean state, and I_4 corresponds to the inequality $u - s > -1$ (which is equivalent to $s \leq u$), we obtain

$$step(u, r_b, s) = (r_b \wedge (s \leq u), \textbf{if true then } u \textbf{ else } 0)$$

as the step function.   □

By combining the procedures above, we can construct the function $step$. After constructing the $step$ function, we test the synthesized recursive function against training data, and check whether the outputs of the synthesized function satisfy all the implication constraints. If some constraints are not satisfied, we re-train the RNN and repeat the synthesis procedure above. To avoid the re-training of the RNN from scratch, however, we first fix the part for computing the hidden integer states. This is because the process of re-scaling the parameters for the hidden integer states as explained above is costly and error-prone. Upon repeated failures, however, we reset all the parameters of the RNN and re-train it from scratch.

5 Implementation and Experiments

We have implemented a tool called NEUGUSR for the synthesis of recursive predicates based on the method described above in OCaml using the machine learning framework ocaml-torch (https://github.com/LaurentMazare/ocaml-torch), which is an OCaml interface for the PyTorch library. Our tool is available at https://github.com/naokikob/neugusR. This section describes the experiments we conducted that confirm the effectiveness of our approaches.

All the experiments below were conducted on a laptop computer with Intel(R) Core(TM) i5-8265U CPU (1.60GHz) and 8 GB memory. Training was done using only CPU.

5.1 Dataset and predicates

We have prepared 11 recursive predicates over integer lists and integers for synthesis. Examples include predicates such as $\max(l, n)$ which says the largest element of l is n, $\mathtt{sumle}(l_1, l_2)$ which says the sum of l_1 is less than or equal to the sum of l_2, and predicates $\mathtt{sorted}(l)$ and $\mathtt{avge}(l, n)$ as already described in Section 1.

For experiments, we consider positive constraints (of the form $\Rightarrow a_k$ where $a_k \in \mathbf{Atoms}_{\mathcal{K}}$ and $\mathcal{K}$ is the corresponding signature of the predicate), negative constraints (of the form $b_k \Rightarrow$), as well as general implication constraints as defined in Section 2.

For each problem (predicate), we performed 3 runs to see if the solver was able to synthesize a program that matches all the training examples. We set the time limit of each run to 1200 seconds. In each run, the neural network is trained for 30000 steps by default. At each step, all the training examples of the predicate were used to optimize the neural network. In each run, the training was terminated early if the accuracy reached 100% on the training examples and the loss was less than a threshold, which in the current setting is 10^{-6}.

If the accuracy did not reach 100% within 30000 steps or there are constraints not satisfied by the synthesized program, the training was set to restart with fresh parameters except for the weights of the hidden integer states. If there are three consecutive failures of convergence, however, we reset all the parameters and restart training from scratch.

We used the Adam optimizer [11] for training with the default setting of ocaml-torch ($\beta_1 = 0.9$, $\beta_2 = 0.999$ without weight decay), and the learning rate was 0.001. Learned parameters are not shared between different problems.

5.2   Evaluation

The specification of RNN used for each problem is as follows. For all the predicates other than updown and max, we used 4 nodes for the second layer of the RNN, 8 nodes for the third layer of the RNN, and 1 node each for the integer hidden state and the boolean hidden state. For updown and max, we used 2 nodes for the boolean hidden states and 16 nodes for the third layer. For max, we also used 8 nodes for the second layer instead of 4.

We report the performance of our tool NEUGUSR with respect to the following metrics.

- #retry: the total number of retries. For each run, up to 10 retries were allowed within the time limit. There can be 3×10 retries for each problem in total in the worst case.
- #success: the number of runs in which a program that correctly classifies the positive and negative examples was constructed.
- time: the average execution time per run. The execution time includes the whole process for training the RNN and synthesizing/testing a program, though it was dominated by the time for training the RNN.

Table 2 shows the performance of NEUGUSR for each predicate. It can be seen that NEUGUSR was able to solve all the problems consistently, with the only exception of max which failed once due to a timeout. The small number of retries triggered during the synthesis of each predicate suggests that our approach is effective. Our RNN was able to classify the positive and negative examples very well, because otherwise multiple restarts of training would have been forced even before entering the extraction phase. Our extraction procedure was also reasonably accurate — while errors could occur, they were quickly fixed within a few retries (3 on average as can be seen in Table 2).

Table 2. Performance on the predicates to be synthesized.

Predicate	# retry	# success (out of 3)	time (s)
sorted (l)	0	3	171.2
sortedrev (l)	1	3	217.5
stairge (l)	5	3	560.6
allge (l, n)	1	3	272.3
allle (l, n)	1	3	355.1
somege (l, n)	1	3	376.2
avge (l, n)	8	3	571.2
listle (l_1, l_2)	0	3	214.4
sumle (l_1, l_2)	2	3	241.4
updown (l)	1	3	226.1
max (l, n)	7	2	557.6

The predicate max is the only predicate that involves equality among the 11 predicates, which probably explains why it is the most difficult one. The fact that max can be synthesized was more of a surprise which demonstrated the generality of our approach to some extent. While our framework was not designed specifically to handle equalities, the neural network, if lucky, might still be able to find clever ways to express equalities using inequalities. This is one of the reasons we specified 8 nodes for the second layer when dealing with max — the more inequalities we have, the more likely a combination of them happens to express certain equality.

Remark 2. We could not find any previous tool that can be directly compared with ours. A possible alternative approach to our synthesis problem would be to prepare a template for the step function, generate constraints on parameters in the template, and use an SMT solver to solve them.

6 Related Work

As already mentioned, the present work may be considered an extension of Kobayashi et al.'s NEUGUS framework [12], where feed-forward neural networks are used as gray-boxes to synthesize formulas of quantifier-free linear integer arithmetic. We have significantly expanded the scope of NEUGUS, by enabling the synthesis of recursive predicates on lists; to that end, we have employed special-purpose recursive neural networks.

Our work has been partially motivated by Shimoda et al.'s work on an extension of symbolic automata called symbolic automatic relations (SARs) [19]. They introduced SARs to express recursive predicates on lists, and used them to express loop invariants on lists (more precisely, to express candidate solutions for the CHC satisfiability problem [1]) for automated verification of list-manipulating programs. They left it to future work how to automatically infer SARs from positive, negative, and implication constraints. Our work fills that gap, since the class of programs synthesized in our framework corresponds to their SARs (more precisely, Σ_1^{sar}-formulas [19]). Further refinement and optimizations would be, however, required for our tool to be effectively used in that context.

Our work is also related to neural network-based approaches to the synthesis of finite automata [16,21]. Our method deals with a much wider class of programs involving integers and integer lists. Also, the problem setting is slightly different; Weiss et al.'s method [21] takes a trained RNN as the ground truth, and aims to construct an automaton whose behavior matches that of the RNN. In contrast, in our approach, we allow the behavior of the synthesized program and that of the RNN to be different for inputs other than those given as training data. This is because in the NEUGUS framework, the trained RNN is supposed to be used just as a hint, and does not necessarily provide the ground truth. The ground truth is determined from the whole verification or synthesis goal [12,13], as discussed at the end of Section 2. In the context of program verification, the synthesized predicate is used as a candidate program invariant, and it is checked whether it is indeed an inductive invariant; if not, then new training data are added and

NEuGuS should be repeated. In the context of oracle-based program synthesis, the synthesized function is used as a component of the whole program, and then it is checked whether the whole program satisfies a specification; if not, then new training data for the function are generated and NEuGuS should be repeated. Recently, the above line of work has also been further extended to infer weighted automata [22,15] and context-free grammars [23], which are incompatible with the class of programs synthesized by our method.

There have been studies of other approaches to program synthesis based on neural networks, most notably, those based on transformers [3,18,17]. Both the problem settings and approaches (the ways in which neural networks are used) are quite different between those studies and our work. Our goal is to synthesize programs from positive/negative/implication constraints (where those constraints are added as necessary in the whole loop of program verification or synthesis), and it is not clear to us how to effectively apply transformers-based approaches to program synthesis for that purpose. Whilst the transformers-based approaches can in principle be used for our program synthesis problem, huge training data (which consist of pairs of positive/negative/implication constraints and a program that satisfies the constraints) would be required and they might not work well for the synthesis of unseen programs. Other neural network-based approaches include that of AlphaTensor [5], which used deep reinforcement learning to discover new matrix multiplication algorithms.

The synthesis of predicates from positive/negative samples (but without implication constraints) is an instance of the well-studied problem of *programming by examples* (PBE). PBE has been successful especially in the synthesis of string-to-string functions in DSL [8], and machine learning has also been recently applied [20]. To our knowledge, however, the synthesis of recursive functions has not been much studied in that context.

7 Conclusion

We have proposed a novel approach to automated synthesis of recursive predicates on lists, as an extension of Kobayashi et al.'s neural-network-guided synthesis (NEuGuS) [12]. We have designed a special-purpose recursive neural network and devised a method to synthesize a recursive predicate by using the trained network as a hint. We have implemented a synthesis tool based on the method and confirmed that the tool works reasonably well for various examples. We plan to further refine the tool and deploy it in the context of automated verification of list-manipulating programs [19] and oracle-based program synthesis [13]. We also plan to extend the method to enable the synthesis of a larger class of recursive programs, including more general list-processing programs that go beyond the "fold" functions, and tree-processing programs.

Acknowledgments

We would like to thank anonymous referees for useful comments. This work was supported by JSPS KAKENHI Grant Number JP20H05703.

References

1. Bjørner, N., Gurfinkel, A., McMillan, K.L., Rybalchenko, A.: Horn clause solvers for program verification. In: Fields of Logic and Computation II - Essays Dedicated to Yuri Gurevich on the Occasion of His 75th Birthday. LNCS, vol. 9300, pp. 24–51. Springer (2015)
2. Champion, A., Chiba, T., Kobayashi, N., Sato, R.: ICE-based refinement type discovery for higher-order functional programs. J. Autom. Reason. **64**(7), 1393–1418 (2020), https://doi.org/10.1007/s10817-020-09571-y
3. Chen, M., et al.: Evaluating large language models trained on code. CoRR **abs/2107.03374** (2021), https://arxiv.org/abs/2107.03374
4. Ezudheen, P., Neider, D., D'Souza, D., Garg, P., Madhusudan, P.: Horn-ICE learning for synthesizing invariants and contracts. Proc. ACM Program. Lang. **2**(OOPSLA), 131:1–131:25 (2018), https://doi.org/10.1145/3276501
5. Fawzi, A., Balog, M., Huang, A., Hubert, T., Romera-Paredes, B., Barekatain, M., Novikov, A., Ruiz, F.J.R., Schrittwieser, J., Swirszcz, G., Silver, D., Hassabis, D., Kohli, P.: Discovering faster matrix multiplication algorithms with reinforcement learning. Nat. **610**(7930), 47–53 (2022). https://doi.org/10.1038/s41586-022-05172-4, https://doi.org/10.1038/s41586-022-05172-4
6. Garg, P., Löding, C., Madhusudan, P., Neider, D.: ICE: A robust framework for learning invariants. In: Proceedings of CAV 2014. LNCS, vol. 8559, pp. 69–87. Springer (2014)
7. Garg, P., Neider, D., Madhusudan, P., Roth, D.: Learning invariants using decision trees and implication counterexamples. In: Proceedings of the 43rd Annual ACM SIGPLAN-SIGACT Symposium on Principles of Programming Languages, POPL 2016. pp. 499–512. ACM (2016), https://doi.org/10.1145/2837614.2837664
8. Gulwani, S.: Automating string processing in spreadsheets using input-output examples. In: Ball, T., Sagiv, M. (eds.) Proceedings of the 38th ACM SIGPLAN-SIGACT Symposium on Principles of Programming Languages, POPL 2011, Austin, TX, USA, January 26-28, 2011. pp. 317–330. ACM (2011). https://doi.org/10.1145/1926385.1926423
9. Hochreiter, S., Schmidhuber, J.: Long short-term memory. Neural Comput. **9**(8), 1735–1780 (1997). https://doi.org/10.1162/neco.1997.9.8.1735, https://doi.org/10.1162/neco.1997.9.8.1735
10. Hojjat, H., Rümmer, P.: The ELDARICA Horn solver. In: 2018 Formal Methods in Computer Aided Design (FMCAD). pp. 1–7 (2018)
11. Kingma, D.P., Ba, J.: Adam: A method for stochastic optimization. In: 3rd International Conference on Learning Representations, ICLR 2015, Conference Track Proceedings (2015), http://arxiv.org/abs/1412.6980
12. Kobayashi, N., Sekiyama, T., Sato, I., Unno, H.: Toward neural-network-guided program synthesis and verification. In: Dragoi, C., Mukherjee, S., Namjoshi, K.S. (eds.) Static Analysis - 28th International Symposium, SAS 2021, Chicago, IL, USA, October 17-19, 2021, Proceedings. Lecture Notes in Computer Science, vol. 12913, pp. 236–260. Springer (2021). https://doi.org/10.1007/978-3-030-88806-0_12
13. Kobayashi, N., Sekiyama, T., Sato, I., Unno, H.: Toward neural-network-guided program synthesis and verification. CoRR **abs/2103.09414** (2021), https://arxiv.org/abs/2103.09414
14. Komuravelli, A., Gurfinkel, A., Chaki, S.: SMT-based model checking for recursive programs. Formal Methods Syst. Des. **48**(3), 175–205 (2016), https://doi.org/10.1007/s10703-016-0249-4

15. Okudono, T., Waga, M., Sekiyama, T., Hasuo, I.: Weighted automata extraction from recurrent neural networks via regression on state spaces. In: The Thirty-Fourth AAAI Conference on Artificial Intelligence, AAAI 2020, The Thirty-Second Innovative Applications of Artificial Intelligence Conference, IAAI 2020, The Tenth AAAI Symposium on Educational Advances in Artificial Intelligence, EAAI 2020, New York, NY, USA, February 7-12, 2020. pp. 5306–5314. AAAI Press (2020), https://ojs.aaai.org/index.php/AAAI/article/view/5977

16. Omlin, C.W., Giles, C.L.: Extraction of rules from discrete-time recurrent neural networks. Neural Networks **9**(1), 41–52 (1996). https://doi.org/10.1016/0893-6080(95)00086-0

17. Poesia, G., Polozov, A., Le, V., Tiwari, A., Soares, G., Meek, C., Gulwani, S.: Synchromesh: Reliable code generation from pre-trained language models. In: The Tenth International Conference on Learning Representations, ICLR 2022, Virtual Event, April 25-29, 2022. OpenReview.net (2022), https://openreview.net/forum?id=KmtVD97J43e

18. Roper, J.: Transformer-based program synthesis for low-data environments. CoRR **abs/2205.09246** (2022). https://doi.org/10.48550/arXiv.2205.09246

19. Shimoda, T., Kobayashi, N., Sakayori, K., Sato, R.: Symbolic automatic relations and their applications to SMT and CHC solving. In: Dragoi, C., Mukherjee, S., Namjoshi, K.S. (eds.) Static Analysis - 28th International Symposium, SAS 2021, Chicago, IL, USA, October 17-19, 2021, Proceedings. Lecture Notes in Computer Science, vol. 12913, pp. 405–428. Springer (2021). https://doi.org/10.1007/978-3-030-88806-0_20

20. Verbruggen, G., Le, V., Gulwani, S.: Semantic programming by example with pre-trained models. Proc. ACM Program. Lang. **5**(OOPSLA), 1–25 (2021). https://doi.org/10.1145/3485477

21. Weiss, G., Goldberg, Y., Yahav, E.: Extracting automata from recurrent neural networks using queries and counterexamples. In: Dy, J.G., Krause, A. (eds.) Proceedings of the 35th International Conference on Machine Learning, ICML 2018, Stockholmsmässan, Stockholm, Sweden, July 10-15, 2018. Proceedings of Machine Learning Research, vol. 80, pp. 5244–5253. PMLR (2018), http://proceedings.mlr.press/v80/weiss18a.html

22. Weiss, G., Goldberg, Y., Yahav, E.: Learning deterministic weighted automata with queries and counterexamples. In: Wallach, H.M., Larochelle, H., Beygelzimer, A., d'Alché-Buc, F., Fox, E.B., Garnett, R. (eds.) Advances in Neural Information Processing Systems 32: Annual Conference on Neural Information Processing Systems 2019, NeurIPS 2019, December 8-14, 2019, Vancouver, BC, Canada. pp. 8558–8569 (2019), https://proceedings.neurips.cc/paper/2019/hash/d3f93e7766e8e1b7ef66dfdd9a8be93b-Abstract.html

23. Yellin, D.M., Weiss, G.: Synthesizing context-free grammars from recurrent neural networks. In: Groote, J.F., Larsen, K.G. (eds.) Tools and Algorithms for the Construction and Analysis of Systems - 27th International Conference, TACAS 2021, Held as Part of the European Joint Conferences on Theory and Practice of Software, ETAPS 2021, Luxembourg City, Luxembourg, March 27 - April 1, 2021, Proceedings, Part I. Lecture Notes in Computer Science, vol. 12651, pp. 351–369. Springer (2021). https://doi.org/10.1007/978-3-030-72016-2_19

Automata

Modular Mix-and-Match
Complementation of Büchi Automata

Vojtěch Havlena[1(✉)] , Ondřej Lengál[1(✉)] , Yong Li[2,3(✉)] ,
Barbora Šmahlíková[1(✉)] , and Andrea Turrini[3,4(✉)]

[1] Faculty of Information Technology, Brno University of Technology, Brno, Czech Republic
ihavlena@fit.vut.cz, lengal@vut.cz, xsmahl00@vut.cz
[2] Department of Computer Science, University of Liverpool, Liverpool, UK
liyong@liverpool.ac.uk
[3] State Key Laboratory of Computer Science, Institute of Software,
Chinese Academy of Sciences, Beijing, People's Republic of China
turrini@ios.ac.cn
[4] Institute of Intelligent Software, Guangzhou, Guangzhou, People's Republic of China

Abstract. Complementation of nondeterministic Büchi automata (BAs) is an important problem in automata theory with numerous applications in formal verification, such as termination analysis of programs, model checking, or in decision procedures of some logics. We build on ideas from a recent work on BA determinization by Li *et al.* and propose a new modular algorithm for BA complementation. Our algorithm allows to combine several BA complementation procedures together, with one procedure for a subset of the BA's strongly connected components (SCCs). In this way, one can exploit the structure of particular SCCs (such as when they are inherently weak or deterministic) and use more efficient specialized algorithms, regardless of the structure of the whole BA. We give a general framework into which partial complementation procedures can be plugged in, and its instantiation with several algorithms. The framework can, in general, produce a complement with an Emerson-Lei acceptance condition, which can often be more compact. Using the algorithm, we were able to establish an exponentially better new upper bound of $O(4^n)$ for complementation of the recently introduced class of elevator automata. We implemented the algorithm in a prototype and performed a comprehensive set of experiments on a large set of benchmarks, showing that our framework complements well the state of the art and that it can serve as a basis for future efficient BA complementation and inclusion checking algorithms.

1 Introduction

Nondeterministic Büchi automata (BAs) [8] are an elegant and conceptually simple framework to model infinite behaviors of systems and the properties they are expected to satisfy. BAs are widely used in many important verification tasks, such as termination analysis of programs [30], model checking [54], or as the underlying formal model of decision procedures for some logics (such as S1S [8] or a fragment of the first-order logic over Sturmian words [31]). Many of these applications require to perform *complementation* of BAs: For instance, in termination analysis of programs within ULTIMATE AUTOMIZER [30], complementation is used to keep track of the set of paths whose termination still needs to be proved. On the other hand, in model checking[5] and decision

---

[5] Here, we consider model checking w.r.t. a specification given in some more expressive logic, such as S1S [8], QPTL [50], or HyperLTL [12], rather than LTL [44], where negation is simple.

S. Sankaranarayanan and N. Sharygina (Eds.): TACAS 2023, LNCS 13993, pp. 249–270, 2023.
https://doi.org/10.1007/978-3-031-30823-9_13

procedures of logics, complement is usually used to implement negation and quantifier alternation. Complementation is often the most difficult automata operation performed here; its worst-case state complexity is $O((0.76n)^n)$ [48,2] (which is tight [55]).

In these applications, efficiency of the complementation often determines the overall efficiency (or even feasibility) of the top-level application. For instance, the success of ULTIMATE AUTOMIZER in the Termination category of the International Competition on Software Verification (SV-COMP) [51] is to a large degree due to an efficient BA complementation algorithm [6,11] tailored for BAs with a special structure that it often encounters (as of the time of writing, it has won 6 gold medals in the years 2017–2022 and two silver medals in 2015 and 2016). The special structure in this case are the so-called *semi-deterministic BAs* (SDBAs), BAs consisting of two parts: (i) an initial part without accepting states/transitions and (ii) a deterministic part containing accepting states/transitions that cannot transition into the first part.

Complementation of SDBAs using one from the family of the so-called NCSB algorithms [6,5,11,28] has the worst-case complexity $O(4^n)$ (and usually also works much better in practice than general BA complementation procedures). Similarly, there are efficient complementation procedures for other subclasses of BAs, e.g., (i) *deterministic BAs* (DBAs) can be complemented into BAs with $2n$ states [35] (or into co-Büchi automata with $n + 1$ states) or (ii) *inherently weak BAs* (BAs where in each *strongly connected component* (SCC), either all cycles are accepting or all cycles are rejecting) can be complemented into DBAs with $O(3^n)$ states using the Miyano-Hayashi algorithm [42].

For a long time, there has been no efficient algorithm for complementation of BAs that are highly structured but do not fall into one of the categories above, e.g., BAs containing inherently weak, deterministic, and some nondeterministic SCCs. For such BAs, one needed to use a general complementation algorithm with the $O((0.76n)^n)$ (or worse) complexity. To the best of our knowledge, only recently has there appeared works that exploit the structure of BAs to obtain a more efficient complementation algorithm: (i) The work of Havlena *et al.* [29], who introduce the class of *elevator automata* (BAs with an arbitrary mixture of inherently weak and deterministic SCCs) and give a $O(16^n)$ algorithm for them. (ii) The work of Li *et al.* [37], who propose a BA determinization procedure (into a deterministic Emerson-Lei automaton) that is based on decomposing the input BA into SCCs and using a different determinization procedure for different types of SCCs (inherently weak, deterministic, general) in a synchronous construction.

In this paper, we propose a new BA complementation algorithm inspired by [37], where we exploit the fact that complementation is, in a sense, more relaxed than determinization. In particular, we present a *framework* where one can plug-in different partial complementation procedures fine-tuned for SCCs with a specific structure. The procedures work only with the given SCCs, to some degree *independently* (thus reducing the potential state space explosion) from the rest of the BA. Our top-level algorithm then orchestrates runs of the different procedures in a *synchronous* manner (or completely independently in the so-called *postponed* strategy), obtaining a resulting automaton with potentially a more general acceptance condition (in general an Emerson-Lei condition), which can help keeping the result small. If the procedures satisfy given correctness requirements, our framework guarantees that its instantiation will also be correct. We also propose its optimizations by, e.g., using round-robin to decrease the amount of nondeterminism, using a shared breakpoint to reduce the size and the number of colours for certain class of partial algorithms, and generalize simulation-based pruning of macrostates.

We provide a detailed description of partial complementation procedures for inherently weak, deterministic, and initial deterministic SCCs, which we use to obtain a *new* exponentially better upper bound of $O(4^n)$ for the class of elevator automata (i.e., the same upper bound as for its strict subclass of SDBAs). Furthermore, we also provide two partial procedures for general SCCs based on determinization (from [37]) and the rank-based construction. Using a prototype implementation, we then show our algorithm complements well existing approaches and significantly improves the state of the art.

2 Preliminaries

We fix a finite non-empty alphabet Σ and the first infinite ordinal ω. An (infinite) word w is a function $w \colon \omega \to \Sigma$ where the i-th symbol is denoted as w_i. Sometimes, we represent w as an infinite sequence $w = w_0 w_1 \ldots$ We denote the set of all infinite words over Σ as Σ^ω; an ω-*language* is a subset of Σ^ω.

Emerson-Lei Acceptance Conditions. Given a set $\Gamma = \{0, \ldots, k-1\}$ of k *colours* (often depicted as ⓪, ①, etc.), we define the set of *Emerson-Lei acceptance conditions* $\mathbb{EL}(\Gamma)$ as the set of formulae constructed according to the following grammar:

$$\alpha ::= \mathsf{Inf}(c) \mid \mathsf{Fin}(c) \mid (\alpha \wedge \alpha) \mid (\alpha \vee \alpha) \tag{1}$$

for $c \in \Gamma$. The *satisfaction* relation $\models$ for a set of colours $M \subseteq \Gamma$ and condition α is defined inductively as follows (for $c \in \Gamma$):

$$M \models \mathsf{Fin}(c) \text{ iff } c \notin M, \qquad M \models \alpha_1 \vee \alpha_2 \text{ iff } M \models \alpha_1 \text{ or } M \models \alpha_2,$$
$$M \models \mathsf{Inf}(c) \text{ iff } c \in M, \qquad M \models \alpha_1 \wedge \alpha_2 \text{ iff } M \models \alpha_1 \text{ and } M \models \alpha_2.$$

Emerson-Lei Automata. A (nondeterministic transition-based[6]) *Emerson-Lei automaton* (TELA) over Σ is a tuple $\mathcal{A} = (Q, \delta, I, \Gamma, \mathsf{p}, \mathsf{Acc})$, where Q is a finite set of *states*, $\delta \subseteq Q \times \Sigma \times Q$ is a set of *transitions*[7], $I \subseteq Q$ is the set of *initial* states, Γ is the set of *colours*, $\mathsf{p} \colon \delta \to 2^\Gamma$ is a *colouring function* of transitions, and $\mathsf{Acc} \in \mathbb{EL}(\Gamma)$. We use $p \xrightarrow{a} q$ to denote that $(p, a, q) \in \delta$ and sometimes also treat δ as a function $\delta \colon Q \times \Sigma \to 2^Q$. Moreover, we extend δ to sets of states $P \subseteq Q$ as $\delta(P, a) = \bigcup_{p \in P} \delta(p, a)$. We use $\mathcal{A}[q]$ for $q \in Q$ to denote the automaton $\mathcal{A}[q] = (Q, \delta, \{q\}, \Gamma, \mathsf{p}, \mathsf{Acc})$, i.e., the TELA obtained from $\mathcal{A}$ by setting q as the only initial state. $\mathcal{A}$ is called *deterministic* if $|I| \leq 1$ and $|\delta(q, a)| \leq 1$ for each $q \in Q$ and $a \in \Sigma$. If $\Gamma = \{⓪\}$ and $\mathsf{Acc} = \mathsf{Inf}(⓪)$, we call $\mathcal{A}$ a *Büchi automaton* (BA) and denote it as $\mathcal{A} = (Q, \delta, I, F)$ where F is the set of all transitions coloured by ⓪, i.e., $F = \mathsf{p}^{-1}(\{⓪\})$. For a BA, we use $\delta_F(p, a) = \{q \in \delta(p, a) \mid \mathsf{p}(p \xrightarrow{a} q) = \{⓪\}\}$ (and extend the notation to sets of states as for δ). A BA $\mathcal{A} = (Q, \delta, I, F)$ is called *semi-deterministic* (SDBA) if for every accepting transition $(p \xrightarrow{a} q) \in F$, the reachable part of $\mathcal{A}[q]$ is deterministic.

A *run* of $\mathcal{A}$ from $q \in Q$ on an input word w is an infinite sequence $\rho \colon \omega \to Q$ that starts in q and respects δ, i.e., $\rho_0 = q$ and $\forall i \geq 0 \colon \rho_i \xrightarrow{w_i} \rho_{i+1} \in \delta$. Let $\inf_\delta(\rho) \subseteq \delta$ denote the set of transitions occurring in ρ infinitely often and $\inf_\Gamma(\rho) = \bigcup \{\mathsf{p}(x) \mid x \in$

---

[6] We only consider transition-based acceptance in order to avoid cluttering the paper by always dealing with accepting states *and* accepting transitions. Extending our approach to state/transition-based (or just state-based) automata is straightforward.

[7] Note that some authors use a more general definition of TELAs with $\delta \subseteq Q \times \Sigma \times 2^\Gamma \times Q$; we only use them as the output of our algorithm, where the simpler definition suffices.

$\inf_\delta(\rho)\}$ be the set of infinitely often occurring colours. A run ρ is *accepting* in $\mathcal{A}$ iff $\inf_\Gamma(\rho) \models$ Acc and the *language* of $\mathcal{A}$, denoted as $\mathcal{L}(\mathcal{A})$, is defined as the set of words $w \in \Sigma^\omega$ for which there exists an accepting run in $\mathcal{A}$ starting with some state in I.

Consider a BA $\mathcal{A} = (Q, \delta, I, F)$. For a set of states $S \subseteq Q$ we use $\mathcal{A}_S$ to denote the copy of $\mathcal{A}$ where accepting transitions only occur between states from S, i.e., the BA $\mathcal{A}_S = (Q, \delta, I, F \cap \delta|_S)$ where $\delta|_S = \{p \xrightarrow{a} q \in \delta \mid p, q \in S\}$. We say that a non-empty set of states $C \subseteq Q$ is a *strongly connected component* (SCC) if every pair of states of C can reach each other and C is a maximal such set. An SCC of $\mathcal{A}$ is *trivial* if it consists of a single state that does not contain a self-loop and *non-trivial* otherwise. An SCC C is *accepting* if it contains at least one accepting transition and *inherently weak* iff either (i) every cycle in C contains a transition from F or (ii) no cycle in C contains any transitions from F. An SCC C is *deterministic* iff the BA $(C, \delta|_C, \{q\}, \emptyset)$ for any $q \in C$ is deterministic. We denote inherently weak components as IWCs, accepting deterministic components that are not inherently weak as DACs (deterministic accepting), and the remaining accepting components as NACs (nondeterministic accepting). A BA $\mathcal{A}$ is called an *elevator automaton* if it contains no NAC.

We assume that $\mathcal{A}$ contains no accepting transition outside its SCCs (no run can cycle over such transitions). We use δ_{SCC} to denote the restriction of δ to transitions that do not leave their SCCs, formally, $\delta_{SCC} = \{p \xrightarrow{a} q \in \delta \mid p \text{ and } q \text{ are in the same SCC}\}$. A *partition block* $P \subseteq Q$ of $\mathcal{A}$ is a nonempty union of its accepting SCCs, and a *partitioning* of $\mathcal{A}$ is a sequence $P_1, \ldots, P_n$ of pairwise disjoint partition blocks of $\mathcal{A}$ that contains all accepting SCCs of $\mathcal{A}$. Given a P_i, let $\mathcal{A}_{P_i}$ be the BA obtained from $\mathcal{A}$ by removing colours from transitions outside P_i. The following fact serves as the basis of our decomposition-based complementation procedure.

Fact 1. $\mathcal{L}(\mathcal{A}) = \mathcal{L}(\mathcal{A}_{P_1}) \cup \ldots \cup \mathcal{L}(\mathcal{A}_{P_n})$

The complement (automaton) of a BA $\mathcal{A}$ is a TELA that accepts the complement language $\Sigma^\omega \setminus \mathcal{L}(\mathcal{A})$ of $\mathcal{L}(\mathcal{A})$. In the paper, we call a state and a run of a complement automaton a *macrostate* and a *macrorun*, respectively.

3   A Modular Complementation Algorithm

In a nutshell, the main idea of our BA complementation algorithm is to first decompose a BA $\mathcal{A}$ into several partition blocks according to their properties, and then perform complementation for each of the partition blocks (potentially using a different algorithm) independently, using either a *synchronous* construction, synchronizing the complementation algorithms for all partition blocks in each step, or a *postponed* construction, which complements the partition blocks independently and combines the partial results using automata product construction. The decomposition of $\mathcal{A}$ into partition blocks can either be trivial—i.e., with one block for each accepting SCC—, or more elaborate, e.g., a partitioning where one partition block contains all accepting IWCs, another contains all DACs, and each NAC is given its own partition block. In this way, one can avoid running a general complementation algorithm for unrestricted BAs with the state complexity upper bound $O((0.76n)^n)$ and, instead, apply the most suitable complementation procedure for each of the partition blocks. This comes with three main advantages:

1. The complementation algorithm for each partition block can be selected differently in order to exploit the properties of the block. For instance, for partition blocks

with IWCs, one can use complementation based on the breakpoint (the so-called Miyano-Hayashi) construction [42] with $O(3^n)$ macrostates (cf. Sec. 4.1), while for partition blocks with only DACs, one can use an algorithm with the state complexity $O(4^n)$ based on an adaptation of the NCSB construction [6,5,11,28] for SDBAs (cf. Sec. 4.2). For NACs, one can choose between, e.g., rank- [34,21,48,10,24,29] or determinization-based [46,43,45] algorithms, depending on the properties of the NACs (cf. Sec. 6).

2. The different complementation algorithms can focus only on the respective blocks and do not need to consider other parts of the BA. This is advantageous, e.g., for rank-based algorithms, which can use this restriction to obtain tighter bounds on the considered ranks (even tighter than using the refinement in [29]).

3. The obtained automaton can be more compact due to the use of a more general acceptance condition than Büchi [47]—in general, it can be a conjunction of any EL conditions (one condition for each partition block), depending on the output of the complementation procedures; this can allow a more compact encoding of the produced automaton allowed by using a mixture of conditions. E.g., a deterministic BA can be complemented with constant extra generated states when using a co-Büchi condition rather than a linear number of generated states for a Büchi condition (see Sec. 5.1).

Those partial complementation algorithms then need to be orchestrated by a top-level algorithm to produce the complement of $\mathcal{A}$.

One might regard our algorithm as an optimization of an approach that would for each partition block P obtain a BA $\mathcal{A}_P$, complement $\mathcal{A}_P$ using the selected algorithm, and perform the intersection of all obtained $\mathcal{A}_P$'s (which would, however, not be able to get the upper bound for elevator automata that we give in Sec. 4.3). Indeed, we also implemented the mentioned procedure (called the *postponed* approach, described in Sec. 5.2) and compared it to our main procedure (called the *synchronous* approach).

3.1 Basic Synchronous Algorithm

In this section, we describe the basic *synchronous* top-level algorithm. Then, in Sec. 4, we provide its instantiation for elevator automata and give a new upper bound for their complementation; in Sec. 5, we discuss several optimizations of the algorithm; and in Sec. 6, we give a generalization for unrestricted BAs. Let us fix a BA $\mathcal{A} = (Q, \delta, I, F)$ and, w.l.o.g., assume that $\mathcal{A}$ is *complete*, i.e., $|I| > 0$ and all states $q \in Q$ have an outgoing transition over all symbols $a \in \Sigma$.

The synchronous algorithm works with partial complementation algorithms for BA's partition blocks. Each such algorithm Alg is provided with a structural condition φ_{Alg} characterizing partition blocks it can complement. For a BA $\mathcal{B}$, we use the notation $\mathcal{B} \models \varphi$ to denote that $\mathcal{B}$ satisfies the condition φ. We say that Alg is a *partial complementation algorithm for a partition block* P if $\mathcal{A}_P \models \varphi_{\text{Alg}}$. We distinguish between Alg, a general algorithm able to complement a partition block of a given type, and Alg_P, its instantiation for the partition block P. Each instance Alg_P is required to provide the following:

- T^{Alg_P} — the type of the macrostates produced by the algorithm;
- $\text{Colours}^{\text{Alg}_P} = \{0, \ldots, k^{\text{Alg}_P} - 1\}$ — the set of used colours;
- $\text{Init}^{\text{Alg}_P} \in 2^{\text{T}^{\text{Alg}_P}}$ — the set of initial macrostates;
- $\text{Succ}^{\text{Alg}_P} : (2^Q \times \text{T}^{\text{Alg}_P} \times \Sigma) \to 2^{\text{T}^{\text{Alg}_P} \times \text{Colours}^{\text{Alg}_P}}$ — a function returning the successors of a macrostate such that $\text{Succ}^{\text{Alg}_P}(H, M, a) = \{(M_1, \alpha_1), \ldots, (M_k, \alpha_k)\}$, where H is the set of all states of $\mathcal{A}$ reached over the same word, M is the Alg_P's

macrostate for the given partition block, a is the input symbol, and each (M_i, α_i) is a pair (*macrostate, set of colours*) such that M_i is a successor of M over a w.r.t. H and α_i is a set of colours on the edge from M to M_i (H helps to keep track of *new runs* coming into the partition block); and

- $\text{Acc}^{\text{Alg}_P} \in \mathbb{EL}(\text{Colours}^{\text{Alg}_P})$ — the acceptance condition.

Let $P_1, \ldots, P_n$ be a partitioning of $\mathcal{A}$ (w.l.o.g., we assume that $n > 0$), and $\text{Alg}^1, \ldots, \text{Alg}^n$ be a sequence of algorithms such that Alg^i is a partial complementation algorithm for P_i. Furthermore, let us define the following auxiliary *renumbering* function λ as $\lambda(c, j) = c + \sum_{i=1}^{j-1} |\text{Colours}^{\text{Alg}_{P_i}^i}|$, which is used to make the colours and acceptance conditions from the partial complementation algorithms disjoint. We also lift λ to sets of colours in the natural way, and also to $\mathbb{EL}$ conditions such that $\lambda(\varphi, j)$ has the same structure as φ but each atom $\text{Inf}(c)$ is substituted with the atom $\text{Inf}(\lambda(c, j))$ (and likewise for Fin atoms). The synchronous complementation algorithm then produces the TELA $\text{MODCOMPL}(\text{Alg}_{P_1}^1, \ldots, \text{Alg}_{P_n}^n, \mathcal{A}) = (Q^C, \delta^C, I^C, \Gamma^C, p^C, \text{Acc}^C)$ with components defined as follows (we use $[S_i]_{i=1}^n$ to abbreviate $S_1 \times \cdots \times S_n$):

- $Q^C = 2^Q \times [\text{T}^{\text{Alg}_{P_i}^i}]_{i=1}^n$,
- $I^C = \{I\} \times [\text{Init}^{\text{Alg}_{P_i}^i}]_{i=1}^n$,
- δ^C and p^C are defined such that if
- $\Gamma^C = \{0, \ldots, \lambda(k^{\text{Alg}_{P_n}^n} - 1, n)\}$,
- $\text{Acc}^C = \bigwedge_{i=1}^n \lambda(\text{Acc}^{\text{Alg}_{P_i}^i}, i)$,[8]and

$$((M_1', \alpha_1), \ldots, (M_n', \alpha_n)) \in [\text{Succ}^{\text{Alg}_{P_i}^i}(H, M_i, a)]_{i=1}^n,$$

then δ^C contains the transition $t: (H, M_1, \ldots, M_n) \xrightarrow{a} (\delta(H, a), M_1', \ldots, M_n')$, coloured by $p^C(t) = \bigcup\{\lambda(\alpha_i, i) \mid 1 \le i \le n\}$, and δ^C is the smallest such a set.

In order for MODCOMPL to be correct, the partial complementation algorithms need to satisfy certain properties, which we discuss below.

For a structural condition φ and a BA $\mathcal{B} = (Q, \delta, I, F)$, we define $\mathcal{B} \models_P \varphi$ iff $\mathcal{B} \models \varphi$, P is a partition block of $\mathcal{B}$, and $\mathcal{B}$ contains no accepting transitions outside P. We can now provide the correctness condition on Alg.

Definition 1. *We say that* Alg *is correct if for each BA $\mathcal{B}$ and partition block P such that $\mathcal{B} \models_P \varphi_{\text{Alg}}$ it holds that $\mathcal{L}(\text{MODCOMPL}(\text{Alg}_P, \mathcal{B})) = \Sigma^\omega \setminus \mathcal{L}(\mathcal{B})$.*

The correctness of the synchronous algorithm (provided that each partial complementation algorithm is correct) is then established by Theorem 1.

Theorem 1. *Let $\mathcal{A}$ be a BA, $P_1, \ldots, P_n$ be a partitioning of $\mathcal{A}$, and $\text{Alg}^1, \ldots, \text{Alg}^n$ be a sequence of partial complementation algorithms such that Alg^i is correct for P_i. Then, we have $\mathcal{L}(\text{MODCOMPL}(\text{Alg}_{P_1}^1, \ldots, \text{Alg}_{P_n}^n, \mathcal{A})) = \Sigma^\omega \setminus \mathcal{L}(\mathcal{A})$.*

4   Modular Complementation of Elevator Automata

In this section, we first give partial algorithms to complement partition blocks with only accepting IWCs (Sec. 4.1) and partition blocks with only DACs (Sec. 4.2). Then, in Sec. 4.3, we show that using our algorithm, the upper bound on the size of the complement of elevator BAs is in $O(4^n)$, which is *exponentially better* than the known upper bound $O(16^n)$ established in [29].

---

[8] If we drop the condition that $\mathcal{A}$ is complete, we also need to add an *accepting sink state* (representing the case for $H = \emptyset$) with self-loops over all symbols marked by a new colour ⑨, and enrich Acc^C with $\ldots \vee \text{Inf}(⑨)$.

4.1 Complementation of Inherently Weak Accepting Components

First, we introduce a partial algorithm MH with the condition φ_{MH} specifying that all SCCs in the partition block P are *accepting* IWCs. Let P be a partition block of $\mathcal{A}$ such that $\mathcal{A}_P \models \varphi_{\text{MH}}$. Our proposed approach makes use of the Miyano-Hayashi construction [42]. Since in accepting IWCs, all runs are accepting, the idea of the construction is to accept words such that all runs over the words eventually leave P.

Therefore, we use a pair (C, B) of sets of states as a macrostate for complementing P. Intuitively, we use C to denote the set of all runs of $\mathcal{A}$ that are in P (C for "*check*"). The set $B \subseteq C$ represents the runs being inspected whether they leave P at some point (B for "*breakpoint*"). Initially, we let $C = I \cap P$ and also sample into breakpoint all runs in P, i.e., set $B = C$. Along reading an ω-word w, if all runs that have entered P eventually leave P, i.e., B becomes empty infinitely often, the complement language of P should contain w (when B becomes empty, we sample B with all runs from the current C). We formalize MH_P as a partial procedure in the framework from Sec. 3.1 as follows:

- $T^{\text{MH}_P} = 2^P \times 2^P$, $\text{Colours}^{\text{MH}_P} = \{\textcircled{0}\}$, $\text{Init}^{\text{MH}_P} = \{(I \cap P, I \cap P)\}$,
- $\text{Acc}^{\text{MH}_P} = \text{Inf}(\textcircled{0})$, and $\text{Succ}^{\text{MH}_P}(H, (C, B), a) = \{((C', B'), \alpha)\}$ where
  - $C' = \delta(H, a) \cap P$,
  - $B' = \begin{cases} C' & \text{if } B^\star = \emptyset \text{ for } B^\star = \delta(B, a) \cap C', \\ B^\star & \text{otherwise, and} \end{cases}$ $\alpha = \begin{cases} \{\textcircled{0}\} & \text{if } B^\star = \emptyset \text{ and} \\ \emptyset & \text{otherwise.} \end{cases}$

We can see that checking whether w is accepted by the complement of P reduces to check whether B has been cleared infinitely often. Since every time when B becomes empty, we emit the colour $\textcircled{0}$, we have that w is not accepted by $\mathcal{A}$ within P if and only if $\textcircled{0}$ occurs infinitely often. Note that the transition function $\text{Succ}^{\text{MH}_P}$ is deterministic, i.e., there is exactly one successor.

Lemma 1. *The partial algorithm* MH *is correct.*

4.2 Complementation of Deterministic Accepting Components

In this section, we give a partial algorithm CSB with the condition φ_{CSB} specifying that a partition block P consists of *DACs*. Let P be a partition block of $\mathcal{A}$ such that $\mathcal{A}_P \models \varphi_{\text{CSB}}$. Our approach is based on the NCSB family of algorithms [6,11,5,28] for complementing SDBAs, in particular the NCSB-MaxRank construction [28]. The algorithm utilizes the fact that runs in DACs are deterministic, i.e., they do not branch into new runs. Therefore, one can check that a run is non-accepting if there is a time point from which the run does not see accepting transitions any more. We call such a run that does not see accepting transitions any more *safe*. Then, an ω-word w is not accepted in P iff all runs over w in P either (i) leave P or (ii) eventually become safe.

For checking point (i), we can use a similar technique as in algorithm MH, i.e., use a pair (C, B). Moreover, to be able to check point (ii), we also use the set S that contains runs that are supposed to be *safe*, resulting in macrostates of the form (C, S, B)[9]. To make sure that all runs are deterministic, we will use δ_{SCC} instead of δ when computing the successors of S and B since there may be nondeterministic jumps between different DACs in P; we will not miss any run in P since if a run moves between DACs of P, it

---

[9] In contrast to MH, here we use $C \cup S$ rather than C to keep track of all runs in P.

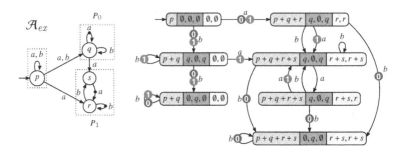

Fig. 1: Left: BA $\mathcal{A}_{ex}$ (dots represent accepting transitions). Right: the outcome of $\text{ModCompl}(\text{CSB}_{P_0}, \text{MH}_{P_1}, \mathcal{A}_{ex})$ with Acc: $\text{Inf}(\mathbf{0}) \wedge \text{Inf}(\mathbf{1})$. States are given as $(H, (C_0, S_0, B_0), (C_1, B_1))$; to avoid too many braces, sets are given as sums.

can be seen as the run leaving P and a new run entering P. Since a run eventually stays in one SCC, this guarantees that the run will not be missed.

We formalize CSB_P in the top-level framework as follows:

- $\text{T}^{\text{CSB}_P} = 2^P \times 2^P \times 2^P$, $\text{Init}^{\text{CSB}_P} = \{(I \cap P, \emptyset, I \cap P)\}$,
- $\text{Colours}^{\text{CSB}_P} = \{\mathbf{0}\}$, $\text{Acc}^{\text{CSB}_P} = \text{Inf}(\mathbf{0})$, and
- $\text{Succ}^{\text{CSB}_P}(H, (C, S, B), a) = U$ such that
  - if $\delta_F(S, a) \neq \emptyset$, then $U = \emptyset$ (Runs in S must be *safe*),
  - otherwise U contains $((C', S', B'), c)$ where
    * $S' = \delta_{\text{SCC}}(S, a) \cap P$, $C' = (\delta(H, a) \cap P) \setminus S'$,
    * $B' = \begin{cases} C' & \text{if } B^\star = \emptyset \text{ for } B^\star = \delta_{\text{SCC}}(B, a), \\ B^\star & \text{otherwise, and} \end{cases}$ $\quad * c = \begin{cases} \{\mathbf{0}\} & \text{if } B^\star = \emptyset, \\ \emptyset & \text{otherwise.} \end{cases}$

    Moreover, in the case $\delta_F(B, a) = \emptyset$, then U also contains $((C'', S'', C''), \{\mathbf{0}\})$ where $S'' = S' \cup B'$ and $C'' = C' \setminus S''$.

Intuitively, when $\delta_F(B, a) \cap \delta_{\text{SCC}}(B, a) = \emptyset$, we make the following guess: (i) either the runs in B all become safe (we move them to S) or (ii) there might be some unsafe runs (we keep them in B). Since the runs in B are deterministic, the number of tracked runs in B will not increase. Moreover, if all runs in B are eventually safe, we are guaranteed to move all of them to S at the right time point, e.g., the maximal time point where all runs are safe since the number of runs is finite.

As mentioned above, w is not accepted within P iff all runs over w either (i) leave P or (ii) become safe. In the context of the presented algorithm, this corresponds to (i) B becoming empty infinitely often and (ii) $\delta_F(S, a)$ never seeing an accepting transition. Then we only need to check if there exists an infinite sequence of macrostates $\hat{\rho} = (C_0, S_0, B_0) \ldots$ that emits $\mathbf{0}$ infinitely often.

Lemma 2. *The partial algorithm* CSB *is correct.*

It is worth noting that when the given partition block P contains all DACs of $\mathcal{A}$, we can still use the construction above, while the construction in [28] only works on SDBAs.

Example 1. In Fig. 1, we give an example of the run of our algorithm on the BA $\mathcal{A}_{ex}$. The BA contains three SCCs, one of them (the one containing p) non-accepting (therefore, it does not need to occur in any partition block). The partition block P_0 contains a single DAC, so we can use algorithm CSB, and the partition block P_1 contains a single accepting IWC, so we can use MH. The resulting $\text{MODCOMPL}(\text{CSB}_{P_0}, \text{MH}_{P_1}, \mathcal{A}_{ex})$ uses two colours, ⓪ from CSB and ① from MH. The acceptance condition is $\text{Inf}(⓪) \wedge \text{Inf}(①)$.   □

4.3 Upper-bound for Elevator Automata Complementation

We now give an upper bound on the size of the complement generated by our algorithm for elevator automata, which significantly improves the best previously known upper bound of $O(16^n)$ [29] to $O(4^n)$, the same as for SDBAs, which are a strict subclass of elevator automata [6] (we note that this upper bound cannot be obtained by a determinization-based algorithm, since determinization of SDBAs is in $\Omega(n!)$ [17,40]).

Theorem 2. *Let $\mathcal{A}$ be an elevator automaton with n states. Then there exists a BA with $O(4^n)$ states accepting the complement of $\mathcal{L}(\mathcal{A})$.*

Proof (Sketch). Let Q_W be all states in accepting IWCs, Q_D be all states in DACs, and Q_N be the remaining states, i.e., $Q = Q_W \uplus Q_D \uplus Q_N$. We make two partition blocks: $P_0 = Q_W$ and $P_1 = Q_D$ and use MH and CSB respectively as the partial algorithms, with macrostates of the form $(H, (C_0, B_0), (C_1, S_1, B_1))$. For each state $q_N \in Q_N$, there are two options: either $q_N \notin H$ or $q_N \in H$. For each state $q_W \in Q_W$, there are three options: (i) $q_W \notin C_0$, (ii) $q_W \in C_0 \setminus B_0$, or (iii) $q_W \in C_0 \cap B_0$. Finally, for each $q_D \in Q_D$, there are four options: (i) $q_D \notin C_1 \cup S_1$, (ii) $q_D \in S_1$, (iii) $q_D \in C_1 \setminus B_1$, or (iv) $q_D \in C_1 \cap B_1$. Therefore, the total number of macrostates is $2 \cdot 2^{|Q_N|} \cdot 3^{|Q_W|} \cdot 4^{|Q_D|} \in O(4^n)$ where the initial factor 2 is due to degeneralization from two to one colour (the two colours can actually be avoided by using our shared breakpoint optimization from Sec. 5.4).   □

5 Optimizations of the Modular Construction

In this section, we propose optimizations of the basic modular algorithm. In Sec. 5.1, we give a partial algorithm to complement initial partition blocks with DACs. Further, in Sec. 5.2, we propose the postponed construction allowing to use automata reduction on intermediate results. In Sec. 5.3, we propose the round-robin algorithm alleviating the problem with the explosion of the size of the Cartesian product of partial successors. In Sec. 5.4, we provide an optimization for partial algorithms that are based on the breakpoint construction, and, finally, in Sec. 5.5, we show how to employ simulation to decrease the size of macrostates in the synchronous construction.

5.1 Complementation of Initial Deterministic Partition Blocks

Our first optimization is an algorithm CoB for a subclass of partition blocks containing DACs. In particular, the condition φ_{CoB} specifies that the partition block P is deterministic and can be reached only deterministically in $\mathcal{A}$ (i.e., $\mathcal{A}_P$ after removing redundant states is deterministic). Then, we say that P is an *initial deterministic* partition block. The algorithm is based on complementation of deterministic BAs into co-Büchi automata.

The algorithm CoB_P is formalized below:

- $T^{\text{CoB}_P} = P \cup \{\emptyset\}$, $\text{Init}^{\text{CoB}_P} = I \cap P$, $\text{Colours}^{\text{CoB}_P} = \{⓪\}$, $\text{Acc}^{\text{CoB}_P} = \text{Fin}(⓪)$,

- $\mathrm{Succ}^{\mathrm{CoB}_P}(H, q, a) = \{(q', \alpha)\}$ where

  - $q' = \begin{cases} r & \text{if } \delta(H, a) \cap P = \{r\} \text{ and} \\ \emptyset & \text{otherwise,} \end{cases}$ • $\alpha = \begin{cases} \{\textcircled{0}\} & \text{if } q \xrightarrow{a} q' \in F \text{ and} \\ \emptyset & \text{otherwise.} \end{cases}$

Intuitively, all runs reach P deterministically, which means that over a word w, at most one run can reach P (so $|\mathtt{Init}^{\mathrm{CoB}_P}| = 1$). Thus, we have $|\delta(H, w_j) \cap P| = 1$ for some $j \geq 0$ if there is a run over w to P, corresponding to $\delta(H, a) \cap P = \{r\}$ in the construction. To check whether w is not accepted in P, we only need to check whether the run from $r \in P$ over w visits accepting transitions only finitely often. We give an example of complementation of a BA containing an initial deterministic partition block in [27].

Lemma 3. *The partial algorithm* CoB *is correct.*

5.2   Postponed Construction

The modular synchronous construction from Sec. 3.1 utilizes the assumption that in the simultaneous construction of successors for each partition block over a, if one partial macrostate M_i does not have a successor over a, then there will be no successor of the $(H, M_1, \ldots, M_n)$ macrostate in δ^C as well. This is useful, e.g., for inclusion testing, where it is not necessary to generate the whole complement. On the other hand, if we need to generate the whole automaton, a drawback of the proposed modular construction is that each partial complementation algorithm itself may generate a lot of useless states. In this section, we propose the *postponed construction*, which complements the partition blocks (with their surrounding) independently and later combines the intermediate results to obtain the complement automaton for $\mathcal{A}$. The main advantage of the postponed construction is that one can apply automata reduction (e.g., based on removing useless states or using simulation [13,18,1,9]) to decrease the size of the intermediate automata.

In the postponed construction, we use product-based BA intersection operation (i.e., for two TELAs $\mathcal{B}_1$ and $\mathcal{B}_2$, a product automaton $\mathcal{B}_1 \cap \mathcal{B}_2$ satisfying $\mathcal{L}(\mathcal{B}_1 \cap \mathcal{B}_2) = \mathcal{L}(\mathcal{B}_1) \cap \mathcal{L}(\mathcal{B}_2)^{10}$). Further, we employ a function Red performing some language-preserving reduction of an input TELA. Then, the postponed construction for an elevator automaton $\mathcal{A}$ with a partitioning $P_1, \ldots, P_n$ and a sequence $\mathtt{Alg}^1, \ldots, \mathtt{Alg}^n$ where $\mathtt{Alg}^i$ is a partial complementation algorithm for P_i, is defined as follows:

$$\mathrm{POSTPCOMPL}(\mathtt{Alg}^1_{P_1}, \ldots, \mathtt{Alg}^n_{P_n}, \mathcal{A}) = \bigcap_{i=1}^{n} \mathrm{Red}\left(\mathrm{MODCOMPL}(\mathtt{Alg}^i_{P_i}, \mathcal{A}_{P_i})\right). \quad (2)$$

The correctness of the construction is then summarized by the following theorem.

Theorem 3. *Let $\mathcal{A}$ be a BA, $P_1, \ldots, P_n$ be a partitioning of $\mathcal{A}$, and $\mathtt{Alg}^1, \ldots, \mathtt{Alg}^n$ be a sequence of partial complementation algorithms such that $\mathtt{Alg}^i$ is correct for P_i. Then, $\mathcal{L}(\mathrm{POSTPCOMPL}(\mathtt{Alg}^1_{P_1}, \ldots, \mathtt{Alg}^n_{P_n}, \mathcal{A})) = \Sigma^\omega \setminus \mathcal{L}(\mathcal{A})$.*

5.3   Round-Robin Algorithm

The proposed basic synchronous approach from Sec. 3.1 may suffer from the combinatorial explosion because the successors of a macrostate are given by the Cartesian product of all successors of the partial macrostates. To alleviate this explosion, we propose

---

[10] Alternatively, one might also avoid the product and generate linear-sized *alternating* TELA, but working with those is usually much harder and not used in practice.

a *round-robin* top-level algorithm. Intuitively, the round-robin algorithm actively tracks runs in only one partial complementation algorithm at a time (while other algorithms stay passive). The algorithm periodically changes the active algorithm to avoid starvation (the decision to leave the active state is, however, fully directed by the partial complementation algorithm). This can alleviate an explosion in the number of successors for algorithms that generate more than one successor (e.g., for rank-based algorithms where one needs to make a nondeterministic choice of decreasing ranks of states in order to be able to accept [34,21,48,10,24,29]; such a choice needs to be made only in the active phase while in the passive phase, the construction just needs to make sure that the run is consistent with the given ranking, which can be done deterministically).

The round-robin algorithm works on the level of *partial complementation round-robin algorithms*. Each instance of the partial algorithm provides *passive types* to represent partial macrostates that are passive and *active types* to represent currently active partial macrostates. In contrast to the basic partial complementation algorithms from Sec. 3.1, which provide only a single successor function, the round-robin partial algorithms provide several variants of them. In particular, SuccPass returns (passive) successors of a passive partial macrostate, Lift gives all possible active counterparts of a passive macrostate, and SuccAct returns successors of an active partial macrostate. If SuccAct returns a partial macrostate of the passive type, the round-robin algorithm promotes the next partial algorithm to be the active one. For instance, in the round-robin version of CSB, the passive type does not contain the breakpoint and only checks that safe runs stay safe, so it is deterministic. Due to space limitations, we give a formal definition and more details about the round-robin algorithm in [27].

5.4 Shared Breakpoint

The partial complementation algorithms CSB and MH (and later RNK defined in Sec. 6) use a breakpoint to check whether the runs under inspection are accepting or not. As an optimization, we consider merging of breakpoints of several algorithms and keeping only a single breakpoint for all supported algorithms. The top-level algorithm then needs to manage only one breakpoint and emit a colour only if this sole breakpoint becomes empty. This may lead to a smaller number of generated macrostates since we synchronize the breakpoint sampling among several algorithms. The second benefit is that this allows us to generate fewer colours (in the case of elevator automata complemented using algorithms CSB and MH, we get only one colour).

5.5 Simulation Pruning

Our construction can be further optimized by a simulation (or other compatible) relation for pruning macrostates.[11] A simulation is, broadly speaking, a relation $\preccurlyeq \subseteq Q \times Q$ implying language inclusion of states, i.e., $\forall p, q \in Q: p \preccurlyeq q \implies \mathcal{L}(\mathcal{A}[p]) \subseteq \mathcal{L}(\mathcal{A}[q])$. Intuitively, our optimization allows to remove a state p from a macrostate M if there is also a state q in M such that (i) $p \preccurlyeq q$, (ii) p is not reachable from q, and (iii) p is smaller than q in an arbitrary total order over Q (this serves as a tie-breaker for

---

[11] This optimization can be seen as a generalization of the simulation-based pruning techniques that appeared, e.g., in [41,28] in the context of concrete determinization/complementation procedures. Here, we generalize the technique to all procedures that are based on run tracking.

simulation-equivalent mutually unreachable states). The reason why p can be removed is that its behaviour can be completely mimicked by q. In our construction, we can then, roughly speaking, replace each call to the functions $\delta(U, a)$ and $\delta_F(U, a)$, for a set of states U, by $pr(\delta(U, a))$ and $pr(\delta_F(U, a))$ respectively in each partial complementation algorithm, as well as in the top-level algorithm, where $pr(S)$ is obtained from S by pruning all eligible states. The details are provided in [27].

6   Modular Complementation of Non-Elevator Automata

A non-elevator automaton $\mathcal{A}$ contains at least one NAC, besides possibly other IWCs or DACs. To complement $\mathcal{A}$ in a modular way, we apply the techniques seen in Sec. 4 to its DACs and IWCs, while for its NACs we resort to a general complementation algorithm Alg. In theory, rank- [34], slice- [32], Ramsey- [50], subset-tuple- [2], and determinization- [46] based complementation algorithms adapted to work on a single partition block instead of the whole automaton are all valid instantiations of Alg. Below, we give a high-level description of two such algorithms: rank- and determinization-based.

Rank-based partial complementation algorithm. Working on each NAC independently benefits the complementation algorithm even if the input BA contains only NACs. For instance, in rank-based algorithms [34,21,48,33,10,24,29], the fact whether all runs of $\mathcal{A}$ over a given ω-word w are non-accepting is determined by *ranks* of states, given by the so-called *ranking functions*. A ranking function is a (partial) function from Q to ω. The main idea of rank-based algorithms is the following: (i) every run is initially nondeterministically assigned a rank, (ii) ranks can only decrease along a run, (iii) ranks need to be even every time a run visits an accepting transition, and (iv) the complement automaton accepts iff all runs eventually get trapped in odd ranks[12]. In the standard rank-based procedure, the initial assignment of ranks to states in (i) is a function $Q \rightharpoonup \{0, \ldots, 2n - 1\}$ for $n = |Q|$. Using our framework, we can, however, significantly restrict the considered ranks in a partition block P to only $P \rightharpoonup \{0, \ldots, 2m - 1\}$ for $m = |P|$ (here, it makes sense to use partition blocks consisting of single SCCs). One can further reduce the considered ranks using the techniques introduced in, e.g., [24,29].

In order to adapt the rank-based construction as a partial complementation algorithm RNK in our framework, we need to extend the ranking functions by a fresh "box state" ∎ representing states outside the partition block. The ranking function then uses ∎ to represent ranks of runs newly coming into the partition block. The box-extension also requires to change the transition in a way that ∎ always represents reachable states from the outside. We provide the details of the construction, which includes the MaxRank optimization from [24], in [27].

Determinization-based partial complementation algorithm. In [52,29] we can see that determinization-based complementation is also a good instantiation of Alg in practice, so, we also consider the standard Safra-Piterman determinization [46,43,45] as a choice of Alg for complementing NACs. Determinization-based algorithms use a layered subset construction to organize all runs over an ω-word w. The idea is to identify a subset $S \subseteq H$ of reachable states that occur infinitely often along reading w such that between every two occurrences of S, we have that (i) every state in the second occurrence of S can be reached

---

[12] Since we focus on intuition here, we use runs rather than the directed acyclic graphs of runs.

Table 1: Statistics for our experiments. The column **unsolved** classifies unsolved instances by the form *timeouts : out of memory : other failures*. For the cases of VBS we provide just the number of unsolved cases. The columns **states** and **runtime** provide *mean : median* of the number of states and runtime, respectively.

tool	solved	unsolved	states	runtime		tool	solved	unsolved	states	runtime
KOFOLA$_S$	39,738	89:10:0	76:3	0.32:0.03		COLA	39,814	21:0:2	80:3	0.17:0.02
KOFOLA$_P$	39,750	76:11:0	86:3	0.41:0.03		RANKER	38,837	61:939:0	45:4	3.31:0.01
VBS$_+$	39,834	3	78:3	0.05:0.01		SEMINATOR	39,026	238:573:0	247:3	1.98:0.03
VBS$_-$	39,834	3	96:3	0.05:0.01		SPOT	39,827	8:0:2	160:4	0.08:0.02

by a state in the first occurrence of S and (ii) every state in the second occurrence is reached by a state in the first occurrence while seeing an accepting transition. According to König's lemma, there must then be an accepting run of $\mathcal{A}$ over w.

The construction initially maintains only one set H: the set of reachable states. Since S as defined does not necessarily need to be H, every time there are runs visiting accepting transitions, we create a new subset C for those runs and remember which subset C is coming from. This way, we actually organize the current states of all runs into a tree structure and do subset construction in parallel for the sets in each tree node. If we find a tree node whose labelled subset, say S', is equal to the union of states in its children, we know the set S' satisfies the condition above and we remove all its child nodes and emit a good event. If such good event happens infinitely often, it means that S' also occurs infinitely often. So in complementation, we only need to make sure those good events only happen for finitely many times. Working on each NAC separately also benefits the determinization-based approach since the number of possible trees will be less with smaller number of reachable states. Following the idea of [37], to adapt for the construction as the partial complementation algorithm, we put all the newly coming runs from other partition blocks in a newly created node without a parent node. In this way, we actually maintain a forest of trees for the partial complementation construction. We denote the determinization-based construction as DET; cf. [37] for details.

7 Experimental Evaluation

To evaluate the proposed approach, we implemented it in a prototype tool KOFOLA [25] (written in C++) built on top of SPOT [16] and compared it against COLA [37], RANKER [28] (v. 2), SEMINATOR [5] (v. 2.0), and SPOT [15,16] (v. 2.10.6), which are the state of the art in BA complementation [29,28,37]. Due to space restrictions, we give results for only two instantiations of our framework: KOFOLA$_S$ and KOFOLA$_P$. Both instantiations use MH for IWCs, CSB for DACs, and DET for NACs. The partitioning selection algorithm merges all IWCs into one partition block, all DACs into one partition block, and keeps all NACs separate. Simulation-based pruning from Sec. 5.5 is turned on, and round-robin from Sec. 5.3 is turned off (since the selected algorithms are quite deterministic). KOFOLA$_S$ employs the *synchronous* and KOFOLA$_P$ employs the *postponed* strategy. We also consider the Virtual Best Solver (VBS), i.e., a virtual tool that would choose the best solver for each single benchmark among all tools (VBS$_+$) and among all tools except both versions of KOFOLA (VBS$_-$). We ran our experiments on an Ubuntu 20.04.4 LTS system running on a desktop machine with 16 GiB RAM and an

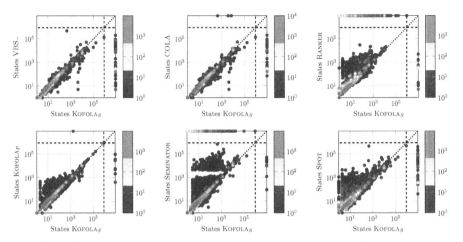

Fig. 2: Scatter plots comparing the numbers of states generated by the tools.

Intel 3.6 GHz i7-4790 CPU. To constrain and collect statistics about the executions of the tools, we used BENCHEXEC [3] and imposed a memory limit of 12 GiB and a timeout of 10 minutes; we used SPOT to cross-validate the equivalence of the automata generated by the different tools. An artifact reproducing our experiments is available as [26].

As our data set, we used 39,837 BAs from the AUTOMATA-BENCHMARKS repository [36] (used before by, e.g., [29,28,37]), which contains BAs from the following sources: (i) randomly generated BAs used in [52] (21,876 BAs), (ii) BAs obtained from LTL formulae from the literature and randomly generated LTL formulae [5] (3,442 BAs), (iii) BAs obtained from ULTIMATE AUTOMIZER [11] (915 BAs), (iv) BAs obtained from the solver for first-order logic over Sturmian words PECAN [31] (13,216 BAs), (v) BAs obtained from an S1S solver [23] (370 BAs), and (vi) BAs from LTL to SDBA translation [49] (18 BAs). From these BAs, 23,850 are deterministic, 6,147 are SDBAs (but not deterministic), 4,105 are elevator (but not SDBAs), and 5,735 are the rest.

In Table 1 we present an overview of the outcomes. Despite being a prototype, KOFOLA can already complement a large portion of the input automata, with very few cases that can be complemented successfully only by SPOT or COLA. Regarding the mean number of states, KOFOLA$_S$ has the **least mean value** from all tools (except RANKER, which, however, had 1,000 unsolved cases) Moreover, KOFOLA **significantly decreased the mean number of states** when included into the VBS: from 96 to 78! We consider this to be a strong validation of the usefulness of our approach. Regarding the runtime, both versions of KOFOLA are rather similar; KOFOLA is just slightly slower than SPOT and COLA but much faster than both RANKER and SEMINATOR (cf. [27]).

In Fig. 2 we present a comparison of the number of states generated by KOFOLA$_S$ and other tools; we omit VBS$_+$ since the corresponding plot can be derived from the one for VBS$_-$ (since RANKER and SEMINATOR only output BAs, we compare the sizes of outputs transformed into BAs for all tools to be fair). In the plots, the number of benchmarks represented by each mark is given by its colour; a mark above the diagonal means that KOFOLA$_S$ generated a BA smaller than the other tool while a mark on the top border means that the other tool failed while KOFOLA$_S$ succeeded, and symmetrically for the bottom part and the right-hand border. Dashed lines represent the maximum number of states generated by one of the tools in the plot, axes are logarithmic.

From the results, KOFOLA$_S$ clearly dominates state-of-the-art tools that are not based
on SCC decomposition (RANKER, SPOT, SEM-
INATOR). The outputs are quite comparable to
COLA, which also uses SCC decomposition
and can be seen as an instantiation of our framework. This supports our intuition that working
on the single SCCs helps in reducing the size
of the final automaton, confirming the validity
of our modular mix-and-match Büchi comple-

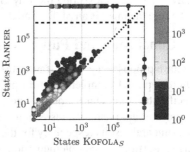

mentation approach. Lastly, in the figure in the right we compare our algorithm for elevator automata with the one in RANKER (the only other tool with a dedicated algorithm for this subclass). Our new algorithm clearly dominates the one in RANKER.

8 Related Work

To the best of our knowledge, we provide the *first general framework* where one can plug-in different BA complementation algorithms while taking advantage of the specific structure of SCCs. We will discuss the difference between our work and the literature.

The breakpoint construction [42] was designed to complement BAs with only IWCs, while our construction treats it as a partial complementation procedure for IWCs and differs in the need to handle incoming states from other partition blocks. The NCSB family of algorithms [6,11,5,28] for SDBAs do not work when there are nondeterministic jumps between DACs; they can, however, be adapted as partial procedures for complementing DACs in our framework, cf. Sec. 4.2. In [29], a deelevation-based procedure is applied to elevator automata to obtain BAs with a fixed maximum rank of 3, for which a rank-based construction produces a result of the size in $O(16^n)$. In our work, we exploit the structure of the SCCs much more to obtain an exponentially better upper bound of $O(4^n)$ (the same as for SDBAs). The upper bound $O(4^n)$ for complementing unambiguous BAs was established in [39], which is orthogonal to our work, but seems to be possible to incorporate into our framework in the future.

There is a huge body of work on complementation of general BAs [8,50,7,34,21,22,10,24,29,48,2,46,43,45,5,52,32,53,19,20]; all of them work on the whole graph structure of the input BAs. Our framework is general enough to allow including all of them as partial complementation procedures for NACs. On the contrary, our framework does not directly allow (at least in the synchronous strategy) to use algorithms that *do not* work on the structure of the input BA, such as the learning-based complementation algorithm from [38]. The recent determinization algorithm from [37], which serves as our inspiration, also handles SCCs separately (it can actually be seen as an instantiation of our framework). Our current algorithm is, however, more flexible, allowing to mix-and-match various constructions, keep SCCs separate or merge them into partition blocks, and allows to obtain the complexity $O(4^n)$, while [37] only allowed $O(n!)$ (which is tight since SDBA determinization is in $\Omega(n!)$ [17,40]).

Regarding the tool SPOT [15,16], it should not be perceived as a single complementation algorithm. Instead, SPOT should be seen as a highly engineered platform utilizing breakpoint construction for inherently weak BAs, NCSB [6,11] for SDBAs, and determinization-based complementation [46,43,45] for general BAs, while using many other heuristics along the way. SEMINATOR uses semi-determinization [14,4,5] to make sure the input is an SDBA and then uses NCSB [6,11] to compute the complement.

9   Conclusion and Future Work

We have proposed a general framework for BA complementation where one can plug-in different partial complementation procedures for SCCs by taking advantage of their specific structure. Our framework not only obtains an exponentially better upper bound for elevator automata, but also complements existing approaches well. As shown by the experimental results (especially for the VBS), our framework significantly improves the current portfolio of complementation algorithms.

We believe that our framework is an ideal testbed for experimenting with different BA complementation algorithms, e.g., for the following two reasons: (i) One can develop an efficient complementation algorithm that only works for a quite restricted sub-class of BAs (such as the algorithm for initial deterministic SCCs that we showed in Sec. 5.1) and the framework can leverage it for complementation of all BAs that contain such a sub-structure. (ii) When one tries to improve a general complementation algorithm, they can focus on complementation of the structurally hard SCCs (mainly the nondeterministic accepting SCCs) and do not need to look for heuristics that would improve the algorithm if there were some easier substructure present in the input BA (as was done, e.g., in [29]). From how the framework is defined, it immediately offers opportunities for being used for on-the-fly BA *language inclusion* testing, leveraging the partial complementation procedures present. Finally, we believe that the framework also enables new directions for future research by developing smart ways, probably based on machine learning, of selecting which partial complementation procedure should be used for which SCC, based on their features. In future, we want to incorporate other algorithms for complementation of NACs, and identify properties of SCCs that allow to use more efficient algorithms (such as unambiguous NACs [39]). Moreover, it seems that generalizing the DELAYED optimization from [24] on the top-level algorithm could also help reduce the state space.

Acknowledgements. We thank the reviewers for their useful remarks that helped us improve the quality of the paper and Alexandre Duret-Lutz for sharing a TikZ package for beautiful automata. This work was supported by the Strategic Priority Research Program of the Chinese Academy of Sciences (grant no. XDA0320000); the National Natural Science Foundation of China (grants no. 62102407 and 61836005); the CAS Project for Young Scientists in Basic Research (grant no. YSBR-040); the Engineering and Physical Sciences Research Council (grant no. EP/X021513/1); the Czech Ministry of Education, Youth and Sports project LL1908 of the ERC.CZ programme; the Czech Science Foundation project GA23-07565S; and the FIT BUT internal project FIT-S-23-8151.

▓ This project has received funding from the European Union's Horizon 2020 research and innovation programme under the Marie Sklodowska-Curie grant no. 101008233.

Data Availability Statement. An environment with the tools and data used for the experimental evaluation in the current study is available in the following Zenodo repository: https://doi.org/10.5281/zenodo.7505210.

References

1. Abdulla, P.A., Chen, Y., Holík, L., Vojnar, T.: Mediating for reduction (on minimizing alternating büchi automata). Theor. Comput. Sci. **552**, 26–43 (2014). https://doi.org/10.1016/j.tcs.2014.08.003, https://doi.org/10.1016/j.tcs.2014.08.003
2. Allred, J.D., Ultes-Nitsche, U.: A simple and optimal complementation algorithm for Büchi automata. In: Dawar, A., Grädel, E. (eds.) Proceedings of the 33rd Annual ACM/IEEE Symposium on Logic in Computer Science, LICS 2018, Oxford, UK, July 09-12, 2018. pp. 46–55. ACM (2018). https://doi.org/10.1145/3209108.3209138, https://doi.org/10.1145/3209108.3209138
3. Beyer, D., Löwe, S., Wendler, P.: Reliable benchmarking: requirements and solutions. Int. J. Softw. Tools Technol. Transf. **21**(1), 1–29 (2019). https://doi.org/10.1007/s10009-017-0469-y, https://doi.org/10.1007/s10009-017-0469-y
4. Blahoudek, F., Duret-Lutz, A., Klokocka, M., Kretínský, M., Strejcek, J.: Seminator: A tool for semi-determinization of omega-automata. In: Eiter, T., Sands, D. (eds.) LPAR-21, 21st International Conference on Logic for Programming, Artificial Intelligence and Reasoning, Maun, Botswana, May 7-12, 2017. EPiC Series in Computing, vol. 46, pp. 356–367. Easy-Chair (2017). https://doi.org/10.29007/k5nl, https://doi.org/10.29007/k5nl
5. Blahoudek, F., Duret-Lutz, A., Strejcek, J.: Seminator 2 can complement generalized Büchi automata via improved semi-determinization. In: Lahiri, S.K., Wang, C. (eds.) Computer Aided Verification - 32nd International Conference, CAV 2020, Los Angeles, CA, USA, July 21-24, 2020, Proceedings, Part II. Lecture Notes in Computer Science, vol. 12225, pp. 15–27. Springer (2020). https://doi.org/10.1007/978-3-030-53291-8_2, https://doi.org/10.1007/978-3-030-53291-8_2
6. Blahoudek, F., Heizmann, M., Schewe, S., Strejček, J., Tsai, M.: Complementing semi-deterministic Büchi automata. In: Chechik, M., Raskin, J. (eds.) Tools and Algorithms for the Construction and Analysis of Systems - 22nd International Conference, TACAS 2016, Held as Part of the European Joint Conferences on Theory and Practice of Software, ETAPS 2016, Eindhoven, The Netherlands, April 2-8, 2016, Proceedings. Lecture Notes in Computer Science, vol. 9636, pp. 770–787. Springer (2016). https://doi.org/10.1007/978-3-662-49674-9_49, https://doi.org/10.1007/978-3-662-49674-9_49
7. Breuers, S., Löding, C., Olschewski, J.: Improved Ramsey-based Büchi complementation. In: Birkedal, L. (ed.) Foundations of Software Science and Computational Structures - 15th International Conference, FOSSACS 2012, Held as Part of the European Joint Conferences on Theory and Practice of Software, ETAPS 2012, Tallinn, Estonia, March 24 - April 1, 2012. Proceedings. Lecture Notes in Computer Science, vol. 7213, pp. 150–164. Springer (2012). https://doi.org/10.1007/978-3-642-28729-9_10, https://doi.org/10.1007/978-3-642-28729-9_10
8. Büchi, J.R.: On a decision method in restricted second order arithmetic. In: Mac Lane, S., Siefkes, D. (eds.) The Collected Works of J. Richard Büchi, pp. 425–435. Springer (1990). https://doi.org/10.1007/978-1-4613-8928-6_23, https://doi.org/10.1007/978-1-4613-8928-6_23
9. Bustan, D., Grumberg, O.: Simulation-based Minimization. ACM Transactions on Computational Logic **4**(2), 181–206 (2003)
10. Chen, Y., Havlena, V., Lengál, O.: Simulations in rank-based Büchi automata complementation. In: Lin, A.W. (ed.) Programming Languages and Systems - 17th Asian Symposium, APLAS 2019, Nusa Dua, Bali, Indonesia, December 1-4, 2019, Proceedings. Lecture Notes in Computer Science, vol. 11893, pp. 447–467. Springer (2019). https://doi.org/10.1007/978-3-030-34175-6_23, https://doi.org/10.1007/978-3-030-34175-6_23

11. Chen, Y., Heizmann, M., Lengál, O., Li, Y., Tsai, M., Turrini, A., Zhang, L.: Advanced automata-based algorithms for program termination checking. In: Foster, J.S., Grossman, D. (eds.) Proceedings of the 39th ACM SIGPLAN Conference on Programming Language Design and Implementation, PLDI 2018, Philadelphia, PA, USA, June 18-22, 2018. pp. 135–150. ACM (2018). https://doi.org/10.1145/3192366.3192405, https://doi.org/10.1145/3192366.3192405

12. Clarkson, M.R., Finkbeiner, B., Koleini, M., Micinski, K.K., Rabe, M.N., Sánchez, C.: Temporal logics for hyperproperties. In: Abadi, M., Kremer, S. (eds.) Principles of Security and Trust - Third International Conference, POST 2014, Held as Part of the European Joint Conferences on Theory and Practice of Software, ETAPS 2014, Grenoble, France, April 5-13, 2014, Proceedings. Lecture Notes in Computer Science, vol. 8414, pp. 265–284. Springer (2014). https://doi.org/10.1007/978-3-642-54792-8_15, https://doi.org/10.1007/978-3-642-54792-8_15

13. Clemente, L., Mayr, R.: Efficient reduction of nondeterministic automata with application to language inclusion testing. Log. Methods Comput. Sci. 15(1) (2019). https://doi.org/10.23638/LMCS-15(1:12)2019, https://doi.org/10.23638/LMCS-15(1:12)2019

14. Courcoubetis, C., Yannakakis, M.: Verifying temporal properties of finite-state probabilistic programs. In: 29th Annual Symposium on Foundations of Computer Science, White Plains, New York, USA, 24-26 October 1988. pp. 338–345. IEEE Computer Society (1988). https://doi.org/10.1109/SFCS.1988.21950, https://doi.org/10.1109/SFCS.1988.21950

15. Duret-Lutz, A., Lewkowicz, A., Fauchille, A., Michaud, T., Renault, E., Xu, L.: Spot 2.0 - A framework for LTL and ω-automata manipulation. In: Artho, C., Legay, A., Peled, D. (eds.) Automated Technology for Verification and Analysis - 14th International Symposium, ATVA 2016, Chiba, Japan, October 17-20, 2016, Proceedings. Lecture Notes in Computer Science, vol. 9938, pp. 122–129 (2016). https://doi.org/10.1007/978-3-319-46520-3_8, https://doi.org/10.1007/978-3-319-46520-3_8

16. Duret-Lutz, A., Renault, E., Colange, M., Renkin, F., Aisse, A.G., Schlehuber-Caissier, P., Medioni, T., Martin, A., Dubois, J., Gillard, C., Lauko, H.: From Spot 2.0 to Spot 2.10: What's new? In: Shoham, S., Vizel, Y. (eds.) Computer Aided Verification - 34th International Conference, CAV 2022, Haifa, Israel, August 7-10, 2022, Proceedings, Part II. Lecture Notes in Computer Science, vol. 13372, pp. 174–187. Springer (2022). https://doi.org/10.1007/978-3-031-13188-2_9, https://doi.org/10.1007/978-3-031-13188-2_9

17. Esparza, J., Kretínský, J., Raskin, J., Sickert, S.: From LTL and limit-deterministic Büchi automata to deterministic parity automata. In: Legay, A., Margaria, T. (eds.) Tools and Algorithms for the Construction and Analysis of Systems - 23rd International Conference, TACAS 2017, Held as Part of the European Joint Conferences on Theory and Practice of Software, ETAPS 2017, Uppsala, Sweden, April 22-29, 2017, Proceedings, Part I. Lecture Notes in Computer Science, vol. 10205, pp. 426–442 (2017). https://doi.org/10.1007/978-3-662-54577-5_25, https://doi.org/10.1007/978-3-662-54577-5_25

18. Etessami, K., Wilke, T., Schuller, R.A.: Fair simulation relations, parity games, and state space reduction for Büchi automata. SIAM J. Comput. 34(5), 1159–1175 (2005). https://doi.org/10.1137/S0097539703420675, https://doi.org/10.1137/S0097539703420675

19. Fogarty, S., Kupferman, O., Vardi, M.Y., Wilke, T.: Profile trees for Büchi word automata, with application to determinization. Inf. Comput. 245, 136–151 (2015). https://doi.org/10.1016/j.ic.2014.12.021, https://doi.org/10.1016/j.ic.2014.12.021

20. Fogarty, S., Kupferman, O., Wilke, T., Vardi, M.Y.: Unifying Büchi complementation constructions. Log. Methods Comput. Sci. 9(1) (2013). https://doi.org/10.2168/LMCS-9(1:13)2013, https://doi.org/10.2168/LMCS-9(1:13)2013

21. Friedgut, E., Kupferman, O., Vardi, M.Y.: Büchi complementation made tighter. Int. J. Found. Comput. Sci. **17**(4), 851–868 (2006). https://doi.org/10.1142/S0129054106004145, https://doi.org/10.1142/S0129054106004145

22. Gurumurthy, S., Kupferman, O., Somenzi, F., Vardi, M.Y.: On complementing nondeterministic Büchi automata. In: Geist, D., Tronci, E. (eds.) Correct Hardware Design and Verification Methods, 12th IFIP WG 10.5 Advanced Research Working Conference, CHARME 2003, L'Aquila, Italy, October 21-24, 2003, Proceedings. Lecture Notes in Computer Science, vol. 2860, pp. 96–110. Springer (2003). https://doi.org/10.1007/978-3-540-39724-3_10, https://doi.org/10.1007/978-3-540-39724-3_10

23. Havlena, V., Lengál, O., Smahlíková, B.: Deciding S1S: down the rabbit hole and through the looking glass. In: Echihabi, K., Meyer, R. (eds.) Networked Systems - 9th International Conference, NETYS 2021, Virtual Event, May 19-21, 2021, Proceedings. Lecture Notes in Computer Science, vol. 12754, pp. 215–222. Springer (2021). https://doi.org/10.1007/978-3-030-91014-3_15, https://doi.org/10.1007/978-3-030-91014-3_15

24. Havlena, V., Lengál, O.: Reducing (to) the ranks: Efficient rank-based Büchi automata complementation. In: Haddad, S., Varacca, D. (eds.) 32nd International Conference on Concurrency Theory, CONCUR 2021, August 24-27, 2021, Virtual Conference. LIPIcs, vol. 203, pp. 2:1–2:19. Schloss Dagstuhl - Leibniz-Zentrum für Informatik (2021). https://doi.org/10.4230/LIPIcs.CONCUR.2021.2, https://doi.org/10.4230/LIPIcs.CONCUR.2021.2

25. Havlena, V., Lengál, O., Li, Y., Šmahlíková, B., Turrini, A.: KOFOLA (2022), https://github.com/VeriFIT/kofola

26. Havlena, V., Lengál, O., Li, Y., Šmahlíková, B., Turrini, A.: Artifact for the TACAS'23 paper "Modular Mix-and-Match Complementation of Büchi Automata" (Jan 2023). https://doi.org/10.5281/zenodo.7505210, https://doi.org/10.5281/zenodo.7505210

27. Havlena, V., Lengál, O., Li, Y., Šmahlíková, B., Turrini, A.: Modular mix-and-match complementation of Büchi automata (technical report). CoRR **abs/2301.01890** (2023). https://doi.org/10.48550/arXiv.2301.01890, https://doi.org/10.48550/arXiv.2301.01890

28. Havlena, V., Lengál, O., Šmahlíková, B.: Complementing Büchi automata with Ranker. In: Shoham, S., Vizel, Y. (eds.) Computer Aided Verification - 34th International Conference, CAV 2022, Haifa, Israel, August 7-10, 2022, Proceedings, Part II. Lecture Notes in Computer Science, vol. 13372, pp. 188–201. Springer (2022). https://doi.org/10.1007/978-3-031-13188-2_10, https://doi.org/10.1007/978-3-031-13188-2_10

29. Havlena, V., Lengál, O., Šmahlíková, B.: Sky is not the limit: Tighter rank bounds for elevator automata in Büchi automata complementation. In: Fisman, D., Rosu, G. (eds.) Tools and Algorithms for the Construction and Analysis of Systems - 28th International Conference, TACAS 2022, Held as Part of the European Joint Conferences on Theory and Practice of Software, ETAPS 2022, Munich, Germany, April 2-7, 2022, Proceedings, Part II. Lecture Notes in Computer Science, vol. 13244, pp. 118–136. Springer (2022). https://doi.org/10.1007/978-3-030-99527-0_7, https://doi.org/10.1007/978-3-030-99527-0_7

30. Heizmann, M., Hoenicke, J., Podelski, A.: Termination analysis by learning terminating programs. In: Biere, A., Bloem, R. (eds.) Computer Aided Verification - 26th International Conference, CAV 2014, Held as Part of the Vienna Summer of Logic, VSL 2014, Vienna, Austria, July 18-22, 2014. Proceedings. Lecture Notes in Computer Science, vol. 8559, pp. 797–813. Springer (2014). https://doi.org/10.1007/978-3-319-08867-9_53, https://doi.org/10.1007/978-3-319-08867-9_53

31. Hieronymi, P., Ma, D., Oei, R., Schaeffer, L., Schulz, C., Shallit, J.O.: Decidability for Sturmian words. In: Manea, F., Simpson, A. (eds.) 30th EACSL Annual Conference on Computer Science Logic, CSL 2022, February 14-19, 2022, Göttingen, Germany (Virtual Conference). LIPIcs, vol. 216, pp. 24:1–24:23. Schloss Dagstuhl - Leibniz-Zentrum für

Informatik (2022). https://doi.org/10.4230/LIPIcs.CSL.2022.24, https://doi.org/10.4230/LIPIcs.CSL.2022.24

32. Kähler, D., Wilke, T.: Complementation, disambiguation, and determinization of Büchi automata unified. In: Aceto, L., Damgård, I., Goldberg, L.A., Halldórsson, M.M., Ingólfsdóttir, A., Walukiewicz, I. (eds.) Automata, Languages and Programming, 35th International Colloquium, ICALP 2008, Reykjavik, Iceland, July 7-11, 2008, Proceedings, Part I: Tack A: Algorithms, Automata, Complexity, and Games. Lecture Notes in Computer Science, vol. 5125, pp. 724–735. Springer (2008). https://doi.org/10.1007/978-3-540-70575-8_59, https://doi.org/10.1007/978-3-540-70575-8_59

33. Karmarkar, H., Chakraborty, S.: On minimal odd rankings for Büchi complementation. In: Liu, Z., Ravn, A.P. (eds.) Automated Technology for Verification and Analysis, 7th International Symposium, ATVA 2009, Macao, China, October 14-16, 2009. Proceedings. Lecture Notes in Computer Science, vol. 5799, pp. 228–243. Springer (2009). https://doi.org/10.1007/978-3-642-04761-9_18, https://doi.org/10.1007/978-3-642-04761-9_18

34. Kupferman, O., Vardi, M.Y.: Weak alternating automata are not that weak. ACM Trans. Comput. Log. 2(3), 408–429 (2001). https://doi.org/10.1145/377978.377993, https://doi.org/10.1145/377978.377993

35. Kurshan, R.P.: Complementing deterministic Büchi automata in polynomial time. J. Comput. Syst. Sci. 35(1), 59–71 (1987). https://doi.org/10.1016/0022-0000(87)90036-5, https://doi.org/10.1016/0022-0000(87)90036-5

36. Lengál, O.: Automata benchmarks (2022), https://github.com/ondrik/automata-benchmarks

37. Li, Y., Turrini, A., Feng, W., Vardi, M.Y., Zhang, L.: Divide-and-conquer determinization of Büchi automata based on SCC decomposition. In: Shoham, S., Vizel, Y. (eds.) Computer Aided Verification - 34th International Conference, CAV 2022, Haifa, Israel, August 7-10, 2022, Proceedings, Part II. Lecture Notes in Computer Science, vol. 13372, pp. 152–173. Springer (2022). https://doi.org/10.1007/978-3-031-13188-2_8, https://doi.org/10.1007/978-3-031-13188-2_8

38. Li, Y., Turrini, A., Zhang, L., Schewe, S.: Learning to complement Büchi automata. In: Dillig, I., Palsberg, J. (eds.) Verification, Model Checking, and Abstract Interpretation - 19th International Conference, VMCAI 2018, Los Angeles, CA, USA, January 7-9, 2018, Proceedings. Lecture Notes in Computer Science, vol. 10747, pp. 313–335. Springer (2018). https://doi.org/10.1007/978-3-319-73721-8_15, https://doi.org/10.1007/978-3-319-73721-8_15

39. Li, Y., Vardi, M.Y., Zhang, L.: On the power of unambiguity in Büchi complementation. In: Raskin, J., Bresolin, D. (eds.) Proceedings 11th International Symposium on Games, Automata, Logics, and Formal Verification, GandALF 2020, Brussels, Belgium, September 21-22, 2020. EPTCS, vol. 326, pp. 182–198 (2020). https://doi.org/10.4204/EPTCS.326.12, https://doi.org/10.4204/EPTCS.326.12

40. Löding, C.: Optimal bounds for transformations of omega-automata. In: Rangan, C.P., Raman, V., Ramanujam, R. (eds.) Foundations of Software Technology and Theoretical Computer Science, 19th Conference, Chennai, India, December 13-15, 1999, Proceedings. Lecture Notes in Computer Science, vol. 1738, pp. 97–109. Springer (1999). https://doi.org/10.1007/3-540-46691-6_8, https://doi.org/10.1007/3-540-46691-6_8

41. Löding, C., Pirogov, A.: New optimizations and heuristics for determinization of Büchi automata. In: Chen, Y., Cheng, C., Esparza, J. (eds.) Automated Technology for Verification and Analysis - 17th International Symposium, ATVA 2019, Taipei, Taiwan, October 28-31, 2019, Proceedings. Lecture Notes in Computer Science, vol. 11781, pp. 317–333. Springer

(2019). https://doi.org/10.1007/978-3-030-31784-3_18, https://doi.org/10. 1007/978-3-030-31784-3_18

42. Miyano, S., Hayashi, T.: Alternating finite automata on omega-words. Theor. Comput. Sci. **32**, 321–330 (1984). https://doi.org/10.1016/0304-3975(84)90049-5, https:// doi.org/10.1016/0304-3975(84)90049-5

43. Piterman, N.: From nondeterministic Büchi and Streett automata to deterministic parity automata. Log. Methods Comput. Sci. **3**(3) (2007). https://doi.org/10.2168/LMCS-3(3: 5)2007, https://doi.org/10.2168/LMCS-3(3:5)2007

44. Pnueli, A.: The temporal logic of programs. In: 18th Annual Symposium on Foundations of Computer Science, Providence, Rhode Island, USA, 31 October - 1 November 1977. pp. 46–57. IEEE Computer Society (1977). https://doi.org/10.1109/SFCS.1977.32, https://doi.org/10.1109/SFCS.1977.32

45. Redziejowski, R.R.: An improved construction of deterministic omega-automaton using derivatives. Fundam. Informaticae **119**(3-4), 393–406 (2012). https://doi.org/10. 3233/FI-2012-744, https://doi.org/10.3233/FI-2012-744

46. Safra, S.: On the complexity of omega-automata. In: 29th Annual Symposium on Foundations of Computer Science, White Plains, New York, USA, 24-26 October 1988. pp. 319–327. IEEE Computer Society (1988). https://doi.org/10.1109/SFCS.1988.21948, https: //doi.org/10.1109/SFCS.1988.21948

47. Safra, S., Vardi, M.Y.: On omega-automata and temporal logic (preliminary report). In: Johnson, D.S. (ed.) Proceedings of the 21st Annual ACM Symposium on Theory of Computing, May 14-17, 1989, Seattle, Washington, USA. pp. 127–137. ACM (1989). https: //doi.org/10.1145/73007.73019, https://doi.org/10.1145/73007.73019

48. Schewe, S.: Büchi complementation made tight. In: Albers, S., Marion, J. (eds.) 26th International Symposium on Theoretical Aspects of Computer Science, STACS 2009, February 26-28, 2009, Freiburg, Germany, Proceedings. LIPIcs, vol. 3, pp. 661–672. Schloss Dagstuhl - Leibniz-Zentrum für Informatik, Germany (2009). https://doi.org/10.4230/LIPIcs. STACS.2009.1854, https://doi.org/10.4230/LIPIcs.STACS.2009.1854

49. Sickert, S., Esparza, J., Jaax, S., Kretínský, J.: Limit-deterministic Büchi automata for linear temporal logic. In: Chaudhuri, S., Farzan, A. (eds.) Computer Aided Verification - 28th International Conference, CAV 2016, Toronto, ON, Canada, July 17-23, 2016, Proceedings, Part II. Lecture Notes in Computer Science, vol. 9780, pp. 312–332. Springer (2016). https://doi.org/10.1007/978-3-319-41540-6_17, https://doi.org/10. 1007/978-3-319-41540-6_17

50. Sistla, A.P., Vardi, M.Y., Wolper, P.: The complementation problem for Büchi automata with applications to temporal logic. Theor. Comput. Sci. **49**, 217–237 (1987). https://doi.org/10.1016/0304-3975(87)90008-9, https://doi.org/10.1016/ 0304-3975(87)90008-9

51. The SV-COMP Community: International competition on software verification (2022), https://sv-comp.sosy-lab.org/

52. Tsai, M., Fogarty, S., Vardi, M.Y., Tsay, Y.: State of Büchi complementation. Log. Methods Comput. Sci. **10**(4) (2014). https://doi.org/10.2168/LMCS-10(4:13)2014, https: //doi.org/10.2168/LMCS-10(4:13)2014

53. Vardi, M.Y., Wilke, T.: Automata: from logics to algorithms. In: Flum, J., Grädel, E., Wilke, T. (eds.) Logic and Automata: History and Perspectives. Texts in Logic and Games, vol. 2, pp. 629–736. Amsterdam University Press (2008)

54. Vardi, M.Y., Wolper, P.: An automata-theoretic approach to automatic program verification (preliminary report). In: Proceedings of the Symposium on Logic in Computer Science (LICS '86), Cambridge, Massachusetts, USA, June 16-18, 1986. pp. 332–344. IEEE Computer Society (1986)

55. Yan, Q.: Lower bounds for complementation of omega-automata via the full automata technique. Log. Methods Comput. Sci. **4**(1) (2008). https://doi.org/10.2168/LMCS-4(1:5)2008, https://doi.org/10.2168/LMCS-4(1:5)2008

Validating Streaming JSON Documents with Learned VPAs*

Véronique Bruyère[1], Guillermo A. Pérez[2], and Gaëtan Staquet[1,2]([✉])

[1] University of Mons (UMONS), Mons, Belgium
{veronique.bruyere,gaetan.staquet}@umons.ac.be
[2] University of Antwerp (UAntwerp) – Flanders Make, Antwerp, Belgium
guillermo.perez@uantwerpen.be

Abstract. We present a new streaming algorithm to validate JSON documents against a set of constraints given as a JSON schema. Among the possible values a JSON document can hold, objects are unordered collections of key-value pairs while arrays are ordered collections of values. We prove that there always exists a visibly pushdown automaton (VPA) that accepts the same set of JSON documents as a JSON schema. Leveraging this result, our approach relies on learning a VPA for the provided schema. As the learned VPA assumes a fixed order on the key-value pairs of the objects, we abstract its transitions in a special kind of graph, and propose an efficient streaming algorithm using the VPA and its graph to decide whether a JSON document is valid for the schema. We evaluate the implementation of our algorithm on a number of random JSON documents, and compare it to the classical validation algorithm.

Keywords: Visibly pushdown automata · JSON · streaming validation

1 Introduction

JavaScript Object Notation (JSON) has overtaken XML as the de facto standard data-exchange format, in particular for web applications. JSON documents are easier to read for programmers and end users since they only have arrays and objects as structured types. Moreover, in contrast to XML, they do not include named open and end tags for all values, but open and end tags (braces actually) for arrays and objects only. *JSON schema* [13] is a simple schema language that allows users to impose constraints on the structure of JSON documents.

In this work, we are interested in the *validation* of *streaming* JSON documents against JSON schemas. Several previous results have been obtained about the formalization of XML schemas and the use of formal methods to validate XML documents (see, e.g., [5, 15, 16, 18, 24, 25]). Recently, a standard to formalize JSON schemas has been proposed and (hand-coded) validation tools for such schemas can be found online [13]. Pezoa et al, in [19], observe that the standard

---

*This work was supported by the Belgian FWO "SAILor" project (G030020N). Gaëtan Staquet is a research fellow (Aspirant) of the Belgian F.R.S.-FNRS.

S. Sankaranarayanan and N. Sharygina (Eds.): TACAS 2023, LNCS 13993, pp. 271–289, 2023.
https://doi.org/10.1007/978-3-031-30823-9_14

of JSON documents is still evolving and that the formal semantics of JSON schemas is also still changing. Furthermore, validation tools seem to make different assumptions about both documents and schemas. The authors of [19] carry out an initial formalization of JSON schemas into formal grammars from which they are able to construct a *batch* validation tool from a given JSON schema.

In this paper, we rely on the formalization work of [19] and propose a *streaming* algorithm for validating JSON documents against JSON schemas. To our knowledge, this is the first JSON validation algorithm that is streaming. For XML, works that study streaming document validation base such algorithms on the construction of some automaton (see, e.g., [25], for XML). In [7], we first experimented with one-counter automata for this purpose. We submit that *visibly-pushdown automata* (VPAs) are a better fit for this task — this is in line with [15], where the same was proposed for streaming XML documents. In contrast to one-counter automata,[3] we show that VPAs are expressive enough to capture the language of JSON documents satisfying any JSON schema.

More importantly, we explain that *active learning à la* Angluin [4] is a good alternative to the automatic construction of such a VPA from the formal semantics of a given JSON schema. This is possible in the presence of labeled examples or a computer program that can answer membership and (approximate) equivalence queries about a set of JSON documents. This learning approach has two advantages. First, we derive from the learned VPA a streaming validator for JSON documents. Second, by automatically learning an automaton representation, we circumvent the need to write a schema and subsequently validate that it represents the desired set of JSON documents. Indeed, it is well known that one of the highest bars that users have to clear to make use of formal methods is the effort required to write a formal specification, in this case, a JSON schema.

Contributions. We present a VPA active learning framework to achieve what was mentioned above — though we fix an order on the keys appearing in objects. The latter assumption helps our algorithm learn faster. Secondly, we show how to bootstrap the learning algorithm by leveraging existing validation and document-generation tools to implement approximate equivalence checks. Thirdly, we describe how to validate streaming documents using our fixed-order learned automata — that is, our algorithm accepts other permutations of keys, not just the one encoded into the VPA. Finally, we present an empirical evaluation of our learning and validation algorithms, implemented on top of LEARNLIB [17].

All contributions, while complementary, are valuable in their own right. First, our learning algorithm for VPAs is a novel gray-box extension of TTT [9] that leverages side information about the language of all JSON documents. Second, our validation algorithm that uses a fixed-order VPA is novel and can be applied regardless of whether the automaton is learned or constructed from a schema. For the validation algorithm, we developed the concept of *key graph*, which allows us to efficiently realize the validation no matter the key-value order in the docu-

---

[3] By nesting objects and arrays, we obtain a set of JSON documents encoding $\{a^n b^m c^m d^n \mid n, m \in \mathbb{N}\}$, a context-free language that requires two counters.

ment, and might be of independent interest for other JSON-analysis applications using VPAs. Finally, we implemented our own batch validator to facilitate approximating equivalence queries as required by our learning algorithm. Both the new validator and the equivalence oracle are efficient, open-source, and easy to modify. We strongly believe the latter can be re-used in similar projects aiming to learn automata representations of sets of JSON documents.

A long version of this work is on arXiv: https://arxiv.org/abs/2211.08891.

2   Visibly Pushdown Languages

First, we recall the definition VPAs [3] and state some of their properties. We also recall how they can be actively learned following Angluin's approach [4].

Visibly Pushdown Automata An *alphabet* Σ is a finite set whose elements are called *symbols*. A *word* w over Σ is a finite sequence of symbols from Σ, with the *empty word* denoted by ε. The length of w is denoted $|w|$; the set of all words, Σ^*. Given two words $v, w \in \Sigma^*$, v is a *prefix* (resp. *suffix*) of w if there exists $u \in \Sigma^*$ such that $w = vu$ (resp. $w = uv$), and v is a *factor* of w if there exist $u, u' \in \Sigma^*$ such that $w = uvu'$. Given $L \subseteq \Sigma^*$, called a *language*, we denote by $\mathrm{Pref}(L)$ (resp. $\mathrm{Suff}(L)$) the set of prefixes (resp. suffixes) of words of L. Given a set Q, we write $\mathbb{I}_Q$ for the *identity relation* $\{(q, q) \mid q \in Q\}$ on Q.

VPA [3] are particular pushdown automata that we recall in this section. The *pushdown alphabet*, denoted $\tilde{\Sigma} = (\Sigma_c, \Sigma_r, \Sigma_i)$, is partitioned into pairwise disjoint alphabets $\Sigma_c, \Sigma_r, \Sigma_i$ such that Σ_c (resp. Σ_r, Σ_i) is the set of *call* symbols (resp. *return* symbols, *internal* symbols). In this paper, we work with the particular alphabet of return symbols $\Sigma_r = \{\bar{a} \mid a \in \Sigma_c\}$. For any such $\tilde{\Sigma}$, we denote by Σ the alphabet $\Sigma_c \cup \Sigma_r \cup \Sigma_i$. Given a pushdown alphabet $\tilde{\Sigma}$, the set $\mathrm{WM}(\tilde{\Sigma})$ of *well-matched* words over $\tilde{\Sigma}$ is defined:

- $\varepsilon \in \mathrm{WM}(\tilde{\Sigma})$, and $a \in \mathrm{WM}(\tilde{\Sigma})$ for all $a \in \Sigma_i$,
- if $w, w' \in \mathrm{WM}(\tilde{\Sigma})$, then $ww' \in \mathrm{WM}(\tilde{\Sigma})$,
- if $a \in \Sigma_c, w \in \mathrm{WM}(\tilde{\Sigma})$, then $aw\bar{a} \in \mathrm{WM}(\tilde{\Sigma})$.

Also, the *call/return balance* function $\beta : \Sigma^* \to \mathbb{Z}$ is defined as $\beta(\varepsilon) = 0$ and $\beta(ua) = \beta(u) + x$ with x being $1, -1,$ or 0 if a is in $\Sigma_c, \Sigma_r,$ or Σ_i respectively. In particular, for all $w \in \mathrm{WM}(\tilde{\Sigma})$, we have $\beta(u) \geq 0$ for each prefix u of w and $\beta(u) \leq 0$ for each suffix u of w. Finally, the *depth* $d(w)$ of a well-matched word w is equal to $\max\{\beta(u) \mid u \in \mathrm{Pref}(\{w\})\}$, that is, the maximum number of unmatched call symbols among the prefixes of w.

Definition 1. *A* visibly pushdown automaton *(VPA) over a pushdown alphabet $\tilde{\Sigma}$ is a tuple $(Q, \tilde{\Sigma}, \Gamma, \delta, Q_I, Q_F)$ where Q is a finite non-empty set of states, $Q_I \subseteq Q$ is a set of initial states, $Q_F \subseteq Q$ is a set of final states, Γ is a stack alphabet, and δ is a finite set of transitions of the form $\delta = \delta_c \cup \delta_r \cup \delta_i$ where $\delta_c \subseteq Q \times \Sigma_c \times Q \times \Gamma$ is the set of call transitions, $\delta_r \subseteq Q \times \Sigma_r \times \Gamma \times Q$ is the set of return transitions, and $\delta_i \subseteq Q \times \Sigma_i \times Q$ is a set of internal transitions. The size of $\mathcal{A}$ is denoted by $|Q|$, and its number of transitions by $|\delta|$.*

Let us describe the *transition system* $T_\mathcal{A}$ of a VPA $\mathcal{A}$ whose vertices are configurations. A *configuration* is a pair $\langle q, \sigma \rangle$ where $q \in Q$ is a state and $\sigma \in \Gamma^*$ a stack content. A configuration is *initial* (resp. *final*) if $q \in Q_I$ (resp. $q \in Q_F$) and $\sigma = \varepsilon$. For $a \in \Sigma$, we write $\langle q, \sigma \rangle \xrightarrow{a} \langle q', \sigma' \rangle$ in $T_\mathcal{A}$ if there is either a call transition $(q, a, q', \gamma) \in \delta_c$ verifying $\sigma' = \gamma\sigma$,[4] or a return transition $(q, a, \gamma, q') \in \delta_r$ verifying $\sigma = \gamma\sigma'$, or an internal transition $(q, a, q') \in \delta_i$ such that $\sigma' = \sigma$.

The transition relation of $T_\mathcal{A}$ is extended to words in the usual way. We say that $\mathcal{A}$ *accepts* a word $w \in \Sigma^*$ if there exists a path in $T_\mathcal{A}$ from an initial configuration to a final configuration that is labeled by w. The *language of* $\mathcal{A}$, denoted by $\mathcal{L}(\mathcal{A})$, is defined as $\mathcal{L}(\mathcal{A}) = \{w \in \Sigma^* \mid \exists q \in Q_I, \exists q' \in Q_F, \langle q, \varepsilon \rangle \xrightarrow{w} \langle q', \varepsilon \rangle\}$, i.e., the set of all words accepted by $\mathcal{A}$. Any language accepted by some VPA is a *visibly pushdown language* (VPL). Notice that such a language is composed of well-matched words only.[5] Given a VPA $\mathcal{A}$ over $\tilde{\Sigma}$, the *reachability relation* $\text{Reach}_\mathcal{A}$ of $\mathcal{A}$ is $\text{Reach}_\mathcal{A} = \{(q, q') \in Q^2 \mid \exists w \in \text{WM}(\tilde{\Sigma}), \langle q, \varepsilon \rangle \xrightarrow{w} \langle q', \varepsilon \rangle\}$.

Finally, we say that $p \in Q$ is a *bin state* if there exists no path in $T_\mathcal{A}$ of the form $\langle q, \varepsilon \rangle \xrightarrow{w} \langle p, \sigma \rangle \xrightarrow{w'} \langle q', \varepsilon \rangle$ with $q \in Q_I$ and $q' \in Q_F$. If a VPA $\mathcal{A}$ has bin states, those states can be removed from Q as well as the transitions containing bin states without modifying the accepted language.

Minimal Deterministic VPAs Given a VPA $\mathcal{A} = (Q, \tilde{\Sigma}, \Gamma, \delta, Q_I, Q_F)$, we say that it is *deterministic* (det-VPA) if $|Q_I| = 1$ and $\mathcal{A}$ does not have two distinct transitions with the same left-hand side. By *left-hand side*, we mean (q, a) for a call transition $(q, a, q', \gamma) \in \delta_c$ or an internal transition $(q, a, q') \in \delta_i$, and (q, a, γ) for a return transition $(q, a, \gamma, q') \in \delta_r$.

Theorem 1 ([3,32]). *For any VPA $\mathcal{A}$ over $\tilde{\Sigma}$, one can construct a det-VPA $\mathcal{B}$ over $\tilde{\Sigma}$ such that $\mathcal{L}(\mathcal{A}) = \mathcal{L}(\mathcal{B})$. Moreover, the size of $\mathcal{B}$ is in $\mathcal{O}(2^{|Q|^2})$ and the size of its stack alphabet is in $\mathcal{O}(|\Sigma_c| \cdot 2^{|Q|^2})$.*

Proof. Let us briefly recall this construction. Let $\mathcal{A} = (Q, \tilde{\Sigma}, \Gamma, \delta, Q_I, Q_F)$. The states of $\mathcal{B}$ are subsets R of the reachability relation $\text{Reach}_\mathcal{A}$ of $\mathcal{A}$ and the stack symbols of $\mathcal{B}$ are of the form (R, a) with $R \subseteq \text{Reach}_\mathcal{A}$ and $a \in \Sigma_c$. Let $w = u_1 a_1 u_2 a_2 \ldots u_n a_n u_{n+1}$ be such that $n \geq 0$ and $u_i \in \text{WM}(\tilde{\Sigma}), a_i \in \Sigma_c$ for all i. That is, we decompose w in terms of its unmatched call symbols. Let R_i be equal to $\{(p, q) \mid \langle p, \varepsilon \rangle \xrightarrow{u_i} \langle q, \varepsilon \rangle\}$ for all i. Then after reading w, the det-VPA $\mathcal{B}$ has its current state equal to R_{n+1} and its stack containing $(R_n, a_n) \ldots (R_2, a_2)(R_1, a_1)$. Assume we are reading the symbol a after w, then $\mathcal{B}$ performs the following transition from R_{n+1}: (1) if $a \in \Sigma_c$, then push (R_{n+1}, a) on the stack and go to the state $R = \mathbb{I}_Q$ (a new unmatched call symbol is read); (2) if $a \in \Sigma_i$, then go to the state $R = \{(p, q) \mid \exists(p, p') \in R_{n+1}, (p', a, q) \in \delta_i\}$ (u_{n+1} is extended to the well-matched word $u_{n+1}a$); (3) if $a \in \Sigma_r$, then pop (R_n, a_n) from the stack if $\bar{a}_n = a$, and go to the state

$$R = \{(p, q) \mid \exists(p, p') \in R_n, (p', a_n, r', \gamma) \in \delta_c, (r', r) \in R_{n+1}, (r, a, \gamma, q) \in \delta_r\}$$

---

[4] The stack symbol γ is pushed on the left of σ.

[5] The original definition of VPA [3] allows acceptance of ill-matched words.

(the call symbol a_n is matched with the return symbol $a = \bar{a}_n$, leading to the well-matched word $u_n a_n u_{n+1} a$). Finally the initial state of $\mathcal{B}$ is $\mathbb{I}_{Q_I}$ and its final states are sets R containing some (p, q) with $p \in Q_I$ and $q \in Q_F$.   □

Though a VPL L in general does not have a unique minimal det-VPA $\mathcal{A}$ accepting L, imposing the following subclass leads to a unique minimal acceptor.

Definition 2 ([2, 9]). *A 1-module single entry VPA[6] (1-SEVPA) is a det-VPA $\mathcal{A} = (Q, \tilde{\Sigma}, \Gamma, \delta, Q_I = \{q_0\}, Q_F)$ such that its stack alphabet Γ is equal to $Q \times \Sigma_c$, and all its call transitions $(q, a, q', \gamma) \in \delta_c$ are such that $q' = q_0$ and $\gamma = (q, a)$.*

Theorem 2 ([2]). *For any VPL L, there exists a unique minimal (with regards to the number of states) 1-SEVPA accepting L, up to a renaming of the states.[7]*

Learning VPAs Let us recall the concept of *learning* a deterministic finite automaton (DFA), as introduced in [4]. Let L be a regular language over an alphabet Σ. The task of the *learner* is to construct a DFA $\mathcal{H}$ such that $\mathcal{L}(\mathcal{H}) = L$ by interacting with the *teacher*. The two possible types of interactions are *membership queries* (does $w \in \Sigma^*$ belong to L?), and *equivalence queries* (does the DFA $\mathcal{H}$ accept L?). For the latter type, if the answer is negative, the teacher also provides a counterexample, i.e., a word w such that $w \in L \Leftrightarrow w \notin \mathcal{L}(\mathcal{H})$. The so-called L^* *algorithm* of [4] learns at least one representative per equivalence class of the Myhill-Nerode congruence of L [8] from which the minimal DFA $\mathcal{D}$ accepting L is constructed. This learning process terminates and it uses a polynomial number of membership and equivalence queries in the size of $\mathcal{D}$, and in the length of the longest counterexample returned by the teacher [4].

In [9], an extension of Angluin's learning algorithm is given for VPLs. The Myhill-Nerode congruence for regular languages is extended to VPLs as follows. Given a pushdown alphabet $\tilde{\Sigma}$ and a VPL L over $\tilde{\Sigma}$, we consider the set of *context pairs* $\mathrm{CP}(\tilde{\Sigma}) = \{(u, v) \in (\mathrm{WM}(\tilde{\Sigma}) \cdot \Sigma_c)^* \times \mathrm{Suff}(\mathrm{WM}(\tilde{\Sigma})) \mid \beta(u) = -\beta(v)\}$, and we define the equivalence relation $\simeq_L \subseteq \mathrm{WM}(\tilde{\Sigma}) \times \mathrm{WM}(\tilde{\Sigma})$ [2,9] such that $w \simeq_L w'$ if and only if $\forall (u, v) \in \mathrm{CP}(\tilde{\Sigma}), uwv \in L \Leftrightarrow uw'v \in L$. The minimal 1-SEVPA accepting L as described in Theorem 2 is constructed from $\simeq_L$ such that its states are the equivalence classes of $\simeq_L$.

Theorem 3 ([9]). *Let L be a VPL over $\tilde{\Sigma}$ and n be the index of $\simeq_L$. queries and a number of membership queries polynomial in n, $|\Sigma|$, and $\log \ell$, where ℓ is the length of the longest counterexample returned by the teacher.*

The learning process designed in [9] extends to VPLs the TTT *algorithm* proposed in [10] for regular languages. TTT improves the efficiency of the L^* algorithm by eliminating redundancies in counterexamples provided by the teacher.

---

[6] The definitions of 1-SEVPA in [2] and [9] differ slightly. We follow the one in [9].

[7] This 1-SEVPA may be exponentially bigger than the size of a VPA accepting L.

3   JSON Format

In this section, we describe JSON documents [6] and JSON schemas [13] that impose some constraints on the structure of JSON documents. We also present the abstractions we make for the purpose of this paper.

JSON Documents We describe the structure of JSON documents. Our presentation is inspired by [19], though some details are skipped for readability (see [14] for a full description). The JSON format defines different types of *JSON values*:

- `true, false, null` are JSON values. Any decimal number (positive, negative) is a JSON value, called a *number*. In particular any number that is an integer is called an *integer*. Any finite sequence of characters starting and ending with " is a *string value*. All those values are called *primitive values*.
- If $v_1, v_2, \ldots, v_n$ are JSON values and $k_1, k_2, \ldots, k_n$ are *pairwise distinct* string values, then $\{k_1 : v_1, k_2 : v_2, \ldots, k_n : v_n\}$ is a JSON value, called an *object*. Each $k_i : v_i$ is called a *key-value pair* such that k_i is the *key*. The collection of these pairs is *unordered*.
- If $v_1, v_2, \ldots, v_n$ are JSON values, then $[v_1, v_2, \ldots, v_n]$ is a JSON value, called an *array*. Each v_i is an *element* and the collection thereof is *ordered*.

In this work, *JSON documents* are supposed to be objects.[8] One can use *JSON pointers* to navigate through a document, e.g., if J is an object and k is a key, then $J[k]$ is the value v such that the key-value pair $k : v$ appears in J.

In this paper, we consider somewhat *abstract* JSON documents. We see JSON documents as well-matched words over the pushdown alphabet $\tilde{\Sigma}_{\mathrm{JSON}}$ that we describe hereafter. We abstract all string values as $\mathbf{s}$, and all numbers as $\mathbf{n}$ (as $\mathbf{i}$ when they are integers). We denote by $\Sigma_{\mathrm{pVal}} = \{\mathtt{true}, \mathtt{false}, \mathtt{null}, \mathbf{s}, \mathbf{n}, \mathbf{i}\}$ the alphabet composed of the six primitive values. Concerning the key-value pairs appearing in objects, each key together with the symbol ":" following the key is abstracted as an alphabet symbol k. We assume knowledge of a *finite* alphabet Σ_{key} of keys. We define the pushdown alphabet $\tilde{\Sigma}_{\mathrm{JSON}} = (\Sigma_c, \Sigma_r, \Sigma_i)$ with $\Sigma_i = \Sigma_{\mathrm{key}} \cup \Sigma_{\mathrm{pVal}} \cup \{\#\}$, where $\#$ is used in place of the comma; $\Sigma_c = \{\prec, \sqsubset\}$, where $\prec$ (resp. $\sqsubset$) is used in place of "{" (resp. "["); and $\Sigma_r = \{\succ, \sqsupset\}$, with $\overline{\prec} = \succ$ and $\overline{\sqsubset} = \sqsupset$. We denote by Σ_{JSON} the set $\Sigma_c \cup \Sigma_r \cup \Sigma_i$.

Example 1. An example of a JSON document is given in Listing 1. We can see that this document is an object containing three keys: `"title"`, whose associated value is a string value; `"keywords"`, whose value is an array containing string values; and `"conf"`, whose value is an object. This inner object contains two keys: `"name"`, whose value is a string value; `"year"`, whose value is an integer. The pointer J[conf][name], where J is the root of the document, retrieves the value `"TACAS"`. The JSON document is abstracted as the word $\prec k_1 \mathbf{s} \# k_2 \sqsubset \mathbf{s} \# \mathbf{s} \# \mathbf{s} \sqsupset \#$ $k_3 \prec k_4 \mathbf{s} \# k_5 \mathbf{i} \succ \succ \in \mathrm{WM}(\tilde{\Sigma}_{\mathrm{JSON}})$ where Σ_{key} contains the keys $k_i, i \in \{1, \ldots, 5\}$.

---

[8]In [6], a JSON document can be any JSON value and duplicated keys are allowed inside objects. In this paper, we follow what is commonly used in practice: JSON documents are objects, and keys are pairwise distinct inside objects.

```
1  { "title": "Validating Streaming JSON Documents with Learned VPAs",
2    "keywords": ["VPA", "JSON documents", "streaming validation"],
3    "conf": { "name": "TACAS", "year": 2023 }
4  }
```

Listing 1: A JSON document.

```
1  { "type": "object",
2    "required": ["title", "conf"],
3    "properties": {
4      "title": { "type": "string" },
5      "keywords": { "type": "array", "items": { "type": "string" } },
6      "conf": {
7        "type": "object",
8        "required": ["name", "year"],
9        "properties":{ "name":{"type": "string"},"year":{"type": "integer"}}}}}
```

Listing 2: A JSON schema.

JSON Schemas A *JSON schema* can impose some constraints on JSON documents by specifying any of the types of JSON values that appear in those documents. We say that a JSON document *satisfies* (or is *valid* for) the schema if it verifies the constraints imposed by this schema. We denote by $\mathcal{L}(S)$ the set of documents that are valid for S. In this section, we give a simplified presentation of JSON schemas and refer to [13] for a complete description and to [19] for a formalization (i.e. a formal grammar with its syntax and semantics).

A JSON schema is itself a JSON document that uses several keywords that help shape and restrict the set of JSON documents that this schema specifies. As we abstract JSON documents, JSON schemas we work on are also abstracted. We do not consider the restrictions that can be imposed on string values and numbers, for instance. We give here a few examples. See [13] for more details.

— Within object schemas, restrictions can be imposed on the key-value pairs of the objects, e.g., the value associated with some key has itself to satisfy a certain schema, or some particular keys must be present in the object.
— Within array schemas, it can be imposed that all elements of the array satisfy a certain schema, or that the array has a minimum/maximum size.
— Schemas can be combined with Boolean operations, e.g., a JSON document must satisfy a conjunction of several schemas.
— A schema can be defined as one referred to by a JSON pointer. This allows a *recursive* structure for the JSON documents satisfying a certain schema.

Example 2. The schema from Listing 2 describes objects that can have three keys: `"title"`, whose associated value must be a string value; `"keywords"`, an array of strings; and `"conf"`, an object. Among these, `"title"` and `"conf"` are required. The JSON document of Example 1 satisfies this JSON schema.

Under these abstractions, we can always construct a VPA that accept the same set of JSON documents than a schema S, as shown in the following theorem. We also extend this construction to the case where we fix an *order* <

on Σ_{key} and consider the set $\mathcal{L}_<(S)$ of documents valid for S whose key order inside objects respects this order $<$. The main idea of the proof is to define a formalism of JSON schemas as *extended context-free grammars*, and show that we can construct a VPA from such a grammar.

Theorem 4. *Let S be a JSON schema. Then, there exists a VPA $\mathcal{A}$ such that $\mathcal{L}(\mathcal{A})$ is the set $\mathcal{L}(S)$ of documents valid with regards to S. Moreover, for any order $<$ of Σ_{key}, there exists a VPA $\mathcal{B}$ such that $\mathcal{L}(\mathcal{B}) = \mathcal{L}_<(S)$.*

Our proof does not give a construction of the grammar from the schema S. The grammar depends on the formal semantics of JSON schemas which are still changing and being debated. Thus, to be more robust to changes in the semantics, we prefer to learn the minimal 1-SEVPA $\mathcal{B}$ accepting $\mathcal{L}_<(S)$ given a fixed order $<$, in the sense of Theorem 3.[9] For learning, equivalence queries require to generate a certain number of random JSON documents.[10] If S and the learner's hypothesis $\mathcal{H}$ disagree on a document, we have a counterexample. Otherwise, we say that $\mathcal{H}$ is correct. In both membership and equivalence queries, we only accept documents whose key order inside objects satisfy the order $<$. The randomness used in the equivalence queries implies that the learned 1-SEVPA may not exactly accept $\mathcal{L}_<(S)$. Setting the number of generated documents to be large would help reducing the probability that an incorrect 1-SEVPA is learned.

4   Validation of JSON Documents

For this section, let us fix a schema S, an order $<$ on Σ_{key}, and a 1-SEVPA $\mathcal{A} = (Q, \tilde{\Sigma}_{\text{JSON}}, \Gamma, \delta, \{q_0\}, Q_F)$ accepting $\mathcal{L}_<(S)$. We present a *streaming* algorithm to decide if a document J is in $\mathcal{L}(S)$. By "streaming", we mean an algorithm that processes the document in a single pass, symbol by symbol. Our new approach is as follows. We learn $\mathcal{A}$ such that $\mathcal{L}(\mathcal{A}) = \mathcal{L}_<(S)$. As $\mathcal{L}_<(S) \neq \mathcal{L}(S)$, we design an algorithm that uses $\mathcal{A}$ in a clever way to allow arbitrary key orders in documents to validate. To do this, we use a *key graph* defined in the sequel.

Key Graph In this section, w.l.o.g. we suppose that $\mathcal{A}$ has *no bin states*. Let $T_{\mathcal{A}}$ be the transition system of $\mathcal{A}$. We explain how to associate to $\mathcal{A}$ its *key graph* $G_{\mathcal{A}}$: an abstraction of the paths of $T_{\mathcal{A}}$ labeled by the contents of the objects appearing in words of $\mathcal{L}_<(S)$. This graph is essential in our validation algorithm.

Definition 3. *The key graph $G_{\mathcal{A}}$ of $\mathcal{A}$ has:*

- *the vertices (p, k, p') with $p, p' \in Q$ and $k \in \Sigma_{\text{key}}$ if there exists in $T_{\mathcal{A}}$ a path $\langle p, \varepsilon \rangle \xrightarrow{kv} \langle p', \varepsilon \rangle$ with $v \in \Sigma_{\text{pVal}} \cup \{au\bar{a} \mid a \in \Sigma_c, u \in \text{WM}(\tilde{\Sigma}_{\text{JSON}})\}$,[11]*

---

[9]We use this automaton in the next section for the validation of JSON documents. We do not use a 1-SEVPA for $\mathcal{L}(S)$ as it could be exponentially larger.

[10]It is common to proceed this way in automata learning, as explained in [4, Sec. 4].

[11]Notice that each vertex (p, k, p') of $G_{\mathcal{A}}$ only stores the key k and not the word kv.

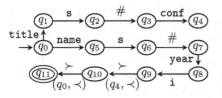

Fig. 1: A 1-SEVPA for the schema from Listing 2, without the key keywords.

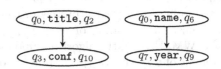

Fig. 2: The key graph for the 1-SEVPA from Figure 1.

– the edges $((p_1, k_1, p'_1), (p_2, k_2, p'_2))$ if there exists $(p'_1, \#, p_2) \in \delta_i$.

We have the following property.

Lemma 1. *There exists a path* $((p_1, k_1, p'_1) \ldots (p_n, k_n, p'_n))$ *in* G_A *with* $p_1 = q_0$ *if and only if there exist a factor* u *of a word in* $\mathcal{L}_<(S)$ *such that* $u = k_1 v_1 \# \ldots \#$ $k_n v_n$ *where each* $k_i v_i$ *is a key-value pair, and a path* $\langle q_0, \varepsilon \rangle \xrightarrow{u} \langle p'_n, \varepsilon \rangle$ *in* T_A *that decomposes as* $\langle p_i, \varepsilon \rangle \xrightarrow{k_i v_i} \langle p'_i, \varepsilon \rangle, \forall i \in \{1, \ldots, n\}$ *and* $\langle p'_i, \varepsilon \rangle \xrightarrow{\#} \langle p_{i+1}, \varepsilon \rangle, \forall i \in \{1, \ldots, n-1\}$. *Furthermore, there is no path* $((p_1, k_1, p'_1) \ldots (p_n, k_n, p'_n))$ *such that* $k_i = k_j$ *for some* $i \neq j$. *That is,* G_A *contains a finite number of paths.*

Hence, paths in G_A focus on contents of objects being part of JSON documents in $\mathcal{L}_<(S)$. Moreover, they abstract paths in T_A in the sense that only keys k_i are stored and the subpaths labeled by the values v_i are implicit.

Example 3. Consider the schema from Listing 2, without the key keywords. A 1-SEVPA A accepting $\mathcal{L}_<(S)$ is given in Figure 1. For clarity, call transitions[12] and the bin state are not represented. In Figure 2, we depict its corresponding key graph G_A. Since we have the path $\langle q_0, \varepsilon \rangle \xrightarrow{\text{title } s} \langle q_2, \varepsilon \rangle$ in T_A, the triplet $(q_0, \texttt{title}, q_2)$ is a vertex of G_A. Likewise, $(q_0, \texttt{name}, q_6)$ and $(q_7, \texttt{year}, q_9)$ are vertices. As we have the path $\langle q_4, \varepsilon \rangle \xrightarrow{\prec} \langle q_0, (q_4, \prec) \rangle \xrightarrow{\text{name } s \# \text{ year } i} \langle q_9, (q_4, \prec) \rangle \xrightarrow{\succ} \langle q_{10}, \varepsilon \rangle$, $(q_3, \texttt{conf}, q_{10})$ is also a vertex of G_A. Finally, as $\langle q_2, \varepsilon \rangle \xrightarrow{\#} \langle q_3, \varepsilon \rangle$, we have an edge from $(q_0, \texttt{title}, q_2)$ to $(q_3, \texttt{conf}, q_{10})$.

Computing the key graph can be done in polynomial time by first computing the reachability relation Reach_A. From this relation, the vertices can be easily found. Since the edges require to check whether a transition reading $\#$ exists, it is obvious that it can be done in polynomial time.

Validation Algorithm In this section, we provide a streaming algorithm that validates JSON documents against a given JSON schema S.

Given a word $w \in \Sigma^*_{\text{JSON}} \setminus \{\varepsilon\}$, we want to check whether $w \in \mathcal{L}(S)$. The main difficulty is that the key-value pairs inside an object are arbitrarily ordered in w while a fixed key order $<$ is encoded in the 1-SEVPA A ($\mathcal{L}(A) = \mathcal{L}_<(S)$).

---

[12]Recall the form of call transitions for 1-SEVPAs, see Definition 2.

Our validation algorithm is inspired by the algorithm computing a det-VPA equivalent to some given VPA [3] (see Theorem 1 and its proof) and uses the key graph $G_{\mathcal{A}}$ to treat arbitrary orders of the key-value pairs inside objects.

During the reading of $w \in \Sigma_{\mathrm{JSON}}^* \setminus \{\varepsilon\}$, in addition to checking whether $w \in \mathrm{WM}(\tilde{\Sigma}_{\mathrm{JSON}})$, the algorithm updates a subset $R \subseteq \mathrm{Reach}_{\mathcal{A}}$ and modifies the content of a stack Stk (push, pop, modify the element on top of Stk).

First, let us explain the information stored in R. Assume that we have read the prefix zau of w such that $a \in \Sigma_c$ is the last unmatched call symbol (thus $za \in (\mathrm{WM}(\tilde{\Sigma}_{\mathrm{JSON}}) \cdot \Sigma_c)^*$ and $u \in \mathrm{WM}(\tilde{\Sigma}_{\mathrm{JSON}})$).

- If a is the symbol $\sqsubset$, then we have $R = \{(p,q) \mid \langle p, \varepsilon \rangle \xrightarrow{u} \langle q, \varepsilon \rangle\}$.
- If a is the symbol $\prec$, then we have $u = k_1 v_1 \# k_2 v_2 \# \ldots k_{n-1} v_{n-1} \# u'$ such that $u' \in \mathrm{WM}(\tilde{\Sigma}_{\mathrm{JSON}})$ and u' is prefix of $k_n v_n$, where each $k_i v_i$ is a key-value pair. Then $R = \{(p,q) \mid \langle p, \varepsilon \rangle \xrightarrow{u'} \langle q, \varepsilon \rangle\}$.

In the first case, by using R as defined previously, we adopt the same approach as for the determinization of VPAs. In the second case, with u, we are currently reading the key-value pairs of an object in some order, not necessarily the one encoded in $\mathcal{A}$. In this case the set R is focused on the currently read key-value pair $k_n v_n$, that is, on the word u'. After reading of the whole object $\prec k_1 v_1 \# k_2 v_2 \# \ldots \succ$, we will use the key graph $G_{\mathcal{A}}$ to update the current set R.

Second, an element stored in the stack Stk is either a pair $(R, \sqsubset)$, or a 5-tuple $(R, \prec, K, k, Bad)$, where R is a set as described previously, $K \subseteq \Sigma_{\mathrm{key}}$ is a subset of keys, $k \in \Sigma_{\mathrm{key}}$ is a key, and Bad is a set containing some vertices of $G_{\mathcal{A}}$.[13]

We now detail our streaming validation algorithm.[14] Before reading w, we initialize R to the set $\mathbb{I}_{\{q_0\}}$ and Stk to the empty stack. Let us explain how to update the current set R and the current content of the stack Stk while reading the input word w. Suppose that we are reading the symbol a in w. In some cases we will also peek the symbol b following a (lookahead of one symbol).

Case (1) Suppose that a is the symbol $\sqsubset$, i.e., we start an array. Hence $(R, \sqsubset)$ is pushed on Stk and R is updated to $R_{Upd} = \mathbb{I}_{\{q_0\}}$. We thus proceed as in the proof of Theorem 1 (with $\mathbb{I}_{\{q_0\}}$ instead of $\mathbb{I}_Q$, since $\mathcal{A}$ is a 1-SEVPA[12]).

Case (2) Suppose that $a \in \Sigma_i$ and $\sqsubset$ appears on top of Stk. We are thus reading the elements of an array. Hence R is updated to $R_{Upd} = \{(p,q) \mid \exists(p,q') \in R, (q',a,q) \in \delta_i\}$. Again we proceed as in the proof of Theorem 1.

Case (3) Suppose that a is the symbol $\sqsupset$. This means that we finished reading an array. If the stack is empty or its top element contains $\prec$, then $w \notin \mathcal{L}(S)$ and we stop the algorithm. Otherwise $(R', \sqsubset)$ is popped from Stk and R is updated to $R_{Upd} = \{(p,q) \mid \exists(p,p') \in R', (p', \sqsubset, q_0, \gamma) \in \delta_c, (q_0, r) \in R, (r, \sqsupset, \gamma, q) \in \delta_r\}$, as in the proof of Theorem 1.

Case (4) Suppose that a is the symbol $\prec$.

---

[13]In the particular case of the object $\prec\succ$, the 5-tuple $(R, \prec, K, k, Bad)$ is replaced by $(R, \prec)$. This situation will be clarified during the presentation of our algorithm.

[14]Note that the algorithm assumes we have a 1-SEVPA.

– Let us first consider the particular case where the symbol b following $\prec$ is equal to $\succ$, meaning that we will read the object $\prec\succ$. In this case, $(R, \prec)$ is pushed on Stk and R is updated to $R_{Upd} = \mathbb{I}_{\{q_0\}}$ as in Case (1).

– Otherwise, if b belongs to Σ_{key}, we begin to read a (non-empty) object whose treatment is different from that of an array as its key-value pairs can be read in any order. Then, R is updated to $R_{Upd} = \mathbb{I}_{P_b}$ where $P_b = \{p \in Q \mid \exists (p, b, p') \in G_{\mathcal{A}}\}$, and $(R, \prec, K, b, Bad)$ is pushed on Stk such that K is the singleton $\{b\}$ and Bad is the empty set. The 5-tuple pushed on Stk indicates that the key-value pair that will be read next begins with key b; moreover $K = \{b\}$ because this is the first pair of the object. The meaning of Bad will be clarified later. The updated set R_{Upd} is equal to the identity relation on P_b since after reading $\prec$, we will start reading a key-value pair whose abstracted state in $G_{\mathcal{A}}$ can be any state from P_b. Later while reading the object whose reading is here started, we will update the 5-tuple on top of Stk as explained below.

– Finally, it remains to consider the case where $b \notin \Sigma_{\text{key}} \cup \{\succ\}$. In this final case, we have that $w \notin \mathcal{L}(S)$ and we stop the algorithm.

Case (5) Suppose that $a \in \Sigma_i \setminus \{\#\}$ and $\prec$ appears on top of Stk. Therefore, we are currently reading a key-value pair of an object. Then R is updated to $R_{Upd} = \{(p, q) \mid \exists (p, q') \in R, (q', a, q) \in \delta_i\}$.

Case (6) Suppose that a is the symbol $\#$ and $\prec$ appears on top of Stk. This means that we just finished reading a key-value pair whose key k is stored in the 5-tuple $(R', \prec, K, k, Bad)$ on top of Stk, and that another key-value pair will be read after symbol $\#$. The set K in $(R', \prec, K, k, Bad)$ stores all the keys of the key-values pairs already read including k.

– If the symbol b following $\#$ does not belong to Σ_{key}, then $w \notin \mathcal{L}(S)$ and we stop the algorithm.

– Otherwise, if b belongs to K, this means that the object contains twice the same key, that is, $w \notin \mathcal{L}(S)$, and we also stop the algorithm.

– Otherwise, the set R is updated to $R_{Upd} = \mathbb{I}_{P_b}$ (as we begin the reading of a new key-value pair whose key is b) and the 5-tuple $(R', \prec, K, k, Bad)$ on top of Stk is updated such that (i) K is replaced by $K \cup \{b\}$, (ii) k is replaced by b, and (iii) all vertices (p, k, p') of $G_{\mathcal{A}}$ such that $(p, p') \notin R$ are added to the set Bad. Recall that the vertex (p, k, p') of $G_{\mathcal{A}}$ is a witness of a path $\langle p, \varepsilon \rangle \xrightarrow{kv} \langle p', \varepsilon \rangle$ in $T_{\mathcal{A}}$ for some key-value pair kv. Hence by adding this vertex (p, k, p') to Bad, we mean that the pair that has just been read does not use such a path.

Case (7) Suppose that a is the symbol $\succ$. Therefore we end the reading of an object. If the stack is empty or its top element contains $\sqsubset$, then $w \notin \mathcal{L}(S)$ and we stop the algorithm. Otherwise the top of Stk contains either $(R', \prec)$ or $(R', \prec, K, k, Bad)$ that we pop from Stk.

– If $(R', \prec)$ is popped, then we are ending the reading of the object $\prec\succ$. Hence, we proceed as in Case (3): R is updated to $R_{Upd} = \{(p, q) \mid \exists (p, p') \in R', (p', \prec, q_0, \gamma) \in \delta_c, (q_0, \succ, \gamma, q) \in \delta_r\}$.[15]

---

[15]Notice that R does not appear in R_{Upd} as $R = \mathbb{I}_{\{q_0\}}$.

– If $(R', \prec, K, k, Bad)$ is popped, we are ending an object whose last seen key is k. As in Case (6), we add to Bad all vertices (p, k, p') such that $(p, p') \notin R$. Let $\text{Valid}(K, Bad)$ be the set of pairs of states (q_0, r') such that there exists a path $((p_1, k_1, p'_1) \ldots (p_n, k_n, p'_n))$ in $G_{\mathcal{A}}$ with $p_1 = q_0$, $p'_n = r'$, $(p_i, k_i, p'_i) \notin Bad$ for all $i \in \{1, \ldots, n\}$, and $K = \{k_1, \ldots, k_n\}$. Then R is updated to $R_{Upd} = \{(p, q) \mid \exists (p, p') \in R', (p', \prec, q_0, \gamma) \in \delta_c, (q_0, r) \in \text{Valid}(K, Bad), (r, \succ, \gamma, q) \in \delta_r\}$. We thus proceed as in Case (3) except that condition $(r', r) \in R$ is replaced by $(r', r) \in \text{Valid}(K, Bad)$. That way, we check that the key-value pairs that have been read as composing an object of w label some path in $T_{\mathcal{A}}$, once ordered by $<$. That is, the corresponding abstract path appears in $G_{\mathcal{A}}$.

Case (8) Suppose that $a \in \Sigma_i$ and Stk is empty, then $w \notin \mathcal{L}(S)$ and we stop the algorithm. Indeed an internal symbol appears either in an array or in an object (see Cases (2), (5), and (6) above).

Finally, when the input word w is completely read, we check whether the stack Stk is empty and the computed set R contains a pair (q_0, q) with $q \in Q_F$. The complexity of our algorithm is given in the following proposition.

Proposition 1. *Let S be a schema and $\mathcal{A}$ be a 1-SEVPA such that $\mathcal{L}(\mathcal{A}) = \mathcal{L}_<(S)$. Deciding if a document J is valid is in time $\mathcal{O}(|J| \cdot (|Q|^4 + |Q|^{|\Sigma_{\text{key}}|} \cdot |\Sigma_{\text{key}}|^{|\Sigma_{\text{key}}|+1}))$, and uses $\mathcal{O}(|\delta| + |Q|^2 \cdot |\Sigma_{\text{key}}| + d(J) \cdot (|Q|^2 + |\Sigma_{\text{key}}|))$ memory.*

5   Implementation and Experiments

We present here our Java implementation of the learning process and the validation algorithm. First, we present classical validation algorithms and explain how to generate documents from a schema. We then explain how the required membership and equivalence queries are implemented. Finally, we present the schemas we evaluated, and the results for the learning, computation of the key graph, and validation experiments. The reader is referred to the code documentation for more details about our implementation [27–31].

In the remaining of this section, let us assume we have a JSON schema S_0.

Classical Validation Algorithm and Documents Generation Let us explain briefly the *classical* algorithm used in many implementations for validating a JSON document J_0 against S_0 [13]. It is a recursive algorithm that follows the constraints of S_0.[16] For instance, if the current value J is an object, we iterate over each key-value pair in J and its corresponding sub-schema in the current schema S. Then, J satisfies S if and only if the values in the key-value pairs all satisfy their corresponding sub-schema. As long as S_0 does not contain any Boolean operations, this algorithm is straightforward and linear in the size of both the initial document J_0 and schema S_0. However, if S_0 contains Boolean operations, then the current value J may be processed multiple times.

---

[16]Such a recursive algorithm is briefly presented in [19].

In order to match the abstractions we defined (see Section 3) and to have options to tune the learning process, we implemented our own classical validator. Alongside the validator, we implemented a tool to generate JSON documents whose structure is dictated by S_0. Due to the Boolean operations S_0 can contain, it may happen that choices must be made during the generation process. We have two generators: a *random* generator that makes a choice at random, and an *exhaustive* generator that exhaustively explores every choice, thus producing every valid document one by one. Moreover, we implemented modifications of these generators to allow the creation of invalid documents, by allowing *deviations*.[17] For instance, if the current schema describes an integer, we can instead decide to generate a string. To ensure we eventually produce a document, we can fix a *maximal depth* (i.e., the maximal number of nested objects or arrays). This is useful for recursive schemas, or when generating invalid documents.

Learning Algorithm Let us now focus on the learning algorithm itself, and in particular on the membership and equivalence queries. We recall that the equivalence queries are performed by generating a certain number of (valid and invalid) JSON documents and by verifying that the learned VPA $\mathcal{H}$ and the given schema S_0 agree on the documents' validity. As said in Section 2, we use the TTT algorithm [9] to learn a 1-SEVPA from S_0, relying on its implementation in the well-known Java libraries LEARNLIB and AUTOMATALIB [11].

We use the random and exhaustive generators of valid and invalid documents as explained above and we fix two constants C and D depending on the schema to be learned.[18] For a *membership* query over a word $w \in \Sigma^*_{\text{JSON}}$, the teacher runs the classical validator on w and S_0. For an *equivalence* query over a learned 1-SEVPA $\mathcal{H}$, the teacher uses a generator to produce documents on which $\mathcal{H}$ is tested. If that generator is random, at each query, C documents are generated for each document depth between 0 and D. If none of the documents leads to a counterexample, the teacher checks whether $G_{\mathcal{H}}$ does not satisfy Lemma 1, i.e., whether there is path $((p_1, k_1, p'_1) \ldots (p_n, k_n, p'_n))$ with $p_1 = q_0$ such that $k_i = k_j$ for some $i \neq j$. In that case, we can create a counterexample.

Evaluated Schemas For the experimental evaluation of our algorithms, we consider the following schemas, sorted in increasing size: (1) A schema that accepts documents defined recursively. Each object contains a string and can contain an array whose single element satisfies the whole schema, i.e., this is a recursive list. (2) A schema that accepts documents containing each type of values, i.e., an object, an array, a string, a number, an integer, and a Boolean. (3) A schema that defines how snippets must be described in *Visual Studio Code* [23]. (4) A recursive schema that defines how the metadata files for *VIM plugins* must be written [22]. (5) A schema that defines how *Azure Functions Proxies* files must look like [20]. (6) A schema that defines the configuration file

---

[17]This is similar to mutation testing [1, 12].
[18]The values of C and D are given below.

for a code coverage tool called *codecov* [21]. Hence, we consider two schemas written by ourselves to test our framework, and four schemas that are used in real world cases. The last four schemas were modified to make all object keys mandatory and to remove unsupported keywords. All used schemas and scripts can be consulted on our repository [30]. In the rest of this section, the schemas are referred to by their order in the previous enumeration.

We present three types of experimental results: (1) the time and number of membership and equivalence queries to learn a 1-SEVPA $\mathcal{A}$ from a JSON schema, (2) the time and memory to compute the reachability relation $\text{Reach}_{\mathcal{A}}$ and the key graph $G_{\mathcal{A}}$, and (3) the time and memory to validate a document using both classical and new algorithms. The server used for the benchmarks ran OpenJDK version 11.0.12 on Debian 10 over Linux 5.4.73-1-pve with a 4-core Intel® Xeon® Silver 4214R Processor with 16.5M cache, and 64GB of RAM.

Learning VPAs First, we learn a 1-SEVPA from a schema. We use an exhaustive generator for the first three schemas (accepting a small set of documents), and a random generator[19] for the remaining three for which we fix $C = 10000$. For both generators, we set $D = depth(S) + 1$, where $depth(S)$ is the maximal number of nested objects and arrays in the schema S, except for the recursive list where $D = 10$, and for the recursive *VIM plugin* schema where $D = 7$.

For the first five schemas, we do not set a time limit and repeat the learning process ten times. For the last schema, we set a time limit of one week and, for time constraints, only perform the learning process once. After that, we stop the computation and retrieve the learned 1-SEVPA at that point. The retrieved automaton is therefore an approximation of this schema. Its key graph has repeated keys along some of its paths, a situation that cannot occur if the 1-SEVPA was correctly learned, see Lemma 1. Results are given in Table 1.

Comparing Validation Algorithms The second part of the preprocessing step is to construct the key graph of the learned 1-SEVPA. For each evaluated schema, we select the learned automaton with the largest set of states, in order to report a worst-case measure. Results after a single experiment are given in Table 2. We can see that the storage of the key graph does not consume more than one megabyte, except for *codecov* schema. That is, even for non-trivial schemas, the key graph is relatively lightweight.

Finally, we compare both classical and new streaming validation algorithms. For the latter, we use the 1-SEVPA (and its key graph) selected as described above. We first generate 5000 valid and 5000 invalid JSON documents using a random generator, with a maximal depth equal to $D = 20$. We then measure the time and memory required by both validation algorithms on these documents.[20]

---

[19]With the random generator, the learned 1-SEVPAS may differ each experiment.

[20]Since obtaining a close approximation of the consumed memory requires Java to stop the execution and destroy all unused objects, we execute each algorithm twice: once to measure time, and a second time to measure memory.

Time (s)	Membership	Equivalence	$|Q|$	$|\Sigma|$	$|\delta_c|$	$|\delta_r|$	$|\delta_i|$	Diameter
2.2	2055.0		5.0	7.0	15.0	14.0	3.0	5.0	3.0
4.5	69514.0		3.0	24.0	20.0	48.0	3.0	26.0	12.0
9.0	21943.0		5.0	16.0	17.0	32.0	7.0	18.0	13.0
9590.3	4246085.0		36.4	150.0	27.0	300.0	2946.5	760.3	9.0
35008.2	4063971.7		30.5	121.0	35.0	242.0	2123.0	752.5	13.3
Timeout	633049534.0		192.0	884.0	77.0	1768.0	89695.0	8557.0	28.0

Table 1: Learning results. For the first five schemas, values are averaged out of ten experiments. For the last schema, a single experiment was conducted.

	Reach$_\mathcal{A}$			G$_\mathcal{A}$		
Time (s)	Memory (kB)	Size	Time (s)	Computation (kB)	Storage (kB)	Size
34	492	31	100	2231	65	3
67	1152	213	234	2623	69	9
67	737	125	118	2223	69	10
1756	10316	5832	1715	11827	419	418
2208	13978	4420	2839	17968	667	541
377141	212970	270886	187659	120398	16335	6397

Table 2: Results for the computation of Reach$_\mathcal{A}$ and G$_\mathcal{A}$. The Computation (resp. Storage) column gives the memory required to compute G$_\mathcal{A}$ (resp. to store G$_\mathcal{A}$).

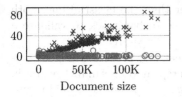

(a) Time usage (ms) for *VIM plugins*.

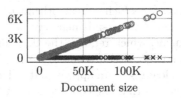

(b) Mem. usage (kB) for *VIM plugins*.

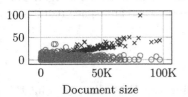

(c) Time usage for *Azure*.

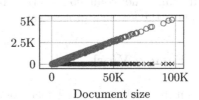

(d) Mem. usage for *Azure*.

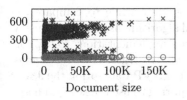

(e) Time usage for *codecov*.

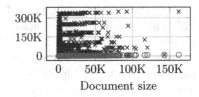

(f) Mem. usage for *codecov*.

Fig. 3: Results of validation benchmarks.

On all considered documents, both algorithms return the same classification output, even for the partially learned 1-SEVPA.

For our algorithm, we only measure the memory required to execute the algorithm, as we do not need to store the whole document to be able to process it. We also do not count the memory to store the 1-SEVPA and its key graph. As the classical algorithm must have the complete document stored in memory, we sum the RAM consumption for the document and for the algorithm itself. This is coherent to what happens in actual web-service handling: Whenever a new validation request is received, we would spawn a new subprocess that handles a specific document. Since the 1-SEVPA and its key graph are the same for all subprocesses, they would be loaded in a memory space shared by all processes.

Experimental results indicate that our algorithm exhibits good performance. Results for the three smaller schemas are not presented here to save space, while they are given in Figure 3 for *VIM plugins*, *Azure Functions Proxies*, and *codecov*. The blue (resp. red) crosses (resp. circles) give the values for our (resp. the classical) algorithm. The x-axis gives the size of each (abstracted) document.

For both *VIM plugins* and *Azure Functions Proxies*, our algorithm consumes less memory than the classical one. For these benchmarks, memory and time usage seemingly trade off as we see that our algorithm usually requires more time to validate a document — a majority of that time is spent computing the set Valid(K, Bad). This tradeoff, however, does not hold in general: There are schemas for which our algorithm performs better than the classical one, both in terms of time and memory, as it does not have to backtrack to validate a document, which reduces the time and memory space required.

For the *codecov* schema, we recall that the learning process was not completed, leading to an approximated 1-SEVPA with repeated keys in its key graph. This means that the computation of Valid(K, Bad) explores some invalid paths, increasing the memory and time consumed by our algorithm. Thus, it appears that, while a not completely learned 1-SEVPA can still be used in our algorithm, stopping the learning process early may increase the time and space required.

6   Future Work

As future work, one could focus on constructing the VPA directly from the schema, without going through a learning algorithm. While this task is easy if the schema does not contain Boolean operations, it is not yet clear how to proceed in the general case. Second, it could be worthwhile to compare our algorithm against an implementation of a classical algorithm used in the industry. This would require either to modify the industrial implementations to support abstractions, or to modify our algorithm to work on unabstracted JSON schemas. Third, in our validation approach, we decided to use a VPA accepting the JSON documents satisfying a fixed key order — thus requiring to use the key graph and its costly computation of the set Valid(K, Bad). It could be interesting to make additional experiments to compare this approach with one where we instead use a VPA accepting the JSON documents and all their key permutations — in this case, reasoning on the key graph would no longer be needed. Finally, motivated by obtaining efficient querying algorithms on XML trees, the authors of [26] have introduced the concept of mixed automata in a way to accept subsets of unranked trees where some nodes have ordered sons and some other have unordered sons. It would be interesting to adapt our validation algorithm to different formalisms of documents, such as the one of mixed automata.

Data-Availability Statement. The source code and experimental results that support the findings of this study are available in Zenodo with the identifier https://doi.org/10.5281/zenodo.7309690 [31].

References

1. Richard A. DeMillo, Richard J. Lipton, Frederick G. Sayward: Hints on Test Data Selection: Help for the Practicing Programmer. Computer **11**(4), 34–41 (1978). https://doi.org/10.1109/C-M.1978.218136
2. Rajeev Alur, Viraj Kumar, Madhusudan, P., Mahesh Viswanathan: Congruences for Visibly Pushdown Languages. In: Luís Caires, Giuseppe F. Italiano, Luís Monteiro, Catuscia Palamidessi, Moti Yung (eds.) Automata, Languages and Programming, 32nd International Colloquium, ICALP 2005, Lisbon, Portugal, July 11-15, 2005, Proceedings. Lecture Notes in Computer Science, vol. 3580, pp. 1102–1114. Springer (2005). https://doi.org/10.1007/11523468_89
3. Rajeev Alur, Madhusudan, P.: Visibly pushdown languages. In: László Babai (ed.) Proceedings of the 36th Annual ACM Symposium on Theory of Computing, Chicago, IL, USA, June 13-16, 2004. pp. 202–211. ACM (2004). https://doi.org/10.1145/1007352.1007390
4. Dana Angluin: Learning Regular Sets from Queries and Counterexamples. Inf. Comput. **75**(2), 87–106 (1987). https://doi.org/10.1016/0890-5401(87)90052-6
5. Iovka Boneva, Radu Ciucanu, Slawek Staworko: Schemas for Unordered XML on a DIME. Theory Comput. Syst. **57**(2), 337–376 (2015). https://doi.org/10.1007/s00224-014-9593-1
6. Tim Bray: The JavaScript Object Notation (JSON) Data Interchange Format. RFC **8259**, 1–16 (2017). https://doi.org/10.17487/RFC8259
7. Véronique Bruyère, Guillermo A. Pérez, Gaëtan Staquet: Learning Realtime One-Counter Automata. In: Dana Fisman, Grigore Rosu (eds.) International Conference on Tools and Algorithms for the Construction and Analysis of Systems. Lecture Notes in Computer Science, vol. 13243, pp. 244–262. Springer (2022). https://doi.org/10.1007/978-3-030-99524-9_13
8. John E. Hopcroft, Jeffrey D. Ullman: Introduction to Automata Theory, Languages and Computation, Second Edition. Addison-Wesley (2000)
9. Malte Isberner: Foundations of active automata learning: an algorithmic perspective. Ph.D. thesis, Technical University Dortmund, Germany (2015), http://hdl.handle.net/2003/34282
10. Malte Isberner, Falk Howar, Bernhard Steffen: The TTT Algorithm: A Redundancy-Free Approach to Active Automata Learning. In: Borzoo Bonakdarpour, Scott A. Smolka (eds.) Runtime Verification - 5th International Conference, RV 2014, Toronto, ON, Canada, September 22-25, 2014. Proceedings. Lecture Notes in Computer Science, vol. 8734, pp. 307–322. Springer (2014). https://doi.org/10.1007/978-3-319-11164-3_26

11. Isberner, M., Howar, F., Steffen, B.: The Open-Source LearnLib. In: Kroening, D., Păsăreanu, C.S. (eds.) Computer Aided Verification. pp. 487–495. Springer International Publishing, Cham (2015)

12. Yue Jia, Mark Harman: An Analysis and Survey of the Development of Mutation Testing. IEEE Trans. Software Eng. **37**(5), 649–678 (2011). https://doi.org/10.1109/TSE.2010.62

13. JSON Schema: JSON Schema website. Online (2015), https://json-schema.org

14. JSON.org: JSON.org website. Online (2013), https://www.json.org

15. Viraj Kumar, Madhusudan, P., Mahesh Viswanathan: Visibly pushdown automata for streaming XML. In: Carey L. Williamson, Mary Ellen Zurko, Peter F. Patel-Schneider, Prashant J. Shenoy (eds.) Proceedings of the 16th International Conference on World Wide Web, WWW 2007, Banff, Alberta, Canada, May 8-12, 2007. pp. 1053–1062. ACM (2007). https://doi.org/10.1145/1242572.1242714

16. Wim Martens, Frank Neven, Matthias Niewerth, Thomas Schwentick: BonXai: Combining the Simplicity of DTD with the Expressiveness of XML Schema. ACM Trans. Database Syst. **42**(3), 15:1–15:42 (2017). https://doi.org/10.1145/3105960

17. Maik Merten, Bernhard Steffen, Falk Howar, Tiziana Margaria: Next Generation LearnLib. In: Parosh Aziz Abdulla, Rustan M. Leino, K. (eds.) Tools and Algorithms for the Construction and Analysis of Systems - 17th International Conference, TACAS 2011, Held as Part of the Joint European Conferences on Theory and Practice of Software, ETAPS 2011, Saarbrücken, Germany, March 26-April 3, 2011. Proceedings. Lecture Notes in Computer Science, vol. 6605, pp. 220–223. Springer (2011). https://doi.org/10.1007/978-3-642-19835-9_18

18. Matthias Niewerth, Thomas Schwentick: Reasoning About XML Constraints Based on XML-to-Relational Mappings. Theory Comput. Syst. **62**(8), 1826–1879 (2018). https://doi.org/10.1007/s00224-018-9846-5

19. Felipe Pezoa, Juan L. Reutter, Fernando Suárez, Martín Ugarte, Domagoj Vrgoc: Foundations of JSON Schema. In: Jacqueline Bourdeau, Jim Hendler, Roger Nkambou, Ian Horrocks, Ben Y. Zhao (eds.) Proceedings of the 25th International Conference on World Wide Web, WWW 2016, Montreal, Canada, April 11 - 15, 2016. pp. 263–273. ACM (2016). https://doi.org/10.1145/2872427.2883029

20. Schema for Azure Functions Proxies. Online, https://json.schemastore.org/proxies.json

21. Schema for codecov configuration. Online, https://json.schemastore.org/codecov.json

22. Schema for VIM plugins. Online, https://json.schemastore.org/vim-addon-info.json

23. Schema for Visual Studio Code snippets. Online, https://raw.githubusercontent.com/Yash-Singh1/vscode-snippets-json-schema/main/schema.json

24. Thomas Schwentick: Foundations of XML Based on Logic and Automata: A Snapshot. In: Thomas Lukasiewicz, Attila Sali (eds.) Foundations of Information and Knowledge Systems - 7th International Symposium, FoIKS 2012, Kiel, Germany, March 5-9, 2012. Proceedings. Lecture Notes in Computer Science, vol. 7153, pp. 23–33. Springer (2012). https://doi.org/10.1007/978-3-642-28472-4_2

25. Luc Segoufin, Victor Vianu: Validating Streaming XML Documents. In: Lucian Popa, Serge Abiteboul, Phokion G. Kolaitis (eds.) Proceedings of the Twenty-first ACM SIGACT-SIGMOD-SIGART Symposium on Principles of Database Systems, June 3-5, Madison, Wisconsin, USA. pp. 53–64. ACM (2002). https://doi.org/10.1145/543613.543622

26. Helmut Seidl, Thomas Schwentick, Anca Muscholl: Counting in trees. In: Jörg Flum, Erich Grädel, Thomas Wilke (eds.) Logic and Automata: History and Perspectives [in Honor of Wolfgang Thomas]. Texts in Logic and Games, vol. 2, pp. 575–612. Amsterdam University Press (2008)

27. Staquet, G.: AutomataLib, https://github.com/DocSkellington/automatalib

28. Staquet, G.: JSON Schema Tools, https://github.com/DocSkellington/JSONSchemaTools

29. Staquet, G.: LearnLib, https://github.com/DocSkellington/learnlib

30. Staquet, G.: Validating JSON Documents With Learned VPA, https://github.com/DocSkellington/ValidatingJSONDocumentsWithLearnedVPA

31. Staquet, G.: Validating Streaming JSON Documents with Learned VPAs (Nov 2022). https://doi.org/10.5281/zenodo.7309689

32. Nguyen Van Tang: A Tighter Bound for the Determinization of Visibly Pushdown Automata. In: Axel Legay (ed.) Proceedings International Workshop on Verification of Infinite-State Systems, INFINITY 2009, Bologna, Italy, 31th August 2009. EPTCS, vol. 10, pp. 62–76 (2009). https://doi.org/10.4204/EPTCS.10.5

Antichains Algorithms for the Inclusion Problem Between ω-VPL[*]

Kyveli Doveri[1,2]([⊠])[iD], Pierre Ganty[1][iD], and Luka Hadži-Đokić[1]

[1] IMDEA Software Institute, Madrid, Spain
{kyveli.doveri,pierre.ganty,luka.hadzi-dokic}@imdea.org
[2] Universidad Politécnica de Madrid, Madrid, Spain

Abstract. We define novel algorithms for the inclusion problem between two visibly pushdown languages of infinite words, an EXPTIME-complete problem. Our algorithms search for counterexamples to inclusion in the form of ultimately periodic words i.e. words of the form uv^ω where u and v are finite words. They are parameterized by a pair of quasiorders telling which ultimately periodic words need not be tested as counterexamples to inclusion without compromising completeness. The pair of quasiorders enables distinct reasoning for prefixes and periods of ultimately periodic words thereby allowing to discard even more words compared to using the same quasiorder for both. We put forward two families of quasiorders: the state-based quasiorders based on automata and the syntactic quasiorders based on languages. We also implemented our algorithm and conducted an empirical evaluation on benchmarks from software verification.

1 Introduction

Visibly pushdown languages [4] (VPL) have applications in various domains including verification [22], theorem proving [27] or XML schema languages reasoning [26] where the inclusion problem plays a crucial role. For instance proving correctness relative to a specification reduces to a language inclusion problem and so does proving correctness of a theorem of the form $\forall x \exists y P(x) \implies Q(y)$. The extension to the case of visibly pushdown languages of infinite words (ω-VPL) has also been studied in the context of program verification [21] and it has applications in word combinatorics [23,25,27].

We distinguish two general approaches to solve the language inclusion problem $L \subseteq M$: (i) complement M, intersect with L and check for emptiness of the result; and (ii) reduce the inclusion check to finitely many *membership queries* asking whether $w \in M$ holds where $w \in L$ and each query aims at finding a counterexample to inclusion.

[*] This work was partially funded by the ESF Investing in your future, the RYC-2016-20281/MCIN/AEI/10.13039/501100011033, the Madrid regional government as part of the program S2018/TCS-4339 (BLOQUES-CM) co-funded by EIE Funds of the European Union, the PRODIGY Project (TED2021-132464B-I00) funded by MCIN and the European Union NextGenerationEU/ PRTR.

S. Sankaranarayanan and N. Sharygina (Eds.): TACAS 2023, LNCS 13993, pp. 290–307, 2023.
https://doi.org/10.1007/978-3-031-30823-9_15

In this paper we focus on the second approach. Previous work in that space leverage relations between words to select a finite subset of words of L on which we run the membership queries. A class of relations that consistently yields good results in practice are *quasiorders* which discard words subsumed (for the quasiorder) by others. A key feature of such quasiorders is that the subset of L selected via the quasiorder must contain a counterexample to inclusion if there exists one. Quasiorders are a versatile heuristic that has been applied to inclusion problems for languages such as languages of finite words [3,10,14] (including visibly pushdown language [6]) or infinite words [1,2,12,13,16,24] and even tree languages [3,5]. Algorithms leveraging quasiorders are commonly referred to as *antichains algorithms*. Subsequent improvements (e.g. [2] improving [1]) often attempt at defining coarser quasiorders because they enable the selection of an even smaller subset of L.

Let us now turn to the inclusion problem between ω-VPL, an EXPTIME-complete problem. For that problem the selection of words of L is limited to *ultimately periodic words*, i.e. words of the form uv^ω, where u and v are called *prefix* and *period* respectively. For an ultimately periodic word uv^ω subsumption (for a quasiorder) simply means subsumption of (u, v) relative to a pair $\leqq_1 \times \leqq_2$ of quasiorders on finite words. The quasiorders found in the literature [17,18] are all equivalences and are all such that $\leqq_1 = \leqq_2$.

In this paper, we propose a new family of algorithms for the inclusion problem between ω-VPL that leverages a subset of the ultimately periodic words, deemed *legitimate decompositions* and is parameterized by a pair of quasiorders and a decision procedure for the membership queries in M. We identify properties that such pair of quasiorders must satisfy so that the resulting algorithm actually decides the inclusion problem between two ω-VPL: (1) be decidable; (2) be well-quasiorders; (3) verify some monotonicity conditions w.r.t. word operations that are characteristic to ω-VPL and (4) satisfy a preservation property intuitively saying that a legitimate decomposition inside M cannot subsume a legitimate decomposition outside of M. We put forward two families of quasiorders satisfying (1) thru (4): the *state-based quasiorders* whose definition rely on a visibly pushdown automaton underlying M and the *syntactic quasiorders* whose definition is based solely on M. The syntactic orders are the "ideal" quasiorders in the sense they are the coarsest, hence they select the "smallest" subset of L. None of our quasiorders is symmetric, hence they are coarser than equivalences and in each and every pair we define the quasiorder on prefixes differs from the one on periods (i.e. $\leqq_1 \neq \leqq_2$). We further prove that when instantiated with the state-based quasiorders and with a state-based decision procedure for membership queries the resulting algorithm, which we call the *state-based algorithm*, has a runtime that matches the corresponding problem complexity.

Finally we implement the state-based algorithm and evaluate it on various benchmarks collected from Friedmann et al. [18] and from SV-COMP[3], the Software Verification competition. The empirical evaluation is carried out against Ultimate [21] which follows a complement, intersect and check for emptiness

---

[3] https://sv-comp.sosy-lab.org

approach. The preliminary conclusion of the empirical results is in favor of our approach as it scales up better.

Related Work. Bruyere et al. [6] proposed an antichain algorithm for the inclusion of VPL but they only tackle the problem for languages of finite words. The same limitation applies to Ganty et al. [19,20] where, moreover, they do not tackle the inclusion problem of VPL into VPL (the closest they tackle is CFL into regular). The extension from the finite to the infinite case was tackled in Doveri et al. [13] but they do not cover the case ω-VPL into ω-VPL (the closest they tackle is ω-CFL into ω-regular). Friedmann et al. [17,18] do tackle the ω-VPL into ω-VPL problem. However they do not leverage the full power of quasiorders (they use equivalence instead); they do not use distinct pruning techniques for prefix and periods; and they do not put forward syntactic quasiorders. A summary comparing our work (omegaVPLinc) with the closest works in the area is given at Table 1.

Table 1. Comparison of the closest work in the area based on the characteristics of the problem tackled (first two columns) and the techniques used (last three columns). N/A means non applicable, $\bigcirc$ means no support and $\bullet$ means full support. The labels ω, VPL, qo, $\leq_1 \neq \leq_2$ and syntactic qo ask respectively whether the work thereof tackles the problem of infinite words, tackles the problem of VPL, leverage quasiorders, defines distinct quasiorders for prefixes and periods, and defines syntactic quasiorders.

	ω	VPL	qo	$\leq_1 \neq \leq_2$	syntactic qo
Bruyere et al. [6]	$\bigcirc$	$\bullet$	$\bullet$	N/A	$\bigcirc$
Ganty et al. [20]	$\bigcirc$	$\bigcirc$	$\bullet$	N/A	$\bullet$
Doveri et al. [13]	$\bullet$	$\bigcirc$	$\bullet$	$\bullet$	$\bigcirc$
Friedmann et al. [18]	$\bullet$	$\bullet$	$\bigcirc$	$\bigcirc$	$\bigcirc$
omegaVPLinc	$\bullet$	$\bullet$	$\bullet$	$\bullet$	$\bullet$

2   Background

Fix $\Sigma \triangleq \Sigma_i \cup \Sigma_c \cup \Sigma_r$ an alphabet (a finite non empty set of symbols) comprising three disjoint alphabets. The set of finite words and the set of infinite words over Σ are denoted by Σ^* and Σ^ω respectively. We denote by ϵ the empty word and define $\Sigma^+ \triangleq \Sigma^* \backslash \{\epsilon\}$. Given a word $u = u_0 u_1 \cdots \in \Sigma^* \cup \Sigma^\omega$ we say that a position j where $j \in \mathbb{N}$, $j < |u|$ and $|u| \in \mathbb{N} \cup \{\omega\}$ is the length of u, is an *internal* (resp. *call*, resp. *return*) position if $u_j \in \Sigma_i$ (resp. $u_j \in \Sigma_c$, resp. $u_j \in \Sigma_r$).

Visibly Pushdown Languages. A Visibly Pushdown Automaton (VPA) over Σ is a tuple $\mathcal{A} = (Q, q_I, \Gamma, \delta, F)$, where Q is a finite set of states including an initial state $q_I \in Q$, $F \subseteq Q$ is the set of final states, Γ is the stack alphabet including a bottom-of-stack symbol $\bot$ and $\delta = \delta_i \cup \delta_c \cup \delta_r$ consists of three transition relations $\delta_i \subseteq Q \times \Sigma_i \times Q$, $\delta_c \subseteq Q \times \Sigma_c \times Q \times \Gamma \backslash \{\bot\}$ and $\delta_r \subseteq Q \times \Sigma_r \times \Gamma \times Q$. *Configurations* in $\mathcal{A}$ are pairs in $Q \times \Gamma^*$. For $a \in \Sigma$ we define the relation $\vdash^a$ between configurations as follows:

- If $a \in \Sigma_i$ and $w \in \Gamma^*$ we have $(p, w) \vdash^a (q, w)$ if $(p, a, q) \in \delta_i$.
- If $a \in \Sigma_c$ and $w \in \Gamma^*$ we have $(p, w) \vdash^a (q, w\gamma)$ if $(p, a, q, \gamma) \in \delta_c$.
- If $a \in \Sigma_r, \gamma \in \Gamma \backslash \{\bot\}$ and $w \in \Gamma^*$ we have $(p, w\gamma) \vdash^a (q, w)$ if $(p, a, \gamma, q) \in \delta_r$.
- If $a \in \Sigma_r$ we have $(p, \bot) \vdash^a (q, \bot)$ if $(p, a, \bot, q) \in \delta_r$.

We lift the relation $\vdash$ to words by transitivity and reflexivity, that is, for all $u \in \Sigma^*$, $(q, w) \vdash^{*u} (p, w')$ when the configurations (q, w) and (p, w') are related by a sequence of transitions such that the concatenation of the corresponding labels is the word u. We write $(q, w) \vdash^{\otimes u} (p, w')$ when such a sequence includes a configuration whose state is final. A *trace* of $\mathcal{A}$ on a infinite word $\xi = a_0 a_1 \cdots \in \Sigma^\omega$ is an infinite sequence $(q_0, w_0) \vdash^{a_0} (q_1, w_1) \vdash^{a_1} \cdots$ It is a *final trace* when $q_j \in F$ for infinitely many j's. It is an *accepting trace* when it is a final trace and $(q_0, w_0) = (q_I, \bot)$. The ω-language accepted by $\mathcal{A}$ is $L^\omega(\mathcal{A}) \triangleq \{\xi \in \Sigma^\omega \mid$ there is an accepting trace of $\mathcal{A}$ on $\xi\}$. A language $L \subseteq \Sigma^\omega$ is ω-VPL if $L = L^\omega(\mathcal{A})$ for some VPA $\mathcal{A}$. Two examples of VPA are given at Fig. 1, $\mathcal{A}$ has an accepting trace on $c\,cr\,cr\,cr \ldots$ and so does $\mathcal{B}$ on $crr\,crr \ldots$

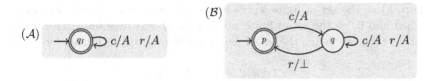

Fig. 1. Two ω-VPA with $\Gamma = \{A, \bot\}$, $\Sigma_i = \emptyset$, $\Sigma_c = \{c\}$ and $\Sigma_r = \{r\}$.

Ultimately Periodic Words. An *ultimately periodic word* is an infinite word $\xi \in \Sigma^\omega$ such that $\xi = uv^\omega$ for some finite *prefix* $u \in \Sigma^*$ and some finite *period* $v \in \Sigma^+$. We call the couple $(u, v) \in \Sigma^* \times \Sigma^+$ a *decomposition* of ξ. Note that ξ admits infinitely many decompositions.

Ultimately periodic words play a central role in our approach as they suffice for the inclusion problem as shown by the following theorem. [4]

Theorem 1. *Let* $L, M \subseteq \Sigma^\omega$ *be* ω-*VPL. Then,* $L \subseteq M$ *iff* $\forall uv^\omega \in L, uv^\omega \in M$.

Matching Relation. The partition of the alphabet $\Sigma = \Sigma_i \cup \Sigma_c \cup \Sigma_r$ induces a unique matching relation between a word's *call* and *return* positions (see [18]). Given $u \in \Sigma^* \cup \Sigma^\omega$ define the *matching relation* of u, denoted $\curvearrowright_u$, as the unique relation on its call and return positions such that for every $j \curvearrowright_u k$ we have $0 \le j < k < |u|$, $u_j \in \Sigma_c$, $u_k \in \Sigma_r$, $|\{n \mid j \curvearrowright_u n\}| \le 1$, $|\{n \mid n \curvearrowright_u k\}| \le 1$ and there are no j', k' with $j' \curvearrowright_u k'$ and $j < j' < k < k'$. Given $j \curvearrowright_u k$ we say that j and k are *matched* positions. A call (resp. return) position j in u is *unmatched*

---

[4] Theorem 1 can be easily obtained by adapting the proof of Fact 1 in [7].

if $j \curvearrowright_u k$ (resp. $k \curvearrowright_u j$) for no k. Furthermore, for every unmatched positions n in u there is no $j \curvearrowright_u k$ such that $j < n < k$, and if $u_n \in \Sigma_c$ (resp. $u_n \in \Sigma_r$) then there is no unmatched return (resp. call) position k with $n < k$ (resp. $k < n$). A word is said to be *well-matched* if it has no unmatched position.

3   Foundations

In this section we outline our approach which, given a VPA $\mathcal{A} = (Q, q_I, \Gamma, \delta, F)$ and an ω-VPL M, reduces the inclusion problem $L^\omega(\mathcal{A}) \subseteq M$ to finitely many membership queries in M. More precisely, we derive a finite subset S_{finite} of ultimately periodic words of $L^\omega(\mathcal{A})$ such that

$$L^\omega(\mathcal{A}) \subseteq M \iff \forall(u, v) \in S_{\text{finite}}, \ uv^\omega \in M \ . \tag{$\dagger$}$$

Reduction to Legitimate Decompositions. Our first step is to reduce the inclusion check to a subset of ultimately words of $L^\omega(\mathcal{A})$ given by legitimate decompositions. To do so, we define W as the set of well-matched finite words, C (resp. R) as the set of finite words where all call (resp. return) positions are matched and U_c as the set of finite words with at least one unmatched call position. In turn, we define the set of *legitimate decompositions* given by

$$\mathsf{Ld} \triangleq \mathsf{C} \times \mathsf{C} \ \cup \ \mathsf{U_c} \times \mathsf{R}$$

which, as shown next, is sufficient for the inclusion problem between ω-VPL.

Theorem 2. *Let* $L, M \subseteq \Sigma^\omega$ *be* ω-*VPL. Then,* $L \subseteq M$ *iff* $\forall(u, v) \in \mathsf{Ld}$, $uv^\omega \in L \implies uv^\omega \in M$.

Next we leverage the relations $\vdash^*$ and $\vdash^\circledast$ of $\mathcal{A}$ to characterize the legitimate decompositions of the ultimately periodic words of $L^\omega(\mathcal{A})$. We start by defining the following languages of finite words for each pair $p, q \in Q$ of state of $\mathcal{A}$: $L_{p,q} \triangleq \{u \in \Sigma^* \mid \exists w \in \Gamma^*, \ (p, \bot) \vdash^{*u} (q, w)\}$ and $L^\circledast_{p,q} \triangleq \{u \in \Sigma^+ \mid \exists w \in \Gamma^*, \ (p, \bot) \vdash^{\circledast u} (q, w)\}$. Finally, define the following subset of Ld:

$$S \triangleq \bigcup_{p \in Q} L_{q_I, p|\mathsf{C}} \times L^\circledast_{p,p|\mathsf{C}} \ \cup \ L_{q_I, p|\mathsf{U_c}} \times L^\circledast_{p,p|\mathsf{R}}$$

where $L_{|K}$ is defined to be $L \cap K$ to emphasize that L is restricted to K.

Example 1. Consider the VPA $\mathcal{A}$ and $\mathcal{B}$ depicted in Fig. 1. We have $L^\omega(\mathcal{A}) = \mathsf{R}^\omega$, $S = (\mathsf{W} \times \mathsf{W}\backslash\{\epsilon\}) \cup (\mathsf{R}\backslash\mathsf{C} \times \mathsf{R}\backslash\{\epsilon\})$ and $L^\omega(\mathcal{B}) = ((\mathsf{W}\backslash\{\epsilon\})r)^\omega$.

Proposition 1. *We have that* $uv^\omega \in L^\omega(\mathcal{A}) \iff \exists(u', v') \in S, \ uv^\omega = u'v'^\omega$.

By Theorem 2 and Proposition 1 the subset S verifies:

$$L^\omega(\mathcal{A}) \subseteq M \iff \forall(u, v) \in S, \ uv^\omega \in M \ . \tag{1}$$

Next we reduce the inclusion check to a finite subset of S using quasiorders.

Reduction to a Finite Basis. A *quasiorder* (qo) on a set E, is a reflexive and transitive relation $\bowtie \ \subseteq E \times E$. Given two subsets $X, Y \subseteq E$ the set Y is said to be a *basis* for X with respect to $\bowtie$ whenever $Y \subseteq X$ and $\forall x \in X, \exists y \in Y, y \bowtie x$. A qo $\bowtie$ is a *well-quasiorder* (wqo) if every subset of E admits a finite basis.

We obtain S_{finite} as a finite basis for S with respect to $\leqslant \times \preccurlyeq$ for a pair $\leqslant, \preccurlyeq$ of wqos.[5] To guarantee the direction $\Leftarrow$ in Eq. (†) we need the pair $\leqslant, \preccurlyeq$ to be *M-preserving*, a notion we introduce below.

A pair $\leqslant, \preccurlyeq$ of qos on Σ^* is said to be *M-preserving* if for all $(u, v), (u', v') \in \text{Ld}$ such that $(u, v), (u', v') \in \mathsf{C} \times \mathsf{C}$ or $(u, v), (u', v') \in \mathsf{U_c} \times \mathsf{R}$,

$$\text{if } uv^\omega \in M, u \leqslant u' \text{ and } v \preccurlyeq v' \text{ then } u'v'^\omega \in M \ .$$

Intuitively, M-preservation guarantees that if the inclusion does not hold then the finite basis S_{finite} contains a counterexample.

Next, we fix a pair of M-preserving wqos $\leqslant, \preccurlyeq$ and show the existence of a subset S_{finite} such that Eq. (†) holds. Since $\leqslant \times \preccurlyeq$ is a wqo, there exist two finite bases S_1 and S_2 for $S_{|\mathsf{C} \times \mathsf{C}}$ and $S_{|\mathsf{U_c} \times \mathsf{R}}$ respectively w.r.t. $\leqslant \times \preccurlyeq$. We define S_{finite} to be the union of such sets S_1, S_2, viz. $S_{\text{finite}} \triangleq S_1 \cup S_2 \subseteq S$. We have that: $\forall(u, v) \in S, \ uv^\omega \in M \implies \forall(u, v) \in S_{\text{finite}}, \ uv^\omega \in M$. We now turn to the converse implication. Assume that $\forall(u, v) \in S_{\text{finite}}, \ uv^\omega \in M$. Let $(u, v) \in S$. If $(u, v) \in S_{|\mathsf{C} \times \mathsf{C}}$ then there is $(u_0, v_0) \in S_1$ such that $(u_0, v_0) \leqslant \times \preccurlyeq (u, v)$. Since $S_1 \subseteq S_{|\mathsf{C} \times \mathsf{C}} \subseteq \mathsf{C} \times \mathsf{C}$ we have that $(u_0, v_0), (u, v) \in \mathsf{C} \times \mathsf{C}$. Since $u_0 v_0^\omega \in M$ and the pair $\leqslant, \preccurlyeq$ is M-preserving, we conclude that $uv^\omega \in M$. The case $(u, v) \in S_{|\mathsf{U_c} \times \mathsf{R}}$ proceeds analogously. It follows that $\forall(u, v) \in S, \ uv^\omega \in M \Longleftarrow \forall(u, v) \in S_{\text{finite}}, \ uv^\omega \in M$. Hence, we derive Equation (†) using Equation (1).

In Section 4, we give a fixpoint characterization of S and in Section 5 we show that under some monotonicity conditions on the wqos $\leqslant$ and $\preccurlyeq$ we can effectively compute a finite basis for S. We then give two examples of monotonic pairs of wqos in Section 6. In Section 7 we present our algorithm which given two VPA $\mathcal{A}$ and $\mathcal{B}$ decides the inclusion problem $L^\omega(\mathcal{A}) \subseteq L^\omega(\mathcal{B})$. Therein we discuss the state-based algorithm and give an upper bound on its running time. Finally in Section 8 we report on an empirical evaluation.

4 Fixpoint Characterization

In this section we give a least fixpoint characterization of S for the VPA $\mathcal{A} = (Q, q_I, \Gamma, \delta, F)$. To this end we work with the complete lattice $(\wp(\Sigma^*)^{n \cdot |Q|^2}, \subseteq \times \cdots \times \subseteq)$, where $n \in \{4, 6\}$ and each Cartesian product consists of $n \cdot |Q|^2$ factors.

For a function $f \colon E \to E$ on a quasiordered set $(E, \bowtie)$ and for all $n \in \mathbb{N}$, we define the *n*-th iterate $f^n \colon E \to E$ of f inductively as follows: $f^0 \triangleq \lambda x.x$; $f^{n+1} \triangleq f \circ f^n$. The denumerable sequence of *Kleene iterates* of f starting from the bottom value $\bot \in E$ is given by $\{f^n(\bot)\}_{n \in \mathbb{N}}$. Recall that when $(E, \bowtie)$ is a complete lattice and $f \colon E \to E$ is a monotone function (i.e. $d \bowtie d' \implies$

---

[5] The qo $\leqslant \times \preccurlyeq$ is a wqo when both $\leqslant$ and $\preccurlyeq$ are wqos.

$f(d) \ltimes f(d'))$ then by the Knaster–Tarski theorem, f has a least fixpoint lfp f given by the supremum of the ascending[6] sequence of Kleene iterates of f.

Given a $n \cdot |Q|^2$-dimensional vector X and a $|Q|^2$-dimensional vector Y on $\wp(\Sigma^*)$ we write $X_{i,p,q}$, for the (i, p, q)-component of X and $Y_{p,q}$ for the (p, q)-component of Y. We define the following equations where $X, X' \in \wp(\mathsf{W})^{|Q|^2}$, $Y, Y' \in \wp(\mathsf{C})^{|Q|^2}$, $Z, Z' \in \wp(\mathsf{R})^{|Q|^2}$, and $T \in \wp(\mathsf{U_c})^{|Q|^2}$:

$$W(X) = \langle L_{p,q \,|\, (\Sigma_i \cup \{\epsilon\})} \cup \bigcup_{\substack{(p,c,p',\gamma) \in \delta_c, \\ (q',r,\gamma,q) \in \delta_r}} cX_{p',q'}{}^r \cup \bigcup_{q' \in Q} X_{p,q'}\, X_{q',q} \rangle_{p,q \in Q}$$

$$C(X, Y) = \langle L_{p,q \,|\, \Sigma_r} \cup X_{p,q} \cup \bigcup_{q' \in Q} Y_{p,q'} Y_{q',q} \rangle_{p,q \in Q}$$

$$R(X, Z) = \langle L_{p,q \,|\, \Sigma_c} \cup X_{p,q} \cup \bigcup_{q' \in Q} Z_{p,q'} Z_{q',q} \rangle_{p,q \in Q}$$

$$U(Y, Z, T) = \langle L_{p,q \,|\, \Sigma_c} \cup \bigcup_{p',q' \in Q,} Y_{p,p'} T_{p',q'} Z_{q',q} \rangle_{p,q \in Q}$$

$$W_{\circledast}(X, X') = \langle L^{\circledast}_{p,q \,|\, \Sigma_i} \cup \bigcup_{\substack{(p,c,p',\gamma) \in \delta_c, \\ (q',r,\gamma,q) \in \delta_r, \\ \{p,q\} \cap F \neq \emptyset}} cX_{p',q'}{}^r \cup \bigcup_{\substack{(p,c,p',\gamma) \in \delta_c, \\ (q',r,\gamma,q) \in \delta_r, \\ \{p,q\} \cap F = \emptyset}} cX'_{p',q'}{}^r \cup \bigcup_{q' \in Q} (X'_{p,q'} X_{q',q} \cup X_{p,q'} X'_{q',q}) \rangle_{p,q \in Q}$$

$$C_{\circledast}(X', Y, Y') = \langle L^{\circledast}_{p,q \,|\, \Sigma_r} \cup X'_{p,q} \cup \bigcup_{q' \in Q} (Y'_{p,q'} Y_{q',q} \cup Y_{p,q'} Y'_{q',q}) \rangle_{p,q \in Q}$$

$$R_{\circledast}(X', Z, Z') = \langle L^{\circledast}_{p,q \,|\, \Sigma_c} \cup X'_{p,q} \cup \bigcup_{q' \in Q} (Z'_{p,q'} Z_{q',q} \cup Z_{p,q'} Z'_{q',q}) \rangle_{p,q \in Q} .$$

The equations W, C, R and U are used to obtain the set of words in W, C, R and $\mathsf{U_c}$ respectively, that connect two configurations of $\mathcal{A}$. The equations $W_{\circledast}$, $C_{\circledast}$ and $R_{\circledast}$ refine those of W, C and R by filtering out words not visiting final states. In turn we define the functions $f_{\mathcal{A}}$ and $r_{\mathcal{A}}$ used to obtain the prefixes u and the periods v respectively for the decompositions $(u, v) \in S$. Define

$$f_{\mathcal{A}} \colon \wp(\Sigma^*)^{4 \cdot |Q|^2} \longrightarrow \wp(\Sigma^*)^{4 \cdot |Q|^2}$$
$$(X, Y, Z, T) \longmapsto (W(X), C(X, Y), R(X, Z), U(Y, Z, T))$$

for the prefixes, and for the periods define

$$r_{\mathcal{A}} \colon \wp(\Sigma^*)^{6 \cdot |Q|^2} \longrightarrow \wp(\Sigma^*)^{6 \cdot |Q|^2}$$
$$(X, Y, Z, X', Y', Z') \longmapsto \big(W(X), C(X,Y), R(X,Z), W_{\circledast}(X,X'), C_{\circledast}(X',Y,Y'), R_{\circledast}(X',Z,Z')\big) .$$

The function $f_{\mathcal{A}}$ (resp. $r_{\mathcal{A}}$) is monotone and the supremum of the ascending sequence of its Kleene iterates starting at the bottom value $\vec{\emptyset} \triangleq (\emptyset, \dots, \emptyset)$ of dimension $4 \cdot |Q|^2$ (resp. $6 \cdot |Q|^2$) is the vector $(\Lambda_{|\mathsf{W}}, \Lambda_{|\mathsf{C}}, \Lambda_{|\mathsf{R}}, \Lambda_{|\mathsf{U_c}})$ (resp. $(\Lambda_{|\mathsf{W}}, \Lambda_{|\mathsf{C}}, \Lambda_{|\mathsf{R}},$ $\Lambda^{\circledast}_{|\mathsf{W}}, \Lambda^{\circledast}_{|\mathsf{C}}, \Lambda^{\circledast}_{|\mathsf{R}})$) where $\Lambda_{|\mathsf{J}} \triangleq \langle L_{p,q|\mathsf{J}} \rangle_{p,q \in Q}$ and $\Lambda^{\circledast}_{|\mathsf{J}} \triangleq \langle L^{\circledast}_{p,q|\mathsf{J}} \rangle_{p,q \in Q}$ for $\mathsf{J} \in \{\mathsf{W}, \mathsf{C}, \mathsf{R}, \mathsf{U_c}\}$. Therefore, by the Knaster–Tarski theorem we obtain the following proposition.

Proposition 2. lfp $f_{\mathcal{A}} = (\Lambda_{|\mathsf{W}}, \Lambda_{|\mathsf{C}}, \Lambda_{|\mathsf{R}}, \Lambda_{|\mathsf{U_c}})$ *and* lfp $r_{\mathcal{A}} = (\Lambda_{|\mathsf{W}}, \Lambda_{|\mathsf{C}}, \Lambda_{|\mathsf{R}}, \Lambda^{\circledast}_{|\mathsf{W}},$ $\Lambda^{\circledast}_{|\mathsf{C}}, \Lambda^{\circledast}_{|\mathsf{R}})$.

---

[6] A sequence $\{s_n\}_{n \in \mathbb{N}} \in E^{\mathbb{N}}$ on an ordered set $(E, \ltimes)$ is ascending if for every $n \in \mathbb{N}$ we have $s_n \ltimes s_{n+1}$.

Finally, by Proposition 2, we obtain the desired fixpoint characterization of S:

$$S = \bigcup_{p \in Q} \Big(\big((\text{lfp } f_A)_{2,q_I,p} \times (\text{lfp } r_A)_{5,p,p}\big) \cup \big((\text{lfp } f_A)_{4,q_I,p} \times (\text{lfp } r_A)_{6,p,p}\big) \Big) \ . \quad (2)$$

Example 2. We derive from the VPA A depicted in Fig. 1 the following functions

$$W(X) \triangleq \{\epsilon\} \cup cXr \cup XX, \qquad C(X,Y) \triangleq X \cup YY,$$
$$R(X,Z) \triangleq \{c\} \cup X \cup ZZ, \qquad U(Y,Z,T) \triangleq \{c\} \cup YTZ \ .$$

Hence, we obtain the function

$$f_A \colon \wp(\Sigma^*)^4 \longrightarrow \wp(\Sigma^*)^4$$
$$(X,Y,Z,T) \longmapsto (W(X), C(X,Y), R(X,Z), U(Y,Z,T)) \ .$$

The first three iterates of the least fixpoint computation of lfp f_A are given by

$$f_A(\vec{\emptyset}) = (\{\epsilon\}, \emptyset, \{c\}, \{c\}),$$
$$f_A{}^2(\vec{\emptyset}) = (\{\epsilon, cr\}, \{\epsilon\}, \{\epsilon, c, c^2\}, \{c\}),$$
$$f_A{}^3(\vec{\emptyset}) = (\{\epsilon, cr, c^2r^2, (cr)^2\}, \{\epsilon, cr\}, \{\epsilon, cr, c, c^2, c^3, c^4\}, \{c, c^2, c^3\})$$

$$\vdots$$

$$\text{lfp } f_A = (\mathsf{W}, \mathsf{W}, \mathsf{R}, \mathsf{R} \backslash \mathsf{C})$$

Since the unique state of A is a final state we have that $L_{q_I,q_I} = L^{\circledast}_{q_I,q_I}$. Consequently, the function f_A suffices to describe both the set of prefixes and the set of periods of S given by $\big((\text{lfp } f_A)_2 \times (\text{lfp } f_A)_2 \backslash \{\epsilon\}\big) \cup \big((\text{lfp } f_A)_4 \times (\text{lfp } f_A)_3 \backslash \{\epsilon\}\big)$.

Each (i, p, q)-component of the Kleene iterates of f_A and r_A keeps a finite set of words. However, if the language $L^{\omega}(A)$ is infinite, the fixpoint computations of lfp f_A and lfp r_A do not terminate in a finite number of steps. Nevertheless, under some monotonicity assumptions on our wqos we show in the following section that we can compute a finite basis for S w.r.t. $\leqslant \times \preccurlyeq$ as a terminating fixpoint computation.

5 Monotonicity Requirements

In order to detect finite bases among the Kleene iterates of the functions defined in the previous section we replace the set inclusion on $\wp(\Sigma^*)$, used so far, with the qo $\sqsubseteq_{\bowtie} \subseteq \wp(\Sigma^*) \times \wp(\Sigma^*)$ defined by $X \sqsubseteq_{\bowtie} Y \stackrel{\triangle}{\Longleftrightarrow} \forall x \in X, \exists y \in Y, y \bowtie x$. The qo $\sqsubseteq_{\bowtie}$ leverage the notion of basis: given $X \in \wp(\Sigma^*)$ a subset $Y \subseteq X$ is a basis for X with respect to $\bowtie$ whenever $X \sqsubseteq_{\bowtie} Y$.

In the following we lift the notion of basis to n-dimensional vectors component wise and work with the quasiordered sets $(\wp(\Sigma^*)^{n \cdot |Q|^2}, \sqsubseteq_{\bowtie}^{n \cdot |Q|^2})$, where $n \in \{4, 6\}$ and the ordering $\sqsubseteq_{\bowtie}^{n \cdot |Q|^2}$ is given by the product $\sqsubseteq_{\bowtie} \times \cdots \times \sqsubseteq_{\bowtie}$ of $n \cdot |Q|^2$

factors. Given a pair $\leqslant, \preccurlyeq$ of wqos, the orderings $\sqsubseteq_{\leqslant}^{4 \cdot |Q|^2}$ and $\sqsubseteq_{\preccurlyeq}^{6 \cdot |Q|^2}$ are used to compare the Kleene iterates of the functions $f_{\mathcal{A}}$ and $r_{\mathcal{A}}$ respectively. For them to be apt to detect finite bases for the least fixpoints of these functions the qos $\leqslant$ and $\preccurlyeq$ need to verify some monotonicity conditions.

We introduce the monotonicity conditions $\mathbf{W}, \mathbf{C}, \mathbf{R}, C_\odot, R_\odot$ and $\mathbf{U}$ on a qo $\ltimes \subseteq \Sigma^* \times \Sigma^*$ as follows: for all $u, u' \in \Sigma^*$ such that $u \ltimes u'$

> (**W**) if $u, u' \in \mathtt{W}$ and $c \in \Sigma_c, r \in \Sigma_r$ then $cur \ltimes cu'r$,
> (**C**) if $u, u' \in \mathtt{C}$ and $s \in \mathtt{C}$, $t \in \Sigma^*$ then $sut \ltimes su't$,
> (**R**) if $u, u' \in \mathtt{R}$ and $s \in \Sigma^*, t \in \mathtt{R}$ then $sut \ltimes su't$,
> (**U**) if $u, u' \in \mathtt{U}_c$ and $s \in \mathtt{C}$, $t \in \mathtt{R}$ then $sut \ltimes su't$,
> ($C_\odot$) if $u, u' \in \mathtt{C}$ and $s \in \mathtt{C}$, $t \in \mathtt{C}$ then $sut \ltimes su't$,
> ($R_\odot$) if $u, u' \in \mathtt{R}$ and $s \in \mathtt{R}$, $t \in \mathtt{R}$ then $sut \ltimes su't$.

A pair of qos $\leqslant, \preccurlyeq$ is *monotonic* if $\leqslant$ verifies $\mathbf{W}, \mathbf{C}, \mathbf{R}, \mathbf{U}$ and $\preccurlyeq$ verifies $\mathbf{W}, C_\odot, R_\odot$.

Proposition 3. *Let $\leqslant, \preccurlyeq$ be a pair of wqos. There is a positive integer n such that $f_{\mathcal{A}}^{n+1}(\vec{\emptyset}) \sqsubseteq_{\leqslant}^{4 \cdot |Q|^2} f_{\mathcal{A}}^n(\vec{\emptyset})$ (resp. $r_{\mathcal{A}}^{n+1}(\vec{\emptyset}) \sqsubseteq_{\preccurlyeq}^{6 \cdot |Q|^2} r_{\mathcal{A}}^n(\vec{\emptyset})$); and, if the pair of wqos is monotonic then $\mathrm{lfp}\, f_{\mathcal{A}} \sqsubseteq_{\leqslant}^{4 \cdot |Q|^2} f_{\mathcal{A}}^n(\vec{\emptyset})$ (resp. $\mathrm{lfp}\, r_{\mathcal{A}} \sqsubseteq_{\preccurlyeq}^{6 \cdot |Q|^2} r_{\mathcal{A}}^n(\vec{\emptyset})$).*

Each Kleene iterate of $f_{\mathcal{A}}$ and $r_{\mathcal{A}}$ is computable and given a decidable qo $\ltimes$ on Σ^* and two finite sets $X, Y \subseteq \Sigma^*$ it is decidable whether $X \sqsubseteq_\ltimes Y$ holds. Thus, given a monotonic pair $\leqslant, \preccurlyeq$ of decidable wqos, by Proposition 3, we can compute a finite basis for $\mathrm{lfp}\, f_{\mathcal{A}}$ w.r.t. $\leqslant$ and a finite basis for $\mathrm{lfp}\, r_{\mathcal{A}}$ w.r.t. $\preccurlyeq$. Hence, by Equation (2) we can compute a finite basis for S w.r.t. $\leqslant \times \preccurlyeq$.

6   Quasiorders for ω-VPL

In the following we present two families of qos to solve the inclusion problem $L^\omega(\mathcal{A}) \subseteq M$, the state-based qos which are derived from a VPA-representation of M and compare words according to the set of configurations each word connects in the VPA, and the syntactic qos which rely on the syntactic structure of M. We say that a pair of qos is *M-suitable* if it is an M-preserving and monotonic pair of decidable wqos. Intuitively, if a pair of qos is M-suitable then it can be used in our algorithm to decide the inclusion $L^\omega(\mathcal{A}) \subseteq M$.

State-based Quasiorders. Given a VPA $\mathcal{B} = (\hat{Q}, \hat{q}_I, \hat{\Gamma}, \hat{\delta}, \hat{F})$ we associate with each word $u \in \Sigma^*$ its *context* $\mathrm{ctx}^{\mathcal{B}}[u]$ and *final context* $\mathrm{ctx}_\odot^{\mathcal{B}}[u]$ *in $\mathcal{B}$* as follows:

$$\mathrm{ctx}^{\mathcal{B}}[u] \triangleq \{(p, q) \in \hat{Q}^2 \mid \exists w \in \hat{\Gamma}^*, (p, \bot) \vdash^{*u} (q, w)\},$$
$$\mathrm{ctx}_\odot^{\mathcal{B}}[u] \triangleq \{(p, q) \in \hat{Q}^2 \mid \exists w \in \hat{\Gamma}^*, (p, \bot) \vdash^{\odot u} (q, w)\} \ .$$

Hence we define the following qos on words in Σ^*:

$$u \leqslant^{\mathcal{B}} u' \overset{\triangle}{\Longleftrightarrow} \mathrm{ctx}^{\mathcal{B}}[u] \subseteq \mathrm{ctx}^{\mathcal{B}}[u'], \quad u \preccurlyeq^{\mathcal{B}} u' \overset{\triangle}{\Longleftrightarrow} u \leqslant^{\mathcal{B}} u' \wedge \mathrm{ctx}_\odot^{\mathcal{B}}[u] \subseteq \mathrm{ctx}_\odot^{\mathcal{B}}[u'] \ .$$

Proposition 4. *Let $\mathcal{B}$ be a VPA. The pair $\leqslant^{\mathcal{B}}, \preccurlyeq^{\mathcal{B}}$ is $L^{\omega}(\mathcal{B})$-suitable.*

Example 3. Consider the pair of qos $\leqslant^{\mathcal{B}}, \preccurlyeq^{\mathcal{B}}$ derived as explained above from $\mathcal{B}$ (Fig. 1) and the set $S = (\mathtt{W} \times \mathtt{W} \backslash \{\epsilon\}) \cup (\mathtt{R} \backslash \mathtt{C} \times \mathtt{R} \backslash \{\epsilon\})$ from Example 1. We have that $\mathrm{ctx}^{\mathcal{B}}[\epsilon] = \{(p,p),(q,q)\}$, $\mathrm{ctx}_{\circledcirc}^{\mathcal{B}}[\epsilon] = \{(p,p)\}$, $\mathrm{ctx}^{\mathcal{B}}[u] = \{(p,q),(q,q)\}$ and $\mathrm{ctx}_{\circledcirc}^{\mathcal{B}}[u] = \{(p,q)\}$ for every $u \in \mathtt{R} \backslash \{\epsilon\}$. We have that $\{c\}$ is a basis for $\mathtt{R} \backslash \{\epsilon\}$ w.r.t. $\preccurlyeq^{\mathcal{B}}$ since $c \preccurlyeq^{\mathcal{B}} u$ for every $u \in \mathtt{R} \backslash \{\epsilon\}$. Since $\mathtt{R} \backslash \mathtt{C} \subseteq \mathtt{R} \backslash \{\epsilon\}$ and $\{c\} \subseteq \mathtt{R} \backslash \mathtt{C}$ we deduce that $\{c\}$ is also a basis for $\mathtt{R} \backslash \mathtt{C}$ w.r.t. $\leqslant^{\mathcal{B}}$. Similarly we deduce that $\{\epsilon, cr\}$ is basis for $\mathtt{W}$ w.r.t $\leqslant^{\mathcal{B}}$ and that $\{cr\}$ is a basis for $\mathtt{W} \backslash \{\epsilon\}$ w.r.t. $\preccurlyeq^{\mathcal{B}}$. Hence, $(\{\epsilon, cr\} \times \{cr\}) \cup (\{c\} \times \{c\})$ is a basis for S w.r.t. $\leqslant^{\mathcal{B}} \times \preccurlyeq^{\mathcal{B}}$.

Syntactic Quasiorders. Given a ω-VPL M we associate with each word $u \in \Sigma^*$ its *context* $\mathrm{ctx}^M[u]$ and *final context* $\mathrm{ctx}_{\circledcirc}^M[u]$ in M as follows:

$$\mathrm{ctx}^M[u] \triangleq \{(s,\xi) \in \Sigma^* \times \Sigma^{\omega} \mid su\xi \in M\},$$
$$\mathrm{ctx}_{\circledcirc}^M[u] \triangleq \{(s,t) \in \Sigma^* \times \Sigma^* \mid s(ut)^{\omega} \in M\} \ .$$

At first glance, we are tempted to define the syntactic qos from ctx^M and $\mathrm{ctx}_{\circledcirc}^M$ in the analogue way we defined the state-based qos from the contexts and final contexts relatively to a VPA. Although, this definition provides a pair of M-preserving qos, it does not guarantee that the pair is M-suitable. To overcome this, we impose the respect of the partition $\mathcal{P} \triangleq \{\mathtt{W}, \mathtt{C} \backslash \mathtt{W}, \mathtt{R} \backslash \mathtt{W}, \mathtt{U}_c \backslash \mathtt{R}\}$ of Σ^*, meaning that two words compare only if they belong to a same subset of $\mathcal{P}$. Additionally, given $\mathtt{J} \in \mathcal{P}$ we compare two words of $\mathtt{J}$ by considering a restriction of their context and final context in M which depends on $\mathtt{J}$. More precisely, we define the qo $\leqslant^M$ on Σ^* as the union $\bigcup_{\mathtt{J} \in \mathcal{P}} \leqslant_{\mathtt{J}}^M$ where for every $\mathtt{J} \in \mathcal{P}$, the qo $\leqslant_{\mathtt{J}}^M \subseteq \mathtt{J} \times \mathtt{J}$ is defined by

$$u \leqslant_{\mathtt{W}}^M u' \overset{\triangle}{\iff} \mathrm{ctx}^M[u] \subseteq \mathrm{ctx}^M[u'],$$
$$u \leqslant_{\mathtt{C} \backslash \mathtt{W}}^M u' \overset{\triangle}{\iff} \mathrm{ctx}^M[u]_{|\mathtt{C} \times \Sigma^{\omega}} \subseteq \mathrm{ctx}^M[u']_{|\mathtt{C} \times \Sigma^{\omega}},$$
$$u \leqslant_{\mathtt{R} \backslash \mathtt{W}}^M u' \overset{\triangle}{\iff} \mathrm{ctx}^M[u]_{|\Sigma^* \times \mathtt{R}^{\omega}} \subseteq \mathrm{ctx}^M[u']_{|\Sigma^* \times \mathtt{R}^{\omega}},$$
$$u \leqslant_{\mathtt{U}_c \backslash \mathtt{R}}^M u' \overset{\triangle}{\iff} \mathrm{ctx}^M[u]_{|\mathtt{C} \times \mathtt{R}^{\omega}} \subseteq \mathrm{ctx}^M[u']_{|\mathtt{C} \times \mathtt{R}^{\omega}} \ .$$

Similarly, we define the qo $\preccurlyeq^M \triangleq \bigcup_{\mathtt{J} \in \mathcal{P}} \preccurlyeq_{\mathtt{J}}^M$ on Σ^* where for every $\mathtt{J} \in \mathcal{P}$, $\preccurlyeq_{\mathtt{J}}^M \subseteq \mathtt{J} \times \mathtt{J}$ is the qo defined by

$$u \preccurlyeq_{\mathtt{W}}^M u' \overset{\triangle}{\iff} u \leqslant_{\mathtt{W}}^M u' \wedge \mathrm{ctx}_{\circledcirc}^M[u] \subseteq \mathrm{ctx}_{\circledcirc}^M[u'],$$
$$u \preccurlyeq_{\mathtt{C} \backslash \mathtt{W}}^M u' \overset{\triangle}{\iff} u \leqslant_{\mathtt{C} \backslash \mathtt{W}}^M u' \wedge \left(\mathrm{ctx}_{\circledcirc}^M[u]_{|\mathtt{C} \times \mathtt{C}} \subseteq \mathrm{ctx}_{\circledcirc}^M[u']_{|\mathtt{C} \times \mathtt{C}}\right),$$
$$u \preccurlyeq_{\mathtt{R} \backslash \mathtt{W}}^M u' \overset{\triangle}{\iff} u \leqslant_{\mathtt{R} \backslash \mathtt{W}}^M u' \wedge \left(\mathrm{ctx}_{\circledcirc}^M[u]_{|\Sigma^* \times \mathtt{R}} \subseteq \mathrm{ctx}_{\circledcirc}^M[u']_{|\Sigma^* \times \mathtt{R}}\right),$$
$$u \preccurlyeq_{\mathtt{U}_c \backslash \mathtt{R}}^M u' \overset{\triangle}{\iff} u, u' \in \mathtt{U}_c \backslash \mathtt{R} \ .$$

Proposition 5. *Let $\mathcal{B}$ be a VPA. The pair $\leqslant^{L^{\omega}(\mathcal{B})}, \preccurlyeq^{L^{\omega}(\mathcal{B})}$ is $L^{\omega}(\mathcal{B})$-suitable.*

Proof (sketch). First we show that the pair $\leqslant^M, \preccurlyeq^M$ is M-preserving, where $M \triangleq L^\omega(\mathcal{B})$. Let $(u,v),(u',v') \in \mathsf{C} \times \mathsf{C}$ (resp. $\mathsf{U_c} \times \mathsf{R}$) such that $u \leqslant^M u'$, $v \preccurlyeq^M v'$ and $uv^\omega \in M$. From $u \leqslant^M u'$ and $uv^\omega \in M$ we deduce that $(\epsilon, v^\omega) \in \mathrm{ctx}^M_{|\mathsf{C} \times \Sigma^\omega}[u] \subseteq \mathrm{ctx}^M_{|\mathsf{C} \times \Sigma^\omega}[u']$ (resp. $(\epsilon, v^\omega) \in \mathrm{ctx}^M_{|\mathsf{C} \times \mathsf{R}^\omega}[u] \subseteq \mathrm{ctx}^M_{|\mathsf{C} \times \mathsf{R}^\omega}[u']$). Thus, $u'v^\omega \in M$. From $v \preccurlyeq^M v'$ and $u'v^\omega \in M$ we deduce that $(u',\epsilon) \in \mathrm{ctx}^M_\circledcirc[v]_{|\mathsf{C} \times \mathsf{C}} \subseteq \mathrm{ctx}^M_{\circledcirc\mathsf{C}}[v']_{|\mathsf{C} \times \mathsf{C}}$ (resp. $(u',\epsilon) \in \mathrm{ctx}^M_\circledcirc[v]_{|\Sigma^* \times \mathsf{R}} \subseteq \mathrm{ctx}^M_{\circledcirc\mathsf{C}}[v']_{|\Sigma^* \times \mathsf{C}}$). Thus, $u'v'^\omega \in M$.

We now show that the qo $\leqslant^M$ satisfies the monotonicity conditions $\mathbf{C}$ and $\mathbf{R}$. Let $u \leqslant^M u'$ such that $u, u' \in \mathsf{C}$ (resp. $u, u' \in \mathsf{R}$). Let $s \in \mathsf{C}$ and $t \in \Sigma^*$ (resp. $s \in \Sigma^*$ and $t \in \mathsf{R}$). If $u, u' \in \mathsf{W}$ then it is easy to check that $sut \leqslant^M su't$. Otherwise $u, u' \in \mathsf{C}\backslash\mathsf{W}$ (resp. $u, u' \in \mathsf{R}\backslash\mathsf{W}$) and we distinguish two cases: if $t \in \mathsf{C}$ (resp. $s \in \mathsf{R}$) then $sut, su't \in \mathsf{C}\backslash\mathsf{W}$ (resp. $sut, su't \in \mathsf{R}\backslash\mathsf{W}$). We show that $sut \leqslant^M_{\mathsf{C}\backslash\mathsf{W}} su't$ (resp. $sut \leqslant^M_{\mathsf{R}\backslash\mathsf{W}} su't$). Let $(s',\xi) \in \mathrm{ctx}^M[sut]_{|\mathsf{C} \times \Sigma^\omega}$ (resp. $(s',\xi) \in \mathrm{ctx}^M[sut]_{|\Sigma^* \times \mathsf{R}^\omega}$). Since $s's \in \mathsf{C}$ (resp. $t\xi \in \mathsf{R}^\omega$), we deduce from $u \leqslant^M_{\mathsf{C}\backslash\mathsf{W}} u'$ (resp. $u \leqslant^M_{\mathsf{R}\backslash\mathsf{W}} u'$) that $(s',\xi) \in \mathrm{ctx}^M[su't]_{|\mathsf{C} \times \Sigma^\omega}$ (resp. $(s',\xi) \in \mathrm{ctx}^M[su't]_{|\Sigma^* \times \mathsf{R}^\omega}$). If $t \in \mathsf{U_c}$ (resp. $s \in \Sigma^*\backslash\mathsf{R}$) then $sut, su't \in \mathsf{U_c}\backslash\mathsf{R}$ and similarly we can show that $sut \leqslant^M_{\mathsf{U_c}\backslash\mathsf{R}} su't$. The proof that $\leqslant^M$ and $\preccurlyeq^M$ are wqos follows from [9, Prop 1.2] by observing that for every J in the partition $\mathcal{P}$ of Σ^* we have $\leqslant^\mathcal{B}_{|\mathsf{J} \times \mathsf{J}} \subseteq \leqslant^M_\mathsf{J}$ and $\preccurlyeq^\mathcal{B}_{|\mathsf{J} \times \mathsf{J}} \subseteq \preccurlyeq^M_\mathsf{J}$, where $\leqslant^\mathcal{B}$ and $\preccurlyeq^\mathcal{B}$ are the state-based qos previously defined. □

Deciding the syntactic qos can be easily shown to be as hard as the inclusion problem between ω-VPL generated by VPA. Nevertheless, the syntactic qos act as a gold standard for quasiorders in the sense formalized in the next proposition.

Proposition 6. *Let $M \subseteq \Sigma^\omega$ be an ω-VPL and $\leqslant, \preccurlyeq$ be a M-suitable pair of qos such that $\preccurlyeq \subseteq \leqslant$. For every $\mathsf{J} \in \mathcal{P}$ we have $\leqslant_{|\mathsf{J} \times \mathsf{J}} \subseteq \leqslant^M$ and $\preccurlyeq_{|\mathsf{J} \times \mathsf{J}} \subseteq \preccurlyeq^M$.*

By Propositions 5 and 6 the pair $\leqslant^{L^\omega(\mathcal{B})}, \preccurlyeq^{L^\omega(\mathcal{B})}$ is the greatest (w.r.t $\subseteq \times \subseteq$) among the $L^\omega(\mathcal{B})$-suitable pairs $\leqslant, \preccurlyeq$ of qos that respect the partition $\mathcal{P}$ and that verify $\preccurlyeq \subseteq \leqslant$.

7   Algorithm

We are now in position to present our algorithm which, given two VPA $\mathcal{A} = (Q, q_I, \Gamma, \delta, F)$ and $\mathcal{B} = (\hat{Q}, \hat{q}_I, \hat{\Gamma}, \hat{\delta}, \hat{F})$ and a pair of $L^\omega(\mathcal{B})$-suitable qos, decides the inclusion problem $L^\omega(\mathcal{A}) \subseteq L^\omega(\mathcal{B})$.

Algorithm 1 computes a finite basis for S w.r.t. $\leqslant \times \preccurlyeq$ (lines 1–2) and afterwards checks membership in $L^\omega(\mathcal{B})$ on every ultimately periodic word uv^ω stemming from this finite basis (lines 3–7).

Theorem 3. *Given the required inputs, Algorithm 1 decides the inclusion problem $L^\omega(\mathcal{A}) \subseteq L^\omega(\mathcal{B})$.*

Proof. As established by Proposition 3, given a monotonic pair $\leqslant, \preccurlyeq$ of decidable wqos, Algorithm 1 computes in line 1 (resp. line 2) a finite basis $f_\mathcal{A}{}^m(\vec{\emptyset})$ (resp.

Algorithm 1: Algorithm for deciding $L^\omega(\mathcal{A}) \subseteq L^\omega(\mathcal{B})$

Data: VPA $\mathcal{A} = (Q, q_I, \Gamma, \delta, F)$ and $\mathcal{B} = (\hat{Q}, \hat{q}_I, \hat{\Gamma}, \hat{\delta}, \hat{F})$.
Data: $L^\omega(\mathcal{B})$-suitable pair $\leqslant, \preccurlyeq$.
Data: Procedure deciding $uv^\omega \in L^\omega(\mathcal{B})$ given (u, v).

1   Compute $f_{\mathcal{A}}{}^m(\vec{\emptyset})$ with least m s.t. $f_{\mathcal{A}}{}^{m+1}(\vec{\emptyset}) \sqsubseteq_{\leqslant}^{4 \cdot |Q|^2} f_{\mathcal{A}}{}^m(\vec{\emptyset})$;

2   Compute $r_{\mathcal{A}}{}^{m'}(\vec{\emptyset})$ with least m' s.t. $r_{\mathcal{A}}{}^{m'+1}(\vec{\emptyset}) \sqsubseteq_{\preccurlyeq}^{6 \cdot |Q|^2} r_{\mathcal{A}}{}^{m'}(\vec{\emptyset})$;

3   **foreach** $p \in Q$ **do**

4   **foreach** $u \in (f_{\mathcal{A}}{}^m(\vec{\emptyset}))_{2, q_I, p}$, $v \in (r_{\mathcal{A}}{}^{m'}(\vec{\emptyset}))_{5, p, p}$ **do**

5   **if** $uv^\omega \notin L^\omega(\mathcal{B})$ **then return** false;

6   **foreach** $u \in (f_{\mathcal{A}}{}^m(\vec{\emptyset}))_{4, q_I, p}$, $v \in (r_{\mathcal{A}}{}^{m'}(\vec{\emptyset}))_{6, p, p}$ **do**

7   **if** $uv^\omega \notin L^\omega(\mathcal{B})$ **then return** false;

8   **return** true;

$r_{\mathcal{A}}{}^{m'}(\vec{\emptyset})$) for lfp $f_{\mathcal{A}}$ (resp. lfp $r_{\mathcal{A}}$) w.r.t. $\leqslant$ (resp. $\preccurlyeq$). Next define:

$$S_{\mathcal{A}}^{m,m'} \triangleq \bigcup_{p \in Q} \left(((f_{\mathcal{A}}{}^m(\vec{\emptyset}))_{2, q_I, p} \times (r_{\mathcal{A}}{}^{m'}(\vec{\emptyset}))_{5, p, p}) \cup ((f_{\mathcal{A}}{}^m(\vec{\emptyset}))_{4, q_I, p} \times (r_{\mathcal{A}}{}^{m'}(\vec{\emptyset}))_{6, p, p}) \right) .$$

Using Equation (2) we deduce that $S_{\mathcal{A}}^{m,m'}$ is a finite basis for S w.r.t. $\leqslant \times \preccurlyeq$. Since the pair $\leqslant, \preccurlyeq$ is $L^\omega(\mathcal{B})$-preserving, by Section 3, we deduce that

$$L^\omega(\mathcal{A}) \subseteq L^\omega(\mathcal{B}) \iff \forall (u, v) \in S_{\mathcal{A}}^{m,m'}, \ uv^\omega \in L^\omega(\mathcal{B}) .$$

$\square$

We remark that Algorithm 1 can be easily adapted to decide the inclusion problem between visibly pushdown languages of finite words. The adaptation to the finite words case omits the fixpoint computation of line 2 and iterates over the components (i, q_I, p) where $i \in \{2, 3, 4\}$ and where $p \in F$ is a final state.

Example 4. Consider the iterates of the function $f_{\mathcal{A}}$ from Example 2. One can check that $f_{\mathcal{A}}{}^4(\vec{\emptyset}) \sqsubseteq_{\leqslant_B}^4 f_{\mathcal{A}}{}^3(\vec{\emptyset})$ (thus also $f_{\mathcal{A}}{}^4(\vec{\emptyset}) \sqsubseteq_{\leqslant_B}^4 f_{\mathcal{A}}{}^3(\vec{\emptyset})$ since $\preccurlyeq^B \subseteq \leqslant^B$). Thus, we check whether the inclusion $L^\omega(\mathcal{A}) \subseteq L^\omega(\mathcal{B})$ holds on the finite set $(\{\epsilon, cr\} \times \{cr\}) \cup (\{c, c^2, c^3\} \times \{cr, c, c^2, c^3, c^4\})$ and find the counterexample $c(cr)^\omega \in L^\omega(\mathcal{A}) \backslash L^\omega(\mathcal{B})$.

Antichains Everywhere. We show next that Algorithm 1 remains correct if, in the sequence of Kleene iterates of $f_{\mathcal{A}}$ or $r_{\mathcal{A}}$, for each application of $f_{\mathcal{A}}$ or $r_{\mathcal{A}}$ we first select a finite basis for their arguments instead (using $\leqslant^{4 \cdot |Q|^2}$ for $f_{\mathcal{A}}$ and $\preccurlyeq^{6 \cdot |Q|^2}$ for $r_{\mathcal{A}}$).

Proposition 7. *Let $\varkappa$ be a qo that verifies the monotonicity conditions **W, C, R, U**. If B is a basis for $(X, Y, Z, T) \in \wp(W)^{|Q|^2} \times \wp(C)^{|Q|^2} \times \wp(R)^{|Q|^2} \times \wp(U_c)^{|Q|^2}$ w.r.t. $\varkappa^{4 \cdot |Q|^2}$, then $f_{\mathcal{A}}(B)$ is a basis for $f_{\mathcal{A}}(X, Y, Z, T)$ w.r.t. $\varkappa^{4 \cdot |Q|^2}$. The analogue result holds for $r_{\mathcal{A}}$ when $\varkappa$ satisfies the monotonicity conditions **W, $C_\oplus$, $R_\odot$**.*

Since every Kleene iterate of f_A belongs to $\wp(\mathsf{W})^{|Q|^2} \times \wp(\mathsf{C})^{|Q|^2} \times \wp(\mathsf{R})^{|Q|^2} \times \wp(\mathsf{U}_c)^{|Q|^2}$ given a basis B for $f_A{}^n(\vec{\emptyset})$ w.r.t. $\leqslant^{4\cdot|Q|^2}$, by Proposition 7, $f_A(B)$ is a basis for $f_A{}^{n+1}(\vec{\emptyset})$ w.r.t. $\leqslant^{4\cdot|Q|^2}$. Hence, at each iteration we can select, for each (i, p, q)-component, a basis w.r.t. $\leqslant$ and then apply f_A. In particular, we can keep antichains for each (i, p, q)-component, that is, finite bases of incomparable words. The analogue result holds for the Kleene iterates of r_A.

7.1 State-based Algorithm

Next we consider Algorithm 1 instantiated with the pair of state-based qos (§ 6).

Data Structures. Comparing two words given a state-based qo requires to compute the corresponding sets of contexts in $\mathcal{B}$. Instead of computing contexts every time we need to compare two words we cache the context information along with each word for faster retrieval. More precisely, we cache $\mathrm{ctx}^{\mathcal{B}}[u]$ along with u when u is a prefix and we cache $(\mathrm{ctx}^{\mathcal{B}}[v], \mathrm{ctx}^{\mathcal{B}}_{\circledcirc}[v])$ along with v when v is a period. Next we go even further and explain that new context information can be computed inductively from already computed context information. Assume we are computing a new word during the fixpoint computation, for instance the word cur that is obtained by flanking c and r to u. We will show that the context information of cur can be computed directly from that of u, c and r instead of computing cur from "scratch".

Fixpoint Computation. Given an input vector the functions f_A and r_A add new words of type uu', and cur to its components, where c and r are fixed letters, and u, u' are words already present in some components of the vector. The following equalities show that we can inductively compute the contexts and final contexts in $\mathcal{B}$ of newly added words in these functions: for every $u, u' \in \mathsf{C} \cup \mathsf{R}$, $c \in \Sigma_c$, $r \in \Sigma_r$, we have

$$\mathrm{ctx}^{\mathcal{B}}[uu'] = \{(p, q) \in \hat{Q}^2 \mid \exists p_i \in \hat{Q}, (p, p_i) \in \mathrm{ctx}^{\mathcal{B}}[u], (p_i, q) \in \mathrm{ctx}^{\mathcal{B}}[u']\},$$
$$\mathrm{ctx}^{\mathcal{B}}[cur] = \{(p, q) \in \hat{Q}^2 \mid \exists(p', q') \in \mathrm{ctx}^{\mathcal{B}}[u], \exists\gamma \in \hat{\Gamma}, (p, c, p', \gamma) \in \hat{\delta}_c, (q', r, \gamma, q) \in \hat{\delta}_r\} \ .$$

The definitions for $\mathrm{ctx}^{\mathcal{B}}_{\circledcirc}[uu']$ and $\mathrm{ctx}^{\mathcal{B}}_{\circledcirc}[cur]$ are left as exercise to the reader.

Example 5. Using the above definition it is routine to check that $\mathrm{ctx}^{\mathcal{B}}[cr] = \{(p, q), (q, q)\}$ because $cr = c\epsilon r$, $\mathrm{ctx}^{\mathcal{B}}[\epsilon] = \{(p, p), (q, q)\}$ (Example 3) and $(p, c, q, A), (q, c, q, A) \in \hat{\delta}_c$, $(q, r, A, q) \in \hat{\delta}_r$.

Using the context information cached along words we check convergence of the fixpoint computations (lines 1–2) using the following qos directly on contexts $\sqsubseteq_{\mathsf{C}}$ on $\wp(\wp(\hat{Q}^2))^4$ for prefixes and $\sqsubseteq_{\mathsf{C} \times \mathsf{C}}$ on $\wp(\wp(\hat{Q}^2) \times \wp(\hat{Q}^2))^6$ for periods.

Incidentally, as we show below, we can perform the membership checks of lines 5 and 7 (asking whether $uv^\omega \in L^\omega(\mathcal{B})$ given u and v) using the context information associated to the prefix u and period v and nothing else.

Membership Check. To decide membership in $L^\omega(\mathcal{B})$ we use the membership predicate $\mathrm{Inc}^{\mathcal{B}}$ defined for $x, y_1, y_2 \in \wp(\hat{Q}^2)$ as follows:

$$\mathrm{Inc}^{\mathcal{B}}(x, y_1, y_2) \triangleq \exists q, p \in \hat{Q}, (\hat{q}_I, q) \in x \wedge (q, p) \in y_1^* \wedge (p, p) \in y_1^* \circ y_2 \circ y_1^* \ ,$$

where, given two binary relations $y, y' \in \wp(\hat{Q}^2)$ on states of $\mathcal{B}$, the notation $y \circ y'$ denotes their composition, and y^* denotes the Kleene closure of y.

Proposition 8. *For all* $(u, v) \in \mathsf{Ld}$, $\mathrm{Inc}^{\mathcal{B}}(ctx^{\mathcal{B}}[u], ctx^{\mathcal{B}}[v], ctx_\circledast^{\mathcal{B}}[v]) \iff uv^\omega \in L^\omega(\mathcal{B})$.

Proof. Let $(u, v) \in \mathsf{Ld}$. Note that if $v \in \mathsf{C}$ (resp. $v \in \mathsf{R}$) then for every positive integer n we have $v^n \in \mathsf{C}$ (resp. $v^n \in \mathsf{R}$) and $(p, q) \in ctx^{\mathcal{B}}[v]^* \iff \exists n, (p, q) \in ctx^{\mathcal{B}}[v^n]$. Therefore, if $\mathrm{Inc}^{\mathcal{B}}(ctx^{\mathcal{B}}[u], ctx^{\mathcal{B}}[v], ctx_\circledast^{\mathcal{B}}[v])$ holds then there are $q, p \in \hat{Q}$ and two positive integers n, m such that $(\hat{q}_I, q) \in ctx^{\mathcal{B}}[u]$, $(q, p) \in ctx^{\mathcal{B}}[v^n]$ and $(p, p) \in ctx_\circledast^{\mathcal{B}}[v^m]$. If $(u, v) \in \mathsf{C} \times \mathsf{C}$ then we deduce an accepting trace of $\mathcal{B}$ on uv^ω of the form $(\hat{q}_I, \bot) \vdash^{*u} (q, \bot) \vdash^{*v^n} (p, \bot) \vdash^{\circledast v^m} (p, \bot)$ for uv^ω. If $(u, v) \in \mathsf{U_c} \times \mathsf{R}$ then we deduce an accepting trace of $\mathcal{B}$ on uv^ω of the form $(\hat{q}_I, \bot) \vdash^{*u} (q, w) \vdash^{*v^n} (p, ww') \vdash^{\circledast v^m} (p, ww'w'')$ for some $w, w', w'' \in \Gamma$.

  Conversely if $uv^\omega \in L^\omega(\mathcal{B})$ then there is an accepting trace of $\mathcal{B}$ on uv^ω.

- If $(u, v) \in \mathsf{C} \times \mathsf{C}$ then this trace is of the form

$$(\hat{q}_I, \bot) \vdash^{*u} (q, \bot) \vdash^{*v} (q_1, \bot) \vdash^{*v} (q_2, \bot) \vdash^{*v} \cdots$$

  Since $\hat{Q}$ is finite, there is $p \in \hat{Q}$ and a sequence $\{n_k\}_{k \in \mathbb{N}}$ such that $q_{n_k} = p$ for all $k \in \mathbb{N}$. Since the trace is accepting there is $m \in \mathbb{N}$ such that $(p, \bot) \vdash^{\circledast v^m} (p, \bot)$.

- If $(u, v) \in \mathsf{U_c} \times \mathsf{R}$ then it is of the form

$$(\hat{q}_I, \bot) \vdash^{*u} (q, w_0) \vdash^{*v} (q_1, w_1) \vdash^{*v} (q_2, w_1 w_2) \vdash^{*v} \cdots$$

  where for each $j \in \mathbb{N}$ no symbol of w_j is popped while reading v in the sequence of transitions $(q_j, w_j) \vdash^{*v} (q_{j+1}, w_j w_{j+1})$. Thus, we can derive sequences $(q_j, \bot) \vdash^{*v} (q_{j+1}, w_{j+1})$ for every $j \in \mathbb{N}$. There is $p \in \hat{Q}$ and a sequence $\{n_k\}_{k \in \mathbb{N}}$ such that $q_{n_k} = p$ for all $k \in \mathbb{N}$ and since the trace is accepting there is $m \in \mathbb{N}$ such that $(p, \bot) \vdash^{\circledast v^m} (p, w_{n_j} \cdots w_{n_{j+m}})$.

In both cases we deduce that $(\hat{q}_I, q) \in ctx^{\mathcal{B}}[u]$, $(q, p) \in ctx^{\mathcal{B}}[v^{n_0}]$ and $(p, p) \in ctx_\circledast^{\mathcal{B}}[v^m]$. Thus, $\mathrm{Inc}^{\mathcal{B}}(ctx^{\mathcal{B}}[u], ctx^{\mathcal{B}}[v], ctx_\circledast^{\mathcal{B}}[v])$ holds. $\qquad\square$

By showing how to reason on contexts directly (for comparisons, for applying functions $f_\mathcal{A}$ and $r_\mathcal{A}$, for convergence check and for membership check) we removed the need to store words altogether since their contexts suffice. To sum up, Algorithm 1 instantiated with the state-based qos can be implemented by manipulating directly subsets of $\wp(\hat{Q}^2)$ (for the prefixes) and pairs of subsets of $\wp(\hat{Q}^2)$ (for the periods) thereby removing the need to store and manipulate words. We call this implementation of Algorithm 1 the *state-based algorithm*. We conclude this section with its complexity.

Proposition 9. *Let* $n \triangleq |Q|$, $\hat{n} \triangleq |\hat{Q}|$ *and* $m \triangleq max\{1, |\Sigma|\}$. *The running time of the state-based algorithm is* $2^{O(\hat{n}^2)} m^2 n^4$.

8   Experiments

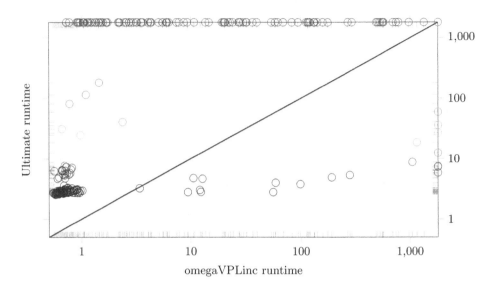

Fig. 2. Scatter plot comparing the runtime (in seconds) of Ultimate and omegaVPLinc on the Ultimate suite. Both axis feature a logarithmic scale. When a tool does not return an answer within 1800 seconds (it runs out of time or memory) the data point is plotted on the edge thereof (top edge for Ultimate, right edge for omegaVPLinc).

We implemented *omegaVPLinc* [11] , a Java prototype of the state-based algorithm and evaluated it against Ultimate from Heizmann et al. [21] which decides inclusion via complementation, intersection and emptiness check.[7]

Benchmarks. Our experiments use two sets of benchmarks. The first stems from [18] and consists of 5 queries $L^\omega(\mathcal{A}) \subseteq L^\omega(\mathcal{B})$ given $\mathcal{A}$ and $\mathcal{B}$. We first translated those VPA into the AutomataScript language that Ultimate and omegaVPLinc can use and then we minimized them with Ultimate. The second set of benchmarks consists of 281 instances of VPA $\mathcal{A}, \mathcal{B}_1, \mathcal{B}_2, \ldots, \mathcal{B}_n$ for which we run the query $L^\omega(\mathcal{A}) \subseteq \bigcup_{i=1}^{n} L^\omega(\mathcal{B}_i)$. These VPA were computed by Ultimate from randomly selected tasks in SV-COMP (Software Verification Competition) termination category. We used Ultimate to compute the unions of $\mathcal{B}_1, \ldots, \mathcal{B}_n$ and then minimize the result before running each query.

---

[7] We excluded FADecider [18] from our evaluation because it returned 22 false positive answers on a randomly chosen subset of 50 from our 286 benchmarks. Counterexamples to inclusion for these benchmarks were validated with Ultimate. The problem has been reported.

Experimental Setup. We ran our experiment in Debian/GNU Linux 11 (Bullseye) 64bit, running on a server with 20 GB of RAM and 2 Xeon E5640 2.6 GHz CPUs. We used Ultimate version 0.2.1, with openJDK 11.0.13, whereas omegaVPLinc uses openJDK 17.0.1. Maximal heap size for both programs was set to 6 GB and they were given a timeout of 30 minutes (or, equivalently, 1800 seconds).

Results. Of the 5 benchmarks in the FADecider suite, omegaVPLinc is faster on 4 of them. Our prototype times out on the remaining one, while Ultimate runs out of memory. Of the 281 benchmarks in the Ultimate suite, omegaVPLinc correctly returns an answer on 253 (165 $\subseteq$ and 88 $\not\subseteq$), times out on 27 and runs out of memory on 1. Ultimate, however, only terminates on 142 benchmarks, running out of memory on the remaining 139 (the red data points on the top edge in Fig. 2). There are 7 benchmarks for which Ultimate terminates, but omegaVPLinc doesn't (the data points on the right edge but not the top one), whereas there are 118 benchmarks for which omegaVPLinc terminates, but Ultimate doesn't (the red data points on the top edge but not the right one). Of the 135 benchmarks on which both tools terminate, omegaVPLinc is faster than Ultimate on 123 (data points touching no edges and above the diagonal). Moreover omegaVPLinc and Ultimate coincide on whether inclusion holds (98) or not (37). This empirical evaluation suggests that omegaVPLinc scales up better than Ultimate on both of these benchmark sets.

9   Conclusion and Future Work

We presented novel algorithms to solve the inclusion problem between visibly pushdown languages of infinite words that leverage antichain-like techniques as well as the use of separate quasiorders for prefixes and periods of ultimately periodic words. Our empirical evaluation suggests that our approach scales up better than the ones relying on an explicit complementation. A future work is to extend our approach to the class of operator-precedence languages [15] which also enjoy an EXPTIME-complete inclusion problem and which is strictly contained in the class of deterministic CFL, and strictly contains VPL [8].

References

1. Abdulla, P.A., Chen, Y.F., Clemente, L., Holík, L., Hong, C.D., Mayr, R., Vojnar, T.: Simulation Subsumption in Ramsey-Based Büchi Automata Universality and Inclusion Testing. In: CAV'10: Proc. 20th Int. Conf. on Computer Aided Verification. Springer (2010). https://doi.org/10.1007/978-3-642-14295-6_14
2. Abdulla, P.A., Chen, Y.F., Clemente, L., Holík, L., Hong, C.D., Mayr, R., Vojnar, T.: Advanced Ramsey-Based Büchi Automata Inclusion Testing. In: CONCUR'11: Proc. 22nd Int. Conf. on Concurrency Theory. Springer (2011). https://doi.org/10.1007/978-3-642-23217-6_13
3. Abdulla, P.A., Chen, Y.F., Holík, L., Mayr, R., Vojnar, T.: When Simulation Meets Antichains. In: TACAS'10: Proc. 16th Int. Conf. on Tools and Algorithms for the Construction and Analysis of Systems. Springer (2010). https://doi.org/10.1007/978-3-642-12002-2_14

4. Alur, R., Madhusudan, P.: Visibly pushdown languages. In: STOC'04: Proc. 36th Ann. ACM Symp. on Theory of Computing. ACM (2004). https://doi.org/10.1145/1007352.1007390

5. Bouajjani, A., Habermehl, P., Holík, L., Touili, T., Vojnar, T.: Antichain-Based Universality and Inclusion Testing over Nondeterministic Finite Tree Automata. In: CIAA'08: Proc. Int. Conf. on Implementation and Applications of Automata. LNCS, Springer (2008). https://doi.org/10.1007/978-3-540-70844-5_7

6. Bruyère, V., Ducobu, M., Gauwin, O.: Visibly Pushdown Automata: Universality and Inclusion via Antichains. In: LATA'13: Proc. Int. Conf. on Language and Automata Theory and Applications. LNCS, Springer (2013). https://doi.org/10.1007/978-3-642-37064-9_18

7. Calbrix, H., Nivat, M., Podelski, A.: Ultimately periodic words of rational ω-languages. In: Proc. Int. Symp. on Mathematical Foundations of Programming Semantics (MFPS). LNCS, Springer (1994). https://doi.org/10.1007/3-540-58027-1_27

8. Crespi Reghizzi, S., Mandrioli, D.: Operator precedence and the visibly pushdown property. Journal of Computer and System Sciences **78**(6), 1837–1867 (2012). https://doi.org/10.1016/j.jcss.2011.12.006

9. de Luca, A., Varricchio, S.: Well quasi-orders and regular languages. Acta Informatica **31**(6), 539–557 (1994). https://doi.org/10.1007/BF01213206

10. De Wulf, M., Doyen, L., Henzinger, T.A., Raskin, J.F.: Antichains: A new algorithm for checking universality of finite automata. In: CAV'06: Proc. 16th Int. Conf. on Computer Aided Verification. Springer (2006). https://doi.org/10.1007/11817963_5

11. Doveri, K., Ganty, P., Hadzi-Djokic, L.: omegavplinc v1.1 (Jan 2023). https://doi.org/10.5281/zenodo.7506895

12. Doveri, K., Ganty, P., Mazzocchi, N.: FORQ-Based Language Inclusion Formal Testing. In: CAV'22: Proc. 32nd Int. Conf. on Computer Aided Verification. Springer (2022). https://doi.org/10.1007/978-3-031-13188-2_6

13. Doveri, K., Ganty, P., Parolini, F., Ranzato, F.: Inclusion Testing of Büchi Automata Based on Well-Quasiorders. In: CONCUR'21: Proc. 32nd Int. Conf. on Concurrency Theory. LIPIcs, Schloss Dagstuhl (2021). https://doi.org/10.4230/LIPIcs.CONCUR.2021.3

14. Doyen, L., Raskin, J.F.: Antichain Algorithms for Finite Automata. In: Tools and Algorithms for the Construction and Analysis of Systems. LNCS, Springer (2010)

15. Floyd, R.W.: Syntactic analysis and operator precedence. J. ACM **10**(3), 316–333 (1963). https://doi.org/10.1145/321172.321179

16. Fogarty, S., Vardi, M.Y.: Efficient Büchi Universality Checking. In: TACAS'10: Proc. 16th Int. Conf. on Tools and Algorithms for the Construction and Analysis of Systems. LNCS, Springer (2010). https://doi.org/10.1007/978-3-642-12002-2_17

17. Friedmann, O., Klaedtke, F., Lange, M.: Ramsey goes visibly pushdown. In: ICALP'13: Proc. 40th Int. Coll. on Automata, Languages, and Programming. LNCS, Springer (2013). https://doi.org/10.1007/978-3-642-39212-2_22

18. Friedmann, O., Klaedtke, F., Lange, M.: Ramsey-based inclusion checking for visibly pushdown automata. ACM Transactions on Computational Logic **16**(4), 1–24 (2015). https://doi.org/10.1145/2774221

19. Ganty, P., Ranzato, F., Valero, P.: Language inclusion algorithms as complete abstract interpretations. In: Static Analysis. Springer (2019). https://doi.org/10.1007/978-3-030-32304-2_8

20. Ganty, P., Ranzato, F., Valero, P.: Complete abstractions for checking language inclusion. ACM Trans. Comput. Logic **22**(4) (2021). https://doi.org/10.1145/3462673
21. Heizmann, M., Chen, Y., Dietsch, D., Greitschus, M., Hoenicke, J., Li, Y., Nutz, A., Musa, B., Schilling, C., Schindler, T., Podelski, A.: Ultimate automizer and the search for perfect interpolants - (competition contribution). In: TACAS'18: Proc. 24th Int. Conf. on Tools and Algorithms for the Construction and Analysis of Systems. LNCS, Springer (2018). https://doi.org/10.1007/978-3-319-89963-3_30
22. Heizmann, M., Hoenicke, J., Podelski, A.: Nested interpolants. SIGPLAN Notices **45**(1), 471–482 (2010). https://doi.org/10.1145/1707801.1706353
23. Hieronymi, P., Ma, D., Oei, R., Schaeffer, L., Schulz, C., Shallit, J.: Decidability for Sturmian Words. In: Manea, F., Simpson, A. (eds.) CSL'22: Proc. 30th EACSL Ann. Conf. on Computer Science Logic. LIPIcs, Schloss Dagstuhl (2022). https://doi.org/10.4230/LIPIcs.CSL.2022.24
24. Meyer, R., Muskalla, S., Neumann, E.: Liveness verification and synthesis: New algorithms for recursive programs. CoRR **abs/1701.02947** (2017), http://arxiv.org/abs/1701.02947
25. Oei, R., Ma, D., Schulz, C., Hieronymi, P.: Pecan: An automated theorem prover for automatic sequences using Büchi automata (2021), https://arxiv.org/abs/2102.01727
26. Picalausa, F., Servais, F., Zimányi, E.: Xevolve: An XML schema evolution framework. In: SAC'11: Proc. ACM Symp. on Applied Computing. p. 1645–1650. ACM (2011). https://doi.org/10.1145/1982185.1982530
27. Rajasekaran, A., Shallit, J., Smith, T.: Additive number theory via automata theory. Theory of Computing Systems **64**(3), 542–567 (2019). https://doi.org/10.1007/s00224-019-09929-9

Stack-Aware Hyperproperties*

Ali Bajwa[2]([✉]), Minjian Zhang[1], Rohit Chadha[2]([✉]), and Mahesh Viswanathan[1]

[1] University of Illinois, Urbana-Champaign, USA
{minjian2,vmahesh}@illinois.edu
[2] University of Missouri, Columbia, USA
{azb9q8,chadhar}@missouri.edu

Abstract. A hyperproperty relates executions of a program and is used to formalize security objectives such as confidentiality, non-interference, privacy, and anonymity. Formally, a hyperproperty is a collection of allowable sets of executions. A program violates a hyperproperty if the set of its executions is not in the collection specified by the hyperproperty. The logic HYPERCTL* has been proposed in the literature to formally specify and verify hyperproperties. The problem of checking whether a finite-state program satisfies a HYPERCTL* formula is known to be decidable. However, the problem turns out to be undecidable for procedural (recursive) programs. Surprisingly, we show that decidability can be restored if we consider restricted classes of hyperproperties, namely those that relate only those executions of a program which have the same call-stack access pattern. We call such hyperproperties, *stack-aware hyperproperties*. Our decision procedure can be used as a proof method for establishing security objectives such as noninference for recursive programs, and also for refuting security objectives such as observational determinism. Further, if the call stack size is observable to the attacker, the decision procedure provides exact verification.

Keywords: Hyperproperties · Temporal Logic · Recursive Programs · Model Checking · Pushdown Systems · Visibly Pushdown Automata.

1 Introduction

Temporal logics HYPERLTL and HYPERCTL* [5] were designed to express and reason about security guarantees that are *hyperproperties* [6]. A hyperproperty [6] is a security guarantee that does not depend solely on individual executions. Instead, a hyperproperty relates multiple executions. For example, non-interference, a confidentiality property, states that any *two* executions of a program that differ only in high-level security inputs must have the same *low*-security observations. As pointed out in [6], several security guarantees are hyperproperties. The logic HYPERCTL* subsumes HYPERLTL, and the problem of checking a finite-state system against a HYPERCTL* formula is decidable [5].

* Ali Bajwa was partially supported by NSF CNS 1553548. Rohit Chadha was partially supported by NSF CNS 1553548 and NSF SHF 1900924. Mahesh Viswanathan and Minjian Zhang were partially supported by NSF SHF 1901069 and NSF SHF 2007428.

S. Sankaranarayanan and N. Sharygina (Eds.): TACAS 2023, LNCS 13993, pp. 308–325, 2023.
https://doi.org/10.1007/978-3-031-30823-9_16

In this paper, we consider the problem of model checking procedural (recursive) programs against security hyperproperties. Recall recursive programs are naturally modeled as a pushdown system. Unlike the case of finite-state transition systems, the problem of checking whether a pushdown system satisfies a HYPERCTL* formula is undecidable [16]. In contrast, CTL* model checking is decidable for pushdown systems [3,18].

Our contributions. We consider restricted classes of hyperproperties for recursive programs, namely those that relate only those executions that have the same *call-stack access pattern*. Intuitively, two executions have the same stack access pattern if they access the call stack in the same manner at each step, i.e., if in one execution there is a push (pop) at a point, then there is a push (pop) at the same point in the other execution. Observe that if two executions have the same stack access pattern, then their stack sizes are the same at all times. We call such hyperproperties, *stack-aware hyperproperties*.

In order to specify stack-aware hyperproperties, we extend HYPERCTL* to sHCTL*. The logic sHCTL* has a two level syntax. At the first level, the syntax is identical to HYPERCTL* formulas, and is interpreted over executions of the pushdown system with the same stack access pattern. At the top-level, we quantify over different stack access patterns. The formula $E\psi$ is true if for some stack access pattern ρ of the system, the pushdown system restricted to executions with stack access pattern ρ satisfies the HYPERCTL* formula ψ. The formula $A\psi$ is true if for each stack access pattern ρ of the system, the pushdown system restricted to executions with stack access pattern ρ satisfies the HYPER-CTL* formula ψ. See Figure 1 on Page 8 for a side-by-side comparison of the syntax for HYPERCTL* and sHCTL*. HYPERLTL is extended to sHLTL similarly. Please note that sHCTL* subsumes sHLTL, and that sHCTL* (sHLTL) coincides with HYPERCTL* (HYPERLTL) for finite state systems as all executions of finite state systems have the same stack access pattern.

We show that the model checking problem for sHCTL* is decidable. We demonstrate three different ways this result can aid in verifying recursive programs. First, for security guarantees such as noninference [14], which are expressible in the $\forall\exists^*$ fragment of HYPERLTL, we can use the model checking algorithm to establish that a recursive program satisfies the HYPERLTL property. Secondly, for the $\forall^*$ fragment of HYPERLTL, the model checking algorithm can be used to detect security flaws by establishing that a recursive program does not satisfy security guarantees. Observational determinism [13,19] is an example of such a property. Finally, when the attacker can observe stack access patterns (or, equivalently, stack sizes), we can get exact verification for several properties. The assumption of the attacker observing stack access patterns holds, for example, in the program counter security model [15] in which the attacker has access to program counters at each step. As argued in [15], the program security model is appropriate to capture control-flow side channels such as those arising from timing behavior and/or disclosure of errors.

The decision procedure uses an automata-theoretic approach inspired by the model checking algorithm for finite state systems and HYPERCTL* given in [10]. Since stack-aware hyperproperties relate only executions with the same stack access-pattern, a set of executions with the same stack access pattern can be encoded as a word over a *pushdown* alphabet, [3] and the problem of model checking a sHCTL* formula can be reduced to the problem of checking emptiness of a *non-deterministic visibly pushdown automaton (NVPA)* over infinite words [1]. The reduction of the model checking problem to the emptiness problem is based on a compositional construction of an automaton for each sub-formula which accepts exactly the set of assignments to path variables that satisfy the sub-formula. For this construction to be optimal, we carefully leverage two equi-expressive classes of automata on infinite words, namely NVPAs and *1-way alternating jump automata (1-AJA)* [4]. The model checking algorithm for sHCTL* against procedural programs has a complexity that is very close to the complexity of model checking finite state systems against HYPERCTL*. If $g(k, n)$ denotes a tower of exponentials of height k, where the top most exponent is $\mathsf{poly}(n)$, then for a formula with formula complexity r, [4] and a system and formula whose size is bounded by n, our algorithm is in $\mathsf{DTIME}(g(\lceil \frac{r}{2} \rceil, n))$. In comparison, model checking finite state systems against HYPERCTL* is in $\mathsf{NSPACE}(g(\lceil \frac{r}{2} \rceil - 1, n))$. This slight difference in complexity is consistent with checking other properties like invariants for finite state systems (NL) versus procedural programs (P).

We also prove that our model checking algorithm is optimal by proving a matching lower bound. Our proof showing $\mathsf{DTIME}(g(\lceil \frac{r}{2} \rceil, n)$-hardness of the model checking problem for formulas with (formula) complexity r, relies on re-ducing the membership problem for $g(\lceil \frac{r}{2} \rceil - 1, n)$ space bounded *alternating Turing machines* (ATM) to the model checking problem. The reduction requires identifying an encoding of computations of ATMs, which are trees, as strings that can be guessed and generated by pushdown systems. The pushdown system we construct for the model checking problem guesses potential computations of the ATM, while the sHCTL* formula we construct checks if the guessed computation is a valid accepting computation.

Related work. Clarkson and Schneider introduced *hyperproperties* [6] and demonstrated their need to capture complex security properties. Temporal logics HYPERLTL and HYPERCTL*, that describe hyperproperties, were introduced by Clarkson et al. [5]. They also characterized the complexity of model checking finite state transition systems against HYPERCTL* specifications by a reduction to the satisfiability problem of QPTL [17]. Subsequently, other model checking algorithms for verifying finite state systems against HYPERCTL* properties have been proposed [10,7]. Tools that check satisfiability [8] and runtime verifi-cation [9] for HYPERLTL formulas have also been developed. Finkbeiner et al. introduced the automata-theoretic approach to model checking HYPERCTL* for finite-state systems [10].

---

[3] A pushdown alphabet is an alphabet that is partitioned into three sets: a set of call symbols, a set of internal symbols, and a set of return symbols. See Section 4.1.

[4] Our definition of formula complexity is roughly double the usual notion of quantifier alternation. For a precise definition, see Definition 4.

The model checking problem for HYPERLTL, and consequently HYPER-CTL*, was shown to be undecidable for pushdown systems in [16]. For restricted fragments of HYPERLTL, Pommellet and Tayssir [16] introduced over-approximations and under-approximations to establish/refute that a pushdown system satisfies a HYPERLTL formula in those fragments. Gutsfeld et al. introduced stuttering H_μ, a *linear* time logic for checking asynchronous hyperproperties for recursive programs in [12]. The authors present complexity results for the model checking problem under an assumption of *fairness*, and a restriction of *well-alignment*. While the restriction to paths with the same *stack access pattern* is similar to the well-alignment restriction, we do not assume any fairness condition to establish decidability. However, as sHCTL* is a branching time logic and only considers synchronous hyperproperties, the two logics are not directly comparable. It is also worth mentioning that the branching nature of sHCTL* requires us to "copy" a potentially unbounded stack, from the most recently quantified path variable, when assigning a path to the "current" quantified path variable. In contrast, all path assignments in [12] start with an empty stack.

For lack of space reasons, some proofs are omitted and can be located in [2].

2   Motivation

Clarkson and Schneider [6] argue that many important *security* guarantees are expressible only as *hyperproperties*. We discuss two examples of security hyperproperties, and the logics HYPERLTL and HYPERCTL* used to specify them.

Hyperproperties and temporal logics. We discuss two variants of non-interference [11] that model confidentiality requirements. In non-interference, the inputs of a system are partitioned into *low*-level input security variables and *high*-level input security variables. The attacker is assumed to know the values of low-level security inputs. During an execution, the attacker can observe parts of the system configuration such as system outputs, or the memory usage. A system satisfies *non-interference* if the attacker cannot deduce the values of high-level inputs from the low-level observations. To formally specify the variants, we use the logic HYPERLTL [5], a fragment of the logic HYPERCTL* [5]. The precise syntax of HYPERLTL and HYPERCTL* is shown in Fig. 1. In the syntax, π is a path variable and the formula a_π is true if the proposition a is true along the path "π". Intuitively, the formula $\exists \pi. \psi$ is existential quantification over paths, and is true if there is a path that can be assigned to π such that ψ is true. Universal quantification ($\forall \pi. \psi$), and other logical connectives such as conjunction ($\wedge$), implication ($\rightarrow$), equivalence ($\leftrightarrow$) and the temporal operators G and F can be defined in the standard way. By having explicit path variables, HYPERLTL and HYPERCTL* allow quantification over multiple paths simultaneously.

Example 1. The first variant, noninference [14], states that for each execution σ of a program, there is another execution σ' such that (a) σ' is obtained from σ by replacing the high-level security inputs by a dummy input, and (b) σ and σ' have the same low-level observations. Noninference is a hyperliveness property [5,6].

Let us assume that the low-level observations of a configuration are determined by the values of the propositions in $L = \{\ell_1, \cdots \ell_m\}$. As shown in [5], non-inference is expressible by the HYPERLTL formula: $\text{NI} \stackrel{\text{def}}{=} \forall \pi. \exists \pi'.(\text{G} \lambda_{\pi'}) \wedge \pi \equiv_L \pi'$. Here $\text{G} \lambda_{\pi'}$ expresses that G*lobally* (or in each configuration of the execution) the high input of π' is the dummy input λ, and $\pi \equiv_L \pi' \stackrel{\text{def}}{=} \text{G}(\wedge_{\ell \in L}(\ell_\pi \leftrightarrow \ell_{\pi'}))$ expresses that π and π' have the same low-level observations.

Example 2. The second variant, observational determinism [13,19], states that any two executions that have the same low-level initial inputs, must have the same low-level output observations. Observational determinism is a hypersafety property [5,6], and is also expressible in HYPERLTL using the formula [5]: $\text{OD} \stackrel{\text{def}}{=} \forall \pi. \forall \pi'.(\pi[0] \equiv_{L,in} \pi'[0]) \to \pi \equiv_{L,out} \pi'$. Here $\equiv_{L,in}$ and $\equiv_{L,out}$ express the fact that π and π' have the same low-security inputs and outputs respectively.

Procedural (recursive) programs and Stack-aware hyperproperties. Pushdown systems model procedural programs that do not dynamically allocate memory, and whose program variables take values in finite domains. Unlike finite-state transition systems, the problem of checking whether a pushdown system satisfies a HYPERCTL* formula is undecidable [16]. However, we identify a natural class of hyperproperties for which the model checking problem becomes decidable. As we shall shortly see, this class of hyperproperties not only enjoys decidability, but is also useful in reasoning about security hyperproperies such as noninference and observational determinism.

We consider a restricted class of hyperproperties for recursive programs, which relate only executions that access the call stack in the same manner, i.e., push or pop at the same time. An execution of a pushdown system $\mathcal{P}$ is a sequence of configurations (control state + stack) $\sigma = c_1 c_2 \cdots$, such that the stacks of consecutive configurations c_i and c_{i+1} differ only due to the possible presence of an additional element at the top of the stack of either c_i or c_{i+1}. For such a sequence, we can associate a sequence $\text{pr}(\sigma) = o_1 o_2 \cdots$ such that $o_i \in \{\text{call}, \text{int}, \text{ret}\}$ such that $o_i = \text{call}$ (ret respectively) if and only if the stack in c_{i+1} has one more (less respectively) element than c_i. The sequence $\text{pr}(\sigma)$ is said to be the *stack access pattern* of σ. Observe that the stack sizes of two executions with the same stack access pattern evolve in a similar fashion. Thus, equivalently, we can consider this class of hyperproperties to be the hyperproperties that relate executions with identical memory usage.

To specify these hyperproperties, we propose the logic sHCTL* which extends HYPERCTL*. sHCTL* has a two level syntax. At the innermost level, the syntax is identical to that of HYPERCTL* formulas, but is interpreted over executions of the pushdown system with the same stack access pattern. At the outer level, we quantify over different stack access patterns. Intuitively, the formula $E\psi$ is true if there is a stack access pattern ρ exhibited by the system such that the set of executions with access pattern ρ satisfy the hyperproperty ψ. The dual formula $A\psi$, defined as $\neg E \neg \psi$, is true if for each stack access pattern ρ exhibited by the system, the set of all executions with stack access pattern ρ

satisfy ψ. The syntax of sHLTL is obtained from HYPERLTL in a similar fashion. Please see Fig. 1 on Page 8 for a side-by-side comparison of the syntax of HYPERCTL* (HYPERLTL) and sHCTL* (sHLTL). Unlike HYPERCTL*, we show that the problem of checking sHCTL* is decidable for pushdown systems (Theorem 3). Formal definitions of stack access patterns, syntax and semantics of sHCTL* are in Section 3.

For the rest of the paper, hyperproperties expressible in sHCTL* will be called *stack-aware hyperproperties*. Restricting to stack-aware hyperproperties is useful in verifying security guarantees of recursive programs as discussed below.

Proving $\forall\exists^*$ hyperproperties. The *noninference* property (Example 1) can be expressed in HYPERLTL as $\mathsf{NI} \overset{\text{def}}{=} \forall\pi.\exists\pi'.(\mathsf{G}\,\lambda_{\pi'})\wedge\pi \equiv_L \pi'$. Consider the sHLTL formula $A(\mathsf{NI})$ obtained by putting an A in front NI. A pushdown system satisfies $A(\mathsf{NI})$ only if for each execution σ of the system, there is another execution σ' with *the same stack access pattern as* σ such that σ, σ' together satisfy $(\mathsf{G}\,\lambda_{\sigma'})\wedge\sigma \equiv_L \sigma'$. Thus, if the pushdown system satisfies the sHLTL formula $A(\mathsf{NI})$, then it also satisfies noninference. Thus, a decision procedure for sHLTL can be used to prove that a recursive program satisfies noninference.

The above observation generalizes to HYPERLTL formulas of the form $\psi = \forall\pi.\exists\pi_1.\ldots.\exists\pi_k.\psi'$ — if a system satisfies the sHLTL formula $A\psi$ then it must also satisfy the HYPERLTL formula ψ. Though the model checking problem is undecidable for pushdown systems even when restricted to such HYPERLTL formulas, we gain decidability by restricting the search space for $\pi, \pi_1, \ldots, \pi_k$.

Refuting $\forall^*$ hyperproperties. *Observational determinism* (Example 2) can be written in HYPERLTL as $\mathsf{OD} \overset{\text{def}}{=} \forall\pi.\forall\pi'.(\pi[0] \equiv_{L,in} \pi'[0]) \to \pi \equiv_{L,out} \pi'$. Consider the sHLTL formula $A(\mathsf{OD})$. A pushdown system *fails* to satisfy the sHLTL formula $A(\mathsf{OD})$ only if there is a stack access pattern ρ and executions σ_1 and σ_2 with stack access pattern ρ such that the pushdown system does not satisfy $(\sigma[0] \equiv_{L,in} \sigma'[0]) \to \sigma \equiv_{L,out} \sigma'$.

This observation generalizes to HYPERLTL formulas of the form $\psi = \forall\pi_1.\ldots.\forall\pi_k.\psi'$ — if a pushdown system fails to satisfy the sHLTL formula $A\psi$ then it does not satisfy ψ. Even though model checking pushdown systems against such restricted specifications is undecidable, our decision procedure can be used to show that a recursive program does not meet such properties.

Exact verification when stack access pattern is observable. Often, it is reasonable to assume that the attacker can observe the stack access pattern. For example, in the program counter security model [15], the attacker has access to the program counter transcript, i.e., the sequence of program counters during an execution. Access to the program counter transcript implies that the attacker can observe stack access pattern. The assumption that the program counter transcript is observable helps model control flow side channel attacks which include timing attacks and error disclosure attacks [15]. sHCTL* can be used to verify security guarantees in this security model. For example, the sHCTL* formula $A(\mathsf{NI})$ models noninference faithfully by introducing a unique proposition for each control state. Observational determinism can also be verified in this model by suitably transforming the pushdown automaton.

Another scenario in which stack access patterns are observable is when the attacker can observe the memory usage of a program in terms of stack size. As observing stack size may lead to information leakage, stack size should be considered a low-level observation. Since the stack size can be unbounded, it cannot be modeled as a proposition. sHCTL*, however, can still be used to verify security guarantees in this case. For example, $A(\mathsf{NI}) = A(\forall \pi. \exists \pi.' (\mathsf{G} \lambda_{\pi'}) \wedge \pi \equiv_L \pi')$ faithfully models non-inference as semantics of sHCTL* forces π and π' to have the same call-stack size in addition to other low-level observations. Once again, observational determinism can also be verified in this model by suitably transforming the pushdown automaton.

3   Stack-aware Hyper Computation Tree Logic (sHCTL*)

Stack-aware Hyper Computation Tree Logic (sHCTL*), and its sub-logic Stack-aware Hyper Linear Temporal Logic (sHLTL) are formally presented. We begin by establishing some conventions over strings.

Strings. A *string/word* w over a finite alphabet Σ is a sequence $w = a_0 a_1 \cdots$ of finite or infinitely many symbols from Σ, i.e., $a_i \in \Sigma$ for all i. The *length* of a string w, denoted $|w|$, is the number of symbols appearing in it — if $w = a_0 a_1 \cdots a_{n-1}$ is finite then $|w| = n$, and if $w = a_0 a_1 \cdots$ is infinite then $|w| = \omega$. The *unique* string of length 0, the *empty string*, is denoted ε. For a string $w = a_0 a_1 \cdots a_i \cdots$, $w(i) = a_i$ denotes the ith symbol, $w[\,:i\,] = a_0 a_1 \cdots a_{i-1}$ denotes the prefix of length i, $w[i\,:\,] = a_i a_{i+1} \cdots$ denotes the suffix of w starting at position i, and $w[i\,:\,j] = a_i a_{i+1} \cdots a_{j-1}$ denotes the substring from position i (included) to position j (not included). Thus $w[0\,:\,] = w$. By convention, when $i \leq 0$, we take $w[\,:i\,] = \varepsilon$. Over Σ, the set of all finite strings is denoted Σ^*, and the set of all infinite strings is denoted Σ^ω. For a finite string u and a (finite or infinite) string v, uv denotes the *concatenation* of u and v.

3.1   Pushdown Systems

Pushdown systems naturally model for sequential recursive programs. Formally, an AP-*labeled pushdown system* is a tuple $\mathcal{P} = (S, \Gamma, s_{\mathsf{in}}, \Delta, L)$, where S is a finite set of *control states*, Γ is a finite set of *stack symbols*, $s_{\mathsf{in}} \in S$ is the *initial control state*, $L : S \rightarrow 2^{\mathsf{AP}}$ is the *labeling function*, and Δ is the transition relation. The transition relation $\Delta = \Delta_{\mathsf{int}} \uplus \Delta_{\mathsf{call}} \uplus \Delta_{\mathsf{ret}}$ is the disjoint union of *internal transitions* $\Delta_{\mathsf{int}} \subseteq S \times S$ where the stack is unchanged, *call transitions* $\Delta_{\mathsf{call}} \subseteq S \times (S \times \Gamma)$ where a single symbol is *pushed* onto the stack, and *return transitions* $\Delta_{\mathsf{ret}} \subseteq (S \times \Gamma) \times S$ where a single symbol is *popped* from the stack. When AP is clear from the context, we simply refer to them as pushdown systems. **Transition System Semantics.** We recall the standard semantics of a pushdown system as a transition system. Let us fix a pushdown system $\mathcal{P} = (S, \Gamma, s_{\mathsf{in}}, \Delta, L)$. A *configuration* c of $\mathcal{P}$ is a pair (s, α) where $s \in S$ and $\alpha \in \Gamma^*$.

$$a \in \mathsf{AP}, \pi \in \mathcal{V}$$

$\psi ::= a_\pi \mid \neg\psi \mid \psi \vee \psi \mid \mathsf{X}\psi$ $\theta ::= E\psi \mid \neg\theta \mid \theta \vee \theta$
$\quad\quad\mid \psi \, \mathsf{U} \, \psi \mid \exists\pi.\psi$ $\psi ::= a_\pi \mid \neg\psi \mid \psi \vee \psi \mid \mathsf{X}\psi \mid \psi \, \mathsf{U} \, \psi \mid \exists\pi.\psi$

(a) HYPERCTL*   (b) sHCTL*

Fig. 1: BNF for HYPERCTL* and sHCTL*. Let $\forall$ denote $\neg\exists\neg$ and A denote $\neg E\neg\psi$. HYPERLTL is the set of HYPERCTL* formulas $Q_1\pi_1.\cdots Q_r\pi_r.\psi$ where $Q_i \in \{\exists, \forall\}$ and ψ is quantifier-free. sHLTL is the set of sHCTL* formulas $\mathbb{E}\varphi$, where $\mathbb{E} \in \{A, E\}$ and φ is in HYPERLTL.

The set of all configurations of $\mathcal{P}$ will be denoted $\mathsf{Conf}_\mathcal{P} = S \times \Gamma^*$. The *labeled transition system* associated with $\mathcal{P}$ is $[\![\mathcal{P}]\!] := (\mathsf{Conf}_\mathcal{P}, c_{\mathsf{in}}, \longrightarrow, \mathsf{AP}, L)$ where $c_{\mathsf{in}} = (s_{\mathsf{in}}, \varepsilon)$ is the *initial configuration*, $\longrightarrow \subseteq \mathsf{Conf}_\mathcal{P} \times (\{\mathsf{call}, \mathsf{ret}, \mathsf{int}\} \times S \times (\Gamma \cup \{\varepsilon\}) \times S) \times \mathsf{Conf}_\mathcal{P}$ is the *transition relation*, and L is the *labeling function* that extends the labeling function of $\mathcal{P}$ to configurations as follows: $L(s, \alpha) = L(s)$. The transition relation $\longrightarrow$ is defined to capture the informal semantics of internal, call, and return transitions — for any $\alpha \in \Gamma^*$, (int) $(s, \alpha) \xrightarrow{(\mathsf{int}, s, \varepsilon, s')} (s', \alpha)$ iff $(s, s') \in \Delta_{\mathsf{int}}$; (call) $(s, \alpha) \xrightarrow{(\mathsf{call}, s, a, s')} (s', a\alpha)$ iff $(s, (s', a)) \in \Delta_{\mathsf{call}}$; and (ret) $(s, a\alpha) \xrightarrow{(\mathsf{ret}, s, a, s')} (s', \alpha)$ iff $((s, a), s') \in \Delta_{\mathsf{ret}}$.

A *path* of $[\![\mathcal{P}]\!]$ is an infinite sequence of configurations $\sigma = c_0, c_1, \ldots$ such that for each i, $c_i \xrightarrow{(\mathsf{o}, s, a, s')} c_{i+1}$ for some $\mathsf{o} \in \{\mathsf{int}, \mathsf{call}, \mathsf{ret}\}$, $s, s' \in S$ and $a \in \Gamma \cup \{\varepsilon\}$. The path σ is said to *start* in configuration c_0 (the first configuration in the sequence). We will use $\mathsf{Paths}([\![\mathcal{P}]\!], c)$ to denote the set of paths of $[\![\mathcal{P}]\!]$ starting in the configuration c and $\mathsf{Paths}([\![\mathcal{P}]\!])$ to denote all paths of $[\![\mathcal{P}]\!]$.

We conclude this section by introducing some notation on configurations. For $c = (s, \alpha)$, its *stack height* is $|\alpha|$, its *control state* is $\mathsf{state}(c) = s$, and its *top of stack symbol* is $\mathsf{top}(c) = a \in \Gamma$ if $\alpha = a\alpha'$ and is undefined if $\alpha = \varepsilon$.

3.2   Syntax of sHCTL*

Let us fix a set of atomic propositions AP, and a set of path variables, $\mathcal{V}$. The BNF grammar for sHCTL* formulas is given in Figure 1(b). In the BNF grammar, $a \in \mathsf{AP}$ is an *atomic proposition*, π is a *path variable*, ψ is a *cognate formula*, and θ is a sHCTL* formula. The syntax has two levels, with the inner level identical to HYPERCTL* formulas, while the outer level allows quantification over different stack access patterns (see Section 3.3). Also, following [5,10], we assume that the until operator U only occurs within the scope of a path quantifier.

Remark 1. We have chosen to not have A, the dual of E, and conjunction as explicit logical operators to keep our exposition simple. This choice does makes the automata constructions presented here less efficient for formulas involving conjunction. Adding them explicitly does not pose a technical challenge to our setup and our automata constructions can be extended to handle them explicitly. In addition, we will sometimes use other quantifiers and logical operators to write formulas. Some standard examples include: $\theta_1 \wedge \theta_2 = \neg(\neg\theta_1 \vee \neg\theta_2)$, where θ_i ($i \in \{1, 2\}$) is either a sHCTL* or cognate formula; $\forall\pi.\psi = \neg\,\exists\pi.\,\neg\psi$; $\mathsf{F}\,\psi = \mathsf{true}\,\mathsf{U}\,\psi$, where $\mathsf{true} = a_\pi \vee \neg a_\pi$; $\mathsf{G}\,\psi = \neg\,\mathsf{F}\,\neg\psi$.

We call formulas of the form $\mathfrak{E}\psi$ (where $\mathfrak{E} \in \{A, E\}$ and ψ is a cognate formula) *basic formulas*. Observe that any sHCTL* formula is a Boolean combination of basic formulas. A sHCTL* formula θ is a *sentence* if in each basic sub-formula $\mathfrak{E}\psi$, ψ is a sentence, i.e., every path variable appearing in ψ is quantified. Without loss of generality, we assume that in any cognate formula ψ, all bound variables in ψ are renamed to ensure that any path variable is quantified at most once. We will only consider sHCTL* sentences in this paper. The logic sHLTL is the sub-logic of sHCTL* consisting of all formulas of the form $\mathfrak{E}Q_1\pi_1.\cdots Q_r\pi_r.\psi$ where $\mathfrak{E} \in \{A, E\}$, $Q_i \in \{\exists, \forall\}$ and ψ is quantifier free.

3.3   Semantics of sHCTL*

The syntax of cognate formulas is identical to that HYPERCTL* formulas. Their semantics will be described in a similar manner, in a context where free path variables in the formula are interpreted as executions of a system. However, we will require that the interpretations of every path variable share a *common* stack access pattern — hence the term *cognate*. Thus, before defining the semantics, we will define what we mean by the *stack access pattern* of a path and a *path environment* that assigns an interpretation to path variables.

For the rest of this section let us fix a pushdown system $\mathcal{P} = (S, \Gamma, s_{\mathsf{in}}, \Delta, L)$. A string $w \in \{\mathsf{call}, \mathsf{int}, \mathsf{ret}\}^*$ is said to be *well matched* if either $w = \varepsilon$ or $w = \mathsf{int}$ or $w = \mathsf{call}\,u\,\mathsf{ret}$ or $w = uv$, where $u, v \in \{\mathsf{call}, \mathsf{int}, \mathsf{ret}\}^*$ are (recursively) well matched. In a string $\rho \in \{\mathsf{call}, \mathsf{int}, \mathsf{ret}\}^\omega$, $\rho(i)$ is an *unmatched return*, if $\rho[\,:\,i+1] = w\,\mathsf{ret}$, where w is well matched. We are now ready to present the definition of a stack access pattern.

Definition 1 (Stack access pattern). *A string $\rho \in \{\mathsf{call}, \mathsf{int}, \mathsf{ret}\}^\omega$ is a stack access pattern if the set $\{i \in \mathbb{N} \mid \rho(i)$ is an unmatched return$\}$ is finite.*

A path $\sigma = c_0 c_1 c_2 \cdots \in \mathsf{Paths}([\![\mathcal{P}]\!])$ is said to have a stack access pattern $\rho = o_0 o_1 \cdots$ (denoted $\mathsf{pr}(\sigma) = \rho$) if for every i: (a) $o_i = \mathsf{call}$ if and only if $\mathsf{stack}(c_{i+1}) = \mathsf{top}(c_{i+1})\,\mathsf{stack}(c_i)$, (b) $o_i = \mathsf{int}$ if and only if $\mathsf{stack}(c_{i+1}) = \mathsf{stack}(c_i)$, and (c) $o_i = \mathsf{ret}$ if and only if $\mathsf{stack}(c_i) = \mathsf{top}(c_i)\,\mathsf{stack}(c_{i+1})$.

We now present the definition of *path environment* that interprets the free path variables in a cognate formula as paths of $[\![\mathcal{P}]\!]$ such that they share a common stack access pattern. This plays a key role in defining the semantics of sHCTL*. For a set of path variables $\mathcal{V}$, let $\mathcal{V}^\dagger$ be defined as the set $\mathcal{V} \cup \{\dagger\}$.

Definition 2 (Path Environment). *A path environment for pushdown system $\mathcal{P}$ over variables $\mathcal{V}$ is function $\Pi : \mathcal{V}^\dagger \to \mathsf{Paths}([\![\mathcal{P}]\!]) \cup \{\mathsf{call}, \mathsf{int}, \mathsf{ret}\}^\omega$ such* *that* $\Pi(\dagger)$ *is a stack access pattern , and for every* $\pi \in \mathcal{V}$, $\Pi(\pi) \in \mathsf{Paths}(\llbracket \mathcal{P} \rrbracket)$ *with* $\mathsf{pr}(\Pi(\pi)) = \Pi(\dagger)$. *When the pushdown system is clear from the context, we will simply refer to it as a path environment over* $\mathcal{V}$.

When $\mathcal{V} = \emptyset$, *we additionally require that there is a path* $\sigma \in \mathsf{Paths}(\llbracket \mathcal{P} \rrbracket, c_{\mathsf{in}})$ *(where* c_{in} *is the initial configuration of* $\llbracket \mathcal{P} \rrbracket$*) such that* $\mathsf{pr}(\sigma) = \Pi(\dagger)$.

We introduce some notation related to path environments. Let us fix a path environment Π over variables $\mathcal{V}$. Given a path $\sigma \in \mathsf{Paths}(\llbracket \mathcal{P} \rrbracket)$, $\Pi[\pi \mapsto \sigma]$ denotes the path environment over $\mathcal{V} \cup \{\pi\}$ such that $\Pi[\pi \mapsto \sigma](\pi) = \sigma$, and $\Pi[\pi \mapsto \sigma](\pi') = \Pi(\pi')$, for any $\pi' \in \mathcal{V}^\dagger$ with $\pi' \neq \pi$. Finally, for $i \in \mathbb{N}$, $\Pi[i:]$ denotes the *suffix* path environment, where every variable is mapped to the suffix of the path starting at position i. More formally, for every $\pi' \in \mathcal{V}^\dagger$, $\Pi[i:](\pi') = \Pi(\pi')[i:]$.

We now define when a pushdown system $\mathcal{P}$ satisfies a sHCTL* sentence θ, denoted $\mathcal{P} \models \theta$. The definition of satisfaction of θ relies on a definition of satisfaction for cognate formulas. To inductively to define the semantics of cognate formulas, we will interpret free path variables using a path environment. Finally, as in HYPERCTL*, it is important to track the most recently quantified path variable because that influences the semantics of $\exists \pi(\cdot)$. Thus satisfaction of cognate formulas takes the form $\mathcal{P}, \Pi, \pi' \models \psi$, where π' is the most recently quantified path variable, and Π is a path environment over the free variables of ψ. Finally, by convention, we will take $\mathsf{Paths}(\llbracket \mathcal{P} \rrbracket, \Pi(\dagger)(0))$ to mean $\mathsf{Paths}(\llbracket \mathcal{P} \rrbracket, c_{\mathsf{in}})$, where c_{in} is the initial configuration of $\llbracket \mathcal{P} \rrbracket$ [5]. Below, θ, θ_1, and θ_2 are sHCTL* sentences, while ψ, ψ_1, ψ_2 are cognate formulas.

$$\mathcal{P} \models \neg\theta \text{ iff } \mathcal{P} \not\models \theta$$
$$\mathcal{P} \models \theta_1 \vee \theta_2 \text{ iff } \mathcal{P} \models \theta_1 \text{ or } \mathcal{P} \models \theta_2$$
$$\mathcal{P} \models E\psi \text{ iff for some path environment } \Pi \text{ over } \emptyset, \mathcal{P}, \Pi, \dagger \models \psi$$
$$\mathcal{P}, \Pi, \pi' \models a_\pi \text{ iff } a \in L(\Pi(\pi)(0))$$
$$\mathcal{P}, \Pi, \pi' \models \neg\psi \text{ iff } \mathcal{P}, \Pi, \pi' \not\models \psi$$
$$\mathcal{P}, \Pi, \pi' \models \psi_1 \vee \psi_2 \text{ iff } \mathcal{P}, \Pi, \pi' \models \psi_1 \text{ or } \mathcal{P}, \Pi, \pi' \models \psi_2$$
$$\mathcal{P}, \Pi, \pi' \models X\psi \text{ iff } \mathcal{P}, \Pi[1:], \pi' \models \psi$$
$$\mathcal{P}, \Pi, \pi' \models \psi_1 U \psi_2 \text{ iff } \exists i \geq 0 : \mathcal{P}, \Pi[i:], \pi' \models \psi_2 \text{ and } \forall j, 0 \leq j < i,$$
$$\mathcal{P}, \Pi[j:], \pi' \models \psi_1$$
$$\mathcal{P}, \Pi, \pi' \models \exists \pi. \psi \text{ iff } \exists \sigma \in \mathsf{Paths}(\llbracket \mathcal{P} \rrbracket, \Pi(\pi')(0)) \text{ with } \mathsf{pr}(\sigma) = \Pi(\dagger),$$
$$\text{such that } \mathcal{P}, \Pi[\pi \mapsto \sigma], \pi \models \psi$$

4 A Decision Procedure for sHCTL*

Given a pushdown system $\mathcal{P}$ and a sHCTL* sentence θ, we present an algorithm that determines if $\mathcal{P} \models \theta$. Our approach is similar to the one in [10]. Given a finite state transition system $\mathcal{K}$ and a HYPERCTL* formula φ, Finkbeiner et. al. [10], construct an alternating (finite state) Büchi automaton $\mathcal{A}_{\mathcal{K},\varphi}$, by induction on φ, such that an input word σ is accepted by $\mathcal{A}_{\mathcal{K},\varphi}$ if and only if σ is the encoding

---

[5] The convention is needed because $\Pi(\dagger)(0)$ is not a configuration but an element of the set $\{\mathsf{call}, \mathsf{int}, \mathsf{ret}\}$.

of a path environment Π such that $\mathcal{K}, \Pi \models \varphi$. Determining if $\mathcal{K} \models \varphi$ then reduces to checking if $\mathcal{A}_{\mathcal{K},\varphi}$ accepts any string.

Extending these ideas to sHCTL* and pushdown systems, requires one to answer two questions: (a) What is an encoding of path environments for cognate formulas where path variables are mapped to sequences of configurations (control state + stack)?; (b) Which automata models can capture the collection of path environments satisfying a cognate formula with respect to a pushdown system? We encode path environments for cognate formulas using strings over a *pushdown alphabet* — pushdown tags on symbols adds structure that helps encode sequences of configurations. And for automata, we consider automata that process such strings and accept *visibly pushdown languages*. A natural generalization of the approach outlined in [10] would suggest the use of alternating visibly pushdown automata (AVPA) on infinite strings [4]. However, using AVPAs results in an inefficient algorithm. To get a more efficient algorithm, we instead rely on a careful use of *nondeterministic visibly pushdown automata (NVPA)* [1] and *1-way alternating jump automata (1-AJA)* [4]. The advantage of using NVPA and 1-AJA can be seen in the case of existential quantification $(\exists \pi.)$ which requires converting an alternating automaton to a nondeterministic one [10]: Converting from 1-AJA to NVPA leads to exponential blowup while converting AVPA to NVPA leads to a doubly exponential blowup [4].

The rest of this section is organized as follows. We begin by introducing the automata models on pushdown alphabets (Section 4.1). Next we present our encoding of path environments, and finally our automata constructions that establish the decidability result (Section 4.2).

4.1 Automata on Pushdown Alphabets

A *pushdown alphabet* is a finite set Σ that is partitioned into three sets $\Sigma_{\mathsf{call}} \uplus \Sigma_{\mathsf{int}} \uplus \Sigma_{\mathsf{ret}}$, where Σ_{call} is the set of *call symbols*, Σ_{int} is the set of *internal symbols*, and Σ_{ret} is the set of *return symbols*. Automata models processing strings over a pushdown alphabet are restricted to perform certain types of transitions based on whether the read symbol is a call, internal, or return symbol. We introduce, informally, two such automata models next. Precise definition and its semantics can be found in the detailed version of this paper [2].

Nondeterministic Visibly Pushdown Büchi Automata. A *nondeterministic visibly pushdown automaton (NVPA)* [1] is like a pushdown system. It has finitely many control states and uses an unbounded stack for storage. However, unlike a pushdown system, it is an automaton that processes an infinite sequence of input symbols from a pushdown alphabet $\Sigma = \Sigma_{\mathsf{call}} \uplus \Sigma_{\mathsf{int}} \uplus \Sigma_{\mathsf{ret}}$. Transitions are constrained to conform to pushdown alphabet — whenever a Σ_{call} symbol is read, a symbol onto the stack, whenever a Σ_{ret} symbol is read, the top stack symbol is popped, and whenever Σ_{int} symbol is read, the stack is unchanged.

1-way Alternating Jump Automata. Our second automaton model is *1-way Alternating Parity Jump Automata (1-AJA)* [4]. 1-AJA are computationally equivalent to NVPAs (i.e., accept the same class of languages) but provide greater flexibility in describing algorithms. 1-AJAs are alternating automata, which means that they can define acceptance based on multiple runs of the machine on an input word. Though they are finite state machines with no auxiliary storage, their ability to spawn a computation thread that jumps to a future portion of the input string on reading a symbol, allows them to have the same computational power as a more conventional machine with storage (like NVPAs).

We present some useful properties of NVPA and 1-AJA. The two models are equi-expressive with the size of automata constructed by the translation known.

Theorem 1 ([4]). *For any NVPA N of size n, there is a 1-AJA $\mathcal{A}_N$ of size $O(n^2)$, such that $\mathcal{L}(\mathcal{A}_N) = \mathcal{L}(N)$. Conversely, for any 1-AJA $\mathcal{A}$ of size n, there is a NVPA $N_\mathcal{A}$ of size $2^{O(n)}$, such that $\mathcal{L}(N_\mathcal{A}) = \mathcal{L}(\mathcal{A})$. Constructions can be carried out in time proportional to the size of the resulting automaton.*

Both 1-AJA and NVPAs are closed for language operations like complementation, union and prefixing. We also recall the following result.

Theorem 2 ([1]). *For NVPAs, the emptiness problem is PTIME-complete.*

4.2   Algorithm for sHCTL*

Let us fix a pushdown system $\mathcal{P} = (S, \Gamma, s_{\text{in}}, \Delta, L)$ and a sHCTL* sentence θ. Our goal is to decide if $\mathcal{P} \models \theta$. We will reduce this problem to checking the emptiness of multiple NVPAs (Theorem 2). Our approach is similar to [10] — for each cognate sub-formula ψ (not necessarily sentence) of θ, we will compositionally construct an automaton that accepts the path environments satisfying ψ. Path environments will be encoded by strings over pushdown alphabets as follows.

For a path $\sigma = c_0 c_1 c_2 \cdots$ of $[\![\mathcal{P}]\!]$, the *trace* of σ, denoted $\text{tr}(\sigma)$, is the (unique) sequence $(o_0, q_0, a_0, q_1)(o_1, q_1, a_1, q_2) \cdots$ such that for every $i \in \mathbb{N}$, $c_i \xrightarrow{(o_i, q_i, a_i, q_{i+1})} c_{i+1}$ where $o_i \in \{\text{call, int, ret}\}$, $q_i, q_{i+1} \in Q$, and $a_i \in \Gamma \cup \{\varepsilon\}$ [6].

While $\text{tr}(\sigma)$ is uniquely determined by the path σ, the converse is not true — different paths may have the same trace. To see this, consider the following example. For configuration c and $\gamma \in \Gamma^*$, let $\gamma(c)$ denote the configuration $(\text{state}(c), \text{stack}(c)\gamma)$, i.e., the configuration with the same control state, but with stack containing the symbols in γ at the bottom. Observe that, for any $\gamma \in \Gamma^*$, if $\sigma = c_0 c_1 c_2 \cdot$ is a path then so is $\gamma(\sigma) = \gamma(c_0)\gamma(c_1)\gamma(c_2)\cdots$. Additionally, $\text{tr}(\sigma) = \text{tr}(\gamma(\sigma))$. Two paths σ_1 and σ_2 of $[\![\mathcal{P}]\!]$ will be said to be equivalent if $\text{tr}(\sigma_1) = \text{tr}(\sigma_2)$ and will be denoted as $\sigma_1 \simeq \sigma_2$. Observe that equivalent paths have the same stack access pattern , i.e. if $\sigma_1 \simeq \sigma_2$ then $\text{pr}(\sigma_1) = \text{pr}(\sigma_2)$. The semantics of sHCTL* doesn't distinguish between equivalent paths.

---

[6] Observe that even when σ is not a path in $[\![\mathcal{P}]\!]$ (i.e., corresponds to an actual sequence of transitions of $\mathcal{P}$), the trace of σ is uniquely defined as long as stacks of successive configurations of σ can be obtained by leaving the stack unchanged, or pushing/popping one symbol.

Proposition 1. *Let φ be a cognate formula with $\mathcal{V}$ as the set of free path variables. Let Π_1 and Π_2 be two path environments such that for every $\pi \in \mathcal{V}$, $\Pi_1(\pi) \simeq \Pi_2(\pi)$. Then, $\mathcal{P}, \Pi_1, \pi \models \varphi$ if and only if $\mathcal{P}, \Pi_2, \pi \models \varphi$.*

The proof of Proposition 1 follows by induction on cognate formulas. Proposition 1 establishes that the set of path environments satisfying a cognate formula is a union of equivalence classes with respect to path equivalence. Thus, instead of constructing automata that accept path environments, we will construct automata that accept mappings from path variables to traces of paths. For $m \in \mathbb{N}$, let $\Sigma[m] = \Sigma[m]_{\mathsf{call}} \uplus \Sigma[m]_{\mathsf{int}} \uplus \Sigma[m]_{\mathsf{ret}}$ be the pushdown alphabet where $\Sigma[m]_{\mathsf{call}} = \{\mathsf{call}\} \times S^m \times \Gamma^m$, $\Sigma[m]_{\mathsf{int}} = \{\mathsf{int}\} \times S^m \times \{\varepsilon\}^m$, and $\Sigma[m]_{\mathsf{ret}} = \{\mathsf{ret}\} \times S^m \times \Gamma^m$. Observe $\Sigma[0]$ is (essentially) the set $\{\mathsf{int}, \mathsf{call}, \mathsf{ret}\}$.

Definition 3 (Encoding Path Environments). *Consider a set of m path variables $\mathcal{V} = \{\pi_1, \pi_2, \ldots \pi_m\}$. A string $w \in \Sigma[m]^{\omega}$ where for any $j \in \mathbb{N}$, $w(j) = (\mathsf{o}_j, (s_1^j, s_2^j, \ldots s_m^j), (a_1^j, a_2^j, \ldots a_m^j))$ encodes all path environments Π such that*

$$\Pi(\dagger) = \mathsf{o}_0 \mathsf{o}_1 \mathsf{o}_2 \cdots \mathsf{o}_j \cdots$$
$$\mathsf{tr}(\Pi(\pi_i)) = (\mathsf{o}_0, s_i^0, a_i^0, s_i^1)(\mathsf{o}_1, s_i^1, a_i^1, s_i^2) \cdots$$

for any $i \in \{1, 2, \ldots m\}$. The string encoding a path environment Π is denoted as $\mathsf{enc}(\Pi)$ ($= w$, in this case).

Based on the definitions, the following observation about traces and encodings can be concluded.

Proposition 2. *For any path $\sigma \in \mathsf{Paths}(\llbracket \mathcal{P} \rrbracket)$ and $i \in \mathbb{N}$, $\mathsf{tr}(\sigma[i:]) = \mathsf{tr}(\sigma)[i:]$. For any path environment Π and $i \in \mathbb{N}$, $\mathsf{enc}(\Pi[i:]) = \mathsf{enc}(\Pi)[i:]$.*

The encoding of path environments as strings over $\Sigma[m]$ (for an appropriate value of m) is used in our decision procedure, which compositionally constructs automata that accept path environments satisfying each cognate formula. The size of our constructed automata, like in [10], will be tower of exponentials that depends on the *formula complexity* of the cognate formula φ.

Definition 4 (Formula Complexity). *The formula complexity of a sHCTL* formula φ, denoted $\mathsf{fc}(\varphi)$, is inductively defined as follows. Let $\mathsf{odd} : \mathbb{N} \to \mathbb{N}$ be the function that maps a number n to the smallest odd number $\geq n$, i.e., $\mathsf{odd}(n) = n$ if n is odd and $\mathsf{odd}(n) = n + 1$ if n is even. Similarly, $\mathsf{even} : \mathbb{N} \to \mathbb{N}$ maps n to the smallest even number $\geq n$, i.e., $\mathsf{even}(n) = \mathsf{odd}(n + 1) - 1$. Below ψ_1, ψ_2 denote cognate formulas, and θ_1, θ_2 denote sHCTL* sentences.*

$$\mathsf{fc}(a_\pi) = 0 \qquad \mathsf{fc}(\neg\psi_1) = \mathsf{even}(\mathsf{fc}(\psi_1)) \qquad \mathsf{fc}(\mathsf{X}\psi_1) = \mathsf{fc}(\psi_1)$$
$$\mathsf{fc}(\psi_1 \vee \psi_2) = \max(\mathsf{fc}(\psi_1), \mathsf{fc}(\psi_2)) \qquad \mathsf{fc}(\psi_1 \, \mathsf{U} \, \psi_2) = \mathsf{even}(\max(\mathsf{fc}(\psi_1), \mathsf{fc}(\psi_2)))$$
$$\mathsf{fc}(\exists\pi. \psi_1) = \mathsf{odd}(\mathsf{fc}(\psi_1)) \qquad \mathsf{fc}(\mathsf{E}\psi_1) = \mathsf{odd}(\mathsf{fc}(\psi_1))$$
$$\mathsf{fc}(\neg\theta_1) = \mathsf{fc}(\theta_1) \qquad \mathsf{fc}(\theta_1 \vee \theta_2) = \max(\mathsf{fc}(\theta_1), \mathsf{fc}(\theta_2))$$

Observe the difference in the definition of $\mathsf{fc}(\neg\theta_1)$ and $\mathsf{fc}(\neg\psi_1)$; for $\neg\theta_1$ there is no change in formula complexity, while for $\neg\psi_1$ we move to the next even level.

Our main technical lemma is a compositional construction of an automaton for cognate formulas ψ. Depending on the parity of $\mathsf{fc}(\psi)$, the automaton we construct will either be a 1-AJA or a NVPA. Before presenting this lemma, we define a function that is a tower of exponentials. For $c, k, n \in \mathbb{N}$, the value $g_c(k, n)$ is defined inductively on k as follows: $g_c(0, n) = cn \log n$, and $g_c(k + 1, n) = 2^{g_c(k,n)}$. We use $g_{O(1)}(k, n)$ to denote the family of functions $\{g_c(k, n) \mid c \in \mathbb{N}\}$.

Lemma 1. *Consider pushdown system $\mathcal{P} = (S, \Gamma, s_{\mathsf{in}}, \Delta, L)$ and* sHCTL* *sentence θ. Let ψ be a cognate subformula of θ with free path variables in the set $\mathcal{V} = \{\pi_1, \ldots \pi_m\}$ for $m \in \mathbb{N}$. We assume, without loss of generality, that the variables $\pi_1, \ldots \pi_m$ are in the order in which they are quantified in θ with π_m being the first free variable of ψ that will be quantified in the context θ. In addition, we assume that the size of both ψ and $\mathcal{P}$ is bounded by n. There is an automaton $\mathcal{A}_\psi$ over pushdown alphabet $\Sigma[m]$ such that for any path environment Π over $\mathcal{V}$,*

$$\mathcal{P}, \Pi, \pi_m \models \psi \text{ if and only if } \mathsf{enc}(\Pi) \in \mathcal{L}(\mathcal{A}_\psi). \text{ [7]}$$

The automaton $\mathcal{A}_\psi$ is a NVPA if $\mathsf{fc}(\psi)$ is odd, and a 1-AJA if $\mathsf{fc}(\psi)$ is even. The size of $\mathcal{A}_\psi$ is at most $g_{O(1)}(\lceil \frac{\mathsf{fc}(\psi)}{2} \rceil, n)^8$.

Before presenting the proof of Lemma 1, we would like to highlight a subtlety about its statement. The result guarantees that for *valid* path environments Π, encoding $\mathsf{enc}(\Pi)$ is accepted by $\mathcal{A}_\psi$ if and only if Π satisfies ψ. It says nothing about path environments that are not valid. In particular, there may be functions that map path variables to traces that do not correspond to actual paths of $[\![\mathcal{P}]\!]$, but which are nonetheless accepted by $\mathcal{A}_\psi$. Notice, however, when $\psi = \exists \pi . \psi_1$ is a cognate sentence, a string over $\{\mathsf{call}, \mathsf{int}, \mathsf{ret}\}$ will, by conditions guaranteed in Lemma 1, be accepted if and only if it corresponds to a stack access pattern of a path from the initial state that satisfies $\exists \pi . \psi_1$.

Proof (Sketch of Lemma 1). Our construction of $\mathcal{A}_\psi$ will proceed inductively. The type of automaton constructed will be consistent with the parity of $\mathsf{fc}(\psi)$, i.e., an NVPA if $\mathsf{fc}(\varphi)$ is odd and a 1-AJA if $\mathsf{fc}(\psi)$ is even. We sketch the main ideas here, with the full proof in [2].

For a_π, $\neg \psi_1$, $\psi_1 \vee \psi_2$, and $X\psi_1$, the construction essentially proceeds by converting $\mathcal{A}_{\psi_i}$ ($i \in \{1,2\}$) if needed, into the type (NVPA or 1-AJA) of the target automaton using Theorem 1, and then using standard closure properties to combine them to get the desired automaton. In case of $\psi = \psi_1 \mathsf{U} \psi_2$, we first convert (if needed) $\mathcal{A}_{\psi_i}$ ($i \in \{1,2\}$) into a 1-AJA. At each step, the automaton for ψ will choose to either run $\mathcal{A}_{\psi_2}$, or run $\mathcal{A}_{\psi_1}$ *and* restart itself. Correctness relies on the fact that our encoding for path environments satisfies Proposition 2.

The most interesting case is that of $\psi = \exists \pi . \psi_1$. We will first convert (if needed) the automaton for ψ_1 into a NVPA $\mathcal{A}_1$. The automaton for ψ will essentially guess the encoding of a path that is consistent with the transitions of

---

[7] When $m = 0$, we take π_m to be $\dagger$.

[8] When the size of the specification ψ is considered constant, the size of $\mathcal{A}_\psi$ is at most $g_{O(1)}(\lceil \frac{\mathsf{fc}(\psi)}{2} \rceil - 1, n)$

$\mathcal{P}$, and check if assigning the guessed path to variable π satisfies ψ_1 by running the automaton $\mathcal{A}_1$. The additional requirement we have is that the guessed path start at the *same configuration* as the current configuration of the path assigned to variable π_m which introduces some subtle challenges. In order to be able to guess a path, $\mathcal{A}_\psi$ will keep track of $\mathcal{P}$'s control state in its control state, and use its stack to track $\mathcal{P}$'s stack operations along the guessed path. Since the stacks of all paths are synchronized, it makes it possible for $\mathcal{A}_\psi$ to use its (single stack) to track the stack of both $\mathcal{P}$ and the stack of $\mathcal{A}_1$. □

Using Lemma 1, we can establish the main result of this section.

Theorem 3. *Given a* $\mathcal{P} = (S, \Gamma, s_{in}, \Delta, L)$ *and a* sHCTL* *sentence* θ, *the problem of determining if* $\mathcal{P} \models \theta$ *is in* $\cup_c DTIME(g_c(\lceil \frac{fc(\theta)}{2} \rceil, n))$, *where* n *is a bound on the size of* $\mathcal{P}$ *and* θ.

Proof. Recall that a sHCTL* sentence is a Boolean combination of formulas of the form $E\psi$, where ψ is a cognate sentence. Results on whether $\mathcal{P} \models E\psi$ for each such subformula can be combined to determine whether $\mathcal{P} \models \theta$. Given this, the time to determine if $\mathcal{P} \models \theta$ is at most the time to decide if $\mathcal{P}$ satisfies each subformula of the form $E\psi$ plus $O(n)$ (to compute the Boolean combination of these results). Next, recall that the construction in Lemma 1 ensures that for a cognate sentence of the form $\exists \pi. \psi$, $\mathcal{L}(\mathcal{A}_{\exists \pi. \psi})$ consists exactly of strings in $\{\mathsf{call}, \mathsf{int}, \mathsf{ret}\}^\omega$ that encode a path environment over $\emptyset$ that satisfy $\exists \pi. \psi$.

Consider a sHCTL* sentence $E\psi$. Let π be a path variable that does not appear in the sentence ψ. Based on the semantics of sHCTL* the following observation holds: $\mathcal{P} \models E\psi$ if and only if for some path environment Π over $\emptyset$, $\mathcal{P}, \Pi, \dagger \models \exists \pi. \psi$. Which is equivalent to saying that $\mathcal{P} \models E\psi$ if and only if $\mathcal{L}(\mathcal{A}_{\exists \pi. \psi}) \neq \emptyset$. Since $fc(E\psi) = fc(\exists \pi. \psi)$, and the emptiness problem of NVPA can be decided in polynomial time (Theorem 2), our theorem follows. □

5 Lower Bound

In this section, we establish a lower bound for the problem of model checking sHCTL* sentences against pushdown systems. Our proof establishes a hardness result for the sHLTL sub-fragment of sHCTL*. Before presenting this lower bound, we introduce the function $h_c(\cdot, \cdot)$, which is another tower of exponentials, inductively defined as follows: $h_c(0, n) = n$, and $h_c(k + 1, n) = h_c(k, n) \cdot c^{h_c(k,n)}$.

Theorem 4. *Let* $\mathcal{P}$ *be a pushdown system and* θ *be a* sHLTL *sentence such that the sizes of both* $\mathcal{P}$ *and* θ *is bounded by* n *and* $fc(\theta) = 2k - 1$ *for some* $k \in \mathbb{N}$. *The problem of checking if* $\mathcal{P} \models \theta$ *is* $DTIME(h_c(k, n))$-*hard, for every* $c \in \mathbb{N}$.

Proof (Sketch). We sketch the main intuitions behind the proof. To highlight the novelties of this proof, it is useful to recall how $NSPACE(h_c(k-1, n))$-hardness for HYPERLTL model checking is proved [5]. The idea is to reduce the language of a nondeterministic $h_c(k-1, n)$ space bounded machine M to the model checking problem by constructing a finite state transition system that guesses a run of M, and a HYPERLTL formula that checks if the path is a valid accepting run.

To get the stricter bound of $\mathsf{DTIME}(h_c(k, n))$, we use the fact that we are checking pushdown systems. The stack of the pushdown system can be used to guess a *tree*, as opposed to a simple trace. Therefore, we reduce a $h_c(k - 1, n)$ space bounded *alternating* Turing machine, instead of a nondeterministic machine. Since $\mathsf{ASPACE}(f(n)) = \mathsf{DTIME}(2^{O(f(n))})$ for $f(n) \geq \log n$, the theorem will follow if the reduction succeeds.

Recall that a run of an alternating Turing machine M is a rooted, labeled tree, where vertices are labeled by configurations of M in a manner that is consistent with the transition function of M. To faithfully encode a tree as a sequence of symbols, we record the DFS traversal of the tree, making explicit the stack operations performed during such a traversal. Consider a labeled, rooted tree T with root r whose label is $\ell(r)$ with T_1 as a the left sub-tree and T_2 as the right sub-tree. The DFS traversal of T will push $\ell(r)$, traverse T_1 recursively, pop $\ell(r)$, push $\ell(r)$, traverse T_2, and then pop $\ell(r)$. We will use such a DFS traversal to guess and encode runs of M. Popping and pushing $\ell(r)$ between the traversals of T_1 and T_2 may seem redundant. Why not simply do nothing between the traversals of T_1 and T_2? For T to be a valid run of M, the configuration labeling of the root of T_2 must be the result of taking one step from $\ell(r)$. Such checks will be encoded in our sHLTL sentence, and for that to be possible, we need successive configurations of M to be consecutive in the string encoding.

To highlight some additional consistency checks, let us continue with our example tree T from the previous paragraph. For a string to be a correct encoding of T, it is necessary that the string pushed before the traversal of T_i ($i \in \{1, 2\}$) be the same as the string popped after the traversal. This can be ensured by the pushdown system by actually pushing and popping those symbols. In addition, the string popped after T_1's traversal must be the same as the string pushed before T_2's traversal. Neither the stack nor the finite control of the pushdown system can be used to ensure this. Instead this must be checked by the sHLTL sentence we construct. But the symbols while popping $\ell(r)$ will be in reverse order of the symbols being pushed, and it is challenging to perform this check in the formula. To overcome this, we push/pop the label *and its reverse* at the same time. This ensures that if we want to check if a string pushed is the same as a string that was just popped, then we can check for string *equality*, and this check is easier to do using formulas in sHLTL. Additional checks to ensure that the tree encodes a valid accepting run are performed by the sHLTL sentence using ideas from [17]. Full details can be found in [2]. □

6 Conclusions

In this paper, we introduced a branching time temporal logic sHCTL* that can be used to specify synchronous hyperproperties for recursive programs modeled as pushdown systems. The primary difference from the standard branching time logic HYPERCTL* for synchronous hyperproperties is that sHCTL* considers a restricted class of hyperproperties, namely, those that relate only executions that the same stack access pattern. We call such hyperproperties stack-aware hyperproperties. We showed that the problem of model checking pushdown systems sHCTL* specifications is decidable, and characterized its complexity. We also showed how this result can potentially be used to aid security verification.

References

1. Alur, R., Madhusudan, P.: Visibly pushdown languages. In: Proceedings of the 36th Annual ACM Symposium on Theory of Computing. pp. 202–211. ACM (2004)
2. Bajwa, A., Zhang, M., Chadha, R., Viswanathan, M.: Stack-aware hyperproperties. https://arxiv.org/abs/2301.11521 (2023)
3. Bouajjani, A., Esparza, J., Maler, O.: Reachability analysis of pushdown automata: Application to model-checking. In: Concurrency Theory, 8th International Conference. pp. 135–150. Springer (1997)
4. Bozzelli, L.: Alternating automata and a temporal fixpoint calculus for visibly pushdown languages. In: Concurrency Theory, 18th International Conference. pp. 476–491. Springer (2007)
5. Clarkson, M.R., Finkbeiner, B., Koleini, M., Micinski, K.K., Rabe, M.N., Sánchez, C.: Temporal logics for hyperproperties. In: Principles of Security and Trust - Third International Conference. pp. 265–284. Springer (2014)
6. Clarkson, M.R., Schneider, F.B.: Hyperproperties. In: Proceedings of the 21st IEEE Computer Security Foundations Symposium. pp. 51–65. IEEE Computer Society (2008)
7. Coenen, N., Finkbeiner, B., Sánchez, C., Tentrup, L.: Verifying hyperliveness. In: Computer Aided Verification - 31st International Conference. pp. 121–139. Springer (2019)
8. Finkbeiner, B., Hahn, C., Stenger, M.: EAHyper: Satisfiability, implication, and equivalence checking of hyperproperties. In: Computer Aided Verification - 29th International Conference. pp. 564–570. Springer (2017)
9. Finkbeiner, B., Hahn, C., Stenger, M., Tentrup, L.: RVHyper: A runtime verification tool for temporal hyperproperties. In: Tools and Algorithms for the Construction and Analysis of Systems - 24th International Conference. pp. 194–200. Springer (2018)
10. Finkbeiner, B., Rabe, M.N., Sánchez, C.: Algorithms for model checking HyperLTL and HyperCTL*. In: Computer Aided Verification - 27th International Conference. pp. 30–48. Springer (2015)
11. Goguen, J.A., Meseguer, J.: Security policies and security models. In: IEEE Symposium on Security and Privacy. pp. 11–20. IEEE Computer Society (1982)
12. Gutsfeld, J.O., Müller-Olm, M., Ohrem, C.: Deciding asynchronous hyperproperties for recursive programs. CoRR **abs/2201.12859** (2022)
13. McLean, J.: Proving noninterference and functional correctness using traces. Journal of Computer Security **1**(1), 37–58 (1992)
14. McLean, J.: A general theory of composition for trace sets closed under selective interleaving functions. In: IEEE Computer Society Symposium on Research in Security and Privacy. pp. 79–93. IEEE Computer Society (1994)
15. Molnar, D., Piotrowski, M., Schultz, D., Wagner, D.: The program counter security model: Automatic detection and removal of control-flow side channel attacks. In: Proceedings of the 8th international conference on Information Security and Cryptology. p. 156–168. Springer-Verlag (2005)

16. Pommellet, A., Touili, T.: Model-checking HyperLTL for pushdown systems. In: Model Checking Software - 25th International Symposium. pp. 133–152. Springer (2018)

17. Sistla, A.P., Vardi, M.Y., Wolper, P.: The complementation problem for büchi automata with appplications to temporal logic. Theoretical Computer Science **49**, 217–237 (1987)

18. Walukiewicz, I.: Pushdown processes: Games and model checking. In: Computer Aided Verification, 8th International Conference. pp. 62–74. Springer (1996)

19. Zdancewic, S., Myers, A.C.: Observational determinism for concurrent program security. In: Proceedings of the 16th IEEE Computer Security Foundations Workshop. p. 29. IEEE Computer Society (2003)

Proofs

Propositional Proof Skeletons*

Joseph E. Reeves[1]([⊠])[iD], Benjamin Kiesl-Reiter[2][iD], and Marijn J. H. Heule[1,2][iD]

[1] Carnegie Mellon University, Pittsburgh, PA, USA
{jereeves,mheule}@cs.cmu.edu
[2] Amazon Web Services, Seattle, WA, USA
benkiesl@amazon.com

Abstract. Modern SAT solvers produce proofs of unsatisfiability to justify the correctness of their results. These proofs, which are usually represented in the well-known DRAT format, can often become huge, requiring
multiple gigabytes of disk storage. We present a technique for semantic
proof compression that selects a subset of important clauses from a proof
and stores them as a so-called proof skeleton. This proof skeleton can
later be used to efficiently reconstruct a full proof by exploiting parallelism. We implemented our approach on top of the award-winning SAT
solver CaDiCaL and the proof checker DRAT-trim. In an experimental
evaluation, we demonstrate that we can compress proofs into skeletons
that are 100 to 5,000 times smaller than the original proofs. For almost
all problems, proof reconstruction using a skeleton improves the solving
time on a single core, and is around five times faster when using 24 cores.

Keywords: SAT solving · proofs · compression.

1 Introduction

Solvers for the Boolean satisfiability problem (SAT) take as input a formula of
propositional logic and decide if the formula is satisfiable. In case of satisfiability,
they usually return an assignment of truth values to the variables of the formula;
by plugging these truth values into the formula, users can easily convince themselves that the solver was right and that the formula is indeed satisfiable. In
case of unsatisfiability, however, things are more complicated: to justify their
answer, solvers need to produce an independently checkable proof that none of
the—exponentially many—potential truth assignments make the formula true.

In practical SAT solving, proofs of unsatisfiability are represented in the
DRAT format [10], and they are often huge, requiring several gigabytes (in some
cases even terabytes [12] or petabytes [11]) of disk storage. Storing proofs is thus
costly, especially since users might not require access to the proofs until sometime
long after solving, at a point when proof verification or further analysis is desired.

* Supported by the U.S. National Science Foundation under grant CCF-2229099, and
supported in part by a fellowship award under contract FA9550-21-F-0003 through
the National Defense Science and Engineering Graduate (NDSEG) Fellowship Program, sponsored by the Air Force Research Laboratory (AFRL), the Office of Naval
Research (ONR) and the Army Research Office (ARO).

S. Sankaranarayanan and N. Sharygina (Eds.): TACAS 2023, LNCS 13993, pp. 329–347, 2023.
https://doi.org/10.1007/978-3-031-30823-9_17

Up to now, the only options to deal with this problem were either to not store proofs and instead recompute them on demand—a laborious but plausible approach considering that proof checking typically takes longer than solving—or to use compression methods to reduce proof size. However, syntactic compression techniques (such as LZMA or DEFLATE, as supported by the ZIP file format) only provide moderate levels of compression. The same can be said about existing semantic compression techniques for proofs in SAT and SMT (c.f. [4, 18, 21]), which only achieve 20% compression on average.

In this paper, we present a novel approach to semantic compression that stores only a small subset of the clauses derived by a solver, called a *proof skeleton*. We can achieve strong compression rates with proof skeletons (around 100 to 5,000 times smaller than the original proof), while still retaining enough information to allow for a quick on-demand reconstruction of a complete proof that might differ from the original proof. This is similar to how a mathematician might put down the most important reasoning steps of a proof in a proof sketch, enabling a moderately talented reader to fill in the gaps. In our case, the gaps can even be filled independently, meaning that multiple readers can work in parallel.

We present both an online version (creating a proof skeleton during solving) and an offline version (creating a proof skeleton from a full proof) of our approach. We select the clauses that end up in a proof skeleton by relying on several heuristics such as *glue* (a heuristic used internally by solvers to estimate the usefulness of clauses) for online and *clause activity* (a measure of how often a clause is used to derive new clauses) for offline. To reconstruct a full proof from a proof skeleton, we utilize multiple incremental SAT solvers that can run in parallel. We implemented all our algorithms on top of the award-winning SAT solver CADICAL [2] and the proof checker DRAT-TRIM [22]. In an extensive empirical evaluation, we demonstrate the feasibility of our approach, with all code and data available at https://github.com/amazon-science/unsat-proof-skeletons.

Beyond being a tool for compression, proof skeletons can also serve as a source of insight into a solver's reasoning. Getting any sort of intuition from a million-line proof is difficult; by computing a skeleton, we obtain a small set of facts—logically implied by the problem—that can give us an idea of how a solver established the unsatisfiability of a formula. This can lead to a feedback loop that improves solver performance. For example, when inspecting skeletons for some bounded-model-checking benchmarks, we observed many unit clauses and binary clauses of a certain type. From this, we hypothesized that the problems required more preprocessing, which did indeed improve performance.

Our main contributions are as follows: (1) We present a semantic approach for proof compression that selects only the most important clauses of a proof. (2) We implemented an online version and an offline version of our approach on top of the SAT solver CADICAL and the proof checker DRAT-TRIM. (3) In an extensive empirical evaluation, we demonstrate that our approach can drastically reduce proof size while still enabling efficient proof reconstruction.

The rest of this paper is structured as follows. In Section 2, we discuss background required to understand our paper and review related work. In Section 3, we outline the main idea behind our proof-compression approach. In Section 4, we show multiple ways to create proof skeletons, and in Section 5 we show how to reconstruct full proofs from skeletons. Finally, in Section 6, we present an empirical evaluation of our approach before concluding in Section 7.

2 Background and Related Work

The Boolean satisfiability problem (SAT) takes as input a formula of propositional logic and asks if there exists a truth assignment under which the formula evaluates to true. As is common in SAT solving, we consider propositional formulas in *conjunctive normal form* (CNF), which are defined as follows. A *literal* is either a variable x (a *positive literal*) or the negation $\bar{x}$ of a variable x (a *negative literal*). The *complement* $\bar{l}$ of a literal l is defined as $\bar{l} = \bar{x}$ if $l = x$ and as $\bar{l} = x$ if $l = \bar{x}$. For a literal l, we denote the variable of l by $var(l)$. A *clause* is a finite disjunction of the form $(l_1 \vee \cdots \vee l_n)$, where $l_1, \ldots, l_n$ are literals. Clauses with only one literal are called *unit clauses* and clauses with two literals are called *binary clauses*. We denote the empty clause by $\bot$. A *formula* is a finite conjunction of the form $C_1 \wedge \cdots \wedge C_m$, where $C_1, \ldots, C_m$ are clauses. For example, $(x \vee \bar{y}) \wedge (z) \wedge (\bar{x} \vee \bar{z})$ is a formula consisting of the clauses $(x \vee \bar{y})$, (z), and $(\bar{x} \vee \bar{z})$.

A *truth assignment* (or *assignment* for short) is a function from a set of variables to the truth values 1 (*true*) and 0 (*false*). A literal l is *satisfied* by an assignment α if l is positive and $\alpha(var(l)) = 1$ or if l is negative and $\alpha(var(l)) = 0$. A literal l is *falsified* by an assignment if its complement $\bar{l}$ is satisfied by the assignment. A clause C is satisfied by an assignment α if α satisfies at least one of C's literals. A formula ψ is satisfied by an assignment α if α satisfies all of ψ's clauses. A formula is *satisfiable* if there exists an assignment that satisfies it, otherwise it is *unsatisfiable*. A clause $C = (l_1 \vee \cdots \vee l_k)$ is *implied* by a formula ψ, denoted by $\psi \models C$, if all satisfying assignments of ψ satisfy C, or equivalently, if $\psi \wedge \bar{C}$ is unsatisfiable, where $\bar{C} = (\bar{l}_1) \wedge \cdots \wedge (\bar{l}_k)$. In case a formula is satisfiable, modern solvers can output a satisfying assignment; in case the formula is unsatisfiable, most solvers can output a proof of unsatisfiability.

Proofs of Unsatisfiability. State-of-the-art SAT solvers produce so-called *clausal proofs*. Intuitively, a clausal proof is a list of clause additions and clause deletions. Formally, a clausal proof is a list of pairs $\langle s_1, C_1 \rangle, \ldots, \langle s_m, C_m \rangle$, where for each $i \in 1, \ldots, m$, $s_i \in \{a, d\}$ and C_i is a clause. If $s_i = a$, the pair is called an *addition*, and if $s_i = d$, it is called a *deletion*. For a given input formula ψ_0, a clausal proof gives rise to *accumulated formulas* ψ_i ($i \in 1, \ldots, m$) as follows:

$$\psi_i = \begin{cases} \psi_{i-1} \cup \{C_i\} & \text{if } s_i = a \\ \psi_{i-1} \setminus \{C_i\} & \text{if } s_i = d \end{cases}$$

The clauses of an accumulated formula ψ_i are also called the *active clauses* at point i. Clause additions must preserve satisfiability, which is usually guaranteed by requiring the added clauses to fulfill some efficiently decidable syntactic criterion that itself implies satisfiability is preserved. Deletions are unrestricted and are not useful for proving unsatisfiability as they only make a formula "more satisfiable"; their main purpose is to speed up proof checking by keeping the set of active clauses small. A valid proof of unsatisfiability must end with the addition of the empty clause. As the empty clause is trivially unsatisfiable, and since all proof steps preserve satisfiability, the unsatisfiability of the original formula can then be concluded.

Clausal proof systems are distinguished by the syntactic criterion they impose on clause additions. The standard SAT solving paradigm *conflict-driven clause learning* (CDCL) [15,16] adds so-called *RUP* (short for *reverse unit propagation*) clauses [20], whose definition is based on the notion of *unit propagation*. Unit propagation is the process of repeatedly applying the *unit-clause rule* to a formula until no unit clauses are left. Given a formula ψ, the unit-clause rule takes a unit clause (l) and makes its literal l true, meaning that (1) all clauses that contain l are removed from ψ, and (2) the negation $\bar{l}$ of l is removed from all remaining clauses. If unit propagation produces the empty clause, we say it derived a *conflict*. For example, unit propagation derives a conflict on $(x) \wedge (\bar{x} \vee y) \wedge (\bar{x} \vee \bar{y})$ as the application of the unit-clause rule for (x) produces the formula $(y) \wedge (\bar{y})$, on which another application of the unit-clause rule, with either of (y) or $(\bar{y})$, produces the empty clause. If unit propagation derives a conflict on a formula, the formula is clearly unsatisfiable, but not vice versa.

A clause $C = (l_1 \vee \cdots \vee l_k)$ is a RUP for a formula ψ if unit propagation derives a conflict on $\psi \wedge \bar{C}$. If C is a RUP for ψ, it is implied by ψ since $\psi \wedge \bar{C}$ is unsatisfiable; we thus sometimes write $\psi \vdash_1 C$ to denote that C is a RUP for ψ. The clausal proof system allowing the addition of RUP clauses together with deletions is called DRUP. Solvers participating in the SAT competition must produce DRAT proofs, but since each DRUP proof is also a DRAT proof (but not vice versa) and since all state-of-the-art solvers actually produce DRUP proofs by default, we restrict this study of proof compression to DRUP proofs.

A *proof checker* is an independent tool that verifies the correctness of proofs. There exist formally verified proof checkers that provide strong correctness guarantees (c.f., [5, 9, 14, 19]). Because these tools are inefficient, proofs are often passed through an—efficient but unverified—intermediary proof checker (such as DRAT-TRIM [22]) that transforms a DRAT proof into a so-called *LRAT proof* [5]. The resulting LRAT proof includes additional information (called *hints*), which allows a formally verified checker to efficiently check the proof.

3   Problem Overview

We want to compress proofs into small representations that can be efficiently decompressed into full proofs. Existing techniques for SAT and SMT focus on transformations and substitutions that preserve validity to generate smaller proofs [4,18,21]. We achieve greater compression by storing only a so-called *proof skeleton*, which itself is not a valid proof.

Tools like SLEDGEHAMMER [3] automatically solve proof obligations from interactive theorem provers, filling gaps in the proof by translating lower-level reasoning into the theorem provers' logic. More recent work proposed a method for constructing proofs for complex SMT rewriting steps on demand in a post-processing step [17]. In a similar way, we use proof skeletons to efficiently reconstruct valid proofs that can differ from the original proofs.

Suppose you solved an unsatisfiable CNF formula ψ, and out of the many facts you learned during solving, there were three facts A, B, and C, which you deem particularly important for showing the unsatisfiability of ψ. You can then build a proof skeleton from A, B, and C. Later, you can rephrase the question $\psi \models \bot$ ("does ψ imply the empty clause?", or equivalently, "is ψ unsatisfiable?") into the following questions:

$$\psi \models A \qquad \psi \wedge A \models B \qquad \psi \wedge A \wedge B \models C \qquad \psi \wedge A \wedge B \wedge C \models \bot$$

Not only do A, B, and C provide a way to partition the proof effort, when ordered carefully, they can be used as assumptions in subsequent questions. Each question can be submitted to a solver independently, and combining the four resulting proofs will give a proof of the original claim that ψ is unsatisfiable.

Our work translates this general schema to the realm of SAT by (1) determining which learned clauses from a SAT solver are most useful and should be stored in a proof skeleton; (2) carefully grouping solver calls to prevent repeated work when producing partial proofs from a proof skeleton; and (3) stitching the partial proofs together to generate a complete proof.

Determining which clauses are stored in a proof skeleton. We co-opt the clause-importance metrics used by CDCL solvers. We give a brief overview of these metrics in the following. CDCL solvers make progress by continuously learning new clauses that help them prune the search space of possible truth assignments. To limit memory usage, they occasionally perform a clause database *reduction*, removing a large portion of learned clauses based on some usefulness heuristics. Most solvers keep clauses that are short, have low *glue* value, are *reason clauses*, or have been used recently. The glue of a clause (also known as its *literal block distance*, or LBD) is a positive integer that estimates the usefulness of a clause. Intuitively, a low glue value means that few decisions are required to falsify the clause, which is considered good. For a more extensive discussion of glue, we refer to the respective literature [1]. A *reason clause* is a clause that was used by the solver when performing unit propagation, meaning that the clause became a unit clause under a partial assignment. The number of times a reason clause is *used* during conflict analysis is considered the clause's *activity*.

Grouping solver calls for partial proofs. We leverage incremental SAT to construct partial proofs. An incremental SAT solver solves a problem with several related steps, with the solver retaining state (e.g., learned clauses and heuristics) between steps; it also allows solving under so-called *assumptions*, which are literals assumed to be true in a step. Solving a sequence of related steps incrementally is often much faster than solving them independently of each other (for more details on incremental SAT see, e.g., [6]).

Given a formula ψ and a sequence $C_1, \ldots, C_n$ of clauses, we want to produce a DRUP proof of $\psi \models C_i$ for each $i \in 1, \ldots, n$. We use an incremental solver to produce partial proofs, with each solving step corresponding to a clause C_i. For the first step, $\psi \models C_1$, we pass the assumptions $\bar{C}_1 = \bar{l}_1 \wedge \cdots \wedge \bar{l}_k$ to the incremental solver. Given the formula ψ, the solver assigns the literals in the assumptions, then runs the CDCL algorithm until it derives the empty clause. During solving, CDCL guarantees that all learned clauses are RUPs for the input formula ψ. Let ϕ_1 denote the sequence of clauses learned by the solver. Then, since unit propagation under the assumptions $\bar{l}_1 \wedge \cdots \wedge \bar{l}_k$ derived the empty clause, C_1 is by definition a RUP for $\psi \wedge \phi_1$. This means that C_1 can be appended to the corresponding proof of the solver (which derives all clauses in ϕ_1) to obtain a valid DRUP derivation of C_1 from ψ.

In the next step, the clause C_2 is handled similarly, except the solver retains the learned clauses $\phi_1 \wedge C_1$ when proving that C_2 is a RUP clause. This continues until all $n + 1$ steps corresponding to the n clauses of the proof skeleton are completed (step $n + 1$ corresponds to the derivation of the empty clause).

To parallelize this reasoning, we use an approach akin to *divide-and-conquer* techniques established in parallel SAT solving [13]. Divide-and-conquer solvers first partition a problem into multiple subproblems and then solve the subproblems in parallel. Similarly, we divide the incremental solver steps into so-called *chunks*, which are independent groups of subsequent solver steps. For example, we can split the solver steps into one chunk containing the first half of steps and another chunk containing the second half of steps. Both chunks can then be solved in parallel by two independent incremental SAT solvers.

Stitching partial proofs together. Once we have partial proofs for all $n+1$ solving steps, a full proof of unsatisfiability can be constructed as the sequence of clause additions arising from $\phi_1, C_1, \phi_2, C_2, \ldots, C_n, \phi_{n+1}, \bot$, where ϕ_i is the sequence of learned clauses by the i-th solver step, as explained above. In general, clauses are added and deleted during solving, so the proof can be augmented with the deletion information contained in the proofs emitted by a solver. But, we need to ensure clauses are not deleted in the proof and then implicitly reintroduced into a solver, which can occur when inprocessing techniques touch variables in the assumptions. We use *variable freezing* [7] to freeze all variables occurring in $C_1, \ldots, C_n$; this avoids any unsound inprocessing [8], and is required to ensure correctness of the proofs.

4   Creating Proof Skeletons

Given a clausal proof $P = \langle s_1, C_1 \rangle, \ldots, \langle s_m, C_m \rangle$, we define a proof skeleton of P to be a sequence of clauses obtained from clause additions in P. Ideally, a skeleton is small but contains enough useful clauses to guide reasoning during proof reconstruction. A proof skeleton can be constructed *online*, during the solver's execution, by applying a filter to clauses as they are traced to a proof. Alternatively, a proof skeleton can be constructed *offline*, after solving, by processing the full proof and selecting important clauses.

4.1 Online Generation of Proof Skeletons

We create proof skeletons online by filtering clause additions as the solver traces them to a proof. Clauses that pass a usefulness threshold are added to the skeleton. As mentioned earlier, the filter applies usefulness heuristics from CDCL including *glue* and *clause activity*. Additionally, at certain intervals we add *reason clauses* to the skeleton. We implemented the filter within the solver CADICAL, giving us access to these values as well as to the reason clauses (through the *trail* of assignments). We also enabled logging, giving every clause a unique identifier, in order to sort the skeletons. We evaluate three different configurations:

- GLUE: Clauses with glue lower than 3.
- GLUE+TRAIL: Clauses with glue lower than 3, and all reason clauses on the trail before each clause-database reduction.
- DYNAMIC: Clauses with glue lower than some dynamically adjusted threshold $glue_d$, and all reason clauses on the trail every 50,000 learned clauses.

The first two configurations combine low-glue clauses with either no or some reason clauses. Increasing the glue value threshold often led to a compression of less than 1,000 times and slower reconstruction. Reason clauses are important because they are actively used by the solver whereas for low-glue clauses this is not guaranteed (although low glue is associated with high usage in general). Clause-database reductions are sparse, so reason clauses (which are added only during these reductions) will be added infrequently. We evaluate the impact of including reason clauses in the skeletons in Section 6.3.

   In the first two configurations, all clauses passing the filter are accepted into the skeleton. For some formulas, a solver will produce many low-glue clauses and the skeleton will become too large, and for others too few low-glue clauses will lead to a small skeleton. Our third configuration accounts for the differences between formulas by adjusting heuristics dynamically to meet a desired compression ratio. The heuristics are updated based on the number of clauses added to the skeleton within some number of conflicts, denoted as $window_c$. For a compression ratio between 500 and 1,000, and a $window_c$ value of 5,000, we tuned the DYNAMIC configuration in the following way: every 5,000 conflicts, if more than 25 ($window_c/200$) lemmas passed the filter, the $glue_d$ value is decreased, and if less than 3 lemmas ($window_c/2,000$) passed the filter, the $glue_d$ value is increased. Reasons from the trail are added every 50,000 conflicts ($window_c \times 10$).

   For configurations using reason clauses, the unique clause IDs are used to sort the skeleton. This is necessary because reason clauses are traced during reductions, so they may initially appear in the skeleton long after they were learned by the solver. During proof reconstruction it is important that clauses appear in the skeleton in an order that corresponds with a solver's reasoning.

We implemented additional configurations using clause activities. For this, we incremented an *activity* field for each clause every time it was used during conflict analysis. An evaluation of these additional configurations is beyond the scope of this paper, but data can be found in the paper's repository.

4.2   Offline Generation of Proof Skeletons

We create proof skeletons offline by processing a full proof and selecting the most active clauses. Given a DRAT proof, the tool DRAT-TRIM uses backwards checking to generate an optimized LRAT proof and, optionally, an UNSAT core (i.e., an unsatisfiable subset of the original formula). From the LRAT proof, we can estimate a clause's *activity* by counting the number of times the clause appears in a hint of a clause-addition step. We then add the clauses with the highest activity to the skeleton until a target compression ratio is met. We found for most problems the target 1,000 provided optimal reconstruction performance. We sort the skeleton by each clause's first use as a hint in the LRAT proof, signifying when a clause is actually used as opposed to when it is learned. We evaluate three configurations for offline generation:

- OFFLINE: Select 1,000 times fewer clauses than in the original DRAT proof.
- OFFLINE+UNITS: Additionally include all unit clauses from the proof.
- OFFLINE-OPT: Select 1,000 times fewer clauses than in the optimized LRAT proof.

The motivation for OFFLINE-OPT is that some optimized LRAT proofs have significantly fewer clauses than the DRAT proofs, resulting from many unused lemmas, which suggests that stronger compression is possible.

Offline construction requires expensive post-processing with DRAT-TRIM. However, during online construction we can only *guess* the future usefulness of clauses when they are derived, by relying on heuristics such as glue, but we cannot know how often a clause will actually be used. For instance, it may be that a clause has low glue (predicting high usefulness) but is learned and then never used in the rest of the proof, making it worthless in the skeleton. In contrast, when constructing a skeleton offline—after solving—we know already how often the clause was actually used in reasoning throughout the proof, and whether it was used to derive the empty clause. Also, we can use the UNSAT core instead of the original formula when reconstructing a proof for the original problem.

5   Reconstructing Proofs from Skeletons

We reconstruct proofs by filling the gaps of a proof skeleton with a SAT solver. Once we have proofs for all gaps, we stitch them together with the clauses of the skeleton to create a complete proof. We can utilize information obtained during proof reconstruction to further shrink skeletons by removing less useful clauses. Finally, we can also use a skeleton to create an optimized LRAT proof.

Proof	Skeleton	Reconstruction	Incremental Reconstruction
C_1	C_2	$\psi \models C_2$	$\psi \models C_2 : \phi_1$
C_2	C_5	C_2	C_2
C_3	$\vdots$	$\psi \wedge C_2 \models C_5$	$\psi \wedge C_2 \wedge \phi_1 \models C_5 : \phi_2$
C_4		C_5	C_5
C_5		$\vdots$	$\vdots$
$\vdots$		$\psi \wedge Skeleton \models \bot$	$\psi \wedge Skeleton \wedge \phi \models \bot$

Fig. 1. Proof reconstruction from a proof skeleton and a formula ϕ by filling in the gaps between skeleton clauses. This can be done with independent SAT calls or with an incremental SAT solver that keeps learned clauses (ϕ_i) between steps.

5.1 Filling Skeletons Using Incremental Solvers

We consider two ways of filling a proof skeleton's gaps—*reconstruction* and *incremental reconstruction*; both are illustrated in Fig. 1. Given a formula ϕ and a skeleton $C_1, \ldots, C_n$, reconstruction fills each gap $\psi \wedge C_1 \wedge \cdots \wedge C_{i-1} \models C_i$ using independent SAT solver calls, with $\psi_1 \wedge C_1 \wedge \cdots \wedge C_n \models \bot$ as the final call. Filling a gap for $C_i = (l_1 \vee \cdots \vee l_k)$ involves assuming $\bar{l}_1 \wedge \cdots \wedge \bar{l}_k$ and deriving the empty clause with proof ϕ, which proves that C_i is a RUP for $\psi \wedge C_1 \wedge \cdots \wedge C_{i-1} \wedge \phi$. Each gap has an associated DRUP proof ϕ_i emitted by the solver. Since RUP is a monotonic property, the clauses added in ϕ_i will not affect the validity of ϕ_j for $i < j$. However, clause deletions could make the proof $\phi_1, \langle a, C_1 \rangle, \phi_2, \langle a, C_2 \rangle, \ldots, \langle a, C_n \rangle, \phi_{n+1}, \bot$ incorrect. For example, if a skeleton clause C_1 is deleted in ϕ_2, then ϕ_3 (stemming from $\psi \wedge C_1 \wedge C_2 \models C_3$) may use C_2—a clause already deleted in the proof. The same problem could occur if formula clauses are deleted. Therefore, we must remove any deletion steps for clauses of the skeleton or of the formula clauses from each ϕ_i.

The second approach, *incremental reconstruction*, uses an incremental SAT solver, which allows the use of learned clauses when filling subsequent gaps. Specifically, we create an incremental problem with the steps $assume(\bar{C}_1), \ldots, assume(\bar{C}_n), assume(\emptyset)$, where each step $assume(\bar{C}_i)$, with $C_i = (l_1 \vee \cdots \vee l_k)$, involves assuming $\bar{l}_1 \wedge \cdots \wedge \bar{l}_k$ and deriving the empty clause. Each step produces a proof ϕ_i, and the complete proof $\phi_1, \langle a, C_1 \rangle, \phi_2, \langle a, C_2 \rangle, \ldots, \langle a, C_n \rangle, \phi_{n+1}, \langle a, \bot \rangle$ is correct as long as variables occurring in skeleton clauses are frozen (as described in Section 3). With this approach, we no longer need to worry about deletions of skeleton clauses or formula clauses because the solver fills each gap using the current clause database, i.e., each gap is proved without clauses formerly deleted by the solver.

To parallelize incremental reconstruction, we partition the incremental problem into several independent incremental problems, which we call *chunks*. We assign k clauses $C_l, \ldots, C_{l+k-1}$ from the skeleton to each chunk, and we then use an incremental solver to compute partial proofs for each of the clauses, starting from the formula $\psi \wedge C_1 \wedge \cdots \wedge C_{l-1}$. For each partial proof corresponding to a clause C_i, we call the solver with the assumptions negating the clause, i.e., with $assume(\bar{C}_i)$. Again, we must remove any deletion steps of skeleton clauses or formula clauses since they may be used in later chunks. All added clauses are then RUPs, and so the concatenation of chunk proofs is a complete proof.

Each chunk can be solved independently in parallel. The more skeleton clauses in each chunk, the more clauses the incremental solver can learn and reuse in subsequent steps. However, gaps might differ in hardness, meaning that some gaps can be filled quickly while others require a significant amount of solving time. A chunk can thus become a bottleneck during parallelization if it includes many difficult gaps. In our evaluation, we partitioned the skeleton into chunks of equal size, one for each core. For instance, on a single core, one incremental problem spanning the entire skeleton was given to a solver instance whereas for 24 cores, the skeleton was partitioned into 24 chunks. In principle, we could partition a skeleton into more chunks than cores, but this would require an intermediary level of problem scheduling that we leave for future work.

5.2   Shrinking Skeletons

The runtimes for filling each gap of a proof skeleton could provide insight into the usefulness of the skeleton clauses. For example, if the solver can quickly fill a gap, the corresponding skeleton clause may be trivially implied, and if the solver takes long, the clause may be useful since its derivation requires a lot of reasoning. Alternatively, the difference in runtime might not be explained by clause usefulness. Take, for example, the two gaps $\psi \models C_2$ and $\psi \wedge C_2 \models C_5$ from Fig. 1, and assume that the solver fills the first gap in a millisecond and the second gap in ten seconds. If the difference is a result of C_2 being trivially implied, it makes sense to remove C_2 from the skeleton; otherwise, if the difference is due to factors unrelated to usefulness, it is better to remove C_5. Based on this observation, we try to shrink a given skeleton by sorting gap reconstruction times and removing a certain share of the slowest or fastest clauses.

Our empirical evaluation in Section 6 indicates that removing the fastest clauses is the right approach for improving compression and (sometimes) reducing reconstruction time. Even though gap runtime and clause usefulness are correlated, the correlation is not perfect. For instance, sometimes the incremental solver is able to quickly fill a gap because of learning from previous steps of the incremental problem. Even if it takes a long time to fill a gap, there is no guarantee that the corresponding skeleton clause is useful for filling future gaps. We examine in detail how shrinking skeletons affects reconstruction time.

5.3   Reconstructing LRAT Proofs from Skeletons

The proof reconstruction described above will produce DRAT proofs. Formally verified checkers typically require LRAT proofs, forcing a conversion via a proof checker such as DRAT-TRIM, which can take much longer than the original solving time. Instead, we can reconstruct DRAT proofs for each chunk, then convert the DRAT proofs to LRAT in parallel, and finally concatenate them.

We use DRAT-TRIM to convert chunk DRAT proofs to LRAT. This required us to modify DRAT-TRIM (e.g., by changing the way it performs backwards checking, and how it handles unit clauses). By default, DRAT-TRIM starts backwards checking at the empty clause. But, only the last chunk will derive the empty clause, and further, we must ensure all skeleton clauses are included in the backwards check, as they may be used in later chunks. To account for this, we mark each skeleton clause in the DRAT proof before performing the backwards check. The backwards check verifies that each marked clause is RAT (or RUP, in our case), including the clauses in the LRAT proof. When combining the chunk LRAT proofs, we map the skeleton clauses in each chunk to the index of the LRAT step where they were initially added. Finally, we remove all deletions from the LRAT proof, but this will not affect proof-checking time, mainly since LRAT checkers perform unit propagation in linear time using hints. While the following evaluation focuses on DRAT proof reconstruction from skeletons, we tested our implementation of parallel LRAT proof reconstruction on 24 cores, and verified several proofs with CAKE-LPR [19].

6 Experimental Evaluation

We evaluated our approach on SAT competition 2021 Main Track benchmarks, using all (65) unsatisfiable formulas that were solved between 500 and 5,000 seconds by the solver CADICAL [2]. By requiring at least 500 seconds of solving time, we ensured that proofs are of reasonable size (around 1 GB) and therefore good candidates for compression. We ran experiments on an AWS EC2 m5d.metal instance, with 96 virtual CPUs and 500 GB of memory, running at most 24 parallel processes at a time. We used a timeout of 5,000 seconds for solving a problem and constructing a DRAT proof. For proof reconstruction on a single core we used a single incremental problem spanning the entire skeleton. For proof reconstruction on 24 cores, we evenly divided the proof skeleton into 24 incremental problems (chunks) passed to 24 instances of CADICAL. We report real time for proof reconstruction, not including skeleton extraction.

6.1 Single-Core Proof Reconstruction

Fig. 2 shows the best configurations on each formula using online skeletons (left) and offline skeletons (right), for the single-core experiments (i.e., the entire skeleton on a single core). Almost all proofs were reconstructed faster than the original solving time (below the red dotted line), and in some cases more than five times faster (below the blue dotted line). Each configuration was the best for some formulas. The GLUE configuration led the online skeletons. With a single incremental problem, learned clauses from earlier incremental calls can be kept for the entire execution, meaning that clauses that occur later in large skeletons (e.g., GLUE+TRAIL) may be trivially implied by previously learned clauses.

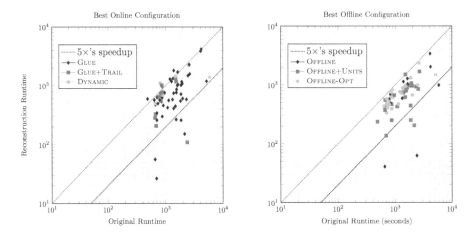

Fig. 2. Runtimes (in seconds) of best online (left) and offline (right) configurations for proof reconstruction using a proof skeleton and a single core.

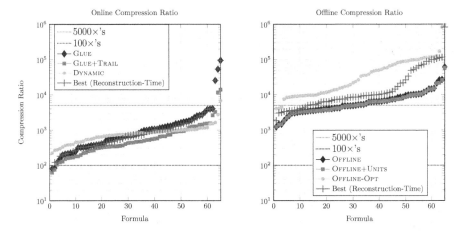

Fig. 3. Proof skeleton compression ratio for online (left) and offline (right).

6.2 Skeleton Compression Ratio

Fig. 3 shows the sorted compression ratios (w.r.t. file size) between proof skeletons and the original DRAT proofs for each configuration as well as the compression ratios for the configuration with the fastest reconstruction time on each formula (Best). For online configurations (left), the DYNAMIC skeletons have the most consistent compression ratios, with a tradeoff in reconstruction times. In some cases, skeletons can have higher compression (10,000 times) without a loss in performance, witnessed by the right-hand-side tail of the plot.

For offline configurations (right), OFFLINE selects 1/1,000 of the clauses from the original DRAT proof. The ratios are much greater than 1,000 because skele-

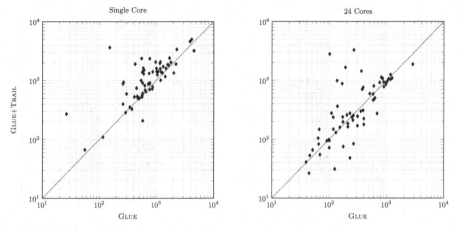

Fig. 4. Runtimes (in seconds) for proof reconstruction of multiple online configurations with a single core (left) and 24 cores (right).

tons have no deletion information and the most active clauses are typically much shorter than the average clause. OFFLINE-OPT provides around a factor 10 more compression, and these smaller skeletons provide faster reconstruction for about half of the formulas. In general, the compression is much better when using *clause activity* as a measure for clause importance as opposed to online heuristics (such as *glue*), with similar reconstruction times seen in Fig. 2.

6.3 Impact of Reason Clauses in Online Skeletons

Fig. 4 shows a comparison of reconstruction times between the GLUE and the GLUE+TRAIL online configurations, both on a single core (left) and on 24 cores (right). On a single core, creating skeletons with only low-glue clauses performs better than creating skeletons with low-glue clauses *and* reasons from the trail. On multiple cores, however, the reason clauses are beneficial for many reconstructions. This may be because for parallel reconstruction, each individual chunk only has access to lemmas earlier in the skeleton during solving. Therefore, having more clauses in the skeleton will aid the later chunks. In contrast, for a single chunk on one core, learned clauses are kept throughout solving, and these learned clauses supplement the smaller skeletons.

6.4 Impact of the UNSAT Core on Offline Skeletons

Fig. 5 shows the effect of using an UNSAT core during reconstruction for offline skeletons on a single core (left) and on 24 cores (right). For the experiments using an UNSAT core, we remove formula clauses that are not in the UNSAT core before passing the formula to the solver during the incremental SAT call for the chunk proof. Using the UNSAT core greatly improves performance during

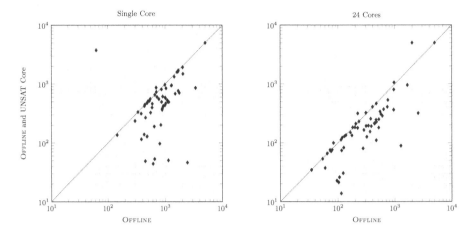

Fig. 5. Runtimes (in seconds) for OFFLINE proof reconstruction with and without an UNSAT core with a single core (left) and 24 cores (right).

reconstruction on a single core. This may be because the skeleton is built from reasoning based on the UNSAT core, so focusing the solver on these specific formula clauses makes filling the gaps in the skeleton easier. The UNSAT core is useful in parallel reconstruction as well, producing the overall best configuration between online and offline skeletons. To give an idea, it takes approximately 125 KB to store an UNSAT core as a bit vector (each bit indicating whether or not a clause is part of the core) for a formula with one million clauses. For most formulas, this data would be dominated by the size of the proof skeleton.

6.5   Skeleton Shrinking after Reconstruction

We discussed in Section 5.2 that it might make sense to shrink a skeleton by removing some amount of the fastest or of the slowest skeleton clauses. Fig. 6 shows results for reconstruction on 24 cores using the online skeleton, removing either the fastest 90% or the slowest 10% of clauses. To perform the shrinking, we performed proof reconstruction from the skeleton and measured the solve times for the incremental calls, with each call corresponding to a skeleton clause. Removing the fastest 90% has a small impact on reconstruction time, performing slower for the majority of formulas. In some cases, shrinking the skeleton even improves performance because redundant or unnecessary clauses are removed from the skeleton. Removing the slowest solved clauses causes a wider variation in reconstruction time. This might be because these clauses are important for guiding the solver during reconstruction, and sometimes they lead the solver into unprofitable search regions that waste time. This shows two things: (1) For some formulas, removing only a fraction of clauses from the skeleton can lead to a big or small improvement, and (2) skeleton clauses are mostly nontrivial and cannot be added or removed randomly without a potentially consequential impact.

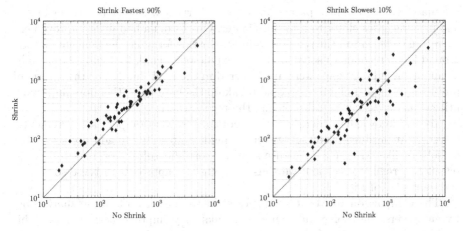

Fig. 6. Runtimes (in seconds) of proof reconstruction on 24 cores after skeleton shrinking for the DYNAMIC online configuration, removing the fastest 90% (left) or the slowest 10% (right) of clauses from the skeleton.

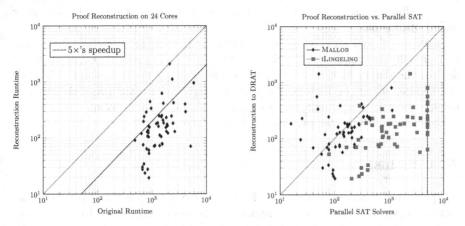

Fig. 7. Left: Runtimes (in seconds) of original solver on a single core against proof reconstruction on 24 cores with the best offline-skeleton configurations OFFLINE+UNITS using UNSAT cores. Right: Runtimes (in seconds) of parallel SAT solvers MALLOB and LINGELING without proof logging against proof reconstruction with the best offline skeleton configurations using an UNSAT core, each using 24 cores.

6.6   Comparison With Sequential and Parallel SAT Solvers

Alternatives to our proof reconstruction could be to compute a proof on demand by solving a formula from scratch (either with a sequential or with a parallel SAT solver) or to run a parallel incremental solver that fills the gaps of a skeleton.

The left plot of Fig. 7 shows the difference between running a sequential solver on a single core versus running our parallel proof reconstruction on 24 cores. For the majority of formulas, parallel proof reconstruction is over five times faster, and in some cases closer to ten times faster. One formula had little improvement for reconstruction (on the red dotted line). For this formula, the final chunk took around 2,000 seconds to solve, and the next slowest chunk took only 24 seconds, meaning the hardest gaps were all clustered in the final chunk. For these sorts of problems, a smaller chunk size could break up the hard gaps, therefore improving utilization across cores and reducing the reconstruction time.

To our knowledge, there exist no portfolio solvers or parallel incremental solvers that produce proofs. However, it might be possible to add proof support to solvers like MALLOB (a clause-sharing portfolio solver) or ILINGELING (a parallel incremental solver); we thus compare our approach to these solvers in the right plot of Fig. 7.

The comparison to MALLOB suggests that some form of clause sharing between solvers that solve independent chunks may improve performance. This could be achieved with *forward clause sharing*, where learned clauses can only be sent to solvers running on subsequent chunks. Also, MALLOB has full core utilization by running each solver until one derives the empty clause, but our proof reconstruction does not since some chunks take longer than others. With smaller chunk sizes and good scheduling, proof reconstruction could get closer to full utilization.

ILINGELING, which is based on LINGELING [2], takes an incremental problem and greedily assigns steps to solver instances, terminating when one instance derives the empty clause. There is no clause sharing between solvers. We ran ILINGELING using the incremental problem derived from the proof skeleton. In proof reconstruction, chunks can use skeleton clauses from previous chunks, leading to consistently better performance than ILINGELING.

7 Conclusion

We presented a semantic approach for compressing propositional proofs by selecting important clauses that summarize the reasoning of a solver. We store these clauses in a so-called proof skeleton, from which we can reconstruct a complete proof in parallel by performing multiple incremental SAT solver calls. We implemented our approach on top of the SAT solver CADICAL and the proof checker DRAT-TRIM. In an empirical evaluation, we showed that our approach can produce skeletons that are 100 to 5,000 times smaller than the original proofs. On a single core, almost all proofs were reconstructed faster than the original solving time, and when using 24 cores, the majority of proofs was reconstructed around five times faster. This is significant since proof checking typically takes longer than solving, and since existing parallel solvers cannot produce proofs while maintaining strong performance. We observed that proof skeletons not only serve as a compression mechanism but also provide insight into a problem. In future work, we thus plan to explore the connection between skeletons, proofs, and solver performance.

References

1. Audemard, G., Simon, L.: Predicting learnt clauses quality in modern SAT solvers. In: Boutilier, C. (ed.) IJCAI 2009, Proceedings of the 21st International Joint Conference on Artificial Intelligence, Pasadena, California, USA, July 11-17, 2009. pp. 399–404 (2009), http://ijcai.org/Proceedings/09/Papers/074.pdf
2. Biere, A., Fazekas, K., Fleury, M., Heisinger, M.: CaDiCaL, Kissat, Paracooba, Plingeling and Treengeling entering the SAT Competition 2020. In: Balyo, T., Froleyks, N., Heule, M., Iser, M., Järvisalo, M., Suda, M. (eds.) Proc. of SAT Competition 2020 – Solver and Benchmark Descriptions. Department of Computer Science Report Series B, vol. B-2020-1, pp. 51–53. University of Helsinki (2020)
3. Blanchette, J.C., Böhme, S., Paulson, L.C.: Extending sledgehammer with SMT solvers. J. Autom. Reason. **51**(1), 109–128 (2013)
4. Boudou, J., Fellner, A., Paleo, B.W.: Skeptik: A proof compression system. In: Demri, S., Kapur, D., Weidenbach, C. (eds.) Automated Reasoning - 7th International Joint Conference, IJCAR 2014, Held as Part of the Vienna Summer of Logic, VSL 2014, Vienna, Austria, July 19-22, 2014. Proceedings. Lecture Notes in Computer Science, vol. 8562, pp. 374–380. Springer (2014), https://doi.org/10.1007/978-3-319-08587-6_29
5. Cruz-Filipe, L., Heule, M.J.H., Jr., W.A.H., Kaufmann, M., Schneider-Kamp, P.: Efficient certified RAT verification. In: de Moura, L. (ed.) Automated Deduction - CADE 26 - 26th International Conference on Automated Deduction, Gothenburg, Sweden, August 6-11, 2017, Proceedings. Lecture Notes in Computer Science, vol. 10395, pp. 220–236. Springer (2017), https://doi.org/10.1007/978-3-319-63046-5_14
6. Eén, N., Sörensson, N.: An extensible SAT-solver. In: Giunchiglia, E., Tacchella, A. (eds.) Theory and Applications of Satisfiability Testing, 6th International Conference, SAT 2003. Santa Margherita Ligure, Italy, May 5-8, 2003 Selected Revised Papers. Lecture Notes in Computer Science, vol. 2919, pp. 502–518. Springer (2003), https://doi.org/10.1007/978-3-540-24605-3_37
7. Eén, N., Sörensson, N.: Temporal induction by incremental SAT solving. Electron. Notes Theor. Comput. Sci. **89**(4), 543–560 (2003), https://doi.org/10.1016/S1571-0661(05)82542-3
8. Fazekas, K., Biere, A., Scholl, C.: Incremental inprocessing in SAT solving. In: Janota, M., Lynce, I. (eds.) Theory and Applications of Satisfiability Testing - SAT 2019 - 22nd International Conference, SAT 2019, Lisbon, Portugal, July 9-12, 2019, Proceedings. Lecture Notes in Computer Science, vol. 11628, pp. 136–154. Springer (2019), https://doi.org/10.1007/978-3-030-24258-9_9
9. Heule, M., Jr., W.A.H., Kaufmann, M., Wetzler, N.: Efficient, verified checking of propositional proofs. In: Ayala-Rincón, M., Muñoz, C.A. (eds.) Interactive Theorem Proving - 8th International Conference, ITP 2017, Brasília, Brazil, September 26-29, 2017, Proceedings. Lecture Notes in Computer Science, vol. 10499, pp. 269–284. Springer (2017), https://doi.org/10.1007/978-3-319-66107-0_18
10. Heule, M.J.H.: The DRAT format and drat-trim checker. CoRR **abs/1610.06229** (2016), http://arxiv.org/abs/1610.06229
11. Heule, M.J.H.: Schur number five. In: McIlraith, S.A., Weinberger, K.Q. (eds.) Proceedings of the Thirty-Second AAAI Conference on Artificial Intelligence, (AAAI-18), the 30th innovative Applications of Artificial Intelligence (IAAI-18), and the 8th AAAI Symposium on Educational Advances in Artificial Intelligence (EAAI-18). pp. 6598–6606. AAAI Press (2018), https://www.aaai.org/ocs/index.php/AAAI/AAAI18/paper/view/16952

12. Heule, M.J.H., Kullmann, O., Marek, V.W.: Solving and verifying the boolean pythagorean triples problem via cube-and-conquer. In: Creignou, N., Le Berre, D. (eds.) Theory and Applications of Satisfiability Testing – SAT 2016. pp. 228–245. Springer International Publishing, Cham (2016)
13. Heule, M.J.H., Kullmann, O., Wieringa, S., Biere, A.: Cube and conquer: Guiding CDCL SAT solvers by lookaheads. In: Eder, K., Lourenço, J., Shehory, O. (eds.) Hardware and Software: Verification and Testing. pp. 50–65. Springer Berlin Heidelberg, Berlin, Heidelberg (2012)
14. Lammich, P.: Efficient verified (UN)SAT certificate checking. J. Autom. Reason. **64**(3), 513–532 (2020), https://doi.org/10.1007/s10817-019-09525-z
15. Marques-Silva, J.P., Sakallah, K.A.: GRASP: A search algorithm for propositional satisfiability. IEEE Trans. Computers **48**(5), 506–521 (1999), https://doi.org/10.1109/12.769433
16. Moskewicz, M.W., Madigan, C.F., Zhao, Y., Zhang, L., Malik, S.: Chaff: Engineering an efficient SAT solver. In: Proceedings of the 38th Design Automation Conference, DAC 2001, Las Vegas, NV, USA, June 18-22, 2001. pp. 530–535. ACM (2001), https://doi.org/10.1145/378239.379017
17. Nötzli, A., Barbosa, H., Niemetz, A., Preiner, M., Reynolds, A., Barrett, C., Tinelli, C.: Reconstructing fine-grained proofs of rewrites using a domain-specific language. In: Griggio, A., Rungta, N. (eds.) Formal Methods in Computer-Aided Design - 22nd Conference, FMCAD 2022, Trento, Italy, October 17-21, 2022, Proceedings. pp. 65–74. Formal Methods in Computer-Aided Design, TU Wien Academic Press (2022)
18. Rollini, S.F., Bruttomesso, R., Sharygina, N., Tsitovich, A.: Resolution proof transformation for compression and interpolation. Formal Methods Syst. Des. **45**(1), 1–41 (2014), https://doi.org/10.1007/s10703-014-0208-x
19. Tan, Y.K., Heule, M.J.H., Myreen, M.O.: cake_lpr: Verified propagation redundancy checking in CakeML. In: Groote, J.F., Larsen, K.G. (eds.) Tools and Algorithms for the Construction and Analysis of Systems - 27th International Conference, TACAS 2021, Held as Part of the European Joint Conferences on Theory and Practice of Software, ETAPS 2021, Luxembourg City, Luxembourg, March 27 - April 1, 2021, Proceedings, Part II. Lecture Notes in Computer Science, vol. 12652, pp. 223–241. Springer (2021), https://doi.org/10.1007/978-3-030-72013-1_12
20. Van Gelder, A.: Verifying RUP proofs of propositional unsatisfiability. In: International Symposium on Artificial Intelligence and Mathematics, ISAIM 2008, Fort Lauderdale, Florida, USA, January 2-4, 2008 (2008), http://isaim2008.unl.edu/PAPERS/TechnicalProgram/ISAIM2008_0008_60a1f9b2fd607a61ec9e0feac3f438f8.pdf
21. Vyskocil, J., Stanovský, D., Urban, J.: Automated proof compression by invention of new definitions. In: Clarke, E.M., Voronkov, A. (eds.) Logic for Programming, Artificial Intelligence, and Reasoning - 16th International Conference, LPAR-16, Dakar, Senegal, April 25-May 1, 2010, Revised Selected Papers. Lecture Notes in Computer Science, vol. 6355, pp. 447–462. Springer (2010), https://doi.org/10.1007/978-3-642-17511-4_25
22. Wetzler, N., Heule, M.J.H., Hunt, W.A.: DRAT-trim: Efficient checking and trimming using expressive clausal proofs. In: Theory and Applications of Satisfiability Testing (SAT). LNCS, vol. 8561, pp. 422–429 (2014)

Unsatisfiability Proofs for Distributed Clause-Sharing SAT Solvers

Dawn Michaelson[2]([⊠]) [iD], Dominik Schreiber[3]([⊠]) [iD], Marijn J. H. Heule[1,4] [iD],
Benjamin Kiesl-Reiter[1] [iD], and Michael W. Whalen[1,2] [iD]

[1] Amazon Web Services, Seattle, USA
[2] University of Minnesota, Minneapolis, USA
micha576@umn.edu
[3] Karlsruhe Institute of Technology, Karlsruhe, Germany
dominik.schreiber@kit.edu
[4] Carnegie Mellon University, Pittsburgh, USA

Abstract. Distributed clause-sharing SAT solvers can solve problems
up to one hundred times faster than sequential SAT solvers by sharing derived information among multiple sequential solvers working on
the same problem. Unlike sequential solvers, however, distributed solvers
have not been able to produce proofs of unsatisfiability in a scalable manner, which has limited their use in critical applications. In this paper,
we present a method to produce unsatisfiability proofs for distributed
SAT solvers by combining the partial proofs produced by each sequential solver into a single, linear proof. Our approach is more scalable and
general than previous explorations for parallel clause-sharing solvers, allowing use on distributed solvers without shared memory. We propose a
simple sequential algorithm as well as a fully distributed algorithm for
proof composition. Our empirical evaluation shows that for large-scale
distributed solvers (100 nodes of 16 cores each), our distributed approach
allows reliable proof composition and checking with reasonable overhead.
We analyze the overhead and discuss how and where future efforts may
further improve performance.

Keywords: SAT solving · proofs · distributed computing.

1   Introduction

SAT solvers are general-purpose tools for solving complex computational problems. By encoding domain problems into propositional logic, users have successfully applied SAT solvers in various fields such as formal verification [31],
automated planning [25], and mathematics [8, 16]. The list of applications has
grown significantly over the years, mainly because algorithmic improvements
have led to orders of magnitude improvement in the performance of the best
sequential solvers (see, e.g., [21] for a comparison).

Despite all this progress, there are still many problems that cannot be solved
quickly with even the best sequential solvers, pushing researchers to explore
ways of parallelizing SAT solving. One approach that has worked well for specific
problem instances is *Cube-and-Conquer* [17, 18], which can achieve near-linear

© The Author(s) 2023
S. Sankararanarayanan and N. Sharygina (Eds.): TACAS 2023, LNCS 13993, pp. 348–366, 2023.
https://doi.org/10.1007/978-3-031-30823-9_18

speedups for thousands of cores but requires domain knowledge about how effectively to split a problem into subproblems. An alternative approach that does not require such knowledge is *clause-sharing portfolio solving*, which has recently led to solvers [12,28] achieving impressive speedups (10x–100x on a 100x16 core cluster) over the best sequential solvers across broad sets of benchmarks.[5]

Although distributed solvers are demonstrably the most powerful tools for solving hard SAT problems, there is an important caveat: unlike sequential solvers, current distributed clause-sharing solvers cannot produce proofs of unsatisfiability. While there has been foundational work in producing proofs for shared-memory clause-sharing SAT solvers [14], existing approaches are neither scalable nor general enough for large-scale distributed solvers. This is not just a theoretical problem—for four problems in the 2020 and 2021 SAT competitions, distributed solvers produced incorrect answers that were not discovered until the 2022 competition because they could not be independently verified.[6]

In this paper, we deal with this issue and present the first scalable approach for generating proofs for distributed SAT solvers. To construct proofs, we maintain *provenance* information about shared clauses in order to track how they are used in the global solving process, and we use the recently-developed LRAT proof format [9] to track dependencies among partial proofs produced by solver instances. By exploiting these dependencies, we are then able to reconstruct a single linear proof from all the partial proofs produced by the sequential solvers. We first present a simple sequential algorithm for proof reconstruction before devising a parallel algorithm that can even be implemented in a distributed way. Both algorithms produce independently-verifiable proofs in the LRAT format. We demonstrate our approaches using an LRAT-producing version of the sequential SAT solver CaDiCaL [5] to turn it into a clause-sharing solver, and then modify the distributed solver Mallob [28] to orchestrate a portfolio of such CaDiCaL instances while tracking the IDs of all shared clauses.

We conduct an evaluation of our approaches from the perspective of efficiency, benchmarking the performance of our clause-sharing portfolio solver against the winners of the cloud track, parallel track, and sequential track from the SAT Competition 2022. Adding proof support introduces several kinds of overhead for clause-sharing portfolios in terms of solving, proof reconstruction, and proof checking, which we examine in detail. We show that even with this overhead, distributed solving and proving is much faster than the best sequential approaches. We also demonstrate that our approach dramatically outperforms previous work on proof production for clause-sharing portfolios [14]. We argue that much of the overhead of our current setup can be compensated, among other measures, by improving support for LRAT in solver backends. We thus hope that our work provides an impetus for researchers to add LRAT support to other solvers.

Our main contributions are as follows:

---

[5] c.f.: the SAT Competition 2022 results:
https://satcompetition.github.io/2022/downloads/sc2022-detailed-results.zip
[6] The incorrectly scored problems were SAT_MS_sat_nurikabe_p08.pddl_71.cnf, randomG-Mix-n18-d05.cnf, php12e12.cnf, and Cake_9_20.cnf.

- We present the first effective and scalable approach for proof generation in distributed SAT solving.
- We implement our approach on top of the state-of-the-art solvers CaDiCaL and Mallob.
- We perform a large-scale empirical evaluation analyzing the overhead introduced by proof production as compared to state-of-the-art portfolios.
- We demonstrate that our approach dramatically outperforms previous work in parallel proof production, and that it remains substantially more scalable than the best sequential solvers.

The rest of this paper is structured as follows. In Section 2, we present the background required to understand the rest of our paper and discuss related work. In Section 3, we describe the general problem of producing proofs for distributed SAT solving and a simple algorithm for proof combination. In Section 4, we describe a much more efficient distributed version of our algorithm before discussing implementation details in Section 5. Finally, we present the results of our empirical evaluation in Section 6 and conclude with a summary and an outlook for future work in Section 7.

2   Background and Related Work

The Boolean satisfiability problem (SAT) asks whether a Boolean formula can be satisfied by some assignment of truth values to its variables. An overview can be found in [6]. We consider formulas in *conjunctive normal form* (CNF). As such, a formula F is a conjunction (logical "AND") of disjunctions (logical "OR") of literals, where a literal is a Boolean variable or its negation. For example, $(\overline{a} \vee b \vee c) \wedge (b \vee \overline{c}) \wedge (a)$ is a formula with variables a, b, c and three clauses. A *truth assignment* $\mathcal{A}$ maps each variable to a Boolean value (true or false). A formula F is *satisfied* by an assignment $\mathcal{A}$ if F evaluates to true under $\mathcal{A}$, and F is *satisfiable* if such an assignment exists. Otherwise, F is called *unsatisfiable*.

If a formula F is found to be satisfiable, modern SAT solvers commonly output a truth assignment; users can easily evaluate F under the assignment in linear time to verify that F is indeed satisfiable. In contrast, if a formula turns out unsatisfiable, sequential SAT solvers produce an independently-checkable proof that there exists no assignment that satisfies the formula.

File Formats in Practical SAT Solving. In practical SAT solving, formulas are specified in the DIMACS format. DIMACS files feature a header of the form 'p cnf #variables #clauses' followed by a list of clauses, one clause per line. For example, the clause $(x_1 \vee \overline{x}_2 \vee x_3)$ is represented as '1 -2 3 0'. An example formula in DIMACS format is given in Figure 1.

The current standard format for proofs is DRAT [15]. DRAT files are similar to DIMACS files, with each line containing a proof statement that is either an *addition* or a *deletion*. Additions are lines that represent clauses like in the DIMACS format; they identify clauses that were derived ("learned") by the solver. Each clause addition must preserve satisfiability by adhering to the so-called

```
DIMACS                 DRAT                LRAT
p cnf 4 8                                  9          -3 0     5  4 0
  1 -2      0                 -3 0         10    1    2 0      3  2 0
     2    -4 0          1     2 0          11        -1 0      6  9 0
  1  2     4 0                -1 0         11 d                   9 0
 -1 -3      0      d          -3 0         12    2 3 -4 0      7 11 0
  1    -3   0          2 3 -4 0            13    1 2 3 0       8 12 0
 -1     3   0          1 2 3 0             14          0    11 10 1 0
  1     3 -4 0                    0
  1     3  4 0
```

Fig. 1: DIMACS formula and corresponding proofs in DRAT and LRAT format.

RAT criterion—as the details of RAT are not essential to our paper, we refer the reader to the respective literature for more details [20]. Deletions are lines that start with a 'd', followed by a clause; they identify clauses that were deleted by the solver because they were not deemed necessary anymore. Clause deletions can only make a formula "more satisfiable", meaning that they aren't required for deriving unsatisfiability, but they drastically speed up proof checking. A valid DRAT proof of unsatisfiability ends with the derivation of the empty clause. As the empty clause is trivially unsatisfiable (and since each proof step preserves satisfiability) the unsatisfiability of the original formula can then be concluded. An example DRAT proof is given in Figure 1.

The more recent LRAT proof format [9] augments each clause-addition step with so-called *hints*, which identify the clauses that were required to derive the current clause. This makes proof checking more efficient, and in fact the usual pipeline for trusted proof checking is to first use an efficient but unverified tool (like DRAT-trim [15]) to transform a DRAT proof into an LRAT proof, and then check the resulting LRAT proof with a formally verified proof checker (c.f., [9, 13, 22, 30]). Figure 1 shows an LRAT proof corresponding to a DRAT proof. Each proof line starts with a clause ID. The numbering starts with 9 because the eight clauses of the original formula are assigned the IDs 1 to 8. Each clause addition first lists the literals of the clause, then a terminating 0, followed by hints (in the form of clause IDs), and finally another 0. For example, clause 9 contains the literal -3 and can be derived from the clauses 4 and 5 of the original formula. Clause deletions just state the clause ID of the clause that is to be deleted, as in the later deletion of clause 9. In our work, we exploit the hints of LRAT to determine dependencies among distributed solvers.

Parallel and Distributed SAT Solving. One way to parallelize SAT solving is to run a portfolio of sequential solvers in parallel and to consider a problem solved as soon as one of the solvers finishes (c.f. [1, 4, 5, 11, 12, 18, 23, 29, 32]). Given that the solvers are sufficiently diverse, portfolio solving is already effective if all of the sequential solvers work independently, but performance and scalability can be boosted significantly by having the solvers share information in the form of learned clauses [4, 12]. This approach is taken by the distributed solver Mallob [28], which won the cloud track of the last three SAT competitions [2, 3, 27]. As opposed to other solvers, Mallob relies on a communication-efficient aggregation strategy to collect the globally most useful learned clauses and to reliably filter duplicates as well as previously shared clauses [27]. With this strategy, which aims to maximize the density and utility of the communicated data, Mallob scored first place in all four eligible subtracks for unsatisfiable problems at the 2022 SAT Competition.

As we discuss in more detail later, the drawback of clause sharing is that a local proof written by an individual solver may contain clauses whose derivations cannot be justified because they rely on clauses imported from another solver. Previous work focuses on writing DRAT proofs for clause-sharing parallel solvers [14]. In that work, solvers write to the same shared proof as they learn clauses. However, since the clauses are shared, one solver deleting a clause could invalidate a later clause-addition by another solver that is still holding the clause. To handle this, the parallel solver moderates deletion statements, only writing them to the proof once all solvers have deleted a clause, which leads to poor scalability during proof search. In our approach, solvers write proof files fully independently—only when the unsatisfiability of the problem has been determined do we combine all proofs into a single valid proof.

Other recent work includes reconstructing proofs from divide-and-conquer solvers [24] and from a particular shared-memory parallel solver [10] whereas we aim to exploit distributed portfolio solving.

3   Basic Proof Production

Our goal is to produce checkable unsatisfiability proofs for problems solved by distributed clause-sharing SAT solvers. We propose to reuse the work done on proofs for sequential solvers by having each solver produce a partial proof containing the clauses it learned. These partial proofs are invalid in general because each sequential solver can rely on clauses shared by other solvers when learning new clauses. For example, when solver A derives a new clause, it might rely on clauses from solvers B and C, which in turn relied on clauses from solvers D and E, and so on. The justification of A's clause derivation is thus spread across multiple partial proofs. We need to combine the partial proofs into a single valid proof in which the clauses are in *dependency order*, meaning that each clause can be derived from previous clauses.

To generate an efficiently-checkable combined proof in a scalable way, we must solve three challenges:

1. Provide metadata to identify which solver produced each learned clause.
2. Efficiently sort learned clauses in dependency order across all solvers.
3. Reduce proof size by removing unnecessary clauses.

Switching from DRAT to the LRAT proof format provides the mechanism to unlock all three challenges. First, we specialize the clause-numbering scheme used by LRAT in order to distinguish the clauses produced by each solver. Second, we use the dependency information from LRAT to construct a complete proof from the partial proofs produced by each solver. Finally, we determine which clauses are unnecessary (or used only for certain parts of the proof) to delete clauses from the proof as soon as they are no longer required.

Algorithm 1 Algorithm for combining partial proofs

1: **function** COMBINE(partial proofs $p_1, p_2, ...p_n$, number of original clauses o)
2:     $i \leftarrow 1$
3:     **while** true **do**
4:         **if** $p_i.hasNext()$ **then**
5:             $\langle id, type, clause, proofHint \rangle \leftarrow p_i.peekNext()$
6:             **if** $dependenciesSatisfied(proofHint)$ **then**
7:                 emit $\langle id, type, clause, proofHint \rangle$
8:                 $p_i.next()$ ▷ Line completed
9:                 **if** $clause = \emptyset$ **then**   ▷ Derived empty clause
10:                     **return**
11:             **else**   ▷ Leave the line and move to next partial proof
12:                 $i \leftarrow (i \mod n) + 1$
13:         **else**   ▷ Move to next partial proof if current is done
14:             $i \leftarrow (i \mod n) + 1$

We update the clause-distribution mechanism in the distributed solver to broadcast the clause ID with each learned clause. A receiving solver stores the clause with its ID and uses the ID in proof hints when the clause is used locally, as it does with locally-derived clauses. Unlike locally-derived clauses, we add no derivation lines for remote clauses to the local proof. Instead, these derivations will be added to the final proof when combining the partial proofs.

3.1 Solver Partial Proof Production

To combine the partial proofs into a complete proof, we modify the mechanism producing LRAT proofs in each of the component solvers. We assign to each clause an ID that is unique across solvers and identifies which solver originally derived it. The following mapping from clauses to IDs achieves this:

Definition 1. *Let o be the number of clauses in the original formula and let n be the number of sequential solvers. Then, the ID of the k-th derived clause ($k \geq 0$) of solver i is defined as $ID^i_k = o + i + nk$.*

Given ID^i_k, we can easily determine the solver ID i using modular arithmetic.

3.2 Partial Proof Combination

Once the distributed solver has concluded the input formula is unsatisfiable, we have n partial proofs. The clause derivations in these proofs refer to clauses of other partial proofs, but they are, locally, in dependency order. We can therefore combine the partial proofs without reordering their clauses beforehand. We can simply interleave their clauses so the resulting proof is also in dependency order, ignoring any deletions in the partial proofs.

Our algorithm goes through the partial proofs round-robin, at each step emitting all the clauses from each file where the dependencies of the clause have

```
INSTANCE 1                    INSTANCE 2                    COMBINED
 9        -3 0    5  4 0       10   1  2 0       3  2 0      9        -3 0    5  4 0
11        -1 0    6  9 0       12 2 3 -4 0       7 11 0     11        -1 0    6  9 0
11 d 9 0                       14       0   11  10  1 0     10   1  2 0       3  2 0
13 1  2  3 0    8 12 0                                      12 2 3 -4 0       7 11 0
                                                            14       0   11  10  1 0
```

Fig. 2: Partial proofs and combined proof of unsatisfiability.

already been emitted. It ends when the empty clause is emitted. The procedure is shown in Algorithm 1. For each partial proof, we maintain an iterator over the learned clauses. We add the next clause from the current partial proof (p_i) to the final proof if its dependencies are satisfied (determined by comparing each hint to the last clause emitted from the partial proof whence it originated); otherwise it cycles to the next partial proof. It emits the line and moves to the next clause in the file. The algorithm terminates when it emits the empty clause (line 10).

Example 1. Suppose that two solver instances (instance 1 and instance 2) determined together that the formula from Figure 1 is unsatisfiable, with the two partial proofs shown in Figure 2. We start with instance 1. As clause 9 only relies on original clauses, we emit it. Clause 11 relies on original clause 6 and emitted clause 9, so we emit it. Clause 13 relies on clauses 8 and 12, which is not emitted, so we cannot emit clause 13 and move to instance 2. Clause 10 can be emitted, as can clause 12, which relies on an original and an emitted clause. Clause 14 relies on emitted clauses 11 and 10 and on original clause 1, so we can emit it as well. Since clause 14 is the empty clause, we finish with a complete proof, shown in Figure 2(c). Notice that clause 13 was not added to the combined proof, since it was not required to satisfy any dependencies of the empty clause.

3.3   Proof Pruning

The combined proof produced by our procedure is valid but not efficiently checkable because (1) it can contain clauses that are not required to derive the empty clause and (2) it does not contain deletion lines, meaning that a proof checker must maintain *all* learned clauses in memory throughout the checking process. To reduce size and to improve proof-checking performance, we prune our combined proof toward a minimal proof containing only necessary clauses, and we add deletion statements for clauses as soon as they are not needed anymore.

Algorithm 2 shows our pruning algorithm that walks the combined proof in reverse (similar to backward checking of DRAT proofs [19]). We maintain a set of clauses *required* in the proof, initialized to the empty clause alone. We then process all clauses in reverse order, including the empty clause, ignoring all clauses not in the required set. For each required clause, we check its dependencies to see if this is the first time (from the proof's end) a dependency is seen; if so, we emit a deletion line for the dependency since it will never be used again in the proof. After checking all its dependencies, we output the clause itself. The

---

Algorithm 2 Algorithm for pruning proofs

1: **function** PRUNE(combined and reversed proof p, number of original clauses o)
2:     $required \leftarrow \{p.peekNextId()\}$ ▷ Must be empty clause, which is required
3:     **while** $p.hasNext()$ **do**
4:         $\langle id, type, clause, proofHint \rangle \leftarrow p.readNext()$
5:         **if** $id \in required$ **then**   ▷ Only process a line if it is required later
6:             **for** $hint \in proofHint$ **do**
7:                 **if** $hint > o \wedge hint \notin required$ **then**   ▷ Not used later
8:                     $required \leftarrow required \cup \{hint\}$
9:                     emit $\langle id, \texttt{delete}, hint \rangle$
10:            emit $\langle id, \texttt{add}, clause, proofHint \rangle$

---

final output of the algorithm is a proof in reversed order, where each clause is required for some derivation and deleted as soon as it is no longer required.

Example 2. Consider the combined proof from Figure 2. After applying Algorithm 2, working backward from clause 14, we determine that clause 12 is not required, so it is removed. Additionally, prior to clause 11, clause 9 is not in the required set, so it can be deleted after processing clause 11. On larger proofs, as discussed in Section 6, pruning can reduce the size of the proof by 10x or more.

4 Distributed Proof Production

The proof production as described above is sequential and may process huge amounts of data, all of which needs to be accessible from the machine that executes the procedure. In addition, maintaining the required clause IDs during the procedure may require a prohibitive amount of memory for large proofs. In the following, we propose an efficient distributed approach to proof production.

4.1 Overview

Our previous sequential proof-combination algorithm first combines all partial proofs into a single proof and then prunes unneeded proof lines. In contrast, our distributed algorithm first prunes all partial proofs in parallel and only then merges them into a single file.

We have m processes with c solver instances each, amounting to a total of $n = mc$ solvers. We make use of the fact that the solvers exchange clauses in periodic intervals (one second by default). We refer to these intervals between subsequent sharing operations as *epochs*. Consider Fig. 3 (left): Clause 118 was produced by S_2 in epoch 1. Its derivation may depend on local clause 114 and on any of the 11 clauses produced in epoch 0, but it cannot depend, e.g., on clause 109 or 111 since these clauses have been produced after the last clause sharing. More generally, a clause c produced by instance i during epoch e can only depend on (i) earlier clauses by instance i produced during epoch e or earlier, and (ii) clauses by instances $j \neq i$ produced *before* epoch e.

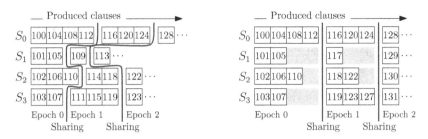

Fig. 3: Four solvers work on a formula with 99 original clauses, produce new clauses (depicted by their ID), and share clauses periodically, without (left) and with (right) aligning clause IDs.

Using this knowledge, we can essentially *rewind* the solving procedure. Each process reads its partial proofs in reverse order, outputs each line which adds a required clause, and adds the hints of each such clause to the required clauses. Required remote clauses produced in epoch e are transferred to their process of origin before any proof lines from epoch e are read. As such, whenever a process reads a proof line, it knows whether the clause is required. The outputs of all processes can be merged into a single valid proof (Section 4.3).

4.2 Distributed Pruning

Clause ID Alignment. To synchronize the reading and redistribution of clause IDs in our distributed pruning, we need a way to decide from which epoch a remote clause ID originates. However, solvers generally produce clauses with different speeds, so the IDs by different solvers will likely be in dissimilar ranges within the same epoch over time. For instance, in Fig. 3 (left) instance S_3 has no way of knowing from which epoch clause 118 originates. To solve this issue, we propose to align all produced clause IDs after each sharing. During the solving procedure, we add a certain offset δ_i^e to each ID produced by instance i in epoch e. As such, we can associate each epoch e with a global interval $[A_e, A_{e+1})$ that contains all clause IDs produced in that epoch. In Fig. 3 (right), $A_0 = 100$, $A_1 = 116$, and $A_2 = 128$. Clause 118 on the left has been aligned to 122 on the right ($\delta_2^1 = 4$) and due to $A_1 \leq 122 < A_2$ all instances know that this clause originates from epoch 1.

Initially, $\delta_i^0 := 0$ for all i. Let I_i^e be the first original (unaligned) ID produced by instance i in epoch e. With the sharing that initiates epoch $e > 0$, we compute the common start of epoch e, $A_e := \max_i\{I_i^e + \delta_i^{e-1} - i\}$, as the lowest possible value that is larger than all clause IDs from epoch $e-1$. We then compute offsets δ_i^e in such a way that $I_i^e + \delta_i^e = A_e + i$, which yields $\delta_i^e := (A_e + i) - I_i^e$. If we then export a clause produced during e by instance i, we add δ_i^e to its ID, and if we import shared clauses to i, we filter any clauses produced by i itself. Note that we do not modify the solvers' internal ID counters or the proofs they output. Later, when reading the partial proof of solver i at epoch e, we need to add δ_i^e to each ID originating from i. All other clause IDs are already aligned.

Rewinding the Solve Procedure. Assume that instance $u \in \{1, \ldots, n\}$ has derived the empty clause in epoch $\hat{e}$. For each local solver i, each process has a *frontier* F_i of required clauses produced by i. In addition, each process has a *backlog* B of remote required clauses. B and F_i are collections of clause IDs and can be thought of as maximum-first priority queues. Initially, F_u contains the ID of the empty clause while all other frontiers and backlogs are empty. Iteration $x \geq 0$ of our algorithm processes epoch $\hat{e} - x$ and features two stages:

1. *Processing:* Each process continues to read its partial proofs in reverse order from the last introduced clause of the current epoch. If a line from solver i is read whose clause ID is at the top of F_i, then the ID is removed from F_i, the line is output, and each clause ID hint h in the line is treated as follows:
   - h is inserted in F_j if local solver j (possibly $j = i$) produced h.
   - h is inserted in B if a remote solver produced h.
   - h is dropped if h is an ID of an original clause of the problem.
Reading stops as soon as a line's ID precedes epoch $e = \hat{e} - x$. Each F_i as well as B now only contain clauses produced *before* e.

2. *Task redistribution:* Each process extracts all clause IDs from B that were produced during $\hat{e} - x - 1$. These clause IDs are aggregated among all processes, eliminating duplicates in the same manner as Mallob's clause sharing detects duplicate clauses [28]. Each process traverses the aggregated clause IDs, and each clause produced by a local solver i is added to F_i.

Our algorithm stops in iteration $\hat{e}$ after the Processing stage, at which point all frontiers and backlogs are empty and all relevant proof lines have been output.

Analysis. In terms of total work performed, all partial proofs are read completely. For each required clause we may perform an insertion into some B, a deletion from said B, an insertion into some F_i, and a deletion from said F_i. If we assume logarithmic work for each insertion and deletion, the work for these operations is linear in the combined size of all partial proofs and loglinear in the size of the output proof. In addition, we have $\hat{e}$ iterations of communication whose overall volume is bounded by the communication done during solving. In fact, since only a subset of shared clauses are required and we only share 64 bits per clause, we expect strictly less communication than during solving. Computing A_e for each epoch e during solving is negligible since the necessary aggregation and broadcast can be integrated into an existing collective operation. Regarding memory usage, the size of each B and each F_i can be proportional to the combined size of all required lines of the according partial proofs. However, we can make use of external data structures which keep their content on disk except for a few buffers.

4.3   Merging Step

For each partial proof processed during the pruning step, we have a stream of proof lines sorted in reverse chronological order, i.e., starting with the highest clause ID. The remaining task is to merge all these lines into a single, sorted proof file. As shown in Fig. 4 (left), we arrange all processes in a tree. We can easily merge a number of sorted input streams into a single sorted output stream

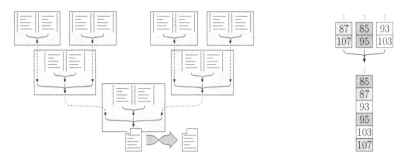

Fig. 4: Left: Proof merging with seven processes and 14 solvers. Each box represents a process with two local proof sources. Dashed arrows denote communication. Right: Example of merging three streams of LRAT lines into a single stream. Each number i represents an LRAT line describing a clause of ID i.

by repeatedly outputting the line with the highest ID among all inputs (Fig. 4 right). This way, we can hierarchically merge all streams along the tree. At the tree's root, the output stream is directed into a file. This is a sequential I/O task that limits the speed of merging. Finally, since the produced file is in reverse order, a buffered operation reverses the file's content.

A final challenge is to add clause deletions to the final proof. Before a line is written to the combined proof file, we can scan its hints and output a deletion line for each hint we did not encounter before (see Section 3.3). However, implementing this in an exact manner requires maintaining a set of clause IDs which scales with the final proof size. Since our proof remains valid even if we omit some clause deletions, we can use an approximate membership query (AMQ) structure with fixed size and a small false positive rate, e.g., a Bloom filter [7].

5   Implementation

We employ a solver portfolio based on the sequential SAT solver CaDiCaL [5]. We modified CaDiCaL to output LRAT proof lines and to assign clause IDs as described in Section 3.1. To ensure sound LRAT proof logging, some features of CaDiCaL currently need to be turned off, such as bounded variable elimination, hyper-ternary resolution, and vivification. Similarly, Mallob's original portfolio of CaDiCaL configurations features several options that are incompatible with our proof logging as of yet. Therefore, we created a smaller portfolio of "safe" configurations that include shuffling variable priorities, adjusted restart intervals, and disabled inprocessing. We also use different random seeds and use Mallob's diversification based on randomized initial variable polarities.

We modified Mallob to associate each clause with a 64-bit clause ID. For consistent bookkeeping of sharing epochs, we defer clause sharing until all processes have fully initialized their solvers. While several solvers may derive the empty clause simultaneously, only one of them is selected to be the "winner" whose empty clause will be traced. The distributed proof production features communication similar to Mallob's clause sharing. To realize the frontier F_i and the backlog B described in Section 4.2, we implemented an external-memory data structure which writes clause IDs to disk, categorized by their epoch. Upon reaching a new epoch, all clause IDs from this epoch are read from disk and inserted into an internal priority queue to allow for efficient polling and insertion. To merge the pruned partial proofs, we use point-to-point messages to query and send buffers of proof lines between processes. We interleave this merging with the pruning procedure in order to avoid writing the intermediate output to disk. We use a fixed-size Bloom filter to add some deletion lines to the final proof.

6   Evaluation

In this section, we present an evaluation of our proof production approaches. We provide the associated software as well as a digital appendix online.[7]

6.1   Experimental Setup

Supporting proofs introduces several kinds of performance overhead for clause-sharing portfolios in terms of solving, proof reconstruction, and proof checking. We wish to examine how well our proof-producing solver performs against (1) best-of-breed parallel and cloud solvers that do not produce proofs, (2) previous approaches to proof-producing parallel solvers, and (3) best-of-breed sequential solvers. We analyze the overhead introduced by each phase of the process, and we discuss how and where future efforts might improve performance.

We use the following pipeline for our proof-producing solvers: First, the input formula is preprocessed by performing exhaustive unit propagation. This is necessary due to a technical limitation of our LRAT-producing modification of CaDiCaL. Second, we execute our proof-producing variant of Mallob on the preprocessed formula. Third, we prune and combine all partial proofs, using either our sequential proof production or our distributed proof production. Fourth, we merge the preprocessor's proof and our produced proof and syntactically transform the result to bring the set of clause IDs into compact shape. Fifth and finally, we run `lrat-check`[8] to check the final proof. Only steps two and three of our pipeline are parallelized (step three depending on the particular experiment). We will refer to the first two steps as *solving*, the third step as *assembly*, the fourth step as *postprocessing*, and the fifth step as *checking*.

To examine performance overhead for proof-producing parallel and distributed solvers, we compare our proof-producing cloud and parallel solvers (`mallob-cacld-p` and `mallob-capar-p`) against six solvers. First, we include the winners of the 2022 SAT competition cloud track (`mallob-kicaliglu`, using Kissat+CaDiCaL+Lingeling+Glucose), parallel track (`parkissat-rs`, using Kissat), and sequential track (`Kissat_MAB-HyWalk`), as well as the second place

---

[7] https://github.com/domschrei/mallob/tree/certified-unsat

[8] https://github.com/marijnheule/drat-trim

Table 1: Overview of solved instances: (S)equential, (P)arallel, and (C)loud

Solver	Type	Solved	SAT	UNSAT	PAR-2 score
Kissat_MAB-HyWalk	S	218	118	100	1065.7
parkissat-rs	P	299	155	144	603.0
mallob-ki	P	260	113	147	827.6
mallob-capar	P	292	145	147	641.6
mallob-capar-p (Seq.)	P	279	140	139	719.8
mallob-capar-p (Par.)	P	276	141	135	731.4
mallob-kicaliglu	C	341	165	176	344.8
mallob-cacld	C	333	163	170	378.0
mallob-cacld-p	C	314	159	155	484.1

solver from the parallel track (`mallob-ki`, using Lingeling[9]). We then run a parallel and cloud version of Mallob that runs our described CaDiCaL portfolio *without* proof production (`mallob-capar` and `mallob-cacld`).

Following the SAT competition setup, each cloud solver runs on 100 m6i.4xlarge EC2 instances (16 core, 64GB RAM), each parallel solver runs on a single m6i.16xlarge EC2 instance (64 core, 256GB RAM), and the sequential `Kissat_MAB-HyWalk` runs on a single m6i.4xlarge EC2 instance. For each solver, we run the full benchmark suite from the SAT-Competition 2022 (400 formulas) containing both SAT and UNSAT examples. The timeout for the solving step is 1000 seconds, and the timeout for all subsequent steps is set to 4000 seconds.

Since earlier work [14] is no longer competitive in terms of solving time, we only compare proof-checking times. Specifically, we measure the overhead of checking un-pruned DRAT proofs as the ones produced by [14]. As such, we can get a picture of the performance of the earlier approach if it was realized with state-of-the-art solving techniques. We generate un-pruned DRAT proofs from the original (un-pruned) LRAT proof by stripping out the dependency information and adding delete lines for the last use of each clause.

6.2   Results

First we examine the performance overhead of changing portfolios to enable proof generation as described in Section 5 on the *solving process only*. Fig. 5 (left) and Table 1 show this data. The PAR-2 metric takes the average time to solve each problem, but counts a timeout result as a 2x penalty (e.g., given our timeout of 1000 seconds, a timeout is scored as taking 2000 seconds). We can see that our CaDiCaL portfolio `mallob-capar` outperforms the Lingeling-based `mallob-ki` significantly and is almost on par with `parkissat-rs`. Similarly, `mallob-cacld` solves eight instances less compared to `mallob-kicaliglu` but performs almost equally well otherwise. In both cases, we have constructed solvers which are,

---

[9] `mallob-ki` employed a Lingeling-based portfolio due to a misconfiguration, see: http://algo2.iti.kit.edu/schreiber/downloads/mallob-ki-mallob-li.pdf

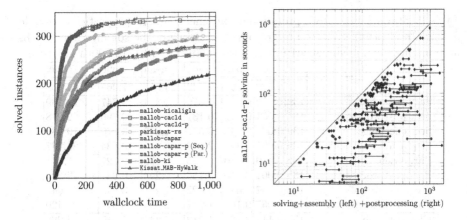

Fig. 5: Left: Comparison of solving times. Right: Relation of solving times to assembly and postprocessing times for `mallob-cacld-p`. Each pair of points corresponds to one instance, the y coordinate denoting the solving time. The left x coordinate denotes solving and assembly time and the right x coordinate denotes solving, assembly, and postprocessing time.

up to a small margin, on par with the state of the art. For our actual proof-producing solvers, `mallob-capar-p` and `mallob-cacld-p`, we noticed a more pronounced decline in solving performance. On top of the overhead introduced by proof logging and our preprocessing, we experienced a few technical problems, including memory issues[10], which resulted in a drop in the number of instances solved and also caused `mallob-capar-p` with parallel proof production to solve three instances less than with sequential proof production. We believe that we can overcome these issues in future versions of our system. That being said, our proof-producing solvers already outperform any of the solvers at a lower scale.

Second, we examine statistics on proof reconstruction and checking, showing results in Table 2. Since we want to investigate our approaches' overhead compared to pure solving, we measure run times as a multiple of the solving time. (We provide absolute run times in the Appendix, Table 1.) The prefix "Seq." denotes `mallob-capar-p` with sequential proof production, "Par." denotes `mallob-capar-p` with distributed proof production run on a single machine, and "Cld." denotes `mallob-cacld-p` with distributed proof production.

DRAT checking succeeded in 81 out of 139 cases and timed out in 58 cases. For the successful cases, DRAT checking took 24.8× the solving time on average whereas our sequential assembly, postprocessing and checking combined succeeded in 139 cases and only took 3.8× the solving time on average. This result confirms that our approach successfully overcomes the major scalability problems of earlier work [14]. In terms of uncompressed proof sizes, our LRAT

---

[10] We disabled Mallob's memory panic mode to ensure consistent proof logging.

Table 2: Statistics on proof production and checking. All properties except for file sizes and pruning factor are given as a multiple of the solving time. We list minima, maxima, medians, arithmetic means, and the 10th and 90th percentiles.

Property	#	min	p10	med	mean	p90	max
DRAT check	81	0.512	1.725	7.442	24.815	67.065	169.869
Seq. assembly	139	0.019	0.305	1.376	2.324	5.747	13.289
Seq. postprocessing	139	0.001	0.012	0.131	0.263	0.790	2.218
Seq. checking	139	0.007	0.043	0.572	1.252	3.970	10.980
Seq. asm+post+chk	139	0.037	0.412	2.110	3.840	10.834	26.487
Par. assembly	135	0.059	0.080	0.365	0.805	2.227	7.475
Par. postprocessing	135	0.001	0.016	0.156	0.293	0.861	2.300
Par. checking	135	0.007	0.042	0.622	1.241	3.540	11.645
Par. asm+post+chk	135	0.067	0.167	1.097	2.339	6.611	21.420
Cld. assembly	155	0.114	0.185	1.412	2.444	5.410	44.268
Cld. postprocessing	155	0.003	0.060	0.696	2.046	4.785	39.096
Cld. checking	155	0.033	0.189	3.291	8.883	21.974	170.378
Cld. asm+post+chk	155	0.168	0.577	5.110	13.373	32.484	253.742
DRAT proof size (GiB)	139	0.012	0.366	1.236	3.246	8.395	29.308
Seq. proof size (GiB)	139	0.016	0.223	2.379	5.384	16.082	46.986
Par. proof size (GiB)	135	0.006	0.173	2.034	5.345	13.164	57.739
Cld. proof size (GiB)	155	0.016	0.342	3.940	10.533	30.130	89.106
Cld. pruning factor	155	2.374	5.379	17.826	293.762	337.486	12466.700

proofs can be about twice as large as the DRAT proofs, which seems more than acceptable considering the dramatic difference in performance. Given that DRAT-based checking was ineffective at the scale of parallel solvers, we decided to omit it in our distributed experiments which feature even larger proofs.

Regarding `mallob-capar-p` with parallel proof production, we can see that the assembly time is reduced from 2.32× down to 0.81× the solving time on average, which also improves overall performance (3.84× to 2.34×).

The results for `mallob-cacld-p` demonstrate that our proof assembly is feasible, taking around 2.5× the solving time on average. We visualized this overhead and how it relates to the postprocessing overhead in Fig. 5 (right). The proofs produced are about twice as large as for `mallob-capar-p`. Considering that the proofs originate from 25 times as many solvers, this increase in size is quite modest, which can be explained by our proof pruning. We captured the *pruning factor* — the number of clauses in all partial proofs divided by the number of clauses in the combined proof — for each instance. Our pruning reduces the derived clauses by a factor of 293.8 on average (17.8 for the median instance), showing that it is a crucial technique to obtain proofs that are feasible to check. As such, we also managed to produce and check a proof of unsatisfiability for a formula whose unsatisfiability has not been verified before (`PancakeVsInsertSort_8_7.cnf`).

Lastly, to compare our approach at the largest scale with the state of the art in sequential solving, we computed speedups of `mallob-cacld-p`, solving times only, over `Kissat_MAB-HyWalk` and arrived at a median speedup of 11.5 (Appendix, Table 2). We also analyzed `drat-trim` checking times of `Kissat_MAB-HyWalk`, kindly provided by the competition organizers, and arrived at a median overhead of 1.1× its own solving time (Appendix, Table 3). Going by these measures, `Kissat_MAB-HyWalk` takes around $11.5 \cdot 2.1 \approx 24.2\times$ the solving time of `mallob-cacld-p` to arrive at a checked result while our complete pipeline only takes 5.1× the solving time for the median instance. This indicates that our approach is considerably faster than the best available sequential solvers.

We can see that the bottleneck of our pipeline shifts from the assembly step further to the postprocessing and checking steps when increasing the degree of parallelism. This is to be expected since the latter steps are, so far, inherently sequential whereas our proof assembly is scalable. While the postprocessing step is a technical necessity in our current setup, we believe that large portions of it can be eliminated in the future with further engineering. For instance, enhancing the LRAT support of our modified CaDiCaL to natively handle unit clauses in the input would allow us to skip preprocessing and simplify postprocessing.

7 Conclusion and Future Work

Distributed clause-sharing solvers are currently the fastest tools for solving a wide range of difficult SAT problems. Nevertheless, they have previously not supported proof-generation techniques, leading to potential soundness concerns. In this paper, we have examined mechanisms to add efficient support for proof generation to clause-sharing portfolio solvers. Our results demonstrate that we can, with reasonable efficiency, add support to these solvers to have full confidence that the results they produce are correct.

Following our research, more work is required to reduce overhead in the different steps involved and to improve scalability of the end-to-end procedure. This may include designing more efficient (perhaps even parallel) LRAT checkers, examining proof-streaming techniques to eliminate most I/O operations, and improving LRAT support in solver backends. In fact, it might be possible to generalize our approach to DRAT-based solvers by adding additional metadata, and this might allow easier retrofitting of the approach onto larger portfolios of solvers. We also intend to investigate producing proofs in Mallob for the case where many problems are solved at once and jobs are rescaled dynamically [26].

Acknowledgments

We would like to thank Mario Carneiro for providing help for his FRAT-supporting variant of CaDiCaL; Markus Iser for providing competition data on proof checking; Andrew Gacek for his suggestions to early drafts of this paper; and the reviewers for their helpful feedback. This project has received funding from the European Research Council (ERC) under the European Union's Horizon 2020 research and innovation programme (grant agr. No. 882500). This project was partially supported by the U.S. National Science Foundation grant CCF-2015445.

References

1. Audemard, G., Simon, L.: Lazy clause exchange policy for parallel SAT solvers. In: Sinz, C., Egly, U. (eds.) Theory and Applications of Satisfiability Testing - SAT 2014 - 17th International Conference, Held as Part of the Vienna Summer of Logic, VSL 2014, Vienna, Austria, July 14-17, 2014. Proceedings. Lecture Notes in Computer Science, vol. 8561, pp. 197–205. Springer (2014). `https://doi.org/10.1007/978-3-319-09284-3_15`

2. Balyo, T., Froleyks, N., Heule, M., Iser, M., Järvisalo, M., Suda, M. (eds.): Proceedings of SAT Competition 2021: Solver and Benchmark Descriptions. Department of Computer Science Report Series B, Department of Computer Science, University of Helsinki, Finland (2021)

3. Balyo, T., Froleyks, N., Heule, M., Iser, M., Järvisalo, M., Suda, M. (eds.): Proceedings of SAT Competition 2020: Solver and Benchmark Descriptions. Department of Computer Science Report Series B, Department of Computer Science, University of Helsinki, Finland (2020)

4. Balyo, T., Sanders, P., Sinz, C.: HordeSat: A massively parallel portfolio SAT solver. In: Heule, M., Weaver, S. (eds.) Theory and Applications of Satisfiability Testing – SAT 2015. pp. 156–172. Springer International Publishing, Cham (2015). `https://doi.org/10.1007/978-3-319-24318-4_12`

5. Biere, A., Fazekas, K., Fleury, M., Heisinger, M.: CaDiCaL, Kissat, Paracooba, Plingeling and Treengeling entering the SAT Competition 2020. In: Balyo, T., Froleyks, N., Heule, M., Iser, M., Järvisalo, M., Suda, M. (eds.) Proc. of SAT Competition 2020 – Solver and Benchmark Descriptions. Department of Computer Science Report Series B, vol. B-2020-1, pp. 51–53. University of Helsinki (2020)

6. Biere, A., Heule, M., van Maaren, H., Walsh, T. (eds.): Handbook of Satisfiability, Frontiers in Artificial Intelligence and Applications, vol. 185. IOS Press (2009), `http://dblp.uni-trier.de/db/series/faia/faia185.html`

7. Bloom, B.H.: Space/time trade-offs in hash coding with allowable errors. Communications of the ACM **13**(7), 422–426 (1970). `https://doi.org/10.1145/362686.362692`

8. Brakensiek, J., Heule, M., Mackey, J., Narváez, D.E.: The resolution of Keller's conjecture. J. Autom. Reason. **66**(3), 277–300 (2022). `https://doi.org/10.1007/s10817-022-09623-5`

9. Cruz-Filipe, L., Heule, M.J.H., Jr., W.A.H., Kaufmann, M., Schneider-Kamp, P.: Efficient certified RAT verification. In: de Moura, L. (ed.) Automated Deduction - CADE 26 - 26th International Conference on Automated Deduction, Gothenburg, Sweden, August 6-11, 2017, Proceedings. Lecture Notes in Computer Science, vol. 10395, pp. 220–236. Springer (2017). `https://doi.org/10.1007/978-3-319-63046-5_14`

10. Fleury, M., Biere, A.: Scalable proof producing multi-threaded SAT solving with Gimsatul through sharing instead of copying clauses. In: Pragmatics of SAT (2022). `https://doi.org/10.48550/arXiv.2207.13577`

11. Gomes, C.P., Selman, B.: Algorithm portfolios. Artif. Intell. **126**(1-2), 43–62 (2001). `https://doi.org/10.1016/S0004-3702(00)00081-3`

12. Hamadi, Y., Jabbour, S., Sais, L.: ManySAT: a parallel SAT solver. J. Satisf. Boolean Model. Comput. **6**(4), 245–262 (2009). `https://doi.org/10.3233/sat190070`

13. Heule, M., Jr., W.A.H., Kaufmann, M., Wetzler, N.: Efficient, verified checking of propositional proofs. In: Ayala-Rincón, M., Muñoz, C.A. (eds.) Interactive Theorem Proving - 8th International Conference, ITP 2017, Brasília, Brazil, September

26-29, 2017, Proceedings. Lecture Notes in Computer Science, vol. 10499, pp. 269–284. Springer (2017). https://doi.org/10.1007/978-3-319-66107-0_18

14. Heule, M., Manthey, N., Philipp, T.: Validating unsatisfiability results of clause sharing parallel sat solvers. In: POS@ SAT. pp. 12–25 (2014)

15. Heule, M.J.H.: The DRAT format and drat-trim checker. CoRR abs/1610.06229 (2016). https://doi.org/10.48550/arXiv.1610.06229

16. Heule, M.J.H.: Schur number five. In: McIlraith, S.A., Weinberger, K.Q. (eds.) Proceedings of the Thirty-Second AAAI Conference on Artificial Intelligence, (AAAI-18), the 30th innovative Applications of Artificial Intelligence (IAAI-18), and the 8th AAAI Symposium on Educational Advances in Artificial Intelligence (EAAI-18). pp. 6598–6606. AAAI Press (2018). https://doi.org/10.1609/aaai.v32i1.12209

17. Heule, M.J.H., Kullmann, O., Marek, V.W.: Solving and verifying the boolean pythagorean triples problem via cube-and-conquer. In: Creignou, N., Berre, D.L. (eds.) Theory and Applications of Satisfiability Testing - SAT 2016 - 19th International Conference, Bordeaux, France, July 5-8, 2016, Proceedings. Lecture Notes in Computer Science, vol. 9710, pp. 228–245. Springer (2016). https://doi.org/10.1007/978-3-319-40970-2_15

18. Heule, M.J.H., Kullmann, O., Wieringa, S., Biere, A.: Cube and conquer: Guiding CDCL SAT solvers by lookaheads. In: Eder, K., Lourenço, J., Shehory, O. (eds.) Hardware and Software: Verification and Testing. pp. 50–65. Springer Berlin Heidelberg, Berlin, Heidelberg (2012). https://doi.org/10.1007/978-3-642-34188-5_8

19. Heule, M.J., Hunt, W.A., Wetzler, N.: Trimming while checking clausal proofs. In: 2013 Formal Methods in Computer-Aided Design. pp. 181–188 (2013). https://doi.org/10.1109/FMCAD.2013.6679408

20. Järvisalo, M., Heule, M.J., Biere, A.: Inprocessing rules. In: Gramlich, B., Miller, D., Sattler, U. (eds.) Automated Reasoning - 6th International Joint Conference, IJCAR 2012, Manchester, UK, June 26-29, 2012. Proceedings. Lecture Notes in Computer Science, vol. 7364, pp. 355–370. Springer (2012). https://doi.org/10.1007/978-3-642-31365-3_28

21. Kissat SAT solver. http://fmv.jku.at/kissat/, accessed: 2022-08-17

22. Lammich, P.: Efficient verified (UN)SAT certificate checking. J. Autom. Reason. 64(3), 513–532 (2020). https://doi.org/10.1007/s10817-019-09525-z

23. Le Frioux, L., Baarir, S., Sopena, J., Kordon, F.: Painless: A framework for parallel SAT solving. In: Gaspers, S., Walsh, T. (eds.) Theory and Applications of Satisfiability Testing – SAT 2017. pp. 233–250. Springer International Publishing, Cham (2017). https://doi.org/10.1007/978-3-319-66263-3_15

24. Nair, A., Chattopadhyay, S., Wu, H., Ozdemir, A., Barrett, C.: Proof-stitch: Proof combination for divide and conquer SAT solvers. In: Formal Methods in Computer-Aided Design. pp. 84–88 (2022). https://doi.org/10.34727/2022/isbn.978-3-85448-053-2

25. Rintanen, J.: Planning and SAT. In: Biere, A., Heule, M., van Maaren, H., Walsh, T. (eds.) Handbook of Satisfiability, Frontiers in Artificial Intelligence and Applications, vol. 185, pp. 483–504. IOS Press (2009). https://doi.org/10.3233/978-1-58603-929-5-483

26. Sanders, P., Schreiber, D.: Decentralized online scheduling of malleable NP-hard jobs. In: European Conference on Parallel Processing. pp. 119–135. Springer (2022). https://doi.org/10.1007/978-3-031-12597-3_8

27. Schreiber, D.: Mallob in the SAT competition 2022. In: Proc. of SAT Competition 2022 – Solver and Benchmark Descriptions. pp. 46–47. Department of Computer Science Report Series B, University of Helsinki (2022)

28. Schreiber, D., Sanders, P.: Scalable SAT solving in the cloud. In: Li, C.M., Manyà, F. (eds.) Theory and Applications of Satisfiability Testing – SAT 2021. pp. 518–534. Springer International Publishing, Cham (2021). https://doi.org/10.1007/978-3-030-80223-3_35

29. Schubert, T., Lewis, M., Becker, B.: Pamiraxt: Parallel SAT solving with threads and message passing. J. Satisf. Boolean Model. Comput. **6**(4), 203–222 (2009). https://doi.org/10.3233/sat190068

30. Tan, Y.K., Heule, M.J.H., Myreen, M.O.: cake_lpr: Verified propagation redundancy checking in cakeml. In: Groote, J.F., Larsen, K.G. (eds.) Tools and Algorithms for the Construction and Analysis of Systems - 27th International Conference, TACAS 2021, Held as Part of the European Joint Conferences on Theory and Practice of Software, ETAPS 2021, Luxembourg City, Luxembourg, March 27 - April 1, 2021, Proceedings, Part II. Lecture Notes in Computer Science, vol. 12652, pp. 223–241. Springer (2021). https://doi.org/10.1007/978-3-030-72013-1_12

31. Vizel, Y., Weissenbacher, G., Malik, S.: Boolean satisfiability solvers and their applications in model checking. Proc. IEEE **103**(11), 2021–2035 (2015). https://doi.org/10.1109/JPROC.2015.2455034

32. Xu, L., Hutter, F., Hoos, H.H., Leyton-Brown, K.: SATzilla: Portfolio-based algorithm selection for SAT. J. Artif. Intell. Res. **32**, 565–606 (2008). https://doi.org/10.1613/jair.2490

CARCARA: An Efficient Proof Checker and Elaborator for SMT Proofs in the Alethe Format*

Bruno Andreotti[1] , Hanna Lachnitt[2] , Haniel Barbosa[1(✉)]

[1] Universidade Federal de Minas Gerais, Belo Horizonte, Brazil
hbarbosa@dcc.ufmg.br
[2] Stanford University, Stanford, USA

Abstract. Proofs from SMT solvers ensure correctness independently from implementation, which is often a requirement when solvers are used in safety-critical applications or proof assistants. Alethe is an established SMT proof format generated by the solvers veriT and cvc5, with reconstruction support in the proof assistants Isabelle/HOL and Coq. The format is close to SMT-LIB and allows both coarse- and fine-grained steps, facilitating proof production. However, it lacks a stand-alone checker, which harms its usability and hinders its adoption. Moreover, the coarse-grained steps can be too expensive to check and lead to verification failures. We present CARCARA, an independent proof checker and elaborator for Alethe, implemented in Rust. It aims to increase the adoption of the format by providing push-button proof-checking for Alethe proofs, focusing on efficiency and usability; and by providing elaboration for coarse-grained steps into fine-grained ones, increasing the potential success rate of checking Alethe proofs in performance-critical validators, such as proof assistants. We evaluate CARCARA over a large set of Alethe proofs generated from SMT-LIB problems and show that it has good performance and its elaboration techniques can make proofs easier to check.

1 Introduction

Satisfiability modulo theories (SMT) solvers are widely used as background tools in various formal method applications, ranging from proof assistants to program verification [9]. Since these applications rely on the SMT solver results, they must trust their correctness. However, state-of-the-art SMT solvers are often found to have bugs, despite the best efforts of developers [30, 38]. One way to address this issue is to formally verify the solvers' correctness ("certifying" them), but this approach can be prohibitively expensive and time consuming, besides often requiring performance compromises [19, 20, 27, 33] and increasing the evolution cost of the systems [14]. Alternatively, solvers can produce proofs: independently checkable certificates that justify the correctness of their results. Since proof checking generally has lower complexity than solving, small and trusted checkers can verify solver results in an scalable manner. Despite the successful adoption

---

* This work was partially supported by an Amazon Research Award (Spring 2021), a gift from Amazon Web Services, and the Stanford Center for Automated Reasoning.

S. Sankaranarayanan and N. Sharygina (Eds.): TACAS 2023, LNCS 13993, pp. 367–386, 2023.
https://doi.org/10.1007/978-3-031-30823-1_19

of this approach by several SMT solvers [7,13,15,24,37], no standard SMT proof format has emerged, with each system using their own format and independent toolchain. The Alethe[1] format [35] for SMT proofs however can be emitted by the veriT solver for several years [10] and recently[2] also by the cvc5 solver [7]. Moreover, Alethe proofs can be reconstructed within the proof assistants Coq [4, 16] and Isabelle/HOL [11,36], which allows leveraging solvers who support the format (namely veriT and CVC4, the latter via a translator [16]) for automatic theorem proving. In Isabelle/HOL in particular this integration has been very successful with the veriT solver, significantly increasing the success rate of the popular Sledgehammer tactic [36]. The format has been refined and extended through the years [6], being now mature and used by multiple systems, with support for core SMT theories, quantifiers, and pre-processing. It allows different levels of granularity, so that solvers can provide coarse-grained proofs (which are easier to produce), or take the effort to produce more detailed, fine-grained proofs (which are often easier to check). It provides a term language close to SMT-LIB [8], facilitating printing from solvers as well as validating the connection between proofs and the corresponding proved problems. An overview of the Alethe proof format is given in Section 2.

A significant drawback of the Alethe format, however, is that it does not have an independent proof checker. This makes it harder for solvers to adopt the format, since to test their proof production they must be directly integrated with the proof assistants with Alethe reconstructions available. Moreover, these reconstruction methods do not check whether proof steps comply to the format's semantics, but rather are used as hints for internal tactics. Finally, the reconstruction techniques struggle with scalability due to well-known performance issues in the proof assistants [12,36].

In this paper we introduce CARCARA[3] (Section 3), an independent proof checker for Alethe proofs, implemented in a high-performance programming language, Rust. CARCARA is open-source and available under the Apache 2.0 license. Proof checking (Section 3.1) is performed by a collection of modules specific for each rule being checked. The presence of coarse-grained steps in Alethe requires special handling in the checker to account for missing information, which are discussed in detail. CARCARA also provides proof elaboration methods (Section 3.2) for particularly impactful coarse-grained steps, so that they can be automatically translated, offline from the solver, into easier-to-check fine-grained steps. We evaluate (Section 4) CARCARA's proof checking on a large set of proofs generated by veriT from SMT-LIB problems, analyzing its performance and effectiveness. The same set of proofs is used to evaluate the proof elaboration methods, where we analyze how checking elaborated proofs compares with the

---

[1] The format was previously known as the "veriT format", but it has recently been renamed to reflect its independence from any individual solver.

[2] cvc5's support for Alethe is still experimental and is under active development. CARCARA can actually be instrumental for improving cvc5's support for Alethe.

[3] We follow on the bird theme of the "Alethe" name. Carcará is the Portuguese word for the crested caracara, a resourceful bird of prey native of South America.

originals. Our analysis shows that CARCARA has performant proof checking and can identify wrong proofs produced by veriT. It also shows that elaboration can in some cases generate proofs significantly easier to check than the original ones.

1.1 Related work

CARCARA is inspired by the highly-successful DRAT-trim [23] proof checker for SAT proofs, which has been instrumental to the extensive usage of proofs in toolchains involving SAT solvers. It has also provided a basis for numerous advances in SAT proofs, with new proof formats and new checking techniques. We see its performant proof checking and elaboration techniques as the key elements to its success, serving both as an independent checker and as a bridge between solvers and performance-critical checkers, such as proof assistants or certified checkers. Providing both these features is the main goal of CARCARA.

The checker for the Logical Framework with Side Conditions (LFSC) [37], an extension of Edinburgh's Logical Framework (LF) [22], written in C++, is also a stand-alone, non-certified, highly efficient proof checker. The logical framework, where new rules can be mechanized in a language understood by the checker, provides great flexibility, and LFSC has been successfully used as a proof format for CVC4 [28] and cvc5 [5]. Similarly, Dedukti [25] is an OCaml checker for the $\lambda\Pi$-calculus, another extension of LF, and has been applied to SMT proofs, including to Alethe[4]. However, we are not aware of any mature implementation for this end. Elaboration techniques have not been the focus in these tools. Another difference is that they are based on dependently-typed languages far-removed from SMT-LIB, and generating proofs from SMT solvers for them can be more challenging, as well as relating the resulting proofs to the original problems.

An independent checker has been proposed for SMT proofs [34] from the OpenSMT [26] solver. The checker targets problems with uninterpreted functions and linear arithmetic, but does not support quantifiers nor pre-processing. It leverages DRAT-trim for the propositional reasoning and employs Python components for checking the other parts of the proof. Different components can use different proof formats, and to the best of our knowledge no comprehensive specification of the overall format is available. Some SMT solvers, such as SMT-Interpol [24] and cvc5 [7], have internal checkers for their proofs. Since these are not independent from the solvers, they are incomparable to our approach.

2   The Alethe Proof Format

Alethe was originally designed [10] as a proof-assistant friendly, easy-to-produce proof format for SMT solvers. A clear specification of the rules in a reference document [2] is provided, facilitating reconstruction within proof assistants by avoiding ambiguous syntax or semantics. To facilitate proof production, Alethe uses a term language that directly extends SMT-LIB, thus not requiring solvers

---

[4] "Verine" library available at https://deducteam.github.io/data/libraries/verine.tar.gz

to translate between different term languages when outputting proofs. More importantly, Alethe's proof calculus provides rules with varying levels of granularity, allowing coarse-grained steps and relying on powerful proof checkers for filling in the gaps. This reduces the burden on developers to track all reasoning steps performed by the solver, a notoriously difficult task [7]. The set of rules in the format captures SMT solving (as generally performed by CDCL($\mathcal{T}$)-based SMT solvers [31]) for problems containing a mix of any of quantifiers, uninterpreted functions, and linear arithmetic, as well as multiple pre-processing techniques. As a testament of the format's success, it has been refined and extended throughout the years [6], and has been used as the basis for the integration, with the proof assistants Isabelle/HOL and Coq, of the SMT solvers veriT [6, 36], CVC4 [16] and cvc5 [5, Sec. 3].

Here we briefly overview the Alethe proof format. For the full description of its syntax and semantics please see [2]. We assume the reader is familiar with basic notions of many-sorted equational first-order logic [17]. Alethe proofs have the form $\pi : \varphi_1 \wedge \cdots \wedge \varphi_n \rightarrow \bot$, i.e., they are refutations, where $\bot$ is derived from assumptions $\varphi_1, \ldots, \varphi_n$ corresponding to the original SMT instance being refuted. Proofs are a series of steps represented as an indexed list of step commands. The command assume is analogous to step but used only for introducing assumptions. The indexed steps induce a directed acyclic graph rooted on the step concluding $\bot$ and with the assumptions $\varphi_1, \ldots, \varphi_n$ as leaves. Steps represent inferences and abstractly have the form

$$c_1, \ldots, c_k \ \triangleright \ i.\ \psi_1, \ldots, \psi_l \ (\texttt{rule}\ p_1, \ldots, p_n)\ [a_1, \ldots, a_m]$$

where rule names the inference rule used in this step. Every step has an identifier i and concludes a clause, represented as a list of literals $\psi_1, \ldots, \psi_l$. The premises are identifiers $p_1, \ldots, p_n$ of previous steps or assumptions, and rule-dependent arguments are terms $a_1, \ldots, a_m$; steps may occur under a *context*, which is defined by bound variables or substitutions $c_1, \ldots, c_k$. Contexts are introduced by the anchor command, which opens subproofs. Subproofs simulate the effect of the $\Rightarrow$-introduction rule of Natural Deduction, where local assumptions are put in context and the last step in a subproof represents its conclusion and the closing of its context. Besides arbitrary formulas, Alethe has support for contexts which put in scope bound variables and substitutions, which are useful for representing pre-processing techniques in the presence of binders [6], such as Skolemization, let elimination and alpha-conversion.

The structure of Alethe proofs is motivated by SMT solvers generally operating with a cooperation of a SAT solver and multiple engines to perform theory reasoning, deriving new facts and applying simplifications. The overall proof may be seen as a ground first-order resolution proof with theory lemmas justified by closed subproofs. Thus the emphasis on steps concluding clauses as term lists, which avoids ambiguity as to what clause a disjunction represents. An example is that whether a resolution step concluding the term $A \vee B$ corresponds to the clause $[A,\ B]$ or $[A \vee B]$ depends on the premises. The use of identifiers for steps allows representing proofs as directed acyclic graphs rather than trees. Similarly,

```
(set-logic LIA)
(assert (forall ((x Int)) (> x 0)))
(assert (not (forall ((y Int)) (> y 0))))
(check-sat)
```

```
(assume h1 (forall ((x Int)) (> x 0)))
(assume h2 (not (forall ((y Int)) (> y 0))))
(anchor :step t3 :args ((y Int) (:= x y)))
(step t3.t1 (cl (= x y)) :rule refl)
(step t3.t2 (cl (= (> x 0) (> y 0))) :rule cong :premises (t3.t1))
(step t3 (cl (= (forall ((x Int)) (> x 0)) (forall ((y Int)) (> y 0))))
   :rule bind)
(step t4 (cl (not (forall ((x Int)) (> x 0))) (forall ((y Int)) (> y 0)))
   :rule equiv1 :premises (t3))
(step t5 (cl) :rule resolution :premises (t4 h1 h2))
```

Fig. 1: A simple SMT-LIB problem and an Alethe proof of its unsatisfiability.

term sharing can be achieved via the SMT-LIB :named attribute or define-fun commands [8, Sec1 4.1.6], which both allow naming subterms. These measures are essential for compact representation of proofs, which can be prohibitively large otherwise. Explicitly providing the conclusion of proof steps aims to both facilitate proof checking (as it allows steps to be verified locally) and proof production, so coarse-grained rules that do not uniquely define their conclusions from premises and arguments can be effectively checked.

Example 1. Figure 1 shows an SMT-LIB problem and an Alethe proof of its unsatisfiability. Note that in Alethe's concrete syntax clauses are represented via the cl operator (the only exception are conclusions of assume commands, which are considered unit clauses) and the context is not explicitly put in the steps, but rather assumed for all steps under (potentially nested) anchors introducing its elements. For this proof to be valid, three conditions need to be met: each assume command must correspond to an assert command in the original problem, every step command must be valid according to the semantics of its rule, and the proof must end with a step that concludes the empty clause (cl). The proof satisfies the first condition, as the terms in the assume commands are precisely the asserted terms in the SMT problem. The third condition holds as t5, the last step, concludes the empty clause. For the second condition, step t4 is a direct consequence of the equivalence in its premise, t3, so it remains to check step t3, which is derived from a subproof. The anchor for t3 introduces a bound variable y and a substitution $\{x \mapsto y\}$. The steps in the subproof contain terms with this new variable and operate under this substitution. The rule refl models reflexivity modulo the cumulative, capture-avoiding substitution in the (potentially nested) context, and thus t3.t1 holds since $x = y\{x \mapsto y\}$. Step t3.t2 is regular congruence with the operator ">" and does not depend on the context. Finally, step t3 holds because its subproof shows the equivalence of the

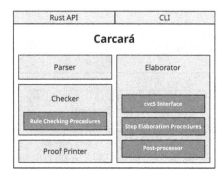

Fig. 2: Overview of the architecture of CARCARA.

bodies of the quantifiers under the renaming, introduced in the context, into a fresh variable relative to the left-hand side quantifier. Since all steps follow the expected semantics, all conditions are met and the proof is valid.

In the next section we show how CARCARA checks the above conditions, highlighting some challenging rules and showing how some coarse-grained steps are elaborated into proofs potentially simpler to check.

3   Architecture and core components

CARCARA is developed in the Rust programming language, and is publicly available[5] under the Apache 2.0 license. Its architecture is shown in Figure 2. It provides both a command line interface and bindings for a Rust API. The main component is the proof checking one, with 6.5k LOC, which is a collection of procedures for each rule to be checked (Section 3.1). The elaborator has 1k LOC and has an interface to the cvc5 solver, as well as a collection of elaboration methods and a post-processing module to knit together the elaborated proof (Section 3.2). The other components together have 6k LOC, including a handwritten 2k LOC SMT-LIB and Alethe parser, and an Alethe printer.

The inputs of CARCARA are an SMT-LIB problem φ and an Alethe proof $\pi : \varphi \to \bot$. In proof-checking mode it checks each step in π with the respective procedure for its rule and prints either valid, when all steps are successfully checked and the proof concludes the empty clause (cl), holey when π is valid but contains steps that are not checked ("holes"), and invalid otherwise, together with an error message indicating the first step where checking failed and why. In proof-elaboration mode it converts π into $\pi' : \varphi \to \bot$, where some steps may be replaced by a series of steps elaborating them, and prints π'.

---

[5] https://github.com/ufmg-smite/carcara

3.1   Checking Alethe proofs

First the original SMT-LIB problem and its Alethe proof are parsed. The problem provides the declaration of sorts and symbols that may be used in the proof, as well as the original assertions, which must match the assumptions in the proof. Symbol definitions in the proof for term sharing are expanded during parsing. Terms are internally represented as directed acyclic graphs, using *hash consing* for maximal sharing and constant-time syntactically-equality tests. The proof is represented internally as an array of command objects, each corresponding either to an Alethe `assume` or `step` command, or a subproof, which is represented as a step with an (arbitrarily) nested array of command objects. Step identifiers are converted into indices for the arrays, so that access is constant-time.

Each command is checked individually by the rule checker corresponding to the rule in that command. That component takes as input the conclusion, the conclusions of its premises, and the arguments of the command, as well as the context it is in. As the Alethe format currently has 90 possible rules, CARCARA has 90 rule checkers. We highlight below some of the rule checkers as well as some challenges for checking Alethe proofs and how we addressed them.

Term equality tests. Terms introduced by Alethe rules may have equality subterms implicitly reordered, but the rules are still valid if the conclusion changes only in this way. This flexibility is motivated by solvers often internally representing equalities ignoring order, which may lead to equalities being implicitly reordered when appearing in facts derived by these components. The congruence closure procedure [29] commonly used in SMT is an example of such a component. Since equality symmetry justifies these reorderings, but keeping track of all the changes can be challenging, the format allows them to be implicit.

As a consequence, syntactic equality cannot be the only test for whether two terms are the same. For example, the terms (and p (= a b)) and (and p (= b a)) may be required to be equal. Thus CARCARA tests equality in two phases: first if they are syntactically equal, in which case they can be compared in constant time; otherwise they are simultaneously traversed and equality subterms in the same position are compared modulo equality reordering, failing as soon as subterms differ. We refer to this as a *polyequal* test. As we will see in Section 4.1, these tests can be a substantial portion of overall checking time in some cases.

Checking initial assumptions. The initial `assume` commands in an Alethe proof must correspond to assertions in the original problem, so their checker searches through the assertions to find a match. In general, this can be done efficiently: assertions are stored in a hash set during parsing, and these `assume` commands are valid if their conclusions occur in the set. However, `assume` commands are also impacted by implicit equality reordering, thus requiring polyequal tests. When an assumption does not occur in the assertions hash set, the checker attempts to match it to each assertion in turn, performing a polyequal test. As a consequence, when the original problem is large and the assertions similar and deep, checking `assume` steps may dominate overall checking time, as our experiments show (Section 4.1).

Checking contextual steps. Steps within subproofs may depend on their context to be valid, so before checking these steps, a context object is built based on the anchor opening the subproof. As shown in Section 2, context elements on which rules may depend are bound variables and substitutions. The former make new symbols available to build terms, while the latter allows steps to be valid modulo applying these substitutions.

Substitutions in Alethe are capture-avoiding, renaming bound variables during application, which facilitates producing proofs with binders [6]. However, it has the side effect of also preventing constant-time equality tests, since we must rather check α-equivalence, i.e., a term with bound variables may be required to be equal[6] to the result of applying a substitution that may have renamed some of these variables. To avoid spurious renaming when applying substitutions, the checker only renames bound variables which occur as free variables in the substitution range. Since computing free variables is itself costly, it is done lazily, only when the substitution is to be applied under a binder, and the result is cached.

Note that, as subproofs can be nested, the substitution in context for a step is the composition of a stack of substitutions $\sigma_1, \ldots, \sigma_n$. To avoid sequential application of substitutions, Alethe requires the substitution σ in context to be a cumulative substitution in which every term t in the range of the substitution σ_{i+1} is replaced by $t\sigma_i$. Thus σ can be applied simultaneously and correspond to a sequential application of $\sigma_1, \ldots, \sigma_n$. As a result of these requirements, handling and applying substitutions can be expensive in Alethe, as shown in Section 4.1.

Finally, the rules enclosing subproofs must be checked to whether their conclusions are valid from the introduced context and resulting subproof. For example, the **bind** rule in Example 1 requires that the bound variable in the quantifier at the right-hand side of the equality matches the range of the substitution put in context for its subproof. The **subproof** rule, which introduces local assumptions $a_1, \ldots, a_n$, and concludes a formula $\neg a_1' \lor \cdots \neg a_n' \lor \varphi$, requires that the enclosed subproof derives φ and that each a_i match a_i'.

We now highlight coarse-grained rules whose checking is more intricate and expensive.

Resolution. The rule **resolution** in Alethe captures hyper-resolution on ground first-order clauses, i.e.,

$$\frac{C_1 \ \cdots \ C_n}{C} \ \text{resolution}, p_1, p_2, \ldots, p_{n-1}$$

where $C_1, \ldots, C_n$ are premises; p_i the pivot for the binary resolution between C_i and C_{i+1}, occurring as is in C_i and as $\neg p_i$ in C_{i+1}; and C the conclusion. While it is simple to check such steps, Alethe allows **resolution** steps to not provide the pivots, for the sake of facilitating proof-production in solvers. Checking such steps requires searching for the pivots and in which binary resolution they are to

---

[6] Since Alethe has bound-variable renaming rules, the checker requires names to be handled properly, rather than normalizing all binders internally via De Brujin indices.

be used, but CARCARA applies an incomplete heuristic where pivots are inferred between the difference of literals in the premises and in the conclusion (i.e., literals not in the conclusion must have been pivots eventually eliminated). If that fails, we apply a reverse unit propagation (RUP) test [21], i.e., the step is valid if we can derive a conflict via Boolean Constraint Propagation from the premises and the negated conclusion. Note that CARCARA also allows the pivots to be provided as arguments, in which case checking is simple, as expected.

AC simplification. Normalization modulo associativity and commutativity for conjunction and disjunction can be represented in Alethe via the `ac_simp` rule, which establishes the equality between a term t and a term t' that is t but with nested occurrences of these connectives flattened and duplicate arguments removed, until a fix-point. While this simplification is performance-critical [6, Sec. 4.6], checking the corresponding rule requires traversing t and performing the normalization, which is proportional to t's depth.

Arithmetic reasoning. Apart from simplification rules, arithmetic reasoning in Alethe is mainly captured by two rules: `la_generic` and `lia_generic`. Both rules conclude a clause of negated linear inequalities, which is valid due to the Farkas' lemma [18] guaranteeing that there exists a linear combination of these inequalities equivalent to $\bot$. The `la_generic` rule takes as arguments the coefficients of this linear combination, with which the rule can be checked by applying simple (but costly) operations on the coefficients to reduce the linear combination to $\bot$ (see [2, Sec 5.4, Rule 9] for the algorithm). The checker uses GMP [1] for efficiently performing the required computations with the coefficients.

While `la_generic` can be checked effectively, `lia_generic` cannot. It provides only the negated inequalities, which would require searching for the coefficients to perform the checking, essentially requiring the arithmetic solving to be repeated in the checker. As a consequence this rule is considered a hole and CARCARA ignores it during proof checking, issuing a warning.

3.2   Elaborating Alethe proofs

In order to mitigate bottlenecks in checking some Alethe steps, CARCARA can also elaborate Alethe proofs into easier-to-check ones by filling in missing details from the original proofs. This is done by replacing coarse-grained steps with fine-grained proofs of their conclusions, producing a new overall proof equivalent to the original, but with some coarse-grained steps broken down into fine-grained ones. Formally, a proof as the one below on the left, with a coarse step concluding ψ from premises $\psi_1, \ldots, \psi_n$, is elaborated into the proof on the right where the coarse step is replaced by a proof π, with *fine-grained* steps, rooted on ψ and with $\psi_1, \ldots, \psi_n$ as leaves:

$$
\cfrac{\cfrac{\psi_1 \ \cdots \ \psi_n}{\psi} \ \text{COARSESTEP} \qquad \cdots}{\Theta} \ \text{RULE} \qquad \Rightarrow_{\text{elab}} \qquad \cfrac{\cfrac{\cfrac{\psi_1 \ \cdots \ \psi_n}{\pi}}{\psi} \qquad \cdots}{\Theta} \ \text{RULE}
$$

```
(step t2.t1 (cl (not (= a b)) (not (= b c)) (not (= c d)) (= a d))
   :rule eq_transitive)
(step t2.t2 (cl (not (= b a)) (= a b)) :rule eq_symmetric)
(step t2.t3 (cl (not (= c b)) (= b c)) :rule eq_symmetric)
(step t2.t4 (cl (not (= c d)) (= a d) (not (= b a)) (not (= c b)))
   :rule resolution :premises (t2.t1 t2.t2 t2.t3))
(step t2 (cl (not (= b a)) (not (= c d)) (not (= c b)) (= a d))
   :rule reordering :premises (t2.t4))
```

Fig. 3: Elaboration of an eq_transitive step. Note the new eq_transitive step is easy to check, and the new t2 step has the same conclusion as the original.

Note the expansion only affects the proof locally, since any step using the conclusion of the coarse step as a premise may use the conclusion of π interchangeably.

There are many Alethe rules whose checking would be simpler if elaborated, but we have focused initially on what we believe can be more impactful: removing implicit equality reordering, and thus polyequal tests, which affects virtually every Alethe rule; and providing checkable justifications for lia_generic steps, to remove holes from proofs. Before detailing these methods, we illustrate the elaboration process with an example.

Elaborating transitivity steps. The eq_transitive rule concludes a valid clause composed of negated equalities followed by a single positive equality, such that the negated equalities form a transitive chain resulting in the final equality. However, the specification does not impose an order on the negated equalities (which can, remember, also be implicitly reordered). So the following step must also be valid, with a "shuffled" chain:

```
(step t2 (cl (not (= b a)) (not (= c d)) (not (= c b)) (= a d))
   :rule eq_transitive)
```

This permissive specification again facilitates proof production (particularly from congruence closure procedures), but requires the eq_transitive checker, for every link in the chain, to potentially traverse the whole clause searching for the next one, performing polyequal tests throughout. The goal of elaborating eq_transitive steps is that steps like t2 are justified in a fine-grained manner. If we changed the conclusion of the step, this would impact the rest of the proof, if t2 is used anywhere as a premise. We instead introduce a fine-grained proof for t2's conclusion, as shown in Figure 3: an easy-to-check eq_transitive step (t2.t1), eq_symmetric steps to flip the equalities (t2.t2, t2.t3), resolution (t2.t4) and reordering (t2.t5) steps to derive the original conclusion.

Elaborating implicit equality reordering. Similarly to above, steps concluding a term t, with some subterm equality implicitly reordered, have their conclusion replaced by t' where that subterm is not reordered and a fine-grained proof of the conversion of t' into t is added. Figure 4 illustrates this process for an assume

```
(set-logic QF_UF)
(declare-const a Bool)
(declare-const b Bool)
(declare-const p Bool)
(assert (not (or p (= a b))))
(assert (or p (= b a)))
(check-sat)
```

Fig. 4a: An example SMT problem instance.

```
(assume h1 (not (or p (= a b))))
(assume h2 (or p (= a b)))
(step t3 (cl) :rule resolution
       :premises (h1 h2))
```

Fig. 4b: An Alethe proof for the SMT problem in Figure 4a. Notice that this proof makes use of implicit reordering of equalities in h2.

```
(assume h1 (not (or p (= a b))))
(assume h2 (or p (= b a)))
(step h2.t1 (cl (= (= b a) (= a b))) :rule equiv_simplify)
(step h2.t2 (cl (= (or p (= b a)) (or p (= a b))))
      :rule cong :premises (h2.t1))
(step h2.t3 (cl (not (or p (= b a))) (or p (= a b)))
      :rule equiv1 :premises (h2.t2))
(step h2.t4 (cl (or p (= a b))) :rule resolution :premises (h2 h2.t3))
(step t3 (cl) :rule resolution :premises (h1 h2.t4))
```

Fig. 4c: The elaborated proof without implicit equality reordering.

Fig. 4: An example of the elaboration to remove implicit equality reordering.

command, where note that step h2.t1 is the rewriting justifying the equality reordering of the subterm and the following steps rebuild the original conclusion.

In the original proof, the assume command h2 introduces the term (or p (= a b)), which is the original assertion (or p (= b a)) with the equality (= b a) implicitly reordered. In the elaborated proof (Figure 4c), the conclusion of h2 is replaced by one without implicit equality reordering, but step t3 expects the original conclusion. The steps h2.t1 to h2.t4 convert the new h2 conclusion into the original one, relying on standard equality reasoning and on resolution to connect the introduced steps. Notice that the t3 step, which originally refered to h2 as a premise, now refers to h2.t4.

When applied to every concluding terms with implicit equality reordering, the result of this elaboration method is a proof where equality tests are only syntactic, erasing the overhead of checking assumptions and polyequal tests.

Elaborating lia_generic *steps.* As discussed in Section 3.1, CARCARA considers lia_generic steps holes in the proof, as their checking is as hard as solving. Since our goal is to keep CARCARA as simple as possible, we rely on an external tool to elaborate the step by solving a problem corresponding to it in a proof-producing manner, then import the proof, checking it and guaranteeing that it is sound to replace the original step. Any tool producing detailed Alethe proofs for linear-integer arithmetic reasoning can be used to this end, but currently only cvc5 can do so [7]. We note that cvc5 currently has the limitation that its Alethe proofs may contain rewrite steps not yet modeled in the Alethe simplification rules [2, Sec 5.11], and are thus not supported by CARCARA. They are considered holes, but since these are generally simple simplification rules, are much less harmful than lia_generic ones.

In detail, the elaboration method, when encountering a lia_generic step S concluding the negated inequalities $\neg l_1 \lor \cdots \lor \neg l_n$, generates an SMT-LIB problem asserting $l_1 \land \cdots \land l_n$ and invokes cvc5 on it, expecting an Alethe proof $\pi : (l_1 \land \cdots \land l_n) \to \bot$. CARCARA will check each step in π and, if they are not invalid, will replace step S in the original proof by a proof of the form:

```
(anchor :step S.t_m+1)
(assume S.h_1 l1)
...
(assume S.h_n ln)
...
(step S.t_m (cl false) :rule ...)
(step S.t_m+1 (cl (not l1) ... (not ln) false) :rule subproof)
(step S.t_m+2 (cl (not false)) :rule false)
(step S (cl (not l1) ... (not ln))
  :rule resolution :premises (S.t_m+1 S.t_m+2))
```

where steps S.h_1 until S.t_m are imported from the cvc5 proof. As a result the lia_generic step S in the original proof will have been replaced by a detailed justification whose correctness can be independently established by CARCARA.

4   Evaluation

We evaluate CARCARA for proof-checking performance and the impact of elaboration methods. We use the veriT solver [13], version 2021.06-40-rmx, to generate Alethe proofs from all problems in the SMT-LIB benchmark library[7] whose logic it supports, with a 120 seconds timeout. We did not consider cvc5 as its support for Alethe is not yet as mature or complete. The veriT solver produced 39,229 proofs. They total 92gb, but vary greatly in size. The biggest proof has 4.5gb, fourteen have at least 1gb and over a hundred have more than 100mb, while almost 90% are under 1mb. All the experiments were run on a server equipped with AWS Graviton2 2.5 GHz ARM CPUs, with 4 GB of memory for each job.

4.1   Proof checking

We ran CARCARA on each proof until checking succeeded or failed. Only 378 had checking failures, which were due to incorrect[8] steps for quantifier simplifications (Skolemization and elimination of one-point quantifiers) and AC normalization. The issues have been communicated to the solver developers. For the successful proofs, a summary is given in Table 1, for each SMT-LIB logic, with the cumulative solving time by veriT and checking time by CARCARA.

---

[7] https://smtlib.cs.uiowa.edu/benchmarks.shtml
[8] In a superficial analysis the steps seemed sound, but the proofs were incorrect.

Logic	Problems	Solving time (s)	Checking time (s)	Ratio
AUFLIA	2135	1094.67	12.51	87.53
AUFLIRA	19200	248.95	144.03	1.73
UF	2885	2858.14	30.95	92.35
UFIDL	55	0.54	0.66	0.82
UFLIA	7221	3547.78	136.21	26.05
UFLRA	10	0.02	0.01	3.05
QF_ALIA	16	0.79	1.39	0.57
QF_AUFLIA	256	0.34	0.11	3.04
QF_IDL	609	3316.08	2240.10	1.48
QF_LIA	1018	5975.36	742.73	8.05
QF_LRA	537	3629.39	258.60	14.03
QF_RDL	81	620.46	123.14	5.04
QF_UF	4180	3857.34	1881.55	2.05
QF_UFIDL	66	396.74	87.58	4.53
QF_UFLIA	167	1194.51	4.70	254.41
QF_UFLRA	415	141.82	65.14	2.18
Total:	38851	26882.93	5729.39	4.69

Table 1: Total solving and proof-checking time per logic for veriT and CARCARA.

As expected, the comparison is heavily logic-dependent. In quantified logics (top of the table), checking is generally significantly cheaper than solving. An outlier is AUFLIRA, which is explained by the problems to which veriT could produce proofs being all both simple to solve and check. In logics such as QF_UF and QF_IDL, which can have very large proofs, overall checking time is comparable to solving time, if still noticeably smaller in total.

When comparing per-problem, for the large majority of proofs (81.61%) the checking time was smaller than the solving time. Furthermore, for 3.96% of the proofs, checking was more than 10 times faster than solving the problem, and for 0.96%, that ratio was of 100 times. There were only 24 instances where the checking time was more than 10 times bigger than the solving time, and, in all of them, the checking time was less than 0.6 seconds.

We also evaluate the per-rule frequency, as shown in Figure 5b, and checking time, with Figure 6a showing the cumulative checking times and Figure 5a a box plot considering individual rule checks. The lower whisker represents the 5th percentile, the lower bound of the box represents the first quartile, the line inside the box represents the median, the upper bound of the box represents the third quartile, and the upper whisker represents the 95th percentile[9]. Rules that are rare and have negligible checking time are omitted. The data is gathered from proof checking in all proofs, even those that failed.

The `assume` commands account for a large proportion of the total time. This is justified by their checking, due to implicit equality reordering, being potentially proportional to both the quantity and the depth of assertions in the original problems. The box plot shows that the worse cases lead to the most expensive rule checks among all rules.

---

[9] The plots follow the same criteria of the evaluation in [36].

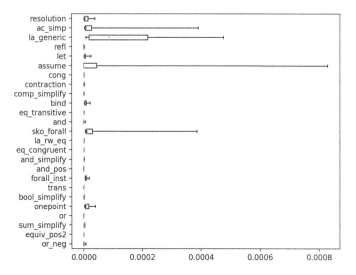

Rule	%
cong	31%
resolution	27%
refl	17%
comp_simplify	5%
eq_transitive	4%
la_rw_eq	2%
ac_simp	1%
and_pos	1%
and	1%
bind	1%
trans	< 1%
or	< 1%
equiv_pos2	< 1%
eq_congruent	< 1%
la_generic	< 1%
...	< 1%

Fig. 5b: Perc. of total steps per rule (only most frequent shown).

Fig. 5a: Box plot for checking time per rule.

Rules with highest overall time are `resolution`, `ac_simp` and `la_generic`. For `resolution` this is explained mainly by its high frequency (this is similarly the case for `cong`), as well as by some more expensive checks (veriT does not provide pivots), as shown in the box plot. As for `ac_simp` and `la_generic`, while they are much less frequent, their checking is expensive (Section 3.1).

Other expensive rules to note are those related to contexts involving substitutions[10], specially `let`, for let elimination, and `refl`. It is common for `let` subproofs to be deeply nested, leading to large cumulative substitutions needing to be computed. As for `refl`, besides being one of the most frequent rules, about a third of its total time is spent on polyequal tests, and most of the rest is related to handling and applying substitutions, as well as checking alpha-equivalence.

4.2   Proof elaboration

We ran CARCARA, on each successfully checked proof, in proof-elaboration mode with the elaboration of transitivity steps and, more importantly, the removal of implicit equality reordering. On average, excluding parsing, elaboration takes 40% of the time required for checking. We focus on the impact on proof checking of the result of elaboration.

In Figure 7 we have the comparison, per proof, of the proof-checking time on the original proof and on the elaborated one (excluding parsing time). There is not a clear winner, but note that for harder proofs (those originally requiring at least 1s), checking the elaborated proof is often significantly faster. A per-rule analysis is shown in Figure 6b, with the proportion of the checking time spent

---

[10] The ones shown in the plots are `let`, `bind`, `sko_forall`, and `onepoint`.

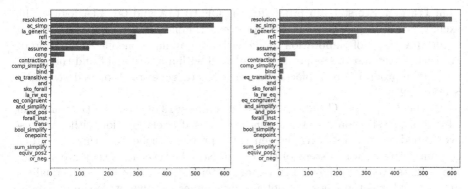

Fig. 6a: Total checking time per rule.   Fig. 6b: Times after elaboration.

in each rule, for the elaborated proofs. Comparing to Figure 6a, the checking time for `assume` steps becomes negligible in the elaborated proofs, as checking them now amounts to checking occurrence in a hash set. The overall time for `refl` also decreases, but only by 10%. This can be explained by the `refl` steps added during elaboration. While checking each `refl` is now potentially cheaper, this is offset by their increased number. Note that these additions also impact other rules, specially `cong`, whose cumulative time increased by 13%. Overall, proof elaboration resulted in a net improvement in checking time of 6%. Parsing time, however, increased, which made the overall runtime for proof-checking the original proofs virtually the same as for the elaborated proofs.

The results indicate that elaborating implicit equality reordering is not always worth it, specially for high-performant tools. However, it successfully yields proofs not requiring polyequal tests, which may help performance in other scenarios. For example, the reconstruction of Alethe proofs in Isabelle/HOL requires equality tests to be done by applying a normalizer to both terms and then testing them for syntactic equality. This leads to performance issues for reconstructing some rules [36], which this elaboration method would avoid.

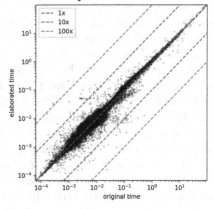

Fig. 7: Before vs after elaboration.

Elaborating `lia_generic` steps. In our benchmark set, 276 proofs contain a total of 127k `lia_generic` steps. As a proof of concept we instrumented CARCARA to apply the elaboration method described in Section 3.2 via a connection with cvc5[11]. Due to the still experimental Alethe proof production in cvc5, we only considered SMT problems derived

---

[11] cvc5-1.0.2, modified for better Alethe support, provided by the cvc5 team.

from lia_generic steps in proofs for the QF_UFLIA and QF_LIA logics. This excluded only 15 proofs, each containing exactly one lia_generic step. We ran CARCARA on proof-elaboration mode with a 30 minute timeout for each proof. For each lia_generic step, cvc5 was invoked with a 30s timeout and the resulting Alethe proof, if any, replaced the original lia_generic step, as described in Section 3.2.

Of the 261 proofs, CARCARA timed out on only 13 of them. Of the remaining 248 proofs, 82 still contained lia_generic steps after elaboration, either because cvc5 timed out when solving the generated problem, or because the cvc5 proofs contained lia_generic steps of their own. Note however that they are still improvements over the original lia_generic steps, since generally less inequalities are involved and the steps are potentially simpler to solve, were the process to be repeated. Similarly, although all elaborated proofs contained holes from cvc5 rewriting steps, these are much simpler than the original lia_generic ones.

As with the elaboration of implicit equality reordering, this elaboration method would be particularly impactful in scenarios such as Alethe reconstruction in Isabelle/HOL. Steps such as lia_generic are reconstructed via limited internal automation for arithmetic reasoning, which is known to fail [36, Sec. 4.3].

5   Conclusion and future work

Our evaluation shows that CARCARA has good performance and can identify shortcomings in the proof-production of established SMT solvers. CARCARA can also elaborate proofs into demonstrably easier-to-check ones, which can have a significant impact, for example, if it is used as a bridge between solvers and proof assistants. Extending CARCARA to convert Alethe proofs into other formats would also allow the elaboration techniques to benefit other toolchains.

As future work, we will add support for parallel proof checking, since steps in the same context can be checked completely independently. We will also add new elaboration methods for resolution and ac_simp, which occasionally are bottlenecks, and will provide elaboration for rewrite rules, which can change significantly between different solvers, complicating proof-production if solvers have to phrase their rewrites with a fixed set of rules. An automatic conversion into a defined set of rewrite rules, as described in [32], would address this issue.

Finally, we expect CARCARA to facilitate improving how we use Alethe proofs. For example, our large-scale evaluation shows the significant time spent on contextual substitutions, which is mainly due to the Alethe requirement of only applying substitutions simultaneously. Extending the proof format to allow other substitution application strategies may be beneficial for different scenarios, as proof production in some solvers has indicated [7, Sec 5.1]. In general, extensions to the format (for example, to other logical theories) can be done in a more informed way with the help of an independent checker.

Acknowledgments. We thank the reviewers for their helpful suggestions to improve this paper as well as CARCARA. We thank Hans-Jörg Schurr for his extensive work in detailing the semantics of Alethe, which greatly facilitated developing CARCARA.

Data Availability Statement. The datasets generated and analyzed during the current study are available in the Zenodo repository: `https://zenodo.org/record/7574451` [3].

References

1. GNU Multiple Precision Arithmetic Library. `http://gmplib.org/`, Oct 2022.
2. The Alethe Proof Format: A Speculative Specification and Reference. `https://verit.loria.fr/documentation/alethe-spec.pdf`, Oct 2022.
3. Bruno Andreotti, Hanna Lachnitt, and Haniel Barbosa. Carcara artifact, 2023. zenodo, `https://doi.org/10.5281/zenodo.7574451`.
4. Michaël Armand, Germain Faure, Benjamin Grégoire, Chantal Keller, Laurent Théry, and Benjamin Werner. A modular integration of SAT/SMT solvers to coq through proof witnesses. In Jean-Pierre Jouannaud and Zhong Shao, editors, *Certified Programs and Proofs - First International Conference, CPP 2011, Kenting, Taiwan, December 7-9, 2011. Proceedings*, volume 7086 of *Lecture Notes in Computer Science*, pages 135–150. Springer, 2011.
5. Haniel Barbosa, Clark W. Barrett, Martin Brain, Gereon Kremer, Hanna Lachnitt, Makai Mann, Abdalrhman Mohamed, Mudathir Mohamed, Aina Niemetz, Andres Nötzli, Alex Ozdemir, Mathias Preiner, Andrew Reynolds, Ying Sheng, Cesare Tinelli, and Yoni Zohar. cvc5: A versatile and industrial-strength SMT solver. In Dana Fisman and Grigore Rosu, editors, *Tools and Algorithms for Construction and Analysis of Systems (TACAS), Part I*, volume 13243 of *Lecture Notes in Computer Science*, pages 415–442. Springer, 2022.
6. Haniel Barbosa, Jasmin Christian Blanchette, Mathias Fleury, and Pascal Fontaine. Scalable fine-grained proofs for formula processing. *Journal of Automated Reasoning*, 64(3):485–510, 2020.
7. Haniel Barbosa, Andrew Reynolds, Gereon Kremer, Hanna Lachnitt, Aina Niemetz, Andres Nötzli, Alex Ozdemir, Mathias Preiner, Arjun Viswanathan, Scott Viteri, Yoni Zohar, Cesare Tinelli, and Clark W. Barrett. Flexible proof production in an industrial-strength SMT solver. In Jasmin Blanchette, Laura Kovács, and Dirk Pattinson, editors, *International Joint Conference on Automated Reasoning (IJCAR)*, volume 13385 of *Lecture Notes in Computer Science*, pages 15–35. Springer, 2022.
8. Clark Barrett, Pascal Fontaine, and Cesare Tinelli. The Satisfiability Modulo Theories Library (SMT-LIB). `www.SMT-LIB.org`, 2016.
9. Clark W. Barrett, Roberto Sebastiani, Sanjit A. Seshia, and Cesare Tinelli. Satisfiability modulo theories. In Armin Biere, Marijn Heule, Hans van Maaren, and Toby Walsh, editors, *Handbook of Satisfiability - Second Edition*, volume 336 of *Frontiers in Artificial Intelligence and Applications*, pages 1267–1329. IOS Press, 2021.
10. Frédéric Besson, Pascal Fontaine, and Laurent Théry. A flexible proof format for SMT: a proposal. In *Workshop on Proof eXchange for Theorem Proving (PxTP)*, 2011.
11. Jasmin Christian Blanchette, Sascha Böhme, and Lawrence C. Paulson. Extending sledgehammer with SMT solvers. *Journal of Automated Reasoning*, 51(1):109–128, 2013.
12. Sascha Böhme, Anthony C. J. Fox, Thomas Sewell, and Tjark Weber. Reconstruction of z3's bit-vector proofs in HOL4 and isabelle/hol. In Jean-Pierre Jouannaud

and Zhong Shao, editors, *Certified Programs and Proofs - First International Conference, CPP 2011, Kenting, Taiwan, December 7-9, 2011. Proceedings*, volume 7086 of *Lecture Notes in Computer Science*, pages 183–198. Springer, 2011.

13. Thomas Bouton, Diego Caminha B. de Oliveira, David Déharbe, and Pascal Fontaine. veriT: An Open, Trustable and Efficient SMT-Solver. In Renate A. Schmidt, editor, *Conference on Automated Deduction (CADE)*, volume 5663 of *Lecture Notes in Computer Science*, pages 151–156. Springer, 2009.

14. Lilian Burdy and David Déharbe. Teaching an old dog new tricks - the drudges of the interactive prover in atelier B. In Michael J. Butler, Alexander Raschke, Thai Son Hoang, and Klaus Reichl, editors, *Abstract State Machines, Alloy, B, TLA, VDM, and Z - 6th International Conference, ABZ 2018, Southampton, UK, June 5-8, 2018, Proceedings*, volume 10817 of *Lecture Notes in Computer Science*, pages 415–419. Springer, 2018.

15. Leonardo Mendonça de Moura and Nikolaj Bjørner. Proofs and refutations, and Z3. In Piotr Rudnicki, Geoff Sutcliffe, Boris Konev, Renate A. Schmidt, and Stephan Schulz, editors, *Logic for Programming, Artificial Intelligence, and Reasoning (LPAR) Workshops*, volume 418 of *CEUR Workshop Proceedings*. CEUR-WS.org, 2008.

16. Burak Ekici, Alain Mebsout, Cesare Tinelli, Chantal Keller, Guy Katz, Andrew Reynolds, and Clark W. Barrett. Smtcoq: A plug-in for integrating SMT solvers into coq. In Rupak Majumdar and Viktor Kuncak, editors, *Computer Aided Verification - 29th International Conference, CAV 2017, Heidelberg, Germany, July 24-28, 2017, Proceedings, Part II*, volume 10427 of *Lecture Notes in Computer Science*, pages 126–133. Springer, 2017.

17. Herbert B. Enderton. *A mathematical introduction to logic*. Academic Press, 2 edition, 2001.

18. G. Farkas. A Fourier-féle mechanikai elv alkamazásai. *Mathematikaiés Természettudományi Értesítö*, 12:457–472, 1894. reference from Schrijver's Combinatorial Optimization textbook (Hungarian).

19. Mathias Fleury. Optimizing a verified SAT solver. In Julia M. Badger and Kristin Yvonne Rozier, editors, *NASA Formal Methods - 11th International Symposium, NFM 2019, Houston, TX, USA, May 7-9, 2019, Proceedings*, volume 11460 of *Lecture Notes in Computer Science*, pages 148–165. Springer, 2019.

20. Mathias Fleury, Jasmin Christian Blanchette, and Peter Lammich. A verified SAT solver with watched literals using imperative HOL. In June Andronick and Amy P. Felty, editors, *Proceedings of the 7th ACM SIGPLAN International Conference on Certified Programs and Proofs, CPP 2018, Los Angeles, CA, USA, January 8-9, 2018*, pages 158–171. ACM, 2018.

21. Allen Van Gelder. Verifying RUP proofs of propositional unsatisfiability. In *International Symposium on Artificial Intelligence and Mathematics (ISAIM)*, 2008.

22. Robert Harper, Furio Honsell, and Gordon D. Plotkin. A framework for defining logics. *J. ACM*, 40(1):143–184, 1993.

23. Marijn J. H. Heule. The DRAT format and drat-trim checker. *CoRR*, abs/1610.06229, 2016.

24. Jochen Hoenicke and Tanja Schindler. A simple proof format for SMT. In David Déharbe and Antti E. J. Hyvärinen, editors, *International Workshop on Satisfiability Modulo Theories (SMT)*, volume 3185 of *CEUR Workshop Proceedings*, pages 54–70. CEUR-WS.org, 2022.

25. Gabriel Hondet and Frédéric Blanqui. The new rewriting engine of dedukti (system description). In Zena M. Ariola, editor, *International Conference on Formal*

Structures for Computation and Deduction (FSCD), volume 167 of *LIPIcs*, pages 35:1–35:16. Schloss Dagstuhl - Leibniz-Zentrum für Informatik, 2020.

26. Antti E. J. Hyvärinen, Matteo Marescotti, Leonardo Alt, and Natasha Sharygina. Opensmt2: An SMT solver for multi-core and cloud computing. In Nadia Creignou and Daniel Le Berre, editors, *Theory and Applications of Satisfiability Testing (SAT)*, volume 9710 of *Lecture Notes in Computer Science*, pages 547–553. Springer, 2016.

27. Shuanglong Kan, Anthony Widjaja Lin, Philipp Rümmer, and Micha Schrader. Certistr: a certified string solver. In Andrei Popescu and Steve Zdancewic, editors, *Certified Programs and Proofs (CPP)*, pages 210–224. ACM, 2022.

28. Guy Katz, Clark W. Barrett, Cesare Tinelli, Andrew Reynolds, and Liana Hadarean. Lazy proofs for dpll(t)-based SMT solvers. In Ruzica Piskac and Muralidhar Talupur, editors, *Formal Methods In Computer-Aided Design (FMCAD)*, pages 93–100. IEEE, 2016.

29. Greg Nelson and Derek C. Oppen. Fast Decision Procedures Based on Congruence Closure. *J. ACM*, 27(2):356–364, 1980.

30. Aina Niemetz, Mathias Preiner, and Clark W. Barrett. Murxla: A modular and highly extensible API fuzzer for SMT solvers. In Sharon Shoham and Yakir Vizel, editors, *Computer Aided Verification (CAV), Part II*, volume 13372 of *Lecture Notes in Computer Science*, pages 92–106. Springer, 2022.

31. Robert Nieuwenhuis, Albert Oliveras, and Cesare Tinelli. Solving sat and sat modulo theories: From an abstract davis–putnam–logemann–loveland procedure to dpll(t). *J. ACM*, 53(6):937–977, November 2006.

32. Andres Nötzli, Haniel Barbosa, Aina Niemetz, Mathias Preiner, Andrew Reynolds, Cesare Tinelli, and Clark Barrett. Reconstructing fine-grained proofs of complex rewrites using a domain-specific language. In Alberto Griggio and Neha Rungta, editors, *Formal Methods In Computer-Aided Design (FMCAD)*, 2022. To appear.

33. Duckki Oe, Aaron Stump, Corey Oliver, and Kevin Clancy. versat: A verified modern SAT solver. In Viktor Kuncak and Andrey Rybalchenko, editors, *Verification, Model Checking, and Abstract Interpretation (VMCAI)*, volume 7148 of *Lecture Notes in Computer Science*, pages 363–378. Springer, 2012.

34. Rodrigo Otoni, Martin Blicha, Patrick Eugster, Antti E. J. Hyvärinen, and Natasha Sharygina. Theory-specific proof steps witnessing correctness of SMT executions. In *58th ACM/IEEE Design Automation Conference, DAC 2021, San Francisco, CA, USA, December 5-9, 2021*, pages 541–546. IEEE, 2021.

35. Hans-Jörg Schurr, Mathias Fleury, Haniel Barbosa, and Pascal Fontaine. Alethe: Towards a generic SMT proof format (extended abstract). In Chantal Keller and Mathias Fleury, editors, *Proceedings Seventh Workshop on Proof eXchange for Theorem Proving, PxTP 2021, Pittsburg, PA, USA, July 11, 2021*, volume 336 of *EPTCS*, pages 49–54, 2021.

36. Hans-Jörg Schurr, Mathias Fleury, and Martin Desharnais. Reliable reconstruction of fine-grained proofs in a proof assistant. In André Platzer and Geoff Sutcliffe, editors, *Conference on Automated Deduction (CADE)*, volume 12699 of *Lecture Notes in Computer Science*, pages 450–467. Springer, 2021.

37. Aaron Stump, Duckki Oe, Andrew Reynolds, Liana Hadarean, and Cesare Tinelli. SMT proof checking using a logical framework. *Formal Methods in System Design*, 42(1):91–118, 2013.

38. Dominik Winterer, Chengyu Zhang, and Zhendong Su. Validating SMT solvers via semantic fusion. In Alastair F. Donaldson and Emina Torlak, editors, *Conference on Programming Language Design and Implementation (PLDI)*, pages 718–730. ACM, 2020.

Constraint Solving/Blockchain

The Packing Chromatic Number
of the Infinite Square Grid is 15*

Bernardo Subercaseaux✉️ and Marijn J. H. Heule

Carnegie Mellon University, Pittsburgh, PA 15203, USA
{bsuberca,mheule}@cs.cmu.edu

Abstract. A packing k-coloring is a natural variation on the standard notion of graph k-coloring, where vertices are assigned numbers from $\{1, \ldots, k\}$, and any two vertices assigned a common color $c \in \{1, \ldots, k\}$ need to be at a distance greater than c (as opposed to 1, in standard graph colorings). Despite a sequence of incremental work, determining the packing chromatic number of the infinite square grid has remained an open problem since its introduction in 2002. We culminate the search by proving this number to be 15. We achieve this result by improving the best-known method for this problem by roughly two orders of magnitude. The most important technique to boost performance is a novel, surprisingly effective propositional encoding for packing colorings. Additionally, we developed an alternative symmetry breaking method. Since both new techniques are more complex than existing techniques for this problem, a verified approach is required to trust them. We include both techniques in a proof of unsatisfiability, reducing the trusted core to the correctness of the direct encoding.

Keywords: Packing coloring · SAT · Verification.

1 Introduction

Automated reasoning techniques have been successfully applied to a variety of coloring problems ranging from the classical computer-assisted proof of the *Four Color Theorem* [1], to progress on the *Hadwiger-Nelson problem* [21], or improving the bounds on Ramsey-like numbers [19]. This article contributes a new success story to the area: we show the *packing* chromatic number of the infinite square grid to be 15, thus solving via automated reasoning techniques a combinatorial problem that had remained elusive for over 20 years.

The notion of *packing coloring* was introduced in the seminal work of Goddard et al. [10], and since then more than 70 articles have studied it [3], establishing it as an active area of research. Let us consider the following definition.

Definition 1. *A packing k-coloring of a simple undirected graph $G = (V, E)$ is a function f from V to $\{1, \ldots, k\}$ such that for any two distinct vertices $u, v \in V$, and any color $c \in \{1, \ldots, k\}$, it holds that $f(u) = f(v) = c$ implies $d(u, v) > c$.*

---

* Both authors are supported by the U.S. National Science Foundation under grant CCF-2015445.

S. Sankaranarayanan and N. Sharygina (Eds.): TACAS 2023, LNCS 13993, pp. 389–406, 2023.
https://doi.org/10.1007/978-3-031-30823-9_20

Note that by changing the last condition to $d(u, v) > 1$ we recover the standard notion of coloring, thus making packing colorings a natural variation of them. Intuitively, in a packing coloring, *larger* colors forbid being reused in a larger region of the graph around them. Indeed, packing colorings were originally presented under the name of *broadcast coloring*, motivated by the problem of assigning broadcast frequencies to radio stations in a non-conflicting way [10], where two radio stations that are assigned the same frequency need to be at distance greater than some function of the power of their broadcast signals. Therefore, a large color represents a powerful broadcast signal at a given frequency, that cannot be reused anywhere else within a large radius around it, to avoid interference. Minimizing the number of colors assigned can thus be interpreted as minimizing the pollution of the radio spectrum. The literature has preferred the name *packing coloring* ever since [3].

Analogously to the case of standard colorings, we can naturally define the notion of *packing chromatic number*, and study its computation.

Definition 2. *Given a graph $G = (V, E)$, define its packing chromatic number $\chi_\rho(G)$ as the minimum value k such that G admits a packing k-coloring.*

Example 1. Consider the infinite graph with vertex set $\mathbb{Z}$ and with edges between consecutive integers, which we denote as $\mathbb{Z}^1$. A packing 3-coloring is illustrated in Figure 1. On the other hand, by examination one can observe that it is impossible to obtain a packing 2-coloring for $\mathbb{Z}^1$.

Fig. 1: Illustration of a packing 3-coloring for $\mathbb{Z}^1$.

While Example 1 shows that $\chi_\rho(\mathbb{Z}^1) = 3$, the question of computing $\chi_\rho(\mathbb{Z}^2)$, where $\mathbb{Z}^2$ is the graph with vertex set $\mathbb{Z} \times \mathbb{Z}$ and edges between orthogonally adjacent points (i.e., points whose ℓ_1 distance equals 1), has been open since the introduction of packing colorings by Goddard et al. [10]. On the other hand, it is known that $\chi_\rho(\mathbb{Z}^3) = \infty$ (again considering edges between points whose ℓ_1 distance equals 1) [9]. The problem of computing $3 \leq \chi_\rho(\mathbb{Z}^2) \leq \infty$ has received significant attention, and it is described as *"the most attractive [of the packing coloring problems over infinite graphs]"* by Brešar et al. [3]. We can now state our main theorem, providing a final answer to this problem.

Theorem 1. $\chi_\rho(\mathbb{Z}^2) = 15$.

An upper bound of 15 had already been proved by Martin et al. [18], who found a packing 15-coloring of a 72×72 grid that can be used for periodically tiling the entirety of $\mathbb{Z}^2$. Therefore, the main contribution of our work consists of proving that 14 colors are not enough for $\mathbb{Z}^2$. Table 1 presents a summary of the historical progress on computing $\chi_\rho(\mathbb{Z}^2)$. It is worth noting that amongst the computer-generated proofs (i.e., all since Soukal and Holub [22] in 2010), ours is the first one to be formally verified, see Section 4.

Table 1: Historical summary of the bounds known for $\chi_\rho(\mathbb{Z}^2)$.

Year	Citation	Approach	Lower bound	Upper bound
2002	Goddard et al. [10]	Manual	9	23
2002	Schwenk [20]	Unkown	9	22
2009	Fiala et al. [8]	Manual + Computer	10	23
2010	Soukal and Holub [22]	Simulated Annealing	10	17
2010	Ekstein et al. [7]	Brute Force Program	12	17
2015	Martin et al. [17]	SAT solver	13	16
2017	Martin et al. [18]	SAT solver	13	15
2022	Subercaseaux and Heule [23]	SAT solver	14	15
2022	**This article**	SAT solver	15	15

For any $k \geq 4$, the problem of determining whether a graph G admits a packing 4-coloring is known to be NP-hard [10], and thus we do not expect a polynomial time algorithm for computing $\chi_\rho(\cdot)$. This naturally motivates the use of satisfiability (SAT) solvers for studying the packing chromatic number of finite subgraphs of $\mathbb{Z}^2$. The rest of this article is thus devoted to proving Theorem 1 by using automated reasoning techniques, in a way that produces a proof that can be checked independently and that has been checked by verified software.

2   Background

We start by recapitulating the components used to obtain a lower bound of 14 in our previous work [23]. Naturally, in order to prove a lower bound for $\mathbb{Z}^2$ one needs to prove a lower bound for a finite subgraph of it. As in earlier work, we consider *disks* (i.e., 2-dimensional balls in the ℓ_1-metric) as the finite subgraphs to study [23]. Concretely, let $D_r(v)$ be the subgraph induced by $\{u \in V(\mathbb{Z}^2) \mid d(u, v) \leq r\}$. To simplify notation, we use D_r as a shorthand for $D_r((0,0))$, and we let $D_{r,k}$ be the instance consisting of deciding whether D_r admits a packing k-coloring. Moreover, let $D_{r,k,c}$ be the instance $D_{r,k}$ but enforcing that the central vertex $(0,0)$ receives color c (Fig. 2).

For example, a simple lemma of Subercaseaux and Heule [23, Proposition 5] proves that the unsatisfiability of $D_{3,6,3}$ is enough to deduce that $\chi_\rho(\mathbb{Z}^2) \geq 7$. We will prove a slight variation of it (Lemma 2) later on in order to prove Theorem 1, but for now let us summarize how they proved that $D_{12,13,12}$ is unsatisfiable.

Encodings. The direct encoding for $D_{r,k,c}$ consists simply of variables $x_{v,t}$ stating that vertex v gets color t, as well as the following clauses:

1. (at-least-one-color clauses, ALOC) $\bigvee_{t=1}^{k} x_{v,t}, \quad \forall v \in V,$
2. (at-most-one-distance clauses, AMOD)

$$\overline{x_{u,t}} \vee \overline{x_{v,t}}, \quad \forall t \in \{1, \ldots, k\}, \forall u, v \in V \text{ s.t. } 0 < d(u, v) \leq t,$$

Fig. 2: Illustration of satisfying assignments for $D_{3,7,3}$ and $D_{3,6,6}$. On the other hand, $D_{3,6,3}$ is not satisfiable.

3. (center clause) $x_{(0,0),c}$.

This amounts to $O(r^2 k^3)$ clauses [23]. The recursive encoding is significantly more involved, but it leads to only $O(r^2 k \log k)$ clauses asymptotically. Unfortunately, the constant involved in the asymptotic expression is large, and this encoding did not give them practical speed-ups [23].

Cube And Conquer. Introduced by Heule et al. [13], the *Cube And Conquer* approach aims to *split* a SAT instance φ into multiple SAT instances $\varphi_1, \ldots, \varphi_m$ in such a way that φ is satisfiable if, and only if, at least one of the instances φ_i is satisfiable; thus allowing to work on the different instances φ_i in parallel. If $\psi = (c_1 \lor c_2 \lor \cdots \lor c_m)$ is a tautological DNF, then we have

$$\text{SAT}(\varphi) \iff \text{SAT}(\varphi \land \psi) \iff \text{SAT}\left(\bigvee_{i=1}^{m}(\varphi \land c_i)\right) \iff \text{SAT}\left(\bigvee_{i=1}^{m}\varphi_i\right),$$

where the different $\varphi_i := (\varphi \land c_i)$ are the instances resulting from the split.

Intuitively, each cube c_i represents a *case*, i.e., an assumption about a satisfying assignment to φ, and soundness comes from ψ being a tautology, which means that the split into cases is exhaustive. If the split is well designed, then each φ_i is a particular case that is substantially easier to solve than φ, and thus solving them all in parallel can give significant speed-ups, especially considering the sequential nature of CDCL, at the core of most solvers. Our previous work [23] proposed a concrete algorithm to generate a split, which already results in an almost linear speed-up, meaning that by using 128 cores, the performance gain is roughly a $\times 60$ factor.

Symmetry Breaking. The idea of *symmetry breaking* [6] consists of exploiting the symmetries that are present in SAT instances to speed-up computation. In particular, $D_{r,k,c}$ instances have 3 axes of symmetry (i.e., vertical, horizontal, and diagonal) which allowed for close to an 8-fold improvement in performance for proving $D_{12,13,12}$ to be unsatisfiable. The particular use of symmetry breaking in our previous approach [23] was happening at the *Cube And Conquer* level, where out of the sub-instances $\varphi_i, \ldots, \varphi_m$ produced by the split, only a $1/8$-fraction of them had to be solved, as the rest were equivalent under isomorphism.

Verification. Arguably the biggest drawback of our previous approach proving a lower bound of 14 is that it lacked the capability of generating a computer-checkable proof. To claim a full solution to the 20-year-old problem of computing $\chi_\rho(\mathbb{Z}^2)$ that is accepted by the mathematics community, we deem paramount a fully verifiable proof that can be scrutinized independently.

The most commonly-used proofs for SAT problems are expressed in the DRAT clausal proof system [11]. A DRAT proof of unsatisfiability is a list of clause addition and clause deletion steps. Formally, a clausal proof is a list of pairs $\langle s_1, C_1 \rangle, \ldots, \langle s_m, C_m \rangle$, where for each $i \in 1, \ldots, m$, $s_i \in \{a, d\}$ and C_i is a clause. If $s_i = a$, the pair is called an *addition*, and if $s_i = d$, it is called a *deletion*. For a given input formula φ_0, a clausal proof gives rise to a set of *accumulated formulas* φ_i $(i \in \{1, \ldots, m\})$ as follows:

$$\varphi_i = \begin{cases} \varphi_{i-1} \cup \{C_i\} & \text{if } s_i = a \\ \varphi_{i-1} \setminus \{C_i\} & \text{if } s_i = d \end{cases}$$

Each clause addition must preserve satisfiability, which is usually guaranteed by requiring the added clauses to fulfill some efficiently decidable syntactic criterion. The main purpose of deletions is to speed up proof checking by keeping the accumulated formula small. A valid proof of unsatisfiability must end with the addition of the empty clause.

3   Optimizations

Even with the best choice of parameters for our previous approach, solving the instance $D_{12,13,12}$ takes almost two days of computation with a 128-core machine [23]. In order to prove Theorem 1, we will require to solve an instance roughly 100 times harder, and thus several optimizations will be needed. In fact, we improve on all aspects discussed in Section 2; we present five different forms of optimization that are key to the success of our approach, which we summarize next.

1. We present a new encoding, which we call the plus *encoding* that has conceptual similarities with the recursive encoding of Subercaseaux and Heule [23], while achieving a significant gain in practical efficiency.
2. We present a new split algorithm that works substantially better than the previous split algorithm when coupled with the plus encoding.
3. We improve on symmetry breaking by using multiple layers of symmetry-breaking clauses in a way that exploits the design of the split algorithm to increase performance.
4. We study the choice of color to fix at the center, showing that one can gain significantly in performance by making instance-based choices; for example, $D_{12,13,6}$ can be solved more than three times as fast as $D_{12,13,12}$ (the instance used by Subercaseaux and Heule [23]).

5. We introduce a new and extremely simple kind of clauses called ALOD clauses, which improve performance when added to the other clauses of any encoding we have tested.

The following subsections present each of these components in detail.

3.1   *"Plus"*: a New Encoding

Despite the asymptotic improvement of the recursive encoding of Subercaseaux and Heule [23], its contribution is mostly of "theoretical interest" as it does not improve solution times. Nonetheless, that encoding suggests the possibility of finding one that is both more succinct than the direct encoding and that speed-ups computation. Our path towards such an encoding starts with *Bounded Variable Addition (BVA)* [16], a technique to automatically re-encode CNF formulas by adding new variables, with the goal of minimizing their resulting size (measured as the sum of the number of variables and the number of clauses). BVA can significantly reduce the size of $D_{r,k,c}$ instances, even further than the recursive encoding. Moreover, BVA actually speeds-up computation when solving the resulting instances with a CDCL solver, see Table 2. Figure 3 compares the number of AMOD clauses between the direct encoding and the BVA encoding; for example in the direct encoding, for D_{14} color 10 would require roughly 30000 clauses, whereas it requires roughly 3500 in the BVA encoding. It can be observed as well in Figure 3 that the direct encoding grows in a very structured and predictable way, where color c in D_r requires roughly r^2c^2 clauses. On the other hand, arguably because of its locally greedy nature, the results for BVA are far more erratic, and roughly follow a $4r^2 \lg c$ curve.

The encoding resulting from BVA does not perform particularly well when coupled with the split algorithm of Subercaseaux and Heule. Indeed, Table 2 shows that while BVA heavily improves runtime under sequential CDCL, it does not provide a meaningful advantage when using *Cube And Conquer*. Furthermore, encodings resulting from BVA are hardly interpretable, as BVA uses

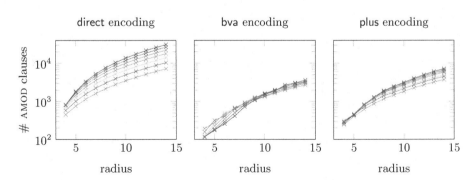

Fig. 3: Comparison of the size of the at-most-one-color clauses between the direct encoding and the BVA-encoding, for D_4 up to D_{14} and colors $\{4, \ldots, 10\}$.

Table 2: Comparison between the different encodings. *Cube And Conquer* experiments were performed with the approach of Subercaseaux and Heule [23] (parameters $F = 5, d = 2$) on a 128-core machine. Hardware details in Section 5.

	direct encoding		bva encoding		plus encoding	
	$D_{5,10,5}$	$D_{6,11,6}$	$D_{5,10,5}$	$D_{6,11,6}$	$D_{5,10,5}$	$D_{6,11,6}$
Number of variables	610	935	973	1559	673	1039
Number of clauses	10688	21086	2313	3928	4063	7548
CDCL runtime (s)	255.12	10774.79	39.88	2539.38	15.90	811.66
Cube-and-conquer wall-clock (s)	0.77	26.20	0.78	17.97	0.50	6.68

a locally greedy strategy for introducing new variables. As a result, the design of a split algorithm that could work well with BVA is a very complicated task. Therefore, our approach consisted of reverse engineering what BVA was doing over some example instances, and using that insight to design a new encoding that produces instances of size comparable to those generated by BVA while being easily interpretable and thus compatible with natural split algorithms.

By manually inspecting BVA encodings one can deduce that a fundamental part of their structure is what we call *regional variables/clauses*. A regional variable $r_{S,c}$ is associated with a set of vertices S and a color c, meaning that at least one vertex in S receives color c. Let us illustrate their use with an example.

Example 2. Consider the instance $D_{6,11}$, and let us focus on the *at-most-one-distance* (AMOD) clauses for color 4. Figure 4a depicts two regional clauses: one in orange (vertices labeled with α), and one in blue (vertices labeled with β), each consisting of 5 vertices organized in a *plus* (+) shape. We thus introduce variables $r_{\text{orange},4}$ and $r_{\text{blue},4}$, defined by the following clauses:

1. $\overline{r_{\text{orange},4}} \vee \bigvee_{v \text{ has label } \alpha} x_{v,4}$,
2. $\overline{r_{\text{blue},4}} \vee \bigvee_{v \text{ has label } \beta} x_{v,4}$,
3. $r_{\text{orange},4} \vee \overline{x_{v,4}}$, for each v with label α,
4. $r_{\text{blue},4} \vee \overline{x_{v,4}}$, for each v with label β.

The benefit of introducing these two new variables and $2 + (5 \cdot 2) = 12$ additional clauses will be shown now, when using them to forbid conflicts more compactly. Indeed, each vertex labeled with α or β participates in $|D_4| - 1 = 40$ AMOD clauses in the direct encoding, which equals a total of $10 \cdot 40 - \binom{10}{2} = 355$ clauses for all of them (subtracting the clauses counted twice). However, note that all 36 vertices shaded in light orange are at distance at most 4 from all vertices labeled with α, and thus they are in conflict with $r_{\text{orange},4}$. This means that we can encode all conflicts between α-vertices and orange-shaded vertices with 36 clauses. The same can be done for β-vertices and the 36 vertices shaded in light blue. Moreover, all pairs of vertices (x, y) with x being an α-vertex and y being a β-vertex are in conflict, which we can represent simply with the clause $(r_{\text{orange},4} \vee r_{\text{blue},4})$, instead of $5 \cdot 5 = 25$ pairwise clauses. We still need,

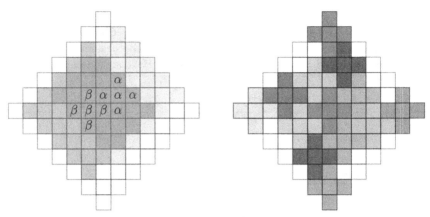

(a) Illustration of regions interacting in $P_{6,11,6}$, for color 4.

(b) Illustration of the placement of regions of the 13 regions in $P_{6,11,6}$.

Fig. 4: Illustrations for $P_{6,11,6}$.

however, to forbid that more than one α-vertex receives color 4, and the same for β-vertices, which can be done by simply adding all $2 \cdot \binom{5}{2} = 20$ AMOD clauses between all pairs. In total, the total number of clauses involving α or β vertices has gone down to $12 + 2 \cdot 36 + 20 + 1 = 105$ clauses, from the original 355 clauses, by merely adding two new variables.

As shown in Example 2, the use of regional clauses can make encodings more compact, and this same idea scales even better for larger instances when the regions are larger. A key challenge for designing a *regional encoding* in this manner is that it requires a choice of regions (which can even be different for every color). After trying several different strategies for defining regions, we found one that works particularly well in practice (despite not yielding an optimal number for the metric #variables + #clauses), which we denote the plus *encoding*. The plus encoding is based on simply using "+" shaped regions (i.e., D_1) for all colors greater than 3, and to not introduce any changes for colors 1, 2 and 3 as they only amount to a very small fraction of the total size of the instances we consider. We denote with $P_{d,k,c}$ the plus encoding of the diamond of size d with k colors, and the centered being colored with c. Figure 4b illustrates $P_{6,11,6}$. Interestingly, the BVA encoding opted for larger regions for the larger colors, using for example D_2's or D_3's as regions for color 14. We have experimentally found this to be very ineffective when coupled with our split algorithms. In terms of the locations of the "+" shaped regions, we have placed them manually through an interactive program, arriving to the conclusion that the best choice of locations consists of packing as many regions as possible and as densely around the center as possible. A more formal presentation of all the clauses involved in the plus encoding is presented in the extended *arXiv* version [24] of this paper, but all its components have been illustrated in Example 2.

The exact number of clauses resulting from the plus encoding is hard to analyze precisely, but it is clear that asymptotically it only improves from the direct encoding by a constant multiplicative factor. Figure 3 and Table 2 illustrate the compactness of the plus encoding over particular instances, and its increase in efficiency both for CDCL solving as well as with the *Cube And Conquer* approach of Subercaseaux and Heule [23].

3.2   Symmetry Breaking

Another improvement of our approach is a static symmetry-breaking technique, while Subercaseaux and Heule [23] achieved symmetry breaking by discarding all but $1/8$ of the cubes. We cannot do this easily since the plus encoding does not have an 8-fold symmetry. Instead it has a 4-fold symmetry (see Figure 4b). We add symmetry breaking clauses directly on top of the direct encoding (i.e., instead of using it after a *Cube And Conquer* split), as $D_{r,k,c}$ has indeed an 8-fold symmetry (see Figure 5b). Concretely, if we consider a color t, it can only appear once in the $D_{\lfloor t/2 \rfloor}$, as if it appeared more than once said appearances would be at distance $\leq t$. Given this, we can assume without loss of generality that if there is one appearance of t in $D_{\lfloor t/2 \rfloor}$, then it appears with coordinates (a, b) such that $a \geq 0 \wedge b \geq a$. We enforce this by adding negative units of the form $\overline{x_{(i,j),t}}$ for every pair $(i,j) \in D_{\lfloor t/2 \rfloor}$ such that $i < 0 \vee j < i$. This is illustrated in Figure 5b for $D_{5,10}$. Note however that this can only be applied to a single color t, as when a vertex in the *north-north-east* octant gets assigned color t, the 8-fold symmetry is broken. However, if the symmetry breaking clauses have been added for color t, and yet t does not appear in $D_{\lfloor t/2 \rfloor}$, then there is still an 8-fold symmetry in the encoding we can exploit by breaking symmetry on some other color t'. This way, our encoding uses $L = 5$ *layers* of symmetry breaking, for colors $k, k-1, \ldots, k-L+1$. At each layer i, where symmetry breaking is done over color $k-i$, except for the first (i.e., $i > 0$), we need to concatenate a clause

$$\text{SymmetryBroken}_i := \bigvee_{t=k-i}^{k} \bigvee_{\substack{(a,b) \in D_{\lfloor t/2 \rfloor} \\ 0 \leq a \leq b}} x_{(a,b),t}$$

to each symmetry breaking clause, so that symmetry breaking is applied only when symmetry has not been broken already. Table 3 (page 14) illustrates the impact of this symmetry breaking approach, yielding close to a $\times 40$ speed-up for $D_{6,11,6}$.

3.3   *At-Least-One-Distance* clauses

Yet another addition to our encoding is what we call *At-Least-One-Distance* (ALOD) clauses, which consist on stating that, for every vertex v, if we consider $D_1(v)$, then at least one vertex in $D_1(v)$ must get color 1. Concretely, the *At-Least-One-Distance* clause corresponding to a vertex $v = (i, j)$ is

$$C_v = x_{(i,j),1} \vee x_{(i+1,j),1} \vee x_{(i-1,j),1} \vee x_{(i,j+1),1} \vee x_{(i,j-1),1}.$$

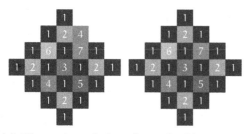
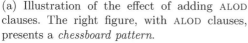
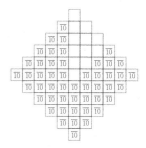

(a) Illustration of the effect of adding ALOD clauses. The right figure, with ALOD clauses, presents a *chessboard pattern*.

(b) Some symmetry-breaking unit clauses added to $D_{5,10}$.

Fig. 5: The effect of adding ALOD clauses (left) and symmetry-breaking (right).

Note that adding these clauses preserves satisfiability since they are *blocked clauses* [15]; this can be seen as follows. If no vertex in $D_1(v)$ gets assigned color 1, then we can simply assign $x_{v,1}$, thus satisfying the new clause C_v.

The purpose of ALOD clauses can be described as *incentives* towards assigning color 1 in a *chessboard pattern* (see Figure 5a), which seems to simplify the rest of the computation. Empirically, their addition improves runtimes; see Table 3.

3.4   Cube And Conquer Using Auxiliary Variables

The split of Subercaseaux and Heule [23] is based on cases about the $x_{v,c}$ variables of the direct encoding, and specifically using vertices v that are close to the center and colors c that are in the top-t colors for some parameter t.

Our algorithm is instead based on cases only around the new regional variables $r_{S,c}$, which appears to be key for exploiting their use in the encoding.

More concretely, our algorithm, which we call PTR, is roughly based on splitting the instance into cases according to which out of the R regions that are closest to the center get which of the T highest colors (noting that a region can get multiple colors). A third parameter P indicates the maximum number of positive literals in any cube of the split. More precisely, there are cubes with i positive literals for $i \in \{0, 1, \ldots, P-1, P\}$, and the set of cubes with i positive literals is constructed by PTR as follows:

1. Let $\mathcal{R}$ be the set of R regions that are the closest to the center, and $\mathcal{T}$ the set consisting of the T highest colors (i.e., $\{k, k-1, \ldots, k-T+1\}$).
2. For each of the R^i tuples $\vec{S} \in \mathcal{R}^i$, we create $\binom{T}{i}$ cubes as described in the next step.
3. For each subset $Q \subseteq \mathcal{T}$ with size $|Q| = i$, let $q_1, \ldots, q_i$ be its elements in increasing order, and then create a cube with positive literals $r_{\vec{S}_j, q_j}$ for $j \in \{1, \ldots, i\}$. Then, if $i < P$, add to the cube negative literals $\overline{r_{\vec{S}_j, q_\ell}}$ for $j \in \{1, \ldots, i\}$ and every $q_\ell \notin Q$.

Lemma 1. *The cubes generated by the* PTR *algorithm form a tautology.*

The proof of Lemma 1 is quite simple, and we refer the reader to the proof of Lemma 7 in Subercaseaux and Heule [23] for a very similar one. Moreover, because our goal is to have a verifiable proof, instead of relying on Lemma 1, we test explicitly that the cubes generated by our algorithm form a tautology in all the instances mentioned in this paper. Pseudo-code for PTR is presented in the extended *arXiv* version of this paper [24].

3.5   Optimizing the Center Color

Our previous work [23] argued that for an instance $D_{r,k}$, one should fix the color of the central vertex to $\min(r, k)$. However, our experiments suggest otherwise. As the proof of Lemma 2 (in extended *arXiv* version [24]) implies, we are allowed to fix any color in the center, and as long as the resulting instance is unsatisfiable, that will allow us to establish the same lower bound. It turns out that the choice of the center color can dramatically affect performance, as shown for instance $D_{12,13}$ (the one used to prove $\chi_\rho(\mathbb{Z}^2) \geq 14$) in Figure 6. Interestingly, performance does not change monotonically with the value fixed in the center. Intuitively, it appears that fixing smaller colors in the center is ineffective as they impose restrictions on a small region around the center, while fixing very large colors in the center does not constrain the center much; for example, on the one hand, fixing a 1 or 2 in the center does not seem to impose any serious constraints on solutions. On the other hand, when a 12 is fixed in the center (as in our previous work [23]), color 6 can be used 5 times in D_6, whereas if color 6 is fixed in the center, it can only be used once in D_6. The apparent advantage of fixing 12 in the center (that it cannot occur anywhere else in $D_{12,13}$), is outweighed by the extra constraints around the center that fixing color 6 imposes; Subercaseaux and Heule already observed that most conflicts between colors occur around the center [23]), thus explaining why it makes sense to optimize in that area.

The main result of Subercaseaux and Heule [23] is the unsatisfiability of $D_{12,13,12}$, which required 45 CPU hours using the same SAT solver and similar hardware. Let $P^\star_{d,k,c}$ denote $P_{d,k,c}$ with ALOD clauses and symmetry-breaking

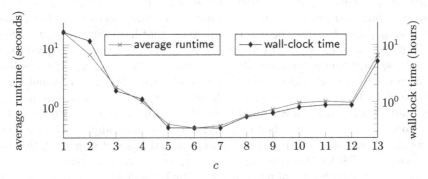

Fig. 6: The impact of the color in the center (c) on the performance for $P^\star_{12,13,c}$.

$$\overbrace{D_{15,14,6} \equiv \underbrace{D^\star_{15,14,6} \equiv P^\star_{15,14,6}}_{\text{re-encoding proof}}}^{\text{symmetry proof}} \overbrace{P^\star_{15,14,6} \vDash \underbrace{N_{15,14,6}}_{\text{tautology proof}}}^{\text{implication proof}} \vDash \bot$$

Fig. 7: Illustration of the verification pipeline.

predicates. We show unsatisfiability of $P^\star_{12,13,12}$ in 1.18 CPU hours and of $P^\star_{12,13,6}$ in 0.34 CPU hours. So the combination of the plus encoding and the improved center reduces the computational costs by two orders of magnitude.

4   Verification

Our pipeline proves that, in order to trust $\chi_\rho(\mathbb{Z}^2) = 15$ as a result, the only component that requires unverified trust is the direct encoding of $D_{15,14,6}$. Indeed, let $P^\star_{15,14,6}$ be the instance $P_{15,14,6}$ with ALOD-clauses and 5 layers of symmetry breaking clauses, and let $\psi = \{c_1, \ldots, c_m\}$ be the set of cubes generated by the PTR algorithm with parameters $P = 6, T = 7, R = 9$. We then prove:

1. that $D_{15,14,6}$ is satisfiability equivalent to $P^\star_{15,14,6}$.
2. the DNF $\psi = c_1 \vee c_2 \vee \cdots \vee c_m$ is a tautology.
3. each instance $(P^\star_{15,14,6} \wedge c_i)$, for $c_i \in \psi$ is unsatisfiable.
4. hence the negation of each cube is implied by $P^\star_{15,14,6}$.
5. since ψ is a tautology, its negation $N_{15,14,6}$ is unsatisfiable.

As a result, Theorem 1 relies only on our implementation of $D_{15,14,6}$. Fortunately, this is quite simple, and the whole implementation is presented in the extended *arXiv* version of this paper [24]. Figure 7 illustrates the verification pipeline, and the following paragraphs detail its different components.

Symmetry Proof. The first part of the proof consists in the addition of symmetry-breaking predicates to the formula. This part needs to go before the re-encoding proof, because the plus encoding does not have the 8-fold symmetry of the direct encoding. Each of the clauses in the symmetry-breaking predicates have the substitution redundancy (SR) property [5]. This is a very strong redundancy property and checking whether a clause C has SR w.r.t. a formula φ is NP-complete. However, since we know the symmetry, it is easy to compute a SR certificate. There exists no SR proof checker. Instead, we implemented a prototype tool to convert SR proofs into DRAT for which formally verified checkers exists. Our conversion is similar to the approach to converted propagation redundancy into DRAT [12]. The conversion can significantly increase the size of the proof, but the other proof parts are typically larger for harder formulas, thus the size is acceptable.

Re-encoding Proof. After symmetry breaking, the formula encoding is optimized by transforming the direct encoding into the plus encoding and adding the ALOD clauses. This part of the proof is easy. All clauses in the plus encoding and all ALOD clauses have the RAT redundancy property w.r.t. the direct encoding. This means that we can add all these clauses with a single addition step per clause. Afterward, the clauses that occur in the direct encoding but not in the plus encoding are removed using deletion steps.

Implication Proof. The third part of the proof expresses that the formula cannot be satisfied with any of the cubes from the split. For easy problems, one can avoid splitting and just use the empty cube as tautological DNF. For harder problems, splitting is crucial. We solve $D_{15,14,6}$ using a split with just over 5 million cubes. Using a SAT solver to show that the formula with a cube is unsatisfiable shows that the negative of the cube is implied by the formula. We can derive all these implied clauses in parallel. The proofs of unsatisfiability can be merged into a single implication proof.

Tautology Proof. The final proof part needs to show that the negation of the clauses derived in the prior steps form a tautology. In most cases, including ours, the cubes are constructed using a tree-based method. This makes the tautology check easy as there exists a resolution proof from the derived clauses to the empty clause using $m - 1$ resolution steps with m denoting the number of cubes. This part can be generated using a simple SAT call.

The final proof merges all the proof parts. In case the proof parts are all in the DRAT format, such as our proof parts, then they can simply be merged by concatenating the proofs using the order presented above.

5   Experiments

Experimental Setup. In terms of hardware, all our experiments were run in the Bridges2 [4] supercomputer. Each node has the following specifications: Two AMD EPYC 7742 CPUs, each with 64 cores, 256MB of L3 cache, and 512GB total RAM memory. Our code and various formulas are publicly available at the repository https://github.com/bsubercaseaux/PackingChromaticTacas. In terms of software, all sequential experiments were run on state-of-the-art solver CaDiCaL [2], while parallel experiments with *Cube And Conquer* were run using a new implementation of parallel iCaDiCaL because it supports incremental solving [13] while being significantly faster than iLingeling.

Effectiveness of the Optimizations. We evaluated the optimizations to the direct encoding as proposed in Section 3: the plus encoding, the addition of the ALOD clauses, and the new symmetry breaking. The results are shown in Table 3. We picked $D_{6,11,6}$ for this evaluation since it is the largest diamond that can still be solved within a couple of hours on a single core.

The main conclusion is that the optimizations significantly improve the runtime. A comparison between the direct encoding without symmetry breaking and the plus encoding with symmetry breaking and the ALOD clauses shows that the latter can be solved roughly 200x faster. Table 3 shows all 8 possible configurations. Turning on any of the optimizations always improves performance. The effectiveness of the plus encoding and ALOD clauses is somewhat surprising: the speed-up factor obtained by re-encoding typically does not exceed the factor by which the formula size is reduced. In this case, the reduction factor in formula size is less than 3, while the speed-up is larger than 13 (see the difference between the first and second row of Table 3). Moreover, we are not aware of the effectiveness of adding blocked clauses. Typically SAT solvers remove them.

We also constructed DRAT proofs of the optimizations (shown as derivation in the table) and the solver runtime. We merged them into a single DRAT proof by concatenating the files. The proofs were first checked with the `drat-trim` tool, which produced LRAT proofs. These LRAT files were validated using the formally-verified `cake-lpr` checker. The size of the DRAT proofs and the checking time are shown in the table. Note that the checking time for the proofs with symmetry breaking is always larger than the solving times. This is caused by expressing the symmetry breaking in DRAT resulting in a 436 Mb proof part.

The Implication Proof. The largest part of the computation consist of showing that $P^\star_{15,4,6}$ is unsatisfiable under each of the $5,217,031$ cubes produced by the cube generator. The results of the experiments are shown in Figure 8 (left). The left plot shows that roughly half of the cubes can be solved in a second or less. The average runtime of cubes was 3.35 seconds, while the hardest cube required 1584.61 seconds. The total runtime was 4851.38 CPU hours.

For each cube, we produced a compressed DRAT proof (the default output of CaDiCaL). Due to the lack of hints in DRAT proofs, they are somewhat complex to validate using a formally-verified checker. Instead, we use the tool `drat-trim` to trim the proofs and add hints. The result are uncompressed LRAT files, which we validate using the formally-verified checker `cake_lpr`. The verification time was 4336.93 CPU hours, so slightly less than the total runtime.

The sizes of each of the implication proofs show a similar distribution, as depicted in Figure 8 (right). Most proofs are less than 10 MB in size. The

Table 3: Evaluating the effectiveness of the optimizations on $D_{6,11,6}$.

sym	ALOD	plus	#var	#cls	runtime	derivation	proof	check
			935	21086	10741.69	0 b	11.99 Gb	31731.20
		x	1039	7548	809.65	149 Kb	1.29 Gb	1720.82
	x		935	21171	8422.38	1.6 Kb	8.11 Gb	21732.74
	x	x	1039	7633	389.71	151 Kb	1.29 Gb	1708.21
x			935	21286	273.19	436 Mb	0.63 Gb	1390.04
x		x	1039	7748	66.74	436 Mb	0.14 Gb	1022.42
x	x		935	21371	252.71	436 Mb	0.68 Gb	1359.05
x	x	x	1039	7833	55.56	436 Mb	0.10 Gb	997.90

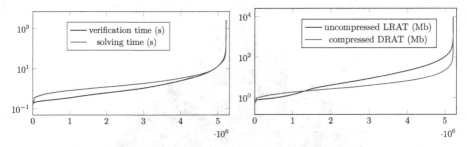

Fig. 8: Cactus plot of solving and verification times in seconds (left) and cactus plot of the size of the compressed DRAT proof and uncompressed LRAT proof in Mb (right).

compressed DRAT proofs are generally smaller compared to the LRAT proofs, but that is mostly due to compression, which reduces the size by around 70%.

The Chessboard Conjecture and its Counterexample. Given that color 1 can be used to fill in $1/2$ of $\mathbb{Z}^2$ in a packing coloring, and the packing colorings found in the past, with $15, 16$ or 17 colors used color 1 with density $1/2$ in a *chessboard pattern* [18], it is tempting to assume that this must always be the case. This way, we conjectured that any instance $D_{r,k,c}$ is satisfiable if and only if it is with the chessboard pattern. The consequence of the conjecture is significant, as if it were true we could fix half of the vertices to color 1, thus massively reducing the size of the instance and its runtime. Unfortunately, this conjecture happens to be false, with the smallest counterexample being $D_{14,14,6}$ as illustrated in Figure 9, which deviates from the chessboard pattern in only 2 vertices. We have proved as well that no solution for $D_{14,14,6}$ deviating in only 1 vertex from the chessboard pattern exists.

Proving the Lower Bound. In order to prove Theorem 1, we require the following 3 lemmas, from where the conclusion easily follows.

Lemma 2. *If $D_{15,14,6}$ is unsatisfiable, then $\chi_\rho(\mathbb{Z}^2) \geq 15$.*

Lemma 3. *If $D_{15,14,6}$ is satisfiable, then $P^\star_{15,14,6}$ is also satisfiable.*

Lemma 4. *$P^\star_{15,14,6}$ is unsatisfiable.*

We have obtained computational proofs of Lemma 3 and Lemma 4 as described above, and thus it only remains to prove Lemma 2, which we include in the appendix. We can thus proceed to our main proof.

Proof (of Theorem 1). Since Martin et al. proved that $\chi_\rho(\mathbb{Z}^2) \leq 15$ [18], it remains to show $\chi_\rho(\mathbb{Z}^2) \geq 15$, which by Lemma 2 reduces to proving Lemma 3 and Lemma 4. We have proved these lemmas computationally, obtaining a single DRAT proof as described in Section 4. The total solving time was 4851.31 CPU hours, while the total checking time of the proofs was 4336.93 CPU hours. The total size of the compressed DRAT proof is 34 terabytes, while the uncompressed LRAT proof weighs 122 terabytes.

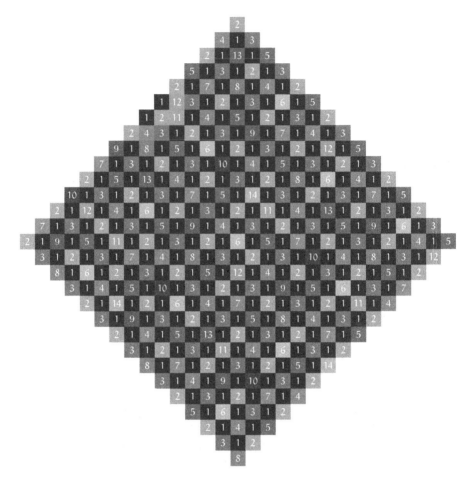

Fig. 9: A valid coloring of $D_{14,14,6}$. No valid coloring exists for this grid with a full chessboard pattern of 1's.

6   Concluding Remarks and Future Work

We have proved $\chi_\rho(\mathbb{Z}^2) = 15$ by using several SAT-solving techniques, in what constitutes a new success story for automated reasoning tools applied to combinatorial problems. Moreover, we believe that several of our contributions in this work might be applicable to other settings and problems. Indeed, we have obtained a better encoding by reverse engineering BVA, and designed a split algorithm that works well coupled with the new encoding; this experience suggests the *split-encoding compatibility* as a new key variable to pay attention to when solving combinatorial problems under the *Cube And Conquer* paradigm. As for future work, it is natural to study whether our techniques can be used to improve other known bounds in the packing-coloring area (see e.g., [3]), as well as to other families of coloring problems, such as *distance colorings* [14].

Acknowledgements We thank the Pittsburgh Supercomputing Center for allowing us to use Bridges2 [4] in our experiments. We thank as well the anonymous reviewers for their comments and suggestions. We also thank Donald Knuth for his thorough comments and suggestions. The first author thanks the Facebook group *"actually good math problems"*, from where he first learned about this problem, and in particular to Dylan Pizzo for his post about this problem.

References

1. Appel, K., Haken, W.: Every planar map is four colorable. Part I: Discharging. Illinois Journal of Mathematics **21**(3), 429 – 490 (1977)
2. Biere, A., Fazekas, K., Fleury, M., Heisinger, M.: CaDiCaL, Kissat, Paracooba, Plingeling and Treengeling entering the SAT Competition 2020. In: Balyo, T., Froleyks, N., Heule, M., Iser, M., Järvisalo, M., Suda, M. (eds.) Proc. of SAT Competition 2020 – Solver and Benchmark Descriptions. Department of Computer Science Report Series B, vol. B-2020-1, pp. 51–53. University of Helsinki (2020)
3. Brešar, B., Ferme, J., Klavžar, S., Rall, D.F.: A survey on packing colorings. Discussiones Mathematicae Graph Theory **40**(4), 923 (2020)
4. Brown, S.T., Buitrago, P., Hanna, E., Sanielevici, S., Scibek, R., Nystrom, N.A.: Bridges-2: A Platform for Rapidly-Evolving and Data Intensive Research, pp. 1–4. Association for Computing Machinery, New York, NY, USA (2021)
5. Buss, S., Thapen, N.: DRAT proofs, propagation redundancy, and extended resolution. In: Janota, M., Lynce, I. (eds.) Theory and Applications of Satisfiability Testing – SAT 2019. pp. 71–89. Springer International Publishing, Cham (2019)
6. Crawford, J., Ginsberg, M., Luks, E., Roy, A.: Symmetry-breaking predicates for search problems. In: Proc. KR'96, 5th Int. Conf. on Knowledge Representation and Reasoning, pp. 148–159. Morgan Kaufmann (1996)
7. Ekstein, J., Fiala, J., Holub, P., Lidický, B.: The packing chromatic number of the square lattice is at least 12. CoRR **abs/1003.2291** (2010), http://arxiv.org/abs/1003.2291
8. Fiala, J., Klavžar, S., Lidický, B.: The packing chromatic number of infinite product graphs. Eur. J. Comb. **30**(5), 1101–1113 (jul 2009)
9. Finbow, A.S., Rall, D.F.: On the packing chromatic number of some lattices. Discrete Applied Mathematics **158**(12), 1224–1228 (2010), traces from LAGOS'07 IV Latin American Algorithms, Graphs, and Optimization Symposium Puerto Varas - 2007
10. Goddard, W., Hedetniemi, S., Hedetniemi, S., Harris, J., Rall, D.: Broadcast chromatic numbers of graphs. Ars Comb. **86** (01 2008)
11. Heule, M.J.H.: The DRAT format and drat-trim checker. CoRR **abs/1610.06229** (2016), http://arxiv.org/abs/1610.06229
12. Heule, M.J.H., Biere, A.: What a difference a variable makes. In: Beyer, D., Huisman, M. (eds.) Tools and Algorithms for the Construction and Analysis of Systems. pp. 75–92. Springer International Publishing, Cham (2018)
13. Heule, M.J.H., Kullmann, O., Wieringa, S., Biere, A.: Cube and conquer: Guiding CDCL SAT solvers by lookaheads. In: Eder, K., Lourenço, J., Shehory, O. (eds.) Hardware and Software: Verification and Testing. pp. 50–65. Springer Berlin Heidelberg, Berlin, Heidelberg (2012)
14. Kramer, F., Kramer, H.: A survey on the distance-colouring of graphs. Discrete Mathematics **308**(2), 422–426 (2008)

15. Kullmann, O.: On a generalization of extended resolution. Discrete Applied Mathematics **96-97**, 149–176 (1999)
16. Manthey, N., Heule, M.J.H., Biere, A.: Automated reencoding of boolean formulas. In: Proceedings of Haifa Verification Conference 2012 (2012)
17. Martin, B., Raimondi, F., Chen, T., Martin, J.: The packing chromatic number of the infinite square lattice is less than or equal to 16 (2015), `http://arxiv.org/abs/1510.02374v1`
18. Martin, B., Raimondi, F., Chen, T., Martin, J.: The packing chromatic number of the infinite square lattice is between 13 and 15. Discrete Applied Mathematics **225**, 136–142 (2017)
19. Neiman, D., Mackey, J., Heule, M.J.H.: Tighter bounds on directed Ramsey number R(7). Graphs and Combinatorics **38**(5), 156 (2022)
20. Schwenk, A.: private communication with Wayne Goddard. (2002)
21. Soifer, A.: The Hadwiger–Nelson Problem, pp. 439–457. Springer International Publishing, Cham (2016)
22. Soukal, R., Holub, P.: A note on packing chromatic number of the square lattice. The Electronic Journal of Combinatorics **17**(1), #N17 (Mar 2010)
23. Subercaseaux, B., Heule, M.J.H.: The Packing Chromatic Number of the Infinite Square Grid Is at Least 14. In: Meel, K.S., Strichman, O. (eds.) 25th International Conference on Theory and Applications of Satisfiability Testing (SAT 2022). Leibniz International Proceedings in Informatics (LIPIcs), vol. 236, pp. 21:1–21:16. Schloss Dagstuhl – Leibniz-Zentrum für Informatik, Dagstuhl, Germany (2022)
24. Subercaseaux, B., Heule, M.J.H.: The packing chromatic number of the infinite square grid is 15 (2023), `https://arxiv.org/abs/2301.09757`

Active Learning for SAT Solver Benchmarking

Tobias Fuchs[✉] [ORCID], Jakob Bach [ORCID], and Markus Iser [ORCID]

Karlsruhe Institute of Technology (KIT), Karlsruhe, Germany
info@tobiasfuchs.de, {jakob.bach,markus.iser}@kit.edu

Abstract. Benchmarking is a crucial phase when developing algorithms. This also applies to solvers for the SAT (propositional satisfiability) problem. Benchmark selection is about choosing representative problem instances that reliably discriminate solvers based on their runtime. In this paper, we present a dynamic benchmark selection approach based on active learning. Our approach predicts the rank of a new solver among its competitors with minimum runtime and maximum rank prediction accuracy. We evaluated this approach on the Anniversary Track dataset from the 2022 SAT Competition. Our selection approach can predict the rank of a new solver after about 10 % of the time it would take to run the solver on all instances of this dataset, with a prediction accuracy of about 92 %. We also discuss the importance of instance families in the selection process. Overall, our tool provides a reliable way for solver engineers to determine a new solver's performance efficiently.

Keywords: Propositional satisfiability · Benchmarking · Active learning

1 Introduction

One of the main phases of algorithm engineering is benchmarking. This also applies to propositional satisfiability (SAT), the archetypal $\mathcal{NP}$-complete problem. Benchmarking is, however, quite expensive regarding the runtime of experiments. While benchmarking a single SAT solver might still be feasible, developing new, competitive SAT solvers requires extensive experimentation with a variety of ideas [8,2]. In particular, a new solver idea is rarely best on the first try. Thus, it is highly desirable to reduce benchmarking time and discard unpromising ideas early, allowing to test more approaches or spend more time on promising ones. The field of SAT solver benchmarking is well established, but traditional benchmark selection approaches do not optimize benchmark runtime. Instead, they focus on selecting a representative set of instances for scoring solvers [10,15]. For the latter, SAT Competitions typically employ the PAR-2 score, i.e., the average runtime with a penalty of 2τ for timeouts with time-limit τ [8].

In this paper, we present a novel benchmark selection approach based on active learning. Our approach can predict the rank of a new solver with high accuracy in only a fraction of the time needed to evaluate the complete benchmark. Definition 1 specifies the problem we address.

S. Sankaranarayanan and N. Sharygina (Eds.): TACAS 2023, LNCS 13993, pp. 407–425, 2023
https://doi.org/10.1007/978-3-031-30823-9_21

Definition 1 (New-Solver Problem). *Given solvers $\mathcal{A}$, instances $\mathcal{I}$, runtimes $r \colon \mathcal{A} \times \mathcal{I} \to [0, \tau]$ with time-limit τ, and a new solver $\hat{a} \notin \mathcal{A}$, incrementally select benchmark instances from $\mathcal{I}$ to maximize the confidence in predicting the rank of $\hat{a}$ while minimizing the total benchmark runtime.*

Note that our scenario assumes knowing the runtimes of all solvers, except the new one, on all instances. One could also imagine a collaborative filtering scenario, where runtimes are only partially known [23,25].

Our approach satisfies several desirable criteria for benchmarking: Rather than outputting a binary classification, i.e., whether the new solver is worse than an existing solver or not, we provide a *scoring* function that shows by which margin a solver is worse and how similar it is to existing solvers. In particular, our approach enables *ranking* the new solver amidst a set of existing solvers. For this ranking, we do not even need to predict exact solver runtimes, which is trickier. Further, we optimize the *runtime* that our strategy needs to arrive at its conclusion. We use instance and runtime *features*. Moreover, we select instances *non-randomly* and *incrementally*. In particular, we consider runtime information from already done experiments when choosing the next. By doing so, we can control the properties of the benchmarking approach, such as its required runtime. Our approach is *scalable* in that it ranks a new solver $\hat{a}$ among any number of known solvers $\mathcal{A}$. In particular, we only subsample the benchmark once instead of comparing pairwise against each other solver [21].

We evaluate our approach with the SAT Competition 2022 Anniversary Track dataset [2], consisting of 5355 instances and runtimes of 28 solvers. We perform cross-validation by treating each solver once as the new solver and learning to predict the PAR-2 rank of that solver. On average, our predictions reach about 92 % accuracy with only about 10 % of the runtime required to evaluate these solvers on the complete set of instances.

Our entire source code[1] and experimental data[2] are available on GitHub.

2   Related Work

Benchmarking is not only of high interest in many fields but also an active research area on its own. Recent studies show that benchmark selection is challenging for multiple reasons. Biased benchmarks can easily lead to fallacious interpretations [7]. Benchmarking also has many interchangeable parts, such as the performance measures used, how measurement points are aggregated, and how missing values are handled. Questionable research practices could alter these elements a-posteriori to meet expectations, thereby skewing the results [27]. In the following, we discuss related work from the areas of static benchmark selection, algorithm configuration, incremental benchmark selection, and active learning. Table 1 compares the most relevant approaches, which all pursue slightly different goals. Thus, our approach is *not* a general improvement over the others but the only one fully aligned with Definition 1.

---

[1] https://github.com/mathefuchs/al-for-sat-solver-benchmarking
[2] https://github.com/mathefuchs/al-for-sat-solver-benchmarking-data

Table 1: Comparison of features of our benchmark-selection approach, the static benchmark-selection approach by Hoos et al. [15], the algorithm configuration system SMAC [16], and the active-learning approaches by Matricon et al. [21].

Feature	Hoos [15]	SMAC [16]	Matricon [21]	Our approach
Ranking/Scoring	✓	✗	(✓)	✓
Runtime Minimization	✗	✓	✓	✓
Incremental/Non-Random	✗	✗	✓	✓
Scalability	✓	✓	✗	✓

Static Benchmark Selection. Benchmark selection is essential for competitions, e.g., the SAT Competition. In such competitions, the organizers define the rules for composing the benchmarks. These selection strategies are primarily static, i.e., they do not depend on particular solvers to distinguish. Balint et al. provide an overview of benchmark-selection criteria in different solver competitions [1]. Froleyks et al. describe benchmark selection in recent SAT competitions [8]. Manthey and Möhle find that competition benchmarks might contain redundant instances and propose a feature-based approach to remove redundancy [20]. Mısır presents a feature-based approach to reduce benchmarks by matrix factorization and clustering [24].

Hoos et al. [15] discuss which properties are most desirable when selecting SAT benchmark instances. The selection criteria are instance variety to avoid over-fitting, adapted instance hardness (not too easy but also not too hard), and avoiding duplicate instances. To filter too similar instances, they use a distance-based approach with the SATzilla features [37,38]. The approach does, however, not optimize for benchmark *runtime* and selects instances *randomly*, apart from constraints on the instance hardness and feature distance.

Algorithm Configuration. Further related work can be found within the field of algorithm configuration [14,32], e.g., the configuration system SMAC [16]. Thereby, the goal is to tune SAT solvers for a given sub-domain of problem instances. Although this task is different from our goal, e.g., we do not need to navigate the configuration space, there are similarities to our approach as well. For example, SMAC also employs an iterative, model-based selection procedure, though for configurations rather than instances. An algorithm configurator, however, cannot be used to *rank/score* a new solver since algorithm configuration solemnly seeks to find the best-performing configuration. Also, while using a model-based selection strategy to sample configurations, instance selection is made *randomly*, i.e., without building a model over instances.

Incremental Benchmark Selection. Matricon et al. present an incremental benchmark selection approach [21]. Their *per-set efficient algorithm selection problem* (PSEAS) is similar to our *New-Solver Problem* (cf. Definition 1). Given a pair of SAT solvers, they iteratively select a subset of instances until the

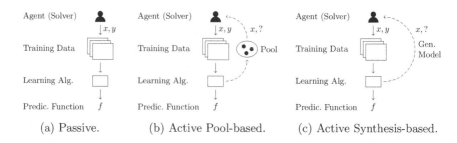

Fig. 1: Types of machine learning (depiction inspired by Rubens et.al. [29]).

desired confidence level is reached to decide which of the two solvers is better. The selection of instances depends on the choice of the solvers to distinguish. They calculate a scoring metric for all unselected instances, run the experiment with the highest score, and update the confidence. Their approach ticks off most of our desired features in Table 1. However, the approach only compares solvers binarily rather than providing a *scoring*. Thus, it is unclear how similar two given solvers are or on which instances they behave similarly. Moreover, a significant shortcoming is the lacking *scalability* with the number of solvers. Comparing only pairs of solvers, evaluating a new solver requires sampling a separate benchmark for each existing solver. In contrast, our approach allows comparing a new solver against a set of existing solvers by sampling only one benchmark.

Active Learning. Prediction models in passive machine learning are trained on datasets with given instance labels (cf. Fig. 1a). In contrast, active learning (AL) starts with no or little labeled data. It repeatedly selects interesting problem instances for which to acquire labels, aiming to gradually improve the prediction model (cf. Fig. 1b). AL methods are especially beneficial if acquiring labels is computationally expensive, like obtaining solver runtimes. Without AL methods, it is not obvious which instances to label and which not. On the one hand, we want to maximize the utility an instance provides to our model, i.e., rank prediction accuracy, and on the other hand, minimize the cost, i.e., predicted runtime, associated with the instance's acquisition. Thus, we strive for an accurate prediction model without having to label every data point.

Rubens et. al. [29] survey active-learning advances. While synthesis-based AL methods [5,9,34] generate instances for labeling, pool-based methods [11,13,19] rely on a fixed set of unlabeled instances to sample from. Recent synthesis-based methods within the field of SAT solving show how to generate problem instances with desired properties [5,9]. This goal is, however, orthogonal to ours. While those approaches want to generate instances on which a solver is good or bad, we want to predict whether a solver is good or bad on an existing benchmark. Volpato and Guangyan use pool-based AL to learn an instance-specific algorithm selector [35]. Rather than benchmarking a solver's overall performance, their goal is to recommend the best solver out of a set of solvers for each SAT instance.

Algorithm 1: Incremental Benchmarking Framework

Input: Solvers $\mathcal{A}$, Instances $\mathcal{I}$, Runtimes $r : \mathcal{A} \times \mathcal{I} \to [0, \tau]$, Solver $\hat{a}$
Output: Predicted Score of $\hat{a}$, Measured Runtimes $\mathcal{R}$

1 $\mathcal{M} \leftarrow$ initModel $(\mathcal{A}, \mathcal{I}, r, \hat{a})$ // cf. Section 3.1

2 $\mathcal{R} \leftarrow \emptyset$

3 **while** not stop $(\mathcal{M})$ **do**   // cf. Section 3.3

4 $\quad$ $e \leftarrow$ selectNextInstance $(\mathcal{M})$ // cf. Section 3.2

5 $\quad$ $t \leftarrow$ runExperiment $(\hat{a}, e)$ // Runs $\hat{a}$ on e with timeout τ

6 $\quad$ $\mathcal{R} \leftarrow \mathcal{R} \cup \{(e, t)\}$

7 $\quad$ updateModel $(\mathcal{M}, \mathcal{R})$ // cf. Section 3.1

8 $s_{\hat{a}} \leftarrow$ predictScore$(\mathcal{M})$ // cf. Section 3.1

9 **return** $(s_{\hat{a}}, \mathcal{R})$

---

3 Active Learning for SAT Solver Benchmarking

Algorithm 1 outlines our benchmarking framework. Given a set of solvers $\mathcal{A}$, instances $\mathcal{I}$ and runtimes r, we first initialize a prediction model $\mathcal{M}$ for the new solver $\hat{a} \notin \mathcal{A}$ (Line 1). The prediction model $\mathcal{M}$ is used to repeatedly select an instance (Line 4) for benchmarking $\hat{a}$ (Line 5). The acquired result is subsequently used to update the prediction model $\mathcal{M}$ (Line 7). When the stopping criterion is met (Line 3), we quit the benchmarking loop and predict the final score of $\hat{a}$ (Line 8). Algorithm 1 returns the predicted score of $\hat{a}$ as well as the acquired instances and runtime measurements (Line 9).

Section 3.1 describes the underlying prediction model $\mathcal{M}$ and specifies how we may derive a solver ranking from it. We discuss criteria for selecting instances in Section 3.2. Section 3.3 concludes with possible stopping conditions.

3.1 Solver Model

The model M provides a runtime-label prediction function $f : \hat{\mathcal{A}} \times \mathcal{I} \to \mathbb{R}$ for all solvers $\hat{\mathcal{A}} := \mathcal{A} \cup \{\hat{a}\}$. This prediction function powers instance selection as described in Section 3.2. During model updates (Algorithm 1, Line 7), f is trained to predict a transformed version of the acquired runtimes $\mathcal{R}$. We describe the runtime transformation in the subsequent section. The features described in Section 4.2 serve as the input to the model. Further, note that we build a new prediction model in each iteration since running experiments (Line 5) dominates the runtime of model training by magnitudes. Finally, we predict the score of the new solver $\hat{a}$ with the prediction function f (Line 8).

Runtime Transformation. For the prediction model M, we transform the real-valued runtimes into discrete runtime labels on a per-instance basis. For each instance $e \in \mathcal{I}$, we use a clustering algorithm to assign the runtimes in $\{r(a, e) \mid a \in \mathcal{A}\}$ to one of k clusters $C_1, \ldots, C_k$ such that the fastest runtimes for the instance e are in cluster C_1 and the slowest are in cluster C_{k-1}. Timeouts τ always form a separate cluster C_k. The runtime transformation function $\gamma_k : \mathcal{A} \times \mathcal{I} \rightarrow \{1, \dots, k\}$ is then specified as follows:

$$\gamma_k(a, e) = j \;\Leftrightarrow\; r(a, e) \in C_j$$

Given an instance $e \in \mathcal{I}$, a solver $a \in \mathcal{A}$ belongs to the $\gamma_k(a, e)$-fastest solvers on instance e. In preliminary experiments, we achieved higher accuracy for predicting such discrete runtime labels than for predicting raw runtimes. Research on portfolio solvers has also shown that discretization works well in practice [4,26].

Ranking Solvers. To determine solver ranks, we use the transformed runtimes $\gamma_k(a, e)$ in the adapted scoring function $s_k : \mathcal{A} \rightarrow [1, 2 \cdot k]$ as follows:

$$s_k(a) := \frac{1}{|\mathcal{I}|} \sum_{e \in \mathcal{I}} \gamma_k'(a, e) \qquad \gamma_k'(a, e) := \begin{cases} 2 \cdot \gamma_k(a, e) & \text{if } \gamma_k(a, e) = k \\ \gamma_k(a, e) & \text{otherwise} \end{cases} \tag{1}$$

I.e., we apply PAR-2 scoring, which is commonly used in SAT competitions [8], on the discrete labels. The scoring function s_k induces a ranking among solvers.

3.2   Instance Selection

Selecting an instance based on the model is a core functionality of our framework (cf. Algorithm 1, Line 4). In this section, we introduce two instance sampling strategies, one that minimizes uncertainty and one that maximizes information gain. Both strategies use the model's label-prediction function f and are inspired by existing work within the realms of active learning [30]. These methods require the model's predictions to include probabilities for the k discrete runtime labels. Let $f' : \hat{\mathcal{A}} \times \mathcal{I} \rightarrow [0, 1]^k$ denote this modified prediction function. In the following, the set $\tilde{\mathcal{I}} \subseteq \mathcal{I}$ denotes the instances that have already been sampled.

Uncertainty Sampling. The uncertainty sampling strategy selects the instance closest to the model's decision boundary, i.e., we select the instance $e \in \mathcal{I} \setminus \tilde{\mathcal{I}}$ that minimizes $U(e)$, which is specified as follows:

$$U(e) := \left| \frac{1}{k} - \max_{n \in \{1, \dots, k\}} f'(\hat{a}, e)_n \right|$$

Information-Gain Sampling. The information-gain sampling strategy selects the instance with the highest expected entropy reduction regarding the runtime labels of the instance. To be more specific, we select the instance $e \in \mathcal{I} \setminus \tilde{\mathcal{I}}$ that maximizes $IG(e)$, which is specified as follows:

$$IG(e) := H(e) - \sum_{n=1}^{k} f'(\hat{a}, e)_n \, \hat{H}_n(e)$$

Here, $H(e)$ denotes the entropy of the runtime labels $\gamma(a, e)$ over all $a \in \mathcal{A}$ and $H(e, n)$ denotes the entropy of these labels plus n as the runtime label for $\hat{a}$. The term $\hat{H}_n(e)$ is computed for every possible runtime label $n \in \{1, \ldots, k\}$. By maximizing information gain, we select instances that identify solvers with similar behavior.

3.3 Stopping Criteria

In this section, we present the two dynamic stopping criteria in our experiments, the Wilcoxon and the ranking stopping criterion (cf. Algorithm 1, Line 3).

Wilcoxon Stopping Criterion. The Wilcoxon stopping criterion stops the active-learning process when we are confident enough that the predicted runtime labels of the new solver are sufficiently different from existing solvers. This criterion is loosely inspired by Matricon et. al. [21]. We use the average p-value $W_{\hat{a}}$ of a Wilcoxon signed-rank test $w(S, P)$ of the two runtime label distributions $S = \{\gamma(a, e) \mid e \in \mathcal{I}\}$ for an existing solver a and $P = \{f(\hat{a}, e) \mid e \in \mathcal{I}\}$ for the new solver $\hat{a}$:

$$W_{\hat{a}} := \frac{1}{|\mathcal{A}|} \sum_{a \in \mathcal{A}} w(S, P)$$

To improve the stability of this criterion, we use an exponential moving average to smooth out outliers and stop as soon as $W_{\exp}^{(i)}$ drops below a fixed threshold:

$$W_{\exp}^{(0)} := 1$$
$$W_{\exp}^{(i)} := \beta W_{\hat{a}} + (1 - \beta) W_{\exp}^{(i-1)}$$

Ranking Stopping Criterion. The ranking stopping criterion is less sophisticated in comparison. It stops the active-learning process if the ranking induced by the model's predictions (Equation 1) remained unchanged within the last l iterations. However, the concrete values of the predicted score $s_{\hat{a}}$ might still change. We are solemnly interested in the induced ranking in this case.

4 Experimental Design

Given all the previously presented instantiations for Algorithm 1, this section outlines our experimental design, including our evaluation framework, used data sets, hyper-parameter choices, and implementation details.

4.1 Evaluation Framework

As stated in the Introduction, this work addresses the *New-Solver Problem* (cf. Definition 1). As described in Section 3.1, a prediction model $\mathcal{M}$ provides us with an estimated scoring $s_{\hat{a}}$ for the new solver $\hat{a}$.

Algorithm 2: Evaluation Framework

Input: Solvers $\mathcal{A}$, Instances $\mathcal{I}$, Runtimes $r : \mathcal{A} \times \mathcal{I} \to [0, \tau]$
Output: Average Ranking Accuracy $\bar{O}_{\text{acc}}$, Average Fraction of Runtime $\bar{O}_{\text{rt}}$

1 $O \leftarrow \emptyset$

2 **for** $\hat{a} \in \mathcal{A}$ **do**

3 $\quad\mathcal{A}' \leftarrow \mathcal{A} \setminus \{\hat{a}\}$

4 $\quad(s_{\hat{a}}, \mathcal{R}) \leftarrow \text{runALAlgorithm}(\mathcal{A}', \mathcal{I}, r, \hat{a})$ $\quad\quad$ *// Refer to Algorithm 1*

$\quad$ *// Determine Ranking Accuracy*

5 $\quad O_{\text{acc}} \leftarrow 0$

6 $\quad$ **for** $a \in \mathcal{A}$ **do**

7 $\quad\quad$ **if** $\left(s_k(a) - s_{\hat{a}}\right) \cdot \left(\text{par}_2(a) - \text{par}_2(\hat{a})\right) > 0$ **then**

8 $\quad\quad\quad O_{\text{acc}} \leftarrow O_{\text{acc}} + \frac{1}{|\mathcal{A}|}$

$\quad$ *// Determine Runtime Fraction*

9 $\quad r \leftarrow \sum_{e \in \mathcal{I}} r(\hat{a}, e)$

10 $\quad O_{\text{rt}} \leftarrow 0$

11 $\quad$ **for** $e \in \mathcal{I}$ **do**

12 $\quad\quad$ **if** $\exists t, (e, t) \in \mathcal{R}$ **then**

13 $\quad\quad\quad O_{\text{rt}} \leftarrow O_{\text{rt}} + \frac{t}{r}$

14 $\quad O \leftarrow O \cup \{(O_{\text{acc}}, O_{\text{rt}})\}$

15 $(\bar{O}_{\text{acc}}, \bar{O}_{\text{rt}}) \leftarrow \text{average}(O)$

16 **return** $(\bar{O}_{\text{acc}}, \bar{O}_{\text{rt}})$

To evaluate a concrete instantiation of Algorithm 1, i.e., a concrete choice for all the sub-routines, we perform cross-validation on our set of solvers. Algorithm 2 shows this. That means each solver plays the role of the new solver $\hat{a}$ once (Line 2). Note that the *new* solver in each iteration is excluded from the set of solvers $\mathcal{A}$ to avoid data leakage (Line 3). After running our active-learning framework for solver $\hat{a}$ (Line 4), we compute the value of both our optimization goals, i.e., ranking accuracy and runtime. We define the *ranking accuracy* $O_{\text{acc}} \in [0, 1]$ (higher is better) by the fraction of pairs $(\hat{a}, a)$ for all $a \in \mathcal{A}$ that are decided correctly regarding the ground-truth scoring par_2 (Lines 5-8). The *fraction of runtime* that the algorithm needs to arrive at its conclusion is denoted by $O_{\text{rt}} \in [0, 1]$ (lower is better). This metric puts the runtime summed over the sampled instances in relation to the runtime summed over all instances in the dataset (Lines 9-13). Finally, we compute averages of the output metrics in Line 15 after we have collected all cross-validation results in Line 14. Overall, we want to find an approach that maximizes

$$O_\delta := \delta O_{\text{acc}} + (1 - \delta)(1 - O_{\text{rt}}) \ , \tag{2}$$

whereby $\delta \in [0, 1]$ allows for linear weighting between the two optimization goals O_{acc} and O_{rt}. Plotting the approaches that maximize O_δ for all $\delta \in [0, 1]$ on an O_{rt}-O_{acc}-diagram provides us with a Pareto front of the best approaches for different optimization-goal weightings.

4.2 Data

In our experiments, we work with the dataset of the SAT Competition 2022 Anniversary Track [2]. The dataset consists of 5355 instances with respective runtime data of 28 sequential SAT solvers. We also use a database of 56 instance features[3] from the Global Benchmark Database (GBD) by Iser et al. [17]. They comprise instance size features and node distribution statistics for several graph representations of SAT instances, among others, and are primarily inspired by the SATzilla 2012 features described in [38]. All features are numeric and free of missing values. We drop 10 out of 56 features because of zero variance. Overall, prediction models have access to 46 instance features and 27 runtime features, i.e., excluding the current new solver $\hat{a}$.

Additionally, we retrieve instance-family information[4] to evaluate the composition of our sampled benchmarks. Instance families comprise instances from the same application domain, e.g., planning, cryptography, etc., and are a valuable tool for analyzing solver performance.

For hyper-parameter tuning, we randomly sample 10 % of the complete set of 5355 instances with stratification regarding the instances' family. All instance families that are too *small*, i.e., 10 % of them corresponds to less than one instance, are put into one meta-family for stratification. This *tuning dataset* allows for a more extensive exploration of the hyper-parameter space.

4.3 Hyper-parameters

Given Algorithm 1, there are several possible instantiations for the three subroutines, i.e., *ranking*, *selection*, and *stopping*. Also, there are different choices for the runtime-label prediction model and runtime discretization. We describe these experimental configurations in the following.

Ranking. Regarding *ranking* (cf. Section 3.1), we experiment with the following approaches and hyper-parameter values:

- Observed PAR-2 ranking of already sampled instances
- Predicted runtime-label ranking
  - History size: Consider the latest 1, 10, 20, 30, or 40 predictions within a voting approach for stability. The latest x predictions for each instance vote on the instance's winning label.
  - Fallback threshold: If the difference of scores between the new solver $\hat{a}$ and another solver drops below 0.01, 0.05, or 0.1, use the partially observed PAR-2 ranking as a tie-breaker.

---

[3] https://benchmark-database.de/getdatabase/base_db
[4] https://benchmark-database.de/getdatabase/meta_db

Selection. For *selection* (cf. Section 3.2), we experiment with the following methods and hyper-parameter values. Since the potential runtime of experiments is by magnitudes larger than the model's update time, we only consider incrementing our benchmark by one instance at a time rather than using batches, which is also proposed in current active-learning advances [31,34]. A drawback of this is the lack of parallel execution of runtime experiments.

- Random sampling
- Uncertainty sampling
  - Fallback threshold: Use random sampling for the first 0 %, 5 %, 10 %, 15 %, or 20 % of instances to explore the instance space.
  - Runtime scaling: Whether to normalize uncertainty scores per instance by the average runtime of solvers on it or use the absolute values.
- Information-gain sampling
  - Fallback threshold: Use random sampling for the first 0 %, 5 %, 10 %, 15 %, or 20 % of instances to explore the instance space.
  - Runtime scaling: Whether to normalize information-gain scores per instance by the average runtime of solvers on it or use the absolute values.

Stopping. For *stopping* decisions (cf. Section 3.3), we experiment with the following criteria and hyper-parameter values:

- Subset-size stopping criterion, using 10 % or 20 % of instances
- Ranking stopping criterion
  - Minimum amount: Sample at least 2 %, 8 %, 10 %, or 12 % of instances before applying the criterion.
  - Convergence duration: Stop if the predicted ranking stays the same for a number of sampled instances equal to 1 % or 2 % of all instances.
- Wilcoxon stopping criterion
  - Minimum amount: Sample at least 2 %, 8 %, 10 %, or 12 % of instances before applying the criterion.
  - Average of p-values to drop below: 5 %.
  - Exponential-moving average: Incorporate previous significance values by using an EMA with $\beta = 0.1$ or $\beta = 0.7$.

Prediction model. Our experiments only use one model configuration for runtime-label prediction since an exhaustive grid search would be infeasible. In preliminary experiments, we compared various model types from *scikit-learn* [28]. In particular, we conducted nested cross-validation, including hyper-parameter tuning, and used Matthews Correlation Coefficient [12,22] to assess the performance for predicting runtime labels. Our final choice is a stacking ensemble [36] of two prediction models, a quadratic-discriminant analysis [33] and a random forest [3]. Both these models can learn non-linear relationships between the instance features and the runtime labels. Stacking means that another prediction model, in our case a simple decision tree, decides which of the two ensemble members makes the prediction on which instance.

Runtime discretization. To define prediction targets, i.e., discrete runtime labels, we use hierarchical clustering with $k = 3$ and a log-single-link criterion, which produced the most *useful* labels in preliminary experiments. We denote this adapted solver scoring function with s_3. In our chosen hierarchical procedure, each non-timeout runtime starts in a separate interval. We then gradually merge intervals whose single-link logarithmic distance is the smallest until the desired number of partitions is reached. Other clustering approaches that we tried include hierarchical clustering with mean-, median-, and complete-link criterion, as well as k-means and spectral clustering.

To obtain *useful* labels, we need to ensure that discretized labels still discriminate solvers and align with the actual PAR-2 ranking. We analyzed the ranking induced by s_3 in preliminary experiments with the SAT Competition 2022 Anniversary Track [2]. According to a Wilcoxon-signed-rank test with $\alpha = 0.05$, 87.83 % of solver pairs have significantly different scores after discretization, only a slight drop compared to 89.95 % before discretization. Further, our ranking approach correctly decides for almost all (about 97.45 %; $\sigma = 3.68$ %) solver pairs which solver is faster. In particular, the Spearman correlation of s_3 and PAR-2 ranking is about 0.988, which is very close to the optimal value of 1 [6]. All these results show that discretized runtimes are suitable for our framework.

4.4   Implementation Details

For reproducibility, our source code and data are available on GitHub (cf. footnotes in Section 1). Our code is implemented in PYTHON using *scikit-learn* [28] for making predictions and *gbd-tools* [17] for SAT-instance retrieval.

5   Evaluation

In this section, we evaluate our active-learning framework. First, we analyze and tune the different sub-routines of our framework on the tuning dataset. Next, we evaluate the best configurations with the full dataset. Finally, we analyze the importance of different instance families to our framework.

5.1   Hyper-Parameter Analysis

Our experiments follow the evaluation framework introduced in Section 4.1. Fig. 2 shows the performance of the approaches from Section 4.3 on O_{rt}-O_{acc}-diagrams for the hyper-parameter-tuning dataset. Evaluating a particular configuration with Algorithm 2 returns a point $(O_{\mathrm{rt}}, O_{\mathrm{acc}})$. We do not show intermediate results of the active-learning procedure but only the final results after stopping. The plotted lines represent the best-performing configurations per ranking approach (Fig. 2a), selection approach (Fig. 2b), and stopping criterion (Fig. 2c). In particular, we show the Pareto front, i.e., of all configurations that share a particular value of the plotted hyper-parameter, we take the maximum ranking accuracy over all remaining hyper-parameters *not* displayed in the corresponding plot.

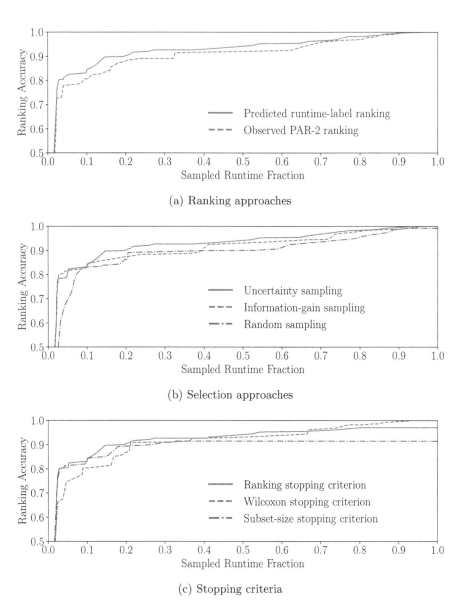

(a) Ranking approaches

(b) Selection approaches

(c) Stopping criteria

Fig. 2: O_{rt}-O_{acc}-diagrams comparing different hyper-parameter instantiations of our active-learning framework on the hyper-parameter-tuning dataset. The x-axis shows the ratio of total solver runtime on the sampled instances relative to all instances. The y-axis shows the ranking accuracy (cf. Section 4.1). Each line entails the front of Pareto-optimal configurations for the respective hyper-parameter instantiation.

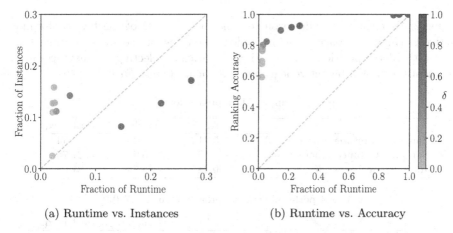

(a) Runtime vs. Instances   (b) Runtime vs. Accuracy

Fig. 3: Scatter plot comparing different instantiations of trade-off parameter δ for our active-learning framework on the hyper-parameter-tuning dataset. The x-axis shows the fraction of runtime O_{rt} of the sample, while the y-axes show the fraction of instances sampled and ranking accuracy, respectively. The color indicates the weighting between different optimization goals $\delta \in [0, 1]$. The larger δ, the more we favor accuracy over runtime.

Regarding ranking approaches (Fig. 2a), using the predicted s_3-induced runtime-label ranking consistently outperforms the partially observed PAR-2 ranking for each possible value of the trade-off parameter δ. This outcome is expected since selection decisions are not random. For example, we might sample more instances of one family if it benefits discrimination of solvers. While the partially observed PAR-2 score is skewed, the prediction model can account for this.

Regarding the selection approaches (Fig. 2b), uncertainty sampling performs best in most cases. However, information-gain sampling is beneficial if runtime is strongly favored (small δ; runtime fraction less than 5 %). This result aligns with our expectations: Information-gain sampling selects instances that maximize the expected reduction in entropy. This means we sample instances revealing similarities between solvers rather than differences, which helps to build a confident model quickly. However, the method cannot select helpful instances for distinguishing solvers later. Random sampling performs reasonably well but is outperformed by uncertainty sampling in all cases, showing the benefit of actively selecting instances based on a prediction model.

Regarding the stopping criteria (Fig. 2c), the ranking stopping criterion performs most consistently well. If accuracy is strongly favored (very high δ), the Wilcoxon stopping criterion performs better. The subset-size stopping criterion performs reasonably well but does not improve beyond a certain accuracy because of sampling a fixed subset of instances.

Fig. 3a shows an interesting consequence of weighting our optimization goals: If we, on the one hand, desire to get a *rough* estimate of a solver's performance

Table 2: Performance comparison (on the full dataset) of the best-performing active-learning approaches (*AL*), random sampling of the same runtime fraction with 1000 repetitions (*Random*), and statically selecting the instances most frequently sampled by active-learning approaches (*Most Freq.*)

(a) Best-performing AL approach for $\delta \in [0.2, 0.7]$

	AL	Random	Most Freq.
Sampled Runtime Fraction (%)	5.41	5.43	5.44
Sampled Instance Fraction (%)	26.53	5.43	27.75
Ranking Accuracy (%)	90.48	88.54	81.08

(b) Best-performing AL approach for $\delta \in (0.7, 0.8]$

	AL	Random	Most Freq.
Sampled Runtime Fraction (%)	10.35	10.37	10.37
Sampled Instance Fraction (%)	5.24	10.37	36.96
Ranking Accuracy (%)	92.33	91.61	84.52

fast (low δ), approaches favor selecting many *easy* instances. In particular, the fraction of sampled instances is larger than the fraction of runtime. By having many observations, it is easier to build a model. If we, on the other hand, desire to get a *good* estimate of a solver's performance in a moderate amount of time (high δ), approaches favor selecting few, *difficult* instances. In particular, the fraction of instances is smaller than the fraction of runtime.

Furthermore, Fig. 3b reveals which values make the most sense for δ. The range $\delta \in [0.2, 0.8]$, thereby, corresponds to the points with a runtime fraction between 0.03 and 0.22 We consider this region to be most promising, analogous to the *elbow* method in cluster analysis [18].

5.2 Full-Dataset Evaluation

Having selected the most promising hyper-parameters, we run our active-learning experiments on the complete Anniversary Track dataset (5355 instances). The aforementioned range $\delta \in [0.2, 0.8]$ only results in two distinct configurations. The best-performing approach for $\delta \in [0.2, 0.7]$ uses the predicted runtime-label ranking, information-gain sampling, and ranking stopping criterion. It can predict a new solver's PAR-2 ranking with 90.48 % accuracy (O_{acc}) in only 5.41 % of the full evaluation time (O_{rt}). The best-performing approach for $\delta \in (0.7, 0.8]$ uses the predicted runtime-label ranking, uncertainty sampling, and ranking stopping criterion. It can predict a new solver's PAR-2 ranking with 92.33 % accuracy (O_{acc}) in only 10.35 % of the full evaluation time (O_{rt}).

Table 2 shows how both active-learning approaches (column *AL*) compare against two static baselines: *Random* samples instances until it reaches roughly the same fraction of runtime as the AL benchmark sets. We repeat sampling 1000 times and report average results. *Most Freq.* uses a static benchmark set

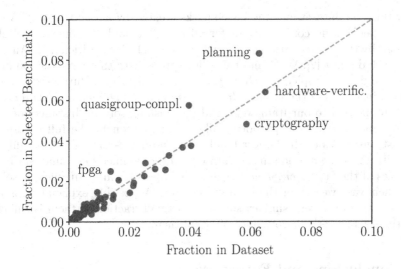

Fig. 4: Scatter plot showing the *importance* of different instance families to our framework on the full dataset. The x-axis shows the frequency of instance families in the dataset. The y-axis shows the average frequency of instance families in the samples selected by active learning. The dashed line represents families that occur with the same frequency in the dataset and samples.

consisting of those instances most frequently sampled by our active learning approach. In particular, we consider the average sampling frequency over all solvers and Pareto-optimal active-learning approaches.

Both our AL approaches perform better than random sampling. However, the performance differences are not significant regarding a Wilcoxon signed-rank test with $\alpha = 0.05$ and also depend on the fraction of sampled runtime (cf. Fig. 2b). A clear advantage of our approach is, though, that it indicates when to stop adding further instances, depending on the trade-off parameter δ. While the active-learning results are less strong on the full dataset than on the smaller tuning dataset, they still show the benefit of making benchmark selection dependent on the solvers to distinguish.

A static benchmark using the most frequently AL-sampled instances performs poorly, though, compared to active learning and random sampling. This outcome is somewhat expected since the static benchmark does not reflect the right balance of instance families: Families whose instances are uniform-randomly selected by AL, e.g., for different solvers, appear less often in this benchmark than families where some instances are sampled more often than others.

5.3   Instance-Family Importance

Selection decisions of our approach also reveal the importance of different instance families to our framework. Fig. 4 shows the occurrence of instance families within the dataset and the benchmarks created by active learning. We use the best-performing configurations for all $\delta \in [0, 1]$ and examine the selection decisions by the active-learning approach on the SAT Competition 2022 Anniversary Track dataset [2]. While most families appear with the same fraction in the dataset and the sampled benchmarks, a few outliers need further discussion. Problem instances of the families *fpga*, *quasigroup-completion*, and *planning* are especially helpful to our framework in distinguishing solvers. Instances of these families are selected over-proportionally in comparison to the full dataset. In contrast, instances of the largest family, i.e., *hardware-verification*, roughly appear with the same fraction in the dataset and the sampled benchmarks. Finally, instances of the family *cryptography* are less important in distinguishing solvers than their vast weight in the dataset suggests. A possible explanation is that these instances are very similar, such that a small fraction of them is sufficient to estimate a solver's performance on all of them.

6 Conclusions and Future Work

In this work, we have addressed the *New-Solver Problem*: Given a new solver, we want to find its ranking amidst competitors. Our approach provides accurate ranking predictions while needing significantly less runtime than a complete evaluation on a given benchmark set. On data from the SAT Competition 2022 Anniversary Track, we can determine a new solver's PAR-2 ranking with about 92 % accuracy while only needing 10 % of the full-evaluation time. We have evaluated several ranking algorithms, instance-selection approaches, and stopping criteria within our sequential active-learning framework. We also took a brief look at which instance families are the most prevalent in selection decisions.

Future work may compare further sub-routines for ranking, instance selection, and stopping. Additionally, one can apply our evaluation framework to arbitrary computation-intensive problems, e.g., other $\mathcal{NP}$-complete problems than SAT, as all discussed active-learning methods are problem-agnostic. Such problems share most of the relevant properties of SAT solving, i.e., there are established instance features, a complete benchmark is expensive, and traditional benchmark selection requires expert knowledge.

From the technical perspective, one could formulate runtime discretization as an optimization problem rather than addressing it empirically. Further, a major shortcoming of our current approach is the lack of parallelization, selecting instances one at a time. Benchmarking on a computing cluster with n cores benefits from having batches of n instances. However, bigger batch sizes n impede *active learning*. Also, it is unclear how to synchronize instance selection and updates of the prediction model without wasting too much runtime.

Acknowledgments. This work was supported by the Ministry of Science, Research and the Arts Baden-Württemberg, project *Algorithm Engineering for the Scalability Challenge (AESC)*.

References

1. Balint, A., Belov, A., Järvisalo, M., Sinz, C.: Overview and analysis of the SAT Challenge 2012 solver competition. Artif. Intell. **223**, 120–155 (2015). https://doi.org/10.1016/j.artint.2015.01.002
2. Balyo, T., Heule, M., Iser, M., Järvisalo, M., Suda, M. (eds.): Proceedings of SAT Competition 2022: Solver and Benchmark Descriptions. Department of Computer Science, University of Helsinki (2022), http://hdl.handle.net/10138/347211
3. Breiman, L.: Random forests. Mach. Learn. **45**(1), 5–32 (2001). https://doi.org/10.1023/A:1010933404324
4. Collautti, M., Malitsky, Y., Mehta, D., O'Sullivan, B.: SNNAP: solver-based nearest neighbor for algorithm portfolios. In: Proc. ECML PKDD. pp. 435–450 (2013). https://doi.org/10.1007/978-3-642-40994-3_28
5. Dang, N., Akgün, Ö., Espasa, J., Miguel, I., Nightingale, P.: A framework for generating informative benchmark instances. In: Proc. CP. pp. 18:1–18:18 (2022). https://doi.org/10.4230/LIPIcs.CP.2022.18
6. De Winter, J.C.F., Gosling, S.D., Potter, J.: Comparing the pearson and spearman correlation coefficients across distributions and sample sizes: A tutorial using simulations and empirical data. Psychol. Methods **21**(3), 273–290 (2016). https://doi.org/10.1037/met0000079
7. Dehghani, M., Tay, Y., Gritsenko, A.A., Zhao, Z., Houlsby, N., Diaz, F., Metzler, D., Vinyals, O.: The benchmark lottery. arXiv:2107.07002 [cs.LG] (2021), https://arxiv.org/abs/2107.07002
8. Froleyks, N., Heule, M., Iser, M., Järvisalo, M., Suda, M.: SAT Competition 2020. Artif. Intell. **301** (2021). https://doi.org/10.1016/j.artint.2021.103572
9. Garzón, I., Mesejo, P., Giráldez-Cru, J.: On the performance of deep generative models of realistic SAT instances. In: Proc. SAT. pp. 3:1–3:19 (2022). https://doi.org/10.4230/LIPIcs.SAT.2022.3
10. Gelder, A.V.: Careful ranking of multiple solvers with timeouts and ties. In: Proc. SAT. pp. 317–328 (2011). https://doi.org/10.1007/978-3-642-21581-0_25
11. Golbandi, N., Koren, Y., Lempel, R.: Adaptive bootstrapping of recommender systems using decision trees. In: Proc. WSDM. pp. 595–604 (2011). https://doi.org/10.1145/1935826.1935910
12. Gorodkin, J.: Comparing two k-category assignments by a k-category correlation coefficient. Comput. Biol. Chem. **28**(5–6), 367–374 (2004). https://doi.org/10.1016/j.compbiolchem.2004.09.006
13. Harpale, A., Yang, Y.: Personalized active learning for collaborative filtering. In: Proc. SIGIR. pp. 91–98 (2008). https://doi.org/10.1145/1390334.1390352
14. Hoos, H.H., Hutter, F., Leyton-Brown, K.: Automated configuration and selection of SAT solvers. In: Handbook of Satisfiability, chap. 12, pp. 481–507. IOS Press, 2 edn. (2021). https://doi.org/10.3233/FAIA200995
15. Hoos, H.H., Kaufmann, B., Schaub, T., Schneider, M.: Robust benchmark set selection for boolean constraint solvers. In: Proc. LION. pp. 138–152 (2013). https://doi.org/10.1007/978-3-642-44973-4_16
16. Hutter, F., Hoos, H.H., Leyton-Brown, K.: Sequential model-based optimization for general algorithm configuration. In: Proc. LION. pp. 507–523 (2011). https://doi.org/10.1007/978-3-642-25566-3_40
17. Iser, M., Sinz, C.: A problem meta-data library for research in SAT. In: Proc. PoS. pp. 144–152 (2018). https://doi.org/10.29007/gdbb

18. Kodinariya, T.M., Makwana, P.R.: Review on determining number of cluster in k-means clustering. Int. J. Adv. Res. Comput. Sci. Manage. Stud. **1**(6), 90–95 (2013), http://www.ijarcsms.com/docs/paper/volume1/issue6/V1I6-0015.pdf

19. Koren, Y., Bell, R.M., Volinsky, C.: Matrix factorization techniques for recommender systems. Computer **42**(8), 30–37 (2009). https://doi.org/10.1109/MC.2009.263

20. Manthey, N., Möhle, S.: Better evaluations by analyzing benchmark structure. In: Proc. PoS (2016), http://www.pragmaticsofsat.org/2016/reg/POS-16_paper_4.pdf

21. Matricon, T., Anastacio, M., Fijalkow, N., Simon, L., Hoos, H.H.: Statistical comparison of algorithm performance through instance selection. In: Proc. CP. pp. 43:1–43:21 (2021). https://doi.org/10.4230/LIPIcs.CP.2021.43

22. Matthews, B.W.: Comparison of the predicted and observed secondary structure of T4 phage lysozyme. Biochim. Biophys. Acta - Protein Struct. **405**(2), 442–451 (1975). https://doi.org/10.1016/0005-2795(75)90109-9

23. Mısır, M.: Data sampling through collaborative filtering for algorithm selection. In: Proc. IEEE CEC. pp. 2494–2501 (2017). https://doi.org/10.1109/CEC.2017.7969608

24. Mısır, M.: Benchmark set reduction for cheap empirical algorithmic studies. In: Proc. IEEE CEC. pp. 871–877 (2021). https://doi.org/10.1109/CEC45853.2021.9505012

25. Mısır, M., Sebag, M.: ALORS: An algorithm recommender system. Artif. Intell. **244**, 291–314 (2017). https://doi.org/10.1016/j.artint.2016.12.001

26. Ngoko, Y., Cérin, C., Trystram, D.: Solving SAT in a distributed cloud: A portfolio approach. Int. J. Appl. Math. Comput. Sci. **29**(2), 261–274 (2019). https://doi.org/10.2478/amcs-2019-0019

27. Nießl, C., Herrmann, M., Wiedemann, C., Casalicchio, G., Boulesteix, A.: Overoptimism in benchmark studies and the multiplicity of design and analysis options when interpreting their results. WIREs Data Min. Knowl. Discov. **12**(2) (2022). https://doi.org/10.1002/widm.1441

28. Pedregosa, F., Varoquaux, G., Gramfort, A., Michel, V., Thirion, B., Grisel, O., Blondel, M., Prettenhofer, P., Weiss, R., Dubourg, V., Vanderplas, J., Passos, A., Cournapeau, D., Brucher, M., Perrot, M., Édouard Duchesnay: Scikit-learn: Machine learning in Python. J. Mach. Learn. Res. **12**(85), 2825–2830 (2011), http://jmlr.org/papers/v12/pedregosa11a.html

29. Rubens, N., Elahi, M., Sugiyama, M., Kaplan, D.: Active learning in recommender systems. In: Recommender Systems Handbook, chap. 24, pp. 809–846. Springer, 2 edn. (2015). https://doi.org/10.1007/978-1-4899-7637-6_24

30. Settles, B.: Active learning literature survey. Tech. rep., University of Wisconsin-Madison, Department of Computer Sciences (2009), http://digital.library.wisc.edu/1793/60660

31. Sinha, S., Ebrahimi, S., Darrell, T.: Variational adversarial active learning. In: Proc. ICCV. pp. 5971–5980 (2019). https://doi.org/10.1109/ICCV.2019.00607

32. Stützle, T., López-Ibáñez, M., Pérez-Cáceres, L.: Automated algorithm configuration and design. In: Proc. GECCO. pp. 997–1019 (2022). https://doi.org/10.1145/3520304.3533663

33. Tharwat, A.: Linear vs. quadratic discriminant analysis classifier: a tutorial. Int. J. Appl. Pattern Recognit. **3**(2), 145–180 (2016). https://doi.org/10.1504/IJAPR.2016.079050

34. Tran, T., Do, T., Reid, I.D., Carneiro, G.: Bayesian generative active deep learning. In: Proc. ICML. pp. 6295–6304 (2019), http://proceedings.mlr.press/v97/tran19a.html
35. Volpato, R., Song, G.: Active learning to optimise time-expensive algorithm selection. arXiv:1909.03261 [cs.LG] (2019), https://arxiv.org/abs/1909.03261
36. Wolpert, D.H.: Stacked generalization. Neural Networks **5**(2), 241–259 (1992). https://doi.org/10.1016/S0893-6080(05)80023-1
37. Xu, L., Hutter, F., Hoos, H.H., Leyton-Brown, K.: SATzilla: Portfolio-based algorithm selection for SAT. J. Artif. Intell. Res. **32**, 565–606 (2008). https://doi.org/10.1613/jair.2490
38. Xu, L., Hutter, F., Hoos, H.H., Leyton-Brown, K.: Features for SAT. Tech. rep., University of British Columbia (2012), https://www.cs.ubc.ca/labs/beta/Projects/SATzilla/Report_SAT_features.pdf

ParaQooba: A Fast and Flexible Framework for Parallel and Distributed QBF Solving*

Maximilian Heisinger[1]([envelope]) [iD], Martina Seidl[1] [iD], and Armin Biere[2] [iD]

[1] JKU Linz, Linz, Austria, {maximilian.heisinger,martina.seidl}@jku.at
[2] ALU Freiburg, Freiburg, Germany, biere@informatik.uni-freiburg.de

Abstract. Over the last years, innovative parallel and distributed SAT solving techniques were presented that could impressively exploit the power of modern hardware and cloud systems. Two approaches were particularly successful: (1) search-space splitting in a Divide-and-Conquer (D&C) manner and (2) portfolio-based solving. The latter executes different solvers or configurations of solvers in parallel. For quantified Boolean formulas (QBFs), the extension of propositional logic with quantifiers, there is surprisingly little recent work in this direction compared to SAT. In this paper, we present ParaQooba, a novel framework for parallel and distributed QBF solving which combines D&C parallelization and distribution with portfolio-based solving. Our framework is designed in such a way that it can be easily extended and arbitrary sequential QBF solvers can be integrated out of the box, without any programming effort. We show how ParaQooba orchestrates the collaboration of different solvers for joint problem solving by performing an extensive evaluation on benchmarks from QBFEval'22, the most recent QBF competition.

1 Introduction

Quantified Boolean formulas (QBFs) extend propositional logic by quantifiers over the Boolean variables [2]. As a consequence, the decision problem of QBF (QSAT) is PSPACE complete, which is potentially harder than the NP-complete decision problem of propositional logic (SAT). Hence, the quantifiers allow for an efficient encoding of many reasoning problems from formal verification, synthesis, and planning [26] that most likely do not have a compact formulation in propositional logic. Over the last decade, considerable progress has been made in sequential QBF solving [22,21]. In contrast to SAT, where conflict-driven clause learning (CDCL) [19] is the predominant solving paradigm, in QBF solving different approaches of orthogonal strength have been presented. Besides QCDCL, the QBF variant of CDCL, which is implemented for example in the solver DepQBF [17], clausal abstraction as implemented in the solver Caqe [23] and abstraction-refinement based expansion as implemented in the solver RaReQs [13] are particularly successful [22,21]. All of these QBF solving approaches considerably benefit from preprocessing, i.e., an extra step before

---

* Supported by the LIT AI Lab funded by the State of Upper Austria.

S. Sankaranarayanan and N. Sharygina (Eds.): TACAS 2023, LNCS 13993, pp. 426–447, 2023.
https://doi.org/10.1007/978-3-031-30823-9_22

the actual solving in which certain redundancies of a formula are eliminated in a satisfiability-preserving way with the aim to make it easier for the solver [10].

Despite the vivid development in sequential QBF solving, only few approaches have been presented for parallel and distributed QBF solving [18]. The most recent parallel QBF solvers are HORDEQBF [1] which integrates sequential QCDCL-based solvers to obtain a parallel QBF solver and, more recently, a basic implementation of a QBF module based on the parallel SAT solver PARA-COOBA [6] with DEPQBF as its only backend solver. To the best of our knowledge, besides these two approaches no other parallel QBF solver has recently been presented. The situation in SAT is different: several very powerful parallel and distributed SAT solvers like MALLOB [24], PAINLESS [5], and the afore mentioned solver PARACOOBA [7] have been released. They show the potential of parallel and distributed approaches impressively by solving hard SAT instances, for example from multiplier verification [15].

In this paper, we present PARAQOOBA, a novel framework for parallel and distributed QBF solving that integrates search-space splitting based on the Divide-and-Conquer paradigm with portfolio solving. Our framework is built on top of the PARACOOBA SAT solving framework and extends its basic non-portfolio QBF solving module. PARAQOOBA reuses most of PARACOOBA's modules providing management and distribution of solver tasks. In addition, we implemented a very generic interface that allows the easy integration of any QBF solver binary into our framework.

Our main contributions are as follows:

- we present a new flexible framework for parallel and distributed QBF solving that combines D&C search-space splitting with portfolio solving;
- we show how different QBF solvers that are based on different solving approaches can be integrated seamlessly into our framework;
- we provide our framework as open-source project;
- we perform an extensive evaluation that demonstrates the power of our approach on various kinds of benchmarks.

PARAQOOBA is integrated into PARACOOBA's and available on GitHub:

https://github.com/maximaximal/paracooba

This paper is structured as follows: First we introduce some preliminaries required for the rest of the paper in the following section. We continue with related work in section 3. After that, section 4 summarizes concepts of the PARACOOBA solver framework used in our work. Then we introduce how we apply Divide-and-Conquer to solving QBF in section 5. Having introduced the background, we present our portfolio PARAQOOBA module in detail in section 6 and provide an extensive evaluation in section 7. Finally, we summarize our findings and conclude in section 8.

2   Preliminaries

We consider QBFs $Q.\varphi$ in *prenex conjunctive normal form* (PCNF) where the *prefix* Q is of the form $Q_1 x_1, \ldots, Q_n x_n$ with $Q \in \{\forall, \exists\}$. The *matrix* φ is a propositional formula over the variables $x_1, \ldots, x_n$ in conjunctive normal form (CNF). A formula in CNF is a conjunction ($\wedge$) of clauses. A *clause* is a disjunction ($\vee$) of literals. A literal is a variable x, a negated variable $\neg x$ or a (possibly negated) truth constant $\top$ (true) or $\bot$ (false). For a literal l, the expression $\bar{l}$ denotes x if $l = \neg x$ and it denotes $\neg x$ otherwise. We sometimes write a clause as a set of literals and a CNF formula as set of clauses. Further, it is often convenient to partition the quantifier prefix into *quantifier blocks*, i.e., maximal sets of consecutive sets of variables with the same quantifier type. For example, for the QBF $\forall x_1 \forall x_2 \exists y_1 \exists y_2.\varphi$ we also write $\forall X \exists Y.\varphi$ with $X = \{x_1, x_2\}$ and $Y = \{y_1, y_2\}$. With upper case letters $X, Y, \ldots$ (possibly subscripted), we usually denote sets of variables, while with lower case letters $x, y, \ldots$ (also possibly subscripted), we denote variables. If φ is CNF formula, then $\varphi_{x \leftarrow t}$ is the CNF formula obtained from φ by replacing all occurrences of variable x by truth constant $t \in \{\top, \bot\}$. Depending on the value of t, variable x is either set to true (if t is $\top$) or to false (if t is $\bot$). We define the semantics of QBFs as follows:

- a QBF $\forall X Q.\varphi$ is true iff both QBFs $\forall X' Q.\varphi_{x \leftarrow \bot}$ and $\forall X' Q.\varphi_{x \leftarrow \top}$ are true where $x \in X$ and $X' = X \setminus \{x\}$;
- a QBF $\exists Y Q.\varphi$ is true iff at least one of $\exists Y' Q.\varphi_{y \leftarrow \bot}$ and $\exists Y' Q.\varphi_{y \leftarrow \top}$ is true where $y \in Y$ and $Y' = Y \setminus \{y\}$.

Note that we assume that all variables of a QBF are quantified, i.e., we are considering closed formulas only. Further, we use standard semantics of conjunction, disjunction, negation, and truth constants. For example, the QBF $\phi_1 = \forall x \exists y.((x \vee y) \wedge (\neg x \vee \neg y))$ is true, while $\phi_2 = \exists y \forall x.((x \vee y) \wedge (\neg x \vee \neg y))$ is false. As we see already by this small example, the semantics impose an ordering on the variables w.r.t. the prefix. Given a QBF $Q.\varphi$, we say that $x <_Q y$ iff x occurs before y in the prefix. If clear from the context, we write $x < y$. In ϕ_1, we have $x < y$, while in ϕ_2, we have $y < x$.

3   Related Work

In practical QBF solving, attempts to parallelize and distribute QBF solvers have a long history (cf. [18] for a survey). Already more than 20 years back, the first distributed QBF solver PQSOLVE [4] was presented, in a time when QCDCL had not been invented yet. With the advent of QCDCL, several attempts have been made to build parallel QCDCL solvers and implement knowledge-sharing mechanisms for learned clauses and cubes. One example of such a solver is PAQuBE [16]. Unfortunately, the code of most of the early approaches is not available anymore. Following the success of Cube-and-Conquer-based search-space splitting, the QBF solver MPIDEPQBF has been presented [14]. While MPIDEPQBF does not implement any sophisticated look-ahead mechanisms, it could demonstrate that even without knowledge-sharing considerable speedup could be achieved. These results serve as motivation for the approach presented in this paper. Unfortunately, MPIDEPQBF is implemented in an older version of OCaml that does not run on recent systems and relies on now deprecated libraries, making a comparison impossible. As indicated by its name, it is tailored around the sequential QBF solver DEPQBF [17]. Another recent MPI-based QBF solver is HORDEQBF [1] which implements knowledge sharing for QCDCL solvers. It is designed in such a way that it allows the integration of any QCDCL solver. In order to integrate a solver, it requires that it implements a certain interface, i.e., programming effort is necessary to add a new solver. To the best of our knowledge, it includes the QBF solver DEPQBF only. HORDEQBF does not perform search-space splitting, but it is a parallel portfolio solver with clause- and cube sharing. It diversifies the parallel solver instances by different parameter settings. This is different than in sequential portfolio solvers as presented in [12], which select among different solvers based on some properties of the input formula. Overall, a very strong focus on QCDCL-based solvers can be observed for parallel QBF solving frameworks. Because of this, many chances for better solving performance are missed, as nowadays there are many other solvers of orthogonal strength. With PARAQOOBA we provide a simple way of exploiting the power of the different solving approaches without any integration effort.

4   PARACOOBA

Our novel framework PARAQOOBA (with q in the middle of its name) builds on top of the SAT solver PARACOOBA (with c in the middle of its name). In this section, we describe the parts of PARACOOBA that are relevant for the remainder of this work for our extension of PARACOOBA to PARAQOOBA.

PARAQOOBA will be made available publicly during the artifact evaluation under the MIT license, similar to PARACOOBA [7,6] which is publicly available on GitHub also under the MIT license[3]. PARACOOBA is a distributed Cube- and-Conquer (C&C) solver that implements a proprietary peer-to-peer based load balancing protocol. In contrast to standard D&C solvers the splitting of the search-space can both be done upfront by using a look-ahead solver that produces n cubes or online during solving by lookahead or other heuristics. Amongst other information, the cubes are stored in a binary tree, the *solve tree*.

Solver module. A *solver module* manages the sequential solver that is responsible for solving a subproblem. Different solver modules have different code-bases, but they also generally share common concepts. A solver module implements a parser task, which is created directly after the module was initiated and serves as its starting point. It parses the input formula in its own worker thread and instantiates a solver manager based on the fully parsed formula. The parser task also creates the first solver task as the root of the solve tree.

---

[3] github.com/maximaximal/Paracooba

Solver Tasks. For PARACOOBA, *solver tasks* are paths in the solve tree, whith a *parser task* being used to generate the tree's root. Solver tasks are usually started as children of other tasks, saving references to their parents, with the root solver task being the only exception. A task's depth in the solve tree represents its priority to be worked on: The greater the depth, the more important a task is to be solved locally and the less important it is to be offloaded to other compute nodes by the broker module. Only tasks that were created locally may be distributed.

Broker module. The *broker module* handles relations between solver tasks and processes their results. While the solver module generates tasks, the broker schedules them based on their priorities (their depths) and offloads them if a different compute node has less load than the current node. A task result is propagated upwards across compute nodes, there is no conceptual difference between locally and remotely solved tasks. The broker module is generic and does not rely on a specific solver module, instead providing the environment a solver module works in. It is already provided by PARACOOBA and stays the same for different solver modules.

Cube Sources. For generating concrete subproblems, *cube sources* provide assumption literals to leaf solver tasks. A cube source decides whether a given solver task should split again, based on the current configuration (mainly the splitting depth) and the given formula. Every solver module can implement its own cube source, hence there are different kinds of cube sources for different solver modules. On this basis, very flexible mechanisms for the selection of splitting variables can be implemented, ranging from a simple count of literal occurrences to advanced look-ahead heuristics.

Task Tree. The *task tree* built lazily, i.e., only once a leaf is visited, the leaf is either expanded into a sub-tree, or solved. We picture such a tree in Figure 1. This tree has a *depth* of 1, because the path from the tree's root solver task to the leaf solver tasks has a length of 1. Once the active cube source stops further splits from being carried out, the tree's maximum depth is reached. The worker thread currently executing a task then lends a solver instance from the solver manager's central store. Each solver instance is created on-the-fly once (normally initialized based on the parser task) for each worker thread, which can also happen for multiple worker threads in parallel. After a solver instance was created, all other tasks solved by the same worker thread use the same solver instance.

Guiding Paths. The cubes that are given to solver instances as assumptions are called *guiding paths*. They are generated from the path to the leaf being solved. The solver instance then handles the solving internally, blocking the worker thread until either result is generated or the task is terminated. Results are not returned to parents, but instead handled by the broker module, which then traverses the solve tree upwards as far as possible, based on the results already in the tree. Different kinds of evaluations can be defined on every level using a user-defined *assessment function*. With the result processed by the broker module, the solver task then finishes and the worker thread can take on the next task, based on the next-highest priority. The broker may delete the solver task after it finished processing, if the result was already used somewhere above it in the tree and no information from the original solver task structure is required anymore. Once the broker module has enough information to solve the root task, the result of the formula was computed successfully.

Solver Handle. A *solver handle* wraps instances of a given solver. It must be able to receive an *Assume* event, directly followed by a *Solve* event. While processing these events, a correctly working handle must block its calling thread until a result is found. Additionally, it must be fully re-entrant after finishing processing, so that the next solver task can apply new assumptions. On top of this, a handle must also be able to process a *Terminate* event, stopping the solver and early-returning control to its calling thread. Such a termination event may happen at any time, as it is generated by other solver tasks. This possibility of random terminations was an issue for our extension to ParaQooba, as it complicated synchronization of all involved threads.

QBF Solver Module. ParaCooba already provided a basic *QBF solver module* similar to the approach seen in MPIDEPQBF. It implemented a QDIMACS-parser in a new solver module based on the SAT module. It realizes a simple cube source that returns the variable at the nth position in the prefix, with n being the current depth of a solver task. The solve tree is built using two adapted assessment functions: one for variables quantified $\forall$ (requiring all sub-trees to be true), one for $\exists$ (requiring at least one sub-tree to be true). The assessment functions also use ParaCooba's cancellation-support to terminate unneeded siblings after results already satisfy the respective subproblem. As backend solver, it exclusively uses DEPQBF that provides an incremental API (which no other recent solver provides, to the best of our knowledge).

Summary. With its already existing tree-based QBF solving module together with its support for distributed solving, ParaCooba provides a stable basis for building an advanced parallel QBF solver. While the existing QBF module is rather uncompetitive with a few exceptions that indicate its potential, its core infrastructure turned out to be very useful to build our novel framework ParaQooba that offers built-in portfolio support.

The networking support mentioned above enables combining multiple compute nodes by giving each peer a connection to the main node. This is achieved with setting the `--known-remote` option. With this feature it becomes possible to easily distribute larger problem instances on a cluster or in the cloud.

5   Architecture of PARAQOOBA: Combining Divide-and-Conquer Portfolio Solving

Our framework PARAQOOBA combines Divide-and-Conquer (D&C) search space splitting with portfolio solving. The key feature of PARAQOOBA compared to PARACOOBA is to allow portfolio solving at different search depths. The idea is illustrated in Figure 1. Both approaches are widely used to realize parallel and distributed SAT and QBF solvers. The D&C approach has been especially successful for hard combinatorial SAT problems [11] in a variant called Cube-and-Conquer (C&C). The C&C approach relies on powerful, but expensive lookahead solvers that heuristically decide which variables shall be considered for splitting. In its original SAT version, PARACOOBA builds upon this idea [7].

For a QBF $Q_1 X Q_2 Y Q.\varphi$ with $Q_1 \neq Q_2$ and $Q_1, Q_2 \in \{\forall, \exists\}$ though, the possible choices for variable selection are more restricted because of the quantifier prefix. In general, only variables from the outermost quantifier block $Q_1 X$ may be considered, because otherwise, the value of the formula might change. Jordan et al. [14] observed that for QBF following the sequential order of the variables in the first quantifier block already leads to improvements compared to the sequential implementation of DEPQBF. The already existing QBF solver module of PARACOOBA (see section 4) relied on this observation: it traverses the prefix of a PCNF and splits each visited leaf into two sub-trees, respecting both universal and existential quantifiers, until a pre-defined maximum depth is reached. Hence, it re-implements the approach of MPIDEPQBF in PARACOOBA.

Our framework PARAQOOBA generalizes the previous QBF module of PARA-COOBA not only by generalizing the interface in such a manner that any QBF solver can be easily (without programming effort) integrated as backend solver. Now it is also possible to run several solvers in the leaves as shown in Figure 2 for one split. Overall, PARAQOOBA realizes the following approach. The search-space is split according to the variable ordering of the prefix until a given depth. Once one of the sub-trees of an existentially quantified variable split is found to be true, the other sibling is terminated. Only when both siblings return false, the whole split returns false. Universal splits work in a dual manner: the result is only true if both sub-trees are found to be true and false otherwise. This property of QBF enables efficient termination of sub-tasks.

In PARAQOOBA, we now also parallelize each solver call over several QBF solvers with orthogonal strategies. Compared to prior approaches [18], we run a portfolio of multiple solvers in the leaves of the solve tree instead of only parallelizing its root. Having just one tree leads to several advantages: We are more flexible and may also call a preprocessor (e.g. BLOQQER) before each solve call. We also only instantiate the tree once, saving memory and enabling early-termination of sibling solver tasks.

6   Implementation

This section describes the extension of the SAT solver PARACOOBA (for an overview see section 4) to our QBF solving framework PARAQOOBA. As PARA-

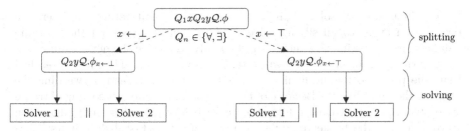

Fig. 1: Divide-and-Conquer with arbitrary-many levels of splitting and sub-formulas on the leaves solved by a portfolio of different sequential solvers

COOBA was originally not designed for portfolio support, several modifications and extensions were necessary. To this end, we first present the new QBF module of PARAQOOBA followed by a discussion of novel search-space pruning facilities.

6.1 The PARAQOOBA QBF Module

We generalized the already existing QBF solver handle to become an abstract base class, which now can be either a single solver handle or a *portfolio handle*. The latter unifies multiple handles into one, emulating a blocking and re-entrant interface. Once a portfolio handle is initialized, it starts one thread per internally wrapped handle. Each such thread implements a small state machine, waiting for events on a shared queue. Once the portfolio handle receives an assumption (a temporary truth assignment of a variable for one solver call), it is forwarded to all internal threads and is worked on by each wrapped solver in parallel.

If a portfolio handle was terminated before a solve call was issued, the internal handles would enter an invalid state. To circumvent this situation, an assumption event also directly triggers the internal state machine to continue into the solve state. Once the solve request actually arrives, it is just translated to an empty event, which, after it finished processing, indicates that a result was computed. A termination event is forwarded to the internal solver handles, but is limited to only one event per solve cycle.

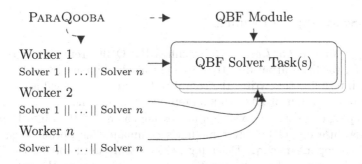

Fig. 2: The PARAQOOBA framework

The first internal solver handle to compute a result returns and sends a termination event to all sibling solvers. The result is saved and the portfolio handle waits for all internal handles to be ready to receive the next assumption, i.e., returning all solvers to a known state. Once every internal handle has reached that, the portfolio handle finally returns to its calling thread, forwarding the result of the inner handle. Because of thread scheduling and fast solving of trivial subproblems, a result can be forwarded even before the other sibling has been started, letting the broker module already complete a task before it itself has created both child tasks. This effect lead to some issues and had to be mitigated by adding some conditions on a task already being terminated even though it did not yet run to completion. Because a task will only be scheduled after the initial call to its assessment function, not many such checks were needed.

As many QBF solvers lack APIs, we have to work with their binaries that generally only read QDIMACS files. For this, we use the QuAPI interfacing library, that adds well-performing assumption-based reasoning support to generic solver binaries [9]. By not relying on specialized modifications of a solver's source code, we are able to plug-in generic third-party solvers, completely composable at runtime. Our PARAQOOBA module provides the `--quapisolver` parameter, that either directly specifies the leaf solver to be used, or automatically generates a portfolio handle to wrap multiple parallel leaf solvers. Note that our approach works for QBFs starting with existential as well as with universal quantification.

In its standard configuration, PARAQOOBA returns whether a given instance is found to be true or false. When enabling trace output using `-t`, it also supports printing the specific solver and the subproblem (including its guiding path) that produced a result. Using this machinery, one obtains an environment to experiment with benchmarks and to see how multiple solvers complement each other for the generated sub-formulas. The trace output is also useful when fully expanding a QBF formula by specifying a tree-depth of -1. While not advised for any real formulas, this was a well-received debugging aid for stress-testing new features. The opposite to this can also be done, by applying a tree-depth of 0. This directly solves the root task, without splitting the formula. This was also how the configuration PQ Portfolio with depth 0 (as discussed in the experimental evaluation below) was executed.

6.2   Search-Space Pruning

Preprocessing in the leaves. We modified the QBF preprocessor BLOQQER to allow forwarding output directly into a given solver binary by adding a `-p` argument. Internally, this writes the complete formula with added assumptions into the standard input of BLOQQER's preprocessing pipeline.

To plug e.g. CAQE into such a processing chain and then into PARAQOOBA, one may use our QBF solver module's command line option `--quapisolver bloqqer-popen@-p=caqe`. Deferring preprocessing until solving the leaves preserves the original formula structure of a formula during the split phase. We discuss the effects of this later in subsection 7.4.

Integer-Split Reduction. In many planning and verification encodings, the variables of a quantifier block QX are interpreted as bitvectors representing m nodes of a graph. Assume that $n = |X|$ bits with $m \leq 2^n$ are used for modeling the states of the graph. Then $2^n - m$ assignments to X are not relevant, but as a solver is agnostic of this information, it has to consider all assignments.

If m is known to the user, PARAQOOBA can be called with the option `--intsplit` (once or multiple times, once for each layer). One integer-split is counted as one layer in the task tree, so a tree-depth of two would split another quantifier into two more tasks for each state encoded in the previous integer-based split. To provide an example: Setting `--intsplit 5` creates 5 child-tasks in the task tree, spanning over the first $\lceil \log_2 5 \rceil = 3$ boolean variables from the quantifier prefix. When not using doing an integer-based split, these 3 variables would have to be expanded over 3 layers in the task tree, each inner task being split into two child tasks, resulting in 8 leaves , opposed to the 5 from before. Thus, integer-based splits require less intermediate splitting tasks to model the same formula, reducing the work to be done by the load-balancing mechanism in the Broker module. These integer splits are efficiently distributed over the network by relying on both the config-system and an extended QBF cube source. The cube source always saves the current guiding path, applying new splits, and in turn new assumptions, by appending to that path. The cube source itself is automatically serialized when a task is chosen to be offloaded to another compute node. While the possible savings are large, one has to exert great caution when using this feature, as it might change the semantics of a formula.

7   Evaluation

In this section, we evaluate PARAQOOBA on recent benchmarks and compare it to (sequential) state-of-the-art QBF solvers. As sequential backend solvers, we use the latest versions of DEPQBF [17] as QCDCL solver, CAQE [23] as clausal-abstraction solver, and RAREQS [13] as recursive abstraction refinement solver. For preprocessing, we use BLOQQER [3] (version 31). All of these solvers were top-ranked in the most recent edition of QBFEval'22 [22]. For our experiments we used the benchmarks of the PCNF-track of this competition. The main questions we want to answer with our evaluation are as follows:

- how does the parallel portfolio-leaf approach of PARAQOOBA perform in comparison to the individual sequential solvers?
- how does the parallel portfolio-leaf approach of PARAQOOBA perform in comparison to the virtual portfolio solver of the sequential solvers?
- what is the impact of performing the preprocessing in the leaves instead on the original input formula?

We ran our experiments on machines with dual-socket 16 core AMD EPYC 7313 processors with 3.7 GHz sustained boost clock speed and 256 GB main memory. Each task was assigned as many physical cores as its setup required, except for tasks with more than 32 concurrent threads, which were exclusively

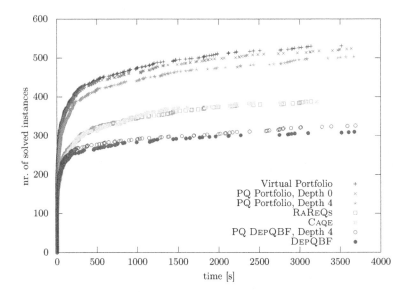

Fig. 3: Full summary of all solved instances with all different solvers without preprocessing. While Divide-and-Conquer (Depth 4) formulas solves 33 instances that no sequential solver solved, it solves 28 instances less in total.

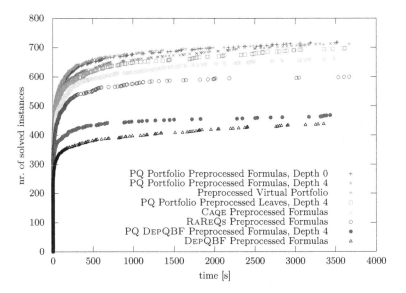

Fig. 4: Full summary of all solved instances with all different solvers with BLO-QQER preprocessing. PQ Portfolio (Depth 4) solves 45 instances no sequential solver could solve and solves 3 more in total.

assigned a whole node each as to not be slowed down by other loads. The effects of over-committing in case of three concurrent portfolio solvers (48 threads running in parallel with only 32 physical cores available) are discussed below in subsection 7.3.

Please note that in this evaluation we do not use the networking features provided by PARACOOBA, as we focus on applicability to QBF and not on the already presented scalability of the networking component (for the details see [3]).

7.1   Overall Performance Comparison

In order to exploit our hardware with 32 physical cores and 64 logical cores in the best possible way, we mainly focus on a *splitting depth of four* in the following. With this depth, 16 worker threads are generated for each problem and with three sequential backend solvers, overall 48 processes are started. We call this configuration *PQ Portfolio, Depth 4*. For understanding the impact of splitting, we also consider other depths as well. With *PQ Portfolio, Depth 0* we refer to the configuration in which splitting is disabled. This configuration is particularly interesting, because compared to the virtual best solver (VBS), it reveals the overhead introduced by our framework (see also the discussion below). In order to show the improvements of PARAQOOBA compared to the QBF module without portfolio solving that was already available in PARACOOBA [6], we also included the configuration *PQ DepQBF, Depth 4*.

Figure 3 shows the overall results of our evaluation *without preprocessing*. Both configurations of PARAQOOBA, *PQ Portfolio, Depth 0* and *PQ Portfolio, Depth 4* are considerably better than the single sequential solvers as well as the basic non-portfolio QBF module of PARACOOBA only solving with DEPQBF (PQ DEPQBF, Depth 4). However, compared to the virtual portfolio, 28 instances less are solved in total (for an explanation see below). On the positive side, 33 formulas can be solved by our new approach that could not be solved by any sequential solver. The situation changes when preprocessing is applied (cf. Figure 4). Now PARAQOOBA in configuration *PQ Portfolio Preprocessed Formulas, Depth 4* is able to solve most formulas. It even solves more formulas than the *Preprocessed Virtual Portfolio*, indicating the potential of our approach.

A detailed analysis is given in Figure 5. By comparing the number of solved instances to the solve time of individual (preprocessed) problem instances, we see a small average speedup when using PARAQOOBA with depth 4 compared to a virtual portfolio solver in Figure 5a. The more trivial instances tend to be solved quicker using a sequential solver, while the harder to solve instances tend to be solved faster with the Divide-and-Conquer approach of PARAQOOBA.

Next, we used the preprocessed leaves functionality introduced in subsection 6.2. Here PARAQOOBA generates its guiding paths using the original formula and applies BLOQQER only in the leaves of the solve tree. In this configuration, some problem instances take longer to solve than when preprocessing the full formula, while others can be solved quicker. We present these results in Figure 5b. Such a result was expected, as it is conceptually similar to inprocessing.

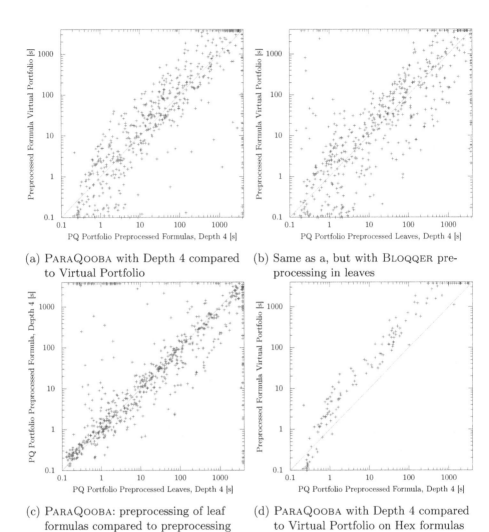

(a) PARAQOOBA with Depth 4 compared to Virtual Portfolio

(b) Same as a, but with BLOQQER preprocessing in leaves

(c) PARAQOOBA: preprocessing of leaf formulas compared to preprocessing of input formula

(d) PARAQOOBA with Depth 4 compared to Virtual Portfolio on Hex formulas

Fig. 5: Detailed comparison of PARAQOOBA against the virtual portfolio of DE-PQBF, CAQE, and RAREQS in a, b, d. In a, PARAQOOBA solves 45 instances that no sequential solver could solve. In b, PARAQOOBA solves 38 instances no sequential solver could solve, 8 of which also could not be solved with portfolio over preprocessed formulas as in a. d focuses only on preprocessed formulas from the Hex benchmark family. In c, we directly compare preprocessing in the leaves to preprocessing in the input formula.

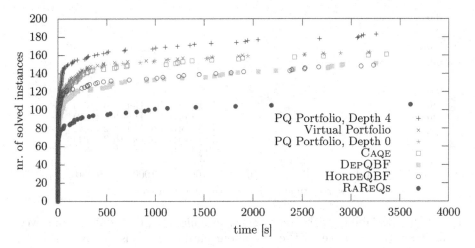

Fig. 6: Preprocessed formulas of the Hex positional game planning [20,25] benchmarks from the QBF22 benchmark set. Also compared to HORDEQBF [1] as available state-of-the-art parallel QBF solver.

When considering the formulas that were exclusively solved by PARAQOOBA, then the variant with preprocessing the full formula up-front performed best followed by the variant with preprocessing in the leaves. These formulas include verification and synthesis benchmarks with 2–3 quantifier alternations as well as many encodings of the game Hex with 13, 15 or 17 quantifier alternations. Table 1 in the appendix lists all instances (48) that were only solved with some variant of PARAQOOBA. It also lists which variant was the fastest.

7.2   Family-Based Analysis

To understand which formula families benefit most from our Divide-and-Conquer solving strategy, we compared the (wall-clock) solve time of PARAQOOBA to the virtual portfolio solver. We calculated the speedup by dividing the solve time of the sequential solver by the solve time of PARAQOOBA. The instances with the highest speedups were some reachability queries (up to 18.09), the Hex game planning family (17.64), multipliers (16.46), and the formula_add family (15.16). More detailed results are appended in Table 2. Together with the number of Hex instances only PARAQOOBA solved (21), this makes Hex game planning the benchmark family with the best overall results in our evaluation. A comparison between PARAQOOBA and other solvers is shown in Figure 6.

7.3   Scalability of our Approach

As already discussed above, using 16 workers leads to overcommitting cores when solving with a portfolio of more than two solvers. To quantify this, we did

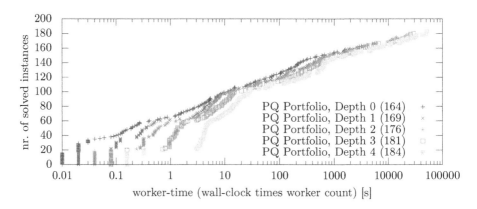

Fig. 7: Hex Scalability with preprocessed formulas. Depth 4 suffers from over-committing the available CPU-cores on our hardware and is relatively slow for the first few problems, but still solves more instances overall.

a scalability experiment with different worker counts. Because the Hex planning benchmarks had the most predictable performance, we focused this experiment on these formulas. Figure 7 shows the scalability graph, where the X-axis has been multiplied by the number of workers used, to visualize the cost of increased CPU-time compared to reduced wall-clock solve time. The impact of over-committing CPU cores can be clearly observed in the results of the portfolio with depth 4. This curve solves more compared to the others and takes longer to solve the first 140 instances, until the curves become more similar again.

7.4   Preprocessed Leaves compared to Preprocessed Formulas

We compared preprocessing the whole formula at once using BLOQQER to calling BLOQQER using `bloqqer-popen` in each leaf after first splitting on the unchanged formula. The first variant modifies the original prefix, including the quantifier ordering. Because the used splitting algorithm generates guiding paths by following this quantifier ordering, the different approaches lead to vastly different results. Figure 5c visualizes these differences by scattering both variants together.

Looking at the specific benchmarks benefiting from the two variants, we often observed improvements to one variant per family. This strongly suggests that adaptive preprocessing and inprocessing techniques could further improve solving performance, even without otherwise changing solvers themselves.

7.5   Lessons Learned

One would expect that for any given problem, parallel portfolio solvers are as fast as the fastest used solver. While this statement is conceptually true, we encountered some formulas where PQ-Portfolio gave comparatively bad results, while a solver alone could solve the same formula quicker or even instantly.

We investigated this in more detail and found several segmentation faults in CAQE and API inconsistencies in DEPQBF that were encountered because of some corner-case structures of the generated subproblems (e.g., by enforcing the values of certain variables). We reported these issues to the solver developers and hope to obtain fixes soon. Having this issues fixed would lead to a more performant general solution and to a more robust user experience. In sequential execution of these solvers, we did not encounter any problems on the unmodified competition benchmarks without added unit clauses.

Currently, we adopt the following work-around. Segmentation faults of the sequential solvers are handled in our QBF module using the indirection provided by QUAPI. Once an unrecoverable error occurs in the solver child process, it exits and returns the error up through QUAPI's factory process and into the solver handle. There, such a result is interpreted as *Unknown*, which is invalid and therefore ignored, letting the portfolio wait for other results. We provide all affected formulas that we found in the artifact submitted alongside this paper.

We also observed that calling a solver via its API might lead to a considerably different behavior than calling a solver from the command line, i.e., different optimizations are activated when calling a solver through its API compared to using the command-line binary. Such behavior can be mitigated by not using the API directly, and instead relying on QUAPI, even if an API would be available. This fixes the issues with DEPQBF, which solves some formulas (with assumptions supplied as unit clauses) in under one second if used as a solver binary, but not when applying assumptions through its API. We also supply all found formulas that triggered this issue in the submitted artifact.

8   Conclusions

We presented PARAQOOBA, a parallel and distributed QBF solving framework that combines search-space splitting with portfolio solving. We designed the framework in such a way that any sequential QBF solver binary can be easily integrated without any implementation effort. Our experiments demonstrate that this approach in combination with sequential preprocessing lead to considerable performance improvements for certain formula families.

With our framework, we provide a stable infrastructure that has the potential for many future extensions. For example, we did not incorporate any advanced splitting heuristics as in modern Cube-and-Conquer solvers. We expect that with more advanced heuristics, combined with adaptive but possibly non-deterministic re-splitting of leaves, even more speedups could be achieved.

In addition to the presented experiments, we also evaluated the novel integer-split feature (cf. subsection 6.2) with the Hex benchmark family. By providing the number of valid game states to PARAQOOBA, we could increase the splitting depth as well as the number of solved instances. We see much potential of providing encoding-specific or domain-specific knowledge to the solver and will investigate this in future work.

Data Availability Statement

Data used for benchmarking the described software, including source code, are made available permanently under a permissive license in a public artifact on Zenodo. Raw source data for the figures presented in this paper are also included [8].

A   Instances Only Solved by PARAQOOBA

Name	Clauses	Variables	QA	Time [s]	Res	Variant
b21_C_3_206	242896	3270	3	265.77	⊤	full
c1_Debug_s3_f1_e1_v1	1775758	379113	3	3164.34	⊤	full
c2_Debug_s3_f1_e1_v2	431970	98425	3	1834.27	⊤	full
cache-coherence-2-fixpoint-2	10648	3686	2	0.56	⊥	leaves
cmu.dme1.B-f3	4540	1795	3	0.2	⊤	leaves
cmu.dme2.B-f3	6151	2342	3	818.3	⊤	leaves
LoginService	21667	5289	2	1086.07	⊥	orig
query64_query42_1344n	3423	1426	2	86.73	⊤	full
hex_compact_goal_witness_based_hein_03_6x6-13.pg	3401	1056	15	2594.27	⊥	leaves
hex_compact_goal_witness_based_hein_05_6x6-13.pg	3493	1071	15	3102.97	⊤	full
hex_compact_goal_witness_based_hein_17_6x6-13.pg	3430	1060	15	1919.64	⊥	full
hex_compact_goal_witness_based_hein_18_7x7-13.pg	4256	1267	15	1401.12	⊥	full
hex_compact_goal_witness_based_hein_02_5x5-13.pg	3134	1007	15	308.99	⊤	full
hex_compact_goal_witness_based_hein_15_5x5-15.pg	3667	1195	17	3063.67	⊤	full
hex_symbolic_explicit_goal_hein_03_6x6-11.pg	3421	902	13	693.11	⊥	full
hex_symbolic_explicit_goal_hein_05_6x6-11.pg	3611	918	13	501.29	⊥	full
hex_symbolic_explicit_goal_hein_18_7x7-11.pg	3084	1021	13	447.7	⊥	leaves
hex_symbolic_explicit_goal_hein_02_5x5-11.pg	2480	739	13	973.33	⊥	full
hex_symbolic_explicit_goal_hein_16_5x5-11.pg	2376	731	13	301.31	⊥	full
hex_symbolic_implicit_goal_hein_03_6x6-13.pg	3069	1001	15	1830.57	⊥	full
hex_symbolic_implicit_goal_hein_17_6x6-13.pg	3097	1005	15	2674.38	⊥	full

hex_symbolic_implicit_goal_ hein_02_5x5-13.pg	2812	952	15	404.36	⊤	full
hex_symbolic_implicit_goal_ hein_15_5x5-15.pg	3106	1072	17	1944.27	⊤	full
hex_witness_based_hein_03_ 6x6-13.pg	7174	1917	13	2050.04	⊥	full
hex_witness_based_hein_05_ 6x6-13.pg	7456	1962	13	1005.06	⊤	full
hex_witness_based_hein_17_ 6x6-13.pg	7353	1936	13	1572.7	⊥	full
hex_witness_based_hein_18_ 7x7-13.pg	9577	2405	13	1102.69	⊥	full
hex_witness_based_hein_20_ 6x6-13.pg	7551	1962	13	3123.99	⊥	full
hex_witness_based_hein_15_ 5x5-15.pg	7423	2136	15	2489.7	⊤	leaves
OrgSynth_mitexams_p02_l_6	83500	23384	3	1852.22	⊤	full
OrgSynth_mitexams_p02_l_7	97214	27239	3	2693.19	⊤	full
OrgSynth_mitexams_p03_l_5	106413	29730	3	2897.47	⊤	full
OrgSynth_mitexams_p07_l_5	165039	46587	3	2469.04	⊥	leaves
OrgSynth_mitexams_p16_l_6	53448	15692	3	2169.18	⊤	full
OrgSynth_mitexams_p16_l_7	62141	18265	3	3054.75	⊤	leaves
OrgSynth_mitexams_p19_l_6	106252	29346	3	3489.44	⊤	full
OrgSynth_mitexams_p20_l_7	74375	21534	3	1782.51	⊥	full
OrgSynth_mitexams_p01_l_4	65294	17864	3	1609.48	⊥	full
OrgSynth_mitexams_p05_l_3	79279	22897	3	2055.46	⊤	leaves
OrgSynth_mitexams_p05_l_4	105042	30409	3	2253.59	⊤	full
OrgSynth_mitexams_p10_l_3	44309	12864	3	870.16	⊤	full
OrgSynth_mitexams_p10_l_4	58490	17046	3	2163.5	⊤	full
OrgSynth_mitexams_p13_l_3	52653	14953	3	1310.32	⊤	full
OrgSynth_mitexams_p13_l_4	69554	19819	3	2592.6	⊤	leaves
OrgSynth_sat18_p09_l_3	52653	14953	3	1765.8	⊤	leaves
OrgSynth_sat18_p09_l_4	69554	19819	3	2328.99	⊤	leaves
OrgSynth_sat18_p11_l_4	85537	23860	3	2123.52	⊥	leaves
OrgSynth_sat18_p12_l_4	82734	23155	3	2803.72	⊥	leaves

Table 1: 48 instances that were only solved by a PARAQOOBA configuration. QA: Quantifier Alternations, Res: Result, Variant: PARAQOOBA configuration that solved the problem the fastest (preprocess full formula, preprocess leaves, original formula).

B   Instances Solved faster by PARAQOOBA

Name	PQ [s]	VPS [s]	Speedup	Res
nreachq_query71_1344n	2.21	39.97	18.09	⊥
hex_witness_based_hein_08_5x5-11.pg	0.22	3.88	17.64	⊤
mult9.sat	2.11	34.73	16.46	⊤
add5_COMPLETE	1.78	26.98	15.16	⊤
hex_symbolic_explicit_goal_hein_10_5x5-11.pg	32.23	465.43	14.44	⊥
hex_compact_goal_witness_based_hein_10_5x5-13.pg	144.98	1853.09	12.78	⊤
hex_symbolic_explicit_goal_hein_11_5x5-09.pg	1.79	22.53	12.59	⊥
hex_symbolic_implicit_goal_hein_03_6x6-11.pg	47.52	538.03	11.32	⊥
reachqu_query60_1344n	7.57	77.4	10.22	⊥
query71_query36_1344n	11.38	105.83	9.30	⊥
hex_symbolic_explicit_goal_hein_08_5x5-09.pg	1.18	10.94	9.27	⊥
hex_symbolic_implicit_goal_hein_20_6x6-11.pg	140.49	1282.38	9.13	⊥
hex_witness_based_hein_06_4x4-11.pg	3.41	30.9	9.06	⊥
hex_compact_goal_witness_based_hein_10_5x5-11.pg	13.97	121.04	8.66	⊥
hex_symbolic_implicit_goal_hein_19_5x5-11.pg	1.69	14.29	8.46	⊤
hex_symbolic_implicit_goal_hein_16_5x5-11.pg	22.26	184.75	8.30	⊥
sortnetsort10.AE.stepl.008	13.33	107.07	8.03	⊥
add7_REDUCED	135.58	1051.44	7.76	⊤
reachqu_query64_1344n	128.4	982.54	7.65	⊥
hex_compact_goal_witness_based_hein_02_5x5-11.pg	39.04	295.57	7.57	⊥
amba4b9y.unsat	10.9	81.72	7.50	⊥
hex_symbolic_implicit_goal_hein_15_5x5-13.pg	95.67	714.78	7.47	⊥
hex_compact_goal_witness_based_hein_15_5x5-13.pg	167.18	1229.74	7.36	⊥
hex_symbolic_implicit_goal_hein_06_4x4-11.pg	1.32	9.67	7.33	⊥
hex_compact_goal_witness_based_hein_16_5x5-13.pg	372.26	2713.59	7.29	⊤

Table 2: Instances that PARAQOOBA (PQ) solved faster compared to a virtual portfolio solver (VPS) that also solved the same problem, ordered by the relative speedup and limited to the top 25 entries. Res: Result, Speedup: $\frac{\text{VPS}[s]}{\text{PQ}[s]}$.

References

1. Balyo, T., Lonsing, F.: HordeQBF: A modular and massively parallel QBF solver. In: Creignou, N., Berre, D.L. (eds.) Proc. of the 19th Int. Conf. on Theory and Applications of Satisfiability Testing (SAT). Lecture Notes in Computer

Science, vol. 9710, pp. 531–538. Springer (2016). https://doi.org/10.1007/978-3-319-40970-2_33

2. Beyersdorff, O., Janota, M., Lonsing, F., Seidl, M.: Quantified boolean formulas. In: Biere, A., Heule, M., van Maaren, H., Walsh, T. (eds.) Handbook of Satisfiability, Frontiers in Artificial Intelligence and Applications, vol. 336, pp. 1177–1221. IOS Press (2021). https://doi.org/10.3233/FAIA201015

3. Biere, A., Lonsing, F., Seidl, M.: Blocked clause elimination for QBF. In: Bjørner, N.S., Sofronie-Stokkermans, V. (eds.) Proc. of the 23rd Int. Conf. on Automated Deduction (CADE). Lecture Notes in Computer Science, vol. 6803, pp. 101–115. Springer (2011). https://doi.org/10.1007/978-3-642-22438-6_10

4. Feldmann, R., Monien, B., Schamberger, S.: A distributed algorithm to evaluate quantified boolean formulae. In: Kautz, H.A., Porter, B.W. (eds.) Proc. of the 17th Nat. Conf. on Artificial Intelligence and 12th Conf. on on Innovative Applications of Artificial Intelligence (AAAI/IAAI). pp. 285–290. AAAI Press / The MIT Press (2000), http://www.aaai.org/Library/AAAI/2000/aaai00-044.php

5. Frioux, L.L., Baarir, S., Sopena, J., Kordon, F.: Modular and efficient divide-and-conquer SAT solver on top of the painless framework. In: Vojnar, T., Zhang, L. (eds.) Proc. of the 25th Int. Conf. on Tools and Algorithms for the Construction and Analysis of Systems (TACAS). Lecture Notes in Computer Science, vol. 11427, pp. 135–151. Springer (2019). https://doi.org/10.1007/978-3-030-17462-0_8

6. Heisinger, M.: Distributed SAT & QBF solving: The paracooba framework. Master Thesis, JKU Linz (2021)

7. Heisinger, M., Fleury, M., Biere, A.: Distributed cube and conquer with paracooba. In: Pulina, L., Seidl, M. (eds.) Proc. of the 23rd Int. Conf. on Theory and Applications of Satisfiability Testing (SAT). Lecture Notes in Computer Science, vol. 12178, pp. 114–122. Springer (2020). https://doi.org/10.1007/978-3-030-51825-7_9

8. Heisinger, M., Seidl, M., Biere, A.: Artifact for Paper ParaQooba: A Fast and Flexible Framework for Parallel and Distributed QBF Solving (Nov 2022). https://doi.org/10.5281/zenodo.7554207

9. Heisinger, M., Seidl, M., Biere, A.: QuAPI: Adding assumptions to non-assuming SAT & QBF solvers. In: Konev, B., Schon, C., Steen, A. (eds.) Proc. of the Workshop on Practical Aspects of Automated Reasoning (FLoC/IJCAR). CEUR Workshop Proceedings, vol. 3201. CEUR-WS.org (2022), http://ceur-ws.org/Vol-3201/paper1.pdf

10. Heule, M., Järvisalo, M., Lonsing, F., Seidl, M., Biere, A.: Clause elimination for SAT and QSAT. J. Artif. Intell. Res. 53, 127–168 (2015). https://doi.org/10.1613/jair.4694

11. Heule, M., Kullmann, O., Wieringa, S., Biere, A.: Cube and conquer: Guiding CDCL SAT solvers by lookaheads. In: Eder, K., Lourenço, J., Shehory, O. (eds.) Proc. of the 7th Int. Conf. on Hardware and Software: Verification and Testing (HVC). Lecture Notes in Computer Science, vol. 7261, pp. 50–65. Springer (2011). https://doi.org/10.1007/978-3-642-34188-5_8

12. Hoos, H.H., Peitl, T., Slivovsky, F., Szeider, S.: Portfolio-based algorithm selection for circuit QBFs. In: Hooker, J.N. (ed.) Proc. of the 24th Int. Conf. on Principles and Practice of Constraint Programming (CP). Lecture Notes in Computer Science, vol. 11008, pp. 195–209. Springer (2018). https://doi.org/10.1007/978-3-319-98334-9_13

13. Janota, M., Klieber, W., Marques-Silva, J., Clarke, E.M.: Solving QBF with counterexample guided refinement. In: Cimatti, A., Sebastiani, R. (eds.) Proc. of

the 15th Int. Conf. on Theory and Applications of Satisfiability Testing (SAT). Lecture Notes in Computer Science, vol. 7317, pp. 114–128. Springer (2012). https://doi.org/10.1007/978-3-642-31612-8_10

14. Jordan, C., Kaiser, L., Lonsing, F., Seidl, M.: MPIDepQBF: Towards parallel QBF solving without knowledge sharing. In: Sinz, C., Egly, U. (eds.) Proc. of the 17th Int. Conf. on Theory and Applications of Satisfiability Testing (SAT). Lecture Notes in Computer Science, vol. 8561, pp. 430–437. Springer (2014). https://doi.org/10.1007/978-3-319-09284-3_32

15. Kaufmann, D., Kauers, M., Biere, A., Cok, D.: Arithmetic verification problems submitted to the SAT Race 2019. In: Heule, M., Järvisalo, M., Suda, M. (eds.) Proc. of SAT Race 2019 – Solver and Benchmark Descriptions. Department of Computer Science Series of Publications B, vol. B-2019-1, p. 49. University of Helsinki (2019)

16. Lewis, M., Schubert, T., Becker, B., Marin, P., Narizzano, M., Giunchiglia, E.: Parallel QBF solving with advanced knowledge sharing. Fundam. Informaticae **107**(2-3), 139–166 (2011). https://doi.org/10.3233/FI-2011-398

17. Lonsing, F., Egly, U.: DepQBF 6.0: A search-based QBF solver beyond traditional QCDCL. In: de Moura, L. (ed.) Proc. of the 26th Int. Conf. on Automated Deduction (CADE). Lecture Notes in Computer Science, vol. 10395, pp. 371–384. Springer (2017). https://doi.org/10.1007/978-3-319-63046-5_23

18. Lonsing, F., Seidl, M.: Parallel solving of quantified boolean formulas. In: Hamadi, Y., Sais, L. (eds.) Handbook of Parallel Constraint Reasoning, pp. 101–139. Springer (2018). https://doi.org/10.1007/978-3-319-63516-3_4

19. Marques-Silva, J., Lynce, I., Malik, S.: Conflict-driven clause learning SAT solvers. In: Biere, A., Heule, M., van Maaren, H., Walsh, T. (eds.) Handbook of Satisfiability, Frontiers in Artificial Intelligence and Applications, vol. 336, pp. 133–182. IOS Press (2021). https://doi.org/10.3233/FAIA200987

20. Mayer-Eichberger, V., Saffidine, A.: Positional games and QBF: The corrective encoding. In: Pulina, L., Seidl, M. (eds.) Proc. of the 23rd Int. Conf. on Theory and Applications of Satisfiability Testing (SAT). Lecture Notes in Computer Science, vol. 12178, pp. 447–463. Springer (2020). https://doi.org/10.1007/978-3-030-51825-7_31

21. Pulina, L., Seidl, M.: The 2016 and 2017 QBF solvers evaluations (QBFEVAL'16 and QBFEVAL'17). Artif. Intell. **274**, 224–248 (2019). https://doi.org/10.1016/j.artint.2019.04.002

22. Pulina, L., Seidl, M., Shukla, A.: QBFEval 2022. http://www.qbflib.org/qbfeval22.php (2022)

23. Rabe, M.N., Tentrup, L.: CAQE: A certifying QBF solver. In: Kaivola, R., Wahl, T. (eds.) Proc. of the Int. Conf. on Formal Methods in Computer-Aided Design (FMCAD). pp. 136–143. IEEE (2015)

24. Sanders, P., Schreiber, D.: Mallob: Scalable SAT solving on demand with decentralized job scheduling. J. Open Source Softw. **7**(77), 4591 (2022). https://doi.org/10.21105/joss.04591

25. Shaik, I., Mayer-Eichberger, V., van de Pol, J., Saffidine, A.: Implicit state and goals in QBF encodings for positional games (extended version) (2023). https://doi.org/10.48550/ARXIV.2301.07345

26. Shukla, A., Biere, A., Pulina, L., Seidl, M.: A survey on applications of quantified boolean formulas. In: Proc. of the 31st IEEE Int. Conf. on Tools with Artificial Intelligence (ICTAI). pp. 78–84. IEEE (2019). https://doi.org/10.1109/ICTAI.2019.00020

Inferring Needless Write Memory Accesses on Ethereum Bytecode*

Elvira Albert[1] , Jesús Correas[1] , Pablo Gordillo[1](✉) ,
Guillermo Román-Díez[2] , and Albert Rubio[1]

[1] Complutense University of Madrid, Madrid, Spain
pabgordi@ucm.es
[2] Universidad Politécnica de Madrid, Madrid, Spain

Abstract. Efficiency is a fundamental property of any type of program, but it is even more so in the context of the programs executing on the blockchain (known as *smart contracts*). This is because optimizing smart contracts has direct consequences on reducing the costs of deploying and executing the contracts, as there are fees to pay related to their bytes-size and to their resource consumption (called *gas*). Optimizing memory usage is considered a challenging problem that, among other things, requires a precise inference of the memory locations being accessed. This is also the case for the Ethereum Virtual Machine (EVM) bytecode generated by the most-widely used compiler, solc, whose rather unconventional and low-level memory usage challenges automated reasoning. This paper presents a static analysis, developed at the level of the EVM bytecode generated by solc, that infers write memory accesses that are needless and thus can be safely removed. The application of our implementation on more than 19,000 real smart contracts has detected about 6,200 needless write accesses in less than 4 hours. Interestingly, many of these writes were involved in memory usage patterns generated by solc that can be greatly optimized by removing entire blocks of bytecodes. To the best of our knowledge, existing optimization tools cannot infer such needless write accesses, and hence cannot detect these inefficiencies that affect both the deployment and the execution costs of Ethereum smart contracts.

1 Introduction

EVM and memory model. Ethereum [27] is considered the world-leading programmable blockchain today. It provides a virtual machine, named EVM (Ethereum Virtual Machine) [21], to execute the programs that run on the blockchain. Such programs, known as Ethereum "smart contracts", can be written in high-level programming languages such as Solidity [6], Vyper [4], Serpent [3] or Bamboo [1] and they are then compiled to EVM bytecode. The EVM bytecode is the code finally deployed in the blockchain, and has become a uniform format to develop analysis and optimization tools. The memory model of EVM programs has been described in previous work [17,19,26,27]. Mainly, there are three

---

* This work was funded partially by the Spanish MCIU, AEI and FEDER (EU) projects PID2021-122830OB-C41 and PID2021-122830OA-C44 and by the CM project S2018/TCS-4314 co-funded by EIE Funds of the European Union.

S. Sankaranarayanan and N. Sharygina (Eds.): TACAS 2023, LNCS 13993, pp. 448–466, 2023.
https://doi.org/10.1007/978-3-031-30823-9_23

regions in which data can be stored and accessed: (1) The EVM is a stack-based virtual machine, meaning that most instructions perform computations using the topmost elements in a machine *stack*. This memory region can only hold a limited amount of values, up to 1024 256-bit words. (2) EVM programs store data persistently using a memory region named *storage* that consists of a mapping of 256-bit addresses to 256-bit words and whose contents persist between external function calls. (3) The third memory region is a local volatile memory area that we will refer to as EVM *memory*, and which is the focus of our work. This memory area behaves as a simple word-addressed array of bytes that can be accessed by byte or as a one-word group. The EVM memory can be used to allocate dynamic local data (such as arrays or structs) and also for specific EVM bytecode instructions which have been designed to require some lengthy operands to be stored in local memory. This is the case of the instructions for computing cryptographic hashes, or for passing arguments to and returning data from external function calls. Compilers use the stack and volatile memory regions in different ways. The most-used Solidity compiler `solc` generates EVM code that uses the stack for storing value-type local variables, as well as intermediate values for complex computations and jump addresses, whereas reference-type local variables such as array types and user-defined struct types are located in memory. For instance, when a Solidity function returns a struct variable, the required memory for the struct is allocated and initialized at the beginning of the function execution. However, the allocated memory is not always accessed as we illustrate in the following function (that belongs to the contract in Fig. 1):

```
1 function _ownershipAt(uint256 i) private returns (TokenOwnership memory) {
2    return c.unpackedOwnership(_packedOwnerships[i]);
3 }
```

Although the execution of `_ownershipAt` allocates memory for the return value declared in the function definition, the execution of the function is reserving a different memory space for the actual returned struct obtained from `unpackedOwnership` and, thus, the first reservation and its initialization are needless. The focus of our work is on detecting such needless write memory accesses on the code generated by `solc`. Nevertheless, as the analysis works at EVM level, it could be easily adapted to EVM code generated by any other compiler.

Optimization. Optimization of Ethereum smart contracts is a hot research topic, see e.g. [9, 10, 12–14, 22, 24] and their references. This is because the reduction of their costs is relevant for three reasons: (1) *Deployment fees.* When the contract is deployed on the blockchain, the owner pays a fee related to the size in bytes of the bytecode. Hence, a clear optimization criterion is the bytes-size of the program. The Solidity compiler `solc` [6] has as optimization target such bytes-size reduction. (2) *Gas-metered execution.* There is a fee to be paid by each client to execute a transaction in the blockchain. This fee is a fixed amount per transaction plus the cost of executing all bytecode instructions within the function being invoked within the transaction. This cost is measured in "gas" (which is then priced in the corresponding cryptocurrency) and this is why the execution is said to be gas-metered. The EVM specification ([27] and more recent updates) provides a precise gas consumption for each bytecode instruction in the language. The goal of most EVM bytecode optimization tools [9, 10, 12–14, 22] is to reduce such gas consumption, as this will revert on reducing the price of all transactions on the smart contract. (3) *Enlarging Ethereum's capability.* Due to the huge volume of transactions that are being demanded, there is a huge interest in enlarging the capability of the Ethereum network to increase the number of transactions that can be handled. Optimization of EVM bytecode in general –and of its memory usage in particular– is an important step contributing into this direction.

Challenges and contributions. Optimizing memory usage is considered a challenging problem that requires a precise inference of the memory locations being accessed, and that usually varies according to the memory model of the language being analyzed, and to the compiler that generates the code to be executed. In the case of Ethereum smart contracts generated by the solc compiler, the memory model is rather unconventional and its low-level memory usage patterns challenge automated reasoning. On one hand, instead of having an instruction to allocate memory, the allocation is performed by a sequence of instructions that use the value stored at address $0x40$ as the *free memory pointer*, i.e., a pointer to the first memory address available for allocating new memory. In the general case, the memory is structured as a sequence of *slots*: a slot is composed of several consecutive memory locations that are accessed in the bytecode from the same initial memory location plus a corresponding offset. A slot might just hold a data structure created in the smart contract but also, when nested data structures are used, from one slot we can find pointers to other memory slots for the nested components. Finally, there are other type of *transient* slots that hold temporary data and that need to be captured by a precise memory analysis as well. These features pose the main challenges to infer needless write accesses and, to handle them accurately, we make the following main contributions: (1) we present a *slot analysis* to (over-)approximate the slots created along the execution and the program points at which they are allocated; (2) we then introduce a *slot usage analysis* which infers the accesses to the different slots from the bytecode instructions; (3) we finally infer *needless write accesses*, i.e., program points where the memory is written but is never read by any subsequent instruction of the program; and (4) we implement the approach and perform a thorough experimental evaluation on real smart contracts detecting needless write accesses which belong to highly optimizable memory usage patterns generated by solc. Finally, it is worth mentioning that the applications of the memory analysis (points 1 and 2) go beyond the detection of needless write accesses: a precise model of the EVM memory is crucial to enhance the accuracy of any posterior analysis (see, e.g., [19] for other concrete applications of a memory analysis).

2   Memory Layout and Motivating Examples

Memory Opcodes. The EVM instruction set contains the usual instructions to access memory: the most basic instructions that operate on memory are MLOAD

```
 4  struct TokenOwnership {           17  contract Running2 {
 5     address addr;                  18    Running1 c;
 6     uint64 startTs;                19    mapping(uint256=>uint256) private _packedOwnerships;
 7     bool burned;                   20    //...
 8  }                                 21    function _ownershipAt(uint256 i) private
 9                                    22 s6      returns (TokenOwnership memory) {
10  contract Running1 {               23 s7    return c.unpackedOwnership(_packedOwnerships[i]);
11     //...                          24    }
12     function unpackedOwnership     25    function explicitOwnershipOf(uint256 tokenId)
13        (uint256 packed) public     26 s3       public returns (TokenOwnership memory) {
14 s1s2    returns (TokenOwnership    27 s4    TokenOwnership memory ownership;
           memory ownership) {        28 s5    if (...) { return ownership; }
15        ownership.addr = ...;       29 s8    ownership = _ownershipAt(tokenId);
16        ownership.startTs = ...;    30    //...
17        ownership.burned = ...;     31 s5    return ownership;
18     }                             32    }
19  }                                33  }
```

Fig. 1: Excerpt of smart contract ERC721A.

and MSTORE, which load and store a 32-byte word from memory, respectively.[3] The solc compiler generates code to handle memory with a cumulative model in which memory is allocated along the execution of the program and is never released. In contrast to other bytecode virtual machines, like the *Java Virtual Machine*, the EVM does not have a particular instruction to allocate memory. The allocation is performed by a sequence of instructions that use the value stored at address 0x40 as the *free memory pointer*, i.e., a pointer to the first memory address available for allocating new memory. In what follows, we use $mem\langle x \rangle$ to refer to the content stored in memory at location x.

Memory Slots. In the general case, memory is structured as a sequence of *slots*. A slot is composed of consecutive memory locations that are accessed by using its initial memory location, which we call the *base reference* (*baseref* for short) of the slot, plus the corresponding offset needed to access a specific location within the slot. Slots usually store (part of) some data structure created in the Solidity program (e.g., an array or a struct) and whose length can be known.

Example 1 (slots). Fig. 1 shows an excerpt of smart contract ERC721A [2] which contains two different contracts Running1 and Running2. We have omitted non-relevant instructions such as those that appear at lines 15-17 (L15-L17 for short). The contract Running1 to the left of Fig. 1 contains the public function unpackedOwnership that returns a struct of type TokenOwnership defined at L4-L7. The contract Running2, shown to the right, contains the public function explicitOwnershipOf that returns, depending on a non-relevant condition, an empty struct of type TokenOwnership (L29) or the TokenOwnership received from a call to function unpackedOwnership of contract Running1 (L23), which is done in the private function _ownershipAt. The execution of function unpackedOwnership in Running1 allocates two different memory slots at L13: s_1, for the returned variable ownership, and s_2, which is used for actually returning from the function the contents of ownership:

---

[3] Although the local memory is byte addressable with instruction MSTORE8, to keep the description simpler, we only consider the general case of word-addressable MSTORE.

The function `explicitOwnershipOf` in `Running2` makes a more intensive use of the memory which can be seen in this graphical representation:

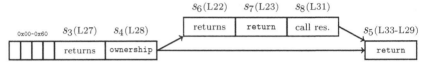

The execution of this function might create up to six different slots. At L27 and L28, it creates two slots, one for the struct declared in the `returns` part of the function header (s_3) and one for the local variable `ownership` (s_4). Depending on the evaluation of the condition in the `if` sentence, it might create the slots needed to perform the call to `_ownershipAt` and, consequently, the external call to `Running1.unpackedOwnership`. The invocation to the private function involves three slots: one for the struct declared in the `returns` part of `_ownershipAt` in L31 (s_6), one slot to manage the external call data in L23 (s_7), and one slot for storing the results of the private function `_ownershipAt` in L31 (s_8). Finally, a new slot (s_5) is created for returning the results of `explicitOwnershipOf`. This new slot might contain the contents of s_4 or s_8, depending on the `if` evaluation.

When an amount of memory t is to be allocated, the slot reservation is made by reading and incrementing the free memory pointer ($mem\langle 0x40 \rangle$) t positions. From this update on, the *base reference* to the slot just allocated is used, and subsequent accesses to the slot are performed by means of this baseref, possibly incremented by an offset.

Example 2 (memory slot reservation). The following excerpt of EVM code allocates a slot of type `TokenOwnership`. The EVM bytecode performs three steps: (i) load the current value of the free memory pointer $mem\langle 0x40 \rangle$ that will be used as the baseref of the new slot; (ii) compute the new free memory address by adding t to the baseref; and (iii), store the new free memory pointer in $mem\langle 0x40 \rangle$. Additionally, in the same block of the CFG, the slot reservation is followed by the slot initialization at `0x19A`, `0x1AB` and `0x1B4`.

```
0x175: JUMPDEST
0x176: PUSH1 0x40
0x178: MLOAD     // (i) baseref
       DUP1
       PUSH1 0x60 // Sizeof "t"
       ADD   // (ii) baseref+0x60
0x17D: PUSH1 0x40
0x17F: MSTORE    // (iii)
       ...
0x19A: MSTORE    // baseref+0x00
       ...
0x1AB: MSTORE    // baseref+0x20
       ...
0x1B4: MSTORE    // baseref+0x40
```

Solidity reference type values such as arrays, struct typed variables and strings are stored in memory using this general pattern, with some minor differences. However, there are some cases in which the steps detailed above vary and the size of the slot is not known in advance, and thus the free memory pointer cannot be updated at this point. For instance, when data is returned by an external call, its length is unknown beforehand and hence the free memory pointer is updated only after the memory pointed to is written. In other cases, the free memory is used as a temporary region with a short lifetime, as in the case of parameter passing to external calls, and the free memory pointer is not updated. These variants of the general schema must be detected by a precise memory analysis. To this end, we consider that a slot is in *transient* state when its baseref has been read from $mem\langle 0x40\rangle$ but the free memory pointer has not been updated, and it is in *permanent* state when the free memory pointer has been pushed forward.

Example 3 (transient slot). Now we focus on the external call in L23 of Running2, which performs a STATICCALL, reading from the stack (see [27] for details) the memory location of the input arguments and the location where the results of the call will be saved. Interestingly, both locations reuse the same slot (it corresponds to s_7) as it can be seen in the following EVM bytecode from _ownerShipAt:

```
        PUSH4 0xb04dd20b // func. selector        PUSH 0x40
        ...                                 0x132: MLOAD      // slot baseref
        PUSH1 0x40                                ...
0x114:  MLOAD      // baseref transient slot 0x139: STATICCALL // external call
        ...                                       ...
        DUP2                                      PUSH1 0x40
        MSTORE  // stores func. selector    0x151: MLOAD      // slot baseref
        PUSH1 0x04                                RETURNDATASIZE
        ADD     // offset of funct. args.          ...
        ... // copy func. args.                   ADD       // baseref + data size
        MSTORE  // stores func. args.              ...
        ...                                 0x15E: PUSH1 0x40
                                            0x160: MSTORE   // permanent slot
```

The call starts by reading the free memory pointer (at 0x114) and storing at that address the arguments' data (which include the function selector as first argument). Importantly, the pointer is not pushed forward when the input arguments are written and thus the slot remains in transient state. Once the call at 0x139 is executed, the result is written to memory from the baseref on (overwriting the locations used for the input arguments) and the slot is finally made permanent by reading the free memory pointer again (0x151) and updating it (0x160) by adding the actual return data size (RETURNDATASIZE).

Transient slots are also used when returning data from a public function to an external caller. In that case, the EVM code of the public function halts its execution using a RETURN instruction. It reads from the stack the memory location where the length and the data to be returned are located. However, it does not change $mem\langle 0x40\rangle$ because the function code halts its execution at this point, as we can see in the EVM code of explicitOwnershipOf (corresponds to slot s_5):

```
        PUSH1 0x40                                 ...
0x4D:   MLOAD   //ret slot baseref          0x5A: MLOAD   //ret slot revisit
        MSTORE  // ret.addr (ret+0x00)             DUP1
        ...                                        SWAP2  //Baseref of ret plus size
        MSTORE  // ret.startTs (ret+0x20)          SUB    //Size of ret data
        ...                                 0x5E: SWAP1
        MSTORE  // ret.burned (ret+0x40)    0x5F: RETURN //ret returned
```

The baseref for the return slot is read (at 0x4D) and it is used as a transient slot to write the struct contents to be returned by adding the corresponding offset for each field contained in the struct (instructions on the left column). The code on the left ends with the baseref plus the size of the stored data on top of the stack. After that, the baseref is read again (top of the right column) and the length of the returned data is computed (by subtracting the baseref to the baseref plus the size of the stored data) before calling the RETURN instruction.

3   Inference of Needless Write Accesses

This section presents our static inference of needless write accesses. We first provide some background in Sec. 3.1 on the type of control-flow-graph (CFG) and static analysis we rely upon. Then, the analysis is divided into three consecutive steps: (1) the slot analysis, which is introduced in Sec. 3.2, to identify the slots created along the execution and the program points at which they are allocated; (2) the slot usage analysis, presented in Sec. 3.3, which computes the read and write accesses to the different slots identified in the previous step; and (3) the detection of needless write accesses, given in Sec. 3.4, which finds those program points where there is a write access to a slot which has no read access later on.

3.1   Context-Sensitive CFG and Flow-Sensitive Static Analysis

The construction of the CFG of Ethereum smart contracts is a key part of any decompiler and static analysis tool and has been subject of previous research [15, 16, 25]. The more precise the CFG is, the more accurate our analysis results will be. In particular, context-sensitivity [16] on the CFG construction is vital to achieve precise results. Our implementation of context-sensitivity is realized by cloning the blocks which are reached from different contexts.

Example 4 (context-sensitive CFG). The EVM code of Running2 creates multiple slots for handling structs of type TokenOwnership. Interestingly, all these slots are created by means of the same EVM code shown in Ex. 2, which corresponds to the CFG block that starts at program point 0x175. As this block is reached from different contexts, the context-sensitive CFG contains three clones of this block: 0x175, which creates s_3 at L27; 0x175_0, which creates s_4 used at L28; and 0x175_1, which reserves s_6, created at L22. Block cloning means that program points are cloned as well, and we adopt the same subindex notation to refer to the program points included in the cloned block: e.g. program point 0x178 contains the MLOAD 0x40 that gets the baseref of the slot reserved at block 0x178, and 0x178_0 to the same MLOAD but at 0x178_0, etc.

In what follows, we assume that cloning has been made and the memory analysis using the resulting CFG (with clones) is thus context-sensitive as well, without requiring additional extensions. As usual in standard analyses [23], one has to define the notion of *abstract state* which defines the abstract information gathered in the analysis and the *transfer function* which models the analysis output for each possible input. Besides context-sensitivity, the two analyses that we will present in the next two sections are *flow-sensitive*, i.e., they make a flow-sensitive traversal of the CFG of the program using as input for analyzing each block of the CFG the information inferred for its callers. When the analysis reaches a CFG block with new information, we use the operation $\sqcup$ to join the two abstract states, and the operator $\sqsubseteq$ to detect that a fixpoint is reached and, thus, that the analysis terminates. The operations $\sqcup$ and $\sqsubseteq$, the abstract state, and transfer function, will be defined for each particular analysis.

3.2   Slot Analysis

The slot analysis aims at inferring the *abstract slots*, which are an abstraction of all memory allocations that will be made along the program execution. The slots inferred are *abstract* because over-approximation is made at the level of the program points at which slots are allocated. Therefore, an abstract slot might represent multiple (not necessarily consecutive) real memory slots, e.g., when memory is allocated within a loop. The slot analysis will look for those program points at which the value stored in $mem\langle 0x40\rangle$ is read for reserving memory space. These program points are relevant in the analysis for two reasons: firstly, to obtain the baseref of the memory slot, and, secondly, because from this point on, the memory reservation of the corresponding slot has started and it is pending to become permanent at some subsequent program point. The output of the slot analysis is a set which contains the allocated abstract slots, named S_{all} in Def. 2 below. Each allocated abstract slot (i.e., each element in S_{all}) is in turn a set of program points, as the same abstract slot might have several program points where $mem\langle 0x40\rangle$ is read before its reservation becomes permanent. In order to obtain S_{all}, the memory analysis makes a flow-sensitive traversal of the (context-sensitive) CFG of the program that keeps at every program point the set of transient slots (i.e. whose baseref has been read but it has not yet made permanent) and applies the transfer function in Def. 1 to each bytecode instruction within the blocks until a fixpoint is reached. An *abstract state* of the analysis is a set $S \subseteq \wp(\mathcal{P}_R)$, where $\mathcal{P}_R$ is the set of all program points at which $mem\langle 0x40\rangle$ is read. The analysis of the program starts with $S = \{\emptyset\}$ at all program points and takes $\sqcup$ and $\sqsubseteq$ as the set union and inclusion operations. Termination is trivially guaranteed as the number of program points is finite and so is $\wp(\mathcal{P}_R)$. In what follows, *Ins* is the set of EVM instructions and, for simplicity, we consider MLOAD 0x40 and MSTORE 0x40 as single instructions in *Ins*.

Definition 1 (slot analysis transfer function). *Given a program point pp with an instruction $I \in Ins$, an abstract state S, and $K = \{MSTORE\ 0x40, RETURN, REVERT, STOP, SELFDESTRUCT\}$, the slot analysis transfer function ν is defined as a mapping $\nu : Ins \times \wp(S) \mapsto \wp(S)$ computed according to the following table:*

	I	$\nu(\mathbf{I}, S)$
(1)	MLOAD 0x40	$\{s \cup \{pp\} \mid s \in S\}$
(2)	$I \in K$	$\{\emptyset\}$
(3)	otherwise	S

Let us explain intuitively how the above transfer function works. As we have seen in Sec. 2, in an EVM program all memory reservations start by reading $mem\langle 0x40\rangle$ by means of a MLOAD instruction preceded by a PUSH 0x40 instruction (case 1 in Def. 1). In this case, the transfer function adds to all sets in S the current program point, since this is, in principle, an access to the same slots that were already open at this program point and are not permanent yet. To properly identify the slots, our analysis also searches for those program points at which slots reservations are made permanent (case 2 in Def. 1), i.e., those program points with instructions $I \in K$. The most frequently used instruction to make a slot reservation *permanent* is a write access to $mem\langle 0x40\rangle$ using MSTORE, that pushes forward the free memory pointer such that any subsequent read access to $mem\langle 0x40\rangle$ will allocate a different slot. The rest of instructions in K finalize the execution in different forms (a normal return, a forced stop, a revert execution, etc.). In all such cases, the slot needs to be considered as a permanent slot so that we can reason later on potential needless write accesses involved in it. The set $\mathcal{S}$ is empty after these instructions since all transient (abstract) slots are made permanent after them. We use the notation $\mathcal{S}_{pp}$ to refer to the abstract state computed at program point pp.

Example 5 (slot analysis). The slot analysis of Running2 starts with $\mathcal{S}_{pp}=\{\emptyset\}$ at all program points. When it reaches the block that starts at 0x175 (see Ex. 2) $\mathcal{S}_{0x175}$ is $\{\emptyset\}$ and it remains empty until 0x178, where the baseref of s_3 is read and hence $\mathcal{S}_{0x178}=\{\{0x178\}\}$. This slot is made permanent when the free memory pointer is updated at 0x17F, thus having $\mathcal{S}_{0x17D}=\{\{0x178\}\}$ and $\mathcal{S}_{0x17F}=\{\emptyset\}$. Following the same pattern, s_4 and s_6 are resp. reserved at instructions 0x178_0 and 0x178_1 and closed at 0x17F_0 and 0x17F_1 (at the cloned blocks). On the other hand, the baseref of s_5 is read at two consecutive program points (0x4D and 0x5A) and updated at 0x5F, and thus, we have $\mathcal{S}_{0x4D}=\{\{0x4D\}\}$ and the same until $\mathcal{S}_{0x5A}=\{\{0x4D,0x5A\}\}$ and again the same until $\mathcal{S}_{0x5F}=\{\emptyset\}$. Finally, after the execution of STATICCALL (see Ex. 3) we have three consecutive reads of $mem\langle 0x40\rangle$ at 0x114, 0x132 and 0x151 that refer to the same slot s_7, which is made permanent at 0x160. Therefore, we have $\mathcal{S}_{0x151}=\{\{0x114,0x132,0x151\}\}$ and $\mathcal{S}_{0x160}=\{\emptyset\}$.

Using the transfer function, as mentioned in Sec. 3.1, our analysis makes a flow-sensitive traversal of the (context-sensitive) CFG of the program that uses as input for analyzing each block the information inferred for its callers. When a fixpoint is reached, we have an abstract state for each program point that we use to compute the set of abstract slots allocated in the program, named $\mathcal{S}_{all}$.

Definition 2. *The set of allocated abstract slots $\mathcal{S}_{all}$ is defined as $\mathcal{S}_{all} = \bigcup_{pp\in\mathcal{P}_W} \mathcal{S}_{pp-1}$, where $\mathcal{P}_W$ is the set of all program points $pp{:}I$ where $I\in\mathcal{K}$.*

Example 6 ($\mathcal{S}_{all}$ computation). With the values of $\mathcal{S}_{0x17F-1}$, $\mathcal{S}_{0x17F\_0-1}$, $\mathcal{S}_{0x17F\_1-1}$, $\mathcal{S}_{0x160-1}$ and $\mathcal{S}_{0x5F-1}$ from Ex. 5, at the end of the slot analysis of Running2, we have:
$\mathcal{S}_{all}=\{\underbrace{\{0x178\}}_{s_3}, \underbrace{\{0x178\_0\}}_{s_4}, \underbrace{\{0x178\_1\}}_{s_6}, \underbrace{\{0x114,0x132,0x151\}}_{s_7}, \underbrace{\{0x5A,0x4D\}}_{s_5}, \dots\}.$

Note that, the cloning of block 0x175 allows our analysis to detect three different slots, s_3, s_4 and s_6, for the same program point, 0x178, in the original EVM code.

The next example shows the behavior of the analysis when the program contains loops, and an abstraction is needed for approximating the slots.

Example 7 (loops). Fig. 2 shows the contract Running3 that includes the function explicitOwnershipsOf from the smart contract at [2] (made through a STATICCALL). This function receives an array of token identifiers as argument and returns an array of TokenOwnership structs that is populated invoking the function explicitOwnershipOf from Running2 inside a loop. The slots identified by the analysis for contract Running3 shown in Fig. 2 are: s_9, which is created for making a copy of parameter tokenIds to memory; s_{10}, which creates the local array ownerships (L44) that contains the array length and pointers to the structs identified initially by s_{11} (and later on by s_{13}); s_{12} for STATICCALL input arguments and return data (L46); s_{13} which abstracts the structs for storing the STATICCALL output results (L46); and s_{14}, which includes the length of ownership

```
37 contract Running3 {
38    Running2 c;
39    //...
40 s9 function explicitOwnershipsOf(uint256[] memory tokenIds)
41      public view returns (TokenOwnership[] memory) {
42      unchecked {
43        uint256 tokenIdsLength = tokenIds.length;
44 s10s11 TokenOwnership[] memory ownerships = new TokenOwnership[](tokenIdsLength);
45        for (uint256 i; i != tokenIdsLength; ++i) {
46 s12s13       ownerships[i] = c.explicitOwnershipOf(tokenIds[i]);
47      }
48 s14    return ownerships;
49    }
50  }
51 }
```

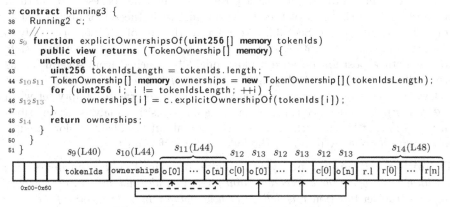

Fig. 2: Solidity code of contract Caller.

and a copy of s_{13} for returning the results (L48). The important point is that, the local array declaration at L44 produces a loop to allocate as many structs as elements are contained in the array. For this reason, s_{11} is an abstract slot that represents all TokenOwnership's initially added to the array. Similarly, s_{12} and s_{13} are created inside the for loop, and each abstract slot represents as many concrete slots as iterations are performed by the loop. Note that, each iteration of the loop creates one instance of s_{12} for getting the results from the call, and it is copied later to s_{13} and pointed by ownerships (s_{10}).

As notation, we will use a unique numeric identifier (1, 2, ...) to refer to each abstract slot (represented in $\mathcal{S}_{all}$ as a set) and retrieve it by means of function $get\_id(a), a \in \mathcal{S}_{all}$. We use $\mathcal{A}$ to refer to the set of all such identifiers in the program. Also, given a program point pp with an instruction MLOAD 0x40, we define the function $get\_slots(pp)$ to retrieve the identifiers of the elements of $\mathcal{S}_{all}$ that might be referenced at pp as follows: $get\_slots(pp) = \{id \mid a \in \mathcal{S}_{all} \wedge pp \in a \wedge id = get\_id(a)\}$.

3.3 Slot Access Analysis

While Sec. 3.2 looked for allocations, the next step of the analysis is the inference of the program points at which the inferred abstract slots might be accessed. To do so, our slot access analysis needs to propagate the references to the abstract slots that are saved at the different positions of the execution stack. Importantly, we keep track, not only of the stack positions, but also, in order to abstract complex data structures stored in memory (e.g., arrays of structs), we need to keep track of the abstract slots that could be saved at memory locations. As seen in Ex. 7, a memory location within a slot might contain a pointer to another memory location of another slot, as it happens when nested data structures are used. Thus, an abstract state is a mapping at which we store the potential slots saved at stack positions or at memory locations within other slots.

Definition 3 (memory analysis abstract state). *A memory analysis abstract state is a mapping π of the form $\mathcal{T} \cup \mathcal{A} \mapsto \wp(\mathcal{A})$.*

$\mathcal{T}$ is the set containing all stack positions, which we represent by natural numbers from 0 (bottom of the stack) on, and $\mathcal{A}$ is the set of abstract slots identifiers computed in Sec. 3.2. We refer to the set of all memory analysis abstract states as AS. Note that, for each entry, we keep a set of potential slots for each stack position because a block might be reached from several blocks with different execution stacks, e.g., in loops or *if-then-else* structures. In what follows, we assume that, given a value k, the map π returns the empty set when $k \notin dom(\pi)$. The inference is performed by a flow-sensitive analysis (as described in Sec. 3.1) that keeps track of the information about the abstract slots used at any program point by means of the following transfer function.

Definition 4 (memory analysis transfer function). *Given an instruction I with n input operands at program point pp and an abstract state π, the* memory analysis transfer function τ *is defined as a mapping $\tau:Ins \times AS \mapsto AS$ of the form:*

	I	$\tau(I, \pi)$		I	$\tau(I, \pi)$
(1)	MLOAD 0x40	$\pi[t \mapsto get\_slots(pp)]$	(4)	SWAPi	$\pi[t \mapsto \pi(t-i), t-i \mapsto \pi(t)]$
(2)	MLOAD	$\pi[t \mapsto \{m \mid s \in \pi(t) \wedge m \in \pi(s)\}]$	(5)	DUPi	$\pi[t+1 \mapsto \pi(t-i+1)]$
(3)	MSTORE	$\pi[s \mapsto \pi(s) \cup \pi(t-1)] \backslash \{t, t-1\}$ $\forall s \in \pi(t)$	(6)	otherwise	$\pi \backslash x$ $t-n < x \leq t$

$t=top(pp)$ *is the numerical position of the top of the stack before executing I.*

Let us explain the above definition. The transfer function distinguishes between two different types of MLOAD: (1) accesses to location $mem\langle 0x40\rangle$, which return the baseref of the slots that might be used, taking them from the previous analysis through $get\_slots(p)$; and (2) other MLOAD instructions, which could potentially return slot baserefs from memory locations. Therefore, we have to consider two possibilities: if we are reading a memory location which reads a generic value (e.g. a number) then $\pi(t) = \emptyset$; if we are reading a memory location that might store an abstract slot, then $\pi(t)$ contains all abstract slots that might be stored at that memory location. Regarding (3), MSTORE has two operands: the operand at t is the memory address that will be modified by MSTORE, and the operand at $t - 1$ is the value to be stored in that address. For each element s in $\pi(t)$, the analysis adds the abstract slots that are in $\pi(t-1)$. Other instructions that are also treated by the analysis are SWAP* and DUP* shown in (4-5), that exchange or copy the elements of the stack that take part in the operation. Finally, all other operations delete the elements of the stack that are no longer used based on the number of elements taken and written to the stack (case 6).

Example 8 (transfer). Now we focus on the analysis of block 0x175, shown in Fig. 3. As we have already explained, this block is responsible for creating the memory needed to work with several structs of type TokenOwnership and it is thus cloned in the CFG. In particular, we focus on the clone 0x175_1. The analysis of the block starts with a stack of size 7 and includes at positions 3 and 4, the abstract slots s_3 and s_4, which were created at L26 and L27 of Fig. 1. At 0x178_1, $mem\langle 0x40\rangle$ is read, and, by means of $get\_slots(0x178\_1)$ and, considering that $top(0x178\_1)=8$, we add to π a new entry $8 \mapsto s_6$. At 0x179_1, 0x180_1, 0x1AA_1, 0x1B3_1 the transfer function duplicates a slot identifier stored in the stack. MSTORE and POP instructions of the example remove a slot identifier from the stack.

PP	Instr	π		PP	Instr	π
0x175_1	JUMPDEST	$\{3\mapsto s_3, 4\mapsto s_4\}$		0x19A_1	MSTORE	$\{3\mapsto s_3, 4\mapsto s_4, 8\mapsto s_6, 9\mapsto s_6\}$
0x176_1	PUSH1 0x40	$\{3\mapsto s_3, 4\mapsto s_4\}$		...		
0x178_1	MLOAD	$\{3\mapsto s_3, 4\mapsto s_4, 8\mapsto s_6\}$		0x1A9_1	AND	$\{3\mapsto s_3, 4\mapsto s_4, 8\mapsto s_6, 9\mapsto s_6\}$
0x179_1	DUP1	$\{3\mapsto s_3, 4\mapsto s_4, 8\mapsto s_6, 9\mapsto s_6\}$		0x1AA_1	DUP2	$\{3\mapsto s_3, 4\mapsto s_4, 8\mapsto s_6, 9\mapsto s_6, 11\mapsto s_6\}$
0x17A_1	PUSH1 0x60	$\{3\mapsto s_3, 4\mapsto s_4, 8\mapsto s_6, 9\mapsto s_6\}$		0x1AB_1	MSTORE	$\{3\mapsto s_3, 4\mapsto s_4, 8\mapsto s_6, 9\mapsto s_6\}$
0x17C_1	ADD	$\{3\mapsto s_3, 4\mapsto s_4, 8\mapsto s_6, 9\mapsto s_6\}$		...		
0x17D_1	PUSH1 0x40	$\{3\mapsto s_3, 4\mapsto s_4, 8\mapsto s_6, 9\mapsto s_6\}$		0x1B2_1	ISZERO	$\{3\mapsto s_3, 4\mapsto s_4, 8\mapsto s_6, 9\mapsto s_6\}$
0x17F_1	MSTORE	$\{3\mapsto s_3, 4\mapsto s_4, 8\mapsto s_6\}$		0x1B3_1	DUP2	$\{3\mapsto s_3, 4\mapsto s_4, 8\mapsto s_6, 9\mapsto s_6, 11\mapsto s_6\}$
0x180_1	DUP1	$\{3\mapsto s_3, 4\mapsto s_4, 8\mapsto s_6, 9\mapsto s_6\}$		0x1B4_1	MSTORE	$\{3\mapsto s_3, 4\mapsto s_4, 8\mapsto s_6, 9\mapsto s_6\}$
...				0x1B5_1	POP	$\{3\mapsto s_3, 4\mapsto s_4, 8\mapsto s_6\}$
0x198_1	AND	$\{3\mapsto s_3, 4\mapsto s_4, 8\mapsto s_6, 9\mapsto s_6\}$		0x1B6_1	SWAP1	$\{3\mapsto s_3, 4\mapsto s_4, 7\mapsto s_6\}$
0x199_1	DUP2	$\{3\mapsto s_3, 4\mapsto s_4, 8\mapsto s_6, 9\mapsto s_6, 11\mapsto s_6\}$		0x1B7_1	JUMP	$\{3\mapsto s_3, 4\mapsto s_4, 7\mapsto s_6\}$

Fig. 3: Block of the CFG that reserves memory slot for struct

As it is flow-sensitive, the analysis of each block of the CFG takes as input the join $\sqcup$ of the abstract states computed with the transfer function for the blocks that jump to it, and keeps applying the memory analysis transfer function until a fixpoint is reached. The operation $A \sqcup B$ is the result of joining, by means of operation $\cup$, all entries from maps A and B. Operation $\sqsubseteq$ is defined as expected, $A \sqsubseteq B$, when B includes entries that are not in $dom(A)$ or when we have an entry $v \in dom(A) \cap dom(B)$ such that $A(v) \subseteq B(v)$. Again, termination of the computation is guaranteed because the domain is finite.

Example 9 (joining abstract states). The EVM code of `explicitOwnershipOf` of Fig. 1 uses s_5 in both `return` sentences at L29 and L33 (see Ex. 1). This EVM code has a single return block which is reachable from two different paths from the `if` statement, and which come with different abstract states: (1) the path that corresponds to L29 comes with $\pi=\{3 \mapsto s_8\}$, and the other path (L33) with $\pi=\{3 \mapsto s_4\}$. Our analysis joins both abstract states resulting in $\pi=\{3 \mapsto \{s_4, s_8\}\}$. Because of this join, we get that the `RETURN` instruction that comes from lines L29 and L33 might return the content of the slots s_4 or s_8.

When the fixpoint is reached, the analysis has computed an abstract state for each program point pp, denoted by π_{pp} in what follows.

Example 10 (complex data structures). The analysis of the code at Fig. 2 shows how it deals with data structures that might contain pointers to other structures, e.g. `ownerships`. The abstract slot that represents variable `ownerships` is s_{10}, which is written, by means of `MSTORE` at two program points, say pp_1 and pp_2 which, resp., come from L44 and L46 of the Solidity code. The input abstract state that reaches pp_1 is $\{2 \mapsto s_9, 6 \mapsto s_{10}, 8 \mapsto s_{10}, 9 \mapsto s_{11}, 10 \mapsto s_{10}\}$, and the transfer function of `MSTORE` leaves the abstract state as $\pi_{pp_1} = \{2 \mapsto s_9, 6 \mapsto s_{10}, 8 \mapsto s_{10}, s_{10} \mapsto s_{11}\}$. At this point, we can see that variable `ownerships` is initialized with empty structs and, to represent it, our analysis includes in π the entry $s_{10} \mapsto s_{11}$ as it is described in instruction `MSTORE` of the transfer function at Def. 4. The second write to s_{10} is performed by another `MSTORE` instruction at pp_2. The input abstract state for pp_2 is $\{2 \mapsto s_9, 5 \mapsto s_{10}, 7 \mapsto s_{13}, 8 \mapsto s_{13}, 9 \mapsto s_{10}, s_{10} \mapsto s_{11}\}$, and thus we get $\pi_{pp_2} = \{2 \mapsto s_9, 5 \mapsto s_{10}, 7 \mapsto s_{13}, s_{10} \mapsto \{s_{11}, s_{13}\}\}$. Interestingly, at pp_2, we detect that s_{11} might also store the structs returned by the call to `c.explicitOwnershipOf(tokenIds[i])`, identified by s_{13}, which is added to

$s_{10} \mapsto \{s_{11}, s_{13}\}$. Finally, s_{10} is read at the end of the method, returning the set $\{s_{11}, s_{13}\}$, to copy the content of ownerships to s_{14}, the slot used in the return.

3.4 Inference of Needless Write Memory Accesses

With the results of the previous analysis, we can compute the maps $\mathcal{R}$ and $\mathcal{W}$, which are of the form $pp \mapsto \wp(\mathcal{A})$ and capture the slots that might be read or written, resp., at the different program points. To do so, as multiple EVM instructions, e.g. RETURN, CALL, LOG, CREATE, ..., might read, or write, memory locations taking the concrete location from the stack, we define functions $mr(I)$ and $mw(I)$ that, given an EVM instruction I, return the position in the stack of the address to be read and written by I, resp. If the instruction does not read/write any memory position, function $mr(I) = \bot / mw(I) = \bot$. For example, $mr(\text{MLOAD}) = 0$ as it reads the top of the stack and $mw(\text{MLOAD}) = \bot$, or $mr(\text{STATICCALL}) = 2$ and $mw(\text{STATICCALL}) = 4$. Now, we define the read/write maps $\mathcal{R}/\mathcal{W}$:

Definition 5 (memory read/write accesses map). *Given an EVM program P, such that $pp \equiv I \in P$ and being $t{=}top(pp)$, we define maps $\mathcal{R}$ and $\mathcal{W}$ as follows:*

$$\mathcal{R}(pp) = \begin{cases} \emptyset & mr(I) = \bot \\ \pi_{pp-1}(t - mr(I)) & otherwise \end{cases} \qquad \mathcal{W}(pp) = \begin{cases} \emptyset & mw(I) = \bot \\ \pi_{pp-1}(t - mw(I)) & otherwise \end{cases}$$

Example 11 ($\mathcal{R}/\mathcal{W}$ maps). Let us illustrate the computation of $\mathcal{R}(\text{0x139})$ and $\mathcal{W}(\text{0x139})$, which contains the STATICCALL of Running2. With the analysis information obtained from the analysis we have that $top(\text{0x139}) = 16$ and $\pi_{\text{0x138}} = \{3 \mapsto s_3, 4 \mapsto s_4, 7 \mapsto s_6, 10 \mapsto s_7, 12 \mapsto s_7, 14 \mapsto s_7\}$, thus we get $\mathcal{R}(\text{0x139}) = \{s_7\}$ and $\mathcal{W}(\text{0x139}) = \{s_7\}$, i.e., the slot used for managing the input and the output of the external call. Analogously, we get that $\mathcal{R}(\text{0x178}) = \{s_3\}$ and $\mathcal{W}(\text{0x178}) = \emptyset$.

The last step of our analysis consists in searching for write accesses to slots which will never be read later. To do so, we use the information computed in $\mathcal{R}$ and $\mathcal{W}$. Given the CFG of the program and two program points p and $p2$, we define function $reachable(p, p2)$, which returns $true$ when there exists a path in the CFG from p to $p2$. We define the set *write leaks* $\mathcal{N}$ as follows:

Definition 6. *Given an EVM program and its $\mathcal{W}$ and $\mathcal{R}$, we define $\mathcal{N}$ as*
$$\mathcal{N} = \{pw{:}s \mid pw \in P \wedge s \in \mathcal{W}(pw) \wedge \neg exists\_read(pw, s)\}$$
where $exists\_read(pw, s) \equiv \exists \, pr \in dom(\mathcal{R}) \mid s \in \mathcal{R}(pr) \wedge reachable(pw, pr)$.

Intuitively, the set $\mathcal{N}$ contains those write accesses, taken from $\mathcal{W}$, that are never read by subsequent blocks in the CFG. As both function *reachable* and the sets $\mathcal{W}$ and $\mathcal{R}$ are over-approximations, the computation of $\mathcal{N}$ provides us those write accesses that can be safely removed, as the next example shows.

Example 12. Our analysis detects that at program points 0x19A, 0x1AB and 0x1B4 there are MSTORE operations that are never read in the subsequent blocks of the CFG. Such operations correspond to the memory initialization of s_3, which is performed at L27 of the code of Fig. 1 (see Ex. 2). Given that these write accesses are the only use of the slot, the whole reservation can be safely removed.

Moreover, the analysis detects that program points 0x19A_1, 0x1AB_1 and 0x1B4_1, which correspond to the reservation of s_6 performed at L22, are detected as needless. In essence, it means that s_3 and s_6 are allocated and initialized but are never used in the program. Note that, all these program points belong to two blocks cloned: (0x175 and 0x175_1). However, the three MSTORE operations of the other clone of the same block (0x175_0), which correspond to the allocation at L28 are not identified as non-read, as they might be used in the return of the function. For this, the precision of the context-sensitive CFG is necessary to identify these MSTORE operations as needless. As a result we cannot eliminate the block because it is needed in one of the clones, but still we can achieve an important optimization on the EVM code by removing the unconditional jumps to this block in the other two cases that would avoid completely the execution of all these instructions (and their corresponding gas consumption [27]).

The soundness of slots and slots access analyses states that, for each concrete slot, there exists an abstract slot in $\mathcal{S}_{all}$ that represents it and, that any access to memory is approximated by an inferred abstract slot. Technical details can be found in an extended report [8].

4 Experimental Evaluation

This section reports on the results of the experimental evaluation of our approach, as described in Sec. 3. All components of the analysis are implemented in Python, are open-source, and can be downloaded from github where detailed instructions for its installation and usage are provided[4]. We use external components to build the CFGs (as this is not a contribution of our work). Our analysis tool accepts smart contracts written in versions of Solidity up to 0.8.17 and bytecode for the Ethereum Virtual Machine v1.10.25[5]. The experiments have been performed on an AMD Ryzen Threadripper PRO 3995WX 64-cores and 512 GB of memory, running Debian 5.10.70. In order to experimentally evaluate the analysis, we pulled from etherscan.io [5] the Ethereum contracts bound to the last 5,000 open-source verified addresses whose source code was available on July 14, 2022. From those addresses, the code of 2.18% of them raises a compilation error from solc. For the code bound to the 4,891 remaining addresses, the generation of the CFG (which is not a contribution of this work) timeouts after 120s on 626 of them. Removing such failing cases, we have finally analyzed 19,199 smart contracts, as each address and each Solidity file may contain several contracts in it. Note that 84.86% of the contracts are compiled with the solc version 0.8, presumably with the most advanced compilation techniques. The whole dataset used will be found at the above github link.

In order to be in a worst-case scenario for us, we run the memory analysis after executing the solc optimizer, i.e, we analyze bytecode whose memory usage may have been optimized already by the optimizer available in solc. This will allow us also to see if we can achieve further optimization with our

---

[4] https://github.com/costa-group/EthIR/tree/memory_optimizer/ethir
[5] The latest versions released up to Oct 2022.

approach. Unfortunately, we have not been able to apply our tool after running the super-optimizer GASOL [9], because it does not generate the optimized bytecode but rather it only reports on the gas and/or size gains for each of the blocks. Nevertheless, a detailed comparison of the techniques that GASOL applies and ours is given in Sec. 5, where we justify that GASOL will not find any of our needless accesses. From the 19,199 analyzed contracts, the analysis infers 679,517 abstract memory slots and detects 6,242 needless write memory accesses in 12,803s. These needless accesses occur within the code bound to 780 different addresses, i.e., 15.95% of the analyzed ones.

We have computed the number of needless accesses identified by our analysis grouped by function and the number of different contracts that contain these functions. Some of them such as transferFrom(1736 accesses in 439 contracts), transfer (1745 aacesses in 441 contracts), reflectionFromToken(105 accesses in 6 contracts) or withdraw(54 accesses in 32 contracts) are functions widely used in the implementation of contracts based on ERC tokens. A manual inspection of the 10 most common public functions with the needless accesses inferred has revealed two different sources for them: some of the needles accesses are due to inefficient programming practices, while others are generated by the compiler and could be improved. As regards compiler inefficiencies, we detected bytecode that allocates memory slots that are inaccessible and cannot be used because the baseref to access them is not maintained in the stack. For example, when a struct is returned by a function, it always allocates memory for this data. However, if the return variable is not named in the header of the function, the compiler allocates memory for this data although it will never be accessed. If programmers are aware of this behavior they can avoid such generation of useless memory but, even better, this memory usage patterns can be changed in the compiler. For instance, it is reflected in L22 and L27 in Fig. 1, where the functions do not name the return variable. Hence, the compiler allocates memory for these *anonymous* data structures which are never used. Similarly, there are various situations involving external calls in which the compiler creates memory that is never used. When there is an external call that does not retrieve any result, the compiler creates two memory slots, one for retrieving the result from the call, and another one for copying a potential result to a memory variable that is never used. Finally, the compiler also creates memory that is never used for low-level plain calls for currency transfer. Even though the contract code does not use the second result returned by the low-level call, the compiler generates code for retrieving it. All these potential optimizations have been detected by means of our inference of needless write accesses and will be communicated to the solc developers.

5   Conclusions and Related Work

We have proposed a novel memory analysis for Ethereum smart contracts and have applied it to infer needless write memory accesses. The application of our implementation over more than 19,000 real smart contracts has detected some compilation patterns that introduce needless write accesses and that can be easily changed in the compiler to generate more efficient code. Let us discuss related work along two directions: (1) memory analysis and (2) memory optimization. Regarding (1), we can find advanced points-to analysis developed for Java-like languages [7, 11, 18, 20]. Focusing on EVM, the static modeling of the EVM memory in [16] has some similarities with the memory analysis presented in Secs. 3.2 and 3.3, since in both cases we are seeking to model the memory although with different applications in mind. There are differences on one hand on the type of static analysis used in both cases: [16] is based on a Datalog analysis while we have defined a standard transfer function which is used within a flow-sensitive analysis. More importantly, there are differences on the precision of both analyses. We can accurately model the memory allocated by nested data structures in which the memory contains pointers to other memory slots, while [16] does not capture such type of accesses. This is fundamental to perform memory optimization since, as shown in the running examples of the paper, it allows detecting needless write accesses that otherwise would be missed. Finally, the application of the memory analysis to optimization is not studied in [16], while it is the main focus of our work.

As regards (2), optimizing memory usage is a challenging research problem that requires to precisely infer the memory positions that are being accessed. Such positions sometimes are statically known (e.g., when accessing the EVM free memory pointer) but, as we have seen, often a precise and complex inference is required to figure out the slot being accessed at each memory access bytecode. Recent work within the super-optimizer GASOL [9] is able to perform some memory optimizations at the level of each block of the CFG (i.e., intra-block). of There are three fundamental differences between our work and GASOL: First, GASOL can only apply the optimizations when the memory locations being addressed refer to the same constant direction. In other words, there is no real memory analysis (namely Secs. 3.2 and 3.3). Second, the optimizations are applied only at an intra-block level and hence many optimization opportunities are missed. These two points make a fundamental difference with our approach, since detected optimizable patterns (see Sec. 4) require inter-block analysis and a precise slot access analysis, and hence cannot be detected by GASOL.

Finally, as mentioned in Sec. 1, in addition to dynamic memory, smart contracts also use a persistent memory called storage. Regarding the application of our approach to infer needless accesses in storage, there are two main points. First, there is no need to develop a static analysis to detect the slots in storage, as they are statically known (hence our inference in Sec. 3.2 and 3.3 is not needed), i.e., one can easily know the read and write sets of Def. 6. Thus, the read and write sets of our analysis can be easily defined for storage. The second point is that, as storage is persistent memory, a write storage access is not removable even if there is no further read access within the smart contract, as it needs to be stored for a future transaction. The removable write storage accesses are only those that are rewritten and not read in-between the two write accesses. Including this in our implementation is straightforward. However, this situation is rather unusual, and we believe that very few cases would be found and hence little optimization can be achieved.

References

1. Bamboo. https://github.com/pirapira/bamboo.
2. ERC721A. https://etherscan.io/address/0xfcd5c0ef90715dc052dad6de08efda758aa09f60#code.
3. Serpent. https://github.com/ethereum/wiki/wiki/Serpent.
4. Vyper. https://github.com/ethereum/vyper.
5. Etherscan. https://etherscan.io, 2018.
6. Solidity documentation, 2021. https://docs.soliditylang.org/en/latest/index.html.
7. Elvira Albert, Puri Arenas, Jesús Correas, Samir Genaim, Miguel Gómez-Zamalloa, and Germán Puebla an d Guillermo Román-Díez. Object-Sensitive Cost Analysis for Concurrent Objects. *Software Testing, Verification and Reliability*, 25(3):218–271, 2015.
8. Elvira Albert, Jesús Correas, Pablo Gordillo, Guillermo Román-Díez, and Albert Rubio. Inferring needless write memory accesses on ethereum bytecode (extended version), 2023. arXiv:2301.04757 [cs.PL].
9. Elvira Albert, Pablo Gordillo, Alejandro Hernández-Cerezo, and Albert Rubio. A Max-SMT Superoptimizer for EVM handling Memory and Storage. In Dana Fisman and Grigore Rosu, editors, *28th International Conference on Tools and Algorithms for the Construction and Analysis of Systems, TACAS 2022. Proceedings*, volume 13243 of *Lecture Notes in Computer Science*, pages 201–219. Springer, 2022.
10. T. Brandstätter, S. Schulte, J. Cito, and M. Borkowski. Characterizing Efficiency Optimizations in Solidity Smart Contracts. In *2020 IEEE International Conference on Blockchain (Blockchain)*, pages 281–290, 2020.
11. Ramkrishna Chatterjee, Barbara G. Ryder, and William Landi. Relevant context inference. In Andrew W. Appel and Alex Aiken, editors, *POPL '99, Proceedings of the 26th ACM SIGPLAN-SIGACT Symposium on Principles of Programming Languages, San Antonio, TX, USA, January 20-22, 1999*, pages 133–146. ACM, 1999.
12. Ting Chen, Youzheng Feng, Zihao Li, Hao Zhou, Xiapu Luo, Xiaoqi Li, Xiuzhuo Xiao, Jiachi Chen, and Xiaosong Zhang. Gaschecker: Scalable analysis for discovering gas-inefficient smart contracts. *IEEE Transactions on Emerging Topics in Computing*, PP(99):1–14, 03 2020.
13. Ting Chen, Zihao Li, Hao Zhou, Jiachi Chen, Xiapu Luo, Xiaoqi Li, and Xiaosong Zhang. Towards saving money in using smart contracts. In *Proceedings of the 40th International Conference on Software Engineering: New Ideas and Emerging Results, ICSE (NIER) 2018, Gothenburg, Sweden, May 27 - June 03, 2018*, pages 81–84, 2018.
14. Bo Gao, Siyuan Shen, Ling Shi, Jiaying Li, Jun Sun, and Lei Bu. Verification assisted gas reduction for smart contracts. In *28th Asia-Pacific Software Engineering Conference, APSEC 2021, Taipei, Taiwan, December 6-9, 2021*, pages 264–274. IEEE, 2021.
15. Neville Grech, Lexi Brent, Bernhard Scholz, and Yannis Smaragdakis. Gigahorse: thorough, declarative decompilation of smart contracts. In Joanne M. Atlee, Tevfik Bultan, and Jon Whittle, editors, *Proceedings of the 41st International Conference on Software Engineering, ICSE 2019, Montreal, QC, Canada, May 25-31, 2019*, pages 1176–1186. IEEE / ACM, 2019.
16. Neville Grech, Sifis Lagouvardos, Ilias Tsatiris, and Yannis Smaragdakis. Elipmoc: Advanced decompilation of ethereum smart contracts. *Proc. ACM Program. Lang.*, 6(OOPSLA):77:1–77:27, 2022.

17. Ákos Hajdu and Dejan Jovanovic. Smt-friendly formalization of the solidity memory model. In Peter Müller, editor, *Programming Languages and Systems - 29th European Symposium on Programming, ESOP 2020, Held as Part of the European Joint Conferences on Theory and Practice of Software, ETAPS 2020, Dublin, Ireland, April 25-30, 2020, Proceedings*, volume 12075 of *Lecture Notes in Computer Science*, pages 224–250. Springer, 2020.

18. George Kastrinis and Yannis Smaragdakis. Hybrid context-sensitivity for points-to analysis. In Hans-Juergen Boehm and Cormac Flanagan, editors, *ACM SIGPLAN Conference on Programming Language Design and Implementation, PLDI '13, Seattle, WA, USA, June 16-19, 2013*, pages 423–434. ACM, 2013.

19. Sifis Lagouvardos, Neville Grech, Ilias Tsatiris, and Yannis Smaragdakis. Precise static modeling of ethereum "memory". *Proc. ACM Program. Lang.*, 4(OOPSLA):190:1–190:26, 2020.

20. Ana Milanova, Atanas Rountev, and Barbara G. Ryder. Parameterized Object Sensitivity for Points-to Analysis for Java. *ACM Transactions on Software Engineering Methodology*, 14:1–41, 2005.

21. Mayukh Mukhopadhyay. *Ethereum Smart Contract Development*. Packt publishing, 2018.

22. Julian Nagele and Maria A Schett. Blockchain superoptimizer. In *Preproceedings of 29th International Symposium on Logic-based Program Synthesis and Transformation (LOPSTR 2019)*, 2019.

23. F. Nielson, H. R. Nielson, and C. Hankin. *Principles of Program Analysis*. Springer, 1999.

24. Maria A. Schett and Julian Nagele. Populating the Peephole Optimizer of a Smart Contract Compiler. In Bruno Bernardo and Diego Marmsoler, editors, *2nd Workshop on Formal Methods for Blockchains (FMBC 2020)*, volume 84 of *OpenAccess Series in Informatics (OASIcs)*, pages 3:1–3:15. Schloss Dagstuhl–Leibniz-Zentrum für Informatik, 2020.

25. Clara Schneidewind, Ilya Grishchenko, Markus Scherer, and Matteo Maffei. eThor: Practical and provably sound static analysis of ethereum smart contracts. In Jay Ligatti, Xinming Ou, Jonathan Katz, and Giovanni Vigna, editors, *CCS '20: 2020 ACM SIGSAC Conference on Computer and Communications Security, USA, November 9-13, 2020*, pages 621–640. ACM, 2020.

26. Petar Tsankov, Andrei Marian Dan, Dana Drachsler-Cohen, Arthur Gervais, Florian Bünzli, and Martin T. Vechev. Securify: Practical Security Analysis of Smart Contracts. In David Lie, Mohammad Mannan, Michael Backes, and XiaoFeng Wang, editors, *Proceedings of the 2018 ACM SIGSAC Conference on Computer and Communications Security, CCS 2018, Toronto, ON, Canada, October 15-19, 2018*, pages 67–82. ACM, 2018.

27. Gavin Wood. Ethereum: A secure decentralised generalised transaction ledger, 2019.

Markov Chains/Stochastic Control

A Practitioner's Guide to
MDP Model Checking Algorithms⋆

Arnd Hartmanns[1] , Sebastian Junges[2] ,
Tim Quatmann[3] , and Maximilian Weininger[4](✉)

[1] University of Twente, Enschede, The Netherlands a.hartmanns@utwente.nl
[2] Radboud University, Nijmegen, The Netherlands sebastian.junges@ru.nl
[3] RWTH Aachen University, Aachen, Germany tim.quatmann@cs.rwth-aachen.de
[4] Technical University of Munich, Munich, Germany maxi.weininger@tum.de

Abstract. Model checking undiscounted reachability and expected-reward properties on Markov decision processes (MDPs) is key for the verification of systems that act under uncertainty. Popular algorithms are policy iteration and variants of value iteration; in tool competitions, most participants rely on the latter. These algorithms generally need worst-case exponential time. However, the problem can equally be formulated as a linear program, solvable in polynomial time. In this paper, we give a detailed overview of today's state-of-the-art algorithms for MDP model checking with a focus on performance and correctness. We highlight their fundamental differences, and describe various optimizations and implementation variants. We experimentally compare floating-point and exact-arithmetic implementations of all algorithms on three benchmark sets using two probabilistic model checkers. Our results show that (optimistic) value iteration is a sensible default, but other algorithms are preferable in specific settings. This paper thereby provides a guide for MDP verification practitioners—tool builders and users alike.

1 Introduction

The verification of MDPs is crucial for the design and evaluation of cyber-physical systems with sensor noise, biological and chemical processes, network protocols, and many other complex systems. MDPs are the standard model for sequential decision making under uncertainty and thus at the heart of reinforcement learning. Many dependability evaluation and safety assurance approaches rely in some form on the verification of MDPs with respect to temporal logic properties. Probabilistic model checking [4,5] provides powerful tools to support this task.

The essential MDP model checking queries are for the *worst-case probability that something bad happens* (reachability) and the *expected resource consumption until task completion* (expected rewards). These are *indefinite (undiscounted)*

⋆ This research was funded by the European Union's Horizon 2020 research and innovation programme under the Marie Skłodowska-Curie grant agreement No. 101008233 (MISSION), and by NWO VENI grant no. 639.021.754.

ⓒ The Author(s) 2023
S. Sankaranarayanan and N. Sharygina (Eds.): TACAS 2023, LNCS 13993, pp. 469–488, 2023.
https://doi.org/10.1007/978-3-031-30823-9_24

horizon queries: They ask about the probability or expectation of a random variable up until an event—which forms the horizon—but are themselves unbounded. Many more complex properties internally reduce to solving either reachability or expected rewards. For example, if the description of *something bad* is in linear temporal logic (LTL), then a product construction with a suitable automaton reduces the LTL query to reachability [6]. This paper sets out to determine the practically best algorithms to solve indefinite horizon reachability probabilities and expected rewards; our methodology is an empirical evaluation.

MDP analysis is well studied in many fields and has lead to three main types of algorithms: *value iteration* (VI), *policy iteration* (PI), and *linear programming* (LP) [55]. While indefinite horizon queries are natural in a verification context, they differ from the standard problem of e.g. operations research, planning, and reinforcement learning. In those fields, the primary concern is to *compute a policy* that (often approximately) optimizes the *discounted* expected reward over an infinite horizon where rewards accumulated in the future are weighted by a discount factor < 1 that exponentially prefers values accumulated earlier.

The lack of discounting in verification has vast implications. The *Bellman operation*, essentially describing a one-step backward update on expected rewards, is a contraction with discounting, but not a contraction without. This leads to significantly more complex termination criteria for VI-based verification approaches [34]. Indeed, VI runs in polynomial time for every fixed discount factor [49], and similar results are known for PI as well as LP solving with the simplex algorithm [60]. In contrast, VI [9] and PI [20] are known to have exponential worst-case behaviour in the undiscounted case.

So, *what is the best algorithm for model checking MDPs?* A polynomial-time algorithm exists using an LP formulation and barrier methods for its solution [12]. LP-based approaches (and their extension to MILPs) are also prominent for multi-objective model checking [21], in counterexample generation [23], and for the analysis of parametric Markov chains [16]. However, folklore tells us that iterative methods, in particular VI, are better for solving MDPs. Indeed, variations of VI are the default choice of all model checkers participating in the QComp competition [14]. This uniformity may be misleading. Indeed, for some stochastic game algorithms, using LP to solve the underlying MDPs may be preferential [3, Appendix E.4]. An application in runtime assurance preferred PI for numerical stability [45, Sect. 6]. A toy example from [34] is a famous challenge for VI-based methods. Despite the prominence of LP, the ease of encoding MDPs, and the availability of powerful off-the-shelf LP solvers, many tools did (until very recently) not include MDP model checking via LP solvers.

With this paper, we reconsider the PI and LP algorithms to investigate whether probabilistic model checking focused on the wrong family of algorithms. We report the results of an extensive empirical study with two independent implementations in the model checkers Storm [42] and mcsta [37]. We find that, in terms of performance and scalability, optimistic value iteration [40] is a solid choice on the standard benchmark collection (which goes beyond competition benchmarks) but can be beat quite considerably on challenging cases. We also emphasize the question of precision and soundness. Numerical algorithms, in particular ones that converge *in the limit*, are prone to delivering wrong results. For VI, the recognition of this problem has led to a series of improvements over the last decade [8,34,40,19,54,56]. We show that PI faces a similar problem. When using floating-point arithmetic, additional issues may arise [36,59]. Our use of various LP solvers exhibits concerning results for a variety of benchmarks. We therefore also include results for *exact* computation using rational arithmetic.

Limitations of this study. A thorough experimental study of algorithms requires a carefully scoped evaluation. We work with flat representations of MDPs that fit completely into memory (i.e. we ignore the state space exploration process and symbolic methods). We selected algorithms that are tailored to converge to *the* optimal value. We also exclude approaches that incrementally build and solve (partial or abstract) MDPs using simulation or model checking results to guide exploration: they are an orthogonal improvement and would equally profit from faster algorithms to solve the partial MDPs. Moreover, this study is on algorithms, not on their implementations. To reduce the impact of potential implementation flaws, we use two independent tools where possible. Our experiments ran on a single type of machine—we do not study the effect of different hardware.

Contributions. This paper contributes a thorough overview on how to model-check indefinite horizon properties on MDPs, making MDP model checking more accessible, but also pushing the state-of-the-art by clarifying open questions. Our study is built upon a thorough empirical evaluation using two independent code bases, sources benchmarks from the standard benchmark suite and recent publications, compares 10 LP solvers, and studies the influence of various prominent preprocessing techniques. The paper provides new insights and reviews folklore statements: Particular highlights are a new simple but challenging MDP family that leads to wrong results on all floating-point LP solvers (Section 2.3), a negative result regarding the soundness of PI with epsilon-precise policy evaluators (Section 4), and an evaluation on numerically challenging benchmarks that shows the limitations of value iteration in a practical setting (Section 5.3).

2   Background

We recall MDPs with reachability and reward objectives, describe solution algorithms and their guarantees, and address commonly used optimizations.

2.1   Markov Decision Processes

Let $D_X := \{ d\colon X \to [0,1] \mid \sum_{x \in X} d(x) = 1 \}$ be the set of distributions over X. A Markov decision process (MDP) [55] is a tuple $\mathcal{M} = (S, A, \delta)$ with finite sets of states S and actions A, and a partially defined transition function $\delta\colon S \times A \rightharpoonup D_S$ such that $A(s) := \{ a \mid (s,a) \in domain(\delta) \} \neq \emptyset$ for all $s \in S$. $A(s)$ is the set of enabled actions at state s. δ maps enabled state-action pairs to distributions over successor states. A Markov chain (MC) is an MDP with $|A(s)| = 1$ for all s. The *semantics* of an MDP are defined in the usual way, see, e.g. [6, Chapter 10]. A (memoryless deterministic) policy—a.k.a. strategy or scheduler—is a function $\pi\colon \mathsf{S} \to \mathsf{A}$ that, intuitively, given the current state s prescribes what action $a \in \mathsf{A}(s)$ to play. Applying a policy π to an MDP induces an MC $\mathcal{M}^\pi$. A path in this MC is an infinite sequence $\rho = s_1 s_2 \ldots$ with $\delta(s_i, \pi(s_i))(s_{i+1}) > 0$. Paths denotes the set of all paths and $\mathbb{P}^\pi_s$ denotes the unique probability measure of $\mathcal{M}^\pi$ over infinite paths starting in the state s.

A *reachability objective* $\mathsf{P}_{\mathsf{opt}}(\mathsf{T})$ with set of target states $\mathsf{T} \subseteq \mathsf{S}$ and $\mathsf{opt} \in \{\max, \min\}$ induces a random variable $X\colon \mathsf{Paths} \to [0, 1]$ over paths by assigning 1 to all paths that eventually reach the target and 0 to all others. $\mathsf{E}_{\mathsf{opt}}(\mathsf{rew})$ denotes an *expected reward objective*, where $\mathsf{rew}\colon \mathsf{S} \to \mathbb{Q}_{\geq 0}$ assigns a reward to each state. $\mathsf{rew}(\rho) := \sum_{i=1}^{\infty} \mathsf{rew}(s_i)$ is the accumulated reward of a path $\rho = s_1 s_2 \ldots$. This yields a random variable $X\colon \mathsf{Paths} \to \mathbb{Q} \cup \{\infty\}$ that maps paths to their reward. For a given objective and its random variable X, the *value of a state* $s \in \mathsf{S}$ is the expectation of X under the probability measure $\mathbb{P}^\pi_s$ of the the MC induced by an optimal policy π from the set of all policies Π, formally $\mathsf{V}(s) := \mathsf{opt}_{\pi \in \Pi} \mathbb{E}^\pi_s[X]$.

2.2 Solution Algorithms

Value iteration (VI), e.g. [15], computes a sequence of value vectors converging to the optimum in the limit. In all variants of the algorithm, we start with a function $x\colon \mathsf{S} \to \mathbb{Q}$ that assigns to every state an estimate of the value. The algorithm repeatedly performs an update operation to improve the estimates. After some preprocessing, this operation has a unique fixpoint when $x = \mathsf{V}$. Thus, value iteration converges to the value in the limit. Variants of VI include interval iteration [34], sound VI [56] and optimistic VI [40]. We do not discuss these in detail, but instead refer to the respective papers.

Linear programming (LP), e.g. [6, Chapter 10], encodes the transition structure of the MDP and the objective as a linear optimization problem. For every state, the LP has a variable representing an estimate of its value. Every state-action pair is encoded as a constraint on these variables, as are the target set or rewards. The unique optimum of the LP is attained if and only if for every state its corresponding variable is set to the value of the state. We provide an in-depth discussion of theoretical and practical aspects of LP in Section 3.

Policy iteration (PI), e.g. [11, Section 4], computes a sequence of policies. Starting with an initial policy, we evaluate its induced MC, improve the policy by switching suboptimal choices and repeat the process on the new policy. As every policy improves the previous one and there are only finitely many memoryless deterministic policies (a number exponential in the number of states), eventually we obtain an optimal policy. We further discuss PI in Section 4.

2.3 Guarantees

Given the stakes in many application domains, we require guarantees about the relation between an algorithm's result $\bar{v}$ and the true value v. First, implementations are subject to floating-point errors and imprecision [59] unless they use exact (rational) arithmetic or safe rounding [36]. This can result in arbitrary

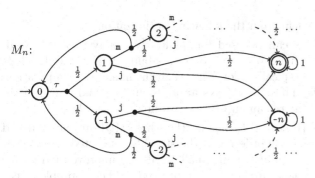

Fig. 1: A hard MDP for all algorithms

Table 1: Correct results

alg.	solver	$n \leq$
PI	–	20
LP	COPT	18
	CPLEX	18
	Glop	25
	GLPK	24
	Gurobi	18
	HiGHS	22
	lp_solve	28
	Mosek	22
	SoPlex	34

differences between $\bar{v}$ and v. Second are the algorithm's inherent properties: VI is an approximating algorithm that converges to the true value only in the limit. In theory, it is possible to obtain the exact result by rounding after exponentially many iterations [15]; in practice, this results in excessive runtime. Instead, for years, implementations used a naive stopping criterion that could return arbitrarily wrong results [33]. This problem's discovery sparked the development of sound variants of VI [8,34,40,19,54,56], including interval iteration, sound value iteration, and optimistic value iteration. A sound VI algorithm guarantees ε-precise results, i.e. $|v - \bar{v}| \leq \varepsilon$ or $|v - \bar{v}| \leq v \cdot \varepsilon$. For LP and PI, the guarantees have not yet been thoroughly investigated. Theoretically, both are exact, but implementations are often not. We discuss the problems in Sections 3 and 4.

The handcrafted MC of [33, Figure 2] highlights the lack of guarantees of VI: standard implementations return vastly incorrect results. We extended it with action choices to obtain the MDP M_n shown in Fig. 1 for $n \in \mathbb{N}$, $n \geq 2$. It has $2n + 1$ states; we compute $P_{\min}(\{n\})$ and $P_{\max}(\{n\})$. The policy that chooses action m wherever possible induces the MC of [33, Figure 2] with $(P_{\min}(\{n\}), P_{\max}(\{n\})) = (\frac{1}{2}, \frac{1}{2})$. In every state s with $0 < s < n$, we added the choice of action j that jumps to n and $-n$. With that, the (optimal) values over all policies are $(\frac{1}{3}, \frac{2}{3})$. In VI, starting from value 0 for all states except n, initially taking j everywhere looks like the best policy for $P_{\max}$. As updated values slowly propagate, state-by-state, m becomes the optimal choice in all states except $-n + 1$. We thus layered a "deceptive" decision problem on top of the slow convergence of the original MC. For $n = 20$, VI with Storm and mcsta deliver the incorrect results $(0.247, 0.500)$. For Storm's PI and various LP solvers, we show in Table 1 the largest n for which they return a ± 0.01-correct result. For larger n, PI and all LP solvers claim $\approx (\frac{1}{2}, \frac{1}{2})$ as the correct solution except for Glop and GLPK which only fail for the maximum at the given n; for the minimum, they return the wrong result at $n \geq 29$ and 52, respectively. Sound VI algorithms and Storm's exact-arithmetic engine produce $(\varepsilon$-$)$correct results, though the former at excessive runtime for larger n. We used default settings for all tools and solvers.

2.4   Optimizations

VI, LP, and PI can all benefit from the following optimizations:

Graph-theoretic algorithms can be used for qualitative analysis of the MDP, i.e. finding states with value 0 or (only for reachability objectives) 1. These qualitative approaches are typically a lot faster than the numerical computations for quantitative analysis. Thus, we always apply them first and only run the numerical algorithms on the remaining states with non-trivial values.

Topological methods, e.g. [17], do not consider the whole MDP at once. Instead, they first compute a topological ordering of the strongly connected components (SCCs)[5] and then analyze each SCC individually. This can improve the runtime, as we decompose the problem into smaller subproblems. The subproblems can be solved with any of the solution methods. Note that when considering acyclic MDPs, the topological approach does not need to call the solution methods, as the resulting values can immediately be backpropagated.

Collapsing of maximal end components (MECs), e.g., [13,34], transforms the MDP into one with equivalent values but simpler structure. After collapsing MECs, the MDP is contracting, i.e. we almost surely reach a target state or a state with value zero. VI algorithms rely on this property for convergence [34,40,56]. For PI and LP, simplifying the graph structure before applying the solution method can speed up the computation.

Warm starts, e.g. [26,46], may adequately initialize an algorithm, i.e., we may provide it with some prior knowledge so that the computation has a good starting point. We implement warm starts by first running VI for a limited number of iterations and using the resulting estimate to guess bounds on the variables in an LP or a good initial policy for PI. See Sections 3 and 4 for more details.

3   Practically solving MDPs using Linear Programs

This section considers the LP-based approach to solving the optimal policy problem in MDPs. To the best of our knowledge, this is the only polynomial-time approach. We discuss various configurations. These configuration are a combination of the LP formulation, the choice of software, and their parameterization.

3.1   How to encode MDPs as LPs?

For objective $P_{\max}(T)$ we formulate the following LP over variables x_s, $s \in S \setminus T$:

$$\text{minimize} \quad \sum_{s \in S} x_s \quad \text{s.t.} \quad lb(s) \leq x_s \leq ub(s) \quad \text{and}$$

$$x_s \geq \sum_{s' \in S \setminus T} \delta(s,a)(s') \cdot x_{s'} + \sum_{t \in T} \delta(s,a)(t) \quad \text{for all } s \in S \setminus T, a \in A$$

---

[5] A set $S' \subseteq S$ is a connected component if for all $s, s' \in S'$, s can be reached from s'. We call S' strongly connected component if it is inclusion maximal.

We assume bounds $lb(s) = 0$ and $ub(s) = 1$ for $s \in S \setminus T$. The unique solution $\eta\colon \{x_s \mid s \in S \setminus T\} \to [0,1]$ to this LP coincides with the desired objective values $\eta(x_s) = V(s)$. Objectives $P_{\min}(T)$ and $E_{opt}(rew)$ have similar encodings: minimizing policies require maximisation in the LP and flipping the constraint relation. Rewards can be added as an additive factor on the right-hand side. For practical purposes, the LP formulation can be tweaked.

The choice of bounds. Any bounds that respect the unique solution will not change the answer. That is, any lb and ub with $0 \leq lb(s) \leq V(s) \leq ub(s)$ yield a sound encoding. While these additional bounds are superfluous, they may significantly prune the search space. We investigate trivial bounds, e.g., knowing that all probabilities are in $[0,1]$, bounds from a structural analysis as discussed by [8], and bounds induced by a warm start of the solver. For the latter, if we have obtained values $V' \leq V$, e.g., induced by a suboptimal policy, then $V'(s)$ is a lower bound on the value x_s, which is particularly relevant as the LP minimizes.

Equality for unique actions. Markov chains, i.e., MDPs where $|A| = 1$, can be solved using linear equation systems. The LP encoding uses one-sided inequalities and the objective function to incorporate nondeterministic choices. We investigate adding constraints for all states with a unique action.

$$x_s \leq \sum_{s' \in S \setminus T} \delta(s,a)(s') \cdot x_{s'} + \sum_{t \in T} \delta(s,a)(t) \quad \text{for all } s \in S \setminus T \text{ with } A(s) = \{a\}$$

These additional constraints may trigger different optimizations in a solver, e.g., some solvers use Gaussian elimination for variable elimination.

A simpler objective. The standard objective assures the solution η is optimal for *every* state, whereas most invocations require only optimality in some specific states – typically the initial state s_0 or the entry states of a strongly connected component. In that case, the objective may be simplified to optimize only the value for those states. This potentially allows for multiple optimal solutions: in terms of the MDP, it is no longer necessary to optimize the value for states that are not reached under the optimal policy.

Encoding the dual formulation. Encoding a dual formulation to the LP is interesting for mixed-integer extensions to the LP, relevant for computing, e.g., policies in POMDPs [47], or when computing minimal counterexamples [58]. For LPs, due to the strong duality, the internal representation in the solvers we investigated is (almost) equivalent and all solvers support both solving the primal and the dual representation. We therefore do not further consider constructing them.

3.2   How to solve LPs with existing solvers?

We rely on the performance of state-of-the-art LP solvers. Many solvers have been developed and are still actively advanced, see [2] for a recent comparison on general benchmarks. We list the LP solvers that we consider for this work in Table 2. The columns summarize for each solver the type of license, whether it uses exact or floating-point arithmetic, whether it supports multithreading,

Table 2: Available LP solvers ("intr" = interior point)

solver	version	license	exact/fp	parallel	algorithms	mcsta	Storm
COPT [24]	5.0.5	academic	fp	yes	intr + simplex	yes	no
CPLEX [44]	22.10	academic	fp	yes	intr + simplex	yes	no
Gurobi [32]	9.5	academic	fp	yes	intr + simplex	yes	yes
GLPK [29]	4.65	GPL	fp	no	intr + simplex	no	yes
Glop [30]	9.4.1874	Apache	fp	no	simplex only	yes	no
HiGHS [35,43]	1.2.2	MIT	fp	yes	intr + simplex	yes	no
lp_solve [10]	5.5.2.11	LGPL	fp	no	simplex only	yes	no
Mosek [52]	10.0	academic	fp	yes	intr + simplex	yes	no
SoPlex [28]	6.0.1	academic	both	no	simplex only	no	yes
Z3 [53]	4.8.13	MIT	exact	no	simplex only	no	yes

and what type of algorithms it implements. We also list whether the solver is available from the two model checkers used in this study[6].

Methods. We briefly explain the available methods and refer to [12] for a thorough treatment. Broadly speaking, the LP solvers use one out of two families of methods. *Simplex*-based methods rely on highly efficient pivot operations to consider vertices of the simplex of feasible solutions. Simplex can be executed either in the *primal* or *dual* fashion, which changes the direction of progress made by the algorithm. Our LP formulation has more constraints than variables, which generally means that the dual version is preferable. *Interior methods*, often the subclass of *barrier methods*, do not need to follow the set of vertices. These methods may achieve polynomial time worst-case behaviour. It is generally claimed that simplex has superior average-case performance but is highly sensitive to perturbations, while interior-point methods have a more robust performance.

Warm starts. LP-based model checking can be done using two types of warm starts. Either by providing a (feasible) basis point as done in [26] or by presenting bounds. The former, however, comes with various remarks and limitations, such as the requirement to disable preprocessing. We therefore used warm starts only by using bounds as discussed above.

Multithreading. We generally see two types of parallelisation in LP solvers. Some solvers support a *portfolio* approach that runs different approaches and finishes with the first one that yields a result. Other solvers parallelize the interior-point and/or simplex methods themselves.

Guarantees for numerical LP solvers. All LP solvers allow tweaking of various parameters, including *tolerances* to manage whether a point is considered feasible or optimal, respectively. The experiments in Table 1 already indicate that these guarantees are *not* absolute. A limited experiment indicated that reducing these tolerances towards zero did remove some incorrect results, but not all.

---

[6] Support for Gurobi, GLPK, and Z3 was already available in Storm. Support for Glop was already available in mcsta. All other solver interfaces have been added.

Exact solving. SoPlex supports exact computations, with a Boost library wrapping GMP rationals [22], after a floating-point arithmetic-based startup phase [27]. While this combination is beneficial for performance in most settings, it leads to crashes for the numerically challenging models. Z3 supports only exact arithmetic (also wrapping GMP numbers with their own interface). We observe that the price of converting large rational numbers may be substantial. SMT solvers like Z3 use a simplex variation [18] tailored towards finding feasible points and in an incremental fashion, optimized for problems with a nontrivial Boolean structure. In contrast, our LP formulation is easily feasible and is a pure conjunction.

4   Sound Policy Iteration

Starting with an initial policy, PI-based algorithms iteratively improve the policy based on the values obtained for the induced MC. The algorithm for solving the induced MC crucially affects the performance and accuracy of the overall approach. This section addresses the solvers available in Storm, possible precision issues, and how to utilize a warm start, while Section 5 discusses PI performance[7].

Markov chain solvers. To solve the induced MC, Storm can employ all linear equation solvers listed in [42] and all implemented variants of VI. In our experiments, we consider (i) the generalized minimal residual method (GMRES) [57] implemented in GMM++ [25], (ii) VI [15] with a standard (relative) termination criterion, (iii) optimistic VI (OVI) [40], and (iv) the sparse LU decomposition implemented in Eigen [31] using either floating-point or exact arithmetic (LU^X). LU and LU^X provide exact results (modulo floating-point errors in LU) while OVI yields ε-precise results. VI and GMRES do not provide any guarantees.

Correctness of PI. The accuracy of PI is affected by the MC solver. Firstly, PI cannot be more precise than its underlying solver: the result of PI has the same precision as the result obtained for the final MC. Secondly, inaccuracies by the solver can hide policy improvements; this may lead to premature convergence with a sub-optimal policy. We show that PI can return arbitrarily wrong results—*even if the intermediate results are ε-precise:*

Consider the MDP in Fig. 2 with objective $P_{max}(\{\,G\,\})$. There is only one nondeterministic choice, namely in state s_0. The optimal policy is to pick b, obtaining a value of 0.5. Picking a only yields 0.1. However, when starting from the initial policy $\pi(s_0) = $ a, an ε-precise MC solver may return $0.1 + \varepsilon$ for both s_0 and s_1 and $\delta/2 + (1 - \delta) \cdot 0.1$ for s_2. This solution is indeed ε-precise. However, when evaluating which action to pick in s_0, we can choose δ such that a seems to obtain a higher value. Concretely, we require $\delta/2 + (1 - \delta) \cdot 0.1 < 0.1 + \varepsilon$. For every $\varepsilon > 0$, this can be achieved by setting $\delta < 2.5 \cdot \varepsilon$. In this case, PI would terminate with the final policy inducing a severely suboptimal value.

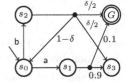

Fig. 2: Example MDP

---

[7] [46] addresses performance in the context of PI for stochastic games.

If every Markov chain is solved precisely, PI is correct. Indeed, it suffices to be certain that one action is better than all others. This is the essence of modified policy iteration as described in [55, Chapters 6.5 and 7.2.6]. Similarly, [46, Section 4.2] suggests to use interval iteration when solving the system induced by the current policy and stopping when the under-approximation of one action is higher than the over-approximation of all other actions.

Warm starts. PI profits from being provided a *good* initial policy. If the initial policy is already optimal, PI terminates after a single iteration. We can inform our choice of the initial policy by providing estimates for all states as computed by VI. For every state, we choose the action that is optimal according to the estimate. This is a good way to leverage VI's ability to quickly deliver good estimates [40], while at the same time providing the exactness guarantees of PI.

5   Experimental Evaluation

To understand the practical performance of the different algorithms, we performed an extensive experimental evaluation. We used three sets of benchmarks: all applicable benchmark instances[8] from the Quantitative Verification Benchmark Set (QVBS) [41] (the *qvbs* set), a subset of hard QVBS instances (the *hard* set), and numerically challenging models from a runtime monitoring application [45] (the *premise* set, named for the corresponding prototype). We consider two probabilistic model checkers, Storm [42] and the Modest Toolset's [37] mcsta. We used Intel Xeon Platinum 8160 systems running 64-bit CentOS Linux 7.9, allocating 4 CPU cores and 32 GB RAM to each experiment unless noted otherwise.

We plot algorithm runtimes in seconds in *quantile plots* as on the left and *scatter plots* as on the right of Fig. 3. The former compare multiple tools or configurations; for each, we sort the instances by runtime and plot the corresponding monotonically increasing line. Here, a point (x, y) on the a-line means that the x-th fastest instance solved by a took y seconds. The latter compare two tools or configurations. Each point (x, y) is for one benchmark instance: the x-axis tool took x while the y-axis tool took y seconds to solve it. The shape of points indicates the model type; the mapping from shapes to types is the same for all scatter plots and is only given explicitly in the first one in Fig. 3. Additional plots to support the claims in this section are provided in the appendix of the full version [39] of this paper.

The depicted runtimes are for the respective algorithm and all necessary and/or stated preprocessing, but do not include the time for constructing the MDP state spaces (which is independent of the algorithms). mcsta reports all time measurements rounded to multiples of 0.1 s. We summarize timeouts, out-of-memory, errors, and incorrect results as "n/a". Our timeout is 30 minutes for the algorithm and 45 minutes for total runtime including MDP construction. We consider a result $\bar{v}$ incorrect if $|v - \bar{v}| > v \cdot 10^{-3}$ (i.e. relative error 10^{-3}) whenever a reference result v is available. We however do not flag a result as incorrect if

---

[8] A *benchmark instance* is a combination of model, parameter valuation, and objective.

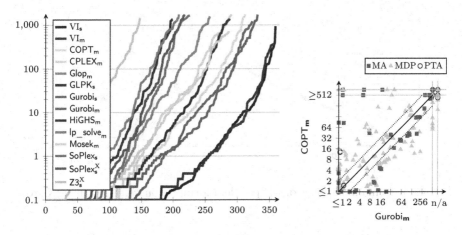

Fig. 3: Comparison of LP solver runtime on the *qvbs* set

v and $\bar{v}$ are both below 10^{-8} (relevant for the *premise* set). Nevertheless, we configure the (unsound) convergence threshold for VI as 10^{-6} relative; among the sound VI algorithms, we include OVI, with a (sound) stopping criterion of relative 10^{-6} error. To only achieve the 10^{-3} precision we actually test, OVI could thus be even faster than it appears in our plots. We make this difference to account for the fact that many algorithms, including the LP solvers, do not have a sound error criterion. We mark exact algorithms/solvers that use rational arithmetic with a superscript [X]. The other configurations use floating-point arithmetic (fp).

5.1 The QVBS Benchmarks

The *qvbs* set comprises all QVBS benchmark instances with an MDP, Markov automaton (MA), or probabilistic timed automaton (PTA) model[9] and a reachability or expected reward/time objective that is quantitative, i.e. not a query that yields a zero or one probability. We only consider instances where both Storm and mcsta can build the explicit representation of the MDP within 15 minutes. This yields 367 instances. We obtain reference results for 344 of them from either the QVBS database or by using one of Storm's exact methods. We found all reference results obtained via different methods to be consistent.

For LP, we have various solvers with various parameters each, cf. Section 3. For conciseness, we first compare all available LP solvers on the *qvbs* set. For the best-performing solver, we then evaluate the benefit of different solver configurations. We do the same for the choice of Markov chain solution method in PI. We then focus on these single, reasonable, setups for LP and PI each in more detail.

LP solver comparison. The left-hand plot of Fig. 3 summarizes the results of our comparison of the different LP solvers. Subscripts $_s$ and $_m$ indicate whether the solver is embedded in either Storm or mcsta. We apply no optimizations or

---

[9] MA and PTA are converted to MDP via embedding and digital clocks [48].

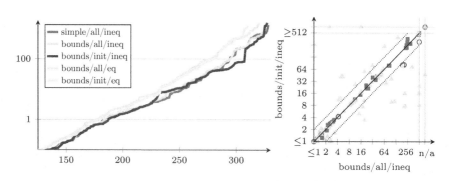

Fig. 4: Performance impact of LP problem formulation variants (using Gurobi$_s$)

reductions to the MDPs except for the precomputation of probability-0 states (and in Storm also of probability-1 states), and use the default settings for all solvers, with the trivial variable bounds $[0, 1]$ and $[0, \infty)$ for probabilities and expected rewards, respectively. We include VI as baseline. In Table 3, we summarize the results.

In terms of **performance** and scalability, Gurobi solves the highest number of benchmarks in any given time budget, closely followed by COPT. CPLEX, HiGHS, and Mosek make up a middle-class group. While the exact solver Z3 is very slow, SoPlex's exact mode actually competes with some fp solvers. However, the quantile plots

Table 3: LP summary

solver	correct	incorr.	no result
VI$_s$	359	8	0
VI$_m$	357	8	2
COPT$_m$	312	12	43
CPLEX$_m$	291	10	66
Glop$_m$	257	4	106
GLPK$_s$	199	5	163
Gurobi$_s$	331	4	32
Gurobi$_m$	323	4	40
HiGHS$_m$	288	10	69
lp_solve$_m$	209	0	158
Mosek$_m$	287	15	65
SoPlex$_s$	226	9	132
SoPlex$_s^X$	218	0	149
Z3$_s^X$	148	0	219

do not tell the whole story. On the right of Fig. 3, we compare COPT and Gurobi directly: each has a large number of instances on which it is (much) better.

In terms of **reliability** of results, the exact solvers as expected produce no incorrect results; so does the slowest fp solver, lp_solve. COPT, CPLEX, HiGHS, Mosek, and fp-SoPlex perform badly in this metric, producing more errors than VI. Interestingly, these are mostly the faster solvers, the exception being Gurobi.

Overall, Gurobi achieves highest performance at decent reliability; in the remainder of this section, we thus use Gurobi$_s$ whenever we apply non-exact LP.

LP solver tweaking. Gurobi can be configured to use an "*auto*" portfolio approach, potentially running multiple algorithms concurrently on multiple threads, a primal or a dual simplex algorithm, or a barrier method algorithm. We compared each option with 4 threads and found no significant performance difference. Similarly, running the *auto* method with 1, 4, and 16 threads (only here, we allocate 16 threads per experiment) also failed to bring out noticeable performance differences. Using more threads results in a few more out-of-memory errors, though. We thus fix Gurobi on *auto* with 4 threads.

Fig. 4 shows the performance impact of supplying Gurobi with more precise bounds on the variables for expected reward objectives using methods from

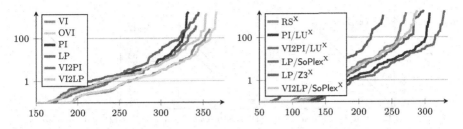

Fig. 5: Comparison of MDP model checking algorithms on the *qvbs* set

[8,51] ("bounds" instead of "simple"), of optimizing only for initial state ("init") instead of the sum over all states ("all"), and of using equality ("eq") instead of less-/greater-than-or-equal ("ineq") for unique action states. More precise bounds yield a very small improvement at essentially no cost. Optimizing for the initial state only results in a little better overall performance (in the "pocket" in the quantile plot around $x = 315$ that is also clearly visible in the scatter plot). However, it also results in 2 more incorrect results in the *qvbs* set. Using equality for unique actions noticeably decreases performance and increases the incorrect result count by 9 instances. For all experiments that follow, we thus use the more precise bounds, but do not enable the other two optimizations.

PI methods comparison. The main choice in PI is which algorithm to use to solve the induced Markov chains. On the right, we show the performance of the different algorithms available in Storm (cf. Section 4). LU^X yields a fully exact PI. This interestingly performs better than the fp version, potentially because fp errors induce spurious policy 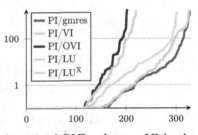 changes. The same effect likely also hinders the use of OVI, whereas VI leads to good performance. Nevertheless, gmres is best overall, and thus our choice for all following experiments with non-exact PI. VI and gmres yield 6 and 4 incorrect results, respectively. OVI and the exact methods are always correct on this benchmark set.

Best MDP algorithms for QVBS. We now compare all MDP model checking algorithms on the *qvbs* set: with floating-point numbers, LP and PI configured as described above, plus unsound VI, sound OVI, and the warm-start variants of PI and LP denoted "VI2PI" and "VI2LP", respectively. Exact results are provided by rational search (RS, essentially an exact version of VI) [50], PI with exact LU, and LP with exact solvers (SoPlex and Z3). All are implemented in Storm.

In a first experiment, we evaluated the impact of using the topological approach and of collapsing MECs (cf. Section 2.4). The results, for which we omit plots, are that the topological approach noticeably improves performance and scalability for *all* algorithms, and we therefore always use it from now on. Collapsing MECs is necessary to guarantee termination of OVI, while for the

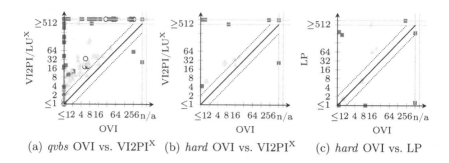

(a) *qvbs* OVI vs. VI2PI^X (b) *hard* OVI vs. VI2PI^X (c) *hard* OVI vs. LP

Fig. 6: Additional direct performance comparisons

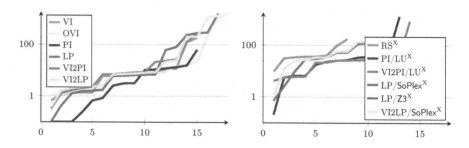

Fig. 7: Comparison of MDP model checking algorithms on the *hard* subset

other algorithms it is a potential optimization; however we found it to overall have a minimal positive performance impact only. Since it is required by OVI and does not reduce performance, we also always use it from now on.

Fig. 5 shows the complete comparison of all the methods on the *qvbs* set, for fp algorithms on the left and exact solutions on the right. Among the fp algorithms, OVI is clearly the fastest and most scalable. VI is somewhat faster but incurs several incorrect results that diminish its appearance in the quantile plot. OVI is additionally special among these algorithms in that it is sound, i.e. provides guaranteed ε-correct results—though up to fp rounding errors, which can be eliminated following the approach of [36]. On the exact side, PI with an inexact-VI warm start works best. The scatter plots in Fig. 6(a) shows the performance impact of computing an exact instead of an approximate solution.

5.2   The Hard QVBS Benchmarks

The QVBS contains many models built for tools that use VI as default algorithm. The other algorithms may actually be important to solve key challenging instances where VI/OVI perform badly. This contribution could be hidden in the sea of instances trivial for VI. We thus zoom in on a selection of QVBS instances that appear "hard" for VI: those where VI takes longer than the prior MDP state

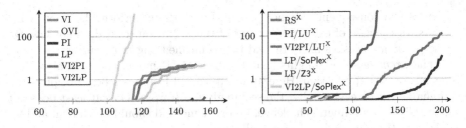

Fig. 8: Comparison of MDP model checking algorithms on the *premise* set

space construction phase in both Storm and mcsta, and additionally both phases together take at least 1 s. These are 18 of the previously considered 367 instances.

In Fig. 7, we show the behaviour of all the algorithms on this *hard* subset. OVI again works better than VI due to the incorrect results that VI returns. We see that the performance and scalability gap between the algorithms has narrowed; although OVI still "wins", LP in particular is much closer than on the full *qvbs* set. We also investigated the LP outcomes with solvers other than Gurobi: even on this set, Gurobi and COPT remain the fastest and most scalable solvers. With mcsta, in the basic configuration, they solve 16 and 17 instances, the slowest taking 835 s and 1334 s, respectively; with the topological optimization, the numbers become 17 and 15 instances with the slowest at 1373 s and 1590 s seconds. We show the detailed comparison of OVI and LP in Fig. 6(c), noting that there are a few instances where LP is much faster, and repeat the comparison between the best fp and exact algorithms (Fig. 6(b)).

5.3   The Runtime Monitoring Benchmarks

While the QVBS is intentionally diverse, our third set of benchmarks is intentionally focused: We study 200 MDPs from a runtime monitoring study [45]. The original problem is to compute the normalized risk of continuing to operate the system being monitored subject to stochastic noise, unobservable and uncontrollable nondeterminism, and partial state observations. This is a query for a conditional probability. It is answered via probabilistic model checking by unrolling an MDP model along an observed history trace of length $n \in \{50, \ldots, 1000\}$ following the approach of Baier et al. [7]. The MDPs contain many transitions back to the initial state, ultimately resulting in numerically challenging instances (containing structures similar to the one of M_n in Section 2.3). We were able to compute a reference result for all instances.

Fig. 8 compares the different MDP model checking algorithms on this set. In line with the observations in [45], we see very different behaviour compared to the QVBS. Among the fp solutions on the left, LP with Gurobi terminates very quickly (under 1 s), and either produces a correct (155 instances) or a completely incorrect result (mostly 0, on 45 instances). VI behaves similarly, but is slower. OVI, in contrast, delivers no incorrect result, but instead fails to terminate on all but 116 instances. In the exact setting, warm starts using VI inherit its relative

484   A. Hartmanns et al.

slowness and consequently do not pay off. Exact PI outperforms both exact LP solvers. In the case of exact SoPlex, out of the 112 instances it does not manage to solve, 98 are crashes likely related to a confirmed bug in its current version.

The *premise* set highlights that the best MDP model checking algorithm depends on the application. Here, in the fp case, LP appears best but produces unreliable (incorrect) results; the seemingly much worse OVI at least does not do so. Given the numeric challenge, an exact method should be chosen, and we show that these actually perform well here.

6   Conclusion

We thoroughly investigated the state of the art in MDP model checking, showing that there is no single best algorithm for this task. For benchmarks which are not numerically challenging, OVI is a sensible default, closely followed by PI and LP with a warm start—although using the latter two means losing soundness as confirmed by a number of incorrect results in our experiments. For numerically hard benchmarks, PI and LP as well as computing exact solutions are more attractive, and clearly preferable in combination. Overall, although LP has the superior (polynomial) theoretical complexity, in our practical evaluation, it almost always performs worse than the other (exponential) approaches. This is even though we use modern commercial solvers and tune both the LP encoding of the problem as well as the solvers' parameters. While we *observed* the behaviour of the different algorithms and have some intuition into what makes the *premise* set hard, an entire research question of its own is to identify and quantify the structural properties that make a model hard.

Our evaluation also raises the question of how prevalent MDPs that challenge VI are in practice. Aside from the *premise* benchmarks, we were unable to find further sets of MDPs that are hard for VI. Notably, several stochastic games (SGs) difficult for VI were found in [46]; the authors noted that using PI for the SGs was better than applying VI to the SGs. However, when we extracted the induced MDPs, we found them all easy for VI. Similarly, [3] used a random generation of SGs of at most 10,000 states, many of which were challenging for the SG algorithms. Yet the same random generation modified to produce MDPs delivered only MDPs easily solved in seconds, even with drastically increased numbers of states. In contrast, Alagöz et al. [1] report that their random generation returned models where LP beat PI. However, their setting is discounted, and their description of the random generation was too superficial for us to be able to replicate it. We note that, in several of our scatter plots, the MA instances from the QVBS (where we check the embedded MDP) appeared more challenging overall than the MDPs. We thus conclude this paper with a call for challenging MDP benchmarks—as separate benchmark sets of unique characteristics like *premise*, or for inclusion in the QVBS.

Data availability statement. The datasets generated and analysed in this study and code to regenerate them are available in the accompanying artifact [38]. For Storm, our code builds on version 1.7.0. We used mcsta version 3.1.213.

References

1. Alagöz, O., Ayvaci, M.U.S., Linderoth, J.T.: Optimally solving Markov decision processes with total expected discounted reward function: Linear programming revisited. Comput. Ind. Eng. **87**, 311–316 (2015). https://doi.org/10.1016/j.cie.2015.05.031
2. Anand, R., Aggarwal, D., Kumar, V.: A comparative analysis of optimization solvers. Journal of Statistics and Management Systems **20**(4), 623–635 (2017). https://doi.org/10.1080/09720510.2017.1395182
3. Azeem, M., Evangelidis, A., Kretínský, J., Slivinskiy, A., Weininger, M.: Optimistic and topological value iteration for simple stochastic games. CoRR **abs/2207.14417** (2022). https://doi.org/10.48550/arXiv.2207.14417
4. Baier, C., de Alfaro, L., Forejt, V., Kwiatkowska, M.: Model checking probabilistic systems. In: Handbook of Model Checking, pp. 963–999. Springer (2018)
5. Baier, C., Hermanns, H., Katoen, J.P.: The 10,000 facets of MDP model checking. In: Computing and Software Science, LNCS, vol. 10000, pp. 420–451. Springer (2019). https://doi.org/10.1007/978-3-319-91908-9_21
6. Baier, C., Katoen, J.P.: Principles of model checking. MIT Press (2008), https://mitpress.mit.edu/books/principles-model-checking
7. Baier, C., Klein, J., Klüppelholz, S., Märcker, S.: Computing conditional probabilities in Markovian models efficiently. In: TACAS. LNCS, vol. 8413, pp. 515–530. Springer (2014). https://doi.org/10.1007/978-3-642-54862-8_43
8. Baier, C., Klein, J., Leuschner, L., Parker, D., Wunderlich, S.: Ensuring the reliability of your model checker: Interval iteration for Markov decision processes. In: CAV (1). LNCS, vol. 10426, pp. 160–180. Springer (2017). https://doi.org/10.1007/978-3-319-63387-9_8
9. Balaji, N., Kiefer, S., Novotný, P., Pérez, G.A., Shirmohammadi, M.: On the complexity of value iteration. In: ICALP. LIPIcs, vol. 132, pp. 102:1–102:15. Schloss Dagstuhl - Leibniz-Zentrum für Informatik (2019). https://doi.org/10.4230/LIPIcs.ICALP.2019.102
10. Berkelaar, M., Eikland, K., Notebaert, P.: Introduction to lp_solve 5.5.2.11, https://lpsolve.sourceforge.net/5.5/, accessed 2023-01-25.
11. Bertsekas, D.P., Tsitsiklis, J.N.: An analysis of stochastic shortest path problems. Math. Oper. Res. **16**(3), 580–595 (1991). https://doi.org/10.1287/moor.16.3.580
12. Boyd, S.P., Vandenberghe, L.: Convex Optimization. Cambridge University Press (2014)
13. Brázdil, T., Chatterjee, K., Chmelik, M., Forejt, V., Kretínský, J., Kwiatkowska, M.Z., Parker, D., Ujma, M.: Verification of Markov decision processes using learning algorithms. In: ATVA. LNCS, vol. 8837, pp. 98–114. Springer (2014). https://doi.org/10.1007/978-3-319-11936-6_8
14. Budde, C.E., Hartmanns, A., Klauck, M., Kretínský, J., Parker, D., Quatmann, T., Turrini, A., Zhang, Z.: On correctness, precision, and performance in quantitative verification – QComp 2020 competition report. In: ISoLA (4). LNCS, vol. 12479, pp. 216–241. Springer (2020). https://doi.org/10.1007/978-3-030-83723-5_15
15. Chatterjee, K., Henzinger, T.A.: Value iteration. In: 25 Years of Model Checking. LNCS, vol. 5000, pp. 107–138. Springer (2008). https://doi.org/10.1007/978-3-540-69850-0_7
16. Cubuktepe, M., Jansen, N., Junges, S., Katoen, J.P., Topcu, U.: Convex optimization for parameter synthesis in MDPs. IEEE Trans. Autom. Control. (2022). https://doi.org/10.1109/TAC.2021.3133265

17. Dai, P., Mausam, Weld, D.S., Goldsmith, J.: Topological value iteration algorithms. J. Artif. Intell. Res. **42**, 181–209 (2011), https://www.jair.org/index.php/jair/article/view/10725

18. Dutertre, B., de Moura, L.M.: A fast linear-arithmetic solver for DPLL(T). In: CAV. LNCS, vol. 4144, pp. 81–94. Springer (2006)

19. Eisentraut, J., Kelmendi, E., Kretínský, J., Weininger, M.: Value iteration for simple stochastic games: Stopping criterion and learning algorithm. Inf. Comput. **285**(Part), 104886 (2022). https://doi.org/10.1016/j.ic.2022.104886

20. Fearnley, J.: Exponential lower bounds for policy iteration. In: ICALP (2). LNCS, vol. 6199, pp. 551–562. Springer (2010). https://doi.org/10.1007/978-3-642-14162-1_46

21. Forejt, V., Kwiatkowska, M.Z., Parker, D.: Pareto curves for probabilistic model checking. In: ATVA. LNCS, vol. 7561, pp. 317–332. Springer (2012). https://doi.org/10.1007/978-3-642-33386-6_25

22. Free Software Foundation: The GNU Multiple Precision Arithmetic Library, https://gmplib.org/, accessed 2023-01-25.

23. Funke, F., Jantsch, S., Baier, C.: Farkas certificates and minimal witnesses for probabilistic reachability constraints. In: TACAS (1). LNCS, vol. 12078, pp. 324–345. Springer (2020)

24. Ge, D., Huangfu, Q., Wang, Z., Wu, J., Ye, Y.: Cardinal Optimizer (COPT) user guide (2022), https://guide.coap.online/copt/en-doc

25. GetFEM project: Gmm++ Library, https://getfem.org/gmm/, accessed 2023-01-25.

26. Giro, S.: Optimal schedulers vs optimal bases: An approach for efficient exact solving of Markov decision processes. Theor. Comput. Sci. **538**, 70–83 (2014). https://doi.org/10.1016/j.tcs.2013.08.020

27. Gleixner, A.M., Steffy, D.E., Wolter, K.: Improving the accuracy of linear programming solvers with iterative refinement. In: ISSAC. pp. 187–194. ACM (2012)

28. Gleixner, A.M., Steffy, D.E., Wolter, K.: Iterative refinement for linear programming. Tech. Rep. 3, ZIB, Takustr. 7, 14195 Berlin (2016). https://doi.org/10.1287/ijoc.2016.0692

29. GNU Project: GLPK (GNU Linear Programming Kit), http://www.gnu.org/software/glpk/glpk.html

30. Google: Glop – linear optimization, https://developers.google.com/optimization/lp, accessed 2023-01-25.

31. Guennebaud, G., Jacob, B., et al.: Eigen v3 (2010), http://eigen.tuxfamily.org

32. Gurobi Optimization, LLC: Gurobi Optimizer Reference Manual (2022), https://www.gurobi.com

33. Haddad, S., Monmege, B.: Reachability in MDPs: Refining convergence of value iteration. In: RP. LNCS, vol. 8762, pp. 125–137. Springer (2014)

34. Haddad, S., Monmege, B.: Interval iteration algorithm for MDPs and IMDPs. Theor. Comput. Sci. **735**, 111–131 (2018). https://doi.org/10.1016/j.tcs.2016.12.003

35. Hall, J., Galabova, I., Gottwald, L., Feldmeier, M.: HiGHS – high performance software for linear optimization, https://www.maths.ed.ac.uk/hall/HiGHS/, accessed 2023-01-25.

36. Hartmanns, A.: Correct probabilistic model checking with floating-point arithmetic. In: TACAS (2). LNCS, vol. 13244, pp. 41–59. Springer (2022). https://doi.org/10.1007/978-3-030-99527-0_3

37. Hartmanns, A., Hermanns, H.: The Modest Toolset: An integrated environment for quantitative modelling and verification. In: TACAS. LNCS, vol. 8413, pp. 593–598. Springer (2014). https://doi.org/10.1007/978-3-642-54862-8_51

38. Hartmanns, A., Junges, S., Quatmann, T., Weininger, M.: A Practitioner's Guide to MDP Model Checking Algorithms (Artefact) (2023). https://doi.org/10.5281/zenodo.7509474

39. Hartmanns, A., Junges, S., Quatmann, T., Weininger, M.: A practitioner's guide to MDP model checking algorithms (2023). https://doi.org/10.48550/ARXIV.2301.10197

40. Hartmanns, A., Kaminski, B.L.: Optimistic value iteration. In: CAV (2). LNCS, vol. 12225, pp. 488–511. Springer (2020). https://doi.org/10.1007/978-3-030-53291-8_26

41. Hartmanns, A., Klauck, M., Parker, D., Quatmann, T., Ruijters, E.: The quantitative verification benchmark set. In: TACAS. LNCS, vol. 11427, pp. 344–350. Springer (2019). https://doi.org/10.1007/978-3-030-17462-0_20

42. Hensel, C., Junges, S., Katoen, J.P., Quatmann, T., Volk, M.: The probabilistic model checker Storm. Int. J. Softw. Tools Technol. Transf. **24**(4), 589–610 (2022). https://doi.org/10.1007/s10009-021-00633-z

43. Huangfu, Q., Hall, J.A.J.: Parallelizing the dual revised simplex method. Math. Program. Comput. **10**(1), 119–142 (2018). https://doi.org/10.1007/s12532-017-0130-5

44. IBM: IBM ILOG CPLEX Optimizer, https://www.ibm.com/analytics/cplex-optimizer, accessed 2023-01-25.

45. Junges, S., Torfah, H., Seshia, S.A.: Runtime monitors for Markov decision processes. In: CAV (2). LNCS, vol. 12760, pp. 553–576. Springer (2021)

46. Kretinsky, J., Ramneantu, E., Slivinskiy, A., Weininger, M.: Comparison of algorithms for simple stochastic games. Inf. Comput. (2022). https://doi.org/10.1016/j.ic.2022.104885

47. Kumar, A., Zilberstein, S.: History-based controller design and optimization for partially observable MDPs. In: ICAPS. vol. 25, pp. 156–164 (2015)

48. Kwiatkowska, M.Z., Norman, G., Parker, D., Sproston, J.: Performance analysis of probabilistic timed automata using digital clocks. Formal Methods Syst. Des. **29**(1), 33–78 (2006). https://doi.org/10.1007/s10703-006-0005-2

49. Littman, M.L., Dean, T.L., Kaelbling, L.P.: On the complexity of solving Markov decision problems. In: UAI. pp. 394–402. Morgan Kaufmann (1995)

50. Mathur, U., Bauer, M.S., Chadha, R., Sistla, A.P., Viswanathan, M.: Exact quantitative probabilistic model checking through rational search. Formal Methods Syst. Des. **56**(1), 90–126 (2020)

51. McMahan, H.B., Likhachev, M., Gordon, G.J.: Bounded real-time dynamic programming: RTDP with monotone upper bounds and performance guarantees. In: ICML. ACM International Conference Proceeding Series, vol. 119, pp. 569–576. ACM (2005). https://doi.org/10.1145/1102351.1102423

52. MOSEK ApS: The MOSEK Optimization Suite 10.0.34, https://docs.mosek.com/latest/intro/index.html, accessed 2023-01-25.

53. de Moura, L.M., Bjørner, N.S.: Z3: an efficient SMT solver. In: TACAS. LNCS, vol. 4963, pp. 337–340. Springer (2008). https://doi.org/10.1007/978-3-540-78800-3_24

54. Phalakarn, K., Takisaka, T., Haas, T., Hasuo, I.: Widest paths and global propagation in bounded value iteration for stochastic games. In: CAV (2). LNCS, vol. 12225, pp. 349–371. Springer (2020), https://doi.org/10.1007/978-3-030-53291-8_19

55. Puterman, M.L.: Markov Decision Processes: Discrete Stochastic Dynamic Programming. Wiley Series in Probability and Statistics, Wiley (1994). https://doi.org/10.1002/9780470316887

56. Quatmann, T., Katoen, J.P.: Sound value iteration. In: CAV (1). LNCS, vol. 10981, pp. 643–661. Springer (2018). https://doi.org/10.1007/978-3-319-96145-3_37

57. Saad, Y., Schultz, M.H.: Gmres: a generalized minimal residual algorithm for solving nonsymmetric linear systems. Siam Journal on Scientific and Statistical Computing **7**, 856–869 (1986), https://epubs.siam.org/doi/10.1137/0907058

58. Wimmer, R., Jansen, N., Vorpahl, A., Ábrahám, E., Katoen, J.P., Becker, B.: High-level counterexamples for probabilistic automata. Log. Methods Comput. Sci. **11**(1) (2015)

59. Wimmer, R., Kortus, A., Herbstritt, M., Becker, B.: Probabilistic model checking and reliability of results. In: DDECS. pp. 207–212. IEEE Computer Society (2008). https://doi.org/10.1109/DDECS.2008.4538787

60. Ye, Y.: The simplex and policy-iteration methods are strongly polynomial for the Markov decision problem with a fixed discount rate. Mathematics of Operations Research **36**(4), 593–603 (2011)

Correct Approximation of
Stationary Distributions

Tobias Meggendorfer[✉][iD]

Institute of Science and Technology Austria, 3400 Klosterneuburg, Austria
tobias.meggendorfer@ista.ac.at

Abstract. A classical problem for Markov chains is determining their
stationary (or steady-state) distribution. This problem has an equally
classical solution based on eigenvectors and linear equation systems.
However, this approach does not scale to large instances, and iterative
solutions are desirable. It turns out that a naive approach, as used by
current model checkers, may yield completely wrong results. We present
a new approach, which utilizes recent advances in partial exploration and
mean payoff computation to obtain a correct, converging approximation.

1 Introduction

Discrete-time Markov chains (MCs) are an elegant and standard framework to
describe stochastic processes, with a vast area of applications such as computer
science [4], biology [28], epidemiology [13], and chemistry [12], to name a few.
In a nutshell, MC comprise a set of states and a transition function, assigning
to each state a distribution over successors. The system evolves by repeatedly
drawing a successor state from the transition distribution of the current state.
This can, for example, model communication over a lossy channel, a queuing
network, or populations of predator and prey which grow and interact randomly.
For many applications, the *stationary distribution* of such a system is of particular
interest. Intuitively, this distribution describes in which states the system is in
after an "infinite" number of steps. For example, in a chemical reaction network
this distribution could describe the equilibrium states of the mixture.

Traditionally, the stationary distribution is obtained by computing the dominant eigenvector for particular matrices and solving a series of linear equation
systems. This approach is appealing in theory, since it is polynomial in the size
of the considered Markov chain. Moreover, since linear algebra is an intensely
studied field, many optimizations for the computations at hand are known.

In practice, these approaches however often turn out to be insufficient. Real-
world models may have millions of states, often ruling out exact solution approaches. As such, the attention turns to iterative methods. In particular, the
popular model checker PRISM [21] employs the *power method* (or *power iteration*)
to approximate the stationary distribution. Similar to many other problems on
Markov chains, such iterative methods have an exponential worst-case, however
obtain good results quickly on many models. (Models where iterative methods
indeed converge slowly are called *stiff*.) However, as we show in this work, the

© The Author(s) 2023
S. Sankaranarayanan and N. Sharygina (Eds.): TACAS 2023, LNCS 13993, pp. 489–507, 2023.
https://doi.org/10.1007/978-3-031-30823-9_25

"absolute change"-criterion used by PRISM to stop the iteration is incorrect. In particular, the produced results may be arbitrarily wrong already on a model with only four states. In [14,7] the authors discuss a similar issue for the problem of *reachability*, also rooted in an incorrect absolute change stopping criterion, and provide a solution through converging lower and *upper* bounds. In our case, the situations is more complicated. The convergence of the power method is quite difficult to bound: A good (and potentially tight) a-priori bound is given by the ratio of first and second eigenvalues, which however is as hard to determine as solving the problem itself. In the case of MC, only a crude bound on this ratio can be obtained easily, which gives an exponential bound on the number of iterations required to achieve a given precision. More strikingly, in contrast to reachability, there is to our knowledge no general *adaptive* stopping criterion for power iteration, i.e. a way to check whether the current iterates are already close to the correct result. Thus, one would always need to iterate for as many steps as given by the a-priori bound to obtain guarantees on the result. In summary, exact solution approaches do not scale well, and the existing iterative approach may yield wrong results or requires an intractable number of steps.

Another, orthogonal issue of the mentioned approaches is that they construct the *complete* system, i.e. determine the stationary distribution for each state. However, when we figure out that, for example, the stationary distribution has a value of at least 99% for one state, all other states can have at most 1% in total. In case we are satisfied with an *approximate* solution, we could already stop the computation here, without investigating any other state. Inspired by the results of [7,18], we thus also want to find such an approximate solution, capable of identifying the relevant parts of the system and only constructing those.

1.1   Contributions

In this work, we address all the above issues. To this end, we

-   provide a characterization of the stationary distribution through mean payoff which allows us to obtain provably correct approximations (Section 3),
-   introduce a general framework to approximate the stationary distribution in Markov chains, capable of utilizing partial exploration approaches (Section 4),
-   as the main technical contribution, provide very general, precise correctness and termination proofs, requiring only minimal assumptions (Theorem 3),
-   instantiate this framework with both the classical solution approach as well as our novel sampling-based interval approximation approach (Section 4.2),
-   evaluate the variants of our framework experimentally (Section 5), and
-   demonstrate with a minimal example that the standard approach of PRISM may yield arbitrarily wrong results (Fig. 2).

1.2   Related Work

Most related is the work of [30], which also try to identify the most relevant parts of the system, however they employ the special structure given by cellular processes to find these regions and estimate the subsequent approximation error. Many other works deal with special cases, such as queueing models [1,17], time-reversible chains [8], or positive rows (all states have a transition to one particular state) [9,11,27]. In contrast, our methods aim to deal with general Markov chains. We highlight that for the "positive row" case, [11] also provides converging bounds, however through a different route. Another topic of interest are continuous time Markov chains, where abstraction- and truncation-based algorithms are applicable [20,3] and computation of the stationary distribution can be used for time-bounded reachability [16].

2   Preliminaries

As usual, $\mathbb{N}$ and $\mathbb{R}$ refer to the (positive) natural numbers and real numbers, respectively. For a set S, $\overline{S}$ denotes its complement, while $S^\star$ and S^ω refer to the set of finite and infinite sequences comprising elements of S, respectively. We write $\mathbb{1}_S(s) = 1$ if $s \in S$ and 0 otherwise for the *characteristic function* of S.

We assume familiarity with basic notions of probability theory, e.g., *probability spaces*, *probability measures*, and *measurability*; see e.g. [6] for a general introduction. A *probability distribution* over a countable set X is a mapping $d : X \to [0,1]$, such that $\sum_{x \in X} d(x) = 1$. Its *support* is denoted by $\mathrm{supp}(d) = \{x \in X \mid d(x) > 0\}$. $\mathcal{D}(X)$ denotes the set of all probability distributions on X. Some event happens *almost surely* (a.s.) if it happens with probability 1.

The central object of interest are Markov chains, a classical model for systems with stochastic behaviour: A (discrete-time time-homogeneous) *Markov chain (MC)* is a tuple $\mathsf{M} = (S, \delta)$, where S is a finite set of *states*, and $\delta : S \to \mathcal{D}(S)$ is a *transition function* that for each state s yields a probability distribution over successor states. We deliberately exclude the explicit definition of an initial state. We direct the interested reader to, e.g., [4, Sec. 10.1], [29, App. A], or [19] for further information on Markov chains and related notions.

For ease of notation, we write $\delta(s, s')$ instead of $\delta(s)(s')$, and, given a function $f : S \to \mathbb{R}$ mapping states to real numbers, we write $\delta(s)\langle f \rangle := \sum_{s' \in S} \delta(s, s') \cdot f(s')$ to denote the weighted sum of f over the successors of s.

We always assume an arbitrary but fixed numbering of the states and identify a state with its respective number. For example, given a vector $v \in \mathbb{R}^{|S|}$ and a state $s \in S$, we may write $v[s]$ to denote the value associated with s by v. In this way, a function $v : S \to \mathbb{R}$ is equivalent to a vector $v \in \mathbb{R}^{|S|}$.

For a set of states $R \subseteq S$ where no transitions leave R, i.e. $\delta(s, s') = 0$ for all $s \in R$, $s' \in S \setminus R$, we define the *restricted Markov chain* $\mathsf{M}|_R := (R, \delta|_R)$ with $\delta|_R : R \to \mathcal{D}(R)$ copying the values of δ, i.e. $\delta|_R(s, s') = \delta(s, s')$ for all $s, s' \in R$.

Paths An *infinite path* ρ in a Markov chain is an infinite sequence $\rho = s_1 s_2 \cdots \in S^\omega$, such that for every $i \in \mathbb{N}$ we have that $\delta(s_i, s_{i+1}) > 0$. We use $\rho(i)$ to refer to the i-th state s_i in a given infinite path. We denote the set of all infinite paths of a Markov chain M by $\mathsf{Paths}_\mathsf{M}$. Observe that in general $\mathsf{Paths}_\mathsf{M}$ is a proper subset of S^ω, as we imposed additional constraints. A Markov chain together with an initial state $\hat{s} \in S$ induces a unique probability measure $\mathsf{Pr}_{\mathsf{M},\hat{s}}$ over infinite paths [4, Sec. 10.1]. Given a measurable random variable $f : \mathsf{Paths}_\mathsf{M} \to \mathbb{R}$, we write $\mathbb{E}_{\mathsf{M},\hat{s}}[f] := \int_{\rho \in \mathsf{Paths}} f(\rho) \, d\mathsf{Pr}_{\mathsf{M},\hat{s}}$ to denote its expectation w.r.t. this measure.

Reachability An important tool in the following is the notion of *reachability probability*, i.e. the probability that the system, starting from a state $\hat{s}$, will eventually reach a given set T. Formally, for a Markov chain M and set of states T, we define the set of runs which reach T (i) at step n by $\Diamond^{=n}T := \{\rho \in \mathsf{Paths_M} \mid \rho(n) \in T\}$ and (ii) eventually by $\Diamond T = \bigcup_{i=1}^{\infty} \Diamond^{=i}T$. (For a measurability proof see e.g. [4, Chp. 10].) For a state $\hat{s}$, the probability to reach T is given by $\mathsf{Pr_{M,\hat{s}}}[\Diamond T]$.

Classically, the reachability probability can be determined by solving a linear equation system, as follows. For a fixed target set T, let S_0 be all states that cannot reach T. Note that S_0 can be determined by simple graph analysis. Then, the reachability probability $\mathsf{Pr_{M,\hat{s}}}[\Diamond T]$ is the unique solution of [4, Thm. 10.19]

$$f(s) = 1 \text{ if } s \in T, \quad 0 \text{ if } s \in S_0, \quad \text{and} \quad \delta(s)\langle f \rangle \text{ otherwise.} \quad (1)$$

Value Iteration A classical tool to deal with Markov chains is *value iteration* (VI) [5]. It is a simple yet surprisingly efficient and extendable approach to solve a variety of problems. At its heart, VI relies, as the name suggests, on iteratively applying an operation to a value vector. This operation often is called "Bellman backup" or "Bellman update", usually derived from a fixed-point characterization of the problem at hand. Thus, VI often can be viewed as fixed point iteration. For reachability, inspired by Eq. (1), we start from $v_1[s] = 0$ and iterate

$$v_{k+1}[s] = 1 \text{ if } s \in T, \quad 0 \text{ if } s \in S_0, \quad \text{and} \quad \delta(s)\langle v_k \rangle \text{ otherwise.} \quad (2)$$

This iteration monotonically converges to the true value in the limit from below [4, Thm. 10.15], [29, Thm. 7.2.12]. Convergence up to a given precision may take exponential time [14, Thm. 3], but in practice VI often is much faster than methods based on equation solving. For further details, see [26, App. A.2].

Strongly Connected Components A non-empty set of states $C \subseteq S$ in a Markov chain is *strongly connected* if for every pair $s, s' \in C$ there is a non-empty finite path from s to s'. Such a set C is a *strongly connected component* (SCC) if it is inclusion maximal, i.e. there exists no strongly connected C' with $C \subsetneq C'$. SCCs are disjoint, each state belongs to at most one SCC. An SCC is *bottom* (BSCC) if additionally no path leads out of it, i.e. for all $s \in C, s' \in S \setminus C$ we have $\delta(s, s') = 0$. The set of BSCCs in an MC M is denoted by $\mathsf{BSCC(M)}$ and can be determined in linear time by, e.g., Tarjan's algorithm [32].

The bottom components fully capture the limit behaviour of any Markov chain. Intuitively, the following statement says that (i) with probability one a run of a Markov chain eventually forever remains inside one single BSCC, and (ii) inside a BSCC, all states are visited infinitely often with probability one.

Lemma 1 ([4, Thm. 10.27]). *For any MC M and state s, we have*

$$\mathsf{Pr_{M,s}}[\{\rho \mid \exists R_i \in \mathsf{BSCC(M)}.\exists n_0 \in \mathbb{N}.\forall n > n_0.\rho(n) \in R_i\}] = 1.$$

For any BSCC $R \in \mathsf{BSCC(M)}$ and states $s, s' \in R$, we have $\mathsf{Pr_{M,s}}[\Diamond\{s'\}] = 1$.

Stationary Distribution Given a state $\hat{s}$, the *stationary distribution* (also known as *steady-state* or *long-run distribution*) of a Markov chain intuitively describes, for each state s, the probability for the system to be at this particular state at an

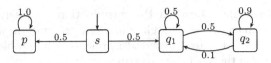

Fig. 1. Example MC to demonstrate the stationary distribution. We have that $\pi^\infty_{M,s} = \{p \mapsto \frac{1}{2}, s \mapsto 0, q_1 \mapsto \frac{1}{2} \cdot \frac{1}{6}, q_2 \mapsto \frac{1}{2} \cdot \frac{5}{6}\}$.

arbitrarily chosen step "at infinity". There are several ways to define this notion. In particular, there is a subtle difference between the *limiting* and *stationary distribution*, which however coincide for *aperiodic* MC. For the sake of readability, we omit this distinction and assume w.l.o.g. that all MCs we deal with are aperiodic. See [26, App. A.1] for further discussion. Our definition follows the view of [4, Def. 10.79]; see [29, Sec. A.4] for a different approach.

Definition 1. *Fix a Markov chain* $M = (S, \delta)$ *and initial state* $\hat{s}$. *Let* $\pi^n_{M,\hat{s}}(s) :=$ $Pr_{M,\hat{s}}[\lozenge^{=n}\{s\}]$ *the probability that the system is at state* s *in step* n. *Then,* $\pi^\infty_{M,\hat{s}}(s) := \lim_{n \to \infty} \frac{1}{n} \sum_{i=1}^n \pi^i_{M,\hat{s}}(s)$ *is the stationary distribution of* M.

See Fig. 1 for an example. Whenever the reference is clear from context, we omit the respective subscripts from $\pi^\infty_{M,\hat{s}}$.

We briefly recall the classical approach to compute stationary distributions (see e.g. [19, Sec. 4.7]). By Lemma 1, almost all runs eventually end up in a BSCC. Thus, $\pi^\infty(s) = 0$ for all states s not in a BSCC, or, dually, $\sum_{s \in B} \pi^\infty(s) = 1$ for $B = \bigcup_{R \in BSCC(M)} R$. Moreover, once in a BSCC, we always obtain the same stationary distribution, irrespective of through which state we entered the BSCC. Formally, for each BSCC $R \in BSCC(M)$ and $s, s' \in R$, we have that $\pi^\infty_{M,s} = \pi^\infty_{M,s'} = \pi^\infty_{M|R,s}$, i.e. each BSCC R has a unique stationary distribution, which we denote by π^∞_R. Note that $supp(\pi^\infty_R) = R$, i.e. $\pi^\infty_R(s) \neq 0$ if and only if $s \in R$. Together, we observe that the stationary distribution of a Markov chain decomposes into (i) the steady state distribution in each BSCC and (ii) the probability to end up in a particular BSCC. More formally, for any state $s \in S$

$$\pi^\infty_{M,\hat{s}}(s) = \sum_{R \in BSCC(M)} Pr_{M,\hat{s}}[\lozenge R] \cdot \pi^\infty_R(s). \tag{3}$$

Consider the example of Fig. 1: We have two BSCCs, $\{p\}$ and $\{q_1, q_2\}$, which both are reached with probability $\frac{1}{2}$, respectively. The overall distribution $\pi^\infty_{M,s}$ then is obtained from $\pi^\infty_{\{p\}} = \{p \mapsto 1\}$ and $\pi^\infty_{\{q_1,q_2\}} = \{q_1 \mapsto \frac{1}{6}, q_2 \mapsto \frac{5}{6}\}$.

As mentioned, we can compute reachability probabilities in Markov chains by solving Eq. (1). Thus, the remaining concern is to compute π^∞_R, i.e. the stationary distribution of $M|_R$. In this case, i.e. Markov chains comprising a single BSCC, the steady state distribution is the unique fixed point of the transition function (up to rescaling). By defining the row transition matrix of M as $P_{i,j} = \delta(i,j)$, we can reformulate this property in terms of linear algebra. In particular, we have that $P \cdot \pi^\infty_R = \pi^\infty_R$, or, in other words, $(P - I) \cdot \pi^\infty_R = \vec{0}$, where I is an appropriately sized identity matrix [29, Thm. A.2]. This equation again can be solved by classical methods from linear algebra. In summary, we (i) compute $BSCC(M)$, (ii) for each BSCC R, compute π^∞_R and $Pr_{M,\hat{s}}[\lozenge R]$, and (iii) combine according to Eq. (3).

However, as also mentioned in the introduction, precisely solving linear equation systems may not scale well, both due to time as well as memory constraints. Thus, we also are interested in relaxing the problem slightly and instead *approximating* the stationary distribution up to a given precision of $\varepsilon > 0$.

Problem Statement Given a Markov chain M and precision requirement $\varepsilon > 0$, compute bounds $l, u : S \to [0, 1]$ such that (i) $\max_{s \in S} u(s) - l(s) \leq \varepsilon$ and (ii) for all $s \in S$ we have $l(s) \leq \pi^\infty_{\mathsf{M}, \hat{s}}(s) \leq u(s)$.

Approximate Solutions Aiming for approximations is not a new idea; to achieve practical performance, current model checkers employ approximate, iterative methods by default for most queries (typically a variant value iteration). In particular, this also is the case for stationary distribution: Instead of solving the equation system for each BSCC R precisely, we can approximate the solution by, e.g., the *power method*. This essentially means to repeatedly apply the transition matrix (of the model restricted to the BSCC) to an initial vector v_0, i.e. iterating $v_{n+1} = P_R \cdot v_n$ (or $v_{n+1} = P_R^n \cdot v_1$). Similarly, the reachability probability for each BSCC then also is approximated by value iteration.

It is known that (for aperiodic MC) $\lim_{n \to \infty} v_n = \pi_R^\infty$ (see e.g. [31,16,27]), however convergence up to a precision of ε may take exponential time in the worst case. Moreover, there is no known stopping criterion which allows us to detect that we have converged and stop the computation early. Yet, similar to reachability [7,14], current model checkers employ this method without a sound stopping criterion, leading to potentially arbitrarily wrong results, as we show in our evaluation (Fig. 2). See [16] for a related, in-depth discussion of these issues in the context of CTMC.

We thus want to find efficient methods to derive safe bounds on the stationary distribution of a BSCC with a correct stopping criterion and combine it with correct reachability approximations to obtain an overall fast and sound approximation. To this end, we exploit two further concepts.

Partial Exploration Recent works [7,2,18,24] demonstrate the applicability of *partial exploration* to a variety of problems associated with probabilistic systems such as reachability. Essentially, the idea is to "omit" parts of the system which can be proven to be irrelevant for the result, instead focussing on important areas of the system. Of course, by omitting parts of the system, we may incur a small error. As such, these approaches naturally aim for approximate solutions.

Mean payoff We make use of another property, namely *mean payoff* (also known as *long-run average reward*). We provide a brief overview and direct to e.g. [29, Chp. 8 & 9] or [2] for more information. Mean payoff is specified by a Markov chain and a *reward function* $r : S \to \mathbb{R}$, assigning a reward to each state. Given an infinite path $\rho = s_1 s_2 \cdots$, this naturally induces a stream of rewards $r(\rho) := r(s_1) r(s_2) \cdots$. The mean payoff of this path then equals the average reward obtained in the limit, $\mathrm{mp}'_r(\rho) := \liminf_{n \to \infty} \frac{1}{n} \sum_{i=1}^n r(s_i)$. (The limit might not be defined for some paths, hence considering the lim inf is necessary.) Finally, the mean payoff of a state s is the *expected mean payoff* according to $\Pr_{\mathsf{M},s}$, i.e. $\mathrm{mp}_r(s) := \mathbb{E}_{\mathsf{M},s}[\mathrm{mp}'_r]$.

Classically, mean payoff is computed by solving a linear equation system [29, Thm. 9.1.2]. Instead, we can also employ value iteration to approximate the mean payoff, however with a slight twist. We iteratively compute the *expected total reward*, i.e. the expected sum of rewards obtained after n steps, by iterating $v_{n+1}(s) = r(s) + \delta(s)\langle v_n \rangle$. It turns out that the *increase* $\Delta_n(s) = v_{n+1}(s) - v_n(s)$ approximates the mean payoff, i.e. $\mathrm{mp}_r(s) = \lim_{n \to \infty} \Delta_n(s)$ [29, Thm. 9.4.5 a)]. Moreover, we have $\min_{s' \in S} \Delta_n(s') \le \mathrm{mp}_r(s) \le \max_{s' \in S} \Delta_n(s')$, yielding a correct stopping criterion [29, Thm. 9.4.5 b)]. Finally, on BSCCs these upper and lower bounds always converge [29, Cor. 9.4.6 b)], yielding termination guarantees. We provide further details on VI for mean payoff in [26, App. A.3].

3 Building Blocks

To arrive at a practical algorithm approximating the stationary distribution, we propose to employ sampling-based techniques, inspired by, e.g. [7,2,18]. Intuitively, these approaches repeatedly sample paths and compute bounds on a single property such as reachability or mean payoff. The sampling is designed to follow probable paths with high probability, hence the computation automatically focuses on the most relevant parts of the system. Additionally, by building the system *on the fly*, construction of hardly reachable parts of the system may be avoided altogether, yielding immense speed-ups for some models (see, e.g., [18] for additional background). We apply a series of tweaks to the original idea to tailor this approach to our use case, i.e. approximating the stationary distribution.

In this section, we present the "building blocks" for our approximate approach. In the spirit of Eq. (3), we discuss how we handle a single BSCC and how to approximate the reachability probabilities of all BSCCs. In the following section, we then combine these two approaches in a non-trivial manner.

3.1 Bounds in BSSCs through Mean Payoff

It is well known that the mean payoff can be computed directly from the stationary distribution [29, Prop. 8.1.1], namely:

$$\mathrm{mp}_r(s) = \sum_{s' \in S} \pi^{\infty}_{\mathsf{M},s}(s') \cdot r(s') \tag{4}$$

In this section, we propose the opposite, namely computing the stationary distribution of a BSCC through mean payoff queries. Fix a Markov chain $\mathsf{M} = (S, \delta)$ which comprises a single BSCC, i.e. $S \in \mathrm{BSCC}(\mathsf{M})$, and define $r(s') = \mathbb{1}_{\{s\}}(s')$, i.e. 1 for s and 0 otherwise. Then, the mean payoff corresponds to the frequency of s appearing, i.e. the stationary distribution. Formally, we have that $\pi^{\infty}_{\mathsf{M},\hat{s}}(s) = \mathrm{mp}_r(s')$ for any state s' (in a BSCC, all states have the same value). This also follows directly by inserting in Eq. (4). So, naively, for each state of the BSCC, we can solve a mean payoff query, and from these results obtain the overall stationary distribution.

Algorithm 1 Approximate Stationary Distribution in BSCC

Input: Markov chain $\mathsf{M} = (S, \delta)$ with $\mathrm{BSCC}(\mathsf{M}) = \{S\}$
Output: Bounds l, u on stationary distribution π_S^∞.

1: $n \leftarrow 1$
2: **for** $s \in S$ **do** $l_1(s) \leftarrow 0$, $u_1(s) \leftarrow 1$
3: **for** $s \in S$ **do**
4:      $m \leftarrow 1$, $v_1 \leftarrow \textsc{InitGuess}(s)$
5:      **while** not $\textsc{ShouldStop}(s, m, \Delta_m)$ **do**   ▷ *Iterate until some stopping criterion*
6:          **for** $s' \in S$ **do** $v_{m+1}(s') \leftarrow \mathbb{1}_{\{s\}}(s') + \delta(s')\langle v_m \rangle$ ▷ *Mean payoff VI for s*
7:          $m \leftarrow m + 1$
8:      $l_n'(s) \leftarrow \max\big(l_n(s), \min_{s' \in S} \Delta_m(s')\big)$, $u_n'(s) \leftarrow \min\big(u_n(s), \max_{s' \in S} \Delta_m(s')\big)$
9:      **for** $s' \in S \setminus \{s\}$ **do** $l_n'(s') \leftarrow l_n(s')$, $u_n'(s') \leftarrow u_n(s')$
10:      **for** $s' \in S$ **do**   ▷ *Update bounds based on current results (optional)*
11:          $l_{n+1}(s') \leftarrow \max\big(l_n'(s'), 1 - \sum_{s'' \in S, s'' \neq s'} u_n'(s'')\big)$
12:          $u_{n+1}(s') \leftarrow \min\big(u_n'(s'), 1 - \sum_{s'' \in S, s'' \neq s'} l_n'(s'')\big)$
13:      $n \leftarrow n + 1$ and copy all unchanged values from n to $n + 1$
14: **return** (l_n, u_n)

At first, this may seem excessive, especially considering that computing the complete stationary distribution is as hard as determining the mean payoff for one state (both can be obtained by solving a linearly sized equation system). However, this idea yields some interesting benefits. Firstly, using the approximation approach discussed in Section 2, we obtain a practical approximation scheme with converging bounds for each state. As such, we can quickly stop the computation if the bounds converge fast. Moreover, we can pause and restart the computation for each state, which we will use later on in order to focus on crucial states. Finally, observe that π_R^∞ is a distribution. Thus, having lower bounds on some states actually already yields upper bounds for remaining states. Formally, for some lower bound $l : S \to [0, 1]$, we have $\pi_R^\infty(s) \leq 1 - \sum_{s' \in S, s' \neq s} l(s')$. If during our computation it turns out that a few states are actually visited very frequently, i.e. the sum of their lower bounds is close to 1, we can already stop the computation without ever investigating the other states. Note that this only is possible since we obtain provably correct bounds.

Combining these ideas, we present our first algorithm template in Algorithm 1. We solve each state separately, by applying the classical value iteration approach for mean payoff until a termination criterion is satisfied. To allow for modifications, we leave the definition of several sub-procedures open. Firstly, $\textsc{InitGuess}$ initializes the value vector for each mean payoff computation. We can naively choose 0 everywhere, obtain an initial guess by heuristics, or re-use previously computed values. Secondly, $\textsc{ShouldStop}$ decides when to stop the iteration for each state. A simple choice is to iterate until $\max \Delta_m(s) - \min \Delta_m(s) < \varepsilon$ for some precision requirement ε. By results on mean payoff, we can conclude that in this case the stationary distribution is computed with a precision of ε. However, as we argue later on, more sophisticated choices are possible. Finally, the order in which states are chosen is not fixed. Indeed, any order yields correct results, however heuristically re-ordering the states may also bring practical benefits.

Before we continue, we briefly argue that the algorithm is correct.

Theorem 1. *The result returned by Algorithm 1 is correct for any MC* $M = (S, \delta)$ *with* $\mathrm{BSCC}(M) = \{S\}$.

Proof (Sketch). Correctness of the mean payoff iteration follows from the definition of the reward function, Eq. (4), and the correctness of value iteration for mean payoff [29, Sec. 8.5]. In particular, note that the states of the MC form a single BSCC and the model is *unichain* (see [29, Chp. A]), implying that all states have the same value. For l and u, we prove correctness inductively. The initial values are trivially correct. The updates based on the mean payoff computation are correct by the above arguments and by induction hypothesis: The maximum of two correct lower bounds still is a lower bound, analogous for the upper bound. The updates based on the bounds are correct since π_R^∞ is a distribution and l', u' are correct bounds.   □

We deliberately omit introducing an explicit precision requirement in the algorithm, since we will use it as a building block later on.

Remark 1. A variant of this approach also allows for memory savings: By handling one state at a time, we only need to store linearly many additional values (in the number of states) at any time, while an explicit equation system may require quadratic space. This only yields a constant factor improvement if the system is represented explicitly (storing δ requires as much space), however can be of significant merit for symbolically encoded systems. Note that this comes at a cost: As we cannot stop and resume the computation for different states, we have to determine the correct result up to the required precision immediately.

3.2   Reachability and Guided Sampling

As mentioned before, the second challenge to obtain a stationary distribution is the reachability probability for each BSCC. We employ a sampling-based approach using insights from [7]. There, the authors considered a single reachability objective, i.e. a single value per state. In contrast, we need to bound reachability probabilities for each BSCC. For now, suppose that all BSCCs are already discovered and their respective stationary distribution is already computed (or approximated). In other words, we have for each BSCC $R \in \mathrm{BSCC}(M)$ bounds $l^R, u^R : R \to [0,1]$ with $l_R(s) \le \pi_R^\infty(s) \le u_R(s)$, and we want to obtain bounds on the stationary distribution, i.e. functions l, u such that $l(s) \le \pi_{M,\hat{s}}^\infty(s) \le u(s)$. We propose to additionally compute bounds on the probability to reach each BSCC R, i.e. functions $l^{\Diamond R}$ and $u^{\Diamond R}$ such that $l^{\Diamond R}(s) \le \mathrm{Pr}_{M,s}[\Diamond R] \le u^{\Diamond R}(s)$. By Eq. (3), we then have for each state s a bound on the stationary distribution

$$\sum\nolimits_{R \in \mathrm{BSCC}(M)} l^{\Diamond R}(\hat{s}) \cdot l^R(s) \le \pi_{M,\hat{s}}^\infty(s) \le \sum\nolimits_{R \in \mathrm{BSCC}(M)} u^{\Diamond R}(\hat{s}) \cdot u^R(s).$$

We take a route similar to [7]. There, the algorithm essentially samples a path through the system, possibly guided by a heuristic, terminates the sampling based on several criteria, and then propagates the reachability value backwards along the path, repeating until termination. We propose a simple modification, namely to sample until a BSCC is reached, and then propagate the reachability

---

Algorithm 2 Approximate BSCC Reachability

Input: Markov chain $M = (S, \delta)$
Output: For each BSCC R bounds $l^{\Diamond R}, u^{\Diamond R}$ on the probability to reach R.
1: $B \leftarrow \bigcup_{R \in \text{BSCC}(M)} R$, $n \leftarrow 1$
2: **for** $R \in \text{BSCC}(M)$ **do**
3:       **for** $s \in R$ **do** $l_1^{\Diamond R}(s) \leftarrow 1$, $u_1^{\Diamond R}(s) \leftarrow 1$
4:       **for** $s \in B \setminus R$ **do** $l_1^{\Diamond R}(s) \leftarrow 0$, $u_1^{\Diamond R}(s) \leftarrow 0$
5:       **for** $s \in S \setminus B$ **do** $l_1^{\Diamond R}(s) \leftarrow 0$, $u_1^{\Diamond R}(s) \leftarrow 1$
6: **while** SHOULDSAMPLE **do**   ▷ *Sample until some stopping criterion*
7:       $P \leftarrow$ SAMPLESTATES   ▷ *Select states to update (e.g. sample a path)*
8:       **for** $R \in$ SELECTUPDATE(P) **do**   ▷ *Select BSCCs to update*
9:             **for** $s \in P$ **do**
10:                 $l_{n+1}^{\Diamond R}(s) \leftarrow \delta(s)\langle l_n^{\Diamond R}\rangle$
11:                 $u_{n+1}^{\Diamond R}(s) \leftarrow \delta(s)\langle u_n^{\Diamond R}\rangle$
12:       **for** $s \in S$ **do**   ▷ *Update bounds based on current results (optional)*
13:             **for** $R \in \text{BSCC}(M)$ **do**
14:                 $l_{n+1}^{\Diamond R}(s) \leftarrow \max\left(l_n^{\Diamond R}(s), 1 - \sum_{R' \in \text{BSCC}(M), R' \neq R} u_n^{R'}(s)\right)$
15:                 $u_{n+1}^{\Diamond R}(s) \leftarrow \min\left(u_n^{\Diamond R}(s), 1 - \sum_{R' \in \text{BSCC}(M), R' \neq R} l_n^{R'}(s)\right)$
16:       $n \leftarrow n + 1$ and copy unchanged values from $l_n^{\Diamond R}$ and $u_n^{\Diamond R}$ to $l_{n+1}^{\Diamond R}$ and $u_{n+1}^{\Diamond R}$
17: **return** $\{(l^{\Diamond R}, u^{\Diamond R}) \mid R \in \text{BSCC}(R)\}$

---

values of that particular BSCC back along the path. Moreover, we can employ a similar trick as above: Due to Lemma 1, the reachability probabilities of BSCCs sum up to one, i.e. $\sum_{R \in \text{BSCC}(M)} \text{Pr}_{M,s}[\Diamond R] = 1$ for every state s. Hence, the sum of lower bounds also yields upper bounds for other BSCCs, even those we have never encountered so far.

Our ideas are summarized in Algorithm 2. As before, the algorithm leaves several choices open. Instead of requiring to sample a path, our algorithm allows to select an arbitrary set of states to update. We note that the exact choice of this sampling mechanism does not improve the worst case runtime. However, as first observed in [7], specially crafted *guidance heuristics* can achieve dramatic practical speed-ups on several models. Later on, we combine our two algorithms and derive such a heuristic. For now, we briefly prove correctness.

Theorem 2. *The result returned by Algorithm 2 is correct for any MC* $M = (S, \delta)$ *with* $\text{BSCC}(M) = \{S\}$.

Proof (Sketch). Similar to the previous algorithm, we prove correctness by induction. The initial values for $l^{\Diamond R}$ and $u^{\Diamond R}$ are correct. Then, assume that $l_n^{\Diamond R}$ and $u_n^{\Diamond R}$ are correct bounds. The correctness of the back propagation updates follows directly by inserting in Eq. (1) (or other works on interval value iteration [7,14]). Updates based on the bounds in other states are correct by Lemma 1 – the sum of all BSCC reachability probabilities is 1. Together, this yields correctness of the bounds computed by the algorithm.   □

To obtain termination, it is sufficient to require that every state eventually is selected "arbitrarily often" by SAMPLESTATES. However, as before, we delegate the termination proof to our combined algorithm in the following section.

4 Dynamic Computation with Partial Exploration

Recall that our overarching goal is to approximate the stationary distribution through Eq. (4). In the previous section, we have seen how we can (i) obtain approximations for a given BSCC and (ii) how to approximate the reachability probabilities of all BSCCs through sampling. However, the naive combination of these algorithms would require us to compute the set of all BSCCs, approximate the stationary distribution in each of them until a fixed precision, and additionally approximate reachability for each of them.

We now combine both ideas to obtain a sampling-based algorithm, capable of partial exploration, that focusses computation on relevant parts of the system. In particular, we construct the system dynamically, identify BSCCs on the fly, and interleave the exploration with both the approximation inside each explored BSCC (Algorithm 1) and the overall reachability computation (Algorithm 2). Moreover, we focus computation on BSCCs which are likely to be reached and thus have a higher impact on the overall error of the result. Together, our approach roughly performs the following steps until the required precision is achieved:

- Sample a path through the system, guided by a heuristic,
- check if a new BSCCs is discovered or sampling ended in a known BSCC,
- refine bounds on the stationary distribution in the reached BSCC, and
- propagate reachability bounds and additional information along the path.

We first formalize a generic framework which can instantiate the classical, precise approach as well as our approximation building blocks and then explain our concrete variant of this framework to efficiently obtain ε-precise bounds.

4.1 The Framework

Since our goal is to allow for both precise as well as approximate solutions, we phrase the framework using lower and upper bounds together with abstract refinement procedures. We first explain our algorithm and how it generalizes the classical approach. Then, we prove its correctness under general assumptions. Finally, we discuss several approximate variants.

Algorithm 3 essentially repeats three steps until the termination condition in Line 4 is satisfied. First, we update the set of known BSCCs through UPDATEB-SCCs. In the classical solution, this function simply computes BSCC(M) once; our on-the-fly construction would repeatedly check for newly discovered BSCCs, dynamically growing the set $\mathcal{B}_n$. Then, we select BSCCs for which we should update the stationary distribution bounds. The classical solution solves the fixed point equation we have discussed in Section 2 for all BSCCs, i.e. SELECTDIS-TRIBUTIONUPDATES yields BSCC(M) and REFINEDISTRIBUTION the precisely computed values both as upper and lower bounds. Alternatively, we could, for example, select a single BSCC and apply a few iterations of Algorithm 1. Next, we update reachability bounds for a selected set of BSCCs. Again, the classical solution solves the reachability problem precisely for each BSCC through Eq. (1). Instead, we could employ value iteration as suggested by Algorithm 2.

Algorithm 3 Stationary Distribution Computation Framework

Input: Markov chain $M = (S, \delta)$, initial state $\hat{s}$, precision $\varepsilon > 0$
Output: ε-precise bounds l, u on the stationary distribution $\pi^{\infty}_{M,\hat{s}}$

1: **for** $s \in S$ **do**   ▷ *Initial bounds for all possible BSCCs that can be discovered*
2: $\quad \lfloor \; l_1^{\lozenge\circ}(s) = 0, u_1^{\lozenge\circ}(s) = 1, l_1^\circ(s) \leftarrow 0, u_1^\circ(s) \leftarrow 1$
3: $n \leftarrow 1, \mathcal{B}_1 \leftarrow \emptyset$
4: **while** $\left(1 - \sum_{R \in \mathcal{B}_n} l_n^{\lozenge R}(\hat{s})\right) + \sum_{R \in \mathcal{B}_n} \left(l_n^{\lozenge R}(\hat{s}) \cdot \max_{s \in S}(u_n^R(s) - l_n^R(s))\right) > \varepsilon$ **do**
5: $\quad n \leftarrow n + 1$
6: $\quad \mathcal{B}_n \leftarrow$ UPDATEBSSCs, $B_n \leftarrow \bigcup_{R \in \mathcal{B}_n} R$ ▷ *Discover new BSCCs*
7: $\quad$ **for** $R \in \mathcal{B}_n \setminus \mathcal{B}_{n-1}, s \in R$ **do**   ▷ *Update trivial reach bounds*
8: $\quad\quad \lfloor \; l_n^{\lozenge R}(s) \leftarrow 1$ ▷ $s \in R$ *surely reaches* R
9: $\quad\quad$ **for** $\circ \neq R$ **do** $u_n^{\lozenge\circ}(s) \leftarrow 0$ ▷ $s \in R$ *reaches no other BSCC*
10: $\quad$ **for** $R \in$ SELECTDISTRIBUTIONUPDATES$(\mathcal{B}_n) \cap \mathcal{B}_n$ **do**
11: $\quad\quad \lfloor \; (l_n^R, u_n^R) \leftarrow$ REFINEDISTRIBUTION(R) ▷ *Update BSCC bounds*
12: $\quad$ **for** $R \in$ SELECTREACHUPDATES$(\mathcal{B}_n) \cap \mathcal{B}_n$ **do**
13: $\quad\quad \lfloor \; (l_n^{\lozenge R}, u_n^{\lozenge R}) \leftarrow$ REFINEREACH(R) ▷ *Update reachability bounds*
14: $\quad\lfloor$ Copy unchanged variables from $n - 1$ to n
15: $L \leftarrow \sum_{R \in \mathcal{B}_n} l_n^{\lozenge R}(\hat{s})$
16: **for** $R \in \mathcal{B}_n, s \in R$ **do**
17: $\quad l(s) \leftarrow l_n^{\lozenge R}(\hat{s}) \cdot l_n^R(s)$
18: $\quad \lfloor \; u(s) \leftarrow \min(u_n^{\lozenge R}(\hat{s}), 1 - L + l_n^{\lozenge R}(\hat{s})) \cdot u_n^R(s)$
19: **for** $s \in S \setminus B_n$ **do** $l(s) \leftarrow 0, u(s) \leftarrow 0$
20: **return** (l, u)

Before we present our variant, we prove correctness under weak assumptions. We note a subtlety of the termination condition: One may assume that upper bounds on the reachability are required to bound the overall error caused by each BSCC. Yet, as we show in the following theorem, *lower* bounds are sufficient. The upper bound is implicitly handled by the first part of the termination condition.

Theorem 3. *The result returned by Algorithm 3 is correct, i.e. ε precise bounds on the stationary distribution, if (i) $\mathcal{B}_n \subseteq \mathcal{B}_{n+1} \subseteq$ BSCC(M) for all n, and (ii) REFINEDISTRIBUTION and REFINEREACH yield correct, monotone bounds.*

The proof can be found in [26, App. B.1].

Remark 2. Technically, the algorithm does not need to track explicit upper bounds on the reachability of each BSCC at all. Indeed, for a BSCC $R \in \mathcal{B}_n$, we could use $1 - \sum_{R' \in \text{BSCC}(M) \setminus \{R\}} l_n^{\lozenge R'}(s)$ as upper bound and still obtain a correct algorithm. However, tracking a separate upper bound is easier to understand and has some practical benefits for the implementation.

We exclude a proof of termination, since this strongly depends on the interplay between the functions left open. We provide a general, technical criterion together with a proof in [26, App. B.2]. Intuitively, as one might expect, we require that eventually UPDATEBSSCs identifies all relevant BSCCs, SELECTDISTRIBUTIONUPDATES and SELECTREACHUPDATES select all relevant BSCCs, and REFINEDISTRIBUTION and REFINEREACH converge to the respective true value. In the following, we present a concrete template which satisfies this criterion.

4.2   Sampling-Based Computation

We present our instantiation of Algorithm 3 using guided sampling and heuristics. Since the details of the sampling guidance heuristic are rather technical, we focus on how the template functions UPDATEBSSCs, SELECTDISTRIBUTIONUPDATES, REFINEDISTRIBUTION, SELECTREACHUPDATES, and REFINEREACH are instantiated. For now, the reader may assume that states are, e.g., selected by sampling random paths through the system.

- UPDATEBSSCs: We track the set of *explored* states, i.e. states which have already been sampled at least once. On these, we search for BSCCs whenever we repeatedly stop sampling due to a state re-appearing.
- SELECTDISTRIBUTIONUPDATES: If we stopped sampling due to entering a known BSCC, we update the bounds of this single one, otherwise none.
- REFINEDISTRIBUTION: We employ Algorithm 1 to refine the bounds until the error over all states is halved.
- SELECTREACHUPDATES: We refine the reach values for all sampled states.
- REFINEREACH: If we stopped sampling due to entering a BSCC, we back-propagate the reachability bounds for this BSCC in the spirit of Algorithm 2, i.e. for all sampled states set $l_{n+1}^{\Diamond R}(s) = \delta(s)\langle l_n^{\Diamond R}\rangle$ and $u_{n+1}^{\Diamond R}(s) = \delta(s)\langle u_n^{\Diamond R}\rangle$.

We prove that this yields correct results and terminates with probability 1 through Theorem 3. Note that this description leaves exact details of the sampling open. Thus, we prove termination using (weak) conditions on the sampling mechanism. For readability, we define the shorthand $\mathrm{err}_n^R = \max_{s \in R} u_n^R(s) - l_n^R(s)$ denoting the overall error of the stationary distribution in BSCC R and $\mathrm{err}_n^{\Diamond R}(s) = u_n^{\Diamond R}(s) - l_n^{\Diamond R}(s)$ the error bound on the reachability of R from s.

Theorem 4. *Algorithm 3 instantiated with our sampling-based approach yields correct results and terminates with probability 1 if, with probability 1,*

   (S.i) the sampled states $P \subseteq S$ satisfy $\mathrm{Pr}_{M,\hat{s}}[\Diamond \overline{P}] < \frac{\varepsilon}{4}$ (P is a $\frac{\varepsilon}{4}$-core [18]),

   (S.ii) the initial state is sampled arbitrarily often, and

   (S.iii) for each state s sampled arbitrarily often, every successor $s' \in P$ with
      $E_n(s') := \max_{R \in \mathcal{B}_n} u_n^{\Diamond R}(s') \cdot \mathrm{err}_n^R + \max_{R \in \mathcal{B}_n} \mathrm{err}_n^{\Diamond R}(s) \geq \frac{\varepsilon}{4(|\mathcal{B}_n|+1)}$ is
      sampled arbitrarily often,

where "arbitrarily often" means that if the algorithm would not terminate, this would happen infinitely often.

The proof can be found in [26, App. B.3].

    Due to space constraints, we omit an in-depth description of our sampling method and only provide a brief summary here. In summary, our algorithm first selects a "sampling target" which is either "the unknown", i.e. states not seen so far, to encourage exploration in the style of [18], or a known BSCC, to bias sampling towards it. We select a choice randomly, weighted by its current potential influence on the precision. The sampling process is guided by the chosen target, taking actions which lead to the respective target with high probability. In technical terms, we sample successors weighted by the upper bound on reachability probability times the transition probability. Once the target is reached, we either explore the unknown, or improve precision in the reached BSCC. Finally, information is back-propagated along the path. Further details, in particular pitfalls we encountered during the design process, together with a complete instantiation of our algorithm can be found in [26, App. C].

5   Experimental Evaluation

In this section, we evaluate our approaches, comparing to both our own reference implementation using classical methods, as well as the established model checker PRISM [21]. (The other popular model checkers Storm [10] and IscasMC/ePMC [15] do not directly support computing stationary distributions.) We implemented our methods in Java based on PET [24], running on consumer hardware (AMD Ryzen 5 3600). To solve arising linear equation systems, we use `Jeigen v1.2`. All executions are performed in a Docker container, restricted to a single CPU core and 8GB of RAM. For approximations, we require a precision of $\varepsilon = 10^{-4}$.

Tools Aside from `PRISM`[1], we consider three variants of Algorithm 3, namely `Classic`, the classical approach, solving each BSCC through a linear equation system and then approximating the reachability through PRISM (using interval iteration), `Naive`, the naive sampling approach, following the transition dynamics, and `Sample`, our sampling approach, selecting a target and steering towards it. The sourcecode of our implementation used to run these experiments as well as all models and our data is available at [25]. Moreover, the current version can be found at GitHub [23].

We mention two points relevant for the comparison. First, as we show in the following, `PRISM` may yield wrong results due to a (too) simple computation. As such, we should not expect that our correct methods are on par or even faster. Second, our implementation employs conservative procedures to further increase quality of the result, such as compensated summation to mitigate numerical error due to floating-point imprecision, noticeably increasing computational effort.

Models We consider the PRISM benchmark suite[2] [22], comprising several probabilistic models, in particular DTMC, CTMC, and MDP. Since there are not too many Markov chains in this set, we obtain further models as follows. For each CTMC, we consider the *uniformized CTMC* (which preserves the steady state distribution), and for MDP we choose actions uniformly at random. Unfortunately, *all* models obtained this way either comprise only single-state BSCCs or the whole model is a single BSCC. In the former case, our approximation within the BSCC is not used at all, in the latter, a sampling based approach needs to invest additional time to discover the whole system. In order to better compare the performance of our mean payoff based approximation approach, in these cases

---

[1] We observed that the default hybrid engine typically is significantly slower than the "explicit" variant and thus use that one, see [26, App. D].

[2] Obtained from `https://github.com/prismmodelchecker/prism-benchmarks`.

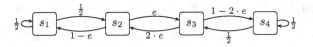

Fig. 2. A small MC where PRISM reports wrong results for $e \leq 10^{-7}$.

we pre-explore the whole system and compute the stationary distribution directly through Algorithm 1. To compare the combined performance, we additionally consider a handcrafted model, named **branch**, which comprises both transient states as well as several non-trivial BSCCs.

We present selected results, highlighting different strengths and weaknesses of each approach. An evaluation of the complete suite can be found in [26, App. D].

Correctness We discovered that PRISM potentially yields wrong results, due to an unsafe stopping criterion. In particular, PRISM iterates the power method until the absolute difference between subsequent iterates is small, exactly as with its "unsafe" value iteration for reachability, as reported by e.g. [7]. On the model from Fig. 2, PRISM (with explicit engine) immediately terminates, printing a result of $\approx (\frac{1}{6}, \frac{1}{6}, \frac{1}{3}, \frac{1}{3})$. However, the correct stationary distribution is $\approx (\frac{1}{9}, \frac{2}{9}, \frac{4}{9}, \frac{2}{9})$ (from left to right), which both of our methods correctly identify. This behaviour is due to the small difference between first and second eigenvalue of the transition matrix, which in turn implies that the iterates of the power method only change by a small amount. We note that on this example, PRISM's default hybrid engine eventually yields the correct result (after $\approx 10^8$ iterations) due to the used iteration scheme. On small variation of the model (included in the artefact) it also terminates immediately with the wrong result.

Results We summarize our results in Table 1. We observe several points. First, we see that the naive sampling approach can hardly handle non-trivial models. Second, our guided sampling approach achieves significant improvements on several models over both the classical, correct method as well as the potentially unsound approach of PRISM, in particular when hardly reachable portions of the state space can be completely discarded. However, on other models, the classical approach seems to be more appropriate, in particular on models with many likely to be reached BSCCs. Here, the sampling approach struggles to propagate the reachability bounds of all BSCCs simultaneously. Finally, as suggested by the **phil** and **rabin** models, using mean payoff based approximation can significantly outperform classical equation solving. In summary, PRISM, Classic, and Sample all can be the fastest method, depending on the structure of the model. However, recall that PRISM's method does not give guarantees on the result.

Further Discussion As expected, we observed that the runtime of approximation can increase drastically for smaller precision requirements (e.g. $\varepsilon = 10^{-8}$) and solving the equation system precisely may actually be faster for some BSCCs. However, especially in the combined approach, if we already have some upper bounds on the reachability probability of a certain BSCC, we do not need to solve it with the original precision. Hence, a future version of the implementation could

Table 1. Overview of our results. For each model, we list its parameters, overall size, and number of BSCCs, followed by the total execution time in seconds for each tool, TO denotes a timeout (300 seconds), MO a memout, and `err` an internal error. On systems comprising a single BSCC, the `Naive` and `Sample` approach coincide.

Model	Parameters	$\lvert S \rvert$	$\lvert$BSCC$\rvert$	PRISM	Classic	Naive	Sample
brp	N=64,MAX=5	5,192	134	1.2	11	TO	4.9
nand	N=15,K=2	56,128	16	4.9	30	TO	64
zeroconf_dl	reset=false,deadline=40,N=1000,K=1	251,740	10,048	99	238	8.0	1.0
phil4		9,440	1	err	TO		51
rabin3		27,766	1	err	MO		178
branch		1,087,079	1,000	155	TO	TO	20

dynamically decide whether to solve a BSCC based on mean payoff approximation or equation solving, combining advantages of both worlds.

Secondly, this also highlights an interesting trade-off implicit to our approach: The algorithm needs to balance between exploring unknown areas and refining bounds on known BSCCs, in particular, since exploring a new BSCC adds noticeable effort: One more target for which the reachability has to be determined. Here, more sophisticated heuristics could be useful.

Finally, for models with large BSCCs, such as **rabin**, we also observed that the classical linear equation approach indeed runs out of memory while a variant of the approximation algorithm can still solve it, as indicated by Remark 1. Thus, the implementation could moreover take memory constraints into account, deciding to apply the memory-saving approach in appropriate cases.

6 Conclusion

We presented a new perspective on computing the stationary distribution in Markov chains by rephrasing the problem in terms of mean payoff and reachability. We combined several recent advances for these problems to obtain a sophisticated partial-exploration based algorithm. Our evaluation shows that on several models our new approach is significantly more performant. As a major technical contribution, we provided a general algorithmic framework, which encompasses both the classical solution approach as well as our new method.

As hinted by the discussion above, our framework is quite flexible. For future work, we particularly want to identify better guidance heuristics. Specifically, based on experimental data, we conjecture that the reachability part can be improved significantly. Moreover, due to the flexibility of our framework, we can apply different methods for each BSCC to obtain the reachability and stationary distribution. Thus, we want to find meta-heuristics which suggest the most appropriate method in each case. For example, for smaller BSCCs, we could use the classical, precise solution method to obtain the stationary distribution, while for larger ones we employ our mean payoff approach, and, in the spirit of Remark 1, for even larger ones we approximate them to the required precision immediately, saving memory. Additionally, we could identify BSCCs that satisfy the conditions of specialized approaches such as [11].

References

1. Adan, I.J.B.F., Foley, R.D., McDonald, D.R.: Exact asymptotics for the stationary distribution of a markov chain: a production model. Queueing Syst. Theory Appl. **62**(4), 311–344 (2009). https://doi.org/10.1007/s11134-009-9140-y
2. Ashok, P., Chatterjee, K., Daca, P., Kretínský, J., Meggendorfer, T.: Value iteration for long-run average reward in markov decision processes. In: Majumdar, R., Kuncak, V. (eds.) Computer Aided Verification - 29th International Conference, CAV 2017, Heidelberg, Germany, July 24-28, 2017, Proceedings, Part I. Lecture Notes in Computer Science, vol. 10426, pp. 201–221. Springer (2017). https://doi.org/10.1007/978-3-319-63387-9_10
3. Backenköhler, M., Bortolussi, L., Großmann, G., Wolf, V.: Abstraction-guided truncations for stationary distributions of markov population models. In: Abate, A., Marin, A. (eds.) Quantitative Evaluation of Systems - 18th International Conference, QEST 2021, Paris, France, August 23-27, 2021, Proceedings. Lecture Notes in Computer Science, vol. 12846, pp. 351–371. Springer (2021). https://doi.org/10.1007/978-3-030-85172-9_19
4. Baier, C., Katoen, J.: Principles of model checking. MIT Press (2008)
5. Bellman, R.: Dynamic programming. Science **153**(3731), 34–37 (1966)
6. Billingsley, P.: Probability and measure. John Wiley & Sons (2008)
7. Brázdil, T., Chatterjee, K., Chmelik, M., Forejt, V., Kretínský, J., Kwiatkowska, M.Z., Parker, D., Ujma, M.: Verification of markov decision processes using learning algorithms. In: Cassez, F., Raskin, J. (eds.) Automated Technology for Verification and Analysis - 12th International Symposium, ATVA 2014, Sydney, NSW, Australia, November 3-7, 2014, Proceedings. Lecture Notes in Computer Science, vol. 8837, pp. 98–114. Springer (2014). https://doi.org/10.1007/978-3-319-11936-6_8
8. Bressan, M., Peserico, E., Pretto, L.: On approximating the stationary distribution of time-reversible markov chains. Theory Comput. Syst. **64**(3), 444–466 (2020). https://doi.org/10.1007/s00224-019-09921-3
9. Busic, A., Fourneau, J.: Iterative component-wise bounds for the steady-state distribution of a markov chain. Numer. Linear Algebra Appl. **18**(6), 1031–1049 (2011). https://doi.org/10.1002/nla.824
10. Dehnert, C., Junges, S., Katoen, J., Volk, M.: A storm is coming: A modern probabilistic model checker. In: Majumdar, R., Kuncak, V. (eds.) Computer Aided Verification - 29th International Conference, CAV 2017, Heidelberg, Germany, July 24-28, 2017, Proceedings, Part II. Lecture Notes in Computer Science, vol. 10427, pp. 592–600. Springer (2017). https://doi.org/10.1007/978-3-319-63390-9_31
11. Fourneau, J., Quessette, F.: Some improvements for the computation of the steady-state distribution of a markov chain by monotone sequences of vectors. In: Al-Begain, K., Fiems, D., Vincent, J. (eds.) Analytical and Stochastic Modeling Techniques and Applications - 19th International Conference, ASMTA 2012, Grenoble, France, June 4-6, 2012. Proceedings. Lecture Notes in Computer Science, vol. 7314, pp. 178–192. Springer (2012). https://doi.org/10.1007/978-3-642-30782-9_13
12. Gillespie, D.T.: A general method for numerically simulating the stochastic time evolution of coupled chemical reactions. Journal of computational physics **22**(4), 403–434 (1976)
13. Gómez, S., Arenas, A., Borge-Holthoefer, J., Meloni, S., Moreno, Y.: Discrete-time markov chain approach to contact-based disease spreading in complex networks. EPL **89**(3), 38009 (feb 2010). https://doi.org/10.1209/0295-5075/89/38009
14. Haddad, S., Monmege, B.: Interval iteration algorithm for MDPs and IMDPs. Theor. Comput. Sci. **735**, 111–131 (2018). https://doi.org/10.1016/j.tcs.2016.12.003

15. Hahn, E.M., Li, Y., Schewe, S., Turrini, A., Zhang, L.: iscasmc: A web-based probabilistic model checker. In: Jones, C.B., Pihlajasaari, P., Sun, J. (eds.) FM 2014: Formal Methods - 19th International Symposium, Singapore, May 12-16, 2014. Proceedings. Lecture Notes in Computer Science, vol. 8442, pp. 312–317. Springer (2014). https://doi.org/10.1007/978-3-319-06410-9_22

16. Katoen, J., Zapreev, I.S.: Safe on-the-fly steady-state detection for time-bounded reachability. In: Third International Conference on the Quantitative Evaluation of Systems (QEST 2006), 11-14 September 2006, Riverside, California, USA. pp. 301–310. IEEE Computer Society (2006). https://doi.org/10.1109/QEST.2006.47

17. Kimura, T., Masuyama, H.: A heavy-traffic-limit formula for the moments of the stationary distribution in GI/G/1-type markov chains. Oper. Res. Lett. **49**(6), 862–867 (2021). https://doi.org/10.1016/j.orl.2021.10.003

18. Kretínský, J., Meggendorfer, T.: Of cores: A partial-exploration framework for markov decision processes. Log. Methods Comput. Sci. **16**(4) (2020), https://lmcs.episciences.org/6833

19. Kulkarni, V.G.: Modeling and analysis of stochastic systems. CRC Press (2016)

20. Kuntz, J., Thomas, P., Stan, G., Barahona, M.: Stationary distributions of continuous-time markov chains: A review of theory and truncation-based approximations. SIAM Rev. **63**(1), 3–64 (2021). https://doi.org/10.1137/19M1289625

21. Kwiatkowska, M.Z., Norman, G., Parker, D.: PRISM 4.0: Verification of probabilistic real-time systems. In: Gopalakrishnan, G., Qadeer, S. (eds.) Computer Aided Verification - 23rd International Conference, CAV 2011, Snowbird, UT, USA, July 14-20, 2011. Proceedings. Lecture Notes in Computer Science, vol. 6806, pp. 585–591. Springer (2011). https://doi.org/10.1007/978-3-642-22110-1_47

22. Kwiatkowska, M.Z., Norman, G., Parker, D.: The PRISM benchmark suite. In: Ninth International Conference on Quantitative Evaluation of Systems, QEST 2012, London, United Kingdom, September 17-20, 2012. pp. 203–204. IEEE Computer Society (2012). https://doi.org/10.1109/QEST.2012.14

23. Meggendorfer, T.: Stationary distribution sampling, https://github.com/incaseoftrouble/stationary-distribution-sampling

24. Meggendorfer, T.: PET - A partial exploration tool for probabilistic verification. In: Bouajjani, A., Holík, L., Wu, Z. (eds.) Automated Technology for Verification and Analysis - 20th International Symposium, ATVA 2022, Virtual Event, October 25-28, 2022, Proceedings. Lecture Notes in Computer Science, vol. 13505, pp. 320–326. Springer (2022). https://doi.org/10.1007/978-3-031-19992-9_20, https://doi.org/10.1007/978-3-031-19992-9_20

25. Meggendorfer, T.: Artefact for: Correct Approximation of Stationary Distributions (Jan 2023). https://doi.org/10.5281/zenodo.7548215

26. Meggendorfer, T.: Correct approximation of stationary distributions. CoRR **abs/2301.08137** (2023). https://doi.org/10.48550/arXiv.2301.08137

27. Nesterov, Y.E., Nemirovski, A.: Finding the stationary states of markov chains by iterative methods. Appl. Math. Comput. **255**, 58–65 (2015). https://doi.org/10.1016/j.amc.2014.04.053

28. Paulsson, J.: Summing up the noise in gene networks. Nature **427**(6973), 415–418 (2004)

29. Puterman, M.L.: Markov Decision Processes: Discrete Stochastic Dynamic Programming. Wiley Series in Probability and Statistics, Wiley (1994). https://doi.org/10.1002/9780470316887

30. Spieler, D., Wolf, V.: Efficient steady state analysis of multimodal markov chains. In: Dudin, A.N., Turck, K.D. (eds.) Analytical and Stochastic Modelling Techniques and Applications - 20th International Conference, ASMTA 2013, Ghent, Belgium,

July 8-10, 2013. Proceedings. Lecture Notes in Computer Science, vol. 7984, pp. 380–395. Springer (2013). https://doi.org/10.1007/978-3-642-39408-9_27

31. Stewart, W.J.: Introduction to the numerical solution of Markov Chains. Princeton University Press (1994)

32. Tarjan, R.E.: Depth-first search and linear graph algorithms. SIAM J. Comput. 1(2), 146–160 (1972). https://doi.org/10.1137/0201010

Robust Almost-Sure Reachability in Multi-Environment MDPs

Marck van der Vegt[✉], Nils Jansen, and Sebastian Junges

Radboud University, Nijmegen, The Netherlands
{marck.vandervegt,nils.jansen,sebastian.junges}@ru.nl

Abstract. Multiple-environment MDPs (MEMDPs) capture finite sets of MDPs that share the states but differ in the transition dynamics. These models form a proper subclass of partially observable MDPs (POMDPs). We consider the synthesis of policies that robustly satisfy an almost-sure reachability property in MEMDPs, that is, *one* policy that satisfies a property *for all* environments. For POMDPs, deciding the existence of robust policies is an EXPTIME-complete problem. We show that this problem is PSPACE-complete for MEMDPs, while the policies require exponential memory in general. We exploit the theoretical results to develop and implement an algorithm that shows promising results in synthesizing robust policies for various benchmarks.

1 Introduction

Markov decision processes (MDPs) are the standard formalism to model sequential decision making under uncertainty. A typical goal is to find a policy that satisfies a temporal logic specification [5]. Probabilistic model checkers such as STORM [22] and PRISM [30] efficiently compute such policies. A concern, however, is the robustness against potential perturbations in the environment. MDPs cannot capture such uncertainty about the shape of the environment.

Multi-environment MDPs (MEMDPs) [36,14] contain a set of MDPs, called environments, over the same state space. The goal in MEMDPs is to find a single policy that satisfies a given specification in *all* environments. MEMDPs are, for instance, a natural model for MDPs with unknown system dynamics, where several domain experts provide their interpretation of the dynamics [11]. These different MDPs together form a MEMDP. MEMDPs also arise in other domains: The guessing of a (static) password is a natural example in security. In robotics, a MEMDP captures unknown positions of some static obstacle. One can interpret MEMDPs as a (disjoint) union of MDPs in which an agent only has partial observation, i.e., every MEMDP can be cast into a linearly larger partially observable MDP (POMDP) [27]. Indeed, some famous examples for POMDPs are in fact MEMDPs, such as *RockSample* [39] and *Hallway* [31]. Solving POMDPs is notoriously hard [32], and thus, it is worthwhile to investigate natural subclasses.

We consider *almost-sure specifications* where the probability needs to be one to reach a set of target states. In MDPs, it suffices to consider memoryless

© The Author(s) 2023
S. Sankaranarayanan and N. Sharygina (Eds.): TACAS 2023, LNCS 13993, pp. 508–526, 2023.
https://doi.org/10.1007/978-3-031-30823-9_26

policies. Constructing such policies can be efficiently implemented by means of a graph-search [5]. For MEMDPs, we consider the following problem:

Compute one *policy that almost-surely reaches the target in* all *environments.*

Such a policy robustly satisfies an almost-sure specification for a set of MDPs.

Our approach. Inspired by work on POMDPs, we construct a belief-observation MDP (BOMDP) [16] that tracks the states of the MDPs and the (support of the) belief over potential environments. We show that a policy satisfying the almost-sure property in the BOMDP also satisfies the property in the MEMDP.

Although the BOMDP is exponentially larger than the MEMDP, we exploit its particular structure to create a PSPACE algorithm to decide whether such a robust policy exists. The essence of the algorithm is a recursive construction of a fragment of the BOMDP, restricted to a setting in which the belief-support is fixed. Such an approach is possible, as the belief in a MEMDP behaves monotonically: Once we know that we are not in a particular environment, we never lose this knowledge. This behavior is in contrast to POMDPs, where there is no monotonic behavior in belief-supports. The difference is essential: Deciding almost-sure reachability in POMDPs is EXPTIME-complete [37,19]. In contrast, the problem of deciding whether a policy for almost-sure reachability in a MEMDP exists is indeed PSPACE-*complete*. We show the hardness using a reduction from the *true quantified Boolean formula problem*. Finally, we cannot hope to extract a policy with such an algorithm, as the smallest policy for MEMDPs may require exponential memory in the number of environments.

The PSPACE algorithm itself recomputes many results. For practical purposes, we create an algorithm that iteratively explores parts of the BOMDP. The algorithm additionally uses the MEMDP structure to generalize the set of states from which a winning policy exists and deduce efficient heuristics for guiding the exploration. The combination of these ingredients leads to an efficient and competitive prototype on top of the model checker STORM.

Related work. We categorize related work in three areas.

MEMDPs. Almost-sure reachability for MEMDPs for exactly two environments has been studied by [36]. We extend the results to arbitrarily many environments. This is nontrivial: For two environments, the decision problem has a polynomial time routine [36], whereas we show that the problem is PSPACE-complete for an arbitrary number of environments. MEMDPs and closely related models such as hidden-model MDPs, hidden-parameter MDPs, multi-model MDPs, and concurrent MDPs [11,2,40,10] have considered for quantitative properties[1]. The typical approach is to consider approximative algorithms for the undecidable problem in POMDPs [14] or adapt reinforcement learning algorithms [3,28]. These approximations are not applicable to almost-sure properties.

POMDPs. One can build an underlying potentially infinite belief-MDP [27] that corresponds to the POMDP – using model checkers [35,7,8] to verify this MDP

---

[1] Hidden-parameter MDPs are different than MEMDPs in that they assume a prior over MDPs. However, for almost-sure properties, this difference is irrelevant.

can answer the question for MEMDPs. For POMDPs, almost-sure reachability is decidable in exponential time [37,19] via a construction similar to ours. Most qualitative properties beyond almost-sure reachability are undecidable [4,15]. Two dedicated algorithms that limit the search to policies with small memory requirements and employ a SAT-based approach [12,26] to this NP-hard problem [19] are implemented in STORM. We use them as baselines.

Robust models. The high-level representation of MEMDPs is structurally similar to featured MDPs [18,1] that represent sets of MDPs. The proposed techniques are called family-based model checking and compute policies for every MDP in the family, whereas we aim to find one policy for all MDPs. Interval MDPs [25,43,23] and SGs [38] do not allow for dependencies between states and thus cannot model features such as various obstacle positions. Parametric MDPs [2,44,24] assume controllable uncertainty and do not consider robustness of policies.

Contributions. We establish PSPACE-completeness for deciding almost-sure reachability in MEMDPs and show that the policies may be exponentially large. Our iterative algorithm, which is the first specific to almost-sure reachability in MEMDPs, builds fragments of the BOMDP. An empirical evaluation shows that the iterative algorithm outperforms approaches dedicated to POMDPs.

2   Problem Statement

In this section, we provide some background and formalize the problem statement.

For a set X, $Dist(X)$ denotes the set of probability distributions over X. For a given distribution $d \in Dist(X)$, we denote its support as $Supp(d)$. For a finite set X, let $\mathsf{unif}(X)$ denote the uniform distribution. $\mathsf{dirac}(x)$ denotes the Dirac distribution on $x \in X$. We use short-hand notation for functions and distributions, $f = [x \mapsto a, y \mapsto b]$ means that $f(x) = a$ and $f(y) = b$. We write $\mathcal{P}(X)$ for the powerset of X. For $n \in \mathbb{N}$ we write $[n] = \{i \in \mathbb{N} \mid 1 \leq i \leq n\}$.

Definition 1 (MDP). *A* Markov Decision Process *is a tuple* $\mathcal{M} = \langle S, A, \iota_{init}, p \rangle$ *where* S *is the finite set of states,* A *is the finite set of actions,* $\iota_{init} \in Dist(S)$ *is the initial state distribution, and* $p \colon S \times A \to Dist(S)$ *is the transition function.*

The transition function is total, that is, for notational convenience MDPs are *input-enabled*. This requirement does not affect the generality of our results. A *path* of an MDP is a sequence $\pi = s_0 a_0 s_1 a_1 \ldots s_n$ such that $\iota_{\mathsf{init}}(s_0) > 0$ and $p(s_i, a_i)(s_{i+1}) > 0$ for all $0 \leq i < n$. The last state of π is $last(\pi) = s_n$. The set of all finite paths is PATH and PATH(S') denotes the paths starting in a state from $S' \subseteq S$. The set of *reachable states* from S' is Reachable(S'). If $S' = Supp(\iota_{\mathsf{init}})$ we just call them *the* reachable states. The MDP restricted to reachable states from a distribution $d \in Dist(S)$ is ReachFragment($\mathcal{M}, d$), where d is the new initial distribution. A state $s \in S$ is *absorbing* if Reachable($\{s\}$) = $\{s\}$. An MDP is *acyclic*, if each state is absorbing or not reachable from its successor states.

Action choices are resolved by a *policy* $\sigma \colon$ PATH $\to Dist(A)$ that maps paths to distributions over actions. A policy of the form $\sigma \colon S \to Dist(A)$ is

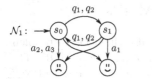
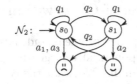
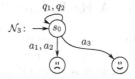

Fig. 1: Example MEMDP

called *memoryless, deterministic* if we have $\sigma\colon \text{PATH} \to A$; and, *memoryless deterministic* for $\sigma\colon S \to A$. For an MDP $\mathcal{M}$, we denote the probability of a policy σ reaching some target set $T \subseteq S$ starting in state s as $\Pr_{\mathcal{M}}(s \to T \mid \sigma)$. More precisely, $\Pr_{\mathcal{M}}(s \to T \mid \sigma)$ denotes the probability of all paths from s reaching T under σ. We use $\Pr_{\mathcal{M}}(T \mid \sigma)$ if s is distributed according to ι_{init}.

Definition 2 (MEMDP). *A Multiple Environment MDP is a tuple* $\mathcal{N} = \langle S, A, \iota_{init}, \{p_i\}_{i\in I}\rangle$ *with* S, A, ι_{init} *as for MDPs, and* $\{p_i\}_{i\in I}$ *is a set of transition functions, where* I *is a finite set of environment indices.*

Intuitively, MEMDPs form sets of MDPs (environments) that share states and actions, but differ in the transition probabilities. For MEMDP $\mathcal{N}$ with index set I and a set $I' \subseteq I$, we define the restriction of environments as the MEMDP $\mathcal{N}_{\downarrow I'} = \langle S, A, \iota_{\text{init}}, \{p_i\}_{i\in I'}\rangle$. Given an environment $i \in I$, we denote its corresponding MDP as $\mathcal{N}_i = \langle S, A, \iota_{\text{init}}, p_i\rangle$. A MEMDP with only one environment is an MDP. Paths and policies are defined on the states and actions of MEMDPs and do not differ from MDP policies. A MEMDP is acyclic, if each MDP is acyclic.

Example 1. Figure 1 shows an MEMDP with three environments $\mathcal{N}_i$. An agent can ask two questions, q_1 and q_2. The response is either 'switch' ($s_1 \leftrightarrow s_2$), or 'stay' (loop). In $\mathcal{N}_1$, the response to q_1 and q_2 is to switch. In $\mathcal{N}_2$, the response to q_1 is stay, and to q_2 is switch. The agent can guess the environment using a_1, a_2, a_3. Guessing a_i leads to the target $\{\ddot{\smile}\}$ only in environment i. Thus, an agent must deduce the environment via q_1, q_2 to surely reach the target. ∎

Definition 3 (Almost-Sure Reachability). *An almost-sure reachability property is defined by a set* $T \subseteq S$ *of target states. A policy* σ *satisfies the property* T *for MEMDP* $\mathcal{N} = \langle S, A, \iota_{init}, \{p_i\}_{i\in I}\rangle$ *iff* $\forall i \in I\colon \Pr_{\mathcal{N}_i}(T \mid \sigma) = 1$.

In other words, a policy σ satisfies an almost-sure reachability property T, called *winning*, if and only if the probability of reaching T *within each MDP* is one. By extension, a state $s \in S$ is winning if there exists a winning policy when starting in state s. Policies and states that are not winning are losing. We will now define both the decision and policy problem:

> Given a MEMDP $\mathcal{N}$ and an almost-sure reachability property T.
> The **Decision Problem** asks to decide if a policy exists that satisfies T.
> The **Policy Problem** asks to compute such a policy, if it exists.

In Section 4 we discuss the computational complexity of the decision problem. Following up, in Section 5 we present our algorithm for solving the policy problem. Details on its implementation and evaluation will be presented in Section 6.

3   A Reduction To Belief-Observation MDPs

In this section, we reduce the policy problem, and thus also the decision problem, to finding a policy in an exponentially larger belief-observation MDP. This reduction is an elementary building block for the construction of our PSPACE algorithm and the practical implementation. Additional information such as proofs for statements throughout the paper are available in the technical report [41].

3.1   Interpretation of MEMDPs as Partially Observable MDPs

Definition 4 (POMDP). *A partially observable MDP (POMDP) is a tuple $\langle \mathcal{M}, Z, O \rangle$ with an MDP $\mathcal{M} = \langle S, A, \iota_{init}, p \rangle$, a set Z of observations, and an observation function $O \colon S \to Z$.*

A POMDP is an MDP where states are labelled with observations. We lift O to paths and use $O(\pi) = O(s_1)a_1 O(s_2) \ldots O(s_n)$. We use observation-based policies σ, i.e., policies s.t. for $\pi, \pi' \in$ PATH, $O(\pi) = O(\pi')$ implies $\sigma(\pi) = \sigma(\pi')$. A MEMDP can be cast into a POMDP that is made up as the disjoint union:

Definition 5 (Union-POMDP). *Given an MEMDP $\mathcal{N} = \langle S, A, \iota_{init}, \{p_i\}_{i \in I} \rangle$ we define its* union-POMDP $\mathcal{N}_{\sqcup} = \langle \langle S', A, \iota'_{init}, p' \rangle, Z, O \rangle$, *with states $S' = S \times I$, initial distribution $\iota'_{init}(\langle s, i \rangle) = \iota_{init}(s) \cdot |I|^{-1}$, transitions $p'(\langle s, i \rangle, a)(\langle s', i \rangle) = p_i(s, a)(s')$, observations $Z = S$, and observation function $O(\langle s, i \rangle) = s$.*

A policy may observe the state s but not in which MDP we are. This forces any observation-based policy to take the same choice in all environments.

Lemma 1. *Given MEMDP $\mathcal{N}$, there exists a winning policy iff there exists an observation-based policy σ such that $\mathrm{Pr}_{\mathcal{N}_{\sqcup}}(T \mid \sigma) = 1$.*

The statement follows as, first, any observation-based policy of the POMDP can be applied to the MEMDP, second, vice versa, any MEMDP policy is observation-based, and third, the induced MCs under these policies are isomorphic.

3.2   Belief-observation MDPs

For POMDPs, memoryless policies are not sufficient, which makes computing policies intricate. We therefore add the information that the history — i.e., the path until some point — contains. In MEMDPs, this information is the *(environment-)belief (support)* $J \subseteq I$, as the set of environments that are consistent with a path in the MEMDP. Given a belief $J \subseteq I$ and a state-action-state transition $s \xrightarrow{a} s'$, then we define $\mathsf{Up}(J, s, a, s') = \{i \in J \mid p_i(s, a, s') > 0\}$, i.e., the subset of environments in which the transition exists. For a path $\pi \in$ PATH, we define its corresponding belief $\mathcal{B}(\pi) \subseteq I$ recursively as:

$$\mathcal{B}(s_0) = I \quad \text{and} \quad \mathcal{B}(\pi \cdot sas') = \mathsf{Up}(\mathcal{B}(\pi \cdot s), s, a, s')$$

The belief in a MEMDP monotonically decreases along a path, i.e., if we know that we are not in a particular environment, this remains true indefinitely.

We aim to use a model where memoryless policies suffice. To that end, we cast MEMDPs into the exponentially larger belief-observation MDPs [16][2].

Definition 6 (BOMDP). *For a MEMDP $\mathcal{N} = \langle S, A, \iota_{init}, \{p_i\}_{i \in I} \rangle$, we define its belief-observation MDP (BOMDP) as a POMDP $\mathcal{G}_\mathcal{N} = \langle \langle S', A, \iota'_{init}, p' \rangle, Z, O \rangle$ with states $S' = S \times I \times \mathcal{P}(I)$, initial distribution $\iota'_{init}(\langle s, j, I \rangle) = \iota_{init}(s) \cdot |I|^{-1}$, transition relation $p'(\langle s, j, J \rangle, a)(\langle s', j, J' \rangle) = p_j(s, a, s')$ with $J' = \mathsf{Up}(J, s, a, s')$, observations $Z = S \times \mathcal{P}(I)$, and observation function $O(\langle s, j, J \rangle) = \langle s, J \rangle$.*

Compared to the union-POMDP, BOMDPs also track the belief by updating it accordingly. We clarify the correspondence between paths of the BOMDP and the MEMDP. For a path π through the MEMDP, we can mimic this path exactly in the MDPs $\mathcal{N}_j$ for $j \in \mathcal{B}(\pi)$. As we track $\mathcal{B}(\pi)$ in the state, we can deduce from the BOMDP state in which environments we can be.

Lemma 2. *For MEMDP $\mathcal{N}$ and the path $\langle s_1, j, J_1 \rangle a_1 \langle s_2, j, J_2 \rangle \dots \langle s_n, j, J_n \rangle$ of the BOMDP $\mathcal{G}_\mathcal{N}$, let $j \in J_1$. Then: $J_n \neq \emptyset$ and the path $s_1 a_1 \dots s_n$ exists in MDP $\mathcal{N}_i$ iff $i \in J_1 \cap J_n$.*

Consequently, the belief of a path can be uniquely determined by the observation of the last state reached, hence the name belief-observation MDPs.

Lemma 3. *For every pair of paths π, π' in a BOMDP, we have:*

$$\mathcal{B}(\pi) = \mathcal{B}(\pi') \quad \text{implies} \quad O(last(\pi)) = O(last(\pi')).$$

For notation, we define $S_J = \{\langle s, j, J \rangle \mid j \in J, s \in S\}$, and analogously write $Z_J = \{\langle s, J \rangle \mid s \in S\}$. We lift the target states T to states in the BOMDP: $T_{\mathcal{G}_\mathcal{N}} = \{\langle s, j, J \rangle \mid s \in T, J \subseteq I, j \in J\}$ and define target observations $T_Z = O(T_{\mathcal{G}_\mathcal{N}})$.

Definition 7 (Winning in a BOMDP). *Let $\mathcal{G}_\mathcal{N}$ be a BOMDP with target observations T_Z. An observation-based policy σ is winning from some observation $z \in Z$, if for all $s \in O^{-1}(z)$ it holds that $\text{Pr}_{\mathcal{G}_\mathcal{N}}(s \to O^{-1}(T_Z) \mid \sigma) = 1$.*

Furthermore, a policy σ is *winning* if it is winning for the initial distribution ι_{init}. An *observation z is winning* if there exists a winning policy for z. The *winning region* $\text{Win}^T_{\mathcal{G}_\mathcal{N}}$ is the set of all winning observations.
Almost-sure winning in the BOMDP corresponds to winning in the MEMDP.

Theorem 1. *There exists a winning policy for a MEMDP $\mathcal{N}$ with target states T iff there exists a winning policy in the BOMDP $\mathcal{G}_\mathcal{N}$ with target states $T_{\mathcal{G}_\mathcal{N}}$.*

Intuitively, the important aspect is that for almost-sure reachability, observation-based memoryless policies are sufficient [13]. For any such policy, the induced Markov chains on the union-POMDP and the BOMDP are bisimilar [16].

BOMDPs make policy search conceptually easier. First, as memoryless policies suffice for almost-sure reachability, winning regions are independent of fixed policies: For policies σ and σ' that are winning in observation z and z', respectively, there must exist a policy $\hat{\sigma}$ that is winning for both z and z'. Second, winning regions can be determined in polynomial time in the size of the BOMDP [16].

---

[2] This translation is notationally simpler than going via the union-POMDP.

3.3   Fragments of BOMDPs

To avoid storing the exponentially sized BOMDP, we only build fragments: We may select any set of observations as *frontier* observations and make the states with those observations absorbing. We later discuss the selection of frontiers.

Definition 8 (Sliced BOMDP). *For a BOMDP* $\mathcal{G}_\mathcal{N} = \langle \langle S, A, \iota_{init}, p \rangle, Z, O \rangle$ *and a set of* frontier *observations* $F \subseteq Z$, *we define a BOMDP* $\mathcal{G}_\mathcal{N} | F = \langle \langle S, A, \iota_{init}, p' \rangle, Z, O \rangle$ *with:*

$$\forall s \in S, a \in A \colon p'(s,a) = \begin{cases} \mathrm{dirac}(s) & \textit{if } O(s) \in F, \\ p(s,a) & \textit{otherwise.} \end{cases}$$

We exploit this sliced BOMDP to derive constraints on the set of winning states.

Lemma 4. *For every BOMDP* $\mathcal{G}_\mathcal{N}$ *with states* S *and targets* T *and for all frontier observations* $F \subseteq Z$ *it holds that:* $\mathsf{Win}^T_{\mathcal{G}_\mathcal{N}|F} \subseteq \mathsf{Win}^T_{\mathcal{G}_\mathcal{N}} \subseteq \mathsf{Win}^{T \cup F}_{\mathcal{G}_\mathcal{N}|F}$.

Making (non-target) observations absorbing extends the set of losing observations, while adding target states extends the set of winning observations.

4   Computational Complexity

The BOMDP $\mathcal{G}_\mathcal{N}$ above yields an exponential time *and* space algorithm via Theorem 1. We can avoid the exponential memory requirement. This section shows the PSPACE-completeness of deciding whether a winning policy exists.

Theorem 2. *The almost-sure reachability decision problem is PSPACE-complete.*

The result follows from Lemmas 11 and 10 below. In Section 4.3, we show that representing the winning policy itself may however require exponential space.

4.1   Deciding Almost-Sure Winning for MEMDPs in PSPACE

We develop an algorithm with a polynomial memory footprint. The algorithm exploits locality of cyclic behavior in the BOMDP, as formalized by an acyclic *environment graph* and *local BOMDPs* that match the nodes in the environment graph. The algorithm recurses on the environment graph while memorizing results from polynomially many local BOMDPs.

The graph-structure of BOMDPs. First, along a path of the MEMDP, we will only gain information and are thus able to rule out certain environments [14]. Due to the monotonicity of the update operator, we have for any BOMDP that $\langle s, j, J \rangle \in \mathsf{Reachable}(\langle s', j, J' \rangle)$ implies $J \subseteq J'$. We define a graph over environment sets that describes how the belief-support can update over a run.

Definition 9 (Environment graph). *Let* $\mathcal{N}$ *be a MEMDP and* p *the transition function of* $\mathcal{G}_\mathcal{N}$. *The environment graph* $GE_\mathcal{N} = (V_\mathcal{N}, E_\mathcal{N})$ *for* $\mathcal{N}$ *is a directed graph with vertices* $V_\mathcal{N} = \mathcal{P}(I)$ *and edges*

$$E_\mathcal{N} = \{\langle J, J' \rangle \mid \exists s, s' \in S, a \in A, j \in I.p(\langle s, j, J \rangle, a, \langle s', j, J' \rangle) > 0 \textit{ and } J \neq J'\}.$$

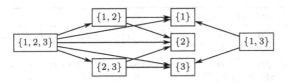

Fig. 2: The environment graph for our running example.

Example 2. Figure 2 shows the environment graph for the MEMDP in Ex. 1. It consists of the different belief-supports. For example, the transition from $\{1,2,3\}$ to $\{2,3\}$ and to $\{1\}$ is due to the action q_1 in state s_0, as shown in Fig. 1. ∎

Paths in the environment graph abstract paths in the BOMDP. Path fragments where the belief-support remains unchanged are summarized into one step, as we do not create edges of the form $\langle J, J \rangle$. We formalize this idea: Let $\pi = \langle s_1, j, J_1 \rangle a_1 \langle s_2, j, J_2 \rangle \ldots \langle s_n, j, J_n \rangle$ be a path in the BOMDP. For any $J \subseteq I$, we call π a *J-local path*, if $J_i = J$ for all $i \in [n]$.

Lemma 5. *For a MEMDP $\mathcal{N}$ with environment graph $GE_\mathcal{N}$, there is a path $J_1 \ldots J_n$ iff there is a path $\pi = \pi_1 \ldots \pi_n$ in $\mathcal{G}_\mathcal{N}$ s.t. every π_i is J_i-local.*

The shape of the environment graph is crucial for the algorithm we develop.

Lemma 6. *Let $GE_\mathcal{N} = (V_\mathcal{N}, E_\mathcal{N})$ be an environment graph for MEMDP $\mathcal{N}$. First, $E_\mathcal{N}(J, J')$ implies $J' \subsetneq J$. Thus, G is acyclic and has maximal path length $|I|$. The maximal outdegree of the graph is $|S|^2|A|$.*

The monotonicity regarding J, J' follows from definition of the belief update. The bound on the outdegree is a consequence from Lemma 9 below.

Local belief-support BOMDPs. Before we continue, we remark that the (future) dynamics in a BOMDP only depend on the current state and set of environments. More formally, we capture this intuition as follows.

Lemma 7. *Let $\mathcal{G}_\mathcal{N}$ be a BOMDP with states S'. For any state $\langle s, j, J \rangle \in S'$, let $\mathcal{N}' = \mathsf{ReachFragment}(\mathcal{N}_{\downarrow J}, \mathrm{dirac}(s))$ and $Y = \{\langle s, i, J \rangle \mid i \in J\}$. Then:*

$$\mathsf{ReachFragment}(\mathcal{G}_\mathcal{N}, \mathrm{unif}(Y)) = \mathcal{G}_{\mathcal{N}'}.$$

The key insight is that restricting the MEMDP does not change the transition functions for the environments $j \in J$. Furthermore, using monotonicity of the update, we only reach BOMDP-states whose behavior is determined by the environments in J.

This intuition allows us to analyze the BOMDP locally and lift the results to the complete BOMDP. We define a local BOMDP as the part of a BOMDP starting in any state in S_J. All observations not in Z_J are made absorbing.

Definition 10 (Local BOMDP). *Given a MEMDP $\mathcal{N}$ with BOMDP $\mathcal{G}_\mathcal{N}$ and a set of environments J. The* local BOMDP *for environments J is the fragment*

$$\mathrm{Loc}\mathcal{G}(J) = \mathsf{ReachFragment}(\mathcal{G}_{\mathcal{N}_{\downarrow J}} | F, \mathrm{unif}(S_J)) \quad \textit{where} \quad F = Z \setminus Z_J .$$

Algorithm 1 Search algorithm

1: **function** SEARCH(MEMDP $\mathcal{N} = \langle S, A, \{p_i\}_{i \in I}, \iota_{\text{init}} \rangle, J \subseteq I, T \subseteq S$)
2:    $T' \leftarrow \{\langle s, j, J \rangle \mid j \in J, s \in T\}$
3:    **for** J' s.t. $E_{\mathcal{N}}(J, J')$ **do**   ▷ Consider the edges in the env. graph (Def. 9)
4:       $W_{J'} \leftarrow$ SEARCH$(\mathcal{N}, J', T)$ ▷ Recursion!
5:       $T' \leftarrow T' \cup \{\langle s, j, J' \rangle \mid j \in J, \langle s, J' \rangle \in W_{J'}\}$
6:    **return** $\text{Win}^{T'}_{\text{Loc}\mathcal{G}(J)} \cap Z_J$ ▷ Construct BOMDP as in Def. 10, then model check
7:
8: **function** ASWINNING(MEMDP $\mathcal{N} = \langle S, A, \{p_i\}_{i \in I}, \iota_{\text{init}} \rangle, T \subseteq S$)
9:    **return** $O(\text{Supp}(\iota_{\text{init}})) \subseteq$ SEARCH$(\mathcal{N}, I, T)$

This definition of a local BOMDP coincides with a fragment of the complete BOMDP. We then mark exactly the winning observations restricted to the environment sets $J' \subsetneq J$ as winning in the local BOMDP and compute all winning observations in the local BOMDP. These observations are winning in the complete BOMDP. The following concretization of Lemma 4 formalizes this.

Lemma 8. *Consider a MEMDP $\mathcal{N}$ and a subset of environments J.*

$$\text{Win}^{T'_{\mathcal{G}_{\mathcal{N}}}}_{\text{Loc}\mathcal{G}(J)} \cap Z_J = \text{Win}^{T_{\mathcal{G}_{\mathcal{N}}}}_{\mathcal{G}_{\mathcal{N}}} \cap Z_J \quad with \quad T'_{\mathcal{G}_{\mathcal{N}}} = T_{\mathcal{G}_{\mathcal{N}}} \cup (\text{Win}^{T_{\mathcal{G}_{\mathcal{N}}}}_{\mathcal{G}_{\mathcal{N}}} \setminus Z_J).$$

Furthermore, local BOMDPs are polynomially bounded in the size of the MEMDP.

Lemma 9. *Let $\mathcal{N}$ be a MEMDP with states S and actions A. $\text{Loc}\mathcal{G}(J)$ has at most $\mathcal{O}(|S|^2 \cdot |A| \cdot |J|)$ states and $\mathcal{O}(|S|^2 \cdot |A| \cdot |J|^2)$ transitions[3].*

A PSPACE algorithm. We present Algorithm 1 for the MEMDP **decision problem**, which recurses depth-first over the paths in the environment graph[4]. We first state the correctness and the space complexity of this algorithm.

Lemma 10. ASWINNING *in Alg. 1 solves the decision problem in PSPACE.*

To prove correctness, we first note that SEARCH$(\mathcal{N}, J, T)$ computes $\text{Win}^{T_{\mathcal{G}_{\mathcal{N}}}}_{\mathcal{G}_{\mathcal{N}}} \cap Z_J$. We show this by induction over the structure of the environment graph. For all J without outgoing edges, the local BOMDP coincides with a BOMDP just for environments J (Lemma 7). Otherwise, observe that T' in line 5 coincides with its definition in Lemma 8 and thus, by the same lemma, we return $\text{Win}^{T_{\mathcal{G}_{\mathcal{N}}}}_{\mathcal{G}_{\mathcal{N}}} \cap Z_J$. To finalize the proof, a winning policy exists in the MEMDP if the observation of the initial states of the BOMDP are winning (Theorem 1). The algorithm must terminate as it recurses over all paths of a finite acyclic graph, see Lemma 6. Following Lemma 9, the number of frontier states is then bounded by $|S|^2 \cdot |A|$. The main body of the algorithm therefore requires polynomial space, and the maximal recursion depth (stack height) is $|I|$ (Lemma 6). Together, this yields a space complexity in $\mathcal{O}(|S|^2 \cdot |A| \cdot |I|^2)$.

---

[3] The number of transitions is the number of nonzero entries in p

[4] In contrast to depth-first-search, we do not memorize nodes we visited earlier.

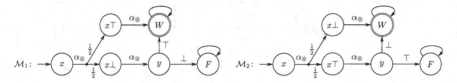

Fig. 3: Constructed MEMDP for the QBF formula $\forall x \exists y \big[(x \vee y) \wedge (\neg x \vee \neg y)\big]$.

4.2   Deciding Almost-Sure Winning for MEMDPs Is PSPACE-hard

It is not possible to improve the algorithm beyond PSPACE.

Lemma 11. *The MEMDP decision problem is PSPACE-hard.*

Hardness holds even for acyclic MEMDPs and uses the following fact.

Lemma 12. *If a winning policy exists for an acyclic MEMDP, there also exists a winning policy that is deterministic.*

In particular, almost-sure reachability coincides with avoiding the sink states. This is a safety property. For safety, deterministic policies are sufficient, as randomization visits only additional states, which is not beneficial for safety.

Regarding Lemma 11, we sketch a polynomial-time reduction from the PSPACE-complete TQBF problem [20] problem to the MEMDP decision problem. Let Ψ be a QBF formula, $\Psi = \exists x_1 \forall y_1 \exists x_2 \forall y_2 \dots \exists x_n \forall y_n [\Phi]$ with Φ a Boolean formula in conjunctive normal form. The problem is to decide whether Ψ is true.

Example 3. Consider the QBF formula $\Psi = \forall x \exists y \big[(x \vee y) \wedge (\neg x \vee \neg y)\big]$. We construct a MEMDP with an environment for every clause, see Figure 3[5]. The state space consists of three states for each variable $v \in V$: the state v and the states $v\top$ and $v\bot$ that encode their assignment. Additionally, we have a dedicated target W and sink state F. We consider three actions: The actions *true* ($\top$) and *false* ($\bot$) semantically describe the assignment to existentially quantified variables. The action *any* $\alpha_\otimes$ is used for all other states. Every environment reaches the target state iff one literal in the clause is assigned true.

In the example, intuitively, a policy should assign the negation of x to y. Formally, the policy σ, characterized by $\sigma(\pi \cdot y) = \top$ iff $x_\bot \in \pi$, is winning. ∎

As a consequence of this construction, we may also deduce the following theorem.

Theorem 3. *Deciding whether a memoryless winning policy exists is NP-complete.*

The proof of NP hardness uses a similar construction for the propositional SAT fragment of QBF, without universal quantifiers. Additionally, the problem for memoryless policies is in NP, because one can nondeterministically guess a (polynomially sized) memoryless policy and verify in each environment independently.

---

[5] We depict a slightly simplified MEMDP for conciseness.

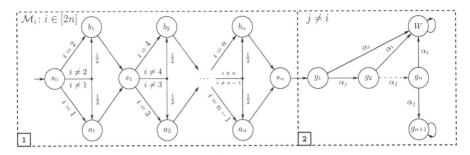

Fig. 4: Witness for exponential memory requirement for winning policies.

4.3   Policy Problem

Policies, mapping histories to actions, are generally infinite objects. However, we may extract winning policies from the BOMDP, which is (only) exponential in the MEMDP. Finite state controllers [34] are a suitable and widespread representation of policies that require only a finite amount of memory. Intuitively, the number of memory states reflects the number of equivalence classes of histories that a policy can distinguish. In general, we cannot hope to find smaller policies than those obtained via a BOMDP.

Theorem 4. *There is a family of MEMDPs $\{\mathcal{N}^n\}_{n \geq 1}$ where for each n, $\mathcal{N}^n$ has $2n$ environments and $\mathcal{O}(n)$ states and where every winning policy for $\mathcal{N}^n$ requires at least 2^n memory states.*

We illustrate the witness. Consider a family of MEMDPs $\{\mathcal{N}^n\}_n$, where $\mathcal{N}^n$ has $2n$ MDPs, $4n$ states partitioned into two parts, and at most $2n$ outgoing actions per state. We outline the MEMDP family in Figure 4. In the first part, there is only one action per state. The notation is as follows: in state s_0 and MDP $\mathcal{N}_1^n$, we transition with probability one to state a_0, whereas in $\mathcal{N}_2^n$ we transition with probability one to state b_0. In every other MDP, we transition with probability one half to either state. In state s_1, we do the analogous construction for environments 3, 4, and all others. A path $s_0 b_1 \ldots$ is thus consistent with every MDP except $\mathcal{N}_1^n$. The first part ends in state s_n. By construction, there are 2^n paths ending in s_n. Each of them is (in)consistent with a unique set of n environments. In the second part, a policy may guess n times an environment by selecting an action α_i for every $i \in [2n]$. Only in MDP $\mathcal{N}_i^n$, action α_i leads to a target state. In all other MDPs, the transition leads from state g_j to g_{j+1}. The state g_{n+1} is absorbing in all MDPs. Importantly, after taking an action α_i and arriving in g_{j+1}, there is (at most) one more MDP inconsistent with the path.

Every MEMDP $\mathcal{N}^n$ in this family has a winning policy which takes $\sigma(\pi \cdot g_i) = \alpha_{2i-1}$ if $a_i \in \pi$ and $\sigma(\pi \cdot g_i) = \alpha_{2i}$ otherwise. Furthermore, when arriving in state s_n, the state of a finite memory controller must reflect the precise set of environments consistent with the history. There are 2^n such sets. The proof shows that if we store less information, two paths will lead to the same memory state, but with different sets of environments being consistent with these paths. As we can rule out only n environments using the n actions in the second part of the MEMDP, we cannot ensure winning in every environment.

5 A Partial Game Exploration Algorithm

In this section, we present an algorithm for the policy problem. We tune the algorithm towards runtime instead of memory complexity, but aim to avoid running out of memory. We use several key ingredients to create a pragmatic variation of Alg. 1, with support for extracting the winning policy.

First, we use an abstraction from BOMDPs to a belief stochastic game (BSG) similar to [45] that reduces the number of states and simplifies the iterative construction[6]. Second, we tailor and generalize ideas from *bounded model checking* [6] to build and model check only a fragment of the BSG, using explicit *partial exploration* approaches as in, e.g., [33,9,42,29]. Third, our exploration does not continuously extend the fragment, but can also prune this fragment by using the model checking results obtained so far. The structure of the BSG as captured by the environment graph makes the approach promising and yields some natural heuristics. Fourth, the structure of the winning region allows to generalize results to unseen states. We thereby operationalize an idea from [26] in a partial exploration context. Finally, we analyze individual MDPs as an efficient and significant preprocessing step. In the following we discuss these ingredients.

Abstraction to Belief Support Games. We briefly recap stochastic games (SGs). See [38,17] for more details.

Definition 11 (SG). *A stochastic game is a tuple* $\mathcal{B} = \langle \mathcal{M}, S_1, S_2 \rangle$, *where* $\mathcal{M} = \langle S, A, \iota_{init}, p \rangle$ *is an MDP and* (S_1, S_2) *is a partition of* S.

S_1 are Player 1 states, and S_2 are Player 2 states. As common, we also 'partition' (memoryless deterministic) policies into two functions $\sigma_1 \colon S_1 \to A$ and $\sigma_1 \colon S_2 \to A$. A Player 1 policy σ_1 is winning for state s if $\Pr(T \mid \sigma_1, \sigma_2)$ for all σ_2. We (re)use $\text{Win}_{\mathcal{B}_\mathcal{N}}^T$ to denote the set of states with a winning policy.

We apply a game-based abstraction to group states that have the same observation. Player 1 states capture the observation in the BOMDP, i.e., tuples $\langle s, J \rangle$ of MEMDP states s and subsets J of the environments. Player 1 selects the action a, the result is Player 2 state $\langle \langle s, J \rangle, a \rangle$. Then Player 2 chooses an environment $j \in J$, and the game mimics the outgoing transition from $\langle s, j, J \rangle$, i.e., it mimics the transition from s in $\mathcal{N}_j$. Formally:

Definition 12 (BSG). *Let* $\mathcal{G}_\mathcal{N}$ *be a BOMDP with* $\mathcal{G}_\mathcal{N} = \langle \langle S, A, \iota_{init}, p \rangle, Z, O \rangle$. *A belief support game* $\mathcal{B}_\mathcal{N}$ *for* $\mathcal{G}_\mathcal{N}$ *is an SG* $\mathcal{B}_\mathcal{N} = \langle \langle S', A', \iota'_{init}, p \rangle, S_1, S_2 \rangle$ *with* $S' = S_1 \cup S_2$ *as usual, Player 1 states* $S_1 = Z$, *Player 2 states* $S_2 = Z \times A$, *actions* $A' = A \cup I$, *initial distribution* $\iota'_{init}(\langle s, I \rangle) = \sum_{i \in I} \iota_{init}(\langle s, i, I \rangle)$, *and the (partial) transition function* p *defined separately for Player 1 and 2:*

$$p'(z, a) = \text{dirac}(\langle z, a \rangle) \qquad \qquad \text{(Player 1)}$$

$$p'(\langle z, a \rangle, j, z') = p(\langle s, j, J \rangle, a, \langle s', j, J' \rangle) \text{ with } z = \langle s, J \rangle, z' = \langle s', J' \rangle \quad \text{(Player 2)}$$

---

[6] At the time of writing, we were unaware of a polytime algorithm for BOMDPs.

Algorithm 2 Policy finding algorithm

1: **function** FINDPOLICY(MEMDP $\mathcal{N} = \langle S, A, \{p_i\}_{i \in I}, \iota_{\text{init}}\rangle$, targets $T \subseteq S$)
2:     $W \leftarrow \{\langle s, J\rangle \mid s \in T, J \subseteq I\}$; $L \leftarrow \emptyset$; $i \leftarrow 1$; $S_{\text{init}} \leftarrow Supp(\iota_{\text{init}}) \times \{I\}$
3:     **while** $S_{\text{init}} \cap W \neq W$ and $S_{\text{init}} \cap L = \emptyset$ **do**
4:         $\langle \mathcal{B}, F\rangle \leftarrow \text{GenerateGameSlice}(\mathcal{N}, W, L, i)$
5:         $W \leftarrow W \cup \text{Win}_{\mathcal{B}}^W$
6:         $L \leftarrow L \cup S \setminus \text{Win}_{\mathcal{B}}^{W \cup F}$
7:         $i \leftarrow i + 1$
8:     **if** $S_{\text{init}} \subseteq W$ **then return** ExtractPolicy(W) **else return** $\bot$

Lemma 13. *An (acyclic) MEMDP $\mathcal{N}$ with target states T is winning if(f) there exists a winning policy in the BSG $\mathcal{B}_{\mathcal{N}}$ with target states T_Z.*

Thus, on acyclic MEMDPs, a BSG-based algorithm is sound and complete, however, on cyclic MDPs, it may not find the winning policy. The remainder of the algorithm is formulated on the BSG, we use sliced BSGs as the BSG of a sliced BOMDP, or equivalently, as a BSG with some states made absorbing.

Main algorithm. We outline Algorithm 2 for the *policy problem*. We track the sets of almost-sure observations and losing observations (states in the BSG). Initially, target states are winning. Furthermore, via a simple preprocessing, we determine some winning and losing states on the individual MDPs.

We iterate until the initial state is winning or losing. Our algorithm constructs a sliced BSG and decides *on-the-fly* whether a state should be a frontier state, returning the sliced BSG and the used frontier states. We discuss the implementation below. For the sliced BSG, we compute the winning region twice: Once assuming that the frontier states are winning, once assuming they are loosing. This yields an approximation of the winning and losing states, see Lemma 4. From the winning states, we can extract a randomized winning policy [13].

Soundness. Assuming that the $\mathcal{B}_{\mathcal{N}}$ is indeed a sliced BSG with frontier F. Then the following invariant holds: $W \subseteq \text{Win}_{\mathcal{B}_{\mathcal{N}}}^T$ and $L \cap \text{Win}_{\mathcal{B}_{\mathcal{N}}}^T = \emptyset$. This invariant exploits that from a sliced BSG we can (implicitly) slice the complete BSG while preserving the winning status of every state, formalized below. In future iterations we only explore the implicitly sliced BSG.

Lemma 14. *Given $W \subseteq \text{Win}_{\mathcal{B}_{\mathcal{N}}}^{T_{\mathcal{B}_{\mathcal{N}}}}$ and $L \subseteq S \setminus \text{Win}_{\mathcal{B}_{\mathcal{N}}}^{T_{\mathcal{B}_{\mathcal{N}}}}$: $\text{Win}_{\mathcal{B}_{\mathcal{N}}}^{T_{\mathcal{B}_{\mathcal{N}}}} = \text{Win}_{\mathcal{B}_{\mathcal{N}}|W \cup L}^{T_{\mathcal{B}_{\mathcal{N}}} \cup W}$*

Termination depends on the sliced game generation. It suffices to ensure that in the long run, either W or L grow as there are only finitely many states. If W and L remain the same longer than some number of iterations, $W \cup L$ will be used as frontier. Then, the new game will suffice to determine if $s \in W$ in one shot.

Generating the sliced BSG. Algorithm 3 outlines the generation of the sliced BSG. In particular, we explore the implicit BSG from the initial state but make every state that we do not explicitly explore absorbing. In every iteration, we first check if there are states in Q left to explore and if the number of explored states

---

Algorithm 3 Game generation algorithm

1: **function** GENERATEGAMESLICE(MEMDP $\mathcal{N}$, W, L, i)
2:      $Q \leftarrow \{s_\iota\}$; $E = \{s_\iota\}$
3:      **while** $s \in Q$ and $|E| \leq$ Bound[i] exists **do**
4:          $E \leftarrow E \cup \{s\}$ ▷ Mark s as explored
5:          $\mathcal{B} \leftarrow \mathcal{B}_\mathcal{N}|(S \setminus E)$ ▷ Extend game, cut-off everything not explored
6:          $Q \leftarrow \mathsf{Reachable}(\mathcal{B}) \setminus (E \cup W \cup L)$ ▷ Add newly reached states
7:      **return** $\mathcal{B}, Q$

---

in E is below a threshold Bound[i]. Then, we take a state from the priority queue and add it to E. We find new reachable states[7] and add them to the queue Q.

Generalizing the winning and losing states. We aim to determine that a state in the game $\mathcal{B}_\mathcal{N}$ is winning without ever exploring it. First, observe:

Lemma 15. *A winning policy in MEMDP $\mathcal{N}$ is winning in $\mathcal{N}_{\downarrow J}$ for any J.*

A direct consequence is the following statement for two environments $J_1 \subseteq J_2$:

$$\langle s, J_2 \rangle \in \mathsf{Win}_{\mathcal{B}_\mathcal{N}}^T \quad \text{implies} \quad \langle s, J_1 \rangle \in \mathsf{Win}_{\mathcal{B}_\mathcal{N}}^T.$$

Consequently, we can store W (and symmetrically, L) as follows. For every MEMDP state $s \in S$, $W_s = \{J \mid \langle s, J \rangle \in W\}$ is downward closed on the partial order $P = (I, \subseteq)$. This allows for efficient storage: We only have to store the set of pairwise maximal elements, i.e., the antichain,

$$W_s^{\max} = \{J \in W_s \mid \forall J' \in W_s \text{ with } J \not\subseteq J'\}.$$

To determine whether $\langle s, J \rangle$ is winning, we check whether $J \subseteq J'$ for some $J' \in W_s^{\max}$. Adding J to $W_s^{\max}$ requires removing all $J' \subseteq J$ and then adding J. Note, however, that $|W_s^{\max}|$ is still exponential in $|I|$ in the worst case.

Selection of heuristics. The algorithm allows some degrees of freedom. We evaluate the following aspects empirically. (1) The maximal size bound[i] of a sliced BSG at iteration i is critical. If it is too small, the sets W and L will grow slowly in every iteration. The trade-off is further complicated by the fact that the sets W and L may generalize to unseen states. (2) For a fixed bound[i], it is unclear how to prioritize the exploration of states. The PSPACE algorithm suggests that going deep is good, whereas the potential for generalization to unseen states is largest when going broad. (3) Finally, there is overhead in computing both W and L. If there is a winning policy, we only need to compute W. However, computing L may ensure that we can prune parts of the state space. A similar observation holds for computing W on unsatisfiable instances.

Remark 1. Algorithm 2 can be mildly tweaked to meet the PSPACE algorithm in Algorithm 1. The priority queue must ensure to always include complete

---

[7] In l. 5 we do not rebuild the game $\mathcal{B}$ from scratch but incrementally construct the data structures. Likewise, reachable states are a direct byproduct of this construction.

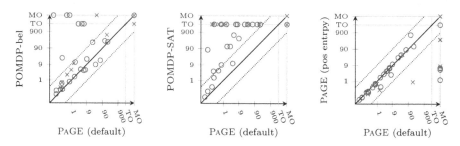

Fig. 5: Performance of baselines and novel PAGE algorithm

(reachable) local BSGs and to explore states $\langle s, J \rangle$ with small J first. Furthermore, W and L require regular pruning, and we cannot extract a policy if we prune W to a polynomial size bound. Practically, we may write pruned parts of W to disk.

6   Experiments

We highlight two aspects: (1) A comparison of our prototype to existing baselines for POMDPs, and (2) an examination of the exploration heuristics. The technical report [41] contains details on the implementation, the benchmarks, and more results.

Implementation. We provide a novel *PArtial Game Exploration* (PAGE) prototype, based on Algorithm 2, on top of the probabilistic model checker STORM [22]. We represent MEMDPs using the PRISM language with integer constants. Every assignment to these constants induces an explicit MDP. SGs are constructed and solved using existing data structures and graph algorithms.

Setup. We create a set of benchmarks inspired by the POMDP and MEMDP literature [26,12,21]. We consider a combination of satisfiable and unsatisfiable benchmarks. In the latter case, a winning policy does not exist. We construct POMDPs from MEMDPs as in Definition 5. As baselines, we use the following two existing POMDP algorithms. For almost-sure properties, a *belief-MDP construction* [7] acts similar to an efficiently engineered variant of our game-construction, but tailored towards more general quantitative properties. A *SAT-based approach* [26] aims to find increasingly larger policies. We evaluate all benchmarks on a system with a 3GHz Intel Core i9-10980XE processor. We use a time limit of 30 minutes and a memory limit of 32 GB.

Results. Figure 5 shows the (log scale) performance comparisons between different configurations[8]. Green circles reflect satisfiable and red crosses unsatisfiable benchmarks. On the x-axis is PAGE in its default configuration. The first plot compares to the belief-MDP construction. The tailored heuristics and representation of the belief-support give a significant edge in almost all cases. The few points

---

[8] Every point $\langle x, y \rangle$ in the graph reflects a benchmarks which was solved by the configuration on the x-axis in x time and by the configuration on the y-axis in y time. Points above the diagonal are thus faster for the configuration on the x-axis.

Table 1: Satisfiable and unsatisfiable benchmark results

	$|I|$	$|S|$	$|A|$	PAGE(posentr) t	n	PAGE(negentr) t	n	Belief t	SAT t
Grid	19	132	4	0.2	3002	0.2	3002	0.6	3.7
	39	152	4	0.4	9007	1.6	41029	12.6	121.3
	199	474	4	6.4	337177	MO		MO	TO
Catch	256	625	4	6.6	93614	5.9	41094	3.8	TO
	256	6561	4	40.1	749295	32.6	337899	9.1	TO
	256	14641	4	82.5	1826922	65.3	338079	16.2	TO
Exp	8	19	9	0.1	349	0.1	349	0.1	75.9
	20	43	21	131.4	192163	197.6	448443	217.6	TO
	24	51	25	TO		MO		MO	TO
Frogger	10	1200	4	0.2	1200	0.2	1200	22.7	1.4
	20	1200	4	0.4	1200	0.5	1200	MO	3.9
	80	4000	4	4.4	4000	4.4	4000	TO	597.3
	99	4000	4	5.9	8001	6.1	8001	TO	TO

	$|I|$	$|S|$	$|A|$	PAGE(posentr) t	n	PAGE(negentr) t	n	Belief t
MMind	16	21	16	0.1	1003	0.2	1445	0.3
	27	17	27	0.5	5167	0.5	7579	2.0
	32	25	32	0.6	7799	0.9	11809	4.2
	81	21	81	41.1	170291	38.6	296407	MO
Exp	20	42	21	0.8	9005	173.8	388127	576.1
	24	50	25	8.3	41022	MO		MO
	32	66	33	347.7	337177	MO		MO

below the line are due to a higher exploration rate when building the state space. The second plot compares to the SAT-based approach, which is only suitable for finding policies, not for disproving their existence. This approach implicitly searches for a particular class of policies, whose structure is not appropriate for some MEMDPs. The third plot compares PAGE in the default configuration – with negative entropy as priority function – with PAGE using positive entropy. As expected, different priorities have a significant impact on the performance.

Table 1 shows an overview of satisfiable and unsatisfiable benchmarks. Each table shows the number of environments, states, and actions-per-state in the MEMDP. For PAGE, we include both the default configuration (negative entropy) and variation (positive entropy). For both configurations, we provide columns with the time and the maximum size of the BSG constructed. We also include the time for the two baselines. Unsurprisingly, the number of states to be explored is a good predictor for the performance and the relative performance is as in Fig. 5.

7 Conclusion

This paper considers multi-environment MDPs with an arbitrary number of environments and an almost-sure reachability objective. We show novel and tight complexity bounds and use these insights to derive a new algorithm. This algorithm outperforms approaches for POMDPs on a broad set of benchmarks. For future work, we will apply an algorithm directly on the BOMDP [16].

Data-Availability Statement

Supplementary material related to this paper is openly available on Zenodo at: https://doi.org/10.5281/zenodo.7560675

References

1. Roman Andriushchenko, Milan Ceska, Sebastian Junges, Joost-Pieter Katoen, and Simon Stupinský. PAYNT: A tool for inductive synthesis of probabilistic programs. In *CAV*, volume 12759 of *LNCS*, pages 856–869. Springer, 2021.
2. Sebastian Arming, Ezio Bartocci, Krishnendu Chatterjee, Joost-Pieter Katoen, and Ana Sokolova. Parameter-independent strategies for pmdps via pomdps. In *QEST*, volume 11024 of *LNCS*, pages 53–70. Springer, 2018.
3. Mohammad Gheshlaghi Azar, Alessandro Lazaric, and Emma Brunskill. Sequential transfer in multi-armed bandit with finite set of models. In *NIPS*, pages 2220–2228, 2013.
4. Christel Baier, Marcus Größer, and Nathalie Bertrand. Probabilistic ω-automata. *J. ACM*, 59(1):1:1–1:52, 2012.
5. Christel Baier and Joost-Pieter Katoen. *Principles of model checking*. MIT Press, 2008.
6. Armin Biere, Alessandro Cimatti, Edmund M. Clarke, Ofer Strichman, and Yunshan Zhu. Bounded model checking. *Adv. Comput.*, 58:117–148, 2003.
7. Alexander Bork, Sebastian Junges, Joost-Pieter Katoen, and Tim Quatmann. Verification of indefinite-horizon pomdps. In *ATVA*, volume 12302 of *LNCS*, pages 288–304. Springer, 2020.
8. Alexander Bork, Joost-Pieter Katoen, and Tim Quatmann. Under-approximating expected total rewards in pomdps. In *TACAS (2)*, volume 13244 of *LNCS*, pages 22–40. Springer, 2022.
9. Tomás Brázdil, Krishnendu Chatterjee, Martin Chmelik, Vojtech Forejt, Jan Kretínský, Marta Z. Kwiatkowska, David Parker, and Mateusz Ujma. Verification of markov decision processes using learning algorithms. In *ATVA*, volume 8837 of *LNCS*, pages 98–114. Springer, 2014.
10. Peter Buchholz and Dimitri Scheftelowitsch. Computation of weighted sums of rewards for concurrent mdps. *Math. Methods Oper. Res.*, 89(1):1–42, 2019.
11. Iadine Chades, Josie Carwardine, Tara G. Martin, Samuel Nicol, Régis Sabbadin, and Olivier Buffet. Momdps: A solution for modelling adaptive management problems. In *AAAI*. AAAI Press, 2012.
12. Krishnendu Chatterjee, Martin Chmelik, and Jessica Davies. A symbolic sat-based algorithm for almost-sure reachability with small strategies in pomdps. In *AAAI*, pages 3225–3232. AAAI Press, 2016.
13. Krishnendu Chatterjee, Martin Chmelik, Raghav Gupta, and Ayush Kanodia. Optimal cost almost-sure reachability in pomdps. *Artif. Intell.*, 234:26–48, 2016.
14. Krishnendu Chatterjee, Martin Chmelík, Deep Karkhanis, Petr Novotný, and Amélie Royer. Multiple-environment markov decision processes: Efficient analysis and applications. In *ICAPS*, pages 48–56. AAAI Press, 2020.
15. Krishnendu Chatterjee, Martin Chmelik, and Mathieu Tracol. What is decidable about partially observable markov decision processes with omega-regular objectives. In *CSL*, volume 23 of *LIPIcs*, pages 165–180. Schloss Dagstuhl - Leibniz-Zentrum für Informatik, 2013.

16. Krishnendu Chatterjee, Martin Chmelik, and Mathieu Tracol. What is decidable about partially observable markov decision processes with ω-regular objectives. *J. Comput. Syst. Sci.*, 82(5):878–911, 2016.
17. Krishnendu Chatterjee, Marcin Jurdzinski, and Thomas A. Henzinger. Simple stochastic parity games. In *CSL*, volume 2803 of *LNCS*, pages 100–113. Springer, 2003.
18. Philipp Chrszon, Clemens Dubslaff, Sascha Klüppelholz, and Christel Baier. Profeat: feature-oriented engineering for family-based probabilistic model checking. *Formal Aspects Comput.*, 30(1):45–75, 2018.
19. Luca de Alfaro. The verification of probabilistic systems under memoryless partial-information policies is hard. Technical report, UC Berkeley, 1999. Presented at ProbMiV.
20. M. R. Garey and David S. Johnson. *Computers and Intractability: A Guide to the Theory of NP-Completeness.* W. H. Freeman, 1979.
21. Arnd Hartmanns, Michaela Klauck, David Parker, Tim Quatmann, and Enno Ruijters. The quantitative verification benchmark set. In *TACAS (1)*, volume 11427 of *LNCS*, pages 344–350. Springer, 2019.
22. Christian Hensel, Sebastian Junges, Joost-Pieter Katoen, Tim Quatmann, and Matthias Volk. The probabilistic model checker storm. *Int. J. Softw. Tools Technol. Transf.*, 24(4):589–610, 2022.
23. Manfred Jaeger, Giorgio Bacci, Giovanni Bacci, Kim Guldstrand Larsen, and Peter Gjøl Jensen. Approximating Euclidean by Imprecise Markov Decision Processes. In *ISoLA (1)*, volume 12476 of *LNCS*, pages 275–289. Springer, 2020.
24. Nils Jansen, Sebastian Junges, and Joost-Pieter Katoen. Parameter synthesis in markov models: A gentle survey. *CoRR*, abs/2207.06801, 2022.
25. Bengt Jonsson and Kim Guldstrand Larsen. Specification and refinement of probabilistic processes. In *LICS*, pages 266–277. IEEE Computer Society, 1991.
26. Sebastian Junges, Nils Jansen, and Sanjit A. Seshia. Enforcing almost-sure reachability in pomdps. In *CAV (2)*, volume 12760 of *LNCS*, pages 602–625. Springer, 2021.
27. Leslie Pack Kaelbling, Michael L. Littman, and Anthony R. Cassandra. Planning and acting in partially observable stochastic domains. *Artif. Intell.*, 101(1-2):99–134, 1998.
28. Robert Kirk, Amy Zhang, Edward Grefenstette, and Tim Rocktäschel. A survey of generalisation in deep reinforcement learning. *CoRR*, abs/2111.09794, 2021.
29. Jan Kretínský and Tobias Meggendorfer. Of cores: A partial-exploration framework for markov decision processes. *Log. Methods Comput. Sci.*, 16(4), 2020.
30. Marta Kwiatkowska, Gethin Norman, and Dave Parker. PRISM 4.0: Verification of probabilistic real-time systems. In *CAV*, volume 6806 of *LNCS*, pages 585–591. Springer, 2011.
31. Michael L. Littman, Anthony R. Cassandra, and Leslie Pack Kaelbling. Learning policies for partially observable environments: Scaling up. In *ICML*, pages 362–370. Morgan Kaufmann, 1995.
32. Omid Madani, Steve Hanks, and Anne Condon. On the undecidability of probabilistic planning and related stochastic optimization problems. *Artif. Intell.*, 147(1-2):5–34, 2003.
33. H. Brendan McMahan, Maxim Likhachev, and Geoffrey J. Gordon. Bounded real-time dynamic programming: RTDP with monotone upper bounds and performance guarantees. In *ICML*, volume 119 of *ACM International Conference Proceeding Series*, pages 569–576. ACM, 2005.

34. Nicolas Meuleau, Leonid Peshkin, Kee-Eung Kim, and Leslie Pack Kaelbling. Learning finite-state controllers for partially observable environments. In *UAI*, pages 427–436. Morgan Kaufmann, 1999.

35. Gethin Norman, David Parker, and Xueyi Zou. Verification and control of partially observable probabilistic systems. *Real Time Syst.*, 53(3):354–402, 2017.

36. Jean-François Raskin and Ocan Sankur. Multiple-environment markov decision processes. In *FSTTCS*, volume 29 of *LIPIcs*, pages 531–543. Schloss Dagstuhl - Leibniz-Zentrum für Informatik, 2014.

37. John H. Reif. The complexity of two-player games of incomplete information. *J. Comput. Syst. Sci.*, 29(2):274–301, 1984.

38. L. S. Shapley. Stochastic games*. *Proceedings of the National Academy of Sciences*, 39(10):1095–1100, 1953.

39. Trey Smith and Reid G. Simmons. Point-based POMDP algorithms: Improved analysis and implementation. In *UAI*, pages 542–547. AUAI Press, 2005.

40. Lauren N. Steimle, David L. Kaufman, and Brian T. Denton. Multi-model markov decision processes. *IISE Trans.*, 53(10):1124–1139, 2021.

41. Marck van der Vegt, Nils Jansen, and Sebastian Junges. Robust almost-sure reachability in multi-environment mdps. *CoRR*, abs/2301.11296, 2023.

42. Matthias Volk, Sebastian Junges, and Joost-Pieter Katoen. Fast dynamic fault tree analysis by model checking techniques. *IEEE Trans. Ind. Informatics*, 14(1):370–379, 2018.

43. Wolfram Wiesemann, Daniel Kuhn, and Berç Rustem. Robust markov decision processes. *Math. Oper. Res.*, 38(1):153–183, 2013.

44. Tobias Winkler, Sebastian Junges, Guillermo A. Pérez, and Joost-Pieter Katoen. On the complexity of reachability in parametric markov decision processes. In *CONCUR*, volume 140 of *LIPIcs*, pages 14:1–14:17. Schloss Dagstuhl - Leibniz-Zentrum für Informatik, 2019.

45. Leonore Winterer, Sebastian Junges, Ralf Wimmer, Nils Jansen, Ufuk Topcu, Joost-Pieter Katoen, and Bernd Becker. Strategy synthesis for pomdps in robot planning via game-based abstractions. *IEEE Trans. Autom. Control.*, 66(3):1040–1054, 2021.

Mungojerrie: Linear-Time Objectives in Model-Free Reinforcement Learning⋆

Ernst Moritz Hahn[1], Mateo Perez[2], Sven Schewe[3],
Fabio Somenzi[2]([✉]), Ashutosh Trivedi[2], and Dominik Wojtczak[3]

[1] University of Twente, Enschede, The Netherlands
[2] University of Colorado Boulder, Boulder, USA
fabio@colorado.edu
[3] University of Liverpool, Liverpool, UK

Abstract. Mungojerrie is an extensible tool that provides a framework to translate linear-time objectives into reward for reinforcement learning (RL). The tool provides convergent RL algorithms for stochastic games, reference implementations of existing reward translations for ω-regular objectives, and an internal probabilistic model checker for ω-regular objectives. This functionality is modular and operates on shared data structures, which enables fast development of new translation techniques. Mungojerrie supports finite models specified in PRISM and ω-automata specified in the HOA format, with an integrated command line interface to external linear temporal logic translators. Mungojerrie is distributed with a set of benchmarks for ω-regular objectives in RL.

1 Introduction

Reinforcement learning (RL) [41] is a sequential optimization approach where a decision maker learns to optimally resolve a sequence of choices based on feedback received from the environment. This feedback often takes the form of rewards and punishments proportional to the fitness of the decisions taken by the agent (or their effects) as judged by the environment towards some higher-level objectives. We call such objectives *learning objectives*. RL is inspired by the way dopamine-driven organisms latch on to past rewarding actions and hence, historically, RL adopted a myopic way of looking at the reward sequences in the form of the discounted-sum of rewards, where the discount factor controls the weight placed toward future rewards. More recently, other forms of reward aggregation, such as limit-average, have also been considered. A key design challenge for users of RL is that of translation: given a class of learning objectives and aggregator functions, design a reward function from the sequence of learner's choices to scalar rewards such that an RL agent maximizing the aggregated sum of rewards converges to an optimal policy for the learning objective.

⋆ Mungojerrie is available at plv.colorado.edu/mungojerrie. This work is supported in part by the National Science Foundation (NSF) grant CCF-2009022 and by NSF CAREER award CCF-2146563. ▨ This project has received funding from the European Union's Horizon 2020 research and innovation programme under grant agreements No 864075 (CAESAR) and 956123 (FOCETA).

© The Author(s) 2023
S. Sankaranarayanan and N. Sharygina (Eds.): TACAS 2023, LNCS 13993, pp. 527–545, 2023.
https://doi.org/10.1007/978-3-031-30823-9_27

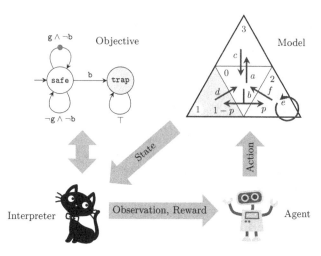

Fig. 1. The reinforcement learning loop implemented within Mungojerrie. The interpreter assigns reward to the agent based on the state of the model and automaton.

The translation of objectives to reward signals has historically been a largely manual process. Such translations not only depend on the expertise of the translator in reward engineering, they also pose obstacles to providing formal guarantees on the faithfulness of the translation. Unsurprisingly, specifying reward manually is prone to error [22,44]. As the practice of model-free RL continues to produce impressive results [38,31,29], the integration of RL in safety-critical system design is inevitable. An alternative to manually programming the reward function is to specify the objective in a formal language and have it "compiled" to a reward function. We call such a translation a *reward scheme*.

In designing reward schemes for RL, one strives to achieve an overall translation that is *faithful* (maximizing reward means maximizing the probability of achieving the objective) and *effective* (RL quickly converges to optimal strategies). While the faithfulness of a reward scheme can be established theoretically, its effectiveness requires experimental evaluation. Experimenting with reward schemes requires a framework for specifying learning objectives, environments, a wide range of RL algorithms, and an interface for connecting reward schemes with these components. In addition, it may be beneficial to have access to a probabilistic model checker to evaluate the quality of the policy computed by RL, and to compare it against ground truth.

> *Mungojerrie is designed to provide this functionality for learning requirements expressible as linear-time objectives (ω-regular languages [32] and linear temporal logic [27,33]) against finite MDPs and stochastic games.*

Features. Mungojerrie is designed with ease of use and extensibility in mind. Models in Mungojerrie can be specified in PRISM [25], which maintains compatibility with existing benchmarks, or by explicitly constructing the model via calls to internal functions. Mungojerrie supports reading ω-automata in the Hanoi Omega Automata (HOA) format [2], and has a command line interface connecting Mungojerrie with performant LTL translators (Spot [7] and Owl [24]). Mungojerrie provides an OpenAI Gym [4] like interface between the RL algorithms (included with the tool) and the learning environment to allow integration with off-the-shelf RL algorithms. The tool also has methods for performing probabilistic model checking (including end-component decomposition, stochastic shortest-path, and discounted-reward optimization) of ω-regular objectives on the same data structures used for learning. Mungojerrie also provides reference implementations of several reward schemes [11,12,14,19,23] proposed by the formal methods community. Mungojerrie is packaged with over 100 benchmarks and outputs GraphViz [8] for easy visualization of small models and automata.

An introductory example. Figure 2 shows an example MDP in which a gambler places bets with the aim of accumulating a wealth of 7 units. In addition the gambler will quit if her wealth wanes to just one unit more than once. This objective is captured by the (deterministic) Büchi automaton of Fig. 3. Mungojerrie computes a strategy for the gambler that maximizes the probability of satisfying her objective. Figure 4 shows the Markov chain that results from following this strategy. This figure was minimally modified from GraphViz output from Mungojerrie. Note that the strategy altogether avoids the state in which $x = 1$; hence it achieves the same probability of success (5/7) as an optimal strategy for the simpler objective of eventually reaching $x = 7$ (without going broke). Mungojerrie computes the strategy of Fig. 4 by RL; it can also verify it by probabilistic model checking.

2   Overview of Mungojerrie

Models. The systems used in Mungojerrie consist of finite sets of states and actions, where states are labeled with atomic propositions. There are at most two strategic players: Max player and Min player. Each state is controlled by one player. We call models where all states are controlled by Max player Markov decision processes (MDPs) [34]. Else, we refer to them as stochastic games [5].

Mungojerrie supports parsing models specified in the PRISM language. The allowed model types are "mdp" (Markov decision process) and "smg" (stochastic multiplayer game) with two players. There should be one initial state. The interface for building the model is exposed, allowing extensions of Mungojerrie to connect with parsers for other languages. The authors of [6] used Mungojerrie in their experiments by extending the tool to support continuous-time MDPs.

Properties. The properties natively supported by Mungojerrie are ω-regular languages. Starting from the initial state, the players produce an infinite sequence of states with a corresponding infinite sequence of atomic propositions: an ω-word. The inclusion of this ω-word in our ω-regular language determines whether or not this particular run satisfies the property. The Max player maximizes the probability that a run is satisfying, while goal of the Min player is the opposite.

We specify our ω-regular language as an ω-automaton, which may be nondeterministic. For model checking and RL, this nondeterminism must be resolved on the fly. Automata where this can be done in any MDP without changing acceptance are said to be Good-for-MDPs (GFM) [13]. Automata where this can be done in any stochastic game without changing acceptance are said to be Good-for-Games (GFG) [21]. In general, nondeterministic Büchi automata are not GFM, but two classes of GFM Büchi automata with limited nondeterminism have been studied: suitable limit-deterministic Büchi automata [10,37] and slim Büchi automata [13].

The user of Mungojerrie can either provide the ω-automaton directly or use one of the supported external translators to generate the automaton from LTL with a single call to Mungojerrie. Mungojerrie reads automata specified in the HOA format. Mungojerrie supports providing the ω-automaton directly for testing the effectiveness of different automata for learning (see Section 4). The LTL translators that can be called from Mungojerrie are the EPMC plugin from [13], SPOT [7], and Owl [24] for generating slim Büchi, deterministic parity, and suitable limit-deterministic Büchi automata. The user is responsible for the ω-automata provided directly having the appropriate property, GFM or GFG.

For use in Mungojerrie, the labels and acceptance conditions for the automaton should be on the transitions. The acceptance conditions supported by

```
0   mdp
1
2   const int Wealth = 5;    // initial gambler's wealth
3   const double p   = 1/2;  // probability of winning one bet
4
5   label "rich" = x = 7;
6   label "poor" = x = 1;
7
8   module gambler
9     x : [0..7] init Wealth;
10
11    [b0] x=0 ∨ x=7 → true;  // absorbing states
12    [b1] x>0 ∧ x<7 → p : (x'=x+1) + (1−p) : (x'=x−1);
13    [b2] x>1 ∧ x<6 → p : (x'=x+2) + (1−p) : (x'=x−2);
14    [b3] x>2 ∧ x<5 → p : (x'=x+3) + (1−p) : (x'=x−3);
15  endmodule
```

Fig. 2. A Gambler's Ruin model in the PRISM language. Line 13, for example, says that when $1 < x < 6$, the gambler may bet two units because action b2 is enabled. The '+' sign does double duty: as addition symbol in arithmetic expressions and as separator of probabilistic transitions.

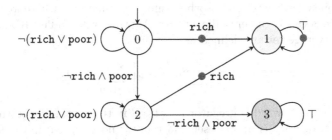

Fig. 3. Deterministic Büchi automaton equivalent to the LTL formula ¬poor U(rich ∨ (poor ∧ X(¬poor U rich))). The transitions marked with the green dots are accepting.

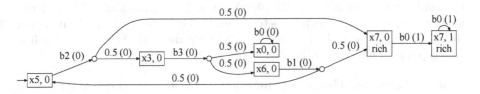

Fig. 4. Optimal gambler strategy for the objective of Fig. 3. Boxes are decision states and circles are probabilistic choice states. For a decision state, the label gives the value of x and the state of the automaton. Transitions are labelled with either an action or a probability, and with the priority (1 for accepting and 0 for non-accepting).

Mungojerrie should be reducible to parity acceptance conditions without altering the transition structure of the automaton. This includes parity, Büchi, co-Büchi, Streett 1 (one pair), and Rabin 1 (one pair) conditions. Nondeterministic automata must have Büchi acceptance conditions. Generalized acceptance conditions are not supported in version 1.1.

Reinforcement Learning. The RL algorithms optimize over MDP/Stochastic game environments equipped with a Markovian reward function. The reward function assigns a reward $R_{t+1} \in \mathbb{R}$ dependent on the state and action at timestep t and the next state at timestep $t+1$. As the players make their choices within the environment, the resulting play produces a sequence of states, actions, and rewards $(S_0, A_0, R_1, S_1, A_1, R_2, \ldots)$. The discounted reward aggregator is

$$\text{disc}_\gamma(\pi, \nu) = \mathbb{E}_{\pi,\nu}\left[\sum_{t \geq 0} \gamma^t R_{t+1}\right],$$

where π is the strategy for Max player, ν is the strategy for Min player, $\gamma \in [0, 1)$ is the discount factor, and R_t is the reward at timestep t. We can set $\gamma = 1$ when with probability 1 we enter an absorbing sink (termination), where we receive no reward. This is called the episodic setting. Another well-studied RL aggregator is the limit-average reward defined as

$$\mathrm{avg}(\pi, \nu) = \limsup_{n \to \infty} \frac{1}{n} \mathbb{E}_{\pi, \nu} \Big[\sum_{n \geq t \geq 0} R_{t+1} \Big].$$

The limit-average reward aggregator is natural in the continuing setting, where the agent's trajectory is never reset and there is no preferred initial state [30]. The objective of RL is to compute the optimal value and policies for a given aggregator. Mungojerrie includes the stochastic game extensions of Q-learning [43], Double Q-learning [20], and Sarsa(λ) [40] for RL in finite state and action models. Mungojerrie also includes Differential Q-learning [42] for average RL in finite communicating MDPs. We collectively refer to parameters that are set by hand prior to running an RL algorithm as hyperparameters. Mungojerrie supports changing all hyperparameters from the command line. As the design of Mungojerrie separates the learning agent(s) from the reward scheme, extending Mungojerrie to include another RL algorithm is easy.

Reward Schemes. The user of Mungojerrie can either select one of the reward schemes included with the tool or extend the tool to include a new reward scheme. Mungojerrie also allows the use of the reward specified in the PRISM model (either state- or action-based). The following reward schemes are included in version 1.1 of Mungojerrie:

- Limit-reachability. The *limit-reachability* scheme [11] uses a GFM Büchi automaton. This reward scheme converts accepting edges in the automaton into a transition to a sink with probability $1 - \zeta$ with a reward of $+1$, where $0 < \zeta < 1$ is a hyperparameter. All other transitions produce zero reward. For a sufficiently large ζ and discount factor γ, strategies that are optimal for the discounted reward maximize the probability of satisfaction of the Büchi objective.
- Multi-discounted. The multi-discounted reward scheme [3] also uses a GFM Büchi automaton. This translation converts accepting edges in the automaton into a transition that gives $1 - \gamma_B$ reward with a discount of γ_B, where $0 < \gamma_B < 1$ is a hyperparameter. All other transitions yield no reward and are discounted by the standard discount factor γ. For suitably large γ_B and γ, discounted reward optimal strategies maximize the probability of satisfaction of the Büchi objective.
- Dense limit-reachability. The dense limit-reachability reward scheme [12] connects the approaches of [11] and [3]. This reward scheme is identical to [11] except for giving a $+1$ reward given every time an accepting transition is seen, instead of only when the transition to the sink succeeds. Since discounting can be thought of as a constant stopping probability [41], this reward scheme is the same in expectation as a scaled version of [3].
- Parity. The parity reward scheme was proposed for stochastic games in [14]. For two-player games, it requires a GFG automaton. This translation utilizes a deterministic parity automaton with a max odd objective. Transitions of priority

i go to a sink with probability ε^{k-i}, where k is the number of priorities and $0 < \varepsilon < 1$ is a hyperparameter. The transition to the sink receives a $+1$ or -1 reward for odd or even priorities, respectively. All other transitions receive a zero reward. For sufficiently small ε, maximizing the cumulative reward results in a strategy maximizing the probability of satisfaction of the parity objective.

– Priority tracker. The priority tracker reward scheme was proposed by Hahn et al. [14]. For MDPs, Hahn et al. introduce a priority tracker gadget that takes a parity objective with a hyperparameter $0 < \varepsilon < 1$. The priority tracker consists of two stages. In stage one, we wait for transients to end by ending the stage with probability ε on each step. In the second stage, we detect the maximum priority occuring infinitely often with a set of wait states, where we accept the current maximum with probability ε on each step. For sufficiently small ε and large discount γ, maximizing the discounted reward also maximizes the probability of satisfaction of the parity objective.

– Lexicographic. Hahn et al.[19] proposed this reward scheme for lexicographic ω-regular objectives. In this reward scheme, there is a tracker gadget that keeps track of which accepting edges for the GFM Büchi automata have been seen. When the tracker indicates that at least one accepting edge has been seen, the learning agent can decide to "cash in" the tracker, which clears the tracker. When this happens, with probability $1 - \zeta$ the learning agent receives a reward which is the weighted sum of seen accepting edges, scaled by powers of f, and transitions to a terminating sink, where $0 < \zeta < 1$ and $f \geq 1$ are hyperparameters. For suitable f, ζ, and γ, maximizing the discounted reward yields the lexicographically optimal strategy.

– Average. The average reward scheme [23] translates absolute liveness ω-regular objectives, which means the objective is concerned with eventual satifaction, to average reward for communicating MDPs. Given a GFM Büchi automaton, transitions from every state in the automaton back to the initial state are introduced, so called "resets". A hyperparameter $c < 0$ is introduced which gives a penalizing reward to these resets. Accepting edges are then given a reward of $+1$. Positional policies that maximize the average reward also maximize the probability of satisfaction of the objective.

– Reward on accept. This reward scheme was proposed in [35]. The translation of [35] picks a pair in a Rabin automaton to satisfy, and gives positive and negative reward for the good and bad states of the pair, respectively. In general, picking the winning pair ahead of time is not possible [11]. For a Büchi automaton, this corresponds to giving positive ($+1$) rewards for accepting edges and zero rewards otherwise. While this reward scheme was shown to be not faithful [11] for general objectives, it is included for comparison purposes.

3   Tool Design

The primary design goal of Mungojerrie is to enable extensibility. To accomplish this, Mungojerrie separates different processing stages as much as possible so that extensions can reuse other components. We begin by presenting the architecture

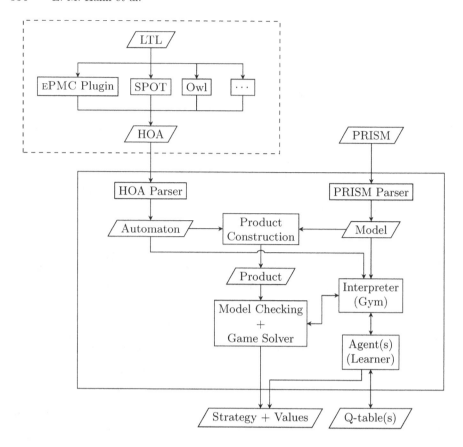

Fig. 5. Architecture of Mungojerrie 1.1.

of Mungojerrie. Afterwards, we take a closer at the novel slim Büchi automata plugin, which is described here in detail for the first time.

Architecture of Mungojerrie. Mungojerrie begins its execution by parsing the input PRISM and HOA (see upper part of Fig. 5). The HOA is either read in from a file or piped from a call to one of the supported LTL translators. In particular the EPMC plugin from [13], an LTL translator capable of producing slim Büchi automata, is packaged with the tool. Requested automaton modifications, such as determinization, are run after this step. If specified, Mungojerrie creates the synchronous product between the automaton and the model, and runs model checking or game solving [1,15,16]. The requested strategy and values are returned. Due to this step, Mungojerrie has been connected to external linear program solvers. This enabled the extension of Mungojerrie to compute reward maximizing policies via a linear program for branching Markov decision processes in [18].

If learning has been specified, the interpreter takes the automaton and model, without explicitly forming the product, and provides an interface akin to OpenAI Gym [4] for the RL agent to interact with the environment and receive rewards. When learning is complete, the Q-table(s) can be saved to a file for later use, and the interpreter forms the Markov chain induced by the learned strategy and passes it to the internal model checker for verification.

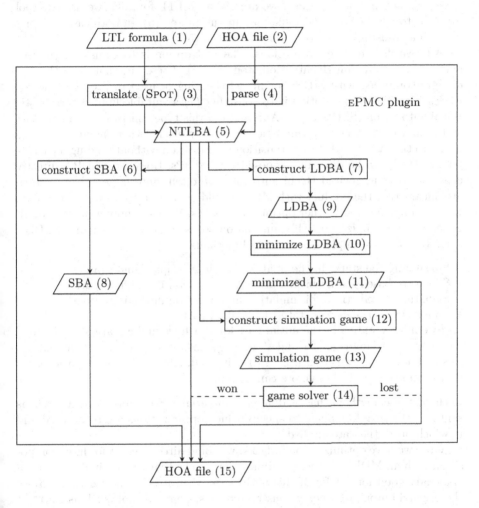

Fig. 6. Automata generation block diagram

Slim Büchi Automata Generation. For reward schemes involving LTL, the ω-regular automata translation is an important part of the design. Certain automata may be more effective for learning than others. Slim Büchi automata [13] were designed with learning considerations in mind. The translator that produces these automata is packaged with Mungojerrie. We will now describe its design in detail for the first time.

We have implemented slim Büchi automata generation as a plugin of the probabilistic model checker EPMC [17]. The process is described in Fig. 6. The starting point is a transition-labeled Büchi automaton in HOA format [2] (2) or an LTL formula (1). In case we are given an automaton in HOA format, we parse this automaton (4) and if we are given an LTL formula, we use the tool SPOT [7] to transform the formula into an automaton (3). In both cases, we end up with a transition-labeled Büchi automaton (5).

Afterwards, we have two options. The first option is to transform (6) this automaton into a slim Büchi automaton (8) [13]. These automata can then be directly composed with MDPs for model checking or used to produce rewards for learning. The other option is to construct (7) a suitable limit-deterministic Büchi automaton (SLDBA) (9). Automata of this type consist of an initial part and a final part. A nondeterministic choice only occurs when moving from the initial to the final part by an ε transition (a transition without reading a character). SLDBA can be directly composed with MDPs. However, SLDBA directly constructed from general Büchi automata are often quite large, which in turn also means that the product with MDPs would be quite large as well. Therefore, we have implemented further optimization steps. We can apply a number of algorithms to minimize (10) this automaton so as to achieve a smaller SLDBA (11). To do so, we implemented several methods:

- Subsuming the states in the final part with an empty language
- Signature-based strong bisimulation minimization in the final part
- Signature-based strong bisimulation minimization in the initial part
- Language-equivalence of states in the final part
- If we have a state s in the initial part for which we find a state s' in the final part where the language of s and s' are the same, we can remove all transitions of s and add an ε transition from s to s' instead. Afterwards, automaton states that cannot be reached anymore can be removed.

Each of these methods has a different potential for minimization as well as runtime. We therefore allow to specify which optimizations are to be used and in which order they are applied.

Once we have optimized the SLDBA, we could directly use it for later composition with an MDP. Another possibility is to prove that the original automaton is already good for MDPs. If this is the case, then it is often preferable to use the original automaton: being constructed by specialized tools such as SPOT, it is often smaller than the minimized SLDBA. The original automaton is good-for-MDPs if it *simulates* the SLDBA [13]. If it does, then it is also composable with MDPs. Otherwise, it is unknown whether it is suitable for MDPs. In this case, sometimes more complex notions of simulation can be used, but existing decision procedures are too expensive to implement [36].

To show simulation, we construct (12) a simulation game, which in our case is a transition-labeled parity game (13) with 3 colors. We solve these games using (a slight variation of) the McNaughton algorithm [28]. (We are aware that specialized algorithms for parity games with 3 colors exist [9]. However, so far the construction of the arena, not solving the game, turned out to be the bottleneck here). If the even player is winning, the simulation holds. Otherwise, more complex notions of simulation can be used, which however lead to larger parity games being constructed. In case the even player is winning for any of them, we can use the original automaton, otherwise we have to use the SLDBA. In any case, we export the result to an HOA file (15). For illustration and debugging , automata and simulation games can be exported to the GraphViz [8].

4 Case Studies

To showcase how Mungojerrie can be used to experiment with different reward schemes, we provide three case studies. In the first case study, we demonstrate how Mungojerrie can be used to compare the effectiveness of two different reward schemes on the same system. In the second case study, we consider the design space of automata, and demonstrate how Mungojerrie can be used to compare how different ω-automata change learning effectiveness. This is important for considering how to design LTL translators that produce automata that are effective for learning. In the last case study, we demonstrate how the different outputs of Mungojerrie can be used. For additional experimental results obtained using Mungojerrie, we refer readers to [11,12,14,19,39,45,23] for case studies testing ω-regular reward schemes, and [13] for the EPMC plugin. We also refer readers to [26, Fig. 3] which examined RL for scLTL properties, [6] for continuous-time MDPs, and [18], which extended Mungojerrie to test model-free reinforcement learning in branching Markov decision processes.

4.1 Comparing Reward Schemes

To demonstrate how Mungojerrie may be used to compare reward schemes, we compare the reward scheme of [11] with a modification of it that assigns a +1 reward on every accepting edge, as introduced in [12]. We compare these two methods on the same problem, where the learner must safely navigate two robots on a slippery gridworld to a goal. We also fix the problem parameters $\zeta = 0.99$ and $\gamma = 0.99999$, and the use of Q-learning. Since we are interested in which method will converge sooner, we fix the amount of training to be relatively low. We allow the two parameters specific to Q-learning, the learning rate α and the exploration rate ε, to be varied in order to find the optimal combination for each method. We average 10 runs for each grid point. This required 32000 runs, which took approximately 79 CPU hours (single-core) on a 2.5GHz Intel Xeon E5-2680 v3. This corresponds to an average of approximately 188000 sampled transitions per second per core, including model checking time. This sampling rate is typical of what was observed in other experiments.

   Figure 7 shows the probability of satisfaction of the learned strategy as computed by the model checker of Mungojerrie. One can see that under these conditions, the reward scheme from [12] is able to consistently learn probability

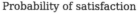

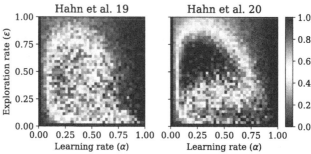

Fig. 7. Probability of satisfaction of learned strategies as computed by the model checker of Mungojerrie. 'Hahn et al. 19' refers to the translation of [11]. 'Hahn et al. 20' refers to the translation of [12] that assigns +1 reward on every accepting edge with reachability parameter ζ. Each grid point is the average of 10 runs.

1 strategies under certain parameter combinations, while [11] does not. Figure 8 shows the difference in the estimated probability of satisfaction, found by taking the value from the initial state of Q-table and renormalizing it appropriately, and the probability of satisfaction of the learned strategy computed by the model checker of Mungojerrie. One can see that the reward scheme of [11] sometimes overestimates and sometimes underestimates when it achieves a high actual probability of satisfaction under these conditions. However, on the same example, the reward scheme of [12] consistently underestimates everywhere. In summary, Mungojerrie allowed us to see that, although the reachability reward scheme of [12] may achieve higher probabilities of satisfaction sooner, it may take longer for the values in the Q-table to properly converge.

4.2 Comparing Automata

An ω-regular objective may be described by different automata, many of which may be good-for-MDPs. Mungojerrie can be used to compare the effectiveness of such automata when used in RL. Consider the two nondeterministic Büchi automata shown in Fig. 9. Both are equivalent to the LTL formula $(\mathsf{F\,G}\,x) \vee (\mathsf{G\,F}\,y)$, but the one on the right should be better for learning: long transient sequences of observations that satisfy $x \wedge \neg y$ may convince the agent to commit to State 1 of the left automaton too soon.

To test this conjecture, we specified a model in PRISM organized in two long chains. In one of them the agent sees many xs for a while, but eventually only sees ys. In the other chain the situation is reversed. Which chain is followed is up to chance. We then used the reward scheme from [3] with Q-learning under the default hyperparameters in Mungojerrie, $\gamma_B = 0.99$, $\gamma = 0.99999$, $\alpha = 0.1$, and $\varepsilon = 0.1$. We then trained for 20000 episodes under each automaton, and used Mungojerrie to compute the probability of satisfaction of the property at periodic

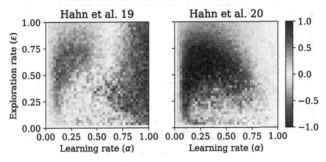

Fig. 8. Estimated probability of satisfaction of learned strategies minus the probability of satisfaction computed by the model checker of Mungojerrie. Blue indicates under-estimation, while red indicates overestimation. Hahn et al. 19 refers to the translation of [11]. Hahn et al. 20 refers to the translation of [12] that assigns +1 reward on every accepting edge with reachability parameter ζ. Each grid point is the average of 10 runs.

intervals. Since learning to control the left automaton requires thorough and deep exploration, we conjectured that optimistic intialization of the Q-table [41] to the value 0.8 will improve performance. We took the average of 1000 runs for each combination.

Figure 10 shows the resulting curve. When using the LDBA without optimistic intialization, the learning agent is unable to learn the optimal strategy under these conditions. While it is worth noting that using the LDBA without optimistic initialization eventually converges to the optimal strategy with enough training, it is clear that the choice of the automaton can have a significant impact on learning performance. Therefore, the design of translations from LTL to automata has a role to play in producing effective reward schemes.

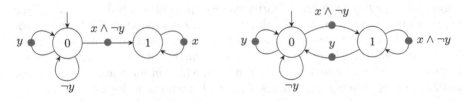

Fig. 9. Equivalent, but not equally effective, Büchi automata. "LDBA" and "Forgiving" refer to the automaton the left and right, respectively.

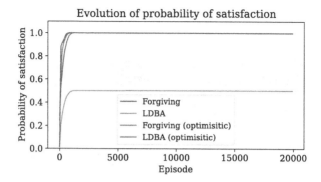

Fig. 10. Plot of the evolution of the probability of satisfaction of learned strategies as computed by the model checker of Mungojerrie. "Forgiving" and "LDBA" refer to the left and right automata in Figure 9, respectively. "(optimistic)" indicates optimistic initialization of the Q-table was used. Each curve is the average of 1000 runs.

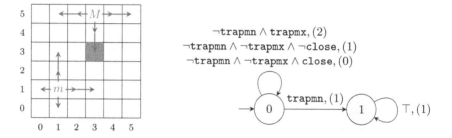

Fig. 11. A grid-world stochastic game arena (left) and a deterministic parity automaton for the objective (right).

4.3 A Game of Pursuit

Figure 11 describes a stochastic parity game of pursuit in which the Max player (M) tries to escape from the Min player (m). At each round, each player in turn chooses a direction to move. If movement in that direction is not obstructed by a wall, then the player moves either two squares or one square with equal probabilities. One square of the grid is a trap, which m must avoid at all times, but M may visit finitely many times. Player M should be at least 5 squares away from player m infinitely often. This objective is described by the LTL property $(\mathsf{F}\,\neg\texttt{trapmn}) \vee ((\mathsf{F}\,\mathsf{G}\,\neg\texttt{trapmx}) \wedge (\mathsf{G}\,\mathsf{F}\,\neg\texttt{close}))$, where $\texttt{trapmn}$ and $\texttt{trapmx}$ are true when m and M visit the trap square, respectively, and $\texttt{close}$ is true when the Manhattan distance between the two players is less than 5 squares. This objective translates to the deterministic parity automaton in Fig. 11, which accepts a word if the maximum recurring priority of its run is odd.

Unlike the example of Fig. 2, inspection of the Markov chain induced by an optimal strategy and manual verification of the optimality of the learned

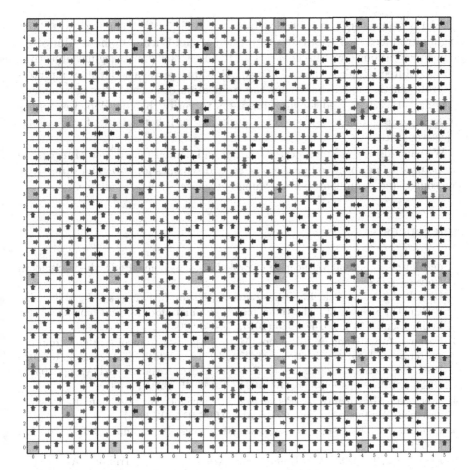

Fig. 12. Max player learned strategy for the game of Fig. 11 when the automaton is in State 0. (Any strategy will do when the automaton is in State 1.) In each 6 × 6 box the rose-colored square is the position of the minimizing player, while the light-blue square marks the trap.

strategy is impractical. Instead, the model checker of Mungojerrie has verified the optimality of this strategy from the intial state. For visualization, Mungojerrie can also save the strategy in CSV format. Postprocessing can then produce a graphical representation like the one of Fig. 12. The color gradient shows that, in the main, M's strategy is to move away from m.

5   Conclusion

We have introduced Mungojerrie, an extensible tool for experimenting with reward schemes for RL, with a focus on ω-regular objectives. Mungojerrie allows the specification of models in PRISM [25] and ω-automata in HOA [2]. Multiple LTL translators can be called from the tool [7,24], including the EPMC plugin introduced in [13] for the construction of slim Büchi automata. Mungojerrie includes various reward schemes [11,3,12,14,19,23,35] for ω-regular objectives and model-free RL algorithms [43,20,40,23]. Mungojerrie also includes an internal probabilistic model checker for the verification of learned strategies against ω-regular objectives, and for allowing users to verify that developed examples are as intended. The tool also comes packaged with benchmarks for ω-regular objectives in RL.

We have discussed Mungojerrie's design and demonstrated how Mungojerrie can be used to perform comparisons of reward schemes for ω-regular objectives. The source and documentation of Mungojerrie are publicly available.

References

1. de Alfaro, L.: Formal Verification of Probabilistic Systems. Ph.D. thesis, Stanford University (1998)
2. Babiak, T., Blahoudek, F., Duret-Lutz, A., Klein, J., Křetínský, J., Müller, D., Parker, D., Strejček, J.: The Hanoi omega-automata format. In: Computer Aided Verification (CAV). pp. 479–486 (2015), LNCS 9206
3. Bozkurt, A.K., Wang, Y., Zavlanos, M.M., Pajic, M.: Control synthesis from linear temporal logic specifications using model-free reinforcement learning. In: 2020 IEEE International Conference on Robotics and Automation (ICRA). pp. 10349–10355 (2020). https://doi.org/10.1109/ICRA40945.2020.9196796
4. Brockman, G., Cheung, V., Pettersson, L., Schneider, J., Schulman, J., Tang, J., Zaremba, W.: OpenAI Gym. CoRR **abs/1606.01540** (2016)
5. Condon, A.: The complexity of stochastic games. Inf. Comput. **96**(2), 203–224 (1992)
6. Dole, K., Gupta, A., Komp, J., Krishna, S.N., Trivedi, A.: Event-triggered and time-triggered duration calculus for model-free reinforcement learning. In: 42nd IEEE Real-Time Systems Symposium, RTSS 2021, Dortmund, Germany, December 7-10, 2021. pp. 240–252. IEEE (2021). https://doi.org/10.1109/RTSS52674.2021.00031,
7. Duret-Lutz, A., Lewkowicz, A., Fauchille, A., Michaud, T., Renault, E., Xu, L.: Spot 2.0 — a framework for LTL and ω-automata manipulation. In: Proceedings of the 14th International Symposium on Automated Technology for Verification and Analysis (ATVA'16). Lecture Notes in Computer Science, vol. 9938, pp. 122–129. Springer (Oct 2016)
8. Ellson, J., Gansner, E.R., Koutsofios, E., North, S.C., Woodhull, G.: Graphviz and dynagraph - static and dynamic graph drawing tools. In: Jünger, M., Mutzel, P. (eds.) Graph Drawing Software, pp. 127–148. Springer (2004)
9. Etessami, K., Wilke, T., Schuller, A.: Fair simulation relations, parity games, and state space reduction for Büchi automata. In: Orejas, F., Spirakis, P.G., van Leeuwen, J. (eds.) Automata, Languages and Programming: 28th International Colloquium. pp. 694–707. Springer, Crete, Greece (Jul 2001), lNCS 2076
10. Hahn, E.M., Li, G., Schewe, S., Turrini, A., Zhang, L.: Lazy probabilistic model checking without determinisation. In: Concurrency Theory, (CONCUR). pp. 354–367 (2015)

11. Hahn, E.M., Perez, M., Schewe, S., Somenzi, F., Trivedi, A., Wojtczak, D.: Omega-regular objectives in model-free reinforcement learning. In: Tools and Algorithms for the Construction and Analysis of Systems. pp. 395–412 (2019), LNCS 11427

12. Hahn, E.M., Perez, M., Schewe, S., Somenzi, F., Trivedi, A., Wojtczak, D.: Faithful and effective reward schemes for model-free reinforcement learning of omega-regular objectives. In: ATVA: Automated Technology for Verification and Analysis. pp. 108–124 (2020), LNCS 12302

13. Hahn, E.M., Perez, M., Schewe, S., Somenzi, F., Trivedi, A., Wojtczak, D.: Good-for-MDPs automata for probabilistic analysis and reinforcement learning. In: Tools and Algorithms for the Construction and Analysis of Systems. pp. 306–323 (2020), LNCS 12078

14. Hahn, E.M., Perez, M., Schewe, S., Somenzi, F., Trivedi, A., Wojtczak, D.: Model-free reinforcement learning for stochastic parity games. In: CONCUR: International Conference on Concurrency Theory. pp. 21:1–21:16 (Sep 2020), LIPIcs 171

15. Hahn, E.M., Schewe, S., Turrini, A., Zhang, L.: A simple algorithm for solving qualitative probabilistic parity games. In: Computer Aided Verification. pp. 291–311. Part II (2016), LNCS 9780

16. Hahn, E.M., Schewe, S., Turrini, A., Zhang, L.: Synthesising strategy improvement and recursive algorithms for solving 2.5 player parity games. In: Verification, Model Checking, and Abstract Interpretation. pp. 266–287 (2017)

17. Hahn, E., Li, Y., Schewe, S., Turrini, A., Zhang, L.: iscasMc: A web-based probabilistic model checker. In: International Symposium on Formal Methods. pp. 312–317 (May 2014)

18. Hahn, E.M., Perez, M., Schewe, S., Somenzi, F., Trivedi, A., Wojtczak, D.: Model-free reinforcement learning for branching markov decision processes. In: Silva, A., Leino, K.R.M. (eds.) Computer Aided Verification. pp. 651–673. Springer International Publishing, Cham (2021)

19. Hahn, E.M., Perez, M., Schewe, S., Somenzi, F., Trivedi, A., Wojtczak, D.: Model-free reinforcement learning for lexicographic omega-regular objectives. In: Formal Methods - 24th International Symposium. pp. 142–159. LNCS 13047 (2021)

20. van Hasselt, H.: Double Q-learning. In: Advances in Neural Information Processing Systems. pp. 2613–2621 (2010)

21. Henzinger, T.A., Piterman, N.: Solving games without determinization. In: 15th Conference on Computer Science Logic. pp. 394–409. Szeged, Hungary (Sep 2006), LNCS 4207

22. Irpan, A.: Deep reinforcement learning doesn't work yet. https://www.alexirpan.com/2018/02/14/rl-hard.html (2018)

23. Kazemi, M., Perez, M., Somenzi, F., Soudjani, S., Trivedi, A., Velasquez, A.: Translating omega-regular specifications to average objectives for model-free reinforcement learning. In: Proceedings of the 21st International Conference on Autonomous Agents and Multiagent Systems. pp. 732–741 (2022)

24. Křetínský, J., Meggendorfer, T., Sickert, S.: Owl: A library for ω-words, automata, and LTL. In: Automated Technology for Verification and Analysis, ATVA. pp. 543–550 (2018), LNCS 11138

25. Kwiatkowska, M., Norman, G., Parker, D.: PRISM 4.0: Verification of probabilistic real-time systems. In: Computer Aided Verification (CAV). pp. 585–591 (Jul 2011), LNCS 6806

26. Lavaei, A., Somenzi, F., Soudjani, S., Trivedi, A., Zamani, M.: Formal controller synthesis for continuous-space mdps via model-free reinforcement learning. In: 11th ACM/IEEE International Conference on Cyber-Physical Systems,

ICCPS 2020, Sydney, Australia, April 21-25, 2020. pp. 98–107. IEEE (2020). https://doi.org/10.1109/ICCPS48487.2020.00017,

27. Manna, Z., Pnueli, A.: The Temporal Logic of Reactive and Concurrent Systems *Specification*. Springer (1991)

28. McNaughton, R.: Testing and generating infinite sequences by a finite automaton. Inf. Control. **9**(5), 521–530 (1966)

29. Mnih, V., Kavukcuoglu, K., Silver, D., et al.: Human-level control through deep reinforcement learning. Nature **518** (2015)

30. Naik, A., Shariff, R., Yasui, N., Sutton, R.S.: Discounted reinforcement learning is not an optimization problem. CoRR **abs/1910.02140** (2019), http://arxiv.org/abs/1910.02140

31. OpenAI, Akkaya, I., Andrychowicz, M., Chociej, M., Litwin, M., McGrew, B., Petron, A., Paino, A., Plappert, M., Powell, G., Ribas, R., Schneider, J., Tezak, N., Tworek, J., Welinder, P., Weng, L., Yuan, Q., Zaremba, W., Zhang, L.: Solving rubik's cube with a robot hand. arXiv preprint (2019)

32. Perrin, D., Pin, J.É.: Infinite Words: Automata, Semigroups, Logic and Games. Elsevier (2004)

33. Pnueli, A.: The temporal semantics of concurrent programs. Theoret. Comput. Science **13**, 45–60 (1981)

34. Puterman, M.L.: Markov Decision Processes: Discrete Stochastic Dynamic Programming. John Wiley & Sons, Inc., New York, NY, USA (1994)

35. Sadigh, D., Kim, E., Coogan, S., Sastry, S.S., Seshia, S.A.: A learning based approach to control synthesis of Markov decision processes for linear temporal logic specifications. In: IEEE Conference on Decision and Control (CDC). pp. 1091–1096 (Dec 2014)

36. Schewe, S., Tang, Q., Zhanabekova, T.: Deciding what is good-for-mdps. CoRR **abs/2202.07629** (2022), https://arxiv.org/abs/2202.07629

37. Sickert, S., Esparza, J., Jaax, S., Křetínský, J.: Limit-deterministic Büchi automata for linear temporal logic. In: Computer Aided Verification (CAV). pp. 312–332 (2016), LNCS 9780

38. Silver, D., et al.: Mastering the game of Go with deep neural networks and tree search. Nature **529**, 484–489 (Jan 2016)

39. Simovec, P.: Transformation of nondeterministic büchi automata to slim automata (2021), https://is.muni.cz/th/nd15g/

40. Sutton, R.S.: Learning to predict by the method of temporal differences. Machine Learning **3**, 9–44 (1998)

41. Sutton, R.S., Barto, A.G.: Reinforcement Learning: An Introduction. MIT Press, second edn. (2018)

42. Wan, Y., Naik, A., Sutton, R.S.: Learning and planning in average-reward markov decision processes. In: International Conference on Machine Learning. pp. 10653–10662. PMLR (2021)

43. Watkins, C.J.C.H., Dayan, P.: Q-learning. In: Machine Learning. pp. 279–292 (1992)

44. Wiewiora, E.: Reward shaping. In: Encyclopedia of Machine Learning, pp. 863–865. Springer (2010)

45. Yang, C., Littman, M., Carbin, M.: Reinforcement learning for general ltl objectives is intractable. arXiv preprint arXiv:2111.12679 (2021)

Verification

A Formal CHERI-C Semantics for Verification

Seung Hoon Park(✉) , Rekha Pai , and Tom Melham

Department of Computer Science, University of Oxford, Oxford, UK
{seunghoon.park,rekha.pai,tom.melham}@cs.ox.ac.uk

Abstract. CHERI-C extends the C programming language by adding *hardware capabilities*, ensuring a certain degree of memory safety while remaining efficient. Capabilities can also be employed for higher-level security measures, such as software compartmentalization, that have to be used correctly to achieve the desired security guarantees. As the extension changes the semantics of C, new theories and tooling are required to reason about CHERI-C code and verify correctness. In this work, we present a formal memory model that provides a memory semantics for CHERI-C programs. We present a generalised theory with rich properties suitable for verification and potentially other types of analyses. Our theory is backed by an Isabelle/HOL formalisation that also generates an OCaml executable instance of the memory model. The verified and extracted code is then used to instantiate the parametric *Gillian* program analysis framework, with which we can perform concrete execution of CHERI-C programs. The tool can run a CHERI-C test suite, demonstrating the correctness of our tool, and catch a good class of safety violations that the CHERI hardware might miss.

Keywords: CHERI-C · Hardware Capabilities · Memory Model · Semantics · Theorem Proving · Verification

1 Introduction

Despite having been developed more than 40 years ago, C remains a widely used programming language owing to its efficiency, portability, and suitability for low-level systems code. The language's lack of inherent memory safety, however, has been the source of many serious issues [18]. While there have been significant efforts aimed at vulnerability mitigation, memory safety issues remain widespread, with a recent study stating that 70% of security vulnerabilities are caused by memory safety issues [31].

The Capability Hardware Enhanced RISC Instructions (CHERI) project offers an alternative model that provides better memory safety [44]. Its main features include a new machine representation of C pointers called *capabilities* and extensions to existing Instruction Set Architectures (ISA) that enable the secure manipulation of capabilities. Capabilities are in essence memory addresses bound to additional safety-related metadata, such as access permissions and bounds on the memory locations that can be accessed. As the hardware performs the safety checks on capabilities, legacy C programs compiled and run

© The Author(s) 2023
S. Sankaranarayanan and N. Sharygina (Eds.): TACAS 2023, LNCS 13993, pp. 549–568, 2023.
https://doi.org/10.1007/978-3-031-30823-9_28

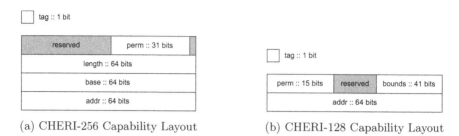

(a) CHERI-256 Capability Layout   (b) CHERI-128 Capability Layout

Fig. 1: Simplified CHERI Capability Layouts

on CHERI architecture, i.e. CHERI-C code, acquire hardware-ensured spatial memory safety, while retaining efficiency. Porting code from one language to another generally requires significant efforts. But porting C codes to CHERI-C requires little, if any, changes to the original code to ensure the code runs on CHERI hardware [36, 39].

In 2019, the UK announced its *Digital Security by Design* programme with £190 million of funding distributed over more than 26 research projects and 5 industrial demonstrators [6] to 'radically update the foundation of our insecure digital computing infrastructure, by demonstrating that mainstream processor technology ... can be updated to include new security technologies based on the CHERI Architecture' [5]. A cornerstone of the programme is Morello [4], a CHERI-enabled prototype developed by Arm.

Over the several years that lead to the realisation of Morello, there were several design revisions made to the hardware; examples are depicted in Fig. 1. The refined designs used methods for compression of bounds that reduced cache footprints and improved overall performance while minimising incompatibility. Morello uses a very similar design to the compressed scheme for capabilities depicted in Fig. 1b, with the overall bit-representation of the layout differing slightly. Future capability designs may possibly incorporate a different bit-representation design, provided there are improvements in performance or compatibility. Due to the ever-changing design of capability bit-representations, it seems best to have an *abstract* representation of capabilities, so that CHERI-based verification tools can remain modular.

Checking for memory safety issues of legacy C code can, of course, be achieved using existing analysis tools for C, but there are new problems that arise when such code is run on CHERI hardware. Because the pointer and memory representations are fundamentally different in a CHERI architecture, there are non-trivial differences in the semantics between C and CHERI-C.

To illustrate this point, consider the C code in Listing 1.1. This code segment performs memcpy twice: once from a to b, where pointers/capabilities are stored misaligned in b, then from b to c, where pointers/capabilities are stored correctly again in c. In standard C, there are no problems accessing the pointer stored in c. But in CHERI-C, misaligned capabilities in memory are invalidated. That means the address and meta-data of the misaligned capabilities are accessible, but such capabilities can no longer be dereferenced [41]. While c will contain the same capability value as that of a, the capability stored in c is invalidated. Thus, the last line will trigger an 'invalid tag' exception when the code is executed on ARM Morello and other CHERI-based machines.

```c
#include <stdlib.h>
#include <string.h>
void main(void) {
    int *n = calloc(sizeof(int), 1);
    int **a = malloc(sizeof(int *));
    *a = n;
    int **b = malloc(sizeof(int *) * 2);
    int **c = malloc(sizeof(int *));
    memcpy((char *) b + 1, a, sizeof(int *));
    memcpy(c, (char *) b + 1, sizeof(int *));
    int x = **c;
}
```

Listing 1.1: C code example

Of course, existing C analysis tools cannot catch these cases, as such tools are not only unaware of the changes in the semantics that capabilities bring, but also the code is not problematic in conventional C. Moreover, while CHERI ensures spatial safety by the hardware, CHERI is still incapable of catching temporal safety violations, such as Use After Free (UAF) violations. There exists work that attempt to address temporal safety [11, 17, 42], but they are either a software-implemented solution [42], where overall performance is inevitably affected, or ongoing work [11]. There is, therefore, a need for program analysis tools that correctly integrate the semantics of CHERI-C.

To the best of our knowledge, there is no prior work on formalising a CHERI-C memory model. The Cerberus C work [30] is primarily designed to capture pointer provenance of C programs and uses CHERI-C as a reference for pointer provenance, but the tool lacks a formal CHERI-C memory model. ESBMC is a verification tool that supports CHERI-C code [15]. But support for tagged memory does not yet exist; ESBMC would not be able to catch the 'invalid tag' exception in the code in Listing 1.1. Furthermore, ESBMC's memory model is not formally verified. Users of ESBMC must trust that the implementation of the memory model and its underlying theory are correct. SAIL formalisations for each CHERI architectures exist [3, 8, 9], but they only capture the low-level semantics of the architecture and not high-level C constructs such as allocation.

In this paper, we introduce a formal CHERI-C memory model that captures the memory semantics of the CHERI-C language. In Sect. 3, We formalise the memory and its operations and prove essential properties that provide correctness guarantees. We provide a rigorous logical formalisation of the CHERI-C memory model in Isabelle/HOL [32] (in Sect. 4.1) and use the code generation feature to generate a verified OCaml instance of the memory model [21]. We then show, in Sect. 4.2, the practical aspects of this work by providing the memory model to, and thereby instantiating, Gillian [20], a general, parametric verification framework that supports concrete and symbolic execution and verification based on separation logic, backed by rich correctness properties. In Sect. 5, we demonstrate that the tool can capture the semantics of CHERI-C programs correctly. A discussion on the existing works can be found in Sect. 6 while Sect. 7 concludes this paper mentioning possible future directions. We first start with an introduction to the CHERI architecture.

2   CHERI

CHERI extends a conventional ISA by introducing *capabilities* which are essentially pointers that come along with metadata to restrict memory access. The ISA now has additional hardware instructions and exceptions that operate over capabilities. Register sets are extended to include capability registers, instructions are added that reference the capability registers, and custom hardware exceptions are added to block operations that would violate memory safety. Designs of CHERI capabilities have refined over the past several years and have been incorporated in several existing architectures, such as MIPS and RISC-V [40]. All CHERI-extended ISAs have been formally defined using the SAIL specification language, in which the logic of machine instructions and memory layout have been defined formally in a first-order language [13].

Regardless of the layout, CHERI capabilities include three important types of high-level information, in addition to a 64-bit address:

- **Permissions.** Permissions state what kind of operations a capability can perform. Loading from memory and storing to memory are examples of permissions a capability may possess.
- **Bounds.** Bounds stipulate the memory region that the address part of a capability can reference. The lower bound stipulates the lowest address that a capability may access, and the upper bound stipulates the highest address.
- **Tag.** Stored separately from the other components of a capability, the tag states the validity of the capability it is attached to. Capabilities with invalid tags can hold data but cannot be dereferenced. Attempts to forge capabilities out of thin air result in a tag-invalidated capability.

Fig. 1a show a 256-bit representation of a capability, which was one of the earlier designs. The lower and upper bounds are represented using the base and length fields. Here, the lower bound is the address stated by the base field, and the upper bound is the address in the base field plus the length field. Permissions and other metadata are stored in the remaining fields as a bit vector. The capability's tag bit exists separately from the capability. Tag bits are, in practice, stored separately from the main memory where capabilities reside, so users cannot manipulate the tag bits of capabilities stored in memory. Furthermore, overwriting capabilities stored in memory with non-capability values invalidates their tag bits, which ensures capabilities cannot be forged out of thin air.

This representation, in theory, exercises a high level of compatibility with existing C code. But performance, particularly with regards to caching, is reduced due to the size of the capability representation [43]. Refined designs ultimately resulted in a capability that utilises a floating-point-based lossy compression technique on the bounds [43], such as the one depicted in Fig. 1b. In many cases, the upper bits of the address fields are most likely to overlap with those of the lower and upper bounds. Knowing this, bounds can be compressed by having the upper bits of their fields depend on that of the address, which means only the lower bits need to be stored.

The lossy compression of bounds may result in some incompatibility. Bounds may no longer be represented exactly, and changes in the address field may result in an unintentional change in the bounds. Nonetheless, such representations give an acceptable level of compatibility, provided aggressive pointer arithmetic optimisations are avoided. The Morello processor incorporates a similar compression-based design in its architecture, though sizes of each field differ [12].

The added capability-aware instructions operate over capabilities. Conventional load and store operations are extended to first check that the tag, permissions, and bounds of the capability are all valid. Violations result in triggering a capability-related hardware exception. There are additional operations to access or change the tag, permissions, and bounds. To ensure spatial memory safety, these operations can, at most, make the conditions for execution more restrictive; they cannot grant that which was not previously available. For instance, one cannot lower the lower bound of a capability to access a region that was inaccessible before, or grant a store permission that was unset beforehand. Because of how tags work for capabilities stored in memory, one cannot grant capabilities larger bounds or more permissions by manipulating the memory—attempting this results in tag invalidation.

Library support for CHERI has grown over the past few years. In particular, a software stack for CHERI-C that utilises a custom Clang compiler now exists [41]. Users can compile their program either in 'purecap' mode, where all pointers in programs are replaced with capabilities, or in 'hybrid' mode, where both pointers and capabilities co-exist within the program. Because operations that change the fields of a capability does not generally exist in standard C, Clang incorporates additional CHERI libraries of operations that users may use to access or mutate capabilities.

3   CHERI-C Memory Model

Incorporating hardware-enabled spatial safety requires significant changes to the C memory model. Pointer designs must be extended to incorporate bounds, metadata, and the out-of-band tag bit. The memory, i.e. heap, must also be able to distinguish the main memory and the tagged memory. Operations with respect to the heap must also be defined such that tag preservation and invalidation are incorporated appropriately.

In this section, we provide a generalised theory for the CHERI-C memory model. We identify the type and value system used by the memory model. We then define the heap and the core memory operations. Finally, we state some essential properties of the heap and the operations that (1) characterises the semantics and (2) states what types of verification or analyses could be supported. We make the assumption that we work on a 'purecap' environment, where all pointers have been replaced with capabilities.

3.1   Design

The CHERI-C memory model is inspired by that of CompCert [26]. The beauty of CompCert is that it is a verified C compiler. The internal components, which include the block-offset based memory model, are formalised in a theorem prover, with many of its essential properties verified. Using CompCert's memory model as a basis, we design the CHERI-C memory model by providing extensions to ensure the modelling of correct semantics and the capture of safety violations:

- **Capability Values.** In addition to the standard primitive types, we incorporate abstract capabilities as values. We also incorporate capability fragments to provide semantics to higher-level memory actions like memcpy, which should preserve tags if copied correctly and invalidate otherwise [41].
- **Extended Operations.** Basic memory actions such as load and store now work on capabilities and will trigger the correct capability-related exception when required.
- **Tagged Memory.** Tags in memory are stored separately from the main heap, as could be seen by the formal CHERI-MIPS SAIL model [9]. So we provide a separate mapping for tagged memory for storing capability tags.
- **Freed Regions.** The standard CompCert memory model can mark which memory regions are valid but lacks the ability to distinguish which regions are marked as 'Freed'. We incorporate freed regions as a means to catch temporal safety violations.

3.2   Type and Value System

Figure 2 shows the formalisation of CHERI-C types and values. Types τ are analogous to chunks in CompCert terms. Types comprise primitive types (e.g. $U8_\tau$,

$$
\begin{aligned}
\tau &\triangleq U8_\tau \mid S8_\tau \mid ... \mid U64_\tau \mid S64_\tau \mid Cap_\tau \\
MCap &\triangleq \mathcal{B} \times \mathbb{Z} \times md \\
Cap &\triangleq MCap \times \mathbb{B} \\
\mathcal{V_C} &\triangleq U8_\mathcal{V} :: 8\ bits \mid ... \\
&\quad \mid S64_\mathcal{V} :: 64\ sbits \\
&\quad \mid Cap_\mathcal{V} :: Cap \\
&\quad \mid CapF_\mathcal{V} :: Cap \times \mathbb{N} \\
&\quad \mid Undef \\
\mathcal{V_M} &\triangleq Byte :: 8\ bits \\
&\quad \mid MCapF :: MCap \times \mathbb{N}
\end{aligned}
$$

Fig. 2: CHERI-C Types and Values

S64$_\tau$, etc.) and a capability type Cap_τ. We define a function $|\cdot| : \tau \to \mathbb{N}$ that returns, in terms of bytes, the size of the type. For Cap_τ, the value is not fixed but requires that it must be divisible by 16. This requirement allows capabilities with 128- and 256-bit representations to have a valid size.

$MCap$ represents a *memory capability* value and is represented as a tuple (b, i, m), which comprises the block identifier $b \in \mathcal{B}$, offset $i \in \mathbb{Z}$, and metadata $m \in md$, where md represents the bounds and permissions. Here, $\mathcal{B}$ must be a countable set. Offsets are represented as integers, as CHERI allows out-of-bounds addresses, where the address may be lower than the lower bound. Because capabilities stored in memory have their tag bit stored elsewhere, we make the distinction between memory capabilities and *tagged capabilities*, Cap, which is a capability $((b, i, m), t)$ that contains the tag bit $t \in \mathbb{B}$.

Unlike those of CompCert, CHERI-C values $\mathcal{V}_C$ are given type distinctions to ensure: (1) types can be inferred directly, and (2) they contain the correct values at all times. From a practical standpoint, this ensures that the proof of correctness of memory operations can be simplified, and bounded arithmetic operations can be implemented correctly. Capability values $Cap_\mathcal{V}$ and capability fragment values $CapF_\mathcal{V}$ also exist as values. Provided some capability value $C \in Cap_\mathcal{V}$, capability fragment values $C_n \in CapF_\mathcal{V}$ correspond to the n-th byte of the capability C. For both cases, instead of fixing their representation concretely, we represent them abstractly using a tuple. This representation ensures that conversion to a compressed representation could be achieved when needed while avoiding the need to fix to one particular bit representation. Furthermore, this approach provides a reasonable way to correctly define memcpy, where capability tags must be preserved if possible. While capability fragments are extended structures of capabilities, operations that can be performed on capability fragments are limited. Finally, we have $Undef$, which represents invalid values. These values may appear when, for example, the user calls malloc and immediately tries to load the undefined contents. The idea behind incorporating capability fragments values is heavily inspired by the work from [25].

Because values are given a type distinction, identifying the types of values is straightforward. For capability fragments, we have two choices: they may either be a $U8_\tau$ or $S8_\tau$ type. Capability fragments are essentially bytes, so operations over capability fragments can be treated as if they were a $U8_\tau$ or $S8_\tau$ type. Since $Undef$ does not correspond to a valid value, it is not assigned a type.

$$
\begin{aligned}
\text{CapErr} &\triangleq \text{TagViolation} \mid \text{PermitLoadViolation} \mid \ldots \\
\text{LogicErr} &\triangleq \text{UseAfterFree} \mid \text{MissingResource} \mid \ldots \\
\text{Err} &\triangleq \text{CapErr} \mid \text{LogicErr} \\
\mathcal{R}\, \rho &\triangleq \mathcal{S}ucc\, \rho \\
&\mid \mathcal{F}ail\, \text{Err}
\end{aligned}
$$

Fig. 3: CHERI-C Errors

Memory operations, such as load and store, are defined so that, upon failure, the operation returns the type of error that lead to the failure. In general, partial functions, or function using the option type, can model function failure but cannot state what caused the failure. As such, the operations use the return type $\mathcal{R}\ \rho$, where ρ is a generic return type. For CHERI-C, we make the distinction between errors caused by capabilities, denoted by CapErr, and errors caused by the language, denoted by LogicErr. Figure 3 depicts the formalised Errors system used by the memory model.

3.3   Memory

We now formalise the memory. We use CompCert's approach of using a union type $\mathcal{V}_{\mathcal{M}}$ that can represent either a byte or a byte fragment of a memory capability. Then it is possible to create a memory mapping $\mathbb{N} \rightharpoonup \mathcal{V}_{\mathcal{M}}$.[1] We also create a separate mapping of type $\mathbb{N} \rightharpoonup \mathbb{B}$ for tagged memory. When the user attempts to store a capability, it will be converted into a memory capability and then stored in the memory mapping. Separately, the tag bit will be stored in the tagged memory. When the tag bit is stored, adjustments are made to ensure tags are only stored in capability-size-aligned offsets.

To ensure we can catch temporal safety violations, we need to be able to make distinctions between blocks that are freed and blocks that are valid. One way to encode this is as follows: a block b may point to either a freed location (i.e. $b \mapsto \varnothing$), or point to the pair of maps we defined earlier. The idea is that if a block identifier points to a freed block, attempts to load such a block will trigger a 'Use After Free' violation and would otherwise point to a valid mapping pair. Ultimately, the heap has the following form:

$$\mathcal{H} : \mathcal{B} \rightharpoonup ((\mathbb{N} \rightharpoonup \mathcal{V}_{\mathcal{M}}) \times (\mathbb{N} \rightharpoonup \mathbb{B}))_{\varnothing}$$

3.4   Operations

We define the core memory operations, or *actions*, of the memory model. We use the same result type $\mathcal{R}$ given in Fig. 3 instead of using a partial function to give the type of error, should the operation fail.

The memory actions $A_C = \{\text{alloc}, \text{free}, \text{load}, \text{store}\}$ are given below with their respective signatures:

- alloc : $\mathcal{H} \rightarrow \mathbb{N} \rightarrow \mathcal{R}\ (\mathcal{H} \times Cap)$
- free : $\mathcal{H} \rightarrow Cap \rightarrow \mathcal{R}\ (\mathcal{H} \times Cap)$
- load : $\mathcal{H} \rightarrow Cap \rightarrow \tau \rightarrow \mathcal{R}\ (\mathcal{V}_C)$
- store : $\mathcal{H} \rightarrow Cap \rightarrow \mathcal{V}_C \rightarrow \mathcal{R}\ (\mathcal{H})$

---

[1] The notation $\rightharpoonup$ denotes a partial map. Offsets in heaps are $\mathbb{N}$, whereas offsets stored in capabilities are $\mathbb{Z}$. Operations check whether the offsets are in bounds, which requires offsets to be non-negative. This means valid offset values can be converted from $\mathbb{Z}$ to $\mathbb{N}$ without issues.

The function $\texttt{alloc}\ \mu\ n = \mathcal{S}ucc\ (\mu', c)$ takes a heap μ and size n input and produces a fresh capability c and the updated heap μ' as output. The bounds of c are determined by n. In the case of compressed capabilities, a sufficiently large n *may* result in the upper bound being larger than what was requested. The capability c is also given the appropriate permissions and a valid tag bit. Like that of CompCert, $\texttt{alloc}$ is designed to never fail, provided that the countable set $\mathcal{B}$ has infinite elements.

The function $\texttt{free}\ \mu\ c = \mathcal{S}ucc\ (\mu', c')$ takes a heap μ and capability $c = ((b, i, m), t)$ as input. Upon success, the operation will return the updated heap, where we now have $b \mapsto \varnothing$. The capability c' is also updated such that the tag bit of c is invalidated. This conforms to the CHERI-C design stated in [41]. We note that c should also be a valid capability, that is—at the very least—the tag bit should be set, and the offset should be within the capability bounds. The function $\texttt{free}$ may fail if the block is invalid or already freed, even if the capability itself was valid. In such case, $\texttt{free}$ returns a logical error.

The function $\texttt{load}\ \mu\ c\ t\ = \mathcal{S}ucc\ v$ takes a heap μ, capability c and type t as input, where t is the type the user wants to load. Upon success, the operation will return the value v from the memory, where v has the corresponding type t.[2] Before $\texttt{load}$ attempts to access the block provided by c, it first checks that c has sufficient permissions to load. We use the CHERI-MIPS SAIL implementation of the CL[C] instruction [40] for the capability checks, implementing the extra checks provided that $t = Cap_\tau$. Once the capability checks are done, the operation attempts to access the blocks and the mappings, failing and returning the appropriate logical error if they do not exist.

When accessing both the main memory and tagged memory, there are a number of cases to consider. When loading primitive values, it is important that the region about to be loaded is all of *Byte* and not of *MCapF* type. Thus, before loading the values, we check whether the contiguous region in memory are all of *Byte* type. If this is not the case, $\texttt{load}$ will return *Undef*. For capability fragments, the cell in memory has to be an *MCapF*. Finally for capabilities, not only do the contiguous cells have to be of *MCapF* type, but (1) they must have the same memory capability value, and (2) the fragment values must all be a sequence forming $\{0, 1, ..., |Cap_\tau| - 1\}$. The idea is that even if the contiguous cells have the same memory capability values, they do not form a valid capability if the fragments are not stored in order. After all the checks, the tagged memory will be accessed, where the tag value is retrieved.[3] The loaded memory capability and tag bit are then combined to form a tagged capability, which $\texttt{load}$ returns.

The function $\texttt{store}\ \mu\ c\ v\ = \mathcal{S}ucc\ \mu'$ takes a heap μ, capability c, and value v. Upon success, the operations will return the updated heap μ'. Like $\texttt{load}$, $\texttt{store}$ performs the necessary capability checks based on CHERI-MIPS' CS[C] instruction and attempts to access the blocks and mappings afterwards, returning the appropriate exception upon failure. For storing primitive values and capability

---

[2] For capability fragments, the corresponding type may be either $U8_\tau$ or $S8_\tau$.

[3] The tagged memory does not need to be accessed if c does not have a capability load permission. In such case, the loaded capability will have an invalidated tag.

fragment values, the main memory mapping will simply be updated to contain the values, and the associated tagged memories will be invalidated. For primitive values that are not bytes, the values will be converted into a sequence of bytes, where each byte in the list will be stored contiguously in memory. For a capability fragment value, it will be stored in the cell as an $MCapF$ type, where the tag value of the fragment will be stripped when storing in memory. Finally, for capability values, the value will be split into a list comprising $|Cap_\tau| - 1$ memory capability fragments, with the fragment value forming a sequence $\{0, 1, .. |Cap_\tau| - 1\}$, and a tag bit. The main memory will store the list of memory fragments contiguously, and the tagged memory will store the tag value in the corresponding capability-aligned tagged memory.

3.5   Properties

In the previous section, we have articulated a formal CHERI-C memory model, explaining how the heap is structured and how the operations are defined. It is essential that the formalisation we provided is correct and is also suitable for verification or other types of analyses. In this section, we first discuss the properties of the memory. We then discuss the properties of the operations themselves, primarily concerned with correctness.

When we observe the memory, it is important that we always work with a valid one, i.e. the memory is *well-formed*. In our formalisation, we require that all tags in the tagged memory are stored in a capability-aligned location. The well-formedness relation $\mathcal{W}_f^{\mathcal{C}}$ is defined as follows:

$$\mathcal{W}_f^{\mathcal{C}}(\mu) \equiv \forall b \in dom(\mu).\ b \mapsto (c, t) \longrightarrow \forall x \in dom(t).\ x \bmod |Cap_\tau| = 0$$

The well-formedness property must hold when the heap is initialised and when memory operations mutate the heap. That is, provided μ_0 is the initialised heap where all mappings are empty, $\alpha \in \mathcal{A}_{\mathcal{C}}$ is a memory action, v are the arguments of the memory operation α and μ' is one of the return values denoting the updated heap, we have the following properties:

$$\mathcal{W}_f^{\mathcal{C}}(\mu_0)$$

$$\mathcal{W}_f^{\mathcal{C}}(\mu) \Longrightarrow \alpha\ \mu\ v = \mathcal{S}ucc\ \mu' \Longrightarrow \mathcal{W}_f^{\mathcal{C}}(\mu')$$

The two properties above ensure that the heap is well-formed throughout the execution of the CHERI-C program.

For the correctness of the operations, we primarily consider soundness and completeness:

- If the inputs are valid for operation $\alpha \in \mathcal{A}_{\mathcal{C}}$ then the action should succeed.
- If the action α succeeds, the inputs provided to the operations are valid.
- If the inputs are invalid for the operation α, then the action should fail and return the correct error.

The first and second points are simple soundness and completeness properties. The third point is important in that the input may be problematic in many ways. For example, the NULL capability has an invalid tag bit, invalid bounds, and no permissions. The function load will fail if provided with the NULL capability, as it violates many of the checks. Because the SAIL specification states that tags are always checked first, the error must be a TagViolation type.

Next, we need to ensure successive operations yield the desired result. The primary properties to consider are the *good variable* laws [26]; examples of properties encoding this law include *load after allocation*, *load after free*, and *load after store*. It is worth mentioning there are some caveats. For example, the *load after store* case no longer guarantees that you will retrieve the same value you stored, unlike CompCert's load after store property in [26], since the value that was stored and to be loaded again could have been either a capability or capability fragment. In such cases, the tag bit may become invalidated due to insufficient permissions on the capability, or because storing capability fragments resulted in the tagged memory being cleared. The solution is to divide the general property into a primitive value case and a capability-related value case. Ultimately, the idea is to prove that the loaded value is *correct* rather than exact, i.e. capability-related values when loaded with have the correct tag value.

Finally, we have properties suitable for verification. We note that the memory $\mathcal{H}$ can be instantiated as a separation algebra by providing the partial commutative monoid (PCM) $(\mathcal{H}, \uplus, \mu_0)$, where $\uplus$ is the disjoint union of two heaps and μ_0 is the empty initialised heap. For tools that rely on using partial memories, it is also imperative to show that the well-formedness property is compatible with memory composition:

$$\mathcal{W}_f^{\mathcal{C}}(\mu_1 \uplus \mu_2) \implies \mathcal{W}_f^{\mathcal{C}}(\mu_1) \wedge \mathcal{W}_f^{\mathcal{C}}(\mu_2)$$

We also note that the current heap design keeps track of *negative* resources [28], which may potentially be useful for incorrectness logic based verification [33].

4 Application

The overall memory model provided in Sect. 3 has been designed to be applicable for verification tools. In this section, we explain how we use the theory provided above to create a verified, executable instance of the memory model. We then explain how this executable model can be used to instantiate a tool called Gillian [20]. Using the instantiated tool, we demonstrate the concrete execution of CHERI-C programs with the desired behaviour.

4.1 Isabelle/HOL

Isabelle/HOL is an interactive theorem prover based on classical Higher Order Logic (HOL) [32]. We use Isabelle/HOL to formalise the entirety of the CHERI-C memory model discussed in Sect. 3. Types, values, heap structure, etc. were implemented, memory operations were defined, and properties relating to the heap and the operations were proven. Memory capabilities, tagged capabilities, and capability fragments were represented using records, a form of tuple with named fields. For code generation, we instantiated the block type $\mathcal{B}$ to be $\mathbb{Z}$. For showing that $\mathcal{H}$ is an instance of a separation algebra, we use the cancellative_sep_algebra class [23] and prove that the heap model is an instance. This proof ultimately shows that $\mathcal{H}$ forms a PCM. Proving that well-formedness is compatible with memory composition is stated slightly differently. The cancellative_sep_algebra class takes in a total operator $\cdot_t$ instead of a partial one and requires a 'separation disjunction' binary operator #, which states disjointedness. Ultimately, the compatibility property can be given as:

$$\mu_1 \mathbin{\#} \mu_2 \implies \mathcal{W}_f^{\mathcal{C}}(\mu_1 \cdot_t \mu_2) \implies \mathcal{W}_f^{\mathcal{C}}(\mu_1) \wedge \mathcal{W}_f^{\mathcal{C}}(\mu_2)$$

For partial mappings of the form $A \rightharpoonup B$, we use Isabelle/HOL's finite mapping type ('a,'b) mapping [22]. To ensure we obtain an OCaml executable instance of the memory model, we use the Containers framework [27], which generates a Red-Black Tree mapping provided the abstract mapping in Isabelle/HOL. All definitions in Isabelle were either defined to be code-generatable to begin with (i.e. definitions should not comprise quantifiers or non-constructive constants like the Hilbert choice operation $SOME$), or code equations were provided and proven to ensure a sound code generation [21]. For bounded machine words, which is required for formalising the primitive values, we use Isabelle/HOL's word type 'a word, where 'a states the length of the word [14]. Types like 'a word, nat, int and string were also transformed to use OCaml's Zarith and native string library for efficiency [21].

4.2 Gillian

Gillian is a high-level analysis framework, theoretically capable of analysing a wide range of languages. The framework allows concrete and symbolic execution, verification based on Separation Logic, and bi-abduction [28]. The crux of the framework lies in its parametricity, where the tool can be instantiated by simply providing a compiler front end and OCaml-based memory models of the language. So far, CompCert C and JavaScript have both been instantiated for Gillian, giving birth to Gillian-C and Gillian-JS.

The underlying theoretical foundation of Gillian has its essential correctness properties like soundness and completeness already proven [20, 29]. Thus, users who instantiate the tool only need to prove the correctness of the implementation of their compiler and memory models to ensure the correctness of the entire tool. From the perspective of someone trying to instantiate Gillian with their compiler and memory models, it is essential to understand the underlying intermediate language GIL and the overall memory model interface used by Gillian.

GIL GIL is the GOTO-based Intermediate Language used by Gillian which is used for all types of analyses the tool supports. For concrete execution, GIL supports basic GOTO constructs and assertions. For symbolic execution, the GIL grammar is extended to support path cutting, i.e. assumptions, and generation of symbolic variables. For separation logic based verification, the GIL grammar is further extended to support core predicates and user-defined predicates [28] that can be utilised to form separation logic based assertions. Furthermore, function specifications in the Hoare-triple form $\{P\}f(\bar{x})\{Q\}$ can be provided, where P and Q are separation logic based assertions.

Note that Gillian uses a value set $\mathcal{V}$ which differs from that used in the CHERI-C memory model. As we are only interested in the values used in the CHERI-C memory model, it is possible to implement a thin conversion layer between the two value systems. We note that a list of GIL values also constitutes a GIL value, so arguments for functions can be expressed as a single GIL value. This is important when understanding the memory model layout of Gillian.

Memory Model Memory Models in Gillian have a specific definition and have properties that state what kind of analysis is supported. Proving that the provided memory models satisfy certain properties is essential in understanding what the instantiated tool supports.

Gillian differentiates between concrete and symbolic memory models, which are used for concrete and symbolic execution, respectively. As we are concerned with concrete execution, we will consider only concrete memory models here.

At the highest level, there are two kinds of memory model properties: *executional* and *compositional*. The *executional* memory model states properties a memory model must have for whole-program execution, and the *compositional* memory model states properties a memory model must have for separation logic based symbolic verification. Each paper in the Gillian literature states slightly different definitions for the memory models [20, 28, 29, 37]—in Definitions 1 and 2 below, we present unified, consistent definitions for each of the memory model properties. We ignore contexts, as there exists only one context in concrete memories, which is the GIL boolean value true.

Definition 1. *(Execution Memory Model). Given the set of GIL values $\mathcal{V}$ and an action set A, an execution memory model $M(\mathcal{V}, A) \triangleq (|M|, \mathcal{W}_f, \underline{ea})$ comprises:*

1. *a set of memories $|M| \ni \mu$*
2. *a well-formedness relation $\mathcal{W}_f \subseteq |M|$, with $\mathcal{W}_f(\mu)$ denoting μ is well-formed*
3. *the action execution function $\underline{ea} : A \to |M| \to \mathcal{V} \to \mathcal{R}\ (|M| \times \mathcal{V})$*

Definition 2. *(Compositional Memory Model). Given the set of GIL values V and core predicate set Γ, a compositional memory model, $M(V, A_\Gamma) \triangleq (|M|, \mathcal{W}_f, \underline{ea}_\Gamma)$ comprises:*

1. *a partial commutative monoid (PCM) $(|M|, \cdot, 0)$*
2. *A well-formedness relation $\mathcal{W}_f \subseteq |M|$ with the following property:*

$$\mathcal{W}_f(\mu_1 \cdot \mu_2) \implies \mathcal{W}_f(\mu_1) \wedge \mathcal{W}_f(\mu_2)$$

3. *the predicate action execution function* $\underline{ea}_\Gamma : A_\Gamma \to |M| \to V \to \mathcal{R}\,(|M| \times V)$

First, we note that for concrete execution, Gillian also uses the return type $\mathcal{R}$ in the action execution function $\underline{ea}$.[4] For $\mathcal{W}_f$ defined in Definition 1, the main properties that must be satisfied are Properties 3.1, 3.2, and 3.6 in [29].

The PCM requirement is required to show that the heap forms a separation algebra [16]. $\mathcal{W}_f$ is extended to state that memory composition must also be well-formed. Finally, the predicate action execution function $\underline{ea}_\Gamma$ provides a way to frame on and off parts of the memory, though they are not required for concrete execution as they are not part of the GIL concrete execution grammar.

Using the CHERI-C memory model we defined earlier, we can show that our model conforms to both Definitions 1 and 2. Let A_C be the set of memory actions, $\mathcal{H}$ be the memory, $\underline{ea}_C$ be the action execution function of the CHERI-C memory model, and $\mathcal{W}_f^C$ be the well-formedness relation. Then we observe that $(\mathcal{H}, \mathcal{W}_f^C, \underline{ea}_C)$ forms an execution memory model. We note that Properties 3.1 and 3.2 in [29] are satisfied, and Property 3.6 is trivial in that operations that return errors do not return an updated heap. We also note that the memory model also conforms to a compositional memory model, as we have the PCM $(\mathcal{H}, \uplus, \mu_0)$ along with the well-formedness property being composition-compatible. The predicate action execution function is not required to be given, as the concrete execution of Gillian does not utilise this feature.

4.3 Compiler

We implemented a CHERI-C to GIL compiler by utilising ESBMC's GOTO language. The idea is that ESBMC uses its own intermediate representation for bounded model checking, which is the GOTO language. CHERI-enabled ESBMC uses Clang as a front end to generate the GOTO language. In our case we can build a GOTO to GIL compiler instead of building a CHERI-C compiler from scratch. The GOTO language is very similar to GIL in that they are both goto-based languages and uses single static assignment. For most parts, the compilation process is straightforward. As ESBMC's GOTO language is typed while the CHERI-C memory model is untyped—untyped in the sense that the memory model does not support user-defined types like `structs`—we make sure that capability arithmetic and casts are applied correctly by inferring the sizes of the user-defined types.

5 Experimental Results

In Sect. 4, we have provided a way to instantiate the Gillian tool, where we obtain a concrete CHERI-C model using Isabelle/HOL and a CHERI-C to GIL

---

[4] In the Gillian literature, it is stated that $\mathcal{R}$ can return both a return value and an error. The OCaml implementation of Gillian slightly differs from this and is more similar to $\mathcal{R}$ used for the CHERI-C memory model.

compiler that utilises ESBMC's GOTO language. Our framework can demonstrate that higher-level memory actions—such as memcpy(), which preserves tags when applicable—can be implemented. Furthermore, we can run concrete instances of programs that use memcpy() to show they emit the expected behaviour. This also means the tool can catch the TagViolation exception that is triggered in Listing 1.1. Our tool also allows capability-related functions defined in cheriintrin.h and cheri.h, to be usable, i.e. it is possible to call operations such as cheri_tag_get() and cheri_tag_clear().

Filename	GC	GCC	AM	BMC
buffer_overflow.c	✓	✓	✓	✓
dangling_ptr.c	✓	✓	✗	✓
double_free.c	✓	✓	✗	✓
invalid_free.c	✗[5]	✓	✓	✓
misaligned_ptr.c	✓	✓	✓	✗
listing_1.c	✗	✓	✓	✗

Table 1: Violation detection

Filename	Time(s)
libc_malloc.c	**8.585**
libc_memcpy.c	1.698
libc_memmove.c	0.318
libc_string.c	0.315

Table 2: GCC runtime performance

Table 1 shows a list of safety violations that Gillian-C, our tool, the ARM Morello hardware, and CHERI-ESBMC—labelled as GC, GCC, AM, and BMC, respectively—all catch. We observe that Morello fails to catch temporal safety violations such as dangling pointers and double frees. For the invalid free case, where we attempt to free a pointer not produced by malloc, we discovered a bug in the Gillian-C tool that fails to catch this violation.[5] Gillian-C does not return any errors for the program in Listing 1.1, which is to be expected, as this is not problematic for conventional C. Finally, we observe that CHERI-ESBMC fails to catch the last two violations that relating to tag invalidation.

Table 2 shows the runtime performance of running the CHERI-C library test suites, based on the Clang CHERI-C test suite [1]. Tests were conducted on a machine running Fedora 34 on an 11th Gen Intel Core i7-1185G7 CPU with 31.1 GB RAM, with trace logging enabled. We note that when the test cases were executed on Morello without any modifications to the code, all of the tests terminated instantaneously without any issues. In the libc_malloc.c test case, we reduced the scope of the test[6] to ensure the tool terminates within a reasonable time, though the performance can be drastically improved by turning logging off, e.g. the libc_malloc.c case would only take 0.686 seconds. For the remaining tests, we made modifications to the code to ensure the compiler can correctly produce the GIL code, and we made sure to preserve all the edge cases covered by the original tests. For example, in libc_memcpy.c we made sure to test all cases where both src and dst capabilities were aligned and misaligned in the beginning and the end, which affected tag preservation. We observed that no assertions were violated, and we also observed that the same

---

[5]The bug has since been fixed after a discussion with the developers [7].

[6]In particular, we reduced max from the libc_malloc.c case in [1] from 20 to 9.

code when run in Morello also resulted in no assertion violations, demonstrating a faithful implementation of CHERI-C semantics.

6 Related Work

The CompCert C memory model [26], CH₂O memory model [24], and Tuch's C memory model [38] are C memory models formalised in a theorem prover, each focusing on different aspects of verification. Our model mostly draws inspiration from these models, extending such work to support CHERI-C programs.

VCC, which internally uses the typed C memory model [19], and CHERI-ESBMC [15] are designed with automated verification of C programs via symbolic execution in mind—in particular, CHERI-ESBMC supports hybrid settings and compressed capabilities in addition to purecap settings and uncompressed capabilities. Both tools rely on a memory model that is not formally verified, so the tools have components that must be trusted.

7 Conclusion and Future Work

We have provided a formal CHERI-C memory model and demonstrated its utility for verification. We formalised the entire theory in Isabelle/HOL and generated an executable instance of the memory model, which was then used to instantiate a CHERI-C tool. The result lead to a concrete execution tool that is robust in terms of the properties that are guaranteed both by the tool and by the memory model. We demonstrated its practicality by running CHERI-C based test suites, capturing memory safety violations, and comparing the results with actual CHERI hardware—namely the physical Morello processor.

Currently there are a number of limitations provided by the memory model. Capability arithmetic is limited only to addition and subtraction, but the heap can be extended to incorporate mappings from blocks to physical addresses and vice versa. This provides a way to extend capability arithmetic. While the theory incorporates abstract capabilities, compression is still under work. We believe, however, that the abstract design itself does not need to change. It may be possible to utilise the compression/decompression work to convert between the two forms [2] when needed whilst retaining our design for the operations.

This theory serves as a starting point for much potential future work. A compositional symbolic memory model can be built from this design to enable symbolic execution and verification in Gillian. As we have already proven the core properties, proving the remaining properties for the extended model will allow automated separation logic based verification of CHERI-C programs.

Acknowledgements We are very grateful to the Gillian team, in particular, Sacha-Élie Ayoun, for providing assistance with instantiating the Gillian tool. We also thank Fedor Shmarov and Franz Brauße for providing assistance with building and modifying the ESBMC tool. This work was funded by the UKRI programme on Digital Security by Design (Ref. EP/V000225/1, SCorCH [10]).

Data-Availability Statement The Isabelle/HOL formalisation of the CHERI-C memory model described in Sect. 4.1 is available in the Isabelle Archive of Formal Proofs [34]. The artefact of the evaluation provided in Sect. 5, which includes Gillian-CHERI-C itself, CHERI-ESBMC, and other tools, is archived in the Zenodo open-access repository [35].

References

1. CHERI C Tests. https://github.com/CTSRD-CHERI/cheri-c-tests
2. cheri-compressed-cap.   https://github.com/CTSRD-CHERI/cheri-compressed-cap
3. CHERI RISC-V Sail model. https://github.com/CTSRD-CHERI/sail-cheri-riscv
4. CHERI: The Arm Morello Board, https://www.cl.cam.ac.uk/research/security/ctsrd/cheri/cheri-morello.html
5. CHERI: The Digital Security by Design (DSbD) Initiative, https://www.cl.cam.ac.uk/research/security/ctsrd/cheri/dsbd.html
6. Digital Security by Design Challenge – UKRI, https://www.ukri.org/our-work/our-main-funds/industrial-strategy-challenge-fund/artificial-intelligence-and-data-economy/digital-security-by-design-challenge/
7. fix the behaviour of free, https://github.com/GillianPlatform/Gillian/commit/6fa87b046f8d8f328c20b89cbdff1a00944da3fe,   GillianPlatform/Gillian@ 6fa87b0
8. Morello Sail specification. https://github.com/CTSRD-CHERI/sail-morello
9. Sail model of CHERI-MIPS ISA. https://github.com/CTSRD-CHERI/sail-cheri-mips
10. SCorCH: Secure Code for Capability Hardware, https://scorch-project.github.io
11. Armv8.5-A Memory Tagging Extension. Tech. rep. (Jun 2021), https://documentation-service.arm.com/static/624ea580caabfd7b3c13e23f?token=
12. ARM Ltd.: Arm Architecture Reference Manual Supplement Morello for A-Profile Architecture (2022), https://documentation-service.arm.com/static/61e577e1b691546d37bd38a0?token=
13. Armstrong, A., Bauereiss, T., Campbell, B., Reid, A., Gray, K.E., Norton, R.M., Mundkur, P., Wassell, M., French, J., Pulte, C., Flur, S., Stark, I., Krishnaswami, N., Sewell, P.: ISA Semantics for ARMv8-a, RISC-v, and CHERI-MIPS. Proc. ACM Program. Lang. 3(POPL) (Jan 2019)
14. Beeren, J., Fernandez, M., Gao, X., Klein, G., Kolanski, R., Lim, J., Lewis, C., Matichuk, D., Sewell, T.: Finite Machine Word Library. Archive of Formal Proofs (Jun 2016), https://isa-afp.org/entries/Word_Lib.html, Formal proof development
15. Brauße, F., Shmarov, F., Menezes, R., Gadelha, M.R., Korovin, K., Reger, G., Cordeiro, L.C.: ESBMC-CHERI: Towards Verification of C Programs for CHERI Platforms with ESBMC. In: Proceedings of the 31st ACM SIGSOFT International Symposium on Software Testing and Analysis. p. 773–776. ISSTA 2022, Association for Computing Machinery, New York, NY, USA (2022)

16. Calcagno, C., O'Hearn, P.W., Yang, H.: Local Action and Abstract Separation Logic. In: 22nd Annual IEEE Symposium on Logic in Computer Science (LICS 2007). pp. 366–378 (2007)
17. Chisnall, D.: Towards a Safe, High-Performance Heap Allocator (Sep 2022), https://soft-dev.org/events/cheritech22/slides/Chisnall.pdf, presented at CHERI Technical Workshop 2022
18. Chisnall, D., Rothwell, C., Watson, R.N., Woodruff, J., Vadera, M., Moore, S.W., Roe, M., Davis, B., Neumann, P.G.: Beyond the PDP-11: Architectural Support for a Memory-Safe C Abstract Machine. SIGPLAN Not. **50**(4), 117–130 (Mar 2015)
19. Cohen, E., Moskal, M., Tobies, S., Schulte, W.: A Precise Yet Efficient Memory Model For C. Electronic Notes in Theoretical Computer Science **254**, 85–103 (2009). https://doi.org/https://doi.org/10.1016/j.entcs.2009.09.061, proceedings of the 4th International Workshop on Systems Software Verification (SSV 2009)
20. Fragoso Santos, J., Maksimović, P., Ayoun, S.E., Gardner, P.: Gillian, Part i: A Multi-Language Platform for Symbolic Execution. In: Proceedings of the 41st ACM SIGPLAN Conference on Programming Language Design and Implementation. p. 927–942. PLDI 2020, Association for Computing Machinery, New York, NY, USA (2020)
21. Haftmann, F.: Code generation from Isabelle/HOL theories (Dec 2021), https://isabelle.in.tum.de/doc/codegen.pdf
22. Haftmann, F., Krauss, A., Kunčar, O., Nipkow, T.: Data Refinement in Isabelle/HOL. In: Blazy, S., Paulin-Mohring, C., Pichardie, D. (eds.) Interactive Theorem Proving. pp. 100–115. Springer Berlin Heidelberg, Berlin, Heidelberg (2013). https://doi.org/10.1007/978-3-642-39634-2_10
23. Klein, G., Kolanski, R., Boyton, A.: Mechanised Separation Algebra. In: Beringer, L., Felty, A. (eds.) Interactive Theorem Proving. pp. 332–337. Springer Berlin Heidelberg, Berlin, Heidelberg (2012). https://doi.org/10.1007/978-3-642-32347-8_22
24. Krebbers, R.: A Formal C Memory Model for Separation Logic. Journal of Automated Reasoning **57**(4), 319–387 (Dec 2016). https://doi.org/10.1007/s10817-016-9369-1
25. Krebbers, R., Leroy, X., Wiedijk, F.: Formal C Semantics: CompCert and the C Standard. In: Klein, G., Gamboa, R. (eds.) Interactive Theorem Proving. pp. 543–548. Springer International Publishing, Cham (2014)
26. Leroy, X., Appel, A.W., Blazy, S., Stewart, G.: The CompCert Memory Model, Version 2. Research Report RR-7987, INRIA (Jun 2012)
27. Lochbihler, A.: Light-Weight Containers for Isabelle: Efficient, Extensible, Nestable. In: Blazy, S., Paulin-Mohring, C., Pichardie, D. (eds.) Interactive Theorem Proving. pp. 116–132. Springer Berlin Heidelberg, Berlin, Heidelberg (2013). https://doi.org/10.1007/978-3-642-39634-2_11
28. Maksimovic, P., Ayoun, S.E., Santos, J.F., Gardner, P.: Gillian, part II: real-world verification for javascript and C. In: Silva, A., Leino, K.R.M. (eds.) Proceedings of the 33rd Computer Aided Verification International Conference, CAV 2021, Virtual Event, July 20-23, 2021, Part II. Lecture Notes in Computer Science, vol. 12760, pp. 827–850. Springer (2021). https://doi.org/10.1007/978-3-030-81688-9_38
29. Maksimovic, P., Santos, J.F., Ayoun, S.E., Gardner, P.: Gillian: A Multi-Language Platform for Unified Symbolic Analysis (2021). https://doi.org/10.48550/ARXIV.2105.14769, https://arxiv.org/abs/2105.14769

30. Memarian, K., Gomes, V.B.F., Davis, B., Kell, S., Richardson, A., Watson, R.N.M., Sewell, P.: Exploring C Semantics and Pointer Provenance. Proc. ACM Program. Lang. **3**(POPL) (Jan 2019)
31. Miller, M.: Trends, challenges, and strategic shifts in the software vulnerability mitigation landscape (Feb 2019), `https://msrnd-cdn-stor. azureedge.net/bluehat/bluehatil/2019/assets/doc/Trends% 2C%20Challenges%2C%20and%20Strategic%20Shifts%20in%20the% 20Software%20Vulnerability%20Mitigation%20Landscape.pdf`, presented at BlueHat IL
32. Nipkow, T., Paulson, L.C., Wenzel, M.: Isabelle/HOL - A Proof Assistant for Higher-Order Logic. [ecture Notes in Computer Science, Springer (2002). `https: //doi.org/10.1007/3-540-45949-9`
33. O'Hearn, P.W.: Incorrectness logic. Proc. ACM Program. Lang. **4**(POPL) (Dec 2019). `https://doi.org/10.1145/3371078`, `https://doi.org/10.1145/ 3371078`
34. Park, S.H.: A Formal CHERI-C Memory Model. Archive of Formal Proofs (Nov 2022), `https://isa-afp.org/entries/CHERI-C_Memory_ Model.html`, Formal proof development
35. Park, S.H., Pai, R., Melham, T.: Artifact for Paper A formal CHERI-C Semantics for Verification (Jan 2023). `https://doi.org/10.5281/zenodo.7504675`, `https://doi.org/10.5281/zenodo.7504675`
36. Richardson, A.: Porting C/C++ software to Morello (Sep 2022), `https:// soft-dev.org/events/cheritech22/slides/Richardson.pdf`, presented at CHERI Technical Workshop 2022
37. Santos, J.F., Maksimovic, P., Ayoun, S.E., Gardner, P.: Gillian: Compositional Symbolic Execution for All. CoRR **abs/2001.05059** (2020), `https://arxiv. org/abs/2001.05059`
38. Tuch, H.: Formal Verification of C Systems Code. Journal of Automated Reasoning **42**(2), 125–187 (Apr 2009). `https://doi.org/10.1007/ s10817-009-9120-2`
39. Watson, R., Laurie, B., Richardson, A.: Assessing the Viability of an Open- Source CHERI Desktop Software Ecosystem. Tech. rep., Capabilities Limited (Sep 2021), `https://www.capabilitieslimited.co.uk/pdfs/ 20210917-capltd-cheri-desktop-report-version1-FINAL.pdf`
40. Watson, R.N.M., Neumann, P.G., Woodruff, J., Roe, M., Almatary, H., Anderson, J., Baldwin, J., Barnes, G., Chisnall, D., Clarke, J., et al.: Capability Hardware Enhanced RISC Instructions: CHERI Instruction-Set Architecture (Version 8). Tech. rep., University of Cambridge, Cambridge, England (Oct 2020), `https://www.cl.cam.ac.uk/techreports/UCAM-CL-TR-951.pdf`
41. Watson, R.N.M., Richardson, A., Davis, B., Baldwin, J., Chisnall, D., Clarke, J., Filardo, N., Moore, S.M., Napierala, E., Sewell, P., Neumann, P.G.: CHERI C/C++ Programming Guide. Tech. rep., University of Cambridge, Cambridge, England (Jun 2020), `https://www.cl.cam.ac.uk/techreports/ UCAM-CL-TR-947.pdf`
42. Wesley Filardo, N., Gutstein, B.F., Woodruff, J., Ainsworth, S., Paul-Trifu, L., Davis, B., Xia, H., Tomasz Napierala, E., Richardson, A., Baldwin, J., Chisnall, D., Clarke, J., Gudka, K., Joannou, A., Theodore Markettos, A., Mazzinghi, A., Norton, R.M., Roe, M., Sewell, P., Son, S., Jones, T.M., Moore, S.W., Neumann, P.G., Watson, R.N.M.: Cornucopia: Temporal Safety for CHERI Heaps. In: 2020 IEEE Symposium on Security and Privacy (SP). pp. 608–625 (2020). `https: //doi.org/10.1109/SP40000.2020.00098`

43. Woodruff, J., Joannou, A., Xia, H., Fox, A., Norton, R.M., Chisnall, D., Davis, B., Gudka, K., Filardo, N.W., Markettos, A.T., Roe, M., Neumann, P.G., Watson, R.N.M., Moore, S.W.: CHERI Concentrate: Practical Compressed Capabilities. IEEE Transactions on Computers **68**(10), 1455–1469 (2019). https://doi.org/10.1109/TC.2019.2914037
44. Woodruff, J., Watson, R.N.M., Chisnall, D., Moore, S.W., Anderson, J., Davis, B., Laurie, B., Neumann, P.G., Norton, R., Roe, M.: The CHERI Capability Model: Revisiting RISC in an Age of Risk. In: 2014 ACM/IEEE 41st International Symposium on Computer Architecture (ISCA). pp. 457–468. IEEE (Jun 2014)

Automated Verification for Real-Time Systems via Implicit Clocks and an Extended Antimirov Algorithm

Yahui Song$^{(\boxtimes)}$ and Wei-Ngan Chin

School of Computing, National University of Singapore, Singapore, Singapore
{yahuis,chinwn}@comp.nus.edu.sg

Abstract. The correctness of real-time systems depends both on the correct functionalities and the realtime constraints. To go beyond the existing Timed Automata based techniques, we propose a novel solution that integrates a modular Hoare-style forward verifier with a term rewriting system (TRS) on *Timed Effects* (*TimEffs*). The main purposes are to: increase the expressiveness, dynamically manipulate clocks, and efficiently solve clock constraints. We formally define a core language C^t, generalizing the real-time systems, modeled using mutable variables and timed behavioral patterns, such as *delay, timeout, interrupt, deadline*. Secondly, to capture real-time specifications, we introduce *TimEffs*, a new effects logic, that extends *regular expressions* with dependent values and arithmetic constraints. Thirdly, the forward verifier reasons temporal behaviors – expressed in *TimEffs* – of target C^t programs. Lastly, we present a purely algebraic TRS, i.e., an extended *Antimirov algorithm*, to efficiently check language inclusions between *TimEffs*. To demonstrate the feasibility of our proposal, we prototype the verification system; prove its soundness; report on case studies and experimental results.

1 Introduction

During the last three decades, a popular approach for specifying real-time systems has been based on Timed Automata (TAs) [1]. TAs are powerful in designing real-time models via explicit clocks, where real-time constraints are captured by explicitly setting/resetting clock variables. A number of automatic verification tools for TAs have proven to be successful [2,3,4,5]. Industrial case studies show that requirements for real-time systems are often structured into phases, which are then composed sequentially, in parallel, alternatively [6,7]. TAs lack high-level compositional patterns for hierarchical design; moreover, users often need to manipulate clock variables with carefully calculated clock constraints manually. The process is tedious and error-prone.

There have been some translation-based approaches on building verification support for compositional timed-process representations. For example, Timed Communicating Sequential Process (TCSP), Timed Communicating Object-Z (TCOZ) and *Statechart* based hierarchical Timed Automata are well suited for presenting compositional models of complex real-time systems. Prior works [8,9] systematically translate TCSP/TCOZ/Statechart models to flat TAs so that the

© The Author(s) 2023
S. Sankaranarayanan and N. Sharygina (Eds.): TACAS 2023, LNCS 13993, pp. 569–587, 2023.
https://doi.org/10.1007/978-3-031-30823-9-29

model checker Uppaal [3] can be applied. However, possible insufficiencies are: the expressiveness power is limited by the finite-state automata; and there is always a gap between the verified logic and the actual code implementation.

In this work, we investigate an alternative approach for verifying real-time systems. We propose a novel temporal specification language, Timed Effects (*TimEffs*), which enables a compositional verification via a Hoare-style forward verifier and a term rewriting system (TRS). More specifically, we specify system behaviors in the form of *TimEffs*, which integrates the Kleene Algebra with dependent values and arithmetic constraints, to provide real-time abstractions into traditional linear temporal logics. For example, one safety property, *"The event Done will be triggered no later than one time unit"*[1], is expressed in *TimEffs* as: $\Phi \triangleq 0 \leq t < 1 \wedge (\_^* \cdot Done)\#t$. Here $\wedge$ connects the arithmetic formula and the timed trace; the operator $\#$ binds time variables to traces (here t is a time bound of $(\_^* \cdot Done)$); $\_$ is a wildcard matching to any event; Kleene star $\star$ denotes a trace repetition. The above formula Φ corresponds to '$\Diamond_{[0,1)} Done$' in metric temporal logic (MTL), reads *"within one time unit, Done finally happens"*. Furthermore, the time bounds can be dependent on the program inputs, as shown in Fig. 1.

```
 1  void addOneSugar ()
 2  /* req: true ∧ _*
 3     ens: t>1 ∧ ϵ # t */
 4  { timeout ((), 1); }
 5
 6  void addNSugar (int n)
 7  /* req: true ∧ _*
 8     ens: t≥n ∧ EndSugar # t */
 9  { if (n == 0) {
10     event ["EndSugar"];}
11     else {
12     addOneSugar ();
13     addNSugar (n-1);}}
```

Fig. 1. Value-dependent specification.

Function addNSugar takes a parameter n, representing the portion of the sugar to add. When n=0, it raises an event EndSugar to mark the end of the process. Otherwise, it adds one portion of the sugar by calling addOneSugar(), then recursively calls addNSugar with parameter n-1. The use of timeout(e, d) is standard [11], which executes a block of code e after the specified time d. Therefore, the time spent on adding one portion of the sugar is more than one time unit. Note that $\epsilon\#t$ refers to an empty trace which takes time t. Both preconditions require no arithmetic constraints and no temporal constraints upon the history traces. The postcondition of addNSugar(n) indicates that the method generates a finite trace where EndSugar takes a no less than n time-units delay to finish.

Although these examples are simple, they show the benefits of deploying value-dependent time bounds, which is beyond the capability of TAs. Essentially, *TimEffs* define symbolic TAs, which stands for a set (possibly infinite) of concrete transition systems. Moreover, we deploy a Hoare-style forward verifier to soundly reason about the behaviors from the source level, with respect to the well-defined operational semantics. This approach provides a *direct* (opposite to the techniques which require manual and remote modeling processes), and modular verification – where modules can be replaced by their already verified properties – for real-time systems, which are not possible by any existing tech-

---

[1] In this paper, we pretend time is discrete and only integral values. However, it's just as easy to represent continuous time by letting time variables assume real values [10].

niques. Furthermore, we develop a novel TRS, which is inspired by Antimirov and Mosses' algorithm[2] [12] but solving the language inclusions between more expressive *TimEffs*. In short, the main contributions of this work are:

1. **Language Abstraction:** we formally define a core language C^t, by defining its syntax and operational semantics, generalizing the real-time systems with mutable variables and timed behavioral patterns, e.g., *delay, timeout, deadline.*
2. **Novel Specification:** we propose *TimEffs*, by defining its syntax and semantics, gaining the expressive power beyond traditional linear temporal logics.
3. **Forward Verifier:** we establish a sound effect system to reason about temporal behaviors of given programs. The verifier triggers the back-end solver TRS.
4. **Efficient TRS:** we present the rewriting rules to (dis)prove the inclusion relations between the actual behaviors and the given specifications, both in *TimEffs*.
5. **Implementation and Evaluation:** we prototype the automated verification system, prove its soundness, report on case studies and experimental results.

2   Overview

An overview of our automated verification system is given in Fig. 2. The system consists of a forward verifier and a TRS, i.e., the rounded boxes. The input of the forward verifier is a C^t program annotated with temporal specifications written in *TimEffs*. The input of the TRS is a pair of effects LHS and RHS, referring to the inclusion LHS $\sqsubseteq$ RHS[3] to be checked

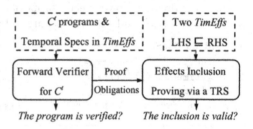

Fig. 2. System Overview.

(LHS and RHS refer to left/right-hand-side effects respectively). The forward verifier calls TRS to solve proof obligations. Next, we use Fig. 3 to highlight our main methodologies, which simulates a coffee machine, that dynamically adds sugar based on the user's input number.

2.1   *TimEffs*. We define Hoare-triple style specifications (enclosed in /*...*/) for each function, which leads to a compositional verification strategy, where static checking can be done locally. The precondition of `makeCoffee` specifies that the input value n is non-negative, and it *requires* that before entering into this function, this history trace must contain the event `CupReady` on the tail. The verification fails if the precondition is not satisfied at the caller sites. Line 17 sets a five time-units deadline (i.e., maximum 5 portion of sugar per coffee) while calling `addNSugar` (defined in Fig. 1); then emits event `Coffee` with a deadline, indicating the pouring coffer process takes no more than four time-units. The precondition of `main` requires no arithmetic constraints (expressed as `true`) and an empty history trace. The postcondition of `main` specifies that before the final

---

[2] Antimirov and Mosses' algorithm was designed for deciding the inequalities of regular expressions based on an axiomatic algorithm of the algebra of regular sets.
[3] The *TimEffs* inclusion relation $\sqsubseteq$ is formally defined in Definition 3.

Done happens, there is no occurrence of Done (! indicates the absence of events); and the whole process takes no more than nine time-units to hit the final event.

```
14  void makeCoffee (int n)
15  /* req: n≥0 ∧ _*· CupReady
16      ens: n≤t≤5 ∧ t'≤4 ∧
            (EndSugar # t) · (Coffee # t') */
17  { deadline (addNSugar(n), 5);
18    deadline (event["Coffee"],4);}
19
20  int main ()
21  /* req: true ∧ ε
22      ens: t≤9 ∧ ((!Done)* # t) · Done */
23  { event["CupReady"];
24    makeCoffee (3);
25    event["Done"];}
```

Fig. 3. To make coffee with three portions of sugar within nine time units.

TimEffs support more features such as *disjunctions, guards, parallelism* and *assertions*, etc (cf. Sec. 3.3), providing detailed information upon: branching properties: different arithmetic conditions on the inputs lead to different effects; and required history traces: by defining the prior effects in precondition. These capabilities are beyond traditional timed verification, and cannot be fully captured by any prior works [8,9,2,3,4,5]. Nevertheless, the increase in expressive power needs support from finer-grind reasoning and a more sophisticated back-end solver, discharged by our forward verifier and TRS.

1. void addOneSugar(){   // initialize the state using the function precondition.
   $\Phi_C = \Phi_{pre}^{addOneSugar(n)} = \{\text{true} \land \_^*\}$ [FV-Meth]
2.   timeout ((), 1);}
   $\Phi'_C = \{t1{>}1 \land \_^* \cdot (\epsilon \# t1)\}$ [FV-Timeout]
3. $\Phi'_C \sqsubseteq \Phi_{pre}^{addOneSugar(n)} \cdot \Phi_{post}^{addOneSugar(n)} \Leftrightarrow t1{>}1 \land \_^* \cdot (\epsilon \# t1) \sqsubseteq t{>}1 \land \_^* \cdot (\epsilon \# t)$

---

4. void addNSugar (int n){   // initialize the state using the function precondition.
   $\Phi_C = \Phi_{pre}^{addNSugar(n)} = \{\text{true} \land \_^*\}$ [FV-Meth]
5.   if (n == 0){
   $\{n{=}0 \land \_^*\}$ [FV-Cond]
6.   event ["EndSugar"];}
   $\{n{=}0 \land \_^* \cdot \text{EndSugar}\}$ [FV-Event]
7.   else {
   $\{n{\neq}0 \land \_^*\}$ [FV-Cond]
8.   addOneSugar();
   $\{n{\neq}0 \land t2{>}1 \land \_^* \cdot (\epsilon \# t2)\}$ [FV-Call]
9.   addNSugar (n-1);}}
   $n{\neq}0 \land t2{>}1 \land \_^* \cdot (\epsilon \# t) \sqsubseteq \Phi_{pre}^{addNSugar(n-1)}$ // TRS: precondition checked.
   $\{n{\neq}0 \land t2{>}1 \land \_^* \cdot (\epsilon \# t2) \cdot \Phi_{post}^{addNSugar(n-1)}\}$ [FV-Call]
10. $\Phi'_C = (n{=}0 \land \_^* \cdot \text{Sugar}) \lor (n{\neq}0 \land t2{>}1 \land \_^* \cdot (\epsilon\#t2) \cdot \Phi_{post}^{addNSugar(n-1)})$ [FV-Cond]
11. $\Phi'_C \sqsubseteq \Phi_{pre}^{addNSugar(n)} \cdot \Phi_{post}^{addNSugar(n)} \Leftrightarrow$ //TRS: postcondition checked, cf. Table 1
    $(n{=}0 \land \text{Sugar}) \lor (n{\neq}0 \land t2{>}1 \land (\epsilon \# t2) \cdot \Phi_{post}^{addNSugar(n-1)}) \sqsubseteq \Phi_{post}^{addNSugar(n)}$

Fig. 4. The forward verification examples (t1 and t2 are fresh time variables).

2.2   Forward Verification.

Fig. 4 demonstrates the forward verification of functions addOneSugar and addNSugar, defined in Fig. 1. The effects states are captured in the form of $\{\Phi_C\}$. To facilitate the illustration, we label the steps by (1) to (11), and mark the deployed forward rules (cf. Sec. 4.1) in [gray]. The initial states (1) and (4) are obtained from the preconditions, by the [*FV-Meth*] rule. States (5)(7)(10) are obtained by [*FV-Cond*], which enforces the conditional constraints into the effects states, and unions the effects accumulated from two branches. State (6) is obtained by [*FV-Event*], which concatenates an event to the current effects. The intermediate states (8) and (9) are obtained by [*FV-Call*]. Before each function call, [*FV-Call*] invokes the TRS to check whether the current effects states satisfy callees' preconditions. If it is not satisfied, the verification fails; otherwise, it concatenates the callee's postcondition to the current states (the precondition check for step (8) is omitted here).

State (2) is obtained by [*FV-Timeout*], which adds a lower time-bound to an empty trace. After these state transformations, steps (3) and (11) invoke the TRS to check the inclusions between the final effects and the declared postconditions.

2.3   The TRS. Having *TimEffs* to be the specification language, and the forward verifier to reason about the actual behaviors, we are interested in the following verification problem: Given a program $\mathcal{P}$, and a temporal specification Φ', does the inclusions $\Phi^{\mathcal{P}} \sqsubseteq \Phi'$ holds? Typically, checking the inclusion/entailment between the concrete program effects $\Phi^{\mathcal{P}}$ and the expected property Φ' proves that: the program $\mathcal{P}$ will never lead to unsafe traces which violate Φ'.

Our TRS is an extension of Antimirov and Mosses's algorithm [12], which can be deployed to decide inclusions of two regular expressions (REs) through an iterated process of checking inclusions of their *partial derivatives* [13]. There are two basic rules: [*Disprove*] infers false from trivially inconsistent inclusions; and [*Unfold*] applies Definition 2 to generate new inclusions.

Definition 1 (Derivative). *Given any formal language S over an alphabet Σ and any string $u \in \Sigma^*$, the derivative of S with respect to u is defined as:*

$$u^{-1}S = \{w \in \Sigma^* \mid uw \in S\}.$$

Definition 2 (REs Inclusion). *For REs r and s, $r \preceq s \Leftrightarrow \forall (\mathsf{A} \in \Sigma).\mathsf{A}^{-1}(r) \preceq \mathsf{A}^{-1}(s)$.*

Definition 3 (*TimEffs* Inclusion). *For* TimEffs *Φ_1 and Φ_2,*

$$\Phi_1 \sqsubseteq \Phi_2 \Leftrightarrow \forall \mathsf{A}.\forall t \geq 0. \ (\mathsf{A}\#t)^{-1}\Phi_1 \sqsubseteq (\mathsf{A}\#t)^{-1}\Phi_2.$$

Similarly, we defined Definition 3 for unfolding the inclusions between *TimEffs*, where $(\mathsf{A}\#t)^{-1}\Phi$ is the partial derivative of Φ w.r.t the event A with the time bound t. Termination of the rewriting is guaranteed because the set of derivatives to be considered is finite, and possible cycles are detected using *memorization* (cf. Table 5) [14]. Next, we use Table 1 to demonstrate how the TRS automatically proves the final effects of `main` satisfying its postcondition (shown at step (11) in Fig. 4). We mark the rewriting rules (cf. Sec. 5) in [gray].

In Table 1, step ① renames the time variables to avoid the name clashes between the antecedent and the consequent. Step ② splits the proof tree into two branches, according to the different arithmetic constraints, by rule [LHS-OR]. In the first branch, step ③ eliminates the event ES from the head of both sides, by rule [UNFOLD]. Step ④ proves the inclusion, because evidently the consequent $\mathsf{tR} \geq 0 \ \wedge \ \epsilon\#\mathsf{tR}$ contains ϵ when $\mathsf{tR}=0$. In the second branch, step ⑤ eliminates a

Table 1. An inclusion proving example. (I) is the right hand side sub-tree of the the main rewriting proof tree. (ES stands for the event EndSugar)

$$\frac{\dfrac{\overline{\text{n=0} \land \epsilon \sqsubseteq \text{tR}{\geq}0 \land \epsilon \; \# \; \text{tR}}\; ④ \; [\text{PROVE}]}{\text{n=0} \land \text{ES} \sqsubseteq \text{tR}{\geq}0 \land \text{ES\#tR}}\; ③ \; [\text{UNFOLD}]}{}$$

$$\frac{(\text{n=0}\land\text{ES}) \lor (\text{n}{\neq}0\land\text{t2}{>}1\land\text{tL}{\geq}(\text{n-1})\land \; \epsilon\#\text{t2} \cdot \text{ES\#tL}) \sqsubseteq \text{tR}{\geq}\text{n} \land \text{ES\#tR}}{(\text{n=0} \land \text{ES}) \lor (\text{n}{\neq}0\land\text{t2}{>}1 \land (\epsilon \; \# \; \text{t2}) \cdot \Phi_{post}^{addNSugar(n-1)}) \sqsubseteq \Phi_{post}^{addNSugar(n)}}$$

(I) \; ② [LHS-OR] \; ① [RENAME]

(I)

$$\frac{\dfrac{\overline{\text{t2}{>}1\land\text{tL}{\geq}(\text{n-1}) \; \Rightarrow \; \text{tR}{\geq}\text{n}}\; ⑦ \; [\text{PROVE}]}{\text{n}{\neq}0\land\text{t2}{>}1\land\text{tL}{\geq}(\text{n-1}) \; \land \; \epsilon \sqsubseteq \text{tR}{\geq}\text{n} \land \epsilon}\; ⑥ \; [\text{UNFOLD}] \; \pi_u\text{:tL=(tR-t2)}}{\dfrac{\text{n}{\neq}0\land\text{t2}{>}1\land\text{tL}{\geq}(\text{n-1}) \; \land \; \text{ES\#tL} \sqsubseteq \text{tR}{\geq}\text{n} \land \text{ES\#(tR-t2)}}{\text{n}{\neq}0\land\text{t2}{>}1\land\text{tL}{\geq}(\text{n-1}) \; \land \; \epsilon\#\text{t2}\cdot \text{ES\#tL} \sqsubseteq \text{tR}{\geq}\text{n} \land \text{ES\#tR}}\; ⑤ \; [\text{UNFOLD}]}}{}$$

time duration $\epsilon\#\text{t2}$ from both sides. Therefore the rule [UNFOLD] subtracts a time duration from the consequent, i.e., (tR-t2). Similarly, step ⑥ eliminates ES#tL from the both sides, adding tL=(tR-t2) to the unification constraints. Step ⑦ proves $\text{t2}{>}1\land\text{tL}{\geq}(\text{n-1})\land\text{tL=(tR-t2)}{\Rightarrow}\text{tR}{\geq}\text{n}$ [4]; therefore, the proof succeed.

2.4 Verifying the Fischer's Mutual Exclusion Protocol.

Fig. 5 presents the classical Fischer's mutually exclusion protocol, in C^t. Global variables x and cs indicate *'which process attempted to access the critical section most recently'* and *'the number of processes accessing the critical section'* respectively. The main procedure is a parallel composition of three processes, where d and e are two constants. Each process attempts to enter the critical section when x is -1, i.e. no other process is currently attempting. Once the process is active (i.e., reaches line 6), it sets x to its identity number i within d

```
1 var x := -1;
2 var cs:= 0;
3
4 void proc (int i) {
5   [x=-1] //block waiting until true
6   deadline(event["Update"(i)]{x:=i},d);
7   delay (e);
8   if (x==i) {
9     event["Critical"(i)]{cs:=cs+1};
10    event["Exit"(i)]{cs:=cs-1;x:=-1};
11    proc (i);
12  } else {proc (i);}}
13
14 void main ()
15 /* req: d<e ∧ ε          ens_c: true∧(cs≤1)*
16    ens_b: true∧ ((_*).Critical.Exit.(_*))* */
17 { proc(0) || proc(1) || proc(2); }
```

Fig. 5. Fischer's mutually exclusion algorithm.

time units, captured by deadline(...,d). Then it idles for e time units, captured by delay(e) and then checks whether x still equals to i. If so, it safely enters the critical section. Otherwise, it restarts from the beginning. Quantitative timing constraint d<e plays an important role in this algorithm to guarantee mutual exclusion. One way to prove mutual exclusion is to show that cs≤1 is always true. Or, using event temporal logic, we can show that the occurrence of Critical always indicates the next event is Exit. We show in Sec. 6 that our prototype system can verify such algorithms symbolically.

---

[4] The proof obligations for arithmetic constraints are discharged by the Z3 solver [15].

3   Language and Specifications

3.1   The Target Language

We define the core language C^t in Fig. 6, which is built based on C syntax and provides support for timed behavioral patterns.

$$
\begin{array}{lll}
(\textit{Program}) & \mathcal{P} ::= (\alpha^*, meth^*) \\
(\textit{Types}) & \iota ::= int \mid bool \mid void \\
(\textit{Method}) & meth ::= \iota \; mn \; (\iota \; x)^* \; \{\textbf{req} \; \Phi_{pre} \; \textbf{ens} \; \Phi_{post}\} \; \{e\} \\
(\textit{Values}) & v ::= () \mid c \mid b \mid x \\
(\textit{Assignment}) & \alpha ::= x := v \\
(\textit{Expressions}) & e ::= v \mid \alpha \mid [v]e \mid mn(v^*) \mid e_1; e_2 \mid e_1 \| e_2 \mid if \; v \; e_1 \; e_2 \mid \textbf{event}[\textbf{A}(v, \alpha^*)] \\
& \quad\; \mid \textbf{delay}[v] \mid e_1 \; \textbf{timeout}[v] \; e_2 \mid e \; \textbf{deadline}[v] \mid e_1 \; \textbf{interrupt}[v] \; e_2 \\
(\textit{Terms}) & t ::= c \mid x \mid t_1 + t_2 \mid t_1 - t_2 \\
\end{array}
$$

| $c \in \mathbb{Z}$ | $b \in \mathbb{B}$ | $mn, x \in \textbf{var}$ | (*Action labels*) $\textbf{A} \in \Sigma$ |

Fig. 6. A core first-order imperative language with timed constructs via implicit clocks.

Here, c and b stand for integer and Boolean constants, mn and x are meta-variables, drawn from **var** (the countably infinite set of arbitrary distinct identifiers). A program $\mathcal{P}$ comprises a list of global variable initializations α^* and a list of method declarations $meth^*$. Here, we use the $*$ superscript to denote a finite list of items, for example, x^* refers to a list of variables, $x_1, ..., x_n$. Each method $meth$ has a name mn, an expression-oriented body e, also is associated with a precondition Φ_{pre} and a postcondition Φ_{post} (specification syntax is given in Fig. 7). C^t allows each iterative loop to be optimized to an equivalent tail-recursive method, where mutation on parameters is made visible to the caller.

Expressions comprise: values v; guarded processes $[v]e$, where if v is true, it behaves as e, else it idles until v becomes true; method calls $mn(v^*)$; sequential composition $e_1; e_2$; parallel composition $e_1 \| e_2$, where e_1 and e_2 may communicate via shared variables; conditionals $if \; v \; e_1 \; e_2$; and event raising expressions $\textbf{event}[\textbf{A}(v, \alpha^*)]$ where the event $\textbf{A}$ comes from the finite set of event labels Σ. Without loss of generality, events can be further parametrized with one value v and a set of assignments α^* to update the mutable variables. Moreover, a number of timed constructs can be used to capture common real-time system behaviors, which are explained via operational semantics rules in Sec. 3.2.

3.2   Operational Semantics of C^t

To build the semantics of the system model, we define the notion of a configuration in Definition 4, to capture the global system state during system execution.

Definition 4 (System configuration). *A system configuration ζ is a pair $(\mathcal{S}, e)$ where $\mathcal{S}$ is a variable valuation function (or a stack) and e is an expression.*

A transition of the system is of the form $\zeta \xrightarrow{l} \zeta'$ where ζ and ζ' are the system configurations before and after the transition respectively. Transition labels l include: d, denoting a non-negative integer; τ, denoting an invisible event; A, denoting an observable event. For example, $\zeta \xrightarrow{d} \zeta'$ denotes a d time-units elapse. Next, we present the firing rules, associated with timed constructs.

Process $\texttt{delay}[v]$ idles for exactly t time units. Rule $[delay_1]$ states that the process may idle for any amount of time given it is less than or equal to t; Rule $[delay_2]$ states that the process terminates immediately when t becomes 0.

$$\frac{d \leq v}{(\mathcal{S}, \texttt{delay}[v]) \xrightarrow{d} (\mathcal{S}, \texttt{delay}[v\text{-}d])} \, [delay_1] \qquad \frac{}{(\mathcal{S}, \texttt{delay}[0]) \xrightarrow{\tau} (\mathcal{S}, ())} \, [delay_2]$$

In $e_1 \; \texttt{timeout}[v] \; e_2$, the first observable event of e_1 shall occur before t time units; otherwise, e_2 takes over the control after exactly t time units. Note that the usage of timeout in Fig. 1 is a special case where e_1 never starts by default.

$$\frac{(\mathcal{S}, e_1) \xrightarrow{A} (\mathcal{S}', e_1')}{(\mathcal{S}, e_1 \; \texttt{timeout}[v] \; e_2) \xrightarrow{A} (\mathcal{S}', e_1')} \, [to_1] \qquad \frac{(\mathcal{S}, e_1) \xrightarrow{\tau} (\mathcal{S}', e_1')}{(\mathcal{S}, e_1 \; \texttt{timeout}[v] \; e_2) \xrightarrow{\tau} (\mathcal{S}', e_1' \; \texttt{timeout}[v] e_2)} \, [to_2]$$

$$\frac{(\mathcal{S}, e_1) \xrightarrow{d} (\mathcal{S}, e_1') \qquad (d \leq v)}{(\mathcal{S}, e_1 \; \texttt{timeout}[v] \; e_2) \xrightarrow{d} (\mathcal{S}, e_1' \; \texttt{timeout}[v\text{-}d] e_2)} \, [to_3] \qquad \frac{}{(\mathcal{S}, e_1 \; \texttt{timeout}[0] e_2) \xrightarrow{\tau} (\mathcal{S}, e_2)} \, [to_4]$$

Process $\texttt{deadline}\,[v]\,e$ behaves exactly as e except that it must terminate before t time units. The guarded process $[v]e$ behaves as e when v is true, otherwise it idles until v becomes true. Process $e_1 \; \texttt{interrupt}[v] \; e_2$ behaves as e_1 until t time units, and then e_2 takes over. We leave the rest rules in [16].

$$\frac{(\mathcal{S}, e) \xrightarrow{A/\tau} (\mathcal{S}', e')}{(\mathcal{S}, \texttt{deadline}[v] \; e) \xrightarrow{A/\tau} (\mathcal{S}', \texttt{deadline}[v] \; e')} \, [ddl_1] \qquad \frac{(\mathcal{S}, e) \xrightarrow{l} (\mathcal{S}', v)}{(\mathcal{S}, \texttt{deadline}[v] \; e) \xrightarrow{l} (\mathcal{S}', v)} \, [ddl_2]$$

$$\frac{\mathcal{S} \models (v\text{=}true)}{(\mathcal{S}, [v]e) \xrightarrow{\tau} (\mathcal{S}, e)} \, [gu_1] \qquad \frac{(\mathcal{S}, e) \xrightarrow{d} (\mathcal{S}, e') \qquad (d \leq v)}{(\mathcal{S}, \texttt{deadline}[v] \; e) \xrightarrow{d} (\mathcal{S}, \texttt{deadline}[v\text{-}d] \; e')} \, [ddl_3]$$

$$\frac{\mathcal{S} \not\models (v\text{=}true)}{(\mathcal{S}, [v]e) \xrightarrow{\tau} (\mathcal{S}, [v]e)} \, [gu_2] \qquad \frac{(\mathcal{S}, e_1) \xrightarrow{A/\tau} (\mathcal{S}', e_1')}{(\mathcal{S}, e_1 \; \texttt{interrupt}[v] \; e_2) \xrightarrow{A/\tau} (\mathcal{S}', e_1' \; \texttt{interrupt}[v] \; e_2)} \, [int_1]$$

$$\frac{(\mathcal{S}, e_1) \xrightarrow{l} (\mathcal{S}', v)}{(\mathcal{S}, e_1 \; \texttt{interrupt}[v] \; e_2) \xrightarrow{l} (\mathcal{S}', v)} \, [int_2] \qquad \frac{}{(\mathcal{S}, e_1 \; \texttt{interrupt}[0] \; e_2) \xrightarrow{\tau} (\mathcal{S}, e_2)} \, [int_3]$$

$$\frac{(\mathcal{S}, e_1) \xrightarrow{d} (\mathcal{S}, e_1') \qquad (d \leq v)}{(\mathcal{S}, e_1 \; \texttt{interrupt}[v] \; e_2) \xrightarrow{d} (\mathcal{S}, e_1' \; \texttt{interrupt}[v\text{-}d] \; e_2)} \, [int_4]$$

3.3   The Specification Language

We plant *TimEffs* specifications into the Hoare-style verification system, using Φ_{pre} and Φ_{post} to capture the temporal pre/post conditions. As shown in Fig. 7, *TimEffs* can be constructed by a conditioned event sequence $\pi \wedge \theta$; or an effects disjunction $\Phi_1 \vee \Phi_2$. Timed sequences comprise *nil* ($\bot$); empty trace ϵ; single event *ev*; concatenation $\theta_1 \cdot \theta_2$; disjunction $\theta_1 \vee \theta_2$; parallel composition $\theta_1 || \theta_2$; a block waiting for a certain constraint to be satisfied $\pi?\theta$. We introduce a new operator #, and $\theta\#t$ represents the trace θ takes t time units to complete, where t

$$(\textit{Timed Effects}) \quad \Phi ::= \pi \wedge \theta \mid \Phi_1 \vee \Phi_2$$
$$(\textit{Event Sequences}) \quad \theta ::= \perp \mid \epsilon \mid ev \mid \theta_1 \cdot \theta_2 \mid \theta_1 \vee \theta_2 \mid \theta_1 \| \theta_2 \mid \pi?\theta \mid \theta\#t \mid \theta^*$$
$$(\textit{Events}) \quad ev ::= \mathtt{A}(v, \alpha^*) \mid \tau(\pi) \mid \overline{\mathtt{A}} \mid \_$$
$$(\textit{Pure}) \quad \pi ::= True \mid False \mid bop(t_1, t_2) \mid \pi_1 \wedge \pi_2 \mid \pi_1 \vee \pi_2 \mid \neg\pi \mid \pi_1 \Rightarrow \pi_2$$
$$(\textit{Real-Time Terms}) \quad t ::= c \mid x \mid t_1 + t_2 \mid t_1 - t_2$$

$c \in \mathbb{Z}$	$x \in$ **var**	(*Real Time Bound*) **#**	(*Kleene Star*) $\star$

Fig. 7. Syntax of *TimEffs*.

is a *real-time term*. A timed sequence also can be constructed by θ^*, representing zero or more times repetition of the trace θ. For single events, $\mathtt{A}(v, \alpha^*)$ stands for an observable event with label $\mathtt{A}$, parameterized by v, and the assignment operations α^*; $\tau(\pi)$ is an invisible event, parameterized with a pure formula π[5].

Events can also be $\overline{\mathtt{A}}$, referring to all events which are not labeled using $\mathtt{A}$; and a wildcard $\_$, which matches to all the events. We use π to denote a pure formula which captures the (Presburger) arithmetic conditions on terms or program parameters. We use $bop(t_1, t_2)$ to represent binary atomic formulas of terms (including $=$, $>$, $<$, $\geq$ and $\leq$). Terms consist of constant integer values c; integer variables x; simple computations of terms, $t_1 + t_2$ and $t_1 - t_2$.

3.4 Semantic Model of Timed Effects

Let $d, \mathcal{S}, \varphi \models \Phi$ denote the model relation, i.e., a stack $\mathcal{S}$, a concrete execution trace φ take d time units to complete, and they satisfy the specification Φ.

$d, \mathcal{S}, \varphi \models \Phi_1 \vee \Phi_2$	iff $d, \mathcal{S}, \varphi \models \Phi_1$ or $d, \mathcal{S}, \varphi \models \Phi_2$
$d, \mathcal{S}, \varphi \models \pi \wedge \epsilon$	iff $d=0$ and $[\![\pi]\!]_s = True$ and $\varphi = [\,]$
$d, \mathcal{S}, \varphi \models \pi \wedge ev$	iff $d=0$ and $[\![\pi]\!]_s = True$ and $\varphi = [ev]$
$d, \mathcal{S}, \varphi \models \pi \wedge (\theta_1 \cdot \theta_2)$	iff $\exists \varphi_1, \varphi_2. \ \varphi_1 {+}{+} \varphi_2 = \varphi$ and $\exists d_1, d_2. \ d_1 + d_2 = d$
	$\quad$ s.t. $d_1, \mathcal{S}, \varphi_1 \models \pi \wedge \theta_1$ and $d_2, \mathcal{S}, \varphi_2 \models \pi \wedge \theta_2$
$d, \mathcal{S}, \varphi \models \pi \wedge (\theta_1 \vee \theta_2)$	iff $d, \mathcal{S}, \varphi \models \pi \wedge \theta_1$ or $d, \mathcal{S}, \varphi \models \pi \wedge \theta_2$
$d, \mathcal{S}, \varphi \models \pi \wedge (ev_1 \cdot \theta_1) \| (ev_2 \cdot \theta_2)$	iff $d, \mathcal{S}, \varphi \models \pi \wedge ev_1 \cdot (\theta_1 \| (ev_2 \cdot \theta_2))$ or
	$\quad d, \mathcal{S}, \varphi \models \pi \wedge ev_2 \cdot ((ev_1 \cdot \theta_1) \| \theta_2)$
$d, \mathcal{S}, \varphi \models \pi \wedge (ev \cdot \theta_1) \| (ev \cdot \theta_2)$	iff $d, \mathcal{S}, \varphi \models \pi \wedge ev \cdot (\theta_1 \| \theta_2)$
$d, \mathcal{S}, \varphi \models \pi \wedge (\epsilon\#t_1) \| (\epsilon\#t_2)$	iff $d, \mathcal{S}, \varphi \models (\pi \wedge t_1 \geq t_2) \wedge (\epsilon\#t_1) \cdot (\epsilon\#(t_1 - t_2))$ or
	$\quad d, \mathcal{S}, \varphi \models (\pi \wedge t_1 < t_2) \wedge (\epsilon\#t_2) \cdot (\epsilon\#(t_2 - t_1))$
$d, \mathcal{S}, \varphi \models \pi \wedge \pi_1?\theta$	iff $[\![\pi_1]\!]_s = True, d, \mathcal{S}, \varphi \models \pi \wedge \theta$ or
	$\quad [\![\pi_1]\!]_s = False, d, \mathcal{S}, \varphi \models \pi \wedge \pi_1?\theta$
$d, \mathcal{S}, \varphi \models \pi \wedge \theta\#t$	iff $[\![\pi \wedge t \geq 0]\!]_s = True, \ \exists \theta_1, \theta_2. \ \theta_1 \cdot \theta_2 = \theta, \ $ fresh $t_1, t_2, s.t.$
	$\quad d, \mathcal{S}, \varphi \models (\pi \wedge t_1 \geq 0 \wedge t_2 \geq 0 \wedge t_1 + t_2 = t) \wedge (\theta_1\#t_1) \cdot (\theta_2\#t_2)$
$d, \mathcal{S}, \varphi \models \pi \wedge \theta^*$	iff $d, \mathcal{S}, \varphi \models \pi \wedge \epsilon$ or $d, \mathcal{S}, \varphi \models \pi \wedge \theta \cdot \theta^*$
$d, \mathcal{S}, \varphi \models false$	iff $[\![\pi]\!]_s = False$ or $\varphi = \perp$

Fig. 8. Semantics of *TimEffs*.

---

[5] The difference between $\tau(\pi)$ and π? is: $\tau(\pi)$ marks an assertion which leads to false ($\perp$) if π is not satisfied, whereas π? waits until π is satisfied.

To define the model, *var* is the set of program variables, *val* is the set of primitive values; and d, $\mathcal{S}$, φ are drawn from the following concrete domains: d: $\mathbb{N}$, $\mathcal{S}$: *var*→*val* and φ: *list of event*. As shown in Fig. 8, ++ appends event sequences; [] describes the empty sequences, $[ev]$ represents the singleton sequence contains event ev; $[\![\pi]\!]_{\mathcal{S}} = True$ represents π holds on the stack $\mathcal{S}$. Notice that, simple events, i.e., without #, are taken to be happening in instant time.

3.5 Expressiveness. *TimEffs* draw similarities to metric temporal logic (MTL), which is derived from LTL, where a set of non-negative real numbers is added to temporal modal operators. As shown in Table 2, we are able to encode MTL operators into *TimEffs*, making it more intuitive and readable. The basic modal operators are: □ for "globally"; ◊ for "finally"; ○ for "next"; $\mathcal{U}$ for "until", and their past time reversed versions: $\overleftarrow{\square}$; $\overleftarrow{\lozenge}$; and ⊖ for "previous"; $\mathcal{S}$ for "since". I in MTL is the time interval with concrete upper/lower bounds; whereas in *TimEffs* they can be symbolic bounds which are dependent on program inputs.

Table 2. Examples for converting MTL formulae into *TimEffs* with $t \in I$ applied.

Φ_{post}	$\square_I A \equiv (A^*)\#t$	$\lozenge_I A \equiv (\_^* \cdot A)\#t$	$\bigcirc_I A \equiv (\_)\#t \cdot A$	$A\mathcal{U}_I B \equiv (A^*)\#t \cdot B$
Φ_{pre}	$\overleftarrow{\square}_I A \equiv (A^*)\#t$	$\overleftarrow{\lozenge}_I A \equiv (A \cdot \_^*)\#t$	$\ominus_I A \equiv A \cdot ((\_)\#t)$	$A\mathcal{S}_I B \equiv B \cdot ((A^*)\#t)$

4   Automated Forward Verification

4.1   Forward Rules

Forward rules are in the Hoare-style triples $\mathcal{S} \vdash \{\Pi, \Theta\}\ e\ \{\Pi', \Theta'\}$, where $\mathcal{S}$ is the stack environment; $\{\Pi, \Theta\}$ and $\{\Pi', \Theta'\}$ are program states, i.e., disjunctions of conditioned event sequence $\pi \wedge \theta$. The meaning of the transition is: $\{\Pi', \Theta'\} = \bigcup_{i=0}^{|\{\Pi,\Theta\}|-1} \{\Pi'_i, \Theta'_i\}$ where $(\pi_i \wedge \theta_i) \in \{\Pi, \Theta\}$ and $\vdash \{\pi_i, \theta_i\}\ e\ \{\Pi'_i, \Theta'_i\}$[6].

We here present the rules for time-related constructs and leave the rest rules in [16]. Rule $[FV\text{-}Delay]$ creates a trace $\epsilon\#t$, where t is fresh, and concatenates it to the current program state, together with the additional constraint $t=v$. Rule $[FV\text{-}Deadline]$ computes the effects from e and adds an upper time-bound to the results. Rule $[FV\text{-}Timeout]$ computes the effects from e_1 and e_2 using the starting state $\{\pi, \epsilon\}$. The final state is an union of possible effects with corresponding time bounds and arithmetic constraints. Note that, $hd(\Theta_1)$ and $tl(\Theta_1)$ return the event *head* (cf. Definition 6), and the tail of Θ_1 respectively.

$$[FV\text{-}Delay]$$
$$\frac{\theta' = \theta \cdot (\epsilon\#t) \quad (t\ is\ fresh)}{\mathcal{S} \vdash \{\pi, \theta\}\ \texttt{delay}[v]\ \{\pi \wedge (t=v), \theta'\}}$$

$$[FV\text{-}Deadline]$$
$$\frac{\mathcal{S} \vdash \{\pi, \epsilon\}\ e\ \{\Pi_1, \Theta_1\} \quad (t\ is\ fresh)}{\mathcal{S} \vdash \{\pi, \theta\}\ \texttt{deadline}[v]\ e\ \{\Pi_1 \wedge (t \leq v), \theta \cdot (\Theta_1\#t)\}}$$

$$[FV\text{-}Timeout]$$
$$\frac{\mathcal{S} \vdash \{\pi, \epsilon\}\ e_1\ \{\Pi_1, \Theta_1\} \quad \mathcal{S} \vdash \{\pi, \epsilon\}\ e_2\ \{\Pi_2, \Theta_2\} \quad (t_1, t_2\ are\ fresh)}{\{\Pi_f, \Theta_f\} = \{\Pi_1 \wedge t_1 < v, (hd(\Theta_1)\#t_1) \cdot tl(\Theta_1)\} \cup \{\Pi_2 \wedge t_2 = v, (\epsilon\#t_2) \cdot \Theta_2\}}$$
$$\frac{}{\mathcal{S} \vdash \{\pi, \theta\}\ e_1\ \texttt{timeout}[v]\ e_2\ \{\Pi_f, \theta \cdot \Theta_f\}}$$

$$[FV\text{-}Interrupt]$$
$$\frac{\mathcal{S} \vdash \{\pi, \epsilon\}\ e_1\ \{\Pi, \Theta\} \quad \Delta = \bigcup_{i=0}^{|\{\Pi,\Theta\}|-1} \mathsf{N}_{Interleave}^{Interrupt(v,\pi_i)}(\theta_i, \epsilon) \quad \mathcal{S} \vdash \{\Delta\}\ e_2\ \{\Pi', \Theta'\}}{\mathcal{S} \vdash \{\pi, \theta\}\ e_1\ \texttt{interrupt}[v]\ e_2\ \{\Pi', \theta \cdot \Theta'\}}$$

---

[6] $|\{\Pi, \Theta\}|$ is the size of $\{\Pi, \Theta\}$, i.e., the count of conditioned event sequence $\pi \wedge \theta$.

[*FV-Interrupt*] computes the interruption interleaves of e_1's effects, which come from the over-approximation of all the possibilities. For example, for trace $A \cdot B$, the interruption with time t creates three possibilities: $(\epsilon\#t) \vee (A\#t) \vee ((A \cdot B)\#t)$. Then the rule continues to compute the effects of e_2; lastly, it prepends the original history θ to the final results. Algorithm 1 presents the interleaving algorithm for *interruptions*, where + unions program states (cf. Definition 7 and Definition 8 for *fst* and D functions).

Algorithm 1: Interruption Interleaving

Input: $v, \pi, \theta, \theta_{his}$
Output: Program States: Δ
1 **function** $\aleph_{Interleave}^{Interrupt(v,\pi)}(\theta, \theta_{his})$
2 $\quad \Delta \leftarrow []$
3 $\quad$ **foreach** $f \in fst_\pi(\theta)$ **do**
4 $\quad\quad \phi \leftarrow \pi \wedge (t < v) \wedge (\theta_{his}\#t)$
5 $\quad\quad \theta' \leftarrow D_f^\pi(\theta)$
6 $\quad\quad \theta'_{his} \leftarrow \theta_{his} \cdot f$
7 $\quad\quad \Delta' \leftarrow \aleph_{Interleave}^{Interrupt(v,\pi)}(\theta', \theta'_{his})$
8 $\quad\quad \Delta \leftarrow \Delta + \phi + \Delta'$
9 $\quad$ **return** Δ

Theorem 1 (Soundness of Forward Rules). *Given any system configuration* $\zeta = (\mathcal{S}, e)$, *by applying the operational semantics rules, if* $(\mathcal{S}, e) \rightarrow^* (\mathcal{S}', v)$ *has execution time* d *and produces event sequence* φ; *and for any history effect* $\pi \wedge \theta$, *such that* $d_1, \mathcal{S}, \varphi_1 \models (\pi \wedge \theta)$, *and the forward verifier reasons* $\mathcal{S} \vdash \{\pi, \theta\} e \{\Pi, \Theta\}$, *then* $\exists (\pi' \wedge \theta') \in \{\Pi, \Theta\}$ *such that* $(d_1 + d), \mathcal{S}', (\varphi_1 {+}{+} \varphi) \models (\pi' \wedge \theta')$. *($\zeta \rightarrow^* \zeta'$ denotes the reflexive, transitive closure of* $\zeta \rightarrow \zeta'$.)*

Proof. See the technical report [16].

5   Temporal Verification via a TRS

The TRS is an automated entailment checker to prove language inclusions between *TimEffs*. It is triggered prior to function calls for the precondition checking; and by the end of verifying a function, for the post condition checking.

Given two effects Φ_1 and Φ_2, the TRS decides if the inclusion $\Phi_1 \sqsubseteq \Phi_2$ is valid. During the effects rewriting process, the inclusions are in the form of $\Gamma \vdash \Phi_1 \sqsubseteq^\Phi \Phi_2$, a shorthand for: $\Gamma \vdash \Phi \cdot \Phi_1 \sqsubseteq \Phi \cdot \Phi_2$. To prove such inclusions is to check whether all the possible timed traces in the antecedent Φ_1 are legitimately allowed in the timed traces described by the consequent Φ_2. Here Γ is the proof context, i.e., a set of effects inclusion hypothesis; and Φ is the history effects from the antecedent that have been used to match the effects from the consequent. The checking is initially invoked with $\Gamma = \emptyset$ and $\Phi = True \wedge \epsilon$.

Effects Disjunctions. An inclusion with a disjunctive antecedent succeeds if both disjunctions entail the consequent. An inclusion with a disjunctive consequent succeeds if the antecedent entails either of the disjunctions.

$$\frac{\Gamma \vdash \Phi_1 \sqsubseteq \Phi \quad \Gamma \vdash \Phi_2 \sqsubseteq \Phi}{\Gamma \vdash \Phi_1 \vee \Phi_2 \sqsubseteq \Phi} \, [LHS\text{-}OR] \qquad \frac{\Gamma \vdash \Phi \sqsubseteq \Phi_1 \quad or \quad \Gamma \vdash \Phi \sqsubseteq \Phi_2}{\Gamma \vdash \Phi \sqsubseteq \Phi_1 \vee \Phi_2} \, [RHS\text{-}OR]$$

Now, the inclusions are disjunction-free formulas. Next we provide the definitions and key implementations of auxiliary functions Nullable, First and Derivative. Intuitively, the Nullable function $\delta_\pi(\theta)$ returns a Boolean value indicating whether $\pi\wedge\theta$ contains the empty trace; the First function $fst_\pi(\theta)$ computes a set of initial *heads*, denoted as h, of $\pi\wedge\theta$; the Derivative function $D_h^\pi(\theta)$ computes a next-state effects after eliminating the head h from the current effects $\pi \wedge \theta$.

Definition 5 (Nullable [7]). *Given any* $\Phi=\pi \wedge \theta$, $\delta_\pi(\theta) : bool= \begin{cases} true & if \ \epsilon \in [\![\pi\wedge\theta]\!] \\ false & if \ \epsilon \notin [\![\pi\wedge\theta]\!] \end{cases}$

$\delta_\pi(\bot)=\delta_\pi(ev)=false \quad \delta_\pi(\epsilon)=\delta(\theta^*)=true \quad \delta_\pi(\pi'?\theta)=\delta_\pi(\theta) \quad \delta_\pi(\theta_1\vee\theta_2)=\delta(\theta_1)\vee\delta(\theta_2)$

$\delta_\pi(\theta \cdot \theta_2)=\delta(\theta_1)\wedge\delta(\theta_2) \quad \delta_\pi(\theta_1||\theta_2)=\delta(\theta_1)\wedge\delta(\theta_2) \quad \delta_\pi(\theta\#t)=SAT(\pi\wedge(t=0)) \wedge \delta_\pi(\theta)$

Definition 6 (Heads). *If* h *is a head of* $\pi \wedge \theta$, *then there exist* π' *and* θ', *such that* $\pi \wedge \theta = \pi' \wedge (h \cdot \theta')$. *A head can be* t, *denoting a pure time passing;* $A(v,\alpha^*)$, *denoting an instant event passing; or* $(A(v,\alpha^*),t)$, *denoting an event passing which takes time* t.

Definition 7 (First). *Given any* $\Phi=\pi \wedge \theta$, $fst_\pi(\theta)$ *returns a set of heads, be the set of initial elements derivable from effects* $\pi \wedge \theta$, *where* $(t'$ *is fresh):*

$fst_\pi(\bot)=fst_\pi(\epsilon)=\{\} \quad fst_\pi(A(v,\alpha^*))=\{A(v,\alpha^*)\} \quad fst_\pi(\epsilon\#t)=\{t\} \quad fst_\pi(\theta^*)=fst_\pi(\theta)$

$fst_\pi(\theta\#t)=\{(A(v,\alpha^*),t') \mid A(v,\alpha^*)\in fst_\pi(\theta)\} \quad fst_\pi(\theta_1\vee\theta_2)=fst_\pi(\theta_1) \cup fst_\pi(\theta_2)$

$fst_\pi(\pi'?\theta)=fst_\pi(\theta) \quad\quad\quad fst_\pi(\theta_1||\theta_2)=fst_\pi(\theta_1) \cup fst_\pi(\theta_2)$

$fst_\pi(\theta_1 \cdot \theta_2)= \begin{cases} fst_\pi(\theta_1) \cup fst_\pi(\theta_2) & if \ \delta(\theta_1)=true \\ fst_\pi(\theta_1) & if \ \delta(\theta_1)=false \end{cases}$

Definition 8 (*TimEffs* Partial Derivative). *Given any* $\Phi=\pi \wedge \theta$, *the partial derivative* $D_h^\pi(\theta)$ *computes the effects for the left quotient* $h^{-1}(\pi \wedge \theta)$, *cf. Definition 1.*

$D_h^\pi(\bot)=D_h^\pi(\epsilon)=False\wedge\bot \quad\quad D_h^\pi(A(v,\alpha^*))=(\pi\wedge(h=A(v,\alpha^*)))\wedge\epsilon \quad\quad D_h^\pi(\theta^*)=D_h^\pi(\theta)\cdot\theta^*$

$D_{\tau(\pi_1)}^\pi(\pi'?\theta)= \begin{cases} \pi\wedge\pi'?\theta & if \ \pi_1\not\Rightarrow\pi' \\ \pi\wedge\theta & if \ \pi_1\Rightarrow\pi' \end{cases} \quad D_h^\pi(\theta_1\cdot\theta_2)= \begin{cases} D_h^\pi(\theta_1)\cdot\theta_2\vee D_h^\pi(\theta_2) & if \ \delta_\pi(\theta_1)=true \\ D_h^\pi(\theta_1)\cdot\theta_2 & if \ \delta_\pi(\theta_1)=false \end{cases}$

$D_{(A(v,\alpha^*),t)}^\pi(\theta) = \bigvee \{D_{A(v,\alpha^*)}^{\pi'}(\theta') \mid (\pi' \wedge \theta') \in D_t^\pi(\theta)\}$

$D_t^\pi(\theta\#t')=(\pi \wedge t+t''=t') \wedge \theta\#t'' \quad (t'' \ is \ fresh) \quad\quad\quad D_h^\pi(\theta_1\vee\theta_2)=D_h^\pi(\theta_1) \vee D_h^\pi(\theta_2)$

$D_{A(v,\alpha^*)}^\pi(\theta\#t)=\bigvee\{(\pi'\wedge(\theta'\#t)) \mid (\pi'\wedge\theta')\in D_{A(v,\alpha^*)}^\pi(\theta)\} \quad D_h^\pi(\theta_1||\theta_2)=\bar{\bar{D}}_h^\pi(\theta_1)||\bar{\bar{D}}_h^\pi(\theta_2)$

Notice that the derivatives of a parallel composition makes use of the *Parallel Derivative* $\bar{\bar{D}}_h^\pi(\theta)$, defined as follows: $\bar{\bar{D}}_h^\pi(\theta)= \begin{cases} \pi\wedge\theta & if \ D_h^\pi(\pi \wedge \theta) = (False\wedge\bot) \\ D_h^\pi(\theta) & otherwise \end{cases}$

5.1 Rewriting Rules.
Given the well-defined auxiliary functions above, we now discuss the key rewriting rules that deployed in effects inclusion proofs.

$$\frac{}{\Gamma \vdash \pi \wedge \bot \sqsubseteq \Phi} \ \text{[Bot-LHS]} \quad\quad \frac{\Phi \neq \pi \wedge \bot}{\Gamma \vdash \Phi \not\sqsubseteq \pi \wedge \bot} \ \text{[Bot-RHS]}$$

$$\frac{\delta_{\pi_1}(\theta_1) \wedge \neg\delta_{\pi_2}(\theta_2)}{\Gamma \vdash \pi_1 \wedge \theta_1 \not\sqsubseteq \pi_2 \wedge \theta_2} \ \text{[DISPROVE]} \quad\quad \frac{\pi_1 \Rightarrow \pi_2 \quad\quad fst_{\pi_1}(\theta_1) = \{\}}{\Gamma \vdash \pi_1 \wedge \theta_1 \sqsubseteq \pi_2 \wedge \theta_2} \ \text{[PROVE]}$$

---

[7] $SAT(\pi)$ stands for querying the Z3 theorem prover to check the satisfiability of π.

Axiom rules [Bot-LHS] and [Bot-RHS] are analogous to the standard propositional logic, $\bot$ (referring to *false*) entails any effects, while no *non-false* effects
entails $\bot$. [DISPROVE] is used to disprove the inclusions when the antecedent is
nullable, while the consequent is not nullable.

We use two rules to prove an inclusion: (i) [PROVE] is used when the antecedent
has no head; and (ii) [REOCCUR] proves an inclusion when there exist inclusion
hypotheses in the proof context Γ, which are able to soundly prove the current
goal. [UNFOLD] is the inductive step of unfolding the inclusions. The proof of the
original inclusion succeeds if all the derivative inclusions succeed.

$$\frac{(\pi_1 \wedge \theta_1 \sqsubseteq \pi_3 \wedge \theta_3) \in \Gamma \quad (\pi_3 \wedge \theta_3 \sqsubseteq \pi_4 \wedge \theta_4) \in \Gamma \quad (\pi_4 \wedge \theta_4 \sqsubseteq \pi_2 \wedge \theta_2) \in \Gamma}{\Gamma \vdash \pi_1 \wedge \theta_1 \sqsubseteq \pi_2 \wedge \theta_2} \text{[REOCCUR]}$$

$$\frac{H = fst_{\pi_1}(\theta_1) \quad \Gamma' = \Gamma, (\pi_1 \wedge \theta_1 \sqsubseteq \pi_2 \wedge \theta_2) \quad \forall h \in H. \ (\Gamma' \vdash D_h^{\pi_1}(\theta_1) \sqsubseteq D_h^{\pi_2}(\theta_2))}{\Gamma \vdash \pi_1 \wedge \theta_1 \sqsubseteq \pi_2 \wedge \theta_2} \text{[UNFOLD]}$$

Theorem 2 (Termination of the TRS). *The TRS is terminating.*

Proof. See the technical report [16].

Theorem 3 (Soundness of the TRS). *Given an inclusion $\Phi_1 \sqsubseteq \Phi_2$, if the
TRS returns TRUE with a proof, then $\Phi_1 \sqsubseteq \Phi_2$ is valid.*

Proof. See the technical report [16].

6 Implementation and Evaluation

To show the feasibility, we prototype our automated verification system using
OCaml ($\sim$5k LOC); and prove soundness for both the forward verifier and the
TRS. We set up two experiments to evaluate our implementation: i) functionality validation via verifying symbolic timed programs; and ii) comparison with
PAT [17] and Uppaal [3] using real-life Fischer's mutual exclusion algorithm. Experiments are done on a MacBook with a 2.6 GHz 6-Core Intel i7 processor. The
source code and the evaluation benchmark are openly accessible from [18].

6.1 Experimental Results for Symbolic Timed Models. We manually
annotate *TimEffs* specifications for a set of synthetic examples (for about 54 programs), to test the main contributions, including: computing effects from symbolic timed programs written in C^t; and the inclusion checking for *TimEffs* with
the parallel composition, block waiting operator and shared global variables.

Table 3 presents the evaluation results for another 16 C^t programs[8], and the
annotated temporal specifications are in a 1:1 ratio for succeeded/failed cases.
The table records: **No.**, index of the program; **LOC**, lines of code; **Forward(ms)**,
effects computation time; **#Prop(✓)**, number of valid properties; **Avg-Prove(ms)**,
average proving time for the valid properties; **#Prop(✗)**, number of invalid properties; **Avg-Dis(ms)**, average disproving time for the invalid properties; **#AskZ3**,
number of querying Z3 through out the experiments.

---

[8] All programs contain timed constructs, conditionals, and parallel compositions.

Table 3. Experimental Results for Manually Constructed Synthetic Examples.

No.	LOC	Forward(ms)	#Prop(✓)	Avg-Prove(ms)	#Prop(✗)	Avg-Dis(ms)	#AskZ3
1	26	0.006	5	52.379	5	21.31	77
2	37	43.955	5	83.374	5	52.165	188
3	44	32.654	5	52.524	5	33.444	104
4	72	202.181	5	82.922	5	55.971	229
5	98	42.706	7	149.345	7	60.325	396
6	134	403.617	7	160.932	7	292.304	940
7	133	51.492	7	17.901	7	47.643	118
8	173	57.114	7	40.772	7	30.977	128
9	182	872.995	9	252.123	9	113.838	1142
10	210	546.222	9	146.341	9	57.832	570
11	240	643.133	9	146.268	9	69.245	608
12	260	1032.31	9	242.699	9	123.054	928
13	265	12558.05	11	150.999	11	117.288	2465
14	286	12257.834	11	501.994	11	257.800	3090
15	287	1383.034	11	546.064	11	407.952	1489
16	337	49873.835	11	1863.901	11	954.996	15505

Observations: i) the proving/disproving time increases when the effect computation time increases because larger **Forward(ms)** indicates the higher complexity w.r.t the timed constructs, which complicates the inclusion checking; ii) while *the number of querying Z3 per property* (**#AskZ3/(#Prop(✓)+#Prop(✗)**)) goes up, the proving/disproving time goes up. Besides, we notice that iii) the disproving times for invalid properties are constantly lower than the proving process, regardless of the program's complexity, which is as expected in a TRS.

6.2 Verifying Fischer's mutual exclusion algorithm. As shown in Fig. 4, the data in columns **PAT(s)** and **Uppaal(s)** are drawn from prior work [19], which indicate the time to prove Fischer's mutual exclusion w.r.t the number of processes (**#Proc**) in PAT and Uppaal respectively. For our system, based on the implementation presented in Fig. 5, we are able to prove the mutual exclusion properties, given the arithmetic constraint d<e. Besides, the system disproves mutual exclusion when d≤e. We record the proving (**Prove(s)**) and disproving (**Disprove(s)**) time and their number of uniquely querying Z3 (**#AskZ3-u**).

Table 4. Comparison with PAT via verifying Fischer's mutual exclusion algorithm

#Proc	Prove(s)	#AskZ3-u	Disprove(s)	#AskZ3-u	PAT(s)	Uppaal(s)
2	0.09	31	0.110	37	≤0.05	≤0.09
3	0.21	35	0.093	42	≤0.05	≤0.09
4	0.46	63	0.120	47	0.05	0.09
5	25.0	84	0.128	52	0.15	0.19

Observations: i) automata-based model checkers (both PAT and Uppaal) are vastly efficient when given concrete values for constants d and e; however ii) our proposal is able to symbolically prove the algorithm by only providing the constraints of d and e, which cannot be achieved by existing model checkers; ii) our verification time largely depends on the number of querying Z3, which is optimized in our implementation by keeping a table for already queried constraints.

6.3 Case Study: Prove it when Reoccur. Termination of TRS is guaranteed because the set of derivatives to be considered is finite, and possible cycles are detected using *memorization* [14], demonstrated in Table 5. In step ②, in order to eliminate the first event B, A*#tR has to be reduced to ϵ, therefore the RHS time constraint has been strengthened to tR=0. Looking at the sub-tree (I), in step ⑤, tL and tR are split into tL^1+tL^2 and tR^1+tR^2. Then in step ⑥, A#tL^1 together with A#tR^1 are eliminated, unifying tL^1 and tR^1 by adding the side constraint tL^1=tR^1. In step ⑧, we observe the proposition is isomorphic with one of the the previous step, marked using (‡). Hence we apply the rule [REOCCUR] to prove it with a succeed side constraints entailment.

Table 5. The reoccurrence proving example. (I) is the left hand side sub-tree of the main rewriting proof tree.

$$
\begin{array}{l}
\text{------------------------ ④ [PROVE]}\\
\text{True} \wedge \epsilon \sqsubseteq \text{tR=0} \wedge \epsilon\\
\text{------------------------ ③ [Normal]}\\
\end{array}
$$

	True $\wedge$ $\cancel{B}$ $\sqsubseteq$ tR=0 $\wedge$ $\cancel{B}$ ② [UNFOLD]
(I)	True $\wedge$ B $\sqsubseteq$ tR<4 $\wedge$ (A*#tR) $\cdot$ B ① [OR–LHS]

tL<3$\wedge$(A*#tL)$\cdot$B $\sqsubseteq$ tR<4$\wedge$(A*#tR)$\cdot$B

(tL<3 $\wedge$ (A*#tL) $\cdot$ B) $\vee$ (True $\wedge$ B) $\sqsubseteq$ tR<4 $\wedge$ (A*#tR) $\cdot$ B

(I) :

tL<3$\wedge$tL^1+tL^2=tL$\wedge$tR=tR^1+tR^2$\wedge$tL^1=tR^1$\wedge$tL^2=tR^2$\Rightarrow$tR<4

tL<3 $\wedge$ (A*#tL^2) $\cdot$ B $\sqsubseteq$ tR<4 $\wedge$ (A*#tR^2) $\cdot$ B   (‡) ⑧ [REOCCUR]

tL<3$\wedge$ $\cancel{A\#tL^1}$ $\cdot$ A*#tL^2$\cdot$B$\sqsubseteq$tR<4$\wedge$ $\cancel{A\#tR^1}$ A*#tR^2$\cdot$B ⑦ [UNFOLD]

tL<3$\wedge$(A#tL^1$\cdot$ A*#tL^2)$\cdot$B$\sqsubseteq$tR<4$\wedge$(A#tR^1$\cdot$ A*#tR^2)$\cdot$B ⑥ [UNFOLD] π_u:tL^1=tR^1

tL<3 $\wedge$ (A*#tL) $\cdot$ B $\sqsubseteq$ tR<4 $\wedge$ (A*#tR) $\cdot$ B   (‡) ⑤ [SPLIT]tL^1+tL^2=tL$\wedge$tR^1+tR^2=tR

6.4 Discussion. Our implementation is the first that proves the inclusion of symbolic TAs, which is considered significant because it overcomes the following main limitations of traditional timed model checking: i) TAs cannot be used to specify/verify incompletely specified systems (i.e., whose timing constants have yet to be known) and hence cannot be used in early design phases; ii) verifying a system with a set of timing constants usually requires enumerating all of them if they are supposed to be integer-valued; iii) TAs cannot be used to verify systems with timing constants to be taken in a real-valued dense interval.

7 Related Work

7.1 Verification Framework. This work draws the most similarities to [20], which also deploys a forward verifier and a TRS for extended regular expressions. The differences are: i) [20] targets general-purpose sequential programs without shared variables, whereas this work targets time-critical programs with the presence of concurrency and global shared states; ii) the dependent values in [20] denote the number of repetitions of a trace, whereas in this work, they abstract the real-time bounds; iii) in this work, the TRS supports inclusion checking for the block waiting operator π? and the concurrent composition ||. These are essential in timed verification (or, more generally, for distributed systems), which are not supported in [20] or any other TRS-related works.

7.2   Specifications and Real-Time Verification. Apart from compositional modelling for real-time systems based on timed-process algebras, such as Timed CSP [8] and CCS+Time [21], there have been a number of translation-based approaches on building verification support for timed-process algebras. For example, in [8], Timed CSP is translated to TAs (TAs) so that the model checker Uppaal [3] can be applied. On the other hand, all the translation-based approaches share the common problem: the overhead introduced by the complex translation makes it particularly inefficient when *disproving* properties. We are of the opinion that in that the goal of verifying real-time systems, in particular safety-critical systems is to check logical temporal properties, which can be done without constructing the whole reachability graph or the full power of model-checking. We consider our approach is simpler as it is based directly on constraint-solving techniques and can be fairly efficient in verifying systems consisting of many components as it avoids to explore the whole state-space [20,22].

This work draws similarities to Real-Time Maude [23], which complements timed automata with more expressive object-oriented specifications.

7.3   Clock Manipulation and Zone-based Bisimulation. The concept of implicit clocks has also been used in time Petri nets, and implemented in a several model checking engines, e.g., [24]. On the other hand, to make model checking more efficient with *explicit* clocks, [25,26,27,28] work on dynamically deleting or merging clocks. Our work also draw connections with region/zone-based bisimulations [29], which is broadly used in reasoning timed automata.

8   Conclusion

This work provides an alternative approach for verifying real-time systems, where temporal behaviors are reasoned at the source level, and the specification expressiveness goes beyond traditional Timed Automata. We define the novel effects logic *TimEffs*, to capture real-time behavioral patterns and temporal properties. We demonstrate how to build axiomatic semantics (or rather an effects system) for C^t via timed-trace processing functions. We use this semantic model to enable a Hoare-style forward verifier, which computes the program effects constructively. We present an effects inclusion checker – the TRS – to efficiently prove the annotated temporal properties. We prototype the verification system and show its feasibility. To the best of our knowledge, our work proposes the first algebraic TRS for solving inclusion relations between timed specifications.

Limitations And Future Work. Our TRS is incomplete, meaning there exist valid inclusions which will be disproved in our system. That is mainly because of insufficient unification in favour of achieving automation. We also foresee the possibilities of adding other logics into our existing trace-based temporal logic, such as separation logic for verifying heap-manipulating distributed programs.

9   Acknowledgements

The authors would like to thank anonymous reviewers for their comments. This work was partially supported by a Singapore Ministry of Education (MoE) Tier 3 grant "Automated Program Repair", MOET32021-0001.

References

1. R. Alur and D. L. Dill, "A theory of timed automata," *Theor. Comput. Sci.*, vol. 126, no. 2, pp. 183–235, 1994. [Online]. Available: https://doi.org/10.1016/0304-3975(94)90010-8

2. X. Wang, J. Sun, T. Wang, and S. Qin, "Language inclusion checking of timed automata with non-zenoness," *IEEE Trans. Software Eng.*, vol. 43, no. 11, pp. 995–1008, 2017. [Online]. Available: https://doi.org/10.1109/TSE.2017.2653778

3. K. G. Larsen, P. Pettersson, and W. Yi, "UPPAAL in a nutshell," *Int. J. Softw. Tools Technol. Transf.*, vol. 1, no. 1-2, pp. 134–152, 1997. [Online]. Available: https://doi.org/10.1007/s100090050010

4. S. Yovine, "KRONOS: A verification tool for real-time systems," *Int. J. Softw. Tools Technol. Transf.*, vol. 1, no. 1-2, pp. 123–133, 1997. [Online]. Available: https://doi.org/10.1007/s100090050009

5. F. Wang, R. Wu, and G. Huang, "Verifying timed and linear hybrid rule-systems with RED," in *Proceedings of the 17th International Conference on Software Engineering and Knowledge Engineering (SEKE'2005), Taipei, Taiwan, Republic of China, July 14-16, 2005*, W. C. Chu, N. J. Juzgado, and W. E. Wong, Eds., 2005, pp. 448–454.

6. K. Havelund, A. Skou, K. G. Larsen, and K. Lund, "Formal modeling and analysis of an audio/video protocol: an industrial case study using UPPAAL," in *Proceedings of the 18th IEEE Real-Time Systems Symposium (RTSS '97), December 3-5, 1997, San Francisco, CA, USA.* IEEE Computer Society, 1997, pp. 2–13. [Online]. Available: https://doi.org/10.1109/REAL.1997.641264

7. K. G. Larsen, M. Mikucionis, B. Nielsen, and A. Skou, "Testing real-time embedded software using UPPAAL-TRON: an industrial case study," in *EMSOFT 2005, September 18-22, 2005, Jersey City, NJ, USA, 5th ACM International Conference On Embedded Software, Proceedings*, W. H. Wolf, Ed. ACM, 2005, pp. 299–306. [Online]. Available: https://doi.org/10.1145/1086228.1086283

8. J. S. Dong, P. Hao, S. Qin, J. Sun, and W. Yi, "Timed automata patterns," *IEEE Trans. Software Eng.*, vol. 34, no. 6, pp. 844–859, 2008. [Online]. Available: https://doi.org/10.1109/TSE.2008.52

9. A. David and M. D. Möller, "From huppaal to uppaal–a translation from hierarchical timed automata to flat timed automata," 2001.

10. L. Lamport, "Real-time model checking is really simple," in *Correct Hardware Design and Verification Methods, 13th IFIP WG 10.5 Advanced Research Working Conference, CHARME 2005, Saarbrücken, Germany, October 3-6, 2005, Proceedings*, ser. Lecture Notes in Computer Science, D. Borrione and W. J. Paul, Eds., vol. 3725. Springer, 2005, pp. 162–175. [Online]. Available: https://doi.org/10.1007/11560548_14

11. P. L. P. Ltd., https://www.programiz.com/javascript/setTimeout, 2022.

12. V. M. Antimirov and P. D. Mosses, "Rewriting extended regular expressions," *Theor. Comput. Sci.*, vol. 143, no. 1, pp. 51–72, 1995. [Online]. Available: https://doi.org/10.1016/0304-3975(95)80024-4

13. V. Antimirov, "Partial derivatives of regular expressions and finite automata constructions," in *Annual Symposium on Theoretical Aspects of Computer Science.* Springer, 1995, pp. 455–466.

14. J. Brotherston, "Cyclic proofs for first-order logic with inductive definitions," in *Automated Reasoning with Analytic Tableaux and Related Methods, International Conference, TABLEAUX 2005, Koblenz, Germany, September 14-17, 2005,*

Proceedings, ser. Lecture Notes in Computer Science, B. Beckert, Ed., vol. 3702. Springer, 2005, pp. 78–92. [Online]. Available: https://doi.org/10.1007/11554554_8

15. L. M. de Moura and N. Bjørner, "Z3: an efficient SMT solver," in *Tools and Algorithms for the Construction and Analysis of Systems, 14th International Conference, TACAS 2008, Held as Part of the Joint European Conferences on Theory and Practice of Software, ETAPS 2008, Budapest, Hungary, March 29-April 6, 2008. Proceedings*, ser. Lecture Notes in Computer Science, C. R. Ramakrishnan and J. Rehof, Eds., vol. 4963. Springer, 2008, pp. 337–340. [Online]. Available: https://doi.org/10.1007/978-3-540-78800-3_24

16. Anonymous, https://www.comp.nus.edu.sg/~yahuis/TACAS2023.pdf, 2023.

17. J. Sun, Y. Liu, J. S. Dong, and J. Pang, "PAT: towards flexible verification under fairness," in *Computer Aided Verification, 21st International Conference, CAV 2009, Grenoble, France, June 26 - July 2, 2009. Proceedings*, ser. Lecture Notes in Computer Science, A. Bouajjani and O. Maler, Eds., vol. 5643. Springer, 2009, pp. 709–714. [Online]. Available: https://doi.org/10.1007/978-3-642-02658-4_59

18. Y. Song, https://zenodo.org/record/7192718#.Y7rTmi8RpOQ, 2022.

19. Y. Liu, J. Sun, and J. S. Dong, "PAT 3: An extensible architecture for building multi-domain model checkers," in *IEEE 22nd International Symposium on Software Reliability Engineering, ISSRE 2011, Hiroshima, Japan, November 29 - December 2, 2011*, T. Dohi and B. Cukic, Eds. IEEE Computer Society, 2011, pp. 190–199. [Online]. Available: https://doi.org/10.1109/ISSRE.2011.19

20. Y. Song and W. Chin, "Automated temporal verification of integrated dependent effects," in *Formal Methods and Software Engineering - 22nd International Conference on Formal Engineering Methods, ICFEM 2020, Singapore, Singapore, March 1-3, 2021, Proceedings*, ser. Lecture Notes in Computer Science, S. Lin, Z. Hou, and B. P. Mahony, Eds., vol. 12531. Springer, 2020, pp. 73–90. [Online]. Available: https://doi.org/10.1007/978-3-030-63406-3_5

21. W. Yi, "CCS + time = an interleaving model for real time systems," in *Automata, Languages and Programming, 18th International Colloquium, ICALP91, Madrid, Spain, July 8-12, 1991, Proceedings*, ser. Lecture Notes in Computer Science, J. L. Albert, B. Monien, and M. Rodríguez-Artalejo, Eds., vol. 510. Springer, 1991, pp. 217–228. [Online]. Available: https://doi.org/10.1007/3-540-54233-7_136

22. W. Yi, P. Pettersson, and M. Daniels, "Automatic verification of real-time communicating systems by constraint-solving," in *Formal Description Techniques VII, Proceedings of the 7th IFIP WG6.1 International Conference on Formal Description Techniques, Berne, Switzerland, 1994*, ser. IFIP Conference Proceedings, D. Hogrefe and S. Leue, Eds., vol. 6. Chapman & Hall, 1994, pp. 243–258.

23. P. C. Ölveczky and J. Meseguer, "Semantics and pragmatics of Real-Time Maude," *Higher-Order and Symbolic Computation*, vol. 20, no. 1-2, pp. 161–196, 2007.

24. B. Berthomieu and F. Vernadat, "Time petri nets analysis with TINA," in *Third International Conference on the Quantitative Evaluation of Systems (QEST 2006), 11-14 September 2006, Riverside, California, USA.* IEEE Computer Society, 2006, pp. 123–124. [Online]. Available: https://doi.org/10.1109/QEST.2006.56

25. C. Daws and S. Yovine, "Reducing the number of clock variables of timed automata," in *Proceedings of the 17th IEEE Real-Time Systems Symposium (RTSS '96), December 4-6, 1996, Washington, DC, USA.* IEEE Computer Society, 1996, pp. 73–81. [Online]. Available: https://doi.org/10.1109/REAL.1996.563702

26. S. Balaguer and T. Chatain, "Avoiding shared clocks in networks of timed automata," *Log. Methods Comput. Sci.*, vol. 9, no. 4, 2013. [Online]. Available: https://doi.org/10.2168/LMCS-9(4:13)2013

27. M. Muñiz, B. Westphal, and A. Podelski, "Detecting quasi-equal clocks in timed automata," in *Formal Modeling and Analysis of Timed Systems - 11th International Conference, FORMATS 2013, Buenos Aires, Argentina, August 29-31, 2013. Proceedings*, ser. Lecture Notes in Computer Science, V. A. Braberman and L. Fribourg, Eds., vol. 8053. Springer, 2013, pp. 198–212. [Online]. Available: https://doi.org/10.1007/978-3-642-40229-6_14

28. S. Guha, C. Narayan, and S. Arun-Kumar, "Reducing clocks in timed automata while preserving bisimulation," in *CONCUR 2014 - Concurrency Theory - 25th International Conference, CONCUR 2014, Rome, Italy, September 2-5, 2014. Proceedings*, ser. Lecture Notes in Computer Science, P. Baldan and D. Gorla, Eds., vol. 8704. Springer, 2014, pp. 527–543. [Online]. Available: https://doi.org/10.1007/978-3-662-44584-6_36

29. L. Luthmann, H. Göttmann, and M. Lochau, "Checking timed bisimulation with bounded zone-history graphs - technical report," *CoRR*, vol. abs/1910.08992, 2019. [Online]. Available: http://arxiv.org/abs/1910.08992

Parameterized Verification under TSO with Data Types

Parosh Aziz Abdulla[1], Mohamad Faouzi Atig[1], Florian Furbach[1]([✉]),
Adwait A. Godbole[3], Yacoub G. Hendi[1], Shankara N. Krishna[2], and
Stephan Spengler[1]

[1] Uppsala University, Uppsala, Sweden
florian.furbach@it.uu.se
[2] Indian Institute of Technology Bombay, Mumbai, India
[3] UC Berkeley, Berkeley, USA

We consider parameterized verification of systems executing according to the total store ordering (TSO) semantics. The processes manipulate abstract data types over potentially infinite domains. We present a framework that translates the reachability problem for such systems to the reachability problem for register machines enriched with the given abstract data type. We use the translation to obtain tight complexity bounds for TSO-based parameterized verification over several abstract data types, such as push-down automata, ordered multi push-down automata, one-counter nets, one-counter automata, and Petri nets. We apply the framework to get complexity bounds for higher order stack and counter variants as well.

1 Introduction

A *parameterized system* consists of a fixed but arbitrary number of identical processes that execute in parallel. The goal of *parameterized verification* is to prove the correctness of the system regardless of the number of processes. Examples for such systems are sensor networks, leader election protocols, and mutual exclusion protocols. The topic has been the subject of intensive research for more than three decades (see e.g. [10,32,13,6]), and it is the subject of one chapter of the Handbook of Model Checking [8]. Research on parameterized verification has been mostly conducted under the premise that (i) the processes run according to the classical Sequential Consistency (SC) semantics, and (ii) the processes are finite-state machines.

Under SC, the processes operate on a set of shared variables through which they communicate *atomically*, i.e., read and write operations take effect immediately. In particular, a write operation is visible to all the processes as soon as the writing process carries out its operation. Therefore, the processes always maintain a uniform view of the shared memory: they all see the latest value written on any given variable, hence we can interpret program runs as interleavings of sequential process executions. Although SC has been immensely popular as an intuitive way of understanding the behaviours of concurrent processes, it is not realistic to assume computation platforms guarantee SC anymore. The reason is that, due to hardware and compiler optimizations, most modern platforms

S. Sankaranarayanan and N. Sharygina (Eds.): TACAS 2023, LNCS 13993, pp. 588–606, 2023.
https://doi.org/10.1007/978-3-031-30823-9_30

allow more relaxed program behaviours than those permitted under SC, leading to so-called *weak memory models*. Weakly consistent platforms are found at all levels of system design such as multiprocessor architectures (e.g., [48,47]), Cache protocols (e.g., [46,21]), language level concurrency (e.g., [41]), and distributed data stores (e.g., [17]). Therefore, in recent years, research on the parameterized verification of concurrent programs under weak memory models have started to become popular. Notable examples are the cases of the TSO semantics [4] and the Release-Acquire semantics of C11 [39].

In a parallel development, several works have extended the basic model of parameterized systems (under the SC semantics) by considering processes that are infinite-state systems. The most dominant such class has been the case where the individual processes are variants of push-down automata [36,33,28,28,40,42,30]

Parameterized verification is difficult, even under the original assumption of both SC and finite-state processes as we still need to handle an infinite state space. The extension to weakly consistent systems is even more complex due to the intricate extra process behaviours. Almost all weak memory models induce infinite state spaces even without parameterization and even when the program itself is finite-state. Therefore, performing parameterized verification under weak consistency requires handling a state space that is infinite in two dimensions; one due to parameterization and one due to the weak memory model. The same applies to the extension of parameterized verification under SC where the processes are infinite-state: in addition to infiniteness due to parameterization, we have a second source of infinity due to the infiniteness of the processes.

In this paper, we combine the above two extensions. We study parameterized verification of programs under the TSO semantics, where the processes use infinite data structures such as stacks and counters. The framework is uniform in that the manipulation can be described using an abstract data type.

We revisit the pivot abstraction technique presented in [4]. As a first contribution, we show that we can capture pivot abstraction precisely, using a class of register machines in which the registers assume values over a finite domain. We show that, for any given abstract data type A, we can reduce, in polynomial time, the parameterized verification problem under TSO and A to the reachability problem for register machines manipulating A. Furthermore, we show that the reduction also holds in the other direction: the reachability problem for register machines over A is polynomial-time reducible to the parameterized verification problem under TSO for A. In particular, the model abstracts away the semantics of TSO (in fact, it abstracts away concurrency altogether) since we are dealing with a single register machine.

We summarize the contributions of the paper as follows:

- We present a register abstraction scheme that captures the behaviour of parameterized systems under the TSO semantics.
- We translate parameterized verification under the TSO semantics when the processes manipulate an ADT A, to the reachability problem for register machines operating over A.
- We instantiate the framework for deciding the complexity of parameterized verification under TSO for different abstract data types. In particular we

show the problem is PSPACE-complete when A is a one-counter, ExpTime-complete if A is a stack, 2-ETime-complete if A is an ordered multi stack, and ExpSpace-complete if A is a Petri net. We obtain further complexity bounds for higher order counter and stacks.

Related Work There has been an extensive research effort on parameterized verification since the 1980s (see [13,8] for recent surveys of the field). Early works showed the undecidability of the general problem (even assuming finite-state processes) [10], and hence the emphasis has been on finding useful special cases. Such cases are characterized by three aspects, namely the system topology (unordered, arrays, trees, graphs, rings, etc.), the allowed communication patterns (shared memory, Rendez-vous, broadcast, lossy channels, etc.), and the process types (anonymous, with IDs, with priorities, etc.) [27,20,31,24,23,43].

Another line of research to counter undecidability are over-approximations based on regular model checking [38,14,16,1], monotonic abstraction [5], and symmetry reduction [37,22,7].

A seminal work in the area is the paper by German and Sistla [32]. The authors consider the verification of systems consisting of an arbitrary number of finite-state processes interacting through Rendez-Vous communication. The paper shows that the model checking problem is ExpSpace-complete. In a series of more recent papers, parameterized verification has been considered in the case where the individual processes are push-down automata. [36,33,28,40,42,30].All the above works assume the SC semantics.

Due to the relevance of weak memory models in parameterized verification, papers on the topic have started to appear in the last two years. The paper [4] considers parameterized verification of programs running under TSO, and shows that the reachability problem is PSPACE-complete. However, the paper assumes that the processes are finite-state and, in particular, the processes do not manipulate unbounded data domains. The model of the paper corresponds to the particular case of our framework where we take the abstract data type to be empty. In this case our framework also implies PSPACE-completeness.

The paper [39] shows PSPACE-completeness when the underlying semantics is the Release-Acquire fragment of C11. The latter semantics gives rise to different semantics compared to TSO. The paper also considers finite-state processes.

The paper [2] considers parameterized verification of programs running under TSO. However, the paper applies the framework of well-structured systems where the buffers of the processes are modeled as lossy channels, and hence the complexity of the algorithm is non-primitive recursive. In particular, the paper does not give any complexity bounds for the reachability problem (or any other verification problems). Conchon et al. [19] address the parameterized verification of programs under TSO as well. They make use of Model Checker Modulo Theories, no decidability or complexity results are given. The paper [15] considers checking the robustness property against SC for parameterized systems running under the TSO semantics. However, the robustness problem is entirely different from reachability and the techniques and results developed in the paper cannot be applied in our setting. The paper shows that the problem is EXPSPACE-hard. All these works assume finite-state processes.

In contrast to all the above works, the current paper is the first paper that studies decidability and complexity of parameterized verification under the TSO semantics when the individual processes are infinite-state.

2   Preliminaries

We denote a function f between sets A and B by $f : A \rightarrow B$. We write $f[a \leftarrow b]$ to denote the function f' such that $f'(a) = b$ and $f'(x) = f(x)$ for all $x \neq a$.

For a finite set A, we use $|A|$ to refer to the size of A. We also use A^* to denote the set of words over A including the empty word ϵ. For a word $w \in A^*$, we use $|w|$ to refer to the length of w. We say a word w is *differentiated* if all symbols in w are pairwise different. The set A^{diff} is the set of all differentiated words over the set A. Finally, for a differentiated word w, we define $\mathrm{pos}(w)(a)$ as the unique position of the letter a in w.

A *labelled transition system* is a tuple $\langle \mathsf{C}, \mathsf{C_{init}}, \mathsf{Labs}, \rightarrow \rangle$, where C is the set of configurations, $\mathsf{C_{init}} \subseteq \mathsf{C}$ is the set of initial configurations, Labs is a finite set of labels and $\rightarrow \subseteq \mathsf{C} \times \mathsf{Labs} \times \mathsf{C}$ is the transition relation over the set of configurations. For a transition $\langle \mathsf{c_1}, \mathsf{lab}, \mathsf{c_2} \rangle \in \rightarrow$, we usually write $\mathsf{c_1} \xrightarrow{\mathsf{lab}} \mathsf{c_2}$ instead. We use $\mathsf{c_1} \rightarrow \mathsf{c_2}$ to denote that $\mathsf{c_1} \xrightarrow{\mathsf{lab}} \mathsf{c_2}$ for some $\mathsf{lab} \in \mathsf{Labs}$. Furthermore, we write $\xrightarrow{*}$ to denote the transitive reflexive closure over $\rightarrow$, and if $\mathsf{c_1} \xrightarrow{*} \mathsf{c_2}$ then we say $\mathsf{c_2}$ is *reachable from* $\mathsf{c_1}$. If $\mathsf{c_1} \in \mathsf{C_{init}}$, then we just say that $\mathsf{c_2}$ is *reachable*. A *run* ρ is an alternating sequence of configurations and labels and is expressed as follows: $\mathsf{c_0} \xrightarrow{\mathsf{lab_1}} \mathsf{c_1} \xrightarrow{\mathsf{lab_2}} \mathsf{c_2} \ldots \mathsf{c_{n-1}} \xrightarrow{\mathsf{lab_n}} \mathsf{c_n}$. Given ρ, we write $\mathsf{c_0} \xrightarrow{n} \mathsf{c_n}$ meaning that $\mathsf{c_n}$ is reachable from $\mathsf{c_0}$ by n steps, and we write $\mathsf{c_0} \xrightarrow{\rho} \mathsf{c_n}$ meaning that $\mathsf{c_n}$ is reachable from $\mathsf{c_0}$ through the run ρ.

3   Abstract Data Types (ADT)

In this section, we introduce the notion of abstract data types (ADTs) which will be used extensively in the paper. An ADT is a labelled transition system $\mathsf{A} = \langle \mathsf{Vals}, \{\mathsf{val_{init}}\}, \mathsf{Ops}, \rightarrow_{\mathsf{A}} \rangle$. Intuitively, this describes the behaviour of some data type such as a stack, or a counter. Vals is the set of configurations of A. It describes the possible values the data type can assume. The initial configuration is $\mathsf{val_{init}} \in \mathsf{Vals}$. The set of labels Ops represents the operations that can be executed on the data type and the transition relation $\rightarrow_{\mathsf{A}} \in \mathsf{Vals} \times \mathsf{Ops} \times \mathsf{Vals}$ describes the semantics of these operations. Below, we give some concrete examples of abstract data types.

Example 1 (Counter). We define a counter, denoted by the ADT CT, as follows. The set of configurations $\mathsf{Vals}^{\mathrm{CT}} = \mathbb{N}$ are the natural numbers. The initial value, denoted by $\mathsf{val_{init}^{\mathrm{CT}}}$, is 0. The set of operations is $\mathsf{Ops}^{\mathrm{CT}} = \{\mathtt{inc}, \mathtt{dec}, \mathtt{isZero}\}$. The transition relation $\rightarrow_{\mathrm{CT}}$ is as follows: The operations $\mathtt{inc}$ and $\mathtt{dec}$ increase or decrease the value of the counter by one, respectively. The latter operation is only enabled if the value of the counter is non-zero, otherwise it blocks. Finally, the transition isZero checks that the value of the counter is zero, i.e. it is only enabled if that condition is true.

Example 2 (Weak Counter). A weak counter differs from a counter in that it cannot be checked for zero. The ADT wCT representing a weak counter is defined as in Example 1, except the operations of wCT are reduced to $\mathsf{Ops}^{\mathrm{wCT}} = \{\mathtt{inc}, \mathtt{dec}\}$.

Example 3 (Stack). Let Γ be a finite set representing the stack alphabet. A *stack* $\mathrm{ST} = \langle \mathsf{Vals}^{\mathrm{ST}}, \{\mathsf{val}_{\mathrm{init}}^{\mathrm{ST}}\}, \mathsf{Ops}^{\mathrm{ST}}, \rightarrow_{\mathrm{ST}} \rangle$ on Γ is defined as follows. The configurations of ST are $\mathsf{Vals}^{\mathrm{ST}} = \Gamma^*$ and the initial configuration is the empty stack $\mathsf{val}_{\mathrm{init}}^{\mathrm{ST}} = \varepsilon$. The set of operations is $\mathsf{Ops}^{\mathrm{ST}} = \{\mathtt{pop}(\gamma), \mathtt{push}(\gamma), \mathtt{isEmpty} \mid \gamma \in \Gamma\}$. The transition relation is as follows. For every word $w \in \Gamma^*$ and every symbol $\gamma \in \Gamma$, $\mathtt{push}(\gamma)$ adds the symbol γ to the top of the stack. Similiarly, the $\mathtt{pop}(\gamma)$ operation removes the topmost symbol from the stack. It is only enabled if the topmost symbol on the stack. The $\mathtt{isEmpty}$ operation does not change the stack, but can only be performed if the stack is the empty word ε.

Example 4 (Petri Nets). Given a Petri net[44], We can define a corresponding ADT PETRI that models its semantics. The values are the markings, the operations are the Petri net transitions and the transition relation is given by the input and output vectors of the Petri net transitions.

Higher Order ADTs We extend the ADT ST to higher order stacks referred to as n-ST. This is done recursively[18,25]. The formal definition is in the full version of our paper [3]. A value of a level n higher order stack n-ST is a stack of level $n-1$ stacks. For level 1, it is the standard stack ST. The operations for level n are $\mathsf{Ops}^{n\text{-}\mathrm{ST}} = \{\mathtt{pop}(\gamma), \mathtt{push}(\gamma), \mathtt{pop}_k, \mathtt{push}_k, \mid \gamma \in \Gamma, 2 \leq k \leq n\}$. The operations $\mathtt{pop}(\gamma)$ and $\mathtt{push}(\gamma)$ are recursively applied to the top element in the stack (which consists of a stack that is one level lower) until the level of the top element is 1. Here, they have the standard stack behaviour. Operations $\mathtt{pop}_k$ and $\mathtt{push}_k$ are recursively applied to the top element until the level of the element is k. Then, a copy of this level k stack is pushed on top of the original.

Since a counter can be seen as a stack with an alphabet of size 1 (and a bottom element $\perp$), we can extend definitions of wCT and CT to n-wCT and n-CT in the same way. We add operations $\mathtt{inc}_k, \mathtt{dec}_k$. All operations are recursively applied to the top counter. For $\mathtt{inc}, \mathtt{dec}, \mathtt{isZero}$, we use standard behaviour once the level is 1. For $\mathtt{inc}_k, \mathtt{dec}_k$, we copy/remove the top element once the level is k.

Example 5 (Ordered Multi Stack). We extend the stack to a numbered list of n many stacks n-OMST [12]. A value of n-OMST consists of list of stacks $\mathsf{val}_1^{\mathrm{ST}} \ldots \mathsf{val}_n^{\mathrm{ST}}$. An operation $\mathsf{Ops}^{n\text{-}\mathrm{OMST}} = \{\mathtt{isZero}_i, \mathtt{pop}_i(\gamma), \mathtt{push}_i(\gamma), \mid \gamma \in \Gamma, i \leq n\}$ works on stack number i in the standard way. One additional condition is that the stacks have to be ordered, meaning an operation $\mathtt{pop}_i(\gamma)$ is only enabled if the stacks $1 \ldots i-1$ are empty.

4   TSO with an Abstract Data Type : TSO(A)

In this section, we introduce concurrent programs running under TSO(A) for an ADT $A = \langle \mathsf{Vals}, \{\mathsf{val_{init}}\}, \mathsf{Ops}, \rightarrow_A \rangle$. These programs consist of concurrent processes where the communication between processes is performed using shared memory under the TSO semantics. In addition, each process maintains a local variable of type A.

Syntax of TSO(A). Let Dom be a finite data domain and Vars be a finite set of shared variables over Dom. Let $d_{init} \in$ Dom be the initial value of the variables. We define the *instruction set* of TSO(A) as Instrs $= \{\mathtt{rd}(x, d), \mathtt{wr}(x, d) \mid x \in$ Vars, $d \in$ Dom$\} \cup \{\mathtt{skip}, \mathtt{mf}\}$, which are called *read, write, skip* and *memory fence*, respectively.

A process is represented by a finite state transition system. It is given by the tuple Proc $= \langle Q, q_{init}, \delta \rangle$, where Q is a finite set of states, $q_{init} \in$ Q is the initial state, and $\delta \subseteq$ Q $\times$ (Instrs $\cup$ Ops) $\times$ Q is the transition relation. We call this tuple the *description* of the process. A concurrent program is a tuple of processes $\mathcal{P} = \langle \mathsf{Proc}_\iota \rangle_{\iota \in \mathcal{I}}$, where $\mathcal{I}$ is some finite set of process identifiers. For each $\iota \in \mathcal{I}$ we have $\mathsf{Proc}^\iota = \langle Q^\iota, q_{init}^\iota, \delta^\iota \rangle$.

Semantics of TSO(A). We describe the semantics of a program $\mathcal{P}$ running under TSO(A) by a labelled transition system $\mathcal{T_P} = \langle C^\mathcal{P}, C_{init}^\mathcal{P}, \mathsf{Labs}^\mathcal{P}, \rightarrow_\mathcal{P} \rangle$. The formal definition is given in [3]. Under TSO(A), there is an unbounded FIFO buffer of writes between each process and the memory. A configuration $c \in C^\mathcal{P}$ of the system consists of the value of each variable in the shared memory as well as for each process: its local state, its value of the ADT, and the content of the corresponding write buffer.

The labelled transitions $\rightarrow_\mathcal{P}$ are as follows: A local skip transition simply updates the state of the corresponding process. An ADT operation additionally updates the ADT value according to ADT behaviour $\rightarrow_A$. When a process executes a write instruction, the operation is enqueued as a *pending write message* into its buffer. A message msg is an assignment of the form msg $= \langle x, d \rangle$, where $x \in$ Vars and $d \in$ Dom. We denote the set of all messages by Msgs $=$ Vars $\times$ Dom. The buffer content for a process is given as a word over Msgs. The messages inside each buffer are moved non-deterministically to the main memory in a FIFO manner. Once a message reaches the memory, it becomes visible to all the other processes. When executing a read instruction on a variable $x \in$ Vars, the process first checks its buffer for pending write messages on x. If the buffer contains such a message, then it reads the value of the most recent one. If the buffer contains no write messages on x, then the process fetches the value of x from the memory. The *initial configuration* is $c_{init}^\mathcal{P}$, where each process is in its initial state, each ADT holds its initial value, each store buffer is empty and the memory holds the initial values of all variables. Note that since FIFO buffer is unbounded, this is an infinite state transition system, even for finite ADT.

A sequence of transitions $c_0 \xrightarrow{\mathsf{lab_1}}_\mathcal{P} c_1 \xrightarrow{\mathsf{lab_2}}_\mathcal{P} c_2 \ldots c_{n-1} \xrightarrow{\mathsf{lab_n}}_\mathcal{P} c_n$ where $c_0 = c_{init}^\mathcal{P}$ is the initial configuration and $\mathsf{lab}_i \in \mathsf{Labs}^\mathcal{P}$ is called a run in the TSO(A) transition system. If there is a run ending in a configuration with state q_{final}, then we say q_{final} is reachable by Proc under TSO(A).

5   Parameterized Reachability in TSO(A)

In this section, we consider the parameterized TSO setting which allows for an a priori unbounded number of processes with the same process description. We begin by formally introducing the parameterized state reachability problem, and then develop a generic construction that allows us to represent the TSO semantics (except for the ADT) in a finite manner.

The Parameterized State Reachability Problem Intuitively, parameterization allows for an arbitrary number of identical processes. The parameterized state reachability problem for TSO(A) called TSO(A)-P-Reach identifies a family of (standard) reachability problem instances. We want to determine whether we have reachability in some member of the family. We now introduce this formally.

For a given process description Proc, we consider the program instance, $\mathcal{P}^n_{\mathsf{Proc}}$ parameterized by a natural number n as follows. For $\mathcal{I} = \{1, \ldots, n\}$, let $\mathcal{P}^n_{\mathsf{Proc}} = \langle \mathsf{Proc}_1, \ldots, \mathsf{Proc}_n \rangle$ with $\mathsf{Proc}_\iota = \mathsf{Proc}$ for all $\iota \in \mathcal{I}$. That is, the nth *slice* of the parameterized family of programs contains n processes, all with identical descriptions Proc. We require that all processes maintain copies of the ADT A.

TSO(A)-P-Reach:
Given: A process $\mathsf{Proc} = \langle \mathsf{Q}, \mathsf{q}_{\mathsf{init}}, \delta \rangle$, an ADT A, and a state $\mathsf{q}_{\mathsf{final}} \in \mathsf{Q}$,
Decide: Is there a $n \in \mathbb{N}$ s.t. $\mathsf{q}_{\mathsf{final}}$ is reachable by $\mathcal{P}^n_{\mathsf{Proc}}$ under TSO(A)?

When talking about a certain family of ADTs, e.g. the family of petri nets, we write TSO(PETRI)-P-Reach and mean the restriction of TSO(A)-P-Reach to petri nets, i.e. to instances where A is a petri net.

The main difference between the non-parameterized case and the parameterized case of the problem is that in the first case the index set $\mathcal{I}$ is *a priori* fixed, while in the second case it can be *arbitrary*. This results in $\mathsf{C}^{\mathcal{P}}_{\mathsf{init}}$ being a singleton in the non-parameterized case while it becomes infinite (one initial state for each n-slice) in the parameterized case.

We determine upper and lower bounds for the complexity of the state reachability problem. The challenge of solving this problem varies with the ADT. This problem for plain TSO without an ADT has been studied in [4]. They showed that the problem can be decided in PSPACE and is in fact PSPACE-complete. The result is based on an abstraction technique called the *pivot* semantics. The pivot semantics is *exact* in the sense that a state q is reachable under parameterized TSO if and only if it is reachable under the pivot semantics.

We show that the dynamics underlying the pivot abstraction can be generalized to our model with ADT. We show that the pivot abstraction can be extended to obtain a register machine. We use this construction to give a general characterization of TSO(A)-P-Reach. First, we recall the pivot abstraction. **The Pivot Abstraction** [4]. For a set of variables Vars and data domain Dom, processes generate pending write messages from the set $\mathsf{Msgs} = \mathsf{Vars} \times \mathsf{Dom}$ by executing **wr** instructions. This set has size $|\mathsf{Vars}| \cdot |\mathsf{Dom}|$ and hence at most as many distinct (variable, value) pairs can be produced in any run. For a run ρ of the program, for each message $\mathsf{msg} = \langle x, d \rangle \in \mathsf{Msgs}$ we can define the first point along ρ at which some write on variable x with value d is propagated to the memory. The pivot abstraction identifies these points as *pivot* points $\mathrm{pvt}(\mathsf{msg})$, for each distinct message in Msgs. For a write message msg under ρ, the pivot point $\mathrm{pvt}(\mathsf{msg})$ is the first point of propagation of msg to the memory under ρ.

The core observation is that if at some point in ρ, a process Proc_ι propagates a message $\mathsf{msg} = \langle x, d \rangle$ from its buffer to the memory, then after that point, the value d will always be available to read on variable x from the shared memory. Technically, this follows from parameterization. There are arbitrarily many processes executing identical descriptions. This means transitions of the original process Proc_ι can be mimicked by a *clone* process $\mathsf{Proc}_{\iota'}$ identical to Proc_ι. Hence, $\mathsf{Proc}_{\iota'}$ can replicate the execution of Proc_ι right up to the point where the message msg is the oldest message in its buffer. Then a single propagate step updates the value of x in the shared memory to d. There can be arbitrarily many such clones and the propagate step can happen at any time. It follows that beyond the $\mathrm{pvt}(\mathsf{msg})$ point in ρ, the value d can always be read from x.

For distinct messages from Msgs, we can order the pivot points corresponding to these messages according to the order in which they appear in ρ. This gives us a *first update sequence*, denoted by ω. No two messages in ω are the same; the set of such sequences is the set of differentiated words $\mathsf{Msgs}_{\mathsf{diff}}$. A message $\mathsf{msg} \in \mathsf{Msgs}$ in ω has the *rank* k if it is the k-th pivot point in ω.

Providers. The pivot abstraction simulates a run ρ under the TSO semantics by running abstract processes called *providers* in a sequential manner. For $1 \leq k \leq |\omega| + 1$, the k-provider simulates the process that generates the write of the rank k message $\langle x, d \rangle$ corresponding to the k-pivot in ρ. The k-provider completes its task when it has simulated this process until the point it generates $\langle x, d \rangle$. At this point, it invokes the $(k+1)$-provider. With this background, we now develop the formal pivot semantics for parameterized $\mathsf{TSO}(\mathsf{A})$.

Formal Pivot semantics for Parameterized $\mathsf{TSO}(\mathsf{A})$. We define the formal operational semantics of the pivot abstraction as a labelled transition system. Given a process description $\mathsf{Proc} = \langle Q, q_{\mathsf{init}}, \delta \rangle$ and ADT $\mathsf{A} = \langle \mathsf{Vals}, \{\mathsf{val}_{\mathsf{init}}\}, \mathsf{Ops}, \rightarrow_{\mathsf{A}} \rangle$, a configuration of the pivot transition system represents the *view* of a provider when simulating a run of the program. A view $v = \langle q, \mathsf{val}, \mathsf{Lw}, \omega, \phi_E, \phi_L, \phi_P \rangle$ is defined as follows. The process state is given by $q \in Q$. The value of the provider's ADT A is $\mathsf{val} \in \mathsf{Vals}$. The function $\mathsf{Lw} : \mathsf{Vars} \rightarrow \mathsf{Dom} \cup \{\oslash\}$ gives for each $x \in \mathsf{Vars}$, the value of the latest (i.e., most recent) write the provider has performed on x. If no such instruction exists (the process has made no writes to x) then $\mathsf{Lw}(x) = \oslash$. Note that Lw abstracts the buffer in terms of read-own-write operations since the process can only read from the most recent pending write in its buffer on each variable (if it exists). We define $\mathsf{Lw}_\oslash$ such that $\mathsf{Lw}_\oslash(x) = \oslash$ for all $x \in \mathsf{Vars}$. The first update sequence of pivot messages is $\omega \in \mathsf{Msgs}_{\mathsf{diff}}$. It is unchanged by transitions and remains constant throughout the pivot run.

The *external pointer*, $\phi_E \in \{0, 1, \ldots, |\omega|\}$ helps the provider keep track of which messages from ω it has observed. These messages have been propagated by other processes. The external pointer is used to identify which variables are still holding their initial values in the memory. If the provider observes an external write on a variable x (by accessing the memory), then this write has overwritten the initial value of x in the memory. The *local pointer* $\phi_L : \mathsf{Vars} \to \{0, 1, \ldots, |\omega|\}$ is a set of pointers, one for each variable $x \in \mathsf{Vars}$. The function $\phi_L(x)$ gives the highest ranked write operation the provider itself has performed (on any variable) before it performed the latest write on x. The local pointer is necessary to know which variables lose their initial values when we need to empty the buffer. In other words, the local pointer abstracts the buffer in terms of update operations. We define $\phi_L^{\max} := \max\{\phi_L(x) \mid x \in \mathsf{Vars}\}$ as the highest value of a local pointer and ϕ_L^0 such that $\phi_L^0(x) = 0$ for all variables $x \in \mathsf{Vars}$, i.e., the pointers are all in the leftmost position. The *progress pointer* $\phi_P \in \{1, 2, \ldots, |\omega| + 1\}$ gives the rank of the process the current provider is simulating.

$$\text{skip} \frac{\langle q, \mathtt{skip}, q' \rangle \in \delta}{\langle q, \mathsf{val}, \mathsf{Lw}, \omega, \phi_E, \phi_L, \phi_P \rangle \xrightarrow{\mathtt{skip}}_{\mathsf{pvt}} \langle q', \mathsf{val}, \mathsf{Lw}, \omega, \phi_E, \phi_L, \phi_P \rangle}$$

$$\text{write(1)} \frac{\langle q, \mathtt{wr}(x,d), q' \rangle \in \delta, \mathsf{pos}(\omega)(\langle x, d \rangle) < \phi_P, \phi'_L = \phi_L[x \leftarrow \max(\mathsf{pos}(\omega)(\langle x, d \rangle), \phi_L^{\max})]}{\langle q, \mathsf{val}, \mathsf{Lw}, \omega, \phi_E, \phi_L, \phi_P \rangle \xrightarrow{\mathtt{wr}(x,d)}_{\mathsf{pvt}} \langle q, \mathsf{val}, \mathsf{Lw}[x \leftarrow d], \omega, \phi_E, \phi'_L, \phi_P \rangle}$$

$$\text{write(2)} \frac{\langle q, \mathtt{wrx}, d, q' \rangle \in \delta, \mathsf{pos}(\omega)(\langle x, d \rangle) = \phi_P}{\langle q, \mathsf{val}, \mathsf{Lw}, \omega, \phi_E, \phi_L, \phi_P \rangle \xrightarrow{\mathtt{wr}(x,d)}_{\mathsf{pvt}} \mathsf{v}_{\mathsf{init}}(\omega, \phi_P + 1)}$$

$$\text{read(1)} \frac{\langle q, \mathtt{rd}(x,d), q' \rangle \in \delta, \mathsf{Lw}(x) = d}{\langle q, \mathsf{val}, \mathsf{Lw}, \omega, \phi_E, \phi_L, \phi_P \rangle \xrightarrow{\mathtt{rd}(x,d)}_{\mathsf{pvt}} \langle q', \mathsf{val}, \mathsf{Lw}, \omega, \phi_E, \phi_L, \phi_P \rangle}$$

$$\text{read(2)} \frac{\langle q, \mathtt{rd}(x,d), q' \rangle \in \delta, d = \mathsf{init}(x), \mathsf{Lw}(x) = \bot, \mathsf{pos}(\omega)(x) > \phi_E}{\langle q, \mathsf{val}, \mathsf{Lw}, \omega, \phi_E, \phi_L, \phi_P \rangle \xrightarrow{\mathtt{rd}(x,d)}_{\mathsf{pvt}} \langle q', \mathsf{val}, \mathsf{Lw}, \omega, \phi_E, \phi_L, \phi_P \rangle}$$

$$\text{read(3)} \frac{\langle q, \mathtt{rd}(x,d), q' \rangle \in \delta, \mathsf{pos}(\omega)(\langle x, d \rangle) < \phi_P, \phi'_E = \max(\phi_E, \phi_L(x), \mathsf{pos}(\omega)(\langle x, d \rangle))}{\langle q, \mathsf{val}, \mathsf{Lw}, \omega, \phi_E, \phi_L, \phi_P \rangle \xrightarrow{\mathtt{rd}(x,d)}_{\mathsf{pvt}} \langle q', \mathsf{val}, \mathsf{Lw}, \omega, \phi'_E, \phi_L, \phi_P \rangle}$$

$$\text{memory-fence} \frac{\langle q, \mathtt{mf}, q' \rangle \in \delta, \phi'_E = \max(\phi_E, \phi_L^{\max})}{\langle q, \mathsf{val}, \mathsf{Lw}, \omega, \phi_E, \phi_L, \phi_P \rangle \xrightarrow{\mathtt{mf}}_{\mathsf{pvt}} \langle q', \mathsf{val}, \mathsf{Lw}, \omega, \phi'_E, \phi_L, \phi_P \rangle}$$

$$\text{data-operation} \frac{\langle q, \mathtt{op}, q' \rangle \in \delta, \mathtt{op} \in \mathsf{Ops}, \mathsf{val} \xrightarrow{\mathtt{op}}_A \mathsf{val}'}{\langle q, \mathsf{val}, \mathsf{Lw}, \omega, \phi_E, \phi_L, \phi_P \rangle \xrightarrow{\mathtt{op}}_{\mathsf{pvt}} \langle q', \mathsf{val}', \mathsf{Lw}, \omega, \phi_E, \phi_L, \phi_P \rangle}$$

Fig. 1: The transition relation of the pivot semantics for a process Proc.

Given an update sequence $\omega \in \mathsf{Msgs}^{\mathsf{diff}}$ and $1 \leq k \leq |\omega| + 1$, we define *the initial view induced by ω and k* denoted by $\mathsf{v}_{\mathsf{init}}(\omega, k)$, as the view $\langle q^{\mathsf{init}}, \mathsf{val}_{\mathsf{init}}, \mathsf{Lw}_\bot, \omega, 0, \phi_L^0, k \rangle$. For a given ω, the k-provider starts with $\mathsf{v}_{\mathsf{init}}(\omega, k)$: $\mathsf{Lw}_\bot$ and ϕ_L^0 imply that the simulated process has not performed any writes and $\phi_E = 0$ means that it has not read/updated from/to the memory.

We define the labeled transition relation $\longrightarrow_{\mathsf{pvt}}$ on the set of views by the inference rules given in Figure 1. The set of labels is $\mathsf{Instrs} \cup \mathsf{Ops}$. We describe the inference rules briefly. The $\mathtt{skip}$ rule only changes the local state of the process. There are two inference rules, write(1) and write(2), to describe the execution of a write operation $\mathtt{wr}(\mathsf{x}, \mathsf{d})$. The rule write(1) describes the situation when the rank of $\langle \mathsf{x}, \mathsf{d} \rangle$ is strictly smaller than the progress pointer ϕ_P. In this case, we update both Lw and ϕ_L. The rule write(2) describes the situation when the rank of $\langle \mathsf{x}, \mathsf{d} \rangle$ equals the progress pointer. This means that the provider has provided the message $\langle \mathsf{x}, \mathsf{d} \rangle$ with rank ϕ_P. Hence it has completed its mission, and initiates the next provider by transitioning to $\mathsf{v}_{\mathsf{init}}(\omega, \phi_P + 1)$.

There are three inference rules that describe a read operation $\mathtt{rd}(\mathsf{x}, \mathsf{d})$. The rule read(1) describes when the last written value to x by the provider is d, $\mathsf{Lw}(\mathsf{x}) = \mathsf{d}$. In this case, the provider simply reads from its local buffer. The rule read(2) describes the read of an initial value. It ensures that the read is possible by checking that no write operation on x is executed by the provider ($\mathsf{Lw}(\mathsf{x}) = \perp$), and by checking that the initial value of the variable has not been overwritten in the memory. This is achieved by checking if the position of $\langle \mathsf{x}, \mathsf{d} \rangle$ in ω, i.e. $\mathsf{pos}(\omega)(\langle \mathsf{x}, \mathsf{d} \rangle)$, is strictly larger than ϕ_E. The rule read(3) describes when the simulated process reads from the memory. It checks that the message $\langle \mathsf{x}, \mathsf{d} \rangle$ has been generated by some previous provider ($\mathsf{pos}(\omega)(\langle \mathsf{x}, \mathsf{d} \rangle) < \phi_P$), and then it updates the external pointer to $\max(\phi_E, \phi_L(\mathsf{x}), \mathsf{pos}(\omega)(\langle \mathsf{x}, \mathsf{d} \rangle))$. The memory fence rule describes when the simulated process does a fence action. The rule updates the external pointer to $\max(\phi_E, \phi_L^{\max})$. Finally, the data-operation rule describes when the simulated process does an ADT operation.

The set of initial views is $\mathsf{V}_{\mathsf{init}} = \{\mathsf{v}_{\mathsf{init}}(\omega, 1) \mid \omega \in \mathsf{Msgs}^{\mathsf{diff}}\}$. This is the set of initial views of the 1-provider and it is finite because $\mathsf{Msgs}^{\mathsf{diff}}$ is finite, unlike the set of initial configurations $\mathsf{C}_{\mathsf{init}}$ in the parameterized case under TSO.

6   Register Machines

Our goal is to design a general method to determine the decidability and complexity of $\mathsf{TSO(A)\text{-}P\text{-}Reach}$ depending on A. We examine the pivot abstraction introduced in the previous chapter. A view $\mathsf{v} = \langle \mathsf{q}, \mathsf{val}, \mathsf{Lw}, \omega, \phi_E, \phi_L, \phi_P \rangle$ of the pivot transition system, can be partitioned into the following two components: (1) $\mathsf{q}, \mathsf{Lw}, \omega, \phi_E, \phi_L, \phi_P$ which contains the local state and also effectively abstracts the unbounded FIFO buffers and shared memory of the TSO system and (2) val which captures the value of the ADT. The first part is finite since each component takes finitely many values. We call this the *book-keeping* state since it keeps track of the progress of the core TSO system. However, the ADT part can be infinite, depending upon the abstract data type.

We will use a register machine in order to represent the book-keeping state in a finite way using states and registers. On the other hand, we will keep the ADT component general and only later instantiate it to some interesting cases.

A *register machine* is a finite state automaton that has access to a finite set of *registers*, each holding a natural number. The register machine can execute two operations on a register, it can write a given value or it can read a given value. A read is blocking if the given value is not in the register. We differ from most definitions of register machines in two significant ways: Since we only require a finite domain to model $\mathsf{TSO(A)}$ semantics, the values of the registers are bound from above by an $N \in \mathbb{N}$. This makes the register assignments finite whereas most definitions allow for an unbounded domain. Further, our register machine is augmented with an ADT.

Given an ADT $\mathsf{A} = \langle \mathsf{Vals}, \{\mathsf{val}_{\mathsf{init}}\}, \mathsf{Ops}, \rightarrow_{\mathsf{A}} \rangle$, let Regs be a finite set of registers and $\mathsf{Dom} = \{0, \ldots, N\}$ their domain. We define the set of actions $\mathsf{Acts} = \{\mathsf{SKP}, \mathtt{WRITE}(r, d), \mathtt{READ}(r, d) \mid r \in \mathsf{Regs}, d \in \mathsf{Dom}\}$. A register machine is then defined as a tuple $\mathcal{R}(\mathsf{A}) = \langle Q, q_{\mathsf{init}}, \delta \rangle$, where Q is a finite set of states, $q_{\mathsf{init}} \in Q$ is the initial state and $\delta \subseteq Q \times (\mathsf{Acts} \cup \mathsf{Ops}) \times Q$ is the transition relation.

The semantics of the register machine are given in terms of a transition system. The set of configurations is $Q \times \mathsf{Dom}^{\mathsf{Regs}} \times \mathsf{Vals}$. A configuration consists of a state, a register assignment $\mathsf{Regs} \rightarrow \mathsf{Dom}$ and a value of A. The initial configuration is $\langle q_{\mathsf{init}}, 0^{\mathsf{Regs}}, \mathsf{val}_{\mathsf{init}} \rangle$, where all registers contain the value 0.

The transition relation $\rightarrow$ is described in the following. SKP only changes the local state, not the registers or the ADT value. $\mathtt{WRITE}(r, d)$ sets the value of the register r to d. $\mathtt{READ}(r, d)$ is only enabled if the value of r is d, it does not change the value. The operations in Ops work as usually, they do not change any register. We define the state reachability problem for register machines as $\mathcal{R}(\mathsf{A})\text{-}\mathbf{Reach}$ in the usual way. A state $q_{\mathsf{final}} \in Q$ is reachable if there is a run of the transition system defined by the semantics of $\mathcal{R}(\mathsf{A})$ that starts in the initial configuration and ends in a configuration with state q_{final}.

6.1   Simulating Pivot Abstraction by Register Machines

In this section we will show how to simulate the pivot abstraction by a register machine. The idea is to save the book-keeping state (except for the local state) in the registers. Given a process description $\mathsf{Proc} = \langle Q^{\mathsf{Proc}}, q_{\mathsf{init}}^{\mathsf{Proc}}, \delta^{\mathsf{Proc}} \rangle$ for an ADT A, we construct a register machine $\mathcal{R}(\mathsf{A}) = \langle Q, q_{\mathsf{init}}, \delta \rangle$ that simulates the pivot semantics as follows. The set of registers is

$$\mathsf{Regs} := \{\mathsf{Lw}(x), \mathsf{rk}_{\mathsf{Vars}}(x), \mathsf{rk}_{\mathsf{Msgs}}(\mathsf{msg}), \phi_E, \phi_L(x), \phi_L^{\max}, \phi_P, \mathsf{rk}_{\mathsf{nxt}} \mid x \in \mathsf{Vars}, \mathsf{msg} \in \mathsf{Msgs}\} \ .$$

The registers $\mathsf{rk}_{\mathsf{Vars}}(x)$ and $\mathsf{rk}_{\mathsf{Msgs}}(\mathsf{msg})$ hold the rank of each variable and message, respectively. This implicitly gives rise to an update sequence. The auxiliary register $\mathsf{rk}_{\mathsf{nxt}}$ is used to initialize the other rank registers, as will be explained later on. The remaining registers correspond to their respective counterparts in the pivot abstraction. Note that the number of registers is linear in the number of messages $|\mathsf{Msgs}|$. The domain of the registers is defined to be $\mathsf{Dom} = \{0, \ldots, |\mathsf{Msgs}| + 1\}$. Since the TSO memory domain is finite, we can assume w.l.o.g. that the memory values are positive integers. If $\mathsf{Lw}(x) = 0$, it means that there has been no write on x and it still holds the initial value. The set of states Q contains $Q^{\mathsf{Proc}} \cup \{q_{\mathsf{init}}^{\mathcal{R}}(\mathsf{A}), q_{\mathsf{init}}^{\mathsf{ptr}}\}$ as well as a number of (unnamed) auxiliary states that will be used in the following.

To simplify our construction, we will use additional operations on registers, instead of just WRITE and READ. We introduce different blocking comparisons between registers and values such as $==, <, \leq, \neq$, register assignments such as $r := r'$, and increments by one denoted as $r{+}{+}$. A more detailed description of these instructions is given in [3].

The Initializer. The pivot semantics define an exponential number of initial states: one per possible update sequence. The register machine instead guesses an update sequence at the start of the execution and stores it in the rank registers. This part of the register machine is the *rank initializer* (shown in Figure 2 (a)). It uses the auxiliary register rk_{nxt} to keep track of the next rank that is to be assigned. In a nondeterministic manner, the rank initializer chooses a so far unranked message and then it assigns the next rank to this message. If the variable of the message has no rank assigned yet, it updates the rank of the variable. Then it increases the rk_{nxt} register and continues. After each rank assignment, the initializer can choose to stop the rank assignment. In that case, it initializes the register ϕ_P to 1 and finishes in the initial state of Proc.

In addition to the rank initializer, we have the *pointer initializer*. It is responsible for resetting all pointers except the process pointer to zero. The process pointer is incremented by one instead. This initializer is not executed in the beginning of the simulation, but between epochs of the pivot abstraction.

The simulator. The main part of this construction handles the simulation of the pivot abstraction. It contains Q^{Proc} as well as several auxiliary states that are described in the following. It simulates each instruction of $\text{TSO}(A)$. The skip instruction and the data instructions are carried out unchanged. A visualization of the remaining instructions is depicted in Figure 2. In case of a write instruction $\text{wr}(x, d)$, we first compare the rank of the write message with the process pointer. If they are equal, it means that the epoch is finished and the next process should start, therefore we jump to the first state of the pointer initializer. Otherwise, we set the last write pointer $\text{Lw}(x)$ to d. Now, we ensure that ϕ_L^{max} is at least as large as the rank of $\langle x, d \rangle$ and finally we update the local pointer $\phi_L(x)$ to be equal to ϕ_L^{max}. For the memory fence instruction, it only needs to be ensured that the external pointer is at least as large as the maximum local pointer ϕ_L^{max}. For a read instruction $\text{rd}(x, d)$, if the last write to x was of value d, we can execute the read directly. Otherwise, after checking that the write can be performed by the current provider, we ensure that the external pointer is at least as large as both the rank of $\langle x, d \rangle$ and the local pointer of x. For the special case that $d = d_{\text{init}}$, there is an additional way in which the read can be performed: We can read d_{init} from the memory if the process has neither already written to x nor observed a write that has higher or equal rank than the rank of x. This gives us the following theorem, proven in Appendix C of the full version [3]:

Theorem 1. $\text{TSO}(A)$-*P-Reach* is polynomial time reducible to $\mathcal{R}(A)$-*Reach*.

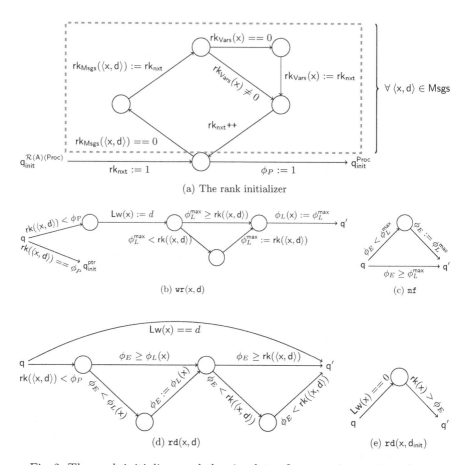

(a) The rank initializer

(b) wr(x, d)

(c) mf

(d) rd(x, d)

(e) rd(x, d_init)

Fig. 2: The rank initializer and the simulator for some instructions instr.

6.2   Simulating Register Machines by TSO

We will now show how to simulate an ADT register machine with a parameterized program running under $\mathsf{TSO}(A)$. The main idea is to save the information about the registers in the last pending write operations, while making sure that not a single write operation actually hits the memory. Thus, the simulator always reads the initial value or its own writes, never writes of other processes.

The TSO program has a variable for each register, and two additional variables x_s and x_c that act as flags: x_s indicates that the verifier should start working, while x_c indicates that the verifier has successfully completed the verification. At the beginning of the execution, each process nondeterministically chooses to be either *simulator*, *scheduler*, or *verifier*. Each role will be described in the following. The complete construction is shown in Appendix C of [3].

The simulator uses the same states and transitions as $\mathcal{R}(A)$, but instead of reading from and writing to registers, it uses the memory. If the simulator reaches the target state q_{target}, it first checks the x_s flag. If it is already set, the simulator stops, never reaching the final state q_{final}. Otherwise, it waits until it observes the flag x_c to be set. It then enters the final state. The scheduler's only responsibility is to signal the start of the verification process. It does so by setting the flag x_s at a nondeterministically chosen time during the execution of the program. The verifier waits until it observers the flag x_s. It then starts the verification process, which consists of checking each variable that corresponds to a register. If all of them still contain their initial value, the verification was successful. The verifier signals this to the simulator process by setting the x_c flag.

Any execution ending in q_{final} must perform a simulation of $\mathcal{R}(A)$ ending in q_{target} first, then a scheduler propagates the setting of flag x_s and afterwards a verifier executes. This ensures that the initial values are read by the verifier after the register machine has been simulated and thus the shared memory is unchanged. This means the simulator only accessed its write buffer and not writes from other threads. It follows that q_{target} is reachable by $\mathcal{R}(A)$ if and only if q_{final} is reachable by Proc under TSO(A). This gives us the following result:

Theorem 2. $\mathcal{R}(A)$-*Reach is polynomial time reducible to* TSO(A)-*P-Reach*.

Theorem 1 and Theorem 2 give us a method of determining upper and lower bounds of the complexity of TSO(A)-P-Reach for different instantiations of ADT. Since we have reductions in both directions, we can conclude that TSO(A)-P-Reach is decidable if and only if $\mathcal{R}(A)$-Reach is decidable. We know TSO(A)-P-Reach is PSPACE-hard for TSO(NoADT)-P-Reach where NoADT is the trivial ADT that models plain TSO semantics [4]. We can immediately derive a lower bound for any ADT: TSO(A)-P-Reach is PSPACE-hard.

7   Instantiations of ADTs

In the following, we instantiate our framework to a number of ADTs in order to show its applicability.

Theorem 3. TSO(CT)-*P-Reach and* TSO(wCT)-*P-Reach are* PSPACE-*complete*.

We know TSO(A)-P-Reach is PSPACE-hard for any ADT A including CT and wCT. Regarding the upper bound for CT, we can show that $\mathcal{R}(CT)$-Reach can be polynomially reduced to $\mathcal{R}(NoADT)$-Reach. The idea is to show that there is a bound on the counter values in order to find a witness for $\mathcal{R}(CT)$-Reach. This bound is polynomial in the number of possible states and register assignments (i.e., this bound is at most exponential in the size of $\mathcal{R}(CT)$.) Assume a run that contains a configuration c with a value that exceeds the bound, then certain state and register assignment are repeated in the run with different values. We can use this to shorten the run such that the counter value in c is reduced.

We can encode the counter value (up to this bound) in a binary way into registers acting as bits. The number of additional registers is polynomial in the size of $\mathcal{R}(CT)$. In order to simulate an inc operation on this binary encoding using WRITE and READ, we only have to go through the bits starting at the least important bit and flip them until one is flipped from 0 to 1. The dec operation works analogously. This only requires a polynomial state and transition overhead.

We know that $\mathcal{R}(\text{NoADT})$-Reach is in PSPACE[4]. It follows from the polynomial reduction that $\mathcal{R}(\text{CT})$-Reach is in PSPACE. Applying Theorem 1 gives us that TSO(CT)-P-Reach is in PSPACE. Since any wCT is a CT, it follows TSO(wCT)-P-Reach is in PSPACE as well. The proof is in [3].

Theorem 4. TSO(ST)-*P-Reach is* ExpTime-*complete.*

For membership, we encode the registers of $\mathcal{R}(\text{ST})$ in the states, which yields a finite state machine with access to a stack, i.e. a pushdown automaton. The construction has an exponential number of states. From [45], we have that checking the emptiness of a context-free language generated by a pushdown automaton is polynomial in terms of the size of the automaton. Combined, we get that state reachability of the constructed pushdown automaton is in ExpTime. It follows that $\mathcal{R}(\text{ST})$-Reach is in ExpTime (thanks to Theorem 1).

To prove the lower bound, we can reduce the problem of checking the emptiness of the intersection of a pushdown with n finite-state automata [35] to $\mathcal{R}(\text{ST})$-Reach. This problem is well-known to be ExpTime-complete. The idea is to use the stack to simulate pushdown automaton and n registers to keep track of the states of the finite-state automata. We apply Theorem 2 and get TSO(ST)-P-Reach is ExpTime-hard. The formal proof is in [3]

Theorem 5. TSO(PETRI)-*P-Reach is* ExpSpace-*complete.*

Proof. Petri net coverability is known to be ExpSpace complete [26]. We show hardness by reducing coverability of a marking m to $\mathcal{R}(\text{PETRI})$-Reach. The idea is to construct a register machine with a Petri net as ADT. This register machine will have two states q_{init} and q_{final}. For every transition t of the original Petri net, we have t: $q_{\text{init}} \xrightarrow{t} q_{\text{init}}$ as a transition of the register machine (we simply simulate the original Petri net). Furthermore, we have $q_{\text{init}} \xrightarrow{t-m} q_{\text{final}}$ as a transition of the register machine. Thus, the state q_{final} can be reached iff m can be covered.

We reduce reachability of $\mathcal{R}(\text{PETRI})$ to Petri net coverability. We construct the Petri net by taking the ADT PETRI and adding a place p_q for every state q and a place $p_{\text{reg},d}$ for every register reg $\in$ Regs and register value $d \in$ Dom. The idea is that a marking with a token in p_q and one in $p_{\text{reg},d}$ but none $p_{\text{reg},d'}$ for $d' \neq d$ corresponds to a configuration of $\mathcal{R}(\text{PETRI})$ with state q and reg $= d$. The value of PETRI is given by the remainder of the marking.

We simulate any $q \xrightarrow{\text{instr}} q'$ with a transition t that takes one token from q and puts one in q'. If instr $\in$ Ops, then instr is a Petri net transition. We simply add the same input and output arcs to t. To simulate a write, we add a new transition $t_{d'}$ for every $d' \in$ Dom with an arc to $p_{\text{reg},d}$ and an arc from $p_{\text{reg},d'}$. The initial marking is consistent with $\text{val}_{\text{init}}^{\text{PETRI}}$ and has one token in $p_{q_{\text{init}}}$. A state q is reachable if a marking with one token in p_q is coverable.

Higher Order ADTs. Let $\mathcal{M}(A)$-Reach problem be the restriction of $\mathcal{R}(A)$-Reach with no registers. The $\mathcal{M}(A)$-Reach problem has been studied for many ADT such as higher order counter and higher order stack variations[34,25].

Theorem 6.

- TSO(n-ST)-*P-Reach is* $(n-1)$-ExpTime-*hard and in* n-ExpTime.
- TSO(n-wCT)-*P-Reach is* $(n-2)$-ExpTime-*hard and in* $(n-1)$-ExpTime.
- TSO(n-CT)-*P-Reach is* $(n-2)$-ExpSpace-*hard and in* $(n-1)$-ExpSpace.

Proof. $\mathcal{M}(n$-ST)-Reach has been shown to be $(n-1)$-ExpTime-complete [25]. We know $\mathcal{M}(n$-wCT)-Reach is $(n-2)$-ExpTime-complete and $\mathcal{M}(n$-CT)-Reach is $(n-2)$-ExpSpace-complete [34]. Since the reduction from $\mathcal{M}(A)$-Reach to $\mathcal{R}(A)$-Reach is trivial, any hardness result can be applied to TSO(A)-P-Reach immediately using Theorem 2. In order to reduce $\mathcal{R}(A)$-Reach to $\mathcal{M}(A)$-Reach, we encode register assignments into the state which results in an exponential state explosion. Then we apply Theorem 1 to obtain our upper bound.

Theorem 7. TSO(n-OMST)-*P-Reach is* 2-ETime-*complete.*

Proof. We know that $\mathcal{M}(n$-OMST)-Reach is 2-ETime-complete [12] and we can apply Theorem 2 to get 2-ETime-hardness. According to Theroem 4.6 in [11], $\mathcal{M}(n$-OMST)-Reach is in $\mathcal{O}(|\mathcal{M}(A)|^{2^{dn}})$ for some constant $d \in \mathbb{N}$. We apply the exponential size reduction to $\mathcal{R}(n$-OMST)-Reach and Theorem 1 and get TSO(n-OMST)-P-Reach is in $\mathcal{O}((2^{|\mathcal{P}|})^{2^{dn}}) = \mathcal{O}(2^{|\mathcal{P}| \cdot 2^{dn}})$ and thus it is also in $\mathcal{O}(2^{2^{|\mathcal{P}| \cdot 2^{dn}}}) = \mathcal{O}(2^{2^{|\mathcal{P}|+dn}})$. Thus, TSO($n$-OMST)-P-Reach is in 2-ETime.

We study well structured ADTs [29,9] as defined in [3]:

Theorem 8. *If ADT* A *is well structured, then* TSO(A)-*P-Reach is decidable.*

A register machine for a well structured ADT A is equivalent to the composition of a well structured transition system (WSTS) modeling A and a finite transition system (and thus a WSTS) that models states and registers. According to [9], the composition is again a WSTS and reachability is decidable. The above theorem is then an immediate corollary of Theorem 1.

8   Conclusions and Future Work

In this paper, we have taken the first step to studying the complexity of parameterized verification under weak memory models when the processes manipulate unbounded data domains. Concretely, we have presented complexity results for parameterized concurrent programs running on the classical TSO memory model when the processes operate on an abstract data type. We reduce the problem to reachability for register machines enriched with the given abstract data type.

State reachability for finite automata with ADT has been extensively studied for many ADTs[34,25]. We have shown in Theorem 6 that we can apply our framework to existing complexity results of this problem. This provides us with decidability and complexity results for the corresponding instances of TSO(A)-P-Reach. However, due to the exponential number of register assignments, the upper bound is exponentially larger than the lower bound. We aim to study these cases further and determine more refined parametric bounds.

A direction for future work is considering other memory models, such as the partial store ordering semantics, the release-acquire semantics, and the ARM semantics. It is also interesting to re-consider the problem under the assumption of having distinguished processes (so-called *leader processes*). Adding leaders is known to make the parameterized verification problem harder. The complexity/decidability of parameterized verification under TSO with a single leader is open, even when the processes are finite-state.

References

1. Parosh Aziz Abdulla. Regular model checking. *STTT*, 14(2):109–118, 2012.
2. Parosh Aziz Abdulla, Mohamed Faouzi Atig, Ahmed Bouajjani, and Tuan Phong Ngo. A load-buffer semantics for total store ordering. *LMCS*, 14(1), 2018.
3. Parosh Aziz Abdulla, Mohamed Faouzi Atig, Florian Furbach, Adwait Godbole, Yacoub G. Hendi, Shankaranarayanan Krishna, and Stephan Spengler. Parameterized verification under tso with data types. *arXiv e-prints*, 2023. arXiv:2302.02163.
4. Parosh Aziz Abdulla, Mohamed Faouzi Atig, and Rojin Rezvan. Parameterized verification under tso is pspace-complete. *Proc. ACM Program. Lang.*, 4(POPL), 2019.
5. Parosh Aziz Abdulla, Yu-Fang Chen, Giorgio Delzanno, Frédéric Haziza, Chih-Duo Hong, and Ahmed Rezine. Constrained monotonic abstraction: A CEGAR for parameterized verification. In *CONCUR 2010*, pages 86–101, 2010.
6. Parosh Aziz Abdulla and Giorgio Delzanno. Parameterized verification. *STTT*, 18(5):469–473, 2016.
7. Parosh Aziz Abdulla, Frédéric Haziza, and Lukás Holík. Parameterized verification through view abstraction. *STTT*, 18(5):495–516, 2016.
8. Parosh Aziz Abdulla, A. Prasad Sistla, and Muralidhar Talupur. Model checking parameterized systems. In *Handbook of Model Checking*, pages 685–725. Springer, 2018.
9. Parosh Aziz Abdulla, Kārlis Čerāns, Bengt Jonsson, and Yih-Kuen Tsay. Algorithmic analysis of programs with well quasi-ordered domains. *Inf. Comput.*, 160:109–127, 2000.
10. Krzysztof R. Apt and Dexter Kozen. Limits for automatic verification of finite-state concurrent systems. *Inf. Process. Lett.*, 22(6):307–309, 1986.
11. Mohamed Faouzi Atig. Model-Checking of Ordered Multi-Pushdown Automata. *LMCS*, Volume 8, Issue 3, 2012.
12. Mohamed Faouzi Atig, Benedikt Bollig, and Peter Habermehl. Emptiness of multi-pushdown automata is 2etime-complete. In *Developments in Language Theory*, pages 121–133. Springer, 2008.
13. Roderick Bloem, Swen Jacobs, Ayrat Khalimov, Igor Konnov, Sasha Rubin, Helmut Veith, and Josef Widder. Decidability in parameterized verification. *SIGACT News*, 47(2):53–64, 2016.

14. Bernard Boigelot, Axel Legay, and Pierre Wolper. Iterating transducers in the large (extended abstract). In *CAV*, volume 2725 of *LNCS*, pages 223–235. Springer, 2003.

15. Ahmed Bouajjani, Egor Derevenetc, and Roland Meyer. Checking and enforcing robustness against TSO. In *ETAPS*, pages 533–553, 2013.

16. Ahmed Bouajjani, Peter Habermehl, Adam Rogalewicz, and Tomás Vojnar. Abstract regular (tree) model checking. *STTT*, 14(2):167–191, 2012.

17. Sebastian Burckhardt. Principles of eventual consistency. *FTPL*, 1(1-2):1–150, 2014.

18. Thierry Cachat and Igor Walukiewicz. The complexity of games on higher order pushdown automata. *CoRR*, abs/0705.0262, 2007.

19. Sylvain Conchon, David Declerck, and Fatiha Zaïdi. Parameterized model checking on the tso weak memory model. *J. Autom. Reason.*, 64(7):1307–1330, 2020.

20. Giorgio Delzanno, Arnaud Sangnier, and Gianluigi Zavattaro. Parameterized verification of ad hoc networks. In *CONCUR*, pages 313–327, 2010.

21. Marco Elver and Vijay Nagarajan. TSO-CC: consistency directed cache coherence for TSO. In *HPCA*, pages 165–176. IEEE, 2014.

22. E. Allen Emerson, John Havlicek, and Richard J. Trefler. Virtual symmetry reduction. In *LICS*, pages 121–131, 2000.

23. E. Allen Emerson and Vineet Kahlon. Exact and efficient verification of parameterized cache coherence protocols. In *CHARME*, volume 2860 of *LNCS*, pages 247–262. Springer, 2003.

24. E. Allen Emerson and Vineet Kahlon. Parameterized model checking of ring-based message passing systems. In *CSL*, volume 3210 of *LNCS*, pages 325–339. Springer, 2004.

25. Joost Engelfriet. Iterated stack automata and complexity classes. *Inf. Comput.*, 95(1):21–75, 1991.

26. Javier Esparza. Decidability and complexity of petri net problems - an introduction. *LNCS*, 1491, 2000.

27. Javier Esparza, Alain Finkel, and Richard Mayr. On the verification of broadcast protocols. In *LICS*, pages 352–359. IEEE Computer Society, 1999.

28. Javier Esparza, Pierre Ganty, and Rupak Majumdar. Parameterized verification of asynchronous shared-memory systems. *J. ACM*, 63(1):10:1–10:48, 2016.

29. A. Finkel and Ph. Schnoebelen. Well-structured transition systems everywhere! *Theoretical Computer Science*, 256(1):63–92, 2001. ISS.

30. Marie Fortin, Anca Muscholl, and Igor Walukiewicz. Model-checking linear-time properties of parametrized asynchronous shared-memory pushdown systems. In *CAV*, pages 155–175, 2017.

31. Pierre Ganty and Rupak Majumdar. Algorithmic verification of asynchronous programs. *ACM Trans. Program. Lang. Syst.*, 34(1):6:1–6:48, 2012.

32. Steven M. German and A. Prasad Sistla. Reasoning about systems with many processes. *J. ACM*, 39(3):675–735, 1992.

33. Matthew Hague. Parameterised pushdown systems with non-atomic writes. In *FSTTCS*, pages 457–468, 2011.

34. Alexander Heußner and Alexander Kartzow. Reachability in higher-order-counters. In *MFCS*, pages 528–539. Springer, 2013.

35. Alexander Heußner, Jérôme Leroux, Anca Muscholl, and Grégoire Sutre. Reachability analysis of communicating pushdown systems. In *FOSSACS*, pages 267–281. Springer, 2010.

36. Vineet Kahlon. Parameterization as abstraction: A tractable approach to the dataflow analysis of concurrent programs. In *LICS*, pages 181–192, 2008.

37. Alexander Kaiser, Daniel Kroening, and Thomas Wahl. Dynamic cutoff detection in parameterized concurrent programs. In *CAV*, volume 6174 of *LNCS*, pages 645–659. Springer, 2010.
38. Yonit Kesten, Oded Maler, Monica Marcus, Amir Pnueli, and Elad Shahar. Symbolic model checking with rich assertional languages. *Theor. Comput. Sci.*, 256(1-2):93–112, 2001.
39. Shankara Narayanan Krishna, Adwait Godbole, Roland Meyer, and Soham Chakraborty. Parameterized verification under release acquire is pspace-complete. In *PODC*, pages 482–492. ACM, 2022.
40. Salvatore La Torre, Anca Muscholl, and Igor Walukiewicz. Safety of parametrized asynchronous shared-memory systems is almost always decidable. In *CONCUR*, pages 72–84, 2015.
41. Ori Lahav, Nick Giannarakis, and Viktor Vafeiadis. Taming release-acquire consistency. In *SIGPLAN-SIGACT*, pages 649–662. ACM, 2016.
42. Anca Muscholl, Helmut Seidl, and Igor Walukiewicz. Reachability for dynamic parametric processes. In *VMCAI*, pages 424–441, 2017.
43. Kedar S. Namjoshi and Richard J. Trefler. Parameterized compositional model checking. In *ETAPS*, volume 9636 of *LNCS*, pages 589–606. Springer, 2016.
44. J. L. Peterson. *Petri Net Theory and the Modeling of Systems*. Prentice Hall PTR, 1981.
45. Ahmed Bouajjani Rajeev Alur and Javier Esparza. *Handbook of Model Checking*, chapter Model Checking Procedural Programs, pages 547–569. Springer, 2018.
46. Alberto Ros and Stefanos Kaxiras. Racer: TSO consistency via race detection. In *MICRO*, pages 33:1–33:13. IEEE Computer Society, 2016.
47. Susmit Sarkar, Peter Sewell, Jade Alglave, Luc Maranget, and Derek Williams. Understanding POWER multiprocessors. In *ACM SIGPLAN, PLDI*, pages 175–186. ACM, 2011.
48. Peter Sewell, Susmit Sarkar, Scott Owens, Francesco Zappa Nardelli, and Magnus O. Myreen. x86-tso: a rigorous and usable programmer's model for x86 multiprocessors. *Commun. ACM*, 53(7):89–97, 2010.

Verifying Learning-Based Robotic Navigation Systems

Guy Amir[1,*(✉)], Davide Corsi[2,*], Raz Yerushalmi[1,3], Luca Marzari[2],
David Harel[3], Alessandro Farinelli[2], and Guy Katz[1]

[1] The Hebrew University of Jerusalem, Jerusalem, Israel
{guyam,guykatz}@cs.huji.ac.il
[2] University of Verona, Verona, Italy
{davide.corsi,luca.marzari,alessandro.farinelli}@univr.it
[3] The Weizmann Institute of Science, Rehovot, Israel
{raz.yerushalmi,david.harel}@weizmann.ac.il

Abstract. Deep reinforcement learning (DRL) has become a dominant deep-learning paradigm for tasks where complex policies are learned within reactive systems. Unfortunately, these policies are known to be susceptible to bugs. Despite significant progress in DNN verification, there has been little work demonstrating the use of modern verification tools on real-world, DRL-controlled systems. In this case study, we attempt to begin bridging this gap, and focus on the important task of mapless robotic navigation — a classic robotics problem, in which a robot, usually controlled by a DRL agent, needs to efficiently and safely navigate through an unknown arena towards a target. We demonstrate how modern verification engines can be used for effective *model selection*, i.e., selecting the best available policy for the robot in question from a pool of candidate policies. Specifically, we use verification to detect and rule out policies that may demonstrate suboptimal behavior, such as collisions and infinite loops. We also apply verification to identify models with overly conservative behavior, thus allowing users to choose superior policies, which might be better at finding shorter paths to a target. To validate our work, we conducted extensive experiments on an actual robot, and confirmed that the suboptimal policies detected by our method were indeed flawed. We also demonstrate the superiority of our verification-driven approach over state-of-the-art, gradient attacks. Our work is the first to establish the usefulness of DNN verification in identifying and filtering out suboptimal DRL policies in real-world robots, and we believe that the methods presented here are applicable to a wide range of systems that incorporate deep-learning-based agents.

1 Introduction

In recent years, *deep neural networks* (DNN) have become extremely popular, due to achieving state-of-the-art results in a variety of fields — such as natural

---

[*] Both authors contributed equally.

© The Author(s) 2023
S. Sankaranarayanan and N. Sharygina (Eds.): TACAS 2023, LNCS 13993, pp. 607–627, 2023.
https://doi.org/10.1007/978-3-031-30823-9_31

language processing [16], image recognition [51], autonomous driving [11], and more. The immense success of these DNN models is owed in part to their ability to train on a fixed set of training samples drawn from some distribution, and then *generalize*, i.e., correctly handle inputs that they had not encountered previously. Notably, *deep reinforcement learning* (DRL) [37] has recently become a dominant paradigm for training DNNs that implement control policies for complex systems that operate within rich environments. One domain in which DRL controllers have been especially successful is robotics, and specifically — robotic navigation, i.e., the complex task of efficiently navigating a robot through an arena, in order to safely reach a target [63, 68].

Unfortunately, despite the immense success of DNNs, they have been shown to suffer from various safety issues [31, 57]. For example, small perturbations to their inputs, which are either intentional or the result of noise, may cause DNNs to react in unexpected ways [45]. These inherent weaknesses, and others, are observed in almost every kind of neural network, and indicate a need for techniques that can supply formal guarantees regarding the safety of the DNN in question. These weaknesses have also been observed in DRL systems [6,21,34], showing that even state-of-the-art DRL models may err miserably.

To mitigate such safety issues, the verification community has recently developed a plethora of techniques and tools [8,10,19,24,28,29,31,35,39,40,64,66] for formally verifying that a DNN model is safe to deploy. Given a DNN, these methods usually check whether the DNN: (i) behaves according to a prescribed requirement for *all* possible inputs of interest; or (ii) violates the requirement, in which case the verification tool also provides a counterexample.

To date, despite the abundance of both DRL systems and DNN verification techniques, little work has been published on demonstrating the applicability and usefulness of verification techniques to real-world DRL systems. In this case study, we showcase the capabilities of DNN verification tools for analyzing DRL-based systems in the robotics domain — specifically, robotic navigation systems. To the best of our knowledge, this is the first attempt to demonstrate how off-the-shelf verification engines can be used to identify both *unsafe* and *suboptimal* DRL robotic controllers, that cannot be detected otherwise using existing, incomplete methods. Our approach leverages existing DNN verifiers that can reason about single and multiple invocations of DRL controllers, and this allows us to conduct a verification-based model selection process — through which we filter out models that could render the system unsafe.

In addition to model selection, we demonstrate how verification methods allow gaining better insights into the DRL training process, by comparing the outcomes of different training methods and assessing how the models improve over additional training iterations. We also compare our approach to gradient-based methods, and demonstrate the advantages of verification-based tools in this setting. We regard this as another step towards increasing the reliability and safety of DRL systems, which is one of the key challenges in modern machine learning [27]; and also as a step toward a more wholesome integration of verification techniques into the DRL development cycle.

In order to validate our experiments, we conducted an extensive evaluation on a real-world, physical robot. Our results demonstrate that policies classified as suboptimal by our approach indeed exhibited unwanted behavior. This evaluation highlights the practical nature of our work; and is summarized in a short video clip [4], which we strongly encourage the reader to watch. In addition, our code and benchmarks are available online [3].

The rest of the paper is organized as follows. Section 2 contains background on DNNs, DRLs, and robotic controlling systems. In Section 3 we present our DRL robotic controller case study, and then elaborate on the various properties that we considered in Section 4. In Section 5 we present our experimental results, and use them to compare our approach with competing methods. Related work appears in Section 6, and we conclude in Section 7.

2   Background

Deep Neural Networks. Deep neural networks (DNNs) [25] are computational, directed, graphs consisting of multiple layers. By assigning values to the first layer of the graph and propagating them through the subsequent layers, the network computes either a label prediction (for a classification DNN) or a value (for a regression DNN), which is returned to the user. The values computed in each layer depend on values computed in previous layers, and also on the current layer's *type*. Common layer types include the *weighted sum* layer, in which each neuron is an affine transformation of the neurons from the preceding layer; as well as the popular *rectified linear unit (ReLU)* layer, where each node y computes the value $y = \text{ReLU}(x) = \max(0, x)$, based on a single node x from the preceding layer to which it is connected. The DRL systems that are the subject matter of this case study consist solely of weighted sum and ReLU layers, although the techniques mentioned are suitable for DNNs with additional layer types, as we discuss later.

Fig. 1 depicts a small example of a DNN. For input $V_1 = [2,3]^T$, the second (weighted sum) layer computes the values $V_2 = [20, -7]^T$. In the third layer, the ReLU functions are applied, and the result is $V_3 = [20, 0]^T$. Finally, the network's single output is computed as a weighted sum: $V_4 = [40]$.

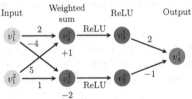

Fig. 1: A toy DNN.

Deep Reinforcement Learning. Deep reinforcement learning (DRL) [37] is a particular paradigm and setting for training DNNs. In DRL, an *agent* is trained to learn a *policy* π, which maps each possible *environment state* s (i.e., the current observation of the agent) to an *action* a. The policy can have different interpretations among various learning algorithms. For example, in some cases, π represents a probability distribution over the action space, while in others it encodes a function that estimates a *desirability score* over all the future actions from a state s.

During training, at each discrete time-step $t \in \{0, 1, 2, \ldots\}$, a *reward* r_t is presented to the agent, based on the action a_t it performed at time-step t. Different DRL training algorithms leverage the reward in different ways, in order to optimize the DNN-agent's parameters during training. The general DNN architecture described above also characterizes DRL-trained DNNs; the uniqueness of the DRL paradigm lies in the training process, which is aimed at generating a DNN that computes a mapping π that maximizes the *expected cumulative discounted reward* $R_t = \mathbb{E}\left[\sum_t \gamma^t \cdot r_t\right]$. The *discount factor*, $\gamma \in [0, 1]$, is a hyperparameter that controls the influence that past decisions have on the total expected reward.

DRL training algorithms are typically divided into three categories [55]:

1. **Value-Based Algorithms.** These algorithms attempt to learn a value function (called the *Q-function*) that assigns a value to each ⟨state,action⟩ pair. This iterative process relies on the *Bellman equation* [44] to update the function: $\mathbb{Q}^\pi(s_t, a_t) = r + \gamma \max_{a_{t+1}} \mathbb{Q}^\pi(s_{t+1}, a_{t+1})$. *Double Deep Q-Network* (DDQN) is an optimized implementation of this algorithm [60].

2. **Policy-Gradient Algorithms.** This class contains algorithms that attempt to directly learn the optimal policy, instead of assessing the value function. The algorithms in this class are typically based on the *policy gradient theorem* [56]. A common implementation is the *Reinforce* algorithm [67], which aims to directly optimize the following objective function, over the parameters θ of the DNN, through a gradient ascent process: $\nabla_\theta J(\pi_\theta) = \mathbb{E}[\sum_t^T \nabla_\theta \log \pi_\theta(a_t|s_t) \cdot r_t]$. For additional details, see [67].

3. **Actor-Critic Algorithms.** This family of hybrid algorithms combines the two previous approaches. The key idea is to use two different neural networks: a *critic*, which learns the value function from the data, and an *actor*, which iteratively improves the policy by maximizing the value function learned by the critic. A state-of-the-art implementation of this approach is the *Proximal Policy Optimization* (PPO) algorithm [50].

All of these approaches are commonly used in modern DRL; and each has its advantages and disadvantages. For example, the value-based methods typically require only small sets of examples to learn from, but are unable to learn policies for continuous spaces of ⟨state,action⟩ pairs. In contrast, the policy-gradient methods can learn continuous policies, but suffer from a low sample efficiency and large memory requirements. Actor-Critic algorithms attempt to combine the benefits of value-based and policy-gradient methods, but suffer from high instability, particularly in the early stages of training, when the value function learned by the critic is unreliable.

DNN Verification and DRL Verification. A DNN verification algorithm receives as input [31]: (i) a trained DNN N; (ii) a precondition P on the DNN's inputs, which limits their possible assignments to inputs of interest; and (iii) a postcondition Q on N's output, which usually encodes the *negation* of the behavior we would like N to exhibit on inputs that satisfy P. The verification algorithm then searches for a concrete input x_0 that satisfies $P(x_0) \wedge Q(N(x_0))$, and returns one of the following outputs: (i) SAT, along with a concrete input x_0 that satisfies the given constraints; or (ii) UNSAT, indicating that no such x_0 exists. When Q encodes the negation of the required property, a SAT result indicates that the property is violated (and the returned input x_0 triggers a bug), while an UNSAT result indicates that the property holds.

For example, suppose we wish to verify that the DNN in Fig. 1 always outputs a value strictly smaller than 7; i.e., that for any input $x = \langle v_1^1, v_1^2 \rangle$, it holds that $N(x) = v_4^1 < 7$. This is encoded as a verification query by choosing a precondition that does not restrict the input, i.e., $P = (true)$, and by setting $Q = (v_4^1 \geq 7)$, which is the *negation* of our desired property. For this verification query, a sound verifier will return SAT, alongside a feasible counterexample such as $x = \langle 0, 2 \rangle$, which produces $v_4^1 = 22 \geq 7$. Hence, the property does not hold for this DNN.

To date, the DNN verification community has focused primarily on DNNs used for a single, non-reactive, invocation [24,28,31,40,64]. Some work has been carried out on verifying DRL networks, which pose greater challenges: beyond the general scalability challenges of DNN verification, in DRL verification we must also take into account that agents typically interact with a reactive environment [6,9,15,21,30]. In particular, these agents are implemented with neural networks that are invoked multiple times, and the inputs of each invocation are usually affected by the outputs of the previous invocations. This fact aggregates the scalability limitations (because multiple invocations must be encoded in each query), and also makes the task of defining P and Q significantly more complex [6].

3 Case Study: Robotic Mapless Navigation

Robotis Turtlebot 3. In our case study, we focus on the *Robotis Turtlebot 3* robot (*Turtlebot*, for short), depicted in Fig. 2. Given its relatively low cost and efficient sensor configuration, this robot is widely used in robotics research [7,46]. In particular, this robotic platform has the actuators required for moving and turning, as well as multiple lidar sensors for detecting obstacles. These sensors use laser beams to approximate the distance to the nearest object in their direction [65]. In our experiments, we used a configuration with seven lidar sensors, each with a maximal range of one meter. Each pair of sensors are 30° apart, thus allowing coverage of 180°. The images in Fig. 3 depict a simulation of the Turtlebot navigating through an arena, and highlight the lidar beams. See the full version of this paper [5] for additional details.

The Mapless Navigation Problem. *Robotic navigation* is the task of navigating a robot (in our case, the Turtlebot) through an arena. The robot's goal is to reach a target destination while adhering to predefined restrictions; e.g., selecting as short a path as possible, avoiding obstacles, or optimizing energy consumption. In recent years, robotic navigation tasks have received a great deal of attention [63,68], primarily due to their applicability to autonomous vehicles.

Fig. 2: The *Robotis Turtlebot 3* platform, navigating in an arena. The image on the left depicts a static robot, and the image on the right depicts the robot moving towards the destination (the yellow square), while avoiding two wooden obstacles in its route.

We study here the popular *mapless* variant of the robotic navigation problem, where the robot can rely only on local observations (i.e., its sensors), without any information about the arena's structure or additional data from external sources. In this setting, which has been studied extensively [58], the robot has access to the *relative location* of the target, but does not have a *complete map* of the arena. This makes mapless navigation a partially observable problem, and among the most challenging tasks to solve in the robotics domain [13,58,70].

DRL-Controlled Mapless Navigation. State-of-the-art solutions to mapless navigation suggest training a DRL policy to control the robot. Such DRL-based solutions have obtained outstanding results from a performance point of view [47]. For example, recent work by Marchesini et al. [43] has demonstrated how DRL-based agents can be applied to control the Turtlebot in a mapless navigation setting, by training a DNN with a simple architecture, including two hidden layers. Following this recent work, in our case study we used the following topology for DRL policies:

- An input layer with nine neurons. These include seven neurons representing the Turtlebot's lidar readings. The additional, non-lidar inputs include one neuron representing the relative angle between the robot and the target, and one neuron representing the robot's distance from the target. A scheme of the inputs appears in Fig. 4a.
- Two subsequent fully-connected layers, each consisting of 16 neurons, and followed by a ReLU activation layer.
- An output layer with three neurons, each corresponding to a different (discrete) action that the agent can choose to execute in the following step: move FORWARD, turn LEFT, or turn RIGHT.[1]

---

[1] It has been shown that discrete controllers achieve excellent performance in robotic navigation, often outperforming continuous controllers in a large variety of tasks [43].

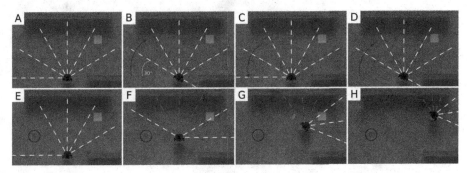

Fig. 3: An example of a simulated Turtlebot entering a 2-step loop. The white and red dashed lines represent the lidar beams (white indicates "clear", and red indicates that an obstacle is detected). The yellow square represents the target position; and the blue arrows indicate rotation. In the first row, from left to right, the Turtlebot is stuck in an infinite loop, alternating between right and left turns. Given the deterministic nature of the system, the agent will continue to select these same actions, ad infinitum. In the second row, from left to right, we present an almost identical configuration, but with an obstacle located 30° to the robot's left (circled in blue). The presence of the obstacle changes the input to the DNN, and allows the Turtlebot to avoid entering the infinite loop; instead, it successfully navigates to the target.

While the aforementioned DRL topology has been shown to be efficient for robotic navigation tasks, finding the optimal training algorithm and reward function is still an open problem. As part of our work, we trained multiple *deterministic* policies using the DRL algorithms presented in Section 2: DDQN [60], Reinforce [67], and PPO [50]. For the reward function, we used the following formulation:

$$\mathbb{R}_t = (d_{t-1} - d_t) \cdot \alpha - \beta,$$

where d_t is the distance from the target at time-step t; α is a normalization factor used to guarantee the stability of the gradient; and β is a fixed value, decreased at each time-step, and resulting in a total penalty proportional to the length of the path (by minimizing this penalty, the agent is encouraged to reach the target quickly). In our evaluation, we empirically selected $\alpha = 3$ and $\beta = 0.001$. Additionally, we added a final reward of +1 when the robot reached the target, or −1 in case it collided with an obstacle. For additional information regarding the training phase, see the full version of this paper [5].

DRL Training and Results. Using the training algorithms mentioned in Section 2, we trained a collection of DRL agents to solve the Turtlebot mapless navigation problem. We ran a stochastic training process, and thus obtained varied agents; of these, we only kept those that achieved a success rate of at least 96% during training. A total of 780 models were selected, consisting of 260 models per each of the three training algorithms. More specifically, for each

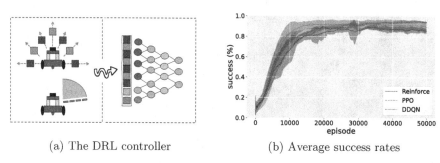

(a) The DRL controller   (b) Average success rates

Fig. 4: (a) The DRL controller used for the robot in our case study. The DRL has nine input neurons: seven lidar sensor readings (blue), one input indicating the relative angle (orange) between the robot and the target, and one input indicating the distance (green) between the robot and the target. (b) The average success rates of models trained by each of the three DRL training algorithms, per training episode.

algorithm, all 260 models were generated from 52 random seeds. Each seed gave rise to a family of 5 models, where the individual family members differ in the number of training episodes used for training them. Fig. 4b shows the trained models' average success rate, for each algorithm used. We note that PPO was generally the fastest to achieve high accuracy. However, all three training algorithms successfully produced highly accurate agents.

4   Using Verification for Model Selection

All of our trained models achieved very high success rates, and so, at face value, there was no reason to favor one over the other. However, as we show next, a verification-based approach can expose multiple subtle differences between them. As our evaluation criteria, we define two properties of interest that are derived from the main goals of the robotic controller: (i) reaching the target; and (ii) avoiding collision with obstacles. Employing verification, we use these criteria to identify models that may fail to fulfill their goals, e.g., because they collide with various obstacles, are overly conservative, or may enter infinite loops without reaching the target. We now define the properties that we used, and the results of their verification are discussed in Section 5. Additional details regarding the precise encoding of our queries appear the full version of this paper [5].

Collision Avoidance. Collision avoidance is a fundamental and ubiquitous safety property [14] for navigation agents. In the context of Turtlebot, our goal is to check whether there exists a setting in which the robot is facing an obstacle, and chooses to move forward — even though it has at least one other viable option, in the form of a direction in which it is not blocked. In such situations, it is clearly preferable to choose to turn LEFT or RIGHT instead of choosing to move FORWARD and collide. See Fig. 5 for an illustration.

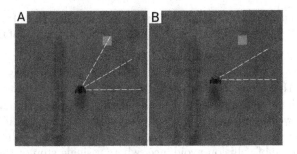

Fig. 5: Example of a single-step collision. The robot is not blocked on its right and can avoid the obstacle by turning (panel A), but it still chooses to move forward — and collides (panel B).

Given that turning LEFT or RIGHT produces an in-place rotation (i.e., the robot does not change its position), the only action that can cause a collision is FORWARD. In particular, a collision can happen when an obstacle is directly in front of the robot, or is slightly off to one side (just outside the front lidar's field of detection). More formally, we consider the safety property *"the robot does not collide at the next step"*, with three different types of collisions:

- FORWARD COLLISION: the robot detects an obstacle straight ahead, but nevertheless makes a step forward and collides with the obstacle.
- LEFT COLLISION: the robot detects an obstacle ahead and slightly shifted to the left (using the lidar beam that is 30° to the left of the one pointing straight ahead), but makes a single step forward and collides with the obstacle. The shape of the robot is such that in this setting, a collision is unavoidable.
- RIGHT COLLISION: the robot detects an obstacle ahead and slightly shifted to the right, but makes a single step forward and collides with the obstacle.

Recall that in mapless navigation, all observations are local — the robot has no sense of the global map, and can encounter any possible obstacle configuration (i.e., any possible sensor reading). Thus, in encoding these properties, we considered a single invocation of the DRL agent's DNN, with the following constraints:

1. All the sensors that are not in the direction of the obstacle receive a lidar input indicating that the robot can move either LEFT or RIGHT without risk of collision. This is encoded by lower-bounding these inputs.
2. The single input in the direction of the obstacle is upper-bounded by a value matching the representation of an obstacle, close enough to the robot so that it will collide if it makes a move FORWARD.
3. The input representing the distance to the target is lower-bounded, indicating that the target has not yet been reached (encouraging the agent to make a move).

The exact encoding of these properties is based on the physical characteristics of the robot and the lidar sensors, as explained in the full version of this paper [5].

Infinite Loops. Whereas collision avoidance is the natural safety property to verify in mapless navigation controllers, checking that progress is eventually made towards the target is the natural liveness property. Unfortunately, this property is difficult to formulate due to the absence of a complete map. Instead, we settle for a weaker property, and focus on verifying that the robot does not enter infinite loops (which would prevent it from ever reaching the target).

Unlike the case of collision avoidance, where a single step of the DRL agent could constitute a violation, here we need to reason about multiple consecutive invocations of the DRL controller, in order to identify infinite loops. This, again, is difficult to encode due to the absence of a global map, and so we focus on *in-place* loops: infinite sequences of steps in which the robot turns LEFT and RIGHT, but without ever moving FORWARD, thus maintaining its current location ad infinitum.

Our queries for identifying in-place loops encode that: (i) the robot does not reach the target in the first step; (ii) in the following k steps, the robot never moves FORWARD, i.e., it only performs turns; and (iii) the robot returns to an already-visited configuration, guaranteeing that the same behavior will be repeated by our deterministic agents. The various queries differ in the choice of k, as well as in the sequence of turns performed by the robot. Specifically, we encode queries for identifying the following kinds of loops:

- ALTERNATING LOOP: a loop where the robot performs an infinite sequence of ⟨LEFT, RIGHT, LEFT, RIGHT, LEFT...⟩ moves. A query for identifying this loop encodes $k = 2$ consecutive invocations of the DRL agent, after which the robot's sensors will again report the exact same reading, leading to an infinite loop. An example appears in Fig. 3. The encoding uses the "sliding window" principle, on which we elaborate later.
- LEFT CYCLE, RIGHT CYCLE: loops in which the robot performs an infinite sequence of ⟨LEFT, LEFT, LEFT, ...⟩ or ⟨RIGHT, RIGHT, RIGHT, ...⟩ operations accordingly. Because the Turtlebot turns at a 30° angle, this loop is encoded as a sequence of $k = 360°/30° = 12$ consecutive invocations of the DRL agent's DNN, all of which produce the same turning action (either LEFT or RIGHT). Using the sliding window principle guarantees that the robot returns to the same exact configuration after performing this loop, indicating that it will never perform any other action.

We also note that all the loop-identification queries include a condition for ensuring that the robot is not blocked from all directions. Consequently, any loops that are discovered demonstrate a clearly suboptimal behavior.

Specific Behavior Profiles. In our experiments, we noticed that the safe policies, i.e., the ones that do not cause the robot to collide, displayed a wide spectrum of different behaviors when navigating to the target. These differences occurred not only between policies that were trained by different algorithms, but also between policies trained by the same reward strategy — indicating that these differences are, at least partially, due to the stochastic realization of the DRL training process.

Specifically, we noticed high variability in the length of the routes selected by the DRL policy in order to reach the given target: while some policies demonstrated short, efficient, paths that passed very close to obstacles, other policies demonstrated a much more conservative behavior, by selecting longer paths, and avoiding getting close to obstacles (an example appears in Fig. 6).

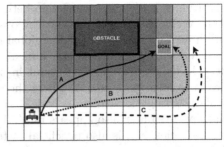

Thus, we used our verification-driven approach to quantify how conservative the learned DRL agent is in the mapless navigation setting. Intuitively, a highly conservative policy will keep a significant safety margin from obstacles (possibly taking a longer route to reach its destination), whereas a "braver" and less conservative controller would risk venturing closer to obstacles. In the case of Turtlebot, the preferable DRL policies are the ones that guarantee the robot's safety (with respect to collision avoidance), and demonstrate a high level of bravery — as these policies tend to take shorter, optimized paths (see path A in Fig. 6), which lead to reduced energy consumption over the entire trail.

Fig. 6: Comparing paths selected by policies with different *bravery* levels. Path A takes the Turtlebot close to the obstacle (red area), and is the shortest. Path B maintains a greater distance from the obstacle (light red area), and is consequently longer. Finally, path C maintains such a significant distance from the obstacle (white area) that it is unable to reach the target.

Bravery assessment is performed by encoding verification queries that identify situations in which the Turtlebot *can* move forward, but its control policy chooses not to. Specifically, we encode single invocations of the DRL model, in which we bound the lidar inputs to indicate that the Turtlebot is sufficiently distant from any obstacle and can safely move forward. We then use the verifier to determine whether, in this setting, a FORWARD output is possible. By altering and adjusting the bounds on the central lidar sensor, we can control how far away the robot perceives the obstacle to be. If we limit this distance to large values and the policy will still not move FORWARD, it is considered conservative; otherwise, it is considered brave. By conducting a binary search over these bounds [6], we can identify the shortest distance from an obstacle for which the policy *safely* orders the robot to move FORWARD. This value's inverse then serves as a bravery score for that policy.

Design-for-Verification: Sliding Windows. A significant challenge that we faced in encoding our verification properties, especially those that pertain to multiple consecutive invocations of the DRL policy, had to do with the local nature of the sensor readings that serve as input to the DNN. Specifically, if the robot is in some initial configuration that leads to a sensor input x, and then chooses to move forward and reaches a successor configuration in which the sensor input is x', some connection between x and x' must be expressed as part of the verification query (i.e., nearby obstacles that exist in x cannot suddenly vanish in x'). In the absence of a global map, this is difficult to enforce.

In order to circumvent this difficulty, we used the *sliding window* principle, which has proven quite useful in similar settings [6, 21]. Intuitively, the idea is to focus on scenarios where the connections between x and x' are particularly straightforward to encode — in fact, most of the sensor information that appeared in x also appears in x'. This approach allows us to encode multistep queries, and is also beneficial in terms of performance: typically, adding sliding-window constraints reduces the search space explored by the verifier, and expedites solving the query.

In the Turtlebot setting, this is achieved by selecting a robot configuration in which the angle between two neighboring lidar sensors is identical to the turning angle of the robot (in our case, $30°$). This guarantees, for example, that if the central lidar sensor observes an obstacle at distance d and the robot chooses to turn RIGHT, then at the next step, the lidar sensor just to the left of the central sensor must detect the same obstacle, at the same distance d. More generally, if at time-step t the 7 lidar readings (from left to right) are $\langle l_1, \ldots, l_7 \rangle$ and the robot turns RIGHT, then at time-step $t + 1$ the 7 readings are $\langle l_2, l_3, \ldots, l_7, l_8 \rangle$, where only l_8 is a new reading. The case for a LEFT turn is symmetrical. By placing these constraints on consecutive states encountered by the robot, we were able to encode complex properties that involve multiple time-steps, e.g., as in the aforementioned infinite loops. An illustration appears in Fig. 3.

5   Experimental Evaluation

Next, we ran verification queries with the aforementioned properties, in order to assess the quality of our trained DRL policies. The results are reported below. In many cases, we discovered configurations in which the policies would cause the robot to collide or enter infinite loops; and we later validated the correctness of these results using a physical robot. We strongly encourage the reader to watch a short video clip that demonstrates some of these results [4]. Our code and benchmarks are also available online [3]. In our experiments, We used the *Marabou* verification engine [33] as our backend, although other engines could be used as well. For additional details regarding the experiments, we refer the reader to the full version of this paper [5].

Model Selection. In this set of experiments, we used verification to assess our trained models. Specifically, we used each of the three training algorithms (DDQN, Reinforce, PPO) to train 260 models, creating a total of 780 models. For each of these, we verified six properties of interest: three collision properties (FORWARD COLLISION, LEFT COLLISION, RIGHT COLLISION), and three loop properties (ALTERNATING LOOP, LEFT CYCLE, RIGHT CYCLE), as described in Section 4. This gives a total of 4680 verification queries. We ran all queries with a

	LEFT COLLISION		FORWARD COLLISION		RIGHT COLLISION	
Algorithm	SAT	UNSAT	SAT	UNSAT	SAT	UNSAT
DDQN	259	1	248	12	258	2
Reinforce	255	5	254	6	252	8
PPO	196	64	197	63	207	53

	ALTERNATING LOOP		LEFT CYCLE		RIGHT CYCLE		INSTABILITY
Algorithm	SAT	UNSAT	SAT	UNSAT	SAT	UNSAT	# alternations
DDQN	260	0	56	77	56	61	21
Reinforce	145	115	5	185	120	97	10
PPO	214	45	26	198	30	198	1

Table 1: Results of the policy verification queries. We verified six properties over each of the 260 models trained per algorithm; SAT indicates that the property was violated, whereas UNSAT indicates that it held (to reduce clutter, we omit TIMEOUT and FAIL results). The rightmost column reports the stability values of the various training methods. For the full results see [3].

TIMEOUT value of 12 hours and a MEMOUT limit of $2G$; the results are summarized in Table 1. The single-step collision queries usually terminated within seconds, and the 2-step queries encoding an ALTERNATING LOOP usually terminated within minutes. The 12-step cycle queries, which are more complex, usually ran for a few hours. 9.6% of all queries hit the TIMEOUT limit (all from the 12-step cycle category), and none of the queries hit the MEMOUT limit.[2]

Our results exposed various differences between the trained models. Specifically, of the 780 models checked, 752 (over 96%) violated at least one of the single-step collision properties. These 752 collision-prone models include *all* 260 DDQN-trained models, 256 Reinforce models, and 236 PPO models. Furthermore, when we conducted a model filtering process based on all six properties (three collisions and three infinite loops), we discovered that 778 models out of the total of 780 (over 99.7%!) violated at least one property. The only two models that passed our filtering process were trained by the PPO algorithm.

Further analyzing the results, we observed that PPO models tended to be safer to use than those trained by other algorithms: they usually had the fewest violations per property. However, there are cases in which PPO proved less successful. For example, our results indicate that PPO-trained models are more prone to enter an ALTERNATING LOOP than those trained by Reinforce. Specifically, 214 (82.3%) of the PPO models have entered this undesired state, compared to 145 (55.8%) of the Reinforce models. We also point out that, similarly to the case with collision properties, *all* DDQN models violated this property.

Finally, when considering 12-step cycles (either LEFT CYCLE or RIGHT CYCLE), 44.8% of the DDQN models entered such cycles, compared to 30.7% of the Reinforce models, and just 12.4% of the PPO models. In computing these results, we

---

[2] We note that two queries failed due to internal errors in *Marabou*.

computed the fraction of violations (SAT queries) out of the number of queries that did not time out or fail, and aggregated SAT results for both cycle directions.

Interestingly, in some cases, we observed a bias toward violating a certain subcase of various properties. For example, in the case of entering full cycles — although 125 (out of 520) queries indicated that Reinforce-trained agents may enter a cycle in either direction, in 96% of these violations, the agent entered a RIGHT CYCLE. This bias is not present in models trained by the other algorithms, where the violations are roughly evenly divided between cycles in both directions.

We find that our results demonstrate that different "black-box" algorithms generalize very differently with respect to various properties. In our setting, PPO produces the safest models, while DDQN tends to produce models with a higher number of violations. We note that this does not necessarily indicate that PPO-trained models perform better, but rather that they are more robust to corner cases. Using our filtering mechanism, it is possible to select the safest models among the available, seemingly equivalent candidates.

Next, we used verification to compute the bravery score of the various models. Using a binary search, we computed for each model the minimal distance a dead-ahead obstacle needs to have for the robot to *safely* move forward. The search range was [0.18, 1] meters, and the optimal values were computed up to a 0.01 precision (see the full version of this paper [5] for additional details). Almost all binary searches terminated within minutes, and none hit the TIMEOUT threshold.

By first filtering the models based on their safe behavior, and then by their bravery scores, we are able to find the few models that are both safe (do not collide), and not overly conservative. These models tend to take efficient paths, and may come close to an obstacle, but without colliding with it. We also point out that over-conservativeness may significantly reduce the success rate in specific scenarios, such as cases in which the obstacle is close to the target. Specifically, of the only two models that survived the first filtering stage, one is considerably more conservative than the other — requiring the obstacle to be twice as distant as the other, braver, model requires it to be, before moving forward.

Algorithm Stability Analysis. As part of our experiments, we used our method to assess the three training algorithms — DDQN, PPO, and Reinforce. Recall that we used each algorithm to train 52 families of 5 models each, in which the models from the same family are generated from the same random seed, but with a different number of training iterations. While all models obtained a high success rate, we wanted to check how often it occurred that a model successfully learned to satisfy a desirable property after some training iterations, only to forget it after additional iterations. Specifically, we focused on the 12-step full-cycle properties (LEFT CYCLE and RIGHT CYCLE), and for each family of 5 models checked whether some models satisfied the property while others did not.

We define a family of models to be *unstable* in the case where a property holds in the family, but ceases to hold for another model from the same family with a higher number of training iterations. Intuitively, this means that the model "forgot" a desirable property as training progressed. The *instability value* of each algorithm type is defined to be the number of unstable 5-member families.

Although all three algorithms produced highly accurate models, they displayed significant differences in the stability of their produced policies, as can be seen in the rightmost column of Table 1. Recall that we trained 52 families of models using each algorithm, and then tested their stability with respect to two properties (corresponding to the two full cycle types). Of these, the DDQN models display 21 *unstable* alternations — more than twice the number of alterations demonstrated by Reinforce models (10), and significantly higher than the number of alternations observed among the PPO models (1).

These results shed light on the nature of these training algorithms — indicating that DDQN is a significantly less stable training algorithm, compared to PPO and Reinforce. This is in line with previous observations in non-verification-related research [50], and is not surprising, as the primary objective of PPO is to limit the changes the optimizer performs between consecutive training iterations.

Gradient-Based Methods. We also conducted a thorough comparison between our verification-based approach and competing gradient-based methods. Although gradient-based attacks are extremely scalable, our results (summarized in [5]) show that they may miss many of the violations found by our complete, verification-based procedure. For example, when searching for collisions, our approach discovered a total of 2126 SAT results, while the gradient-based method discovered only 1421 SAT results — a 33% decrease (!). In addition, given that gradient-based methods are unable to return UNSAT, they are also incapable of proving that a property always holds, and hence cannot formally guarantee the safety of a policy in question. Thus, performing model selection based on gradient-based methods could lead to skewed results. We refer the reader to the full version of this paper [5], in which we elaborate on gradient attacks and the experiments we ran, demonstrating the advantages of our approach for model selection, when compared to gradient-based methods.

6   Related Work

Due to the increasing popularity of DNNs, the formal methods community has put forward a plethora of tools and approaches for verifying DNN correctness [20, 24, 26, 28, 31–33, 36, 39, 52, 59]. Recently, the verification of systems involving multiple DNN invocations, as well as hybrid systems with DNN components, has been receiving significant attention [6, 9, 17, 18, 22, 34, 54, 61]. Our work here is another step toward applying DNN verification techniques to additional, real-world systems and properties of interest.

In the robotics domain, multiple approaches exist for increasing the reliability of learning-based systems [48, 62, 69]; however, these methods are mostly heuristic in nature [1, 23, 42]. To date, existing techniques rely mostly on Lagrangian multipliers [38, 49, 53], and do not provide formal safety guarantees; rather, they optimize the training in an attempt to learn the required policies [12]. Other, more formal approaches focus solely on the systems' input-output relations [15, 41], without considering multiple invocations of the agent and its interactions with the environment. Thus, existing methods are not able to provide rigorous guarantees regarding the correctness of multistep robotic systems, and do not take into account sequential decision making — which renders them insufficient for detecting various safety and liveness violations.

Our approach is orthogonal and complementary to many existing safe DRL techniques. Reward reshaping and shielding techniques (e.g., [2]) improve safety by altering the training loop, but typically afford no formal guarantees. Our approach can be used to complement them, by selecting the most suitable policy from a pool of candidates, post-training. Guard rules and runtime shields are beneficial for preventing undesirable behavior of a DNN agent, but are sometimes less suited for specifying the *desired* actions it should take instead. In contrast, our approach allows selecting the optimal policy from a pool of candidates, without altering its decision-making.

7   Conclusion

Through the case study described in this paper, we demonstrate that current verification technology is applicable to real-world systems. We show this by applying verification techniques for improving the navigation of DRL-based robotic systems. We demonstrate how off-the-shelf verification engines can be used to conduct effective model selection, as well as gain insights into the stability of state-of-the-art training algorithms. As far as we are aware, ours is the first work to demonstrate the use of formal verification techniques on multistep properties of actual, real-world robotic navigation platforms. We also believe the techniques developed here will allow the use of verification to improve additional multistep systems (autonomous vehicles, surgery-aiding robots, etc.), in which we can impose a transition function between subsequent steps. However, our approach is limited by DNN-verification technology, which we use as a black-box backend. As that technology becomes more scalable, so will our approach. Moving forward, we plan to generalize our work to richer environments — such as cases where a memory-enhanced agent interacts with moving objects, or even with multiple agents in the same arena, as well as running additional experiments with deeper networks, and more complex DRL systems. In addition, we see probabilistic verification of stochastic policies as interesting future work.

Acknowledgements. The work of Amir, Yerushalmi and Katz was partially supported by the Israel Science Foundation (grant number 683/18). The work of Amir was supported by a scholarship from the Clore Israel Foundation. The work of Corsi, Marzari, and Farinelli was partially supported by the "Dipartimenti di Eccellenza 2018-2022" project, funded by the Italian Ministry of Education, Universities, and Research (MIUR). The work of Yerushalmi and Harel was partially supported by a research grant from the Estate of Harry Levine, the Estate of Avraham Rothstein, Brenda Gruss and Daniel Hirsch, the One8 Foundation, Rina Mayer, Maurice Levy, and the Estate of Bernice Bernath, grant 3698/21 from the ISF-NSFC (joint to the Israel Science Foundation and the National

Science Foundation of China), and a grant from the Minerva foundation. We thank Idan Refaeli for his contribution to this project.

References

1. J. Achiam, D. Held, A. Tamar, and P. Abbeel. Constrained Policy Optimization. In *Proc. 34th Int. Conf. on Machine Learning (ICML)*, pages 22–31, 2017.
2. M. Alshiekh, R. Bloem, R. Ehlers, B. Könighofer, S. Niekum, and U. Topcu. Safe Reinforcement Learning via Shielding. In *Proc. 32th AAAI Conf. on Artificial Intelligence (AAAI)*, pages 2669–2678, 2018.
3. G. Amir, D. Corsi, R. Yerushalmi, L. Marzari, D. Harel, A. Farinelli, and G. Katz. Supplementary Artifact, 2022. `https://doi.org/10.5281/zenodo.7496352`.
4. G. Amir, D. Corsi, R. Yerushalmi, L. Marzari, D. Harel, A. Farinelli, and G. Katz. Supplementary Video, 2022. `https://youtu.be/QIZqOgxLkAE`.
5. G. Amir, D. Corsi, R. Yerushalmi, L. Marzari, D. Harel, A. Farinelli, and G. Katz. Verifying Learning-Based Robotic Navigation Systems, 2023. Technical Report. `https://arxiv.org/abs/2205.13536`.
6. G. Amir, M. Schapira, and G. Katz. Towards Scalable Verification of Deep Reinforcement Learning. In *Proc. 21st Int. Conf. on Formal Methods in Computer-Aided Design (FMCAD)*, pages 193–203, 2021.
7. R. Amsters and P. Slaets. Turtlebot 3 as a Robotics Education Platform. In *Proc. 10th Int. Conf. on Robotics in Education (RiE)*, pages 170–181, 2019.
8. G. Avni, R. Bloem, K. Chatterjee, T. Henzinger, B. Konighofer, and S. Pranger. Run-Time Optimization for Learned Controllers through Quantitative Games. In *Proc. 31st Int. Conf. on Computer Aided Verification (CAV)*, pages 630–649, 2019.
9. E. Bacci, M. Giacobbe, and D. Parker. Verifying Reinforcement Learning Up to Infinity. In *Proc. 30th Int. Joint Conf. on Artificial Intelligence (IJCAI)*, 2021.
10. T. Baluta, S. Shen, S. Shinde, K. Meel, and P. Saxena. Quantitative Verification of Neural Networks and its Security Applications. In *Proc. ACM SIGSAC Conf. on Computer and Communications Security (CCS)*, pages 1249–1264, 2019.
11. M. Bojarski, D. Del Testa, D. Dworakowski, B. Firner, B. Flepp, P. Goyal, L. Jackel, M. Monfort, U. Muller, J. Zhang, X. Zhang, J. Zhao, and K. Zieba. End to End Learning for Self-Driving Cars, 2016. Technical Report. `http://arxiv.org/abs/1604.07316`.
12. L. Brunke, M. Greeff, A. Hall, Z. Yuan, S. Zhou, J. Panerati, and A. Schoellig. Safe Learning in Robotics: From Learning-Based Control to Safe Reinforcement Learning. *Annual Review of Control, Robotics, and Autonomous Systems*, 5, 2021.
13. H. Chiang, A. Faust, M. Fiser, and A. Francis. Learning Navigation Behaviors End-to-End with AutoRL. *IEEE Robotics and Automation Letters (RA-L/ICRA)*, 4(2):2007–2014, 2019.
14. E. Clarke, T. Henzinger, H. Veith, and R. Bloem. *Handbook of Model Checking*, volume 10. Springer, 2018.
15. D. Corsi, E. Marchesini, and A. Farinelli. Formal Verification of Neural Networks for Safety-Critical Tasks in Deep Reinforcement Learning. In *Proc. 37th Conf. on Uncertainty in Artificial Intelligence (UAI)*, pages 333–343, 2021.
16. L. Deng and Y. Liu. *Deep Learning in Natural Language Processing*. Springer, 2018.

17. S. Dutta, X. Chen, and S. Sankaranarayanan. Reachability Analysis for Neural Feedback Systems using Regressive Polynomial Rule Inference. In *Proc. 22nd ACM Int. Conf. on Hybrid Systems: Computation and Control (HSCC)*, pages 157–168, 2019.

18. S. Dutta, S. Jha, S. Sankaranarayanan, and A. Tiwari. Learning and Verification of Feedback Control Systems using Feedforward Neural Networks. *IFAC-PapersOnLine*, 51(16):151–156, 2018.

19. S. Dutta, S. Jha, S. Sankaranarayanan, and A. Tiwari. Output Range Analysis for Deep Feedforward Neural Networks. In *Proc. 10th NASA Formal Methods Symposium (NFM)*, pages 121–138, 2018.

20. R. Ehlers. Formal Verification of Piece-Wise Linear Feed-Forward Neural Networks. In *Proc. 15th Int. Symp. on Automated Technology for Verification and Analysis (ATVA)*, pages 269–286, 2017.

21. T. Eliyahu, Y. Kazak, G. Katz, and M. Schapira. Verifying Learning-Augmented Systems. In *Proc. Conf. of the ACM Special Interest Group on Data Communication on the Applications, Technologies, Architectures, and Protocols for Computer Communication (SIGCOMM)*, pages 305–318, 2021.

22. N. Fulton and A. Platzer. Safe Reinforcement Learning via Formal Methods: Toward Safe Control through Proof and Learning. In *Proc. 32nd AAAI Conf. on Artificial Intelligence (AAAI)*, 2018.

23. J. Garcıa and F. Fernández. A Comprehensive Survey on Safe Reinforcement Learning. *Journal of Machine Learning Research*, 16(1):1437–1480, 2015.

24. T. Gehr, M. Mirman, D. Drachsler-Cohen, E. Tsankov, S. Chaudhuri, and M. Vechev. AI2: Safety and Robustness Certification of Neural Networks with Abstract Interpretation. In *Proc. 39th IEEE Symposium on Security and Privacy (S&P)*, 2018.

25. I. Goodfellow, Y. Bengio, and A. Courville. *Deep Learning*. MIT Press, 2016.

26. D. Gopinath, G. Katz, C. Păsăreanu, and C. Barrett. DeepSafe: A Data-driven Approach for Assessing Robustness of Neural Networks. In *Proc. 16th. Int. Symposium on Automated Technology for Verification and Analysis (ATVA)*, pages 3–19, 2018.

27. D. Gunning. Explainable Artificial Intelligence (XAI), 2017. Defense Advanced Research Projects Agency (DARPA) Project.

28. X. Huang, M. Kwiatkowska, S. Wang, and M. Wu. Safety Verification of Deep Neural Networks. In *Proc. 29th Int. Conf. on Computer Aided Verification (CAV)*, pages 3–29, 2017.

29. R. Ivanov, T. Carpenter, J. Weimer, R. Alur, G. Pappas, and I. Lee. Verifying the Safety of Autonomous Systems with Neural Network Controllers. *ACM Transactions on Embedded Computing Systems (TECS)*, 20(1):1–26, 2020.

30. P. Jin, J. Tian, D. Zhi, X. Wen, and M. Zhang. Trainify: A CEGAR-Driven Training and Verification Framework for Safe Deep Reinforcement Learning. In *Proc. 34th Int. Conf. on Computer Aided Verification (CAV)*, pages 193–218, 2022.

31. G. Katz, C. Barrett, D. Dill, K. Julian, and M. Kochenderfer. Reluplex: An Efficient SMT Solver for Verifying Deep Neural Networks. In *Proc. 29th Int. Conf. on Computer Aided Verification (CAV)*, pages 97–117, 2017.

32. G. Katz, C. Barrett, D. Dill, K. Julian, and M. Kochenderfer. Reluplex: a Calculus for Reasoning about Deep Neural Networks. *Formal Methods in System Design (FMSD)*, 2021.

33. G. Katz, D. Huang, D. Ibeling, K. Julian, C. Lazarus, R. Lim, P. Shah, S. Thakoor, H. Wu, A. Zeljić, D. Dill, M. Kochenderfer, and C. Barrett. The Marabou Frame-

work for Verification and Analysis of Deep Neural Networks. In *Proc. 31st Int. Conf. on Computer Aided Verification (CAV)*, pages 443–452, 2019.

34. Y. Kazak, C. Barrett, G. Katz, and M. Schapira. Verifying Deep-RL-Driven Systems. In *Proc. 1st ACM SIGCOMM Workshop on Network Meets AI & ML (NetAI)*, pages 83–89, 2019.

35. B. Könighofer, F. Lorber, N. Jansen, and R. Bloem. Shield Synthesis for Reinforcement Learning. In *Proc. Int. Symposium on Leveraging Applications of Formal Methods, Verification and Validation (ISoLA)*, pages 290–306, 2020.

36. L. Kuper, G. Katz, J. Gottschlich, K. Julian, C. Barrett, and M. Kochenderfer. Toward Scalable Verification for Safety-Critical Deep Networks, 2018. Technical Report. https://arxiv.org/abs/1801.05950.

37. Y. Li. Deep Reinforcement Learning: An Overview, 2017. Technical Report. http://arxiv.org/abs/1701.07274.

38. Y. Liu, J. Ding, and X. Liu. Ipo: Interior-Point Policy Optimization under Constraints. In *Proc. 34th AAAI Conf. on Artificial Intelligence (AAAI)*, pages 4940–4947, 2020.

39. A. Lomuscio and L. Maganti. An Approach to Reachability Analysis for Feed-Forward ReLU Neural Networks, 2017. Technical Report. http://arxiv.org/abs/1706.07351.

40. Z. Lyu, C. Y. Ko, Z. Kong, N. Wong, D. Lin, and L. Daniel. Fastened Crown: Tightened Neural Network Robustness Certificates. In *Proc. 34th AAAI Conf. on Artificial Intelligence (AAAI)*, pages 5037–5044, 2020.

41. E. Marchesini, D. Corsi, and A. Farinelli. Benchmarking Safe Deep Reinforcement Learning in Aquatic Navigation. In *Proc. IEEE/RSJ Int. Conf on Intelligent Robots and Systems (IROS)*, 2021.

42. E. Marchesini, D. Corsi, and A. Farinelli. Exploring Safer Behaviors for Deep Reinforcement Learning. In *Proc. 35th AAAI Conf. on Artificial Intelligence (AAAI)*, 2021.

43. E. Marchesini and A. Farinelli. Discrete Deep Reinforcement Learning for Mapless Navigation. In *Proc. IEEE Int. Conf. on Robotics and Automation (ICRA)*, pages 10688–10694, 2020.

44. V. Mnih, K. Kavukcuoglu, D. Silver, A. Graves, I. Antonoglou, D. Wierstra, and M. Riedmiller. Playing Atari with Deep Reinforcement Learning, 2013. Technical Report. https://arxiv.org/abs/1312.5602.

45. S. M. Moosavi-Dezfooli, A. Fawzi, O. Fawzi, and P. Frossard. Universal Adversarial Perturbations. In *Proceedings IEEE Conf. on Computer Vision and Pattern Recognition (CVPR)*, pages 1765–1773, 2017.

46. C. Nandkumar, P. Shukla, and V. Varma. Simulation of Indoor Localization and Navigation of Turtlebot 3 using Real Time Object Detection. In *Proc. Int. Conf. on Disruptive Technologies for Multi-Disciplinary Research and Applications (CENTCON)*, 2021.

47. M. Pfeiffer, S. Shukla, M. Turchetta, C. Cadena, A. Krause, R. Siegwart, and J. Nieto. Reinforced Imitation: Sample Efficient Deep Reinforcement Learning for Mapless Navigation by Leveraging Prior Demonstrations. *IEEE Robotics and Automation Letters*, 3(4):4423–4430, 2018.

48. A. Ray, J. Achiam, and D. Amodei. Benchmarking Safe Exploration in Deep Reinforcement Learning, 2019. Technical Report. https://cdn.openai.com/safexp-short.pdf.

49. J. Roy, R. Girgis, J. Romoff, P. Bacon, and C. Pal. Direct Behavior Specification via Constrained Reinforcement Learning, 2021. Technical Report. https://arxiv.org/abs/2112.12228.

50. J. Schulman, F. Wolski, P. Dhariwal, A. Radford, and O. Klimov. Proximal Policy Optimization Algorithms, 2017. Technical Report. http://arxiv.org/abs/1707.06347.
51. K. Simonyan and A. Zisserman. Very Deep Convolutional Networks for Large-Scale Image Recognition, 2014. Technical Report. http://arxiv.org/abs/1409.1556.
52. G. Singh, T. Gehr, M. Puschel, and M. Vechev. An Abstract Domain for Certifying Neural Networks. In *Proc. 46th ACM SIGPLAN Symposium on Principles of Programming Languages (POPL)*, 2019.
53. A. Stooke, J. Achiam, and P. Abbeel. Responsive Safety in Reinforcement Learning by Pid Lagrangian Methods. In *Proc. 37th Int. Conf. on Machine Learning (ICML)*, pages 9133–9143, 2020.
54. X. Sun, H. Khedr, and Y. Shoukry. Formal Verification of Neural Network Controlled Autonomous Systems. In *Proc. 22nd ACM Int. Conf. on Hybrid Systems: Computation and Control (HSCC)*, 2019.
55. R. Sutton and A. Barto. *Reinforcement Learning: An Introduction*. MIT press, 2018.
56. R. Sutton, D. McAllester, S. Singh, and Y. Mansour. Policy Gradient Methods for Reinforcement Learning with Function Approximation. In *Proc. Advances in Neural Information Processing Systems (NeurIPS)*, 1999.
57. C. Szegedy, W. Zaremba, I. Sutskever, J. Bruna, D. Erhan, I. Goodfellow, and R. Fergus. Intriguing Properties of Neural Networks, 2013. Technical Report. http://arxiv.org/abs/1312.6199.
58. L. Tai, G. Paolo, and M. Liu. Virtual-to-Real Deep Reinforcement Learning: Continuous Control of Mobile Robots for Mapless Navigation. In *Proc. IEEE/RSJ Int. Conf. on Intelligent Robots and Systems (IROS)*, pages 31–36, 2017.
59. V. Tjeng, K. Xiao, and R. Tedrake. Evaluating Robustness of Neural Networks with Mixed Integer Programming, 2017. Technical Report. http://arxiv.org/abs/1711.07356.
60. H. Van Hasselt, A. Guez, and D. Silver. Deep Reinforcement Learning with Double Q-Learning. In *Proc. 30th AAAI Conf. on Artificial Intelligence (AAAI)*, 2016.
61. M. Vasić, A. Petrović, K. Wang, M. Nikolić, R. Singh, and S. Khurshid. MoËT: Mixture of Expert Trees and its Application to Verifiable Reinforcement Learning. *Neural Networks*, 151:34–47, 2022.
62. A. Wachi and Y. Sui. Safe Reinforcement Learning in Constrained Markov Decision Processes. In *Proc. 37th Int. Conf. on Machine Learning (ICML)*, pages 9797–9806, 2020.
63. A. Wahid, A. Toshev, M. Fiser, and T. Lee. Long Range Neural Navigation Policies for the Real World. In *Proc. IEEE/RSJ Int. Conf. on Intelligent Robots and Systems (IROS)*, pages 82–89, 2019.
64. S. Wang, K. Pei, J. Whitehouse, J. Yang, and S. Jana. Formal Security Analysis of Neural Networks using Symbolic Intervals. In *Proc. 27th USENIX Security Symposium*, pages 1599–1614, 2018.
65. K. Yoneda, H. Tehrani, T. Ogawa, N. Hukuyama, and S. Mita. Lidar Scan Feature for Localization with Highly Precise 3-D Map. In *Proc. IEEE Intelligent Vehicles Symposium (IV)*, pages 1345–1350, 2014.
66. H. Zhang, M. Shinn, A. Gupta, A. Gurfinkel, N. Le, and N. Narodytska. Verification of Recurrent Neural Networks for Cognitive Tasks via Reachability Analysis. In *Proc. 24th European Conf. on Artificial Intelligence (ECAI)*, pages 1690–1697, 2020.

67. J. Zhang, J. Kim, B. O'Donoghue, and S. Boyd. Sample Efficient Reinforcement Learning with REINFORCE, 2020. Technical Report. https://arxiv.org/abs/2010.11364.
68. J. Zhang, J. Springenberg, J. Boedecker, and W. Burgard. Deep Reinforcement Learning with Successor Features for Navigation across Similar Environments. In *Proc. IEEE/RSJ Int. Conf. on Intelligent Robots and Systems (IROS)*, 2017.
69. L. Zhang, R. Zhang, T. Wu, R. Weng, M. Han, and Y. Zhao. Safe Reinforcement Learning with Stability Guarantee for Motion Planning of Autonomous Vehicles. *IEEE Transactions on Neural Networks and Learning Systems*, 32(12):5435–5444, 2021.
70. O. Zhelo, J. Zhang, L. Tai, M. Liu, and W. Burgard. Curiosity-Driven Exploration for Mapless Navigation with Deep Reinforcement Learning, 2018. Technical Report. https://arxiv.org/abs/1804.00456.

Make Flows Small Again: Revisiting the Flow Framework

Roland Meyer[1] , Thomas Wies[2] , and Sebastian Wolff[2(✉)]

[1] TU Braunschweig, Braunschweig, Germany, roland.meyer@tu-bs.de
[2] New York University, New York, USA, {wies,sebastian.wolff}@cs.nyu.edu

Abstract We present a new flow framework for separation logic reasoning about programs that manipulate general graphs. The framework overcomes problems in earlier developments: it is based on standard fixed point theory, guarantees least flows, rules out vanishing flows, and has an easy to understand notion of footprint as needed for soundness of the frame rule. In addition, we present algorithms for automating the frame rule, which we evaluate on graph updates extracted from linearizability proofs for concurrent data structures. The evaluation demonstrates that our algorithms help to automate key aspects of these proofs that have previously relied on user guidance or heuristics.

Keywords: Separation Logic · Graph Algorithms · Frame Inference.

1 Introduction

The flow framework [23, 24] is an abstraction mechanism based on separation logic [5, 32, 40] that enables reasoning about global inductive invariants of general graphs in a local manner. The framework has proved useful to verify intricate algorithms that are difficult to handle by other techniques, such as the Priority Inheritance Protocol, object-oriented design patterns, and complex concurrent data structures [22, 24, 27, 34]. However, these efforts have also exposed some rough corners in the underlying meta theory that either limit expressivity or automation. In this paper, we propose a new meta theory for the flow framework that aims to strike a balance between these conflicting requirements. In addition, we present algorithms that aid proof automation.

Background. The central notion of the flow framework is that of a *flow*. Given a commutative monoid $(\mathbb{M}, +, 0)$ (e.g. natural numbers with addition), and a graph with nodes X and an *edge function* $E \colon X \times X \to \mathbb{M} \to \mathbb{M}$, a flow is a function $\mathit{fl} \colon X \to \mathbb{M}$ that satisfies the *flow equation*:

$$\forall x \in X. \quad \mathit{fl}(x) = in_x + \sum_{y \in X} E_{(y,x)}(\mathit{fl}(y)) \ .$$

That is, fl is a fixed point of the function that assigns every node x an initial value $in_x \in \mathbb{M}$, its *inflow*, and then propagates these values through the graph according to the edge function. This is akin to a forward data flow analysis where the monoid operation $+$ is used as the join. By choosing an appropriate flow monoid, inflow, and edge function, one can express inductive properties of graphs (reachability, sortedness, etc.) in terms of conditions that refer only to each node's flow value $\mathit{fl}(x)$.

A graph endowed with an inflow and associated flow is a *flow graph*. An example flow graph h is shown on the right-hand side of Fig. 1a. Here, the flow value $\mathit{fl}(w)$ for

© The Author(s) 2023
S. Sankaranarayanan and N. Sharygina (Eds.): TACAS 2023, LNCS 13993, pp. 628–646, 2023.
https://doi.org/10.1007/978-3-031-30823-9_32

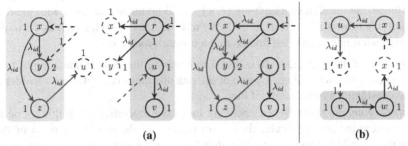

Figure 1. (a) Two flow graphs h_1 with nodes $h_1.X = \{x, y, z\}$ (left) and h_2 with nodes $h_2.X = \{r, u, v\}$ (center) for the flow monoid of natural numbers with addition. The edge label λ_{id} stands for the identity function. Omitted edges are labeled by the constant 0 function. Dashed edges represent the inflows. Nodes are labeled by their flow, respectively, outflow. The right side shows the composition $h = h_1 * h_2$. **(b)** Two flow graphs h_1 with $h_1.X = \{u, x\}$ (top) and h_2 with $h_2.X = \{v, w\}$ (bottom) whose composition is undefined due to vanishing flows.

a node w counts the number of paths from r to w. A flow graph can be partial and have edges to nodes outside of X like the node u for h_1 in Fig. 1a. If we include these nodes in the computation of the flow, then their flow values constitute the *outflow* of the flow graph. For instance, the outflow of h_1 for u is 1.

Flow graphs are equipped with a notion of disjoint composition, $h = h_1 * h_2$. An example is given in Fig. 1a. The composition is only defined if the union of the flows of h_1 and h_2 is again a flow of h. This may not always be the case. For instance, the inflows and outflows of h_1 and h_2 may be mutually incompatible such as h_1 sending outflow 2 to u whereas the inflow to u in h_2 is only 1.

Flow graph composition yields a *separation algebra*. That is, if we use flow graphs as an abstraction of program states (e.g., the heap), then we can use separation logic to reason locally about properties of programs that are expressed in terms of the induced flow graphs. For example, suppose the program updates the flow graph h in Fig. 1a to a new flow graph h' by inserting a new edge labeled λ_{id} between the nodes r and u. This increases the flow of u and v from 1 to 2. We can break this update down as follows. First, we decompose h into h_1 and h_2. Next, we obtain h'_2 from h_2 by inserting the edge and updating the flow of u and v to 2. Finally, we compose h'_2 again with h_1 to obtain h'. Note that the composition $h_1 * h'_2$ is still defined. This means that any property expressed over the flow in the h_1-portion of h still holds in h'. This is the well-known *frame rule* of separation logic, instantiated for flow graphs.

The crux in applying the frame rule is to show that the composition $h_1 * h'_2$ is indeed defined. One can do this locally by showing that the update $h_2 \rightsquigarrow h'_2$ is *frame-preserving*, i.e., for *any* h_1 such that $h_1 * h_2$ is defined, $h_1 * h'_2$ is also defined.

Typically, the flow subgraphs involved in a frame-preserving update $h_2 \rightsquigarrow h'_2$ include more nodes than those immediately affected by the update. For instance, consider the subgraphs of h and h' in our example that consist only of the nodes $\{r, u\}$ directly affected by inserting the edge. These subgraphs do not constitute a frame-preserving update because inserting the edge between r and u also changes the outflow to v from

1 to 2. Hence, the updated subgraph for $\{r, u\}$ would no longer compose with the rest of h where v's flow is still 1 instead of 2. We refer to a set of nodes such as $\{r, u, v\}$ that identifies a frame-preserving update as the update's *footprint*.

Meta theories of flow graphs. In addition to ensuring that flow graph composition yields a separation algebra, there are two desiderata that one has to take into consideration when designing a meta theory of flow graphs:

– *Obtaining unique flows.* When encoding inductive properties using flows, one is often interested in a particular flow, most commonly the least fixed point of the flow equation for a given inflow. One therefore needs a way to focus the reasoning on the particular flow of interest.
– *Identifying frame-preserving updates.* In order to enable the application of the frame rule, one needs a way to effectively compute candidate footprints and check whether they identify frame-preserving updates.

The first subgoal is crucial for expressivity and the second one for proof automation. Achieving one subgoals makes it more difficult to achieve the other. Specifically, consider the meta theory proposed in [24]. It requires that the flow monoid $(\mathbb{M}, +, 0)$ is also cancellative ($m + n_1 = o$ and $m + n_2 = o$ implies $n_1 = n_2$). Requiring cancellativity has the advantage that it is easy to check if an update $h \rightsquigarrow h'$ is frame-preserving: it suffices to show that h and h' have the same inflow and outflow. Cancellativity also ensures that for each flow fl, there exists a unique inflow that produces fl. Hence, it is sufficient to track only fl since the inflow is a derived quantity. However, the converse does not hold.

In fact, obtaining unique flows for cancellative $\mathbb{M}$ becomes more difficult. A natural requirement that one would like to impose on $\mathbb{M}$ is that the pre-order induced by $+$ forms a complete partial order (cpo) or even a complete lattice. This way, one can focus on the least flow, which is guaranteed to exist if one applies standard fixed point theorems, imposing only mild assumptions on the edge functions. However, cancellativity is inherently incompatible with standard domain-theoretic prerequisites. For instance, the only ordered cancellative commutative monoid that is a directed cpo is the trivial one: $\mathbb{M}_0 = \{0\}$. Similarly, $\mathbb{M}_0$ is the only such monoid that has a greatest element.

For cases where unique flows are desired, [24] imposes additional requirements on the edge functions (nil-potent) or the graph structure (effectively acyclic). The former is quite restrictive in terms of expressivity. The latter again complicates the computation of frame-preserving updates: one now has to ensure that no cycles are introduced when the updated graph h_2' is composed with its frame h_1. In fact, for the effectively acyclic case, [24] only provides a sufficient condition that a given footprint yields a frame-preserving update but it gives no algorithm for computing such a footprint.

Contributions. In this paper, we propose a new meta theory of flows based on flow monoids that form ω-cpos (but need not be cancellative). The cpo requirement yields the desired least fixed point semantics. The differences in the requirements on the flow monoid necessitate a new notion of flow graph composition. In particular, for a least fixed point semantics of flows, $h = h_1 * h_2$ is only defined if the flows of h_1 and h_2 do not vanish. An example of such a situation is shown in Fig. 1b, where the flows in h_1 and h_2 would vanish to 0 in $h_1 * h_2$ because the created cycle has no external inflow. Moreover, an update $h \rightsquigarrow h'$ is frame-preserving if h and h' route inflows to outflows in the same way. We formalize this condition using a notion of contextual equivalence of the graphs' *transfer functions*, which are the least fixed points of the flow equation, parameterized by the inflows and restricted to the nodes outside the graphs. We then identify conditions on the edge functions that are commonly satisfied in practice and that allow us to effectively check contextual equivalence of transfer functions. This result is remarkable because the flow monoid can have infinite ascending chains and the flow graphs can be cyclic. Building on this equivalence check, we propose an iterative algorithm for computing footprints of updates. This algorithm enables the automation of the frame rule for reasoning about programs manipulating flow graphs. We evaluate the presented algorithms on a benchmark suite of flow graph updates that are extracted from linearizability proofs for concurrent search structures constructed by the tool plankton [26,27]. The evaluation demonstrates that our algorithms help to automate key aspects of these proofs that have previously relied on user guidance or heuristics.

2 Flow Graph Separation Algebra

We start with the presentation of our new separation algebra of flow graphs.

Given a commutative monoid $(\mathbb{M}, +, 0)$, we define the binary relation $\leq$ on $\mathbb{M}$ by $n \leq m$ if there is $o \in \mathbb{M}$ with $m = n + o$. Flow values are drawn from a *flow monoid*, a commutative monoid for which the relation $\leq$ is an ω-cpo. That is, $\leq$ is a partial order and every ascending chain $K = m_0 \leq m_1 \leq \ldots$ in $\mathbb{M}$ has a least upper bound, denoted $\bigsqcup K$. We expect $n + \bigsqcup K = \bigsqcup(n + K)$. In the following, we fix a flow monoid $(\mathbb{M}, +, 0)$.

Let $ContFun(\mathbb{M} \to \mathbb{M})$ be the continuous functions in $\mathbb{M} \to \mathbb{M}$. Recall that a function $f : \mathbb{M} \to \mathbb{M}$ is *continuous* [43] if it commutes with limits of ascending chains, $f(\bigsqcup K) = \bigsqcup f(K)$ for every chain K in $\mathbb{M}$. We lift $+$ and $\leq$ to functions $\mathbb{M} \to \mathbb{M}$ in the expected way. An empty iterated sum $\sum_{i \in \varnothing} m_i$ is defined to be 0.

Lemma 1. $(ContFun(\mathbb{M} \to \mathbb{M}), \circ, id)$ *is a monoid. Moreover, if* $(\mathbb{M}, \leq)$ *is an* ω-cpo, *so is* $(ContFun(\mathbb{M} \to \mathbb{M}), \leq)$.

A *flow graph* is a tuple $h = (X, E, in)$ consisting of a finite set of nodes $X \subseteq \mathbb{N}$, a set of edges $E : X \times \mathbb{N} \to ContFun(\mathbb{M} \to \mathbb{M})$ labeled by continuous functions, and an *inflow* $in : (\mathbb{N} \setminus X) \times X \to \mathbb{M}$. We use FG for the set of all flow graphs and denote the empty flow graph by $h_\varnothing \triangleq (\varnothing, \varnothing, \varnothing)$.

We define two derived functions for flow graphs. First, the *flow* is the least function $flow : X \to \mathbb{M}$ satisfying the flow equation: $flow(x) = in_x + rhs_x(flow)$, for all $x \in X$. Here, $in_x \triangleq \sum_{y \in (\mathbb{N} \setminus X)} in(y, x)$ is a monoid value and $rhs_x \triangleq \sum_{y \in X} E_{(y,x)}$ is a function of type $ContFun((X \to \mathbb{M}) \to \mathbb{M})$. Finally, we also define the *outflow* $out : X \times (\mathbb{N} \setminus X) \to \mathbb{M}$ by $out(x, y) \triangleq E_{(x,y)}(flow(x))$.

Example 1. For linearizability proofs of concurrent search structures one can use a flow that labels every data structure node x with its *inset*, the set of keys k' such that a thread searching for k' may traverse the node x [22,23]. Translated to our setting, the relevant flow monoid is the powerset of keys, $\mathbb{P}(\mathbb{Z} \cup \{-\infty, \infty\})$, with set union as addition. Figure 2 shows two keyset flow graphs that abstract potential states of a concurrent set implementation based on sorted linked lists. When a key k is removed from the set, the node x that stores k is first marked to indicate that x has been logically deleted. In

Figure 2. Two flow graphs h_1 (left) and h_2 (right) with $h_1.X = h_2.X = \{l, t, r\}$ for the keyset flow monoid $\mathbb{P}(\mathbb{Z} \cup \{-\infty, \infty\})$. The edge label λ_k for a key k denotes the function $\lambda m.(m \setminus [-\infty, k])$.

a second step, x is then physically unlinked from the list. The idea of the abstraction is that an edge leaving a node x that stores a key k is labeled by the function λ_k if x is unmarked and otherwise by $\lambda_{-\infty}$. This is because a search for $k' \in \mathbb{Z}$ will traverse the edge leaving x iff $k < k'$ or x is marked. In the figure, l and r are assumed to be unmarked, storing keys 6 and 8, respectively. Node t is assumed to be marked. Flow graph h_2 is obtained from h_1 by physically unlinking the marked node t. Using the keyset flow one can then express the crucial data structure invariants that are needed for a linearizability proof based on local reasoning (e.g., the invariant that the logical contents of a node is always a subset of its inset).

We note that the inflow of the global flow graph that abstracts the program state can be used in the specification. In the example, one lets $in_r = \mathbb{Z}$ for the root r of the data structure and $in_x = \varnothing$ for all other nodes to indicate that all searches start at r. □

Composition without vanishing flows. To define the composition of flow graphs, $h_1 * h_2$, we proceed in two steps. We first define an auxiliary composition that may suffer from *vanishing* flows, local flows that disappear in the composition. That is, this composition is defined for the flow graphs shown in Fig. 1b. In the composed graph the flow of each node is 0 where it was 1 before the composition—the flow vanishes. This means that the auxiliary composition does not allow to lift lower bounds on the flow values from the individual components to the composed graph. Hence, the actual composition restricts the auxiliary composition to rule out such vanishing flows. Definedness of the auxiliary composition requires disjointness of the nodes in h_1 and h_2. Moreover, the outflow of one flow graph has to match the inflow expectations of the other:

$$h_1 \#\# h_2 \quad \text{if} \quad X_1 \cap X_2 = \varnothing \ \land \ \forall x \in X_1, y \in X_2.\ out_1(x, y) = in_2(x, y) \land$$
$$out_2(y, x) = in_1(y, x).$$

The auxiliary composition $h_1 \uplus h_2$ removes the inflow provided by the other component:

$$h_1 \uplus h_2 \quad \triangleq \quad (X_1 \uplus X_2, E_1 \uplus E_2, (in_1 \uplus in_2)|_{(\mathbb{N} \setminus (X_1 \uplus X_2)) \times (X_1 \uplus X_2)}).$$

To rule out vanishing flows, we incorporate a suitable equality on the flows:

$$h_1 \# h_2 \quad \text{if} \quad h_1 \#\# h_2 \ \land \ h_1.flow \uplus h_2.flow = (h_1 \uplus h_2).flow.$$

Only if the latter equality holds, do we have the composition $h_1 * h_2 \triangleq h_1 \uplus h_2$. It is worth noting that $h_1.flow \uplus h_2.flow \geq (h_1 \uplus h_2).flow$ always holds. What definedness really asks for is the reverse inequality.

Recall from [5] that a *separation algebra* is a partial commutative monoid $(\Sigma, *, \mathsf{emp})$ with a set of units $\mathsf{emp} \subseteq \Sigma$.

Lemma 2. $(FG, *, \{h_\varnothing\})$ *is a separation algebra.*

3   Frame-Preserving Updates

Since flow graphs form a separation algebra, we can use separation logic assertions to describe sets of flow graphs as in [24] and then use them to prove separation logic Hoare triples. A key proof rule used in such proofs is the frame rule. Given separation logic assertions P_1 and P_2, and a command c, the frame rule states: if the Hoare triple $\{P_1\} \, c \, \{P_2\}$ is valid, then so is $\{P_1 * F\} \, c \, \{P_2 * F\}$ for any *frame* F. The remainder of the paper focuses on developing algorithms for automating this proof rule.

The flow graphs described by an assertion may have unbounded size (e.g., due to the use of *iterated separating conjunctions*). We only consider bounded flow graphs in the following; the unbounded case is known to be a challenge for which orthogonal techniques are being developed (cf. Sect. 6). However, even if the flow graphs have bounded size, there may still be infinitely many of them because the inflows and edge functions are encoded symbolically in a logical theory of the flow monoid. For pedagogy, we present our algorithms in terms of concrete flow graphs rather than symbolic ones. However, our development readily extends to symbolic representations assuming the underlying flow monoid theory is decidable. In fact, our implementation discussed in Sect. 5 works with symbolic flow graphs.

The soundness of the frame rule relies on the assumption that the state update induced by the command c satisfies a certain locality condition. In our setting, this condition amounts to checking that the update of P_1 under c is *frame-preserving* with respect to flow graph composition. For the flow graphs h_1 described by P_1 and all flow graphs h_2 in the post image of h_1 under c, this means that $h_1 \# h$ implies $h_2 \# h$ for all h. Intuitively, $h_2 \# h$ still holds if h_1 and h_2 transfer inflows to outflows in the same way.

Formally, for a flow graph h we define its *transfer function* $tf(h)$ mapping inflows to outflows, $tf(h) : ((\mathbb{N} \setminus X) \times X \to \mathbb{M}) \to X \times (\mathbb{N} \setminus X) \to \mathbb{M}$, by

$$tf(h)(in') \triangleq h[in \mapsto in'].out \, .$$

For a given inflow in, we also write $tf(h_1) =_{in} tf(h_2)$ to mean that for all inflows $in' \leq in$, $tf(h_1)(in') = tf(h_2)(in')$.

Definition 1. *Flow graphs* h_1, h_2 *are* contextually equivalent, *denoted* $h_1 =_{ctx} h_2$, *if we have* $h_1.X = h_2.X$, $h_1.in = h_2.in$, *and* $tf(h_1) =_{h_1.in} tf(h_2)$.

Theorem 1 (Frame Preservation). *For all flow graphs* $h_1 =_{ctx} h_2$ *and* h, $h_1 \# h$ *if and only if* $h_2 \# h$ *and, in case of definedness,* $h_1 * h =_{ctx} h_2 * h$.

To automate the frame rule for a command c and a precondition P, we need to identify a decomposition $P = P_1 * F$ so as to infer $\{P_1\} \, c \, \{P_2\}$ and then apply the frame rule to derive $\{P\} \, c \, \{Q\}$ for the postcondition $Q = P_2 * F$. This is closely related to the *frame inference problem* [4]. When a command modifies a flow graph h_1 to h_2, our goal is to identify a (hopefully small) set of nodes Y in h_1 that are affected by this update, the *flow footprint*. That is, Y captures the difference between the flow graphs before and after the update and the complement of Y defines the frame. To make this formal, we need the restriction of flow graphs to subsets of nodes, which then gives us a notion of flow graph decomposition. Towards this, consider h and $Y \subseteq \mathbb{N}$. We define

$$h|_Y \triangleq (h.X \cap Y, h.E|_{(h.X \cap Y) \times \mathbb{N}}, in)$$

such that the inflow in satisfies $in(z, y) \triangleq h.in(z, y)$ for all $z \in \mathbb{N} \setminus h.X$, $y \in h.X \cap Y$ and $in(x, y) \triangleq h.E_{(x,y)}(h.flow(x))$ for all $x \in h.X \setminus Y$, $y \in h.X \cap Y$.

Definition 2. *Consider h_1 and h_2 with $X \triangleq h_1.X = h_2.X$ and $h_1.in = h_2.in$. A flow footprint for the difference between h_1 and h_2 is a subset of nodes $Y \subseteq X$ so that $h_1|_Y =_{ctx} h_2|_Y$ and $h_1|_{X \setminus Y} = h_2|_{X \setminus Y}$. The set of all such footprints is $FFP(h_1, h_2)$.*

Flow graphs over different sets of nodes or inflows never have a flow footprint. The former requirement merely simplifies the presentation. To that end, we assume that all nodes that will be allocated during program execution are already present in the initial flow graph. This assumption can be lifted. The latter requirement is motivated by the fact that the global inflow is part of the specification as noted earlier in Example 1.

Before we proceed with the problem of how to compute flow footprints, we highlight some of their properties.

Lemma 3 (Footprint Monotonicity). *If $Z \in FFP(h_1, h_2)$ and $Z \subseteq Y \subseteq h_1.X$, then $Y \in FFP(h_1, h_2)$.*

A consequence of monotonicity is the existence of a canonical flow footprint: if there is a flow footprint at all, then the set of all nodes will work as a footprint. Of course this canonical footprint is undesirably large. It corresponds to the case where one reasons about flow graph updates globally, forgoing the application of the frame rule. Unfortunately, an inclusion-minimal flow footprint does not exist.

Proposition 1 (Canonical Footprints). *We have: $FFP(h_1, h_2) \neq \varnothing$ if and only if $h_1.X \in FFP(h_1, h_2)$. There is no inclusion-minimal flow footprint; in particular, the set $FFP(h_1, h_2)$ is not closed under intersection.*

The proof of monotonicity requires a better understanding of the restriction operator, as provided by the following lemma.

Lemma 4 (Restriction). *Consider h and $Y, Z \subseteq \mathbb{N}$. Then (i) $h|_Y.flow = h.flow|_Y$, (ii) $h|_Y \# h|_{X \setminus Y}$ and $h|_Y * h|_{X \setminus Y} = h$, and (iii) $(h|_Y)|_Z = h|_{Y \cap Z}$.*

Since flow footprints are defined via restriction, the lemma also shows that flow footprints are well-behaved. For example, the restriction to the footprint Y does not change the flow of a node $y \in Y$ nor that of a node $x \in h.X \setminus Y$. More formally, this means $h|_Y.flow(y) = h.flow(y)$ and $h|_{X \setminus Y}.flow(x) = h.flow(x)$, by Lemma 4(i).

For our development, it will be convenient to have a more operational formulation of the transfer function. Towards this, we understand the flow graph as a function that takes an inflow as a parameter and yields a transformer of flow approximants:

$$h : ((\mathbb{N} \setminus X) \times X \to \mathbb{M}) \to (X \to \mathbb{M}) \to X \to \mathbb{M}$$

defined by $\quad h[in](\sigma)(x) = in_x + rhs_x(\sigma)$.

Recall $in_x \triangleq \sum_{y \in \mathbb{N} \setminus X} in(y, x)$ and $rhs_x(\sigma) = \sum_{y \in X} E_{(y,x)}(\sigma(y))$. The least fixed point of $h[in]$ is $\bigsqcup_{i \in \mathbb{N}} h[in]^i(\bot)$ with $h^0 = id_{X \to \mathbb{M}}$ and $h^{i+1} = h^i \circ h$, by Kleene's theorem. Define $out : (X \to \mathbb{M}) \to X \times (\mathbb{N} \setminus X) \to \mathbb{M}$ by $out(\sigma)(y, z) \triangleq E_{(y,z)}(\sigma(y))$. This yields the following characterization of transfer functions and flows.

Lemma 5 (Transfer). *For all flow graphs h we have (i) $tf(h) = out \circ (lfp.h[-])$ and (ii) $lfp.h[h.in]) = h.flow$.*

4 Computing Footprints

We present an algorithm for computing a footprint for the difference between two given flow graphs. We proceed in two steps. We first give a high-level description of the algorithm that ignores computability problems. In a second step, we show how to solve the computability problems. Throughout the development, we will assume to have flow graphs h_1 and h_2 over the same nodes $X \triangleq h_1.X = h_2.X$ and with the same inflow $h_1.in = h_2.in$. If this assumption fails, a flow footprint does not exist by definition.

4.1 Algorithm

We compute the flow footprint as a fixed point. We start with the footprint candidate Z consisting of the nodes whose outgoing edges differ in h_1 and h_2. Then, we iteratively add the nodes whose outflow leaving the current footprint candidate Z differs in $h_1|_Z$ and $h_2|_Z$. That the outflow differs means that the transfer functions $tf(h_1|_Z)$ and $tf(h_2|_Z)$ differ and thus the candidate Z is not a footprint. In turn, if all outflows match, the transfer functions coincide and Z is a footprint as desired.

Technically, we compute the fixed point over the powerset lattice of nodes endowed with a distinguished top element: $(\mathbb{P}(X)^\top, \sqsubseteq)$ with $\mathbb{P}(X)^\top \triangleq \mathbb{P}(X) \uplus \{\top\}$. Element $\top$ indicates a failure of the footprint computation. This may arise if the footprint is not covered by X, i.e., extends beyond the flow graphs h_1, h_2.

Our fixed point computation starts from $Z = odif_{h_1,h_2} \subseteq X$ as defined by

$$odif_{h_1,h_2} \triangleq \{ x \in X \mid \exists z \in \mathbb{N}.h_1.E(x,z) \neq h_2.E(x,z) \}.$$

The fixed point then proceeds to extend Z as long as the transfer functions associated with $h_1|_Z$ and $h_2|_Z$ do not match. To define the extension, we let the *transfer failure* of $Z \subseteq X$ be the successor nodes of Z that may receive different outflow from h_1 and h_2:

$$tfail_{h_1,h_2}(Z) \triangleq \left\{ x \in \mathbb{N} \setminus Z \; \middle| \; \begin{array}{l} \exists \, in \leq h_1|_Z.in \; \exists \, z \in Z. \\ [tf(h_1|_Z)(in)](z,x) \neq [tf(h_2|_Z)(in)](z,x) \end{array} \right\}.$$

This set is the *reason* why the current footprint candidate Z is not a footprint, that is, $Z \notin FFP(h_1, h_2)$. Extending Z with the transfer failure yields a new candidate. We check that the new candidate is covered by X (i.e., does not include nodes outside of h_1, h_2). If the check fails, the new candidate is $\{\top\}$ to indicate that no footprint could be computed. The following definition makes the extension procedure precise.

Definition 3. *The function* $ext_{h_1,h_2} : \mathbb{P}(X)^\top \to \mathbb{P}(X)^\top$ *is defined by*

$$ext_{h_1,h_2}(Z) \triangleq tfail_{h_1,h_2}(Z) \not\subseteq X \; ? \; \top \; : \; Z \sqcup odif_{h_1,h_2} \sqcup tfail_{h_1,h_2}(Z).$$

Iteratively extending the candidate Z with the transfer failure eventually produces a footprint for the difference of h_1 and h_2, or fails with $\top$. The approach is sound.

Theorem 2 (Soundness). *Let* $F \triangleq lfp.ext_{h_1,h_2}$. *If* $F \neq \top$, *then* $F \in FFP(h_1, h_2)$.

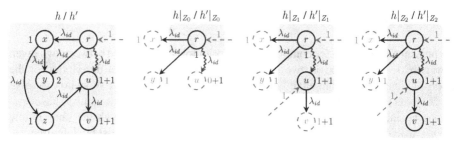

Figure 3. Computing a footprint for the difference of h and h' iterates through the sets $Z_0 \triangleq \{r\}$, $Z_1 \triangleq \{r, u\}$, and $Z_2 \triangleq \{r, u, v\}$. The latter is the least fixed point of $ext_{h,h'}$ and a footprint as desired, $Z_2 \in FFP(h, h')$.

Example 2. For an illustration consider Fig. 3. There, we apply the fixed point computation to find a footprint for the difference of h and h'. As alluded to in Sect. 1, h' is the result of inserting into h a new edge between nodes r and u labeled with λ_{id}.

The fixed point computation starts from $Z_0 \triangleq \{r\} = odif_{H,H'}$ as it is the only node whose outgoing edges have changed. Next, we compute $tfail_{h,h'}(Z_0)$. This yields $\{u\}$ because u receives 0 from Z_0 in h but 1 in h' due to the new edge. The outflow from Z_0 to the remaining nodes coincides in h and h'. Hence, the extension of Z_0 with the transfer failure yields $Z_1 \triangleq ext_{h,h'}(Z_0) = \{u, r\}$. Similarly, we compute $tfail_{h,h'}(Z_1)$ and obtain $Z_2 \triangleq ext_{h,h'}(Z_1) = \{r, u, v\}$. Since v has no outgoing edges, Z_2 is the least fixed point of $ext_{h,h'}$. Because Z_2 is a subset of the nodes of h and h', it is a footprint, $Z_2 \in FFP(h, h')$.   □

To obtain Theorem 2, we have to prove that the fixed point $F \triangleq lfp.ext_{h_1,h_2}$ is indeed a footprint if $F \neq \top$. That is, we have to establish the following two properties according to Definition 2: (i) $h_1|_F =_{ctx} h_2|_F$ and (ii) $h_1|_{X \setminus F} = h_2|_{X \setminus F}$.

To see the latter one, note that the graph structures (the nodes and edges) of $h_1|_{X \setminus F}$ and $h_2|_{X \setminus F}$ coincide because $odif_{h_1,h_2} \subseteq F$. The inflows coincide as well because they are, intuitively, comprised of the flow graph's overall inflow $h_1.in = h_2.in$ and the outflow of the footprint, which is equal in both flow graphs due to $h_1|_F =_{ctx} h_2|_F$.

The interesting part of the soundness proof is to establish property (i), the contextual equivalence $h_1|_F =_{ctx} h_2|_F$. Since F is a fixed point of ext_{h_1,h_2}, we know that $tfail_{h_1,h_2}(Z) = \varnothing$ and thus the transfer functions of $h_1|_F$ and $h_2|_F$ coincide. Hence, it suffices to establish $h_1|_F.in = h_2|_F.in$ to obtain the desired contextual equivalence, Definition 1. This key step in the proof is obtained with the help of the following lemma.

Lemma 6. *Let $odif_{h_1,h_2} \subseteq F \subseteq X$ with $tfail_{h_1,h_2}(F) = \varnothing$. Then $h_1|_F.in = h_2|_F.in$.*

To establish the lemma one has to show that the inflow into F from the non-footprint part $Y \triangleq X \setminus F$ coincides in h_1 and h_2. The challenge is a cyclic dependency in the flow: the inflow from Y depends on the outflow of F, which depends on the inflow from Y. To tackle this, we rephrase the flow equation for h_i as a pairing of the two separate flow equations for $h_i|_F$ and $h_i|_Y$, for $i \in \{1, 2\}$. Intuitively, the pairings compute the flow locally in $h_i|_F$ and $h_i|_Y$ for a fixed inflow (initially $h_i.in$). Then, the inflow to $h_i|_F$

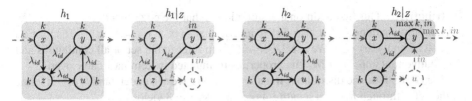

Figure 4. Counterexample to completeness using the monoid $(\mathbb{N} \cup \{\infty\}, \max, 0)$. While the set $\{x, y, z, u\}$ is a footprint for the difference between flow graphs h_1 and h_2, our fixed point will produce the candidates $\{x\}$ and $Z \triangleq \{x, y, z\}$ and then fail with $\{\top\}$.

is updated to the inflow from outside h_i and the inflow from $h_i|_Y$, and similarly for the inflow to $h_i|_Y$. This is repeated until a fixed point is reach. Technically, we rely on Bekić's Lemma [1] to compute the pairings. Then, we observe $tf(h_1|_F) = tf(h_2|_F)$ because $tfail_{h_1,h_2}(F) = \varnothing$ as well as $tf(h_1|_Y) = tf(h_2|_Y)$ because $odif_{h_1,h_2} \subseteq F$. Roughly, this means that the flow pairings for h_1 and h_2 must coincide as the individual parts propagate the same values. Put differently, the updated inflow for $h_1|_F$ and $h_2|_F$ as well as $h_1|_Y$ and $h_2|_Y$ coincide in each iteration. Overall, we get $h_1|_F.in = h_2|_F.in$.

Our computation of a flow footprint is forward, it starts from the nodes where the flow graphs differ and follows the edges. It may therefore fail if predecessor nodes of an iterate Z need to be considered to determine a flow footprint. For an example refer to Fig. 4. Using the monoid $(\mathbb{N} \cup \{\infty\}, \max, 0)$, it is easy to see that the set $\{x, y, z, u\}$ is a footprint for the difference between h_1 and h_2. Our fixed point, however, will start with $\{x\}$ and extend this to $Z \triangleq \{x, y, z\}$. Let v be the node outside the flow graphs that y is pointing to. Then, the next transfer failure is $tfail_{h_1,h_2}(Z) = \{v\}$ because for $in < k$ the outflow of y to v differs in $h_1|_Z$ and $h_2|_Z$. Our approach fails to compute a footprint.

Fact 3 (Incompleteness) *There are flow graphs h_1 and h_2 for which our algorithm is not able to determine a flow footprint although one exists.*

4.2   Comparing Transfer Functions

When implementing the above fixed point computation, the challenge is to prove the equivalence between given transfer functions in order to obtain the transfer failure: $[tf(h_1|_Z)(-)](-, x) = [tf(h_2|_Z)(-)](-, x)$? Already the comparison of two functions is known to be difficult to do algorithmically. What adds to the problem is that transfer functions are defined as least fixed points, meaning we do not have a closed-form representation of the functions to compare.

Our approach is to impose additional requirements on the set of edge functions. The requirements are met in all our experiments, and so do not mean a limitation for the applicability of our approach. We show that if the edge functions are not only continuous but also distributive, then the transfer functions can be understood in terms of paths through the underlying flow graphs. If the edge functions are additionally decreasing and the underlying monoid's addition is idempotent, then acyclic paths are sufficient. Both results do not hold for merely continuous edge functions.

Distributivity. Our first additional assumption is that the edge functions $f : \mathbb{M} \to \mathbb{M}$ are not only continuous, but also *distributive* in that $f(m + n) = f(m) + f(n)$ for all $m, n \in \mathbb{M}$ and $f(0) = 0$. We use $DistFun(\mathbb{M})$ to refer to the set of all continuous and distributive functions over $\mathbb{M}$. The properties formulated in Lemma 1 carry over.

For continuous and distributive transfer functions, we can understand $h[in]^i$ in terms of the paths through $h[in]$ of length i. For example, $i = 3$ yields

$$[h[in]^3](\bot)(z) = in_z + \sum_{y \in X} E_{(y,z)}(\; in_y + \sum_{x \in X} E_{(x,y)}(in_x + \sum_{u \in X} E_{(u,x)}(\bot(u)) \;)$$

$$= in_z + \sum_{y \in X} E_{(y,z)}(in_y) + \sum_{y \in X} \sum_{x \in X} E_{(y,z)}(E_{(x,y)}(in_x)) \; .$$

The first equality is by definition, the second is where distributivity comes in. In particular, $\bot(u) = 0$ and so $E_{(y,z)}(\; E_{(x,y)}(\; E_{(u,x)}(\; \bot(u) \;) \;) \;) = 0$. The last term shows that we forward the inflow given at a node x to an intermediary node y and from there to the node z of interest. For higher powers of $h[in]$, we take longer paths. For $h[in]^*$, we thus obtain the sum over all nodes x and all paths from x to z through the flow graph. We need some definitions to make this precise.

A *path* p through flow graph h is a finite, non-empty sequence of nodes all of which belong to the flow graph except the last which lies outside:

$$p = x_0 \cdot \ldots \cdot x_n \cdot z \in X^+ \cdot (\mathbb{N} \setminus X)$$

where $\cdot$ denotes path concatenation. We use $first(p) = x_0$ resp. $last(p) = x_n$ to extract the first resp. last node from within the flow graph h. By $Paths(h, x, y, z)$ we denote the set of all paths through flow graph h that start in node $first(p) = x$ and leave h from node $last(p) = y$ to move to $z \in \mathbb{N} \setminus X$. Given a set of nodes $X' \subseteq X$, we use $Paths(h, X', y, z)$ for the union over all $x \in X'$ of the sets $Paths(h, x, y, z)$. The path induces the function $E_p : \mathbb{M} \to \mathbb{M}$ that composes the edge functions along the path:

$$E_x = id \qquad\qquad E_{x.p} = E_p \circ E_{(x,first(p))} \; .$$

Together with Lemma 5, the above analysis yields the first closed-form representation of a flow graph's transfer function, which so far has involved a fixed point computation.

Theorem 4 (Closed-Form Representation). *If h is labeled over $DistFun(\mathbb{M})$, then:*

$$[tf(h)(in)](y, z) = \sum_{x \in X} \sum_{p \in Paths(h,x,y,z)} E_p(in_x) \; .$$

Theorem 4 pushes the fixed point computation of transfer functions into the sets $Paths(h, x, y, z)$ which are themselves defined inductively and potentially infinite. In the following, we alleviate this problem without requiring acyclicity of the flow graph.

Idempotence. Our second assumption is that addition in the monoid is idempotent, meaning $m + m = m$ for all $m \in \mathbb{M}$. Idempotence ensures the addition degenerates to a join for comparable elements: $m + n = m \sqcup n = n$ for all $m \leq n \in \mathbb{M}$. Unless stated otherwise, we hereafter assume an idempotent addition.

With Theorem 4, it remains to compare sums over paths. With idempotence, we show that we can further reduce the problem and reason over single paths rather than sums. We show that every path in h_1 can be replaced by a set of paths in h_2, and vice versa. Even more, we only have to consider the paths from nodes where the edges changed. The precise formulation of the path replacement condition is the following.

Definition 4. *The path replacement condition for flow graphs h_1 by h_2 over the same set of nodes X and labeled by $DistDecFun(\mathbb{M})$ requires that for every $x \in odif_{h_1,h_2}$, for every $y \in X$, and for every $z \in \mathbb{N} \setminus X$ we have*

$$\forall p \in Paths(h_1, x, y, z) \ \exists\, P \subseteq Paths(h_2, x, y, z). \quad E_p \leq E_P \triangleq \sum_{q \in P} E_q \,.$$

Example 3. For the flow graphs h_1 and h_2 from Fig. 4, we have path replacement of h_1 by h_2, and vice versa. To see this, consider the path $p \triangleq x \cdot z \cdot u \cdot y \cdot v$ in h_1 and $q \triangleq x \cdot y \cdot v$ in h_2, where v is the node outside of h_1, h_2 that y points to. Since all edges are labeled with λ_{id}, we have $E_p = \lambda_{id} = E_q$. It is worth noting that, in this example, we can ignore the cycles in h_1 and h_2. In a moment, we will introduce restrictions on edge functions in order to do avoid cycles in general.

Similarly, we have path replacement for the flow graphs from Fig. 2. To be precise, $E_p = \lambda_8 = E_q$ for the paths $p \triangleq l \cdot t \cdot r \cdot v$ in h_1 and $q \triangleq l \cdot r \cdot v$ in h_2.   □

The main result is that path replacement is sound and complete for proving equivalence of transfer functions.

Theorem 5 (Path Replacement Principle). *We have $tf(h_1) = tf(h_2)$ if and only if path replacement of h_1 by h_2 and of h_2 by h_1 hold.*

The theorem is remarkable in several respects. First, one would expect we have to replace the paths from all nodes in h_1. Instead, we can focus on the nodes where the outgoing edges changed. Second, one would expect the replacing paths P start from arbitrary nodes in h_2. Such a set of paths would yield a transfer function of type $(Y \to \mathbb{M}) \to \mathbb{M}$. Instead, we can work with a function of type $\mathbb{M} \to \mathbb{M}$. Even more, we can focus on paths starting in the same node as the path we intend to replace. Finally, the paths we use for replacement come without any constraints, leaving room for heuristics.

The proof starts from a *full path replacement condition* of h_1 by h_2, both over X and labeled by $DistFun(\mathbb{M})$. Full path replacement coincides with Definition 4 but draws x from full X rather than $x \in odif_{h_1,h_2}$. Full path replacement characterizes equivalence of the transfer functions in a monoid with idempotent addition in the case of continuous and distributive edge functions.

Lemma 7. *Full path replacement of h_1 by h_2 and h_2 by h_1 hold iff $tf(h_1) = tf(h_2)$.*

The result is a consequence of Theorem 4, which equates $tf(h_1)$ with the sum of the E_p for all paths $p \in Paths(h_1, x, y, z)$ for all $x \in X$. Full path replacement allows us to sum over E_P instead, for some $P \subseteq Paths(h_2, x, y, z)$. Over-approximating P with all paths $Paths(h_2, x, y, z)$, we obtain an upper bound for $tf(h_1)$. It is easy to see that the resulting sum can be rewritten into the form of Theorem 4, yielding $tf(h_1) \leq tf(h_2)$. Analogously, we get $tf(h_1) \geq tf(h_2)$ and thus $tf(h_1) = tf(h_2)$ as required. The reverse direction of the lemma is similar.

To conclude the proof of the path replacement principle in Theorem 5, we show that full path replacement and (ordinary) path replacement of h_1 by h_2 coincide. To see this, consider a path $p \in Paths(h_1, x, y, z)$ for any $x \in X$. The goal is to show $E_p \leq E_P$ for some $P \in Paths(h_2, x, y, z)$. To that end, decompose the path into $p = p_1 \cdot p_2$ such that $x' \triangleq first(p_2)$ is the first node in p from $odif_{h_1, h_2}$. Ordinary path replacement yields $Q \in Paths(h_2, x', y, z)$ with $E_{p_2} \leq E_Q$. Now, choose $P \triangleq \{ p_1 \cdot q \mid q \in Q \}$. Because p_1 exists in h_1 and h_2 with the exact same edge labels, we obtain the desired $E_p \leq E_P$.

Lemma 8. *Full path replacement of h_1 by h_2 holds if and only if path replacement of h_1 by h_2 holds.*

Decreasingness. We assume that the edge functions $f : \mathbb{M} \to \mathbb{M}$ are not only continuous and distributive, but also *decreasing*: $f(m) \leq m$ for all $m \in \mathbb{M}$. The assumption of decreasing edge functions is justified by the fact that a program that traverses the flow graph builds up information about the status of the structure, and smaller flow values mean more information (as in classical data flow analysis). We use $DistDecFun(\mathbb{M})$ to refer to the set of all continuous, distributive, and decreasing transfer functions over $\mathbb{M}$; Lemma 1 carries over to this set. Addition in the monoid is still assumed idempotent.

If all edge functions are decreasing, every cycle in the flow graph is decreasing as well. The key observation is that, given an idempotent addition, cycles with decreasing edge functions can be avoided when forming sums over sets of paths.

Lemma 9. *Let h be labeled over $DistDecFun(\mathbb{M})$ and $p_1 \cdot p \cdot p_2 \in Paths(h, x, y, z)$ with $last(p) = first(p)$. Then $p_1 \cdot p_2 \in Paths(h, x, y, z)$ and $E_{p_1 \cdot p \cdot p_2} \leq E_{p_1 \cdot p_2}$.*

Call a path *simple* if it does not repeat a node and let $SimplePaths(h, x, y, z)$ denote the set of all simple paths through h from x to y and leaving the flow graph towards z. Note that a finite graph only admits finitely many simple paths.

Theorem 6 (Simple Paths). *Assuming continuous, distributive, and decreasing edge functions, and assuming idempotent addition, Theorem 4 and Theorem 5 hold with every occurrency of $Paths(h, x, y, z)$ replaced by $SimplePaths(h, x, y, z)$.*

In practice, path-counting flows, keyset flows, reachability flows, shortest-path flows, and priority inheritance flows are relevant [22–24, 27] and compatible with our theory.

5   Evaluation

We substantiate the practicality of our new approach by evaluating it on a real-world collection of flow graphs extracted from the literature. We explain how we obtained our benchmarks and how we implemented and evaluated our approach.

Benchmark Suite. As alluded to in Sect. 1, the flow framework has been used to verify complex concurrent data structures. More specifically, it has been used for automated proof construction by the plankton tool [26, 27]. plankton performs an exhaustive proof search over a separation logic with support for flows—and further advanced features for establishing linearizability that do not matter for the present evaluation. In order to handle heap updates, plankton generates a footprint h for the flow graph $h_1 = h * h_{frame}$ of the current proof state (represented as an assertion in separation logic). It then frames the non-footprint part h_{frame} of the flow graph h_1 to compute the post state h' of the heap update locally for the footprint h. The result is the new flow graph $h_2 = h' * h_{frame}$. We consider the pair (h_1, h_2) a *benchmark* for our evaluation.

We adapt plankton to export the flow graph pairs for which a footprint is constructed. This way, we obtain 1272 benchmarks from the heap updates occurring during proof construction for a collection of 10 concurrent set data structures. All flow graphs in this benchmark suite contain at most 4 nodes.

Our benchmark suite is limited by the capabilities and restrictions of plankton. In particular, we inherit the confinement to concurrent search structures. This is due to the fact that plankton integrates support only for the keyset flow (cf. Example 1). Our evaluation will compute footprints with respect to this flow.

Implementation. We implement the fixed point computation to find footprints for two given flow graphs h_1, h_2 from Sect. 4 in a tool called krill [28]. It integrates three methods for computing the transfer failure $tfail_{h_1,h_2}(Z)$ of a footprint candidate Z:

1. **NAIVE:** A naive method that computes the flow within the footprint Z. Following [24], we require acyclicity of flow graphs for this method to avoid solving a fixed point equation when computing the flow.
2. **NEW:** Our new approach leveraging the path replacement condition (cf. Theorem 5) for simple paths (cf. Theorem 6). This method requires distributive and decreasing edge functions as well as idempotent addition in the underlying monoid.
3. **DIST:** A variation of our new approach leveraging the closed-form representation (cf. Theorem 4). We require distributive edge functions and acyclicity of the flow graphs to avoid an unbounded sum over all paths in the closed-form representation.

Our benchmark suite satisfies the requirements for all three methods. The NAIVE and DIST methods include a (sufficient) check to ensure acyclicity in the updated flow graph to guarantee soundness of the resulting footprint.

All three methods encode the necessary equivalence checks among transfer functions as SMT formulas which are then discharged using the off-the-shelf SMT solver Z3 [31]. Our encodings use the theory of integers with quantifiers. The NAIVE method additionally uses free functions to encode sets of integers.

Experiments. We ran krill on our benchmark suite and compared the runtime of the three different methods for computing the transfer failure. Our results are summarized in Fig. 5(left). For every search structure that we extracted benchmarks from, the figure lists: (i) the number #FG of flow graph pairs extracted, (ii) each method's total runtime for computing the footprints of all flow graph pairs, and (iii) the speedup of NEW over NAIVE in percent. The experiments were conducted on an Apple M1 Pro.

Figure 5(left) shows that the runtime for all methods is roughly linear in the number of computed footprints. Moreover, the absolute time for computing footprints is small, making the approaches practical. The figure also shows that our NEW and DIST methods have a performance advantage over the NAIVE method. The NEW method is between 22% and 39% faster than the NAIVE method. We believe that the difference is relatively small only because the acyclicity assumption avoids a potentially non-terminating fixed point computation. Avoiding this fixed point in the presence of cycles is a major advantage that our NEW method has over the NAIVE and DIST methods. The performance difference for DIST and NEW are negligible because the acyclicity check is negligible.

Structure	#FG	NAIVE	DIST	NEW	Speedup
Fine set [13]	12	75 ms	48 ms	46 ms	39%
Lazy set [12]	14	73 ms	52 ms	51 ms	30%
ORVYY set [33]	20	106 ms	76 ms	74 ms	30%
VY DCAS set [46]	19	109 ms	74 ms	73 ms	33%
VY CAS set [46]	28	139 ms	104 ms	102 ms	27%
Michael set [29]	225	1216 ms	887 ms	874 ms	28%
Michael set (wait-free)	186	996 ms	731 ms	721 ms	27%
Harris set [11]	352	2242 ms	1490 ms	1443 ms	36%
Harris set (wait-free)	296	1859 ms	1242 ms	1205 ms	35%
FEMRS tree [10]	120	519 ms	409 ms	407 ms	22%
Total	1272	7335 ms	5114 ms	4996 ms	32%

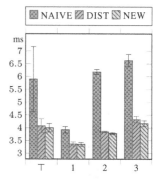

Figure 5. Experimental results averaged over 1000 repeated runs, conducted on an Apple M1 Pro. **(left)** Total runtime for computing footprints for flow graphs occurring during automated proof construction for highly concurrent set data structures. The speedup gives the relative performance improvement of NEW over NAIVE. **(right)** Average runtime for computing a single footprint, partitioned by footprint size ($\top$ indicates failure).

We also factorized the runtimes of our benchmarks along the size of the resulting footprint. Figure 5(right) gives the average runtime and standard deviation for computing a single footprint, broken down by footprint size. If no footprint could be found, its size is listed as $\top$. These failed footprint constructions are consistent with plankton's method and would not lead to verification failure.

6   Related Work

Two alternative meta theories for the flow framework have been proposed in prior work [23, 24]. Like in our setup, the original flow framework [23] demands that the flow domain is an ω-cpo to obtain a least fixed point semantics. However, it proposes a different flow graph composition that leads to a notion of contextual equivalence relying on inflow equivalence classes. This complicates proof automation. In addition, the flow domain is assumed to be a semiring and edge functions are restricted to multiplication with a constant. This limits expressivity.

As discussed in Sect. 1, the revised flow framework proposed in [24] requires that the flow monoid is cancellative but not an ω-cpo. This means that uniqueness of flows is not guaranteed per se. Instead, uniqueness is obtained by imposing additional conditions on the edge functions. However, these conditions are more restrictive than those imposed in our framework. The *capacity* of a flow graph introduced in [24] closely relates to our notion of transfer function. A closed-form representation based on sums over paths is used to check equivalence of capacities. However, this reasoning is restricted to acyclic graphs. Also, [24] provides no algorithm for computing flow footprints.

In a sense, our work strikes a balance between the two prior meta theories by guaranteeing unique flows without sacrificing expressivity and, at the same time, enabling better proof automation. That said, we believe that the framework proposed in [24] remains of independent interest, in particular if the application does not require unique flows (i.e., does not impose lower bounds on flows that may trivially hold in the presence of vanishing flows). Cancellativity allows one to aggregate inflows and outflows to unary functions, which can lead to smaller flow footprints (i.e., more local proofs).

The benchmark suite for our evaluation is obtained from plankton [26,27], a tool for verifying concurrent search structures using keyset flows. When the program mutates the symbolic heap, plankton creates a flow graph for the mutated nodes plus all nodes with a distance of k or less from those nodes. This flow graph is considered to be the footprint and contextual equivalence is checked. The check is basically the same as for NAIVE. However, the paper does not present the meta theory for the underlying notion of flow graphs, nor does it provide any justification for the correctness of the implemented algorithms used to reason about flow graphs.

Flow graphs form a separation algebra. Hence, the developed theory can be used in combination with any existing separation logic that is parametric in the underlying separation algebra such as [5, 7, 18, 27, 41, 44]. Identifying footprints of updates relates to the frame inference problem in separation logic, which has been studied extensively [4, 6, 15, 25, 35, 36, 42]. However, existing work focuses on frame inference for assertions that are expressed in terms of inductive predicates. These techniques are not well-suited for reasoning about programs manipulating general graphs, including overlayed structures, which are often used in practice and easily expressed using flows. A common approach to reason about general heap graphs in separation logic is to use iterated separating conjunction [14, 39, 44, 47] to abstract the heap by a *pure* graph that does not depend on the program state. Though, the verification of specifications that rely on inductive properties of the pure graph then resorts back to classical first-order reasoning and is difficult to automate. An exception is [45] which uses SMT solvers to frame binary reachability relations in graphs that are described by iterated separating conjunctions. However, the technique is restricted to such reachability properties only.

Unbounded footprints have been encountered early on when computing the post image for recursive predicates [8]. This has spawned interest in separation logic fragments for which the reasoning can be efficiently automated [2, 3, 9, 17, 20, 35, 38]. A limitation that underlies all these works is an assumption of tree-regularity of the heap, in one way or another, which flows have been designed to overcome. In cases where the program (or ghost code) traverses the unbounded footprint (before or after the update), recent works [24, 27] have found a way to reduce the reasoning to bounded footprint chunks.

The definition of a flow closely resembles the classical formulation of a forward data flow analysis. The fact that the least fixed point of the flow equation for distributive edge functions can be characterized as a join over all paths in the flow graph mirrors dual results for greatest fixed points in data flow analysis [19,21]. In a similar vein, the notion of contextual equivalence of flow graphs relates to contextual program equivalence and fully abstract models in denotational semantics [16, 30, 37]. In fact, Bekić's Lemma [1], which we use in the proofs of Theorem 1 and lemma 6, was originally motivated by the study of such models. Flow graphs can serve as abstractions of programs (rather than just program states). We therefore believe that our results could also be of interest for developing incremental and compositional data flow analysis frameworks.

Data Availability Statement

The krill artifact and dataset generated and/or analysed in the present paper are available in the Zenodo repository [28], https://zenodo.org/record/7566204.

Acknowledgments

This work is funded in part by NSF grant 1815633. The first author was supported by the DFG project *EDS@SYN: Effective Denotational Semantics for Synthesis*. The third author is supported by a Junior Fellowship from the Simons Foundation (855328, SW).

References

1. Bekić, H.: Definable operation in general algebras, and the theory of automata and flowcharts. In: Programming Languages and Their Definition. Lecture Notes in Computer Science, vol. 177, pp. 30–55. Springer (1984)
2. Berdine, J., Calcagno, C., O'Hearn, P.W.: A decidable fragment of separation logic. In: FSTTCS. Lecture Notes in Computer Science, vol. 3328, pp. 97–109. Springer (2004)
3. Berdine, J., Calcagno, C., O'Hearn, P.W.: Smallfoot: Modular automatic assertion checking with separation logic. In: FMCO. Lecture Notes in Computer Science, vol. 4111, pp. 115–137. Springer (2005)
4. Berdine, J., Calcagno, C., O'Hearn, P.W.: Symbolic execution with separation logic. In: APLAS. Lecture Notes in Computer Science, vol. 3780, pp. 52–68. Springer (2005)
5. Calcagno, C., O'Hearn, P.W., Yang, H.: Local action and abstract separation logic. In: LICS. pp. 366–378. IEEE (2007)
6. Calcagno, C., Distefano, D., O'Hearn, P.W., Yang, H.: Compositional shape analysis by means of bi-abduction. In: POPL. pp. 289–300. ACM (2009)
7. Dinsdale-Young, T., Birkedal, L., Gardner, P., Parkinson, M.J., Yang, H.: Views: compositional reasoning for concurrent programs. In: POPL. pp. 287–300. ACM (2013)
8. Distefano, D., O'Hearn, P.W., Yang, H.: A local shape analysis based on separation logic. In: TACAS. Lecture Notes in Computer Science, vol. 3920, pp. 287–302. Springer (2006)
9. Enea, C., Lengál, O., Sighireanu, M., Vojnar, T.: SPEN: A solver for separation logic. In: NFM. Lecture Notes in Computer Science, vol. 10227, pp. 302–309 (2017)
10. Feldman, Y.M.Y., Enea, C., Morrison, A., Rinetzky, N., Shoham, S.: Order out of chaos: Proving linearizability using local views. In: DISC. LIPIcs, vol. 121, pp. 23:1–23:21. Schloss Dagstuhl - Leibniz-Zentrum für Informatik (2018)
11. Harris, T.L.: A pragmatic implementation of non-blocking linked-lists. In: DISC. Lecture Notes in Computer Science, vol. 2180, pp. 300–314. Springer (2001)
12. Heller, S., Herlihy, M., Luchangco, V., Moir, M., III, W.N.S., Shavit, N.: A lazy concurrent list-based set algorithm. In: OPODIS. Lecture Notes in Computer Science, vol. 3974, pp. 3–16. Springer (2005)
13. Herlihy, M., Shavit, N.: The art of multiprocessor programming. Morgan Kaufmann (2008)
14. Hobor, A., Villard, J.: The ramifications of sharing in data structures. In: POPL. pp. 523–536. ACM (2013)
15. Holík, L., Peringer, P., Rogalewicz, A., Soková, V., Vojnar, T., Zuleger, F.: Low-level bi-abduction. In: ECOOP. LIPIcs, vol. 222, pp. 19:1–19:30. Schloss Dagstuhl - Leibniz-Zentrum für Informatik (2022)
16. Hyland, J.M.E., Ong, C.L.: On full abstraction for PCF: i, ii, and III. Inf. Comput. **163**(2), 285–408 (2000)

17. Iosif, R., Rogalewicz, A., Vojnar, T.: Deciding entailments in inductive separation logic with tree automata. In: ATVA. Lecture Notes in Computer Science, vol. 8837, pp. 201–218. Springer (2014)

18. Jung, R., Krebbers, R., Jourdan, J., Bizjak, A., Birkedal, L., Dreyer, D.: Iris from the ground up: A modular foundation for higher-order concurrent separation logic. J. Funct. Program. **28**, e20 (2018)

19. Kam, J.B., Ullman, J.D.: Monotone data flow analysis frameworks. Acta Informatica **7**, 305–317 (1977)

20. Katelaan, J., Zuleger, F.: Beyond symbolic heaps: Deciding separation logic with inductive definitions. In: LPAR. EPiC Series in Computing, vol. 73, pp. 390–408. EasyChair (2020)

21. Kildall, G.A.: A unified approach to global program optimization. In: POPL. pp. 194–206. ACM Press (1973)

22. Krishna, S., Patel, N., Shasha, D.E., Wies, T.: Verifying concurrent search structure templates. In: PLDI. pp. 181–196. ACM (2020)

23. Krishna, S., Shasha, D.E., Wies, T.: Go with the flow: compositional abstractions for concurrent data structures. Proc. ACM Program. Lang. **2**(POPL), 37:1–37:31 (2018)

24. Krishna, S., Summers, A.J., Wies, T.: Local reasoning for global graph properties. In: ESOP. Lecture Notes in Computer Science, vol. 12075, pp. 308–335. Springer (2020)

25. Le, Q.L., Sun, J., Qin, S.: Frame inference for inductive entailment proofs in separation logic. In: TACAS (1). Lecture Notes in Computer Science, vol. 10805, pp. 41–60. Springer (2018)

26. Meyer, R., Wies, T., Wolff, S.: Artifact for "A Concurrent Program Logic with a Future and History" (Sep 2022). https://doi.org/10.5281/zenodo.7080459

27. Meyer, R., Wies, T., Wolff, S.: A concurrent program logic with a future and history. Proc. ACM Program. Lang. **6**(OOPSLA) (2022)

28. Meyer, R., Wies, T., Wolff, S.: Artifact for "Make flows small again: revisiting the flow framework" (Jan 2023). https://doi.org/10.5281/zenodo.7566204

29. Michael, M.M.: High performance dynamic lock-free hash tables and list-based sets. In: SPAA. pp. 73–82. ACM (2002)

30. Milner, R.: Fully abstract models of typed *lambda*-calculi. Theor. Comput. Sci. **4**(1), 1–22 (1977)

31. de Moura, L.M., Bjørner, N.S.: Z3: an efficient SMT solver. In: TACAS. Lecture Notes in Computer Science, vol. 4963, pp. 337–340. Springer (2008)

32. O'Hearn, P.W., Reynolds, J.C., Yang, H.: Local reasoning about programs that alter data structures. In: CSL. Lecture Notes in Computer Science, vol. 2142, pp. 1–19. Springer (2001)

33. O'Hearn, P.W., Rinetzky, N., Vechev, M.T., Yahav, E., Yorsh, G.: Verifying linearizability with hindsight. In: PODC. pp. 85–94. ACM (2010)

34. Patel, N., Krishna, S., Shasha, D.E., Wies, T.: Verifying concurrent multicopy search structures. Proc. ACM Program. Lang. **5**(OOPSLA), 1–32 (2021)

35. Piskac, R., Wies, T., Zufferey, D.: Automating separation logic using SMT. In: CAV. Lecture Notes in Computer Science, vol. 8044, pp. 773–789. Springer (2013)

36. Piskac, R., Wies, T., Zufferey, D.: Automating separation logic with trees and data. In: CAV. Lecture Notes in Computer Science, vol. 8559, pp. 711–728. Springer (2014)

37. Plotkin, G.D.: LCF considered as a programming language. Theor. Comput. Sci. **5**(3), 223–255 (1977)

38. Qiu, X., Wang, Y.: A decidable logic for tree data-structures with measurements. In: VMCAI. Lecture Notes in Computer Science, vol. 11388, pp. 318–341. Springer (2019)

39. Raad, A., Hobor, A., Villard, J., Gardner, P.: Verifying concurrent graph algorithms. In: APLAS. Lecture Notes in Computer Science, vol. 10017, pp. 314–334 (2016)

40. Reynolds, J.C.: Separation logic: A logic for shared mutable data structures. In: LICS. pp. 55–74. IEEE Computer Society (2002)

41. da Rocha Pinto, P., Dinsdale-Young, T., Gardner, P.: Tada: A logic for time and data abstraction. In: ECOOP. Lecture Notes in Computer Science, vol. 8586, pp. 207–231. Springer (2014)

42. Rowe, R.N.S., Brotherston, J.: Automatic cyclic termination proofs for recursive procedures in separation logic. In: CPP. pp. 53–65. ACM (2017)

43. Scott, D.: Outline of a mathematical theory of computation. Tech. Rep. PRG02, Oxford University Computing Laboratory (1970)

44. Sergey, I., Nanevski, A., Banerjee, A.: Mechanized verification of fine-grained concurrent programs. In: PLDI. pp. 77–87. ACM (2015)

45. Ter-Gabrielyan, A., Summers, A.J., Müller, P.: Modular verification of heap reachability properties in separation logic. Proc. ACM Program. Lang. 3(OOPSLA), 121:1–121:28 (2019)

46. Vechev, M.T., Yahav, E.: Deriving linearizable fine-grained concurrent objects. In: PLDI. pp. 125–135. ACM (2008)

47. Yang, H.: An example of local reasoning in BI pointer logic: the Schorr-Waite graph marking algorithm. In: Proceedings of the SPACE Workshop (2001)

ALASCA: Reasoning in Quantified Linear Arithmetic

Konstantin Korovin[3] , Laura Kovács[1] , Giles Reger[3],
Johannes Schoisswohl[1 (✉)] , and Andrei Voronkov[2,3]

[1] TU Wien, Vienna, Austria
johannes.schoisswohl@tuwien.ac.at
[2] EasyChair, Manchester, UK
[3] University of Manchester, Manchester, UK

Abstract. Automated reasoning is routinely used in the rigorous construction and analysis of complex systems. Among different theories, arithmetic stands out as one of the most frequently used and at the same time one of the most challenging in the presence of quantifiers and uninterpreted function symbols. First-order theorem provers perform very well on quantified problems due to the efficient superposition calculus, but support for arithmetic reasoning is limited to heuristic axioms. In this paper, we introduce the ALASCA calculus that lifts superposition reasoning to the linear arithmetic domain. We show that ALASCA is both sound and complete with respect to an axiomatisation of linear arithmetic. We implemented and evaluated ALASCA using the VAMPIRE theorem prover, solving many more challenging problems compared to state-of-the-art reasoners.

Keywords: Automated Reasoning · Linear Arithmetic · SMT · Quantified First-Order Logic · Theorem Proving

1 Introduction

Automated reasoning is undergoing a rapid development thanks to its successful use, for example, in mathematical theory formalisation [15], formal verification [16] and web security [13]. The use of automated reasoning in these areas is mostly driven by the application of SMT solving for quantifier-free formulas [6, 12, 29]. However, there exist many use case scenarios, such as expressing arithmetic operations over memory allocation and financial transactions [1, 18, 20, 32], which require complex first-order quantification. SMT solvers handle quantifiers using heuristic instantiation in domain-specific model construction [10, 28, 30, 36]. While being incomplete in most cases, instantiation requires instances to be produced to perform reasoning, which can lead to an explosion in work required for quantifier-heavy problems. What is rather needed to address the above use cases is a reasoning approach able to handle both theories and complex applications of quantifiers. Our work tackles this challenge and designs a *practical, low-cost methodology* for proving first-order quantified linear arithmetic properties.

© The Author(s) 2023
S. Sankaranarayanan and N. Sharygina (Eds.) TACAS 2023, LNCS 13993, pp. 647–665, 2023.
https://doi.org/10.1007/978-3-031-30823-9_33

The problem of combining quantifiers with theories, and especially with arithmetic, is recognised as a major challenge in both SMT and first-order proving communities. In this paper *we focus on first-order, i.e. quantified, reasoning with linear arithmetic and uninterpreted functions*. In [26], it is shown that the validity problem for first-order reasoning with linear arithmetic and uninterpreted functions is Π_1^1-complete even when quantifiers are restricted to non-theory sorts. Therefore, there is no sound and complete calculus for this logic.

Quantified Reasoning in Linear Arithmetic – Related Works. In practice, there are two classes of methods of reasoning in first-order theory reasoning, and in particular with linear real arithmetic. SMT solvers use *instance-based methods*, where they repeatedly generate ground, that is quantifier-free, instances of quantified formulas and use decision procedures to check satisfiability of the resulting set of ground formulas [10, 28, 36]. Superposition-based first-order theorem provers use *saturation algorithms* [14, 27, 37]. In essense, they start with an initial set of clauses obtained by preprocessing the input formulas (initial search space) and repeatedly apply inference rules (such as superposition) to clauses in the search space, adding their (generally, non-ground) consequences to the search space. These two classes of methods are very different in nature and complement each other.

The superposition calculus [4, 31] is a refutationally complete calculus for first-order logic with equality that is used by modern first-order provers, for example, Vampire [27], E [37], iProver [17] and Zipperposition [14]. There have been a number of practical extensions to this calculus for reasoning in first-order theories, in particular for linear arithmetic [9, 11, 24]. Superposition theorem provers have become efficient and powerful on theory reasoning after the introduction of the AVATAR architecture [33, 38], which allows generated ground clauses to be passed to SMT solvers. Yet, superposition theorem provers have a major source of inefficiency. To work with theories, one has to add *theory axioms*, for example the transitivity of inequality $\forall x \forall y \forall z (x \leq y \wedge y \leq z \rightarrow x \leq z)$. In clausal form, this formula becomes $\neg x \leq y \vee \neg y \leq z \vee x \leq z$ where $\neg x \leq y$ can be resolved against *every* clause in which an inequality literal $s \leq t$ is selected. This, with other prolific theory axioms, results in a very significant growth of the search space. Note that SMT solvers do not use and do not need such theory axioms.

A natural solution is to try to eliminate some theory axioms, but this is notoriously difficult both in theory and in practice. In [26], the LASCA calculus was proposed, which replaced several theory axioms of linear arithmetic, including transitivity of inequality, by a new inference rule inspired by Fourier-Motzkin elimination and some additional rules. LASCA was shown to be complete for the ground case. But, after 15 years, LASCA is still not implemented, due to its complexity and lack of clear treatment for the non-ground case. As we argue in Sect. 5, lifting LASCA to the non-ground setting is nearly impossible as a non-ground extension of the underlining ordering is missing in [26].

Lifting Lasca to Alasca– Our contributions. In this paper we introduce a new non-ground version of LASCA, which we call Abstracting LASCA (ALASCA). Our ALASCA calculus comes with new abstraction mechanisms (Sect. 4), inference

rules and orderings (Sect. 5), which all together are proved to yield a sound
and complete approach with respect to a natural partial axiomatisation of linear
arithmetic (Theorem 5)[4]. In a nutshell, we make ALASCA both work and scale
by introducing (i) a novel variable elimination rule within saturation-based proof
search (Fig. 3b); (ii) an analogue of *unification with abstraction* [34] needed for
non-ground reasoning (Sect. 4); and (iii) a new non-ground ordering and powerful
background theory for unification, which is not restricted to arithmetic but can be
used with arbitrary theories (Sect. 5). As a result, ALASCA improves [26] by ground
modifications and lifting of LASCA in a finitary way, and complements [3, 40] with
variable elimination rules that are competible with standard saturation algorithms.
We also *demonstrate the practicality and efficiency* of ALASCA (Sect. 6). To this
end, we implemented ALASCA in Vampire and show that it solves overall more
problems than existing theorem provers.

2 Motivating Example

Consider the following mathematical property:

$$\forall x, y.\big(f(2x, y) > 2x + y \vee f(x + 1, y) > x + 2y\big) \to \forall x.\exists y.f(2, y) > x \qquad (1)$$

where f is an uninterpreted function. While property (1) holds, deriving its
validity is hard for state-of-the-art reasoners: only veriT [2] can solve it. Despite
its seeming simplicity, this problem requires non-trivial handling of quantifiers
and arithmetic. Namely, one would need to unify (modulo theory) the terms
$2x$ and $x + 1$ (which can be done by instantiating x with 1) and then derive
$f(2, y) > 2 + y \vee f(2, y) > 1 + 2y$. Further, one also needs to prove that $f(2, y)$ is
always greater than the minimum of $2 + y$ and $1 + 2y$, for arbitrary y.

Vampire with ALASCA finds a remarkably short proof as shown in Fig. 1. To
prove (1) its negation is shown unsatisfiable by first negating and translating into
clausal form (by using skolemization and normalisation, which shifts arithmetic
terms to be compared to 0), as listed in lines 1–4. Next a lower bound for $f(2x, y)$ is
established: In line 5, using our new inequality factoring (IF) rule with unification
with abstraction (see Fig. 3a), the constraint $2x \not\approx x + 1$ is introduced, and
establishing thereby that if $2x \approx 1 + x$ and $y + 2x \leq 2y + x$, then $f(2x, y) > 2x + y$.
After further normalisation, the inequalities $sk \geq f(2, y)$ and $f(2x, y) > 2x + y$
are used to derive $sk > 2x + y$ in line 7, using the Fourier-Motzkin Elimination
rule (FM), while still keeping track of the constraint $2x \not\approx x + 1$. By applying the
Variable Elimination rule (VE) twice, the empty clause $\square$ is derived in line 10,
showing the unsatisfiability of the negation of (1).

The key steps in the proof (and the reason why it was found in a short time)
are: (1) the use of the theory rules (FM), and (IF); (2) the use of the new variable
elimination rule (VE), and finally, a consistent use of unification with abstraction.
These rules give a significant reduction compared to the number of steps required
using theory axioms. In particular, not using (FM) would require the use of
transitivity and generation of several intermediate clauses. As well as shortening

---

[4] proofs and further details of our results can be found in [23]

1. $f(2x, y) > 2x + y \vee f(x + 1, y) > x + 2y$ Hypothesis
2. $\neg f(2, y) > sk$ Skolemized, Neg. Conj.
3. $f(2x, y) - 2x - y > 0 \vee f(x + 1, y) - x - 2y > 0$ Normalisation 1
4. $-f(2, y) + sk \geq 0$ Normalisation 2
5. $f(2x, y) - 2x - y > 0 \vee y + 2x - 2y - x > 0 \vee 2x \not\approx x + 1$ (IF) 3
6. $f(2x, y) - 2x - y > 0 \vee x - y > 0 \vee 0 \not\approx x - 1$ Normalisation 5
7. $-2x - y + sk > 0 \vee x - y > 0 \vee 0 \not\approx x - 1 \vee 2x \not\approx 2$ (FM) 6,4
8. $-2x - y + sk > 0 \vee x - y > 0 \vee 0 \not\approx x - 1$ Normalisation 7
9. $0 \not\approx x - 1$ (VE) 8
10. $\square$ (VE) 9

Fig. 1. A refutational proof using the calculus introduced in this paper. Variables x, y are implicitly universally quantified, and sk is an uninterpreted constant.

the proof, we eliminate the fatal impact on proof search from generating a large number of irrellevant formulas from theory axioms.

Indeed, such short proofs are also found quickly. Similar our previous example, $\forall x, y.\big(f(g(x) + g(a), y) > 2x + y \vee f(2g(x), y) > x + 2y\big) \rightarrow \exists k. \forall x \exists z. f(2g(k), z) > x$ has a short proof of 7 steps, excluding CNF transformation and normalisation steps, found by Vampire with ALASCA. This proof was found in almost no time (only 37 clauses were generated) but cannot be solved by any other solver. This shows the power of the calculus.

3 Background and Notation

Multi-Sorted First-Order Logic. We assume familiarity with standard first-order logic with equality, with all standard boolean connectives and quantifiers in the language. We consider a multi-sorted first-order language, with sorts $\tau_{\mathbb{Q}}, \tau_1, \ldots, \tau_n$. The sort $\tau_{\mathbb{Q}}$ is the *sort of rationals*, whereas $\tau_1, \ldots, \tau_n$ are *uninterpreted sorts*. We write $\approx_\tau$ for the equality predicate of τ. We denote the set of all terms as **T**, variables as **V**, and literals as **L**. Throughout this paper, we denote terms by s, t, u, variables by x, y, z, function symbols by f, g, h, all possibly with indices. Given a term t such that t is $f(\ldots)$, we write $\mathrm{sym}(t)$ for f, referring that f is the top level symbol of t. We write $t : \tau$ to denote that t is a term of sort τ. A term, or literal is called *ground*, when it does not contain any variables. We refer to the sets of all ground terms, and literals as $\mathbf{T}^\theta$, and $\mathbf{L}^\theta$ respectively.

We denote predicates by P, Q, literals by L, clauses by C, D, formulas by F, G, and sets of formulas (axioms) by $\mathcal{E}$, possibly with indices. We write $F \models G$ to denote that whenever F holds in a model, then G does as well. We call a function (similarly, for predicates) f uninterpreted wrt some set of equations $\mathcal{E}$ if whenever $\mathcal{E} \models f(s_1 \ldots s_n) \approx f(t_1 \ldots t_n)$, then $\mathcal{E} \models s_1 \approx t_1 \wedge \ldots \wedge s_n \approx t_n$. A function f is interpreted wrt $\mathcal{E}$ if it is not uninterpreted.

Rational Sort. We assume the signature contains a countable set of unary functions $k : \tau_{\mathbb{Q}} \mapsto \tau_{\mathbb{Q}}$ for every $k \in \mathbb{Q}$ and refer to k as *numeral multiplications*. In addition, the signature is assumed to also contain a constant $1 : \tau_{\mathbb{Q}}$, a function

$+ : \tau_{\mathbb{Q}} \times \tau_{\mathbb{Q}} \mapsto \tau_{\mathbb{Q}}$, and predicate symbols $>, \geq : \mathbf{P}(\tau_{\mathbb{Q}} \times \tau_{\mathbb{Q}})$, as well as an arbitrary number of other function symbols. For every numeral multiplication $k \in \mathbb{Q} \setminus \{1\}$, we simply write k to denote the term $k(1)$ obtained by the numeral multiplication k applied to 1; in these cases, we refer to k as *numerals*. Throughout this paper, we use j, k, l to denote numerals, or numeral multiplications, possibly with indices.

We write $-t$ to denote the term $-1(t)$. If j, k are two numeral multiplications, by (jk) and $(j + k)$ we denote the numeral multiplication that corresponds to the result of multiplying and adding the rationals/numerals j and k, respectively. For applications of numeral multiplications $j(t)$ we may omit the parenthesis and write jt instead. If we write $+k$, or $-k$ for some numeral k, we assume k itself is positive. We write $\pm$ (and $\mp$) to denote either of the symbols $+$ or $-$ (and respectively $-$ or $+$). For $q \in \mathbb{Q}$ we define $\mathbf{sign}(q)$ to be 1 if $q > 0$, -1 if $q < 0$, and 0 otherwise. We call $+, \geq, >, 1$, and the numeral multiplications the $\mathbb{Q}$ *symbols*. Finally, an *atomic term* is either a logical variable, or the term 1, or a term whose top level function symbol is not a $\mathbb{Q}$ symbol.

A $\mathbb{Q}$-*model* interprets the sort $\tau_{\mathbb{Q}}$ as $\mathbb{Q}$, and all $\mathbb{Q}$ symbols as their corresponding functions/predicates on $\mathbb{Q}$. We write $\mathbb{Q} \models C$ iff for every $\mathbb{Q}$-model M, $M \models C$ holds. If $\mathcal{E}$ is a set of formulas, we call a model M a $\mathcal{E}$-*model* if $M \models \mathcal{E}$.

Term Orderings. We write $u[s]$ to denote that s is a subterm of u, where the subterm relation is denoted via $\trianglelefteq$. That is, $s \trianglelefteq u$; similar notation will also be used for literals $L[s]$ and clauses $C[s]$. We denote by $u[s \mapsto t]$ the term resulting from replacing all subterms s of u by t.

Multisets (of term, literals) are denoted with $\{\ldots\}$. For a multiset S and natural number $n \in \mathbb{N}$, we define $0 * S = \emptyset$, and $n * S = (n - 1 * S) \cup S$ for $n > 0$.

Let $\prec$ be a relation and $\equiv$ be an equivalence relation. By $\prec_{\equiv}^{\mathsf{mul}}$ we denote the *multiset extension* of $\prec$, defined as the smallest relation satisfying $M \cup \{s_1, \ldots, s_n\} \prec_{\equiv}^{\mathsf{mul}} N \cup \{t\}$, where $M \equiv N$, $n \geq 0$, and $s_i \prec t$ for $1 \leq i \leq n$. For $n, m \in \mathbb{N}$, by $\prec_{\equiv}^{\mathsf{wmul}}$ we denote the *weighted multiset extension*, defined by $\langle \frac{1}{n}, S \rangle \prec_{\equiv}^{\mathsf{wmul}} \langle \frac{1}{m}, T \rangle$ iff $m * S \prec_{\equiv}^{\mathsf{mul}} n * T$. We omit the equivalence relation $\equiv$ if it is clear in the context.

Let s, t, t_i be terms, θ, θ' be ground substitutions and $\mathcal{E}$ be a set of axioms. We write $s \equiv_{\mathcal{E}} t$ for $\mathcal{E} \models s \approx t$ and $\theta \equiv_{\mathcal{E}} \theta'$ iff for all variables x we have $x\theta \equiv_{\mathcal{E}} x\theta'$. We say that s is a $\mathcal{E}$-subterm of t ($s \trianglelefteq_{\mathcal{E}} t$) if $s \equiv_{\mathcal{E}} t$, or $t \equiv_{\mathcal{E}} f(t_1 \ldots t_n)$ and $s \trianglelefteq_{\mathcal{E}} t_i$. We also say that s is a strict $\mathcal{E}$-subterm of t ($s \triangleleft_{\mathcal{E}} t$) if $s \trianglelefteq_{\mathcal{E}} t$ and $s \not\equiv_{\mathcal{E}} t$.

4   Theoretical Foundation for Unification with Abstraction

Our motivating example from Sect. 2 showcases that first-order arithmetic reasoning requires (i) establishing syntactic difference among terms (e.g. $2x$ and $x + 1$), while (ii) deriving they have instances that are semantically equal in models of a background theory $\mathcal{E}$ (e.g. the theory $\mathbb{Q}$).

A naive approach addressing (i)-(ii) would be to use an axiomatisation of the background theory $\mathcal{E}$, and use this axiomatisation for proof search in uninterpreted first-order logic. Such an approach can however be very costly. For example, even a relatively simple background theory **AC** axiomatizing commutativity and

```
 1  fn uwa(s,t)
 2  │   eqs ← {s ≈ t}; σ ← ∅; C ← ∅;
 3  │   while eqs ≠ ∅
 4  │   │   ṡ ≈ ṫ ← eqs.pop();
 5  │   │   if ṡ ≈ ṫ ∈ {x ≈ u, u ≈ x} for some x ∈ V, x ⊀ u
 6  │   │   │   ⟨σ, eqs, C⟩ ← ⟨σ ∪ {x ↦ u}, eqs, C⟩{x ↦ u};
 7  │   │   else if canAbstract(ṡ, ṫ)
 8  │   │   │   C.push(ṡ ≉ ṫ);
 9  │   │   else if ṡ = f(s_1 ... s_n), ṫ = f(t_1 ... t_n)
10  │   │   │   eqs.push({s_1 ≈ t_1 ... s_n ≈ t_n})
11  │   │   else
12  │   │   │   return ⊥;
13  │   return ⟨σ, C⟩;
```

Algorithm 1: Computing an abstracting unifier uwa.

associativity of $\approx$, that is $\mathbf{AC} = \{x+y \approx y+x, x+(y+z) \approx (x+y)+z\}$, would make a superposition-based theorem prover derive a vast amount of useless/redundant formulas as equational tautologies. An approach to circumvent such inefficient handling of equality reasoning is to use *unification modulo* $\mathbf{AC}$, or in general *unification modulo* $\mathcal{E}$, as already advocated in [22, 34, 40]. In this section we describe the adjustments we made towards unification modulo $\mathcal{E}$, allowing us to introduce *unification with abstraction* (Sect. 4.1). We also show under which condition our method can be used to turn a complete superposition calculus using unification modulo $\mathcal{E}$ into a complete superposition calculus using unification with abstraction. Concretely, we show how this can be used for the specific theory of arithmetic $\mathcal{A}_{eq}$ in the calculus ALASCA (Sect. 4.2).

4.1 Unification with Abstraction – UWA

In a nutshell, unification modulo $\mathcal{E}$ finds substitutions σ that make two terms s, t equal in the background theory, i.e. $\mathcal{E} \models s\sigma \approx t\sigma$. While unification modulo $\mathcal{E}$ removes the need for axiomatisation of $\mathcal{E}$ during superposition reasoning, it comes with some inefficiencies. Most importantly, in contrast to syntactic unification, there is no unique most general unifier $\mathsf{mgu}(s, t)$ when unifying modulo $\mathcal{E}$ but only minimal complete sets of unifiers $\mathsf{mcu}_{\mathcal{E}}(s, t)$, which can be very large; for example, unification modulo $\mathbf{AC}$ is doubly exponential in general [22].

Bypassing the need for unification modulo $\mathcal{E}$, *fully abstracted clauses* are used in [40], without the need for axiomatisation of the theory $\mathcal{E}$ and without compromising completeness of the underlining superposition-based calculus. Our work extends ideas from [40] and adjusts *unification with abstraction* (uwa) from [34], allowing us to prove completeness of a calculus using uwa (Theorem 3).

Example 1. Let us first consider the example of factoring the clause $p(2x) \vee p(x+1)$, a simplified version of the unification step performed in line 5 in Fig. 1. That is, unifying the literals $p(2x)$ and $p(x + 1)$, in order to remove duplicate literals. Within the setting of [40], these literals would only exist in their fully abstracted form, which can be obtained by replacing every subterm $t : \tau_{\mathbb{Q}}$ that is not a variable by a fresh variable x, and adding the constraint $x \not\approx t$ to the corresponding clause. Hence, the clause $p(2x) \vee p(x+1)$ is transformed to $p(y) \vee p(z) \vee y \not\approx 2x \vee z \not\approx x+1$ in [40]. Unification then becomes trivial: we would derive the clause $p(y) \vee y \not\approx 2x \vee y \not\approx x + 1$ by factoring, from which $p(2x) \vee 2x \not\approx x + 1$ is inferred using equality factoring and resolution.

Within unification with abstraction, we aim at cutting out intermediate steps of applying abstractions, equality resolution and factoring. As a result, we skip unnecessary consequences of intermediate clauses, and derive the conclusion $p(2x) \vee 2x \not\approx x + 1$ straight away. To this end, we introduce constraints only for those $s, t : \tau_{\mathbb{Q}}$ on which unification fails. We thus gain the advantage that clauses are not present in the search space in their abstracted forms, increasing efficiency in proof search. Further, our unification with abstraction approach is parametrized by a predicate canAbstract to control the application of abstraction, as listed in Algorithm 1. This is yet another significant difference compared to fully abstracted clauses, as in the latter, abstraction is performed for every subterm $t : \tau_{\mathbb{Q}}$ without considering the terms with which t might be unified later.

Our uwa method can be seen as a lazy approach of full abstraction from [40]. We compute so-called abstracting unifiers $\mathsf{uwa}(s, t) = \langle \sigma, \mathcal{C} \rangle$ in Algorithm 1, allowing us to replace unification modulo $\mathcal{E}$ by unification with abstraction.

Definition 1 (Abstracting Unifier). *Let σ be a substitution and $\mathcal{C}$ a set of literals. A partial function uwa that maps two terms s, t either to $\bot$ or to a pair $\langle \sigma, \mathcal{C} \rangle = \mathsf{uwa}(s, t)$ is called an abstracting unifier.*

The abstracting unifier $\mathsf{uwa}(s, t)$ computed by Algorithm 1 is parametrized by the relation canAbstract. The intuition of this relation is that $\mathsf{canAbstract}(s, t)$ holds for terms s and t, when $s \approx t$ might hold in the background theory $\mathcal{E}$. To ensure that unification with abstraction can replace unification modulo $\mathcal{E}$, we impose the following additional properties over the abstract unifier $\mathsf{uwa}(s, t)$.

Definition 2 (uwa Properties). *Let σ be a substitution and $\mathcal{C}$ a set of literals. Consider $s, t \in \mathbf{T}$ be such that $\mathsf{uwa}(s, t) = \langle \sigma, \mathcal{C} \rangle$ and let θ be an arbitrary ground substitution. We say uwa is*

- *$\mathcal{E}$-sound iff $\mathcal{E} \models (s \approx t)\sigma \vee \mathcal{C}$;*
- *$\mathcal{E}$-general iff $\forall \mu \in \mathsf{mcu}_{\mathcal{E}}(s, t).\exists \rho.\sigma\rho \equiv_{\mathcal{E}} \mu$;*
- *$\mathcal{E}$-minimal iff $\mathcal{E} \models (s \approx t)\sigma\theta \implies \mathcal{E} \models (\neg\mathcal{C})\theta$;*
- *subterm-founded with respect to the clause ordering $\prec$, iff for every uninterpreted function or predicate f, every literal $L[\circ]$, it holds that $\mathcal{E} \models (s \approx t)\theta \implies \mathcal{C}\theta \prec L[f(s)]\theta$ or $\mathcal{C}\theta \prec L[f(t)]\theta$.*

Further, uwa is $\mathcal{E}$-complete if, for all $s, t \in \mathbf{T}$ with $\mathsf{uwa}(s, t) = \bot$, we have $\mathsf{mcu}_{\mathcal{E}}(s, t) = \emptyset$.

Definition 2 is necessary to lift inferences using unification with abstraction. We thereby want to assure that, whenever C does not hold, then s and t are equal; hence abstracting unifiers $\mathsf{uwa}(x, y) = \langle \emptyset, x + y \not\approx y + x \rangle$ would be unsound. The $\mathcal{E}$-generality property enforces that substitutions introduced by uwa are general enough in order to still be turned into a complete set of unifiers. As such, $\mathcal{E}$-generality is needed to rule out cases like $\mathsf{uwa}(x + y, 2) = \langle \{x \mapsto 0, y \mapsto 2\}, \emptyset \rangle$, which would not be able to capture, for example, the substitution $\{x \mapsto 1, y \mapsto 1\}$. We note that we use uwa to extend counterexample-reducing inference systems (see Definition 4), allowing inductive completeness proofs. As these inference systems need to derive conclusions that are smaller than the premises, we need the subterm-foundedness property to make sure to only introduce constraints that are smaller than the premises as well. If we have a look at the previous properties, we see that all of them are fulfilled if $\mathsf{uwa}(s, t) = \bot$. Therefore we need to make sure that uwa only returns $\bot$ when s and t are not unifiable modulo $\mathcal{E}$; this is captured by $\mathcal{E}$-completeness.

In addition to properties of abstract unifiers $\mathsf{uwa}(s, t)$, we also impose conditions over the $\mathsf{canAbstract}$ relation that parametrizes $\mathsf{uwa}(s, t)$. As Algorithm 1 only introduces equality constraints for subterm pairs that should be unified, a resulting abstracting unifier $\mathsf{uwa}(s, t)$ is sound. Further, under the assumption that the clause ordering is defined as in standard superposition (e.g. using multiset extensions of a simplification ordering that fulfills the subterm property), the abstracting unifier $\mathsf{uwa}(s, t)$ is also subterm-founded. However, to ensure that $\mathsf{uwa}(s, t)$ is also minimal, interpreted functions should not be treated as uninterpreted ones; hence the $\mathsf{canAbstract}$ relation needs to always trigger abstraction on interpreted functions. Finally, we require that $\mathsf{canAbstract}$ does not skip terms which are potentially equal modulo $\mathcal{E}$, in order to guarantee completeness. Hence, we define the following properties for $\mathsf{canAbstract}$.

Definition 3 (canAbstract **Properties**). *Let* $s, t \in \mathbf{T}$. *The* $\mathsf{canAbstract}$ *relation*

- captures $\mathcal{E}$, *iff for all* s, t, *it holds that* $\exists \rho . \mathcal{E} \vDash (s \approx t)\rho \implies \mathsf{canAbstract}(s, t)$;
- guards interpreted functions, *iff for all* s, t, *where* $\mathsf{sym}(s) = \mathsf{sym}(t)$ *is an interpreted function*, $\mathsf{canAbstract}(s, t)$ *holds*.

Based on the above, we derive the following result.

Theorem 1. *The abstracting unifier* uwa *computed by Algorithm 1 is subterm-founded and sound. If* $\mathsf{canAbstract}$ *guards interpreted functions, then* uwa *is* $\mathcal{E}$-*general and* $\mathcal{E}$-*minimal. If* $\mathsf{canAbstract}$ *guards interpreted functions and captures* $\mathcal{E}$, *then* uwa *is* $\mathcal{E}$-*complete.*

4.2 UWA Completeness

We now show how unification with abstraction (uwa) can be used to replace unification modulo $\mathcal{E}$ in saturation-based theorem proving [3]. We recall from [3] that in order to show refutational completeness of an inference-system Γ, one constructs a *model functor* I that maps sets of ground clauses N to candidate models I_N. In order to show that Γ is refutationally complete, one needs to show that if N is saturated with respect to Γ, then $I_N \vDash N$. For this, the notion of a counterexample-reducing inference system is introduced.

Definition 4. *We say an inference system Γ is* counterexample reducing, *with respect to a model functor I and a well-founded ordering on ground clauses $\prec$, if for every ground set of clauses N and every minimal $C \in N$ such that $I_N \not\models C$, there is an inference*

$$\frac{C_1 \quad \cdots \quad C_n \quad C}{D}$$

where $\forall i. I_N \models C_i$, $\forall i. C_i \prec C$, $D \prec C$, and $I_N \not\models D$.

We then have the following key result.

Theorem 2 (Bachmair&Ganzinger [3]). *Let $\prec$ be a well-founded ordering on ground clauses and I be a model functor. Then, every inference system that is counterexample-reducing wrt $\prec$ and I is refutationally complete.*

This result also holds for an inference system being refutationally complete wrt $\mathcal{E}$ if for every N it holds that $I_N \models \mathcal{E}$. When constructing a refutationally complete calculus, one usually first defines a ground counterexample-reducing inference system and then lifts this calculus to a non-ground inference system. Lifting is done such that, if the ground inference system is counterexample reducing, then its lifted non-ground version is also counterexample reducing.

We next show how to transform a lifting of a counterexample-reducing inference system that uses unification modulo $\mathcal{E}$ into a lifting using unification with abstraction. That is, given a counterexample-reducing inference-system using unification modulo $\mathcal{E}$ to define its rules, we construct another counterexample-reducing inference system that uses uwa instead. As we only transform rules that use unification, we introduce the notion of a unifying rule.

Definition 5. *An inference rule γ is a* unifying rule *if it is of the form*

$$\frac{C_1 \quad \cdots \quad C_n \quad C}{D\sigma} , \quad \textit{where } \sigma \in \mathsf{mcu}_{\mathcal{E}}(s,t).$$

We also define the mapping $\circ_{\mathsf{uwa}}$ that maps unifying inferences γ to γ_{uwa} as

$$\gamma_{\mathsf{uwa}} = \left(\frac{C_1 \quad \cdots \quad C_n \quad C}{D\sigma \vee \mathcal{C}} , \text{ where } \langle \sigma, \mathcal{C} \rangle = \mathsf{uwa}(s,t) \right)$$

Soundness of the unifying rule γ alone however does not suffice to show soundness of γ_{uwa}. Therefore we introduce a stronger notion of soundness that holds for all the rules we will consider to lift.

Definition 6. *Let γ be a unifying rule. We say γ is* strongly sound *iff $\mathcal{E}, C_1 \ldots C_n, C \models s \approx t \to D$.*

Lemma 1. *Assume that γ is strongly sound and uwa is sound. Then, γ_{uwa} is sound.*

We note that not every inference can be transformed using $\circ_{\mathsf{uwa}}$, without compromising completeness. To circumvent this problem, we consider the notion of compatibility with respect to transformations.

Definition 7. *Let γ be a unifying inference. Then, γ unifies strict subterms iff for every grounding θ, $u \in \{s, t\}$ there is an uninterpreted function or predicate f, a literal $L[f(u)]$, and clause $C' \in \{C_1 \ldots C_n, C\}$, such that $L[f(u)]\theta \preceq C'\theta$.*

Note that in the above definition we usually have that $L[f(s)]$ or $L[f(t)]$ is some literal of one of the premises.

Definition 8 (uwa-Compatibility). *We say an inference γ is uwa compatible if it is a unifying inference, strongly sound, and unifies strict subterms.*

Theorem 3. *Let uwa be a general, compatible, subterm-founded, complete, and minimal abstracting unifier. If Γ is the lifting of a counterexample-reducing inference system Γ^ϑ with respect to a model functor I, and clause ordering $\prec$, then $\Gamma_{\mathsf{uwa}} = \{\gamma_{\mathsf{uwa}} \mid \gamma \in \Gamma, \ \gamma \text{ is uwa-compatible}\} \cup \{\gamma \in \Gamma \mid \ \gamma \text{ is not uwa-compatible}\}$ is the lifting of an inference system $\Gamma^\vartheta_{\mathsf{uwa}}$ that is counterexample-reducing with respect to I and $\prec$.*

Theorem 1 and Theorem 3 together imply that, given a compatible inference system, we need to only specify the right canAbstract predicate in order to perform a lifting using uwa. In Sect. 5 we introduce the calculus ALASCA, a concrete inference system with the desired properties, for which a suitable predicate canAbstract can easily be found.

5   ALASCA Reasoning

We use the lifting results of Sect. 4 to introduce our ALASCA calculus for reasoning in quantified linear arithmetic, by combining superposition reasoning with Fourier-Motzkin type inference rules. While an instance of such a combination has been studied in the LASCA calculus of [26], LASCA is restricted to ground, i.e. quantifier-free, clauses. Our ALASCA extends LASCA with uwa and provides an altered ground version ALASCA$^\theta$ (Sect. 5.1) which efficiently can be lifted to the quantified domain (Sect. 5.2). As quantified reasoning with linear real arithmetic and uninterpreted functions is inherently incomplete, we provide formal guarantess about what ALASCA can prove. Instead of focusing on completeness with respect to $\mathbb{Q}$-models as in [26], we show that ALASCA is complete with respect to a partial axiomatisation $\mathcal{A}_{\mathbb{Q}}$ of $\mathbb{Q}$-models (Sect. 5.2).

5.1   The ALASCA Calculus – Ground Version

The ALASCA calculus uses a partial axiomatisation $\mathcal{A}_{\mathbb{Q}}$ of $\mathbb{Q}$-models, and handles some $\mathbb{Q}$-axioms via inferences and some via uwa. We therefore split the axiom set $\mathcal{A}_{\mathbb{Q}}$ into $\mathcal{A}_{\mathsf{eq}}$ and $\mathcal{A}_{\mathsf{ineq}}$, as listed in Fig. 2.

Our ALASCA calculus modifies the LASCA framework [26] to enable an efficient lifting for quantified reasoning. For simplicity, we first present the ground version of ALASCA, which we refer to as ALASCA$^\theta$, whose one key benefit is illustrated next.

$$\mathcal{A}_{\mathbb{Q}} = \mathcal{A}_{eq} \cup \mathcal{A}_{ineq} \qquad\qquad \mathcal{A}_{ineq} = \{x > y \wedge y > z \rightarrow x > z\}$$

$$\mathcal{A}_{eq} = \mathbf{AC} \qquad\qquad\qquad\quad \cup \{x > y \rightarrow x + z > y + z\}$$

$$\cup \{jx + kx \approx (j + k)x \mid j, k \in \mathbb{Q}\} \qquad \cup \{x > y \vee x \approx y \vee y > x\}$$

$$\cup \{j(k(x)) \approx (jk)x \mid j, k \in \mathbb{Q}\} \qquad\quad \cup \{\neg(x > x)\}$$

$$\cup \{1(x) \approx x\} \qquad\qquad\qquad\qquad \cup \{x \geq y \leftrightarrow (x > y \vee x \approx y)\}$$

$$\cup \{k(x + y) \approx kx + ky \mid k \in \mathbb{Q}\} \qquad \cup \{x > y \rightarrow +kx > +ky \mid +k \in \mathbb{Q}\}$$

$$\cup \{x + 0 \approx x, 0x \approx 0\} \qquad\qquad\quad \cup \{x > y \rightarrow -ky > -kx \mid -k \in \mathbb{Q}\}$$

Fig. 2. Axioms handled by the ALASCA calculus. All are implicity universally quantified.

Example 2. One central rule of ALASCA is the Fourier-Motzkin variable elimination rule (FM). We use (FM) in line 7 of Fig. 1, when proving the motivating example of Sect. 2, given in formula (1). Namely, using (FM), we derive $-2x - y + sk > 0$ from $f(2x, y) - 2x - y > 0$ and $-f(2, y) + sk \geq 0$, under the assumption that $2x \approx 2$. The (FM) rule can be seen as a version of the inequality chaining rules of [3], chaining the inequalities $sk \geq f(2, y)$ and $f(2x, y) > 2x + y$. Moreover, the (FM) rule can also be considered a version of binary resolution, as it resolves the positive summand $f(2x, y)$ with the negative summand $-f(2, y)$, mimicking thus resolution over subterms, instead of literals. The main benefit of (FM) comes with its restricted application to maximal atomic terms in a sum (instead of its naive application whenever possible).

ALASCA$^\theta$ Normalization and Orderings. Compared to LASCA [26], the major difference of ALASCA$^\theta$ comes with focusing on which terms are being considered equal within inferences; this in turn requires careful adjustments in the underlying orderings and normalization steps of ALASCA$^\theta$, and later also in unification within ALASCA. In LASCA terms are rewritten in their so-called $\mathbb{Q}$-normalized form, while equality inference rules exploit equivalence modulo **AC**. Lifting such inference rules is however tricky. Consider for example the application of the rewrite rule $j(ks) \rightarrow (jk)s$ (triggered by $j(ks) \approx (jk)s$) over the clause $C[jx, x]$. In order to lift all instances of this rewrite rule, we would need to derive $C[(jk)x, kx]$ for every $k \in \mathbb{Q}$, which would yield an infinite number of conclusions. In order to resolve this matter, ALASCA$^\theta$ takes a different approach to term normalization and handling equivalence. That is, unlike LASCA, we formulate all inference rules using equivalence modulo $\mathcal{A}_{eq}$, and do not consider the normalization of terms as simplification rules.

As ALASCA$^\theta$ rules use equivalence modulo $\mathcal{A}_{eq}$, we also need to impose that the simplification ordering used by ALASCA$^\theta$ is $\mathcal{A}_{eq}$-compatible. Intuitively, $\mathcal{A}_{eq}$-compatibility means that terms that are equivalent modulo $\mathcal{A}_{eq}$ are in one equivalence class wrt the ordering. This allows us to replace terms by an arbitrary normal form wrt these equivalence classes before and after applying any inference rules, allowing it to use a normalization similar to $\mathbb{Q}$-normalization that does not need to be lifted. Hence, we introduce $\mathcal{A}_{eq}$-*normalized terms* as being terms whose sort is not $\tau_\mathbb{Q}$ or of the form $\frac{1}{k}(k_1 t_1 + \cdots + k_n t_n)$, such that $\forall i.k_i \in \mathbb{Z} \setminus 0$, $\forall i \neq j.t_i \not\equiv t_j$, $\forall i.t_i$ is atomic, k is positive, and $\gcd(\{k, k_1 \ldots k_n\}) = 1$. Obviously every term can be turned into a $\mathcal{A}_{eq}$-normalized term. For the rest of this section we assume terms are $\mathcal{A}_{eq}$-normalized, and write $\equiv$ for $\equiv_{\mathcal{A}_{eq}}$. We also assume that literals with interpreted predicates $\diamond$ are being normalized (during preprocessing) and to be of the form $t \diamond 0$. We write $s \stackrel{.}{\approx} t$ for equalities, with sorts different from $\tau_\mathbb{Q}$, and for equalities of sort $\tau_\mathbb{Q}$ that can be rewritten to $s \approx t$ such that s is an atomic term. Finally, ALASCA^θ also extends LASCA by not only handling the predicates $>$ and $\approx$, but also $\geq$, and $\not\approx$, which has the advantage that inequalities are not being introduced in purely equational problems in ALASCA^θ.

As discussed in Example 2, the (FM) rule of ALASCA^θ is similar to binary resolution, as it can be seen as "resolving" atomic subterms instead of literals. To formalize such handling of terms in (FM), we distinguish so-called $\text{atoms}(t)$, atoms of some term t. Doing so, given an $\mathcal{A}_{eq}$-normalized term $t = \frac{1}{k}(\pm_1 k_1 t_1 + \ldots \pm_n k_n t_n)$, we define $\text{atoms}^\pm(t) = \langle k, k_1 * \{\pm_1 t_1\} \cup \ldots \cup k_n * \{\pm_n t_n\}\rangle$ and $\text{atoms}(t) = \langle k, k_1 * \{t_1\} \cup \ldots \cup k_n * \{t_n\}\rangle$. We extend both of these functions $f \in \{\text{atoms}, \text{atoms}^\pm\}$ to literals as follows: $f(t \diamond 0) = f(t)$, assuming that the term t has been normalised to $\frac{1}{k} = 1$ before. For (dis)equalities $s \approx t$ ($s \not\approx t$) of uninterpreted sorts, we define atoms to be $\langle 1, \{s, t\}\rangle$. Further we define $\text{maxAtoms}(t)$, to be the set of maximal terms in $\text{atoms}(t)$ with respect to $\prec$, and $\text{maxAtom}(t) = t_0$ if $\text{maxAtoms}(t) = \{t_0\}$.

ALASCA^θ Inferences. The inference rules of ALASCA^θ are summarized in Fig. 3a. All rules are parametrized by a $\mathcal{A}_{eq}$-compatible ordering relation $\prec$ on ground terms, literals and clauses. Underlining a literal in a clause or an atomic term in a sum means that the underlined expression is non-strictly maximal wrt to the other literals in the clause, or atomic terms in the sum. We use double-underlining to denote that the expression is strictly maximal. We call $\mathbf{L}^\theta_+$ the set of potentially productive literals, defined as all equalities and inequalities with strictly maximal atomic term with positive coefficient.

Finding a right ordering relation is non-trivial, as many different requirements, like compatibility, subterm property, well-foundedness, and stability under substitutions, need to be met [25, 26, 39, 41]. For ALASCA, we use a modified version of the QKBO ordering of [26], with the following two modifications.

(i) Firstly, the ALASCA ordering is defined for non-ground terms. This means that the ordering needs to handle subterms with sums where there is no maximal atomic summand, like the term $x + y$. In addition, our ordering needs to be stable under substitutions in order to work with non-ground terms. Note however that our atom functions atoms and $\text{atoms}^\pm$ are not stable under substitutions, as the term $f(x) - f(y)$ and the substitution $\{x \mapsto y\}$ demonstrates. Therefore, we parametrize our ALASCA ordering by the relation subSafe. The subSafe relation fulfils the property that if $\text{subSafe}(\frac{1}{k}(\pm_1 k_1 t_1 + \cdots \pm_n k_n t_n))$, then there is no substitution θ such that $\pm_i k_i t_i \theta \equiv \mp_j k_j t_j \theta$, for any i, j. In general, checking the existence of such a θ is as hard as unifying modulo $\mathcal{A}_{eq}$. Nevertheless, we can overapproximate the subSafe relation using the canAbstract predicate.

Fourier-Motzkin Elimination

$$\frac{C_1 \vee +j\underline{s} + t_1 \gtrsim_1 0 \qquad C_2 \vee -k\underline{s'} + t_2 \gtrsim_2 0}{C_1 \vee C_2 \vee kt_1 + jt_2 > 0} \text{ (FM)}$$

where – $js + t_1 > 0 \succ C_1$
– $-ks' + t_2 > 0 \succeq C_2$
– $s \equiv s'$
– $\{>\} \subseteq \{\gtrsim_1, \gtrsim_2\} \subseteq \{>, \geq\}$

Tight Fourier-Motzkin Elimination

$$\frac{C_1 \vee +j\underline{s} + t_1 \geq 0 \qquad C_2 \vee -k\underline{s'} + t_2 \geq 0}{C_1 \vee C_2 \vee kt_1 + jt_2 > 0 \vee -ks' + t_2 \approx 0} \text{ (FM}^{\geq})$$

where – $js + t_1 > 0 \succ C_1$
– $-ks' + t_2 > 0 \succeq C_2$
– $s \equiv s'$

Inequality Factoring

$$\frac{C \vee +j\underline{s} + t_1 \gtrsim_1 0 \vee +k\underline{s'} + t_2 \gtrsim_2 0}{C \vee kt_1 - jt_2 \gtrsim_3 0 \vee +ks' + t_2 \gtrsim_2 0} \text{ (IF)}$$

where – $s \equiv s'$
– $\forall L \in (C \vee js + t_1 \gtrsim_1 0).ks' + t_2 \gtrsim_2 0 \succeq L$ or
  $\forall L \in (C \vee ks' + t_2 \gtrsim_2 0).js + t_1 \gtrsim_1 0 \succeq L$
– $\gtrsim_i \in \{>, \geq\}$
– $\gtrsim_3 = \begin{cases} \geq & \text{if } \gtrsim_1 = \geq, \text{ and } \gtrsim_2 = > \\ > & \text{else} \end{cases}$

Term Factoring

$$\frac{C \vee j\underline{s} + k\underline{s'} + t \diamond 0}{C \vee (j+k)s' + t \diamond 0} \text{ (TF)}$$

where – $s \equiv s'$
– $\diamond \in \{>, \geq, \hat{\approx}, \not\approx\}$
– $s, s' \in \mathsf{maxAtoms}(C \vee js + ks' + t \diamond 0)$
– there is no uninterpreted literal in C

Contradiction

$$\frac{C \vee \pm k \diamond 0}{C} \text{ (Triv)}$$

where – $\diamond \in \{>, \geq, \approx, \not\approx\}$
– $k \in \mathbb{Q}$
– $\mathbb{Q} \not\models \pm k \diamond 0$

Superposition

$$\frac{C_1 \vee \underline{s} \hat{\approx} t \qquad C_2 \vee L[s']}{C_1 \vee C_2 \vee L[s' \rightarrow t]} \text{ (Sup)}$$

where – $s \equiv s'$
– $s \hat{\approx} t \succ C_1$
– $L[s'] \in \mathbf{L}^\theta_+ \ \& \ L[s'] \succ C_2$ or
  $L[s'] \notin \mathbf{L}^\theta_+ \ \& \ L[s'] \succeq C_2$
– $s' \trianglelefteq x \in \mathsf{maxAtoms}(L[s'])$
– $s \approx t \vee C_1 \prec C_2 \vee L[s']$

Equality Resolution

$$\frac{C \vee s \not\approx s'}{C} \text{ (ER)}$$

where – $s \equiv s'$
– $s \not\approx s' \succeq C$

Equality Factoring

$$\frac{C \vee \underline{s} \hat{\approx} t_1 \vee \underline{s'} \hat{\approx} t_2}{C \vee t_1 \not\approx t_2 \vee s \approx t_1} \text{ (EF)}$$

where – $s \equiv s'$
– $s' \approx t_2 \succeq C \vee s \approx t_1$

(a) Rules of the ground calculus ALASCA$^\theta$.

Variable Elimination

$$\frac{C \vee \bigvee_{i \in I} x + b_i \gtrsim_i 0 \vee \bigvee_{j \in J} -x + b_j \gtrsim_j 0 \vee \bigvee_{k \in K} x + b_k \approx 0 \vee \bigvee_{l \in L} x + b_l \not\approx 0}{\bigwedge_{K^+ \subseteq K} \left(\begin{array}{l} C \vee \bigvee_{i \in I, j \in J} b_i + b_j \gtrsim_{i,j} 0 \vee \bigvee_{i \in I, k \in K^-} b_i - b_k \geq 0 \vee \bigvee_{i \in I, l \in L} b_i - b_l \gtrsim_i 0 \\ \vee \bigvee_{j \in J, k \in K^+} b_j + b_k \geq 0 \vee \bigvee_{j \in J, l \in L} b_j + b_l \gtrsim_j 0 \\ \vee \bigvee_{k_1 \in K^+, k_2 \in K^-} b_{k_1} - b_{k_2} \approx 0 \vee \bigvee_{k \in K^+, l \in L} b_k - b_l \geq 0 \\ \vee \bigvee_{k \in K^-, l \in L} b_l - b_k \geq 0 \\ \vee \bigvee_{l_1, l_2 \in L} b_{l_1} - b_{l_2} \not\approx 0 \end{array} \right)} \text{ (VE)}$$

where

– x is an unshielded variable
– $K^- = K \setminus K^+$
– C does not contain x

– $\gtrsim_i, \gtrsim_j \in \{\geq, >\}$
– $(\gtrsim_{i,j}) = \begin{cases} (\geq) & \text{if } \geq \in \{\gtrsim_i, \gtrsim_j\} \\ (>) & \text{otherwise} \end{cases}$

(b) Variable elimination rule used for lifting ALASCA$^\theta$.

Fig. 3. Inference rules used to define the calculus ALASCA.

(ii) Secondly, we adjusted the ALASCA ordering to be $\mathcal{A}_{\mathsf{eq}}$-compatible, instead of **AC**-compatible. We modified the literal ordering of ALASCA, such that literals are ordered by all their atoms using the weighted multiset extension of $\prec$, instead of only using the maximal one of each literal L as in [26].

We define a model functor $\mathcal{I}^{\cdot}_{\infty}$ mapping clauses to $\mathcal{A}_{\mathbb{Q}}$-models (see [23] for details) and conclude the following.

Theorem 4. ALASCA$^{\theta}$ *is a counterexample-reducing inference system with respect to* $\mathcal{I}^{\cdot}_{\infty}$ *and* $\prec$.

5.2   ALASCA Lifting and Completeness

Variable Elimination. Theorem 4 establishes completeness of ALASCA$^{\theta}$ for ground clauses wrt $\mathcal{A}_{\mathbb{Q}}$. We next lift this result (and calculus) to non-ground clauses.

We introduce the concept of an *unshielded variable*. We say a term $t : \tau_{\mathbb{Q}}$ is a top level term of a literal L if $t \in \mathsf{atoms}(L)$. We call a variable x *unshielded* in some clause C if x is a top level term of a literal in C, and there is no literal with an atomic top level term $t[x]$. Observe that within the ALASCA$^{\theta}$ rules, only maximal atomic terms in sums are being used in rule applications. This means, lifting ALASCA$^{\theta}$ to ALASCA is straightforward for clauses where all maximal terms in sums are not variables. Further, due to the subterm property, if a variable is maximal in a sum then it must be unshielded. Hence, the only variables we have to deal within ALASCA rule applications are unshielded ones.

The work of [40] modifies a standard saturation algorithm by integrating it with a variable elimination rule that gets rid of unshielded variables, without compromising completeness of the calculus. Based on [40] and the variable elimination rule of [3], we extend ALASCA$^{\theta}$ with the Variable Elimination Rule (VE), as given in Fig. 3b. In what follows, we show that the handling of unshielded variables in Fig. 3b can naturally be done within a standard saturation framework.

The (VE) rules replaces any clause with a set of clauses that is equivalent and does not contain unshielded variables. We assume that the clause is normalized, such that in every inequality x only occurs once with a factor 1 or -1, whereas for for equalities, x only occurs with factor 1. A simple example for the application of (VE) is the clause $a - x > 0 \vee x - b > 0 \vee a + b + x \geq 0$, where $x \in \mathbf{V}$, and a, b are constants. By reasoning about inequalities, it is easy to see that this is equivalent to $a > x \vee a + b \geq x \vee x > b$, thus further equivalent to $a > b \vee a + b \geq b$, which illustrates the benefit of variable elimination through (VE).

Lemma 2. *The conclusion of* (VE) *is equivalent to its premise.*

ALASCA Calculus - Non-Ground Version with Unification with Abstraction. We now define our lifted calculus ALASCA, as follows. Let ALASCA^{-} be the calculus ALASCA$^{\theta}$ being lifted for clauses without unshielded variables. We define ALASCA to be ALASCA^{-} chained with the variable elimination rule. That is, the result of every rule application is simplified using (VE) as long as applicable.

Theorem 5. *ALASCA is the lifting of a counterexample-reducing inference system for sets of clauses without unshielded variables.*

Theorem 5 implies that ALASCA is refutationally complete wrt $\mathcal{A}_\mathbb{Q}$ for sets of clauses without unshielded variables. As (VE) can be used to preprocess arbitrary sets of clauses to eliminate all unshielded variables, we get the following.

Corollary 1. *If N is a set of clauses that is unsatisfiable with respect to $\mathcal{A}_\mathbb{Q}$, then N can be refuted using ALASCA.*

We conclude this section by specifying the lifting of ALASCA^θ to get ALASCA^-. To this end, we use our uwa results and properties for unification with abstraction (Sect. 4). We note that using unification modulo $\mathcal{A}_{\text{eq}}$ would require us to develop an algorithmic approach that computes a complete set of unifiers modulo $\mathcal{A}_{\text{eq}}$, which is a quite challenging task both in theory and in practice. Instead, using Theorem 1 and Theorem 3, we need to only specify a canAbstract predicate that guards interpreted functions and captures $\mathcal{A}_{\text{eq}}$ within uwa. This is achieved by defining canAbstract(s,t) if any function symbol $f \in \{\text{sym}(s), \text{sym}(t)\}$ is an interpreted function $f \in \mathbb{Q} \cup \{+\}$. This choice of the canAbstract predicate is a slight modification of the abstraction strategy one_side_interpreted of [34]. We note that this is not the only choice for the predicate to fulfil the canAbstract properties. Consider for example the terms $f(x) + a$, and $a + b$. There is no substitution that will make these two terms equal, but our abstraction predicate introduces a constraint upon trying to unify them. In order to address this, we introduce an alternative canAbstract predicate that compares the atoms of a term, instead of only looking at the outer most symbol (Sect. 6).

We believe more precise abstraction predicates can improve proof search, as evidenced by our experiments using second abstraction predicate (Sect. 6).

6 Implementation and Experiments

We implemented ALASCA [5] in the extension of the VAMPIRE theorem prover [27].

Benchmarks. We evaluated the practicality of ALASCA using the following six sets of benchmarks, resulting all together in 6374 examples, as listed in Table 1 and detailed next. (i) We considered all sets of benchmarks from the SMT-LIB repository [7] set that involve real arithmetic and uninterpreted functions, but no other theories. These are the three benchmark sets corresponding to the LRA, NRA, and UFLRA logics in SMT-LIB. (ii) We further used Sledgehammer examples generated by [15], using the SMT-LIB syntax. From the examples of [15], we selected those benchmarks that involve real arithmetic but no other theories. We refer to this benchmark set as SH. (iii) Finally, we also created two new sets of benchmarks, TRIANGULAR, and LIMIT, exploiting various mathematical properties. The TRIANGULAR suite contains variations of our motivating example from Sect. 2, and thus comes with reasoning challenges about triangular inequalities

---

[5] available at https://github.com/vprover/vampire/tree/alasca

Benchmarks (#)	ALASCA	CVC5	VAMPIRE	YICES	ULTELIM	SMTINT	VERIT	solved
all (6374)	**5744**	5626	5585	5531	5218	828	465	5988
LRA (1722)	1572	1401	1396	**1722**	1469	623	89	1722
NRA (3814)	3800	3804	3803	**3809**	3669	0	0	3812
UFLRA (10)	10	10	10	0	0	10	10	10
TRIANGULAR (34)	**24**	10	13	0	0	0	6	25
LIMIT (280)	100	90	81	0	80	0	90	100
SH (514)	238	**311**	282	0	0	195	270	319

Table 1. Experimental results, showing the numbers of solved problems.

and continuous functions. The LIMIT benchmark set is comprised of problems that combine various limit properties of real-valued functions.

Experimental Setup. We compared our implementation against the solvers from the `Arith` (arithmetic) division of the SMT-COMP competition 2022. These solvers, given in columns 3–8 of Table 1, are: CVC5 [5], VAMPIRE [35], YICES [19], ULTELIM [8], SMTINT [21], and VERIT [2]. We note that VAMPIRE is run in its competition portfolio mode, which includes the work from [34]. ALASCA uses the same portfolio but implements our modified version of unification with abstraction (Sect. 4), disabling the use of theory axioms relying on our new ALASCA rules (Sect. 5). We ran our experiments using the SMT-COMP 2022 competition setup: based on the StarExec Iowa cluster, with a 20 minutes timeout and using 4 cores. Benchmarks, solvers and results are publicly available[6].

Experimental Results. Table 1 summarizes our experimental findings and indicates the overall best performance of ALASCA. For example, ALASCA outperforms the two best arithmetic solvers of SMT-COMP 2022 by solving 118 more problems than CVC5 and 159 more problems than VAMPIRE.

7   Conclusions and Future Work

We introduced the ALASCA calculus and drastically improved the performance of superposition theorem proving on linear arithmetic. ALASCA eliminates the use of theory axioms by introducing theory-specific rules such as an analogue of Fourier-Motzkin elimination. We perform unification with abstraction with a general theoretical foundation, which, together with our variable elimination rules, serves as a replacement for unification modulo theory. Our experiments show that ALASCA is competitive with state-of-the-art theorem provers, solving more problems than any prover that entered the arithmetic division in SMT-COMP 2022. Future work includes designing an integer version of ALASCA, developing different versions for the `canAbstract` predicate, and improving literal/clause selections within ALASCA.

Acknowledgements. This work was partially supported by the ERC Consolidator Grant ARTIST 101002685, the TU Wien Doctoral College SecInt, the FWF SFB project SpyCoDe F8504, and the EPSRC grant EP/V000497/1.

---

[6] https://www.starexec.org/starexec/secure/explore/spaces.jsp?id=535817

References

1. Alt, L., Blicha, M., Hyvärinen, A.E.J., Sharygina, N.: SolCMC: Solidity Compiler's Model Checker. In: CAV, LNCS, vol. 13371, pp. 325–338, Springer (2022), https://doi.org/10.1007/978-3-031-13185-1_16
2. Andreotti, B., Barbosa, H., Fontaine, P., Schurr, H.J.: veriT at SMT-COMP 2022. https://smt-comp.github.io/2022/system-descriptions/veriT.pdf (2022)
3. Bachmair, L., Ganzinger, H.: Ordered Chaining Calculi for First-Order Theories of Transitive Relations. J. ACM **45**(6), 1007–1049 (1998), https://doi.org/10.1145/293347.293352, URL **https://doi.org/10.1145/293347.293352**
4. Bachmair, L., Ganzinger, H.: Resolution Theorem Proving. In: Handbook of Automated Reasoning, pp. 19–99, Elsevier and MIT Press (2001), https://doi.org/10.1016/b978-044450813-3/50004-7
5. Barbosa, H., Barrett, C., Brain, M., Kremer, G., Lachnitt, H., Mohamed, A., Mohamed, M., Niemetz, A., Nötzli, A., Ozdemir, A., Preiner, M., Reynolds, A., Sheng, Y., Tinelli, C., , Zohar, Y.: CVC5 at the SMT Competition 2022. https://smt-comp.github.io/2022/system-descriptions/cvc5.pdf (2022)
6. Barbosa, H., Barrett, C.W., Brain, M., Kremer, G., Lachnitt, H., Mann, M., Mohamed, A., Mohamed, M., Niemetz, A., Nötzli, A., Ozdemir, A., Preiner, M., Reynolds, A., Sheng, Y., Tinelli, C., Zohar, Y.: cvc5: A Versatile and Industrial-Strength SMT Solver. In: TACAS, LNCS, vol. 13243, pp. 415–442, Springer (2022), https://doi.org/10.1007/978-3-030-99524-9_24
7. Barrett, C., Fontaine, P., Tinelli, C.: The Satisfiability Modulo Theories Library (SMT-LIB). www.SMT-LIB.org (2016)
8. Barth, M., Dietsch, D., Heizmann, M., Podelski, A.: Ultimate Eliminator at SMT-COMP 2022. https://smt-comp.github.io/2022/system-descriptions/UltimateEliminator%2BMathSAT.pdf (2022)
9. Baumgartner, P., Bax, J., Waldmann, U.: Beagle - A Hierarchic Superposition Theorem Prover. In: CADE, LNCS, vol. 9195, pp. 367–377, Springer (2015), https://doi.org/10.1007/978-3-319-21401-6_25
10. Bonacina, M.P., Graham-Lengrand, S., Shankar, N.: Satisfiability Modulo Theories and Assignments. In: CADE, LNCS, vol. 10395, pp. 42–59, Springer (2017), https://doi.org/10.1007/978-3-319-63046-5_4
11. Bromberger, M., Fleury, M., Schwarz, S., Weidenbach, C.: SPASS-SATT - A CDCL(LA) solver. In: CADE, LNCS, vol. 11716, pp. 111–122, Springer (2019), https://doi.org/10.1007/978-3-030-29436-6_7
12. Bruttomesso, R., Pek, E., Sharygina, N., Tsitovich, A.: The OpenSMT Solver. In: TACAS, LNCS, vol. 6015, pp. 150–153, Springer (2010), https://doi.org/10.1007/978-3-642-12002-2_12
13. Cook, B.: Formal Reasoning About the Security of Amazon Web Services. In: CAV, LNCS, vol. 10981, pp. 38–47, Springer (2018), https://doi.org/10.1007/978-3-319-96145-3_3
14. Cruanes, S.: Extending Superposition with Integer Arithmetic, Structural Induction, and Beyond. Ph.D. thesis, Ecole Polytechnique, Paris, France (2015)
15. Desharnais, M., Vukmirovic, P., Blanchette, J., Wenzel, M.: Seventeen Provers Under the Hammer. In: ITP, LIPIcs, vol. 237, pp. 8:1–8:18 (2022), https://doi.org/10.4230/LIPIcs.ITP.2022.8
16. Distefano, D., Fähndrich, M., Logozzo, F., O'Hearn, P.W.: Scaling Static Analyses at Facebook. Commun. ACM **62**(8), 62–70 (2019), https://doi.org/10.1145/3338112

17. Duarte, A., Korovin, K.: Implementing Superposition in iProver (System Description). In: IJCAR, LNCS, vol. 12167, pp. 388–397, Springer (2020), https://doi.org/10.1007/978-3-030-51054-1_24

18. Elad, N., Rain, S., Immerman, N., Kovács, L., Sagiv, M.: Summing up Smart Transitions. In: CAV, LNCS, vol. 12759, pp. 317–340, Springer (2021), https://doi.org/10.1007/978-3-030-81685-8_15

19. Graham-Lengrand, S.: Yices-QS 2022, an extension of Yices for quantified satisfiability. https://smt-comp.github.io/2022/system-descriptions/YicesQS.pdf (2022)

20. Gurfinkel, A.: Program Verification with Constrained Horn Clauses (Invited Paper). In: CAV, LNCS, vol. 13371, pp. 19–29, Springer (2022), https://doi.org/10.1007/978-3-031-13185-1_2

21. Hoenicke, J., Schindler, T.: SMTInterpol with Resolution Proofs. https://smt-comp.github.io/2022/system-descriptions/smtinterpol.pdf (2022)

22. Kapur, D., Narendran, P.: Double-exponential Complexity of Computing a Complete Set of AC-Unifiers. In: LICS, pp. 11–21, IEEE Computer Society (1992), https://doi.org/10.1109/LICS.1992.185515

23. Korovin, K., Kovács, L., Schoisswohl, J., Reger, G., Voronkov, A.: ALASCA:Reasoning in Quantified Linear Arithmetic (Extended Version). EasyChair Preprint no. 9606 (2023)

24. Korovin, K., Tsiskaridze, N., Voronkov, A.: Conflict Resolution. In: CP, LNCS, vol. 5732, pp. 509–523, Springer (2009), https://doi.org/10.1007/978-3-642-04244-7_41

25. Korovin, K., Voronkov, A.: An AC-Compatible Knuth-Bendix Order. In: CADE, LNCS, vol. 2741, pp. 47–59, Springer (2003), https://doi.org/10.1007/978-3-540-45085-6_5

26. Korovin, K., Voronkov, A.: Integrating Linear Arithmetic into Superposition Calculus. In: CSLs, LNCS, vol. 4646, pp. 223–237, Springer (2007), https://doi.org/10.1007/978-3-540-74915-8_19

27. Kovács, L., Voronkov, A.: First-Order Theorem Proving and Vampire. In: CAV, LNCS, vol. 8044, pp. 1–35, Springer (2013), https://doi.org/10.1007/978-3-642-39799-8_1

28. de Moura, L.M., Bjørner, N.S.: Efficient E-Matching for SMT Solvers. In: CADE, LNCS, vol. 4603, pp. 183–198, Springer (2007), https://doi.org/10.1007/978-3-540-73595-3_13

29. de Moura, L.M., Bjørner, N.S.: Z3: an efficient SMT solver. In: TACAS, LNCS, vol. 4963, pp. 337–340, Springer (2008), https://doi.org/10.1007/978-3-540-78800-3_24

30. de Moura, L.M., Jovanovic, D.: A Model-Constructing Satisfiability Calculus. In: VMCAI, LNCS, vol. 7737, pp. 1–12, Springer (2013), https://doi.org/10.1007/978-3-642-35873-9_1

31. Nieuwenhuis, R., Rubio, A.: Paramodulation-Based Theorem Proving. In: Handbook of Automated Reasoning, pp. 371–443, Elsevier and MIT Press (2001), https://doi.org/10.1016/b978-044450813-3/50009-6

32. Passmore, G.O.: Some Lessons Learned in the Industrialization of Formal Methods for Financial Algorithms. In: FM, LNCS, vol. 13047, pp. 717–721, Springer (2021), https://doi.org/10.1007/978-3-030-90870-6_39

33. Reger, G., Bjørner, N.S., Suda, M., Voronkov, A.: AVATAR Modulo Theories. In: GCAI, EPiC Series in Computing, vol. 41, pp. 39–52, EasyChair (2016), https://doi.org/10.29007/k6tp

34. Reger, G., Suda, M., Voronkov, A.: Unification with Abstraction and Theory Instantiation in Saturation-Based Reasoning. In: TACAS, LNCS, vol. 10805, pp. 3–22, Springer (2018), https://doi.org/10.1007/978-3-319-89960-2_1

35. Reger, G., Suda, M., Voronkov, A., Kovács, L., Bhayat, A., Gleiss, B., Hajdu, M., Hozzova, P., Evgeny Kotelnikov, J.R., Rawson, M., Riener, M., Robillard, S.,

Schoisswohl, J.: Vampire 4.7-SMT System Description. `https://smt-comp.github.io/2022/system-descriptions/Vampire.pdf` (2022)

36. Reynolds, A., King, T., Kuncak, V.: Solving Quantified Linear Arithmetic by Counterexample-Guided Instantiation. FMSD **51**(3), 500–532 (2017), https://doi.org/10.1007/s10703-017-0290-y

37. Schulz, S., Cruanes, S., Vukmirovic, P.: Faster, Higher, Stronger: E 2.3. In: CADE, LNCS, vol. 11716, pp. 495–507, Springer (2019), https://doi.org/10.1007/978-3-030-29436-6_29

38. Voronkov, A.: AVATAR: The Architecture for First-Order Theorem Provers. In: CAV, LNCS, vol. 8559, pp. 696–710, Springer (2014), https://doi.org/10.1007/978-3-319-08867-9_46

39. Waldmann, U.: Extending Reduction Orderings to ACU-Compatible Reduction Orderings. Inf. Process. Lett. **67**(1), 43–49 (1998), https://doi.org/10.1016/S0020-0190(98)00084-2

40. Waldmann, U.: Superposition for Divisible Torsion-Free Abelian Groups. In: CADE, LNCS, vol. 1421, pp. 144–159, Springer (1998), https://doi.org/10.1007/BFb0054257

41. Yamada, A., Winkler, S., Hirokawa, N., Middeldorp, A.: AC-KBO Revisited. Theory Pract. Log. Program. **16**(2), 163–188 (2016), https://doi.org/10.1017/S1471068415000083

A Matrix-Based Approach to Parity Games

Saksham Aggarwal, Alejandro Stuckey de la Banda, Luke Yang, and
Julian Gutierrez$^{(\boxtimes)}$

Monash University, Faculty of Information Technology, Melbourne, Australia
{sagg0005,astu0006,lyan0042}@student.monash.edu
julian.gutierrez@monash.edu

Abstract. Parity games are two-player zero-sum games of infinite duration played on finite graphs for which no solution in polynomial time is still known. Solving a parity game is an NP∩co-NP problem, with the best worst-case complexity algorithms available in the literature running in quasi-polynomial time. Given the importance of parity games within automated formal verification, several practical solutions have been explored showing that considerably large parity games can be solved somewhat efficiently. Here, we propose a new approach to solving parity games guided by the efficient manipulation of a suitable matrix-based representation of the games. Our results show that a sequential implementation of our approach offers very competitive performance, while a parallel implementation using GPUs outperforms the current state-of-the-art techniques. Our study considers both real-world benchmarks of structured games as well as parity games randomly generated. We also show that our matrix-based approach retains the optimal complexity bounds of the best recursive algorithm to solve large parity games in practice.

Keywords: Parity games · Formal verification · Parallel computing.

1 Introduction

Parity games are one of the most useful and effective algorithmic tools used in automated formal verification [18,5,2]. Indeed, several computational problems, such as model checking and automated synthesis using temporal logic specifications, can be reduced to the solution of a parity game [5,2]. More formally, a parity game is a two-player zero-sum game of infinite duration played on a finite graph. Since these games are determined [14,8], solving them is equivalent to finding a winning strategy for one of the two players in the game; or, similarly, deciding from which vertices in the graph one of the two players in the game can force a win no matter the strategy that the other player makes use of. The main question regarding parity games is that of the computational complexity of finding a solution of the game, a problem that is known to be in NP ∩ co-NP [11]. However, despite decades of research, a polynomial-time algorithm to solve such games remains elusive. The best-known decision procedures to solve parity games, most of them recently developed [4,13], run in quasi-polynomial time, which provide better worst-case complexity upper bounds than previous exponential-time approaches [18] found in the parity games literature.

S. Sankaranarayanan and N. Sharygina (Eds.): TACAS 2023, LNCS 13993, pp. 666–683, 2023.
https://doi.org/10.1007/978-3-031-30823-9_34

The importance of parity games in the solution of real-life automated verification problems, and the lack of a polynomial-time decision procedure to solve such games, has motivated the development and implementation of algorithms that can solve parity games somewhat efficiently in practice, despite their known worst-case exponential time complexity. In the quest for developing such decision procedures, several different approaches have been investigated in the last two decades, ranging from solutions that try to improve/optimise on the choice of high-level algorithm to reason about parity games, the programming language used to implement such a solution, the concrete data structures used to represent the games, or the type of hardware architecture used for deployment [7,6,17,9].

Progress solving parity games in practice has been made in different directions. In [7], a state-of-the-art implementation of the best-known algorithms for solving parity games was presented. In this work, two algorithms were found to deliver the best performance in practice, namely, Zielonka's recursive algorithm (ZRA [18]) and priority promotion [3], with the former showing slightly better performance when solving random games and a selection of structured games for model checking, and the latter outperforming ZRA when solving a selection of structured games for equivalence checking. But, overall, the two algorithms expose extremely similar performance in practice, including that of a parallel implementation of ZRA. Another attempt to improve the performance of solving parity games is presented in [6]. In this work, better performance is sought through a parallel implementation of ZRA, known to consistently expose the best performance in different platforms and for different types of games.

These two works [7,6] contain two strikingly opposing conclusions. While in [7] the parallel implementation of ZRA is even outperformed by the best sequential implementation of the same algorithm, in [6] significant gains in performance are observed when parallelising the computation of ZRA – which may solve a large set of random parity games between 3.5 and 4 times faster than the sequential implementation of the same algorithm. These two results, arguably, both conforming with the state of the art in the solution of parity games in practice, indicate that no definitive conclusion can be made into what the best approach to solving parity games in practice is, let alone whether considering a parallel implementation would necessarily produce better results than its sequential version. In this paper, we present a new approach to solving parity games, and investigate some of the issues exposed by the two above papers.

More specifically, motivated by the need to find effective new techniques for solving parity games, in particular in large practical settings, in this paper we:

1. propose a novel matrix-based approach to solving parity games, based on ZRA [18,13], arguably, the best-performing algorithm in practice [7];
2. study the complexity of our matrix-based procedure, and show that it retains the optimal complexity bounds of the best algorithms for parity games [13];
3. develop a parallel implementation, which takes advantage of methods and hardware for matrix manipulation using sophisticated GPU technologies;
4. investigate a number of alternative implementations of our matrix-based approach in order to better assess its usefulness in practical settings.

Our matrix-based approach, whose parallel implementation outperforms the state-of-the-art solvers for parity games, consists in the reduction of key operations on parity games as simple computations on large matrices, which can be significantly accelerated in practice using sophisticated techniques for matrix manipulation, specifically, using modern GPU technologies. Firstly, our matrix-based approach partly builds on the observation that most of the computation time when using ZRA is spent running a particular subroutine called the "attractor" function, which we can parallelise. Secondly, we also rely on the observation that computations on matrices – which guide the search for the solution of parity games within our approach – can be efficiently parallelised using a combination of both algorithmic techniques for parallel computation and GPU devices.

2   Preliminaries

A parity game is two-player zero-sum infinite-duration game played over a finite directed graph $G = (V_0, V_1, E, \Omega)$, where $V = V_0 \cup V_1$ is a set of vertices/nodes partitioned into vertices V_0 controlled by Player Even/0 and vertices V_1 controlled by Player Odd/1. Whenever a statement about both players is made, we may use the letter q ($\in \{0, 1\}$) to refer to either player, and $1 - q$ to refer to the other player in the game. Without any loss of generality, we also assume that every vertex in the graph has at least one successor. Moreover, the function $\Omega : V \to \mathbb{N}$ is a labelling function on the set of vertices of the graph which assigns each vertex a *priority*. Intuitively, the way a parity game is played is by moving a token along the graph (starting from some designated node in V), with the owner of the node of which the token is on selecting a successor node in the graph. Because every vertex has a successor, this process continues indefinitely, producing a infinite sequence of visited nodes, and consequently an infinite sequence of seen priorities. The winner of a particular play is determined by the highest priority that occurs infinitely often: Player 0 wins if the highest infinitely recurring priority is even, while Player 1 wins if the highest infinitely recurring priority is odd. Parity games are determined, which means that it always the case that one of the two players has a strategy (called a winning strategy) that wins against all possible strategies of the other player. Solving a parity game amounts to deciding, for every node in the game, which player has a winning strategy for the game starting in such a node. That is computing disjoint sets $W_0 \subseteq V$ and $W_1 \subseteq V$ such that Player q has a winning strategy to win every play in the game that starts from a node in W_q, with $q \in \{0, 1\}$.

Somewhat surprisingly, the best performing algorithm to solve parity games in practice is Zielonka's Recursive Algorithm (ZRA [18]), which runs in exponential time in the number of priorities, bounded by $|V|$. This algorithm is rather simple, and mostly relies on the computation of *attractor* sets, which are sets of vertices $A = Attr_q(X)$ inductively defined for each Player q as shown below – and used to computing both W_0 and W_1 recursively. Formally, the attractor function $Attr_q : \mathcal{P}(V) \to \mathcal{P}(V)$ for Player q, computes the attractor set of a given set of vertices $U \subseteq V$, and is defined inductively as follows:

Algorithm 1 *Zielonka(G)*

---

if $V = \emptyset$ then
    $(W_0, W_1) \leftarrow (\emptyset, \emptyset)$
else
    $m \leftarrow \max\{\Omega(v) \mid v \in V\}$
    $q \leftarrow m \bmod 2$
    $U \leftarrow \{v \in V \mid \Omega(v) = m\}$
    $A \leftarrow Attr_q(U)$
    $(W'_0, W'_1) \leftarrow Zielonka(G \setminus A)$
    if $W'_{1-q} = \emptyset$ then
        $(W_q, W_{1-q}) \leftarrow (A \cup W'_q, \emptyset)$
    else
        $B \leftarrow Attr_{1-q}(W'_{1-q})$
        $(W'_0, W'_1) \leftarrow Zielonka(G \setminus B)$
        $(W_q, W_{1-q}) \leftarrow (W'_q, W'_{1-q} \cup B)$
    end if
end if
return (W_0, W_1)

$$Attr_q^0(U) = U$$
$$Attr_q^{n+1}(U) = Attr_q^n(U)$$
$$\cup \{u \in V_q \mid \exists v \in Attr_q^n(U) : (u, v) \in E\}$$
$$\cup \{u \in V_{1-q} \mid \forall v \in V : (u, v) \in E \Rightarrow v \in Attr_q^n(U)\}$$
$$Attr_q(U) = Attr_q^{|V|}(U)$$

As shown in Algorithm 1, ZRA [18] finds disjoint sets of vertices W_0/W_1 from which Player $0/1$ has a winning strategy. Through the computation of attractor sets, the algorithm works by recursively decomposing the graph, finding sets of nodes that could be forced towards the highest priority node(s), and hence building the winning regions W_0 and W_1 for each player in the game.

3 A matrix-based approach

Experimental results from [7] motivated us to investigate whether ZRA can be improved in practice, since such an algorithm shows the best performance both in random games as well as in several structured games found in practical settings. This finding is complemented by the observation made in [6], that when running ZRA most of the time is spent in the computation of attractor sets, reported to be about 99% in [6] (with experiments considering random games only), and found to be of about 77% in our study (which considers larger classes of games).

Our observation, and working hypothesis, not found in previous work [7,6], is that the basic ZRA can be highly optimised in practice if its main computation component – the attractor set subroutine – is accelerated using efficient

Algorithm 2 $Attr(A, \mathbf{t}, q, \mathbf{g}, \mathbf{o})$

$\mathbf{d} \leftarrow A\mathbf{g}$
$\mathbf{t}' \leftarrow \mathbf{0}$
while $\|\mathbf{t} \neq \mathbf{t}'\|_1 \neq 0$ **do**
    $\mathbf{t}' \leftarrow \mathbf{t}$
    $\mathbf{v} \leftarrow A\mathbf{t}$
    $\mathbf{t} \leftarrow \mathbf{g} \odot ((\mathbf{o} = q) \odot (\mathbf{v} > 0) + (\mathbf{o} = (1 - q)) \odot (\mathbf{v} = \mathbf{d}))$
end while
return t

---

techniques for matrix manipulation, should a representation of the attractor set procedure was based on computations/operations on matrices encoding the attractor set subroutine in ZRA. This is precisely what we do in this section, which in turn makes our approach incredibly appropriate for an implementation in parallel using modern GPUs technologies for efficient matrix manipulation.

To achieve a matrix-based encoding of ZRA, and in particular of its attractor set subroutine, we redefine the representation of the graph in terms of a sparse adjacency matrix A, a vector defining the ownership of every node $\mathbf{o}$, and a vector $\boldsymbol{\omega}$ defining the priority of every node. Due to the potentially high computational cost of copying A, we maintain a vector $\mathbf{g}$ representing which nodes are still included in the game (a subgame being computed at that point in the algorithm), which is copied and updated as Zielonka's algorithm recurses and decomposes the graph into ever smaller parts. As such, we are able to find $\mathbf{d} = A\mathbf{g}$, a vector containing the maximum out-degree of every node. More specifically:

- $(A)_{ij} = 1$, if edge exists connecting i and j; $(A)_{ij} = 0$, otherwise;
- $(\mathbf{o})_i = q$, if node i belongs to player q;
- $(\boldsymbol{\omega})_i = \Omega(V_i)$;
- $(\mathbf{g})_i = 1$, if node i is in the game; $(\mathbf{g})_i = 0$, otherwise.

With these definitions in place, we can make the necessary modifications to the attractor function presented before – see Algorithm 2. The input/output vector $\mathbf{t}$ contains 1 at position $(\mathbf{t})_i$ where a node i is part of the attractor set and 0 otherwise. We thus define vectorised operations where if a vector is compared to another vector, then the comparisons are done element-wise. If a vector is compared to a scalar, then the scalar s is implicitly converted, $\mathbf{s} = s\mathbf{1}$. The $\odot$ operator denotes the Hadamard product, which is used primarily as a Boolean **And** operation. The argument q is the player: 0 for Player 0 and 1 for Player 1.

This algorithm works by first finding the number of outbound edges each node has ($\mathbf{d} \leftarrow A\mathbf{g}$), and at each iteration finding how many ways each node can enter the attractor set ($\mathbf{v} \leftarrow A\mathbf{t}$). It then finds nodes that q owns that may enter the attractor set $((\mathbf{o} = q) \odot (\mathbf{v} > 0))$, and nodes that q do not own that are forced to enter the attractor set $((\mathbf{o} = (1 - q)) \odot (\mathbf{v} = \mathbf{d}))$. It then filters the nodes to include into the attractor set depending on which nodes are still included in the subgraph ($\mathbf{g} \odot (\cdots)$), and breaks the loop when there is no difference between $\mathbf{t}$ and $\mathbf{t}'$. To illustrate this procedure, take as an example the graph below.

Algorithm 3 $MatZielonka(A, \mathbf{g}, \mathbf{o})$

---

if $\|\mathbf{g}\|_1 = 0$ **then**
    $(W_0, W_1) \leftarrow (\mathbf{0}, \mathbf{0})$
else
    $m \leftarrow \max(\mathbf{g} \odot \boldsymbol{\omega})$
    $q \leftarrow m \mod 2$
    $\mathbf{t} \leftarrow (\boldsymbol{\omega} = m)$
    $\mathbf{t} \leftarrow Attr(A, \mathbf{t}, q, \mathbf{g}, \mathbf{o})$
    $(W_0', W_1') \leftarrow MatZielonka(A, \mathbf{g} - \mathbf{t}, \mathbf{o})$
    if $\|W_{1-q}'\|_1 = 0$ **then**
        $(W_q, W_{1-q}) \leftarrow (\mathbf{t} + W_q', \mathbf{0})$
    else
        $\mathbf{t} \leftarrow Attr(A, W_{1-q}', 1 - q, \mathbf{g}, \mathbf{o})$
        $(W_0', W_1') \leftarrow MatZielonka(A, \mathbf{g} - \mathbf{t}, \mathbf{o})$
        $(W_p, W_{1-p}) \leftarrow (W_q', W_{1-q}' + \mathbf{t})$
    end if
end if
return (W_0, W_1)

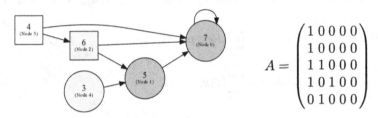

$$A = \begin{pmatrix} 1 & 0 & 0 & 0 & 0 \\ 1 & 0 & 0 & 0 & 0 \\ 1 & 1 & 0 & 0 & 0 \\ 1 & 0 & 1 & 0 & 0 \\ 0 & 1 & 0 & 0 & 0 \end{pmatrix}$$

For this example, assume that $\mathbf{g} = \mathbf{1}$ and that we are computing the attractor set for the player that own the circle nodes, starting from the node with priority 7. After 1 (or some arbitrary number of iteration(s)), the current state is reached. Green nodes denote nodes included in the previous iteration's attractor set, and yellow nodes denote nodes that will be included in this iteration. The calculations that may be performed are as follows. Define the adjacency matrix of the graph (A), the currently included nodes in the attractor set, $\mathbf{t} = (1\ 1\ 0\ 0\ 0)^\top$, the ownership of every node, $\mathbf{o} = (0\ 0\ 1\ 1\ 0)^\top$, and the degree – number of outbound edges – of every node, $\mathbf{d} = A\mathbf{g} = (1\ 1\ 2\ 2\ 1)^\top$. Now, compute the number of edges from each node leading to an element in the current attractor set, that is, $\mathbf{v} = A\mathbf{t} = (1\ 1\ 2\ 1\ 1)^\top$, and with that, update $\mathbf{t}$, to obtain: $\mathbf{t} \leftarrow (1\ 1\ 1\ 0\ 1)^\top$, which exactly represents the value of the attractor function one step later. Similar changes for ZRA in terms of the representation of the game must also be made, so that it becomes, fully, a matrix manipulation algorithm (Algorithm 3).

The correctness of the algorithm remains unchanged from that of ZRA since our encoding into matrix operations is functional. Less clear is whether our algorithm retains the ZRA's complexity, since using a functional mapping does not necessarily imply that the encoding (our representation) has the complexity of the encoded instance (*i.e.*, the original problem). We study this question next.

3.1   Complexity

Using the algorithms defined before, we derive a function $R(d, n)$ that bounds the maximum number of recursive calls to ZRA, given a d number of distinct priorities and n nodes: $R(d, n) = 1 + R(d - 1, n - 1) + R(d, n - 1)$. The 1 is the original call; the 1st recursive call is made with at least the vertex with the largest priority removed, and the second is made with at least one vertex removed. Hence, the construction above. There are two base cases $R(d, 0) = R(0, n) = 1$. Firstly, we observer that based on the algorithms herein defined, we get:

$$R(d, n) = 1 + R(d - 1, n - 1) + R(d, n - 1)$$

$$= (n + 1) + \sum_{i=1}^{n} [R(d - 1, n - i)]$$

Moreover, $R(d, n)$ is then given by: $f(d, n) = 2 \sum_{j=0}^{d} \binom{n}{j} - 1$. For the base case, when $d = 1$, we note that $R(1, n) = (n + 1) + \sum_{i=1}^{n} [R(0, n - i)] = 2n + 1$ and $f(1, n) = 2 \sum_{j=0}^{1} \binom{n}{j} - 1 = 2(n + 1) - 1 = 2n + 1 = R(1, n)$, as required, for all n. For the inductive case, assume that $R(d, n) = f(d, n)$, for $d = k$ and all n.

$$R(k + 1, n) = (n + 1) + \sum_{i=1}^{n} [R(k, n - i)]$$

$$= (n + 1) + \sum_{i=1}^{n} [f(k, n - i)]$$

$$= 1 + 2 \sum_{i=1}^{n} \sum_{j=0}^{k} \binom{n - i}{j} = 2 \sum_{j=0}^{k+1} \binom{n}{j} - 1 = f(k + 1, n)$$

Hence, the statement is true for the base case $d = 1$ and all n, while the inductive case $d = k$ implies $d = k + 1$. Thus, by induction, $R(d, n) = f(d, n)$ for $d \geq 1$ and all n. We now observe that the worst case number of calls occurs, as expected, at $d = n$ where $R(n, n) = 2^{n+1} - 1$. Note that the complexity of a single call to *MatZielonka* has time complexity $O(n^3)$ (dominated by the complexity of calls to the matrix-based *Attr* subroutine[1]) and space complexity $O(n)$, delivering worst-case complexities of $O(n^3 \cdot 2^n)$ time and $O(n \cdot 2^n)$ space.

This result, negative in theory, is consistent with that of the worst-case complexity of ZRA, which indicates that our matrix-based encoding retains the same complexity properties of the original algorithm. More interestingly, is the fact that the quasi-polynomial extension of ZRA by Parys [16], and later improved by Lehtinen et al [13], can also be tackled with our approach while retaining the quasi-polynomial complexity. However, a matrix-based extension of the latter algorithm was not evaluated. Thus, its practical usefulness is yet to be studied.

---

[1] In practice, this is dominated by the complexity of performing matrix multiplication operations, which is just slightly larger than $O(n^2)$ and happens to be a vibrant topic of research recently due to improvements made through the use of Deep learning.

4   Implementation and evaluation

Several factors influence the practical performance of a computational solution to a problem: for instance, (1) the algorithm used to solve the problem, (2) the programming language to implement the solution, (3) the concrete data structures used to represent it, and (4) the hardware where the solution is deployed. Our solution tries to optimise 1–4 using both lessons learnt from previous research and properties of our own matrix-based approach. Details are given later, but in short, in this section, five parity game solvers are implemented and evaluated[2]:

I1 our basic matrix-based approach, presented in the previous section;
I2 its parallel implementation for deployment using GPU technologies;
I3 the improved implementation of the attractor function of ZRA in [6];
I4 the highly optimised C++ implementation of ZRA presented in [7];
I5 the unoptimised version of the above algorithm, also in [7].

Apart from (2), the five implementations above (I1–I5) will allow you to have a comprehensive evaluation of our approach, both against different versions of our own work and against previous research. The only aspect that all the solutions we present in this section have in common is the programming language used for implementation, which is C++, at present the language offering the most efficient practical implementation of parity games solutions; cf. [9,17,6,7]. We first present the characteristics of our matrix-based approach, deployed both as a sequential algorithm and as a parallelised procedure. After that, we will describe key features of the solutions originally developed elsewhere, and continue with the results of the evaluation using different types of parity games.

Matrix-based approach.[3] Whilst it is important to find performance from parallelisable operations, it is equally important to avoid the loss of performance from executing inefficient or slow operations. Specific algorithmic design choices such as maintaining a vector **g** to track nodes that are in or out of the graph are done to avoid otherwise necessary operations such as copying the adjacency matrix, which would otherwise be slow, especially when solving very large games.

Additionally, all values in vectors and matrices are stored as single precision floating point values in practice. This is due to the software limitations of the Compute Unified Device Architecture (CUDA) [15] library, which are likely limitations of the underlying hardware itself. In particular, this limits the maximum out-degree of a node to 2^{24}, which corresponds to the number of bits in the mantissa of a single precision floating point number (23), plus one. Beyond this limit, the accuracy of the values computed in operations such as computing the maximum out-degree of a node with $A\mathbf{g}$ would no longer be guaranteed, along with the correctness of the algorithm. We note that this limitation may be overcome by splitting a single node into multiple nodes, thus curbing the maximum out degree to an acceptable range. We do not do this for these experiments as this transformation has unknown impacts on the performance of the algorithm.

---

[2] All files (implementations, experiments, input games, etc.) can be found in [1].

[3] The description here applies to the first two solutions described above.

Algorithm 4 $Attr(A, \mathbf{t}, q, \mathbf{g}, \mathbf{o})$

$\cdots$

   while $\|\mathbf{t} \neq \mathbf{t}'\|_1 \neq 0$ **do**

      for $i \in (1..3)$ **do**

        $\cdots$

      end for

   end while

   return t

The invocation of functions that run on the GPU (known as *kernels*) have an overhead, with the overhead duration varying somewhat between devices. As a consequence, tuning for a particular problem depends on the functions being executed and the GPUs themselves. Thus, there are periods where the device is idle, and this is a result of the overheads. Also note that in practice, it is usually faster to perform multiple iterations of the attractor computation as performing an iteration when the full attractor set has already been computed does not alter the results (Algorithm 4). This is because queueing multiple kernel invocations has the same overhead as calling one kernel alone. The main difference between our sequential and parallel implementations of the matrix-based method is the function computing attractor sets, which is as in Algorithm 2 in the sequential case, and as in Algorithm 4 in the parallel case. The code in ... is the same in both implementations, and the key difference is that we set the execution of the parallel implementation to make 3 kernel invocations per execution of the attractor function – which in lucky cases may require only 1 kernel invocation, while in unlucky cases may require more than 3 kernel invocations, increasing overheads; for our problem, we found that 3 kernel invocations was appropriate.

We find that there is another possible point of optimisation as the time taken for the attractor computation would be approximately equal to $ct_c + nt_o$, where c is the number of attractor computations (the inside section of the for loop), n is the number of times the outer while loop will run, t_c is the time to run the for loop once, and t_o is the overhead incurred by switching execution from device (GPU) to host (CPU) as the condition is checked in the while loop. Ideally, $c = C+1$, and $n = 1$, where C is the (unknown) number of attractor computations required. Our implementation loops the inner for loop an arbitrary constant number of times (3 times here). As such, $C + 1 \leq c \leq C + 3$, and $n = \lceil \frac{C}{3} \rceil$.

Importantly, requirements for the efficient parallelisation of the algorithm on the GPU require us to select the 'Naive attractor' implementation as the underlying algorithm (Algorithm 2) to be parallelised (leading to Algorithm 4) rather than the 'Improved attractor' implementation in [6]. The concepts of 'Naive' and 'Improved' attractors are presented by Arcucci et al in [6]. In short, the 'Naive' attractor loops over each node and checks if it can be included in the attractor set, and repeats this until no further nodes can be added. The 'Improved' attractor starts from the original attractor set, performing backpropagation on their inbound edges to find other nodes that may be included in the set.

GPU deployment. Our GPU implementation works by parallelising the "attract" operation.[4] Whilst the sequential version may be executed as such:

- (Loop 1) While attracting new nodes...
    - (Loop 2) For each node, check if it can be included in the attractor set.

And the runtime operations may look like:

- While attracting new nodes...
    - Can node 1 be included in the attractor set?
    - ...
    - Can node N be included in the attractor set?
- If attracted new nodes, repeat loop. Else break.

Performance is found through the inner loop being efficiently parallelised on the GPU. Additional specifics include the following GPU deployment features. When asking "Can node X be included ...?", the computation taking place is:

- Let J be the set of nodes in the current attractor set.
- Let K be the set of nodes that X can move to.
- If X is on the "friendly" team, and $K \cap J \neq \emptyset$, then $J \leftarrow J \cup \{X\}$.
- If X is on the "enemy" team, and $K \subseteq J$, then $J \leftarrow J \cup \{X\}$.

Key to our approach is that these operations are efficiently parallelised through means of matrix multiplication operations on the GPU. It is done as such:

- Compute $\mathbf{t} = A\mathbf{1}$. Hence, t_i is the number of nodes node i can move to.
- Let $\mathbf{j}$ be a vector of size N (where N is the size of the parity game), such that $\mathbf{j}_i = 1$ if and only if node i is in the current attractor set. Default 0.
- Let A be an adjacency matrix (usually, a sparse matrix) of the parity game.
- Compute the vector $\mathbf{k} = A\mathbf{j}$. Hence, the value $\mathbf{k}_i$ in the vector is the number of nodes node i can move to and that are in the current attractor set.
- Then, for each node i, if it is on the friendly team, and $\mathbf{k}_i \neq 0$, then $\mathbf{j}_i = 1$; otherwise, if it is on the enemy team, and $\mathbf{k}_i = t_i$, then $\mathbf{j}_i = 1$.

Note we convert the previous logic on sets to suit the new form using vectors:

$$K \cap J \neq \emptyset \Leftrightarrow \mathbf{k}_i \neq 0 \text{ and } K \subseteq J \Leftrightarrow \mathbf{k}_i = \mathbf{t}_i.$$

Improved attractor implementation by Arucci et al [6]. The third parity game solver we evaluate is a custom, C++, implementation of the ZRA using the 'Improved attractor' algorithm in [6], originally implemented in JAVA there.

ZRA implementations in Oink [7]. The fourth and fifth implementations we evaluate and compare against are the most highly optimised implementation of ZRA developed in [7], and its unoptimised version – without pre-processing routines. We include this implementation since our matrix-based ('Naive') implementation is not optimised in terms of the pre-processing routines used for implementation. These solvers in Oink are referred to as zlk and uzlk in [7]. We note that the parallel implementation of this algorithm is not included since in [7] is shown that it usually is outperformed by zlk, which we include here.

---

[4] A very different approach, leading to a very different GPU deployment is done in [10].

4.1   Evaluation

The implementations evaluated in this paper were tested on a wide repository of parity games, and against state-of-the-art parity game solvers in the literature. The games used for performance evaluation include the suite by Keiren [12] (of games representing model checking and equivalence checking problems) and an additional set of variably sized random games generated by PGSolver [9].[5]

We evaluate the performance in terms of solve time of each of the solvers and for each of the games. As it is common practice when evaluating different solvers for parity games, the overheads incurred due to startup and game loading are not included; this is done in order to obtain numbers that estimate only the running time of the algorithms, and nothing else. With the same aim, we ensured that at most one solver is running at any time, with CPU utilisation not exceeding more than one core. Finally, in order to allow for a fair comparison of running times *only* – rather than combining such results with the robustness of the algorithms – we measured the time solving an instance only in case all implementations successfully compute a solution. This allows for a fairer comparison with respect to runtime performance purely, because failing a game usually implies an extremely disproportionately (and arbitrary) high runtime. Such failures include timeouts (at 5 minutes) or being unable to load the game, sometimes due to factors having little to do with the running time of the algorithms. Our experiments were conducted in the Google Cloud Platform (GCP) using a T4 n1-highmem-2.[6]

Profile of the input parity games. Our study includes more than 2000 parity games, with sizes ranging from only a few dozens of states to games with millions of states. Both nodes' out-degrees and number of distinct priorities also cover a wide range of dimensions. However, both random games and structured ones (model checking and equivalence checking) typically are represented by sparse graphs, a feature that we will leverage for implementation purposes.

5   Analysis of results

As can be seen from Tables 1, 2, and 3, we evaluate the main five implementations, all of them following the ZRA philosophy, using two types of parity games: structured and random. Both types of benchmarks are as in [7] and [6], arguably, the two best implementations of ZRA. The focus of this evaluation is to understand the usefulness and scalability of the 'GPU matrix' algorithm, which is the one embodying more cleanly our working hypothesis, namely, that the combination of a matrix-based representation of ZRA and the use of modern GPU technologies can outperform the state of the art in the design of algorithms for parity games – a hypothesis for which we provide strong evidence here.

---

[5] These random games were generated using parameters that are identical to those of the random games in the 'PGSolver' collection in the suit of benchmarks by Keiren.

[6] In order to compare performance in different hardware (GPU) architectures, we use a different technology for experiments presented in a forthcoming section.

Implementation	Model checking Time	P/F	Equiv checking Time	P/F	Random games Time	P/F
GPU matrix	**94**	313/0	**332**	209/7	**20**	1750/0
Naive (matrix) attractor	566	313/0	2190	216/0	88	1750/0
Improved attractor	212	313/0	1310	216/0	113	1750/0
Oink's `zlk`	143	313/0	578	216/0	39	1750/0
Oink's `uzlk`	150	313/0	917	216/0	69	1750/0

Table 1: Times are in milliseconds (ms) representing the average time taken to solve games that all implementations passed (*i.e.*, if *any* implementation fails to solve a game, the game is excluded from the time average of *all* five solvers, including an additional GPU implementation on an RTX2060S, presented later). Failures occur with a small number of large equivalence checking games only. Failures include a few timeouts (at 5 mins), and usually being unable to load the game in memory due to hardware limitations posed by the GPU architectures. Columns P/F show the number of games passed/failed for every type of game.

Implementation	Model checking Time	P/F	Equiv checking Time	P/F	Random games Time	P/F
GPU matrix	**814**	33/0	**2612**	29/7	**283**	50/0
Naive (matrix) attractor	4565	33/0	17610	36/0	1059	50/0
Improved attractor	1832	33/0	10411	36/0	1446	50/0
Oink's `zlk`	1263	33/0	4568	36/0	547	50/0
Oink's `uzlk`	1316	33/0	7332	36/0	952	50/0

Table 2: Results in this table are formatted as in Table 1. In this table, we report the performance (average time in milliseconds taken to solve a single game) for the 5 algorithms on large (>1M nodes) parity games only.

Implementation	Model checking Time	P/F	Equiv checking Time	P/F	Random games Time	P/F
GPU matrix	**9**	280/0	**22**	180/0	**12**	1700/0
Naive (matrix) attractor	95	280/0	172	180/0	59	1700/0
Improved attractor	21	280/0	119	180/0	74	1700/0
Oink's `zlk`	11	280/0	56	180/0	24	1700/0
Oink's `uzlk`	13	280/0	77	180/0	43	1700/0

Implementation	Nodes 4K	8K	12K	16K	20K	40K	80K	320K	640K
GPU matrix	1	1	2	**2**	**2**	**5**	**11**	**43**	**78**
Naive (matrix) attractor	1	1	2	4	5	17	37	208	469
Improved attractor	1	1	3	5	7	19	45	264	557
Oink's `zlk`	1	1	2	3	4	7	15	76	186
Oink's `uzlk`	1	2	3	4	5	11	25	142	354

Table 3: Results in this table are formatted as in Table 1. In this table, we report the performance (average time in milliseconds taken to solve a single game) for the 5 algorithms on "small" (<1M nodes) parity games only: results for structured and random games appear in the top table and for random games (detailed) at the bottom. In the bottom table, there are 200 games per column, apart from column 640K which has 100 games; there are no failures.

The results above also show that going from the sequential version of our approach, 'Naive (matrix) attractor' to its parallel implementation using GPU technologies finds significant improvements. These two main "internal" results are then compared with the state of the art in the algorithmic design of solutions based on ZRA, namely, using the improved attractor in [6] and using the highly optimised procedure zlk in Oink [7], which even outperforms its own parallel implementation; cf. [7]. Finally, the unoptimised version in Oink of this procedure, uzlk, is also included simply because our matrix-based procedure does not contain any of the pre-processing routines that differentiate zlk from uzlk. Thus, in a way, uzlk provides results for a somewhat fairer comparison.

GPU matrix vs Naive (matrix) attractor. Results in all tables show that the parallel implementation using GPU technologies outperforms its own sequential implementation ('Naive matrix attractor') by several orders of magnitude, with some exceptions, usually ranging from 5 times faster in some cases (e.g., model checking of large games) to more than 10 times faster (e.g., model checking of small games). This, we believe, is due to the fact that the bigger the input instances to be analysed the more any losses in the associated overheads of running the procedure in parallel are compensated later on. A trend going in that direction can be observed in detail when comparing the performance of these two algorithms over small random games. But, in any case, our matrix-based approach is always at least as good as its sequential implementation.

GPU matrix vs Improved attractor. The results show that the parallel matrix-based approach can outperform the improved attractor procedure by Arcucci et al [6] by 2-7 orders of magnitude, depending on the type of game being solved, and with the best results obtained when solving random games, whether large or small. However, the sequential version of 'GPU matrix', that is, the Naive implementation, usually is twice slower than the improved attractor implementation in structured games. Contrarily, even the (sequential) Naive implementation of the matrix-based method outperforms the improved attractor procedure over random games, being about 30% overall in that case. When looking at all the tables of results together, one can see that this is in fact an indicator of the fact that the improved attractor approach performs somewhat poorly over random graphs, at least when compared to its performance over structured games.

GPU matrix vs Oink. Even thought the GPU matrix-based implementation outperforms Oink's zlk, it usually does it only by a 1.5 to 2.0 factor, with the GPU implementation performing more efficiently over (large) random games than over structured ones. This result actually speaks very highly of the optimised sequential implementation of ZRA. However, as shown in [7], zlk performs even better than its own parallel implementation (called zlk-8 in [7]) when solving model checking parity games (by a very small margin) and when solving random games, where it is nearly twice faster; cf. Table 3 of [7]. Only when solving equivalence checking parity games zlk-8 outperforms zlk, but only by about a 13% margin.

In contrast, the GPU implementation here outperforms zlk by more than a 70% margin, and is even twice faster when solving small equivalence checking games.

However, as we can see from all tables, the GPU matrix-based implementation has some failures (running timeout or failure to upload the game in memory, mainly due to their size), while the improved attractor method never fails in the considered set of benchmarks. This indicates that in this particular case, there may be a choice to be made between some potentially marginal gain in efficiency and more reliability offered by zlk. On the other hand, zlk clearly outperforms the sequential (Naive) implementation of the matrix-based approach, with better efficiency going from twice faster when solving random games to about four times faster when solving structured games. Regarding performance against Oink's uzlk, all analyses above remain similar, only that a better factor is usually obtained in favour of the GPU matrix-based approach.

Improved attractor vs Oink's zlk. Despite these two procedures being originally developed previously, we would like to comment on their comparative performance, for the sake of completeness of the analysis. As can be seen from our results, both offer the same reliability as they do not fail to solve any instance. Regarding runtime efficiency, we can observe that, on average, Oink's zlk implementation tends to be 1.5 to 3.0 times faster than the improved attractor method, with the worst/best comparative performance being enacted when solving model checking/random parity game instances, and in that way making zlk perhaps the most efficient sequential implementation of ZRA currently available in the literature, and being outperformed only when a parallel approach is considered.

6   Special cases

In this section, we analyse in more details two special cases of our results: performance when solving large parity games and performance on random games.

6.1   Solving large parity games

For the purposes of this section, a *large* parity game is a game with more than 1 million nodes. Our results show that for games that are not large (Table 3), all solvers may be regarded as running efficiently from a human perspective, with some random games with more than 500K nodes being solved in about half a second by the slowest implementation on random games (the improved attractor implementation). In most other instances, solutions may be obtained in just a few milliseconds. For instance, model checking parity games in the suite of benchmarks can be solved in less than 0.1 minutes by any studied solver, and even in less than 10 milliseconds on average using the parallel GPU matrix-based approach, with Oink implementation taking virtually the same time (just a little more than 10 milliseconds on average). Then, the real challenge when solving parity games in practice is solving large parity games, where the relative performances between different solvers can be much better exposed (Table 2).

Our results show (Tables 1 and 2) that, despite the raw data being different in about 9 orders of magnitude, nearly the same relative performance is obtained when looking at performance over all games with respect to performance over large games only, which account for no more than 15% of the games for equivalence checking games, 10% for model checking games and less than 5% for random games. This result indicates that in order to evaluate the performance of parity games solvers in practice, one should better focus on large games only. As the data shows, in that case that parallel GPU matrix-based approach outperforms the second-best technique by, approx., a 1.5-2.0 factor, and its own sequential implementation by a factor of 4 to 5, in each case, depending on the type of parity game under consideration. The analysis holds across all solvers.

6.2   Solving random parity games

Random parity games are a common benchmark for parity games solvers, being the focus of the study on [6]. Our detailed experiments on random parity games show that the parallel GPU implementation of the matrix-based approach is comparable to the parallel implementation of the improved attractor implementation in [6] (see Table 3 there), in the sense that a similar relative *gain* in performance is achieved, overall, performing about 3.5-4.0 times faster over random games of up to 20K nodes. The gain in performance increases in our case when considering larger random graphs, perhaps indicating that our approach may be more scalable in terms of running time; however, in [6], only results on random games of up to 20K nodes are presented. We note that, in this case, only by changing the programming language of choice (JAVA in [6] and C++ here), performance is improved going from games of 20K size being solved in more than 5 seconds to the same type of games being solved in just 7ms on average here.

7   Alternative implementations

In this section, we explore two alternative implementations, one focused on a change of programming environment and another one based on a change of computer architecture. Our results show that while the former is well outperformed by the original C++ implementation, the latter shows even better performance than the already reported can be achieved when using other GPU technologies.

A MATLAB *implementation.* Given its facility to perform matrix operations, we investigated a MATLAB of our matrix-based approach to understand if it could perform better than our original C++ implementation. The results were negative. The MATLAB implementation of our approach, although simple, performed significantly worse than other methods, including our own using C++. A summary of the results, which require little discussion, can be found in Table 4.

Using a different GPU technology. We conducted experiments using the exact same implementation of the GPU matrix solver (run on a GCP) on a different

Implementation	Model checking		Equiv checking		Random games	
	Time	P/F	Time	P/F	Time	P/F
GPU matrix	**94**	313/0	**332**	209/7	**20**	1750/0
Naive (matrix) attractor	566	313/0	2190	216/0	88	1750/0
MATLAB matrix	2462	311/2	2338	198/18	3496	1750/0

Table 4: Results in this table are formatted as in Table 1. We report results on all games, and in each case, independently, remove the time of unsolved instances.

Implementation	Model checking		Equiv checking		Random games	
	Time	P/F	Time	P/F	Time	P/F
GPU matrix (RTX2060S)	**63**	313/0	**203**	205/11	25	1750/0
GPU matrix	94	313/0	332	209/7	**20**	1750/0

Table 5: Results in this table are formatted as in Table 1. We report results on all games, which show an improvement of a 1.5x factor for structured games, while performing approximately 25% slower over random parity games.

GPU architecture, namely, on an RTX2060 Super (Ryzen 5 3600). We found that by simply changing to this alternative hardware specification, the results on all types of games were significantly better, as shown in the Table 5.

8 Concluding remarks and related work

We have shown that a new method for solving parity games using a matrix-based approach can outperform the state-of-the-art techniques, both sequential and parallel, currently available. As such, our results become a new point of comparison when evaluating modern solvers for parity games. Previous research [7,6,17,9] has shown that ZRA is potentially the best performing algorithm to solve parity games in practice, and here we provide more evidence that this is indeed the case. We also give evidence that C++ implementations for this task are hardly ever outperformed in practice. Finally, we also show that choosing the right computer architecture is key to achieve optimal performance, and in particular that in the case of modern GPU technologies, such a choice can make a significant difference in practice – in our study, leading to the development of the, as of today, most efficient parallel implementation/solver for parity games.

Acknowledgement. This research was funded by the Monash Laboratory for the Foundations of Computing (MLFC) and the Monash Faculty of Information Technology (FIT). Parts of this research were developed as FIT3144 projects ("Advanced computer science research project") at Monash in 2022. Preliminary results on the matrix-based approach to parity games were also developed by Henri Urpani during his FIT3144 project under Gutierrez's supervision in 2021. Finally, we thank the reviewers for helpful comments that improved this paper.

References

1. Aggarwal, S., Stuckey de la Banda, A., Yang, L., Gutierrez, J.: Parity games benchmarks: Implemenation and experiments. https://drive.google.com/drive/folders/1z2eAGxU9jyn2ngnhM8c6f4Py4reW3toB?usp=sharing (January 2023)
2. Baier, C., Katoen, J.: Principles of model checking. MIT Press (2008)
3. Benerecetti, M., Dell'Erba, D., Mogavero, F.: Solving parity games via priority promotion. Formal Methods Syst. Des. **52**(2), 193–226 (2018)
4. Calude, C.S., Jain, S., Khoussainov, B., Li, W., Stephan, F.: Deciding parity games in quasi-polynomial time. SIAM J. Comput. **51**(2), 17–152 (2022)
5. Clarke, E.M., Grumberg, O., Kroening, D., Peled, D.A., Veith, H.: Model checking, 2nd Edition. MIT Press (2018)
6. D'Amore, L., Murano, A., Sorrentino, L., Arcucci, R., Laccetti, G.: Toward a multilevel scalable parallel zielonka's algorithm for solving parity games. Concurr. Comput. Pract. Exp. **33**(4) (2021)
7. van Dijk, T.: Oink: An implementation and evaluation of modern parity game solvers. In: Tools and Algorithms for the Construction and Analysis of Systems - 24th International Conference, TACAS 2018. LNCS, vol. 10805, pp. 291–308. Springer (2018)
8. Emerson, E.A., Jutla, C.S.: Tree automata, mu-calculus and determinacy (extended abstract). In: 32nd Annual Symposium on Foundations of Computer Science. pp. 368–377. IEEE (1991)
9. Friedmann, O., Lange, M.: Solving parity games in practice. In: Automated Technology for Verification and Analysis, 7th International Symposium, ATVA 2009. LNCS, vol. 5799, pp. 182–196. Springer (2009)
10. Hoffmann, P., Luttenberger, M.: Solving parity games on the GPU. In: Hung, D.V., Ogawa, M. (eds.) Automated Technology for Verification and Analysis - 11th International Symposium, ATVA 2013, Hanoi, Vietnam, October 15-18, 2013. Proceedings. Lecture Notes in Computer Science, vol. 8172, pp. 455–459. Springer (2013)
11. Jurdzinski, M.: Deciding the winner in parity games is in UP $\cap$ co-UP. Inf. Process. Lett. **68**(3), 119–124 (1998)
12. Keiren, J.J.A.: Benchmarks for parity games. In: Dastani, M., Sirjani, M. (eds.) Fundamentals of Software Engineering. pp. 127–142. Springer (2015)
13. Lehtinen, K., Parys, P., Schewe, S., Wojtczak, D.: A recursive approach to solving parity games in quasipolynomial time. Log. Methods Comput. Sci. **18**(1) (2022)
14. Martin, D.: Borel determinacy. Annals of Mathematics **102**(2), 363–371 (1975)
15. Nickolls, J., Buck, I., Garland, M., Skadron, K.: Scalable parallel programming with cuda: Is cuda the parallel programming model that application developers have been waiting for? Queue **6**(2), 40–53 (2008)
16. Parys, P.: Parity Games: Another View on Lehtinen's Algorithm. In: Fernández, M., Muscholl, A. (eds.) 28th EACSL Annual Conference on Computer Science Logic (CSL 2020). Leibniz International Proceedings in Informatics (LIPIcs), vol. 152, pp. 32:1–32:15. Schloss Dagstuhl–Leibniz-Zentrum fuer Informatik, Dagstuhl, Germany (2020)
17. Stasio, A.D., Murano, A., Prignano, V., Sorrentino, L.: Solving parity games in scala. In: Lanese, I., Madelaine, E. (eds.) Formal Aspects of Component Software - 11th International Symposium, FACS 2014. LNCS, vol. 8997, pp. 145–161. Springer (2014)
18. Zielonka, W.: Infinite games on finitely coloured graphs with applications to automata on infinite trees. Theor. Comput. Sci. **200**(1-2), 135–183 (1998)

A GPU Tree Database for
Many-Core Explicit State Space Exploration

Anton Wijs[(⊠)] [iD] and Muhammad Osama [iD]

Eindhoven University of Technology, Eindhoven, The Netherlands
{a.j.wijs,o.m.m.muhammad}@tue.nl

Abstract. Various techniques have been proposed to accelerate explicit-state model checking with GPUs, but none address the compact storage of states, or if they do, at the cost of losing completeness of the checking procedure. We investigate how to implement a tree database to store states as binary trees in GPU memory. We present fine-grained parallel algorithms to find and store trees, experiment with a number of GPU-specific configurations, and propose a novel hashing technique, called Cleary-Cuckoo hashing, which enables the use of Cleary compression on GPUs. We are the first to assess the effectiveness of using a tree database, and Cleary compression, on GPUs. Experiments show processing speeds of up to 131 million states per second.

Keywords: Explicit state space exploration, finite-state machines, GPU.

1 Introduction

Major advances in computation increasingly need to be obtained via parallel software, as Moore's Law is ending [30]. In the last decade, GPUs have been successfully applied to accelerate various computations relevant for model checking, such as probability computations for probabilistic model checking [8, 25, 48], counter-example construction [54], state space decomposition [52], parameter synthesis for stochastic systems [12], and SAT solving [34–38, 40, 43, 56, 57]. VoxLogicA-GPU applies model checking to analyse (medical) images [9].

In the earliest work on GPU explicit state space exploration, GPUs performed part of the computation, specifically successor generation [18, 19] and property checking once the state space has been generated [5]. This was promising, but the data copying between main and GPU memory and the computations on the CPU were detrimental for performance. The first tool that performed the entire exploration on a GPU was GPUExplore [33, 50, 51, 53]. It was later extended to support LTL model checking [49]. A similar exploration engine was later proposed in [55]. An approach that applied a GPU to explore the state space of Promela models, i.e., the models for the Spin model checker [21], was presented in [6]. This was later adapted to the swarm checker Grapple [16], which can efficiently explore very large state spaces, but at the cost of losing completeness. Finally, the model checker ParaMoC for pushdown systems was presented in [46, 47].

S. Sankaranarayanan and N. Sharygina (Eds.): TACAS 2023, LNCS 13993, pp. 684–703, 2023.
https://doi.org/10.1007/978-3-031-30823-9_35

The above techniques demonstrate the potential for GPU acceleration of state space exploration and (explicit-state) model checking, being able to accelerate those procedures *tens* to *hundreds* of times, but they all have serious practical limitations. Several limit the size of state vectors to 64 bits [6, 55] or the size of transition encodings to 64 bits [46, 47]. GPUEXPLORE does not efficiently support models with variables [50, 53]. When adding variables, the amount of memory needed rapidly grows, due to the growing input model and inefficient state storage. GRAPPLE requires less memory, but uses bitstate hashing. This rules out the ability to detect that all reachable states have been explored, which is crucial to prove the absence of undesired behaviour. PARAMOC verifies push-down systems, but does not support concurrency, and abstracts away data.

Contributions. We propose how to perform memory-efficient complete state space exploration on a GPU for concurrent *Finite-State Machines (FSMs) with data*. To make this possible, we are the first to investigate the storage of binary trees in GPU hash tables, propose new algorithms to find and store trees in a fine-grained parallel fashion, experiment with a number of GPU-specific config-urations, and propose a novel hashing technique called *Cleary-Cuckoo hashing*, which enables the use of *Cleary compression* [13,15] on GPUs. To achieve this, we have to tackle the following challenges: 1) CPU-based algorithms are recursive, but GPUs are not suitable for recursion, and 2) accessing GPU global memory, in which the hash tables reside, is slow. This work marks an important step to pioneer practical GPU accelerated model checking, as it can be extended to checking functional properties of models with data, and paves the way to inves-tigate the use of *Binary Decision Diagrams* [29] for symbolic model checking.

The structure of the paper is as follows. In Section 2, we discuss related work on GPU hash tables. Section 3 presents background information on GPU programming, and Section 4 contains an overview of the state space exploration engine. Section 5 addresses the challenges when designing a GPU tree table, and presents our new algorithms. Experimental results are given in Section 6, and in Section 7, conclusions and our future work plans are discussed.

2   Related Work

An overview of related work on GPU acceleration of model checking is given in Section 1. In the current section, we focus on *hash tables* [14] for the GPU. In explicit state space exploration, states are typically stored in a hash table. Such a table is often implemented as an array, where the elements represent the hash table *buckets*. A recent survey of GPU hash tables [31] identifies that when using integer data items and unordered insertions and queries, *Cuckoo hashing* [41] is (currently) the best option, compared to techniques such as *chaining* [3] or *robin hood hashing* [20], and the Cuckoo hashing of [1] is particularly effective. In Cuckoo hashing, collisions, i.e., situations where a data item e is hashed to an already occupied bucket, are resolved by evicting the encountered item e', storing e, and moving e' to another bucket. A fixed number of m hash functions is used to have multiple storage options for each item. Item look-up and storage is therefore limited to m memory accesses, but can lead to chains of evictions. In [1], it is demonstrated that with four hash functions, a hash table needs around $1.25N$ buckets to store N items.[1] Recent research [4] has demonstrated that using larger buckets, spanning multiple elements, that still fit in the GPU cache line is beneficial for performance, and increases the average load factor, i.e., how much the hash table can be filled until an item cannot be inserted, to 99%. We address this in detail in Section 3. However, in [4], an older NVIDIA GPU of the VOLTA architecture was used (2017), while more recent GPUs are supposedly less susceptible to optimisations exploiting the cache line. In this work, we experimentally assess this for hash table buckets.

Besides buckets, we also consider Cuckoo hashing as used in [1,4], but we are the first to investigate the storage of *binary trees*, and the use of Cleary compression to store more data in less space. Libraries offering GPU hash tables, such as [23], do not offer these capabilities. Furthermore, we are the first to investigate the impact of using larger buckets for binary tree storage embedded in a state space exploration engine.

The model checker GPUEXPLORE [11,50,53] uses multiple hash functions to store a state. State evictions are never performed, as each state is stored in a sequence of integers, making it not possible to store states atomically. This can lead to storing duplicate states, which tends to be worsened when states are evicted, making Cuckoo hashing not practical [51]. Besides compact state storage, a second benefit of using trees with each node being stored in a single integer is that it allows arbitrarily large states to be stored atomically, i.e., a state is stored the moment the root of its tree is stored.

Because we store trees, with the individual nodes referencing each other, we do not consider alternative storage approaches, such as using a list that is repeatedly sorted, even though Alcantara *et al.* identified that using *radix-sort* [32] is competitive to hashing [1].

3   GPU programming

CUDA[2] is a programming interface that enables general purpose programming for a GPU. It has been developed and continues to be maintained by NVIDIA since 2007. In this work, we use CUDA with C++. Therefore, we use CUDA terminology when we refer to thread and memory hierarchies.

The left part of Fig. 1 gives an overview of a GPU architecture. For now, ignore the bold-faced words and the pseudo-code. A GPU consists of a finite number of *streaming multiprocessors* (SM), each containing hundreds of *cores*. For instance, a Titan RTX, which we used for this work, has 72 SMs containing together 4,608 cores. A programmer can implement functions, named *kernels*, to

---

[1] This refers to the *single-level* version of their Cuckoo hashing [1], which we consider in this work. Their two-level version is more complex and less efficient.

[2] https://developer.nvidia.com/cuda-zone.

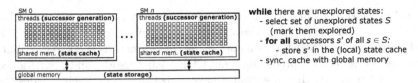

Fig. 1: State space exploration on a GPU architecture.

be executed by a predefined number of GPU threads. Parallelism is achieved by having these threads work on different parts of the data.

When a kernel is launched, threads are grouped into *blocks*, usually of a size equal to a power of two, often 512 or 1,024. Each block is executed by one SM, but an SM can interleave the execution of many blocks. When a block is executed, the threads inside are scheduled for execution in smaller groups of 32 threads called *warps*. A warp has a single program counter, i.e., the threads in a warp run in lock-step through the program. This concept is referred to as *Single Instruction Multiple Threads* (SIMT): each thread executes the same instructions, but on different data. The threads in a warp may also follow *diverging* program paths, leading to a reduction in performance. For instance, if the threads of a warp encounter an `if C then P1 else P2` construct, and for some, but not all, `C` holds, all threads will step through the instructions of both `P1` and `P2`, but each thread only executes the relevant instructions.

GPU threads can use atomic instructions to manipulate data atomically, such as a *compare-and-swap* on 32- and 64-bit integers: ATOMICCAS(`addr`, `compare`, `val`) atomically checks whether at address `addr`, the value `compare` is stored. If so, it is updated to `val`, otherwise no update is done. The actual value read at `addr` is returned.

There are various types of memory on a GPU. The *global memory* is the largest of these, 24 GB in the case of the Titan RTX, and is used to copy data between the *host* (CPU-side) and the *device* (GPU-side). It can be accessed by all GPU threads, and has a high bandwidth, but also a high latency. Having many threads executing a kernel helps to hide this latency; the cores can rapidly switch contexts to interleave the execution of multiple threads, and whenever a thread is waiting for the result of a memory access, the core uses that time to execute another thread. Another way to improve memory access times is by ensuring that the accesses of a warp are *coalesced*: if the threads in a warp try to fetch a consecutive block of memory in size not larger than the cache line (128 bytes for a Titan RTX), then the time needed to access that block is the same as the time needed to access an individual memory address.

Other types of memory are *shared memory* and *registers*. Shared memory is fast on-chip memory with a low latency, that can be used as block-local memory; the threads of a block can share data with each other via this memory. In a Titan RTX, each block can use up to 49,152 bytes of shared memory. Register memory is the fastest, and is used to store thread-local data. It is very small, though, and allocating too much memory for thread-local variables may result in data spilling over into global memory, which can dramatically limit the performance.

Finally, the threads in a warp can communicate very rapidly with each other by means of *intra-warp instructions*. There are various instructions, such as SHUFFLE to distribute register data among the threads and BALLOT to distribute the results of evaluating a predicate. Since CUDA 9.0, threads can be partitioned into *cooperative groups*. If these groups have a size that completely divides the warp size, i.e., it is a power of two smaller than or equal to 32, then the threads in a group can use intra-warp instructions among themselves.

In Section 2, we mentioned the use of buckets in a GPU hash table. When a hash table is divided into buckets, each containing $1 < n \le 32$ elements, that still fit in the cache line, then cooperative groups of n threads each can be created, and the threads in a group can work together for the fetching and updating of buckets. This results in more coalesced memory accesses and reduces thread divergence. However, it also means that fewer tasks can be performed in parallel, and starting with the TURING architecture (2018), which the Titan RTX is built on, NVIDIA has been working on making computations less reliant on coalesced memory accessing.

4   GPU state space exploration

SLCO. For this work, we extended the state space exploration engine of GPU-EXPLORE 2.0 [53] to support models of finite-state concurrent systems written in the *Simple Language of Communicating Objects* (SLCO), version 2.0 [44]. An SLCO model consists of a finite number of FSMs. The FSMs can communicate via globally shared variables, and each FSM can have its own local variables. Variables can be of type `Bool`, `Byte` and (32-bit) `Integer`, and there is support for arrays of these types. We refer with *(system) states* $s, s', \ldots$ to entire states of the system, and with *FSM states* $\sigma, \sigma', \ldots$ to the states of an individual FSM. A system state is essentially a vector, containing all the information that together defines a state of the system, i.e., the current states of the FMSs and the values of the variables.

An FSM transition $tr = \sigma \xrightarrow{st} \sigma'$ indicates that the FSM can change state from σ to σ' iff the associated *statement st* is *enabled*. A statement is either an *assignment*, an *expression* or a *composite*. Each can refer to the variables in the scope of the FSM. An assignment is always enabled, and assigns a value to a variable, an expression is a predicate that acts as a guard: it is enabled iff it evaluates to **true**. Finally, a composite is a finite sequence of statements $st_0; \ldots; st_n$, with st_0 being either an expression or an assignment, and $st_1, \ldots, st_n$ being assignments. A composite is enabled iff its first statement is enabled. A transition $tr = \sigma \xrightarrow{st} \sigma'$ can be *fired* if it is enabled, which results in the FSM atomically moving from state σ to state σ', and any assignments of st being executed in the specified order. When tr is fired while the system is in a state s, then after firing, the system is in state s', which is equal to s, apart from the fact that σ has been replaced by σ', and the effect of st has been taken into account. We call s' a *successor* of s.

The formal semantics of SLCO defines that each transition is executed atomically, i.e., cannot be interrupted by the execution of other transitions. The FSMs execute concurrently, using an interleaving semantics. Finally, the FSMs may have non-deterministic behaviour, i.e., at any point of execution, an FSM may have several enabled transitions.

State space exploration. Given an SLCO model with n FSMs, first, CUDA functions $f_1, \ldots f_n$ are generated, using a new code generator, that take as input a state s, and produce as output the successors of s which can be reached by firing a transition enabled in s of the ith FSM. When the state space is generated, each state s can be analysed in parallel by n threads $t_1, \ldots, t_n$, where each t_i executes f_i to obtain some of the successors of s.

Fig. 1 presents how the different components of the state space exploration engine map on a GPU. We explain how the engine works insofar is needed. For more details, we refer the reader to [50, 51, 53]. Even though the type of input model has changed, as GPUEXPLORE only supports models without data variables, the core of the engine has remained the same.

In the global memory, a large hash table (we call it $\mathcal{G}$) is maintained to store the states visited so far. At the start, the initial state of the input model is stored in $\mathcal{G}$. Each state in $\mathcal{G}$ has a Boolean flag *new*, indicating whether the state has already been explored, i.e., whether or not its successors have been constructed.

On the right in Fig. 1, the state space exploration algorithm is explained from the perspective of a *thread block*. While the block can find unexplored states in $\mathcal{G}$, it selects some of those for exploration. In fact, every block has a *work tile* residing in its shared memory, of a fixed size, which the block tries to fill with unexplored states at the start of each exploration iteration. Such an iteration is initiated on the host side by launching the exploration kernel. States are marked as explored when added by threads to their tile.

Next, every block processes its tile. For this, each thread in the block is assigned to a particular state/FSM combination. Each thread accesses its designated state in the tile, and analyses the possibilities for its designated FSM to change state, as explained before. Hence, the threads in a group can generate successors for a single state in parallel.

The generated successors are stored in a *block-local state cache*, which is a hash table in the shared memory. This avoids repeated accessing of global memory, and local duplicate detection filters out any duplicate successors generated at the block-level. Once the tile has been processed, the threads in the block together scan the cache once more, and store the new states in $\mathcal{G}$ if they are not already present. When states require no more than 32 or 64 bits in total (including the *new* flag), they can simply be stored atomically in $\mathcal{G}$ using compare-and-swap. However, sufficiently large systems have states consisting of more than 64 bits. In this paper, we therefore focus on working with these larger states, and consider storing them as binary trees.

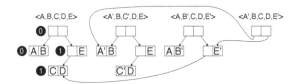

Fig. 2: An example of storing state vectors as binary trees.

5   A Compact GPU Tree Database

5.1   CPU Tree Storage

The number of data variables in a model, and their types, can have a drastic effect on the size of the states of that model. For instance, each 32-bit integer variable in a model requires 32 bits in each state. As the amount of global memory on a GPU is limited, we need to consider techniques to store states in a memory-efficient way. One technique that has proven itself for CPU-based model checkers is *tree compression* [7], in which system states are stored as binary trees. A single hash table can be used to store all tree nodes [27]. Compression is achieved by having the trees share common subtrees. Its success relies on the observation that states and their successors tend to be different in only a few data elements. In [27], it is experimentally assessed that tree compression compresses better than any other compression technique identified by the authors for explicit state space exploration. They observe that the technique works well for a multi-threaded exploration engine. Moreover, they propose an *incremental* variant that has a considerably improved runtime performance, as it reduces the number of required memory accesses to a number logarithmic in the length of the state vector.

Fig. 2 shows an example of applying tree compression to store four state vectors. The black circles should be ignored for now. Each letter represents a part of the state vector that is k bits in length. We assume that in k bits, also a pointer to a node can be stored, and that each node therefore consists of $2k$ bits. The vector <A,B,C,D,E> is stored by having a root node with a left leaf sibling <A,B>, and the right sibling being a non-leaf that has both a left leaf sibling <C,D>, and the element E. In total, storing this tree requires $8k$ bits. To store the vector <A',B,C',D,E>, we cannot reuse any of these nodes, as <A',B> and <C',D> have not been stored yet. This means that all pointers have to be updated as well, and therefore, a new root and a new non-leaf containing E are needed. Again, $8k$ bits are needed. For <A,B',C,D,E'>, we have to store a new node <A,B'> and a new root, and a new non-leaf storing E', but the latter can point to the already existing node <C,D>. Hence, only $6k$ bits are needed to store this vector. Finally, for <A',B,C,D,E'>, we only need to store a new root node, as all other nodes already exist, resulting in only needing $2k$ bits. It has been demonstrated that as more and more state vectors are stored, eventually new vectors tend to require $2k$ bits each [26, 27].

To emphasise that GPU tree compression has to be implemented vastly differently from the typical CPU approach, we first explain the latter, and the incremental approach [27]. Checking for the presence of a tree and storing it if

---

Algorithm 1: Tree-based Find-or-put, CPU version.

```
1  function FINDORPUT-CPU(node_t* G, node_t node):
2      if HAS-LEFT-SIBLING(node) and IS-UPDATED(LEFT-SIBLING(node)) then
3          node.left ← FINDORPUT-CPU(G, LEFT-SIBLING(node))
4      if HAS-RIGHT-SIBLING(node) and IS-UPDATED(RIGHT-SIBLING(node)) then
5          node.right ← FINDORPUT-CPU(G, RIGHT-SIBLING(node))
6      addr ← STORE(G, node)
7      return addr
```

---

not yet present is typically done by means of recursion (outlined by Alg. 1). For now, ignore the red underlined text. The STORE function returns the address of the given node in G, if present, otherwise it stores the node and returns its address, and the FINDORPUT-CPU function first recursively checks whether the siblings of the node are stored, and if not, stores them, after which the node itself is stored. A node has pointers left and right to addresses of G, and there are functions to check for the existence of, and retrieve the siblings of a node.

In the incremental approach, when creating a successor s' of a state s, the tree for s, say $T(s)$, is used as the basis for the tree $T(s')$. When $T(s')$ is created, each node inside it is first initialised to the corresponding node in $T(s)$, and the leaves are updated for the new tree. This 'updated' status propagates up: when a non-leaf has an updated sibling, its corresponding G pointer must be updated when $T(s')$ is stored in G, but for any non-updated sibling, the non-leaf can keep its G pointer. When incorporating the red underlined text in Alg. 1, the incremental version of the function is obtained. With this version, tree storage often results in fewer calls to STORE, i.e., fewer memory accesses.

There are two main challenges when considering GPU incremental tree storage: 1) Recursion is detrimental to performance, as call stacks are stored in global memory (and with thousands of threads, a lot of memory would be needed for call stacks), and 2) The nodes of a tree tend to be spread all over the hash table, potentially leading to many random accesses. To address these, we propose a procedure in which threads in a block store sets of trees together in parallel.

5.2 GPU Tree Generation

When states are represented by trees, the tile of each thread block cannot store entire states, but it can store the roots of trees. To speed up successor generation, and avoid repeated uncoalesced global memory accessing, the trees of those roots are retrieved and stored in the shared memory (state cache) by the thread block. Once this has been done, successor generation can commence.

Fig. 3 shows an example of the state cache evolving over time as a thread generates the successor $s' = <A,B',C,D,E'>$ of $s = <A,B,C,D,E>$, with the trees as in Fig. 2. Each square represents a k-bit cache entry. In addition to two entries needed to store a node, we also use one (grey) entry to store two *cache pointers* or indices, and assume that k bits suffice to store two pointers (in practice, we use $k = 32$, which is enough, given the small size of the state cache). Hence, every pair of white squares followed by a grey square constitutes one cache slot. Initially (shown at the top of the figure), the tile has a cache pointer to the root of s, of

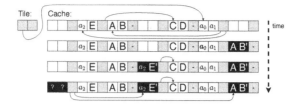

Fig. 3: Successor generation: deriving <A,B',C,D,E'> from <A,B,C,D,E>.

which we know that it contains the $\mathcal{G}$ addresses a_0 and a_1 to refer to its siblings. In turn, this root points, via its cache pointers, to the locally stored copies of its siblings. The non-leaf one contains the global address a_2. A leaf has no cache pointers, denoted by '-'. When creating s', first, the designated thread constructs the leaf <A,B'>, by executing the appropriate generated CUDA function (see Section 4), and stores it in the cache. In Fig. 3, it is coloured black, to indicate that it is marked as new. Next, the thread creates a copy of <a_2,E>, together with its cache pointers, and updates it to <a_2,E'>. Finally it creates a new root, with cache pointers pointing to the newly inserted nodes. This root still has global address gaps to be filled in (the '?' marks), since it is still unknown where the new nodes will be stored in $\mathcal{G}$.

The reason that we store global addresses in the cache is not to access the nodes they point to, but to achieve incremental tree storage: in the example, as the global address a_2 is stored in the cache, there is no need to find <C,D> in $\mathcal{G}$ when the new tree is stored; instead, we can directly construct <a_2,E'>. This contributes to limiting the number of required global memory accesses.

Note that there is no recursion. Given a model, the code generator determines the structure of all state trees, and based on this, code to fetch all the nodes of a tree and to construct new trees is generated. As we do not consider the dynamic creation and destruction of FSMs, all states have the same tree structure.

5.3   GPU Tree Storage at Block Level

Once a block has finished generating the successors of the states referred to by its tile, the state cache content must be synchronised with $\mathcal{G}$. Alg. 2 presents how this is done. The FINDORPUT-MANY function is executed by all threads in the block simultaneously. It consists of an outer **while**-loop (l.5-28), that is executed as long as there is work to be done. The code uses a cooperative group called **bg**, which is created to coincide with the size of a bucket (**bucketsize**). When no buckets are used, these groups can be interpreted as consisting of only a single thread each. At l.4, the **offset** of each thread is determined, i.e., its ID inside its group, ranging from 0 to the size of the group.

Every thread that still has *work to do* (l.5) enters the **for**-loop of l.7-27, in which the content of the state cache is scanned. The parallel scanning works as follows: every thread first considers the node at position tid − **offset** of the cache, with tid being the thread's block-local ID. This node is assigned to the thread with **bg** ID 0. If that index is still within the cache limits, all threads of

Algorithm 2: Tree-based Find-or-put-many, at thread block level.

```
1   device function FINDORPUT-MANY(node_t* 𝒢):
2       node_t p, q; index_t addr; bool work_to_do ← true; bool ready; byte ballot_result
3       auto bg ← TILED-PARTITION(bucketsize)(THIS-THREAD-BLOCK())
4       byte offset ← bg.THREAD-RANK()
5       while work_to_do do
6           work_to_do ← false
7           for i ← tid − offset; i < CACHE_SIZE; i ← i + BLOCK_SIZE do
8               ready ← false
9               if i + offset < CACHE_SIZE then
10                  p ← cache[i + offset]
11                  if IS-NEW-LEAF(p) then ready ← true
12                  else if IS-NEW-NONLEAF(p) then
13                      if LEFT-GAP(p) then
14                          cache[i + offset] ← SET-LEFT-GADDR(p, cache[LEFT-CADDR(p)])
15                      if RIGHT-GAP(p) then
16                          cache[i + offset] ← SET-RIGHT-GADDR(p, cache[RIGHT-CADDR(p)])
17                      if ¬(LEFT-OR-RIGHT-GAP(p)) then ready ← true
18                      else work_to_do ← true
19              ballot_result ← bg.BALLOT(ready)
20              while ballot_result do
21                  lane ← FIND-FIRST-SET(ballot_result) - 1; q ← bg.SHUFFLE(p, lane)
22                  addr ← FINDORPUT-SINGLE(bg, 𝒢, q)
23                  if offset = lane then
24                      ready ← false
25                      if addr = FULL then signal hash table full
26                      else SET-GADDR(cache[i], addr)
27                  ballot_result ← bg.BALLOT(ready)
28          work_to_do ← bg.BALLOT(work_to_do)
```

bg have to move along, regardless of whether they have a node to check or not. At the next iteration of the for-loop, the thread jumps over BLOCK_SIZE nodes as long as the index is within the cache limits.

The main goal of this loop is to check which nodes are ready for synchronisation with $\mathcal{G}$. Initially, this is the case for all nodes without global address gaps (see Subsection 5.2). Each thread first checks whether its own index is still within the cache limits (l.9). If so, the node p is retrieved from the cache at l.10. If it is a new leaf, ready is set to true, to indicate that the active thread is ready for storage (l.11). If the node is a new non-leaf (l.12), it is checked whether the node still has global address gaps. If it has a gap for the left sibling (l.13), this left sibling is inspected via the cache pointer to this sibling (retrieved with the function LEFT-CADDR (l.14)). The function SET-LEFT-GADDR checks whether the cache pointers of that sibling have been replaced by a global memory address, and if so, uses that address to fill the gap. The same is done for the right sibling at l.15-16. If, after these operations, the node p contains no gaps (l.17), ready is set to true. If the node still contains a gap, another loop iteration is required, hence work_to_do is set to true (l.18).

At l.19, the threads in the group perform a ballot, resulting in a bit sequence indicating for which threads ready is true. As long as this is the case for at least one thread, the while-loop at l.20-27 is executed. The function FIND-FIRST-SET identifies the least significant bit set to 1 in ballot_result (l.21), and the SHUFFLE instruction results in all threads in bg retrieving the node of the corresponding bg thread. This node is subsequently stored by bg, by calling

FINDORPUT-SINGLE (l.22) (explained later). Finally, the thread owning the node (l.23) resets its `ready` flag (l.24), and if the hash table is considered full, reports this globally (l.25). Otherwise, it records the global address of the stored node (l.26). After that, `ballot_result` is updated (l.27). Finally, once the `for`-loop is exited, the `bg` threads determine whether they still have more work to do (l.28).

5.4   Single Node Storage at Bucket Group Level

In this section, we address how individual nodes are stored by a cooperative group `bg`. Before we explain the algorithm for this, Alg. 3, in detail, we consider our options for hashing, and propose a novel combination of existing techniques.

In Section 2, we argued that Cuckoo hashing is very effective on a GPU. However, as it frequently moves elements, it is not suitable for a single hash table, since the non-leaves of a tree refer to the positions of other nodes. We address this by maintaining two hash tables, one for tree roots, and one for the other nodes, as done in [26]. The roots are then not referred to, and hence Cuckoo hashing can be applied on the root table.

In fact, when using two hash tables, we can be even more memory-efficient. In [26], it was shown that *Cleary tables* [13, 15] can be very effective to store state spaces. To handle collisions in Cleary tables, *order-preserving bidirectional linear probing* [2] is used, which involves moving nodes to preserve their order. This makes Cleary tables, like Cuckoo hashing, not suitable to store entire trees, but they can be used to store the *roots* of the trees. In a Cleary table for roots of size $2k$, each root r is hashed (bit scrambled) with a hash function h to a $2k$ bit sequence, from which $w < k$ bits are taken to be used as the *address* to store r in a table with exactly 2^w buckets, and at this position, the remaining $2k - w$ bits (the *remainder*) are actually stored. To enable decompression, h must be invertible; given a remainder and an address, h^{-1} can be applied to obtain r.

In a multi-threaded CPU context, this approach scales well [26], but the parallel approach of [26,45] divides a Cleary table into *regions*, and sometimes, a region must be locked by a thread to safely reorder nodes. Unfortunately, the use of any form of locking, also fine-grained locking implemented with atomic operations, is detrimental for GPU performance. Further, the absence of coherent caches in GPUs means that expensive global memory accesses may be needed when a thread repeatedly checks the status of an acquired lock.

As an elegant alternative, we propose *Cleary-Cuckoo hashing*, which combines Cleary compression with Cuckoo hashing. We use m hash functions that are invertible (as with Cuckoo hashing) and capable of scrambling the bits of a root to a $2k$ bit sequence (as in Cleary tables). When we apply a function h_i ($0 \le i < m$) on a root r, we get a $2k$ bit sequence, of which we use w bits for an address d, and store at d the remainder r' consisting of $2k - w + \lceil \log_2(m) \rceil + 1$ bits. The $\lceil \log_2(m) \rceil$ bits are needed to store the ID of the used hash function (i), and the final bit is needed to indicate that the root is *new* (unexplored). It is possible to retrieve r by applying h_i^{-1} on d and r' without the hash function ID and the *new* bit. When a collision occurs, the encountered root is evicted,

---

Algorithm 3: Single node find-or-put, at bucket group level.

---

1 **device function** $index\_t$ FINDORPUT-SINGLE($tile\_t$ bg, $node\_t^*$ $\mathcal{G}$, $node\_t$ p):
2    $node\_t$ q; $index\_t$ addr
3   (q, addr) ← FOP-CUCKOO-ROOT(bg, $\mathcal{G}$, p)
4   **for** i ← 0; q $\neq$ p **and** i < MAX_EVICT; i ← i + 1 **do**
5   (q, addr) ← FOP-CUCKOO-ROOT(bg, $\mathcal{G}$, q)
6   **return** (i = MAX_EVICT? FULL; addr)

7 **device function** ($node\_t$, $index\_t$) FOP-CUCKOO-ROOT($tile\_t$ bg, $node\_t^*$ $\mathcal{G}$, $node\_t$ p):
8    $comprnode\_t$ cp, cq; $node\_t$ q
9   hs ← GET-HASH-START(p); $byte$ offset ← bg.THREAD-RANK()
10   **for** i ← 0; i < NUM_HASH_FUNCTIONS; i ← i + 1 **do**
11   (addr, cp) ← ADDR-COMPR-ROOT(p, $h_{(hs+i)}$ mod NUM_HASH_FUNCTIONS)
12   (cq, pos) ← HT-FIND(bg, offset, $\mathcal{G}$, addr, cp)
13   **if** cq = cp **then return** (p, addr + pos)
14   **if** cq = EMPTY **then**
15   hs ← $h_{(hs+i)}$ mod NUM_HASH_FUNCTIONS
16   **break**
17   **if** i = NUM_HASH_FUNCTIONS **then** (cp, addr) ← ADDR-COMPR-ROOT(p, hs)
18   (cq, pos) = HT-INSERT-CUCKOO(bg, offset, $\mathcal{G}$, addr, cp)
19   **if** cq $\neq$ EMPTY **and** cq $\neq$ cp **then**
20   q ← GET-DECOMPR-ROOT(cq, addr)
21   **return** (q, addr + pos)
22   **return** (p, addr + pos)

---

decompressed, and stored again using the hash function next in line for that root. We refer to the application of Cleary compression to roots as *root compression*.

Alg. 3 presents one version of the FINDORPUT-SINGLE function, to which a call in Alg. 2 is redirected when a root is provided. Here, $\mathcal{G}$ is a Cleary-Cuckoo table that is only used to store roots. In FINDORPUT-SINGLE, a second function FOP-CUCKOO-ROOT (l.7-22) is called repeatedly, as long as nodes are evicted or until the pre-configured MAX_EVICT has been reached, which prevents infinite eviction sequences (l.4). The function FOP-CUCKOO-ROOT returns the address where the given node was found or stored, and a node, which is either the node that had to be inserted or the one that was already present.

In the FOP-CUCKOO-ROOT function, lines highlighted in purple are specific for root compression, i.e., Cleary compression of roots, while the green highlighted lines concern Cuckoo hashing, addressing node eviction. The ID of the first hash function to be used for node p, encoded in p itself, is stored in hs (l.9), and each thread determines its bg offset. Next, the thread iterates over the hash functions, starting with function hs (l.10-16). The $\mathcal{G}$ address and node remainder are computed at l.11. If the node is new, the remainder is marked as new. If root compression is not used, we have p = cp. Then, the function HT-FIND is called to check for the presence of the remainder in the bucket starting at addr (l.12). If HT-FIND returns the remainder, then it was already present (l.13), and this can be returned. Note that the returned address is (addr + pos), i.e., the offset at which the remainder can be found inside the bucket is added to addr. Alternatively, if EMPTY is returned, the node is not present and the bucket is not yet full. In this case, a bucket has been found where the node can be stored. The used hash function is stored in hs (l.15) and the for-loop is exited (l.16).

At l.17, if a suitable bucket for insertion has not been found, the initial hs is selected again. At l.18, the function HT-INSERT-CUCKOO is called to insert cp.

Algorithm 4: Single node insertion, at bucket group level.

---

1   **device function** ($comprnode\_t$, $index\_t$) HT-INSERT-CUCKOO($tile\_t$ bg, $byte$ offset, $node\_t*$
    $\mathcal{G}$, $index\_t$ addr, $comprnode\_t$ cp):

2     $comprnode\_t$ cq ← $\mathcal{G}$[addr + offset]; $byte$ ballot_result ← bg.BALLOT(cq = cp)

3   **if** ballot_result **then return** (cp, FIND-FIRST-SET(ballot_result) - 1)

4   **while** ballot_result ← bg.BALLOT(cq = EMPTY) **do**

5   **if** offset = FIND-FIRST-SET(ballot_result) - 1 **then**

6   cq ← ATOMICCAS($\mathcal{G}$[addr + offset], EMPTY, cp)

7   cq ← bg.SHUFFLE(cq, FIND-FIRST-SET(ballot_result) - 1)

8   **if** cq = EMPTY **or** cq = cp **then return** (cq, FIND-FIRST-SET(ballot_result) - 1)

9   cq ← $\mathcal{G}$[addr + offset]

10     $byte$ i ← GET-EVICTION-POS(cp)

11   **if** offset = i **then**   cq ← ATOMICEXCH($\mathcal{G}$[addr + offset], cp)

12   cq ← bg.SHUFFLE(cq, i)

13   **return** (cq, i)

This function is presented in Alg. 4. Finally, if a value other than the original remainder cp or EMPTY is returned, another (remainder of a) node has been evicted, which is decompressed and returned at l.20-21. Otherwise, p is returned with its address (l.22). When Cuckoo hashing is not used, evictions do not occur, and at l.20-21, it is returned that the bucket is full.

Finally, we present HT-INSERT-CUCKOO in Alg. 4. The function HT-FIND is not presented, but it is almost equal to l.2-3 of Alg. 4. At l.2, each thread in bg reads its part of the bucket $\mathcal{G}$[addr + offset], and checks if it contains cp, the remainder of p. If it is found anywhere in the bucket, the remainder with its position is returned (l.3). In the while-loop at l.4-9, it is attempted to insert cp in an empty position. In every iteration, an empty position is selected (l.5) and the corresponding thread tries to atomically insert cp (l.6). At l.7, the outcome is shared among the threads. If it is either EMPTY or the remainder itself, it can be returned (l.8). Otherwise, the bucket is read again (l.9). If insertion does not succeed, l.10 is reached, where a hash function is used by GET-EVICTION-POS to hash cp to a bucket position. The corresponding thread exchanges cp with the node stored at that position (l.11). After the evicted node has been shared with the other threads (l.12), it is returned together with its position (l.13).

6   Experiments

We implemented a code generator in PYTHON, using TEXTX [17] and JINJA2,[3] that accepts an SLCO model and produces CUDA C++ code to explore its state space. The code is compiled with CUDA 11.4 targeting compute capability 7.5. Experiments were conducted on a machine running LINUX MINT 20 with a 4-core INTEL CORE i7-7700 3.6 GHz, 32GB RAM, and a Titan RTX GPU.

The goal of the experiments is to assess how fast GPU next state computation with the tree database is w.r.t. 1) the various options we have for hashing, 2) state-of-the-art CPU tools, and 3) other GPU tools. For 2), we compare with multi-core Depth-First Search (DFS) of SPIN 6.5.1 [22] and (explicit-state) multi-core Breadth-First Search (BFS) of LTSMIN 3.0.2 [24, 28].

---

[3] https://palletsprojects.com/p/jinja/.

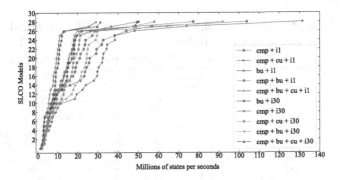

Fig. 4: Speed obtained by different GPU configurations.

In our implementation, we use 32 invertible hash functions. *Root compression* (CMP) can be turned on or off. When selected, we have a root table with 2^{32} elements, 32 bits each, and a non-root table with 2^{29} elements, 64 bits each. This enables storing 58-bit roots (two pointers to the non-root table) in $58 - 32 + \lceil \log_2(32) \rceil + 1 = 32$ bits. When using *buckets with more than one element* (CMP+BU), we have root buckets of size 8, and non-root buckets of size 16. The non-root buckets make full use of the cache line, but the root buckets do not. Making the latter larger means that too many bits for root addressing are lost for root compression to work (the remainders will be too large).

Root compression allows turning *Cuckoo hashing* on (CMP(+BU)+CU) or off (CMP(+BU)). When it is off, essentially Cleary-Cuckoo is still performed, except that evictions are not allowed, meaning that hashing fails as soon as all possible 32 buckets for a node are occupied.

In the configuration BU, neither root compression nor Cuckoo hashing is applied. We use one table with 2^{30} 64-bit elements and buckets of size 16. For reasons related to storing global addresses in the state cache, we cannot make the table larger. The 32 hash functions are used without allowing evictions.

Finally, *multiple iterations* can be run per kernel launch. Shared memory is wiped when a kernel execution terminates, but the state cache content can be reused from one iteration to the next when a kernel executes multiple iterations, by which trees already in the cache do not need to be fetched again from the tree database. We identified 30 iterations to be effective in general (i30), and experimented with a single iteration per kernel launch (i1).

With the CPU tools, we performed reachability analysis on 1- and 4-core configurations, denoted by SP-1 and SP-4 for SPIN, and LM-1 and LM-4 for LTSMIN. We only enabled state compression and basic reachability (without property checking), to favour fast exploration of large state spaces.

For benchmarks, we used models from the BEEM benchmarks [42] of concurrent systems, translated to SLCO and PROMELA (for SPIN). We scaled some of them up to have larger state spaces. Those are marked in Table 1 with '+'. Timeout is set to 3600 seconds for all benchmarks.

Table 1: Millions of states per second for various reachability tools and configurations. Pink cells: out of memory. Yellow cells: timeout. Green cell: best average. O.M.: out of memory at initialisation. SU: speedup of (CMP + i30) vs. (LM-1).

Model	States	SP-1	SP-4	LM-1	LM-4	BITS	CR	BU +i1	CMP +i1	CMP+BU +i1	CMP+CU +i1	CMP +i30	CMP+CU +i30	SU
adding.20+	84,709,120	1.128	3.223	1.211	3.938	100	1.96	49.597	56.793	48.879	36.934	74.026	47.694	61x
adding.50+	529,767,730	0.856	O.M.	1.354	5.356	100	1.96	48.403	103.872	77.243	49.625	131.444	57.968	97x
anderson.6	18,206,917	0.623	1.362	0.516	1.309	122	1.82	14.814	16.035	13.647	11.265	34.111	17.649	62x
anderson.7	538,699,029	0.599	O.M.	0.448	1.583	141	2.75	9.309	21.192	14.244	10.426	22.326	10.435	41x
at.5	31,999,440	0.646	1.495	0.653	1.880	85	1.86	19.894	29.158	23.633	18.204	38.457	21.375	59x
at.6	160,589,600	0.454	0.869	0.695	2.387	85	1.90	17.901	38.275	27.275	19.498	38.418	20.359	55x
at.7	819,243,816	0.527	O.M.	0.666	2.372	97	1.98	12.415	23.629	17.381	13.194	22.329	13.378	34x
at.8+	3,739,953,204	0.534	O.M.	0.555	1.817	97	1.97	5.452	7.246	7.593	11.698	7.287	11.854	13x
bakery.5	7,866,401	1.400	2.570	0.410	0.904	140	2.51	11.504	7.838	7.585	6.407	19.362	12.782	47x
bakery.7	29,047,471	1.228	2.592	0.580	1.618	140	2.49	13.236	9.361	9.021	7.698	29.783	17.456	51x
bakery.8	841,696,300	0.760	1.269	0.690	2.436	140	2.40	3.745	29.410	23.957	17.116	32.778	18.215	48x
elevator2.3	7,667,712	0.554	1.099	0.463	0.985	189	3.96	4.890	3.259	3.185	2.817	6.261	4.827	14x
elevator2.4	91,226,112	0.263	0.561	0.623	1.945	213	3.97	3.025	3.746	2.907	3.087	3.267	2.703	5x
elevator2.5+	1,016,070,144	0.189	O.M.	0.473	1.630	317	5.95	1.540	1.871	1.545	1.520	1.839	1.491	4x
frogs.4	17,443,219	1.044	2.228	0.553	1.423	219	3.49	8.423	10.253	8.686	7.767	11.549	8.168	21x
frogs.5	182,772,126	0.531	1.048	0.751	2.630	251	3.84	6.766	9.573	8.214	6.898	9.846	6.943	13x
lamport.6	8,717,688	1.277	1.375	0.490	1.096	96	1.91	11.813	5.126	5.225	4.697	27.966	19.335	57x
lamport.7	38,717,846	1.001	1.822	0.672	1.979	116	1.98	18.176	23.205	18.915	16.170	34.321	20.641	51x
lamport.8	62,669,317	0.917	1.776	0.698	2.194	116	1.98	17.717	25.947	21.015	17.132	35.387	20.864	50x
loyd.2	362,880	1.278	0.758	0.255	0.497	90	1.05	7.339	4.204	4.220	3.723	3.243	3.930	13x
loyd.3	239,500,800	0.633	O.M.	0.650	2.338	114	1.96	18.268	44.073	28.970	26.556	48.328	28.248	74x
mcs.5	60,556,519	0.706	0.615	0.453	1.489	148	2.97	14.504	24.498	19.537	14.710	29.635	15.912	65x
mcs.6	332,544	1.240	0.244	0.181	0.331	145	2.63	6.037	3.003	3.097	2.751	3.446	3.131	19x
peterson.5	131,064,750	0.711	1.617	0.727	2.435	140	2.98	16.034	31.975	21.394	17.813	32.331	16.681	42x
peterson.6	174,495,861	0.852	0.756	0.720	2.451	140	2.98	15.503	32.725	22.975	17.198	34.902	17.030	45x
peterson.7	142,471,098	0.683	1.496	0.652	2.269	175	2.63	13.077	25.667	18.603	13.868	26.183	13.120	37x
phils.6	14,348,906	0.208	0.422	0.240	0.670	150	1.49	4.410	7.458	5.528	4.789	7.084	4.543	30x
phils.7	71,934,773	0.179	0.297	0.246	0.764	151	1.49	3.585	5.702	4.762	4.064	5.382	3.885	22x
phils.8	43,046,720	0.160	0.361	0.243	0.788	160	1.49	4.842	9.151	6.987	5.119	8.973	5.089	37x
szymanski.5	79,518,740	0.665	1.571	0.535	1.815	180	2.91	11.944	17.803	14.416	11.653	18.357	11.674	33x
Average		0.728	1.309	0.58	1.844	n/a		13.139	21.068	16.355	12.813	26.621	15.246	40x

Fig. 4 compares the speeds of the different GPU configurations in millions of states per second, averaged over 5 runs. For each configuration, we sorted the data to observe the overall trend. The higher the speed the better. The CMP + i30 mode (without Cuckoo hashing or larger buckets) is the fastest for the majority of models. On the other hand, it fails to complete exploration for at.8, the largest state space with 3.7 billion states, due to running out of memory. If Cuckoo hashing is enabled with root compression, all state spaces are successfully explored, which confirms that higher load factors can be achieved [4]. However, Cuckoo hashing negatively impacts performance, which contradicts [4]. Although it is difficult to pinpoint the cause for this, it is clear that it results from our hashing being done in addition to the exploration tasks, while in papers on GPU hash tables [1,4], hashing is analysed in isolation. With the extra variables and operations needed for exploration, hashing should be lightweight, and Cuckoo hashing introduces handling evictions. The more complex code is compiled to a less performant program, even when evictions do not occur.

Table 1 compares GPU performance with SPIN and LTSMIN. We refer to our tool as GPUEXPLORE + SLCO. From the results of Fig. 4, we selected a set of configurations demonstrating the impact of the various options. For each model, BITS and CR gives the state vector length in bits and the compression ratio, defined as (number of roots × number of leaves per tree) / (number of nodes). With the compression ratio, we measure how effective the node sharing is, compared to if we had stored each state individually without sharing. In

Table 2: Millions of states per second for various GPU tools.

Tool	anderson.6	anderson.7	lamport.8	peterson.5	peterson.6	peterson.7	szymanski.5
GRAPPLE	2.138	14.299	n/a	10.941	9.074	8.967	n/a
GPUEXPLORE 2.0	15.863	8.737	33.063	16.874	16.705	13.581	26.454
GPUEXPLORE + SLCO (CMP+i30)	34.111	22.326	35.387	32.331	34.902	26.183	18.357

addition, the speed in millions of states per second is given. Regarding out of memory, we are aware that SPIN has other, slower, compression options, but we only considered the fastest, to favour the CPU speeds. Times are restricted to exploration; code generation and compilation always take a few seconds. The best GPU results are highlighted in bold. To compute the speedup (SU), the result of CMP + i30, the overall best configuration, has been divided by the LM-1 result (the single-core configuration that completely explored all state spaces except one). All GPU experiments have been done with 512 threads per block, and 3,240 blocks (45 blocks per SM). We identified this configuration as being effective for **anderson.6**, and used it for all models.

While LTSMIN tends to achieve near-linear speed-ups (compare LM-1 and LM-4), the speed of GPUEXPLORE + SLCO heavily depends on the model. For some models, as the state spaces of instances become larger, the speed increases, and for others, it decreases. The exact cause for this is hard to identify, and we plan to work on further optimisations. For instance, the branching factor, i.e., average number of successors of a state, plays a role here, as large branching factors favour parallel computation (many threads will become active quickly).

Our overall fastest configuration does not use larger buckets, nor Cuckoo hashing. Regarding buckets, as already noted in Section 3, starting with the TURING architecture, NVIDIA GPUs are less sensitive to uncoalesced accesses, and our results confirm that. Performing fewer tasks in parallel seems to be more harmful for performance than a larger number of uncoalesced accesses.

Finally, Table 2 compares GPUEXPLORE + SLCO with GPUEXPLORE 2.0 and GRAPPLE. A comparison with PARAMOC was not possible, as it targets very different types of (sequential) models. The models we selected are those available for at least two of the tools we considered. Unfortunately, GRAPPLE does not (yet) support reading PROMELA models. Instead, a number of models are encoded directly into its source code, and we were limited to checking only those models. It can be observed that in the majority of cases, our tool achieves the highest speeds, which is surprising, as the trees we use tend to lead to more global memory accesses, but it is also encouraging to further pursue this direction.

7   Conclusions and Future Work

We discussed new algorithms to achieve a GPU tree database, which enables memory-efficient explicit state space exploration for FSMs with data. We proposed Cleary-Cuckoo hashing, which makes it possible to use, for the first time, Cleary compression on GPUs. Experiments show processing speeds of up to 131 million trees per second. In the last decade, new GPUs have been increasingly effective for state space exploration [10], and in the future, they are expected to be more capable of handling thread divergence, which still heavily occurs when accessing $\mathcal{G}$. Therefore, we are optimistic about further improvements. In the future, we will focus on optimisations and verifying temporal logic formulae.

Data Availability Statement. The datasets generated and analysed during the current study are available in the Zenodo repository [39].

References

1. Alcantara, D.A., Volkov, V., Sengupta, S., Mitzenmacher, M., Owens, J.D., Amenta, N.: Building an Efficient Hash Table on the GPU. In: GPU Computing Gems Jade Edition, pp. 39–53. Morgan Kaufmann Publishers Inc. (2012). https://doi.org/10.1016/B978-0-12-385963-1.00004-6
2. Amble, O., Knuth, D.: Ordered Hash Tables. The Computer Journal **17**(2), 135–142 (1974). https://doi.org/10.1093/comjnl/17.2.135
3. Ashkiani, S., Farach-Colton, M., Owens, J.: A Dynamic Hash Table for the GPU. In: IPDPS. pp. 419–429. ACM (2018). https://doi.org/10.1109/IPDPS.2018.00052
4. Awad, M., Ashkiani, S., Porumbescu, S., Farach-Colton, M., Owens, J.: Better GPU Hash Tables. Tech. Rep. 2108.07232, arXiV (2021). https://doi.org/10.48550/arXiv.2108.07232
5. Barnat, J., Bauch, P., Brim, L., Češka, M.: Designing Fast LTL Model Checking Algorithms for Many-Core GPUs. JPDC **72**(9), 1083–1097 (2012). https://doi.org/10.1016/j.jpdc.2011.10.015
6. Bartocci, E., DeFrancisco, R., Smolka, S.A.: Towards a GPGPU-parallel SPIN Model Checker. In: SPIN 2014. pp. 87–96. ACM, New York, NY, USA (2014). https://doi.org/10.1145/2632362.2632379
7. Blom, S., Lisser, B., van de Pol, J., Weber, M.: A Database Approach to Distributed State Space Generation. Electron. Notes Theor. Comput. Sci. **198**(1), 17–32 (2008). https://doi.org/10.1016/j.entcs.2007.10.018
8. Bošnački, D., Edelkamp, S., Sulewski, D., Wijs, A.: Parallel Probabilistic Model Checking on General Purpose Graphics Processors. STTT **13**(1), 21–35 (2011). https://doi.org/10.1007/s10009-010-0176-4
9. Bussi, L., Ciancia, V., Gadducci, F.: Towards a Spatial Model Checker on GPU. In: FORTE. LNCS, vol. 12719, pp. 188–196. Springer (2021). https://doi.org/10.1007/978-3-030-78089-0_12
10. Cassee, N., Neele, T., Wijs, A.: On the Scalability of the GPUexplore Explicit-State Model Checker. In: GaM. EPTCS, vol. 263, pp. 38–52. Open Publishing Association (2017). https://doi.org/10.4204/EPTCS.263.4
11. Cassee, N., Wijs, A.: Analysing the Performance of GPU Hash Tables for State Space Exploration. In: GaM. pp. 1–15. EPTCS, Open Publishing Association (2017). https://doi.org/10.4204/EPTCS.263.1
12. Češka, M., Pilař, P., Paoletti, N., Brim, L., Kwiatkowska, M.: PRISM-PSY: Precise GPU-Accelerated Parameter Synthesis for Stochastic Systems. In: TACAS. LNCS, vol. 9636, pp. 367–384. Springer (2016). https://doi.org/10.1007/978-3-642-54862-8
13. Cleary, J.: Compact Hash Tables Using Bidirectional Linear Probing. IEEE Trans. on Computers **c-33**(9), 828–834 (1984). https://doi.org/10.1109/TC.1984.1676499
14. Cormen, T.H., Leiserson, C.E., Rivest, R.L., Stein, C.: Introduction to Algorithms, 3rd Edition. MIT Press (2009)

15. Darragh, J., Cleary, J., Witten, I.: Bonsai: A Compact Representation of Trees. Software - Practice and Experience **23**(3), 277–291 (1993). https://doi.org/10.1002/spe.4380230305

16. DeFrancisco, R., Cho, S., Ferdman, M., Smolka, S.A.: Swarm model checking on the GPU. Int. J. Softw. Tools Technol. Transf. **22**(5), 583–599 (2020). https://doi.org/10.1007/s10009-020-00576-x

17. Dejanović, I., Vaderna, R., Milosavljević, G., Vuković, Ž.: TextX: A Python tool for Domain-Specific Language implementation. Knowledge-Based Systems **115**, 1–4 (2017). https://doi.org/10.1016/j.knosys.2016.10.023

18. Edelkamp, S., Sulewski, D.: Efficient Explicit-State Model Checking on General Purpose Graphics Processors. In: SPIN. LNCS, vol. 6349, pp. 106–123. Springer (2010). https://doi.org/10.1007/978-3-642-16164-3_8

19. Edelkamp, S., Sulewski, D.: External memory breadth-first search with delayed duplicate detection on the GPU. In: MoChArt. LNCS, vol. 6572, pp. 12–31. Springer (2010). https://doi.org/10.1007/978-3-642-20674-0_2

20. García, I., Lefebvre, S., Hornus, S., Lasram, A.: Coherent Parallel Hashing. ACM Trans. Graph. **30**(6), 161 (2011). https://doi.org/10.1145/2070781.2024195

21. Holzmann, G.: The Model Checker Spin. IEEE Trans. Software Eng. **23**(5), 279–295 (1997). https://doi.org/10.1109/32.588521

22. Holzmann, G., Bošnački, D.: The Design of a Multicore Extension of the SPIN Model Checker. IEEE Trans. on Software Engineering **33**(10), 659–674 (2007). https://doi.org/10.1109/TSE.2007.70724

23. Jünger, D., Kobus, R., Müller, A., Hundt, C., Xu, K., Liu, W., Schmidt, B.: WarpCore: A Library for Fast Hash Tables. In: HiPC. pp. 11–20. IEEE (2020). https://doi.org/10.1109/HiPC50609.2020.00015

24. Kant, G., Laarman, A., Meijer, J., Pol, J.v., Blom, S., Dijk, T.: LTSmin: High-Performance Language-Independent Model Checking. In: TACAS. LNCS, vol. 9035, pp. 692–707. Springer (2015). https://doi.org/10.1007/978-3-662-46681-0_61

25. Khan, M., Hassan, O., Khan, S.: Accelerating SpMV Multiplication in Probabilistic Model Checkers Using GPUs. In: ICTAC. LNCS, vol. 12819, pp. 86–104. Springer (2021). https://doi.org/10.1007/978-3-030-85315-0_6

26. Laarman, A.: Optimal Compression of Combinatorial State Spaces. Innov. Syst. Softw. Eng. **15**, 235–251 (2019). https://doi.org/10.1007/s11334-019-00341-7

27. Laarman, A., van de Pol, J., Weber, M.: Parallel Recursive State Compression for Free. In: SPIN. LNCS, vol. 6823, pp. 38–56. Springer (2011). https://doi.org/10.1007/978-3-642-22306-8_4

28. Laarman, A.: Scalable Multi-Core Model Checking. Ph.D. thesis, University of Twente (2014). https://doi.org/10.3990/1.9789036536561

29. Lee, C.: Representation of Switching Circuits by Binary-Decision Programs. Bell System Technical Journal **38**, 985–999 (1959). https://doi.org/10.1002/j.1538-7305.1959.tb01585.x

30. Leiserson, C.E., Thompson, N.C., Emer, J.S., Kuszmaul, B.C., Lampson, B.W., Sanchez, D., Schardl, T.B.: There's Plenty of Room at the Top: What Will Drive Computer Performance After Moore's Law? Science **368**(6495) (2020). https://doi.org/10.1126/science.aam9744

31. Lessley, B.: Data-Parallel Hashing Techniques for GPU Architectures. IEEE Trans. Parallel Distributed Syst. **31**(1), 237–250 (2019). https://doi.org/10.1109/TPDS.2019.2929768

32. Merrill, D., Grimshaw, A.: High Performance and Scalable Radix Sorting: a Case Study of Implementing Dynamic Parallelism for GPU Computing. Parallel Process. Lett. **21**(2), 245–272 (2011). https://doi.org/10.1142/S0129626411000187

33. Neele, T., Wijs, A., Bošnački, D., van de Pol, J.: Partial Order Reduction for GPU Model Checking. In: ATVA. LNCS, vol. 9938, pp. 357–374. Springer (2016). https://doi.org/10.1007/978-3-319-46520-3_23

34. Osama, M.: GPU Enabled Automated Reasoning. Ph.D. thesis, Eindhoven University of Technology (2022), ISBN: 978-90-386-5445-4

35. Osama, M., Gaber, L., Hussein, A.I., Mahmoud, H.: An Efficient SAT-Based Test Generation Algorithm with GPU Accelerator. J. Electron. Test. **34**(5), 511–527 (2018). https://doi.org/10.1007/s10836-018-5747-4

36. Osama, M., Wijs, A.: Parallel SAT Simplification on GPU Architectures. In: TACAS. LNCS, vol. 11427, pp. 21–40. Springer (2019). https://doi.org/10.1007/978-3-030-17462-0_2

37. Osama, M., Wijs, A.: SIGmA: GPU Accelerated Simplification of SAT Formulas. In: IFM. LNCS, vol. 11918, pp. 514–522. Springer (2019). https://doi.org/10.1007/978-3-030-34968-4_29

38. Osama, M., Wijs, A.: GPU Acceleration of Bounded Model Checking with ParaFROST. In: CAV, Part II. LNCS, vol. 12760, pp. 447–460. Springer (2021). https://doi.org/10.1007/978-3-030-81688-9_21

39. Osama, M., Wijs, A.: Artifact for A GPU Tree Database for Many-Core Explicit State Space Exploration (2023). https://doi.org/10.5281/zenodo.7509129

40. Osama, M., Wijs, A., Biere, A.: SAT Solving with GPU Accelerated In-processing. In: TACAS. LNCS, vol. 12651, pp. 133–151. Springer (2021). https://doi.org/10.1007/978-3-030-72016-2_8

41. Pagh, R., Rodler, F.F.: Cuckoo hashing. In: ESA. LNCS, vol. 2161, pp. 121–133. Springer (2001). https://doi.org/10.1007/3-540-44676-1_10

42. Pelánek, R.: BEEM: Benchmarks for Explicit Model Checkers. In: SPIN 2007. LNCS, vol. 4595, pp. 263–267 (2007). https://doi.org/10.1007/978-3-540-73370-6_17

43. Prevot, N., Soos, M., Meel, K.: Leveraging GPUs for Effective Clause Sharing in Parallel SAT Solving. In: SAT. LNCS, vol. 12831, pp. 471–487. Springer (2021). https://doi.org/10.1007/978-3-030-80223-3_32

44. de Putter, S., Wijs, A., Zhang, D.: The SLCO Framework for Verified, Model-driven Construction of Component Software. In: FACS. Lecture Notes in Computer Science, vol. 11222, pp. 288–296. Springer (2018). https://doi.org/10.1007/978-3-030-02146-7_15

45. van der Vegt, S., Laarman, A.: A Parallel Compact Hash Table. In: MEMICS. LNCS, vol. 7119, pp. 191–204. Springer (2011). https://doi.org/10.1007/978-3-642-25929-6_18

46. Wei, H., Chen, X., Ye, X., Fu, N., Huang, Y., Shi, J.: Parallel Model Checking on Pushdown Systems. In: ISPA/IUCC/BDCloud/SocialCom/SustainCom. pp. 88–95. IEEE (2018). https://doi.org/10.1109/BDCloud.2018.00026

47. Wei, H., Ye, X., Shi, J., Huang, Y.: ParaMoC: A Parallel Model Checker for Pushdown Systems. In: ICA3PP. LNCS, vol. 11945, pp. 305–312. Springer (2019). https://doi.org/10.1007/978-3-030-38961-1_26

48. Wijs, A., Bošnački, D.: Improving GPU Sparse Matrix-Vector Multiplication for Probabilistic Model Checking. In: SPIN. LNCS, vol. 7385, pp. 98–116. Springer (2012). https://doi.org/10.1007/978-3-642-31759-0_9

49. Wijs, A.: BFS-Based Model Checking of Linear-Time Properties With An Application on GPUs. In: CAV, Part II. LNCS, vol. 9780, pp. 472–493. Springer (2016). https://doi.org/10.1007/978-3-319-41540-6_26
50. Wijs, A., Bošnački, D.: GPUexplore: Many-Core On-the-Fly State Space Exploration Using GPUs. In: TACAS. LNCS, vol. 8413, pp. 233–247 (2014). https://doi.org/10.1007/978-3-642-54862-8_16
51. Wijs, A., Bošnački, D.: Many-Core On-The-Fly Model Checking of Safety Properties Using GPUs. STTT **18**(2), 169–185 (2016). https://doi.org/10.1007/s10009-015-0379-9
52. Wijs, A., Katoen, J.P., Bošnački, D.: Efficient GPU Algorithms for Parallel Decomposition of Graphs into Strongly Connected and Maximal End Components. Formal Methods Syst. Des. **48**(3), 274–300 (2016). https://doi.org/10.1007/s10703-016-0246-7
53. Wijs, A., Neele, T., Bošnački, D.: GPUexplore 2.0: Unleashing GPU Explicit-State Model Checking. In: FM. LNCS, vol. 9995, pp. 694–701. Springer (2016). https://doi.org/10.1007/978-3-319-48989-6_42
54. Wu, Z., Liu, Y., Liang, Y., Sun, J.: GPU Accelerated Counterexample Generation in LTL Model Checking. In: ICFEM. LNCS, vol. 8829, pp. 413–429. Springer (2014). https://doi.org/10.1007/978-3-319-11737-9_27
55. Wu, Z., Liu, Y., Sun, J., Shi, J., Qin, S.: GPU Accelerated On-the-Fly Reachability Checking. In: ICECCS. pp. 100–109 (2015). https://doi.org/10.1109/ICECCS.2015.21
56. Youness, H., Osama, M., Hussein, A., Moness, M., Hassan, A.M.: An Effective SAT Solver Utilizing ACO Based on Heterogenous Systems. IEEE Access **8**, 102920–102934 (2020). https://doi.org/10.1109/ACCESS.2020.2999382
57. Youness, H.A., Ibraheim, A., Moness, M., Osama, M.: An Efficient Implementation of Ant Colony Optimization on GPU for the Satisfiability Problem. In: PDP. pp. 230–235. IEEE (2015). https://doi.org/10.1109/PDP.2015.59

Author Index

S. Sankaranarayanan and N. Sharygina (Eds.): TACAS 2023, LNCS 13993, pp. 705–708, 2023.
https://doi.org/10.1007/978-3-031-30823-9

Printed in the United States
by Baker & Taylor Publisher Services